The Cognitive Processes

PRENTICE-HALL INTERNATIONAL, INC., *London*
PRENTICE-HALL OF AUSTRALIA, PTY., LTD., *Sydney*
PRENTICE-HALL OF CANADA, LTD., *Toronto*
PRENTICE-HALL OF INDIA (PRIVATE) LIMITED, *New Delhi*
PRENTICE-HALL OF JAPAN, INC., *Tokyo*

The Cognitive Processes
READINGS

Robert J. C. Harper · *Charles C. Anderson*
Clifford M. Christensen · *Steven M. Hunka*

Prentice-Hall, Inc.   Englewood Cliffs, New Jersey

PRENTICE-HALL PSYCHOLOGY SERIES
John C. Wright, *Editor*

© 1964 by Prentice-Hall, Inc., Englewood Cliffs, N. J.

Second printing............August, 1965

LIBRARY OF CONGRESS
CATALOG CARD NO.: 64-15595

PRINTED IN THE UNITED STATES OF AMERICA
13947-C

PREFACE

D. O. Hebb's article, *The American Revolution,* should be regarded as part of the preface. His views, which we share fully, have served as a guide for the selection of articles. According to Hebb the first phase of the revolution of psychological thought, behaviorism and learning, has been completed and the resulting S-R paradigm can indeed make sense out of much of the simpler behavior. However, another stage of development is essential, consisting of a more systematic and vigorous attack on the thought process. Admittedly only a start has been made on such an analysis, and this book represents an attempt to bring together in one volume some recent contributions to our understanding of the cognitive processes.

If psychological theory has not been developed to a point where it can deal adequately with complex human activities, then the applied psychologist, who attempts to manipulate complex behavior, is confronted with the dilemma that what is most adequately developed in psychology is least relevant in practice. As educational psychologists we feel this keenly, particularly in training young men and women to become teachers. Central to the activities of the teacher are the cognitive processes of the student, and it seems reasonable to conclude that the teacher's effectiveness depends to some extent on her understanding of these processes. Hebb [1] has pointed out that we are not ready to apply theories to complex behavior. In his words:

> The practical problem in this field is to know how to study better, or how to teach in the classroom. Studying and teaching are complicated by many factors, so the general principles of learning, as we know them today, are subject to exceptions when applied in the kind of information that would enable us to take any intelligent student and make a good teacher of him. As to the art of study, some acquire it with little aid, others need advice; for these latter, there are no specific rules to be given that guarantee success, and each one should regard himself as an experimental problem and find out what particular procedures work in his case.

Does this mean then that the teaching of educational psychology should be abandoned until adequate, applicable theories have been developed? Our reasons for opposing such a view are based on our approach to teaching educational psychology and our experiences with a large group of education students.

---

[1] D. O. Hebb, *A Textbook of Psychology* (Philadelphia, W. B. Saunders Co., 1958), p. 153.

One of the most surprising and disturbing features of contemporary educational psychology is that it has virtually nothing to say about theories of cognition, a topic which is clearly central to human learning. While it is difficult to isolate all of the factors that may account for this unhappy state of affairs, it would appear that the principal one is a problem that seems to pervade the field as a whole. This problem is based on the misconception that, as an applied science, educational psychology must concern itself only with "facts." But the truth of the matter is that, whether or not we subscribe to the unrealistic notion that there are enough psychological "facts" that can be applied to education, theory plays an indispensable part in any applied science. To deny theory is to deny the promotion of that sort of cognitive economy and transfer whose great importance is so eloquently argued by Bruner.[2] Indeed this need is so fundamental that all students naturally construct their own rough and inexact models if left to their own devices, and if their textbooks merely disseminate a number of unrelated and questionable "facts."

Therefore, the editors of these readings take the position that, since teachers are actually hypothesis-makers, they should be able to draw on a thorough acquaintance with the best theories. One great advantage of this position is that it discriminates between the function of the educational psychologist and that of the educational methodologist. The business of the former is to help the future teacher to acquire a way of thinking about behavior. Actual teaching procedures are not his primary concern.

Rather than teaching something that is directly and specifically applicable, we experimented with teaching a few general conceptual models. Our main concern was to get the student of education to think about educational problems in a way similar to that in which a psychologist thinks about these problems. A conceptual model surely encourages an individual to make observations that he would not ordinarily make and aids one in formulating fruitful hypotheses that can be checked against additional observations. We were concerned that the student think in terms of more than one model lest he conclude that all the answers have been given to the problems he will face in the classroom. We do not consider it unwise to send out a teacher who is a bit doubtful of his understanding and deeply aware of his ignorance of human behavior.

Obviously a student must be thoroughly versed in a model before he can use it to think about educational problems. We were fortunate that in Alberta all education students are required to complete four semesters of educational psychology. The first two semesters consist of general psychology oriented toward education. The course is taught by educational psychologists, and most of the examples illustrating principles are drawn from a school setting. The final two semesters comprise an advanced educational psychology course and it was here that we tried out the material contained in this book.

Our students were able to comprehend the conceptual models and make use of them in thinking about educational problems, but this was not an easy matter

[2] J. S. Bruner, *The Process of Education* (Cambridge, Mass.: Harvard University Press, 1960), p. 5.

either for the student or for the instructor. During the first third of the course the student appeared confused and bewildered. The most frequently voiced complaint concerned the relevance of the material for education. Part of the difficulty was due to a mental set: the student expected to obtain unambiguous *ad hoc* recipes on how to teach and deal with children. Terminology caused the greatest difficulty, and here the instructor's role was crucial. We found it necessary to translate the psychological terms into familiar terms, and then to translate the familiar terms back to the psychological terms. Finding illustrative examples probably put the greatest strain on the instructor. Our experience convinced us of two things: (1) the instructor must thoroughly understand the material before he can teach it, and (2) the ideas contained in this book are simple, but the articulation and implementation are difficult.

Students were quite comfortable with our approach during the second half of the course and they were able to enter into intelligent discussion; they wrote meaningful term papers, and showed considerable understanding of examination questions. For example, students of average competence found it possible to tackle with equanimity questions of the following sort: "Explain theoretically the following results: A teacher discovers that a pupil's attitude toward the Chinese, Japanese and Negroes changed as a result of a study of Indians, in which no mention was made of the Chinese, Japanese or Negroes," or "Explain how a stimulus, for example the word 'cup,' becomes a sign of a significate? What suggestions would follow from your explanation regarding a child who has difficulty in learning the meaning of a word?" Significant, too, was the interest that many students developed in thinking about educational problems at a level never before attempted by them. This approach also generated an enthusiasm in the student about psychology that we had never seen before and which augured well for their performance at the graduate level. Our impressions are, of course, tentative, and we have not yet followed up any of the students who have left the University and accepted teaching positions.

We are aware that a host of educational psychologists are convinced that their students cannot comprehend the material in this book. We can only point to the results with our students who may be unique in a unique setting. Many educational psychologists may also question the relevance of this material for the future teacher, but we wonder if those psychologists have considered the alternatives and seriously faced the dilemma that they cannot escape. When a beginning teacher first faces a class, he cannot resort to a recall of detailed research findings in order to understand the behavior of the students. The teacher is forced to fall back on the cognitive economy of a theory and, accordingly, would profit in the long run far more from a course in educational psychology if he were encouraged to learn and try out one or more of the theories which are concerned with symbolic behavior and are, therefore, relevant to educational practice.

A few remarks on the organization of the articles are in order. Part One, dealing with a general arousal theory of motivation, is central to the neo-behavioristic and cognitive processes proposed by psychologists like Hebb and Osgood, presented in Part Two. Nonassociative approaches to cognition comprise Part Three, while the computer model and computer simulation of cognitive processes are presented in Part Four. In Part Five the generality of cognitive theory is demonstrated in the context of personality and motivation. Part Six deals with development and cognition in children.

Although we, because of our professional interests, have dealt exclusively with educational psychology, it goes without saying that psychologists in other areas may find the book useful, e.g., instructors of courses on thinking and cognition.

We are deeply grateful to the many authors and publishers who generously permitted the reproduction of their articles. To them belongs the real credit for attempting to increase our understanding of a complex and important process.

This is a joint work and the order of names is irrelevant. The editors wish to express their appreciation to Mr. Frederick Bessai and Mrs. Patricia Bendiksen for valuable assistance in the preparation of the manuscript.

R.J.C.H.

C.C.A.

C.M.C.

S.M.H.

CONTENTS

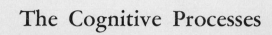

The Cognitive Processes

The American Revolution *

D. O. Hebb

The revolution to which my title refers is not, of course, the political one of 1776, though the parallel is drawn deliberately. A revolution of psychological thought and practice was made by Thorndike, Watson, Holt, Hunter, Lashley, Cattell, Terman, Yerkes (Yerkes the applied psychologist), Tolman, and Skinner between 1898 and 1938. Like the revolution of 1776, however, it turned out to be only the first of two stages of development. I shall urge that the first stage has been complete for some time, largely in the form of Behaviorism and the study of learning, and that it is high time for the rebels to get on with the second one: a behavioristic or learning-theory analysis of the thought process. I propose then to consider a particular aspect of the problem, namely, self-awareness and certain fantasies about the self. This is a topic which has recently assumed practical significance and which has more theoretical interest than may be apparent at first.

The political reference of my title is also meant to suggest that I am taking a detached point of view. Being a foreigner, born in the fourteenth colony (Nova Scotia, the little one that got away in 1776), where skepticism

is endemic concerning the ability, good faith, and morals of all Englishmen, Americans, or Canadians whomsoever, I may, as the first foreign President of this association, take the occasion to look at American psychology in perspective, and the parallel with 1776 is enlightening in more than one way.

To a great extent, American psychology today *is* psychology. Its pre-eminence inevitably invites a kind of criticism that it would not otherwise be subject to—quite in line with the fact that the United States as a dominant power in world affairs can no longer hope to be loved and admired in quite the same way as it may have been in 1910, or even 1920. Power generates hostility. It need not corrupt, evidently, for the unprecedented power held by the United States in 1945 was accompanied by an unprecedented magnanimity, in an extraordinary program of aid to others. But there seem to be, from time to time, errors of judgment, all the more prominent in contrast with the rest of the record; and here again I draw the parallel with American psychology, whose pre-eminence leads others to demand perfection. Should we say, a vain expectation?

Thus I propose no eulogy, but evaluation. The rest of the world is just now learning how to live with the United States politically, these last fifteen years, but Canada like Latin America has been working at it for a century or more. Living in close friendship with the United States is

* From D. O. Hebb, "The American Revolution," *American Psychologist*, 15 (1960), 735-45. Reprinted by permission of the author and the American Psychological Association.

Address of the President to the sixty-eighth Annual Convention of the American Psychological Association, Chicago, September 4, 1960.

1

like making love to an elephant; though your affection is returned you must watch out, not to get stepped on in the excitement. Still, you learn a lot about elephants. We are, after all, as "American" as you are, shaped by the same environmental influences and deriving from the same varied cultures, and yet we retain a separate identity, and thus some detachment. In particular, our distinctive French-plus-English cultural structure we consider to be a greater source of strength than the melting-pot idea, especially for the long run; and whatever we can learn in Canada about protecting cultural diversity, in unity of general purpose, will have value in that urgent business of achieving a supranational sense of unity in mankind.

In psychology Canada has less detachment than in politics, but it is not entirely lacking. My own introduction to the subject was a deep immersion in Freud, Pavlov, and Köhler—none of them American—before taking on my present protective coloring of pseudo-behaviorism. It was no accident of birth or involuntary exposure to the ideas of the American Revolution in psychology that leads me to the conclusion that it was a tremendous achievement —to which some of you at least do not give adequate recognition. On these grounds you will concede, perhaps, that my analysis has hope of detachment; on these, and the ground (as I have implied) that no Canadian is disposed to be uncritical toward anything American, though mostly willing to give the devil his due.

SETTING AND SCOPE

Revolutions do not occur *in vacuo*, and your psychological revolution had support from France (Binet) and Germany (Ebbinghaus and Külpe) with some later necessary needling (the Gestalt group); it was paralleled by the Russian Revolution (Pavlov), and had its roots in a long development of English thought (from Locke and Berkeley to Galton and Lloyd Morgan). You will recognize that this statement is somewhat sketchy; it serves only to say that the revolution did not suddenly appear full-blown, as if La Mettrie and Loeb and James and McDougall had not existed. Recognizing this, however, you may still recognize the achievement of the small group of Americans who for the first time attempted a comprehensive theory of *behavior*, and in so doing set the main lines of the problems we still face.

All this occurred in what was truly an age of revolutions, but coincided particularly with the psychoanalytic revolution: inseparable from psychology, and yet still curiously discrete. As Boring says, Freud is the great man of the psychological world, for he *was* a great man, and he *was* concerned with psychological phenomena. But psychoanalysis is still not part of the main stream of psychological thought, and I think the reason is clear.

Psychoanalysis, as such, has shown no real interest in the mechanics of behavior: in the problems of learning, of sensation and perception, of concept formation, of the nature of mind or the validity of introspective data, and so on. An analogy is made with a conflict of three agents, operating on an upper and lower level, but without detail concerning the nature of their existence or their mode of operation. In short, the analogy is still analogy; a genuine discontinuity with academic theory exists, one such as to make Tolman and Hull in comparison look like blood brothers.

It is salutary, however, to keep in mind the source of the discontinuity. Academic psychology, when Freud began, had nothing but trivialities to offer as far as his problems were concerned. He had to fill in, provisionally, the great gap where motivation—a dynamics of human thought—should have been. That was 1890. Would the situation be so different today? Psychoanalysis is still, I think, a provisional solution, but we are in no position to look down our noses at it. Psychology, also, has made little progress with the mechanics of thought; if we do not like the looks of psychoanalytic theory, what better tools have we to offer the psychiatrist?

You may recall that the political revolution of 1776 was only a beginning. Not till 1865 was it clear that the United States of America was a viable political entity, not subject to progressive fission. In the psychological revolution, the second phase is just now getting under way. The first banished thought, imagery, volition, attention, and other such seditious notions. The sedition of one period, however, may be the good sense of another. These notions relate to a vital problem in the understanding of man, and it is the task of the second phase to bring them back, brainwashed as necessary. In other words: my thesis in this address is that an outstanding contribution to psychology was made in the establishment of a thoroughgoing behavioristic mode of thinking. But this has been achieved, too frequently, only by excluding the chief problem of human behavior. The second contribution must be to establish an equally thoroughgoing behavioristics of the thought process.

Now let us look at the stimulus-response formula, the principal ingredient in this whole development, and its relation to the theory of behavior.

THEORY AND THE S-R FORMULA

The essence of the psychological revolution was the serious, systematic application of the stimulus-response formula to all aspects of behavior, with a consequent development of rigor in experimental analysis. As we have seen, the stimulus-response idea in itself was not very original. What Thorndike and Watson did in the United States, together with Pavlov in Russia, was to get the S-R formula taken seriously in all domains of behavior. They made learning the fundamental issue in psychology, as it still is, by the simple device of denying that there was anything else to be accounted for. Needless to say, the reaction was vigorous, but the upshot of reaction and counterreaction was a development of factual knowledge and rigor—in concept and method—that we should not have had otherwise.

Thought, perception, instinct, emotion, motivation—there is no area of theoretical importance that was not profoundly influenced. On the one hand, analysis of phenomena, to reduce them to stimulus-response connections; on the other, counteranalysis, and devising of new experiments to show that the phenomena could *not* be reduced to S-R terms. Thorndike and Watson in these early years were as wrong as they could be, in some ways, but they had none of that compulsive need to be *right* that rules out the bold conception and cripples speculative inquiry—and as a result, experimental inquiry also. They understood what theory is for, or acted as if they did: which is, first and last, to organize the present facts and lead to the discovery of new facts. In this they succeeded superbly, and it is time that all of us—including us cognitivists—should adequately acknowledge our debt to them.

It has been suggested that Behaviorism was a monstrous perversion, so bad that only a brilliant man could have thought it up. Behaviorism has also been considered to be imperceptive instead of brilliantly perverse, an obvious line of thought, which suffered only from not going far enough in its analysis. From either point of view Gestalt psychology (or the later critiques of Lashley and Tolman) provided a better account of the real nature of behavior. Seeing this, the cognitivist has not always seen how necessary the part played by Behaviorism was in the total picture, and how great its contribution to his own position. Gestalt theory is, actually, a disconnected and self-contradictory set of theoretical suggestions, and the only connected, consistent attempts at explanation in psychology are to be found in one form or other of learning theory: earlier, the "association of ideas"; later, the association of stimulus with response (Hebb, 1953; Humphrey, 1951).

Thus Gestalt psychology was not an alternative to learning theory, but a complement and corrective. We have two themes in the development of knowledge and method, each vital: the search for consistent explanation, characteristic of learning theory, and the search for a more adequate statement of the problem, with the emphasis on the "cognitive" and the innate.[1] The debate was intemperate and engendered loyalties that still exist, but we must see today that this was no true opposition and that the loyalties are no longer relevant. One's preference, one's taste, may be for systematizing with as much economy of theoretical ideas as possible, or it may be for the isolation and analysis of phenomena which fall outside the pur-

view of systematic theory and make difficulty for it; but these are complementary functions, and no basis for "schools" of psychology in the old sense.

Set these loyalties aside, then, and we can see better what was going on. It is not true that learning theory (nor for that matter, the Republican party) had to be dragged kicking and screaming into the twentieth century. Instead the learning theorist was the first cause of the twentieth century, as far as psychology is concerned. It is true that he now has his heels dug in and is hard to move, but my whole argument is that this attitude of "make haste slowly" has been vital to the success of American psychology in the present century. I do not need to remind you of the substantive part of this success, the many additions to knowledge that have been made by both sides; my interest here is in the nature of the sophistication of thought and method that has taken place, often without being recognized by us.

Look first at the stimulus-response formula. It began life as a sweeping explanatory conception, in the idea that all behavior could be accounted for by simple S-R connections. We know today that this is not so, but some of us instead of taking the knowledge calmly, have overreacted, in one of those irrelevant loyalties. It may even be thought that the stimulus-response idea was a mistake in the first place, and is no part of good psychology now (a good cognitive psychology, that is). This is absurd; the whole meaning of the term *cognitive* depends on it, though cognitive psychologists seem unaware of the fact. The term is not a good one, but it does have meaning as a reference to features of behavior that do not fit the S-R formula; and no other meaning at all as far as one can discover. The formula then

---

[1] Though this opposition of aims may seem oversimplified, I believe it is fundamentally sound. How understand otherwise the learning theorist's bland refusal even to discuss attention or purpose, or the cognitive psychologist's happy preference for phenomena he cannot explain—so long as the other cannot explain them either?

has two values: first, it provides a reasonable explanation of much reflexive human behavior, not to mention the behavior of lower animals; and secondly, it provides a fundamental analytical tool, by which to distinguish between lower (noncognitive) and higher (cognitive) forms of behavior.

As recently as twenty years ago "set" and "attention" were mysterious entities (Gibson, 1941), but only because this point was not understood. Either the S-R formula was the whole story of behavior, or else it was irrelevant. When the formula is used instead as an analytical conception, the meaning of these "cognitive" terms becomes clear. They are applied when behavior does not fit the formula, when the animal's response is not sense-dominated (Hebb, 1949). Something else has entered the picture.

Schneirla's (1946) distinction of biosocial from psychosocial communication is another example. Here again the S-R formula is a means of classification. Clearly the biosocial communication of wasp or termite, sense-dominated and reflexive, differs in mechanism from the purposive (psychosocial) communications of ape or man. This leaves us still with the problem of accounting for that "something else" that produces systematic deviation from the S-R formula in some of the behavior of the higher animal, but we have now reached a stage when it is increasingly possible to extend the deterministic and analytic mode of thought, characteristic of learning theory, to the realm of the higher processes. There need result no more discontinuity than in the chemist's distinction of organic from inorganic: two sets of phenomena, one set of principles.

Is all this obvious? Perhaps it is, today; but it certainly was not thirty or thirty-five years ago, when cog-nitivist and learning theorist were charging blindly, ripping and tearing but fortunately not striking mortal blows. Sophistication *has* increased, as an example from Tolman's early work will show. Tolman of course was a cognitivist, and in 1925 he wrote a paper to show that purpose could be made a part of an objective psychology. His definition at that time, however, was such as to identify purpose with behavior, instead of a determinant of behavior. Even more, it was identified with any adaptive behavior, explicitly including the case of a child pulling back from a hot stove, and that of *Stentor* avoiding a noxious stimulus. In both the response is reflexive; calling it purposive only confuses things. Later discussions show that Tolman had something quite different in mind, and that any behavior that fits the S-R formula should have been excluded from the definition. It seems evident that here he was groping for the formulation he made later, in which "mental" processes were identified with intervening variables (Tolman, 1932).

One more example. Romanes was a man of great ability who has not received justice because of our own failure to see the nature of the development of psychological thought. He tried to do a job for which the tools were lacking, but his attempt is one of the reasons why the tools became available later. If nowhere else, his ability appears in his introductory discussion of terms (Romanes, 1883, pp. 1-15). He made, for example, a lucid distinction between instinct and reflex, still not understood by some contemporary writers though it was repeated by Lashley (1938), and between instinct and "reason," the latter being found in behavior which today we would call purposive. The later pages often seem, and are, absurd; but instead of thinking of Romanes as a credulous jackass we might ask what has happened in psychology to make the absurdities so apparent.

Contrary to what is usually said, it is not his anecdotalism that is the primary fault. Remember that many of the "anecdotes" came from trained scientists; and for that matter, that some of the more improbable ones (concerning the ants and the bees) are now known to be true. His real difficulty was a lack of adequate analytical ideas; and to think that these ideas should be obvious, instead of having to be painfully won by a long series of later workers, including Hobhouse, Pfungst ("Clever Hans," 1911), Hunter, and Hull in addition to others already discussed, is simply to misunderstand the achievements of modern psychology.

What Romanes shows us is how far we have moved, especially in the separation of descriptive from inferential entities, in the period from Lloyd Morgan to Fred Skinner. This was not a one- or two-step process. Even Morgan (1900) took for granted that where there is learning there is consciousness. Hence, for Morgan as much as for Romanes, consciousness occurs as far down in the animal scale as the frog, the wasp, and even—it seems—the earthworm. No one thinks of the astringent Morgan as credulous; here instead is evidence of how far comparative psychology has come in this century.

Those cat lovers who abhor Thorndike for denying understanding to their pets, and the humanitarians who feel the same way about Watson and human consciousness, should go back and read some of the contemporary literature again. They might, I think, have more sympathy for the too-simple notions of stimulus-response associationism. There is something wrong about discussing an earthworm's thoughts of the past and hopes for the future; if you cannot quite say why, and yet are impeded at every step in the analysis of behavior by a *deus ex machina*—animal consciousness—it is not entirely indefensible to throw the whole question out.

As a strategy, at least, it was highly effective. It put the onus on others to define behavioral criteria for the higher processes they talked about and to develop the means of objective analysis that exist today.

MIND, CONSCIOUSNESS, AND MEDIATING PROCESS

Let us turn now to those "higher processes," and the behavioristic treatment of mind or consciousness.

First, on using such terms. Neimark (1959) has suggested that I do it only to annoy the bull-headed behaviorist. Enjoyable as that might be, it is not my object. The terms are useful still, or again, and can be used not to encourage but to extirpate the latent animism of the student entering psychology. They originally had an objective reference (animism is a theory of behavior) to which they should be restored. They are not precise terms, but it must not be forgotten how constantly science uses molar and grossly defined terms as well as molecularly precise ones. "Mind" and "consciousness" are useful as loose designations of the complex interaction of mediating processes in the intact, waking higher animal; "cognitive processes" would do also, but is it any improvement?

The analysis that we have just been considering says that it is necessary to distinguish between sense-dominated behavior (comprised under the S-R formula) and a broad spectrum of behavior not so dominated. If you insist on burying your head in the sand

and not seeing this rather rough division, we stop communicating at this point; but if you can agree that the old animosities of the thirties and forties are irrelevant today and, whatever his interpretation may be, that the learning theorist must deal with both levels of behavior, you can at least see that a reference to mental processes is not inconsistent with a fully behavioristic analysis. In the end this comes down to a classification of behavior, as meaningful for Spence or Estes or Neal Miller as it is for Krech or Bruner. Whether one wishes to designate the causal factor underlying one class, or how one is to designate it, is a logically separate question.

Now the fact is that the student comes to us with notions about mind and consciousness deeply engrained. As psychologists, surely, we know that putting a taboo on these words will not get rid of the kind of thinking to which they relate. If we avoid them, develop objective thinking only in the context of new terms and the well-controlled laboratory experiment (incidentally avoiding some important aspects of human behavior), all we succeed in doing is to compartmentalize the student's thinking. At the Yerkes Laboratories it used to be both entertaining and discouraging to see the hard-boiled visiting behaviorist trying on the one hand to describe what he saw clearly in the chimpanzee's behavior, and on the other to avoid terms that seemed subjective and anthropomorphic. He was either reduced to silence, or had to resort to circumlocutions: "It was *just as though* Bimba was thinking. . . ." or *"If she was a person I would say that* Kambi wanted . . . ," or "hoped," or "intended," with elaborate apologies for the improper language. But the language conveys behavioral information; though it is imprecise, synonyms and circumlotions are no

better. As things stand now, we either use the terms available and attack the problem of improving the underlying ideas, or we shut our eyes to the real dimensions of the problem of behavior, whether chimpanzee or human. Should we not teach undergraduate and graduate alike that the whole domain of behavior comes within the scope of objective psychology; that "mind," "consciousness," and so on are references to crudely conceived intervening variables—no more, no less—about which we do not know nearly as much as we might be expected to, after fifty years of Behaviorism and the proscription of animistic notions?

For the idea that these are subjective assumes the validity of introspective observation, as clasically understood, and it is now evident that introspection in this sense is illusory. It has long been clear that it does not reveal a knower, or the process of knowing: nothing is found but sensations (or perceptions). This conclusion goes as far back as Locke, and was reiterated by Hume, Ward, and James, among others. Humphrey (1951) has now shown that what the trained introspector described was not his sensations, as mental content, but the thing sensed. Boring (1953), also, concludes that introspection, as immediate knowledge of conscious content, does not exist; consciousness is wholly a construct. In other words, the introspector engages in inference, not observation.

A recent view of Peirce's pragmatism shows that this idea, radical as it may sound, is not really new and unseasoned. At least one brilliant mind in the nineteenth century, on less evidence than we have today, reached this essentially behavioristic position and recognized its implications. Gallie (1952, p. 81) observes that Peirce's position "seems highly paradoxical: chiefly perhaps because it seems to put our knowledge of our own minds, thoughts and attitudes, etc., on all fours with our knowledge of the minds, thoughts and attitudes of other people." But this is exactly the proposition that I put to you now, and one that is hard to escape on the existing evidence. Mind and consciousness, sensations and perceptions, feelings and emotions, all are intervening variables or constructs and properly part of a behavioristic psychology.

Supposing however that you concede the point, unwilling to argue with my references because you would have to read them first, you may still feel that the point is unimportant: that these conceptions are unrelated to current problems, or that the means are lacking by which to attack such complexities. Either conclusion would be wrong, as I shall try to show you in a moment. There are recent results that demand, here and now, that we find better ways of dealing with man's thought processes, and provide a number of suggestions that doing so is not beyond our experimental ingenuity.

Let me remind you first, however, that the camel already has his nose inside the tent—the learning theorist's tent, I mean. Seward (1947), Lawrence (1950), Meehl and MacCorquodale (1951), Osgood (1953), Berlyne (1954), and Kendler and Kendler (1959) suffice to show that the mediating process is quite compatible with Hullian theory. The choice is whether to prosecute the attack, or to go on with the endless and trivial elaboration of the same set of basic experiments (on pain avoidance, for example); trivial, because they have added nothing to knowledge for some time, though the early work was of great value. A continued reluctance to face problems realistically may mean the slow death of learning theory, as structuralism died when it could not

adjust to new ways of thinking. It is becoming apparent from such work as that of Broadbent (1958) and of Miller, Galanter, and Pribram (1960) that the computer analogy, which can readily include an autonomous central process as a factor in behavior, is a powerful contender for the center of the stage. Learning theory still has certain advantages in dealing with real behavior, however, especially where motivation is concerned. Also, it has some gift for cognitive dissonances (Festinger, 1957) which, unless my notions about creativity are all wrong, ought to make it a continuing stimulant to new ideas. We can still use that argumentative, even dogmatic, preoccupation with scientific rigor.

HALLUCINATION, BODY IMAGE, AND THE SELF

We come then to the question of whether there is any real significance for a tough-minded experimentalist in the problems of thought, and whether there is any practical way of getting at them. Here I propose to take the bull by the horns and consider the most esoteric problem of all, that of the self. There are several reasons for doing so.

One is that the failure of experimental psychology to deal with the "I" or "ego" is a cause of its continued inadequacy with regard to clinical matters. Another is that here, better than anywhere else, one can show the practical importance of understanding thought, even for the engineering psychologist and not only for the clinician. And finally, it seems possible, by bringing together some of the relevant facts from different areas of investigation, to throw new light on the problems of mind and consciousness —or if you prefer, of the complex function of mediating processes.

First, the meaning of the term *self*.

Self or ego, the knower or perceiver or doer, today presents a peculiar problem. Introspective psychology took it for granted as a real entity though, as Hume observed, its existence could only be inferred. In modern objective psychology the self or knower has become the whole organism, thus any designation of a special entity within is superfluous and misleading. Or so it would seem. Now, however, evidence is accumulating to show that there is something here after all. The "something" is a mental construct or set of mediating processes arising out of experience, in part consisting of the so-called body image, in part what seems to be a pure fantasy of an immaterial self which in certain circumstances separates itself from the body. This is fantasy, but a *real* fantasy, with effects on behavior.

The evidence of its practical significance is, first, in the "break-off" phenomenon experienced by pilots at high altitude (Clark and Graybiel, 1957), which clearly involves the subject's self-awareness, his construct of personal identity. The reports are sometimes obscure, partly because the experience is really strange, partly because the pilot does not want to be judged incapable (or to sound like a fool). In some new way he feels detached, disconnected, and may develop a personal identification with his aircraft, with other objects in space, or with the whole of space itself. An accompaniment may be either euphoria or anxiety. The pilots interviewed denied that their efficiency was affected, but one may doubt this, reading between the lines, and Melvill Jones (1960) has obtained evidence that there is a disruptive effect. He has also provided clear evidence of the fantasy referred to. For example:

A pilot on routine high-altitude test flying was forced to descend by "a feeling of dissociation from earth and machine." He had the impression of being detached from the aircraft, of *looking at himself and the machine from outside* and of the aircraft itself being greatly diminished in size like a "toy suspended in space."

Such reports are not from mystics but from practical men, reluctantly given. Further, quite similar effects can be produced experimentally, by the isolation procedure of Bexton, Heron, and Scott (1954). The same conditions that produce (*a*) elaborate visual hallucinations, produce also (*b*) disturbance of the body image and (*c*) the fantasy of a separate mind: one subject's head felt detached from his body, for example, and to another it seemed that his mind was like "a ball of cottonwool floating above my body." All three phenomena therefore seem to be related. Considered singly, each is a puzzling effect, refractory to analysis; but taken together, especially in view of what is known about the body image, a more meaningful picture emerges.

As you know, each of you has his body image, though its existence as a mental construct may be overlooked by the normal person because it is congruent, part by part, with somesthetic and visual perceptions of segments of the body. It comes to attention only when something, such as an amputation, makes a discrepancy between image and the real body. The phantom limb following amputation is the simplest, clearest demonstration that the normal awareness of the body is not a direct perception. (One might better say that your awareness of yourself, at this moment, is a hallucination that happens to agree with reality.) The "sensations" from the phantom are in themselves fully convincing, so that a patient who has not been told that his leg has been removed and who does not see the stump may remain unaware of the loss.

(For the patient who is not prepared in advance, this mystifying phenomenon can be very disturbing indeed; and equally so for the surgeon who wants to concern himself only with physical reality and not to be upset by unrealistic complaints. Consequently one surgeon whom I knew used to prepare his patients psychologically. Before the operation he would visit the patient and tell him: "Tomorrow morning I am going to cut your leg off, and it's going to be *off,* understand? And no damned nonsense about it." He received significantly fewer reports of phantoms; at the 1 per cent level, at least.)

For our purpose here, it is important to note that the body image acts like a product of learning, on the whole fitting very well into learning theory. Simmel (1956) has reviewed the relevant evidence, and provided new data on the question. She has shown that the phantom depends on previous experience, since it does not appear if a limb is lost at birth. There probably is a phantom when the loss occurs in early childhood, but it disappears early if so. The phantom at maturity is extremely persistent, having been reinforced during the whole period of growth, and there is evidence indicating that this learned product is suppressed only by further learning—that is, by retroactive inhibition and not by disuse. If a limb segment wastes away, the slowly modified sensory input permits relearning, and there is no phantom; amputate it, and a phantom ensues (Simmel, 1956). Also, if an injury to the spinal cord prevents sensory input from the stump of an earlier amputation, it stops the fading and shrinkage of the phantom (Bors, 1951). Let me add to this a clinical history, which throws some further light on the functioning of the body image and its relation to the learning process. This is the case history of a Mr. X.

X, aged 56, an apparently undernourished white male; occupation, academic; history of previous hospitalizations. At the age of 22, having failed as a teacher, X got a job as a harvest hand and eight-horse teamster (the latter under false pretenses), where he contracted the bovine TB which caught up with him at age 26 and put him to bed for 15 months. TB of the hip is not supposed to cause mental disturbances, but in this case some confusion was observed in X's self-perceptions.

First, on repeated occasions in an early stage of the illness, when X still had a good deal of discomfort, he saw walking ahead of him, just as he was falling asleep, another person, limping along as X did—though now, in his dream, X himself was quite erect. X would then say to himself, that's a poor way to walk, and straighten the other person up (in the illogical way one has in dreams); whereupon a sharp pain in his *own* hip waked X, who thus could record the dream content.

Second observation: when X got out of bed he had a completely ankylosed hip and had to learn to live with it. He was not at first aware of how extensive the learning was. Besides not doing things that are physically impossible with a stiff hip, he did not even think of doing them; they no longer existed as possible actions. This was brought dramatically to X's attention when he saw a friend walk up to a low couch, without arms or back, bend in the middle, and sit down on it. The momentary shock can hardly be described; the universe had suddenly gone out of order (a real cognitive dissonance). Then things came together again, with hardly an instant's delay in time. Of course, X thought, others can do it, *I* am the one that can't.

There were several such observations over a period of a month or two, after which the confusion in X's mind (as between his body and others') was finally extinguished. The body image returned to normal; X afterward perceived himself as walking and standing normally except when by chance he observed himself by reflection from a shop window, causing mild surprise each time at the abnormality of his walk.

These observations have some interest concerning the effects of learning on the body image at maturity—the hallucination in X's case is remarkably resistant to a changed sensory input—but considerably more interest for our present purposes as a clue to what may be going on in other misperceptions of the self. X's confusion of the properties of his own body with those of another can only mean that *the mental processes of self-perception are the same processes, in large part, that constitute the perception of another person.* And this conclusion need not rest on X's case alone.

Identification with another is, in short, *empathy:* a common property of mental function, as the older literature shows. Also, Rabinovitch (1960) has found an equally clear-cut example of such identification occurring in normal persons, which can easily be set up for experimental study. This is the situation in which an adult attempts to persuade a reluctant baby, 12 to 18 months of age, to open his mouth so he can be given a spoonful of food. Rabinovitch's data show that it is impossible for the adult to avoid opening his own mouth compulsively at least some of the time. Concentration on the idea of baby-opening-mouth causes one's own jaw to move, even if one feels ridiculous and tries to keep it still.

As neural processes therefore, the construct of self, and the perception of another, have a large segment in common, tending to produce the same motor effects. I shall not labor the common sensory cues in the two cases —the visual similarity of one's own hand or foot to another's, or of one's appearance in the mirror to that of someone else a few feet away—nor the fact that these "common" cues are associated by prolonged learning, during growth, with the noncommon, private cues of somesthesis: the sight of a hand making some movement being inevitably associated closely with the corresponding somesthetic sensations, when the hand is one's own, so that the sight of another making the same movement must arouse the same central process that caused one's own movement—and tend to produce imitation.

Contextual sensory cues, of course, mean that the mediating process, as a totality, is not the same in the two cases, and these extra cues may inhibit the imitation (though the facts of "muscle reading" suggest that inhibition is never complete). But this approach implies that the inhibition, also, is learned, and thus may be absent in an unfamiliar context. It is consistent with this that X in his new circumstances took some time to get over his misidentifications, and Rabinovitch's data indicate that uncontrolled jaw movements by the baby feeder are inversely related to length of experience in feeding babies (fathers, for example, are especially susceptible).

Seeing these proposals as a form of Woodworth's (1938) schema-with-correction may make them clearer, and also shows how we can apply them to disturbances of self-awareness by the airplane pilot or the subject in isolation. The "schema" is the indefinite construct of a person; the "correction" in one case is the cues which, coming from one's own body, combine with the schema to be the perception of *person here*, or the self; in the other case, the chiefly visual cues which distinguish *person there*, or the other. The normally complete dichotomy of self from other depends entirely on the efficacy of the distinguishing sensory cues. But we know that the efficacy with which central processes are controlled by sensory processes depends on variation of the sensory input (Sharpless and Jasper, 1956). Such control is seriously impaired in prolonged monotony; and if, as these ideas suggest, a central inhibition is essentially a function of the sensory control, it is not surprising that there should be disturbances of personal identity in the isolation procedure, even if one cannot at present work out the details of the process.

We can put this in still another way. It is not difficult at any time to imagine yourself as seen from some other point in space, nor difficult to imagine prehistoric monsters ploughing through a prehistoric forest. Normally in either case there are sensory cues from one's environment to inhibit the full development of the mental process concerned, so the scene remains "imagination," has not the full characteristic of reality. But let the inhibition lose its effectiveness through habituation and either of these constructs, or products of the imagination, may begin to seem real. In the second case, the subject reports having a hallucination, but in the first he reports being somehow detached from his body, which is inherently a more disturbing event (in this culture). Dream memories, and folklore of "seeing things" in delirium, may have prepared him to some extent for seeming to be where he knows he is not, but so to speak all in one piece. Seeming to observe from

one place with his body in another is a different matter, readily leading to the hypothesis that his mind is capable of wandering through space. To an investigator such reports may sound mystical, or suggest a personality disorder; it is worth emphasizing therefore that all these phenomena seem to have a common basis.

Let me just note, in concluding this part of my discussion, that the argument finds further support in the phenomena of polyopia (Dashiell, 1959; Teuber and Bender, 1949), and reduplication of body parts following brain injury (for example, Weinstein, Kahn, Malitz, and Rozanski, 1954). It would take us too far afield to consider them in detail, but here again are phenomena that can be accounted for by the failure of an inhibition which is normally present and necessary for the integration of higher processes. The perceptual process of the present moment, with its actual sensory input, should inhibit the afterdischarge of preceding ones (as an object moves across the visual field, or a hand changes its position), and the potential activity of others not sensorily aroused (that is, hallucinatory). Lacking that inhibition, a moving object may be seen as a series of "stills" or a patient might find that his bed had become "a nestful of left hands." The integration of the thought process, the attainment of veridical perception, and a unified control of response, evidently depends as much on the suppression of some central activities as on the excitation of others.

THE PROBLEM OF ANALYSIS

Now to put this in the perspective of my more general thesis, as I approach conclusion. The argument is that the serious analytical study of the thought process cannot be postponed any longer. The reconnaissance has been completed, the screens are penetrated, the strong points lie open to attack. No more advantage is to be got from those descriptive studies of thinking, innocent of theory or designed only to destroy S-R theory. There is no advantage in cautiously showing—all over again—that the mediational postulate is justified. This is a powerful tool, and the time has come to use it. In my discussion of the self, I have chosen one aspect of the problem of thought to show that it is both important in a practical sense here and now, and not entirely refractory to analysis even in one of its more esoteric forms. (This of course in addition to my special interest in the case of poor X.) The self is only one line of attack, and probably not the most fertile one, but it is a practicable line and likely to grow rather than diminish in significance.

The self is neither mythical nor mystical, but a complex mental process. It can be manipulated and analyzed by the isolation procedure, and certain clinical phenomena will anatomize it for our inspection. It has a developmental course that is influenced by learning, as seen in the changes or lack of change of the phantom limb or in the acquired immunity of the experienced baby feeder to movements that imitate the baby. It is not really remote and inaccessible in the laboratory, any more than in the clinic. I suspect, further, that it will be found to be involved in the initiation of performance in the ordinary serial learning experiment: part of the "Metaplan" of Miller, Galanter, and Pribram (1960), and related to the difference between incidental and intentional learning. It would be surprising indeed if the subject's intention to repeat a series of syllables—an intention set up by the instructions before any of the

syllables has been presented—did not involve the imagined action of the self making certain sounds, and if this mental process in turn had nothing to do with initiating the later series of responses.

In this situation, therefore, there may be convergence with the fundamentally important line of analysis developed by Lashley (1951) as the problem of serial order, and by Miller, Galanter, and Pribram in their conception of Plan and Metaplan. This concerns the control of skilled performances extended in time, such as speech, typing, or violin playing. Lashley characteristically posed the problem without attempting theoretical explanation; Miller, Galanter, and Pribram have now laid down the general lines of an explanation, using the computer model (Plan and Metaplan correspond to program tapes). The essence of this proposal is, first, that the control of sequential behavior is preformed, centrally—in the brain, not only in the temporal sequence of sensory input—and second, that the control is dual or hierarchical. Plan and Metaplan coexist; the Plan determines the moment-to-moment course of behavior, the Metaplan determines which Plan shall be in effect at any one time (and so is capable of changing Plans in mid-stream). These relatively simple propositions have a greater explanatory power than one might suspect; they handle the general problem raised by Lashley very well, especially in the analysis of speech production, and they provide a new approach to some major puzzles of human behavior.

Before the theory can go much further, however, it may have to be more specific about details: about the nature of the Plan itself, its relation to sensory input and past experience, and how it controls response. It seems, for example, that the Plan is thought of as disjunctive, as a connected series of more or less discrete processes rather than a steady flow like James's stream of thought. What are the properties of the links in the chain? These determine the properties of the chain itself (the Plan), and this is the point at which some physiologizing may become necessary. The theory already has a kinship with the theoretical proposals that Lashley (1958) did make later, and with my own theory of cell-assembly and phase sequence (Hebb, 1949). At least, I see no contradiction, and these more physiologically formulated ideas may bridge the gap between the very molar conceptions of Plan and Metaplan and the more molecular knowledge that is available concerning the relation of receptor and effector function to central processes. Cell-assembly theory has recently received strong support from perceptual studies using Pritchard's method of stabilized retinal images (Pritchard, Heron, and Hebb, 1960). Perception is the area in which the theory originally seemed weakest, so its physiological proposals concerning the nature of the link in the chain of thought may be accepted with increased confidence.

Perhaps I should say again that this does not advocate our becoming neurophysiologists. It is not possible to substitute neurophysiological conceptions for psychological ones, either now or in the future (Hebb, 1958), but it is possible to maintain liaison (translatability of terms) between the two universes of discourse. The stimulating and clarifying value of doing so, for psychology, has been repeatedly demonstrated. The S-R formula, the cornerstone of modern theory as I have tried to show here, was a purely neurological conception, and the last ten years have demonstrated that the stimulant still has its value. Our task is enormously difficult, and we cannot afford to neglect any possible aid—even the physiologist's.

The analysis of thought, the inference from behavior to the interaction of mediating processes or to the functioning of Plan and Metaplan, is still beyond our powers in many respects, but much more progress has been made with it than is sometimes thought. Much of the progress that has been made in this century is evident in the codification of ideas and terminology. The extent to which there is a common behavioral language today is remarkable, in contrast to the pet terms of the various schools of forty years ago. This partly reflects and partly creates an increased agreement concerning the facts, what the essential problems are, and what would constitute crucial evidence in one or other of our arguments about interpretation. In this address I have tried to show that the clarification originated with Behaviorism, broadly speaking: on the one hand from the devoted effort to reduce all to the S-R formula, and on the other to search for the unambiguous experiment by which to refute that effort and on which to base the postulate of an ideational process.

We now have such experiments, and the codification of ideas that is needed to interpret the results. This phase of the Revolution is surely completed; let us press on with the serious, persistent, and if necessary daring, exploration of the thought process, by all available means. I conclude with Conant's (1947) quotation from Bridgman: "The scientific method, as far as it is a method, is nothing more than doing one's damnedest with one's mind, no holds barred."

REFERENCES

Berlyne, D. E., "A Theory of Human Curiosity," *British Journal of Psychology,* **45** (1954), 180-91.

Bexton, W. H., W. Heron, and T. H. Scott, "Effects of Decreased Variation in the Sensory Environment," *Canadian Journal of Psychology,* **8** (1954), 70-76.

Boring, E. G., "A History of Introspection," *Psychological Bulletin,* **50** (1953), 169-89.

Bors, E. "Phantom Limbs of Patients with Spinal Cord Injury," *Archives of Neurological Psychiatry,* **66** (1951), 610-31.

Broadbent, D. E., *Perception and Communication.* New York: Pergamon Press Ltd., 1958.

Clark, B. and A. Graybiel, "The Break-off Phenomenon: A Feeling of Separation from the Earth Experienced by Pilots at High Altitude," *Journal of Aviation Medicine,* **28** (1957), 121-26.

Conant, J. B., *On Understanding Science.* New Haven: Yale University Press, 1947.

Dashiell, J. F., "Monocular Polyopia Induced by Fatigue," *American Journal of Psychology,* **72** (1959), 375-83.

Festinger, L., *A Theory of Cognitive Dissonance.* Evanston, Ill.: Row, Peterson, 1957.

Gallie, W. B., *Peirce and Pragmatism.* Harmondsworth, Middlesex: Penguin, 1952.

Gibson, J. J., "A Critical Review of the Concept of Set in Contemporary Experimental Psychology," *Psychological Bulletin,* **38** (1941), 781-817.

Hebb, D. O., *Organization of Behavior.* New York: John Wiley & Sons, Inc., 1949.

———, "On Human Thought," *Canadian Journal of Psychology,* **7** (1953), 99-110.

———, *A Textbook of Psychology.* Philadelphia: W. B. Saunders Co., 1958.

Humphrey, G., *Thinking.* London: Methuen & Co., Ltd., 1951.

Jones, G. M., personal communication, 1960.

Kendler, Tracy S. and H. H. Kendler, "Reversal and Nonreversal Shifts in Kindergarten Children," *Journal of Experimental Psychology,* **58** (1959), 55-60.

Lashley, K. S., "Experimental Analysis of Instinctive Behavior," *Psychological Review,* **45** (1938), 445-71.

———, "The Problem of Serial Order in Behavior," in *Cerebral Mechanisms in Behavior; The Hixon Symposium,* ed. L. A. Jeffress. New York: John Wiley & Sons, Inc., 1951.

———, "Cerebral Organization and Behavior," *Res. Publ. Assn. Nerv. Ment. Dis.,* **36** (1958), 1-14.

Lawrence, D. H., "Acquired Distinctiveness of Cues: II. Selective Association in a Constant Stimulus Situation," *Journal of Experimental Psychology,* **40** (1950), 175-88.

Meehl, P. E. and K. MacCorquodale, "Some Methodological Comments Concerning Expectancy Theory," *Psychological Review,* **58** (1951), 230-33.

Miller, G. A., E. Galanter, and K. H. Pribram, *Plans and the Structure of Behavior.* New York: Holt, Rinehart & Winston, Inc., 1960.

Morgan, C. L., *Animal Behaviour.* London: Arnold, Ltd., 1900.

Neimark, Edith, "Bones in the Oatmeal," *Psychological Record,* **9** (1959), 115-18.

Osgood, C. E., *Method and Theory in Experimental Psychology.* New York: Oxford University Press, Inc., 1953.

Pritchard, R. M., W. Heron, and D. O. Hebb, "Visual Perception Approached by the Method of Stabilized Images," *Canadian Journal of Psychology,* **14** (1960), 67-77.

Rabinovitch, M. S., personal communication, 1960.

Romanes, G. J., *Animal Intelligence.* New York: Appleton-Century-Crofts, Inc., 1883.

Schneirla, T. C., "Problems in the Biopsychology of Social Organization," *Journal of Abnormal Social Psychology,* **41** (1946), 385-402.

Seward, J. P., "A Theoretical Derivation of Latent Learning," *Psychological Review,* **54** (1947), 83-98.

Sharpless, S. K. and H. Jasper, "Habituation of the Arousal Reaction," *Brain,* **79** (1956), 655-80.

Simmel, Marianne L., "Phantoms in Patients with Leprosy and in Elderly Digital Amputees," *American Journal of Psychology,* **69** (1956), 529-45.

Teuber, H. L. and M. B. Bender, "Alterations in Pattern Vision following Trauma of Occipital Lobes in Man," *Journal of Genetic Psychology,* **40** (1949), 37-57.

Tolman, E. C., "Behaviorism and Purpose," *Journal of Philosophy,* **22** (1925), 36-41.

————, *Purposive Behavior in Animals and Men.* New York: Appleton-Century-Crofts, Inc., 1932.

Weinstein, W. A., R. L. Kahn, S. Malitz, and J. Rozanski, "Delusional Reduplication of Parts of the Body," *Brain,* **77** (1954), 45-60.

Woodworth, R. S., *Experimental Psychology.* New York: Holt, Rinehart & Winston, Inc., 1938.

PART ONE

MOTIVATION

We have two main reasons for including articles on motivation in a book of readings on cognitive processes: first, some concept of motivation is essential to round out the Hebb-Osgood behavioristic explanations of cognitive processes; second, the distinction between motivation and cognition becomes less and less clear as both processes are studied more intensively. This integration of motivation and cognition becomes particularly apparent in Part Five, but it is also evident in Razran's discussion of the orienting reflex.

A number of psychologists have found it convenient to begin their theorizing with conceptual models of the nervous system. These models, which may be regarded as an intermediate step to the theory proper, frequently draw on whatever physiological knowledge happens to be available at the time. Recent work on the neurophysiology of the reticular formation of the brain stem suggests that this structure is the central locus of motivational states and that it is related to the functioning of the cortex and of the skeletal musculature. This relationship, which appears to involve facilitatory and inhibitory functions, has prompted some theorists to incorporate *arousal,* the hypothesized behavioral correlate of reticular activity, as the motivational aspect of their cognitive theories. For this reason, a number of the basic articles on this topic were included. Although the most exhaustive paper is that by Lindsley, the student is advised to begin with the contributions of Hebb and Malmo, which are shorter, less technical, and more psychologically oriented. Hebb's notion of an optimum level of arousal is widely accepted and has many implications for the teacher in the classroom. It has been particularly difficult for teachers to realize that students can be too highly aroused or motivated to learn efficiently. A teacher might well reflect on the possibility that some of her interactions with students have in fact increased the motivation of a student who is already too highly motivated.

17

Lindsley clearly shows that the reticular formation plays an important and complex role in the regulation of behavior. It is, first of all, involved in the general arousal or activation of the organism, and in the facilitation and inhibition of skeletal muscular activity. In addition a two-way relationship between cortex and reticular formation exists: cortical activity can induce arousal, and the activation of the arousal system facilitates cortical activity within upper and lower limits. Hebb and Berlyne, among others, have been stimulated by these neurological findings to theorize about the relationship between cognition and motivation at the behavioral level.

Most of the work on arousal is still at the theoretical stage, but some experimentation has already been undertaken. Blatt reports supporting evidence for a direct relationship between efficiency in problem-solving and one index of arousal.

Included in this section are two papers on the orienting reflex, a set of complex reactions to a new or novel stimulus that have a preparatory rather than an executive function, preparing the organism to deal with new sources of stimulation. Before an organism can learn a response to a new stimulus it must first orient to that stimulus, and thus the orienting reflex plays an important role in all learning. Razran describes the dynamics of the orienting reflex and summarizes considerable research. Berlyne discusses some of the stimulus variables that evoke the orienting reflex. Both authors provide a new approach to the old problem of attention. These articles clearly indicate that the student will learn what he orients to, but this may not be what the teacher has specified.

The papers comprising Part One have many implications for classroom practice. For example, the teacher might consider the possibility that extremely high motivation will have effects on learning that are just as deleterious as those of undermotivation. Furthermore, if the directive and energizing functions of a given teaching situation vary with the child, she might entertain the hypothesis that by catering to individual differences in arousal level (for example, by reassuring the anxious, and giving arousal jags to the undermotivated), there will be a resultant increase in class performance as a whole. Teachers might also consider the possible value of developing a sensitivity to their *own* level of arousal and its relationship to classroom effectiveness. Finally, the suggestion that an orientation response is a prerequisite of adaptive behavior should stimulate discussion on the value of novelty in lesson presentations and pre-training procedures to insure that relevant cues are attended to, before the learning proper is undertaken.

Drives and the C. N. S. (conceptual nervous system)*

D. O. Hebb

The problem of motivation of course lies close to the heart of the general problem of understanding behavior, yet it sometimes seems the least realistically treated topic in the literature. In great part, the difficulty concerns that c.n.s., or "conceptual nervous system," which Skinner disavowed and from whose influence he and others have tried to escape. But the conceptual nervous system of 1930 was evidently like the gin that was being drunk about the same time; it was homemade and none too good, as Skinner pointed out, but it was also habit-forming; and the effort to escape has not really been successful. Prohibition is long past. If we *must* drink, we can now get better liquor; likewise, the conceptual nervous system of 1930 is out of date and—if we must neurologize—let us use the best brand of neurology we can find.

Though I personally favor both alcohol and neurologizing, in moderation, the point here does not assume that either is a good thing. The point

*From D. O. Hebb, "Drives and the C. N. S. (conceptual nervous system)," *Psychological Review,* **62** (1955), 243-354. Reprinted by permission of the author and the American Psychological Association.

Presidential address, Division 3, at American Psychological Association, New York, September 1954.

The paper incorporates ideas worked out in discussion with fellow students at McGill, especially Dalbir Bindra and Peter Milner, as well as with Leo Postman at California, and it is a pleasure to record my great indebtedness to them.

is that psychology is intoxicating itself with a worse brand than it need use. Many psychologists do not think in terms of neural anatomy; but merely adhering to certain classical frameworks shows the limiting effect of earlier neurologizing. Bergmann (2) has recently said again that it is logically possible to escape the influence. This does not change the fact that, in practice, it has not been done.

Further, as I read Bergmann, I am not sure that he really thinks, deep down, that we should swear off neurologizing entirely, or at least that we should all do so. He has made a strong case for the functional similarity of intervening variable and hypothetical construct, implying that we are dealing more with differences of degree than of kind. The conclusion *I* draw is that both can properly appear in the same theory, using intervening variables to whatever extent is most profitable (as physics, for example, does), and conversely not being afraid to use some theoretical conception merely because it might become anatomically identifiable.

For many conceptions, at least, MacCorquodale and Meehl's (26) distinction is relative, not absolute; and it must also be observed that physiological psychology makes free use of "dispositional concepts" as well as "existential" ones. Logically, this leaves room for some of us to make more use of explicitly physiological constructs than others and still lets us stay in communication with one another. It also shows how one's views concerning motivation, for example, might be more influenced than one thinks by earlier physiological notions, since it means that an explicitly physiological conception might be restated in words that have—apparently—no physiological reference.

What I propose, therefore, is to look at motivation as it relates to the c.n.s. —or conceptual nervous system—of three different periods: as it was before 1930, as it was, say, ten years ago, and as it is today. I hope to persuade you that some of our current troubles with motivation are due to the c.n.s. of an earlier day, and ask that you look with an open mind at the implications of the current one. Today's physiology suggests new psychological ideas, and I would like to persuade you that they make psychological sense, no matter how they originated. They might even provide common ground— not necessarily agreement, but communication, something nearer to agreement—for people whose views at present may seem completely opposed. While writing this paper I found myself having to make a change in my own theoretical position, as you will see, and though you may not adopt the same position, you may be willing to take another look at the evidence and consider its theoretical import anew.

Before going on, it is just as well to be explicit about the use of the terms *motivation* and *drive*. *Motivation* refers here in a rather general sense to the energizing of behavior, and especially to the sources of energy in a particular set of responses that keep them temporarily dominant over others and account for continuity and direction in behavior. *Drive* is regarded as a more specific conception about the way in which this occurs: a hypothesis of motivation, which makes the energy a

function of a special process distinct from those S-R or cognitive functions that are energized. In some contexts, therefore, *motivation* and *drive* are interchangeable.

MOTIVATION IN THE CLASSICAL (PRE-1930) C.N.S.

The main line of descent of psychological theory, as I have recently tried to show (20), is through associationism and the stimulus-response formulations. Characteristically, stimulus-response theory has treated the animal as more or less inactive unless subjected to special conditions of arousal. These conditions are first, hunger, pain, and sexual excitement; and second, stimulation that has become associated with one of these more primitive motivations.

Such views did not originate entirely in the early ideas of nervous function but certainly were strengthened by them. Early studies of the nerve fiber seemed to show that the cell is inert until something happens to it from outside; therefore, the same would be true of the collection of cells making up the nervous system. From this came the explicit theory of drives. The organism is thought of as like a machine, such as the automobile, in which the steering mechanism—that is, stimulus-response connections—is separate from the power source, or drive. There is, however, this difference: the organism may be endowed with three or more different power plants. Once you start listing separate ones, it is hard to avoid five: hunger, thirst, pain, maternal, and sex drives. By some theorists, these may each be given a low-level steering function also, and indirectly the steering function of drives is much increased by the law of effect. According to the law, habits— steering functions—are acquired only in conjunction with the operation of drives.

Now, it is evident that an animal is often active and often learns when there is little or no drive activity of the kinds listed. This fact has been dealt with in two ways. One is to postulate additional drives—activity, exploratory, manipulatory, and so forth. The other is to postulate acquired or learned drives, which obtain their energy, so to speak, from association with primary drives.

It is important to see the difficulties to be met by this kind of formulation, though it should be said at once that I do not have any decisive refutation of it, and other approaches have their difficulties, too.

First, we may overlook the rather large number of forms of behavior in which motivation cannot be reduced to biological drive plus learning. Such behavior is most evident in higher species, and may be forgotten by those who work only with the rat or with restricted segments of the behavior of [the] dog or cat. (I do not suggest that we put human motivation on a different plane from that of animals [7]; what I am saying is that certain peculiarities of motivation increase with phylogenesis and, though most evident in man, can be clearly seen with other higher animals.) What is the drive that produces panic in the chimpanzee at the sight of a model of a human head; or fear in some animals, and vicious aggression in others, at the sight of the anesthetized body of a fellow chimpanzee? What about fear of snakes, or the young chimpanzee's terror at the sight of strangers? One can accept the idea that this is "anxiety," but the anxiety, if so, is not based on a prior association of the stimulus object with pain. With the young chimpanzee reared in the nursery of the Yerkes Laboratories, after separation from the

mother at birth, one can be certain that the infant has never seen a snake before, and certainly no one has told him about snakes; and one can be sure that a particular infant has never had the opportunity to associate a strange face with pain. Stimulus generalization does not explain fear of strangers, for other stimuli in the same class, namely, the regular attendants, are eagerly welcomed by the infant.

Again, what drive shall we postulate to account for the manifold forms of anger in the chimpanzee that do not derive from frustration objectively defined (22)? How account for the petting behavior of young adolescent chimpanzees, which Nissen (36) has shown is independent of primary sex activity? How deal with the behavior of the female who, bearing her first infant, is terrified at the sight of the baby as it drops from the birth canal, runs away, never sees it again after it has been taken to the nursery for rearing, and who yet, on the birth of a *second* infant, promptly picks it up and violently resists any effort to take it from her?

There is a great deal of behavior, in the higher animal especially, that is at the very best difficult to reduce to hunger, pain, sex, and maternal drives, plus learning. Even for the lower animal it has been clear for some time that we must add an exploratory drive (if we are to think in these terms at all), and presumably the motivational phenomena recently studied by Harlow and his colleagues (16, 17, 10) could also be comprised under such a drive by giving it a little broader specification. The curiosity drive of Berlyne (4) and Thompson and Solomon (46), for example, might be considered to cover both investigatory and manipulatory activities on the one hand, and exploratory, on the other. It would also comprehend the "problem-seeking" behavior recently studied by Mahut and Havelka at McGill (unpublished studies). They have shown that the rat which is offered a short, direct path to food, and a longer, variable and indirect pathway involving a search for food, will very frequently prefer the more difficult, but more "interesting," route.

But even with the addition of a curiosity-investigatory-manipulatory drive, and even apart from the primates, there is still behavior that presents difficulties. There are the reinforcing effects of incomplete copulation (43) and of saccharin intake (42, 11), which do not reduce to secondary reward. We must not multiply drives beyond reason, and at this point one asks whether there is no alternative to the theory in this form. We come, then, to the conceptual nervous system of 1930 to 1950.

MOTIVATION IN THE C.N.S. OF 1930–1950

About 1930 it began to be evident that the nerve cell is not physiologically inert, does not have to be excited from outside in order to discharge (19, p. 8). The nervous system is alive, and living things by their nature are active. With the demonstration of spontaneous activity in c.n.s. it seemed to me that the conception of a drive system or systems was supererogation.

For reasons I shall come to later, this now appears to me to have been an oversimplification; but in 1945 the only problem of motivation, I thought, was to account for the *direction* taken by behavior. From this point of view, hunger or pain might be peculiarly effective in guiding or channeling activity but not needed for its arousal. It was not surprising, from this point of view, to see human beings liking intellectual work, nor to find evidence that an animal might learn something without pressure of pain or hunger.

The energy of response is not in the stimulus. It comes from the food, water, and oxygen ingested by the animal; and the violence of an epileptic convulsion, when brain cells for whatever reason decide to fire in synchrony, bears witness to what the nervous system can do when it likes. This is like a whole powder magazine exploding at once. Ordinary behavior can be thought of as produced by an organized series of much smaller explosions, and so a "self-motivating" c.n.s. might still be a very powerfully motivated one. To me, then, it was astonishing that a critic could refer to mine as a "motivationless" psychology. What I had said in short was that any organized process in the brain is a motivated process, inevitably, inescapably; that the human brain is built to be active, and that as long as it is supplied with adequate nutrition will continue to be active. Brain activity is what determines behavior, and so the only behavioral problem becomes that of accounting for *in*activity.

It was in this conceptual frame that the behavioral picture seemed to negate the notion of drive, as a separate energizer of behavior. A pedagogical experiment reported earlier (18) had been very impressive in its indication that the human liking for work is not a rare phenomenon, but general. All of the 600-odd pupils in a city school, ranging from 6 to 15 years of age, were suddenly informed that they need do no work whatever unless they wanted to, that the punishment for being noisy and interrupting others' work was to be sent to the playground to play, and that the reward for being good was to be allowed to do more work. In these circumstances, *all* of the pupils discovered within a day or two that, within limits, they preferred work to no work (and incidentally learned more arithmetic and so forth than in previous years).

The phenomenon of work for its own sake is familiar enough to all of us, when the timing is controlled by the worker himself, when "work" is not defined as referring alone to activity imposed from without. Intellectual work may take the form of trying to understand what Robert Browning was trying to say (if anything), to discover what it is in Dali's paintings that can interest others, or to predict the outcome of a paperback mystery. We systematically underestimate the human need of intellectual activity, in one form or another, when we overlook the intellectual component in art and in games. Similarly with riddles, puzzles, and the puzzle-like games of strategy such as bridge, chess, and *Go;* the frequency with which man has devised such problems for his own solution is a most significant fact concerning human motivation.

It is, however, not necessarily a fact that supports my earlier view, outlined above. It is hard to get these broader aspects of human behavior under laboratory study, and when we do we may expect to have our ideas about them significantly modified. For my views on the problem, this is what has happened with the experiment of Bexton, Heron, and Scott (5). Their work is a long step toward dealing with the realities of motivation in the well-fed, physically comfortable, adult human being, and its results raise a serious difficulty for my own theory. Their subjects were paid handsomely to do nothing, see nothing, hear or touch very little, for 24 hours a day. Primary needs were met, on the whole, very well. The subjects suffered no pain and were fed on request. It is true that they could not copulate, but, at the risk of impugning the virility of

Canadian college students, I point out that most of them would not have been copulating anyway and were quite used to such long stretches of three or four days without primary sexual satisfaction. The secondary reward, on the other hand, was high: $20 a day plus room and board is more than $7000 a year, far more than a student could earn by other means. The subjects then should be highly motivated to continue the experiment, cheerful and happy to be allowed to contribute to scientific knowledge so painlessly and profitably.

In fact, the subject was well motivated for perhaps four to eight hours and then became increasingly unhappy. He developed a need for stimulation of almost any kind. In the first preliminary exploration, for example, he was allowed to listen to recorded material on request. Some subjects were given a talk for 6-year-old children on the dangers of alcohol. This might be requested, by a grown-up male college student, 15 to 20 times in a 30-hour period. Others were offered, and asked for repeatedly, a recording of an old stock-market report. The subjects looked forward to being tested but paradoxically tended to find the tests fatiguing when they did arrive. It is hardly necessary to say that the whole situation was rather hard to take, and one subject, in spite of not being in a special state of primary drive arousal in the experiment but in real need of money outside it, gave up the secondary reward of $20 a day to take up a job at hard labor paying $7 or $8 a day.

This experiment is not cited primarily as a difficulty for drive theory, although three months ago that is how I saw it. It *will* make difficulty for such theory if exploratory drive is not recognized; but we have already seen the necessity, on other grounds, of including a sort of exploratory-curiosity-manipulatory drive, which essentially comes down to a tendency to seek varied stimulation. This would on the whole handle very well the motivational phenomena observed by Heron's group.

Instead, I cite their experiment as making essential trouble for my own treatment of motivation (19) as based on the conceptual nervous system of 1930 to 1945. If the thought process is internally organized and motivated, why should it break down in conditions of perceptual isolation, unless emotional disturbance intervenes? But it did break down when no serious emotional change was observed, with problem-solving and intelligence-test performance significantly impaired. Why should the subjects themselves report (a) after four or five hours in isolation that they could not follow a connected train of thought, and (b) that their motivation for study or the like was seriously disturbed for 24 hours or more after coming out of isolation? The subjects were reasonably well adjusted, happy, and able to think coherently for the first four or five hours of the experiment; why, acording to my theory, should this not continue, and why should the organization of behavior not be promptly restored with restoration of a normal environment?

You will forgive me perhaps if I do not dilate further on my own theoretical difficulties, paralleling those of others, but turn now to the conceptual nervous system of 1954 to ask what psychological values we may extract from it for the theory of motivation. I shall not attempt any clear answer for the difficulties we have considered— the data do not seem yet to justify clear answers—but certain conceptions can be formulated in sufficiently definite form to be a background for

new research, and the physiological data contain suggestions that may allow me to retain what was of value in my earlier proposals while bringing them closer to ideas such as Harlow's (16) on one hand and to reinforcement theory on the other.

MOTIVATION AND C.N.S. IN 1954

For psychological purposes there are two major changes in recent ideas of nervous function. One concerns the single cell, the other an "arousal" system in the brain stem. The first I shall pass over briefly; it is very significant, but does not bear quite as directly upon our present problem. Its essence is that there are two kinds of activity in the nerve cell: the spike potential, or actual firing, and the dendritic potential, which has very different properties. There is now clear evidence (12) that the dendrite has a "slow-burning" activity which is not all-or-none, tends not to be transmitted, and lasts 15 to 30 milliseconds instead of the spike's one millisecond. It facilitates spike activity (23) but often ocurs independently and may make up the greater part of the EEG record. It is still true that the brain is always active, but the activity is not always the transmitted kind that conduces to behavior. Finally, there is decisive evidence of primary inhibition in nerve function (25, 14) and of a true fatigue that may last for a matter of minutes instead of milliseconds (6, 9). These facts will have a great effect on the hypotheses of physiological psychology, and sooner or later on psychology in general.

Our more direct concern is with a development to which attention has already been drawn by Lindsley (24): the nonspecific or diffuse projection system of the brain stem, which was shown by Moruzzi and Magoun (34) to be an *arousal* system whose activity in effect makes organized cortical activity possible. Lindsley showed the relevance to the problem of emotion and motivation; what I shall attempt is to extend his treatment, giving more weight to cortical components in arousal. The point of view has also an evident relationship to Duffy's (13).

The arousal system can be thought of as representing a second major pathway by which all sensory excitations reach the cortex, as shown in the upper part of Fig. 1; but there is also feedback from the cortex and I shall urge that the *psychological* evidence further emphasizes the importance of this "downstream" effect.

In the classical conception of sensory function, input to the cortex was via

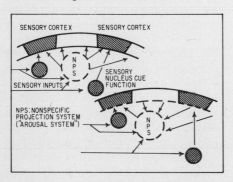

FIGURE 1

the great projection systems only: from sensory nerve to sensory tract, thence to the corresponding sensory nucleus of the thalamus, and thence directly to one of the sensory projection areas of the cortex. These are still the direct sensory routes, the quick efficient transmitters of information. The second pathway is slow and inefficient; the excitation, as it were, trickles through a tangled thicket of fibers and synapses, there is a mixing up of messages, and the scrambled messages are delivered indiscriminately

to wide cortical areas. In short, they are messages no longer. They serve, instead, to tone up the cortex, with a background supporting action that is completely necessary if the messages proper are to have their effect. Without the arousal system, the sensory impulses by the direct route reach the sensory cortex, but go no farther; the rest of the cortex is unaffected, and thus learned stimulus-response relations are lost. The waking center, which has long been known, is one part of this larger system; any extensive damage to it leaves a permanently inert, comatose animal.

Remember that in all this I am talking conceptual nervous system: making a working simplification, and abstracting for psychological purposes; and all these statements may need qualification, especially since research in this area is moving rapidly. There is reason to think, for example, that the arousal system may not be homogeneous but may consist of a number of subsystems with distinctive functions (38). Olds and Milner's (37) study, reporting "reward" by direct intracranial stimulation, is not easy to fit into the notion of a single, homogeneous system. Sharpless' (40) results also raise doubt on this point, and it may reasonably be anticipated that arousal will eventually be found to vary qualitatively as well as quantitatively. But in general terms, psychologically, we can now distinguish two quite different effects of a sensory event. One is the *cue function,* guiding behavior; the other, less obvious but no less important, is the *arousal* or *vigilance function.* Without a foundation of arousal, the cue function cannot exist.

And now I propose to you that, whatever you wish to call it, arousal in this sense is synonymous with a general drive state, and the conception of drive therefore assumes anatomical and physiological identity. Let me remind you of what we discussed earlier: the drive is an energizer, but not a guide; an engine, but not a steering gear. These are precisely the specifications of activity in the arousal system. Also, learning is dependent on drive, according to drive theory, and this too is applicable in general terms —no arousal, no learning; and efficient learning is possible only in the waking, alert, responsive animal, in which the level of arousal is high.

Thus I find myself obliged to reverse my earlier views and accept the drive conception, not merely on physiological grounds but also on the grounds of some of our current psychological studies. The conception is somewhat modified, but the modifications may not be entirely unacceptable to others.

Consider the relation of the effectiveness of cue function, actual or poten-

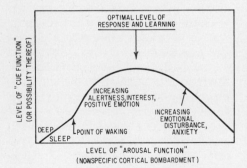

FIGURE 2

tial, to the level of arousal (Fig. 2). Physiologically, we may assume that cortical synaptic function is facilitated by the diffuse bombardment of the arousal system. When this bombardment is at a low level an increase will tend to strengthen or maintain the concurrent cortical activity; that is, when arousal or drive is at a low level, a response that produces in-

creased stimulation and greater arousal will tend to be repeated. This is represented by the rising curve at the left. But when arousal is at a high level, as at the right, the greater bombardment may interfere with the delicate adjustments involved in cue function, perhaps by facilitating irrelevant responses (a high D arouses conflicting $_sH_R$'s?). Thus there will be an optimal level of arousal for effective behavior, as Schlosberg (39) has suggested. Set aside such physiologizing completely, and we have a significant behavioral conception left, namely, that the same stimulation in mild degree may attract (by prolonging the pattern of response that leads to this stimulation) and in strong degree repel (by disrupting the pattern and facilitating conflicting or alternative responses).

The significance of this relation is in a phenomenon of the greatest importance for understanding motivation in higher animals. This is the *positive attraction of risk-taking,* or mild fear, *and of problem-solving,* or mild frustration, which was referred to earlier. Whiting and Mowrer (49) and Berlyne (4) have noted a relation between fear and curiosity—that is, a tendency to seek stimulation from fear-provoking objects, though at a safe distance. Woodworth (50) and Valentine (48) reported this in children, and Woodworth and Marquis (51) have recently emphasized again its importance in adults. There is no doubt that it exists. There is no doubt, either, that problem-solving situations have some attraction for the rat, more for Harlow's (16) monkeys, and far more for man. When you stop to think of it, it is nothing short of extraordinary what trouble people will go to in order to get into more trouble at the bridge table, or on the golf course; and the fascination of the murder story, or thriller, and the newspaper accounts of real-life adventure or tragedy, is no less extraordinary. This taste for excitement *must* not be forgotten when we are dealing with human motivation. It appears that, up to a certain point, threat and puzzle have positive motivating value, beyond that point negative value.

I know this leaves problems. It is not *any* mild threat, *any* form of problem, that is rewarding; we still have to work out the rules for this formulation. Also, I do not mean that there are not secondary rewards of social prestige for risk-taking and problem-solving—or even primary rewards when such behavior is part of lovemaking. But the animal data show that it is not always a matter of extrinsic reward; risk and puzzle can be attractive in themselves, especially for higher animals such as man. If we can accept this, it will no longer be necessary to work out tortuous and improbable ways to explain why human beings work for money, why school children should learn without pain, why a human being in isolation should dislike doing nothing.

One other point before leaving Fig. 2: the low level of the curve to the right. You may be skeptical about such an extreme loss of adaptation, or disturbance of cue function and S-R relations, with high levels of arousal. Emotion is persistently regarded as energizing and organizing (which it certainly is at the lower end of the scale, up to the optimal level). But the "paralysis of terror" and related states do occur. As Brown and Jacobs (8, p. 753) have noted, "the presence of fear may act as an energizer . . . and yet lead in certain instances to an increase in immobility." Twice in the past eight months, while this address was being prepared, the Montreal newspapers reported the behavior of a human being who, suddenly finding himself in extreme danger but with time to escape, simply made no move whatever. One of the two was killed; the other was not, but only because a truck driver chose to wreck his truck and another car instead. Again, it is reported by Marshall (27), in a book that every student of human motivation should read carefully, that in the emotional pressure of battle no more than 15 to 25 percent of men under attack even fire their rifles, let alone use them efficiently.

Tyhurst's (47) very significant study of behavior in emergency and disaster situations further documents the point. The adult who is told that his apartment house is on fire, or who is threatened by a flash flood, may or may not respond intelligently. In various situations, 12 to 25 percent did so; an equal number show "states of confusion, paralyzing anxiety, inability to move out of bed, 'hysterical' crying or screaming, and so on." Three-quarters or more show a clear impairment of intelligent behavior, often with aimless and irrelevant movements, rather than (as one might expect) panic reactions. There seems no doubt: the curve at the right must come down to a low level.

Now back to our main problem: If we tentatively identify a general state of drive with degree of arousal, where does this leave hunger, pain, and sex drives? These may still be anatomically separable, as Stellar (45) has argued, but we might consider instead the possibility that there is just one general drive state that can be aroused in different ways. Stellar's argument does not seem fully convincing. There are certainly regions in the hypothalamus that control eating, for example; but is this a *motivating* mechanism? The very essence of such a conception is that the mechanism in question should energize *other* mechanisms, and Miller, Bailey, and Stevenson (31) have shown that the opposite is true.

But this issue should not be pressed too far, with our present knowledge. I have tried to avoid dogmatism in this presentation in the hope that we might try, for once, to see what we have in common in our views on motivation. One virtue of identifying arousal with drive is that it relates differing views (as well as bringing into the focus of attention data that may otherwise be neglected). The important thing is a clear distinction between cue function and arousal function, and the fact that at low levels an increase of drive intensity may be rewarding, whereas at high levels it is a decrease that rewards. Given this point of view and our assumptions about arousal mechanisms, we see that what Harlow has emphasized is the exteroceptively aroused, but still low-level, drive, with cue function of course directly provided for. In the concept of anxiety, Spence and Brown emphasize the higher-level drive state, especially where there is no guiding cue function that would enable the animal to escape threat. The feedback from cortical functioning makes intelligible Mowrer's (35) equating anxiety aroused by threat of pain, and anxiety aroused in some way by cognitive processes related to ideas of the self. Solomon and Wynne's (44) results with sympathectomy are also relevant, since we must not neglect the arousal effects of interoceptor activity; and so is clinical anxiety due to metabolic and nutritional disorders, as well as that due to some conflict of cognitive processes.

Obviously these are not explanations that are being discussed, but possible lines of future research; and there is one problem in particular that I would urge should not be forgotten. This is the cortical feedback to the arousal system, in physiological terms: or in psychological terms, the *immediate drive value of cognitive processes,* without intermediary. This is psychologically demonstrable and *has* been demonstrated repeatedly.

Anyone who is going to talk about acquired drives, or secondary motivation, should first read an old paper by Valentine (48). He showed that with a young child you can easily condition fear of a caterpillar or a furry animal but cannot condition fear of opera glasses, or a bottle; in other words, the fear of some objects, that seems to be learned, was there, latent, all the time. Miller (29) has noted this possibility but he does not seem to have regarded it very seriously, though he cited a confirmatory experiment by Bregman; for in the same passage he suggests that my own results with chimpanzee fears of certain objects, including strange people, may be dealt with by generalization. But this simply will not do, as Riesen and I noted (21). If you try to work this out, for the infant who is terrified on *first* contact with a stranger, an infant who has never shown such terror before, and who has always responded with eager affection to the only human beings he has made contact with up to this moment, you will find that this is a purely verbal solution.

Furthermore, as Valentine observed, you cannot postulate that the cause of such fear is simply the strange event, the thing that has never occurred before. For the chimpanzee reared in darkness, the first sight of a human being is of course a strange event, by definition; but fear of strangers does not occur until later, until the chimpanze has had an opportunity to learn to recognize a few persons. The fear is not "innate" but depends on some sort of cognitive or cortical conflict of learned responses. This is clearest when the baby chimpanzee, who knows and welcomes attendant *A* and attendant *B*, is terrified when he sees *A* wearing *B*'s coat. The role of learning is inescapable in such a case.

The cognitive and learning element may be forgotten in other motivations, too. Even in the food drive, some sort of learning is fundamentally important: Ghent (15) has shown this, Sheffield and Campbell (41) seem in agreement, and so does the work of Miller and his associates (3, 32, 30) on the greater reinforcement value of food by mouth, compared to food by stomach tube. Beach (1) has shown the cortical-and-learning element in sex behavior. Melzack (28) has demonstrated recently that even pain responses involve learning. In Harlow's (16) results, of course, and Montgomery's (33), the cognitive element is obvious.

These cortical or cognitive components in motivation are clearest when we compare the behavior of higher and lower species. Application of a *genuine* comparative method is essential, in the field of motivation as well as of intellectual functions (22). Most disagreements between us have related to so-called "higher" motivations. But the evidence I have discussed today need not be handled in such a way as to maintain the illusion of a complete separation between our various approaches to the problem. It *is* an illusion, I am convinced; we still have many points of disagreement as to relative emphasis, and as to which of several alternative lines to explore first, but this does not imply fundamental and final opposition. As theorists, we have been steadily coming together in respect of ideational (or representative, or mediating, or cognitive) processes; I believe that the same thing can happen, and is happening, in the field of motivation.

REFERENCES

1. Beach, F. A., "The Neutral Basis at Innate Behavior. III. Comparison of Learning Ability and Instinctive Behavior in the Rat," *Journal of Comparative Physiological Psychology,* **28** (1939), 225-62.

2. Bergmann, G., "Theoretical Psychology," *Annual Review of Psychology,* **4** (1953), 435-58.

3. Berkun, M. M., Marion L. Kessen, and N. E. Miller, "Hunger-Reducing Effects of Food by Stomach Fistula Versus Food by Mouth Measured by a Consummatory Response," *Journal of Comparative Physiological Psychology,* **45** (1952), 550-54.

4. Berlyne, D. E., "Novelty and Curiosity as Determinants of Exploratory Behavior," *British Journal of Psychology,* **41** (1950), 68-80.

5. Bexton, W. H., W. Heron, and T. H. Scott, "Effects of Decreased Variation in the Sensory Environment," *Canadian Journal of Psychology,* **8** (1954), 70-76.

6. Brink, F., "Excitation and Conduction in the Neuron," in *Handbook of Experimental Psychology,* ed. S. S. Stevens, pp. 50-93. New York: John Wiley & Sons, Inc., 1951.

7. Brown, J. S., "Problems Presented by the Concept of Acquired Drives," in *Current Theory and Research in Motivation: A Symposium,* pp. 1-21. Lincoln: University of Nebraska Press, 1953.

8. —— and A. Jacobs, "The Role of Fear in the Motivation and Acquisition of Responses," *Journal of Experimental Psychology,* **39** (1949) 747-59.

9. Burns, B. D., "The Mechanism of Afterbursts in Cerebral Cortex," *Journal of Physiology,* **127** (1955), 168-88.

10. Butler, R. A., "Discrimination Learning by Rhesus Monkeys to Visual-Exploration Motivation, *Journal of Comparative Physiological Psychology,* **46** (1953), 95-98.

11. Carper, J. W. and F. A. Polliard, "Comparison of the Intake of Glucose and Saccharin Solutions under Condi-

tions of Caloric Need," *American Journal of Psychology,* **66** (1953), 479-82.

12. Clare, M. H. and G. H. Bishop, "Properties of Dendrites; Apical Dendrites of the Cat Cortex," *EEG Clinical Neurophysiology,* **7** (1955), 85-98.

13. Duffy, Elizabeth, "An Explanation of the 'Emotional' Phenomena without the Use of the Concept 'Emotion,'" *Journal of Genetic Psychology,* **25** (1941), 283-93.

14. Eccles, J. C., *The Neurophysiological Basis of Mind.* London: Oxford University Press, 1953.

15. Ghent, Lila, "The Relation of Experience to the Development of Hunger," *Canadian Journal of Psychology,* **5** (1951), 77-81.

16. Harlow, H. F., "Mice, Monkeys, Men, and Motives," *Psychological Review,* **60** (1953), 23-32.

17. ———, Margaret K. Harlow, and D. R. Meyer, "Learning Motivated by a Manipulation Drive," *Journal of Experimental Psychology,* **40** (1950), 228-34.

18. Hebb, D. O., "Elementary School Methods," *Teachers' Magazine* (Montreal), **12** (1930), 23-26.

19. ———, *Organization of Behavior.* New York: John Wiley & Sons, Inc., 1949.

20. ———, "On Human Thought," *Canadian Journal of Psychology,* **7** (1953), 99-110.

21. ——— and A. H. Riesen, "The Genesis of Irrational Fears," *Bulletin of the Canadian Psychological Association,* **3** (1943), 49-50.

22. ——— and W. R. Thompson, "The Social Significance of Animal Studies," in *Handbook of Social Psychology,* ed. G. Lindzey, pp. 532-61. Cambridge, Mass.: Addison-Wesley, 1954.

23. Li, Choh-Luh and H. Jasper, "Microelectrode Studies of the Cerebral Cortex in the Cat," *Journal of Physiology,* **121** (1953), 117-40.

24. Lindsley, D. B., "Emotion," in *Handbook of Experimental Psychology,* ed. S. S. Stevens, pp. 473-516. New York: John S. Wiley & Sons, Inc., 1951.

25. Lloyd, D. P. C., "A Direct Central Inhibitory Action of Dromically Conducted Impulses," *Journal of Neurophysiology,* **4** (1941), 184-90.

26. MacCorquodale, K. and P. E. Meehl, "A Distinction Between Hypothetical Constructs and Intervening Variables," *Psychological Review,* **55** (1948), 95-107.

27. Marshall, S. L. A., *Men Against Fire.* New York: William Morrow & Co., Inc., 1947.

28. Melzack, R., "The Effects of Early Experience on the Emotional Responses to Pain." Unpublished doctoral dissertation, McGill University, 1954.

29. Miller, N. E., "Learnable Drives and Rewards," in *Handbook of Experimental Psychology,* ed. S. S. Stevens, pp. 435-72. New York: John S. Wiley & Sons, Inc., 1951.

30. Miller, N. E., "Some Studies of Drive and Drive Reduction," a paper read at the American Psychological Association, Cleveland, September, 1953.

31. ———, C. J. Bailey, and J. A. F. Stevenson, "Decreased 'Hunger' but Increased Food Intake from Hypothalamic Lesions," *Science,* **112** (1950), 256-59.

32. ——— and Marion L. Kessen, "Reward Effects of Food via Stomach Fistula Compared with Those via Mouth," *Journal of Comparative Physiological Psychology,* **45** (1952), 555-64.

33. Montgomery, K. C., "The Effect of Activity Deprivation upon Exploratory Behavior," *Journal of Comparative Physiological Psychology,* **46** (1953), 438-41.

34. Moruzzi, G. and H. W. Magoun, "Brain Stem Reticular Formation and Activation of the EEG," *EEG Clinical Neurophysiology,* **1** (1949), 455-73.

35. Mowrer, O. H., "Motivation," *Annual Review of Psychology,* **3** (1952), 419-38.

36. Nissen, H. W., "Instinct as Seen by a Psychologist," *Psychological Review,* **60** (1953), 291-94.

37. Olds, J. and P. Milner, "Positive Reinforcement Produced by Electrical

Stimulation of Septal Area and Other Regions of Rat Brain," *Journal of Comparative Physiological Psychology,* **47** (1954), 419-27.

38. Olzewski, J., "The Cytoarchitecture of the Human Reticular Formation," in *Brain Mechanisms and Consciousness,* eds. E. D. Adrian, F. Bremer, and H. H. Jasper. Oxford: Blackwell, 1954.

39. Schlosberg, H., "Three Dimensions of Emotion," *Psychological Review,* **61** (1954), 81-88.

40. Sharpless, S. K., "Role of the Reticular Formation in Habituation." Unpublished doctoral dissertation, McGill University, 1954.

41. Sheffield, F. D., and B. A. Campbell, "The Role of Experience in the 'Spontaneous' Activity of Hungry Rats," *Journal of Comparative Physiological Psychology,* **47** (1954), 97-100.

42. ——— and T. B. Roby, "Reward Value of a Non-Nutritive Sweet Taste," *Journal of Comparative Physiological Psychology,* **43** (1950), 471-81.

43. ———, J. J. Wulff, and R. Backer, "Reward Value of Copulation without Sex Drive Reduction," *Journal of Comparative Physiological Psychology,* **44** (1951), 3-8.

44. Solomon, R. L. and L. C. Wynne, "Avoidance Conditioning in Normal Dogs and in Dogs Deprived of Normal Autonomic Functioning," *American Psychologist,* **5** (1950), 264 (abstract).

45. Stellar, E., "The Physiology of Motivation," *Psychological Review,* **61** (1954), 5-22.

46. Thompson, W. R. and L. M. Solomon, "Spontaneous Pattern Discrimination in the Rat," *Journal of Comparative Physiological Psychology,* **47** (1954), 104-7.

47. Tyhurst, J. S., "Individual Reactions to Community Disaster: the Natural History of Psychiatric Phenomena," *American Journal of Psychiatry,* **107** (1951), 764-69.

48. Valentine, C. W., "The Innate Bases of Fear," *Journal of Genetic Psychology,* **37** (1930), 394-419.

49. Whiting, J. W. M. and O. H. Mowrer, "Habit Progression and Regression—a Laboratory Study of Some Factors Relevant to Human Socialization," *Journal of Comparative Psychology,* **36** (1943), 229-53.

50. Woodworth, R. S., *Psychology.* New York: Holt, Rinehart & Winston, Inc., 1921.

51. ——— and D. G. Marquis, *Psychology* (5th ed.). New York, Holt, Rinehart & Winston, Inc., 1947.

Activation: A Neuropsychological Dimension *

Robert B. Malmo

There have been three main lines of approach to the problem of activation: (*a*) through electroencephalography and neurophysiology, (*b*) through physiological studies of "behavioral energetics," and (*c*) through the learning theorists' search for a satisfactory measure of drive. Before attempting a formal definition of acivation, I shall briefly describe these three different approaches to the concept.

* From R. B. Malmo, "Activation: A Neuropsychological Dimension," *Psychological Review,* **66** (1959), 367-86. Reprinted by permission of the author and the American Psychological Association.

Support for some of the research reported herein has come from the following sources: National Institute of Mental Health, National Institutes of Health, United States Public Health Service: Grant Number M-1475; Medical Research and Development Division, Office of the Surgeon General, Department of the United States Army: Contract Number DA-49-007-MD-626; Defense Research Board, Department of National Defense, Canada: Grant Number 9425-04; and National Research Council of Canada: Grant Number A. P. 29.

Grateful acknowledgment is made to A. Amsel, R. C. Davis, S. M. Feldman, P. Milner, M. M. Schnore, R. G. Stennett, D. J. Ehrlich and L. R. Pinneo for constructive criticism of the manuscript.

The main parts of this paper were presented in a Symposium entitled, "Experimental Foundations of Clinical Psychology," under the chairmanship of Arthur J. Bachrach, at the University of Virginia, April 1-2, 1959. To Ian P. Stevenson, who was the discussant of my paper on that Symposium, I owe a debt of gratitude for his very helpful comments.

Neurophysiological Approach: Lindsley's Activation Theory [1]

The neurophysiological approach to activation had its origin in electroencephalography (EEG). Early workers in the EEG field soon discovered that there were distinctive wave patterns characterizing the main levels of phychological functioning in the progression from deep sleep to highly alerted states of activity (Jasper, 1941). In deep sleep large low-frequency waves predominate. In light sleep and drowsy states the frequencies are not as low as in deep sleep, but there are more low-frequency waves than in the wakeful states. In relaxed wakefulness there is a predominance of waves in the alpha (8–12 c.p.s.) range that gives way to beta frequencies

[1] I am using neuropsychology in a rather broad sense, meaning to include the work often referred to by the term "psychophysiology." This usage implies that the chief problems being studied are psychological ones, and it also stresses the importance of neurophysiological techniques. It is true that, strictly speaking, many of the physiological techniques in use are not neurophysiological ones; yet our main interest lies in the central neural control of the physiological functions under study rather than in the peripheral events themselves.

Later on in the paper I shall attempt a formal definition of activation. For the first section of the paper, I believe that it will be sufficient to say that in using the term *activation* I am referring to the intensive dimension of behavior. *Arousal* is often used interchangeably with activation; and level of drive is a very similar concept. For instance, a drowsy *S* is low, an alert *S* is high in activation.

(approximately 18–30 c.p.s.) when the S is moderately alert. Under highly alerting and exciting conditions beta waves predominate. In addition to the increased frequency of the waves under these conditions of heightened alertness there is also a change from a regular synchronized appearance of the tracing to an irregular desynchronized tracing, usually of reduced amplitude.

For Lindsley's theory, desynchronization (called "activation pattern") became the single most important EEG phenomenon. My use of the term *desynchronization* is purely descriptive. Desynchronization or "flattening" in the EEG tracing was consistently found associated with increased alertness in a large variety of experiments with animal and human Ss. The consistency and generality of this phenomenon suggested the existence of mechanisms in the brain mediating behavioral functions having to do with levels of alertness, although at the time that the original observations were made it was not at all clear what these neural mechanisms were.

With the discovery of the ascending reticular activating system (ARAS), however, there was rapid and very significant advance in theory and experimentation. Some of the most important general findings have been as follows: (a) Lesions in the ARAS abolished "activation" of the EEG and produced a behavioral picture of lethargy and somnolence (Lindsley, 1957). (b) The "activation pattern" in the EEG was reproduced by electrical stimulation of the ARAS. Furthermore, in the monkey, Fuster (1958) recently found that concurrent ARAS stimulation of moderate intensity improved accuracy and speed of visual discrimination reaction. He also found that higher intensities had the opposite effect, producing diminution of correct responses and increase of

reaction times. Interpretation of these latter findings is complicated by the fact that they were obtained with stimulation intensities higher than the threshold for the elicitation of observable motor effects such as generalized muscular jerks. It is not stated whether intensity of stimulation was systematically studied. In any event, these observations of deleterious effect from high intensity stimulation are of considerable interest because they are what might be expected according to the activation theory.

The activation theory as first stated by Lindsley (1951)—although introduced in the handbook chapter on emotion—was, from the outset, conceived by him to be broader than an explanatory concept for emotional behavior. The theory was elaborated by Hebb (1955) in an attempt to solve the problem of drives. With the continuous flow of new experimental data on the ARAS (Lindsley, 1957), this area of neuropsychological investigation appears to be heading toward an important breakthrough. I shall attempt to state very briefly the main points of the current theory, drawing upon the ideas of several authors. According to this theory, the continuum extending from deep sleep at the low activation end to "excited states" [2] at the high activation end is very largely a function of cortical bombardment by the ARAS, such that the greater the cortical bombardment the higher the activation. Further, the relation between activation and behavioral efficiency (cue function or level of performance) is described by an inverted

[2] The expression "excited states" is frequently used to refer to the upper end of the activation continuum. In using this term I do not wish to imply increased overt activity. In fact, overt activity may be reduced to a very low level at the high end of the continuum, when—for example—a person is immobilized by terror.

U curve. That is, from low activation up to a point that is optimal for a given function, level of performance rises monotonically with increasing activation level, but beyond this optimal point the relation becomes nonmonotonic: further increase in activation beyond this point produces a fall in performance level, this fall being directly related to the amount of the increase in level of activation.

Principles of neural action that could account for the reversal in the effects of nonspecific neural bombardment of the cortex by the ARAS have long been known (Lorente de Nó, 1939, p. 428). Circulation of neural impulses in a closed chain of neurons (or "cell assembly" to use Hebb's [1949] term) may be facilitated by impulses arriving outside the chain (e.g. from the ARAS). According to Lorente de Nó's schema, such extraneous impulses have the effect of stimulating certain neurons subliminally thus making it possible for an impulse from within the chain to finish the job, that is make it fire at the appropriate time in the sequence, when alone, without the prior hit, it would have failed to fire it.

Again, according to the same account by Lorente de Nó (1939, p. 428), the deleterious effects of overstimulation from impulses outside the chain can be explained. A neuron in the chain may fail to respond to stimulation if owing to repeated activity it acquires a high threshold, and this failure to transmit the circulating impulses would mean cessation of activity in a cell assembly. I proposed this kind of explanation previously (1958) to account for the downturn in the inverted U curve as an alternative to Hebb's suggestion that "the greater bombardment may interfere with the delicate adjustments involved in cue function, perhaps by facilitating irrelevant responses (a high D arouses conflicting $_sH_R$'s?)" (Hebb, 1955, p. 250).

It seems reasonable to suppose that as diffuse bombardment from the ARAS greatly exceeds an amount that is optimal for some simple psychological function being mediated by a particular cell assembly, the operation of that cell assembly will be impaired, and that the performance being mediated by it will suffer accordingly. This line of reasoning suggests that the inverted U relation should be found in quite simple psychological functions. Present evidence appears to support this suggestion. A recent (unpublished) experiment by Bélanger and Feldman, that I shall describe later in this paper, indicates that in rats the inverted U relation is found with simple bar pressing performance, and an experiment by Finch (1938) suggests that even such a simple response as the unconditioned salivary response yields the inverted U curve when plotted against activation level.

It may be noted that according to a response competition hypothesis, the inverted U relation should appear most prominently in complex functions where opportunities for habit interference are greater than they are in the case of simple functions. According to the response competition hypothesis, in the limiting case where response is so simple that habit interference is negligible, the relation between response strength and activation level should be monotonic. Therefore, finding the nonmonotonic relation in such simple responses as bar pressing and salivation raises strong doubts that the habit interference explanation can account for the seemingly pervasive phenomenon of the inverted U curve.

Principle of Activation Growing Out of Work on Behavioral Intensity

Even before the EEG work on

desynchronization, the behavioral evidence had suggested the existence of some brain mechanism like the ARAS. The writings of Duffy (1951, 1957), Freeman (1948), and others of the "energetics" group have long stressed the importance of an intensity dimension in behavior.

In an attempt to obtain a measure of this intensity variable, Duffy relied mainly on records of muscular tension (1932) while Freeman's favorite indicator was palmar conductance (1948). These workers concluded from their experiments that there was a lawful relationship between a state of the organism, called "arousal," "energy mobilization," "activation," or simply "intensity," and level of performance. Moreover, they suggested that the relationship might be described by an inverted U curve (Duffy, 1957). This suggestion has proved heuristic as indicated by the current experimental attack on the inverted U hypothesis (Stennett, 1957a; Bindra, 1959; Cofer, 1959; Kendler, 1959).

The inverted U-shaped curve has been shown to hold in numerous learning and performance situations where the amount of induced muscle tension was varied systematically (Courts, 1942). It is tempting to conclude that tension induction is simply one of the many ways to increase activation level, but, as Courts' (1942) discussion suggests, this conclusion would be premature. It is possible that squeezing on a dynamometer, a typical means of inducing tension in these experiments, may produce generalized activation effects as some data from Freeman indicate (1948, p. 71). But Freeman's data are insufficient to establish this point, and there are alternative explanations for the relationship between the performance data and induced tension (Courts, 1942). By repeating the induced-tension experiments with

simultaneous recordings of EEG and other physiological functions it would be possible to determine how general the effects of inducing tension actually are. Such direct tests of the activation hypothesis are very much needed.

Drive and Activation

A third approach to the activation principle was made by learning theorists, especially those of the Hull school. I have argued elsewhere (Malmo, 1958) that general drive (D), without the steering component, became identical in principle with activation or arousal. Set aside for the moment the attractive possibility of using ARAS as a neural model for mediation of D, and consider only the methodological advantages of physiological measures in the quantification of D. It seems that none of the other attempts to measure D has been really satisfactory, and that physiological indicants where applied have been surprisingly effective. Learning theorists up to the present time have made only very occasional use of physiological measures. For instance, in arguing that a previously painful stimulus had lost its drive properties, Brown (1955) cited the absence of physiological reaction when the stimulus was applied. More recently, Spence (1958) has reported some success with physiological measures in his studies of "emotionally-based" drive.

In keeping with traditional views concerning the place of physiological measures in psychology, on those few occasions that they were employed at all they were applied to aversive or emotionally based drive. According to the activation principle, however, it should be possible to use physiological measures to gauge appetitionally based as well as aversively based drive. This means, for instance, that in a water deprivation experiment there should be close correspondence between number of hours of deprivation and physiological level. That is, heart rate, for example, should be higher in an animal performing in a Skinner box after 36 hours of deprivation than after 24, higher still after 48 hours of deprivation and so on. In my Nebraska Symposium paper I stated that, as far as I was aware, this kind of experiment had not been reported (Malmo 1958, p. 236).

Bélanger and Feldman in Montreal have recently completed such an experiment, and, as can be seen by inspecting Fig. 1, the results were as

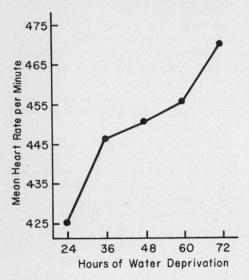

FIG. 1. *Data from Bélanger and Feldman showing relation between water deprivation and heart rate in rats* (N = 7).

predicted by the activation hypothesis. Heart rate in rats showed progressive change corresponding with increasing hours of water deprivation. Although there were only seven rats in the group, this change in heart rate was highly significant. Deprivations were carried out serially on the same group of animals, commencing at 12 hours and

proceeding to 24, 48 hours and so on with sufficient hydration (four to seven days) between deprivation periods to prevent any cumulative effects from affecting the experiments. Heart rate was picked up by means of wire electrodes inserted in the skin of the animals and was amplified and registered graphically by means of a Sanborn electrocardiograph. Particular

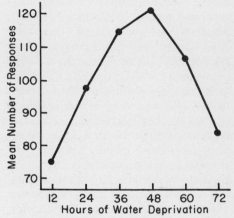

FIG. 2. *Data from Bélanger and Feldman showing relation between water deprivation and Skinner box performance in rats* (N = 7).

care was taken to record heart rate under nearly the same conditions of stimulation each time, that is, when the animal was pressing on the lever in the Skinner box or during drinking from the dispenser immediately after pressing. Under these conditions it was not possible to obtain sufficient heart-rate data at the 12-hour deprivation interval. Testing the animal under constant stimulating conditions is a very important methodological consideration. Some exploratory observations indicated that heart-rate measurements taken in a restraining compartment did not agree with those taken under the carefully controlled stimulus conditions provided by the Skinner box. I shall return to this finding later on because, aside from its methodological importance, I believe that it has considerable theoretical significance as well.

Figure 2 presents the behavioral data which are again in remarkably good agreement with prediction from the activation hypothesis. Up to the 48-hour deprivation interval there is an increasing monotonic relationship between number of bar presses and hours of deprivation, which is strictly in accordance with Hullian theory. The accompanying rise in heart rate suggests that for this part of the curve, hours of deprivation and the physiological indicant are roughly equivalent as measures of drive. But after the 48-hour point on the curves, the combined heart rate and behavioral data support predictions previously made from activation theory (Malmo, 1958) and suggest that the Hullian position requires revision. This kind of downward turn in the response curve has usually been attributed to a physical weakening of the animal due to the deprivation of food or water. In the absence of physiological data such an assumption appeared reasonable in many cases, although it did not account for response decrement in certain experiments where physical weakening seemed to be ruled out (Finan, 1940; Freeman, 1940; Fuster, 1958; Kaplan, 1952; Stennett, 1957a). Attack on this problem with physiological methods should soon provide a definitive answer concerning the main determinants of this response decrement. The present experiment respresents an important first step in a program of animal studies that should go a long way towards solving this problem. It is not claimed that this one experiment demolishes the inanition hypothesis, but it does seem that the results are opposed to it. Heart rate in the Minnesota starvation experiments was found lowered in the weakened individuals (Malmo, 1958, p. 252), whereas heart rate in the present experiment was markedly increased during the period when number of responses was declining. Moreover, Bélanger was careful to record the weights of the animals all through the experiments, and he observed only very slight changes in weight, even at the 72-hour deprivation interval. Again, it should be stressed that all through the experiment the animals received four to seven days of hydration between conditions. Furthermore, it is interesting to note that the animals continued to press the bar at fairly regular intervals in the high-deprivation conditions (with response decrement). That is, their behavior did not appear as though they had "given up." The acts of pressing continued to occur regularly, only they were separated by longer temporal intervals than under more optimal conditions of deprivation.

The increasing monotonic curve for heart rate did not seem to be simply due to the physical conditions of exertion associated with the act of bar pressing. It is true that up to the peak of the performance curve increasing heart rate was accompanied by increasing frequency of bar pressing, but past this point, heart rate continued to show rise despite the decline in exertion due to bar pressing. One might conjecture that exercise may have had greater effect on heart rate under extreme deprivation, but this would be counterbalanced—to some extent, at least—by the reduced number of presses.

To control for possible serial effects in this experiment there were two checks. First, he obtained similar findings from a second group of rats in

which the order of deprivation conditions was reversed, commencing
with the 72-hour deprivation condition, and finishing with the 12-hour
condition. Second, the group of rats
that had the ascending order of deprivation intervals were tested one
week after the end of the experiment
under the 60-hour deprivation condition. Mean number of responses was
96.7 and mean heart rate was 458.9
beats per minute, thus providing good
agreement with the results that were
obtained in the main experiment.

Finally, it is possible to speculate
along various lines about how the
heart-rate data could be accounted
for without involving the concept of
activation. Obviously, further experimentation is needed, but it is encouraging nonetheless that the first animal
experimentation specifically designed
to explore the relation between appetitional drive and activation turned out
according to prediction.

CHARACTERISTICS
OF ACTIVATION

The three approaches described in
the previous section appear to lead to
the same fundamental concept of activation. It will, of course, be difficult
to state a precise definition of activation that will satisfy everyone.
Neurophysiologically oriented workers
will maintain a healthy skepticism
concerning the so-called "peripheral"
indicants of activation. The "energetics" group, while welcoming the extended use of what is essentially their
own methodology, will in company
with some learning theorists look ask-
ance at theoretical models that verge
on neurologizing. Despite differences
in point of view, however, it seems
worthwhile to attempt to deal with
certain major characteristics of acti-

vation on which we may expect a large
measure of agreement.

Activation Level a Product of
Multiple Factors

When a man is deprived of sleep
for some 60 hours his activation level
appears higher than it was before he
had suffered sleep loss. Physiological
indicants reveal an upward shift in
activation level that is gradual and
progressive throughout the vigil
(Malmo, 1958). Having once demonstrated these physiological changes it
is tempting to dispense with physiological recording in further work, assuming that 60 hours of deprivation
will invariably produce a heightened
state of activation. Such an assumption, however, cannot be made. An example will make clear why this
assumption is untenable. A sleep-deprived S requires constant stimulation
to prevent him from going to sleep. It
is a general finding in such studies
that despite the best intentions of the
S to remain awake he will "catnap"
if left alone. When he is working at a
task trying to keep his efficiency from
falling, the effect of major sleep loss
is to produce a large increase in activation level. The important point to
see here, however, is that the higher
activation level is a combined product
of the stimuli and their demands on
him plus the condition of sleep loss.
Without such stimulation, the S would
surely fall asleep, and we know from
our studies of sleep that physiological
levels drop very rapidly as one drifts
into sleep. It is obvious, therefore,
that in the absence of the task, physiological indicants at 60 hours' deprivation would show lower, not higher,
activation in comparsion with the
rested condition.

That the "drive state" is in large
part determined by environmental
stimulating factors is indicated also by

the observations of Bélanger and Feldman in their water-deprivation experiments. Incidental observations suggested that, in addition to being more variable, heart rates recorded from the animal in a restraining compartment seemed to be consistently lower than those that were recorded when the animal was pressing the lever or drinking. In the restraining compartment the animal could view the lever through glass so that apparently mere sight of the lever was insufficient stimulation to produce the full effect upon heart rate that was produced by the acts of pressing on the lever and drinking. It thus appeared that, with deprivation time approximately the same, activation level differed appreciably depending upon the conditions of external stimulation. These observations were merely incidental ones in this experiment, and they should be repeated; but they encourage the point of view that activation level is in large part a function of environmental stimulating conditions. The experiments of Campbell and Sheffield (1953) seem to point in the same direction. In the absence of sufficient environmental stimulation, food-deprived rats are no more active than satiated ones, but with stimulation they are much more active than the satiated controls.

Returning to the example of the water-deprived rat in the Skinner box, the two major factors determining the level of activation in that situation are (*a*) the internal conditions produced by deprivation and (*b*) the environmental stimulating conditions. To restate a point previously made, level of activation does not seem to be simply determined by the condition of deprivation alone. This would mean that depriving an animal of water per se could not produce some direct effect on motor mechanisms such as a simple discharge into the cardiac accelerating

mechanism, leading to increased heart rate. Instead of some direct effect of this kind leading immediately over to some observable effector action, deprivation appears to have a sensitizing effect that is undetectable (or latent). According to this view, when appropriate stimulation does occur, the previously latent effect of deprivation will show itself in the heart rate: within limits, the longer the period of deprivation the higher the heart rate. Furthermore, according to activation theory, the same central mechanism that increases heart rate also acts to increase bombardment of the cerebral cortex. As previously stated, this central mechanism is presumed to be the ARAS.[3]

What could be the means of sensitizing cells in the ARAS by a condition such as deprivation of water or food? If some hormone like epinephrine were released by deprivation, it is conceivable that this hormone could act to sensitize the ARAS cells in degree proportional to the amount of time that the animal had been deprived. As a matter of fact, hormonal sensitization of neural mechanisms is a currently active area of research (Saffran, Schally, and Benfey, 1955; Dell, 1958).

There are some real difficulties in defending the position that the ARAS is a unitary intensity-mediating mechanism, because the ARAS does not appear to be a homogeneous anatomical system. Indeed, as Olszewski (1954) has shown, these central brain stem structures appear very complex and highly differentiated. This unreassuring fact must not be forgotten,

---

[3] It is very likely that the descending reticular activating system is involved here too, but, at the present stage of knowledge in this field, it does not seem wise to introduce further complications into the neuropsychological model.

but neither should it be accepted as precluding the unitary function. As Lashley points out in the discussion of Olszewski's paper, structural differences are not reliable indices of function when unsupported by other evidence.

As a matter of fact, there is some important functional evidence which encourages the unitary view despite the structural complexity of the ARAS. Dell (1958) has found that: "Epinephrine does not activate selectively mammillothalamocingular systems . . . but instead activates the ascending reticular system *en masse*, thus leading to a generalized cortical arousal" (p. 370). Control experiments showed that the activation effect was due to a direct action of the epinephrine at the reticular level and not to an effect on the cerebral cortex. Similar results have been obtained by Rothballer (1956).

Another kind of difficulty for the quantitative view would be posed by showing that patterned discharge from the ARAS to the cortex (not merely total quantity of discharge) was the crucial factor in supporting some behavioral action. Don't the effector patterns of standing, walking, and righting pose just such a difficulty? The relation of midbrain mechanisms to posture seems to be clearly one in which patterns of discharge from the midbrain are important. But the decorticate mammal (guinea pig, rabbit, cat, dog) in which the cortex of both hemispheres has been removed shows approximately normal postural and progressional activities (Dusser de Barenne, 1934, p. 229). Since the activation concept under review deals with bombardment of the cerebral cortex, it appears that these noncortically mediated response patterns fall outside of phenomena under present consideration.

I should add, finally, that my admittedly speculative suggestion concerning hormonal sensitization is by no means essential to the main point which is that the behavioral evidence clearly shows the effects of deprivation to be latent (that is, unobservable) under certain conditions. Moreover, this stress placed on the latent effects of deprivation is not mere hairsplitting. In addition to being required for an explanation of the Montreal experiments, this concept of latent deprivation effects appears to account in large measure for the findings of Campbell and Sheffield (1953), and more generally for the failure of random activity to adequately serve as a measure of drive or activation (Malmo, 1958).

Activation and the S-R Framework

As the product of interaction between internal (perhaps hormonal) conditions and external stimulating ones, activation cannot be very reasonably classified as either stimulus or response. This means that the physiological measurements that are used to gauge level of activation do not fit very well into the S-R formula. It is perhaps useful to think of these physiological conditions as part of O in the S-O-R formula (Woodworth and Schlosberg, 1954, p. 2).

The momentary physiological reaction to a discrete stimulus like the sudden rise in palmar conductance accompanying pinprick is not of primary concern to us in our study of activation. This kind of S-R reaction, important as it undoubtedly is for investigating other problems, is of little relevance for the study of activation, compared with the longer-lasting changes. As Schlosberg has put it to me in personal communication, in employing skin conductance to gauge level of activation, one observes the "tides" and not the "ripples." I do not mean to disparage studies that use physiological reactions as R terms in the strict S-R sense. It is just that in this paper I am concerned with physiological functions only insofar as they are related to activation.

It may be queried whether we are dealing with a needless and hair-splitting distinction by saying that activation is not a response. However, the kind of difference I have in mind appears quite distinct and useful to keep in mind, though it should not be stressed unduly. Basically, it is the same distinction which Woodworth and Schlosberg (1956) make when they draw particular attention to the difference between slow and rapid changes in skin conductance. As examples of rapid changes in skin conductance, there are the "GSRs" as R terms in conditioned responses, and in free association tests. Examples of slow skin-conductance changes, on the other hand, are the gradual downward drifts that occur over hours during sleep (see Fig. 4, page 46), the slow downward changes in skin conductance in Ss as they become gradually habituated to an experimental situation (Davis, 1934; Duffy and Lacey, 1946), and (going up the activation scale) the progressive upward changes in conductance during a vigil (Malmo, 1958).

I would not deny that there are stimuli and responses going on in the physiological systems, but at the present time I see no way of identifying and handling them. It should be added, however, that this does not give one license to completely disregard the antecedents of physiological changes. For instance, if the hand of a sleeping S becomes hot by being covered with heavy bedclothing, the local thermal sweating induced thereby will bring about a sudden rise in palmar conductance which has nothing to do with activation. Or sleep may be induced by certain drugs which have a specific stimulating effect on respiration, such that respiration rate will not fall during sleep as it usually does (see Fig. 5 for curve obtained under nondrug conditions). Furthermore, artifacts due to movement and postural shifts may prevent muscle potentials from serving as reliable indicants of activation level.

Limitations of the Activation Concept

I am not attempting to solve the problem of selection, that is, the problem of finding the neurophysiological mechanisms that determine which cues in the animal's environment are prepotent in the sense of winning out over other cues in triggering off a pattern of effector action. This point seems clear enough, especially when it is stressed that activation has no steering function; and yet there is still the risk that some critics may misunderstand and state as one shortcoming of this theory that it does not adequately handle the problem of selection. The theory may be open to criticism on the grounds that it is limited, but it should not be criticized for failing to do something which it was not intended to do.

It will be noted that in general an attempt is made to raise theoretical questions that stand a good chance of being answered by available experimental techniques. Schematically, the experimental paradigm is as follows:

Activation
    level   : Low Moderate High
Expected perform-
    ance level : Low Optimal Low

It is important to stress that the measure denoted by "moderate activation level" has meaning only in relative (not in absolute) terms. That is, the level is "moderate" because it is higher than that of the low-activation condition, and lower than the level of the high-activation condition. Comparisons are invariably of the within-individual, within-task kind, which means that the level of activation which is found to be optimal for one task is not directly compared with the level of activation which is found to be optimal for a different task. Thus, at the present stage of theorizing, no attempt is made to deal with the question of whether tasks which differ in complexity, for example, also differ with respect to the precise level of activation which is optimal for each one. However, I have dealt elsewhere (Malmo, 1958) with the related question of response competition, suggesting an alternative to the response competition explanation for decrement in performance with increased activation (or D).

Again, the theoretical formulations may be criticized for being too narrow. But it must be kept in mind that their narrowness is due to the close nexus between theory and experiment in this program. These formulations may also be criticized for an unjustifiable assumption in the postulation of a communal drive mechanism. One may well ask where the evidence is that proves the existence of a state of general drive. In dealing with this kind of question, it is essential to refer back to the outline of the experimental paradigm. The experimental induction of the three discriminable activation levels referred to in the outline depends upon the controlled variation of certain conditions in the S's environment. The fact that by varying conditions as dissimilar as appetitional deprivations and verbal incentives it is possible to produce similar shifts in physiological indicants provides a sound basis for introducing the operationally defined concept of activation level that cuts across traditional demarcation lines of specific drives. All

this, of course, does not constitute final proof for a communal drive mechanism. Certainly further data are required before it is even safe to conclude equivalence of drive conditions in the alteration of physiological levels, to say nothing of proving the existence of a communal drive mechanism.

INTERRELATIONS BETWEEN PHYSIOLOGICAL INDICANTS OF ACTIVATION

Criticism directed against physiological measures as indicants of activation usually involves one or both of the following points. The first objection is that intercorrelations between physiological measures are so low that it is unreasonable to consider their use for gauging a single dimension of behavior. A second objection is that activation properly refers to events in the brain and that the correspondence between these central events and what may be observed in such peripheral functions as heart rate, respiration, muscle tension and the like is not close enough to permit valid inferences from the peripheral events to the central ones. In the following section, I shall attempt to answer these criticisms.

Intra- and Interindividual Correlations among Physiological Indicants of Activation

In an unpublished paper, Schnore and I have discussed certain misconceptions that have confused some critics of physiological methods. The most serious misunderstanding concerns correlations among physiological measures. It is true that *inter*individual correlations are low, but this fact is actually irrelevant insofar as using these measures to gauge activation is concerned. The important question is whether significant *intra*-individual correlations are found in a sufficiently high proportion of individuals, and the answer appears to be yes (Schnore, 1959).

What the low *inter*individual correlations mean, of course, is that an individual in any given situation may have a heart rate that is high relative to the mean heart rate for the group, and at the same time have a respiration rate or a blood pressure that is low relative to the group mean. These findings are in line with the principle of physiological specificity that is now supported by several lines of evidence.[4] Physiological specificity is a separate problem that is in no way crucial for the activation hypothesis. An illustration will make this clear. Take a rather extreme example of an individual with very *high* heart rate (say 95 when the mean for his group under specified conditions is 75) and very *low* palmar conductance (50 micromhos when the group mean is 100). In an experiment with varied incentive, in going from a low-incentive to a high-incentive condition this *S* will likely show an increase in heart rate from 95 to say 110 and an increase in palmar conductance from 50 to say 60 micromhos. The main point is that even though the *S*'s heart rate is already high compared with the mean for his group, it goes still higher (concordantly with palmar conductance) when the stimulating situation increases the level of activation. This is the kind of intra-individual correlation between phys-

iological measures [5] that is required for gauging the dimension of activation and, to repeat, the evidence strongly indicates that the intra-individual correlations are sufficiently high for this purpose.

RELATIONS BETWEEN CENTRAL AND PERIPHERAL INDICANTS OF ACTIVATION

As previously noted, the pioneer EEG workers observed definite changes in EEG pattern accompanying major shifts in the conscious state of the *S*. Moreover, they recognized a continuum of increasing activation usually referred to as the sleep-waking-excitement continuum, just as other workers (like Freeman [1948] and Duffy [1957]) employing peripheral measures of palmar sweating and muscular tension recognized it. Among the early workers in this field, Darrow (1947) studied EEG and other measures simultaneously, but only very recently have techniques been made available that can provide the kind of quantitative EEG measurements required for critical comparisons along the activation continuum. That is, from simple inspection of the raw EEG tracing it is possible to see gross differences between sleeping and waking, or between a drowsy, relaxed state and one of extreme alertness. But for experiments on activation it is necessary to have an instrument that will reveal measurable differences for "points" lying closer to each other on the activation continuum. For example, it is

---

[4] The general principle of physiological specificity states that under significantly different conditions of stimulation individuals exhibit idiosyncratic but highly stereotyped patterns of autonomic and somatic activation. I use the term *physiological specificity* as a generic reference to autonomic-response stereotypy (Lacey and Lacey, 1958) to symptom specificity (Malmo and Shagass, 1949), and to stereotypy of somatic and autonomic activation patterns (Schnore, 1959).

[5] It is not claimed, however, that all physiological measures are equally useful for the purpose of gauging activation level. On the contrary, as Schnore's experiments have suggested, some measures appear superior to others, and eventually we may be able to select the most discriminating ones and thus improve our measurement (Schnore, 1959).

essential to have a measure that will discriminate reliably between a moderately alert and a highly alert state. For such discriminations the method of inspection will not do, and a device for objective quantification of the wave forms is required.

Because of its complexity the EEG tracing has been difficult to quantify, and although gross differences in activation level could be detected by simple inspection of the tracing, this method was too crude for more detailed work. However, with the advent of EEG frequency analyzers, quantification of the EEG looked promising because these analyzers were designed to provide quantified EEG data for each of many different narrow frequency bands. Unfortunately, these instruments have not proved useful because of insufficient stability. In our laboratory we have been trying band-pass filters to provide stable quantification of various selected frequency bands in which we are primarily interested (Ross and Davis, 1958). Results thus far appear highly encouraging.

Data Indicating Relationships between EEG and Other Physiological Functions

In a recent sleep-deprivation experiment, we found that palmar conductance and respiration showed progressive rise during the vigil, indicating increasing activation with deprivation of sleep. In the same experiment we recorded EEG and, by means of a band-pass filter, obtained a quantified write-out of frequencies from 8–12 per second, in the alpha range. It will be recalled that the classical picture of activation is reduction in the amount of alpha activity. Therefore, what we might expect to find in this experiment is progressive decrease in the amount of alpha activity. As a matter of fact, this is exactly what was found (Malmo, 1958, p. 237).

As Stennett (1957b) has shown, however, the relationship between EEG alpha activity and other physiological variables is sometimes curvilinear. In the sleep-deprivation experiments physiological measurements were taken under highly activating conditions and at this high end of the continuum further increase in activation seems invariably to decrease the amount of alpha activity. But at the lower end of the continuum with the S in a drowsy state, increased activation has the opposite effect on alpha activity. An alerting stimulus, instead of producing a flattening of the EEG tracing, will actually produce an augmentation of the alpha activity. This has sometimes been referred to as a "paradoxical" reaction, although it seems paradoxical only when it is assumed that the relaton between activation level and alpha amplitude is a decreasing monotonic one throughout the entire activation continuum. But Stennett (1957b) has shown that the relationship is not monotonic. From his data he plotted a curve which has the shape of an inverted U. From this curve it would be predicted that with a drowsy S, stimulation should *increase* alpha amplitude. From the same inverted U curve it would also be predicted that an S whose activation level was sufficiently high (past the peak of the curve) before stimulation would show a *decrease* in alpha amplitude. Actually, some unpublished experiments on startle by Bartoshuk fit these predictions very well.

Recent data indicate the usefulness of a 2–4 c.p.s. band-pass filter in experiments on sleep. The data in the figures that follow represent mean values from three men who slept all night in our laboratory after serving as Ss in our sleep-deprivation experiments.

Bipolar sponge electrodes, soaked in

electrode jelly and attached to the *S*
by Lastonet bands, were used for the
parietal EEG placement (two-thirds
of the distance from nasion to inion,
and 3 cm from the midline on each
side). The primary tracing was recorded by an Edin Electroencephalo-
graph, and the two secondary tracings
were integrations of the EEG potentials that were passed through band-
pass filters for selective amplification
of signals in the 2–4 and 8–12 c.p.s.
frequency bands. Measurements on the
secondary tracings were carried out
with special rulers, and these measurements were converted to microvolt
values by reference to calibration
standards.

Method of recording and measuring
palmar conductance was similar to that
described by Stennett (1957a).

Electrocardiograms were picked up
from electrodes placed on contralateral
limbs, and heart rates were determined
from measurements of electrocardio-
tachometric tracings. Respiration rates
were obtained by means of a Phipps
and Bird pneumograph.

All three *S*s slept well throughout
the night (approximately from 10 P.M.
to 9 A.M. after some 60 hours without
sleep). Physiological recordings were
carried out continuously during the
whole period of sleep in each case, and
except for occasional attention to electrodes (for example, application of
electrode jelly and saline to electrodes),
the *S*s were undisturbed.

Four pairs of cellulose sponge electrodes were attached to the four limbs
(to the pronator teres muscles of the
arms and the peroneal muscles of the
legs) for the purpose of recording
muscle potentials. Primary muscle-
potential tracings were recorded on
the chart of a custom-built Edin elec-
tromyograph (EMG). Electronic integrators (employing the condenser
charge-discharge principle, like those

used for the secondary EEG tracings),
attached in parallel across the galva-
nometers of this EMG unit, integrated
the muscle potentials over successive
4-second periods.

These muscle-potential tracings
were used to record movements and
periods of restlessness during sleep.
Five-minute periods free from muscle-
potential activity and preceded by at
least 5 minutes of movement-free tracings were chosen for measurement in
order to provide the values plotted in
Figs. 3–5. The actual times plotted on
the baseline represent the medians for
the three *S*s. In each instance the three
times were close to one another.

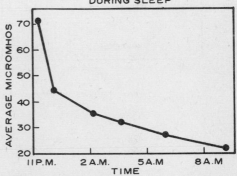

Fig. 3. *Mean EEG values from three
healthy young male* Ss *during a night's
sleep. Subjects had been sleep-deprived.
Band-pass filters were used in connection with electronic integrators to provide quantitative data in the two different frequency bands.*

In Fig. 3 observe that following a
brief rise early in sleep the upper curve
for 2–4 c.p.s. falls continuously during
the entire period of sleep. This curve
is consistent with published accounts
of changes in EEG during sleep noted
by inspection of the raw tracings
(Lindsley, 1957, p. 68). Early in sleep
there is an increase in slow waves

around 2–4 cycles per second, but as sleep continues these waves are replaced by even slower ones. As far as I am aware, the data in Fig. 3 represent the first use of a 2–4 band-pass filter to quantify the EEG. The curve for 8–12 c.p.s. EEG also shows some fall, and the voltage is low in accordance with the well-known disappearance of alpha waves from the raw tracings during sleep.

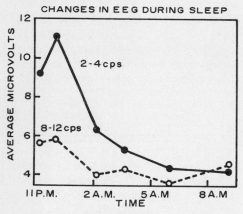

FIG. 4. *Mean palmar conductance values from the same Ss, at the same times during sleep as in Fig. 3.*

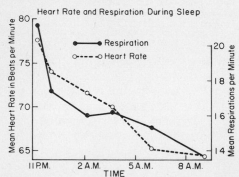

FIG. 5. *Mean values for heart rate and respiration from the same Ss at the same times during sleep as in Figs. 3 and 4.*

Figures 4 and 5 show data for palmar conductance, heart rate, and respiration that were recorded at the same time as the EEG data. From the second plotted point on, there is rather close resemblance between these curves and the one for 2–4 c.p.s. EEG. It seems likely that a band-pass filter for fast frequencies in the beta range might yield a continuously falling curve commencing with drowsiness and continuing through the onset and early stages of sleep. There are serious technical difficulties in quantifying the next step of frequencies above the alpha band, but we are hopeful that a band-pass filter that has recently been constructed in our laboratory will overcome these difficulties.

Direct Alteration of ARAS Activity by Means of Electrical Stimulation and Related Animal Experimentation

The most relevant experiment on direct stimulation of the ARAS is, as far as I know, the one by Fuster (1958) that was mentioned earlier. By stimulating in the same part of the ARAS that produces the EEG picture of activation, Fuster was able to produce improved discrimination performance in the monkey. Presumably, this effect was achieved by causing a larger number of impulses from the ARAS to bombard the cortex. The assumption would be that before the onset of electrical stimulation the cortex was not receiving sufficient bombardment for optimal performance (Hebb, 1955) and that ARAS stimulation brought total bombardment in the cortex closer to the optimal value. The situation may not be as simple as this, but the success of the Fuster experiment encourages further experimentation along these same lines. Finding that level of performance can be altered by electrical stimulation of the ARAS opens up the exciting possibility that if the amount of neural activity in the ARAS can be measured, we might find a direct correlation between a central measure of activation and level of performance. For instance, the Bélanger and Feldman experiment described earlier might be repeated with the addition of recordings from the ARAS. The aim of such an experiment would be to determine whether the continuous rise in the heart rate curve with increasing deprivation times could be matched by a similar rise in amplitude of deflections from recording in the ARAS with implanted electrodes. Recent neurophysiological experiments appear encouraging with respect to the feasibility of such an approach (Li and Jasper, 1953, pp. 124–125; Magoun, 1958, p. 68).

EFFECTS OF INCREASED ACTIVATION ON LOCALIZED SKELETAL-MUSCLE TENSION IN PSYCHIATRIC PATIENTS

The implication of activation theory for various clinical phenomena might very well be the topic of a separate paper. Certainly there is not space to deal at length with the topic here. I have chosen, therefore, to present a few recent observations, chiefly in order to suggest how level of activation may be studied in relation to a clinical phenomenon.

The graph in Fig. 6 illustrates what appears to be a general finding in patients complaining of tensional discomfort in a localized muscular site. The data for the curves plotted in the figure were obtained from a psychiatric patient, a 42-year-old woman who complained of muscular discomfort localized in the left thigh. In the session when these data were taken, electromyograms (EMGs) were recorded from various muscles over the body; those from the left and right thighs are shown in the figure. The patient was engaged in pursuit tracking using an apparatus similar to the one em-

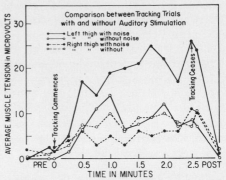

FIG. 6. *Mean muscle tension from left thigh and right thigh from patient with complaint of tensional discomfort in the left thigh. Note that when patient was performing the tracking task under distraction (loud noise), tension rose in the left thigh but not in the right.*

ployed by Surwillo (1955, 1956). Figure 6 shows that when a loud distracting noise, of the kind described by Schnore (1959), was presented during tracking, the tension in the left thigh was very much higher than that of the right thigh. When tracking was carried out under distraction-free conditions this tensional difference between thighs was not observed.

Interpretation of these data seems quite straightforward. When level of activation was increased by presenting a loud distracting noise, the effect was shown entirely in one muscle group, the left thigh, which was the symptom area in this patient. Simultaneous recordings of tension from other parts of the body showed that the tension was specific to the left thigh and was not merely increased on the whole left side of the body.

The specificity of the left thigh in indicating the higher activation is quite clear. Observe that tension in the thigh muscles on the opposite side of the body actually fell slightly under the activating condition.

The same procedure was carried out

with a second patient, a young girl of 28, who complained of a distressing feeling of tightness in the neck on the right side. Results were similar to the ones obtained in the previous case, with activation again showing its effect specifically in the symptom area. When the loud distracting noise was turned on during tracking, tension in this area showed marked increase, whereas tension in the muscles on the left side of the neck showed no rise whatever.

Very similar results were obtained from two additional patients whose areas of tensional discomfort were localized in still different parts of the body. One woman with complaint of tension on the left side of her neck served as a useful control for the patient previously described with tension localized in the opposite side of the neck. No tracking experiment was carried out with this patient. Apparently the sight of the EMG recording room for the first time was itself sufficient to increase the amplitude of muscle potentials from the symptom area so that they become appreciably higher than those on the opposite side of her neck. The other woman (fourth patient in this series) complained of tensional discomfort that appeared to originate in the left shoulder. EMGs were recorded from the left and right shoulders of this patient while she lay in bed listening to the playback of a recorded interview. During the first part of the playback, tension was about the same on the two sides of the body. But when the topic concerning her dead sister commenced to come over the speaker, tension in the left shoulder became much greater than that in the right.

As far as could be determined, the EMG data from all these patients were consistent in suggesting that for skeletal-muscle tension in patients with well-developed tensional symptoms, in-

creasing the activation level up to a certain point has the effect of raising muscle tension in one localized muscle group, the one in which the patient complained of tensional discomfort. It was not necessary for the patient to actually feel the discomfort during the experimental session for this differential result to appear. I have been using the term *symptom area* to refer to the muscle group where the discomfort was localized when present.

Interesting findings that appear to parallel those from the patients were obtained from three young male nonpatient Ss in our recent investigation of sleep deprivation. As previously mentioned, evidence from EEG, palmar conductance, and respiration indicated that activation during tracking increased progressively with hours of sleep deprivation. In addition to these other physiological tracings, EMGs from various areas over the body were also recorded. One muscle area, a different one for each S, showed significant rise in tension over the vigil. It was the neck muscles in one S, the forehead in another, and the biceps muscle of the right arm in the third. In each case the one muscle showed statistically significant rise in tension, and in none of the Ss was there signficant tensional rise in any other muscle. In fact, there was regularly progressive and very significant fall in the tension of the left forearm in all three Ss. As far as I know, none of the men actually complained of tensional discomfort in the areas showing rise in tension during the vigil.

Where high-level activation is long continued as in a vigil or in certain psychoneurotic patients, it appears that skeletal tension may become localized to a single muscle group. The discomfort associated with this tension in some patients can become extremely severe. It should be noted that in one-session experiments, where rise in activation was for relatively short intervals of time, tensional rise occurred in more than one muscle group (Surwillo, 1956; Stennett, 1957a).

Methodologically, these results are important because they reveal a difference between EMGs and some other physiological measures with respect to gauging activation. Unlike heart rate or respiration rate that invariably yields one measure no matter how it is recorded, there are as many measures of muscle tension as there are muscles that can be recorded from. It appears that when sufficient care is taken, EMGs may be very valuable in helping to gauge activation, but that considerable caution is required in the interpretation of results, and especially in the interpretation of negative results.

From the clinical point of view it seems an interesting speculation that the patient's localized muscle tension may itself actually increase the general activation level. (I do not mean the level of muscle tension all over the body.) Two main assumptions are involved in this suggestion. The first one is that the area of localized muscle tension in the patient acts like tension that is induced, for example, by having an S squeeze on a dynamometer. From the generalized effects of tension induction on learning and performance it is clear that the effects of increased muscle tension are quite general ones. Though crucial physiological data are missing in these experiments, as previously mentioned, one very likely explanation of these results is that the local increase in muscle tension somehow produces an increase in the general level of activation, with rise in heart rate and blood pressure, with fall in level of EEG alpha, and so on. This is the second assumption. The results of two recent experiments are

in line with this assumption. Meyer and Noble (1958) found that induced tension interacted with "anxiety" in verbal-maze learning ("anxiety" measured by means of the MAS [Taylor, 1953]), while Kuethe and Eriksen (1957) in a study of stereotypy likewise reported a significant interaction between these two variables when "anxiety" was experimentally produced by means of electric shocks. The MAS appears to select individuals who are significantly above the mean in activation, and from the results of Schnore (1959) and Feldman (1958) it seems safe to conclude that anticipation of shock also leads to increased levels of physiological activity. In short, generalizing from the induced tension experiments, it seems reasonable to suppose that a patient's muscular tension in a small focal area might have the general effect of increasing activation. If such is the case, symptomatic treatment might have significant general as well as specific effects. Although based on only one patient, Yates' (1958) results from symptomatic treatment of tics seems encouraging with respect to the feasibility of research in this general area.

SUMMARY

The neuropsychological dimension of activation may be briefly described as follows. The continuum extending from deep sleep at the low-activation end to "excited" states at the high-activation end is a function of the amount of cortical bombardment by the ARAS, such that the greater the cortical bombardment the higher the activation. The shape of the curve relating level of performance to level of activation is that of an inverted U: from low activation up to a point that is optimal for a given performance or function, level of performance rises monotonically with increasing activation level; but past this optimal point the relation becomes nonmonotonic: further increase in activation beyond this point produces fall in performance level, this fall being directly related to the amount of the increase in level of activation.

Long before the discovery of the ARAS, the behavioral evidence of Duffy, Freeman, and others of the "energetics" group had suggested the existence of some such brain mechanism. Moreover, learning theorists of the Hull school have in their concept of the general drive state come very close to the activation principle. Up to the present time they have employed physiological measures only sparingly and have restricted their use to the aversive aspects of drive. But with evidence that such measures may also be applied to nonaversive (appetitional) drive, it seems likely that the present rather unsatisfactory measures of drive may eventually be replaced by physiological indicants.

Activation has a number of main characteristics that may be listed as follows: (a) Activation has no steering function in behavior. (b) It is considerably broader than emotion. (c) Activation is not a state that can be inferred from knowledge of antecedent conditions alone, because it is the product of an interaction between internal conditions such as hunger or thirst, and external cues. (d) Activation does not fit very well into the S-R formula. It is a phenomenon of slow changes, of drifts in level with a time order of minutes (even hours), not of seconds or fractions thereof. (e) Activation is a quantifiable dimension, and the evidence indicates that physiological measures show a sufficiently high intra-individual concordance for quantifying this dimension.

It is suggested that activation is mediated chiefly through the ARAS, which seems, in the main, to be an intensity system. Neurophysiological findings strongly suggest that it may be possible to achieve more precise measurement of activation through a direct recording of discharge by the ARAS into the cerebral cortex. Research on this problem is urgently needed.

The concept of activation appears to have wide application to phenomena in the field of clinical psychology. As one illustration, in this paper, activation was applied to clinical phenomena of tensional symptoms.

REFERENCES

Bindra, D., *Motivation. A Systematic Re-interpretation*. New York: The Ronald Press Company, 1959.

Brown, J. S., "Pleasure-Seeking Behavior and the Drive-Reduction Hypothesis," *Psychological Review,* **62** (1955), 169-79.

Campbell, B. A. and F. D. Sheffield, "Relation of Random Activity to Food Deprivation," *Journal of Comparative Physiological Psychology,* **46** (1953), 320-26.

Cofer, C. N., "Motivation," *Annual Review of Psychology,* **10** (1959), 173-202.

Courts, F. A., "Relations Between Muscular Tension and Performance," *Psychological Bulletin,* **39** (1942), 347-67.

Darrow, C. W., "Psychological and Psychophysiological Significance of the Electroencephalogram," *Psychological Review,* **54** (1947), 157-68.

Davis, R. C., "Modification of the Galvanic Reflex by Daily Repetition of a Stimulus," *Journal of Experimental Psychology,* **17** (1934), 504-35.

Dell, P. C., "Humoral Effects on the Brain Stem Reticular Formations," in *Reticular Formation of the Brain,* eds. H. H. Jasper, L. D. Proctor, R. S.

C. Shagass, "Physiologic
tom Mechanisms in Psy-
ts Under Stress," *Psycho-
ine,* **11** (1949), 25-29.

. and M. E. Noble, "Sum-
nifest Anxiety and Muscu-
Journal of Experimental
5 (1958), 599-602.

., "The Cytoarchitecture of
Reticular Formation," in
anisms and Consciousness,
Delafresnaye, pp. 54-75.
Ill.: Charles C. Thomas,
954.

R. D. and J. F. Davis,
nd-pass Filters of Electro-
aphy," *I. R. E. Canadian
Record 1958,* Paper No.

er, A. B., "Studies on the
-Sensitive Component of the
Activating System," *Electro-
gram Clinical Neurophysiol-
956), 603-21.

M., A. V. Schally, and B. G.
Stimulaton of the Release of
pin from the Adenohypophysis
urohypophysial Factor," *Endo-
,* **57** (1955), 439-44.

e, M. M., "Individual Patterns
ological Activity as a Function
Differences and Degree of
" *Journal of Experimental Psy-*
58 (1959), 117-28.

Spence, K. W., "Theory of Emotionally-Based Drive (D) and Its Relation to
Performance in Simple Learning Situations," *American Psychologist,* **13**
(1958), 131-41.

Stennett, R. G., "The Relationship of
Performance Level to Level of Arousal,"
Journal of Experimental Psychology, **58**
(1959), 117-28. (a)

———, "The Relationship of Alpha
Amplitude to the Level of Palmar Conductance," *Electroencephalogram Clinical Neurophysiology,* **9** (1957), 131-38.
(b)

Surwillo, W. W., "A Device for Re-
cording Variations in Pressure of Grip
During Tracking," *American Journal of
Psychology,* **68** (1955), 669-70.

———, Psychological Factors in
Muscle-Action Potentials: EMG Gradients," *Journal of Experimental Psychology,* **52** (1956), 263-72.

Taylor, Janet A., "A Personality Scale
of Manifest Anxiety," *Journal of Abnormal Psychology,* **48** (1953), 285-90.

Woodworth, R. S., and H. Schlosberg,
Experimental Psychology. New York:
Holt, Rinehart & Winston, Inc., 1954.

Yates, A. J., "The Application of
Learning to the Treatment of Tics,"
Journal of Abnormal Psychology, **56**
(1958), 175-82.

Knighton, W. C. Noshay, and R. T. Costello, pp. 365-79. Toronto: Little, Brown & Co., 1958.

Duffy, Elizabeth, "The Measurement of Muscular Tension as a Technique for the Study of Emotional Tendencies," *American Journal of Psychology*, **44** (1932), 146-62.

————, "The Concept of Energy Mobilization," *Psychological Review*, **58** (1951), 30-40.

————, "The Psychological Significance of the Concept of 'Arousal' or 'Activation,'" *Psychological Review*, **64** (1957), 265-75.

———— and O. L. Lacey, "Adaptation in Energy Mobilization: Changes in General Level of Palmar Skin Conductance," *Journal of Experimental Psychology*, **36** (1946), 437-52.

Dusser de Barenne, J. G., "The Labyrinthine and Postural Mechanisms," in *A Handbook of General Experimental Psychology*, ed. C. Murchison, pp. 204-46. Worcester, Mass.: Clark University Press, 1934.

Feldman, S. M., "Differential Effect of Shock as a Function of Intensity and Cue Factors in Maze Learning." Unpublished doctoral dissertation, McGill University, 1958.

Finan, J. L., "Quantitative Studies of Motivation. I. Strength of Conditioning in Rats under Varying Degrees of Hunger," *Journal of Comparative Physiological Psychology*, **29** (1940), 119-34.

Finch, G., "Hunger as a Determinant of Conditional and Unconditional Salivary Response Magnitude," *American Journal of Physiology*, **123** (1938), 379-82.

Freeman, G. L., "The Relationship Between Performance Level and Bodily Activity Level," *Journal of Experimental Psychology*, **26** (1940), 602-8.

————, *The Energetics of Human Behavior*. Ithaca, N. Y.: Cornell University Press, 1948.

Fuster, J. M., "Effects of Stimulation of the Brain Stem on Tachistoscopic Perception," *Science*, **127** (1958), 150.

———— and Study of Sym chiatric Patien *somatic Medic*

(lo

ph tio pp. Tho

K Stim Interi Behav *iologic*

Ken *Review*

Kueti "Person sion as Stereotyp *Psycholo*

Li, C. electrode ity of the *Journal of* 40.

Lindsley, *book of E* S. S. Stevens John Wiley &

————, "P vation," in *Motivation 19* 44-105. Lincoln Press, 1957.

Lorente De Impulses Throu clei," *Journal* (1939), 402-64.

Magoun, H. W Springfield, Ill.: Publishers, 1958.

Malmo, R. B Drive: An Unsolv chology," in *Nebr Motivation 1958*, e 229-65. Lincoln: Un Press, 1958.

Meyer, D. mation of Ma lar Tension," *Psychology*,

Olzewski, the Human *Brain Mech* ed. J. F. Springfield, Publishers,

Ross, W "Stable Ba encephalogr *Convention* 860, 202-6.

Rothball Adrenaline Reticular *encephalo ogy*, **8** (1

Saffran Benfey, Corticotr by a Ne *crinology*

Schno of Physi of Task Arousal, *chology*

Psychophysiology and Motivation *

Donald B. Lindsley

A visitor from outer space, granted an understanding of the English language, would no doubt be amazed by many things upon this Earth, but I would wager that when he got around to examining psychology he would be confused. He would no doubt wonder about the relationships among and between the various chapter headings in our texts of psychology, but when he came to the topic of motivation I have a feeling he really would be in a quandary. He would find no lack of elegant prose on this subject, ranging from the most esoteric of theories to the most prosaic of experiments. He would discover too that the ordinary English language could not be stretched sufficiently to encompass the full range of vocabulary to which he would be exposed. But after all, why should we worry about him? This happens to our majors and graduate students all of the time, and, if the truth were known, it happens to us.

A cursory scanning of the last two volumes of this symposium series will reveal a wide diversity of subject matter labeled *motivation*. Each of the contributions seems to "belong" according to our usual traditions, and a careful reading will show that each chapter deals very ably with some facet of a many-sided concept or of a series of concepts. We find many terms being used, sometimes synonymously, sometimes with sharp distinctions being drawn. For example, some do not distinguish between drives, needs, motivation, and incentives, or if they do, inevitably talk most about one or another, rather than all, after the introductory formalities are over.

In the 1955 volume, we find a consideration of the physiological mechanisms of "reward" and "punishment" representing opposite aspects of drive and all subsumed under motivational processes. The unique technique of self-stimulation seemingly gives rise to unlimited potentialities of exploration of drive mechanisms and perhaps, eventually, a clarification of terminology. This stimulating chapter is preceded and followed by others of equal interest and ingenuity of experimentation, but now motivation appears in the garb of "Social Consequences of Achievement" and "Attitude." We see a most interesting concept of "needs" developing from deprivation and deficit, and of "needs" which seek gratification as a function of the normal growth process. Two other significant contributions of the 1955 volume

* From D. B. Lindsley, "Psychophysiology and Motivation," in *Nebraska Symposium on Motivation 1957*, ed. M. R. Jones (Lincoln: University of Nebraska Press, 1957), pp. 44-105. Reprinted by permission of the author and publisher.

Support for some of the research reported herein has come from the following sources: USPHS B-362; Department of Army, Contract DA-49-007-MD-722; Carnegie Corporation of New York; Office of Naval Research, Contract NR-144-102 (Nonr-233) (32). Grateful acknowledgment is made to the following, who have participated in various phases of the work: William Emmons, Roy Griffiths, Robert Lansing, and Edward Schwartz.

dealt with the importance of affective processes as determinants of motivation, and the role of the situation external to the individual in determining his behavior potential, his expectancy and the nature of the reinforcement value of the situation to him.

In the 1956 volume, Frustration, Conflict, and Anxiety come into the picture; an excellent review of the latter topic presents no less than nine techniques for producing experimental aversion and emphasizes the importance of temporal factors in aversive and avoidance conditioning. Another chapter attempted a neurological conception of "approach"-"withdrawal" behavior. Still another took an analytic approach to a so-called "basic drive" mechanism, emphasizing the probable existence of two separate mechanisms in the mating behavior of the male rat. A final contribution, of no less importance than the others, took a masterful crack at the inconsistencies of the motivational theorists and, perhaps most importantly, so far as I am concerned, brought out the need for direction in our thinking with regard to psychological problems generally. I agree wholeheartedly with this admonition, for I feel that we need less thought and activity associated with so-called "chapter headings" and more concentrated upon an empirical elaboration of the underlying processes and mechanisms and their integration in relation to better defined problems.

Let me say at the outset that I am not an expert on motivation and have never claimed to be. Whatever contribution I may be able to make to this Symposium on Motivation, if any, will not depend upon a detailed knowledge of past results in the field, nor upon the adherence to any theory of motivation espoused by a so-called "school of psychology." Rather than

become enmeshed in polemics or tangential issues and with the semantic problems growing out of them, I feel it might be better to back up and attempt to think more carefully about the problem we start with, namely, what is motivation? What do we mean by it? And where shall we start to measure or control it? Is it an independent or dependent variable, or a so-called intervening variable? Is it stimulus, response, or a stimulus-response relationship, or is it simply a construct inferred from stimulus, response, or both? These seem to be some of the dilemmas we have been facing, and, as far as I can see from reading the literature, including a number of the presentations in preceding symposia, there is a great deal of confusion. Even some of the most avid proponents of "motivational theories" and the designers of clever experiments to support them eventually "run down" and become discouraged. In other words, they lose their "motivation" for pursuing the problem.

But what is meant by the term *motivation*? Apparently it derives from the Latin word *movere*, meaning "to move." It is said by Webster to be "that within the individual, rather than without, which incites him to action; any idea, need, emotion, or organic state that prompts to action." At least this tells us that one commonplace conception is that it is a process (or processes)—something going on within the individual which moves him to action. But what creates internal conditions? Obviously, change or lack of change of external conditions, as a function of time, is involved.

We often treat motivation as if it were a construct, some hypothetical something, which can be added to or subtracted from, like so much gasoline in the tank of an automobile. But we can't measure it by dropping a stick into the tank or by looking at the gauge. Nor do we attempt to analyze or measure its constituents, or consider the steps in the process by which it is produced. In general we tend to be concerned mainly with the output or performance—how much effort, or work, or learning, in how much time or how many trials. As in the case of the car and its performance—how many miles per gallon, how fast, what horsepower—these are products of many things. Looked at in this way, motivation becomes a function of rate, direction, and amount of pull or push toward a goal. But even the goal, like the processes which underlie action toward it, is inferred. By the time we make a few more assumptions or inferences about secondary goals and reinforcements, we are "out of gas" on an uncharted road—stranded! That seems to be about what has happened to us in recent years with our theorizing about motivation. We have concerned ourselves very little with operational steps in the process, or with possible understanding of the mechanisms of drive and motivation.

Without presuming to understand or even know all of the operational steps in the process, and certainly not presuming to know the intricacies of the mechanism, I should nevertheless like to review some of the empirical observations of behavior and some of the possible neural mechanisms evolving from neurophysiology which seem to have a bearing on the problems of drive and motivation. Coupled with these, I should like to include the concept of homeostasis (regulation or balance) and the role of feedback circuits in the regulation of input and output. The observations I will make, stemming from facts, but obviously going beyond them, will attempt to present some possible mechanisms recently revealed in neurophysiologic

studies which I feel cannot be ignored, either in formulating a conception of motivation or in planning experiments bearing upon it.

SOME DEFINITIONS

First it may be well to review some terms frequently used in discussing the problem of motivation. And we may as well start with a commonly accepted definition of motivation.

Motivation is generally defined as the combination of forces which initiate, direct, and sustain behavior toward a goal. This may be much too broad and inclusive to be useful, and we will see that this definition needs further qualifications.

Needs are often dealt with under two broad categories: *Biological needs*, and *Personal-Social needs*. *Biological needs* are basic conditions (usually chemical) which are necessary to the maintenance of life and normal processes of health, growth, and reproduction. Specifically, these might be the need for oxygen, calcium, carbohydrates, etc. *Personal-Social* needs can be less objectively described by such concepts as personal security, self-confidence, group status, prestige, aggression, and so forth.

Drives are generally defined as the internal stimuli or organic states which initiate activity and predispose an animal toward making differential responses which presumably aid in attaining satisfaction of needs but may well go beyond this. These we are told may be primary and unlearned, or secondary and acquired.

Incentives or *goals* are the external stimuli (or their surrogates) toward which or away from which the animal orients himself in seeking satisfaction of needs.

From these definitions it will be seen that Drives and Incentives or Goals are only special aspects of motivation and are not to be construed as independent factors. These concepts necessarily overlap and constantly interact. The separation of motivational forces into drives and incentives is arbitrary and tends to delude us when we think only about end results, or behavior. Presumably it is done to facilitate and simplify the design of experiments. But do we necessarily have to simplify at this stage? Sometimes it is better to look at a problem in its broadest context in order to map or conceive a plan before attacking it. Have we considered all we know in relation to this problem? Are we looking far enough afield, for example, to other disciplines, as perforce we must with respect to other problems? Have we settled too soon upon our parameters of measurement? Have we become overly preoccupied with the need for finding a simple method of measuring and evaluating drive and motivation? Do we have to find in a specific technique of behavioral measurement the one and only approach to this problem? Obviously not, for the problem is a broad and complex one. To be sure we are interested in all promising behavioral methods of assessing motivation, but we should not overlook clinical and subjective evaluations, for what they may contribute. Nor should we overlook the role of social factors. If endocrinology, biochemistry, neurophysiology, or other disciplines can be of help, we should not spurn knowledge so derived.

SOME BASIC BIOLOGICAL CONSIDERATIONS

For a biological orientation bearing on this problem, two distinguished companion volumes published in 1924 might well be read or reread by psychologists. These are *Physiological Foundations of Behavior* by C. M. Child (10) and *Neurological Foundations of Animal Behavior* by C. J. Herrick (35).

If we are examining a concept of motivation which represents it as "a combination of forces which initiate, sustain, and direct behavior toward a goal," we must consider those forces or conditions which excite or activate an organism, as well as those that sustain and channel its activities. With regard to activation, we must consider more than the external stimulus or stimulating situation; we must also consider the *physiological state* of the organism. Concerning physiological state and its modifiability, Child (10) has this to say:

Any particular type of reaction of an organism to an external factor involves the integration of various mechanisms, and the character of the reaction as a whole depends on the integration pattern in each particular case. . . . That this pattern is modifiable through differences in the direct action of external factors is demonstrated by universal everyday experience. . . . Such modifiability evidently depends primarily upon changes in what Jennings has called the physiological state of the organism. . . . Physiological state represents the sum total of the physiological factors which determine the excito-motor integration pattern at any particular moment. As Jennings has pointed out, many factors may be concerned in determining physiological state. Among such factors, for example, [are] the persistent effects of previous reactions, such as altered irritability, morphological alteration in pattern, memory, etc., the effect of different excitations occurring simultaneously, metabolic condition as determined by nutrition, respiratory, endocrine and other factors, physiological age and other periodicities, in short all factors, external and internal, which affect the organism.

Years before, Claude Bernard had pointed out the significance of the blood and lymph which bathe the cells and tissues of an organism, thus constituing a "milieu interne," the relative constancy of which is a necessity to the survival of at least the higher animals. Cannon (7) referred to the internal environment as a fluid-matrix and called attention to the many mechanisms which operate to maintain it. The ability of the organism, or any part or system within it, to approximate, though not actually achieve, a steady-state equilibrium he termed *homeostasis*. Not unrelated to this concept is that of *regulation* or *equilibration* used by Child (10) in the following manner:

> The persistence and continuity of the individual organism in a changing environment is unquestionably a fact of great interest and significance. . . . When we investigate the physiological conditions on which their maintenance and persistence is based, we see that when these are disturbed by external factors they commonly react in a way that appears to be useful in that it makes maintenance possible. The reaction may be a compensation of the disturbance, an escape from it by locomotion, or some other reaction, but the effect in general is some sort and degree of equilibration of the system as a whole. . . . Functional regulations, that is, regulations of special function in mature organisms, show similar characteristics. In the mammal a rise in internal temperature brings into play mechanisms which tend to decrease the internal temperature; life in high altitudes brings about increased production of red blood corpuscles; similarly in motor reactions, the organism encountering unfavorable or injurious conditions commonly moves away, and the useful reflexes such as the withdrawal of a part from painful stimulation, the

closure of the eyelid in excessive light, and so on, are familiar to all.

Thus we see that there are various short, and immediate, adjustment mechanisms operating in the face of environmental stimuli, and there are various longer, more delayed adjustments to persisting effects in the environment; these assume the form of *homeostatic mechanisms* or *regulatory* or *equilibratory mechanisms*. The balance or adjustment achieved may be useful or harmful so far as the organism is concerned; it is not implied that the balance is always returned to a so-called "normal" state, or even to a previous level prior to stimulation. These internal adjustments are not without external manifestations at times and in any case may so modify conditions of tension, excitability, and the like that they have a direct influence on behavior as well as an indirect one.

Herrick (35) discusses *behavior regulation* as follows:

> The most distinctive characteristics of living things . . . are those concerned with the maintenance of the individuality of the organism, so that the forces of surrounding nature do not corrode and disintegrate it but on the other hand are incorporated into its organization to furnish the driving energy of the machine. The material and energy of the living body are in constant flux, yet the pattern of their manifestation persists. When this pattern is deformed by external violence or by changes of internal state it is said in current biological descriptions that there is a tendency to return to the typical condition. This restoration of the original pattern after deformation is termed regulation. . . . Though each regulatory act is a strictly individual adjustment, the mechanism of regulation and the pattern which is restored are parts of the hereditary organization. In view of the fact that the ordinary conditions of life involve

constant changes in the relations of the body to its environment, regulation in the broad sense means simply the continuous readjustment of the organism to the flux of the surrounding conditions. . . . So in behavior the disturbance of the usual conditions may be corrected either by a return to the former state or by the acquisition of some quite different form of compensating activity, as, for instance, migration from a given locality after exhaustion of local food supply. In each case after disturbance of the vital equilibrium a physiological readjustment occurs until a new equilibrium is established which is not necessarily the same as the original condition but which in general is adaptive or useful. The organism responds as whole, in some measure, even to local disturbance, and in more complex adjustments the nervous system plays a leading role.

With regard to modifiability of behavior, Herrick states:

Individual modifications of behavior, of course, can occur only if there is a certain capital of innate action system or reflex pattern with which to work. . . . The innate patterns . . . have developed very slowly through biological agencies like natural selection which are able to effect relatively permanent changes in the organization of the protoplasmic "physical basis of life" and so are heritable. The individual modifications, on the other hand, are relatively quickly acquired and, while enduring for a time, do not involve any so permanent changes in the organization. . . . Modifiability in this wide sense includes fatigue, acclimation, associative memory, and many other effects of past experience, in short, all of the internal factors of behavior except those immediately consequent upon the stimulus. Some modifications are evanescent, while others may persist throughout the life of the individual. This persistence of internal change is a true mnemonic function, ranging all the way from a transitory facilitation by use, through the so-called physiological memories of lower animals slowly acquired by numberless repetitions, to the lifelong memories of single events so characteristic of human experience.

As a prelude to the next section dealing with new developments in neurophysiology, perhaps one final quotation from Herrick may be made which will attest to his prescience about the future, particularly in the realm of mechanisms of correlation in the nervous system. Although the modern field of neurophysiology was then only, one might say, in its infancy, and though one of its most powerful tools, electrical recording of potential changes in the central nervous system, had scarcely been dreamed of and certainly not implemented, Herrick exhibited unusual insight into the organization of the nervous system and its role in behavior.

He states,

But the concept of the reflex is not a general master key competent to unlock all of the secrets of the brain and mind, as some seem to suppose . . . attention should be especially directed to the futility of attempting to derive intelligence and the higher mental faculties in general from reflexes, habits, or any other form of fixed or determinate behavior. On the contrary, these owe their origin to the more labile and plastic components of behavior, which are determined, if you like, though not by rigid innate organization but rather by individual experience acting through and upon the innate units and recombining these in new patterns. The nervous system is more than an aggregate of reflex arcs and life is more than reaction to stimuli. . . . In actual practice each reflex center is usually a region where more or less complex compounding of simple reflexes is effected, where a single afferent impulse is distributed to all of the synergic muscles necessary for the complex motor response, where antagonistic impulses meet and struggle for possession of a final common path (Sherrington, 1906), or some other correlation of higher order is effected. . . . In searching for the probable mechanisms of these central correlations attention may again be directed to the neural rhythms . . . the activities of the centers of nervous adjustment are in part determined by functional variations in synaptic refractory periods and neuronic rhythms.

It is commonly believed that the acquired correlations and associations of higher animals are effected by opening up of new connections between previously established conduction systems so that the simpler elements of behavior may be linked in new combinations. . . . On this view learning and indeed the whole course of the development of individual behavior patterns depend structurally upon the spread of nervous impulses out of the already established channels across the barriers into unfamiliar paths and then the preservation and strengthening of these newly acquired nervous conductors by further use. There is anatomical evidence that all main nervous circuits are related by collateral cross-connections permitting such overflow, presumably, however, only under stress of strong excitation or block of the usual paths of more open and free discharge. There is, it must be admitted, little specific evidence of the mode of formation of such collateral connections. . . . The term *correlation* is applied to those combinations of the afferent impulses within the sensory centers and of mnemonic vestiges of previous reactions which determine which of several possible efferent pathways will be activated or what is the appropriate reaction to the situation: . . . Every reaction, even the simplest actual reflex, involves the combined action of several different

muscles or other effectors, and the ordering of these so as to effect the appropriate response is *co-ordination*. . . . But within the central nervous system the main conduction pathways, the highways of through traffic which serve the great fundamental reflex systems of the routine activities of each animal species, are not detached fiber tracts like the insulated wires of a telephone system. On the contrary, all of the parts of each such reflex system are so intimately and variously connected with one another and with parts of other systems by collateral branches of the nerve fibers and by correlation neurons that anatomical mechanisms are provided for innumerable modifications of any typical or primary reflex pattern. Which, if any, of these cross-connections will be activated in any particular response will be determined by the aggregate of external and internal factors at the moment operating.

Any simple cross-connection between afferent and efferent paths in lower centers may be blocked by fatigue, by intercurrent stimuli, or otherwise, so that a present reaction is suspended while an overflow from the lower sensory centers passes up to the higher centers of correlation, there to be redirected, perhaps into the same, perhaps into some different motor system, with reinforcement, inhibition, or other modifications. The lower centers in this event do not cease to work, but they are no longer the sole arbiters of the problem of conduct. . . . Conversely, an activity directed from the cerebral cortex may be in process when a strong intercurrent stimulus short-circuits the lower centers and perhaps discharges into the same motor system which was before in action, thus capturing the final common path and transforming the deliberative act into a reflex one, or it may be that it discharges into a different motor system replacing the first activity by a totally different one.

The tissue of the reticular formation which intervenes between sensory and motor centers is chiefly concerned with adjustments of the administrative type on the efferent side of the arc, that is to say with co-ordination rather than with correlation. Apparently many of these bulbar reflex systems "turn the corner" from afferent to efferent type at the first synaptic junction. . . . The reticular formation . . . is a mixture of gray and white matter which contains the intercalary neurons and the connecting tracts through which primary sensory centers are connected with one another and with motor centers from which peripheral motor nerves arise.

As the following account will suggest, Herrick's concept of the reticular formation and its role was limited to its descending influence and did not envisage the important integrating role it serves as an ascending activating system in sleep-waking, attentiveness, perception, and so forth.

These extensive quotations abstracted from the work of Child (10) and Herrick (35) have been presented, first, because it is believed that they are relevant as a background for the activity systems underlying motivation; second, because through phylogenetic and ontogenetic approaches they instructively document the concept of *regulation* (and *homeostasis* of Cannon) in the organism; third, they emphasize the degree of interaction between internal and external factors in the understanding of behavior, thus helping to obviate in some degree the mysterious "black box" concept of the organism and the central nervous system; and finally, because they represent historically a remarkable insight into, and a presaging of, the most recent neurophysiological discoveries to be elaborated in the following section. The books of these authors are not, of course, replete with

the details, nor do they provide the evidence and full significance, of modern findings, but they point the way.

RECENT NEUROPHYSIOLOGICAL CONCEPTS

During the past thirty years a number of new concepts of the nervous system have evolved from neurophysiology and electroencephalography. In the sections which follow, an attempt will be made to present some of these in relation to the problem of motivation, keeping in mind the matter of induction, maintenance and direction of activity or behavior which may be said to be motivated. From the foregoing sections it may be concluded that homeostasis or regulation constitutes a basic concept of an organism in continuous activity in some degree, where material exchanges and energy transformations are continually going on and are reflected in some state or activity of the organism as a whole. In what follows we will be concerned mainly with those aspects of the nervous system which play a part in the integration of such activity and in its regulation, control, and direction.

Briefly, we shall concern ourselves with the following factors:

1. Mechanisms of Efferent Control
2. Mechanisms of Afferent Control
3. Mechanisms of Central Control

Intimately related to each of these mechanisms of control is the *brain stem reticular formation*.

Structurally the reticular formation has been known for many years (viz., Herrick) but its functional role was poorly understood and has been largely overlooked, apparently, in deference to the ascending sensory and descending motor pathways, and the cranial nerve and other nuclei surrounding it. The reticular formation consists of a rather dense network of neurons which forms a kind of central core extending from the medulla of the lower brain stem to the thalamus in the diencephalon. It extends through the region of the pons and the midbrain tegmentum upward through the caudal portions of the hypothalamus and subthalamus.

From the reticular formation and other brain stem nuclei there are descending fibers which pass into the spinal cord and serve to regulate postural and motor activities of the body musculature. In addition to this efferent somatic influence there may also be a regulatory influence on the autonomic system. The ascending fibers originating in the reticular formation consist of both long and short fibers, but the latter predominate and form multineuronal and multisynaptic relays within the substance of the reticular formation itself. The course of these pathways through the brain stem, hypothalamus, and subthalamus is fairly clear, but from there the upward projections are less certain. Some (51) believe that the ascending fibers from the reticular formation take an extrathalamic route via the internal capsule; others (27) believe they proceed via a thalamic route connecting with the diffuse thalamic projection system in the region of the intralaminar, reticular, and other nonspecific thalamic nuclei. It seems probable that both views may be correct. In any case, it is known that the upward influence of the ascending reticular activating system (ARAS) upon the cortex is a diffuse one as has been shown by its widespread effects upon electrocortical potentials, and evidence for this will be presented later.

Mechanisms of Efferent Control

There are a long history and extensive literature on the centers of the brain which control motor activity and maintain postural relationships. These include sites in the cortex, basal ganglia, brain stem, and cerebellum, and in addition there are spinal reflexes at various segmental levels. For the most part the mechanisms of efferent control may be found in any up-to-date physiology text, such as that of Fulton (19). Suffice to say that the pyramidal tracts which originate in the primary motor areas of the cortex are concerned with voluntary control, whereas the extrapyramidal pathways originating in the premotor cortex, basal ganglia, lower brain stem, and cerebellum form the basis for involuntary control of posture, locomotion, and skilled movements. All of these pathways pass through the region of the lower brain stem; all are subject to inhibitory or excitatory control at their points of origin and at one or more stations along their extent to the muscles of the body. We shall be concerned here primarily with the role of the reticular formation and some new conceptions of its influence on spinal motor activity.

Magoun and Rhines (52) summarized extensive observations which demonstrated distinct regions of the brain stem reticular formation for inhibition and facilitation of spinal motor neurons and the muscles they control. Lindsley (42) has reviewed a number of the recent studies which have a bearing on the brain stem control of spinal motor activity. Briefly, it may be pointed out that the brain stem reticular formation consists of two functionally distinct portions so far as motor control is concerned. These are illustrated in Fig. 1, which shows diagrammatically the regions of the lower brain stem reticular formation having facilitatory (region 5, symbolized by plus sign) and inhibitory (region 4, with minus sign) influences

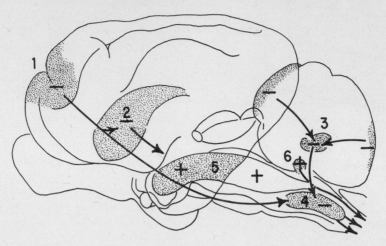

FIG. 1. *Reconstruction of cat's brain showing inhibitory (minus) and facilitory (plus) pathways influencing spinal motor activity. Inhibitory or suppressor pathways: 1, cortico-bulbo-reticular; 2, caudato-spinal; 3, cerebello-bulbo-reticular; 4, reticulo-spinal; Facilitatory pathways; 5, reticulo-spinal; 6, vestibulo-spinal. (From Lindsley, Schreiner, and Magoun [47].)*

upon spinal motor activity. Eliminating the inhibitory region by lesion leads to a marked increase in tonicity and hyperreflexia and spasticity; lesions of the upper facilitatory portion of the reticular formation, on the other hand, produce a profound inhibition with suppression of spinal reflexes and cortically induced movements. Lindsley, Schreiner, and Magoun (47) demonstrated that lesions of any of the so-called supressor areas (marked with a minus sign) produced increased spasticity and hyperreflexia and facilitated cortical-induced movements. Lesions of all of them, including the cortex (1), caudate nucleus (2), and cerebellar regions (3) produced a more profound inhibition.

Thus we see that in addition to the traditional and well-known modes of efferent control, the brain stem reticular formation provides a descending influence capable of providing balance or regulation of spinal motor activity.

This balance can be upset, not only by experimental or naturally occurring lesions, but also by instinctive reflex patterns, learned modes of behavior, and by sensory or cortical impulses which are known to have ready access to the reticular formation. Part of our problem is to determine how habituation and learning, and how emotional or other stimuli, affect the reticular formation, or those cortical and peripheral structures which give rise to impulses which feed into it. One of the outstanding characteristics of the reticular formation, whether we are considering its ascending or descending influences, is the tonic or persistent character of its effects once excited. Although this effect may be less pronounced peripherally than centrally, it probably aids greatly in smoothing and maintaining bodily sets and postures; where repetitive, rhythmic, and skilled movements are concerned, it might be a handicap to quick and successive adjustments. However, there appear to be adaptive mechanisms in the reticular formation for adjusting to repetitive influences. In fact, these may play a significant role in the process of learning. Such effects of adjustment in the reticular formation to centrally directed sensory messages will be discussed later. The relation of such adaptations to efferent function are certainly evident in the adjustments to a repeated stimulus of startling character, as revealed both by behavior or posture and by the adapting response of the galvanic skin reflex. No doubt many other examples of observed behavior could be marshaled to support such an explanation. As yet, however, these behavioral examples have not been properly correlated with electrical changes in the reticular formation or other parts of the central nervous system under its influence.

Mechanisms of Sensory Control

Until fairly recently the mechanisms of sensory control were thought to reside solely in the *classical afferent pathways* to the thalamus and cortex. These were thought of as the *specific sensory pathways*, each of which conveyed its own individual kind of message to a specific nucleus of the thalamus and to a special zone of the cortex concerned with analysis, discrimination, and integration. For example, the stimulation of a given region of peripheral skin receptors would initiate impulses in a cutaneous nerve which could be followed along the course of the peripheral nerve by the electrical signs associated with the nerve impulse volley, and could be further traced through the spinothalamic tracts of the cord to the somato-sensory relay nucleus (ventralis postero-lateralis) in the thalamus and thence to the postcentral convolution of the somato-sensory cortex in the parietal lobe of the brain. The

arrival of the impulse volley in the cortex is typically signaled by a surface-positive potential which can be recorded electrically from the cortex. Such an electric change is known as an *evoked potential*, and the locus of arrival of sensory messages in the cortex can be mapped reasonably well in terms of the distribution of evoked potentials elicited by stimuli presented to the different sensory receptors. The type of message carried by the *specific sensory system* is typically a fairly discrete and short-lasting one, although, of course, repeated messages may continue to represent the reactions of the receptor field to continued or changing stimulation.

The existence of a second or an *unspecific sensory system* has gradually become evident as a result of a chance observation of Moruzzi and Magoun (55). In 1949 while exploring the effect of electrical stimulation delivered to various points in the brain stem of the cat by means of the Horsley-Clark stereotaxic instrument, which enabled them to guide insulated needle electrodes to desired regions, they found that electrical shocks in the region of the reticular formation gave rise to a generalized desynchronization of electrical activity of the cortex. If the brain of the animal was "asleep" as indicated by slow random waves and so-called sleep spindles consisting of synchronized, moderately high-voltage waves, the activity of this type changed immediately upon electrical stimulation of the reticular formation to a low-amplitude, desynchronized, or fast activity. This change was general over the surface of the cortex and indicated the widespread nature of the effect. This effect they referred to as electrocortical activation, and hence the term *activation* came to be applied eventually to any influence, either direct electrical stimulation or natural sensory stimulation, which was transmitted to the cortex via the reticular formation. Thus also the phrase *ascending reticular activating system* (ARAS) arose.

At about the same time as the Moruzzi and Magoun study, Lindsley, Bowden, and Magoun (45) studied the effect of the reticular formation and the ARAS upon the electroencephalogram of cats. Under deep ether anesthesia, the spinal cord was transected at the C-1 (first cervical) level, thus making a so-called *encéphale isolé* (isolated brain) preparation after the method of Bremer. All cut surfaces were injected with procaine hydrochloride and the ether anesthesia was discontinued. After a suitable time for elimination of ether effects, electrocortical recordings were made in the unanesthetized, isolated brain preparation. Under these conditions the EEG picture was typical of that of a normal unoperated cat, showing low-amplitude fast waves of relatively desynchronized pattern, characteristic of the waking state. Progressively higher transections of the brain stem were made with increasingly more synchronized slow waves and spindle formations appearing as more and more of the reticular formation and its collaterals from the classical afferent pathways were eliminated. With lesions of the central reticular core in the rostral midbrain region, but with lateral afferent pathways intact, or with lesions in the hypothalamus in the region of the projections of the reticular formation, the EEG of the cat showed an electrocortical picture characteristic of deep sleep or somnolence. With lesions of the specific sensory pathways (medial and lateral lemnisci) bilaterally, but with the reticular formation intact, the EEG picture remained one of wakefulness with desynchronized, low-amplitude fast waves. With a lesion of the reticular formation or the hy-

pothalamus which produced sleep waves and spindle bursts, it was found that with recording electrodes placed in the nonspecific nuclei of the thalamus (center median, intralaminar, and ventromedial regions) the same type of activity could be recorded there as in the cortex, and the bursts of activity were relatively synchronous. Decortication of one hemisphere abolished the spindle bursts in the thalamus on that side; likewise with local lesions of the responding areas in the thalamus, the widespread spindling of the ipsilateral cortex was abolished. Thus there appears to be an interdependence of these thalamic and cortical structures, at least so far as the timing of their activities is concerned.

Bremer (5) was the first to demonstrate that separation of the forebrain from its lower portions by a midbrain transection (*cerveau isolé*) produces not only a somnolent animal, but an electrocortical picture comparable to that of natural sleep. He interpreted this incorrectly, however, for he thought it was due to deafferentation, whereas the preceding studies have shown that it is the interruption of the ARAS rather than the classical afferent pathways which eliminates the waking activity of the EEG and shifts the pattern to one of sleep. Lindsley, Schreiner, Knowles, and Magoun (46) made chronic cat preparations in which there were lesions interrupting either the afferent pathways or the ARAS. Figure 2 shows the EEG and the behavior of such animals. It will be noted that cat *A* with a midbrain lesion of the specific sensory pathways is able to stand and move about in a wakeful state, and its EEG is that of a waking animal. In contrast, cat *B* is continually somnolent and has a deep-sleep-type EEG. This animal could be aroused only momentarily to the extent of

A   B

AWAKE = MIDBRAIN LESION AFFERENT PATHS

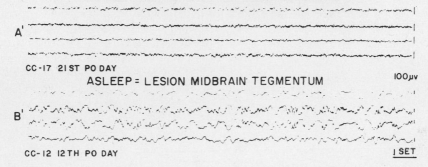

FIG. 2. *(A) Cat awake and alert with classical sensory pathways in midbrain severed; (A′) EEG record of waking type. (B) Cat somnolent with lesions of reticular formation, but with classical afferents intact; (B′) EEG record of somnolence or deep sleep. (From Lindsley, Schreiner, Knowles, and Magoun [46].)*

lifting its head slightly and partially opening its eyes upon intense somatic stimulation.

Figure 3 shows a typical sleep EEG in a normal cat; midway in the record the cat was awakened by a loud handclap. The shift in the EEG from sleep-type to waking-type was accompanied by the usual signs of behavioral arousal. Note the persistence of this effect mediated by the ARAS. After one and one-half to two and one-half minutes of waking and low-amplitude fast activity in the EEG, there was a gradual return of synchronized slow waves suggesting the return of drowsiness. French and Magoun (18) repeated in monkeys the type of study described for the cat and found even more profound somnolence and lack of responsiveness resulting from lesions in the ARAS. French, Amerongen, and Magoun (16) recorded the electrical potentials elicited in the monkey throughout the ARAS when peripheral stimuli were

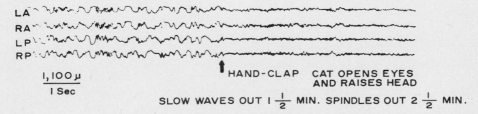

FIG. 3. *Activation of the EEG of a normal sleeping cat by auditory stimulation. EEG records from anterior (top) and posterior (bottom) regions of brain. Note persistence of desynchronization. (From Lindsley, Schreiner, Knowles, and Magoun [46].)*

applied to somatic, visual, auditory, and visceral systems. Their results, as did those of Starzl, Taylor, and Magoun (62) in the cat, showed that potentials recorded in the ARAS were produced interchangeably by the different sense modalities, through branches or collaterals of the primary sensory fibers which entered the ARAS throughout its length from the region of the medulla low in the brain stem to the thalamic relay nuclei in the diencephalon.

and with a projection to a specific area of the sensory cortex. In the region of the lower brain stem, branches or collaterals are given off from the afferent pathways to the reticular formation, represented in the central core by multisynaptic and multineuronal ascending pathways. These are shown at the cephalic end of the system spreading out to all areas of the cortex. As previously mentioned, electrical stimulation of this ARAS arouses an animal from sleep and produces a general

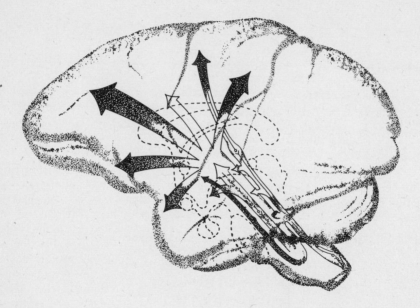

FIG. 4. *Schema projected upon monkey brain showing ARAS, including reticular formation in central core of lower brain stem with multi-synaptic relays, and its upward diffuse projections to all parts of cortex. To right a single afferent pathway with a relay in thalamus proceeds to post-central cortex, but gives off collaterals (arrows) to reticular formation. These are respectively the* unspecific *and the* specific *sensory systems.*

Figure 4 illustrates schematically on a phantom projection of the monkey brain what has heretofore been discussed in connection with these experiments. To the right of the figure and ascending from below is a primary or classical sensory pathway with a synaptic relay shown in the thalamus

alerting of the behavior of an animal already awake. Similarly, stimulation of any of the sense modalities feeds impulses into this system and arouses, alerts, and produces attentive behavior. Relative absence of peripheral stimulation, and with bodily needs generally satisfied, tends to lead to quiescent behavior and eventually to sleep. Not only are these behavioral signs of sleep or wakefulness noted, but electrical recording from the cortex, either directly or through scalp and skull as is usually the case in human subjects, shows transitions in the EEG ranging from large, random

TABLE 1

PSYCHOLOGICAL STATES AND THEIR EEG, CONSCIOUS AND BEHAVIORAL CORRELATES

Behavioral Continuum	Electro-encephalogram	State of Awareness	Behavioral Efficiency
Strong, Excited Emotion (Fear) (Rage)(Anxiety)	Desynchronized: Low to moderate amplitude; fast, mixed frequencies.	Restricted awareness; divided attention; diffuse, hazy; "Confusion."	Poor: (lack of control, freezing-up, disorganized).
Alert Attentiveness	Partially synchronized: Mainly fast, low-amplitude waves.	Selective attention, but may vary or shift. "Concentration" anticipation, "set."	Good: (efficient, selective, quick, reactions). Organized for serial responses.
Relaxed Wakefulness	Synchronized: Optimal alpha rhythm.	Attention wanders — not forced. Favors free association.	Good: (routine reactions and creative thought).
Drowsiness	Reduced alpha and occasional low-amplitude slow waves.	Borderline, partial awareness. Imagery and reverie. "Dream-like states."	Poor: (unco-ordinated, sporadic, lacking sequential timing).
Light Sleep	Spindle bursts and slow waves (larger). Loss of alphas.	Markedly reduced consciousness (loss of consciousness). Dream state.	Absent
Deep Sleep	Large and very slow waves (synchrony but on slow time base). Random, irregular pattern.	Complete loss of awareness (no memory for stimulation or for dreams).	Absent
Coma	Isoelectric to irregular large slow waves.	Complete loss of consciousness (little or no response to stimulation); amnesia.	Absent
Death	Isoelectric: Gradual and permanent disappearance of all electrical activity.	Complete loss of awareness as death ensues.	Absent

From D. B. Lindsley, Psychological Phenomena and the Electroencephalogram. *EEG Clinical Neurophysiology*, **4** (1952), 443-56.

waves of long duration characteristic of deep sleep to low-amplitude fast waves of alert attentiveness or of excited emotion (see Lindsley [41] [43]).

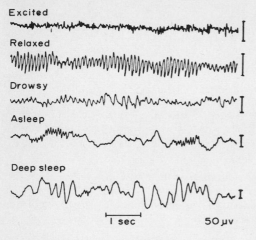

Excited

Relaxed

Drowsy

Asleep

Deep sleep

1 sec   50 μv

FIG. 5. *Different patterns of EEG in normal subject, from sleep to wakefulness to excitement. (From Jasper, 1941), in Penfield & Erickson:* Epilepsy and cerebral localization. *Springfield: Thomas.)*

Figure 5 shows in part some of the range of patterns of the EEG in the normal human subject, extending from deep sleep to excited emotion. Table 1 illustrates some of the correspondences between such a continuum of behavior and the EEG patterns, together with the state of awareness and the behavioral efficiency typically exhibited.

Can we explain all behavioral levels from sleep to waking, from relaxed wakefulness to a problem-solving set, and from affective moderation to emotional arousal and excitement, in terms of the influx of somatic, visual, auditory, olfactory, and visceral impulses into the ARAS? Apparently not. These are all contributory influences and operate somewhat interchangeably so far as general arousal

and alerting are concerned. But what about the mother who, despite being very tired, retires with her baby's welfare in mind and is aroused by the slightest cry in the night, whereas her husband sleeps soundly through it all? What about the busy husband who late in the afternoon realizes that tomorrow is his wife's birthday and he hasn't bought her a present? The memory or idea alerts him to action obviously, whether triggered by an unconscious stimulus cue or a set, or simply by a change of state due to fatigue, boredom, or inability to attend to his routine duties for a long period of time. To describe this process as a spontaneous, or a deliberate, association of past experiences and the ideas and memories they have generated explains nothing in terms of the arousal and alerting mechanism we have discussed.

However, it has been demonstrated by French, Hernandez-Peon, and Livingston (17) that stimulation of various cortical areas in the monkey gives rise to potentials recordable in the reticular formation. Figure 6 is a schematic illustration of this corticifugal influence. Thus the perceptual discriminations of the present, or those of the past stored as memories, the ideations and imagery, the higher-level symbolization and thinking of man, all are presumably capable of generating impulses in the cortical matrix. These impulses may, according to their findings, result in excitation of the ARAS, which in turn reflects its influence upon the cortex in the form of electrocortical change in the direction of "activation," "desynchronization," or "differentiation." The end result behaviorally may be action or suppression of action. To quote these investigators, "It seems logical to conclude that under normal physiological conditions influences exerted upon the reticular activating

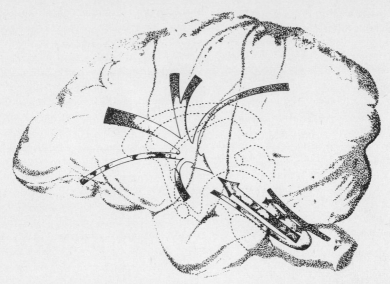

FIG. 6. *Schema projected on monkey brain showing cortico-reticular influence upon reticular formation and the ARAS. Cortical stimulation produces potential changes in reticular formation, thus cortical events can presumably influence the cortex via the ARAS as well as lower centers. (From French, Hernandez-Peon, and Livingston [17].)*

system by these specific cortical zones may be functionally allied to arousal. For consideration in this regard is the possibility that these cortico-subcortical mechanisms might participate in such aspects of consciousness as voluntary alerting, maintenance of the aroused state, focusing of attention, vigilance or perhaps 'set,' and meditation or introspection. While these processes would appear at first glance to be facilitatory in nature, inhibitory patterns are by no means excluded. Certainly focusing of attention and introspection may be associated with inhibition of somatic movement. Moreover, the 'startle reaction' is characterized by hyo-kinesis or even motor collapse."

We have seen thus far that the reticular formation serves as a kind of pool for incoming impulses of two general classes: those that come by way of collaterals from classical sensory pathways, and those that originate in the cortex. Furthermore, the ARAS, when excited by incoming impulses, serves to modify the electrical activity of the cortex on a widespread scale, producing "desynchronization" or "differentiation" of the electrical pattern. This change in the electrical pattern of the cortex may be identified as a shift from the more synchronized patterns of sleep (or relaxed wakefulness) to the less synchronized ones of waking (or alert attentiveness), and it is accompanied by corresponding changes in the behavior of the animal or human subject. Thus peripheral (or visceral) stimulation or centrally aroused impulses (ideation) are capable of producing action or a readiness for action. What holds this action in check? What prevents sensory stimuli from overexciting the reticular formation and in turn the cortex? And what prevents them from persistently keeping the cortex and behavior at a high pitch of activity?

Mechanisms of Central Control

Centrifugal regulation of afferent influx has now been demonstrated for all sense modalities. There is a kind of efferent sensory-controlling mechanism which helps to keep the sensory influx within bounds. These feedback control systems may be either negative or positive in effect, thus limiting or restricting input of sensory messages, or in some instances reinforcing and facilitating others. These corticifugal-controlling mechanisms extend to the reticular formation, but also to the first synaptic level of sensory path involved. For a brief review of the corticifugal regulation of afferent influx and references to the literature on this subject, see Lindsley (44). Granit and Kaada (23) and Eldred, Granit, and Merton (15) have shown that control of the muscle spindle proprioceptor and its sensory discharges takes place at the receptor level through the gamma-efferent system and may be triggered at the reticular level. Similar influences have been demonstrated at the first synaptic level or at other relays by Gernandt and Thulin (21) for the vestibular system, for the retina by Granit (22), and for the olfactory system by Hagbarth and Kerr (26). Thus a new principle of feedback control has been uncovered for regulating sensory influx, and this is important, for it amounts to a kind of automatic volume control like that of the modern radio. What, or how much of what, one hears, sees, feels, and so forth, may thus be determined by central factors of discrimination, habituation, and perhaps even specific conditioning. At least the lines of communication appear to be a reality, and the evidence to date clearly indicates an inhibitory

control; that central facilitation may also occur in connection with sensory input seems likely. At least at the level of the reticular formation, Hernandez-Peon and Hagbarth (32) and Scheibel, Scheibel, Mollica, and Moruzzi (59) have observed interaction between afferent impulses, and between afferent impulses and cortico-reticular impulses. Again this may take the form of inhibition or facilitation; in the case of the former, blocking of the ARAS through this kind of interaction upon its neurons could lead to disturbances in awareness and to distractibility and lack of general or specific alerting. Examples in the emotional realm of everyday experience come to mind where behavior and awareness may be blocked presumably by a flooding of the reticular system with strong and diverse interacting inputs. Immobilization and often generalized confusion result from sudden and intense barrages from afferent and corticifugal sources. Electrocortical blocking frequently is associated with sudden, intense, novel, and unexpected stimulation such as is often associated with fear or startle.

Thalamo-cortical integrating mechanisms. Jasper and Ajmone-Marsan (36) have reviewed some of the evidence of the interrelations of thalamus and cortex and the possibility of feedback control existing within these systems. This information is important to us in several ways, including the cues this may provide with regard to the mechanisms which make it possible for specific sensory messages to reach specific loci in the cortex, with respect to the possibilities of elaboration of these messages within the associational zones of a given sense modality, with respect to the integration of these messages with those of other sense modalities, and finally in relation to the manner in which stimuli of a given sense modality may dominate attention and consciousness and also how a particular stimulus may dominate others within the same modality.

The projection nuclei of the thalamus are of two general types: those which are *specific* and project from thalamic relay nuclei concerned with a specific sense mode, and those which are *diffuse* or *unspecific* and which project from thalamic nuclei subserving all sense modalities. The nuclei of the first type, such as the medial geniculate (auditory), lateral geniculate (visual), and posteroventral (somesthetic), project somewhat topographically upon the primary sensory zones of the temporal, occipital, and parietal cortex, respectively, thus preserving certain spatial attributes. The *diffusely* projecting nuclei, such as the dorsomedial, intralaminar, center median, ventralis anterior, and reticular, are apparently widely distributed to all areas, even the primary receiving centers of the cortex. A possible third type of thalamo-cortical connection is that which projects to the second sensory zone of each sense modality. Presumably this is more specific than diffuse, but it may have some of the characteristics of each type.

What then is the role of each of these systems and how do they interact in order to provide elaboration and integration? Under deep anesthesia and particularly under barbiturate (nembutal) anesthesia, the ARAS and its electrocortical activating role are reduced or abolished. Under these conditions, however, evoked potentials may be elicited as well as before. Therefore, the anesthesia and the elimination of the ARAS have not prevented the transmission of sensory messages over the classical sensory pathways and via the specific relay nuclei of the thalamus and their topographical projections to the primary receiving areas. However, behaviorally

(and subjectively, in the case of humans) the animal does not respond to the messages in a discriminative way. Thus one may draw the inference that elaboration and integration of messages received at the cortex in order for perception to occur are dependent upon the ARAS, and probably also the diffuse projection nuclei of the thalamus. It should be remembered at this point that the action of the ARAS may be mediated in whole or in part by the extra-thalamic route, in which case diffuse thalamo-cortical projections might subserve none, or only part, of the *general arousal and alerting functions* initiated through the ARAS as previously discussed.

Everyday experience provides many examples of differences between *general alerting* or readiness and *specific alerting* or focused attentiveness. It seems possible that either the diffuse thalamo-cortical projection system or some combination of it and the thalamo-cortical (semispecific) projections to the second sensory areas of the cortex may be involved in the specific alerting, including the focusing of attention upon a given type of stimulus within a modality. As indicated above, the spatial characteristics of the stimulating environment seem to be preserved by a more or less point-to-point projection system from the periphery to the receiving cortex. The qualitative nature of the stimulus, such as a specific color in the visual modality, seems not to be preserved on the basis of a topographical representation in the cortex. Chang (9) has presented evidence of a three-fiber conduction system in vision which he believes subserves the three primary colors, but he does not find a topographical representation of them on the visual cortex. He feels that the fibers of each of these three systems are distributed over the whole of the visual receiving area, and the qualitative aspect is preserved in terms of the individual fiber projections themselves.

Another aspect of the thalamo-cortical relations involves the possibility of feedback loops, or at least some cortico-thalamic connections which may facilitate or inhibit the transmission of sensory impulses through the thalamic relays. That such cortico-thalamic fibers from most areas of the cortex exist has been demonstrated in several ways. Just what function they serve remains speculative. Experimental evidence has made one thing clear, namely, that stimulation of specific relay nuclei gives rise to an evoked potential more prominent in one localized area of the cortex than in others nearby. Following such an evoked potential there are often after-discharges in the cortex. These may have a repetitive sequence, with a recurrence rate of the so-called spontaneous rhythms of the cortex, or the alpha waves. In my opinion these are due to an interruption of and a resetting of the timing characteristics masses of cells in the neighborhood, with the result that the sources of the spontaneous potentials (whether from dendrites or cell body) become synchronized and persist this way briefly until other factors cause them to diverge and fall out of step again. The nature of the organizing and time-synchronizing factor for cortical rhythms is not known, but there is some evidence to suggest that the nuclei of diffuse projection may have something to do with it, along with the ARAS. Stimulating repetitively some of these nuclei in the thalamus, such as the intralaminar group, gives rise to the "recruiting response" first described by Morison and Dempsey (54) (14), and further elaborated and utilized by Starzl and Magoun (61) and by Verzeano, Lindsley, and Magoun (64).

It consists of a small surface-positive wave followed by a large surface-negative wave. The large wave follows the shock by 15 to 50 msec which in itself suggests that it is dependent upon the exciting of activity in cortical neurons only after several synaptic relays. With repetitive stimulation in the thalamic nucleus the recruiting response grows steadily until it reaches maximal height after three to five stimulations. It is believed that the "recruiting" involves bringing greater numbers of neurons into the sphere of influence of the exciting stimulus, perhaps increased participation of both thalamic and cortical neurons. Two things are of particular interest about this response, one being the fact that there is an optimal rhythm or frequency of stimulation, perhaps due to temporal characteristics of reverberating circuits, or perhaps due to a respiratory or metabolic optimum of the individual neurons of the cortex. Apart from the actual phasic discharge of a neuron, there appears to be a rhythmical property of the cell body depending upon the rate of chemical reactions taking place in it. Such a rhythmic waxing and waning of activity seems to be accompanied by an electrical effect, the summation of which in many neurons, somehow synchronized, gives rise to the spontaneous (alpha) rhythms of the cortex. The optimal rate of recruiting responses and the recurrence rate of after-potentials following a single evoked potential, together with the decay period for such rhythms, suggest that both phenomena are functions of the so-called spontaneous rhythms of the cortex. The second thing of significance about the recruiting phenomena is that they have been reported to be most prominent in associational and motor cortex regions (61), a fact which would tend to link them with integrative functions.

Cortical Rhythms as a Control Mechanism

Among the various cortical rhythms, the most prominent and most studied is the alpha rhythm first reported upon by Berger (3) in 1929. The importance of Berger's discovery of the Electroencephalogram (EEG) cannot be overemphasized, for it provided an entirely new concept of the functional properties of the cortex. We see that, instead of being a static stand-by mechanism waiting to be excited by incoming impulses, the cortex is an active, dynamic thing with constantly shifting patterns of electric activity playing over it. As indicated above, this activity appears to be of a different type than that associated with the discharge of a neuron when it is excited and conducts an impulse. The latter type of activity is known as a spike discharge and begins with a sharp detonation. The electrical changes upon which the alpha or spontaneous activity is based seem to be related to constant fluctuations in the cell body or its dendrites.

An important principle, first elaborated by Bishop (4) and Bartley and Bishop (2), hinges upon the alpha rhythm and the electrical activity underlying it. They found upon stimulating the cut optic nerve of the rabbit that an impulse volley thus set up would produce an evoked potential in the visual cortex only when its time of arrival was properly synchronized with alpha (or spontaneous electrical) waves of the cortex. Apparently the waxing and waning of these potentials reflected a similar change in the excitability of the underlying cortical cellular matrix. Thus the alpha rhythm seemed to be associated with an excitability rhythm.

Lindsley (43) reviewed some of the indirect evidence for such a mechanism, pointing out that some of the limitations imposed upon psychological processes and behavior have time characteristics which would correspond with those of a ten-per-second alpha rhythm and excitability cycle. Chang (8) has shown, neurophysiologically, that after-potentials have temporal characteristics like those of the alpha rhythm and that an excitability cycle accompanies them. Gradually more and more fragments of evidence in support of such a concept have arisen, so that it appears that the alpha rhythm of the electroencephalogram (and perhaps other rhythms as well) plays a significant role not only in the regulation of sensory input to the cortex, but likewise in the timing of central integrations which result in action or behavior. It was proposed by Meister (53) that the alpha rhythm and its excitability cycle might operate like the shutter on a movie projector, alternately passing and blocking information—a kind of neuronic shutter mechanism. Those impulses arriving at a favorable time in the excitability cycle would excite the neurons involved, but at the opposite phase of the wave would not. This would tend to chop us or break up the continuity of a continuous train of incoming impulses and hence not only would preserve a continuing sensitivity but might provide a kind of central coding device. In any case a mechanism which can produce discrete signals out of more or less continuous trains of them would seem to provide for greater flexibility of adjustments. Thus the shifting of attention from one stimulus to another, from one set to another, is undoubtedly a function of a mechanism which permits separation and discreteness of the incoming signals, and perhaps also helps to establish some kind of synchrony with other diverse areas or other sense modes. The influence of the ascending reticular activating system upon cortical rhythms, desynchronizing them, and differentiating the domains of cortical neurons from which such rhythms arise, appears to be one of the really significant roles in the whole integrative process which makes consciousness, perception, and other processes possible.

Admittedly the preceding views are speculative and undocumented, but not in their entirety. There are a number of bits of evidence which offer some encouraging support for pursuing further the concept of the cortical excitability cycle. Figure 7 is an attempt to illustrate the manner in which well-known phenomena of electroencephalography might be explained in terms of homogeneous and differentiated brain fields. It has been known for a long time, in fact since Berger discovered the EEG, that the optimal alpha rhythm is obtained when a person is relaxed and at rest with his mind free of problems and disturbing thoughts. In the upper right of this figure is schematically illustrated a rhythmic alpha pattern at ten per second. In the upper left is a homogeneous brain field from which it might arise. Assuming that each individual neuron gives a minute electrical oscillation at about ten per second as a function of its own waxing and waning metabolism, then it may be further assumed that the electrical activity of

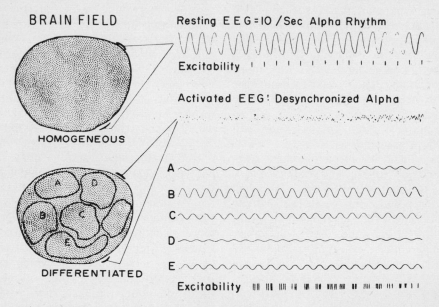

FIG. 7. *Hypothetical brain fields and type of EEG assumed to be associated with them. Ten-per-second alpha waves characterizing the "homogeneous" or relaxed condition, and a desynchronized, ARAS-activated EEG associated with a "differentiated" state of brain function. The latter EEG is characteristic of attention and problem-solving and, in general, more efficient perception and performance. According to concept that an excitability cycle is associated with waxing and waning phases of waves, there would be one per each wave peak or every tenth of a second in the case of the resting EEG, whereas for dynamic aggregates of neurons, each with its own rhythm, and out of phase with one another, there would be many periods of excitability throughout as shown below. (From Lindsley, D. B. Basic perceptual processes and the EEG*, Psychiat. Res. Reports 6, 1956.)

literally hundreds of thousands of such cells in a given region may well become synchronized, so that their potentials summate. However this comes about, we will assume that synchronization gives rise to larger potentials of the same basic frequency—ten per second. According to our hypothesis, we will arbitrarily assume that the peaks of the alpha waves are associated with excitability and the troughs, inexcitability. Drawing a vertical line below each peak to mark the periods of excitability, we note that these occur once in every tenth of a second.

When a person is given a "set" to attend, or is given a problem to solve, it is well known to electroencephalographers that the EEG becomes one of low-amplitude fast activity rather than alpha waves. We say that the alpha pattern becomes "desynchronized" or "differentiated." The differentiated brain field is meant to illustrate the formation of dynamically changing aggregates of brain cells which are synchronized as subgroups, each still presumably giving rise to the same ten-per-second electrical rhythm as the individual cell is assumed to have. These aggregates, A, B, C, D, E, and so forth, generate electrical rhythms which are not in phase with one another, and hence the summated picture is that shown in the center of the figure. The individual rhythms for each of the aggregates is shown below. Now, if a vertical line is drawn below the peaks of all of the waves in each tracing, it will be seen that instead of once every tenth of a second, there is almost continuous excitability of one aggregate or another. Such a condition would mean that incoming messages would always find some aggregate in readiness to respond, and the speed and efficiency of response would be greatly enhanced. This is precisely what happens when a person has been alerted or given a problem set. His EEG is activated, his problem-solving ability is apt to be better and his reaction time faster, and in general his efficiency is improved.

Such a conception as the above is probably closer to modern viewpoints of brain function, for much clinical and experimental neurological evidence suggests that the functions of the brain are not strictly localized, and that one part may serve somewhat interchangeably with others. If we were considering learning or the development of a particular habit sequence, it is likely that the stimulus cue as a message would at one time find one aggregate ready, and at another time a different one. As a consequence of dynamically shifting aggregates, the probability that any given neuron would have participated in the formation of the habit would be a statistical matter. Some neurons would have been involved many more times than others, but these would be distributed throughout the brain field. Hebb's (31) concept of cell assemblies might be substituted here for aggregates if one wished, and a phase sequence might be included to represent the linkage of neural elements at any given time of activation. The destruction of brain tissue after the formation of such a habit might cause disruption of it if those elements which had been involved more and carried the heaviest burden for the habit were damaged, but many other neurons would also have been activated a lesser number of times and would still represent some degree of the habit. Restitution of function following a brain injury might represent in part this kind of process, and the aphasic with partially returning speech abilities would be a case in point. One final speculative point might be mentioned. The process of "differentiation," which seems to be necessary to perception and the formation of habits and also in the intellectual application of these, may be a process which is lacking or improperly timed in the mentally deficient person. It is conceivable that some innate property of organization of the ARAS is lacking in such persons; furthermore, it is likely that growth, maturation, and experience are necessary to the formation of differentiated brain fields. Is it possible that a better understanding of the mechanism of activation might someday lead to the application of rehabilitative and retraining procedures for developing the ARAS and the diffuse projection system to a point where suitable differentiation could take place? An investigation of the EEG of mentally deficient persons from this point of view might be indicated. The traditional measurements of the EEG (frequency, voltage, and percent time of alpha) do not correlate with intelligence to any significant degree, but the reaction of the EEG to activation procedures might prove to be a different story.

In support of the excitability cycle concept, Lansing (39), working in my laboratory, sought to determine the relationship between the phase of the alpha activity in which a visual stimulus fell and reaction time. It is well known that in a series of reaction times there is great variability, visual reaction time ranging roughly from 150 to 300 milliseconds. The question may legitimately be raised as to why such a wide variation occurs, even in successive reactions, although presumably the subject is ready for each stimulus, or at least has been asked to be attentive and alert and to respond quickly. Figure 8 shows some typical records. The occipital and motor area alpha waves were recorded, as well as the finger tremor of the extended finger

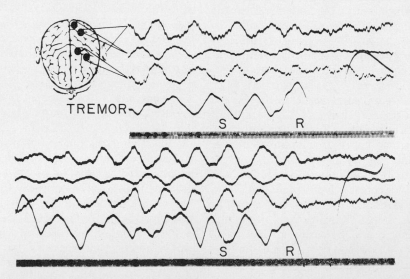

FIG. 8. *Oscillographic records of alpha waves from capital (top two lines) and motor (third from top) areas, and tremor of extended finger (bottom trace). Stimulus (S) indicated by "pip" on tremor trace, and response (R) by sharp depression of trace as finger moves downward. Stimulus onset related to phase of occipital alpha wave (top EEG) and response onset to phase of motor alpha wave. Time line: 250 cycles per second. (From Lansing [39].)*

which was to make the response. The finger was held extended and attached to a very light and balanced rocker arm which extended into a beam of light focused on a photocell through a V-shaped opening. The variation in voltage across the photocell due to very slight rhythmic tremors of the finger, and also the response which produced depression of the finger, were amplified and recorded.

With a dim red light for a fixation point, the subject responded to the onset of blue-white light produced by an electronic photoflash stimulator (Grass Instrument Co.). The stimulus onset is indicated by a small pip on one of the recording lines, and the response is seen where the tremor recording line moves sharply downward. The duration between the two is the reaction time. The purpose of the experiment was to measure in what phase of the occipital alpha wave the light stimulus occurred and then relate this to the reaction time. Similarly, the onset of the motor response was related to the phase of the motor alpha wave in which it occurred. When the briefest reaction times were selected, it was found that the stimulus had occurred predominantly in one phase of the alpha wave; likewise for the response. When corrections were made for the latency from eye to visual cortex, and for the time from motor cortex to finger movement, it turned out that both the stimulus and the response occurred in the same phase of their respective waves. These, however, might be at least 100 milliseconds apart. This suggested that in the case of the greatest speed or efficiency of response, the stimulus message arrived in the cortex at an optimal excitability period in a certain phase of the occipital alpha wave, and the motor discharge originated in the motor area in a similar optimal phase of the motor alpha wave.

Despite the fact that several other neural centers, such as the thalamic relay nucleus (lateral geniculate body), the primary sensory cortex, the motor horn-cell pool of the spinal cord, and perhaps others, may have been subject to similar excitability cycles, the results based on two of these seemed to show that excitability cycles (phase of the spontaneous alpha wave) do have some bearing on central transmission and elaboration time. Only about 50 to 60 milliseconds are required for impulses to get to and from the brain in the reaction-time situation, which means that from 100 to 200 milliseconds or more are utilized in central integration time.

In another reaction-time study (40), an attempt was made to present the visual stimuli under two general conditions, nonalerted and alerted. In the nonalert condition there were good alpha waves, poor alpha waves, or none at all, as a function of spontaneous variation, when the stimulus to respond occurred. In the alerted condition an auditory warning signal was presented prior to the visual stimulus so as to "activate" the EEG of the subject. The results show that the mean reaction time for all trials under the nonalert condition was 280 milliseconds, whereas that for the alerted state was 225 milliseconds. This much is not new, for we have known for years that reaction time may be decreased by a "set" or forewarning of the stimulus. What is new is the relation of the state of the alpha waves, for example, blocking or desynchronizing time as an index of "activation" via ARAS, to the reaction time.

With a forewarning of 50 to 250 milliseconds, insufficient time for the auditory signal to have produced alpha wave blocking or EEG activation, the mean reaction time was 255 milliseconds, a reduction, but not nearly so much as when the forewarning came 300 to 1000 milliseconds prior to the visual stimulus and accordingly had time to produce alpha blocking. These trials gave a mean reaction time of 206 milliseconds. Of special interest was the plotting of curves for reaction time and the percentage of trials in which alpha blocking was complete against duration of forewarning period. These two curves have almost identical form and reach an asymptote at about four-tenths of a second. (See Fig. 9.) In other words, if alpha blocking is complete (actually, EEG activation via ARAS has had time to occur and produce a differentiation state of one or more brain fields), reaction time is at a minimum, and this occurs when the fore-period is 300 to 400 milliseconds or more. This seems to be evidence that stimulation of the reticular formation,

and hence the ARAS, through afferent influx from tense muscles or other peripheral sensory sources, and from impulses generated in the cortex by "mental set," "anticipation," readiness instructions, or a desire to compete with someone or oneself, produces facilitation somewhere centrally which reduces the "central time" of reaction.

Still another example of the influence of the reticular formation and the ARAS in facilitating response may be given. Fuster (20), who has kindly permitted me to use some of his data, has been able to show in monkeys that visual discrimination reaction time can be reduced by stimulation of the reticular formation concurrently with the discrimination reaction. Figure 10 shows the apparatus in which he trained monkeys to discriminate between a smooth cone and a cone with flat sides.

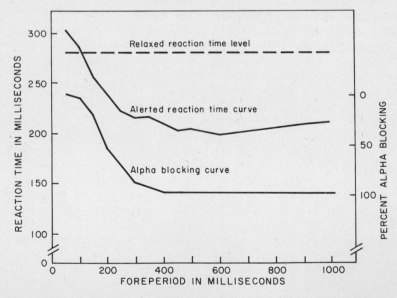

FIG. 9. *Reaction time and activation time (alpha blocking) as a function of fore-period alerting*. Relaxed reaction time level: *280 msec.* Alerted reaction time curve *decreases as a function of foreperiod, from 300 with a 50 msec. foreperiod, to 205 msec. with a 400 msec. foreperiod.* Alpha blocking curve: *percent of trials in which blocking was just complete by time visual stimulus was presented. Note that minimal reaction time level occurs when blocking is complete, namely, at about 400 msec. (From Lansing, Schwartz, and Lindsley.)*

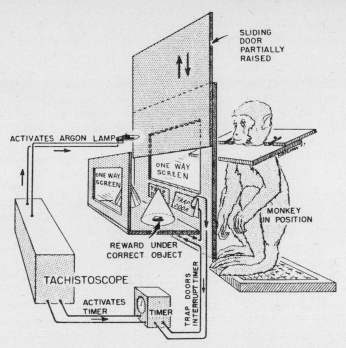

FIG. 10. *Visual-discrimination reaction-time apparatus. Animal trained to discriminate objects. Timer starts with brief tachistoscopic exposure of objects, animal makes choice, reaches through trap door, opening switch and stopping clock. Duration of exposure may be varied. Animal lives in special stock, comfortably fastened in cage, which is not shown in figure. Animal can move back and forth and feed self, but cannot reach wires to electrodes implanted in reticular formation of brain. (By courtesy of Dr. Joaquin Fuster, UCLA Medical School, Visiting Research Fellow from Spain.)*

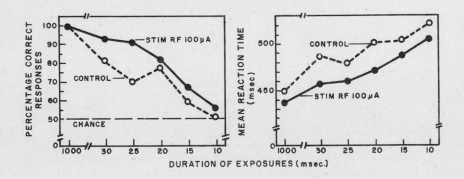

FIG. 11. *Percentage of correct responses and mean reaction time as a function of duration of tachistoscopic exposure. Dotted lines: Control; solid lines: reticular formation stimulation during visual-discrimination reaction. Each point on curves represents 100 trials for this monkey. (By courtesy Dr. Joaquin Fuster.)*

After being trained to make the discrimination and reach through a hinged door in front of the proper stimulus cue to get food under the object, the animals were confronted with a one-way vision screen through which they could see the objects to be discriminated only when a light on the other side illuminated them. As the light flashed on, it started a timer which was stopped (thus providing a measure of reaction time) when opening of a hinged door stopped the clock. This light could be flashed for durations ranging from one second to ten milliseconds. At one second the monkey could make 100 percent correct choices, but for tachistoscopic durations of 50 to ten milliseconds the percentage of correct responses decreased to a chance level at ten milliseconds. With reticular formation stimulation during the period of discrimination and reaction, the percentage of correct choices was improved at all levels.

(See Fig. 11.) Similarly, the reaction time for the discrimination ranged from 400 msec with a one-second duration of exposure to 520 msec at ten msec exposure. Under reticular stimulation the reaction times were consistently 15 to 20 milliseconds less. Hence in both accuracy and speed of visual discrimination reaction, concurrent stimulation of the reticular formation facilitated or improved performance.

In the human subject two brief 20-microsecond flashes of light presented 150 msec apart are easily seen as two, and similarly at 100 msec separation. At 50 msec separation they are seen as one. In the cat and monkey, while recording from various stations along the visual pathways from eye to cortex, the same two flashes of light at 150 and 100 msec separation produce two distinct evoked potentials, but at 50 msec separation only one such evoked potential pattern can be detected. In Fig. 12, pairs of flashes 50 msec apart

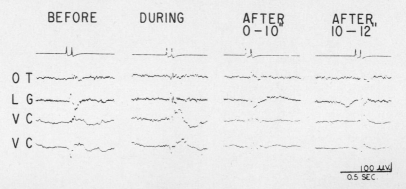

EFFECT OF RET. FORM. STIM. ON CORTICAL RESPONSE
TO PAIRED LIGHT FLASHES 50 MSEC. APART   (CAT)

FIG. 12. *Electrical recordings in cat from OT (optic tract), LG (lateral geniculate), VC (visual cortex). Top line shows paired light flashes, each 20 microseconds in duration and 50 milliseconds apart. Flashes came at one-second intervals before, during reticular formation stimulation, and after. Note in bottom VC tracing only* one evoked potential per pair of flashes *before reticular stimulation with a three volt, one msec. square wave pulse, at 300 per second for five seconds; after stimulation for about ten seconds* two evoked potentials *are recorded for each pair of flashes; beyond ten to twelve seconds after stimulation there is a return to a single evoked potential per flash pair. (D. B. Lindsley and R. S. Griffiths.)*

were presented at one-second intervals and, as the bottom tracing from the visual cortex shows, only one evoked potential appears. Then the reticular formation was stimulated electrically by electrodes lowered into it by means of the Horsley-Clarke stereotaxic instrument. For the next ten seconds, as may be seen on the lower tracing (VC), there are two distinct evoked potentials; thereafter the response reverts to a single evoked potential as before reticular stimulation. Thus it is evident that stimulation of the ARAS has in some way facilitated the visual cortex so that it can resolve two brief flashes which it could not do without stimulation of the reticular formation.

We have seen in several instances how the ARAS facilitates performance involving some aspect of cortical elaboration and integration as in reaction time, perceptual discrimination, and the handling of evoked potentials under the influence of time-limited stimulation. Attention should be drawn to still another role it seems to play. Earlier I have mentioned *general* and *specific alerting* or *attention mechanisms*. Evidence that one activity may displace or reduce another is clearly shown in an experiment by Hernandez-Peon, Scherrer, and Jouvet (34). Figure 13 (A) shows a cat sitting quietly and apparently relaxed, but with electrodes chronically implanted in the cochlear nucleus. With each auditory "click" stimulus there is an evoked potential recorded from the cochlear nucleus. In (B) two mice in a glass jar

CLICK RESPONSES IN COCHLEAR NUCLEUS

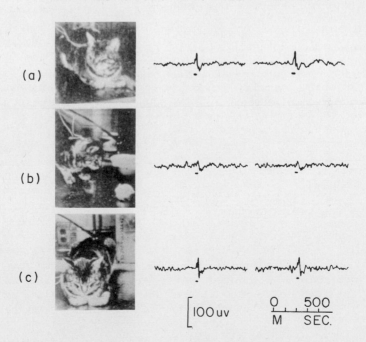

(a)

(b)

(c)

100 uv   0   500
          M   SEC.

FIG. 13. *Cat with indwelling electrodes in cochlear nucleus for recording response to click stimuli. When cat is relaxed and resting (top and bottom photos) cochlear nucleus response is large; when cat watches mice in jar, cochlear response is depressed (inhibited). (From Hernandez-Peon, Scherrer, and Jouvet,* Science, *1956,* Vol. 123, *pp. 331-32.)*

are brought before the cat, and, as the cat's behavior indicates, it is distinctly interested and attending visually to the mice. The electrical response of the cochlear nucleus to the auditory stimulus during this "activation" by a novel and unique visual stimulus which commands the cat's attention may be seen to be markedly reduced almost to the point of abolition. During state (C), after the mouse has been removed and the cat is quietly settled down again, the response returns at its original magnitude. Similarly, an olfactory stimulus (fish smell) of definite interest to the cat caused the cochlear response to subside; the cochlear response was essentially blocked also by a nociceptive stimulus (shock) to its paw.

The authors point out that

> Attention involves the selective awareness of certain sensory messages with the simultaneous suppression of others. . . . During the attentive state, it seems as though the brain integrates for consciousness only a limited amount of sensory information, specifically, those impulses concerned with the object of attention. . . . It is conceivable not only that such a selective sensory inhibition might operate simultaneously for various sensory modalities, leaving one or more unaffected but that the selectivity could extend to some discriminable aspects of any single modality—for example to one tone and not to others.

The authors mention another experiment by Hernandez-Peon and Scherrer (33) in which the repetition of a tone many times gradually produced a reduction in the cochlear nucleus response. This they referred to as "habituation" and likened it to learning. The adjustment was selective to that tone only, for a new and novel tone immediately restored the response. These investigators have also

found that direct electrical stimulation of the reticular formation depresses the cochlear nucleus response, so that it would appear that the reticular formation may have something to do with the selective control of sensory messages by inhibiting old and repeated ones and giving preference to new and unique ones. This suggests that the curiosity drive of animals described by Harlow (28) (29), and the hyperactivity, playfulness, and curiosity of young children, although perhaps maintained in part by the reticular system, will in and of itself tend to reactivate the system. Such a cycle of events tends to perpetuate activity and behavior until other factors and needs of greater moment intervene, or until the sheer repetition of the activity and the resultant cycle of behavior-activation-behavior leads to inhibition which breaks a link in the cycle. It appears that the phenomena exhibited in the reticular formation, in the cochlear nucleus, and other stations along classical afferent pathways is about as close as we have yet come to a neural representation of habit and learning, and deserves much more study.

The Role of the Limbic System

In his chapter in a previous volume in this series, Olds (56) has discussed the Limbic System quite extensively from the point of view of its subsystems anatomically, physiologically, and behaviorally. Only brief comment will be made here dealing with experiments which bear upon reticular formation-hippocampal and cortical relationships. Much work is going on with respect to the hippocampus, amygdala, and related structures of the cortex, hypothalamus, and the reticular formation. On the whole, comparatively little can be said at this point with certainty concerning these relationships. In 1939 Klüver and Bucy (38) described a series of behavioral changes in the monkey resulting from bilateral removal of the temporal lobes, including invasions of the uncus and hippocampus. The behavioral modifications included "psychic blindness," excessive oral tendencies, compulsive attentiveness to visual stimuli, decreased aggressiveness and loss of fear, increased and bizarre sex activity, and changes in dietary habits.

On the basis of subsequent studies by Bard and Mountcastle (1), Schreiner and Kling (60), Green and Arduini (25), MacLean (49) (50), and others, there is little doubt that in addition to olfactory functions, the hippocampus and related rhinencephalic structures play a significant role in emotional behavior and affective states, and are particularly related to sex behavior. Klüver (37) has presented an interesting and lucid account of brain mechanisms and behavior associated with the rhinencephalon.

Green and Arduini (25) have proposed three interesting hypotheses about the role of the hippocampus in terms of its possible relationships with the cortex. These are that 1) the hippocampus facilitates or induces changes in the cerebral cortex, 2) the hippocampus exerts a restraining or controlling influence on cortical activity, and 3) the hippocampus is affected by the same afferent modalities as the cerebral cortex but, subserving an entirely different function, is related to other levels of activity. They have found in their experiments with rabbits, cats, and monkeys that afferent stimuli capable of arousing or alerting an animal and desynchronizing its cortical activity produce series of rhythmic slow waves of three to six per second in the hippocampus. A reciprocal or inverse relationship obtains between the activity of the hippocampus and cortex, for with subsidence of synchronized activity in one it begins in the other. They conclude that the arousal response of the hippocampus (rhythmic synchronized waves) has many features in common with EEG arousal in the cortex (desynchronization), and therefore also with behavioral arousal or alerting. They point out that both the hippocampal and cortical responses, though of opposite type, are induced by all modalities of sensory stimulation. Both are generalized in their respective cortices and persist for relatively long periods after cessation of the stimulus which initiated them. Both accommodate or "habituate" to repetition of a given stimulus, and are reinstated by slight changes in the mode or type of stimulation.

The sensitivity, persistence, and adaptivity of the cortical and hippocampal arousal-response mechanisms, both activated on the afferent side through the reticular system (ARAS), suggest that they may both play a significant role in motivation, particularly with regard to initiation and maintenance of activity. The main efferent connections of the hippocampus are to the posterior hypothalamus, but its arousal response appears to be transmitted to both the hypothalamus and the thalamus. Green and Arduini associate this response with both pleasant and threatening stimuli, and other investigators (1) (60) (65) have observed marked affective changes such as anger, pleasure, placidity, and so forth in relation to stimulation and lesions in rhinencephalic structures. The amygdala appears to be a particularly sensitive region in this regard.

Terzian and Ore (63) in bilateral removal of the temporal lobes in man, including most of the uncus and hippocampus, reproduced the Klüver and Bucy syndrome of monkeys. Their case showed loss of recognition of people, including relatives, loss of fear and rage reaction, increased sexual activity, marked changes in dietary habits, and deficiency of memory. Penfield (58) associates memory functions with the temporal cortex, and has not been able to elicit memories from hippocampal stimulation in man. This leads Terzian and Ore to conclude that the changes in memory in their patient may be due to removal of the temporal cortex, and the emotional changes to interference with the hippocampus.

Delgado, Roberts, and Miller (12) observed that stimulation of tectal, lateral thalamic, and hippocampal regions produces fear-like reactions which have all the drive properties of a true emotion:

a) it could be used to establish a conditioned response; b) it could motivate the trial-and-error learning and performance of an instrumental response; c) it could be used to condition an emotional disturbance to a distinctive compartment, and after this, during trials without any further stimulation, the animals would learn to escape from that compartment; d) it could serve as a punishment to teach hungry animals to avoid food.

The fact that each of these areas is in some way linked with the reticular formation, the diffuse projection system, and the hippocampus may be of significance because of overlapping connections and functions. In a more extensive survey of areas of stimulation in the monkey, Delgado, Rosvold, and Looney (13) have found that subcortical stimulation in amygdala, medial midbrain reticular formation, ventral lateral thalamus, and other regions related to the limbic system produce the fear response which may be adapted to external circumstances. However, they also found a number of closely related regions which did

not. Weiskrantz (65), studying monkeys with lesions of the amygdala, found increased tameness and decreased fear response, more rapid extinction of conditioned avoidance and conditioned depression, a slow rate of acquisition of the behaviors (as had also been observed by Brady, Schreiner, Geller, and Kling [6] in cats), and no change in retention of avoidance behavior.

Cohen, Brown, and Brown (11) have demonstrated that hypothalamic stimulation could serve as an "unconditioned stimulus" for instrumental avoidance conditioning. They interpret this as an instance of hypothalamic stimulation producing emotionality, its termination giving rise to reinforcement of escape behavior. Pairing of a tone with hypothalamic stimulation caused it to acquire ability to elicit emotionality and avoidance behavior. They believe the central stimulation serves as a drive-arousing operation with motivational properties of energizing nature. The work of Olds (57) with self-stimulation techniques in an operant response situation illustrates the tremendous drive properties of stimulation in some areas and not in others within the general subcortical regions of the hypothalamus, septum, hippocampus, and reticular formation, regions either identified or linked in some way with the limbic system. Whether these stimulations are "pleasurable" and therefore rewarding or "painful" and perhaps also rewarding when terminated remains to be seen.

The important thing at the moment seems to be that a number of subcortical regions are beginning to emerge as having either positive or negative energizing properties. Not only does stimulation of some of these areas directly elicit behavior patterns of innate and acquired nature, but the behavior can be conditioned to other types of stimuli. The fact that some of the structures concerned have to do with affective and emotional behavior, some with arousal and alerting behavior, some with perceptual discrimination, and perhaps some with the formation of habits and learning, begins to form a pattern of understanding with regard to motivation and learning. Much remains to be done to clarify the picture, and we must proceed with caution. The temptations to speculate are great indeed, but it is an area where much wisdom and experience is needed from several disciplines. Neurophysiology is providing some opening wedges, but the behavioral data of psychology will be equally important in pointing the way. There should be no attempt to displace psychological investigation by neurophysiological or to substitute neurophysiologic explanations and mechanisms for those of behavioral science. A close liaison should exist between these disciplines so that the benefits from one might help subserve those of the other.

Green (24), in a signficant paper on the rhinencephalon and the physiology of needs, associates this paleocortical region of the brain with such basic needs as thirst, hunger, sleep and arousal, reproduction, and defense. In a concluding statement which should be important to psychologists he says,

The rhinencephalon, undoubtedly, plays an important role in behavior. However, its role is at a very high integrative level and the results to be expected from lesions or stimulation must be expected to be highly variable and capable of conditioning by past experience. Future progress is likely to be made chiefly by experimental psychological techniques combined with physiological procedures.

Along these same lines, Klüver (37) has said,

Despite the paucity of experimental data, there has never been a lack of speculations concerning the functional significant of the rhinencephalon or, more particularly, of the hippocampus. . . . There is little doubt that further progress depends less on building up more elaborate theories than on analysis and ever more analysis along behavioral, physiological and biochemical lines.

SUMMARY

An attempt has been made to present a point of view which deals with the more biologically oriented aspects of motivation. It is taken as a tacit assumption that life itself, in terms of cells, tissues, organs, organ systems, and even whole organisms, implies a continual shifting of materials and energies. This process may be referred to as *homeostasis* or *regulation,* for it is going on constantly in order to maintain physiochemical balances of smaller or larger scope within the organism and between the organism and its environment. These seem to constitute a backdrop of activity against which special increases or decreases may arise from time to time. The mechanisms underlying homeostasis appear to be built into the organism, and although subject to modification, are relatively inflexible. Their unity and integrity are products of a long history of natural selection.

Superimposed upon the homeostatic background are neural mechanisms of varying degree of lability and plasticity. Some serve predominantly homeostatic demands, others are more directly concerned with organism-environment relationships. Since conceptions of the controlling and organizing features of the central nervous system have changed in the past thirty years, an attempt has been made to deal with some of the newer views, particularly as these may be relevant to an understanding of motivation, and especially those conditions which initiate, maintain, and direct activity.

Among important new concepts of brain organization and function are the following:

Brain Rhythms and Excitability Cycles

The cortex and other nuclear masses in the brain are continually active electrically, due to autochthonous activity of its neurons. Apart from the electrical change which occurs when a neuron is excited and conducts an impulse, its cell body and/or dendrites generate minute electrical currents of rhythmical nature. These are believed to be a product of chemical change probably associated with cellular metabolism. The waxing and waning of these currents, recorded as potential variations, from thousands of cells beating in unison, are believed to represent fluctuations in the excitability of the neuron and the aggregate of neurons of which it may temporarily be a part. According to the excitability hypothesis, this may have a controlling influence upon sensory messages entering the cortex. The summation of the currents from many neurons in synchrony gives rise to measurable brain rhythms. In the relaxed state, the waking brain of an adult human has a ten-per-second rhythm, but the pattern of the EEG shows wide variations from sleep to waking, and from relaxed wakefulness to attentive alertness, or excited emotion. These changes constitute a kind of continuum, paralleled by behavioral changes, and both appear to be regulated by the ARAS (ascending reticular activating system) of the brain stem.

Ascending Reticular Activating System (ARAS)

In addition to the well-known classical or specific sensory pathways which carry messages to the brain via direct routes with few synaptic relays, there is a second sensory system, or an *unspecific sensory system*. This system is rooted in the *reticular formation* of the lower brain stem, which forms a central core extending from the medulla to the thalamus. It is composed of multineuronal, multisynaptic paths which slow conduction through it. Branches from classical afferent pathways lead into it. The reticular formation and its upward extensions project upon widespread areas of the cortex in contrast to the specific sensory system, and when activated it causes desynchronization or differentiation of electrocortical activity. This unspecific or diffuse influence of the ARAS upon the cortex has as its primary role the maintenance of a waking state. This is its *general arousal function* which causes the electrical activity of the cortex to shift from a sleep picture (with synchronized slow waves) to waking (with alpha waves). There is also believed to be a *general alerting function* which causes a shift from synchronized alpha waves of the relaxed waking state to low-amplitude fast waves of a desynchronized pattern, and creates a general attentive state. Differential excitation in the reticular formation and/or some combination of interaction between thalamus and cortex may give rise to a *specific alerting function*, in which attention may be focused on a single sense modality or upon a specific stimulus within a modality. The alerting functions, both general and specific, appear to play a role in perception, including the elaboration and integration of incoming messages. The ARAS and its activating functions are supported by impulses feeding into the reticular pool from collaterals of all sensory paths, and also from cortico-reticular fibers. Thus cortical events, as well as sensory events, enter into the energizing of the ARAS, with resulting changes in consciousness, attention, perception, and perhaps learning.

Descending Influences from Reticular Formation

The more rostral portion of the reticular formation has a facilitatory influence upon spinal motor outflow to muscles, whereas the caudal portion is a region of inhibitory influence. Certain regions of the cortex, caudate nucleus and cerebellum connect with the inhibitory portion of the brain stem reticular formation and maintain a tonic influx into it. Normally this maintains a balance with the facilitatory portion and spinal motor reflexes and muscle tension are properly controlled. If any of the regions concerned with the inhibitory system are interfered with by lesions, there is a loss of inhibitory control, and spasticity, hyperreflexia, and abnormal tone of bodily musculature ensues.

Feedback Mechanisms Controlling Afferent Conduction

All sensory avenues have been shown to be subject to inhibitory or negative feedback control. Sensory influx can be reduced by stimulation of the reticular formation or by cortical stimulation of fibers leading into it. This inhibitory control may take place at any synaptic level but takes effect on the first synaptic level, and perhaps even at the receptor in some instances. The cortico-thalamic fibers exercise some inhibitory control at a thalamic level. The inhibitory influences during the waking state appear to act tonically upon the sensory channels, for during sleep or anesthesia there may be enhancement of afferent conduction. Selective inhibitory control

may be a possibility. There is some indication that positive feedback or facilitation may also occur. Such controlling influences upon the sensory input provide a much greater flexibility and range of adjustment centrally than had heretofore been realized.

ARAS and the Limbic System

Like the ARAS, the limbic system, and especially the hippocampus, is aroused by any sensory stimulus, but whereas the effect of ARAS upon the cortex is to desynchronize its electrical activity, such stimuli produce a rhythmic synchronized activity in the hippocampus and related structures. Both show persistence of activity once activated. The limbic system, especially amygdala and hippocampus, is closely associated with emotional behavior and persistent drive states. It has afferent connections from the reticular formation and efferent connections with the posterior hypothalamus, as well as other structures. These rhinencephalic structures, originally only associated with smell and taste sensations, now appear to be intimately linked with the reticular formation, hypothalamus, and cortex, and are sensitive to arousal by all modalities.

Motivation requires an activator. The reticular formation has been shown to have such a function. It is sensitive to all types of internal and external sensory stimulation; it is also sensitive to events originating in the cortex. Its excitation leads to changes in the electrical activity of the cortex; such changes are often accompanied by changes in posture and behavior, but also they are capable of modifying the receptivity of the cortex to incoming messages, thus permitting selective discrimination and selective action. The reticular formation has inhibitory and facilitatory control of somatic motor outflow, and has influence upon autonomic activity. The multisynaptic nature of the reticular formation delays its action beyond that of primary sensory pathways to the cortex, apparently permitting differentiation and elaboration of cortical integrating functions, probably through the agency of control of cortical rhythms and excitabilities. The rhythmic beat may be stopped and reset or reconstituted in various areas, with or without a synchronous beat. The timing of these rhythms and the conducted disturbances in the cortical matrix make for integration of diverse areas, and also permit associations on the basis of an optimal interval such as that for a conditioning process.

Motivation requires persistence of action or its surrogates. The ARAS set in action manifests some persistence; the hippocampus which is activated by it may show a longer perseveration. Habits and memories established by virtue of its complementary action, and perhaps that of the hippocampus, to excitations in the cortex which are marked by discrimination, provide relatively indefinite persistence.

Motivation *may* require direction and a goal or goal-surrogate (witness Harlow [29] [30] on curiosity and manipulatory motives; O. R. Lindsley [48] on free operants). Sheer activity, with or without direction, may be a goal in itself. The perception and definition of a goal and the establishment of direction toward it seem to call for selective discriminatory control and imply specific alerting based on novel or unique stimulus cues. The ARAS and the diffuse thalamo-cortical projection system presumably play an important role, but the reticular formation seems to have a way of dealing with and eliminating routine and repetitive stimuli by "habituation" or "adaptation."

REFERENCES

1. Bard, P. and V. B. Mountcastle, "Some Forebrain Mechanisms Involved in Expression of Rage with Special Reference to Suppression of Angry Behavior," *Research Publications of the Association for Nervous and Mental Disease,* **27** (1948), 362-402.

2. Bartley, S. H. and G. H. Bishop, "The Cortical Response to Stimulation of the Optic Nerve in the Rabbit," *American Journal of Physiology,* **103** (1933), 159-72.

3. Berger, H., "Über das Electrenkephalogramm des Menschen," *Archives of Psychiatry,* **87** (1929), 527-70.

4. Bishop, G. H., "Cyclic Changes in Excitability of the Optic Pathway of the Rabbit," *American Journal of Physiology,* **103** (1933), 213-24.

5. Bremer, F., "Cerveau isole et physiologie du sommeil," *C. R. Soc. Biol.* (Paris), **118** (1935), 1235-42.

6. Brady, J. V., L. Schreiner, I. Geller, and A. Kling, "Subcortical Mechanisms in Emotional Behavior: The Effect of Rhinencephalic Injury Upon the Acquisition and Retention of a Conditioned Avoidance Response in Cats," *Journal of Comparative Physiological Psychology,* **47** (1954), 179-86.

7. Cannon, W. B., *The Wisdom of the Body.* New York: W. W. Norton & Company, Inc., 1932.

8. Chang, T.-T., "Changes in Excitability of Cerebral Cortex Following Single Electric Shock Applied to Cortical Surface," *Journal of Neurosphysiology,* **14** (1951), 95-112.

9. ———, "Functional Organization of Central Visual Pathways," *Research Publications of the Association for Nervous and Mental Disease,* **30** (1952), 430-53.

10. Child, C. M., *Physiological Foundations of Behavior.* New York: Holt, Rhinehart & Winston, Inc., 1924.

11. Cohen, B. D., G. W. Brown, and M. Brown, "Avoidance Learning Motivated by Hypothalamic Stimulation,"

Journal of Comparative Physiological Psychology. See also Brown, G. W., and B. D. Cohen, "Avoidance and Approach Learning Motivated by Stimulation of Identical Hypothalamic Loci," *Fed. Proc.,* **16** (1956), 16.

12. Delgado, J. M. R., W. W. Roberts, and N. E. Miller, "Learning Motivated by Electrical Stimulation of the Brain," *American Journal of Physiology,* **179** (1954), 587-93.

13. Delgado, J. M. R., H. E. Rosvold, and E. Looney, "Evoking Conditioned Fear by Electrical Stimulation of Subcortical Structures in the Monkey Brain," *Journal of Comparative Psychology,* **49** (1956), 373-80.

14. Dempsey, E. W. and R. S. Morrison, "The Production of Rythmically Recurrent Cortical Potentials after Localized Thalamic Stimulation," *American Journal of Physiology,* **135** (1942), 293-300.

15. Eldred, E., R. Granit, and P. A. Merton, "Observations on 'Intact,' De-afferented, and De-efferented Muscle Spindles," *Acta Physiol. Scand.,* **29** (1953), 83-85.

16. French, J. D., F. K. Amerongen, and H. W. Magoun, "An Activating System in Brain Stem of Monkey," *Arch. Neurological Psychiatry* (Chicago), **68** (1952), 577-90.

17. French, J. D., R. Hernandez-Peon, and R. B. Livingston, "Projections from Cortex to Cephalic Brain Stem (Reticular Formation) in Monkey," *Journal of Neurophysiology,* **18** (1955), 44-55.

18. French, J. D. and H. W. Magoun, "Effects of Chronic Lesions in Central Cephalic Brain Stems of Monkeys," *Archives of Neurological Psychiatry* (Chicago), **68** (1952), 591-604.

19. Fulton, J. F., *A Textbook of Physiology.* Philadelphia: W. B. Saunders Co., 1949.

20. Fuster, J. M., "Tachistoscopic Perception in Monkeys," *Fed. Proc.,* **16** (1957), 43.

21. Gernandt, B. E. and C. A. Thulin,

"Vestibular Connections of the Brain Stem," *American Journal of Physiology,* **171** (1952), 121-27.

22. Granit, R., "Centrifugal and Antidromic Effects on Ganglion Cells of Retina," *Journal of Neurophysiology,* **18** (1955), 388-411.

23. Granit, R. and B. R. Kaada, "Influence of Stimulation of Central Nervous Structures on Muscle Spindles in Cat," *Acta Physiol. Scand.,* **27** (1952), 130-60.

24. Green, J. D., "Rhinencephalon and the Physiology of Needs," *Semaine de la Salpetrere* (Paris, 1956).

25. Green, J. D. and A. A. Arduini, "Hippocampal Electrical Activity in Arousal," *Journal of Neurophysiology,* **17** (1954), 533-57.

26. Hagbarth, K. E. and D. I. B. Kerr, "Central Influences on Spinal Afferent Conduction," *Journal of Neurophysiology,* **17** (1954), 295-307.

27. Hanberry, J. and H. Jasper, "Independence of Diffuse Thalamo-cortical Projection System Shown by Specific Nuclear Destructions," *Journal of Neurophysiology,* **16** (1953), 252-71.

28. Harlow, H. F., "Learning and Satiation of Response in Intrinsically Motivated Complex Puzzle Performance in Monkeys," *Journal of Comparative Physiological Psychology,* **43** (1950), 289-94.

29. ———, "Mice, Monkeys, Men and Motives," *Psychological Review,* **60** (1953), 23-32.

30. Harlow, H. F., N. C. Blazek, and G. E. McClearn, "Manipulatory Motivation in the Infant Rhesus Monkey," *Journal of Comparative Physiological Psychology,* **49** (1956), 444-48.

31. Hebb, D. O., *The Organization of Behavior.* New York: John Wiley & Sons, Inc., 1949.

32. Hernandez-Peon, R. and K. E. Hagbarth, "Interaction Between Afferent and Cortically Induced Reticular Responses," *Journal of Neurophysiology,* **18** (1955), 44-55.

33. Hernandez-Peon, R. and H. Scherrer, "'Habituation' to Acoustic Stimuli

in Cochlear Nucleus," *Fed. Proc.*, **14** (1955), 44-55.

34. Hernandez-Peon, R., H. Scherrer, and M. Jouvet, "Modification of Electric Activity in Cochlear Nucleus During 'Attention' in Unanesthetized Cats," *Science*, **123** (1956), 331-32.

35. Herrick, C. J., *Neurological Foundations of Animal Behavior*. New York: Holt, Rinehart & Winston, Inc., 1924.

36. Jasper, H. H. and C. Ajmone-Marsan, "Thalamo-cortical Integrating Mechanisms," *Research Publications of the Association for Nervous and Mental Disease*, **30** (1952), 493-512.

37. Kluver, H., "Brain Mechanisms and Behavior with Special Reference to the Rhinencephalon," *Journal Lancet* (Minneapolis), **72** (1952), 567-77.

38. Kluver, H. and P. Bucy, "Preliminary Analysis of Functions of the Temporal Lobes in Monkeys," *Archives of Neurological Psychiatry* (Chicago), **42** (1939), 979-1000.

39. Lansing, R. W., "The Relationship of Brain and Tremor Rhythms to Visual Reaction Time." (Doctoral thesis, University of California at Los Angeles, 1954.)

40. Lansing, R. W., E. Schwartz, and D. B. Lindsley, "Reaction Time and EEG Activation," *American Psychologist*, **11** (1956), 433.

41. Lindsley, D. B., "Emotion," in *Handbook of Experimental Psychology*, ed. S. S. Stevens, pp. 473-516. New York: John Wiley & Sons, Inc., 1951.

42. ———, "Brain Stem Influences on Spinal Motor Activity," in *Patterns of Organization in the Central Nervous System*, **30**, pp. 174-95. Baltimore: The Williams & Wilkins Co., 1952.

43. ———, "Psychological Phenomena and the Electroencephalogram," *EEG Clinical Neurophysiology*, **4** (1952), 443-56.

44. ———, "Physiological Psychology," *Annual Review of Psychology*, **7** (1956), 323-48.

45. Lindsley, D. B., J. Bowden, and H. W. Magoun, "Effect upon EEG of Acute Injury to the Brain Stem Activating System," *EEG Clinical Neurophysiology*, **1** (1949), 475-86.

46. Lindsley, D. B., L. H. Schreiner, W. B. Knowles, and H. W. Magoun, "Behavioral and EEG Changes Following Chronic Brain Stem Lesions in the Cat," *EEG Clinical Neurophysiology*, **2** (1950), 483-98.

47. Lindsley, D. B., L. M. Schreiner, and H. W. Magoun, "An Electromyographic Study of Spasticity," *Journal of Neurophysiology*, **12** (1949), 197-205.

48. Lindsley, O. R., "Operant Conditioning Methods Applied to Research in Chronic Schizophrenia," *Psychiatric Research Reports*, **5** (1956), 118-39.

49. MacLean, P. D., "The Limbic System and Its Hippocampal Formation. Studies in Animals and Their Possible Application to Man," *Journal of Neurosurgery*, **11** (1954), 29-44.

50. ———, "The Limbic System ('visceral brain') in Relation to Central Gray and Reticulum of the Brain Stem," *Psychosomatic Medicine*, **17** (1955), 355-66.

51. Magoun, H. W., "The Ascending Reticular System and Wakefulness," *Brain Mechanisms and Consciousness*, pp. 1-20. Oxford: Blackwell, 1954.

52. Magoun, H. W. and R. Rhines, *Spasticity: The Stretch Reflex and Extrapyramidal Systems*. Springfield, Ill.: Charles C Thomas, Publishers, 1948.

53. Meister, R. K., "A Hypothesis Concerning the Function of the Occipital Alpha Rhythm in Vision with Special Reference to the Perception of Movement." (Unpublished doctoral dissertation, University of Chicago, 1951.)

54. Morison, R. S. and E. W. Dempsey, "A Study of Thalamo-cortical Relations," *American Journal of Physiology*, **135** (1942), 281-92.

55. Moruzzi, G. and H. W. Magoun, "Brain Stem Reticular Formation and Activation of the EEG," *EEG Clinical Neurophysiology*, **1** (1949), 455-73.

56. Olds, J., "Physiological Mechanisms of Reward," *Nebraska Symposium on Motivation 1955*, ed. Marshall R. Jones, pp. 73-139. Lincoln: University of Nebraska Press, 1955.

57. ———, "A Preliminary Mapping of Electrical Reinforcing Effects in the Rat Brain," *Journal of Comparative Physiological Psychology*, **49** (1956), 281-85.

58. Penfield, W., "Observations on the Anatomy of Memory," *Folia Psychiat., neurol. et neurochir, neerl.* Brouwer Memorial Volume, (1950), p. 348.

59. Scheibel, M., A. Scheibel, A. Mollica, and G. Moruzzi, "Patterns of Convergence and Interaction of Afferent Impulses on Single Units of the Reticular Formation," *Journal of Neurophysiology*, **18** (1955), 309-331.

60. Schreiner, L. H. and A. Kling, "Behavioral Changes Following Rheinencephalic Injury in Cat," *Journal of Neurophysiology*, **16** (1953), 643-59.

61. Starzl, T. E. and H. W. Magoun, "Organization of the Diffuse Thalamic Projection System," *Journal of Neurophysiology*, **14** (1951), 133-46.

62. Starzl, T. E., C. W. Taylor, and H. W. Magoun, "Collateral Afferent Excitation of Reticular Formation of Brain Stem," *Journal of Neurophysiology*, **14** (1951), 479-96.

63. Terzian, H. and G. D. Ore, "Syndrome of Klüver and Bucy: Reproduced in Man by Bilateral Removal of the Temporal Lobes," *Neurology*, **5** (1955), 373-80.

64. Verzeano, M., D. B. Lindsley, and H. W. Magoun, "Nature of Recruiting Response," *Journal of Neurophysiology*, **16** (1953), 183-95.

65. Weiskrantz, L., "Behavioral Changes Associated with Ablation of the Amygdaloid Complex in Monkeys," *Journal of Comparative Physiological Psychology*, **49** (1956), 381-91.

Patterns of Cardiac Arousal During Complex Mental Activity *

S. J. Blatt

In recent years, trends in such divergent fields as motivational theory, experimental psychology, and psychoanalytic ego psychology have reflected converging emphasis on the organism's capacity and desire to interact effectively with its environment. This adaptive motivational force was noticed early in animal research in the animal's exploration, search, and observation of its surroundings. The adaptive aspect of this behavior has been demonstrated by the research on latent learning and incidental learning. Extensive recent research on exploration, curiosity, activity, and the need for novelty in animals has been well summarized (Berlyne, 1960; Hebb, 1955; White,

* From S. J. Blatt, "Patterns of Cardiac Arousal During Complex Mental Activity," *Journal of Abnormal Social Psychology*, 63 (1961), 272-82. Reprinted by permission of the author and the American Psychological Association.

The author wishes to express his appreciation to Roy R. Grinker, Sheldon J. Korchin, Sara K. Polka, and Morris I. Stein for their comments during this study and for making available funds and equipment. The author also expresses appreciation to Helen Heath for aid with the statistical analysis, to Paul Cekan for assistance in the polygraph instrumentation, and to Charles Greenberg for aid in scoring the data.

1959) and indicates the basic need of the organism to explore a novel situation or to create a stimulus change in a repetitive and bland environment (Zimbardo & Miller, 1958). These findings, as well as the research on the severe effects of sensory deprivation (Hebb, 1958; Lilly, 1956), have compelled many theorists to formulate the organism's need for effective interaction with its environment as a motivational force that is relatively independent of any primary drive or tissue need (White, 1959; Woodworth, 1958).

A similar trend and emphasis has also been apparent in the development of psychoanalytic theory (Gill, 1959), where the ego theorists all have highlighted the autonomous ego functions: those aspects of the personality structure concerned with adaptation[1] which are functionally independent of instinctual drives and derive in part from an independent source. Hendrick (1942) also wrote of an "instinct to master," an "inborn drive to do and to learn how to do," a "pleasure in exercising a function successfully regardless of its sensual value." Fenichel (1945) wrote of mastery as a "general aim of every organism but not a specific instinct," "a pleasure of enjoying one's abilities" that derives from the pleasure of functioning without anxiety. Actually this motivational force for exploration and adaptive functioning was discussed by Bühler (1930) as the *Funktionlust* and by Freud (1927, 1949) when he alluded to the fact that ego functions are supplied with their own energy independent of instincts, and that there is pleasure in their exercise. Intrinsic satisfaction in functioning and the desire for stimulation and growth are

seen in many personality theories (Goldstein, 1939; Maslow, 1954; Rogers, 1951) as the *sine qua non* of mental health and psychological maturity. It is these factors that are impaired in pathology, distorted by conflict, and thwarted by defensive maneuvers. For some theorists, such as Woodworth (1958) and White (1959), coping or dealing with the environment is viewed as a fundamental element in motivation.

Cognitive processes are an essential component of adaptive functioning. Curiosity, exploration, and the need for novelty all imply a need for intellectual stimulation. Playful exploration, the desire to effect a stimulus change, the enjoyment of work and of novelty all stress intrinsic satisfaction in cognitive functioning. As Hebb (1955) has insistently pointed out, we "underestimate the human need of intellectual activity" and the degree to which man's activity is spent in raising the level of stimulation and excitement. Hebb (1955) has conceptualized excitement and exploration in physiological terms and views it as serving an arousal or vigilance function that establishes a level of cortical excitation without which learning could not occur. Arousal serves as a drive, as an energizer, and efficient learning or functioning is only possible when the level of arousal is high. In extreme situations, however, such as those provoking paralysis from terror or fright, excessive arousal interferes with functioning. Such an "inverted U-shaped" relationship between arousal (as measured by autonomic variables) and level of performance has been frequently demonstrated (Duffy, 1951, 1957; Freeman, 1940; Malmo, 1957). There is an optimal level of arousal for efficient performance, and levels of arousal either below or (in extreme situations) above this optimal level

---

[1] *Adaptation* as used in this paper is more than just a passive conformity; it rather includes an active, creative, constructive coping and interaction with the environment.

interfere with effective functioning. The inverted U-shaped curve, however, has been demonstrated mainly in the relationship between arousal and functioning in relatively simple tasks such as reaction time, rotary pursuit, and mirror tracing. Scant data are available about the relationship between arousal and efficiency of thought in complex problems. From the conceptualization of the arousal continuum, similar relationships should exist between autonomic arousal and complex problem-solving. The purpose of the present study is to explore the relationships between a measure of autonomic arousal (cardiac rate) and the efficiency of complex mental activity.

Duffy (1951, 1957) proposes two major dimensions of arousal: intensity and direction. Direction, expressed in dynamic characteristics of the behavior that occur concomitant with arousal, indicates the degree to which the arousal and behavior are goal-directed. Thus not only should autonomic arousal be high in efficient functioning, but the arousal reactions should also have direction and should occur in response to important points in the behavior or thought process.

In prior research (Blatt, 1958; Blatt & Stein, 1959), a model was developed of the process by which subjects solve a complex logical problem. In this model of the problem-solving process two crucial points were identified: where the subject had available, implicitly at least, the necessary and sufficient information for solution, and where the subjects' predominant activity shifts from questions of analysis about one-to-one relationships to the more complex questions of synthesis that attempt to organize and integrate information to achieve solution (analysis-synthesis shift). These two points, which subjects are not able to report, delineate three phases of the problem-

solving process. The initial phase extends from the beginning of the problem to the point at which the subject has available implicitly the necessary and sufficient information for solution. This is followed by the lag phase, in which the subject gathers additional information prior to shifting from analysis to synthesis. In the synthesis phase the subject's behavior reflects primary concern with co-ordinating the information he has obtained.

The body of research and theory reviewed at the outset leads to the expectation that efficiency in complex mental activity should be characterized by heightened arousal, which should occur, in part, at important points in the thought process. The following hypotheses were the focus of the present study:

1. Efficient problem-solvers have a higher level of cardiac rate and a greater variability of cardiac rate than inefficient ones during complex mental activity.

2. Among efficient problem-solvers, elevations in the cardiac rate occur at those points in the thought process at which necessary and sufficient information for solution has become available, at which the predominant activity has changed from analysis to synthesis, and at solution.

METHOD

Concurrent recordings of cardiac rate were obtained as subjects attempted to solve problems on the John-Rimoldi Problem-Solving Apparatus (PSI). Since a more detailed description of the PSI apparatus is available (Blatt & Stein, 1959; John, 1957), only a brief description of the apparatus is presented here. A diagrammatic representation of the demonstration problem and its solution are presented in Figure 1.

On the apparatus the subject is pre-

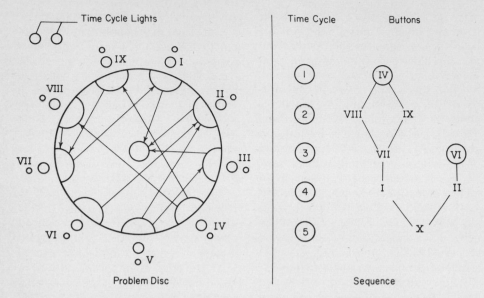

FIG. 1. *Diagrammatic representation of the disc and the solution sequence of the demonstration problem.*

sented with a panel containing a circular array of nine lights, plus a center light. Next to each of the nine outer lights there is a button, which, when pressed, lights up its corresponding light. Some of the lights are interrelated, so that when Button A is pressed, Light A comes on, followed in the next time cycle (three seconds later) by Light B, with which it was related. The existence of a relationship between the lights is indicated by arrows on a removable disc, and there are different discs for each problem. An arrow indicates one of three types of relationships:

1. A direct one-to-one effect—such that the activation of A causes B to light in the next time interval.
2. A facilitatory or combiner effect —such that A plus another light, X, which also has an arrow going to B, can light B if, and only if, A and X are lit simultaneously.
3. A blocking effect—such that A prevents X (which has an arrow to B) from lighting B, that is, X can

light B only if A has not been activated. The subject is instructed about the types of relationships that exist on the apparatus, but he is left to discover or infer the specific relationships within each problem.

In each problem the subject's task is to discover the one correct sequence of the three buttons at the bottom of the circle that will light the center light, which has no activating button. The subject may use any of the buttons that he wishes to discover relationships, but may use only the three buttons at the bottom in the final solution.

Thus, on the apparatus the subject must press buttons to gather information about the logical relationships within the problem and must also press buttons when testing his various attempts to integrate this information. All button presses are automatically recorded, creating a complete record of the problem-solving performance.

The subject's problem-solving process can be reconstructed sequentially, step by step, and each of the subject's responses identified as necessary for solution or not. Each sequence of interacting button presses is regarded as putting a question to the apparatus, and the number of unnecessary questions the subject asks while solving the problem measures his problem-solving efficiency. Also in the sequential analysis of the responses, the crucial points of necessary and sufficient information and analysis-synthesis shift can be identified for each subject. The analysis-synthesis shift point is the point that best meets the following two conditions: most of the analytic questions have already been asked, and most of the synthetic questions still remain to be asked. Analytic questions are defined as those in which one side of the question is unity and the question is asked to find the constituent parts of that unity (Duncker, 1945); there is one cause and one effect, or one cause and multiple effects, or multiple causes with a single effect. Synthetic questions are those in which there are multiple causes and multiple effects, where the question involves an attempt to integrate information. The analysis-synthesis shift point is located where the difference between the percentage of analytic questions asked and the percentage of synthetic questions asked is maximum ($a/A — s/S =$ Maximum). (a and s are, respectively, the number of preceding analytic and synthetic questions.) This maximum value also indicates the degree to which the problem-solving process was organized into these two phases. For example, if all the analytic questions had already occurred before a specific point ($a/A = 100$) and all the synthesis questions were still to be asked ($s/S = 0$), then the separation of the phases would be perfect or 100. A less clear separation between the two phases would be correspondingly indicated by smaller values.

Cardiac rate was recorded by chest leads throughout the entire experimental procedure of instructions, practice problem (presented to the subjects as first experimental problem), experimental problem, and four interposed rest periods (ten minutes each). Cardiac rate was measured for each 30-second interval during the entire experiment, the measure of heart rate being prorated to one-tenth beat at each end of these intervals. The mean and standard deviation of these values were obtained for each of the experimental periods. Though the issue of response specificity (Lacey, 1950) arises, recent research (Schnore, 1959) indicates that heart rate reflects most consistently the general level of arousal. Cardiac rate was selected as the physiological measure of arousal in the present study also because it is among the more reliable autonomic measures, responds rapidly, and can be recorded continuously without drastically limiting the subject's activity and movement.

Eighteen first- and second-year male graduate students who had volunteered to take part in a study of problem-solving served as subjects. They were paid $6.00 each for participating in the study, which at the maximum required three hours. After the experimental procedures the subjects were asked for retrospective accounts of their problem-solving process, their conceptualization of the problem, the methods by which they attempted to solve it, their awareness of any crucial moments, their feelings about the problem, and the degree of arousal they experienced during the course of the experimental problem.

RESULTS

Efficient vs. Inefficient Problem-Solvers

On the basis of the problem-solving performance on the experimental problem, the 18 subjects were divided into two groups of nine "efficient" (11–50 unnecessary questions) and nine "inefficient" subjects (73–161 unnecessary questions). All subjects completed the practice problem; two of the nine inefficient subjects did not solve the experimental problem in the allotted time of one hour.

nificant ($<.001$), indicating that the different experimental occasions evoke changes in rate for both the efficient and inefficient subjects.

Table 2 presents the mean cardiac rate for the two groups during each experimental occasion and a comparison by t test of the groups during each of the occasions. The two groups did not differ significantly in mean cardiac rate during the early experimental conditions of initial rest and instructions. After the instructions, however, the cardiac rate of the efficient subjects

TABLE 1

ANALYSIS OF VARIANCE OF MEAN CARDIAC RATE
FOR EFFICIENT AND INEFFICIENT SUBJECTS

Subjects	Source	df	MS	F	p
Total ($N = 18$)	Groups	1	445.41	3.05	.10
	Error term	16	145.96		
	Occasions	6	43.79	10.85	$<.001$
	Group $\times$ Occasion	6	18.68	4.63	$<.001$
	Error term	96	4.04		
Efficient ($N = 9$)	Occasion	6	28.22	7.68	$<.001$
	Error term	48	3.67		
Inefficient ($N = 9$)	Occasion	6	34.25	7.78	$<.001$
	Error term	48	4.40		

The mean and the standard deviation of cardiac rate for each of the seven experimental occasions were obtained from the 30-second measures of cardiac rate. Table 1 presents a comparison of the mean cardiac rates, using a Lindquist (1953) Type I analysis of variance. The total between-group difference in cardiac rate for the entire experimental procedure approached significance at the .10 level, suggesting that the efficient group had a higher over-all cardiac rate. There was a significant total between-occasion difference ($<.001$), indicating that the various experimental occasions evoked different levels of cardiac rate. The between-occasion difference within each of the groups was highly significant

became significantly greater than that of the inefficient subjects. The difference between the two groups reached statistical significance during the practice problem and continued significant for the remainder of the experiment, being particularly marked during the experimental problem.

To test the differences in level of cardiac rate within each group between the different occasions, the Lindquist (1953) procedure for testing simple effects in Type I analysis of variance with significant Group $\times$ Occasion interaction was used. Within the efficient group the cardiac rate during the practice and experimental problems was significantly greater ($<.05$) than it was in the other conditions. Within

TABLE 2

MEAN CARDIAC RATE OF EFFICIENT AND INEFFICIENT SUBJECTS

Occasion	Efficient subjects (N = 9)	Inefficient subjects (N = 9)	p (one-tailed)
Initial rest (A)	87.32	84.18	ns
Instructions	88.60	85.26	ns
Rest (B)	88.18	83.82	ns
Practice problem	96.24	87.92	<.10
Rest (C)	89.28	80.82	<.05
Experimental problem	94.16	80.80	<.01
Rest (D)	87.50	75.84	<.01

the inefficient groups the mean cardiac rate during the practice problem was significantly greater ($<.05$) than during all the other occasions except the initial rest and the instructions. However, the cardiac rate of the inefficient group during the experimental problem was significantly lower ($<.05$) than it was during the initial rest, instructions, and practice problem.

In comparing the variability of heart rate of the two groups during the seven occasions, the same statistical procedures were employed. The standard deviation of each subject's cardiac rate was obtained for each of the experimental occasions from the 30-second measures of cardiac rate. Table 3 presents a comparison of these standard deviations of cardiac rate, using a Lindquist Type I analysis of variance.

The total between-group difference was significant at less than the .025 level, indicating a greater over-all *intra-*individual variability of cardiac rate for the efficient group. There was a significant total between-occasion difference ($<.001$), indicating that the various experimental occasions evoked different levels of variability. The between-occasion difference within each group was obtained since there was a significant Group $\times$ Occasion interaction. The between-occasion difference within the efficient group was highly significant ($<.001$); however, the between-occasion difference for the inefficient group was not significant and, in fact, approached zero.

Table 4 presents the mean standard deviation of cardiac rate for the two groups during each of the experimental

TABLE 3

ANALYSIS OF VARIANCE OF STANDARD DEVIATION OF CARDIAC RATE
FOR EFFICIENT AND INEFFICIENT SUBJECTS

Subjects	Source	df	MS	F	p
Total (N = 18)	Groups	1	13.71	7.01	<.025
	Error term	16	1.96		
	Occasions	6	3.01	5.28	<.001
	Group × Occasion	6	2.85	5.00	<.001
	Error term	96	.57		
Efficient (N = 9)	Occasion	6	5.69	5.95	<.001
	Error term	48	.96		
Inefficient (N = 9)	Occasion	6	.16	.88	ns
	Error term	48	.18		

TABLE 4

MEAN STANDARD DEVIATION OF CARDIAC RATE
FOR EFFICIENT AND INEFFICIENT SUBJECTS

Occasion	Efficient subjects (N = 9)	Inefficient subjects (N = 9)	p (one-tailed)
Initial rest (A)	3.628	3.380	ns
Instructions	3.850	3.366	ns
Rest (B)	4.112	3.882	ns
Practice problem	7.530	3.866	<.01
Rest (C)	4.274	3.678	ns
Experimental problem	6.794	3.180	.005
Rest (D)	3.934	3.534	ns

occasions and a comparison by t test of the groups during each of the occasions. Though efficient subjects were significantly more variable in cardiac rate over the entire experiment, this difference resulted mainly from the significant difference in variability between the two groups on the practice problem ($<.01$) and the experimental problem ($<.005$).

To test the differences in variability of cardiac rate between the different occasions within each of the groups, the Lindquist (1953) procedure for testing simple effects in Type I analysis of variance with significant Group $\times$ Occasion interaction was used. Within the efficient group the same pattern was found for variability of cardiac rate as was observed in the analysis of the levels of cardiac rate: variability was significantly greater ($<.05$) during the practice and experimental problems than during the other experimental occasions. Within the inefficient group there were no significant differences in variability between any of the occasions.

The results thus far support the hypothesis that efficient problem-solvers are significantly more rapid and variable than inefficient subjects in cardiac rate while attempting to cope with a complex cognitive problem.

Cardiac Arousal at Crucial Points in Problem-Solving

The second hypothesis states that the cardiac arousal of efficient subjects should occur at crucial points in the problem-solving process. The three crucial points and the three phases of the problem-solving process that they demark identify six occasions for analysis. By a Lindquist (1953) Type I analysis of variance, the cardiac rates for the two groups of subjects during each of the six occasions were compared (Table 5).[2] The total between-group difference of cardiac rate during the experimental problem was significant ($<.005$), and, as was indicated earlier, the efficient subjects had a higher cardiac rate. There was also a significant total between-occasion difference ($<.001$). Examination of the between-occasion differences for each group separately showed them to be

[2] A comparison of the intra-individual variation of cardiac rate during these six conditions of the experimental problem was not possible since the measure of cardiac rate at the three points of the process is based on heart rate during one 30-second interval measure. In each of the three phases of the process, however, efficient subjects had significantly greater variability of cardiac rate than inefficient subjects and there were no significant within-group differences in variability for the three phases.

TABLE 5

ANALYSIS OF VARIANCE OF CARDIAC RATE OF EFFICIENT AND INEFFICIENT SUBJECTS
DURING SIX OCCASIONS OF THE PROBLEM-SOLVING PROCESS
(Experimental problem only)

Subjects	Source	df	MS	F	p
Total ($N = 18$)	Groups	1	2002.26	10.04	.005
	Error term	16	199.41		
	Occasions	5	46.32	4.68	<.001
	Group $\times$ Occasion	5	44.09	4.46	<.005
	Error term	80	9.89		
Efficient ($N = 9$)	Occasion	5	89.20	5.42	<.001
	Error term	40	16.45		
Inefficient ($N = 9$)	Occasion	5	1.21	.36	ns
	Error term	40	3.32		

almost wholly attributable to the efficient group. These findings are presented graphically in Fig. 2.

Using a t test for correlated distributions (McNemar, 1955), the cardiac rate at the points of necessary and sufficient information, analysis-synthesis shift, and solution were compared with the mean cardiac rate of the phase before and after each of these points. As indicated in Fig. 2, efficient subjects had elevations in cardiac rate at all

three points which were significantly greater than the mean heart rate of the phase that preceded and the phase that followed each point. For the inefficient group, on the other hand, only one significant difference was noted, between the point of necessary and sufficient information and the mean value of the lag phase. Figure 3 presents individual records of the two efficient subjects who most clearly demonstrate the phenomena. Figure 4 presents in-

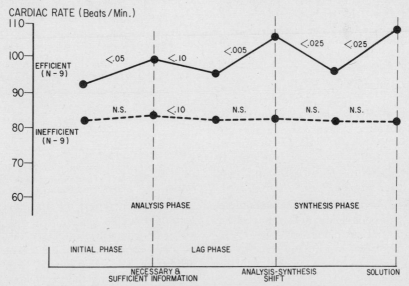

FIG. 2. *Cardiac rate of efficient and inefficient groups during the three phases and three points of the experimental problem.*

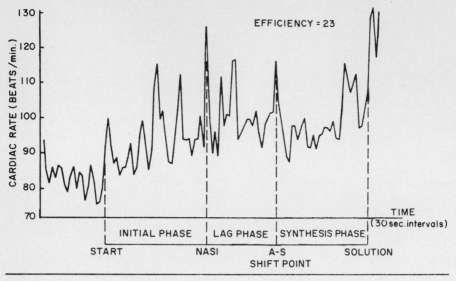

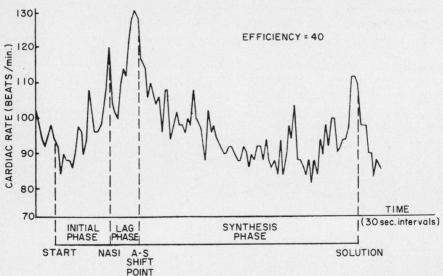

FIG. 3. *Cardiac rate of two efficient subjects during the experimental problem.*

dividual records of two inefficient subjects. These data support the hypothesis that elevations in cardiac rate of efficient subjects accompany crucial developments in their problem-solving processes.

At the end of the experimental problem each subject was asked for a retrospective report of his problem-solving. None of the subjects was aware of, or conceptualized, the crucial points of the process. Subjects were also asked for a description of their feelings while solving the problem and to rate, on a six-point scale, their degree of "arousal, anxiety, or tension" while

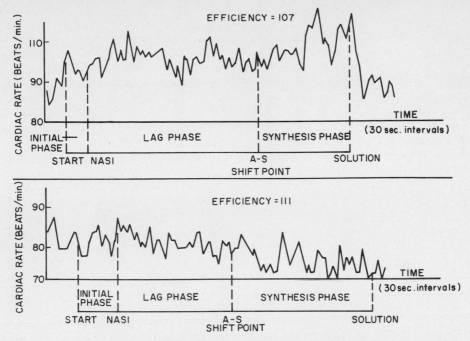

F IG. 4. *Cardiac rate of two inefficient subjects during the experimental problem.*

solving the experimental problem.[3] With the score of 6 indicating maximum arousal, anxiety, or tension, the mean score for the efficient group was 2.71, lower, though insignificantly so, than the mean score of 3.57 for the inefficient group.

DISCUSSION

Arousal, as measured by elevations in cardiac rate, is clearly related to the efficiency with which subjects solve the complex logical problems of the present study. Efficient subjects had significant increases in cardiac rate and variability of cardiac rate during problem-solving both in comparison to their own resting baseline and in comparison to the pattern of cardiac response of inefficient subjects. These findings support the hypothesis that arousal is characteristic of efficient functioning and that arousal seems to have an adaptive or facilitating effect. The facilitating effect of arousal may be, as Hebb (1955) postulates, "to tone up the cortex with a background supporting action that is completely necessary if messages are to have their effect"; for "without a foundation of arousal the cue (or learning) function cannot exist." In a recent exploratory study, Beckman and Stein (1961) report that efficiency on the PSI apparatus correlates significantly with reduced amounts of alpha in resting EEG records. Their findings of a general "cortical excitation" in the efficient subject are consistent with those of the present study and tend to support the interpretation that autonomic arousal during efficient functioning reflects the general tendency toward higher levels of cortical excitation.

[3] Four of the 18 subjects were not given the questionnaire about their feelings of arousal during the experiment; for this analysis there are seven rather than nine subjects in each group.

The results of the present study also indicate that arousal is not a total reaction but, rather, occurs differentially and, in part, at crucial points in the problem-solving process. Efficient subjects had significant elevations of cardiac rate at three crucial points in the problem-solving process even though they could not identify or conceptualize such points or stages in retrospective report.[4] Arousal at these crucial points in the problem-solving process may not only be indicative of the implicit understanding that efficient subjects have of the problem but may also serve as a stimulus through which the subject begins to make more explicit his implicit conceptualization of the problem. Thus in addition to facilitating the cue or learning function, arousal, or variations in arousal, may also have cue properties. The stimulus properties of autonomic responses have been extensively discussed by Lacey and Lacey (1958).

In the relationship between problem-solving efficiency and autonomic arousal, the variability of autonomic response seems to be as important as the level of arousal. Lacey and Lacey (1958) have discussed the degree of autonomic fluctuation as a reliable individual characteristic. They found that fluctuations in heart rate and skin resistance during a resting state were significantly related to motor impulsivity and to the length of time an individual could maintain maximal readiness for response. They concluded that though autonomic variability may have disruptive effects in motor tasks, there are also indications that it has a facilitatory effect on receptor-cortical

functions. In a variable arousal pattern, subjects can respond differentially to various aspects and elements within a situation, and these differential reactions may serve to facilitate functioning. If the facilitating effect of arousal is to "tone up the cortex" (Hebb, 1955), a constant state of arousal, regardless of level, may reach habituation. Changes and variations in arousal level may be more effective in maintaining a general level of cortical excitation. At the extreme ends of the arousal continua where arousal is exceedingly low or exceedingly high, there is relatively little variability of response. It is only in the middle ranges of the arousal continua where reactions can vary and fluctuate. Therefore, this capacity for differential reaction and response may be the important facilitating effect rather than the absolute level of the arousal.

Some of the psychological and motivational counterparts of autonomic arousal seem to be the positive attraction of a complex and challenging task. In response to a questionnaire about their feelings during the experimental problem, efficient subjects frequently commented in retrospect about the "satisfaction of working out the problem—it was like trying to play a musical instrument," "elation as solution was reached—the problem was rather stimulating," "the problem was lots of fun, I enjoyed it." Inefficient subjects frequently wrote of "frustration, but I knew I would solve it if I kept thinking in terms of it," "annoyance that you must go along only one path and continually get stuck at the same point along that path," "elation when pressing a button caused a reaction which fitted into my preconceived ideas, but determination when I saw the end in sight," "interesting, required concentration all throughout." Though the cardiac arousal and comments of in-

---

[4] Cardiac arousal at these crucial points in the thought process which are not reported by subjects has been discussed in an earlier paper (Blatt, 1960) as the intuitive, sensitive, effect-laden functioning frequently conceptualized as preconscious.

trigue, elation, stimulation and excitement of the efficient subjects can be interpreted as indicative of a greater level of involvement, motivation, or a feeling of success, in many ways inefficient subjects seemed equally well motivated. Subjects had no idea of their relative degree of efficiency, for no information was given them through which they could judge their performance other than having been told of the time limit and that this was a "reasonable amount of time." On reaching solution, inefficient subjects frequently expressed great satisfaction at having solved the problem. In terms of the output of physical energy, inefficient subjects pressed more buttons at a much faster rate than the efficient subjects and, in this sense, worked harder. Inefficient subjects also tended to report a higher degree of experienced arousal or tension.

Thus the difference in arousal patterns of efficient and inefficient subjects does not seem to be simply an issue of the degree of motivation, but rather more one of the type of motivation. As suggested in their spontaneous comments, efficient subjects seemed freer from internal needs and pressures and were better able to attend to and appreciate the nuances and subtleties of the problem and to see it as an exciting and intriguing puzzle. Inefficient subjects seem to express in their comments a need to master, control, or impose their own preconceived structure on the problem rather than naturally following the leads that evolve from the problem. The playful exploration and feelings of discovery of the efficient subjects seem more conducive to an appreciation of the subtleties and complexities of the problem and to more efficient functioning. In earlier research (Blatt & Stein, 1959), efficiency on the PSI was found to have a highly significant positive correlation with the esthetic value of the Allport-Vernon-Lindzey Scale of Values. The esthetic value, with its emphasis on form and harmony, seems to typify this playful exploration and the freedom to attend to and appreciate the enjoyable and exciting aspects of the environment.

The importance of playful exploration and the "conflict-free" exercise of ego functions has become a major focus of recent developments in experimental psychology and in personality theories. In developmental processes the role of play is seen as a crucial aspect for the objective recognition of the environment. As Schachtel (1954) states, it is

. . . only thought which is sufficiently free from urgent needs or fears that can contemplate its objects fully and recognize it in relative independence from the thinker's needs and fears— that is, as something objective. In thinking about a problem one is usually successful only if one does not press too hard for solution; that is, one is more likely to be successful if the thought is truly object-centered, free to contemplate the object from all sides, than if the thought is goal-centered, under the pressure of having to produce a solution immediately.

It is this playful exploration, this exciting appreciation of the problem from all sides, and the intrinsic satisfaction in functioning, which seems to be the psychological counterpart of the adaptive arousal indicated by the elevations in cardiac rate during efficient problem-solving.

SUMMARY

Concomitant recordings of heart rate were obtained from 18 male young-adult subjects during complex problem-solving on the John-Rimoldi PSI apparatus. The level of cardiac rate and its variability were compared for relatively efficient and inefficient subjects. Though the two groups of efficient and inefficient subjects were initially similar in cardiac patterns, there was a highly significant increase in cardiac rate and variability in the efficient subjects while they were attempting to solve the problems. These increases in cardiac rate and variability of cardiac rate of efficient subjects were significantly greater than their own initial resting baseline as well as being significantly greater than the changes in cardiac patterns of the inefficient subjects. The elevations of cardiac rate of efficient subjects occurred, in part, at crucial moments in the thought process: where necessary and sufficient information for solution was available, where the subject's predominant activity changed from analysis to synthesis, and at solution.

These findings were discussed in terms of the role of autonomic arousal in efficient functioning and in terms of some of the possible psychological or motivational counterparts.

REFERENCES

Beckman, F. H. and M. I. Stein, "A Note on the Relationship between Per Cent Alpha Time and Efficiency in Problem Solving," *Journal of Psychology,* **51** (1961), 169-72.

Berlyne, D. E., *Conflict, Arousal, and Curiosity.* New York: McGraw-Hill Book Company, Inc., 1960.

Blatt, S. J., "Experimental Evidence of Preconscious Functioning in Efficient Problem Solving." Presented at the Easter Psychological Association meetings, New York, 1960.

Blatt, S. J. and M. I. Stein, "Efficiency in Problem Solving," *Journal of Psychology,* **48** (1959), 193-213.

Buhler, K., *Die Geistige Entwicklung des Kindes* (6th ed.). Jena: G. Fischer, 1930.

Duffy, Elizabeth, "The Concept of Energy Mobilization," *Psychological Review,* **58** (1951), 30-40.

————, "The Psychological Significance of the Concept of 'Arousal' or 'Activation,'" *Psychological Review,* **64** (1957), 265-75.

Duncker, K., "On Problem Solving (trans. L. S. Lees), *Psychology Monograph,* **58** (**5,** Whole No. 270 [1945]).

Fenichel, O., *The Psychoanalytic Theory of Neurosis.* New York: W. W. Norton & Company, Inc., 1945.

Freeman, G. L., "The Relationship between Performance Level and Bodily Activity Level," *Journal of Experimental Psychology,* **26** (1940), 602-608.

Freud, S., *The Ego and the Id* (trans. J. Riviere). London: Hogarth, 1927.

————, *An Outline of Psychoanalysis* (trans. J. Strachey). New York: W. W. Norton & Company, Inc., 1949.

Gill, M., "The Present State of Psychoanalytic Theory," *Journal of Abnormal Psychology,* **58** (1959), 1-8.

Goldstein, K., *The Organism.* New York: American Book Company, 1939.

Hebb, D. O., "Drive and the C.N.S. (Conceptual Nervous System)," *Psychological Review,* **62** (1955), 243-54.

————, "The Motivating Effects of Exteroceptive Stimulation," *American Psychologist,* **13** (1958), 109-13.

Hendrick, I., "Instinct and the Ego during Infancy," *Psychoanalytic Quarterly* **11** (1942), 33-58.

John, E. R., "Contributions to the Study of the Problem-Solving Process," *Psychology Monograph,* **71** (**18,** Whole No. 447 [1957]).

Lacey, J. I., "Individual Differences in Somatic Response Patterns," *Journal of Comparative Physiological Psychology,* **43** (1950), 338-50.

Lacey, J. I. and B. C. Lacey, "The Relationship of Resting Autonomic Activity to Motor Impulsivity," in *Brain and Human Behavior.* Baltimore: The William & Wilkins Co., 1958.

Lilly, J. C., "Mental Effects of Reduction of Ordinary Levels of Physical Stimuli on Intact Healthy Persons," *Psychiatric Research Proceedings,* **5** (1956).

Lindquist, E. F., *Design and Analysis of Experiments in Psychology and Education.* Boston: Houghton Mifflin Company, 1953.

McNemar, Q., *Psychological Statistics* (2nd ed.). New York: John Wiley & Sons, Inc., 1955.

Malmo, R. B., "Anxiety and Behavioral Arousal," *Psychological Review,* **64** (1957), 276-87.

Maslow, A. H., *Motivation and Personality.* New York: Harper & Row, Publishers, 1954.

Rogers, C. R., *Client-centered Therapy.* Boston: Houghton Mifflin Company, 1951.

Schactel, E. G., "The Development of Focal Attention and the Emergence of Reality," *Psychiatry,* **17** (1954), 309-24.

Schnore, M. M., "Individual Patterns of Physiological Activity as a Function of Task Differences and Degree of Arousal," *Journal of Experimental Psychology,* **58** (1959), 117-28.

White, R. W., "Motivation Reconsidered: The Concept of Competence," *Psychological Review,* **66** (1959), 297-333.

Woodworth, R. S., *Dynamics of Behavior.* New York: Holt, Rinehart & Winston, Inc., 1958.

Simbardo, P. G. and N. E. Miller, "Facilitation of Exploration by Hunger in Rats," *Journal of Comparative Physiological Psychology,* **51** (1958), 43-46.

The Orienting Reflex *

Gregory Razran

HISTORICAL BACKGROUND

The conditioned stimuli—the sounds of bells, buzzers, whistles, metronomes; the flashes of lights and the sights of rotating whirligigs and other objects; the rhythmical scratchings, touchings, and so forth; the different thermal stimulations; and the various odors—which Pavlov used to condition the food reactions, and later also the de-

* From G. Razran, "The Observable Unconscious and the Inferable Conscious in Current Soviet Psychophysiology: Interoceptive Conditioning, Semantic Conditioning, and the Orienting Reflex," *Psychological Review,* **68** (1961), 109-19. Reprinted by permission of the author and the American Psychological Association.

fense reactions, of his dogs were what we call sensory stimuli: that is, stimuli that are accompanied in human subjects by sensory experience, indeed, that *are* the body-material of almost all our ordinary experience. Pavlov, however, was no more concerned with the stimuli's preconditioning sensory experiences than with their postconditioning image experiences—both sensations and images were left in limbo in 1902 when he decided to abandon the term "psychic" (notably, psychic secretion used by him since 1886) for that of "conditioned." Still, the stimuli evoked in the dogs some overt, though often not very pronounced, reactions, and these reactions Pavlov named the "orienting" or the "what-is-it" or the "investigatory" or the "attitudinal" (in Russian, *ustanovychny*) reflex, using the particular names nondifferentially. The stimuli themselves Pavlov called "indifferent stimuli"—added evidence that he did not accord their original preconditioned reactions any particular per se significance in his system.

Later on, in the laboratory, Pavlov noted that conditioning proceeded best when the orienting reflex (for convenience, it will abbreviated as OR) is neither too large nor minimal or absent, and that in the course of CR training the OR tends to disappear— characteristics that might have been correlated with conscious experience by saying, for instance, that the conditioned stimuli must arouse adequate but not overwhelming consciousness and that consciousness tends to disappear as habit develops. But, again, such formulations became, after 1902, wholly alien to Pavlov. Dedicating his entire program of experimentation to, we might say, an isomorphic study of two Cs, the Cortex and Conditioning, he had no use for the isomorphism of the third C, that of Cognition or Consciousness. And, although less radical with respect to the general status of consciousness than early American behaviorists and, unlike them, in no way involved in any attempt to "explain it away," he, nonetheless, was very militant about its invalid methodology. Years before the rise of American behaviorism, in 1904, Pavlov stated that "one must renounce completely psychological formulations and remain standing upon a purely objective ground" (Pavlov, 1928, p. 75; 1949a, Vol. 3, p. 51). And in 1910 he wrote:

> Why had we formerly, like cowards, embraced the subjective method? . . . The subjective method is a method of causeless thinking, psychological reasoning is indeterminate reasoning,

recognizing phenomena but not knowing whether they come from here or there. To be content with saying "the dog thought," "the dog wishes" is a fiction, not a disclosure of the cause of the phenomenon. Our [former] psychological explanations were fictitious and groundless. Our [present] objective explanation is truly scientific, always turning to causes, always seeking causes (Pavlov, 1928, p. 165; 1949a, Vol. 3, p. 138).

This total Pavlovian rejection of psychology and of special psychological cognitive-perceptual problems continued for a number of years after Pavlov's death (1936). In time, however, changes occurred in the wake of special problems, new techniques, and modified general points of view. The special problems which contributed to the extension of Pavlovianism to the cognitive-perceptual dimension fall, interestingly, into two contrasting categories: those dealing with predominantly conscious reactions and emphasizing the dimension directly, and those dealing with unconscious ones and emphasizing it by contrast. The extensive and very successful investigations of the Lazarev-Kravkov school of sensory interactions (Razran, 1958, p. 1187), the highly original Makarov experiments (1950a, 1950b, 1952) on interoceptive sensibility, and the aforementioned studies of verbal-semantic conditioning are the outstanding examples of the first category of special problems. Gershuni's experiments (1947, 1955, 1957a, 1957b; Gershuni, Klass, Lukomskaya, Linyuchev, & Segal, 1959) on subliminal auditory conditioning and Pshonik's (1949a, 1949b, 1949c, 1952) on subliminal thermal conditioning, as well as the entire area of interoceptive conditioning, are cases of the second category of problems.

Again, post-Pavlovian CR and OR techniques and methodologies began to move rapidly from what might be called a "monoeffector" to what the Russians call a "polyeffector" stage. That is to say, as may be judged from what has been said so far, the old Pavlov and Bekhterev way of measuring changes in reactivity and conditionability in only one effector such as salivation or paw-withdrawal was replaced by simultaneous recordings of changes in a wide, almost an all-possible, variety of effectors, a state of affairs which almost automatically inducted series of correlations among differing indices of organismic change, and thus also of correlations with the cognitive index. Indeed, in very recent years Russian psychophysiologists have even resorted to such traditional devices as correlating subjects' rankings of stimulations and stimulation changes with objective pointer readings. And spectacular Russian engineering advances multiplied of course the number of possible pointer readings of psychophysiological processes.

Finally, with respect to modified points of view and cognition, one should mention that Pavlov's immediate successor, the late L. A. Orbeli, was a student of the German psychophysicist Hering; that J. S. Beritov (Beritashvili) became much interested in what he called "psychonervous behavior" in his later experiments; and that K. M. Bykov, P. K. Anokhin, and E. A. Asratyan have in general been friendly to psychological approaches and have tended to introduce some innovations in the Pavlovian system (the last two more than the first). And last, but by no means least, there is the fact of the rapprochements between psychophysiology and psychology since 1950—rather, the since-1950 Pavlovianization of psychology—and the deeper penetration of Marxism-Leninism and its emphasis on the emergent efficacy of consciousness, which Pavlov

resisted but which his successors could not or would not resist in the same way.

Just how the Russian psychophysiologists' experimental interest in problems of cognition and perception has become, and is continuing to become, closely connected with experimental problems of the orienting reflex is the subject of the last section of the present article. Suffice it to say here only that a recent Russian book, *Perception and the Conditioned Reflex* (Sokolov, 1958c), might as well, and indeed more appropriately, have been named "The Orienting Reflex and the Conditioned Reflex" or "The Orienting Reflex, Perception, and the Conditioned Reflex."

CHARACTERISTICS

Two collections of experiments wholly devoted to the study of the OR appeared in the Soviet Union recently, one in 1958 and one in 1959. The 1958 collection, entitled *The Orienting Reflex and Orienting-Investigatory Activity* (Voronin, Leont'yev, Luria, Sokolov, and Vinogradova, 1958) consists of 48 reports of experiments divided into six parts: General Problems; the Orienting Reflex and Problems of Reception (Perception); the Phylogeny of the Orienting Reflex; Its Ontogeny, Pathology, and Special Problems in Man. The 1959 collection, named *The Orienting Reflex and Problems of Higher Nervous Activity* (Sokolov, 1959a), comprises only 14 experiments but is nonetheless quite comprehensive; it contains, for instance, a total of 116 figures and a bibliography of 385 titles. And to these 62 OR experiments, should be added at least as many that have been reported in the periodical literature, mostly in the last five or six years. There is thus no doubt that the OR is a prime focusing center in current Soviet psychophysiological and psychological research and thought, particularly if one remembers that its experiments purport to provide not only new information but a new look at old information: that is, the OR is put forward as a new concept, although, as will be seen later, in a number of aspects it is really only a renovated one and in some respects it is one that under different names is not at all new to American and Western students of behavior.

The total material of the OR, unlike that of interoceptive and semantic conditioning, does not lend itself readily to summing up and discussing through sample experiments. A better way of presenting it would seem to be an unfolding enumeration and discussion of experimentally established and indicated OR characteristics. Six sets of such characteristics will be considered:

Reactional Primacy
and Holistic Specificity

The OR is the organism's normal first reaction to any adequate normal stimulus or, in terms of the stimulus, it is the organism's normal reaction to a normal *novel* stimulus. Novelty does not mean no previous presentations of the stimulus but merely that the stimulus possesses the OR-evoking novelty for only a limited number of presentations—the exact number depending upon a variety of parameters to be discussed later—after which the stimulus either evokes no reaction at all or a reaction that is different from an OR. And novelty includes also change, that is, it extends liberally to inherent or acquired discriminable changes in attributes of the stimulus. A human subject who has shown consistent defensive reactions to electric stimulation (unless the shock was very strong, its first reaction—or first sev-

eral reactions—was an OR) will react fully in OR fashion when the shock is changed discriminably in intensity or locus (Vinogradova, 1958), a dog will manifest a clear-cut OR when his food is changed in kind (Anokhin, 1958, p. 17), and a rabbit fully accustomed to a hammock as a vivarium will resume all old OR action upon shock administration (Anokhin, 1958, p. 15).

The OR is in no sense a single reflex but is in all respects a centrally organized, holistic system of a variety of specifically distinguishable visceral, somatic, cognitive, neural, and neuromotor reactions (Sokolov, 1958c). The specificity of the OR reactions pertains to kind, amplitude, latency, and general pattern, and the Russians have been working at full speed to detect and ascertain each distinctness experimentally. At least in human subjects, they seem to have clearly established, as was already indicated earlier, that the dilatation of the blood vessels of the forehead accompanied by the constriction of the digital blood vessels is an OR reaction and only an OR one (Vinogradova, 1958, 1959a, 1959b; Vinogradova and Eysler, 1959; Vinogradova and Sokolov, 1955). Figure 1 (Luria and Vinogradova, 1959), based upon data of a large number of experiments and subjects, illustrates fully this vascular distinctness of the OR in response to stimuli of all modalities, and shows as well the reactional primacy of the OR, its modifiability through repetition, and its reappearance in novel settings. The Russians have also experimented extensively with pupillary dilatation as an OR component. Their data show dilatation to be almost invariably the first reaction to nonvisual stimuli and to occur in about 20 per cent of first reactions to visual stimulations; the 80 per cent of pupil constriction to visual stimuli are interpreted as cases of inhibition of the dilatative OR reaction by the constrictive local-adaptive reflex (Liberman, 1958; Shakhnovich, 1958).

Likewise, the galvanic skin reflex,

Stimulus	Initial applications	Next applications	After extra-stimulus
Sound, light, etc.	◡	══	◡
Cold	◡	◠◡	◡
Warmth	◡	◠	◡
Pain	◡	◠◡	◡

FIG. 1. *Vasomotor pattern of the orienting reflex in human subjects. (Concave arc above convex arc—constriction of digital blood vessels plus dilatation of forehead blood vessels; double line —no observable vascular change in either digital or forehead blood vessels; two concave arcs—constriction of both digital and forehead blood vessels; two convex arcs—dilatation of both digital and forehead blood vessels.) (Reproduced from the* British Journal of Psychology *by permission.)*

electroencephalographic desynchronizations, a variety of respiratory changes, and special oculomotor, digital, manual, pedal, and general bodily motor and proprioceptive reactions are being studied carefully and delimited as OR components. Figure 2 (Shakhnovich, 1958, p. 197) shows an OR dilatation of the pupils of a cat's eyes in response to sound, with the muscles of the left iris sympathectomized, and Fig. 3 is an oculomotor chart of a subject looking at a Repin painting *"Nye Zhdali"* [They Did Not Expect Him] under three conditions: without instructions, thinking of what the family was doing when the visitor arrived, and estimating ages of members of the family. Figure 4 (Bronshteyn, Itina, Kamenet-

skaya, and Sitova, 1958, p. 239) is a record of cessation of respiration in a 72-hour-old human neonate in response to stimulation with a light,

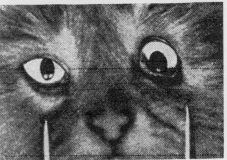

FIG. 2. *Pupillary dilatation to sound in cats as part of the orienting reflex. (Left eye is sympathectomized.)*

which, too, is held to be a specific OR component (non-OR respiratory changes are allegedly characterized not by cessation but by alterations of amplitude, frequency, and pattern). Characteristic stimuli-produced cessations of reactions must in general, it is argued, be placed alongside evocations of reactions in determining OR patterns—for example, the "listening to" of birds and mammals and the "frozen-in-thought" states of apes and children during the solving of problems (Dolin, Zborovskaya, & Zamakhover, 1958). And of course there is in the fully developed OR the specific molar reaction of "turning towards the source of stimulation," a reaction which the

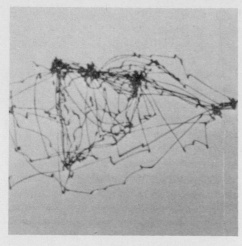

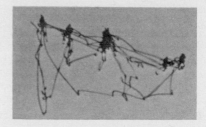
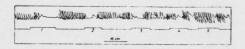

FIG. 3. *Eye movement chart of a subject watching painting "Nye Zhdali" (They Did Not Expect Him) by Repin for 10 minutes under three conditions. (Left—uninstructed; lower left—told to think what family was doing when the visitor arrived; lower right—told to estimate ages of members of family.)*

author would like to name versive, with a note that this reaction is outside the much-used dichotomy of approaching-avoiding or adient-abient reactions —the versive reaction is neither and may indeed precede either.

On the other hand, it should be noted

FIG. 4. *Respiratory change in human neonate 72 hours after birth, upon stimulation with lights, as part of the orienting reflex. (Note extinction of response after four trials.)*

that the OR is specific only to the novelty and change characteristics of the stimuli that evoke it but not to their intrinsic nature, and that in general it might be said that, unlike the alimentary or defensive or sexual reaction patterns of the organism, the OR pattern does not really "manage" the stimuli that come to it but merely reacts to their presence, its reactions thus being more preparatory than consummatory and preadaptive than adaptive. Yet these very characteristics impart a general controlling role to the OR and a function not unlike that of cognition, about which more will be said later.

Evolutionary, Ecological, and
Pathological Aspects

Phyletically, the lowest animals the ORs of which the Russians have studied are fish (Chumak, 1958; Gusel'nokov, 1958; Vedyayev and Karmanova, 1958), and it was already mentioned that the Russians hold that in human ontogeny ORs are present right after birth. However, they have also reported near-absence of ORs in the early ontogeny of such animals as dogs, cats, and rabbits (Chumak, 1955; Nikitina, 1954; Nikitina and Novikova, 1958), and there is no doubt that the assumption is that the OR is a phyletically recent reaction pattern. And it is of course a pattern that manifests the greatest amount of evolutionary plasticity with respect to type, variety, and duration of its reactions (Dolin *et al.*, 1958; Vedyayev and Karmanova, 1958). Clear-cut differences were found, for instance, in one experiment between the ORs of monkeys and of dogs, the former showing invariably more and longer-lasting reactions and in addition a much greater ratio of somatic to visceral components (Nikitna and Novikova, 1958). And similar results were obtained in comparing the ORs in the first months of normal and of prematurely born children (Polikanina and Probatova, 1955, 1958; Voronin *et al.*, 1958), and in age-specific comparisons of infants (Karlova, 1959) and of baby rats, rabbits, dogs, and monkeys (Volokhov, Nikitina, and Novikova, 1959). Yet, with respect to effectiveness of stimuli that evoke ORs, differences between animals appear to be often more a matter of ecological than of purely phyletic factors. Rustling sounds which are very weak OR stimuli in dogs are very powerful ones with hares. Figure 5 (Klimova, 1958, p. 79) shows that 240 applications of a rustling sound failed to extinguish completely a hare's

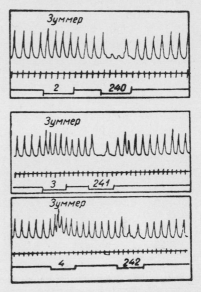

Fig. 5. *Persistent (highly resistant to extinction) respiratory reaction of a hare to a rustling sound, and the conditioning of this reaction to the sound of a buzzer. (Lines from above: respiration, time in seconds, application of buzzer and of rustling sound. Numbers denote ordinal trials.)*

respiratory OR changes to it, and that furthermore the sound of a buzzer which originally was ineffective became conditioned to the rustle reaction in three trials. Other specific and particularly effective OR-evoking stimuli were found to be: the sight of a cat for owls, the odor of rosemary and hunters' decoy sounds for ducks, the displacements of objects in the field of vision and sucking sounds for hares, the sound of wood splintering for beavers, and the sound of waves splashing for fish (Klimova, 1958, p. 77). While it is possible that some of the effectiveness of the particular stimuli was due to "natural" pre-experimental reinforcements, the consistency of the results and the fact that young animals

were used in some cases point to con-
genital ecological differences.

The relation of the OR to human
pathology is evident in the difficulty of
arousing it in schizophrenic and head-
injured patients and in feeble-minded
children. Figure 6 (Gamburg, 1958,

only on the eighth presentation. The
results with feeble-minded children,
compared with normal ones, run in the
same direction. In one experiment, all
20 normal children manifested vascular
OR reactions to the flash of a light, the
sound of a metronome, and the sound

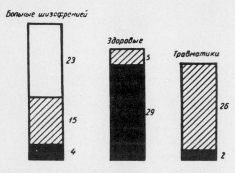

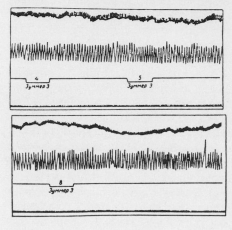

FIG. 6. *First reactions of 42 schizophrenics, 28 head-injured patients, and
34 normal subjects to equal auditory
stimulation. (Blackened area, orienting
reflex pattern; diagonal-line area, defensive pattern of reactions; clear area, no
reactions. Left bar, schizophrenics; middle bar, normal; right bar, head injured.
Numbers of subjects showing each reaction pattern are indicated to the right
of the bars.)*

FIG. 7. *Absence of vascular and respiratory reactions of a schizophrenic
patient to the sound of a buzzer and the
appearance of a vascular change only on
the eighth stimulation. (No data are
given on the first appearance of the
respiratory reaction.)*

pp. 273, 277) demonstrates that a con-
cealed sound (experimenter does not
state its nature) which evoked consistent OR somatic and visceral reaction patterns in 29 of 34 healthy subjects aroused the pattern in only 4 of
42 schizophrenic and in 2 of 28 head-
injured patients. (As may be seen in
the figure, the 5 remaining healthy subjects and the 26 remaining head-injured
patients responded to the stimulus with
defensive reactions, while 15 of the
schizophrenics reacted defensively and
23 did not react at all.) Figure 7
(Dolin *et al.*, 1958, p. 57) shows that
the sound of a buzzer produced a vascular change in a schizophrenic patient

of spoken words, but of 40 feeble-
minded children, only 20, 31, and 35
reacted so to the three respective
stimuli (Vinogradova, 1959b, p. 172).
Similarly, in another experiment, with
12 feeble-minded children and the use
of pure tones as stimuli, it was found
that one child produced a psychogalvanic OR reaction only on the fifth
presentation, a second child on the
ninth, and a third on the twenty-third
presentation of the tone (Paramanova,
1959, p. 78). This disruption of the
OR in pathology is obviously of considerable theoretical and practical-
clinical significance; but, unfortunately,
evidence for it is as yet very meager.

Extinguishability and Transformability

The ready extinguishability of the OR in dogs in contrast to the persistence of other unconditioned reactions was noted early—at least as far as reactions observable to the naked eye are concerned—in Pavlov's laboratory. Pavlov himself stated that the extinction of the OR "is analogous in details to the extinction of conditioned reflexes" (Pavlov, 1927, p. 256; 1949a, Vol. 4, p. 269) and that "this reflex has points of applications [representations] in both the cortex and the lower-lying regions of the brain (*ibid.*), and later Orbeli (1949) declared: *"There exist reflexes* [in reference to the OR] *that are innate in origin yet function fully as acquired reactions"* (p. 736). And while present-day data suggest the need of qualifying considerably the generalization of the ready extinguishability of the OR with respect to some stimuli, reactions, and subjects, the same qualification applies equally to the extinguishability of the CR which, too, may be very difficult with largely similar types of stimuli, reactions, and subjects. In other words, Pavlov's original statement about the extinction similarity of the OR and the CR—and we might add also, as will be seen later, his view of the combined cortical-subcortical neural basis of the OR—is in the main still quite valid, although one might well argue with Orbeli and say that extinction similarity of reactions does not mean total functional similarity.

The main indicated parameters of OR extinguishability are: (*a*) direct relationships with the phyletic position of the subjects (Obraztsova, Pomazanskaya, Stel'mach, and Troshikhin, 1958, p. 251; Vedyayev and Karmanova, 1958, p. 204) and the phyletic recency of the specific OR component (Sokolov, 1958b, p. 113)—animals higher in the phyletic scale extinguish their ORs more readily, and the PGR component of the OR extinguishes much more quickly than the respiratory component; (*b*) inverse relationships with intensity of the OR stimulus (Petelina, 1958), amount of brain extirpation in animals (Karamyan, 1958), and organic and functional psychopathology in human subjects (Lichko, 1952; Sokolov, 1959b, p. 48; Usov, 1952)—lesser extinguishability in each of the three cases. And to these should be added: (*c*) the inverse relationship with the ecological significance of the OR stimulus; and (*d*) the unsettled—sometimes direct, sometimes inverse—relationship with intelligence of children as subjects (Polikanina and Probatova, 1958). The first two sets of parameters as well as the fourth parameter operate equally in CR extinguishability (Razran, 1956); while the parameter of ecological significance is not readily applicable to conditioning situations. Little more can be said here about extinction, except for a general statement that our best empirically based hypothesis is that extinction is a phyletically more recent function than is conditioning and that the wholesale bracketing of the two in American laboratories may well be more a matter of experimental convenience than of an empirical and logical cogency.

OR transformability refers to the fact that while, as seen in Fig. 1 (the first figure in this section), repeated presentations of some stimuli (and some intensities of stimuli) extinguish the OR, repeated presentations of other stimuli (and other intensities of stimuli) transform the OR into another type of reaction (or, we might say, the OR gives way to another type of reaction). So far, quantitative relations have been worked out only with respect to the transformation of the OR into a defensive reaction, when 20 repeated applications of each of 20 discriminable shock stimuli were administered to adult human subjects (Sokolov, 1958c, p. 64). The criterion of the appearance of the OR was a *disparate* vascular reaction, that is, dilatation of the blood vessels of the forehead plus the constriction of the digital blood vessels; the criterion of the defense reaction was a *conjoint* vascular reaction, that is, constriction of both the digital and the forehead blood vessels. The experiment was performed by E. N. Sokolov, by all tokens the most active student of the topic, and the data are all presented in Fig.

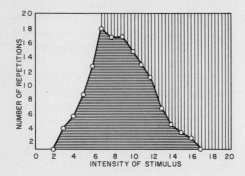

FIG. 8. *The transformation of OR vascular patterns upon electrical stimulation into defensive ones as a function of the intensity of stimulus and the number of repetitions. (Clear area, no reaction; horizontal-line area, OR pattern; vertical-line area, defensive pattern.)*

8. As may be seen from the figure, the OR first appeared at 2 units of shock but disappeared after the first trial; at 4 units the disappearance took 6 trials, at 6 it took 13 trials, but at 7 units a defense reaction emerged after 17 trials, while at 13 units the defense reaction came after 6 trials, and at 17 units of shock the first reaction was defensive. Quantitative find-

ings on the transformation of the OR into other types of reaction have to date not been reported but are of course very much needed.

Conditionability and Reinforceability

That ORs which are difficult to extinguish could act as URs and be readily conditioned to other stimuli was demonstrated, it will be remembered, by the case of the hare whose respiratory OR to a rustling sound was conditioned to a previously inadequate sound of a buzzer (Figure 5). However, even more normal and quickly extinguished ORs could be thus effective. Children's turning to the source of a flash of light could be conditioned to a preceding sound provided the latter is not too loud (Karlova, 1959; Lebedinskaya, 1958; Kasatkin, Mirzoyants, and Khokhitiva, 1953; Mirzoyants, 1954), and conversely dogs' or apes' turning to a sound of a buzzer has been known to become conditioned to a preceding change in illumination (Rokotova, 1952). Indeed, it is the contention of Soviet experimenters that all sensory preconditioning or what the Russians call associative conditioning is mediated through OR conditioning (Anokhin, 1958, p. 18; Voronin, 1957, pp. 99–103), while according to Anokhin (1958) and to Polezhayev (1958, 1960) the OR operates in all conventional (food or shock) classical conditioning to complex stimuli as an afferent and feedback central integrator of the stimuli before their actual conditioning to the peripheral food or shock reaction. Moreover, there is the study by Vinogradova (1959a) in which the administration of unavoidable electric shocks to human subjects was preceded by sounds of a metronome or of a pure 50-db 1,024-cps tone and the resultant vascular conditioning was for a number of trials orienting and not defensive in nature (disparate and not conjoint). Anokhin's views and Vinogradova's findings are clearly of special relevance to American theories of learning which maintain that classical conditioning is a central, sensory, anticipatory, or expectancy event (Woodworth, Tolman, Hilgard), insofar as the OR may well be conceived in such terms. However, the Anokhin-Vinogradova claims extend only to the OR as an intervening preparatory-guiding aid in conditioning, and not as its final idiopathic mechanism.

The reinforceability of the OR refers to the feasibility of strengthening it through some subsequent event in the manner of operant conditioning (though the OR could not readily be conceived of as an operant). Two kinds of experiments are available as evidence. In one, fox cubs were brought to the laboratory to listen to squeaks of mice. The squeaks evoked in the young animals clear ORs which, however, extinguished rather quickly upon repetition. Yet when the cubs were permitted to eat the mice, one meal sufficed to make the OR to the squeaks almost unextinguishable (Biryukov, 1958, p. 24). In the other kind of studies, weakened ORs of human subjects to auditory sensory and verbal stimuli became very much strengthened when the subjects were told that they had to do something such as push a button, count the beats of the metronomes or the letters of the words, and so forth when they heard the stimuli—that is, when the stimuli were "functionalized" or "signalized" (Russian term) in a simple "voluntary" reaction time design (Sokolov, 1958c).

Moreover, as has already been indicated in the preceding paragraph, reinforcement of CS-evoked ORs continues for some time even in typical classical CR designs. Indeed, it might even be argued that the commonly noted final reduction of the OR in classical conditioning is not unrelated to the loss in rate of CR elicitation in operant conditioning when reinforcement is continuous (100 per cent)—a matter which raises the whole problem of the relation of the two types of CR modifications and which, together with other more general problems of theory, will be discussed in the final section of this article.

Cortical-subcortical Basis—Vigilance versus Investigation

Pavlov's view that the OR is rooted in both the cortex and the subcortex is being supported by a number of—although as yet still few—experiments on the effects of brain extirpation and specific drugs on OR manifestations. The fact is of course that the very conception of the OR as involving the psychogalvanic reflex (see Schwartz' experiment, 1936, 1937, on the relation of Cortex Area 6 to its elicitation), the desynchronization of alpha rhythm, and molar-versive reactions, on the one hand, and pupillary, respiratory, oculomotor, vascular reactions, on the other, means a cortex-subcortex neural expanse—and Pavlov's perspicacity in the matter can only be applauded. In addition, there have been recent attempts by Anokhin as well as by Sokolov to relate the OR also to the action of the reticular formation (Anokhin, 1958, p. 15; Sokolov, 1958b, p. 112). Figure 9 (Lagutina, 1958, p. 84) is a localization map of the OR in the brains of 28 cats and 4 apes, obtained by Lagutina with the use of implanted electrodes. The animals were moving freely in the experimental room, and the electrode stimulations of the points marked on the map produced typical ORs of head turning, pupillary dilatation, respiratory and vascular

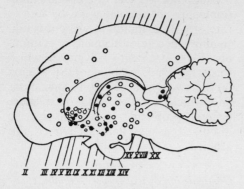

FIG. 9. *Localization map of ORs in the brains of 28 cats and 4 apes, with the use of implanted electrodes. (Dots indicate stimulation points which evoked ORs of the "vigilance" type; circles, ORs of the "investigatory" type.)*

changes, as well as exploratory and manipulative reactions.

As may be seen from the figure, Lagutina divides the evoked ORs into "general vigilance" and "investigatory" types. Other experimenters have sometimes distinguished between "what-is-it" and "what-to-do" ORs (Kvasov, 1956) or between generalized and specified ones (Sokolov, 1958a, p. 171) or assumed separate orienting and investigatory reflexes or preadaptive and adaptive ones (Bykov, 1958). As yet, however, these divisions and distinctions are far from experimental validation or even clear delineation and are fraught with the difficulty that adaptive and specified reactions are normally integral parts of nutritive, defensive, sexual-reproductive, and other non-OR reaction patterns. Hence, at least for the time being, the reviewer would favor subsuming under the OR only reactions that, it might be said, "hold" but do not "manage" stimuli—thus including investigatory-exploratory reactions but not adaptive-specified ones.

Cognitivity

Discussion of the cognitive nature of innate behavior patterns in animals —for that matter, also of acquired patterns—must obviously relate to indirect arguments and assumptions, and be more than a mere analysis of experimental data. Yet, there is little doubt that if any such pattern is accorded cognitive status, the OR pattern is surely the most likely candidate. Consider the indications of its relatively recent phyletic emergence and its dependence upon the relatively newer regions of the encephalon and of encephalization, its high evolutionary plasticity in both phylogeny and ontogeny, its ready functional lability and modifiability, its disruption in human organic and functional psychopathology, its central organized unity and cohesiveness coupled with its peripheral variety of reactions and, notably, its general function as a preparatory and controlling mechanism of what is to come. Moreover, in human subjects there is also considerable evidence to show that the elicitation of the OR is paralleled by a significant decrease in thresholds of conscious sensitivities (Sokolov, 1958a) and that, in general, positive correlations may be found between the scope and duration of elicited ORs and the scope and duration of conscious experiences (Asafov, 1958; Mikhalevskaya, 1958; Sokolov, 1958a, pp. 170–182; 1958c, p. 7–38). To be sure, there is also evidence that ORs may operate in human subjects without awareness, particularly in interoceptive stimulations (Mysyashchikova, 1952). However, on the one hand, it is by no means claimed that cognition is a *sine qua non* of OR action but only that fully developed ORs are cognitive, or that cognition "emerges" from the OR as "the material basis." And, on the other hand, as was already indicated, Russian theoreticians are quite friendly to the view of *unbewusste Bewusstseinslagen* and have always been avowed adherents of the concept of levels. Hence, there may well be: reactions without ORs, ORs without cognition, cognition without awareness, and, for that matter, levels of "awarenesses."

REFERENCES

Anokhin, P. K., "The Role of Orienting-Investigatory Reactions in the Formation of the Conditioned Reflex," in *Orientirovochny refleks i orientirovochnoissledovatel'skaya deyatel'nost'* (*The Orienting Reflex and Orienting-Investigatory Activity*), eds. L. G. Voronin, A. N. Leont'yev, A. R. Luria, E. N. Sokolov, and O. S. Vinogradova, pp. 9-20. Moscow: Akad. Pedag. Nauk RSFSR, 1958.

Asafov, B. D., "Changes of the Dynamics of the Vegetative Components of the Orienting Reflex in the Course of Application of Auditory Stimuli of Increasing Intensity," in *The Orienting Reflex*, pp. 123-28.

Biryukov, D. A., "The Nature of Orienting Reactions," in *The Orienting Reflex*, pp. 20-25.

Bronshteyn, A. I., N. A. Itina, A. D. Kamenetskaya, and V. A. Sitova, "Orienting Reactions of Human Neonates," in *The Orienting Reflex*, pp. 237-41.

Bykov, V. D., "The Dynamics of Orienting-Investigatory Reactions During the Formation of Positive and Inhibitory Conditioned Refleves and Their Transformation," in *The Orienting Reflex*, pp. 25-33.

Chumak, V. I., "Extinction of the Orienting Reflex of Cats in the Early Postnatal Period," *Zh. vyssh. vervn. Deyatel.*, 5 (1955), 863-72.

———, "Orienting Reactions During the Formation of Conditioned Reflexes to a Simultaneous Application of a Positive and a Differential Stimulus," in *The Orienting Reflex*, pp. 231-34.

Dolin, A. O., I. I. Zborovskaya, and Sh. M. Zamakhover, "The Role of the Orienting-Investigatory Reflex in Conditioned-Reflex Activity," in *The Orienting Reflex*, pp. 270-81.

Gamburg, A. L., "Orienting and Defensive Reactions in Simple and Paranoid Forms of Schizophrenia," in *The Orienting Reflex*, pp. 270-81.

Gershuni, G. V., "The Study of Subsensory Reactions in Action of Sensory Organs," *Fiziol. Zh. SSSR.* 33 (1947), 393-412.

———, "Conditioned Galvanic-Skin Reactions and Alpha-rhythm-Depression Reactions During Subliminal and Supraliminal Auditory Stimulations of Human Subjects," *Zh. vyssh. nervn. Deyatel.*, 5 (1955), 665-76.

———, "General Results of the Study of the Activity of the Auditory Analyzer by Means of Various Reactions," *Zh. vyssh. nervn. Deyatel.*, 7 (1957), 13-23. (a)

———, "Human Auditory Discrimination of Complex Stimuli with Increasing Amount of Information, *Fiziol. Zh. SSSR,* 43 (1957), 1086-97. (b)

Gershuni, G. V., Yu. A. Klass, N. Ya. Lukomskaya, M. N. Linyuchev, and A. A. Segal, "Evaluation of Human Discrimination of Auditory Stimuli with Increased Information and Its Utilization in the Study of the Effect of Certain Pharmacological Substances, *Biofizika,* 4 (2) (1959), 158-65.

Gusel'nokov, V. E., "The Reflection of Orienting Reactions in the Fluctuations of Bio-electric Potentials in the Forebrain of Fish, Turtles, and Pigeons," in *The Orienting Reflex*, pp. 209-20.

Karamyan, A. I., "Orienting Reactions in Animals during Organic Pathology of the Central Nervous System," in *The Orienting Reflex*, pp. 69-75.

Karlova, A. N., "Orienting Reflexes in Young Children," *Zh. vyssh. nervn. Deyatel.*, 9 (1959), 37-44.

Kasatkin, N. I., N. S. Mirzoyants, and A. P. Khokhitiva, "Conditioned Orienting Reflexes in Children under One Year," *Zh. vyssh. nervn. Deyatel.*, 3 (1953), 192-202.

Klimova, V. I., "The Characteristics of Components of Some Orienting Reactions," in *The Orienting Reflex*, pp. 76-80.

Kvasov, D. G., "The Muscular Apparatus of Analyzers," *Fiziol. Zh. SSSR*, **42** (1956), 621-31.

Lagutina, N. I., "The Structure of Orienting Reflexes," in *The Orienting Reflex*, pp. 80-85.

Lebedinskaya, E. I., "The Interrelations between Conditioned-Orienting and Conditioned Reflexes during the Formation of a Temporary Connection between Two Indifferent Stimuli," in *The Orienting Reflex*, pp. 86-92.

Liberman, A. E., "New Data on the Pupillary Component of the Orienting Reflex in Man," in *The Orienting Reflex*, pp. 145-51.

Luria, A. R. and O. S. Vinogradova, "An Objective Investigation of the Dynamics of Semantic Systems," *British Journal of Psychology*, **50** (1959), 89-105.

Marakov, P. O., "The Effect of Interoceptive Gastric Signalizations on the Electroencephalogram of Man," *Fiziol. Zh. SSSR*, **38** (1952), 281-87.

————, "Pre-excitation and Presensation," *Uchen. Zap. Leningr. U., Ser. Biol.*, **22** (123) (1950), 369-99. (b)

————, "A Study of Interoception in Human Subjects," *Uchen. Zap. Leningr. Ser. Biol.*, **22** (123), 345-68. (b)

Mikhalevskaya, M. B., "The Interrelations of the Orienting and the Conditioned Motor Reactions of Man During the Determination of Thresholds of Visual Sensitivity," in *The Orienting Reflex*, pp. 151-58.

Mirozyants, N. S., "The Conditioned Orienting Reflex and Its Differentiation in Children," *Zh. vyssh. nervn. Deyatel.*, **5** (1954), 616-19.

Mysyashchikova, S. S., "The Extinction of Vegetative Reactions During the Stimulation of the Peripheral Apparatus of Various Analyzers," in *Voprosy fiziologii interotseptsii*, ed. K. M. Bykov, pp. 411-27. Moscow: Akad. Nauk SSSR, 1952.

Nikitina, G. M., "Interrelations in the Development of Orienting and Conditioned Motor Reactions in Ontogeny," *Zh. vyssh. nervn. Deyatel.*, **4** (1954), 406-13.

Nikitina, G. M. and E. G. Novikova, "The Characteristics of the Manifestation of Orienting Reactions in Animal Ontogeny," in *The Orienting Reflex*, pp. 242-48.

Obraztsova, G. A., L. F. Pomazanskaya, L. N. Stel'mach, and V. A. Troshikhin, "Orienting Reactions to Indifferent and to Conditioned Stimuli in Ontogeny of Dogs and Rabbits," in *The Orienting Reflex*, pp. 248-53.

Orbeli, L. A., *Problems of Higher Nervous Activity*. Moscow: Akad. Nauk SSSR, 1949.

Paramanova, N. P., "The Characteristics of the Participation of the Orienting Reflex in the Formation of Conditioned Connections in Oligophrenia," in *Orientirovochny refleks i voprosy vyssheyn nervnoy deyatel'nost'* (*The Orienting Reflex and Problems of Higher Nervous Activity*), ed. E. N. Sokolov, pp. 77-85. Moscow: Akad. Pedag. Nauk RSFSR, 1959.

Pavlov, I. P., *Conditioned Reflexes: An Investigation of the Physiological Activity of the Cerebral Cortex*. London: Oxford University Press, 1927.

————, *Lectures on Conditioned Reflexes*. New York: Liveright Publishing Corp., 1928.

————, "The Physiological Mechanisms of So-called Voluntary Movements," *Trud. Fiziol. Lab. Pavlova*, **6** (1) (1936), 115-18.

————, *Complete Works*. Moscow-Leningrad: Akad. Nauk SSSR, 1949. 5 vols. (a)

Petelina, V. V., "The Vegetative Component of Orienting Reactions of the Vestibular, Visual, and Auditory Analyzers," in *The Orienting Reflex*, pp. 158-64.

Polezhayev, E. F., "The Role of the

Orienting Reflex in the Coordination of the Activity of the Cerebral Cortex," in *The Orienting Reflex,* pp. 97-111.

—————, "The Problems of the Physiological Conditions of Linkage," *Dokl. Akad. Nauk SSSR,* **130** (1960), 469-72.

Polikanina, P. I. and Probatova, L. E., "The Problem of the Development of the Orienting Reflex in Premature Infants," in *The Orienting Reflex,* pp. 258-61.

Pshonik, A. T., "Interaction of Extero- and Interoceptive Conditioned Vasomotor Reflexes," in *Problemy Sovetskoy fiziologii, biokhimii i farmakologii,* pp. 269-74. Moscow: Akad. Nauk SSSR, 1949. (b)

—————, "Interaction of Extero- and Interoceptive Conditioned Vasomotor Reflexes," *Dokl. Akad. Nauk SSSR,* **67** (1949), 1175-78. (a)

—————, "The Problem of the Interaction between Exteroceptive and Interoceptive Vasomotor Reflexes," in *Problemy Kortikovistseral'noy patologii,* ed. K. M. Bykov, pp. 255-69. Moscow: Akad. Nauk SSSR, 1949. (c)

—————, *The Cerebral Cortex and the Receptor Functions of the Organisms.* Moscow: GIZ, 1952.

Razran, G., "Extinction Re-examined and Re-analyzed: A New Theory," *Psychological Review,* **63** (1956), 39-52.

Rokotova, N. A., "The Formation of Temporary Connections in the Cerebral Cortex of Dogs during the Action of Several Indifferent Stimuli," *Zh. vyssh. nervn. Deyatel.,* **2** (1952), 753-59.

Schwartz, H. G., "The Effect of Experimental Lesions of the Cortex upon the 'Psychogalvanic Reflex,' " *Anatomical Record Supplement,* **64** (1936), 42.

—————, "Effect of Experimental Lesions of the Cortex on the 'Psychogalvanic Reflex in the Cat," *Archives of Neurological Psychiatry* (Chicago), **38** (1937), 308-20.

Shakhnovich, A. R., "The Pupillary Component of the Orienting Reflex during the Action of Specific and Nonspecific Visual Stimuli," in *The Orienting Reflex,* pp. 191-98.

Sokolov, E. N., "Measuring the Sensitivity and the Reactivity of the Conditioned Reflex in Connection with Interrelations between Orienting and Defensive Reactions," in *The Orienting Reflex,* pp. 170-82. (a)

—————, "The Orienting Reflex, Its Structure and Mechanism," in *The Orienting Reflex,* pp. 111-20. (b)

Sokolov, E. N., ed., *The Orienting Reflex and Problems of Higher Nervous Activity.* Moscow: Akad. Pedag. Nauk RSFSR, 1959. (a)

Usov, A. G., "Cortical Regulation of Respiration in Senility," *Fiziol. Zh. SSSR,* **38** (1952), 576-83.

Vedyayev, F. P. and I. G. Karmanova, "Comparative Physiology of the Orienting Reflex," in *The Orienting Reflex,* pp. 201-204.

Vinogradova, O. S., "The Dynamics of the Orienting Reflex in the Process of the Formation of Conditioned Connections," in *The Orienting Reflex,* pp. 40-47.

—————, "The Role of the Orienting Reflex in the Formation of Conditioned Connections in Man," in *The Orienting Reflex and Problems of Higher Nervous Activity,* pp. 86-160.

—————, "A Study of the Orienting Reflex in Oligophrenic Children by Plethysmographic Technique," in *The Orienting Reflex and Problems of Higher Nervous Activity,* pp. 161-206. (b)

Vinogradova, O. S. and N. A. Eysler, "The Manifestations of Verbal Connections in Recording Vascular Reactions," *Vop. Psikhol.,* **2** (1959), 101-16.

Vinogradova, O. S. and E. N. Sokolov, "Extinction of the Vascular Component of the Orienting Reflex," *Zh. vyssh. nervn. Deyatel.,* **5** (1955), 344-50.

Volokhov, A. A., G. M. Nikitina, and E. G. Novikova, "The Development of the Vegetative Components of the Orienting and Defensive Conditioned Reflex in the Ontogeny of a Comparative Series of Animals," *Zh. vyssh. nervn. Deyatel,* **9** (1959), 420-28.

Voronin, L. G., *Comparative Physiology of Higher Nervous Activity*. Moscow: Moscow University, 1957.

Voronin, L. G., A. N. Leont'yev, A.

R. Luria, E. N. Sokolov, and O. S. Vinogradova, eds. *The Orienting Reflex and Orienting-Investigatory Activity*. Moscow: Akad. Pedag. Nauk RSFSR, 1958.

The Influence of Complexity and Novelty in Visual Figures on Orienting Responses *

D. E. Berlyne

The present experiments were meant to continue a line of investigation initiated in a previous series (10). In the earlier experiments, undergraduate Ss performed key-pressing responses which produced tachistoscopic exposures of visual figures. They were free to give themselves as many exposures of each figure as they wished before the next figure was made available, and the number of responses was regarded as a measure of the "perceptual curiosity" aroused by each figure. It was found, in accordance with predictions from a theory of human curiosity (7, 8), that incongruous and surprising figures, which, it was postulated, would give rise to conflict between implicit responses,

* From D. E. Berlyne, "The Influence of Complexity and Novelty in Visual Figures on Orienting Responses," *Journal of Experimental Psychology,* 55 (1958), 289-296. Reprinted by permission of the author and the American Psychological Association.

The author is greatly indebted to Leonard Hommel, who acted as assistant in preparing for the experiments and as second E during the collection of the data, as well as to Olga McNemar and D. H. Lawrence, who kindly arranged for Ss and facilities at the Psychology Department of Stanford University.

were more curiosity-arousing than others. A positive relation also emerged between perceptual curiosity and certain other attributes of figures, which can jointly be described by some such term as *complexity*. Some of these attributes, equivalent to the amount of variety in a figure, were ones that Attneave (2) has identified with the information-theory measures, redundancy and relative uncertainty ($= 1 -$ redundancy). Another was *amount of material,* which can be associated with (absolute) uncertainty or with measures of structural information (15).

The aim of the present experiments was to supplement these findings by determining whether variables that affect perceptual curiosity also affect attention. The word "attention" has had a variety of meanings in psychology (4). In a wide sense, it refers to the problem of selective response in general: an organism is usually surrounded by numerous stimulus objects with the power to evoke responses, and the factors favoring response to one stimulus rather than another need to be identified. In a narrower sense, attention refers to the selective evocation of observing responses (21) in particular, that is, responses that expose the organism to stimuli or aspects of stimuli that were not accessible before. A still narrower sense, which is pertinent to the present inquiry, refers to the direction of observing responses of a special sort, namely, receptor-orienting movements. In the previous experiments, pressing the key was an observing response, but only one figure was available at once, so that there was no competition between stimuli for attention. In the present experiments, two figures were presented side by side on a screen for ten seconds, and eye movements were recorded. Which figure S looked at first and how much time he spent looking at each were the data of interest.

The two experiments tested the influence on attention of two kinds of factors that have been shown to influence perceptual curiosity. Experiment I was concerned with the complexity or information-theory factors that were studied in the previous project. These factors were to be examined more closely by isolating a number of more precisely definable variables and investigating their effects separately.

Experiment II was devoted to a second factor, which has often been found conducive to perceptual curiosity in lower animals, namely, stimulus change or relative novelty. Rats, for example, will spend more time sniffing at an object that was not present a short time ago than at one that was (3). In human beings, change seems to draw attention in the widest sense: when given a free choice between pressing a key corresponding to a recently changed stimulus and pressing another key corresponding to a stimulus that has remained unchanged, Ss show a preference for the former response (5). Experiment II investigated further this apparent link between perceptual curiosity and attention by testing the hypothesis that changing features of the environment will come to attract more visual fixation than recurrent features. For a number of training trials, the same figure kept on reappearing on one side of the screen, while the other side bore a different figure every time. Three test trials, in each of which new figures appeared on both sides, were then given to ascertain whether any tendency to concentrate attention away from the side of the constant stimulus persisted after the constant stimulus was superseded.

METHOD

Procedure

The S sat facing a cardboard screen at a distance of about 4 ft. He was told: "This is an experiment on number estimation. We want to find out what factors determine how well people can estimate number. Some pictures will be shown on the screen, two at a time. When you hear the word 'Ready!' you are asked to fixate the cross in the middle of the screen. When the pictures appear, you can look at them if you like, but we should like you to be looking at the cross just before they appear. At the end, you will be asked to estimate how many pairs of pictures there were."

The stimulus material was then presented. Two figures at a time were projected on the screen by means of an overhead projector, operated by the first E. Each pair of figures was visible for 10 sec; there was an interval of 20 sec between successive pairs, and the warning was given 3 sec before the figures appeared. The slides were projected as 6 × 4-in. rectangles, 12 in.

apart. The fixation cross was midway between them.

The second *E,* sitting behind the screen, observed *S* through a hole situated below the level at which the figures appeared. He recorded the time spent looking at each figure in units of .2 sec by means of two Morse keys connected with stop clocks. He also noted which figure in each pair was fixated first.

This way of timing fixations was not infallibly accurate, but any errors were prevented from becoming constant errors by the design of the experiment and by the fact that the *E* responsible for the recording was kept ignorant of the experimental conditions allotted to each *S* and thus of the nature of the figure presented on a particular side during a particular trial. The two *E*s alternated between the tasks of observing eye movements and operating

the projector. Although the instructions were designed to make any fixation of a figure as spontaneous as possible by disguising the purpose of the experiment, the recording apparatus made an audible click with each make and break, and *S*s invariably realized after a few trials that their eye movements were being registered.

The material for Exp. II was presented immediately after the material for Exp. I without any interruption of the procedure or warning.

Subjects

Ten male and ten female undergraduates took part in both experiments.

Stimulus Material

Experiment I. Twenty-two pairs of slides were prepared, falling into six categories. Categories A, B, C, D, and

EXPERIMENT I

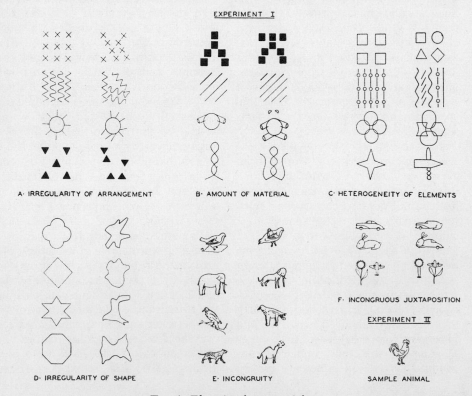

A· IRREGULARITY OF ARRANGEMENT   B· AMOUNT OF MATERIAL   C· HETEROGENEITY OF ELEMENTS

D· IRREGULARITY OF SHAPE   E· INCONGRUITY   F· INCONGRUOUS JUXTAPOSITION

EXPERIMENT II

SAMPLE ANIMAL

FIG. 1. *The stimulus material.*

E contained four pairs each, and Category F the remaining two pairs (Fig. 1). One member of each pair of slides bore a "less complex" and the other a "more complex" figure, and different forms of complexity were represented by the different categories of material:

A. Irregularity of arrangement. The two figures in each pair consisted of exactly the same elements, but in the one case they were arranged in a regular geometrical pattern, and in the other they were irregularly scattered. As far as spatial location is concerned, there is more redundancy in the former. A view of part of the figure would enable the probable arrangement of the remaining material to be guessed, given the assumption, based on past experience, that one part of a visual pattern is more likely than not to resemble another.

B. Amount of material. One figure in each pair consisted of part of the material in the accompanying figure. The latter can be considered to belong to a class of figures with more absolute uncertainty, since more material implies greater possibilities of variation and therefore more information, on the average, to be absorbed before a member of the class can be identified. Alternatively, and perhaps more fruitfully, the concept of structural information content, introduced by MacKay (15) after Gabor and supplementing Shannon's theory of selective information (20), might be applied. Figures with more elements contain more "distinguishable groups or clusters" or more degrees of freedom and hence more "logons."

C. Heterogeneity of elements. One figure in each pair consisted of a number of identical elements, whereas the other figure consisted of the same number of different elements in a similar spatial arrangement. Redun-

dancy is an appropriate concept here as in Category A.

D. Irregularity of shape. Each pair contained one regular geometrical shape, symmetrical along two or more axes, and one irregular nonsymmetrical shape. The variable involved here is one whose relation to redundancy is discussed at length by Attneave (2). It may be said, in brief, that regularity of contour and symmetry imply similarity of parts and predictability of changes in curvature, all of which means high redundancy.

E. Incongruity. Each pair consisted of a picture of a normal animal and a picture of an incongruous animal, that is, one with parts appropriate to different species or with three heads. The latter thus possessed attributes which *S*s' past training would have led them to regard as incompatible and which would consequently lead to conceptual conflict (7). The perception of one part could similarly be assumed to conflict with expectations or redintegrative responses aroused by other parts (6). The difference between the pictures in each pair could also be expressed in information-theory terms. A picture of a well-known animal is highly redundant, as the sight of one characteristic feature makes it easy to reconstruct the rest. One feature of an incongruous animal, on the other hand, gives little hint of what the rest will be like. Each feature has a high information content, since the probability of its appearing together with the other features is low.

F. Incongruous juxtaposition. This category was added as a control for Category E. If it were found that the incongruous animals attracted more attention than the others, it would still not be clear whether the decisive factor was merely the unusual combination of elements or whether the spatial arrangement also played a part, for example, whether it was a matter of seeing a bird's head and an elephant's forelegs in unwonted proximity or a matter of seeing a bird's head where an elephant's head would be expected. Each pair belonging to Category F had, therefore, one slide bearing adjacent pictures of two objects not usually seen together and one slide bearing the same material but with the halves of the two objects incongruously juxtaposed.

The twenty pairs of figures in Categories A-E were arranged in a sequence, such that each successive set of five comprised one pair from each category in a randomized order. The two pairs of Category F were then inserted into the sequence in randomly selected positions. For half the pairs in each category, the "more complex" figure was assigned an odd number and the "less complex" an even number; the reverse held for the remaining half.

The twenty Ss were divided into five subgroups of four. One S in each subgroup received the material in the original order with odd-numbered figures on the right, one in the original order with odd-numbered figures on the left, one in the original order reversed with odd-numbered figures on the right, and one in the reversed order with odd-numbered figures on the left. Two subgroups contained men only and two contained women only. The fifth subgroup contained two men and two women, the men taking the original-order odd-right and the reversed-order odd-left conditions.

Experiment II. Seventeen slides bearing pictures of animals were prepared and arranged in a random order. Slides 1–11 were designated as training slides and Slides 12–17 as test slides. Whereas every figure used in Exp. I had a rectangular white background, those used in Exp. II had less extensive white backgrounds leaving only narrow margins around their contours.

Half of the Ss received ten training trials and the remainder five training trials. Each of the slides numbered 1–5 served as a recurring stimulus for a different subgroup of four Ss. It was presented on one side of the screen during every training trial. Other training slides, varying from trial to trial, appeared on the other side. In each subgroup, the conditions 10R, 10L, 5R, and 5L were allotted to one S each, where ten and five represent the number of training trials and L and R the side on which the recurring stimulus appeared. When there were ten training trials, the varying stimuli were Slides 1–11 except for the recurring picture. When there were five, the varying stimuli were Slides 7–11. The varying stimuli always appeared in numerical order. Immediately after the training trials, Slides 12–17 were projected, two at a time, for the three test trials. They appeared in the same order and locations for all Ss.

RESULTS

First Fixations

Which figure of a pair was fixated first bore no consistent relation to the experimental variables. The Ss generally began with the left-hand figure about twice as often as with the right-hand figure, a consequence, presumably, of reading habits. What follows is therefore confined to the other dependent variable, that is, the amount of time spent looking at each figure in the course of the ten-second exposure.

Fixation Times

Experiment I. The mean fixation time for each of the 44 figures was calculated, as well as the over-all means for "more complex" and "less complex" figures in each category.

TABLE 1

MEAN FIXATION TIMES IN SECONDS: EXP. I

Category	Variable	"Less Complex" Figures	"More Complex" Figures	Wilcoxon's T	P
A	Irregularity of arrangement	3.36	4.56	22	<.01
B	Amount of material	3.40	4.29	28	<.01
C	Heterogeneity of elements	3.16	4.95	7	<.01
D	Irregularity of shape	3.05	4.67	8	<.01
E	Incongruity	3.46	4.97	6	<.01
F	Incongruous juxtaposition	3.46	4.83	14	<.01

The latter are displayed in Table 1. Every single pair showed a greater mean fixation time for the "more complex" figure than for the "less complex" figure. The over-all means for each category were subjected to Wilcoxon's T test (17) for paired replicates. The tendency to spend more time on "more complex" figures was significant beyond the .01 level with every category.

Experiment II. Figure 2 shows the mean fixation times for varying and recurring figures during the training trials of Exp. II. It will be seen that the ten-trial Ss spend more and more time on the former and less and less on the latter. The decline in fixation time for the recurring stimuli was subjected to an analysis of variance for trend

(1). Since the fixation times for recurring and varying stimuli were necessarily interdependent, there was no point in analyzing both. Both the linear trend and the deviation from linearity turned out to be significant, as Table 2 makes clear. The five-trial group had exactly the same stimuli during their training trials as the ten-trial group had during their last five training trials. Their curves show a similar divergence but, as was to be expected, are not so far apart as the corresponding portions of the curves for the ten-trial group. An analysis of variance for trend was carried out on the recurring-stimulus data for the five-trial group but failed to produce any significant F values. Moreover, the difference between the mean fixation times for re-

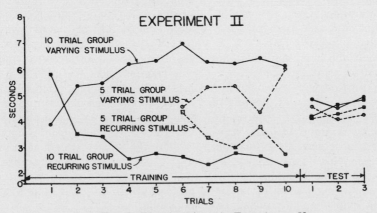

FIG. 2. *Fixation times in Experiment II.*

TABLE 2

ANALYSIS OF VARIANCE OF FIXATION TIMES FOR RECURRING STIMULUS
IN TRAINING TRIALS, 10-TRIAL Ss, EXP. II

Source	df	MS	F	P	Error Term
A. Trials	9	11.23	6.93	<.001	E
A1. Linear trend	1	56.11	11.74	<.01	E1
A2. Deviation from linearity	8	5.62	4.57	<.001	E2
B. Sexes	1	2.79			D
C. Sexes × Trials	9	0.71			E
D. Individuals within sexes	8	7.65	4.72	<.001	E
E. Individuals × Trials	72	1.62			
E1. Individual linear trends	8	4.78			
E2. Individual deviations from linearity	64	1.23			
Total	99				

curring stimuli on Trials 1–5 for the
five-trial group and Trials 6–10 for
the ten-trial group did not turn out to
be significant according to a t test,
although it was in the expected direction, the means being 3.37 and
2.50, respectively.

As for the test trials, the graph
shows that Ss reverted to fixating both
sides about equally. There was no consistent tendency to devote more time
to the side formerly occupied by the
varying stimuli.

DISCUSSION

The findings can be discussed either
in information-theory or in behavior-
theory terms, the field of exploratory
behavior and observing responses being one where the two approaches can
be expected to converge (11).

When S is faced with a definite discriminative task, such as naming a
stimulus or pressing an appropriate
key as quickly as possible, it has regularly been observed that reaction
time increases with information-theory
measures such as the initial uncertainty
or the amount of transmitted information (9). And when letter sequences
are exposed in brief flashes of con-

stant duration, the likelihood of mis-
identification increases with information content (16). These facts have
often been taken to mean that the
human being is a communication
channel with a limited capacity and
requires more time to absorb more information. In the light of such an assumption, it may not be surprising
that Ss spent more time on the inspection of more complex or conflict-arous-
ing, that is, more uncertainty-laden,
stimuli in the preceding series of experiments with the tachistoscope (10).
What is interesting, however, is that Ss
of their own accord spent more time
looking at the more uncertainty-laden
figures, when no specific task requiring
identification of the figures was imposed on them and any persistence in
absorbing the information completely
was spontaneous. The present experiments illustrate quite a different, if related, point, which does not necessarily
follow at all from the postulate that
the rate of taking in information is
limited; they reveal a tendency to fixate
a part of the environment that is a
relatively rich source of information in
preference to one that is a relatively
poor one.

To turn from information theory to

behavior theory, the data yielded by the present experiments do not by themselves call for any such intervening variable as "curiosity" or "exploratory drive." Since we have a movement focussing a sense organ on a stimulus object that has already been perceived peripherally, the investigatory-reflex theory of Pavlov (19) provides a parsimonious explanation. We should have to conclude that "more complex" stimuli elicit the investigatory reflex more strongly than others, as well as that new stimuli elicit it more than stimuli that have been present for some time, which is a fact frequently noted by Pavlov and his school. In the preceding set of experiments (10), on the other hand, the response was an arbitrary one, namely, pressing a key, and the stimulus was not visible at all until the response had been performed. The probability of repeating the response can thus be attributed to an intervening variable, which can be called "perceptual curiosity." The strength of the perceptual curiosity aroused by different figures, judged by the number of times Ss exposed themselves to them, increased with the same "complexity" variables as were found to influence attention in Exp. I of the present series. Experiment II showed that more attention will be given to stimuli that have newly come on to the scene, just as lower animals have been found repeatedly (for example, [3]) to devote more exploration to them. By verifying that eye movements are influenced by two sorts of variable that apparently affect perceptual curiosity, we have confirmed that attention in the narrowest sense depends on, among other things, the curiosity-arousing properties of stimuli. This is in line with a theory of attention in the widest sense that was outlined in an earlier article (4). A further hypothesis (7, 8, 11)—that

complex or novel stimuli attract observing responses and other investigatory behavior because incomplete perception of them arouses a drive which continued examination of them reduces—is therefore admissible and deserving of consideration.

Of the "more complex" stimuli in Exp. I, those in Categories E (incongruity) and F (incongruous juxtaposition) can plausibly be held to produce *conceptual conflict*. Since the forms of complexity represented by the other categories have evidently much the same effects on curiosity and attention, since they, like incongruity, admit of an information-theory analysis, and since information-theory measures, as used in psychology, seem to relate to conflict situations, the possibility that all forms of stimulus complexity involve conflict is worth entertaining (11). The conflict could be between various incompatible perceptual responses (4), for example, between the classifying responses or "connotative meanings" (18) evoked by different parts or aspects of a pattern, or between the perception of one part or aspect and an expectation aroused by another (6, 14).

It may be objected that "less complex" figures are likely to resemble familiar stimulus patterns to a greater degree than "more complex" ones, and that this difference in novelty could be responsible for our results. This point is well taken. But the suggestion (7) that stimulus complexes evoke conflict to the extent that they are complex or unfamiliar is offered as a possible explanation of the fact, among others, that new stimuli and well-known stimuli affect organisms differently.

In conclusion, some limitations of the present study must be indicated. One is that the "more complex" figures were not tremendously complex. Much more complex patterns might conceivably have been shunned rather than preferentially inspected. Aestheticians have often asserted that an intermediate degree of complexity ("unity in diversity") makes for maximum appeal, the exact degree depending on personality traits (13). Too little complexity means insipidity, and too much means bewilderment.

Shortening or lengthening the time of exposure might have brought about different results.[1] The failure of the independent variables to affect the direction of the initial fixation was probably due to the fact that, with a 10-sec exposure, Ss knew they had ample time to examine both figures, no matter with which they started. A brief flash, such as Brandt (12) used, would have allowed no more than one figure in each pair to be fixated, and differences in power to attract attention or arouse perceptual curiosity might have overcome reading habits.

SUMMARY

Undergraduate Ss were presented with a succession of pairs of visual figures, projected on a screen for 10 sec each. Which figure was fixated first and how long each member of a pair was fixated were the data recorded. In Exp. I, one figure of each pair was "more complex" or, in information-theory language, higher in relative or absolute uncertainty than the other. Six different variables which may be regarded as forms of complexity were investigated separately. In all cases, significantly more time was spent looking at the "more complex" figure. In Exp. II, the same figure recurred on one side of the screen for a number of training trials, while a new figure

---

[1] In a more recent experiment with 2-min exposures, 51 per cent of the time was spent fixating "more complex" figures and 36 per cent fixating "less complex" figures.

appeared every time on the other side. The fixation time for the varying stimuli progressively increased at the expense of the fixation time for the recurring stimulus. During subsequent test trials, when new material appeared on both sides, Ss reverted to fixating both figures about equally. Which figure was fixated first bore no consistent relation to the independent variables.

The implications of the findings are discussed in terms of psychological information theory and of behavior theory, with special reference to the relation between attention and perceptual curiosity.

REFERENCES

1. Alexander, H. W., "A General Test for Trend," *Psychological Bulletin,* **43** (1946), 533-57.

2. Attneave, F., "Some Informational Aspects of Visual Perception," *Psychological Review,* **61** (1954), 183-93.

3. Berlyne, D. E., "Novelty and Curiosity as Determinants of Exploratory Behavior," *British Journal of Psychology,* **41** (1950), 68-80.

4. ———, "Attention, Perception and Behavior Theory," *Psychological Review,* **58** (1951), 137-46.

5. ———, "Attention to Change," *British Journal of Psychology,* **42** (1951), 269-78.

6. ———, "Knowledge and Stimulus-Response Psychology," *Psychological Review,* **61** (1954), 245-54.

7. ———, "A Theory of Human Curiosity," *British Journal of Psychology,* **45** (1954), 180-91.

8. ———, "An Experimental Study of Human Curiosity," *British Journal of Psychology,* **45** (1954), 256-65.

9. ———, "Conflict and Choice Time," *British Journal of Psychology,* **48** (1957), 106-18.

10. ———, "Conflict and Information-

Theory Variables as Determinants of Human Perceptual Curiosity," *Journal of Experimental Psychology,* **53** (1957), 399-404.

11. ———, "Uncertainty and Conflict: A Point of Contact between Information-Theory and Behavior-Theory Concepts," *Psychological Review,* **64** (1957), 329-39.

12. Brandt, H. F., *The Science of Seeing.* New York: Philosophical Library, 1944.

13. Eysenck, H. J., "The Experimental Study of the 'Good Gestalt'—a New Approach," *Psychological Review,* **49** (1942), 344-64.

14. Hebb, D. O., *The Organization of Behavior.* New York: John Wiley & Sons, Inc., 1949.

15. MacKay, D. M., "Quantal Aspects of Scientific Information," *Philosophy Magazine,* **41** (1950), 289-311.

16. Miller, G. A., J. S. Bruner, and L. Postman, "Familiarity of Letter Sequences and Tachistoscopic Identification," *Journal of Genetic Psychology,* **50** (1954), 129-311.

17. Mosteller, F. and R. R. Bush, "Selected Quantitative Techniques," in *Handbook of Social Psychology,* ed. G. Lindzey. Cambridge, Mass.: Addison Wesley, Publishing Co., Inc., 1954.

18. Osgood, C. E., "The Nature and Measurement of Meaning," *Psychological Bulletin,* **49** (1952), 197-237.

19. Pavlov, I. P., *Conditioned Reflexes.* Oxford: Oxford University Press, 1927.

20. Shannon, C. E. and W. Weaver, *The Mathematical Theory of Communication.* Urbana: University of Illinois Press, 1949.

21. Wyckoff, L. B., "The Role of Observing Responses in Discrimination Learning," Part I, *Psychological Review,* **59** (1952), 431-42.

PART TWO

NEO-BEHAVIORISTIC APPROACHES
TO COGNITION

As Hebb stated in the introductory article, the S–R paradigm can explain most simple, reflexive behavior but leaves unexplained complex processes such as thought. An attempt to correct this deficiency has been made by adding an additional stage or level, labeled mediation, to the S–R model.

The first stage of this model has reference to associations between external stimuli and overt responses. The second stage refers to implicit or internal stimuli and responses. Many, if not most, associations between stimuli and responses in human behavior are not direct connections between external stimuli and overt responses but rather are mediated by implicit stimuli and responses. As Kendler and Kendler * put it, mediation theory "assumes that the external stimulus evokes an implicit response which produces an implicit cue that is connected to the overt response." They have also stated clearly that "the basic assumption of the mediational hypothesis is that implicit stimulus and response events obey the same principles that operate in observable S–R relationships." Readers are reminded that such an assumption need not be made, may be misleading, and is in fact rejected along with associative models in general, by psychologists represented in Part Three of this book.

A detailed analysis of mediation responses with special emphasis on verbal mediation is made by Goss. After examining several paradigms, Goss concludes that a two-stage paradigm appears most useful in ordering known facts. Staats devotes his attention to the elaboration of Hull's concept of habit-families and its relevance for concept formation and function.

The most comprehensive model of this kind has been developed by Osgood, who has referred to his approach as Hullian theory spiced with Hebbian notions. Therefore it might be helpful if the student first looked at Hebb's "cell assem-

---

* Their article can be found in Part Six.

131

blies" and "phase sequences," which are of course to be regarded as hypothetical constructs rather than as neurological realities. The reader might at this
point recall the material in Part One on the arousal or activating system. One
way to forge a link between the material on motivation and learning is to
recognize that level of arousal influences the firing of neurons which in turn
determines the formation of cell assemblies and phase sequences.

Osgood's theory, liberally interpreted, can be regarded as a summary of the
S–R approach to cognition. A great many behavioral observations are given
a coherent structure by Osgood's model, and the teacher should find it useful
in thinking about educational problems. Many complex behaviors, such as
attitude change, concept formation, generalization, transfer, development of
personality traits, and so forth are comprehensible in terms of Osgood's model.
The question remains, however, whether there are other more fruitful ways of
conceptualizing the activities of concern to the teacher.

The last article in this section is Razran's discussion of semantic conditioning which, as Goss suggests, is essentially verbal mediation, and which is
very similar to Pavlov's "second signal system," a concept to be covered in a
later section.

Verbal Mediating Response and Concept Formation *

Albert E. Goss

Over the past five decades, verbal mediating responses and stimuli have figured as important elements in a number of stimulus-response analyses of concept formation. This paper briefly reviews these analyses as a prelude to carrying out its main purpose, which is the further explication of the role of verbal mediating responses in conceptual behavior. More specifically, spelled out first are criteria for concept-formation tasks, particularly as compared with those for conventional paired-associates tasks. Then described in considerable detail are some paradigms of presumed stimulus-response relationships in concept formation. Finally, the paradigms are considered in con-

* From A. E. Goss, "Verbal Mediating Response and Concept Formation," *Psychological Review*, **68** (1961), 248-74. Reprinted by permission of the author and the American Psychological Association.

An earlier version of this paper was presented as part of a symposium on Mediating Processes in Transfer at the 1958 meetings of the American Psychological Association in Washington, D. C.

The proposals in this paper owe much to the ideas and experimental work of Janice E. Carey, James D. Fenn, Harvey Lacey, Marie C. Moylan, and Alvin J. Simmons. An opportunity to read an analysis by Arnold H. Buss aided development of the present treatment of reversal and nonreversal shifts. In their readings of earlier drafts, Barbara S. Musgrave and Charles N. Cofer offered many useful suggestions. Finally, Mary E. W. Goss, though not responsible for the infelicities of presentation which remain, was responsible for the elimination of many others.

junction with certain variables and learning principles, and sample predictions are generated.

Probably the earliest explicit stimulus-response analysis of the role of verbal mediating responses in conceptual behavior is that which Max Meyer illustrated with the concept "food" in his *Fundamental Laws of Human Behavior* (1911, pp. 213–214). The same example of the essential features of concepts was used subsequently by Weiss (1925), Dashiell (1928), and Gray (1931). Although Watson (1920, p. 102) chose a different example, his treatment of conceptual behavior also emphasized verbal mediating responses. The primary purpose of these early analyses was to show that conceptual phenomena—which had previously been thought to be impervious to behavioristic treatment—could be dealt with in stimulus-response terms. Understandably for the time, such analyses were only incidentally combined with learning principles to derive predictions about the effects of potentially significant variables on conceptual behavior, and none of the predictions was tested experimentally.

Early in the forties, Birge (1941), Miller and Dollard (1941), and Cofer and Foley (1942) made suggestions concerning the possible significance of verbal mediating responses for conceptual behavior. These treatments, however, were more concerned with defining and applying the mechanism of response-mediated similarity and generalization than with analyzing in detail the role of this mechanism in concept formation. The same is true of Gibson's (1940) development and use of the somewhat parallel notion of internal generalization and its complement, internal differentiation.

A decade later, Osgood (1953) offered *post factum* analyses of the conceptual tasks and results described by Hull (1920), Smoke (1932), Heidbreder (1946a, 1946b), and Reed (1946). These analyses, along with those of Baum (1951) and Mandler (1954), emphasized the mechanism of response-mediated similarity and generalization to the virtual exclusion of the complementary mechanism of response-mediated dissimilarity and discrimination. During the same period, Goss and his students extended their studies of the latter mechanism (for example, Goss and Greenfeld, 1958) to the analysis and investigation of the effects of experimentally controlled verbal pretraining on conceptual sorting (for example, Fenn and Goss, 1957), conceptual naming (Lacey, 1959), and animistic thinking (for example, Simmons and Goss, 1957).

Hypotheses about the role of verbal mediating processes in reversal and nonreversal shifts of conceptual phenomena have been proposed and tested by Kendler and his students (for example, Kelleher, 1956; Kendler and D'Amato, 1955), as well as by Buss (1956), Gormezano and Grant (1958), and Harrow and Friedman (1958). These proposals apparently evolved primarily from the considerable body of data and theory concerning the simple discriminative behaviors of infrahuman and preverbal human organisms to which Spence (1936) has been the major contributor, rather than from existing hypotheses and data

concerning response-mediated similarity and dissimilarity. Of similar origin is Wickens' (1954) analysis of the strengthening of discriminative responses to values along one dimension of multidimensional stimuli, and his subsequent more explicit hypotheses as to how verbal mediating responses might be the vehicles of "perceptual sets" (Wickens and Eckstrand, 1954).

Pavlov's "second signal system" is essentially equivalent to mediating responses and stimuli, and it has been the basis for recent analyses of "higher nervous activity" by Soviet psychologists (for example, Elkonin, 1957). Within this framework, Liublinskaya (1957) has described theoretical and experimental work on the role of the second signal system in the conceptual behaviors of preschool children.

Of the many analyses and studies that bear directly or indirectly on the role of verbal mediating responses and stimuli in concept formation, some have been supported solely by informal examples rather than by experimental data and principles. Those which do refer to experimental materials have often been limited to one or two relatively specific situations. And there has been a tendency to consider the nature and implications of only a few of the many possible patterns of relationships that can exist among initiating stimuli, mediating responses and stimuli, and terminating responses (Goss, 1955, 1956).[1] There is clearly need for a

---

[1] A temporal sequence of stimulus-response events in which a mediating response and stimulus may be distinguished can be represented as $S_{Initiating} - R_{Mediating} \sim S_{Mediating} - R_{Terminating}$. Social situations or experimental tasks are conceived as beginning with or initiated by some stimulus "element" or "compound" and as terminating with a response which is reinforced or punished; is instrumental in altering a subject's environment; or, more generally, has simply been designated the terminating,

more comprehensive yet experimentally rooted analysis; within the limitations to be described, such an analysis is offered in this paper.

CRITERIA FOR CONCEPT-FORMATION TASKS

General specification of the nature of concept-formation tasks is a logical starting point. Because many concept-formation tasks have much in common with conventional paired-associates learning tasks, differentiation of the two types of tasks is also required.

General Criteria

Fundamental to the definition of concept-formation tasks (conceptual behaviors) are patterns of relationships between initiating stimuli and terminating responses. More particu-

reference, or criterion response. Any stimulus event or receptor activation might be the initiating stimulus of a sequence, though usually and practically such stimuli are social and physical events.

Ideally, two criteria must be met in order for responses and the stimuli they produce to be considered mediating responses and stimuli. The first criterion is the observation of or grounds for inferring the occurrence of one or more responses subsequent to the initiating stimulus and before the terminating response. The second criterion is the demonstration that such temporally intermediate responses and stimuli have actual or potential facilitative or inhibitory effects on one or more measures of the occurrence and strength of the terminating response. Relative covertness and some particular topography as additional criteria seem unnecessarily restrictive. However, because of the presumed greater functional significance for most complex behaviors of postverbal humans of mediating responses originally or presently involving the vocal musculature, the focus of the analyses developed here will be on such responses and the stimuli they produce—verbal mediating responses and stimuli. A more exhaustive treatment of the definition of mediating responses and stimuli and of the bases for inferring or confirming their occurrences and effects can be found in Goss (1956).

larly, such tasks involve patterns in which two or more independently presented initiating stimuli evoke the same terminating response. It is the independent presentation of stimuli that distinguishes concept-formation tasks from convergent stimulus-compound situations. Thus crudely characterized, of course, the simplest concept-formation tasks are essentially identical to phenomena more often labeled primary stimulus generalization and response-mediated generalization (Dollard and Miller, 1950; Goss, 1955). Indeed, the latter phenomena might be looked on as limiting cases of the former.

Those situations *commonly* regarded as concept-formation tasks, however, are more complex. Sets of initiating stimuli are partitioned into two or more subsets, at least one of which has two or more independently presented members. Usually each of the subsets has two or more members, and the learning requirement is acquisition of the same response to all members of a particular subset and of a different response for each subset.

At a descriptive level, the sets of initiating stimuli in concept formation studies have been markedly heterogeneous. Because some sets apparently require paradigms different from those for other sets, and also for simplicity, sets of initiating stimuli are divided here into three types. These three types seem sufficient both for the development of adequate one-stage and two-stage paradigms and for the representation of all sets of initiating stimuli.

In the first type of set, all members are either variations in values along one physical or psychophysical dimension, or they are combinations of values along two or more dimensions. The dimensions may be primary or derived; the combinations may be completely or incompletely orthogonal.

Illustrative of such sets are four squares which are red-small, red-large, blue-small, and blue-large.

Initiating stimuli in the second type of set can be partitioned into two or more subsets on the basis that all stimuli of each subset have some physically specifiable element or relation in common. The stimuli within each of these subsets differ from each other with respect to additional features. Thus, the stimuli of each subset consist of both common and variable features, neither of which has been (or perhaps could be) completely reduced to combinations of physical or psychophysical dimensions. Four stimuli, two of which have an S-shaped form in common and two of which have a sword-shaped form in common, but whose other features differ, are representative of this type of set of initiating stimuli.

Sets of initiating stimuli which are less readily or not at all reducible to combinations of values along dimensions, or to subsets defined by common elements or relations, constitute the third type of set. Illustrative of this type are sets of words for objects, properties, or relations. Subsets of words are usually, but not necessarily, specified on the basis of observations or assumptions that all of the stimuli of each subset evoke one or more common responses, some of which differ from the common responses evoked by the stimuli of each of the other subsets. An example of such sets of initiating stimuli is provided subsequently.[2]

With this type of initiating stimuli the bases for partitioning into subsets and for assigning responses to those subsets might be entirely arbitrary or random. For example, eight consonant-vowel-consonant initiating stimuli, none of which has any letters in common, might be randomly partitioned into four subsets of two members each. As stimuli for responses, a different one of four two-digit numbers, none of which has any digit in common, might then be randomly assigned to each of the subsets of initiating stimuli, with the requirement that a different response be conditioned to each subset of initiating stimuli.

Paired-Associates Learning Tasks and Concept-Formation Tasks

Paired-associates learning can be regarded as referring either to a particular kind of task or to a more general *procedure* for establishing and changing stimulus-response associations. Many concept-formation *tasks,* however, have employed the paired-associates *procedure* for strengthening associations between stimulus members and responses elicited by response members. Both conventional paired-associates tasks and such concept-formation tasks may therefore be regarded as complementary special cases of patterns of stimulus-response associations which are strengthened by the paired-associates procedure (Metzger, 1958; Richardson, 1958).

---

[2] The first and possibly the second of the three types of sets of initiating stimuli distinguished here and the relationships with terminating responses into which these types of stimuli enter are equivalent to what have been labeled elsewhere as conjunctive categories or concepts (Bruner, Goodnow, and Austin, 1956, pp. 41-43, 244-245). The third of the present types seems approximately equivalent to Bruner, Goodnow, and Austin's disjunctive categories or concepts. From Bruner, Goodnow, and Austin's definition of relational concepts or categories and the accompanying examples, it cannot be determined whether such relational categories overlap with the first and second of the types noted here or whether such categories involve some additional type of initiating stimuli not distinguished here.

There is only one essential difference between conventional paired-associates learning tasks and concept-formation tasks in which stimulus-response associations are established by the paired-associates procedure. That difference is in the ratio of stimulus members to responses which are to be conditioned to those stimuli. For conventional paired-associates learning tasks, the ratio of stimulus members to response members has been 1:1; that is, separate associations are established between each of mn_s different stimulus members and each of the mn_r different responses elicited by mn_r response members.

For the formation of concepts by the paired-associates procedure, however, the ratio of stimulus members to the responses which are conditioned to those stimuli has been greater than 1:1, that is, for at least one, and usually for all of m subsets of stimulus members, $n_{sj} > 1$, where n_{sj} is the number of stimuli in the jth subset. Regardless of the type of sets of initiating stimuli, by increasing the numbers of responses to equal the number of initiating stimuli, concept-formation tasks in which stimulus-response associations are established by the paired-associates procedure can be transformed into conventional paired-associates learning tasks. Conversely, by decreasing the number of responses from equality with the number of initiating stimuli the latter can be transformed into concept-formation tasks.

PARADIGMS

The role of verbal mediating responses in concept-formation tasks can be developed most easily and clearly by means of two-stage paradigms of presumed relationships among initiating stimuli, mediating responses and stimuli, and terminating responses for each of the three types of initiating stimuli which were distinguished in the preceding section. Inferences regarding mediating responses and stimuli are usually based on characteristics of relationships between initiating stimuli and terminating responses. Accordingly, in the first part of this section, the two-stage paradigms are developed within the framework of one-stage paradigms which involve only initiating stimuli and terminating responses. Noted in connection with the description of these paradigms are some explanatory consequences, in particular, for reversal and nonreversal shifts.

Concept-formation tasks are usually complex, and mediating responses and stimuli are commonly inferred rather than observed directly. Two-stage paradigms of conceptual behaviors should, therefore, be proposed cautiously. Emphasized in the second part of this section are some precautions in the development and use of two-stage paradigms.

"Abstract set or attitude," "hypotheses," and "strategies" are notions often advanced as central to any explanations of conceptual behaviors. Moreover, they are often regarded as opposed to stimulus-response analyses of concept-formation tasks. The thesis elaborated in the last part of this section, however, is that these are not opposing notions, but rather are already embodied or can be readily assimilated within the one-stage and two-stage paradigms of the present analysis.

One-Stage and Two-Stage Paradigms

One-stage paradigms of conceptual situations and behaviors involve relationships between initiating stimuli and terminating responses. Such paradigms provide baselines for the development of two-stage paradigms, which introduce verbal mediating responses and stimuli. One-stage paradigms are not merely steppingstones, however; they are useful in themselves, in that they appear to represent adequately some of the conceptual behaviors of infrahuman organisms, of preverbal humans, and of humans under conditions which preclude or short-circuit verbal mediating responses.

Combinations of Values along Dimensions

One-stage paradigms. A set of stimuli consisting of combinations of two values along each of two dimensions is the simplest case of possible sets of stimuli containing complete orthogonal combinations of m values along each of n dimensions. The four initiating stimuli of the one-stage paradigm shown in Fig. 1 are combinations of two values (x_1, x_2) along an X dimension, and of two values (y_1, y_2) along a Y dimension. For ex-

ample, x_1 and x_2 might be the values giving rise to the colors red and blue, respectively, along a dimension of wave length; y_1 and y_2 might be small and large areas, respectively, along a (derived) dimension of size.

The two terminating responses could be naming by means of familiar words, nonsense syllables, or manipulanda representing two different names. Or they could be sorting by placing the stimuli in groups, matching them with other stimuli, or approaching-avoiding. The two patterns of relationships between initiating stimuli and terminating responses depict the associations whose strengthening or occurrence are referred to here as concept formation. That both animals and humans can acquire such differential responses to one or some of the dimensions of multidimensional stimuli has been amply demonstrated (Kelleher, 1956; Kendler and D'Amato, 1955; Woodworth, 1958).

Determinants of the actual and potential patterns of relationships that will be learned include the number of fixed, relevant, and irrelevant dimensions presented, as well as the number of values selected along the relevant and irrelevant dimensions. A *fixed* dimension is exemplified by but one value along the dimension for all of the members of the set of initiating stimuli. For the stimuli shown in Fig. 1, form, dimensionality, number of forms, and location of the forms on the presentation cards might be the same for each of the four initiating stimuli. They are among the fixed dimensions of those stimuli.

Should the task be to respond on the basis of red or blue, disregarding size, or to respond on the basis of small and large, disregarding color, the relevant dimensions would be color and size, respectively. More generally, the dimensions of the combinations of

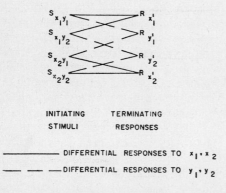

INITIATING   TERMINATING
STIMULI   RESPONSES

———————— DIFFERENTIAL RESPONSES TO $x_1 \cdot x_2$
— — —— DIFFERENTIAL RESPONSES TO $y_1 \cdot y_2$

FIG. 1. *One-stage paradigm of relationships involving initiating stimuli which are combinations of two values,* x_1, x_2 *along an* X *dimension and two values,* y_1, y_2 *along a* Y *dimension. (The differential terminating responses* $R_{x'_1}$, $R_{x'_2}$ *are to* x_1, x_2, *while* $R_{y'_1}$, $R_{y'_2}$ *are to* y_1, y_2. *The* X *dimension might be color with values of red,* x_1, *and blue,* x_2, *and the* Y *dimension might be size with values of small,* y_1, *or large,* y_2.)

values to which discriminative responses are to be conditioned are the *relevant* dimensions. *Irrelevant* dimensions are those which, in the formation of some particular concept (s), involve values which must be disregarded. Such dimensions—or, more precisely, the values along such dimensions—may be completely or incompletely orthogonal with respect to combinations of values along the relevant dimensions.[3]

Once the component associations of particular patterns of relationships, such as those in Fig. 1, are at a given level of strength, changes may occur either *singly* or *jointly,* in the initiating stimuli, the terminating responses, and the stimulus-response relationships. Such changes are important, because they are the bases for concept generalization and for reversal and nonreversal shifts.

The initiating stimulus can be changed by adding or shifting to new values along the original dimensions of the stimuli, or by adding or subtracting dimensions and values along those dimensions. The degree of occurrence of previously learned differential responses to altered sets of stimuli is the measure of *concept generalization.* Except where concept generalization has been used as a criterion of concept formation (for example, Heidbreder, 1946a, 1946b), however, this phenomenon has not been of great experimental interest. For this reason, to elaborate on concept generalization here is considered premature.

[3] As is suggested by the overlap of the terminology employed here and that employed in classifying analysis of variance designs (for example, Federer, 1955), such designs provide models of some of the many possible relationships between terminating responses and sets of initiating stimuli which are combinations of values along dimensions.

Both the initiating stimuli and the terminating responses can remain the same, but their relationships, or the relevant and irrelevant dimensions and values, can be changed by reversal or nonreversal shifts. The effects of such shifts on conceptual behaviors, and explanations of those effects, have been among the major concerns of many recent studies of concept formation (for example, Kendler and Kendler, 1959). It is important, therefore, to describe reversal and nonreversal shifts within one-stage paradigms for this type of initiating stimuli. Also, such description is prerequisite to the subsequent analysis of the role of verbal mediating responses and stimuli in reversal and nonreversal shifts.

With reversal shifts the values or combinations of values to which differential responses are learned remain the same, but the responses to values or combinations of values are interchanged. In Fig. 1, for example, $R_{x'_1}$ might be shifted from $S_{x_1y_1}$ and $S_{x_1y_2}$ to $S_{x_2y_1}$ and $S_{x_2y_2}$; and $R_{x'_2}$ would become the reinforced response to $S_{x_1y_1}$ and $S_{x_1y_2}$ instead of to $S_{x_2y_1}$ and $S_{x_2y_2}$. Specifically, the response to red-small and red-large would be shifted to blue-small and blue-large, and the response to blue-small and blue-large would be made to red-small and red-large.

A complete nonreversal shift entails a change from differential pairings of responses with combinations of values along one or more dimensions to differential pairings of those responses with combinations of values along one or more entirely different dimensions. Thus, the pattern of relationships in Fig. 1 might be changed from responding in terms of x_1 and x_2 along X, disregarding y_1 and y_2 along Y, to responding differentially to y_1 and y_2, disregarding x_1 and

x_2. Only the relationships of the two responses to the initiating stimuli and not the responses themselves are changed. The relationship between $S_{x_1y_1}$ (red-small) and $R_{x'_1}$ would remain the same but that response would be changed from $S_{x_1y_2}$ (red-large) to $S_{x_2y_1}$ (blue-small). The relationship between $S_{x_2y_2}$ (blue-large) and $R_{x'_2}$ would remain the same but that response would be changed from $S_{x_2y_1}$ (blue-small) to $S_{x_1y_2}$ (red-large).

New terminating responses can be introduced. Should the old and the new responses have the same topography and, because of time limitations imposed by the task, be prohibited from occurring in sequence, the old responses must be inhibited for the new responses to occur. Such a state of affairs has been described as a condition, if not the optimum condition, for *negative transfer*. What results is simply a shift from one one-stage paradigm to another one-stage paradigm. But if the old and new responses do not interfere with each other (have separate topographies or can occur in sequence), the old responses may not drop out but instead constitute relatively stable links—mediating responses and stimuli—between initiating stimuli and the new terminating responses. Thus, a two-stage paradigm would have emerged. This is, of course, the sequence of events which has been presumed in investigations of the effect of verbal pretraining on subsequent conceptual sorting and naming (for example, Fenn and Goss, 1957).

Despite the usefulness and greater simplicity of one-stage paradigms, there are considerations which suggest that such paradigms are less adequate than two-stage paradigms for explanation and prediction of the conceptual behavior of verbal humans in many concept-formation tasks and even,

perhaps, of some of the conceptual behaviors of infrahuman organisms and nonverbal humans. These considerations include: (*a*) observations of positive transfer from verbal pretraining to subsequent conceptual sorting or naming and of facilitation due to instructions or instruction-induced sets (Carey and Goss, 1957; Fenn and Goss, 1957; Gelfand, 1958; Goss and Moylan, 1958; Hunter and Ranken, 1956; Lacey and Goss, 1959), (*b*) the relatively greater ease of reversal than of nonreversal shifts for human adults (Buss, 1956; Gormazano and Grant, 1958; Harrow and Friedman, 1958; Kendler and, D'Amato, 1955; Kendler and Mayzner, 1956) and for children who are fast learners (Kendler and Kendler, 1959) in contrast to the superiority of nonreversal shifts for animals (Kelleher, 1956) and for children who are slow learners (Kendler and Kendler, 1959), and (*c*) verbal humans' reports of the occurrence and use of names for dimensions and value of stimuli in the conceptual sorting of stimuli (for example, Lacey and Goss, 1959). An additional consideration rests primarily on the results of studies employing the third type of sets of stimuli (for example, Reed, 1946). Without the postulation of common verbal or other responses to subsets of stimuli whose members are highly dissimilar physically, generalization of a common terminating response from one stimulus of a subset to other stimuli of the subset would be precluded. Each of the associations between initiating stimuli and terminating responses would have to be strengthened separately, with a consequent increase in difficulty of mastering the task.

Two-stage paradigms. Shown in Fig. 2 are some of the possible stimulus-response relationships in a two-stage expansion of the one-stage responses; between mediating stimuli and terminating responses; and between initiating stimuli and terminating responses.

Within the first of these subsets of relationships, variations in the strength of two subpatterns of relationships between initiating stimuli and mediating responses may have somewhat different effects on conceptual behaviors. The first subpattern represents relationships in which responses of naming the dimensions occur. These are the associations between the initating stimuli and R_x, R_y. The second subpattern represents responses of naming the specific values along the dimensions. The responses of these associations are R_{x1} for x_1; R_{x2} for x_2; R_{y1} for y_1; and R_{y2} for y_2.

When the relationships between mediating stimuli and mediating responses are added, variations in the strengths of three more subpatterns of relationships can be distinguished. The first of these subpatterns is sequences of responses of naming the dimensions. These appear in the lower half of Fig. 2 under "Dimensions" as R_xS, R_yS and R_yS, R_xS. The second subpattern is sequences of responses of naming values along dimensions. The eight sequences of combinations and orders of two of such responses are shown in the lower half of Fig. 2 under "Values." The third of these subpatterns is sequences of responses of naming both dimensions and values along dimensions. For example, combining one of the two responses of naming a dimension with one of the four responses of naming a value would generate 16 permutations of a particular dimension response with a particular value response.

Variation in the strength of each of these five subpatterns of relationships between initiating stimuli and mediating responses might have some-

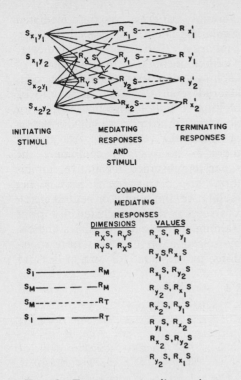

INITIATING STIMULI   MEDIATING RESPONSES AND STIMULI   TERMINATING RESPONSES

COMPOUND MEDIATING RESPONSES

DIMENSIONS	VALUES
R_xS, R_yS	$R_{x1}S$, $R_{y1}S$
R_yS, R_xS	$R_{y1}S$,$R_{x1}S$
	$R_{x1}S$, $R_{y2}S$
S_I————R_M	$R_{y2}S$,$R_{x1}S$
S_M— — — —R_M	$R_{x2}S$, $R_{y1}S$
S_M----------R_T	$R_{y1}S$, $R_{x2}S$
S_I—— ——R_T	$R_{x2}S$,$R_{y2}S$
	$R_{y2}S$, $R_{x1}S$

FIG. 2. *Two-stage paradigm of some of the relationships possible between initiating stimuli and mediating responses, between mediating stimuli and mediating responses, between mediating stimuli and terminating responses, and between initiating stimuli and terminating responses. (In order to simplify the possible relationships of the diagram, relationships involving compound mediating responses for dimensions and compound mediating responses for values along dimensions are listed separately. The mediating responses might be differential with respect to* x_1, x_2 *along the X dimension or to* y_1, y_2 *along the Y dimension which is also the case for the terminating responses.)*

paradigm presented in Fig. 1. The four subsets of these relationships which should be distinguished are those: between initiating stimuli and mediating responses; between mediating stimuli and mediating responses or, more simply, between mediating what different effects on the direction and degree of: extralist response interference with both mediating responses and terminating responses, trial-to-trial variability of the stimulus patterns immediately prior to the terminating responses, response-mediated similarity, and response-mediated dissimilarity. In turn, these conditions should influence direction and degree of transfer to acquisition of associations between initiating stimuli and terminating responses. Table 1 summarizes assumptions about the effects of each of the first four subpatterns on extralist response interference, trial-to-trial variability of

stimulus patterns, response-mediated similarity, and response-mediated dissimilarity. Table 1 also indicates whether these four consequences of each of the four subpatterns considered separately are expected to be facilitative (+), inhibitory (—), or neutral with respect to the formation of particular concepts. At present there is no way of combining the separate presumed facilitative, inhibitory, or neutral effects into a net facilitative, inhibitory, or neutral effect.

Except where precluded by prior training in the experimental situation, by selection on the basis of associations to the same or similar sets of

TABLE 1

SPECIFIC PATTERNS OF STIMULUS-RESPONSE RELATIONSHIPS

Specific Patterns Involving	Extralist Response Interference	Stimulus Variability	Response-Mediated Similarity	Response-Mediated Dissimilarity
Dimensions:				
R_x, R_y	Reduce (+)	Reduce (+)	Increase (—)	Decrease (—)
$R_x R_y$, $R_y R_x$	Reduce (+)	Reduce (+)	Increase (—)	Decrease (—)
Values along single dimensions:				
R_{x1}, R_{x2}	Reduce (+)	Reduce (+)	Increase for $S_{x_1y_1}$, $S_{x_1y_2}$ and for $S_{x_2y_1}$, $S_{x_2y_2}$ (+ for $R_{x'_1}$, $R_{x'_2}$ and — for $R_{y'_1}$, $R_{y'_2}$)	Increase for $S_{x_1y_1}$, $S_{x_1y_2}$ in relation to $S_{x_2y_1}$, $S_{x_2y_2}$ (+ for $R_{x'_1}$, $R_{x'_2}$ and — for $R_{y'_1}$, $R_{y'_2}$)
R_{y1}, R_{y2}	Reduce (+)	Reduce (+)	Increase for $S_{y_1x_1}$, $S_{y_1x_2}$ and for $S_{y_2x_1}$, $S_{y_2x_2}$ (+ for $R_{y'_1}$, $R_{y'_2}$ and — for $R_{x'_1}$, $R_{x'_2}$)	Increase for $S_{y_1x_1}$, $S_{y_1x_2}$ in relation to $S_{y_2x_1}$, $S_{y_2x_2}$ (+ for $R_{y'_1}$, $R_{y'_2}$ and — for $R_{x'_1}$, $R_{x'_2}$)
Combinations of values along dimensions:				
$R_{x1}R_{y1}$, $R_{y1}R_{x1}$, etc.	Reduce (+) to Increase (—)	Reduce (+) to Increase (—)	No differential effects among initiating stimuli	

Note. The directions of these effects are shown along with whether they are expected to have facilitative (+) or inhibitory (—) consequences. In the case of responses to values along single dimensions, whether particular initiating stimulus-mediating response relationships are facilitative or inhibitory is contingent on the relationships between initiating stimuli and terminating responses which are to be acquired.

initiating stimuli, or by instructions, each of these four subpatterns might occur both within trials and in successive trials during a good part of the course of acquiring associations between the initiating stimuli and the terminating responses. Their relative strengths at any point in learning—and, therefore, their effects on acquisition of initiating stimulus-terminating response associations—will be contingent on factors which include the following: their initial relative strengths, the values or combinations of values along one or more dimensions to which the differential terminating responses are being strengthened, time permitted to make the terminating responses, and degree of mastery of the terminating responses.

The fifth subpattern, which involves sequences of mediating responses of naming the dimension and of naming values along the dimension, may also influence acquisition of terminating responses. For example, fairly strong bidirectional associations might exist or be established between R_xS and R_{x1}, R_{x2}, and between R_yS and R_{y1}, R_{y2}. Should R_x be stronger than R_Y, R_{x1} and R_{x2} would occur and be available for mediating discriminative terminating responses to S_{x1y1}, S_{x1y2} and to S_{x2y1}, S_{x2y2} rather than to S_{x1y1}, S_{x2y1}, and S_{x1y2}, S_{x2y2}. Contingent on the relationships between initiating stimuli and terminating responses which were being differentially reinforced, facilitation or inhibition of these associations might be occasioned.

The remaining two subsets of relationships, those between mediating stimuli and terminating responses and those between initiating stimuli and terminating responses, are of primary importance here because of their presumed roles in reversal and non-

reversal shifts. The upper diagram of Fig. 3 shows the relationships among initiating stimuli, mediating responses and stimuli, and terminating responses which might exist at appreciable levels of strength upon attainment of differential responses to the x_1 and x_2 values along the X dimension. Should there be introduction of differential reinforcement of R_{x2} to S_{x1y1}, S_{x1y2}, and of R_{x1} to S_{x2y1}, S_{x2y2} to bring about a reversal shift, six associations might be changed: the four between the initiating stimuli and the terminating responses, and the two between the mediating stimuli and the terminating responses. In contrast, 14 associations might be affected by a nonreversal shift to the differential reinforcement of responses to the y_1 and y_2 values of Y. These are the four between initiating stimuli and R_{x1}, R_{x2}, which might be weakened; the four between those stimuli and R_{y1}, R_{y2}, which might be strengthened; the two between S_{x1} and S_{x2} and the terminating responses which might be extinguished while the two between S_{y1} and S_{y2} and those responses are established and strengthened; and the two associations between initiating stimuli and terminating responses (S_{x1y2} and $R_{x'1}$; S_{x2y1} and $R_{x'2}$), which must be reversed.

If equal weights are assumed for the component associations of two-stage paradigms, and if shifting is inversely related to the number of associations which must or may have to be changed, reversal shifts should be accomplished more rapidly than nonreversal shifts. Within one-stage paradigms, reversal shifts will affect more associations and therefore be more difficult than nonreversal shifts. Thus, as Kendler and his associates (Kendler and D'Amato, 1955) have suggested, but without detailed development of the basis for this proposal, one-stage and two-stage paradigms generate opposing

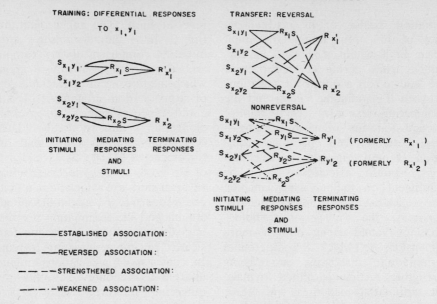

FIG. 3. *The paradigm for training shows conceptual responses, $R_{x'_1}$ and $R_{x'_2}$ to $S_{x_1y_1}$, $S_{x_1y_2}$ and $S_{x_2y_1}$, $S_{x_2y_2}$, respectively, after whose strengthening to some criterion level, reversal and nonreversal shifts are made. (As shown in the two paradigms for transfer, a reversal shift requires changes in only 6 associations, while a nonreversal shift may affect up to 14 associations. The terminating responses remain the same with respect to general topography and specific form—only the stimulus-response relationship into which they enter are altered. $R_{y'_1}$ and $R_{y'_2}$ of the nonreversal shift are the same responses as $R_{x'_1}$ and $R_{x'_2}$, respectively. However, the subscripts were changed to indicate that differences along the Y dimension, y_1, y_2, are the new bases for differential responses.)*

predictions about the relative ease of reversal and nonreversal shifts.

In general, as the number of dimensions and values increases, the number of associations involved in nonreversal shifts becomes increasingly greater than the number altered by reversal shifts. Other factors equal, therefore, with greater numbers of dimensions and values, the relative disadvantage of nonreversal shifts should become greater. Other factors, however, are not likely to be equal. As Buss (1956) has noted, with nonreversal shifts responses on the basis of the previously reinforced values along the no-longer-relevant dimension continue to be reinforced on 50 per cent of the trials. The weakening of such differ-

ential responses will, therefore, be retarded, and will further contribute to the disadvantage of nonreversal shifts. But four additional conditions may serve to reduce the relative disadvantage of nonreversal shifts.

First, once some of the initiating stimuli begin to elicit the new mediating responses, when other initiating stimuli are presented these mediating responses should generalize extensively among those stimuli. One basis of such generalization would be the presence of stimuli common to each trial: that is, those arising from the experimental situation, from postural and receptor-orienting responses, and from responses to instructions other than those aspects referring to more specific associations between initiating stimuli and mediating responses.

Second, because each of the values along the new dimension of the nonreversal shift is an element common to a subset of stimuli, the new mediating response for a subset of initiating stimuli should generalize among the members of the subset. Simultaneously, of course, the same two conditions should result in the generalization of inhibition of the relationships between initiating stimuli and the old mediating responses.

Third, though not included in the paradigms of Fig. 3, the response R_x, which represents the response of naming the X dimension, might be replaced by the comparable response, R_y, for the Y dimension. The increased frequencies of occurrence of stimuli produced by R_{y1} and R_{y2}, which are presumably already associated with R_y, would be the bases of the initial evocations of R_y. Because R_y is only one response, however, its strengthening and generalization among the initiating stimuli should be even faster and more extensive than the strengthening and generalization of R_{y1} and R_{y2}. Therefore, R_y should begin to occur first and, because of the pre-established associations between the stimuli it produced and R_{y1} and R_{y2}, their probabilities of occurrence relative to R_{x1} and R_{x2} should be increased markedly.

Fourth, successive reversal or nonreversal shifts should increase the probabilities of occurrence of mediating responses referring to a change in task. With successive reversal and nonreversal shifts, number of trials to learn the new concepts of each shift usually decreases. Some of this increasingly more rapid formation of new concepts is probably due in part to warm-up or performance set in the form of familiarization with mode and rate of presentation of the initiating stimuli. Such familiarization should eliminate irrelevant competing responses as well as lead to greater stability of postural and receptor-orienting responses to thus assure more effective reception of the initiating stimuli and lower the variability of response-produced stimuli. Also, with experience, subjects should learn to recognize with greater confidence and greater accuracy that they have reached perfect or near perfect performance of discriminative responses to some subsets of stimuli. Consequently, any error then made would serve as a cue that the experimenter has shifted the concepts rather than that the concepts have not yet been learned. Further, subjects will be increasingly familiar with whether the shifts are reversal or nonreversal shifts and, if the latter, with how many dimensions have probably been shifted and even to what dimensions the shifts have probably been made. Thus, mediating responses of the form "He's changed the task" or "Something has changed" should come to control whole sets of further mediating responses which name dimensions and values along dimensions. These four conditions should reduce the net disadvantage of nonreversal to reversal shifts to margins which are much less than those suggested by simply counting the numbers of equally weighted associations which such shifts might affect.

Common Elements or Relations

One-stage paradigms. Figure 4 is a one-stage paradigm for concept formation with sets of stimuli, such as those constructed by Hull (1920), in which each subset requiring a common response consists of a common element accompanied by other features which vary unsystematically from instance

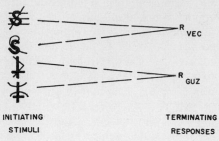

FIG. 4. *One-stage paradigm of relationships between nonsense syllable terminating responses and initiating stimuli which consists of two different common elements each of which is accompanied by features which differ from figure to figure.*

to instance. Furthermore, the common elements are neither completely nor incompletely orthogonal combinations of values along one or more discernible physical or psychophysical dimensions. If common "relations" among the parts of complex forms are regarded as separable from the features which vary among instances exemplifying the same relation, Smoke's (1932) set of initiating stimuli and other sets that resemble his can also be represented by this paradigm.

Two-stage paradigms. The two-stage paradigm for the second type of initiating stimuli is shown in Fig. 5. The letters or word subscripts of the mediating responses are possible specific pre-established mediating responses to the indicated initiating stimuli. Worth noting, because of their predictive consequences, are three major differences between this paradigm and the two-stage paradigm for sets of stimuli composed of combinations of values along dimensions shown in Fig. 2.

First, no responses of naming the component dimensions are present. However, should the common elements of two or more subsets be at

the same spatial position, responses of orienting-toward and naming that position might occur and be strengthened. Although such responses and the stimuli they produce would be nondifferential with respect to the relationships between initiating stimuli and terminating responses, their occurrence might reduce extralist intrusions and stimulus variability as well as assure more frequent reception of the elements which distinguish one subset of figures from another.

Second, both the common element of members of a subset and the variable features of those members are likely to be made up of a fairly large number of discriminable features, each of which elicits naming responses. If the common element or relation which defines a particular subset of stimuli does elicit some response which is the same for all members of the subset, that response to each member is likely to have considerable competition from the responses to other parts of the common element as well as from responses to the variable features of

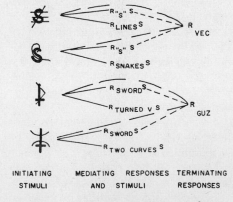

FIG. 5. *Two-stage paradigm of the relationships possible between initiating stimuli, which consists of two different common elements and variable features; both mediating and terminating responses and also between mediating stimuli and terminating responses.*

each member. Such responses and the further responses which they may evoke may interfere, not only with any common mediating response to all stimuli of a subset, but also with the terminating response for that subset. Further, few, if any, pre-established stable patterns of associations among mediating responses might exist. Such conditions should also foster high trial-to-trial stimulus variability.

Third, the variable features of stimuli with a given common element or relation may have little or no phys-

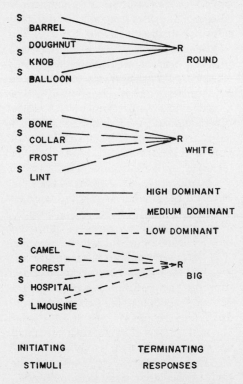

INITIATING   TERMINATING
STIMULI   RESPONSES

FIG. 6. *One-stage paradigm of relationships between subsets of initiating stimuli each of which is defined by elicitation of a common terminating response by the stimuli. (The words used are from Underwood and Richardson's —1956—first list and are of three levels of dominance with respect to their elicitation of the terminating responses.)*

ical similarity to those features of the other subsets of stimuli with common elements. And, as already suggested, the naming responses evoked by one subset may have little overlap with those evoked by the other subsets. While reversal shifts could be instituted, such characteristics of the stimuli would severely limit or obviate nonreversal shifts.

Elicitation of Common Responses

One-stage paradigms. The third kind of stimuli are those whose subsets are distinguished from each other on the basis of their members' elicitation of some common response that differs from the common responses defining each of the other subsets. Figure 6 is a one-stage paradigm and Fig. 7 is a two-stage paradigm of the stimulus-response relationships presumed to be involved in the formation of concepts with such stimuli.

In the one-stage paradigm, increased frequency of arousal of each one of the common terminating responses by the stimuli of the subset is viewed as strengthening of the concept. The stronger the initial associations between the stimuli of subsets and their terminating response, and the higher the variance of those associations, the more rapid the formation of concepts (Freedman and Mednick, 1958; Underwood and Richardson, 1956). The limiting case of the formation of such concepts is the acquisition, from zero levels of initial strength, of common responses which have each been assigned to a different subset of physically dissimilar stimuli.

Two-stage paradigms. The mediating responses of the two-stage paradigm (Fig. 7) are those which define each of the subsets of initiating stimuli. In general, though not necessarily, the associations between initiating stimuli and terminating responses

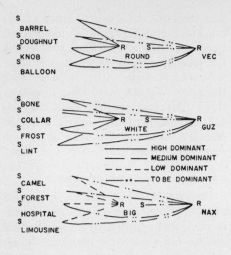

INITIATING   MEDIATING RESPONSES   TERMINATING
STIMULI   AND STIMULI   RESPONSES

FIG. 7. *Two-stage paradigm of relationships possible between subsets of initiating stimuli defined by the elicitation of common responses which now function as mediating responses and stimuli in the acquisition of new associations between each of the subsets of initiating stimuli and their common nonsense syllable terminating responses. (The mediating responses should increase the similarity of stimuli within subsets and decrease the similarity of stimuli of each subset to those of the other subsets.)*

would be at zero levels initially, as would those between mediating stimuli and those responses. To the degree that each stimulus of a subset elicits the common mediating response, there will be a response-mediated increase in the similarity of those largely dissimilar stimuli; and, once the mediating stimulus is associated with the terminating response, acquisition of the concept should be facilitated by response-mediated generalization. Griffith and Spitz (1958) and Griffith, Spitz, and Lipman (1959) obtained direct relationships between correct abstractions made by normal and mentally retarded children and number of

words defined by the same possible common abstractions. From these relationships they inferred that the common definition mediated the common abstractions.

The presence of different mediating response-produced stimuli, each associated with a different terminating response, might also increase the response-mediated dissimilarity and discrimination of stimuli which are members of different subsets (Fenn and Goss, 1957). Such an increase would counteract any generalization of terminating responses among subsets due to fortuitous physical resemblances among stimuli belonging to different response-defined subsets.

The relationships between initiating stimuli and terminating responses which are to be strengthened need not be isomorphic with the relationships between initiating stimuli and mediating responses. With increasing departures from isomorphism, the acquisition of terminating responses might be retarded, possibly to a degree sufficient to produce some negative transfer. Because the mediating responses might also reduce extralist response interference and stimulus variability, however, the net transfer might still be positive.

If each of the initiating stimuli belongs to two or more response-defined subsets, each stimulus would be expected to evoke two or more different mediating responses, at least during the initial trials. Unless each terminating response is then isomorphic with the two or more responses defining each of the other combinations of subsets, multiple mediating responses to initiating stimuli can be expected to increase generalization among subsets; thus some retardation of the learning of terminating responses would be occasioned. Because of greater trial-to-trial variability in stimulation preceding terminating responses, multiple mediating responses to initiating stimuli may always produce some retardation relative to the maximum positive transfer that is achievable with a single mediating response to each initiating stimulus.

Use of Two-Stage Paradigms

Each of the preceding two-stage paradigms represents a different general case of relationships among the particular type of sets of initiating stimuli, mediating responses and stimuli, and terminating responses. The members of each of these types of sets of initiating stimuli may differ with respect to their complexity, their similarity and other properties, their number, and their probabilities of occurrence (Goss, 1955). Thus, it should be obvious that each particular concept-formation task, and its attendant conditions, requires detailed analysis in terms of presumed stimulus-response elements and initial relationships among these elements, and also in terms of the changes in those elements and relationships which are expected to occur. The nature and strengths of both initial and changed relationships should be expressed as completely and precisely as possible. Association techniques or training controlled by the experimenter are the means of specifying the strengths of initial relationships. It should also be remembered that—except when isolated and controlled—changes in many or all of the stimulus-response relationships present probably occur, if not simultaneously, within rather small blocks of trials.

Finally, some subjects who have formed concepts correctly may not provide verbal reports of the bases for their conceptual behaviors which correspond to experimenters' specifications of the basis for forming particular concepts. When verbal mediating responses do not occur, or occur only partially, sporadically, or during the earlier phases of concept formation, appropriate verbal reports would not be expected. Should the words which constitute subjects' mediating responses differ from the labels preferred by experimenters, subjects' reports might be considered wrong or incomplete. Further, during the course of acquisition the sets of verbal mediating responses may have changed. Should subjects have failed to distinguish such changes or to indicate when they took place, their reports would seem inaccurate and confused. In addition, if subjects described the terminating responses or both mediating and terminating responses as bases for their conceptual behaviors, while experimenters' specifications were only in terms of verbal mediating responses, subjects' verbal reports would seem unsatisfactory. This would also be the case were the subjects' mediating responses nonverbal.

Differences between the labels used by subjects and those preferred by experimenters can only be determined by careful, detailed analyses of the labeling habits of subjects from a given population. Confusions between mediating and terminating responses can be minimized by ascertaining the temporal sequences of subjects' responses. Only by careful observation of locomotor-manipulative responses (and even this may be inadequate) will it be possible to determine the presence of nonverbal mediating responses.

PLACE OF "ABSTRACT SET OR ATTITUDE," "HYPOTHESES," AND "STRATEGIES" IN THE FRAMEWORK OF THIS ANALYSIS

"Abstract set or attitude" (Goldstein and Scheerer, 1941; Hanfmann and Kasinin, 1942), "hypotheses"

(Woodworth, 1958), and "strategies" (Bruner, Goodnow, and Austin, 1956) are terms frequently used to label some aspects of the behavior involved in acquiring concepts as well as to explain success or failure in this process. Unfortunately, these notions have certain features that limit both their experimental usefulness and their explanatory power. In general, their presence or absence is ordinarily determined on the basis of characteristics of the conceptual behaviors observed. Thus, they are *post hoc* descriptions which usually cannot be used predictively. Often, too, the notions are treated as primary or sole explanations of conceptual behavior when, in fact, other factors— such as types of sets of initiating stimuli, specific attributes of each type of stimuli, and amount and conditions of practice—appear to be of equal or greater importance. And, on the whole, the relationship of these terms to more general theories of behavior is tenuous at best.

In the face of such shortcomings, one course for a stimulus-response analysis of concept formation consists of ignoring the terms entirely. Another course, followed here, is to attempt to assimilate what is meaningful and useful about the terms within the rather rigorous framework that this paper has presented. More specifically, it is suggested that the most meaningful and useful aspects of such notions as abstract set or attitude, hypotheses, and strategies are in part already present in this analysis, and that what is valuable but not present requires only certain translations in order to be assimilated. These aspects are considered below under the following headings: verbal mediating responses and stimuli, strengths of reactions to occurrences and extent of reversal or nonreversal shifts, sequences in which verbal mediating responses occur on

single and successive trials, sequences of receptor-orienting responses, and prior habits and persistence of covert or overt verbalization and rehearsal.

Verbal Mediating Responses and Stimuli

Following Fenn and Goss (1957), perhaps the simplest as well as the most common meaning of abstract set or attitude and hypotheses in concept formation is, conceived narrowly, the occurrence of verbal mediating responses and stimuli. Conceived more broadly, this meaning subsumes the largely pre-experimentally established patterns of relationships: (*a*) between initiating stimuli and mediating responses, where the latter are names for dimensions and values as well as for common elements or variable features, or where they are common responses or meanings that define subsets of initiating stimuli; (*b*) between such mediating responses and other mediating responses; and (*c*) between such mediating responses and terminating responses. The first part of this section on paradigms was largely devoted to an analysis of the role of these patterns of relationships in concept formation. The functional significance for concept formation of this meaning of abstract set or attitude and hypotheses has, therefore, already been considered.

Reactions to Shifts

Also considered earlier were mediating responses that identify shifts in the task. Such responses, it was suggested, should increase in strength with successive reversal or nonreversal shifts and thus mediate changes in whole sets of further mediating responses which name dimensions and values along dimensions. These changes might be called shifts in hypotheses or strategies. And their occurrence could be taken as evidence of the presence of an abstract set or attitude.

Sequences in Which Verbal Mediating Responses Occur

Bruner, Goodnow, and Austin (1956, pp. 81–103, 126–147) have suggested that conditions of presentation of initiating stimuli influence trial-to-trial sequences of choice and "guess" responses. Thus, when subjects could select each successive initiating stimulus, the four sequences or strategies which were distinguished logically were simultaneous scanning, successive scanning, conservative focussing, and focus gambling. When the successive occurrences of initiating stimuli were controlled by the experimenter, they distinguished wholist (whole, focussing) and part-scanning (part) strategies or sequences. Under the condition of presentation in which subjects could select each successive initiating stimulus, the responses which were recorded were terminating responses, first in the form of a choice and then as a guess. Presumably these choices and guesses were preceded, most immediately, by mediating responses consisting of names for the combinations of values of the stimulus selected and the names of the consequent guess of the correct concept. Therefore, the sequences or strategies they distinguished, and which were found to occur to some degree in various subjects, could be regarded as providing some information about sequences of mediating responses through successive selections of stimuli. Under the condition of presentation in which the experimenter determined each successive initiating stimulus, each hypothesis written during the ten-second period following each initiating stimulus could be regarded as congruent with the just-preceding mediating response. The sequences of such hypotheses,

therefore, probably reflected trial-to-trial sequences of the last mediating response of each trial. No information about intratrial sequences was reported.

The two-stage paradigms of the first part of this section show each initiating stimulus as eliciting only one mediating response, which is either the name for a dimension or value along a dimension, or a single combination of names for dimensions or values. Contingent on both the time subjects have to respond and on subjects' prior experiences with the same or similar stimuli, each initiating stimulus may elicit not one name or combination of names, but a sequence of names or combinations of names. For example, the subject might respond to a particular initiating stimulus with the sequence "red, small, color, size," in which "size" was the last response to occur prior to the appearance of the stimulus eliciting the terminating response to be conditioned to the initiating stimulus. Because of the shorter time interval, the terminating response might be more strongly conditioned to stimuli produced by size than to stimuli produced by the earlier mediating responses. More generally, should terminating responses be most strongly conditioned to stimuli produced by mediating responses which occurred just prior to elicitation of the terminating responses, the sequences with which mediating responses occur and whether those responses are names of values or of dimensions might have marked effects on concept formation.

Whether the effects are facilitative or inhibitory will be contingent on particular conditions. Thus, were size the relevant dimension and large and small the two values along that dimension, the sequence "color, red (or blue), size, large (or small)" should produce greater facilitation than the sequence "size, large (or small), color, red (or blue)." Similarly, sequences in which the last mediating responses were names for common elements of the initiating stimuli rather than names for their variable features should facilitate acquisition of different terminating responses to each subset of initiating stimuli with common features. Inhibitory consequences would be predicted for sequences ending with mediating responses which were names for variable features rather than for common elements. Also, occurrence of the common response to a subset of initiating word stimuli, after more specific associations to those words rather than before such associations, should facilitate; the opposite sequence should inhibit.

A further consideration would be whether the same sequence or different sequences of mediating responses occurred on each presentation of each initiating stimulus or of each member of particular subsets of initiating stimuli. With the sequence, "color, red (or blue), size, large (or small)," for example, constancy of the sequence should be most facilitative, were size the relevant dimension, and most inhibitory, were color the relevant dimension. A reduction in the percentage of times "size, large (or small)" occurred last, and a concomitant increase in the percentage of times "color, red (or blue)" occurred last, should be relatively less facilitative or less inhibitory in the formation of size or color concepts, respectively.

Modes of systematic variation of the components of sequences and of the order in which the components occur can be learned. Therefore, subjects can be expected to differ in the degree to which they have learned to vary the nature and sequences of mediating responses through successive trials. As a result subjects will not only differ with respect to the abstract set or attitude, hypotheses, and strategies with which they began but also with respect to those which are present through successive trials. Whether particular sequences or ways of varying such sequences are facilitative or inhibitory will be contingent on the particular concepts to be formed.

Sequences of Receptor-Orienting Responses

Receptor-orienting responses and their consequences may sometimes be functionally equivalent to mediating responses and stimuli (Goss, 1955). For this reason, abstract set or attitude, hypotheses, or strategies may also be conceived as sequences of receptor-orienting responses.

When initiating stimuli which are relatively small in size are presented at the same place, one at a time, receptor-orienting responses may be of little importance. Possible exceptions are initiating stimuli composed of combinations of common elements or relations and variable features for which the common element or relation of all members of a particular subset have the same location. Should there be some favored point of initial fixation for individual subjects, or for groups of subjects, whether the common element or relation of a particular subset was at that location or at other locations might influence acquisition of the concepts.

Simultaneous presentation of all initiating stimuli or groups thereof, however, might increase the importance of sequences of receptor-orienting responses. Both arrangement of initiating stimuli on the display, and the subjects' pre-experimental and subsequent experimental experiences, should determine the particular sequence of receptor-orienting responses

on a given trial. The initial and subsequent fixation points might maximize
focusing on successive stimuli whose
combinations of values and changes in
those combinations were optimal for
the formation of particular concepts.
If so, such sequences of receptor-
orienting responses should facilitate
concept formation. For other arrangements of initiating stimuli the same
sequences might be inhibitory.

*Prior Habits of Verbalization, Rehearsal,
and Persistence Therein*

Included in Dollard and Miller's
(1950, pp. 118–119) set of factors
in "social training in the use of higher
mental processes" is "training to stop
and think." Adolescent and adult subjects explicitly instructed to use verbal
mediating responses may differ little,
if at all, in the degree to which such
responses are activated. However,
without such explicit instructions—
and therefore largely dependent on the
subjects' past experiences with similar
tasks—they may or may not stop and
think: that is, they may or may not
make overt or covert verbal mediating
responses prior to occurrences of terminating responses to the initiating
stimulus. Furthermore, some subjects
may rehearse such responses between
trials while others may think of other
things; the latter subjects may, in other
words, fail to attend to the task continuously. Finally, in the face of initial
failures, some subjects may persist in
stopping and thinking and in rehears-
ing while other subjects may temporarily or permanently stop both activities. Up through adolescence the
strengths of such habits should be directly related to age. Awaiting detailed determination, however, are both
the nature of the relationships of habits of verbalization and rehearsal to
age and the effects of such habits on

probabilities of occurrence of verbal
mediating responses.

In summary, conceived analytically rather than simply as names for
certain instructions or for certain
changes in terminating responses, the
notions of abstract set or attitude, hypotheses, and strategies apparently
refer to one or more of the preceding
classes of relationships among the stimuli and responses of concept-formation
tasks. Some of the classes of relationships include mediating responses and
stimuli; those which do not can be expected to have indirect effects on relationships that do involve mediating
responses and stimuli.

PRINCIPLES AND PREDICTIONS

Though referred to occasionally—
and always assumed—in the preceding
section, little direct attention has yet
been given to the classes of variables
and of general principles involving
those variables which enter into explanations of the strengthening, generalization, and weakening of the stimulus-
response associations entailed in the
one- and two-stage paradigms that
have been described. Of obvious relevance are the classes of principles
that concern effects on associations or
on performance of classes of variables
such as: schedules of practice and reinforcement-punishment, the number
and both absolute and relative strengths
of conflicting responses, the number of
stimuli associated with the same response and the strengths of those associations, and the degree of similarity
among initiating stimuli and among
mediating stimuli. Setting limits to the
operation of these classes of variables
are the patterns of relationships among
initiating stimuli, mediating responses
and stimuli, and terminating responses
and also conditions of stimulus presentation, such as whether initiating

stimuli are presented simultaneously or successively (Bruner *et al.*, 1956) and whether they are all positive, negative, or both positive and negative (Hovland, 1952; Hovland and Weiss, 1953).

It is not the purpose of this paper to make an exhaustive enumeration of the consequences predicted by the application of each class of potentially relevant variables and the principles involving them to the several paradigms or to the various patterns of relationships the paradigms contain. In order to show explicitly how such variables and principles may be profitably combined with the paradigms, however, this final section deals with certain aspects of predictions of the effects of three important classes of variables for which some data are available. These are: strength of associations between initiating stimuli and mediating responses; patterns of relationships among initiating stimuli, mediating responses and stimuli, and terminating responses; and similarity of initiating stimuli. In each case, pertinent experimental studies are described.[4]

---

[4] Not considered, however, are those studies of the relative effects of reversal and nonreversal shifts which were noted in the first part of the second section. Also ignored are studies (Bensberg, 1958; Carey and Goss, 1957; Fenn and Goss, 1957; Hunter and Ranken, 1956; Wickens and Eckstrand, 1954) which were primarily demonstrations of positive transfer from verbal pretraining to subsequent conceptual behaviors; these demonstrations served as bases for inferences about the functional significance of verbal mediating responses in conceptual behaviors. Several additional experiments (Attneave, 1957; Rhine and Silun, 1958; Shepard and Shaeffer, 1956; Sigel, 1953, 1954; Solley and Messick, 1957; Staats and Staats, 1957; Wulff and Stolurow, 1957) have been excluded because they did not involve either experimentally controlled verbal pretraining or conventional concept-formation criterion tasks.

Strengths of Associations between Initiating Stimuli and Mediating Responses

The strengths of associations between initiating stimuli and verbal mediating responses will be determined by conditions of practice such as the number and distribution of trials or degree of mastery of those relationships prior to undertaking transfer or criterion tasks. In general, any condition of practice and reinforcement-punishment known to increase or decrease the strengths of stimulus-response associations of multiunit tasks are, through their effects on strengths of associations between initiating stimuli and mediating responses, potential determinants of subsequent performance on transfer or criterion tasks.

In Figs. 2 and 7, the relationships between initiating stimuli and mediating responses, and between the initiating stimuli in combination with mediating stimuli and terminating responses, can be described as isomorphic. Put another way, for each different mediating response to a subset of initiating stimuli, there is one and only one terminating response, each of which is different from the terminating response paired with any other mediating response. For such isomorphic patterns of relationships, it is predicted that rate of acquisition of associations between initiating stimuli and terminating responses would be a direct function of strengths of associations between initiating stimuli and mediating responses. Because of generalized responses (errors of generalization, confusions, intralist intrusions), trials to learn associations between initiating stimuli and terminating responses should be related to trials in learning associations between initiating stimuli and mediating responses by an ogival function or by curves showing some slight initial negative transfer rather than being negatively accelerated throughout (Goss, 1955).[5]

Pertinent to this prediction are two recent investigations (Goss and Moylan, 1958; Lacey and Goss, 1959) of the relationship between transfer to conceptual behaviors and strengths of associations between initiating stimuli and presumed verbal mediating responses. In both investigations, the initiating stimuli were 16 blocks, each of which was tall or short, black or white, in combination with top and bottom areas which were large or small, square or circular. In the Goss and Moyland study, nonsense-syllable responses or familiar-word responses were conditioned to subsets of tall-large, tall-small, short-large, and short-small initiating stimuli. Lacey and Goss used only nonsense-syllable responses. The transfer task of both studies was sorting by height-size, and in both the number of blocks sorted by height-size was directly related to degree of mastery of associations between initiating stimuli and presumed mediating responses, as well as to numbers of trials in learning those associations. Unfortunately the resultant curves were not adequate for more precise specification of functions relating direction and degree of transfer to degree of mastery of associations between initiating stimuli and mediating responses, or to trials in learning these associations.[6] As suggested else-

where for paired-associates learning tasks (Goss, 1955), such specifications are further complicated by the likelihood that the functions are contingent on parameters such as patterns of relationships among initiating stimuli, mediating responses and stimuli, and terminating responses, as well as on the degree of similarity of initiating stimuli.

Patterns of Relationships

Within two-stage paradigms, regardless of the type of sets of initiating stimuli, it is useful to distinguish four extreme patterns of relationships among subsets of initiating stimuli, mediating responses and stimuli, and terminating responses, because each pattern should result in somewhat different conceptual behaviors involving the terminat-

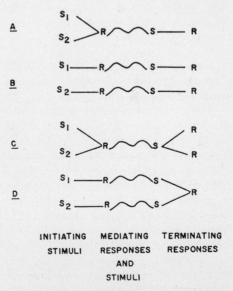

INITIATING   MEDIATING   TERMINATING
STIMULI   RESPONSES   RESPONSES
              AND
              STIMULI

FIG. 8. *Four possible extreme patterns of relationships among subsets of initiating stimuli, mediating responses and stimuli, and terminating responses.*

Such names might then serve as the actual verbal mediating responses of the transfer or criterion task.

---

[5] Murdock (1958) argues that with appropriate allowance for generalization responses, the function is negatively accelerated throughout.

[6] An alternative suggestion (Lacey and Goss, 1959) is that greater mastery of experimentally established associations between initiating stimuli and nonsense-syllable responses increases the likelihood of arousal of pre-experimentally established associations between initiating stimuli and names for dimensions and values along dimensions.

ing responses. Figure 8 shows these four patterns. In Patterns *A* and *B*, the relationships between mediating responses and subsets of initiating stimuli are isomorphic with those between terminating responses and subsets of initiating stimuli plus mediating stimuli. This isomorphism does not hold for Patterns *C* and *D*. Pattern *C* is characterized by a common mediating response to both subsets of initiating stimuli and by two terminating responses, one of which is to stimulus compounds consisting of stimuli from the first subset plus the mediating stimulus, and the other of which is to stimulus compounds consisting of stimuli from the second subset plus the mediating stimulus. Pattern *D* is characterized by a different mediating response to each subset of initiating stimuli, and by a common terminating response both to compounds consisting of the stimuli in the first subset plus the stimulus produced by the mediating response to those stimuli, and to compounds consisting of the stimuli in the second subset plus the stimulus produced by the mediating response to those stimuli.

For concept-formation tasks involving the relationships of Patterns *A* and *B*, prior acquisition of the associations between subsets of initiating stimuli and a common mediating response should facilitate acquisition of associations between the subsets of initiating stimuli and a common terminating response; prior acquisition of different mediating responses should facilitate acquisition of associations between initiating stimuli subsets and different terminating responses. Greater response-mediated similarity and generalization is the basis for the prediction for Pattern *A,* and greater response-mediated dissimilarity and discrimination is the basis for the prediction for Pattern *B*.

For Pattern *C*, in contrast, the greater similarity of the subsets of initiating stimuli (based on the presence of a common mediating stimulus) should retard acquisition of a different terminating response to each subset. For Pattern *D*, greater dissimilarity of the subsets of initiating stimuli (based on the presence of a different mediating stimulus for the stimuli of each subset) should slow the learning of a common terminating response to each subset.

Lacey (1959) tested each of these predictions. His stimuli were eight line drawings of faces or houses, each of which was printed on pink, light blue, light yellow, and light green paper. Eight- to 11-year-old children first learned either a common or different nonsense-syllable mediating response to two subsets of initiating stimuli. The transfer or criterion task was acquisition of a new set of nonsense-syllable responses as either a common or different terminating response to those same subsets of initiating stimuli. Thus the relationships of terminating responses to initiating stimuli and to mediating responses and stimuli were those of Patterns *A, B, C,* or *D*.

Measured against the performance of control groups, whose prior training controlled for facilitation due to warm-up and receptor-orienting responses, positive transfer was obtained with Patterns *A* and *B* and negative transfer occurred with Patterns *C* and *D*. Therefore, as predicted, the pattern of relationships among subsets of initiating stimuli, mediating responses and stimuli, and terminating responses determined whether positive or negative transfer occurred. Lacey's results also suggested that Pattern *B* might produce greater relative positive transfer, though no greater absolute positive transfer, than Pattern *A*. Patterns *C* and *D*, however, did not seem to differ with respect to either relative or absolute amounts of negative transfer.

Similarity of Initiating Stimuli

For Patterns A, B, C, and D, similarity of sets of initiating stimuli might influence amount and perhaps direction of transfer from verbal pretraining to subsequent conceptual behaviors. For Patterns A and D, disregarding mediating responses and stimuli, similarity within and between subsets of initiating stimuli should be directly related to ease of learning associations between those stimuli and a common terminating response. Patterns B and C involve acquisition of discriminative terminating responses to initiating stimuli. Rate of acquisition of those associations should be directly related to similarity of stimuli within subsets of initiating stimuli and inversely related to similarity between those subsets. When verbal mediating responses and stimuli are considered, similarity of initiating stimuli might modify the expected positive transfer with Patterns A and B and the expected negative transfer with Patterns C and D.

Present data and theory do not warrant attempts to develop more exact predictions of the influence of similarity of initiating stimuli on direction and amount of transfer. However, since the second variable of Lacey's (1959) experiment was two degrees of similarity of the members of the sets of face and house stimuli, some pertinent data are available.

For Patterns A and D together, disregarding verbal mediating responses and stimuli, similarity was directly related to mastery of associations between initiating stimuli and terminating responses; inverse relationships were obtained with Patterns B and C together. For Pattern A, while absolute amount of positive transfer was directly related to similarity, an inverse relationship

was obtained for relative amount of transfer. For Pattern D, both absolute and relative amounts of positive transfer were inversely related to similarity. For Patterns B and C, both absolute and relative amounts of positive transfer were directly related to similarity. However, since most of the relationships for each pattern separately were not statistically significant, at best they provide hypotheses for replicatory investigations.

In general, for concept-formation tasks involving prior strengthening of presumed mediating responses, the findings presently available suggest that conceptual behaviors involving terminating responses are influenced by: strengths of associations between initiating stimuli and mediating responses; patterns of relationships among initiating stimuli, mediating responses and stimuli, and terminating responses; and similarity of initiating stimuli. Furthermore, these findings are reasonably consistent with predictions based on two-stage paradigms in combination with principles of the role of these and other classes of variables in the strengthening, generalization, and weakening of stimulus-response associations.

SUMMARY

The purpose of this paper was to analyze the role of verbal mediating responses in concept formation. First summarized was the historical development of stimulus-response analyses of conceptual behaviors which have emphasized the role of mediating responses and stimuli, particularly verbal mediating responses. The influence of Max Meyer and Watson on the behavioristic analyses of the 1920s was noted. Although Birge, Miller and Dollard, Cofer and Foley, and Gibson furthered such analyses in the early 1940s, only the more detailed recent analyses of Baum, Osgood, Mandler, Goss, Kendler, and others have led to hypotheses which have been tested experimentally.

The first section provided a general specification of concept-formation tasks and described the relationship between concept formation and conventional paired-associates tasks. The second section first described the structures and some explanatory consequences of one-stage and two-stage paradigms of conceptual behaviors with each of three types of sets of initiating stimuli. Some precautions in the use of these paradigms were then noted, and assimilation within the present analysis of the notions of abstract set or attitude, hypotheses, and strategies was proposed. The third section showed the complementary relationship between the one-stage and two-stage paradigms and classes of variables and principles involving those variables which enter into explanations of the strengthening, generalization, and weakening of the component stimulus-response associations. Two-stage paradigms in combination with some of these principles were then used to generate sample predictions of effects on concept formation of: strengths of relationships between initiating stimuli and mediating responses; some patterns of relationships among initiating stimuli, mediating responses and stimuli, and terminating responses; and relative similarity of initiating stimuli.

REFERENCES

Attneave, F., "Transfer of Experience with a Class-Schema to Identification-Learning of Patterns and Shapes," *Journal of Experimental Psychology,* **54** (1957), 81-88.

Baum, M. H., "A Study in Concept Attainment and Verbal Learning." (Unpublished Doctoral dissertation, Yale University, 1951.)

Bensberg, G. J., Jr., "Concept Learning in Mental Defectives as a Function of Appropriate and Inappropriate 'Attention Sets,' " *Journal of Educational Psychology,* **49** (1958), 137-43.

Birge, J. S., "The Role of Verbal Responses in Transfer." (Unpublished Doctoral dissertation, Yale University, 1941.)

Brunner, J. S., J. J. Goodnow, and G. A. Austin, *A Study of Thinking.* New York: John Wiley & Sons, Inc., 1956.

Buss, A. H., "Reversal and Nonreversal Shifts in Concept Formation with Partial Reinforcement Eliminated," *Journal of Experimental Psychology,* **52** (1956), 162-66.

Carey, J. E. and A. E. Goss, "The Role of Verbal Labeling in the Conceptual Sorting Behavior of Children," *Journal of Genetic Psychology,* **90** (1957), 69-74.

Cofer, C. N. and J. P. Foley, Jr., "Mediated Generalizations and the Interpretation of Verbal Behavior: I. Prolegomena," *Psychological Review,* **49** (1942), 513-40.

Dashiell, J. F., *Fundamentals of Objective Psychology.* Boston: Houghton Mifflin Company, 1928.

Dollard, J. and N. E. Miller, *Personality and Psychotherapy.* New York: McGraw Hill Book Company, Inc., 1950.

Elkonin, D. B., "The Physiology of Higher Nervous Activity and Child Psychology," in *Psychology in the Soviet Union,* ed., B. Simon. Stanford, Cal.: Stanford University Press, 1957.

Federer, W. T., *Experimental Design: Theory and Application.* New York: The Macmillan Company, 1955.

Fenn, J. D. and A. E. Goss. "The Role of Mediating Verbal Responses in the Conceptual Sorting Behavior of Normals and Schizophrenics," *Journal of Genetic Psychology,* **90** (1957), 59-67.

Freedman, J. L. and S. A. Mednick, "Ease of Attainment of Concepts as a Function of Response Dominance Variance," *Journal of Experimental Psychology*, **55** (1958), 463-66.

Gelfand, S., "Effects of Prior Associations and Task Complexity upon the Identification of Concepts," *Psychological Report*, **4** (1958), 568-74.

Gibson, E. J., "A Systematic Application of the Concepts of Generalization and Differentiation to Verbal Learning," *Psychological Review*, **47** (1940), 196-229.

Goldstein, K. and M. Scheerer, "Abstract and Concrete Behavior: An Experimental Study with Special Tests," *Psychology Monograph*, **53** (2, Whole No. 239 [1941]).

Gormezano, I and D. A. Grant, "Progressive Ambiguity in the Attainment of Concepts on the Wisconsin Card Sorting Test," *Journal of Experimental Psychology*, **55** (1958), 621-27.

Goss, A. E., "A Stimulus-Response Analysis of the Interaction of Cue-Producing and Instrumental Responses," *Psychological Review*, **62** (1955), 20-31.

————, University of Massachusetts Conference on Problem Solving, Amherst, Massachusetts, June 19-21, 1956.

Gray, J. S., "A Behavioristic Interpretation of Concept Formation," *Psychological Review*, **38** (1931), 65-72.

Gross, A. E. and N. Greenfield, "Transfer to a Motor Task as Influenced by Conditions and Degree of Prior Discrimination Training," *Journal of Experimental Psychology*, **55** (1958), 258-69.

Gross, A. E. and M. C. Moylan, "Conceptual Block-sorting as a Function of Type and Degree of Mastery of Discriminative Verbal Responses," *Journal of Genetic Psychology*, **93** (1958), 191-98.

Griffith, B. C. and H. H. Spitz, "Some Relationships between Abstraction and Word Meaning in Retarded Adolescents," *American Journal of Mental Deficiency*, **63** (1958), 247-51.

Griffith, B. C., H. H. Spitz, and R. S. Lipman, "Verbal Mediation and Concept Formation in Retarded and Normal Subjects," *Journal of Experimental Psychology*, **58** (1959), 247-51.

Hanfmann, E. and J. Kasinin, "Conceptual Thinking in Schizophrenia," *Nervous and Mental Disease Monograph*, No. 67 (1942).

Harrow, M. and G. B. Friedman, "Comparing Reversal and Nonreversal Shifts in Concept Formation with Partial Reinforcement Controlled," *Journal of Experimental Psychology*, **55** (1958), 592-98.

Heidbreder, E., "The Attainment of Concepts: I. Terminology and Methodology," *Journal of Experimental Psychology*, **35** (1946), 173-89. (a)

————, "The Attainment of Concepts: II. The Problem," *Journal of Genetic Psychology*, **35** (1946), 191-223. (b)

Hovland, C. I., "A 'Communication Analysis' of Concept Learning," *Psychological Review*, **59** (1952), 461-72.

Hovland, C. I. and W. Weiss, "Transmission of Information Concerning Concepts through Positive and Negative Instances," *Journal of Experimental Psychology*, **45** (1953), 157-82.

Hull, C. L., "Quantitative Aspects of the Evolution of Concepts," *Psychology Monograph*, **28** (**1**, Whole No. 123 [1920]).

Hunter, G. F. and H. B. Ranken, "Mediating Effects of Labeling on Sorting Behavior and Judgments of Similarity." Paper presented at Eastern Psychological Association, Atlantic City, March 1956.

Kelleher, R. T. "Discrimination Learning as a Function of Reversal and Nonreversal Shifts," *Journal of Experimental Psychology*, **51** (1956), 379-84.

Kendler, H. H. and M. F. D'Amato, "A Comparison of Reversal Shifts and Nonreversal Shifts in Human Concept Formation Behavior," *Journal of Experimental Psychology*, **48** (1955), 165-74.

Kendler, H. H. and T. S. Kendler, "Reversal and Nonreversal Shifts in Kindergarten Children," *Journal of Experimental Psychology*, **58** (1959), 56-60.

Kendler, H. H. and M. S. Mayzner, Jr., "Reversal and Nonreversal Shifts in Card-Sorting Tests with Two and Four Categories," *Journal of Experimental Psychology*, **51** (1956), 244-48.

Lacey, H., "Mediating Verbal Responses and Stimulus Similarity as Factors in Conceptual Naming by School-age Children." (Unpublished Doctoral dissertation, University of Massachusetts, 1959.)

Lacey, H. and A. E. Goss, "Conceptual Block Sorting as a Function of Number, Pattern of Assignment, and Strength of Labeling Responses," *Journal of Genetic Psychology*, **94** (1959), 221-32.

Liublinskaya, A. A., "Development of Children's Speech and Thought," in *Psychology in the Soviet Union*, ed., B. Simon. Stanford, Cal.: Stanford University Press, 1957.

Mandler, G., "Response Factors in Human Learning," *Psychological Review*, **61** (1954), 235-44.

Metzger, R., "A Comparison between Rote Learning and Concept Formation," *Journal of Experimental Psychology*, **56** (1958), 226-31.

Meyer, M. F., *The Fundamental Laws of Human Behavior*. Boston: Gorham, 1911.

Miller, N. E. and J. Dollard, *Social Learning and Imitation*. New Haven, Conn.: Yale University Press, 1941.

Murdock, B. B., Jr., "Intralist Generalization in Paired-Associate Learning," *Psychological Review*, **65** (1958), 306-14.

Osgood, C. E., *Method and Theory in Experimental Psychology*. New York: Oxford University Press, 1953.

Reed, H. B., "Factors Influencing the Learning and Retention of Concepts: I. The Influence of Set," *Journal of Experimental Psychology*, **36** (1946), 71-87.

Rhine, R. J. and B. A. Silun, "Acquisition and Change of a Concept Attitude as a Function of Consistency of Reinforcement," *Journal of Experimental Psychology*, **55** (1958), 524-29.

Richardson, J., "The Relationship of

Stimulus Similarity and Numbers of Responses," *Journal of Experimental Psychology*, **56** (1958), 478-84.

Shepard, W. O. and M. Shaeffer, "The Effect of Concept Knowledge on Discrimination Learning," *Child Development*, **26** (1956), 173-78.

Sigel, I., "Developmental Trends in the Abstraction Ability of Children," *Child Development*, **24** (1953), 131-44.

————, "The Dominance of Meaning," *Journal of Genetic Psychology*, **85** (1954), 201-207.

Simmons, A. J. and A. E. Goss, "Animistic Responses as a Function of Sentence Contexts and Instructions," *Journal of Genetic Psychology*, **91** (1957), 181-89.

Smoke, K. L., "An Objective Study of Concept Formation," *Psychology Monograph*, **42** (**4**, Whole No. 191 [1932]).

Solley, C. M. and S. J. Messick, "Probability, Learning, the Statistical Structure of Concepts, and the Measurement of Meaning," *American Journal of Physiology*, **70** (1957), 161-73.

Spence, K. W., "The Nature of Discrimination Learning in Animals," *Psychological Review*, **43** (1936), 427-49.

Staats, C. K. and A. W. Staats, "Meaning Established by Classical Conditioning," *Journal of Experimental Physiology*, **54** (1957), 74-80.

Underwood, B. J. and J. Richardson, "Verbal Concept Learning as a Function of Instructions and Dominance Level," *Journal of Experimental Psychology*, **51** (1956), 229-38.

Watson, J. B., "Is Thinking Merely the Action of Language Mechanisms?" Part V, *British Journal of Psychology*, **11** (1920), 87-104.

Weiss, A. P., *A Theoretical Basis of Human Behavior*. Columbus, Ohio: Adams, 1925.

Wickens, D. D. and G. A. Eckstrand, "Stimulus-Response Theory as Applied to Perception," in *Kentucky Symposium: Learning Theory, Personality Theory, and Clinical Research*. New York: John Wiley & Sons, Inc., 1954.

Woodworth, R. S., *Dynamics of Behavior.* New York: Holt, Rinehart & Winston, Inc., 1958.

Wulff, J. J. and L. M. Stolurow, "The

Role of Class-descriptive Cues in Paired-Associates Learning," *Journal of Experimental Psychology,* **53** (1957), 199-206.

Verbal Habit Families, Concepts, and the Operant Conditioning of Word Classes *

Arthur W. Staats

In several papers Hull (1934a, 1934b) has described the concept of the habit-family which he felt would

prove to have an extremely wide application as an explanatory principle in many subtle and otherwise inexplicable forms of behavior at present usually designated indiscriminately as intelligence (1943b, p. 147).

The concept has already been applied by Hull and others, and this paper falls into the category of additionally, or more specifically, making applications to certain complex human behaviors. Before discussing the applications, it would seem useful to give a short summary of the concept of habit-families.

* From A. W. Staats, "Verbal Habit Families, Concepts, and the Operant Conditioning of Word Classes," *Psychological Review,* **68** (1961), 190-204. Reprinted by permission of the author and the American Psychological Association.

This article arose from research sponsored by the Office of Naval Research under Contract Nonr-2794(02) and the National Institute of Mental Health under Contract M-2381. A longer version of this article was issued August 1959, under the same title, as *ONR Technical Report* Number 10. The author wishes to thank Charles E. Osgood and Carolyn K. Staats for critically reading the manuscript and for their ensuing suggestions.

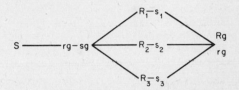

FIG. 1. *A habit-family. (Direct associations between S and the instrumental responses are not depicted in this and the next figure.)*

Figure 1 schematizes a habit-family in a somewhat simplified way. In the figure a part of the response which originally was elicited by the final stimuli in a sequence becomes elicitable by earlier stimuli in the sequence. This partial response is called the fractional anticipatory goal response, rg. Since rg may be elicited by the stimulus at the beginning of a sequence this rg may precede other, instrumental, responses elicited by the stimulus. When this occurs the rg and the stimuli it produces are contiguous with the instrumental responses, and these stimuli will come to elicit the instrumental responses R_1, R_2 and R_3 in a divergent mechanism. The stimuli produced by these three responses will be associated with the goal response, R_g, and tend to elicit the goal response (including the portion which becomes the rg) in a convergent mechanism. Thus, a simple habit-family could be summarized as a stimulus which has tendencies to elicit an anticipatory goal response which in turn has tendencies to elicit a hierarchy of responses, each of which tends to elicit a common final response, part of which is the anticipatory response. This summary ignores the direct associations between the original stimulus and the instrumental responses.

Mediated generalization would occur from one instrumental response to the others.

THE CONCEPT
OF THE HABIT-FAMILY
IN LANGUAGE BEHAVIOR

Cofer and associates (Cofer, 1951, 1957; Judson and Cofer, 1956; Judson, Cofer, and Gelfand, 1956) in a series of papers on reasoning use the term habit-families in respect to language behavior in describing the course of reasoning, but the term is never given elaboration, and sometimes seems to be of varying nature. Thus, Cofer seems to conceive of habit-families in thinking both on the basis of semantic characteristics of the words and also in terms of the direct associations between the words. In this sense, clusters of words which are related to each other in any way could be termed habit-families.[1]

Osgood (1953, 1957a, 1957b; Osgood, Suci, and Tannenbaum, 1957) has applied Hullian mechanisms to language in frequently using the concepts of the convergent and divergent mechanisms. He has stated (1957a) that different environmental stimuli could become associated with the same

mediating response, a convergent mechanism, and that this mediating response (or its stimuli) could have tendencies to elicit various instrumental responses, a divergent mechanism. In addition, a sensory signal may come to elicit more than one mediating response in a divergent hierarchy. As an example, he cites homophones like *"case, bear,* and *right"* (1957a, p. 98) since they each elicit more than one meaning. Thus, much of the development of the habit-family in its application to language has been made by Osgood. However, his model differs from the fuller application of Hull's concept to be developed herein in certain important respects, and the detailed description of the verbal habit-family and its development and function, must still be made. Greater clarity and detail of the verbal habit-family model should have significant heuristic value.

The principles of language learning which are relevant to verbal habit-families will first be summarized and then organized to illustrate the concept. Then the concept will be applied to concepts, concept formation, and the operant conditioning of word classes.

VERBAL HABIT-FAMILIES

Classical Conditioning of Word Meaning

Cofer and Foley (1942), Mowrer (1954), Osgood (1953), and Staats and Staats (1959a, 1959b) have discussed word meaning in terms of Hullian concepts as an implicit, mediating response. A distillation of these views for the present purposes might state, as the first principle in which this paper will be interested, that when a word is contiguously presented with a stimulus object some of the unconditioned responses elicited by the object will be conditioned to the word. These responses when stably conditioned be-

---

[1] Direct associations between words will not be discussed herein. However, it is realized that these associations have an effect upon the organizational aspects of language.

come the meaning of the word. First-order conditioning of meaning has been demonstrated by Staats, Staats, and Crawford (1958). Additional support for the contention that the concept of meaning may be treated as a conditioned response is given by a series of studies by Staats and Staats and associates (Staats, 1959; Staats and Staats, 1957, 1958, 1959a, 1959b; Staats, Staats, and Biggs, 1958; Staats, Staats, and Heard, 1959, 1960). A higher-order conditioning paradigm was involved in the studies since conditioning was accomplished by pairing a word which already elicited a meaning response with the verbal stimulus which was conditioned to elicit that meaning. Both connotative and denotative meaning responses were conditioned in this manner.

Osgood's concept of a representational mediating response which may form the meaning of a word is an elaboration of Hull's (1930) rg, or "pure stimulus act." According to Osgood (1953) this concept includes conditioned autonomic responses and implicit motor responses. The present account elaborates this conception to include conditioned sensory responses. That is, it is suggested that some stimulus objects elicit sensory responses in organisms, parts of which may be conditioned. Thus, parts of the "seeing," "hearing," or "feeling" responses, for example, elicited by the appropriate stimulus on an unconditioned basis may be conditioned to other neutral stimuli, including verbal stimuli.

Studies (for example, Leuba, 1940; Lipton & Blanton, 1957; Phillips, 1958)[2] indicate that sensory responses

may be conditioned. Skinner discusses in detail (1953, pp. 266-270) how sensory responses can come to be elicited by formerly neutral stimuli on the basis of classical conditioning.

A man may see or hear "stimuli which are not present" on the pattern of the conditioned reflexes: he may see X, not only when X is present, but when any stimulus which has frequently accompanied X is present. The dinner bell not only makes our mouth water, it makes us see food (p. 266). (Quoted by permission of the Macmillan Company.)

More recently, Mowrer (1960) has also discussed the conditioning of sensory responses in describing sensory preconditioning studies.

We may confidently assume that the light . . . produces a light *sensation* . . . which is conditionable in the form of a light *image*. Such a reaction to be sure, is central or "cognitive," rather than overt, behavioral; but emotions also are covert, nonbehavioral, yet we have not refused . . . to admit them to our theoretical system (p. 282).

Following the conception that sensory responses may be conditioned, the pairing of the auditory presentation of the word BALL and the visual presentation of the object *ball,* as an example, would be expected to condition the child to respond to the auditory verbal stimulus with part of the visual responses elicited by the ball itself. The word stimulus would now be meaningful. Additionally, the child's own speech response BALL can be considered to be equivalent to the words as a stimulus since it produces the same type of sound. Thus, after the conditioning experience, both the presentation of the word by some other person or the saying of it himself would elicit the meaning response.

---

[2] Mowrer (1960) and Staats, Staats, and Heard (1960) have concluded that sensory preconditioning depends upon the conditioning of sensory responses. This interpretation allows a rapprochement between S-S and S-R theoretical orientations.

Operant Conditioning of Word Responses

In addition to the learning of word meanings, the individual learns through operant conditioning to emit verbal responses. Skinner (1957) has developed at length the principles by which these responses are acquired, and a number of experimental studies as summarized elsewhere (Krasner, 1958; Salzinger, 1959) have shown that verbal responses may be strengthened through the action of reinforcement. It might be expected that precise speech responses, for example, are shaped up by selective reinforcement in the manner described as successive approximation. Thus, at an early age, any sound emitted by the child that sounds like an English word is reinforced. Later only more and more precise utterings receive reinforcement and so on.

Skinner also described the principles by which environmental stimuli come to control certain verbal responses of the individual, or, in common sense terms, the way the child learns to name objects. The principle involved is that of operant discrimination. If, in the presence of a stimulus object, the child is reinforced when he utters a particular name or word, the stimulus object when presented will tend to elicit that verbal response from the individual.[3] Emitting a labeling response under the control of the appropriate environmental stimulus is called "tacting" by Skinner.

Meaning as an Anticipatory Response

According to the conventions of this paper the conditionable sensory com-

ponent elicited by the object ball may be conditioned to the stimulus word BALL. In addition, if the child is reinforced after saying BALL while responding to the object, as occurs in the operant conditioning of verbal behavior, an association is established between the stimuli produced by the sensory responses to the ball and the speech response. The formation of both of these associations is depicted in Fig. 2. Thus, through classical con-

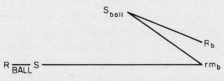

2a. *The conditioning of a meaning response to the stimuli produced by a word response. (When the mother says* BALL, *R*BALL–*S, and presents the ball* S_{ball}, *part of the sensory responses elicited by the object,* rm_b, *are conditioned to the auditory stimuli. Part of the responses elicited by the ball,* R_b, *are not conditionable.)*

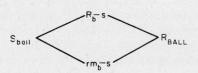

2b. *The conditioning of a word response to the stimuli produced by the conditionable sensory response components. (When the child is reinforced for saying* BALL *in the presence of the ball, the speech response,* RBALL, *comes under the control of the stimuli produced by the conditionable sensory response components,* rm_b—*sm.)*

FIG. 2. *The conditioning of meaning and word responses.*

ditioning, the conditionable sensory responses elicited by the ball, rm_b–s, are conditioned to the word response

---

[3] It is cumbersome to repeatedly use the terminology concerned with operant conditioning, that is, a discriminative stimulus gains control over the emission of the verbal response reinforced in its presence. In the present paper it may be simply stated that a stimulus tends to elicit a response whether the principle involved is classical or operant conditioning.

BALL, R~BALL~-S. In addition, when the child is reinforced for saying BALL while looking at the ball, the verbal response is conditioned to the same sensory responses, rm~b~–s. Thus, the word response R~BALL~–S tends to elicit rm~b~–s, but rm~b~–s also tends to elicit the word response.

When the meaning response (conditionable sensory response), which has been conditioned to a word response, has also become anticipatory to the word response, the meaning response is analogous to Hull's rg. That is, an rg is conditioned to the stimuli produced by preceding instrumental responses but also comes to elicit those instrumental responses in the process of short-circuiting.

Divergent Mechanism

It will be remembered that Hull's habit-family consisted of a stimulus which would elicit an anticipatory response which had tendencies to elicit a divergent hierarchy of responses, each of these responses having tendencies to elicit the same goal response, part of which was the anticipatory goal response. To continue with the example, not only will the naming response BALL be reinforced in the presence of the stimulus object ball (and similar stimulus objects), but in addition a number of other word responses will receive the same treatment, for example, ROUND, CIRCULAR, SPHERICAL. That is, in the presence of the ball, the child will be reinforced if he says, "It is round, it is spherical, and so on." Because of this experience, the sensory responses produced by the object (actually a class of similar objects) will come to tend to elicit each of these speech responses in a divergent hierarchy of responses. Thus, the sensory responses elicited by an object, including the portion which is condi-

tionable, come to control more than one tacting response.

Convergent Mechanism

In addition, each of these stimulus words (or word responses, through the stimuli they produce) will have been conditioned to elicit the same end response component, their common meaning. This forms a convergent hierarchy. Each of the sets of words or word responses of the individual comes to elicit the common meaning in the manner previously described as the first-order conditioning of meaning, for example, through being paired with the object ball when someone says, "This is round," in the presence of the object.

The Mechanisms as a Verbal Habit-Family

These divergent and convergent hierarchies (including both meaning and word responses) actually compose a habit-family, united by the common meaning response component. That is, an "anticipatory" response (rm~r~–s in Fig. 3) has been formed which when

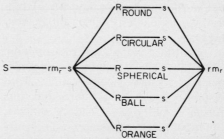

FIG. 3. *The verbal habit-family for "roundness."*

elicited by a stimulus will tend to elicit a class of responses (R~ROUND~, R~CIRCULAR~, R~SPHERICAL~, R~BALL~, and R~ORANGES~) all of which (through the stimuli they produce) culminate in the elicitation of a common response. In terms of the language responses, a verbal habit-family exists when an anticipatory meaning response component elicited by a stimulus has tendencies to elicit a class of word responses and each of these word responses has tendencies to elicit the same common meaning response component. The verbal habit-family in the example is depicted in Fig. 3.

Many different stimuli could tend to arouse the verbal habit-family through eliciting the anticipatory meaning response, for example, verbal and nonverbal stimuli conditioned to elicit the anticipatory meaning response, the objects involved in the original conditioning since they elicit the conditionable sensory components, and objects which elicit similar sensory components. Thus, there could well be a hierarchy of stimulus situations with varying strengths for eliciting the anticipatory meaning response and, thus the verbal habit-family. This would be analagous to Maltzman's (1955) compound habit-family. Any variable which strengthened the association of the anticipatory meaning response to a stimulus (where this is appropriate) would strengthen each of the individual word responses in the verbal habit-family, mediated by the anticipatory meaning.

To further complicate the situation, since meaning is composed of independent response components, a word response could be in more than one verbal habit-family. And a stimulus situation (or stimulus word) could elicit more than one unconditioned or conditioned anticipatory meaning component, and thus have tendencies to elicit more than one verbal habit-family.

CONCEPTS

Hull (1920) originally posited that concepts are developed by abstracting the common stimulus elements in a series of stimulus objects. In his ex-

perimental demonstration of this approach he used as stimulus objects groups of Chinese characters. For each group there was a common component imbedded in each individual character. The subjects' task was to respond with a particular nonsense syllable to a group of characters. It was found that the subjects improved in anticipating correctly the syllable name of a new character, after having experience with other characters containing the same element. That is, they were able to "abstract" the common elements.

Osgood (1953), however, feels that consideration of concept formation as the abstraction of identical stimulus elements would not distinguish the process from all learning, making the term useless. He states that even most lower animals could learn to do what Hull showed in his experiment.

Fields . . . showed that rats could learn to jump toward a triangular form. . . . Yet, should we conclude that the rat can understand the *abstract* concept of triangularity? Would the rat respond positively to three dots in a triangular arrangement versus four dots arranged in a square? Or react positively to three people, three places on a map, a three-cornered block, as "triangles." . . . It would seem that the only *essential* condition for concept formation is the learning of a common mediating response (which is the meaning of the concept) for a group of objects or situations, identical elements and common perceptual relations merely facilitating the establishment of such mediators (pp. 667-668).

Osgood, while rejecting the notion that concepts are based upon identical stimulus elements, does not adequately specify how the objects come to elicit a common response or what the common response is. If the three dots, for example, do not elicit a response like that elicited by a triangle on an unconditioned basis, how do they come to do so? How is the power of abstraction gained? The processes involved must be specified to a much greater extent before concepts can be accounted for in S-R terms.

Kendler and associates (Kendler and D'Amato, 1955; Kendler and Karasik, 1958; Kendler and Mayzner, 1956; Kendler and Vineberg, 1954) have also considered concept formation to be the acquisition of a common implicit response to different stimuli. In addition, Kendler and Karasik (1958) have extended this to verbal concept formation which they assume occurs "when S learns to respond to a set of different words with the same implicit response" (p. 278). The conceptualization that words which elicit a common implicit response are involved in a verbal concept begins to focus on the verbal aspect of concepts in the "two-stage" S-R framework. However, further specification as to the processes of the development and function of verbal concepts is necessary, since the common meaning response to the words used by Kendler and Karasik had been acquired by the subjects prior to the experiment.

The following discussion will attempt the necessary elaborations. A concept may be regarded as a verbal habit-family formed usually on the basis of a class of stimulus objects having identical elements. Take, for example, the "animal" concept. The individual words in the concept will gain their meaning through classical conditioning where the word is paired with the appropriate stimulus object (actually a number of stimulus objects having closely common characteristics). DOG is paired with dogs, COW with cows, and so on, and the conditionable sensory components elicited by the stimulus objects are conditioned to the word involved.

Now each of the stimulus objects in the class has certain identical elements (for example, legs, head, spontaneous movement, furry, and so forth) and the objects in the class will thus elicit sensory response components which also have identical elements. Consequently, part of the meaning response component conditioned to the word DOG will be identical to those which, in the same manner, are conditioned to the words COW, HORSE, and PIG, and so forth. This common response could be called the animal meaning response component, rm_a in Fig. 4.

In addition, however, each stimulus object elicits conditionable sensory response components which the other objects in the class do not. Since these conditionable sensory responses are characteristically elicited only by the specific animal, they are only conditioned to the specific animal word with which the object contiguously occurs. Thus, each of the animal words comes to elicit an animal meaning response component shared by the others, and also a specific meaning response component which none of the others elicit, rm_d, rm_c, rm_b, or rm_p in the figure.

Now, each of the stimulus objects will also occur in the presence of the word ANIMAL. For example, in the presence of each animal the child will be told, "That is an animal." In this process the common conditionable sensory response component elicited by all the animals, the animal component, will be strongly conditioned to the word ANIMAL, and each of the specific conditionable response components elicited by only one of the animals will be weakly conditioned to the word ANIMAL.

The meaning responses which are conditioned to the words will also become anticipatory to the words through

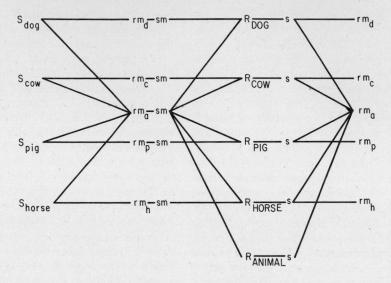

FIG. 4. *The "animal" concept.*

the tacting process which has been described. Thus, the animal meaning response and the animal word responses form a verbal habit-family as Fig. 4 indicates.

The associations depicted in Fig. 4 indicate why, in the presence of a particular stimulus object in the class, the individual is likely to specifically "label" the stimulus object rather than to say ANIMAL, or one of the other words. For example, the stimulus object cow would elicit the sensory response component, rm_a, which in turn would equally tend to elicit all of the animal word responses, including COW and ANIMAL. Thus, all of the words would have an equal probability of occurring simply on the basis of this association. The stimulus object cow would elicit in addition, however, the characteristic sensory response, rm_c, which in turn would strongly tend to elicit the word response COW and, also, though not so strongly, the word response ANIMAL—but none of the other word responses. Thus in the presence of the stimulus object cow there are

two strong associations for the elicitation of the word response COW, one strong and one weak association for the word response ANIMAL, and only one strong association for the elicitation of any other word in the concept class.

But this does not yet account for abstraction, that is, how the individual comes to respond in the same manner to a new object which does not have identical stimulus elements with the other objects in the class and so does not elicit the common response, for example, how one responds to three dots as a triangle. It would seem that abstraction first comes from the verbal habit-family hierarchy. To realize the explanatory value of the verbal habit-family, the principles of communication which have been presented by Mowrer (1954) must first be summarized.

Using a conception of meaning such as had been described herein, that is, an implicit mediating response, Mowrer has suggested that a sentence is a conditioning device and that communication takes place when the meaning response which has been elicited by the predicate is conditioned to the subject of the sentence.[4] In addition, since the subject of the sentence will also elicit a meaning response which has stimulus properties, the meaning response elicited by the predicate will be conditioned to the stimuli produced by the meaning response elicited by the subject of the sentence. That a meaning response may be conditioned to the stimuli produced by another meaning response has been shown by Staats and Staats (1959a, 1959b). Using Mowrer's example, Fig. 5 demonstrates this process and the resulting associations and mediated generalization.

The function of the verbal habit-family in making abstraction possible may now be described, that is, how stimulus objects get into the concept class when they do not have identical stimulus elements and so do not elicit responses common to the objects which are in the class. Returning to the animal concept example, the individual having learned a meaning response to the word ANIMAL will be conditioned to make this same response to the word WORM if told, "a worm is an animal." When the animal meaning response has become anticipatory to the word WORM in the manner already described, the word would be fully in the concept verbal habit-family.

5a. *As a result of the sentence, the meaning of* THIEF, rm_{TH}, *is conditioned to the word* TOM *and also to the stimuli produced by the meaning response elicited by* TOM, rm_T,—*sm.*

$$S_{TOM} \quad\text{———}\quad rm_T\text{-sm} \quad\text{———}\quad rm_{TH}$$

5b.*The word* TOM, S_{TOM}, *now elicits the meaning of the word* THIEF, *mediated by* rm_T—*sm.*

$$S_{Tom} \quad\text{———}\quad rm_T\text{-sm} \quad\text{———}\quad rm_{TH}$$

5c. *The same is true for the person himself,* S_{TOM}, *since he also elicits* rm_T—*sm on an unconditioned basis.*

FIG. 5. *Mowrer's conception of communication.*

Following Mowrer's conception the sentence would also condition the meaning of ANIMAL to the meaning of WORM, that is, form an rm_w-sm—rm_a association. Thus, the object worm (and any object eliciting rm_w, for example, caterpillar) would now elicit the animal meaning response and so be in the animal class of objects.

It is also likely that backward conditioning would broaden the animal concept through the same sentence by conditioning the meaning of worm to the word ANIMAL and its meaning. This would generalize to the other animal words. Dostálek (1959) discusses the importance of backward conditioning in verbal learning.

Whether or not this backward conditioning takes place, the concept animal could be further broadened on the basis of language conditioning. For example, the sentence, "animals consume oxygen," would condition the responses elicited by the predicate of the sentence to the meaning response elicited by the word ANIMALS, with the

---

[4] The view of communication taken by Osgood, Suci, and Tannenbaum (1957) would consider the above interpretation of communication to be oversimplified. It is beyond the scope of the present paper to discuss the process of communication in detail. However, the final principles accepted concerning communication can be incorporated into the present model of concept formation.

expected generalizations occurring.[5]

Thus, with continued verbal experience, the verbal habit-family (concept) grows in terms of the objects and words which elicit the concept meaning. In addition, the concept meaning is broadened to include parts of the response made to new objects and words.

On the basis of verbal habit-families and language conditioning and generalization, learning which is originally derived from experience with a relatively small class of objects, usually having identical elements, may be transferred to many new situations and tasks.[6] The child first learns the "triangle" verbal habit-family on the basis of direct experience with a few stimulus objects, that is, on the basis of the common stimulus elements and the common responses they elicit. Later, however, he is told that three dots, or three people, are a TRIANGLE; and through the meaning which has previously been conditioned to the word TRIANGLE, the concept meaning, the new objects, and other objects which are similar to them enter the concept class. It is suggested that these are the processes which underlie the progression from concrete to abstract thinking which has frequently been said to occur in child development (Brown, 1958), and which are involved in "understanding" a concept.

Osgood was correct in stating that a rat cannot understand a concept—not, however, because it cannot form a common response to a class of stimulus objects. This part of concept learning the animal would be capable of. However, the rat is not capable of acquiring verbal habit-families to correspond to such concept mechanisms and the power of abstraction is thus lost to the animal. The process of concept formation is seen as one which involves complicated principles of learning, communication, and mediated generalization. The relationships between the language processes and the environmental process are complex. The language processes arise from response to the environment but then in turn effect response to other aspects of the environment.

Actually, concepts would not usually be as simple as portrayed. Figure 6 makes one elaboration of the animal concept to include a subconcept, the "dog" concept. Although all of the stimulus objects in the general concept elicit the common animal meaning component, rm_a, three of the objects (the dogs) also elicit a meaning component (rm_d) common to them but not the other stimulus objects. This component comes to elicit the dog word reponses, including the concept word DOG itself, and is conditioned also to each of the dog word responses and becomes part of the meaning of each of these word responses. Each of these dog stimulus objects, in addition to the rm_a and rm_d conditionable sensory response components, would also elicit a specific response component which is common to none of the other dog

---

[5] It is also true that the concept word (that is, ANIMAL) in a concept could gain its meaning on a language basis rather than through being paired with the various objects in the original stimulus class. That is, it should be possible for the concept word to gain its meaning through being paired with subordinate words in the verbal habit-family which had already been conditioned to their meanings. Or the concept word could be presented in sentences with appropriate adjectives and the meanings of the adjectives conditioned in this manner to the concept word. These processes would be higher-order conditioning.

[6] The class of stimulus objects in a concept usually has identical elements, but the same process could start with just one object and through conditioning meaning to meaning as in Mowrer's communication paradigm, grow to a class of objects which elicit a common meaning response and a class of words, and so forth.

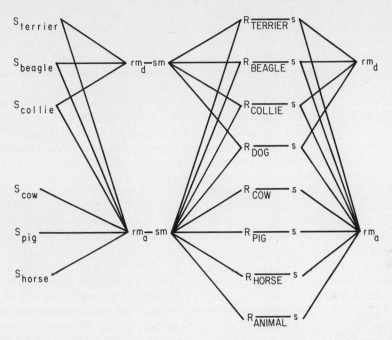

FIG. 6. *This diagram depicts a concept ("dog") which is included in a larger concept ("animal").*

stimulus objects. This would also be true of the other stimulus objects. The figure is simplified by not showing these associations.

It would be expected that the greater the extent of overlap in meaning response components between any two habit-families, or any two words, the greater the amount of generalization that would occur. Thus, following Fig. 6, if one said "Animals are dangerous," the meaning of DANGEROUS would be conditioned to the meaning of the word ANIMALS, and consequently equally to all of the words and objects in the figure. If, however, one said, "Dogs are dangerous," there would be greater generalization to the dog objects and words than to the other animal objects and words. In a semantic generalization paradigm, a response conditioned to the CS DOG should generalize more to TERRIER than it would

to ANIMAL since the two dog words share two strongly conditioned meaning components, rm_a and rm_d as shown in Fig. 6. This has been shown by Razran (1949).

OPERANT CONDITIONING OF WORD CLASSES

A number of recent experiments as summarized by Krasner (1958) and Salzinger (1959) have shown that reinforcement of individual words emitted by individuals will result in the strengthening of a class of words containing the individual words. There are some questions which seem unresolved in these studies—and there is little articulation of these studies to the principles and studies concerning the semantic properties of language. Primarily, there is not adequate rationale concerning the operant conditioning of classes of responses which are as diverse as the classes of verbal response which have been conditioned, for example, travel words (Wilson and Verplanck, 1956), living thing words (Wilson and Verplanck, 1956), animal words (Ball, 1952), action words (Wickes, 1956). In his article on the conditioning of verbal behavior, Salzinger (1959) seems to recognize the need for such a rationale in discussing the definition of verbal response classes, stating that responses in a class may be substituted for one another, are followed by the same reinforcement, or are emitted in the presence of the same discriminative stimulus.

It is not the case, however, that a word in one of the verbal response classes which has been conditioned may be substituted for any other word in the class. In language usage individual words of a word class are not functionally equivalent as are the rat's bar press responses. Substitution of class words into a sentence would make the sentence meaningless. Nor can it be said that all words in the classes which have been operantly conditioned are followed by the same reinforcement in language usage. Most words, regardless of what class they are in, are followed by the same reinforcers, for example, tacting living objects with living thing words is reinforced by the same generalized reinforcers, as is tacting transportation objects. Nor can it be said that the words in a class are emitted in the presence of the same discriminative stimulus. For example, one is reinforced for saying the specific, living thing word in the presence of the specific living thing, not for saying any living thing word. On closer examination, the conclusions made by Salzinger are thus untenable. Salzinger, however, is quite correct in recognizing the need to explain why verbal response classes are strengthened when

individual members are reinforced. The paradox is that as responses these words in the word classes may be very discrepant, and cannot be considered as functionally equivalent, yet response induction occurs nevertheless.

As would be expected from the above analysis, it is not possible to predict what words will operantly condition as a class from an operate conditioning rationale, as Salzinger (1959) admits:

Generally, investigators have had to rely upon their common sense knowledge of verbal behavior to decide upon the constitution of response classes (p. 70).

He continues to suggest that studies of semantic generalization or measurements of the connotative meaning of words may be used to discover response classes. Thus, in both cases, this implicitly recognizes that the commonality of words in the classes which have been operantly conditioned concerns the semantic properties of the words. Notwithstanding this, the account of verbal behavior offered by Skinner eschews the concept of meaning and his example appears to be followed by other investigators interested in the application of operant conditioning principles to language behavior. At any rate, it does not seem to be defensible to exclude the concept of meaning in accounting for the operant conditionability of classes of word responses, and then suggest that meaning properties be used to choose classes of words which *will* condition. In conclusion, this suggests that a combination of operant principles of conditioning along with the semantic properties of words such as has been offered herein will offer a more complete explanation of language behavior.

Osgood (1957b), while not having dealt with the operant conditioning of word responses in any detail, has briefly suggested a way of accounting for the operant conditioning of word response classes which may be further detailed using the concept of the verbal habit-family:

In dealing with adult subjects, we must assume that these associations between mediators and appropriate vocalizations are all available and considerably overlearned. Nevertheless we can temporarily change the relative availability or probability of alternative mediators themselves by manipulating reinforcement conditions. What we observe then is a shift in the emission frequency of certain forms relative to others. This is the way I would interpret the results of many recent experiments on the operant conditioning of verbal behavior (p. 375).

This brief statement can be elaborated in necessary detail through application of the concept of verbal habit-families. In short, it is thought that word response classes which will condition are verbal habit-family hierarchies. Subjects in the verbal conditioning studies are reinforced when they utter a word from a certain class of words. The verbal habit-family (that is, concept) depicted in Fig. 6 will be used as an example. In this example, if the subject spoke an animal word the rm_a meaning response would be elicited. If a social reinforcer was then presented, it would be expected that the rm_a meaning response as well as the verbal response itself would be conditioned to the cues of the situation. The strengthening of the individual speech response would not generalize to different topological speech responses even though they were in the same class of words. However, if only animal words are reinforced, the strongest meaning association to the situation will become that of the animal meaning response

component. Since the animal meaning response component is also the anticipatory response for the class of animal words, it would be expected that the whole class of animal words would be strengthened, that is, the frequency of their occurrence would be heightened. It is the strengthening of the common anticipatory meaning response in the verbal habit-family that mediates the generalized strengthening.

In Fig. 6, which is used as the example, some of the words are in subconcept classes, which actually have aspects of separate verbal habit-families. Reinforcing a word in one of the subclasses would strengthen all the meaning responses elicited by the word. In the case of the word TERRIER, for example, both rm_a and rm_d would be strengthened. Because of this there would be a greater tendency for another word in the subconcept to be emitted than one only in the general concept. This might lead to the strengthening of classes of words other than those the experimenter had intended to strengthen, and this apparently occurs, according to Salzinger (1959):

The problem which arises here is the discrepancy between the experimenter's definition of the response class and the response class which is actually being affected by the experimental manipulations. In one study . . . for example, the experimenter tried to condition plural nouns but actually caused an increase in a subset, i.e., names of tribes (p. 68).

This result is accounted for by the present model, that is, the experimenter strengthened all the meaning response components elicited by the word responses he reinforced. A few reinforcements of the names of tribes could so strengthen all the meaning components so that only these types of responses would be elicited.

One implication involved in this discussion is that if classes of words can be operantly conditioned, then they are members of a verbal habit-family, and therefore have a common meaning response component. Thus, semantic generalization should be possible between individual members of the words in a class which can be operantly conditioned, as Salzinger has implied. And, on the other hand, any concept, or verbal habit-family, should be capable of being operantly conditioned. Thus, for example, each of the concept classes of words found by Underwood and Richardson (1956) should be capable of operant conditioning as a class since each group of words shares a common meaning response component.

The many variables concerned with the strength of the concept meaning response, the extent to which the response produces distinctive cues, the dominance of the concept meaning response in the total meaning elicited by the words in the class, and so on, should be factors in the ease of the operant conditioning of the word class.

SUMMARY

A detailed model of verbal habit-families was described which more fully utilizes Hull's habit-family conception. Additional specifications of the responses involved in verbal habit-families were made as well as of the manner of development and function of verbal habit-families.

This model was then used to indicate how concepts develop and function in a process involving complex learning, communication, and mediated generalization. Complex relationships between language processes and environmental processes were described in concept formation, that is, language processes arise from

response to the environment but then in turn effect response to other aspects of the environment. Abstraction which is based on concept learning was seen to depend on verbal habit-families.

An adequate account of the operant conditioning of word classes was said to require knowledge of both the principles of operant conditioning and the semantic properties of word responses. Such a combined account was given through the use of the verbal habit-family model.

REFERENCES

Ball, R. S., "Reinforcement Conditioning of Verbal Behavior by Verbal and Non-Verbal Stimuli in a Situation Resembling a Clinical Interview." (Unpublished Doctoral dissertation, Indiana University, 1952.)

Brown, R. W., *Words and Things.* New York: Free Press of Glencoe, Inc., 1958.

Cofer, C. N., "Verbal Behavior in Relation to Reasoning and Values," in *Groups, Leadership, and Men,* ed. H. Guetzkow. Pittsburgh: Carnegie, 1951.

———, "Reasoning as an Associate Process: III. The Role of Verbal Responses in Problem Solving," *Journal of Genetic Psychology,* **57** (1957), 55-68.

Cofer, C. N. and J. P. Foley, "Mediated Generalization and the Interpretation of Verbal Behavior: I. Prologemena," *Psychological Review,* **49** (1942), 513-40.

Dostálek, C., "Formation of a Temporary Connection in Man between Two 'Indifferent' Stimuli of Equal Intensity, with Different Time Intervals between Commencements of Both Stimuli," *Physiol. Bohemoslov,* **8** (1959), 47-54.

Hull, C. L., "Quantitative Aspects of the Evolution of Concepts," *Psychology Monograph,* **28** (**1,** Whole No. 123 [1920]).

———, "Knowledge and Purpose as Habit Mechanisms," *Psychological Review,* **37** (1930), 511-25.

———, "The Concept of the Habit-

Family Hierarchy and Maze Learning. Part I," *Psychological Review*, **41** (1934), 33-54. (a)

————, "The Concept of the Habit-Family Hierarchy and Maze Learning. Part II," *Psychological Review*, **41** (1934), 134-52.

Judson, A. J., and C. N. Cofer, "Reasoning as an Associative Process: I. 'Direction' in a Simple Verbal Problem," *Psychological Report*, **1** (1956), 469-76.

Judson, A. J., C. N. Cofer, and S. Gelfland, "Reasoning as an Associative Process: II. 'Direction' in Problem Solving as a Function of Prior Reinforcement of Relevant Responses," *Psychological Report*, **2** (1956), 501-507.

Kendler, H. H. and M. F. D'Amato, "A Comparison of Reversal Shifts and Nonreversal Shifts in Human Concept Formation Behavior," *Journal of Experimental Psychology*, **49** (1955), 165-74.

Kendler, H. H. and A. D. Karasik, "Concept Formation as a Function of Competition between Response Produced Cues," *Journal of Experimental Psychology*, **55** (1958), 278-83.

Kendler, H. H. and M. S. Mayzner, "Reversal and Nonreversal Shifts in Card-Sorting Tests with Two or Four Sorting Categories," *Journal of Experimental Psychology*, **51** (1956), 244-48.

Kendler, H. H. and R. Vineberg, "The Acquisition of Compound Concepts as a Function of Previous Training," *Journal of Experimental Psychology*, **48** (1954), 252-58.

Krasner, L., "Studies of the Conditioning of Verbal Behavior," *Psychological Bulletin*, **55** (1958), 148-70.

Leuba, C., "Images as Conditioned Sensations," *Journal of Experimental Psychology*, **26** (1940), 345-51.

Lipton, L. and R. L. Blanton, "The Semantic Differential and Mediated Generalization as Measures of Meaning," *Journal of Experimental Psychology*, **54** (1957), 431-37.

Maltzman, I., "Thinking: From a Behavioristic Point of View," *Psychological Review*, **62** (1955), 275-76.

Mowrer, O. H., "The Psychologist Looks at Language," *American Journal of Psychology*, **9** (1954), 660-94.

————, *Learning Theory and Behavior*. New York: John Wiley & Sons, Inc., 1960.

Osgood, C. E., *Method and Theory in Experimental Psychology*. New York: Oxford University Press, 1953.

————, "A Behavioristic Analysis of Perception and Language as Cognitive Phenomena," in *Contemporary Approaches to Cognition*. Cambridge, Mass.: Harvard University Press, 1957. (a)

————, "Motivational Dynamics of Language Behavior," in *Nebraska Symposium on Motivation, 1957*, ed. M. R. Jones. Lincoln: University of Nebraska Press, 1957. (b)

Osgood, C. E., G. J. Suci, and P. H. Tannenbaum, *The Measurement of Meaning*. Urbana: University of Illinois Press, 1957.

Phillips, L. W., "Mediated Verbal Similarity as a Determinant of Generalization of a Conditioned GSR," *Journal of Experimental Psychology*, **55** (1958), 56-62.

Razran, G.H.S., "Semantic and Phenetographic Generalization of Salivary Conditioning to Verbal Stimuli," *Journal of Experimental Psychology*, **39** (1949), 642-53.

Salzinger, K., "Experimental Manipulation of Verbal Behavior: A Review," *Journal of Genetic Psychology*, **61** (1959), 65-94.

Skinner, B. F., *Science and Human Behavior*. New York: The Macmillan Company, 1953.

————, *Verbal Behavior*. New York: Appleton-Century-Crofts, Inc., 1957.

Staats, A. W., "Use of the Semantic Differential in Research on S-R Mediational Principles of Learning Word Meaning." Paper presented at Western Psychological Association, San Diego, California, April 1959.

Staats, A. W. and C. K. Staats, "Attitudes Established by Classical Conditioning," *Journal of Abnormal Social Psychology*, **57** (1958), 37-40.

————, "Effect of Number of Trials on the Language Conditioning of Meaning," *Journal of Genetic Psychology*, **61** (1959), 211-23. (a)

————, "Meaning and *M:* Separate but Correlated," *Psychological Review*, **66** (1959), 136-44. (b)

Staats, A. W., C. K. Staats, and D. H. Biggs, "Meaning of Verbal Stimuli Changed by Conditioning," *American Journal of Psychology*, **71** (1958), 429-31.

Staats, A. W., C. K. Staats, and H. L. Crawford, "First-Order Conditioning of Word Meaning and the Parallel Conditioning of a GSR," *ONR Technical Report*, No. 6 (1958). (Contract No. Nonr-2305-00.)

Staats, A. W., C. K. Staats, and W. G. Heard, "Language Conditioning of Meaning to Meaning Using a Semantic Generalization Paradigm," *Journal of Experimental Psychology*, **57** (1959), 187-92.

————, "Language Conditioning of Denotative Meaning," *ONR Technical Report*, No. 13 (1960). (Contract No. Nonr-2794-02.)

Staats, C. K. and A. W. Staats, "Meaning Established by Classical Conditioning," *Journal of Experimental Psychology*, **54** (1957), 74-80.

Underwood, B. J. and J. Richardson, "Some Verbal Materials for the Study of Concept Formation," *Psychological Bulletin*, **53** (1956), 84-95.

Wickes, T. A., Jr., "Examiner Influence in a Testing Situation," *Journal of Consulting Psychology*, **20** (1956), 23-26.

Wilson, W. C. and W. S. Verplanck, "Some Observations on the Reinforcement of Verbal Operants," *American Journal of Psychology*, **69** (1956), 448-51.

Diffuse Conduction:
The Basis of Higher Behavior *

D. O. Hebb

Earlier . . . it was noted that there are two quite different kinds of conduction systems in the CNS: parallel and diffuse. Where cells are laid down in parallel, their fibers beginning and ending close together, there is a high probability that an excitation in the path will be transmitted from one synaptic level to the next. In other regions, conduction is diffuse; cells

* From D. O. Hebb, *A Textbook of Psychology* (Philadelphia: W. B. Saunders Co., 1958), pp. 100-108. Reprinted by permission of the author and publisher.

may start out together but travel in different directions, so that the impulses cannot sum their effects at the next synapse. Such transmission seems inefficient and must often fail to carry through the network to reach the effectors, thus not influencing behavior. However, it is not desirable that every stimulation should be responded to— inattention to the trivial is necessary for concentrating on what is important —and the cortical organization that is inefficient in this sense is very efficient indeed in others. Let us see now how the diffuse conduction of the cortex allows us to understand, in principle, the selectivity of higher behavior (that is, responding to some stimuli, not to others); the holding process, or the delay of transmission that permits a stimulus to have its effect at the proper moment; and, in general terms, the lack of a complete sensory dominance of the behavior of the higher animal.

The distinction between sense-dominated and voluntary behavior has been made earlier. If all conduction in the CNS were in parallel, all behavior would be in the first of these two classes. As we have seen, sensory afferents are laid down in parallel, and even when an animal is asleep or under anesthesia a sensory excitation reliably reaches the cortical projection area. This means that environmental stimulation can control the activity of sensory cortex completely. Each change of pressure on the skin, for example, must be reflected in the pattern of firing in the somesthetic cortex. If a neural cell is not stimulated from without it tends eventually to fire by itself, spontaneously, because it is a living thing and must be active; but this would not be expected to happen unless the neuron was left a rather long time without stimulation. Thus when the sense organ is exposed to the varying stimulation of the environment, as it normally is, the whole afferent pathway must remain under environmental control.

Now if conduction from the sensory cortex onward were also in parallel, the same conclusions would apply elsewhere in the CNS. The whole nervous system would be under direct control of sensory events and the organism would become an automaton, all of its actions being determined by the stimuli of the moment. Each sudden stimulation would produce a convulsive jerk of the muscles with which the sense

organ was connected; the high efficiency of parallel conduction would guarantee that the excitation would reach the muscle and have its effects immediately. No delay of response until a more appropriate moment would be possible. There could be no thought process, and no voluntary behavior. Thought and "volition," as we have seen, are the occurrence of processes which, themselves independent of the immediate sensory input, collaborate with that input to determine which of the various possible responses will be made, and when. Such collaboration could hardly occur if all conduction, throughout the CNS, were in parallel.

Instead, the rules of transmission change as the excitation leaves the sensory projection cortex, and whether it goes further or not, and where it goes, is determined now by what other events are going on in the system. We can now see the significance of the nonspecific projection system and arousal, in relation to cortical function. Its activity provides a diffuse bombardment of widespread cortical regions, increasing the likelihood of summation at the synapse, and thus makes cortical transmission more feasible.

Summation must occur also between cortical cells. Two cells that lie side by side in sensory cortex, and send their axons out into the neighboring association cortex, are not likely to send them to the same point; but the axons of cells that are not close together may converge (as D and E do in Fig. 1), and this must happen very frequently among the thousands or hundreds of thousands of cells involved. In Fig. 1, A may or may not be able to fire C with summation from the arousal system; but if B is active also the probability of firing C would be greatly increased. If sensory stimulation is

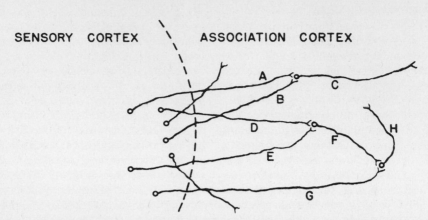

FIG. 1. *Convergence of excitation in association cortex. A and B converge on C; D and E on F; F and G on H. These are assumed to be chance convergences, the diagram representing those, among the thousands of cells in the region, which have such relations.*

such as to fire *D* and *E* at the same time, they are likely to fire *F*; and if the same sensory activity is firing *G*, so *G* sums with *F*, transmission would include *H* also. Whether *H* fires or not therefore depends on the timing of activity in *D*, *E*, *F*, and *G*. If *H* had been fired immediately before by some other neurons not shown in the figure, or were now exposed to inhibition from other cells in the same region, it would not fire now, so that neural transmission of activity through this tangled network must be a function of all the other complex activity going on in the same tissue.

So much is a reasonably direct inference from the available anatomical and physiological evidence and is also in general agreement with the behavioral evidence of set: the response made to a stimulus is a function of what is already going on in the nervous system.

But the behavioral evidence also indicates, as we have seen, that the brain is able to hold an excitation, without its dying out, so that it has its effect on behavior after an appreciable period of time. The only explanation that seems to account for the facts is the presence of the closed pathways, or loop circuits, which are found throughout the nervous system. Theoretically, excitation might continue for some time in such pathways. We have no direct physiological evidence concerning their actual functioning in behavior and learning. Such ideas are therefore in the realm of theory, but they have considerably clarified our problems, and in the laboratory have led to new and significant research. Consequently this line of analysis may be taken with some degree of seriousness even though we must expect that the physiological details, as they can be suggested at present, are not always correct.

What we are discussing here is a physiological hypothesis about the mediating processes previously defined. In brief, the hypothesis is that a mediating process consists of activity in a group of neurons, arranged as a set of closed pathways (cf. Fig. 2), which will be referred to as a *cell-assembly*, or of a series of such activities, which will be referred to as a *phase sequence*. Here the terms "cell-assembly" (or just "assembly") and "phase sequence" will be used when it is intended to refer to the specific physiological hypothesis that is about to be presented, "mediating process" when no such reference is intended. The student should note that it is often desirable in psychology to use ideas that may have derived originally from physiological considerations, but in a more general way and without specific physiological implications. Current physiological knowledge is of course incomplete, and some flexibility is needed when we apply it to psychological problems.

The loop circuits which are supposed to be the basis of the cell-assembly exist anatomically, laid down from the first by the growth processes that determine the whole structure of the CNS. We might suppose that they are ready to function from the first as holding mechanisms (or mediating processes) as already described. As

we shall see, however, the evidence of behavior suggests that a prolonged learning process is involved also. Let us see how this might occur.

The fundamental physiological assumption of learning is that whenever an impulse crosses a synapse it becomes easier for later impulses to do so. More precisely: when a neuron *A* fires, or takes part in firing, another neuron *B*, some change occurs in *A* or *B* or both which increases *A*'s capacity to fire *B* in the future. The change might be an enlargement of a synaptic knob; or it might be some chemical change. The student should note that this is a purely theoretical assumption, but one which is apparently necessary if we are to understand learning as a physiological process.

Now let us suppose that cells *A*, *B* and *C* in Fig. 2 are being fired repeatedly as a result of a particular sensory stimulation. *A* delivers impulses to *B* at the moment when other cells(not shown) are doing so; thus *A* contributes to the firing, and the

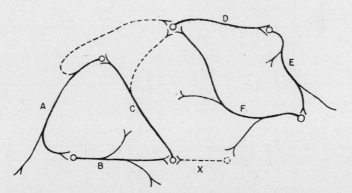

FIG. 2. *To illustrate the way in which learning might modify the functioning of cortical circuits and establish a cell-assembly. It is assumed that A-B-C and D-E-F, in association cortex, are excited by the same sensory event (axons from the sensory cortex are not shown, but it is assumed that they excite these cells separately). If A then delivers impulses to B at the moment when B is being fired by axons from sensory cortex, the synapse A-B will be "strengthened," and similarly with the other synapses. As a result of this strengthening the excitation of one cell may become able to set up reverberation in the circuit. Broken lines show possible connections between the two circuits, which would permit them to function as one system.*

synaptic connection *A-B* is strengthened. Similarly with synapses *B-C* and *C-A*. Each of these neurons thus becomes more efficient at firing the next in the series; and eventually (with the background bombardment from the arousal system) excitation of one of them alone may be enough to set off a reverberation *A-B-C-A-B-C* and so on. At this point the system has become capable of an "autonomous" activity: the activity corresponds to a particular sensory event but can continue after the stimulation has ceased, or if some other event in the cortex should trigger firing in one of the three cells, the whole system will respond just as if the external stimulation were occurring.

It is not likely, however, that one such circuit would function in isolation. Any one sensory event would excite a number of similar circuits, which theoretically would tend to establish interconnections with each other and thus merge in one larger system. The way in which this might occur is suggested in Fig. 2. *D-E-F* is another circuit in which the individual cells are fired by the same stimulus event that fired *A*, *B*, and *C*, and in which the same kind of internal synaptic changes would occur and make reverberation possible. When two such closed pathways lie close to one another there is a rather high probability of chance connections between them, as represented by broken lines in the figure. If then the two circuits are active at the same time, excited by the same sensory event, *A* and *C* will deliver impulses to *D* when *D* is being fired. According to our assumption about learning, the synaptic connections *A-D* and *C-D* will be strengthened. If a cell such as *X* is also being fired by the sensory event, or if for any reason the synaptic connection *F-X* is well established beforehand so

that *X* is fired whenever *F* is fired, *F* will similarly become capable of firing C. *A-B-C* and *D-E-F* will then be fused in one system, together with other circuits in the region which are fired by the same sensory event. This is the cell-assembly.

The formation of such an assembly is assumed to depend on the original chance interconnection among its parts (the connections then being reinforced by the learning process). The neurons involved in an assembly would be those, and only those, that happened to have the kind of interconnection described above. This would mean, perhaps, a tenth of 1 per cent of the neurons in the region. Two assemblies therefore may lie closely intertwined with each other, and yet function as separate systems, unless they are repeatedly active at the same time; in this case, they would establish effective synaptic connection in the same way as *A-B-C* and *D-E-F*.

All this is highly speculative, and such detail is given here only to show the student one direction in which psychological theory can establish meaningful direct relations with physiological and anatomical conceptions. But there are different forms such theory can take, and we do not have enough information, either physiological or psychological, to decide which of the various possible forms is right. Instead of getting completely lost in the details of one theory, or in the details of the firing of the hundreds of millions of individual neurons that must be involved in almost any action by a higher animal, we can make some general assumptions that will help us to keep things in perspective. These can be treated as dealing with the more specifically physiological conception of the "cell-assembly," or the less physiological "mediating process."

ASSUMPTION *1*. A cell-assembly

(or mediating process) is established in the first place as a slow development resulting from the repetition of a particular kind of sensory event, usually in infancy. (Anatomically, this may be set up in the cortex alone, but it is more likely that some of the loop circuits involved would be subcortical as well.)

ASSUMPTION 2. If two assemblies A and B are repeatedly active at the same time they will tend to become "associated," so that A excites B and vice versa. If they are always active at the same time they will tend to merge in a single system—that is, form a single assembly—but if they are also active at different times they will remain separate (but associated) systems. (This means that exciting part of A, for example, has a very high probability of exciting all of A, but a definitely lower probability of exciting a separate assembly, B; A may be able to excite B only when some other assembly, C, also facilitates activity in B).

ASSUMPTION 3. An assembly that is active at the same time as an efferent pathway from the same region will tend to establish connections with it, just as with another assembly. Most of the sensory events that form assemblies are accompanied by motor activities, so this amounts to assuming that most assemblies will have motor components: that is, they tend to produce overt behavior, visual assemblies producing eye movements, somesthetic assemblies movements of hand or foot, and so forth.

ASSUMPTION 4. Each assembly corresponds to a relatively simple sensory input, such as a particular vowel sound or syllable instead of a whole word, an increase of brightness, a simple odor, pressure on a particular skin area, a line of a particular slope in the visual field, and so on. Thus the perception of an actual object will involve not one but a number of assemblies. Activity of assemblies $ABCDE$ is the perception of one object, of $ABCDX$ a different object.

. . . these assumptions bear on a number of behavioral problems. The present discussion may be concluded, however, by outlining the sort of picture that is provided concerning the direction of the thought process, and attention.

It is implied, for example, that transmission of excitations through the cortex occurs by means of a series of assembly activities, or phase sequence. How would this work? An excitation cannot be reliably transmitted by a series of single assemblies, A-B-C-D, since each one has a limited probability of exciting the next (Assumption 2), and if the transmission succeeds at one point in the series it is likely to fail at another. But there are many assemblies active in the brain at the same time. If some of these others are also connected with B, C, and D, so that each is excited by more than one assembly, transmission is much more probable. In other words, a stimulus has a good probability of affecting behavior if it fits into the processes already going on in the brain.

This sort of relation is diagrammed in Fig. 3. The actual activities that occur (C_1, C_2, C_3) are those that are aroused both sensorily and centrally. The sight of a stimulus object might arouse many different trains of thought; which one it does arouse is determined by the already-existing central processes, which (so to speak) select among these possibilities. This selective influence is what is referred to by the term *attention*.

Attention and *set* are closely related terms, both referring to the same sort of selective action by central processes. *Set* is commonly used to refer to selec-

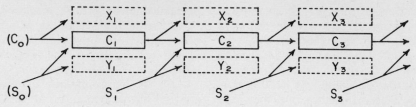

FIG. 3. *To illustrate the selective process in thinking. C, central processes (simultaneously active assemblies) at three successive moments in time; S, corresponding sensory inputs; X and Y, subliminally excited assemblies. X receives excitation from one source (central) only. Y from one source (sensory) only, so these have lower probabilities of being active. C consists of the assemblies which receive excitations from both sources and which consequently are active. Thus* C_1 *selectively determines which of the assemblies will be active, from among those that* S_1 *tends to excite; and contrariwise. This selective central influence is* attention, *represented by the horizontal arrows of the diagram.*

tivity among motor outputs (which of two possible responses will be made to a given stimulus?), *attention* to refer to selectivity between sensory inputs (which aspects of the stimulus object will be responded to), but both imply the same kind of central mechanism.

Figure 3 shows how the course of thought can have some continuity and directedness, since at each moment the processes now going on tend to pick out, from among the many perceptions of the environment that are possible, those that are relevant to the activities that have gone before. Response to environmental stimulation will not be made at random.

However, this does not mean that the train of thought cannot be interrupted. If some sensory event occurs which has strongly established central processes, if it arouses its own group of cell-assemblies which facilitate one another's activities strongly, it is quite capable of setting up a new phase sequence which has no relevance to preceding phase sequences. In Fig. 3, S_3 may have central connections which do not overlap with those of C_3, but there may be sufficient overlap in the connections of the assemblies it *does*

arouse to make possible a new phase sequence, and this in turn may perhaps inhibit other activities. An unexpected event, that is, may interrupt the present train of thought and begin a new one, with the consequent effects on overt behavior. This would be the case in which we speak of an environmental event as "catching one's attention."

SUMMARY

. . . the present discussion focusses on the interaction between individual neurons. The nerve impulse is a tiny electrochemical storm that sweeps across cell-body and axon; it obeys the all-or-none principle. Excitation of a dendrite may facilitate the occurrence of an impulse starting at the cell-body, but is not itself an impulse since it does not obey the all-or-none principle and can occur without firing the cell-body and axon. The all-or-none principle means that intensity in the stimulus must be transformed into frequency of impulses—not bigger impulses.

The probability of transmission at the synapse is increased by summation of two or more impulses delivered by separate neurons at the same time; a single impulse has a low probability of transmission. This makes the timing of impulses very important. Also, neurons fire at different rates. These facts make it possible for two different "messages" to use the same lines: a difference in timing means that they are sorted out at the synapse, taking different routes from there on. The distinctive effects of sensory inputs ("specific energies") are partly determined in this way, partly by separate routes all the way from the sensory surface to the cortex.

The EEG shows that timing of neural firing in consciousness is primarily asynchronous; any great synchrony of firing is likely to cause a convulsion. In unconsciousness there is some firing, but the large EEG potentials are mostly dendritic in origin.

The need of summation at the synapse for reliable transmission means that parallel and divergent conduction systems are very different. Parallel conduction from sense organ to brain guarantees that an excitation will get to the sensory cortex; but conduction from there onward is divergent, and whether it will occur depends on what other activities are going on, and whether these activities provide summation at the synapses in the association area. This, apparently, is why the arousal system must be active if the animal is to be conscious: the bombardment of the whole cortex increases the probability of summation at any synapse.

Another implication of these facts is that the divergent-conduction regions of the brain are necessary if the higher animal is not to be an automaton under complete environmental control. If all transmission were in parallel, each sensory stimulation would have an immediate effect on the musculature, no delay of response being possible; any strong, widespread stimulation would tend to produce a convulsion. The divergent conduction makes possible a screening of sensory inputs, and a selective response to those stimuli that are related to the animal's present behavior.

A physiological mechanism of formation of cell-assemblies (mediating processes) is proposed but these ideas, being very speculative, are not elaborated in great detail; instead, the kinds of properties they might have, suggested by present anatomical, physiological and psychological evidence, are summarized in four generally stated working assumptions. The assumptions are then applied to the problems of thinking and of set and attention.

NOTES

A number of chapters in Stevens (*General References*, Chap. 1, p. 19) deal with the various topics which have been discussed here: see especially Brink, Chaps. 2 and 3; Lindsley, Chap. 14; Morgan, Chap 20; Pfaffman, Chap. 29; and Jenkins, Chap. 30. These chapters may be supplemented by the more up-to-date but also more difficult writings of J. C. Eccles, *The Neurophysiological Basis of Mind* (Oxford University Press, 1953) and R. Granit, *Receptors and Sensory Perception* (Yale University Press, 1955).

The theory of cell-assemblies is developed in Hebb, *Organization of Behavior* (John Wiley & Sons, Inc., 1949); a more adequate form of the theory is proposed by P. M. Milner, *Psychological Review,* **64** (1957), 242–52.

A Behavioristic Analysis of Perception
and Language as Cognitive Phenomena *

Charles E. Osgood

Psychologists, when they are behaving like psychologists, limit themselves to observing what goes into the organism (stimuli) and what comes out (responses). Between these two observation points lies a Great Unknown, the nervous system. Nowadays it is fashionable to refer to this region as "a little black box." In any case, psychological theory, as distinct from psychological observation, is made up of hunches about what goes on in this little black box. Theories of hearing and color vision, principles of association, generalization, and reinforcement, notions about cohesive forces between like processes in a visual field —all imply certain conceptions about how the nervous system works. If these conceptions are made explicit, as Hebb (8) has done, for example, one is said to "neurologize," but, explicit or not, psychological theories select from among neurophysiological alternatives.

Behavior theories are often divided into two general classes—the S-S and S-R models. Each of these models is insufficient, an incomplete theory. The S-S model may adequately handle rela-

tions among input events and between these and central, "meaningful" events, but it says little or nothing about how they eventuate in behavior. For example, we are not told by Köhler (13) how a pattern of direct currents in the visual brain elicits those responses in vocal muscles which constitute saying "circle" or "square." Similarly, the S-R model may adequately handle rather simple relations between stimulus and response variables, but it says little or nothing about either the integration of sensory events (perception) or the integration of response events (motor skill). And neither model has had much to contribute to an understanding of symbolic processes.

Language is challenging to the behavior theorist because it includes at once the most complex organizations of perceptual and motor skills and the most abstract, symbolic processes of which the human animal is capable. It is also a necessary first step in the application of psychological principles to social behavior, because it is mainly via language that one nervous system establishes relationship with others. Perception presents equally difficult problems. Phenomena that have been called perceptual range the gamut from projection-system dynamics to meaningful processes, and certainly the integrational character of perception, which Gestalt psychologists have stressed, has been the Waterloo

* From C. E. Osgood, "A Behavioristic Analysis of Perception and Language as Cognitive Phenomena," in *Contemporary Approaches to Cognition* (Cambridge, Mass.: Harvard University Press, 1957), pp. 75-118. Reprinted by permission of the author and publisher.

of contemporary behaviorism—I know of no S-R model that gives a convincing interpretation of standard perceptual phenomena. It is my hope that a combined analysis of language and perception may shed some light on both.

In the body of this paper I shall describe a highly speculative conception of behavior, which at least pretends to be a complete theory, in scope although certainly not in detail. It will necessarily imply a conception of how the nervous system operates— how it determines the relations we observe between stimulus inputs and response outputs—but I shall try to phrase the theory itself in psychological terms. It is a model that has gradually developed in the course of my work on language behavior. It envisages two stages and three levels of organization between stimulus and response in the complete behavioral act. The first stage is what I shall call *decoding*, the total process whereby physical energies in the environment are interpreted by an organism. The second stage is what I shall call *encoding*, the total process whereby intentions of an organism are expressed and hence turned again into environmental events. The three levels of organization are assumed to apply to both sides of the behavioral equation, to both decoding and encoding: (1) a *projection level* of organization, which relates both receptor and muscle events to the brain via "wire-in" neural mechanism; (2) an *integration level*, which organizes and sequences both incoming and outgoing neural events; and (3) a *representation* or *cognitive level,* which is at once the termination of decoding operations and the initiation of encoding operations. We have evidence for all three of these levels, but the principles that apply most parsimoniously to one do not apply easily to the others.

PROJECTION

The receptor surface of the organism is rather precisely mapped upon the sensory cortex. Similarly, the voluntary muscle system is rather precisely mapped upon the motor cortex. The most direct evidence for these statements is the predictability of experienced sensations or muscle contractions when the sensory or motor cortex is explored electrically. One general principle of the projection level, then, is *isomorphism*. This does not mean that the projection level is simply an uncomplicated relay system. At the successive synaptic junctures between periphery and cortex, transverse connections make possible lateral interactions of limited scope and kind. For example, across any band of impulse-bearing fibers at any synaptic level there seems to be in operation a principle of lateral facilitation and inhibition—more rapidly firing elements in the band are further facilitated by summation with impulses received laterally from more slowly firing elements, and conversely the firing of the slower elements is relatively damped by receiving laterally a more rapid, subthreshold barrage. Something of this sort seems to underlie sharpening of contours and segregation of figure from ground in vision, as well as the phenomenon of masking in audition.

One can also, I think, handle the major characteristics of both color and brightness contrast, such phenomena as the apparent solidity of objects viewed binocularly, the continuity of optimum visual movement, and figural aftereffects with projection level mechanisms. This argument has been given in more detail in my book (23) and in the paper by Heyer and myself (24), which proposed an interpretation of figural aftereffects alternative to that offered by Köhler and Wallach

(13). It relies heavily on the work of Marshall and Talbot (16) and others on the functioning of the projection system.

The main point here is that there are many so-called perceptual phenomena that will probably be shown to depend upon projection mechanisms and hence be entirely predictable from knowledge of the stimulus and knowledge of projection dynamics. Such phenomena represent changes in the sensory signal itself, as I have defined it, rather than subsequent utilization of it in interaction with other signals.

Another characteristic of the projection level is that *its functioning is not modifiable by experience*. I know of no evidence showing that "what leads to what" in either sensory or motor projection systems can be modified by learning. The projection system is a perpetual *tabula rasa*—a centrally fixated object produces the same activity in Area 17 at twenty years as it did at twenty months, even though the subsequent utilization of these signals may be quite different. The experiments of Sperry (30) and others, in which segments of either sensory or motor projection systems are transplanted in embryo, also provide impressive evidence for the absence of functional modifications at this level—an animal operated upon in this manner will continue to lift the left limb when the right limb is shocked, for example, with no evidence of learning. Appropriately, the work of Senden (29), with human adults recovering sight for the first time, and Riesen (27), with chimpanzees reared in darkness, shows that certain so-called perceptual functions are independent of experience—primitive isolation of figure from ground, fixation of an object in space, contour formation, color and brightness differ-

entiation, and certain others.

The salient point for the behavior theorist is this: because the projection systems do display these two characteristics—isomorphism and inability to modify through experience—we can depend on stimulus-and-response observations as faithful indices of the sensory and motor signals with whose more central interactions I think our science of behavior is concerned.

INTEGRATION

Even the crudest observations of behavior reveal that certain patterns and sequences of responses are more readily executed than others and that certain patterns and sequences of stimuli have priority over others. Apparently both motor and sensory signals are capable of becoming structured or organized. I think there is a very simple property of nervous tissues that accounts for such structuring, and D. O. Hebb (8) has already put his finger on it. *Whenever central neural correlates of projection-level signals are simultaneously active and in fibrous contact, either directly or mediately, an increased dependence of one upon the other results*. A few explanatory comments are in order about this statement. First, we must say that it is the more central neural correlates, rather than the sensory or motor signals themselves, which can thus be associated, because the projection systems are not modifiable through experience, as we have seen. There is no requirement that the central correlates of signals be isomorphic with these signals; in fact, existing evidence indicates that strict isomorphism breaks down beyond the sensory projection level. Secondly, strict simultaneity among the signals whose more central correlates are to be associated is not necessary; the work of Lorente de No and others describes reverberatory circuits which would prolong activation and hence make possible integration over time.

In a greatly oversimplified way, Fig. 1 attempts to illustrate what I have in mind here. The isomorphic relations between stimuli and sensory signals and between responses and motor signals are shown on lower left and lower right respectively. It is assumed that cells at the termination of the projection system (for example, sensory or motor signals, as I have called them) have ample synaptic contacts with certain more central cells to guarantee exciting them (in the case of this organism the contingency of events A and B is greater than that between events A and C, and similarly for responses A and B versus A and C. This means that the resultant tendency for central correlate a to activate central correlate b should be greater than its tendency to activate c. I have indicated this in the diagram by a thicker band of contacts on cell b from a than on cell c from a.

Now, as I said before, I wish to outline a psychological theory, not a neurological one. What kind of psychological principle seems to be embodied here? Given isomorphism between observables and signals, which

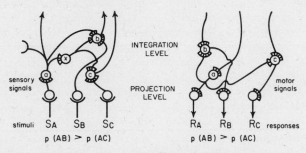

sensory signals

INTEGRATION LEVEL

PROJECTION LEVEL

motor signals

stimuli S_A S_B S_C

$p (AB) > p (AC)$

R_A R_B R_C responses

$p (AB) > p (AC)$

FIGURE 1

sensory decoding) or being excited by them (in the case of motor encoding). These are the cells in the integration level, a, b, and c, which I call "central correlates." This utilizes what I believe is a general principle of central nervous tissue: the probability of an antecedent neuron being a sufficient condition for the firing of a subsequent neuron is some direct function of the density of fibrous contact at their synapse. The control exercised by one cell over the firing of another may be increased, of course, by determining bombardment via mediate, circuitous routes; this is illustrated by cell x in the sensory integration system.

The conditions given in this diagram are such that *in the stimulus input to* makes it possible for me to deal directly with observable stimuli and responses, I can phrase the following pair of principles: *sensory integration—the greater the frequency with which stimulus events* A *and* B *are associated in the input to an organism, the greater will be the tendency for the central correlates of one,* a, *to activate the central correlates of the other,* b. This principle says, in effect, that patternings, regularities, and orderings of events in the stimulating environment of an organism come to be mirrored in the structuring of its sensory nervous system. *Motor integration—the greater the frequency with which response events* A *and* B *are associated in the output of an organism, the greater will be the tendency for the central correlates of one, a, to activate the central correlates of the other, b.* This says, in effect, that patternings, regularities, and orderings of the overt behavior of an organism, no matter how established, will come to be paralleled by equivalent organizations within its motor nervous system.

It should be stressed that what I am calling sensory and motor integrations function as classes of intervening variables, anchored directly to antecedent and subsequent observables, respectively, via a simple frequency-of-co-occurrence function. How would varying this frequency factor be expected to affect what is observed?

I suggest that *with high frequency of stimulus or response pairing, the central correlates of one will become a sufficient condition for the excitation of the correlates of the other.* I shall call this an *evocative relation.* Behaviorally it means that the occurrence of some of a set of related stimulus events will produce the central experience of the others as well and be reported or responded to as such, without their external correlates necessarily being given at all; it means that the initiation of some elements of a response pattern will set the whole pattern going. *With a lower frequency of stimulus or response pairing, the central correlates of one will become merely a condition for "tuning up" the correlates of the other.* I shall call this a *predictive relation.* Perhaps here the energies delivered from the antecedent cell to the dependent cell, while not adequate to fire that cell, are available for summation with energies being delivered via the direct path. Behaviorally this would mean an experience-determined increase in the *stability* of both decoding and encoding processes by the organism—perception of certain cues would increase the probability of

also perceiving others, in competition with many simultaneous stimuli; initiating certain responses would increase the probability of also initiating others, again in competition with many simultaneous action tendencies. In a sense we would have here a mechanism for reducing the "noise" in both decoding and encoding.

Let us look into some of the behavioral implications of this principle. In ordinary perceiving we seldom receive complete information—the environment is inspected with rapid, flighty samplings, and intensity-duration factors in the projection system certainly imply that these samplings must yield only partial signals—nevertheless, perceptual experiences are usually wholistic. I assume that what I have called *evocative relations,* based on high frequencies of input pairing or redundancy, underlie the well-documented closure and "filling in" phenomena. Directly relevant are some recent papers by Fred Attneave (1) in which he demonstrates that "various Gestalt-factors including symmetry, good continuation, and other forms of regularity may all be considered to constitute redundancy in visual stimulation and be quantified accordingly within a framework of information theory." I have not attempted myself the application of information-theory statistics to the phenomena subsumed under this integration principle, but I suspect they would be quite appropriate. We refer to "closure" when actual stimulus events, as independently measured, correspond to what is perceived, but the same tendency toward completion of an integrational unit lies at the base of many perceptual illusions, where the actual stimulus events do *not* correspond to what is integrated. I have an electric clock at home which can't be reset after the current has gone off briefly; I have to stop it and wait a day until time catches up. Every once in a while I glance up to find the time, and momentarily I see the sweep-second hand moving! Considering the thousands of times clock-face signals have been followed in my experience by sweeping second-hand signals, this illusion becomes understandable.

Merely *predictive relations* in perceptual decoding are also familiar in everyday experience. It is easier to follow a familiar juke-box tune than an unfamiliar tune against the uproar in a local tavern; the more familiar the camouflaged object in a complex picture, the more readily its contour can be traced. On the experimental side, I would interpret the findings of Bruner and Postman on the perception of incongruity (4) along these lines—the most common response to trick cards, say a *black* six of hearts, presented tachistoscopically, was to complete the integration set in motion by either the color *or* the form, but, as would be expected from the lack of reciprocal "tuning up," exposure times for decoding trick cards were significantly longer than for normal cards. Similarly, Hake and Hyman (7) have found that subjects will come to reflect in their predictions about successive stimuli the sequential dependencies built into the series, even though they may be unaware that these dependencies exist. Hake says (6), "It appears that the mechanism by which we develop expectancies about the occurrence of probabilistic events operates such that over longer series of trials or choice points we [come to] expect events about as often as they appear."

Turning now to integrations in *ordinary motor encoding,* it may be noted first that S–R behaviorists have always relied upon proprioceptive feedback as the mechanism for organizing motor

skills—and this despite the fact that as long ago as 1917 Lashley pointed out that there simply wasn't enough time in rapidly executed skills for impulses to be carried to and from the sequentially activated muscle groups. In a more recent and very stimulating paper given in the Hixon Symposium (14), he makes this point again (p. 123):

> Sensory control of movement seems to be ruled out in such acts. They require the postulation of some central nervous mechanism which fires with predetermined intensity and duration or activates different muscles in predetermined order. The mechanism might be represented by a chain of effector neurons, linked together by internuncials to produce successive delays in firing.

This does not mean that proprioceptive feedback mechanisms are unimportant. On the contrary, I think that three stages in skill formation could be traced: (1) a very slow and uncertain patterning or ordering of responses on the basis of exteroceptive controls, as in imitating the seen movements of another person; this makes possible (2) a transfer gradually to proprioceptive controls (feedback), accompanied by considerably increased speed of execution; and this more rapid and stable organization in turn makes possible (3) a transfer to central programming in the integrational motor system which we are discussing.

Here again, a very high frequency of pairing should result in the formation of *evocative relations* among motor events. I call such tightly integrated patterns "motor skill components." All the complex acts with which we deal as psychologists seem to be compounded of such components—"opening the door," for example, is a complex act involving an arm-extending-and-hand-opening component, a hand-closing component, a wrist-twisting component, and an arm-flexing component. These same elements, just like the syllables of spoken language, enter in various combinations into the myriad activities of everyday life. Motor integrations may lead to errors of completion analogous to perceptual illusions—in typing, my favorite error is regularly to add an "n" to the word *ratio,* presumably because of the tendency to complete the very common "ion" that terminates words like *action, fashion,* and of course, *ration.* Based on lower orders of frequency, many response-response integrations become merely *predictive motor relations*—unbuttoning one's shirt is predictive of peeling it off, lighting one's cigarette is predictive of blowing out the match (much to my occasional embarrassment when someone just then indicates the need of a light!). I do not mean that stimulus controls are absent in such predictive motor sequences; rather, the motor preparation decreases the probability of disturbance through ordinary stimulus changes. In other words, there seems to be a syntax of behavior just as there is a syntax of language, and this provides a stability of customary action that frees it from constant voluntary supervision.

The integrative mechanisms we have been discussing appear even more clearly in *language behavior,* and this is because the units of both decoding and encoding have been more sharply etched by linguists than have the units of nonlanguage behavior by psychologists. Generally speaking, we find evocative integrations in the smallest skill units of both speaking and listening, and predictive integrations in the grammatical mechanisms that interrelate larger message events.

The minimal units in language decoding are called *phonemes.* These are classes of similar sounds having a common significance in the code—for example, this initial sounds in "key" and "cool" are both members of the "k" phoneme, and their differences in auditory quality are entirely predictable from the message environment, in this case the following vowel. There are only some 32 phonemes in the English code; in other words, on the basis of amazingly high frequency of occurrence we have developed about 32 evocative auditory integrations, each one of which is set in motion by a *class* of input signals that varies in the elements actually present in any instance. Testimony to the general validity of our principle is the fact that ordinarily we are incapable of perceiving the differing members of these phoneme classes—*allophones,* as they are called. Only by adopting the analytic attitude of the linguist, which means listening to our language as sounds rather than meanings, can most of us hear the differences between the allophones of, say, the "p" in "pin," "spin," and "nip," in the allophones of "t" in "I bough*t* a bi*tt*er bo*ttl*e," yet these auditory distinctions are in themselves sufficient for speakers of other languages to arrange separate phoneme categories upon them. It is also interesting in this connection that our decoding of phonemes is on an all-or-nothing basis—when I say "he was a *trader,*" some of you heard "traitor" (to his country) and others heard "trader" (on the stock market), but none of you heard both at once or any compromise between the "t" and "d" phonemes. In other words, evocative integrations function as all-or-nothing units.

In language encoding, the smallest functional units are probably *syllables.* This is at least suggested by the work of Grant Fairbanks on delayed auditory feedback (6), in which he finds the interval of maximum interference to correspond to the rate of syllable production in ordinary speech (about 4/sec); it is also suggested by the fact that slowing down one's speech is usually accomplished by prolongation of syllabic boundaries, for example, "syll-a-ble pro-duct-ion." Here again we have a limited number—much larger than the number of phonemes, to be sure—of motor patterns and sequences used with such high frequency that they become evocative integrations. Think of the number of word units in which the syllable "bit" appears—the word "bit" itself, "habit," "arbitrary," "bitter," "prohibit," "bitsy," and so on. These syllables involve both simultaneous and sequential integrations of many motor elements in the vocal system, and they come to function as units in behavior.

The operation of *predictive integrations* in language has a number of excellent experimental demonstrations. Postman, Bruner, and Walk (26), for example, have shown that imbedding a single reverse-printed letter in a meaningful word lengthens the tachistoscopic exposure time at which that letter can be reported *as* reversed more than imbedding it in a series of unrelated consonants—the normal configuration of the familiar word is thus highly predictive of its components—and this was true despite the fact that the average exposure time for letters in meaningful words was very much shorter than for letters in nonsense sequences, which also follows from the integration hypothesis. An experiment by Miller, Postman, and Bruner (18) shows that varying the sequential probabilities of orthographic materials affects their recognition times in the expected way. And we may add Shannon's finding that the guesses of subjects as to what letters should follow sequences of varying

length matched very closely redundancy measurements made on large samples of English texts.

But it is in the *grammar* of a language that one observes the most remarkable predictions over time—a phenomenon which, interestingly enough, Lashley, in the Hixon Symposium mentioned earlier, took as his jumping-off point for an analysis of serial order in behavior. While in the rapidly flowing tide of conversation, both speakers and listeners attend to the lexical units in messages that represent semantic choices, leaving the complex grammatical and syntactical regularities to take care of themselves. It would be safe to say that the lay user of a language is almost never aware of its grammatical structure, couldn't possibly describe its laws, and yet follows them faithfully. When analyzed linguistically, the rules of grammar prove to be elaborate cases of redundancy or predictiveness. One such grammatical redundancy mechanism is *congruence:* in the present tense in English, the occurrence of a singular subject sets up a readiness for a verb ending in *s* (The boy run*s* but the boy*s* run): a time marker sets up a readiness for the appropriate tense tag on the verb (*Yesterday* in the city I *bought* a hat); a dependent clause marker sets up a readiness for the major clause (*When I come, open the door*). In terms of our model it is the frequency with which such grammatical redundancies have been heard and produced that sets up in the nervous system predictive integrations that match the structure of the language. As would be expected, the longer the interval between congruent elements, the weaker becomes the set and the more likely errors.

Being a relatively uninflected language, English depends heavily upon syntactical *ordering* mechanisms, another grammatical redundancy. "John loves Mary" is quite a different proposition from "Mary loves John," as many a jilted lover had discovered. In Latin these words could be kept in the same order and the difference in implication borne by inflectional endings. If I say "the happy, little ———," all of you feel a strong tendency to fill in *some* noun. If I say "the farmer killed the ———," you have essentially two structural alternatives, a noun or a noun phrase (for example, *duck* or *ugly duckling*). If I say "the old man eats ———," the set of structural alternatives is larger, but still limited (a noun, *dinner, meat;* an adverb, *swiftly, heartily;* a prepositional phrase, *with his hands, on the table,* and so on). At each point in a language message, then, we have a hierarchy of structural alternatives, this hierarchy varying in its probabilistic character with the grammatical restrictions in the language as a whole. The closer the language user's nervous system can come to matching these restrictions with its own predictive integrations, the smoother become both decoding and encoding processes and the fewer decisions have to be handled by the semantic system.

By way of evidence that these grammatical redundancies do facilitate decoding and encoding, we might cite the following: Wilson Taylor (31), using his "cloz" procedure in which the subject fills in the gaps in mutilated messages, finds that with both sides of the gap given as in his method structural determinism is almost perfect (for example, in filling in "the old man ——— along the road," all subjects will fill in a verb form even though they vary semantically in what verb they choose). Miller and Selfridge (19) and others have demonstrated that ease of learning and retention of meaningful materials varies

with the degree of approximation to English structure. Along similar lines, one of my students, Mr. Albert Swanson, compared the ease of learning nonsense sequences that retained the structure of the English sentences from which they were derived, for example,

The maff vlems oothly um the glox nerfs.

with matched materials in which the grammatical cues had been eliminated, for example,

maff vlem ooth um glox nerf.

Despite the greater absolute amount of material in the structured forms, they were learned significantly more easily than the matched strings of nonsense items.

Before leaving this international level, we should deal at least briefly with a problem raised by the existence of these *hierarchies of alternatives.* In grammatical-ordering mechanisms we have seen that at each choice-point in a message the speaker or hearer has available a set of alternative constructions, having different probabilities attached to them; similarly in perceptual decoding a particular subset of signals will be predictive of a hierarchy of potential integrations, each having a different probability associated with it. Take as examples the two sets of letters shown in Fig. 2. Based on the absolute frequencies of occurrence in this type-face, integrations associated with O, C, Q, and G will have varying conditional probabilities upon occurrence of the subset of signals from the lefthand, which are common to all; their *absolute frequencies* of occurrence, however, are all probably sufficient to produce what I have called evocative integrations. Yet, given the arc as a stimulus set in the tachistoscope, one never sees all of these possibilities at once—perception would be a perpetual jumble if

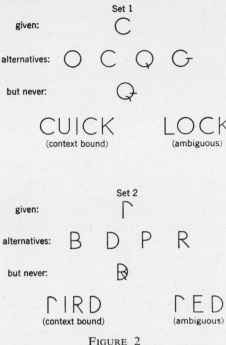

FIGURE 2

such were the case! Rather, we experience one alternative or another, that having the highest over-all momentary conditional probability. The larger context may select among alternatives —C is the only possibility in QUICK, but C and O are competitive in the ambiguous context of LOCK. The same arguments can be made on the basis of the second set of letters—B, D, P, R—where the composite jumble would be even more unlikely.

These facts require some extension of our notion of how the integrational level operates. In the first place, I think we must distinguish between frequency of co-occurrence of signals and redundancy within hierarchies of alternative integrations. The former seems to be the basis for setting up integrations, while the latter is the basis for selection among alternative integrations containing the same subset of initiating signals. Two integration hierarchies may have identical redundancy characteristics (for exam-

ple, a .50, .30, .10, .05, .05 probability structure), and yet on the basis of absolute frequencies of occurrence one may be evocative throughout and the other merely predictive throughout; in either case, only that alternative which is momentarily dominant will be effective. And this implies this notion: *Selection of the momentarily most probable integration among the hierarchy of alternatives based upon the same subset of signals serves to inhibit all other potential integrations.* I am not going to speculate upon the possible neural basis for such selection among alternatives, except to point out that there are known to be in the cortex "suppressor areas," whose excitation produces generalized spread of inhibition and Ruch tentatively identifies them with "attentional" functions (Area 19 seems to exert such an effect upon the visual system). I might also point out that many thoughtfully introspective people, psychologists among them, have reported the "singleness" of awareness or consciousness—as if at any one moment we are capable of handling only one item of information, the apparent multiplicity of attention being in reality a rapid succession. The integrational system seems to operate in such a way that many are called but only one is chosen.

REPRESENTATION

Let's take a moment to see what kind of organism we've constructed so far. On the input side it is capable of rather faithfully recording as signals what events take place on its receptor surface; it is also able, on the basis of experience, to integrate these motor signals into evocative and predictive units that reflect redundancies in its own past behavior. But something is obviously missing: this organism does not connect with its own activities events that are happening in the world; it is completely "mindless" in the colloquial sense. In other words, we have so far dealt exclusively with S-S and with R-R relations, and what are missing are S-R relations.

Stimulus events may be related to response events at all levels of organization, and these associations may be either innate or acquired. Some sensory signals have an innate "wired-in" connection with specific responses (unconditioned reflexes) and additional classes of signals may acquire such direct connection with motor signals (conditioned reflexes). Similarly, at the integrational level, associations between complex patterns of sensory and motor signals may be innate—certainly, the complicated organization of instinctual sex behavior falls in this rubric, as does the "freezing" reaction of baby birds to certain complex retinal patterns. It also seems to be a general characteristic of the central nervous system that S-R relations *originally* organized on the "voluntary" level will, if repeated sufficiently often, become autonomous integrations—most sensory-motor skills seem to suffer this fate, reading aloud and typing as well as tying one's shoes and brushing one's teeth.

But the most important mechanism for associating sensory events with motor events—certainly in the human, and I suspect in the higher vertebrates in general—is via a *two-stage mediation process*. The essential notion here is that in the course of associating external stimuli with overt behavior some representation of this overt behavior becomes anticipatory, producing self-stimulation that has a symbolic function. There is nothing highly original about postulating such mediation processes. My own use of the notion stems directly from Hull's conception of the "pure-stimulus-act," which incidentally

he suggested (11) would prove to be the basis of abstraction and symbolism in behavior; the same idea is used by Guthrie as "movement-produced-stimuli," and Tolman's basic conception of a "sign-significate-expectation" can, I think, be shown to be functionally identical. But whereas Hull and Guthrie, at least, only called upon this device in dire extremities, when single-stage mechanisms proved insufficient, I consider it to be the usual form of S-R learning. And furthermore, taking Hull's suggestion about symbolism very seriously, I have tried to show that the representational character of the mediation process provides the basis for a theory of sign behavior—or, if you will, of cognition.

We may start with the fact that certain stimulus events have a "wired-in" association with certain response events; for the hungry infant the taste and feel of warm milk in the mouth are reflexly associated with swallowing, salivating, and digestive activities, and the pressure of a yielding object against the lips is reflexly associated with sucking and head-turning. This type of stimulation I call a *significate*. However, since I want this class to include previously learned as well as wired-in relations, I would define a significate as *any stimulus that, in a given situation, reliably elicits a predictable pattern of behavior*. Thus all unconditional stimuli in Pavlov's sense are significates, but the reverse is not true. Now, there is an infinitude of stimuli that are *not* initially capable of eliciting specific patterns of behavior—the sight of the breast or the infant's bottle does not initially produce salivating, for example. Under what conditions will such a pattern of stimulation become a *sign*?

I would state the conditions this way: *Whenever a non-significate stimulus is associated with a significate, and this event is accompanied by a reinforcing state of affairs, the non-significate will acquire an increment of association with some fractional portion of the total behavior elicited by the significate.* I call such fractional behavior a representational mediation process. It is representational because although now elicited by another stimulus it is part of the behavior produced by the significate itself—this is why the bottle becomes a sign of milk–food object and not any of a thousand other things. It is mediational because the self-stimulation it produces can become associated with various overt responses appropriate to the object signified—sight of the bottle can thus mediately evoke "yum-yum" noises and reaching out the arms. Just what portions of the total behavior to the significate will appear redintegratively in the mediation process? At least the following determinants should be operating: (1) *energy expenditure*— the less the effortfulness of any component of the total behavior elicited by the significate, the more likely is this component to appear in the portion elicited by the sign; (2) *interference* —the less any component interferes with on-going instrumental (goal-directed) behavior, the more likely it is to be included; (3) *discrimination*— the more discriminable any component

from those elicited by other signs, the more likely it is to be included. There is considerable evidence in the conditioning literature that certain components of UR, particularly "light-weight" and autonomic components, appear earlier in the CR than other components.

Figure 3 diagrams the theoretical development of *perceptual and linguistic decoding.* We may take as illustration the object, BALL. The large *S* at the top of the diagram refers to those stimulus characteristics of this object (its resilience, its shape, its weight, and so on) which reliably produce certain total behavior (rotary eye-movements, grasping, bouncing, squeezing, and even the pleasurable autonomic reactions associated with play-behavior), all of which are symbolized by RT. Now, according to the mediation hypothesis, the sight of this ball as a visual sensory integration, *initially meaningless,* will come to elicit some distinctive portion of the total behavior to the object as a representational mediation process ($r_m — s_m'$). To the extent that this process occurs, the visual pattern becomes a *perceptual sign* (*S*) signifying BALL object, for example, this is *a unit in perceptual decoding.* In other words, here at the ground floor in the development of meaning is the development of per-

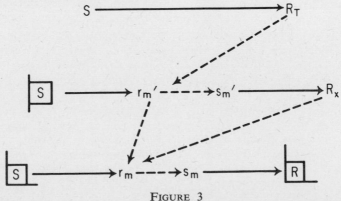

FIGURE 3

ceptual significance. Long before the child begins to use language, most of the sensory signals from its familiar environment have been lifted from their original Jamesian chaos, have become perceptual signs of objects by virtue of association with representational portions of the same behavior the objects themselves produce. Incidentally, this seems to carry back one step further the philosophical argument about the nature of meaning; the visual images of objects, rather than being "the things themselves," as is usually assumed, are actually signs whose significance must be acquired.

Now, whereas perceptual signs bear a necessary physical relation to the objects they represent, linguistic signs bear an arbitrary relation. It is characteristic of human societies that adults, when interacting with children, often vocalize those lexical items in their language code which refer to the objects being used and the activities underway. Thus Johnny is likely to hear the noise "ball," a linguistic sign $(\bar{S})$, in frequent and close continuity with the visual sign of this object. As

shown, on the lower portion of this figure, the linguistic sign must acquire, as its own mediation process $(r_m — s_m)$, some part of the total behavior to the perceptual sign and/or object— presumably the mediation process already established in perceptual learning includes the most readily short-circuited components of the total behavior and hence should tend to be transferred to the linguistic sign. Thus, a socially arbitrary noise becomes associated with a representational process and acquires meaning, for example, *a unit in linguistic decoding.*

Figure 4 diagrams the theoretical development of *instrumental and linguistic encoding.* Stage *a,* called "circular reflex," is a necessary first step, because syllable units must become integrated into skills by the practice babbling provides, and the child must be able to repeat its own vocalizations on an auditory feedback basis before it can imitate others. The second step, "imitation," involves nothing more than primary generalization—the tendency to repeat a heard sound spreads from self-produced cues to other-pro-

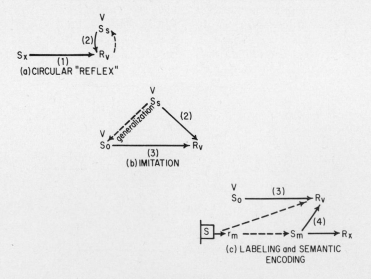

(a) CIRCULAR "REFLEX"

(b) IMITATION

(c) LABELING and SEMANTIC ENCODING

FIGURE 4

duced cues—and upon hearing mother say "ball" the child says "bah," his nearest skill unit. Now, as shown in stage *c,* let us assume that the visual stimuli from BALL object already have significance for the child, that is, constitute a perceptual sign by virtue of eliciting a mediation process (r_m — s_m) derived from BALL-manipulating behavior. Then the pairing of the heard label "ball" with the perception of the object should have at least the following consequences: (1) a single-stage association between the sight of the object and imitative labeling and (2) a two-stage, mediated association between sight of the object and imitative labeling, as shown by the starred arrow. Whereas the first of these is a meaningless process—sheer labeling that requires the physical presence of the object—the second represents the formation of *a unit of linguistic encoding.* The association of a representational process frees the child's language from the immediate here-and-now—*any* antecedent condition —desire for the object when it is missing, for example—which elicits the critical representational process is now

capable of mediating the correct, socially communicative vocalization. This is the essence of abstraction in the use of language, I think. Also indicated in this figure is the fact that mediation processes can become associated with nonlinguistic instrumental reactions (the RX in the diagram); under appropriate conditions of differential reinforcement, the child learns to crawl toward, reach for, and smile at objects perceived as having "play" significance, like this BALL object.

Perhaps the single most important function of representational processes in behavior is as the common term in mediated generalization and transfer. As shown in Fig. 5, whenever various stimuli accompany the same significate, they must become associated with a common mediation process and hence acquire a common significance. Thus, for the rat, the cluster of stimuli surrounding a food object (its appearance and odor, the auditory "click" that announces its coming, the corner around which it is found, and so on) become roughly equivalent signs of the food object. To the extent that signs have varied in their frequency of

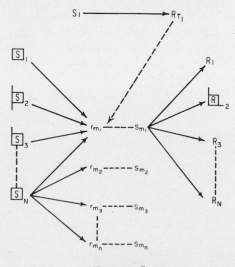

FIGURE 5

pairing with this common significate, they will constitute a *convergent hierarchy of signs* yielding the same significance but with varying strength or *probability*. Similarly, when a number of different overt responses are reinforced in association with a particular sign or class of signs, they will constitute a *divergent hierarchy of instrumental acts* associated with the same mediator. With any sign having a danger-significance for the rat will be associated a hierarchy of alternatives—running, freezing, turning a ratchet-wheel, and so on. These instrumental alternatives will also vary in their habit strengths or probabilities, and selection among them will depend particularly upon contextual cues. Finally, I have indicated toward the bottom of this figure that signs may come to be associated with *divergent hierarchies of mediators*. If the same set of sensory signals accompanies food significates often, sex significates occasionally, and pain significates seldom, this set of signals will become a somewhat ambiguous sign, in that different representational processes will tend to occur with varying probabilities. In language, homophones like *case, bear,* and *right* are merely extreme examples; here again, as whenever divergent hierarchies are operating, selection depends on context (for example, conditional probabilities).

The availability of such hierarchies to the mature organism makes possible the tremendous flexibility we observe in behavior. If to a particular sign having a certain significance, the subject learns a new instrumental adjustment, such as pressing a lever or saying "Please," this immediately becomes available to any other sign having the same significance. Here we speak of *mediated generalization*. If a novel set of sensory signals, such as a flickering light in the rat's box or

some unusual dark spots on the human's skin, acquire a danger significance, all the previously learned instrumental acts associated with this significance immediately become available to this new sign—the rat will shift quickly to running, to turning the ratchet-wheel, and the like, and the human will immediately call the doctor, talk to his wise old grandmother, rub his arm with bacon grease, or whatever he has already learned to do in situations having this significance. Here we speak of *mediated transfer*. The processes we call cognitive—concept formation and utilization, attitudes, personality traits, problem-solving—fit this mediational model, in the sense that they involve a class of stimulus situations associated with a common significance that mediates a class of alternative behaviors.

There are several difficult questions that arise with respect to the mediation hypothesis. One is this: *is such a two-stage process necessary?* Even at the rat level, there is a great deal of experimental evidence requiring a two-stage interpretation: the separation of learning from performance in many of the investigations inspired by Tolman (33); the role of secondary reinforcement mechanisms in experiments by Mowrer (21), Neal Miller (20), and others; the evidence for "learning to pay attention" in discrimination studies like those of Lawrence (15). At the human level: in the many studies of semantic generalization, the measured generalization between stimuli like JOY and GLEE obviously depends upon some common (and unobservable) mediating reaction to them, not to any physical similarities in the stimuli themselves (JOY and BOY are much more similar physically); the separation between learning and performance is even more clear in human behavior—witness the changes in attitude that may be produced by quietly watching a television program —and, as far as I can see, the phenomena of meaning and intention so obviously displayed in human language behavior, entirely escape a single-stage conception. Another question arises: *What is the real nature of representational processes?* Here I have little to say. Following Hull, I have attributed stimulus-producing response characteristics to the process, because in this way it is possible to transfer all the conceptual machinery of single-stage S-R psychology—generalization, inhibition, habit strength, habit competition, and the like—to both the decoding and encoding sides of my two-stage model. However, this does not require a peripheral view as against a central one; the representational process could be entirely cortical, although I suspect it involves peripheral events in its development, at least. And I have no idea as to what might be the neurological basis or locus of such a process. In other words, for the present I am quite content to use the mediation process as a convenient intervening variable in theory, having response-like properties in decoding and stimulus-like properties in encoding.

Another critical problem is that of *indexing these representational processes*, particularly in humans. If we index the occurrence and nature of representational processes by the very behavior presumably mediated by them, we run full tilt into the circularity which I believe characterized Tolman's theory. What we need is some index of representational states that is *experimentally* independent of the behavior to be predicted. In other words, we need some way of measuring *meaning*. Most of my own experimental work at Illinois over the past five years has been devoted to this problem, and what follows is a very concise summary.

To measure anything that goes on within the little black box, it is necessary to use as an index some observable output from it. From a previous survey (22) of varied outputs that are to greater or lesser degree indicative of meaning states—ranging from minute changes in glandular secretion and motor tension to total acts of approach, avoidance, and the like—we conclude that language output itself provides the most discriminative and valid index of meaning. After all, this is supposed to be the function of language. But what linguistic output gains in sensitivity and validity it seems to lose on other grounds; casual introspections are hardly comparable and do not lend themselves to quantification. What we need is a carefully devised *sample* of linguistic responses, a sample representative of the major ways in which meanings can vary.

The *semantic differential*, as our measuring technique has come to be called, is a combination of association and scaling procedures. We provide the subject with a standardized sample of bipolar associations to be made to each concept whose meaning is being measured, and his only task is to indicate the direction of his association and its intensity on a seven-step scale, for example, the concept LADY might be checked at step "6" on a *rough-smooth* scale, signifying "quite smooth." The crux of the method, of course, lies in selecting the sample of descriptive polar terms. Fortunately— and contrary to the assumptions of some philosophers—the myriad dimensions available in language are not unique and independent; our basic assumption is that *a limited number of specific scales, representative of underlying factors, can be used to define a semantic space within which the meaning of any concept can be specified.*

This points to *factor analysis* as the logical mathematical tool. Two factor analyses have already been reported (25); although they were based on the same set of 50 descriptive scales (selected in terms of frequency of usage) one involved Thurstone's Centroid Method and the judgment of 20 concepts against these scales by 100 subjects and the other, by 40 subjects, involved forced pairing among the verbal opposites themselves, with no concepts specified, and a new factoring method developed by my colleague, George Suci. Both analyses yielded the same first three factors: *an evaluative factor,* identified by scales like *good-bad, clean-dirty*, and *valuable-worthless*; a *potency factor*, characterized by scales like *strong-weak, large-small*, and *heavy-light*; and an activity factor characterized by scales like *active-passive* and *fast-slow*. A third factor analysis, based on a sample of 300 scales drawn from Roget's *Thesaurus*, 20 varied concepts, and the judgments thereof by 100 subjects, has just been completed (with the aid of ILLIAC, the Illinois digital computer, without which this work would have been impossible), and again exactly the same first three factors appear in order of magnitude. The regularity with which the same factors keep appearing in diverse judgmental contexts encourages us to believe that we are getting at something fairly basic in human thinking.

Although this factor work is interesting in its own right, its purpose is to devise efficient measuring instruments for meaning. In practice, small sets of scales, heavily and purely loaded on each of the factors isolated so far, are combined as an instrument against which subjects rate signs of any type—ordinary verbal concepts, the self-concept and other-concepts, cartoons, art objects, TAT or Rorschach cards,

attitude objects, and so on. As shown in Fig. 6, application of such an instru-

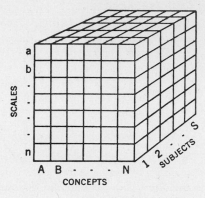

FIGURE 6

ment to a group of subjects yields a cube of data, each cell of which contains a number from 1 to 7 (the seven-step scales), each column of which contains a profile for a given concept, and each slice of which represents the complete profiles for all concepts for a given subject. The *meaning of a concept* to a given individual or group is operationally defined as the profile of numbers, or means, in a single column or, more efficiently, as the point in the factor space determined by this profile. *Difference in meaning* (between two concepts for a given subject or group, between two individuals or groups for a given concept, or between two testings) is operationally defined by D (distance) $= \sqrt{\Sigma d^2}$, the generalized distance formula. Figure 7 illustrates allocation and distances among three concepts—HERO, SUCCESS, and SLEEP—within the three-factor space so far derived. All three concepts are favorable evaluatively, but whereas HERO and SUCCESS are simultaneously quite *potent* and *active*, SLEEP is quite *impotent* and *passive*. The use of multivariate D has

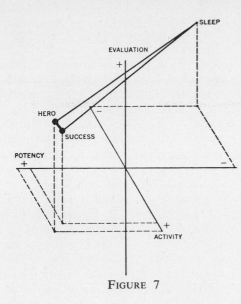

FIGURE 7

the additional advantage that all distances between concepts judged against the same set of scales can be represented simultaneously in the space defined by the scale factors. Computing the D-values between each concept and every other concept yields a distance matrix which, when only three factors are involved, can be plotted as a solid model. Such models represent, if you will, bits of "semantic geography," and the changes in such structures over time and across individuals or groups yield interesting descriptive data.

Is this instrument a valid index of representational processes in human subjects? Information on this point is much harder to come by. There is no doubt that this instrument, as far as it goes, measures meaning in the colloquial sense: the meanings of common adjectives are differentiated in obvious ways, expected differences between Republicans and Democrats are revealed, and so on. We also have some evidence that the dimensions we have isolated by factor analysis correspond to those used spontaneously by subjects

in making meaningful judgments—an experiment by Rowan (28) showed that the similarity relations within a set of concepts obtained with the semantic differential corresponded closely with those obtained for the same subjects by the method of triads (where dimensions of judgment are not specified), and other studies of this sort are in progress. But this offers only the most tenuous connection between our measurement procedures and the representational mediator as a construct in learning theory.

Let me suggest what I think this relation may be and then what may be some possible ways of tying it down experimentally. Our factor analytic work indicates a number of bipolar semantic dimensions—and such bipolar opposition in thinking, by the way, appears to be characteristic of all human cultures. My hunch is that *the representational mediator is a complex reaction made up of a number of components, these reaction components corresponding to the semantic factors we have isolated.* Now, we have been able to show that extremity of judgment on our semantic scales (for example, away from the midpoint, "4," toward "1" or "7") is linearly related to judgmental latency, when the same subjects judge the same concepts against the same scales in a reaction-time device. Since latency is an index of habit strength, it is reasonable to assume that *more polarized judgments on the semantic differential correspond to stronger habits associating sign with mediator components.* In other words, I am saying that the location of a sign in the space defined by the semantic differential is an index of the nature and intensity of the component reactions making up the mediation process elicited by that sign.

Do these identifications make sense in terms of what data we do have?

For one thing, the profile similarities we obtain between signs are obviously dependent upon some implicit, meaningful reaction to the signs and not upon their physical characteristics— profiles for LADY and GIRL are very similar, but those for LADY and LAZY are not (in other words, the instrument is indexing a two-stage, semantic process). Secondly, note the responselike nature of the three factors we have isolated so far—*evaluation* (general autonomic reaction?), *potency*, and *activity*. If representational mediators were in truth fractional portions of total behavior, one would expect them to have responselike characteristics. In this connection, I may mention another factor analysis we have done, on the communicative meanings of 40 posed facial expressions. Again three factors accounted for most of the common variance, and these were identified as *pleasantness* (for example, from GLEE down to ACUTE SORROW), *control* (from CONTEMPT over to HORROR) and *expressiveness* (from COMPLACENCY out to the whole array of active expressions like CONTEMPT, RAGE, and HORROR). These *look like* the same factors, and they are clearly related to the reactive natures of emotional states.

We have planned a number of experiments to check this bridge between semantic measurement and representational process. One is a straightforward *mediated generalization* study—if my hunch is valid, then the measured similarity between signs, as obtained with the semantic differential, should predict the amount of mediated generalization between them under the usual conditions. Another variant of the same design will compare two types of *bilinguals:* compound bilinguals (who have learned two languages in such a way that translation-equiva-

lent signs are associated with a single set of meanings) against co-ordinate bilinguals (who have learned two languages in such a way that translation-equivalent signs are associated with a double set of somewhat different meanings). Again, profile similarities between translation-equivalent signs obtained with the semantic differential should predict mediated generalization, compound bilinguals showing greater generalization than co-ordinate bilinguals.

Figure 8 provides a summary picture of the model I have been describing. Projection, integration (both evocative and predictive), and representation levels on both decoding and encoding sides of the behavioral equation are indicated, as well as the S-R relations within each level. The labels given to each type of association or "pathway," such as "pure semantic decoding" and "grammatical encoding," reflect my major interest in language behavior, but, as I have implied throughout this paper, to the extent that this picture is valid it should hold for perceptuo-motor sequences as well. This is admittedly a complicated conception of behavior, but I doubt that any conception sufficient to handle the complexities of language is going to be very simple. Although I have not indicated it in the diagram, for reasons of clarity, it should be assumed that there are hierarchies of alternatives of varying probability at each locus of S-S, R-R, and S-R relations.

We have made one check on the over-all validity of this model. This was an attempt to predict the greater-than or less-than contingencies between various language disturbance in *aphasia*. Suppose that we were able to get inside the full-blown mechanism shown here and cut one or more of the pathways—perhaps right across pathways 5 and 9, connecting grammatical pre-

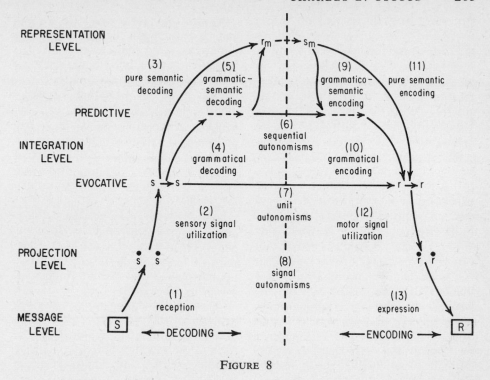

FIGURE 8

dictive integrations with representational processes—what should happen? On the decoding side, all language performances requiring one to get the significance of sequences of signs should be lost (for example, undertaking complex commands, reading interpretively, and the like); on the encoding side, the grammatical correctness of intentional speech should be lost, producing *telegraphia*. On the other hand, both the significance and the ability to produce isolated semantic units should be preserved (pathways 3 and 11), as should previously learned automatisms, like reading aloud mechanically and reciting a familiar poem. Working with the detailed reports of some 35 classic aphasia cases, two clinical graduate students (who were completely unfamiliar with the theory) and I noted in each case the presence and absence of disturbance in some 20 different language performances (such as reading aloud, labeling, written-word recognition, speech, skills, and so on). Empirical contingencies between performances over these cases were then computed and compared with contingencies predicted from theoretical analysis of the "pathways" essential to each performance—the greater the overlap in "pathway" utilization, the more likely it is that disturbance of one would be accompanied by disturbance in the other. A nonparametric test of correspondence between predicted and obtained contingencies was significant beyond the .001 level. While such results do not confirm the details of our theoretical model, they do seem to substantiate the general analysis into several levels of organization and two stages of decoding and encoding, and they have also encouraged us to work on some new aphasia tests based on the model.

PERCEPTION AND MEANING

I would identify as "perceptual" those phenomena characteristic of both evocative and predictive *integrations in decoding*, including direct effects upon this level from the projection system and indirect, "feedback" effects upon this level from the representational system. Actually, this way of thinking about perception agrees pretty well with the ideas of other psychologists: Bruner (3) draws a distinction between "autochthonous" and "behavioral" determinants, the former referring to retinally dependent events and the latter to cognitively dependent events like values and meanings, as I understand it; Hebb (8) distinguishes between "sensory" and "nonsensory" figures on what appears to be the same ground; and Gibson (5) distinguishes the "anatomical visual field" from the "ordinal visual world," again on the same grounds, as I read him. And although I deliberately have not as yet read Floyd Allport's new book on perception, I expect that the same distinction will be found there.

Why *is* there this agreement about dual control over perceptual process? It is perfectly clear from empirical data that what the subject reports as his experience depends both upon the stimulus information given to his senses and upon the store of information derived from past experience. Stimulus information, as operated upon by mechanisms in the projection system itself, determines what sensory signals are present at any moment. These sensory signals set limits upon the possible integrations that can occur. *Stored information* is of two sorts: (1) the entire past history of sensory signal pairing has resulted in hierarchies of evocative and predictive integrations within this level itself, integrations that tend to fill out sketchy sensory information

(closure) and predict synchronous and successive events in proportion to their environmental probabilities; (2) because certain cognitive states have accompanied some but not all integrations within competing hierarchies, the self-stimulation arising from such cognitive states will facilitate or increase the probability of these perceptual integrations as against others. I imagine that these "feedback" effects from the representational system operate just like other sensory signals, and exert their selective effect upon alternative integrations simply by virtue of their past contingencies with exteroceptive signals. Effects of motivational states upon perception could be handled in similar fashion.

A beautiful demonstration of this is to listen to an unfamiliar chorus from Gilbert and Sullivan, alternately following the printed libretto or merely listening without the printed guide. While the reader is seeing the printed words, the *auditory* information seems perfectly intelligible, yet the moment he looks away from the text it degenerates into gibberish. I believe it is feedback from decoding of the printed words that operates selectively among alternative auditory integrations. Now let me apply this type of analysis to two specific perceptual problems, recognition and constancy.

Identity and Recognition in Perceiving

Identifying or recognizing something requires that sensory signals activate a representational process; this must be so, it seems to me, because it is this process that mediates encoding of the words by which the subject reports his perceptions. Before he can express any "hypothesis" as to *what* the input information represents, some cognitive process must occur. I think Ames, Cantril, Kilpatrick, and the others associated with the "transactional" point of view have the same thing in mind when they say (12, p. 4), ". . . we can only have a sense of objective 'thatness' when the impingements on our organism give rise to differentiated stimulus-patterns to which differentiated significances can be related." What is missing from their treatment of perception, however, is any analysis of the nature and development of such signifying processes. Earlier in this paper I described one conception of how stimulus patterns acquire significance or meaning.

Accepting the notion that recognition of "thatness" depends upon the arousal of a representational process in the perceiver, we may now ask what classes of variables should, in theory, influence the probability of recognition. The first class of variables is so obvious that most students of perception have taken it for granted, although the human engineering people have been very much concerned—this is *the availability of the sensory signals themselves* (projection level). The probability of "detection" (usually a kind of recognition) varies with the intensity of sensory signals generated by the physical stimulus, which can be modified by manipulating exposure time, changing the receptor population, moving the stimulus, and so on. The laws operating here are those characteristic of the projection system. What subsequent integrations can occur is limited by this sensory information—a circular pattern of high intensity has about zero probability of being decoded as a vertical line.

For just this reason, in studying the effects of higher-level determinants upon recognition we usually reduce the clarity of the sensory input. A second class of variables concerns *the availability of alternative sensory integrations* (integration level). As has been demonstrated repeatedly (compare

Howes [9]; Howes and Solomon [10]; and others), with intensity-duration factors held constant, the probability of printed-word recognition is a very regular function of frequency of usage, which is another way of saying frequency of sensory signal pairing in past decoding experience. George Miller and others at M.I.T. (17) have demonstrated the same sort of thing for intelligibility (recognition) of spoken words, and I believe one could interpret Gestalt data on "goodness of form" in the perception of figures along similar lines. The laws operating here would be those characteristic of the integrational system.

We can also specify *availability of representational processes themselves* as a class of variables. One relevant experiment is reported by Brown and Lenneberg (2). These investigators first measured the availability of labels in the English language code for various patches of color (a patch of one wave length would be consistently and quickly labeled, yet one of a different wave length would be inconsistently and slowly labeled); they then demonstrated that in a recall situation ease of recognition of color patches by different subjects was predictable from the previously measured availability of their labels. Many other experiments (which I shall not cite in detail) illustrate how *representational feedback* selects among alternative perceptual organizations, how significance helps determine recognition. When frequency-of-usage factors are held constant—a necessary control—it can still be shown that recognition times for words and visual forms vary with such things as values, attitudes, previous rewards or punishments, and the like.

I would like to say something, however, about "perceptual defense." The obvious problem is this—how can an organism defend itself against perceiving a threatening stimulus when the threat depends upon first decoding the significance of the stimulus? Earlier in this paper I suggested that mediation processes are composed of a number of reaction *components*, corresponding to the factors of meaning, and that the associations of these components with a sign will vary in habit strength. Now, since probability of reaction is a function of habit strength, it follows that those meaning components having the strongest habit strength will tend to be elicited at shorter exposure time than those having weaker habit strength. In general, since *fully* discriminated meaning (recognition) depends upon the total semantic profile, this implies that as exposure time is increased the meaning of any sign should develop gradually: the blur produced by H-A-P-P-Y should first yield a vaguely favorable impression, then a more specific favorable-active impression, and should finally be recognized. With signs that have a dominantly threatening significance, this component should be aroused first, prior to complete decoding. If the subject is set for complete decoding, the resultant flood of anxiety self-stimulation could well muddy up the sensory waters and delay further decoding operations (perceptual defense). On the other hand, should the subject be alerted for danger signals, the same prerecognition anxiety stimulation could serve as a distinctive cue in selecting among alternatives (vigilance). And for *any* sign, the dominant component should, through its feedback signals, facilitate alternative integrations of "hypotheses" having similar significance (value resonance). These notions are testable in a number of ways.

The Perceptual Constancies

I have already discussed how a perceptual sign, such as the visual image of an object, may acquire its significance. Now, by virtue of the fact that physical objects and the organisms that explore them are changeable and moveable, the sensory signals deriving from objects will be variable through certain dimensions. The infant's bottle will appear in various sizes as distance changes, in various shapes as the angle of regard changes, in various brightnesses and hues as the intensity and composition of illumination changes. However, the variable sensory integrations arising from the same physical object under different conditions eventuate in the same terminal behavior and hence acquire a *common significance*—retinal images of various sizes, shapes, qualities, and intensities which derive from the infant's bottle as an object are repeatedly followed by milk-in-mouth, and hence aquire a common representational process. According to this view, then, *constancy in perception is the association of a common representational process* (significance) *with a class of stimulus patterns variable through a number of physical dimensions*. In the language of the "Transactional School," this is a common "thatness" shared by a class of stimulus patterns.

This is by no means the whole story. In the course of interaction with environmental objects, the members of such stimulus classes become associated with different instrumental sequences and hence with *differential motor dispositions*. Figure 9 may clarify what I have in mind. The sensory integration arising from an APPLE very close to the face $(s - s_1)$ is identified as this edible object (common significance), but comes to be associated with mouth-opening and biting sequences, and hence the motor integration or disposition toward such behavior $(r - r_1)$. The integration character-

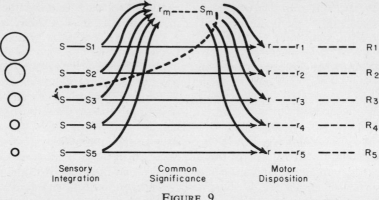

Sensory   Common   Motor
Integration   Significance   Disposition

FIGURE 9

istic of APPLE held at crooked arm's length $(s - s_3)$ has the same perceptual meaning but is associated with dispositions toward grasping or flexing the arm. And the tiny retinal image characteristic of APPLE across the room $(s - s_5)$—again signifying this same edible object—has become most strongly associated with locomotor approach movements. In other words, the sensory integrations deriving from familiar objects become associated with both common representational processes and differential motor dispositions; the former constitute identity or "thatness" in perception, and the latter constitute "thereness" in perception, part of the unconscious syntax of adjustive behavior.

It should be noted that, as shown in this diagram, selection among alternative "therenesses" or behavioral dispositions depends upon signals from both the integrational and representational systems. The disposition toward grasping requires both that the visual angle be of a certain size *and* that it be identified as a particular known object— given the same visual angle, an apple will be grasped at and a beach ball run after. On the other hand, sensory integrations arising from meaningless, abstract, or unfamiliar objects, or objects of variable size like balloons,

will be associated ambiguously with various motor dispositions. The many observations by the Princeton group, summarized by Kilpatrick (12), on absolute distance judgments are consistent with this view. Familiar and standard-sized objects like playing cards and cigarette packs were accurately judged as to distance when only size cues were available, but unfamiliar or abstract stimulus objects like star points and oak leaves were not. Similarly, when size and distance cues are put in conflict, apparent size will tend to be constant while apparent distance varies *if* the object is identified as a familiar thing having a "real" size.

But what, psychologically, *is* the "real" size of an object? Thouless (32), for example, says that constancy always consists in a "regression toward the real object," but he says little indeed about what this "real object" is or how it is established. Let me suggest an experiment and its result. We will project lifelike images of various objects onto an invisible screen at an unknown distance from the observer so that they seem to hang out there in empty space. By some optical means, we will allow the observer to adjust the physical size of these images until they seem "natural" or "just right" in apparent size. Knowing the actual distance of the screen and the final objective size of the image, we will compute the visual angle subtended by each object-image when judged to be "natural-looking." We will find that these visual angles correspond very closely to those subtended by these same objects at their ordinary inspection distances. We inspect and compare horses and automobiles at a distance of some 20 feet; we compare cigarette packages at crooked arm's length; we inspect the sharpness of record needles at a distance of about 6 inches. In other words, *the "real" or "natural" size of an object will be found to be the visual angle subtended at which the finest visual discriminations for that class of objects can be made.* I would also be willing to bet that this "natural" visual angle will approximate a constant for all objects, dependent upon retinal characteristics. The same argument would apply to all other dimensions along which constancy operates —the "real" color and brightness of an object will be that experienced under white light of normal daylight intensity; the "real" shape of an object will be that experienced when held perpendicular to the line of regard (because this is the condition for finest shape discriminations); and so on.

Now, from all this it follows that the representational mediation process associated with a particular class of signs, which gives them their "appleness," "horseness," "pack-of-cigarettes-ness," or what-have-you, will be most frequently and strongly elicited by that sensory integration corresponding to the "real" object. This is to say that we will most often be decoding the perceptual significance of an object when it is being inspected in that portion of the visual field where the finest discriminations can be made, when we are "paying attention to it." By the same token, as shown by the dashed arrow in Fig. 9, *the feedback self-stimulation from this representational process must be most strongly associated with "tuning-up" or predicting this "real" or normative sensory integration.* From this we can derive a number of the standard phenomena of constancy. (1) What is perceived is usually a compromise between the "real" behavioral object and the actual sensory information. Recognition of a meaningful object will itself, through feedback, change the sensory signals in such a way as to increase the probability of occurrence of a more "normal" perceptual integration. Obviously, the less intense and clearly defined the retinal signals, or the more intense the feedback signals from the cognitive system, the greater should be this tendency toward normalizing. Therefore, (2) the phenomenal characteristics of familiar, meaningful objects should show greater constancy than those of nonsensical, unfamiliar, or abstract objects. "Object-colors" show constancy, but "film-colors" do not; a dinner plate held at various angles shows more constancy than forms cut from white cardboard. And similarly, (3) the more natural the situation in which constancy is measured, or the more motivated the subject toward behaving with respect to "things," the greater is the constancy shown. Adults, children, monkeys, and even fish display almost perfect constancy in going about their everyday affairs. In other words, the ordinary behavior of organisms is concerned with decoding the *significance* of signs, regardless of their momentary physical characteristics, and with encoding intentional behavior that takes account of these signficances.

SUMMARY

I said this paper would be speculative, and I think I have kept my word.

In order to discuss the topic I originally proposed, I found it necessary to present a rather general theory of behavior, and despite the length of this paper my treatment has been a very sketchy one. The theory conceives of behavior as a two-stage process, decoding the significance of received signals and encoding intentions into overt acts. Both decoding and encoding processes are assumed to involve three interactive levels of organization—a projection level, an integration level, and a representation or cognitive level—but the principles governing one level do not seem to apply to the others. Throughout this paper I have tried to demonstrate the essential identities of perceptuo-motor behavior and language behavior when viewed within this framework, and I at least feel that both become more understandable by virtue of being compared.

I am not unaware of the crudeness of this kind of theorizing. It is certainly more programmatic than rigorous and more qualitative than quantitative, but, on the other hand, I think that for some time to come rigorous, quantitative theories in psychology are going to be feasible only in very restricted areas. And in the meantime, many of us are going to want to do what we can with such complex problems as perception and language. Theories such as the one I have outlined can help to systematize what information we do have, can provide an impetus to new research, and can give us at least the illusion of some understanding.

REFERENCES

1. Attneave, F., "Some Informational Aspects of Visual Perception," *Psychological Review*, **61** (1954), 183-93.

2. Brown, R. and E. Lenneberg, "A Study in Language and Cognition," *Journal of Abnormal Social Psychology*, **49** (1954), 454-62.

3. Bruner, J. S. and C. C. Goodman, "Value and Need as Organizing Factors in Perception," *Journal of Abnormal Social Psychology*, **42** (1947), 33-44.

4. Bruner, J. S. and L. Postman, "On the Perception of Incongruity: A Paradigm," *Journal of Personality*, **18** (1949), 206-23.

5. Fairbanks, G., "Selected Vocal Effects of Delayed Auditory Feedback," *Journal of Speech and Hearing Disorders*. (In press.)

6. Gibson, J. J., *The Perception of the Visual World*. Boston: Houghton Mifflin Company, 1951.

7. Hake, H. W. and Hyman, R., "Perception of the Statistical Structure of a Random Series of Binary Symbols," *Journal of Experimental Psychology*, **45** (1953), 64-74.

8. Hebb, D. O., *The Organization of Behavior*. New York: John Wiley & Sons, Inc., 1949.

9. Howes, D. H., "On the Interpretation of Word Frequency as a Variable Affecting Speed of Recognition," *Journal of Experimental Psychology*, **48** (1954), 106-12.

10. Howes, D. H. and R. L. Solomon, "Visual Duration Thresholds as a Function of Word-probability," *Journal of Experimental Psychology*, **41** (1951), 401-10.

11. Hull, C. L., "Knowledge and Purpose as Habit Mechanism," *Psychological Review*, **37** (1930), 511-25.

12. Kilpatrick, F. P., ed., *Human Behavior from the Transactional Point of View*. Hanover, N. H.: Institute for Associated Research, 1952.

13. Köhler, W. and H. Wallach, "Figural After-effects," *Proceedings of the American Philosophical Society*, **88** (1944), 269-357.

14. Lashley, K., "The Problem of Serial Order in Behavior," in *Cerebral Mechanisms in Behavior*. (The Hixon Symposium) ed. L. A. Jeffress. New York: John Wiley & Sons, Inc., 1951.

15. Lawrence, D. H., "Acquired Distinctiveness of Cues: II. Selective Association in a Constant Stimulus Situation," *Journal of Experimental Psychology*, **40** (1950), 175-88.

16. Marshall, W. H. and S. A. Talbot, "Recent Evidence for Neural Mechanisms in Vision Leading to a General Theory of Sensory Acuity," in *Visual Mechanisms*, ed. H. Kluver. Lancaster, Pa.: Cattell, 1942.

17. Miller, G. A., G. A. Heise, and W. Lichten, "The Intelligibility of Speech as a Function of the Context of the Test Material," *Journal of Experimental Psychology*, **41** (1951), 329-35.

18. Miller, G. A. and J. A. Selfridge, "Verbal Context and the Recall of Meaningful Material," *American Journal of Psychology*, **63** (1950), 176-85.

19. Miller, G. A., L. Postman, and J. S. Bruner, "Familiarity of Letter Sequences and Tachistoscopic Identification," *Journal of Genetic Psychology*, **50** (1954), 129-39.

20. Miller, N. E., "Studies of Fear as an Acquirable Drive: I. Fear as Motivation and Fear-reduction as Reinforcement in the Learning of New Responses," *Journal of Experimental Psychology*, **38** (1948), 89-101.

21. Mowrer, O. H., *Learning Theory and Personality Dynamics*. New York: The Ronald Press Company, 1950.

22. Osgood, C. E., "The Nature and Measurement of Meaning," *Psychological Bulletin*, **49** (1952), 197-237.

23. ———, *Method and Theory in Experimental Psychology*. New York: Oxford University Press, 1953.

24. Osgood, C. E. and A. W. Heyer, "A New Interpretation of Figural After-effects," *Psychological Review*, **59** (1951), 98-118.

25. Osgood, C. E. and G. J. Suci, "Factor Analysis of Meaning," *Journal of Experimental Psychology*, **50** (1955), 325-38.

26. Postman, L., J. S. Bruner, and R. D. Walk, "The Perception of Error," *British Journal of Psychology*, **42** (1951), 1-10.

27. Riesen, A. H., "The Development of Visual Perception in Man and Chimpanzee," *Science*, **106** (1947), 107-108.

28. Rowan, T. C., "Some Developments in Multidimensional Scaling Applied to Semantic Relationships." (Doctoral dissertation, University of Illinois, 1954.)

29. Senden, M. von, *Raum-und Gestaltauffassung bei operierten Blindge boren vor und nach der Operation*. Leipzig: Barth, 1932.

30. Sperry, K. W., "Mechanisms of Neural Maturation," in *Handbook of Experimental Psychology*, ed. S. S. Stevens. New York: John Wiley & Sons, Inc., 1951.

31. Taylor, W., "Application of 'Cloze' and Entropy Measures to the Study of Contextual Constraint in Samples of Continuous Prose." (Doctoral dissertation, University of Illinois, 1955.)

32. Thouless, R. H., "Phenomenal Regression to the Real Object," *British Journal of Psychology*, **21** (1931), 339-59.

33. Tolman, E. C., *Collected Papers in Psychology*. Berkeley: University of California Press, 1951.

Semantic Conditioning *

Gregory Razran

PROBLEM AND HISTORY

Semantic conditioning may be defined as the conditioning of a reflex to a word or sentence irrespective of the particular constituent letters or sounds of the word or the particular constituent words of the sentence: that is, conditioning to meaning (more specifically, to sense or meaning since some semanticists accord the status of meaning only to sentences or propositions). Its experimental analysis is an outgrowth of the object-word (or sensory stimulus-word) and word-object (or word-sensory stimulus) CR transfer noted in the Russian laboratories of Krasnogorsky and Ivanov-Smolensky in the late '20s and early '30s, when, for instance, a conditioned reflex to the sound of a metronome carried over to the sound of the word metronome or vice versa. However, studies of phonetographically unrelated word transfer of conditioning, and indeed of any word-word CR transfer, originated in this country, as did also the term semantic conditioning itself. The author used the term first in *Science* (Razran, 1939b) when he had found that three college students, conditioned to secrete a mean of 249 mg of saliva

* From G. Razran, "The Observable Unconscious and the Inferable Conscious," in *Current Soviet Psychophysiology: Interoceptive Conditioning, Semantic Conditioning, and the Orienting Reflex, Psychological Review,* **68** (1961), 99-109. Reprinted by permission of the author and the American Psychological Association.

per minute to the sight of the words style, urn, freeze, and surf, had transferred their conditioning more to words fashion, vase, chill, and wave than to stile, earn, frieze, and serf.

The author's results were almost wholly duplicated by Riess (1940) who used the galvanic skin reflex and who, in addition, uncovered a positive correlation between semantic conditioning and age (Riess, 1946). In later experiments, the author reported: a crude semantic gradient to traditional association categories (subordinate, contrasts, part-whole, whole-part, co-ordinate, and supraordinate—Razran, 1949a, 1949b, 1949d, 1949e); more salivary CR transfer from the sentence "Poverty is degrading" to "Wealth is uplifting" than to "Poverty is not degrading" (Razran 1949c); and a sentential distribution of conditioning in accordance with parts of speech (Razran, 1952). Several other American experimenters engaged in the problem, notably Lacey and his collaborators (Lacey and Smith, 1954; Lacey, Smith, and Green, 1955) with highly instructive results and implications. But, in general, there has been little concerted effort in the area in this country, while the Russians have, in recent years (1952 on), advanced it with special speed and planning.

SAMPLE RUSSIAN EXPERIMENTS

I. Yuri K., 13 years old, was conditioned to secrete a considerable amount

TABLE 1

SALIVATION OF 13-YEAR-OLD BOY TO VARIOUS WORDS AND PHRASES AFTER HE HAD
BEEN CONDITIONED POSITIVELY TO THE WORD *Khorosho* [Well, Good] AND
NEGATIVELY TO THE WORD *Plokho* [Poorly, Badly, Bad]

Trial No.	Time of experimentation		Words or phrases tested	Test No.	Saliv. dps. in 30 sec.
	Date	Exact Time			
1	6/26/52	11:20'00"	*khorosho*	47	9
2		11:25'15"	*Uchenik prekrasno zanimayet-sya* [The pupil studies excellently.]	1	14
3		11:29'15"	*Deti igrayut khorosho* [The children are playing well.]	1	19
4		11:31'15"	*plokho*	11	2
5		11:32'45"	*khorosho*	48	15
6		11:37'00"	*Sovet-skaya Armiya pobedila* [The Soviet Army was victorious.]	1	23
7		11:42'00"	*Uchenik nagrubil ychitel'nilse* [The pupil was fresh to the teacher.]	1	0
8		11:45'15"	*khorosho*	49	18
9		11:49'45"	*Pioner pomogayet tovarischu* [The pioneer helps his comrade.]	1	23
10	7/31/52	10:10'00"	*khorosho*	50	18
11		10:14'00"	*plokho*	12	1
12		10:17'00"	*khorosho*	51	16
13		10:21'00"	*Leningrad—zamechatel'ny gorod* [Leningrad is a wonderful city.]	1	15
14		10:24'30"	*Shkol'nik ne sdal ekzamen* [The pupil failed to take the examination.]	1	2
15		10:26'00"	*khorosho*	52	15
16		10:29'30"	*Brat obizhayet sestru* [Brother is insulting sister.]	1	1
17	8/1/52	11:20'00"	*khorosho*	54	12
18		11:25'30"	*Rybaky poymali mnogo ryby* [The fisherman caught many fish.]	1	18
19		11:31'30"	*Sovet-skaya konstitutsiya—samaya demokraticheskaya* [The Soviet Constitution is the most democratic (of all).]	1	17
20		11:36'30"	*Fashisty razrushili mnogo gorodov* [The Fascists destroyed many cities.]	1	2
21	8/1/52	11:40'30"	*Uchenik razbil steklo* [The pupil broke the glass.]	1	2
22		11:41'30"	*Sovet-sky narod lyubit svoyu Rodinu* [The Soviet people love their Motherland.]	1	17
23		11:45'30"	*Moy drug tyazhelo zabolel* [My friend is seriously ill.]	1	2
24		11:47'30"	*Vrazheskaya armiya byla razbita i unichtozhena* [The enemy army was defeated and annihilated.]	1	24
25		11:51'30"	*Uchenik sdal ekzamen na posredstvenno* [The pupil passed the examination with a mediocre grade.]	1	10

of saliva when the word *khorosho* [well, good] was pronounced and to differentiate from it the sound of the word *plokho* [poorly, badly, bad]. Fig. 1 shows that when the two words were

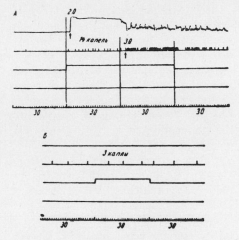

FIG. 1. *Positive salivary conditioning to the word* khorosho *[good, well] negative salivary conditioning to the word* plokho *[poorly, badly, bad] in a 13-year-old boy. (Upper figure data are for* khorosho, *lower for* plokho. *Lines from above in each figure are: motor action of jaw, drops of saliva, conditioned stimulus, unconditioned stimulus, time in seconds; arrow in second line of upper figure refers to beginning of eating. Russian words in the second line of the upper figure mean "14 drops"; in lower figure, "3 drops.")*

put in sentences *Khorosho uchenik otvechayet* and *Plokho vorobey poyot,* Yuri secreted, respectively, 14 and 3 drops of saliva in 30 seconds. (The literal translation of the two sentences is: "Well the student answers" and "Poorly the sparrow sings"—Russian word-order is wholly flexible and each of the two adverbs could have been in any position without appearing at all unusual.) Table 1 includes data on the subject's 30-second conditioned salivation to the words *khorosho* and

plokho and to 16 sentences. Nine of the 16 sentences must have evoked in the subject attitudes of approval (*khorosho*); six, attitudes of disapproval or condemnation (*plokho*); and one (the last sentence) was most likely of an intermediate or indeterminate attitude category.

As seen from the table, the conditioned salivation during the action of the "approval" sentences ranged from 14 to 24 drops in 30 seconds. During the action of the "condemnation" sentences, the range was from 0 to 2 drops, and during the action of the "intermediate" sentences the salivation amounted to 10 drops for the 30 seconds. No secretion was evident when the experimental sentence was "The pupil was fresh to the teacher," but 24 drops were produced when the sentence was "The enemy army was defeated and annihilated," and 23 drops when it was "The pioneer helps his comrade."

Later, in a second experiment, the same subject formed a positive salivary CR to the word *desyat'* [ten] from which he differentiated the word *vosem'* [eight], and was then confronted with 19 arithmetical problems, to 11 of which the answer was "ten" and to 8 of which the answer was "eight." The results are presented in Table 2, from which it may be seen that the "answer ten" problems produced from 7 to 25 drops of saliva in 30 seconds, with a median of 17 drops, whereas none of the "answer eight" problems yielded more than 3 drops in testing periods of the same duration. The "answer ten" problems were effective even when "eight" was a part of them (Problems 9, 12, and 17).

Finally, in a third experiment, the boy was conditioned positively to the word *vosemnadtsat'* [eighteen] from which he differentiated the word *chetyrnadtsat'* [fourteen], and then presented with arithmetical problems: $9 + 9$, $90 \div 5$, $72 \div 4$, and $2,232 \div 124$. His results are given in Figure 2. As may be noted in the figure, $9 + 9$ yielded 18 drops of saliva in 30 seconds

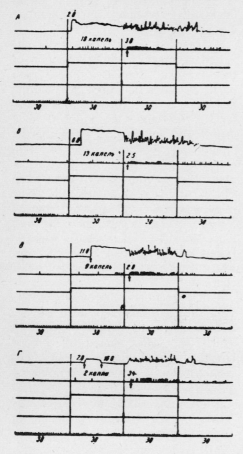

with a latency of 2 seconds; $90 \div 5$ produced 13 drops with a 6-second latency; $72 \div 4$ evoked 9 drops at an 11-second latency; and $2,232 \div 124$, 2 drops and a latency of 7.8 seconds (Volkova, 1953).

The extremely fine reflection of the subject's thoughts, and no doubt subvocal speech, in the conditioned salivation is indeed very striking.

II. Conditioned vasoconstriction was formed in nine adult human subjects to the words *dom* [house] and *doctor* [doctor] by combining the words with the application of a 10°C round lead disc to the dorsal side of the subjects' left arms and recording the conditioned vasoconstriction in both arms photoplethysmographically. CR transfers to phonetographically related words *dym* [smoke] and *diktor* [announcer] and to the semantically related and phonetographically unrelated English word house (subjects knew the language) and Russian word *vrach* [physician] were tested at early and late stages of CR training, and after the administration of 1 gm of chloral hydrate. Figure 3 shows that the phonetographic

FIG. 2. *Semantic salivary transfer in a 13-year-old boy conditioned to the sound of the word* vosemnadtsat' *[eighteen]. (Figures from above down show results when the transfer stimuli were, respectively: $9 + 9$, $90 \div 5$, $72 \div 4$, $2,232 \div 124$. Lines in each figure from above are: motor action of jaw, drops of saliva, verbal stimulus, unconditioned stimulus, time in seconds; arrows refer to beginning of eating. Russian words in the figures from above down mean: "18 drops," "13 drops," "9 drops," and "2 drops.")*

FIG. 3. *CR transfer of vasoconstriction from conditioned word* dom *[house] to phonetographically related word* dym *[smoke]. (Left figure—transfer after 8 conditioned trials; middle figure—loss of transfer after 25 conditioned trials; right figure—recovery of transfer 30 minutes after administration of chloral hydrate.)*

TABLE 2

SALIVATION OF 13-YEAR-OLD BOY TO DIFFERENT ARITHMETICAL OPERATIONS AFTER
HE HAD BEEN CONDITIONED POSITIVELY TO "10" AND NEGATIVELY TO "8"

Trial No.	Time of experimentation		Arithmetical operations tested	Test No.	Saliv. dps. in 30 sec.
	Date	Exact time			
1	8/12/52	11:10′00″	83 − 73	1	15
2		11:14′00″	5 + 5	1	16
3		11:18′30″	20 − 12	1	2
4		11:20′30″	1000 ÷ 100	1	18
5		11:24′30″	5 × 2	1	19
6		11:28′00″	56 ÷ 7	1	2
7		11:32′00″	24 − 14	1	19
8	8/14/52	13:15′00″	19 − 9	1	7
9		13:19′00″	8 + 2	1	19
10		13:22′30″	48 ÷ 6	1	3
11		13:23′30″	4 × 2	1	2
12		13:24′00″	80 ÷ 8	1	17
13		13:27′30″	112 − 102	1	11
14		13:29′30″	4 + 4	1	3
15		13:31′30″	470 ÷ 47	1	11
16	8/14/52	13:33′00″	99 − 91	1	3
17		13:35′00″	80 ÷ 8	2	21
18		13:38′00″	88 ÷ 11	1	3
19		13:40′30″	35 − 25	1	25

CR transfer to the word *dym* was evident only in the early stage of training (8 trials); that it disappeared when the CR was well established (after 25 trials); and that, strikingly, the transfer reappeared 30 minutes after the administration of chloral hydrate to the subjects. Figure 4 brings out the finding that the semantic CR transfer from the Russian word *dym* to the English word *house* disappeared 30 minutes after administration of the same dose of the drug. The results with the words *diktor* and *vrach* are said to have been quite similar (Shvarts, 1954, 1960).

The experiment thus demonstrates, first, that semantic conditioning is a manifestation of a higher level of our learning potentialities and, second and moreover, that the lower level, the phonetographic manifestation, is not nonexistent in us but is held in abeyance and reasserts itself in periods of lower

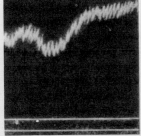

FIG. 4. *The effect of the administration of chloral hydrate upon semantic CR transfer of vasoconstriction from conditioned word* dom *to English equivalent* house *(subjects knew English). (Left figure—transfer before administration of the chloral hydrate; right figure —loss of transfer after the administration of the depressant.)*

organismic functioning. As such, the results are seemingly in line with those of Riess (1940, 1946) on the positive correlation between semantic conditioning and age, with Luria and Vinogradova's (1959) comparisons of semantic conditioning in normal and feebleminded children, with some of my own findings, and with what might be expected on general principles.

III. Markosyan (1953) has demonstrated that the reduction in time of blood coagulation produced by the administration of an electric shock could be conditioned in nine rabbits to the sound of a whistle or of a metronome of three beats per second, and that the CR to the metronome could be differentiated so that it was not evoked by beats of one per second. In a later experiment (1958), Markosyan reported that human subjects (he does not state how many) formed coagulation CRs to the sound of a metronome and that these CRs transferred from the sound of the metronome to the sound of the word metronome and to the phonetographically related words *metrostroy*, *metropol'*, *mikrotom*, and *mikroskop*. When now he had conditioned the blood coagulation to the flash of an electric lamp, he found CR transfer to the words *lampochka* [lamp], *fonar'* [lantern], *svet* [light] but not to the word *svist* [whistle], and, again, that after a while the subjects manifested clear-cut reductions in time of blood coagulation when he merely told them "[you're getting a shock]" or "[it is going to hurt]."

The experiment is obviously important in disclosing experimental evidence on the presence of semantic factors in such a phyletically old function as blood coagulation, a function which Western hematologists, unlike Russian ones, tend to regard as not within neural control. The obtained data are, however, too scanty to be accorded more than a tentative and suggestive status.

IV. Seven university students formed vasoconstrictive CRs, recorded by means of a special photoplethysmo-graph from the fingers and forehead, to the sound of the word *skripka* [violin], by combining the presentation of the word with the administration of an electric shock to the subjects. After the CR was well stabilized (18–27 trials), three varieties of words were tested for CR transfer: words related in different phonetographic degrees to *skripka* such as *skrepka* [paper clip], *strizhka* [hair cutting, shearing], and *skrytnost'* [reticence, secrecy]; words related in different semantic degrees such as *smichok* [violin bow], *gitara* [guitar], *struna* [string], *mandolina* [mandolin], *arfa* [harp], *baraban* [drum], *orkestr* [orchestra], *sonata,* and several others; and wholly unrelated words such as *stakan* [glass], *lenta* [ribbon], *voda* [water], and so forth. The main results show transfer to all the semantically related words, phonetographic transfer to only the word *skrepka*, and, of course, no transfer to the unrelated words. The semantic transfer was of two kinds: one in which the transfer words duplicated the vasomotor changes of the conditioned word, viz., vasoconstriction of both the finger and the forehead blood vessels, and one in which the transfer words elicited vasoconstriction of the vessels of the fingers but vasodilatation of the vessels of the forehead. The phonetographic transfer to *skrepka* was only of the second, vasoconstriction plus vasodilatation, kind—a kind which the Russians identify with the arousal of the orienting reflex. By and large, with respect to the semantically related words, the duplicative kind of transfer was manifest when the transfer words were closely related to the conditioned word, and the orienting kind when the relationship was less close.

Other results of the study might be summed up as follows. (*a*) The amount of the CR transfer—that is, the magnitude of the vasomotor change—was largely a positive function of the degree of semantic relationship of the transfer words to the conditioned word. (*b*) In the course of CR training, the transfer became restricted in scope, duplicative transfer changing into the orienting variety and orienting transfer disappearing altogether. (*c*) The scope of the transfer readily widened when a semantically related transfer word was reinforced with the electric shock. (*d*) However, when the reinforced word was unrelated to the conditioned word such as the word *korova* [cow], a new family of semantic-transfer words such as *telyonok* [calf], *loshad'* [horse], *byk* [bull], and *stado* [herd] came into being. (*e*) When a word had a double meaning, one related to the conditioned word and one unrelated, the word manifested transfer when it was applied after related words and no transfer when it was applied after the unrelated words. (*f*) Subjects' knowledge of the purpose of the experiment and experimenter's instruction modified considerably the course of the conditioning and the transfer but did not wholly nullify or reverse it. (*g*) Postexperimentally, subjects sometimes reported that transfer words had been accompanied by shock stimulations, and there was in general little correlation between postexperimental recall of a word and CR transfer to it during the experiment; indeed, some subjects reported words that had not been used by the experimenter.

Figure 5 presents data for two subjects (upper four strips for one, lowest strip for the other). As may be seen from the figure, none of the seven unrelated words—*plat'ye* [clothes], *pugovitsa* [button], *kastryula* [saucepan], *vilka* [fork], *stul* [chair], *kamin* [fireplace] and *pechka* [stove]—nor the phonetographically related word *strizhka* [hair cutting, shearing] evoked any transfer, whereas all the eight

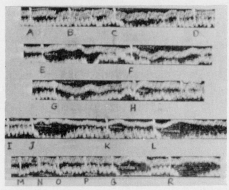

FIG. 5. *Verbal transfer of vasomotor CR formed to word* skripka *[violin], with electric shock as the US. (Two subjects—upper four strips, one subject; lowest strip, the other. Lower record— finger plethysmogram; upper record— forehead plethysmogram. Words from upper left:* strizhka *[hair cutting, shearing],* plat'ye *[clothes],* pianino *[piano],* pugovitsa *[button],* truba *[trumpet, chimney],* skripach *[violinist],* smychok *[violin bow],* arfa *[harp],* vilka *[fork],* mandolina *[mandolin],* fleyta *[flute],* violonchel' *[violoncello],* stul *[chair],* kamin *[fireplace],* pechka *[stove],* truba *[trumpet, chimney],* baraban *[drum],* truba *[trumpet, chimney].)*

words that were semantically related to the conditioned word *skripka* [violin] produced it. The word *truba*, meaning either trumpet or chimney, produced transfer when it was tested after *baraban* [drum] but was ineffective when tested after *pechka* [stove] preceded by tests for *kamin* [fireplace] and *stul* [chair]. Again, it may be noted in the figure that in the early stages of the CR training the words for piano, violinist, and violin bow elicited duplicative transfer while the words for trumpet and harp evoked the orienting kind (upper three strips of figure); and that in later stages (fourth strip) the magnitude of the transfer for the words meaning mandolin and violoncello was larger than that for the word meaning flute (Vinogradova and Eysler, 1959).

The cited experiment no doubt contains a comprehensive array of significant findings on semantic conditioning. Unfortunately, however, because of a total absence of statistical treatment of data, only the main results of the existence of semantic CR transfer, the near-absence of phonetographic transfer, the existence of the semantic transfer in both a duplicative and an orienting form, and perhaps also the positive effects of context on semantic CR transfer could be considered demonstrated with any degree of significance.

V. Ten normal school children, 11 to 15 years of age, and 15 feeble-minded children of different degrees of feeble-mindedness, 13 to 17 years of age, were told to press a button when they heard the word *koshka* [cat], which resulted in consistent constriction of the blood vessels of the children's fingers and dilatation of the vessels of their forehead, in response to the mere sound of the word. A large number of words related semantically or phonetographically to *koshka*, and some neutral unrelated words, were now presented to each child to test for resulting transfers of the vascular reactions. Clear-cut differences are stated to have been obtained between the normal and the feeble-minded children and among the children of different degrees of feeble-mindedness. The normal children transferred their vascular reactions only to semantically related words. The children of moderate degrees of feeble-mindedness manifested both semantic and phonetographic transfers, while the transfer of the children of extreme feeble-mindedness was only phonetographic. (There are no IQs in the USSR.) Again, it is stated that in the moderately feeble-minded children repeated reinforced presentations of the instructional word

koshka increased the amount of semantic transfer; that a presentation of the word *okoshko* [window] in its own semantic context—after the words *derevo* [tree], *dom* [house], *dver* [door], and *stena* [wall]—decreased phonetographic transfer; and that fatigue in general decreased semantic transfer and increased the phonetographic kind.

The experimenters (Luria and Vinogradova, 1959) present data for 6 of their 25 subjects in six figures. Figure 6 is a composite of four of these fig-

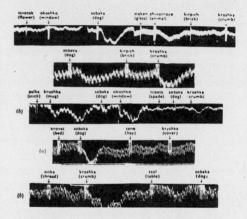

FIG. 6. *Verbal transfer of a vascular orienting reaction to word* koshka *[cat] in four school children. (Upper strip— normal 11–12-year-old child; upper middle strip—16-year-old "mild oligophrenic" or "debile"; middle strip—16-year-old "imbecile," greater degree of feeblemindedness; lower middle strip— 17-year-old "debile" at beginning of school day; lowest strip—same subject after 6 hours of schoolwork, effects of fatigue.) (Reproduced from the* British Journal of Psychology *by permission.)*

ures. The upper strip of the figure shows that a normal child, 11 to 12 years of age, manifested semantic but not phonetographic transfer—to the words *sobaka* [dog] and *zhivotnoye* [animal] but not to the words *okoshko* [window] and *kroshka* [crumb]. The upper middle strip of the figure shows that the transfer of a 16-year-old "mild oligophrenic" or "debile" child was both semantic and phonetographic— to both *sobaka* [dog] and *kroshka* [crumb]; while the lower middle strip shows that the transfer of a 16-year-old "imbecile" (greater degree of feeble-mindedness) was only phoneto-graphic—to *kryshka* [cover] and *kroshka* [crumb] but not to *sobaka* [dog]. The lowest strip of the figure demonstrates that a "17-year-old debile," who transferred his vascular reaction to *sobaka* [dog] but not to *kryshka* [cover] before his school day began, reversed the transfer—to *kryshka* but not to *sobaka*—after 6 hours of schoolwork. (Experimenters' figures not represented in the composite figure pertain to effects of context and of repetition of reinforcement.)

As in the preceding experiment, the data are not reported to have been treated statistically and, as indicated, records of only one subject of each of the three groups varying in intelligence —normal, "debile," and "imbecile"— are presented. Yet, it might be pointed out that the results on the relation of semantic conditioning to intelligence are quite in line with those of Riess (1946) on the relation of this conditioning to age, with some of my own studies, and with common sense; and that the results on the effects of fatigue are quite similar to those of the administration of chloral hydrate in the study by Shvarts (1954) discussed earlier. Moreover, the experiment is of special methodological significance in offering a simple way of studying semantic transfer without recourse to laboratory conditioning. A full report of this experiment and a comprehensive summary of the one preceding appeared in the May 1959 issue of the *British Journal of Psychology*.

VI. Thirty university students, 20 to 29 years of age, were conditioned to withdraw their fingers when they heard any of three short Russian sentences by combining each of the sentences with the administration of an electric shock to the subjects' fingers. The three sentences were: *Vklyuchayu tok* [I am switching on / the shock], *Rukopis' prochitana* [The manuscript / was read], and *Student vyderzhal ekzamen* [The student / passed / the examination]. (The diagonal bars in the parentheses mark off the equivalents of each Russian word.) After the withdrawal CRs to the sentences were stabilized, CR transfer to the separate words of each sentence was tested. It was found that in the first sentence each of the two words acquired 100 per cent transfer on the first trial; that in the second sentence neither word showed any immediate transfer; while in the third sentence, the word *vyderzhal* [passed] manifested transfer in 87 per cent of the cases, the word *ekzamen* in 50 per cent, and the word *student* in only 10 per cent of the tests. The experimenter attributes the results to differences in total sentential "meaning load" carried by the separate words of the respective sentences: that is to say, in the first sentence the total sentential meaning was implied in each of the two words, in the second it was implied in neither, while in the third the sentential meaning was differentially distributed among the three words (Elkin, 1955).

In a previously reported experiment the writer studied the semantic role of parts of speech in salivary conditioning (Razran, 1952). He used three five-word Russian sentences, the meaning of which the subjects learned pre-experimentally, and eight subjects, four of whom were conditioned to the sentences and tested with separate words, and four for whom the sequence was reversed. The sentences were:

Ona khocket kupit' serry koshelyok [She / wants / to buy / a gray / purse], *Belokuraya devochka nashla zolotoye pero* [The blond / girl / found / a gold / pen], and *Ya dal yemu novy myach* [I / gave / him / a new / ball]. As might be expected, the results of the three sentences did not fully correspond. Yet, they did indicate the preponderant semantic role of verbs and direct objects, the considerable role of infinitive complements, and the rather small role of subjects, indirect objects, and qualifying adjectives. Figure 7

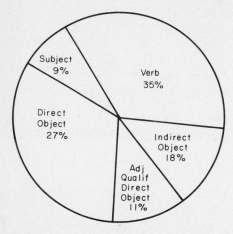

FIG. 7. *CR semantic analysis of "I gave him a new ball" and "Ya dal yemu novy myach." (Relative CR weights of individual syntactical units.)*

shows such an analysis for one sentence. No doubt many more sentences need to be thus conditioned and tested to settle the finding, the ruling out of differences due to lexical rather than to sentence-membership factors being a particularly laborious task.

Significance and Implications

The number of experiments on semantic conditioning is considerably smaller than that on interoceptive conditioning. Yet in a way these experiments uncover an area of even wider significance, a vast realm of experimentally separable meaning-units continually entering in complex functional relationships with each other and with nonmeaning-units, existing both in and out of consciousness, and normally, whether conscious or unconscious, forming controlling rather than controlled systems. Small wonder that the significance of semantic conditioning extends to such varied fields as: the psychology of thinking, ranging from the *unbewusste Bewusstseinslagen* of the Würtzburg school to modern views of cognition as a high level, controlling mechanism of which we may not be aware; Freud's symbolisms, secondary processes, and conscious-unconscious ego relations; cultural anthropology; clinical observations on aphasia and agnosia; practical problems in psychotherapy; general linguistics; general semantics; and such applications as education techniques and the psychology of advertising and of propaganda.

Unfortunately, space permits only a very brief and basic discussion of the topic. Moreover, it seems desirable to postpone the discussion until the topic of the orienting reflex will have been considered. Still, we might mention here that current Russian psychophysiology, quoting Pavlov, accords a *sui generis* status to verbal conditioning in general, regarding it as not merely a case of simple second-order conditioning but as a special higher level "signal-of-signals" CR basis of abstraction of high-level generalization. That a word is by its very nature an abstraction, a statement found in Pavlov's writings, is taken very seriously in both its genetic and its ontological aspects as a problem fit for both experimental analysis and clinical research.

REFERENCES

Elkin, D. G., "The Characteristics of Conditioned Reflexes to a Complex Verbal Stimulus," *Vop. Psikhol.*, **1** (4) (1955), 79-89.

Lacey, J. I. and R. L. Smith, "Conditioning and Generalization of Unconscious Anxiety," *Science*, 120 (1954), 1045-52.

Lacey, J. I., R. L. Smith, and A. Green, "The Use of Conditioned Autonomic Responses in the Study of Anxiety," *Psychosomatic Medicine*, **17** (1955), 208-17.

Luria, A. R. and O. S. Vinogradova, "An Objective Investigation of the Dynamics of Semantic Systems," *British Journal of Psychology*, **50** (1959), 89-105.

Markosyan, A. A., "Conditioned-Reflex Changes of Blood Coagulation," *Zh. vyssh. nervn. Deyatel.*, 3 (1953), 911-18.

———, "The Interaction of Signal Systems in the Process of Blood Coagulation," *Zh. vyssh. nervn. Deyatel.*, **8** (1958), 167-67.

Razran, G., "A Quantitative Study of Meaning by a Conditioned Salivary Technique (Semantic Conditioning)," *Science*, **90** (1939), 89-91.

———, "Attitudinal Determinants of Conditioning and of Generalization of Conditioning," *Journal of Experimental Psychology*, **39** (1949), 820-29. (a)

———, "Semantic and Phonetographic Generalizations of Salivary Conditioning to Verbal Stimuli," *Journal of Experimental Psychology*, **39** (1949), 642-52.

———, "Sentential and Propositional Generalizations of Salivary Conditioning to Verbal Stimuli," *Science*, **109** (1949), 447-48.

———, "Some Psychological Factors in the Generalization of Salivary Conditioning to Verbal Stimuli," *American Journal of Psychology*, **62** (1949), 247-56.

———, "Experimental Semantics," *Transactions of the New York Academy of Science*, **14** (1952), 171-77.

Riess, B. F., "Semantic Conditioning Involving the Galvanic Skin Reflex," *Journal of Experimental Psychology*, **26** (1940), 238-40.

———, "Genetic Changes in Semantic Conditioning," *Journal of Experimental Psychology*, **36** (1946), 143-52.

Shvarts, L. A., "The Problems of Words as Conditioned Stimuli," *Byull. eksp. (Biol. Med.)*, **38** (1954), 15-18.

———, "Conditioned Reflexes to Verbal Stimuli," *Vop. Psikhol.*, **6** (1) (1960), 86-98.

Vinogradova, O. S. and N. A. Eysler, "The Manifestations of Verbal Connections in Recording Vascular Reactions," *Vop. Psikhol.*, **2** (1959), 101-16.

Volkova, V. D., "On Certain Characteristics of the Formation of Conditioned Reflexes to Speech Stimuli in Children," *Fiziol. Zh. SSSR*, **39** (1953), 540-48.

PART THREE

INFORMATION PROCESSING
APPROACH TO COGNITION

An alternative to the S–R approach to cognition is that taken by Bruner and his co-workers. Although some psychologists (Goss, for example) have with difficulty attempted to integrate Bruner's approach with the S–R learning theory approach, it might well prove more fruitful to contrast the two approaches and emphasize differences. Bruner does not accept the assumption that learning or knowing is the same at all levels, that is, that principles applicable to the forming of associations between external stimuli and overt responses are equally relevant for associations at a cognitive or mediational level. Many of the learning theory principles, for example, reinforcement, are considered inadequate to account for cognitive activity of the kind studied by Bruner. His conceptualization does not include associations between stimuli and responses and the S–R paradigm in general.

The emphasis here is on stimulus inputs, which are better regarded as information, and the structuring of information into definite forms or models. Perception then is not distinguishable from other cognitions or thought processes. Central to such higher-level processes as perceiving, knowing, thinking, learning, and problem-solving, is the development of a symbolic model, structure, system of categories, or generic coding system which represents environmental information in an economical manner and which can be used, not only to order information, but also to transform it in such a manner that new information is generated.

In his article on perceptual readiness Bruner defines perception as an "act of categorizing." Thus perception "depends upon the construction of a set of organized categories in terms of which stimulus inputs may be sorted, given identity, and given more elaborated, connotative meaning." The problem of categorization is given considerable attention by Wallach in his article on psychological similarity. Bruner, Wallach, and Galanter discuss identification of "recurrent regularities in the environment" and the necessity of constructing models and strategies. A summary statement can be found in Bruner's article "On Going Beyond the Information Given." Here a number of examples are given showing how the development of a generic coding system can be used to go beyond the immediate information. It is as if a coding system or model, once constructed, achieves an autonomy (that is, is no longer stimulus-bound) that permits the generation of new information. This is, to say the least, an interesting alternative explanation for complex learning and problem-solving.

Bruner * has discussed the implications of his theory for educational practice. Quite logically he concludes that teaching should be concerned with the teaching of the structure of subject matter which will provide a model or coding system that the pupil can use to generate new information. Interestingly enough, the goal and process of education become identical.

Piaget's extensive investigations, a small portion of which are summarized by Berlyne, bear a kinship to that of Bruner and his co-workers. Here we have also a model, symbolic logic, that makes possible operations upon or transformation of information. Piaget's attention to developmental aspects is of significance for learning and teaching at the age levels suggested but must be treated cautiously. Additional research has not always replicated Piaget's findings successfully, but in spite of vastly changed (and often improved) methods, the basic outlines of his stages of cognitive development have been more often confirmed than not.

---

* Jerome S. Bruner, *The Process of Education* (Cambridge, Mass.: Harvard University Press, 1960).

On Perceptual Readiness *

Jerome S. Bruner

About ten years ago I was party to the publication of an innocent enough paper entitled "Value and Need as Organizing Factors in Perception." It was concerned with what at that time was the rather obscure problem of how extrastimulus factors influenced perception, a subject then of interest to only a small band of us—Gardner Murphy, Nevitt Sanford, Muzafer Sherif, and a few others. Obviously, Professor Boring is quite right about the mischievousness of the *Zeitgeist,* for the appearance of this paper seemed to coincide with all sorts of spirit-like rumblings within the world of psychology that were soon to erupt in a most unspirit-like torrent of research on this very topic—perhaps three hundred research reports and theoretical explications in the ten years since then. F. H. Allport (1) and M. D. Vernon (81) have each recently had a fresh look at the field, sorting out the findings and evaluating the theoretical positions, and they have done superb service. Their labors free me to pursue

a more relaxed course. What I should like to do in this paper is to set forth what seem to me to be the outlines of an approach to perception congruent with this body of new (and often contradictory) findings and to sketch out what appear to me to be the persistent problems still outstanding.

ON THE NATURE OF PERCEPTION

Perception involves an act of categorization. Put in terms of the antecedent and subsequent conditions from which we make our inferences, we stimulate an organism with some appropriate input and he responds by referring the input to some class of things or events. "That is an orange," he states, or he presses a lever that he has been "tuned" to press when the object that he "perceives" is an orange. On the basis of certain defining or criterial attributes in the input, which are usually called cues although they should be called clues (35), there is a selective placing of the input in one category of identity rather than another. The category need not be elaborate: "a sound," "a touch," "a pain," are also examples of categorized inputs. The use of cues in inferring the categorial identity of a perceived object, most recently treated by Bruner, Goodnow, and Austin (9) and by Binder (4), is as much a feature of perception as the sensory stuff from which percepts are made. What is interesting about the nature of the inference from

* From J. S. Bruner, "On Perceptual Readiness," *Psychological Review,* 64 (1957), 123-52. Reprinted by permission of the author and the American Psychological Association.

The present paper was prepared with the invaluable assistance of Mr. Michael Wallach. I also benefited from the comments of Professors W. C. H. Prentice, Karl Pribram, and M. E. Bitterman, and from various associates at Princeton University, Kansas University, and the University of Michigan, where versions of this paper were presented.

cue to identity in perception is that it is in no sense different from other kinds of categorial inferences based on defining attributes. "That thing is round and nubbly in texture and orange in color and of such-and-such size—therefore an orange; let me now test its other properties to be sure." In terms of process, this course of events is no different from the more abstract task of looking at a number, determining that it is divisible only by itself and unity, and thereupon categorizing it in the class of prime numbers. So at the outset, it is evident that one of the principal characteristics of perceiving is a characteristic of cognition generally. There is no reason to assume that the laws governing inferences of this kind are discontinuous as one moves from perceptual to more conceptual activities. In no sense need the process be conscious or deliberate. A theory of perception, we assert, needs a mechanism capable of inference and categorizing as much as one is needed in a theory of cognition.

Let it be plain that no claim is being made for the utter indistinguishability of perceptual and more conceptual inferences. In the first place, the former appear to be notably less docile or reversible than the latter. I may know that the Ames distorted room that looks so rectangular is indeed distorted, but unless conflicting cues are put into the situation, as in experiments to be discussed later, the room still looks rectangular. So too with such compelling illusions as the Miller-Lyer: in spite of knowledge to the contrary, the line with the extended arrowheads looks longer than the equal-length one with those inclined inward. But these differences, interesting in themselves, must not lead us to overlook the common feature of inference underlying so much of cognitive activity.

Is what we have said a denial of the classic doctrine of sense-data? Surely, one may argue (and Hebb [36] has done so effectively) that there must be certain forms of primitive organization within the perceptual field that make possible the differential use of cues in identity categorizing. Both logically and psychologically, the point is evident. Yet it seems to me foolish and unnecessary to assume that the sensory "stuff" on which high-order categorizations are based is, if you will, of a different sensory order than more evolved identities with which our perceptual world is normally peopled. To argue otherwise is to be forced into the contradictions of Locke's distinction between primary and secondary qualities in perception. The rather bold assumption that we shall make at the outset is that all perceptual experience is necessarily the end product of a categorization process.

And this for two reasons. The first is that all perception is generic in the sense that whatever is perceived is placed in and achieves its "meaning" from a class of percepts with which it is grouped. To be sure, in each thing we encounter, there is an aspect of uniqueness, but the uniqueness inheres in deviation from the class to which an object is "assigned." Analytically, let it be noted, one may make a distinction, as Gestalt theorists have, between a pure stimulus process and the interaction of that stimulus process with an appropriate memory trace— the latter presumably resulting in a percept that has an identity. If indeed there is a "pure stimulus process," it is doubtful indeed that it is ever represented in perception bereft of identity characteristics. The phenomenon of a completely unplaceable object or event or "sensation"—even unplaceable with respect to modality—is sufficiently far from experience to be uncanny. Categorization of an object or event—

placing it or giving it identity—can be likened to what in set theory is the placement of an element from a universe in a subset of that universe of items on the basis of such ordered dimensional pairs, triples, or n-tuples as man-woman, mesomorph-endomorph-ectomorph, or height to nearest inch. In short, when one specifies something more than that an element or object belongs to a universe, and that it belongs in a subset of the universe, one has categorized the element or object. The categorization can be as intersecting as "this is a quartz crystal goblet fashioned in Denmark," or as simple as "this is a glassy thing." So long as an operation assigns an input to a subset, it is an act of categorization.

More serious, although it is "only a logical issue," is the question of how one could communicate or make public the presence of a nongeneric or completely unique perceptual experience. Neither language nor the tuning that one could give an organism to direct any other form of overt response could provide an account, save in generic or categorial terms. If perceptual experience is ever had raw, that is, free of categorial identity, it is doomed to be a gem serene, locked in the silence of private experience.

Various writers, among them Gibson (26), Wallach (83), and Pratt (66), have proposed that we make a sharp distinction between the class of perceptual phenomena that have to do with the identity or object-meaning of things and the attributive or sensory world from which we derive our cues for inferring identities. Gibson, like Titchener (78) before him, urges a distinction between the visual field and the visual world, the former the world of attributive sense impressions, the latter of objects and things and events. Pratt urges that motivation and set and past experience may affect the things of the visual world but not the stuff of the visual field. And Wallach too reflects this ancient tradition of his Gestalt forebears by urging the distinction between a stimulus process pure and the stimulus process interacting with a memory trace of past experience with which it has made a neural contact on the basis of similarity. The former is the stuff of perception; the latter the fiinished percept. From shirtsleeves to shirtsleeves in three generations: we are back with the founding and founded content of the pre-Gestalt Gestalters. If one is to study the visual field freed of the things of the visual world, it becomes necessary—as Wallach implies—to free oneself of the stimulus error: dealing with a percept not as an object or as a thing with identity, but as a magnitude or a brightness or a hue or a shape to be matched against a variable test patch.

If we have implied that categorizing is often a "silent" or unconscious process, that we do not experience a going-from-no-identity to an arrival-at-identity, but that the first hallmark of *any* perception is some form of identity, this does not free us of the responsibility of inquiring into the origin of categories. Certainly, Hebb (36) is correct in asserting like Immanuel Kant, that certain primitive unities or identities within perception must be innate or autochthonous and not learned. The primitive capacity to categorize "things" from "background" is very likely one such, and so too the capacity to distinguish events in one modality from those in others—although the phenomena of synesthesia would suggest that this is not so complete a juncture as it might seem; for example, von Hornbostel (39). The sound of a buzz saw does rise and fall phenomenally ˀs one switches room illumination on and off. The full repertory of innate categories—a favorite topic for philosophical debate in the 19th century—is a topic on which perhaps much ink and too little empirical effort have been spilled. Motion, causation, intention, identity, equivalence, time, and space, it may be persuasively argued, are categories that must have some primitive counterpart in the neonate. And it may well be, as Piaget (65) implies, that certain primitive capacities to categorize in particular ways depend upon the existence of still more primitive ones. To identify something as having "caused" something else requires, first, the existence of an identity category such that the two things involved each may conserve identity in the process of "cause" producing "effect." Primitive or unlearned categories —a matter of much concern to such students of instinctive behavior as Lashley (51) and Tinbergen (77)— remain to be explicated. In what follows, we shall rather cavalierly take them for granted. As to the development of more elaborated categories in terms of which objects are placed or identified, it involves the process of learning how to isolate, weigh, and use criterial attribute values, or cues for grouping objects in equivalence classes. It is only as mysterious, but no more so, than the learning of any differential discrimination, and we shall have occasion to revisit the problem later.

A second feature of perception, beyond its seemingly categorial and inferential nature, is that it can be described as varyingly veridical. This is what has classically been called the "representative function" of perception: what is perceived is somehow a representation of the external world —a metaphysical hodgepodge of a statement but one which we somehow manage to understand in spite of its confusion. We have long since given

up simulacral theories of representation. What we generally mean when we speak of representation or veridicality is that perception is predictive in varying degrees. That is to say, the object that we *see* can also be *felt* and *smelled* and there will somehow be a match or a congruity between what we see, feel, and smell. Or, to paraphrase a younger Bertrand Russell, what we see will turn out to be the same thing should we take a "closer look" at it. Or, in still different terms, the categorial placement of the object leads to appropriate consequences in terms of later behavior directed toward the perceived object: it appears as an apple, and indeed it keeps the doctor away if consumed once a day.

Let it be said that philosophers, and notably the pragmatist C. S. Peirce, have been urging such a view for more years than psychologists have taken their urgings seriously. The meaning of a proposition, as Peirce noted in his famous essay on the pragmatic theory of meaning (63), is the set of hypothetical statements one can make about attributes or consequences related to that proposition. "Let us ask what we mean by calling a thing *hard*. Evidently, that it will not be scratched by many other substances" (White, [84]). The meaning of a thing, thus, is the placement of an object in a network of hypothetical inference concerning its other observable properties, its effects, and so on.

All of this suggests, does it not, that veridicality is not so much a matter of representation as it is a matter of what I shall call "model building." In learning to perceive, we are learning the relations that exist between the properties of objects and events that we encounter, learning appropriate categories and category systems, *learning to predict and to check what goes with what*. A simple example illustrates the point. I present for tachistoscopic recognition two nonsense words, one a 0-order approximation to English constructed according to Shannon's rules, the other a 4-order approximation: YRULPZOC and VERNALIT. At 500 milliseconds of exposure, one perceives correctly and in their proper place about 48 percent of the letters in 0-order words, and about 93 percent of the letters in 4-order words. In terms of the amount of information transmitted by these letter arrays, that is, correcting them for redundancy, the subject is actually receiving the same informational input. The difference in reportable perception is a function of the fact that the individual has learned the transitional probability model of what goes with what in English writing. We say that perception in one case is more "veridical" than in the other—the difference between 93 percent correct as contrasted with 48 percent. What we mean is that the model of English with which the individual is working corresponds to the actual events that occur in English, and that if the stimulus input does not conform to the model, the resulting perception will be less veridical. Now let us drop the image of the model and adopt a more sensible terminology. Perceiving accurately under substandard conditions consists in being able to refer stimulus inputs to appropriate coding systems; where the information is fragmentary, one reads the missing properties of the stimulus input from the code to which part of the input has been referred. If the coding system applied does not match the input, what we read off from the coding system will lead to error and nonveridical perception. I would propose that perceptual learning consists not of making finer and finer discriminations as the Gibsons (27) would have us believe, but that it consists rather in the learn-ing of appropriate modes of coding the environment in terms of its object character, connectedness, or redundancy, and then in allocating stimulus inputs to appropriate categorial coding systems.

The reader will properly ask, as Prentice (67) has, whether the notion of perceptual representation set forth here is appropriate to anything other than situations where the nature of the percept is not "clear"—perceptual representation under peripheral viewing conditions, in tachistoscopes, under extreme fatigue. If I am given a very good look at an object, under full illumination and with all the viewing time necessary, and end by calling it an orange, is this a different process from one in which the same object is flashed for a millisecond or two on the periphery of my retina with poor illumination? In the first and quite rare case the cues permitting the identification of the object are super-abundant and the inferential mechanism operates with high probability relationships between cues and identities. In the latter, it is less so. The difference is of degree. What I am trying to say is that under *any* conditions of perception, what is achieved by the perceiver is the categorization of an object or sensory event in terms of more *or* less abundant and reliable cues. Representation consists of knowing how to utilize cues with reference to a system of categories. It also depends upon the creation of a system of categories-in-relationship that fit the nature of the world in which the person must live. In fine, adequate perceptual representation involves the learning of appropriate categories, the learning of cues useful in placing objects appropriately in such systems of categories, and the learning of what objects are likely to occur in the environment, a matter to which we will turn later in the course of study.

We have neglected one important feature of perceptual representation in our discussion: representation in perception of the space-time-intensity conditions of the external world. Perceptual magnitudes correspond in some degree to the metrical properties of the physical world that we infer from the nature of our perception. That is to say, when one line *looks* longer than another, it is likely to *be* longer as measured by the ruler. There are constant errors and sampling errors in such sensory representation, but on the whole there is enough isomorphism between perceiving without aids (psychology) and perceiving with aids (physics) to make the matter perennially interesting.

Is this form of representation subject to the kinds of considerations we have been passing in review? Does it depend upon categorizing activities and upon the construction of an adequate system of categories against which stimulus inputs can be matched? There is probably one condition where perceptual acts are relatively free of such influences, and that is in the task of discriminating simultaneously presented stimuli as alike or different— provided we do not count the "tuning of the organism" that leads one to base his judgment on one rather than another feature of the two stimuli. Ask the person to deal with one stimulus at a time, to array it in terms of some magnitude scale, and immediately one is back in the familiar territory of inferential categorizing. Prentice, in his able defense of formalism in the study of perception (67), seems to assume that there is a special status attached to perceptual research that limits the set of the observer to simple binary decisions of "like" and "different" or "present" and "absent," and to research that also provides the subject with

optimal stimulus conditions, and Graham (31) has recently expressed the credo that no perceptual laws will be proper or pure laws unless we reduce perceptual experimentation to the kinds of operations used in the method of constant stimuli.

There was at one time a justification for such a claim on the grounds that such is the best strategy for getting at the sensory-physiological processes that underlie perception. As we shall see in a later section, current work in neurophysiology brings this contention into serious doubt. In any case, the point must be made that many of the most interesting phenomena in sensory perception are precisely those that have been uncovered by departing from the rigid purism of the method of constants. I have in mind such pioneering studies as those of Stevens on sensory scales, where the organism is treated as an instrument whose sensory categorizations and scalar orderings are the specific object of study (74). Add to this the advances made by Helson on adaptation level (37) and by Volkmann on the anchoring of sensory scales (82)—both using the "sloppy" method of single stimuli —and one realizes that the nature of representation in perception of magnitudes is very much subject to categorizing processes, and to perceptual readiness as this is affected by subjective estimates of the likelihood of occurrence of sensory events of different magnitudes. Indeed, Helson's law of adaptation level states that the subjective magnitude of a singly presented stimulus depends upon the weighted geometric mean of the series of stimuli that the subject has worked with, and the ingenious experiments of Donald Brown (7) have indicated that this adaptation level is influenced only by those stimuli that the subject considers to be within the category of objects being considered. Ask the subject to move a weight from one side of the table to the other with the excuse that it is cluttering up the table, and the weight does not serve as an anchor to the series, although it will show a discernible effect if it is directly included in the series being judged. In short, the category systems that are utilized in arraying magnitudes are also affected by the requirement of matching one's model of the world to the actual events that are occurring—even if the categories be no more complicated than "heavy," "medium," and "light."

The recent work of Stevens (75) on "the direct estimation of sensory magnitudes" highlights the manner in which veridicality in sensory judgment depends upon the prior learning of an adequate category set in terms of which sensory input may be ordered. Subjects are presented a standard tone of 1000 cps at 80 db sound-pressure-level and are told that the value of this loudness is 10. Nine variable loudnesses all of the 1000 cps are then presented, varying 70 db on either side of the standard, each one at a time being paired with the standard. "If the standard is called 10, what would you call the variable? Use whatever numbers seem to you appropriate—fractions, decimals, or whole numbers." If one then compares the categorial judgments made with the sound pressure level of the various tones presented, using a log-log plot (log of the magnitude estimation against log of sound-pressure-level), the resulting function is a straight line, described by the empirical formula

$$L = kI^{0.3},$$

where L is loudness and I intensity. In short, categorial sorting of sensory magnitudes provides one with a mapping or representation of physical intensity. There are, to be sure, many problems connected with such a procedure, but the point remains: the magnitude categories in terms of which we scale sensory events represent a good fit to the physical characteristics of the world. Call this "veridicality" if you wish—although I do not see what is gained thereby; yet whatever one calls it, one must not lose sight of the fact that the judgments made are predictive of other features of the sensory inputs. Given the empirical conversion formula, one can predict from categorial judgment to physical meter readings.

To summarize, we have proposed that perception is a process of categorization in which organisms move inferentially from cues to categorial identity and that in many cases, as Helmholtz long ago suggested, the process is a silent one. If you will, the inference is often an "unconscious" one. Moreover, the results of such categorizations are representational in nature: they represent with varying degrees of predictive veridicality the nature of the physical world in which the organism operates. By predictive veridicality I mean simply that perceptual categorization of an object or event permits one to "go beyond" the properties of the object or event perceived to a prediction of other properties of the object not yet tested. The more adequate the category systems constructed for coding environmental events in this way, the greater the predictive veridicality that results.

Doubtless, the reader will think of any number of examples of perceptual phenomena not covered by the simple picture we have drawn. Yet a great many of the classic phenomena are covered—psychophysical judgment, constancy, perceptual identification, perceptual learning, and so on. This will become clearer in the following sections. What must now be dealt with are the phenomena having to do with selectivity: attention, set, and the like.

CUE UTILIZATION
AND CATEGORY ACCESSIBILITY

A fruitful way of thinking of the nature of perceptual readiness is in terms of the accessibility of categories for use in coding or identifying environmental events. Accessibility is a heuristic concept, and it may be defined in terms of a set of measures. Conceive of a person who is perceptually ready to encounter a certain object—an apple, let us say. *How* he happens to be in this state we shall consider later. We measure the accessibility of the category "apples" by the amount of stimulus input of a certain pattern necessary to evoke the perceptual response "there is an apple," or some other standardized response. We can state the "minimum" input required for such categorization by having our observer operate with two response categories, "yes" and "no," with the likelihood of occurrence of apples and nonapples at 50:50, or by using any other definition of "maximum readiness" that one wishes to employ. The greater the accessibility of a category, (*a*) the less the input necessary for categorization to occur in terms of this category, (*b*) the wider the range of input characteristics that will be "accepted" as fitting the category in question, (*c*) the more likely that categories that provide a better or equally good fit for the input will be masked. To put it in more ordinary language: apples will be more easily and swiftly recognized, a wider range of things will be identified or mis-identified as apples, and in consequence the correct or best fitting identity of these other inputs will be masked. This is what is

intended by accessibility.

Obviously, categories are not isolated. One has a category "apples," to be sure, but it is imbedded by past learning in a network of categories: "An apple a day keeps the doctor away" is one such category system. So too, are "apples are fruits" and other placements of an object in a general classification scheme. Predictive systems are of the same order: for example, "The apple will rot if not refrigerated." We have spoken of these systems before as the "meaning" of an object. We mention them again here to indicate that though we speak analytically of separate or isolated categories as being accessible to inputs, it is quite obvious that category systems vary in accessibility as a whole.

It follows from what has just been said that the most appropriate pattern of readiness at any given moment would be that one which would lead on the average to the most "veridical" guess about the nature of the world around one at the moment—best guess here being construed, of course, as a response in the absence of the necessary stimulus input. And it follows from this that the most ready perceiver would then have the best chances of estimating situations most adequately and planning accordingly. It is in this general sense that the ready perceiver who can proceed with fairly minimal inputs is also in a position to use his cognitive readiness not only for perceiving what is before him but in foreseeing what is likely to be before him. We shall return to this point shortly.

We must turn now to the question of cue utilization, the "strategies" in terms of which inferences are made (by the nervous system, of course) from cue to category and thence to other cues. I prefer to use the term strategy for several reasons. Perceiving, since it involves inference, rests upon a decision process, as Brunswick (17), Tanner and Swets (76) and others have pointed out. Even in the simplest threshold-measurement test, the subject has the task of deciding whether what he is seeing or hearing is noise only or signal-plus-noise. Given a set of cues, however presented, my nervous system must "decide" whether the thing is an airplane or a sea gull, a red or a green, or what not.

There appears, moreover, to be a sequence of such decisions involved in categorizing an object or event. A common-sense example will make this clear. I look across to the mantelpiece opposite my desk and see a rectangular object lying on it. If I continue this pursuit, subsequent decisions are to be made: is it the block of plastic I purchased for some apparatus or is it a book? In the dim light it can be either. I remember that the plastic is downstairs in one of the experimental rooms: the object "is" a book now, and I search for further cues on its dark red surface. I see what I think is some gold: it is a McGraw-Hill book, probably G. A. Miller's *Language and Communication* that I had been using late this afternoon. If you will, the process is a "bracketing" one, a gradual narrowing of the category placement of the object.

Let us attempt to analyze the various stages in such a decision sequence.

PRIMITIVE CATEGORIZATION. Before any more elaborate inferential activity can occur, there must be a first, "silent" process that results in the perceptual isolation of an object or an event with certain characteristic qualities. Whether this is an innate process or one depending upon the prior construction of a cell-assembly, in the manner of Hebb (36), need not concern us. What is required simply is that an environmental event has been perceptually isolated and that the event is marked by certain spatio-temporal-qualitative characteristics. The event may have no more "meaning" than that it is an "object," a "sound," or a "movement."

CUE SEARCH. In highly practiced cases or in cases of high cue-category probability linkage, a second process of more precise placement based on additional cues may be equally silent or "unconscious." An object is seen with phenomenal immediacy as a "book" or an "ash tray." In such instances there is usually a good fit between the specifications of a category and the nature of the cues impinging on the organism —although "fit" and "probability of linkage" may stand in a vicarious relation to each other. Where the fit to accessible categories is not precise, or when the linkage between cue and category is low in probability in the past experience of the organism, the conscious experience of cue searching occurs. "What is that thing?" Here, one is scanning the environment for data in order to find cues that permit a more precise placement of the object. Under these circumstances, the organism is "open" to maximum stimulation, in a manner described below.

CONFIRMATION CHECK. When a tentative categorization has occurred, following cue search, cue search changes. The "openness" to stimulation decreases sharply in the sense that now, a tentative placement of identity having occurred, the search is narrowed for additional confirmatory cues to check this placement. It is this feature of perceptual identification that Woodworth (85) in his paper on the "Reenforcement of Perception" speaks of as "trial-and-check." We shall speak of a selective gating process coming into operation in this stage, having the effect of reducing the effective input of stimulation not relevant to the confirmatory process.

CONFIRMATION COMPLETION. The

last stage in the process of perceptual identification is a completion, marked by termination of cue searching. It is characteristic of this state that openness to additional cues is drastically reduced, and incongruent cues are either normalized or "gated out." Experiments on the perception of incongruity (14), error (69), and the like (15), suggest that once an object has been categorized in a high-probability, good-fit category, the threshold for recognizing cues contrary to this categorization increases by almost an order of magnitude.

The question of fit between cue and category specification brings us to the key problem of the nature of categories. By a category we mean a rule for classing objects as equivalent. The rule specifies the following about the instances that are to be comprised in the category.

a. The properties or *criterial attribute values* required of an instance to be coded in a given class.

b. The manner in which such attribute values are to be combined in making an inference from properties to category membership: whether conjunctively (for example, a_i *and* b_i), relationally (for example, a_i bears a certain *relation* to b_i), or disjunctively (for example, a_i *or* b_i).

c. The weight assigned various properties in making an inference from properties to category membership.

d. The acceptance limits within which properties must fall to be criterial. That is to say, from what range of attribute values may a_i, b_i . . . k_i be drawn.

When we speak of rules, again it should be made clear that "conscious rules" are not intended. These are the rules that govern the operation of a categorizing mechanism.

The likelihood that a sensory input will be categorized in terms of a given category is not only a matter of fit between sensory input and category specifications. It depends also on the accessibility of a category. To put the matter in an oversimplified way, given a sensory input with equally good fit to two nonoverlapping categories, the more accessible of the two categories would "capture" the input. It is in this sense that mention was earlier made about the vicarious relationship between fit and accessibility.

We have already noted that the accessibility of categories reflects the learned probabilities of occurrence of events in the person's world. The more frequently in a given context instances of a given category occur, the greater the accessibility of the category. Operationally, this means that less stimulus input will be required for the instance or event to be categorized in terms of a frequently used category. In general, the type of probability we are referring to is not absolute probability of occurrence, where each event that occurs is independent of each other. Such independence is rare in the environment. Rather, the principal form of probability learning affecting category accessibility is the learning of contingent or transitional probabilities—the redundant structure of the environment. That either the absolute or the contingent probability of events makes a crucial difference in determining ease of perceptual identification is readily supported by research findings: in the former case by studies like those of Howes (40) and Solomon and Postman (72), and in the latter by the work of Miller, Heise, and Lichten (62) and Miller, Bruner, and Postman (61).

But the organism to operate adequately must not only be ready for likely events in the environment, the better to represent them, and in order to perceive them quickly and without undue cognitive strain: it must also be able to search out unlikely objects and events essential to its maintenance and the pursuit of its enterprises. If I am walking the streets of a strange city and find myself hungry, I must be able to look for restaurants regardless of their likelihood of occurrence in the environment where I now find myself. In short, the accessibility of categories I employ for identifying the objects of the world around me must not only reflect the environmental probabilities of objects that fit these categories but must also reflect the search requirements imposed by my needs, my ongoing activities, my defenses, etc. And for effective search behavior to occur, the pattern of perceptual readiness during search must be realistic: tempered by what one is likely to find in one's perceptual world at that time and at that place as well as by what one seeks to find.

Let me summarize our considerations about the general properties of perception with a few propositions. The first is that *perception is a decision process*. Whatever the nature of the task set, the perceiver or his nervous system decides that a thing perceived is one thing and not another. A line is longer or shorter than a standard, a particular object is a snake and not a fallen branch, the incomplete word L*VE in the context MEN L*VE WOMEN is the word LOVE and not LIVE.

The second proposition is that *the decision process involves the utilization of discriminatory cues,* as do all decision processes. That is to say, the properties of stimulus inputs make it possible to sort these inputs into categories of best fit.

Thirdly, *the cue utilization process involves the operation of inference.* Going from cue to an inference of identity is probably the most ubiquitous and primitive cognitive activity. The utilization of inference presupposes the learning of environmental probabilities and invariances relating cues to cues, and cues to behavioral consequences. Cue utilization involves various stages: a primitive step of isolating an object or event from the flux of environmental stimulation, stages of cue searching where the task is to find cues that can be fitted to available category specifications, a tentative categorization with more search for confirming cues, and final categorization, when cue searching is severely reduced.

Fourth, *a category may be regarded as a set of specifications* regarding what events will be grouped as equivalent—rules respecting the nature of criterial cues required, the manner of their combining, their inferential weight, and the acceptance limits of their variability.

Fifth, *categories vary in terms of their accessibility,* the readiness with which a stimulus input with given properties will be coded or identified in terms of a category. The relative accessibility of categories and systems of categories seems to depend upon two factors: the expectancies of the person with regard to the likelihood of events to be encountered in the environment; and the search requirements imposed on the organism by his needs and his ongoing enterprises. To use the functionalist's language, perceptual readiness or accessibility serves two functions: *to minimize the surprise value of the environment* by matching category accessibility to the probabilities of events in the world about one, and *to maximize the attainment of sought-after objects and events.*

Veridical perception, so our sixth proposition would run, *consists of the coding of stimulus inputs in appropriate categories* such that one may go from cue to categorial identification, and thence to the correct inference or prediction of other properties of the object so categorized. Thus, veridical perception requires the learning of categories and category systems appropriate to the events and objects with which the person has commerce in the physical world. When we speak of the representative function of perception, we speak of the adequacy of the categorizing system of the individual in permitting him to infer the nature of events and to go beyond them to the correct prediction of other events.

Seventh, *under less than optimal conditions, perception will be veridical in the degree to which the accessibility of categorizing systems reflects the likelihood of ocurrence of the events that the person will encounter.* Where accessibility of categories reflects environmental probabilities, the organism is in the position of requiring less stimulus input, less redundancy of cues for the appropriate categorization of objects. In like vein, nonveridical perception will be systematic rather than random in its error insofar as it reflects the inappropriate readiness of the perceiver. The more inappropriate the readiness, the greater the input or redundancy of cues required for appropriate categorization to occur— where "appropriate" means that an input is coded in the category that yields more adequate subsequent predictions.

MECHANISMS MEDIATING PERCEPTUAL READINESS

Having considered some of the most general characteristics of perceiving, particularly as these relate to the phenomena of perceptual readiness, we must turn next to a consideration of the kinds of mechanisms that mediate

such phenomena. Four general types of mechanisms will be proposed: *grouping and integration, access ordering, match-mismatch signaling, and gating.* They will be described in such a form that they may be considered as prototypes of neural mechanisms and, where possible, neurophysiological counterparts will be described briefly. Six years ago, Edward Tolman (79) proposed that the time was perhaps ripe for reconsidering the neural substrate of perception. Perhaps he was right, or perhaps even now the enterprise is somewhat premature. Yet, the body of perceptual data available makes it worth while to consider the kinds of mechanisms that will be required to deal with them. To use Hebb's engaging metaphor, it is worth while to build a bridge between neurophysiology and psychology provided we are anchored at both ends, even if the middle of the bridge is very shaky.

Grouping and Integration

It is with the neural basis of the categorizing process that Hebb's *Organization of Behavior* (36) is principally concerned. Little is served by recapitulating his proposals here, for the reader will be familiar with the concise account in Chapters 4 and 5 of that book, where the concepts of cell-assembly and phase sequence are set forth with a clarity that permits one to distinguish what is neurophysiological fact and what speculation. In essence, Hebb's account attempts to provide an anatomical-physiological theory of how it is that we distinguish classes of events in the environment, and how we come to recognize new events as exemplars of the once established classes. The theory seeks also to provide a mechanism for integration of sorting activity over time: the formation of phase sequences for the conservation of superordinate classes of events and superordinate sequences. Basically, it is an associational or an "enrichment" theory of perception at the neural level, requiring that established neural associations facilitate perception of events that have gone together before. The expectancies, the centrally induced facilitations that occur prior to the sensory process for which they are appropriate, are learned expectancies based on the existence of frequency integrators. These frequency integrators may be neuroanatomical in the form of synaptic knobs, or they may be any process that has the effect of making activity in one locus of the brain increase or decrease the likelihood of activity in another. To be sure, Hebb's theory depends upon some broad assumptions about convergence of firing from area 17 outward, about synchronization of impulses, and about the manner in which reverberatory circuits can carry organization until the much slower process of anatomical change can take place. But this is minor in comparison with the stimulation provided by facing squarely the question of how the known facts of categorization and superordination in perception *could* be represented in the light of present knowledge.

While it is difficult indeed to propose a plausible neural mediator to account for category formation and the development of elaborated categorial systems (for example, our knowledge of the relations between classes of events in the physical world which we manipulate in everyday life), it is less difficult to specify what such mechanisms must account for in perceptual behavior.

At the level of the individual category or cell-assembly, the phenomena of object identity must be accounted for. Moreover, identity conservation or object constancy requires explanation in terms common with the explanation of identity. Experiments by Piaget (65) suggest that the capacity to maintain the phenomenal identity of an object undergoing change is the hard-won result of maturation-and-learning. In connection with the later discussion of gating processes, we shall have occasion to consider the manner in which, at different stages in cue utilization, the required fit between an input and a cell-assembly changes.

Where integration is concerned, there must be a process capable of conserving a record of the likely transitions and contingencies of the environment. The moment-to-moment programming of perceptual readiness depends upon such integrations. In short, the relation between classes of events is conserved in such a way as to be subject to change by learning. Several things can be guessed about integration processes. It is unlikely that it is a simple autocorrelation device. Clearly, the conceptions of transitional probabilities that are established in dealing with sequences of events show biases that no self-respecting autocorrelation computer would be likely to operate with. One of these is a strong and early tendency to treat events as nonindependent of each other over time. In the absence of evidence, or even in the presence of contrary evidence, humans—as their behavior has been observed in choice tasks, for example, Estes (23), Goodnow (29)—treat random sequences of events as though they were governed by dependent probabilities. The spate of research on two-choice decision behavior has made us quite sharply aware of this characteristic of cognitive functioning. The typical pattern is the gambler's fallacy or, more properly, the negative recency effect. Given two equiprobable events whose occurrences are random, the repetition of one event progressively leads to the expectancy of the other. As in the elegant experiments of Jarvik (44) and Goodnow (29), the probability that a person will predict one of two events increases directly as a function of the number of repetitions of the other event. Such behavior persists over thousands of opportunities for testing, and it appears under a variety of testing conditions (9).

The second feature of sequential probability integration mechanisms is that, in establishing a conception of the probability with which events will occur, the typical human subject will bias his estimate in terms of desired or feared outcomes. As in the experiments of Marks (60) on children and of Irwin (41) on adults, the subjectively estimated probability of strongly desired events will be higher per previous encountered occurrence than the estimated likelihood of less desired events. Quite clearly, then, the establishment of estimates depends upon more than frequency integrations biased by assumptions of nonindependence. The "something more" is a motivational or personality process, and we shall have more to say about it in considering phenomena of so-called "perceptual sensitization" and "perceptual defense."

Access Ordering

The term "accessibility" has been used in preceding pages to denote the *ease* or speed with which a given stimulus input is coded in terms of a given category under varying conditions of instruction, past learning, motivation, etc. It has been suggested, moreover, that two general sets of conditions affect accessibility: subjective probability estimates of the likelihood of a given event, and certain kinds of search sets induced by needs and by a variety of other factors.

Let us consider a few relevant facts about perception. The first of these is that the threshold of recognition for stimuli presented by visual, auditory, or other means is not only a function of the time, intensity, or "fittingness" of the stimulus input, but also varies massively as a function of the number of alternatives for which the perceiver is set. The size of the expected array, to say it another way, increases the identification threshold for any item in the array. Typical examples of this general finding are contained in papers by Miller, Heise, and Lichten (62) and by Bruner, Miller, and Zimmerman (10). The actual shape of the function need not concern us, save that it is quite clear that it is not what one would expect from a simple binary system with a fixed channel capacity. What we are saying holds, of course, only for the case where the perceiver has learned that all the items in the expected array are (*a*) equiprobable and (*b*) independent, one of the other, in order of appearance.

The first hunch we may propose, then, about access-ordering mechanisms is that degree of accessibilty of coding categories to stimulus inputs is related to regulation of the number of preactivated cell-assemblies that are operative at the time of input. In an earlier paper (8), discussing factors that strengthen an hypothesis in the sense of making it more easily confirmable, I proposed that one of the major determinants of such strength was monopoly: where one and only one hypothesis is operative with no competing alternatives, it tends to be more readily confirmable. It is the same general point that is being made here. Accessibility, then, must have something to do with the resolution of competing alternatives.

As between two arrays of expected alternatives, each of the same size, we may distinguish between them in terms of the bias that exists in terms of expected likelihood of occurrence of each alternative. If one could characterize the expected alternatives in terms of probability values, one could conceive of the array ranging in values from a figure approaching 1.0 at one extreme, to another approaching 0.0 at the other. The findings with respect to perceptual readiness for the alternatives represented in such an array are well known. For a constant-sized array, the greater the estimated likelihood of occurrence of an alternative, the more readily will the alternative be perceived or identified. This is known to be true for large arrays, such as the ensemble of known words in the English language, whose likelihood may be roughly judged by their frequency of occurrence in printed English (for example, 40). It is not altogether clear that it is the case for arrays of expected alternatives that are within the so-called span of attention—that is, less than seven or eight alternatives. That the principle holds for middling arrays of about twenty items has been shown by Solomon and Postman (72).

What is particularly interesting about change of accessibility, under conditions where estimates of the likelihood of occurrence of alternatives become biased, is that the biasing can be produced either by a gradual learning process akin to probability learning *or* by instruction. Thus, Bitterman and Kniffin (5), investigating recognition thresholds for taboo and neutral words, show that as the experiment progresses, there is a gradual lowering of threshold for the taboo words as the subject comes to expect their occurrence. Bruner and Postman (14) have similarly shown that repeated presentation of stimulus materials containing very low-probability incongruities leads to a marked decrease in threshold time required for recognizing the incongruous features. At the same time, both Cowen and Bier (20) and Postman and Crutchfield (70) have shown that if a subject is forewarned that taboo words are going to be presented, his threshold for them will tend to be lower than for neutral words, whereas it will be higher if no instruction is given. In short, preactivation of cell-assemblies—assuming for a moment that *degree of preactivation* is the mechanism that represents subjective estimates of likelihood of occurrence of an event—such preactivation can be produced by gradual learning or quantally by instruction. Moreover, biasing may be produced by the nature of the situation in which the perceiver is operating. A recent study by Bruner and Minturn (11) illustrates the point. Subjects are presented at brief exposure a broken capital B with a small separation between the vertical and the curved component of the letter so that it may be perceived as a B or as a 13. The manner in which it is reported is determined by whether the subject has previously been presented with letters or with numbers to recognize. In short, expectancy of one or the other context preactivates a related array of categories or cell-assemblies, not just a single, isolated one.

What the neural correlates of access ordering will look like is anybody's guess. Lashley (52) has remarked that, for all our searching, we have not located a specific memory trace—either in the form of a reverberatory circuit, a definite change in fiber size as proposed by J. Z. Young (88) and Eccles (21), a synaptic knob—in the manner of Lorente de No (57) or in any known form. To be sure, Penfield (64) has activated memories by punctate electrical stimulation of the cortex, but this is a long remove from a definition of the neural properties of the trace. For the time being, one does better to deal in terms of the formal properties that a trace system must exhibit than to rest one's psychological model on any neurophysiological or anatomical conception of the memory trace.

And, quite clearly, one of the formal properties of a trace system is that its elements vary in accessibility to stimulus input with the kinds of conditions we have considered. It is instructive to note that when a theory of traces lacks this feature, it ceases to be useful in dealing with the wide range of perceptual categorizing phenomena of which we now have knowledge. Gestalt theory is a case in point. According to Köhler's view (48), a stimulus process "finds" its appropriate memory trace, resulting in identification of the stimulus process, on the basis of distinctive similarity between stimulus process and memory trace. The theory has been criticized, justly I think, for failing to specify the nature of this similarity save by saying that it is a neural isomorph of phenomenal similarity. But since similarity may be highly selective—two objects may be alike in color but differ in dozens of other respects—there is obviously some *tertium quid* that determines the basis of similarity. More serious still is the inability of such a theory to deal with the increased likelihood of categorization in terms of particular traces as a function of changes in search set or subjective likelihood estimates. The Bruner-Minturn results would require that, as between two traces with which a stimulus process may make contact, each equally "similar" to the stimulus, the stimulus process will make contact with the one having a higher probability of being matched by environmental events. This is interesting, but it is far from the spirit of Gestalt theory.

Match-Mismatch Processes

One may readily conceive of and, indeed, build an apparatus that will accept or reject inputs on the basis of whether or not they fulfill certain specifications. Selfridge (71) has constructed a machine to read letters, Fry (24) has one that will discriminate various phonemes, and Uttley (80) has constructed one that, like Tinbergen's grey lag geese, will recognize the flying silhouette of a predator hawk. All such machines have in common that they require a match between a stimulus input and various specifications required by the sorting mechanism of the machine.

In the examples just given, there is no consequence generated by whether a given input fulfills the specifications required by the identifying machine. It fits or it doesn't fit. But now let us build in two other features. The first is that the machine emit a signal to indicate how closely any given input comes to fulfilling the specifications required: either by indicating how many attributes the object has in common with the specifications, or by indicating how far off the mark on any given attribute dimension a given input is. The second is that the machine do something on the basis of these signals: to increase sensitivity if an object is within a given distance of specifications for a closer look, or to decrease it if the object is further than a certain amount from specifications, or to stop registering further if the input fits.

In short, one can imagine a nervous system that emits all-or-none match-mismatch signals or graded match-mismatch signals, and one can also imagine that these signals could then feed into an effector system to regulate activity relevant to continuing search behavior for a fitting object, or to regulate other forms of activity. Mac-

Kay (59) has recently proposed such a model.

We must return for a moment to an earlier discussion. In the discussion of cue utilization, a distinction was made between three phases of "openness" in cue search. The first was one in which a given input was being scanned for its properties so as to place it in one of a relatively large set of possible alternative categories. Here one would register on as many features of an object as possible. In a second stage, the input has been tentatively placed, and the search is limited to confirming or infirming criterial cues. Finally, with more definite placement, cue search is suspended and deviations from specification may even be "normalized." It is for the regulation of such patterns of search or cue utilization that some mechanism such as match-mismatch signaling is postulated.

Let it be said that while match-mismatch signaling-effector systems are readily conceivable and readily constructed, there is no knowledge available as to how a system like the nervous system might effect such a process. That there is feedback all over the system is quite apparent from its detailed anatomy, and this is the process out of which a larger-scale system such as we have described would be constructed.

Gating Processes

The picture thus far presented is of a conceptual nervous system with a massive afferent intake that manages somehow to sort inputs into appropriate assemblies of varying accessibility. It seems unlikely that this is the nature of the nervous system, that there should be no gating or monitoring of stimulus input short of what occurs at higher centers. It is with this more peripheral form of screening of inputs that we shall now be concerned.

It has long been known that the concept of the "adequate stimulus" could not simply be defined as a change in environmental energy sufficient to stimulate a receptor. For quite evidently, a stimulus could be peripherally adequate in this sense and not be "centrally" adequate at all, either in eliciting electrical activity in the cortex or in producing a verbal report of a change in experience by the subject. Indeed, the very nature of such complex receptor surfaces as the retina argues against such a simple notion of "adequate stimulus." For the reactivity of even a retinal cell at the fovea seems to be "gated" by the state of stimulation of neighboring cells. Thus, if cells A, B, and C lie next to each other in that order in a row, stimulation of B suppresses the sensitivity of C. If A now be stimulated, B is suppressed and C is released or heightened in sensitivity. So even at the level of the first synapse of a sensory system, there is mediation *outward* or gating from internuncial to receptor cells that programs the nature of the input that can come into the sensory system. And to be sure, there are many phenomena in perception itself that speak for this same kind of gating. When we are fixated upon the vase in the Rubin reversible figure, the background recedes, is less surfacy, and in general seems to provide a generally less centrally adequate form of sensory input. So too with the studies of Yokoyama (87) and Chapman (19) where subjects, set to report on one of several attributes of briefly presented stimuli, accomplished their selective task with a loss of ability to discriminate on the attributes for which they had not been set. We shall propose that such phenomena are very likely mediated by a gating process which "filters" input before ever it reaches the cortex.

There is now a growing body of neurophysiological evidence that part of this screening process is relegated to peripheral levels of the nervous system—even as far out as the second synapse of specialized sensory systems. In an earlier paper I used the rather fanciful phrase that "perception acts sometimes as a welcoming committee and sometimes as a screening committee." It now appears that both these committees are closer to the entrance port than previously conceived.

Consider first the evidence of Kuffler and Hunt (50) on so simple a "reflex" as the stretch reflex of the biceps femoris muscle of the cat in an isolated spinal nerve-muscle preparation. Recall a little anatomy first. Muscle tissue contains special cells called spindles that are receptors in function, discharging with contraction or stretch of the muscle in which they are imbedded. The muscle itself is innervated by an efferent nerve trunk emerging from the ventral horn of the spinal cord and, in turn, an afferent nerve travels to the dorsal root of the spinal cord. According to the classical law of Bell and Magendie, the ventral root of the spinal cord carries efferent-motor impulses down to the muscles, while the dorsal root carries sensory impulses up to the cord. Now, it has been known for a long time that the presumed efferent nerve going to muscles carries fibers of large and of small diameter. A quarter-century ago Eccles and Sherrington showed that the ventral nerve branch supplying the biceps femoris of the cat shows a "striking division of the fibers into two diameter groups" (49), one group centering around 5 μ in diameter, the other around 15 or 16 μ. The large fibers are, of course, fast conductors, the small ones slow. Leksell (55) has shown that stimulation of the slow-conducting smaller fibers did not cause detectable contradic-

tions or propagated muscle impulses. When the larger and fast-conducting fibers are stimulated, the usual motor-unit twitch occurred. Kuffler and Hunt (50) state that, in the lumbosacral outflow, about two-thirds of the fibers are of the large-diameter, fast-conduction type; the other third are of the small type that in mammalia are "ineffective in directly setting up significant muscular contraction." There has been much speculation about what these fibers are there for, and the answer is now fairly clear. It is revolutionary in its implications and brings deeply into question both the classical Bell-Magendie law and the simplistic notion of the reflex arc on which so much of American learning theory is based.

It is this. The small fibers of the presumably motor trunk go to the spindle cells, and the activity in these fibers serve to modulate or gate the receptivity of these specialized sensory endings. For example, if the small-diameter fibers are firing into the muscle spindle it may speed up the amount of firing from this cell into the afferent nerve that is produced by a given amount of stretch tension on the muscle. We need not go into detail here. It suffices to note that the state of presumed motor discharge does not simply innervate the muscle; it also regulates the amount and kind of kinesthetic sensory discharge that the sensory cells in the muscle will send back to the central nervous system. Instead of thinking of a stimulus-response reflex arc, it becomes necessary even at this peripheral level to think of the efferent portion of the arc acting back on sensory receptors to change the nature of the stimulus that can get through.

Two additional pieces of evidence on gating mechanisms at higher levels of integration may be cited. Where vision is concerned, Granit (32) has recently shown that pupillary changes produced by the ciliary muscle of the eye create changes in the pattern of firing of the retina: changes in muscular state working its way back through the nervous system into the visual system and back outward to the retina. There is also evidence of gating working from the visual system backward in the opposite direction: during binocular rivalry, the nondominant eye shows a less sensitive pupillary reflex than the dominant eye.

Finally, we may cite the recent evidence of Hernandez-Péon, Scherrer, and Jouvet (38) working in Magoun's laboratory, work confirmed by analogous findings of Golambos, Sheatz, and Vernier (28) at the Walter Reed Hospital. If one stimulates the cat with auditory clicks, it is possible to record an evoked spike potential from the cochlear nucleus. Repetition of the clicks leads to a gradual diminution of the evoked potential, as if the organism were adapting. It is quite extraordinary that such adaptation should be registered as far out peripherally as the cochlear nucleus, which is, after all, only the second synapse of the VIIIth nerve. Now, if the clicks are previously used as conditioned stimuli signaling shock, the diminution of the evoked potential no longer occurs upon repetition of the clicks. Evidence that the response from the brain is not being produced by the muscular activity produced by the click as a conditioned stimulus is provided by the fact that the same kind of effects are obtained from cats with temporarily induced muscular paralysis. Further, if one take a cat whose cochlear nucleus is still firing upon click stimulation and introduce a mouse into its visual field, the clicks no longer evoke a spike potential. A fish odor or a shock to the paw has the same effect of inhibiting spike potentials at the cochlear nucleus, if these distracting stimuli occur concurrently with the click. "Distraction" or "shifting of attention" appears to work its way outward to the cochlear nucleus.[1]

Perhaps the foregoing account has been needlessly detailed on the side of neurophysiology. Yet, the interesting implications of the findings for perceptual theory make such an excursion worth while. That the nervous system accomplishes something like gating is quite clear, even without the neurophysiological evidence. The data of behavior are full of examples, and the phenomena of attention require some such mechanism to be explained. Indeed, it is quite clear that the nervous system must be capable of more selective gating than physiology has yet been able to discover. That is to say, there must be a filter somewhere in the cat's nervous system that will "pass" the squeak of the mouse in the Hernandez-Péon experiment but not the cough of the experimenter. And it is to this problem that we turn now.

I would propose that one of the mechanisms operative in regulating search behavior is some sort of gating or filtering system. In the preceding section, it was proposed that the "openness" of the first stage of cue utilization, the "selectivity" of the second stage, and the "closedness" of the third stage were probably regulated by a match-mismatch mechanism. What may be proposed here is that the degree of "openness" or "closedness" to sensory input during different phases of cue utilization is likely effected by the

[1] Since the above was written, evidence has been presented by Golambos indicating that efferently controlled inhibition operates as far out to the periphery as the hair cells of the organ of Corti and fibers carrying such inhibitory impulses have been traced as far centrally as the superior olivary nucleus—not very far, but a start.

kind of gating processes we have been considering. How these work in intimate detail is far from known, yet the work of the last years in neurophysiology suggests that we are drawing closer to an answer.

Having considered some general properties of perception and some possible mechanisms underlying these, we turn now to some selected problems in perception better to explore the implications of what has thus far been proposed.

ON FAILURE OF READINESS

From the foregoing discussion, it is clear that veridical perception under viewing or listening conditions that are less than ideal depends upon a state of perceptual readiness that matches the probability of occurrence of events in the world of the perceiver. This is true, of course, only in a statistical sense. What is most likely to occur is not necessarily what will occur, and the perceiver whose readiness is well matched to the likelihoods of his environment may be duped. In Farquhar's handsome seventeenth-century phrase: "I cou'd be mighty foolish, and fancy myself mighty witty; reason still keeps its Throne—but it nods a little, that's all." The only assurance against the nodding of reason or probability, under the circumstances, is the maintenance of a flexibility of readiness: an ability to permit one's hypotheses about what it is that is to be perceptually encountered to be easily infirmed by sensory input. But this is a topic for later.

There appear to be two antidotes to nonveridical perception, two ways of overcoming inappropriate perceptual readinesses. The one is a re-education of the misperceiver's expectancies concerning the events he is to encounter. The other is the "constant close look." If the re-education succeeds in producing a better match between internal expectancies and external event-probabilities, the danger of misperception under hurried or substandard conditions of perceiving is lessened. But the matter of re-educating perceptual expectancies is complex. For where consequences are grave, expectancy concerning what may be encountered does not change easily, even with continued opportunity to test the environment. In this concluding section we shall consider some of the factors that contribute to states of perceptual "unreadiness" that either fail to match the likelihood of environmental events or fail to reflect the requirements of adjustment or both.

Before turning to this task, a word is in order about the "constant close look" as an antidote to inappropriate perceptual readiness. There is for every category of objects that has been established in the organism a stimulus input of sufficient duration and cue redundancy such that, if the stimulus input fits the specifications of the category, it will eventually be correctly perceived as an exemplar of that category. With enough time and enough testing of defining cues, such "best fit" perceiving can be accomplished for most but not all classes of environmental events with which the person has contact. There are some objects whose cues to identity are sufficiently equivocal so that no such resolution can be achieved, and these are mostly in the sphere of so-called interpersonal perception: perceiving the states of other people, their characteristics, intentions, and so forth, on the basis of external signs. And since this is the domain where misperception can have the most chronic if not the most acute consequences, it is doubtful whether a therapeutic regimen of "close looking" will aid the misperceiver much in dealing with more complex cue patterns. But the greatest difficulty rests in the fact that the cost of close looks is generally too high under the conditions of speed, risk, and limited capacity imposed upon organisms by their environment or their constitutions. The ability to use minimal cues quickly in categorizing the events of the environment is what gives the organism its lead time in adjusting to events. Pause and close inspection inevitably cut down on this precious interval for adjustment.

Inappropriate Categories

Perhaps the most primitive form of perceptual unreadiness for dealing with a particular environment is the case in which the perceiver has a set of categories that are inappropriate for adequate prediction of his environment. A frequently cited example of such a case is Bartlett's account (3) of the African visitors in London who perceived the London bobbies as especially friendly because they frequently raised their right hand, palm forward, to the approaching traffic. The cue-category inference was, of course, incorrect, and they should have identified the cue as a signal for stopping traffic. The example, however, is not particularly interesting because it is a transient phenomenon, soon corrected by instruction.

A more interesting example, because it is far less tractable, is provided by second-language learning and the learning of a new phonemic system. Why is it, we may ask, that a person can learn the structure of a new language, its form classes, morphemes, lexemes, and so on, but still retain a "foreign accent" which he cannot, after a while, distinguish from the speech flow of native speakers around him? And why is it that a person

learning a new language can follow the speech of a person with his own kind of foreign accent more readily than he can follow a native speaker? The answer lies, I think, in the phenomenon of postcategorization sensory gating: once an utterance has been "understood" or decoded in appropriate categories, on the basis of some of the diacritica of the speech flow, the remaining features are assimilated or normalized or screened out. The phonemic categories that are used, moreover, are modifications of those in the first language of the speaker. Normalization is in the direction of these first-language phonemic categories. It is only by a special effort that, after having achieved adequate comprehension of the second language, one can remain sensorially "open" enough to register on the deviation between his own phonemic pattern and that of native speakers. And since there is common categorization of the "meaning" of utterances by the native speaker and the fluent foreigner, there is no built-in incentive for the foreigner to maintain a cognitively strainful regimen of attending further to speech sounds.

Lenneberg (56) has recently shown the difficulties involved in learning new modes of categorizing such continua as chromatic colors. He taught subjects various nonsense languages, explaining to them that the words were Hopi names for colors and that their task was to learn what colors they stood for. His stimulus materials were graded Munsell colors going in a circle from *brown,* through *green,* through *blue,* through *pink,* and then back to *brown.* A standardized group was used to find the frequency distribution of color naming over the circle when the English color names mentioned above were used. Experimental groups, six in number, were then run, each being exposed to the use of the nonsense color names "as these are used by the Hopi." Then they were tested on their usage of the names. A first group was taught the nonsense words with exact correspondence to the usage found for the standardizing group on *brown, blue, green,* and *pink.* The other groups were given distorted usage training—distorted from English usage. The distortions were both in the slopes of the frequency of usage and in the points on the color continua where the highest usage frequencies fell. That is to say, the mode of a distribution in some cases would fall at a color which in English had no specific name, or fall between two English categories.

The principal results of the experiment are these. If the reference and probability relationship is the same for a nonsense language as it is for English, relearning is very rapid. The slightest deviation from this correspondence increases difficulty of learning quite markedly. It is disturbing either to shift the center of the categories on the color continuum or to change the shape of the frequency-of-calling functions, even when these are made *more* determinative (that is rectilinear) than they normally are. A shift in the shape of the frequency-of-calling functions is more disruptive than a shift in placement on the color continuum. What is quite striking is that a highly determinative frequency-of-calling function can be learned much more rapidly than one in which there is a gradual transition in color naming from one color to another on the color continuum.

Now, I suspect that the difficulty in learning a set of neighboring categories with a state of equivocality prevailing in the area between the "typical instances" of each category comes precisely from the tendency to normalize in the direction of the center of one category or the other. If there is a sharp transition between one color category and another, this tendency aids learning. If the transition is gradual, it hinders it. For it is noteworthy, as in the experiment of Bruner, Postman, and Rodrigues (16) that equivocal colors are readily subject to assimilation in the direction of expected value.

It is perhaps in the realm of social perception, where the problem of validating one's categorizations is severe, that one finds the most striking effects of inappropriate category systems. What is meant here by validation is the testing of the predictions inherent in a categorization. If, on the basis of a few cues of personal appearance, for example, one categorizes another person as dishonest, it is extremely difficult in most cases to check for the other cues that one would predict might be associated with instances of this category. There is either a delay or an absence of opportunity for additional cue checking. Moreover, there is also the likelihood, since cues themselves are so equivocal in such a case, that available equivocal signs will be distorted in such a manner as to confirm the first impression. It is much as in the experiments of Asch (2) and of Haire and Grunes (33) on the formation of first impressions, where later cues encountered are cognitively transformed so as to support the first impression. The reticence of the man we categorize as dishonest is seen as "caginess"; the "honest" man's reticence is seen as "integrity" and "good judgment."

It is perhaps because of this difficulty of infirming such categorial judgments that an inappropriate category system can be so hard to change. The slum boy who rises to the top in science can change his categories for coding the events of the physical world quite readily. He has much more difficulty in altering the socially related category system with which he codes the phenomena of the social world around him.

Inappropriate Accessibility Ordering

Perhaps the most noticeable "perceptual unreadiness" comes from interference with good probability learning by wishes and fears. I have in mind the kind of distorted expectancies that arise when the desirability or undesirability of events distorts the learning of their probability of occurrence. The experiments of Marks (60) and of Irwin (41), cited earlier, are simplified examples of the way in which desired outcomes increase estimates of their likelihood of occurrence. Certain more persistent general personality tendencies also operate in this sphere. It is indeed the case that some people are readier to expect and therefore quicker to perceive the least desirable event among an array of expected events, and others the most desired. This is quite clearly a learned adjustment to the events one is likely to encounter, even if it may be supported by temperamental characteristics. How such learning occurs, and why it is so resistant to correction by exposure to environmental events, are hardly clear. But one matter that becomes increasingly clear is that before we can know much about how appropriate and inappropriate perceptual readiness is produced, we shall have to know much more about how organisms learn the probabilistic structure of their environments. This is a point that Brunswik has made for some years (17), and it is one that is now being taken seriously by such students of probability learning as Bush and Mosteller (18), Bruner, Goodnow, and Austin (9), Estes (23), Galanter and Gerstenhaber (25), Hake and Hyman

(34), Edwards (22), and others.

There is another important feature of learning that affects perceptual readiness. It has to do with the range of alternatives for which organisms learn to be set perceptually. Put the matter this way. It is a matter of common observation that some people are characteristically tuned for a narrow range of alternatives in the situations in which they find themselves. If the environment is banal in the sense of containing only high probability events and sequences or, more properly, events and sequences that are strongly expected, then the individual will do well and perceive with a minimum of pause for close looking. But should the environment contain unexpected events, unusual sequences, then the result will be a marked slowdown in identification and categorizing. Cue search must begin again. We speak of such people as "rigid" or "stuck." George Klein's work (46) on shifting category judgments suggests that, in general, people who are not able to shift categorization under gradually changing conditions of stimulation tend also to show what he describes as "over-control" on other cognitive and motivational tasks. At the other extreme is specialization upon diversity, and how such specialization is learned is equally puzzling. I can perhaps best illustrate the phenomenon by a commonly observed pattern found in subjects in tachistoscopic experiments. There are subjects who show rather high thresholds of identification generally, and who seem to be "weighing" the stimulus in terms of a wide array of interpretive categories. Jenkin (45) has recently described such perception as "rationalized," the subject describing what he sees as "like a so-and-so" rather than, as in the "projective" response, reporting it "as a so-and-so." It is as if the former type of response involved a greater cue searching of stimulus inputs for a fit to a wide range of things that it "could be." It is also very likely that premature sensory gating occurs in individuals with a tendency to be set for a minimum array of alternatives, leading them into error. The topic is one that bears closer investigation. To anyone who has had much experience in observing subjects in tachistoscopic work, it seems intuitively evident that there are large and individual differences possibly worth examining here.

We come finally to the vexing problem of "perceptual defense"—the manner in which organisms utilize their perceptual readiness to ward off events that are threatening but about which there is nothing they can do. There has been foolish and some bitter ink spilled over this topic, mostly because of a misunderstanding. The notion of perceptual defense does not require a little homuncular ego, sitting behind a Judas-eye, capable of ruling out any input that is potentially disruptive— as even so able a critic as F. H. Allport (1) seems to think. Any preset filtering device can do all that is required.

Let me begin with the general proposition that failure to perceive is most often not a *lack* of perceiving but a matter of *interference* with perceiving. Whence the interference? I would propose that the interference comes from categorizations in highly accessible categories that serve to block alternative categorizations in less accessible categories. As a highly speculative suggestion, the mechanism that seems most likely to mediate such interference is probably the broadening of category acceptance limits when a high state of readiness to perceive prevails; or, in the language of the preceding section, the range of inputs that will produce a match signal for a category increases in such a way that more accessible categories are likely to "capture" poorfitting sensory inputs. We have already considered some evidence for increase in acceptance limits under high readiness conditions: the tendency to see a red four of clubs as either a four of diamonds or a four of clubs, with color-suit relationship rectified (14), the difficulty of spotting reversed letters imbedded in the middle of a word (69), and so on.

Let us examine some experimental evidence on the role of interference in perceptual failure. Wyatt and Campbell (86) have shown that if a subject develops a wrong hypothesis about the nature of what is being presented to him for perception at suboptimal conditions, the perception of the object in terms of its conventional identity is slowed down. This observation has been repeated in other studies as well. Postman and Bruner (68), for example, have shown that if a subject is put under pressure by the experimenter and given to believe that he is operating below standard, then he will develop premature hypotheses that interfere with correct perception of the word stimuli being presented to him. The authors refer to "perceptual recklessness" as characterizing the stressed subjects in contrast to those who operated under normal experimental conditions. It may well be, just in passing, that stress has not only the specific effect of leading to premature, interfering hypotheses but that it disrupts the normal operation of match-mismatch signaling systems in the nervous system. Unpublished studies from our own laboratory carried out by Bruner, Postman, and John (15) have shown the manner in which subjects misperceive low-probability contingencies in terms of higher probability categories. For example, a subject in the experimental group is shown tachistoscopically a picture of a discus thrower, wound up and ready to throw. In his balancing arm and placed across the front of him is a large bass viol. A control subject is shown the same picture, the exact space filled by the bass viol now being occupied by the crouching figure of a track official with his back to the camera. The brightness, shading, and area of the viol and the official are almost identical. Subjects begin by identifying the first flash of the picture as an athlete with a shadow across him. The subjects faced with the incongruous picture then go on with reasonable hypotheses—including the hypothesis of a crouching human figure, "probably an official," as one subject put it—and in the process of running through the gamut of likely hypotheses, correct perception is interfered with. It will not surprise you if I report that the threshold for the incongruous stimulus picture is markedly higher than that for the more conventional one.

Hypotheses and states of readiness may interfere with correct perception in yet another way: by creating a shifting "noise" background that masks the cues that might be used for identifying an environmental event. At the common-sense level this can best be illustrated by reference to perceptual-motor learning where kinesthetic cues are of importance. In teaching a person how to cast a fly, it is necessary for him to guide his forward delivery by feeling the gentle pressure release that occurs when the line reaches the end of its uncurving on the backcast. If your flycasting pupil is too eager to spot this cue, he will be rather tense, and his own muscular tension will mask the gentle pressure release that he must use as a signal.

A good instance is provided by the experiment of Goodnow and Pettigrew (30) at Harvard. It is concerned with the ability of subjects to perceive a regularity in a sequence of events —a very simple regularity, like the alternation left-right-left-right. . . . The experiment is done on a conventional two-armed bandit, the subject having the task of betting on whether a light will appear on the left or on the right. The task is simple. A subject is first given some pretraining, in one of four pretraining groups. One is given pretraining by learning a simple alternation pattern of payoff, another is trained to find the payoff all on one side (not easy for all subjects), a third is trained to find the pattern LLRLLR . . . and a final group is given no pretraining. Following the pretraining and without pause, all subjects are given a series of 60 choices in which the payoff is randomly arranged, the two sides totaling out to 50:50. Immediately following this random phase, and again without pause, the payoffs now go into a stage of simple alternation, LRLR. . . . How long does it take the subject to perceive the regularity of the final temporal pattern? The speed of discovery depends, it turns out, upon the kinds of behavioral hypotheses a subject develops during the phase of random payoff. If he develops any regularity of response—like win-stay-lose-shift or win-shift-lose-stay—then he will quickly spot the new pattern. Pretraining on a constant one-side payoff or on single alternation both produce such regularity, and both forms of pretraining produce equally good results—the subject requiring but eight or nine exposures to the pattern introduced after the random phase to begin responding without error. No pretraining, or pretraining on the pattern LLRLLR . . . , does not produce the regularity of response required. Instead, the subject works on odd and constantly shifting hypotheses during the random period. When the single-alternation regularity is introduced, the result is a marked reduction in ability to spot the new pattern—some subjects failing to discover the pattern in 200 trials. What we are dealing with here is interference—hypotheses and responses serve to mask the regularity of events in the environment. In order for an environmental regularity to be perceived, there has to be a certain amount of steadiness in the hypotheses being employed and in the response pattern that is controlled by it. Short of this, masking and clumsy perceptual performance results.

Now what has all this to do with "perceptual defense"? The concept was introduced some years ago by Postman and myself as a description of the phenomenon of failure to perceive and/or report material known by independent test to be regarded as inimical by the subject. It was proposed (13) that there was a hierarchy of thresholds, and that an incoming stimulus could be responded to without its reaching the level of reportable experience—as in the McGinnies (58) and Lazarus and McCleary (54) studies, where autonomic response followed presentation of a potentially traumatic stimulus without the subject's being able to give a report of the nature of the stimulus. The study of Bricker and Chapanis (6) threw further light on the concept of a hierarchy of thresholds by demonstrating that, though subjects could not report spontaneously on the identity of the shock syllables used by Lazarus and McCleary, they could guess them well in excess of chance if given a restricted choice regarding what word had been presented. I would like to propose two additional factors that might lead to a failure of perception of emotionally negative material.

It is conceivable that the estimates of probability of occurrence of disval-

ued events are, in some individuals, reduced—essentially the obverse of what was observed in the experiments of Marks (60) and Irwin (41), where probability estimates were inflated by desirability. If accessibility is decreased by such disvaluation, then a cognitive counterpart of what is clinically called "repression" can be posited. It is known, however, that not everyone shows this tendency to be unready for objects and events that are anxiety-arousing. Others seem to *inflate* their estimate of the likelihood of occurrence of inimical events. Certainly one finds clinical evidence for such a pattern among anxiety neurotics. In an early paper, Postman and Bruner (68) described two types of performance with respect to known anxiety-producing stimuli, defense and vigilance, the former a heightened threshold of identification for such stimuli, the latter a lowered threshold. In a carefully designed experiment contrasting the performance of clinically diagnosed "intellectualizers" and "repressors," Lazarus, Eriksen, and Fonda (53) have shown that the former group indeed are faster in recognizing negatively charged material than they are in recognizing neutral material, while the latter show the reverse tendency. Again, I find it necessary to revert to a point made earlier. I do not think that we are going to get much further ahead in understanding hyper- and hyporeadiness for encountering anxiety-evoking stimuli short of doing studies of the learning of environmental probabilities for sequences containing noxious and beneficial events.

One additional mechanism that may be operative in lowering or generally in altering readiness to perceive material that in some way may be threatening. I hesitate to speak of it in detail, since it is of such a speculative order, and do so only because some experiments suggest themselves. It is this. Conceivably, categories for classes of objects that are pain-arousing are set up with narrow acceptance limits for stimulus inputs related to them. That is to say, what we speak of as "repression" may be the establishment of very narrow category limits that prevent the evocation of match signals for inputs that do not fit category specifications very precisely. I am mindful that as far as autonomic reactivity is concerned potentially traumatic stimuli work in quite the reverse direction. If anything, a wide range of objects, appropriate and inappropriate, arouse autonomic reactions, without leading to verbalizable report concerning the categorial identity of the eliciting objects. Yet it is conceivable that with respect to one kind of threshold (autonomic) the acceptance limits are broad, and with respect to another (reportable awareness) very narrow. I think it would be worth while in any case to investigate the acceptance limits of inimical stimulus inputs by altering the characteristics of objects so that, in essence, one gets a generalization gradient for recognition. My guess is that the gradient will be much steeper for anxiety-arousing stimuli than for neutral ones. All that remains is to do the experiment.

Finally, it may also be the case that category accessibility reflects the instrumental relevance of the environmental events they represent. There is evidence that the recognition threshold for noxious objects about which one can do something is lower than normal, whereas for ones about which nothing instrumental can be done, the threshold is higher. That is to say, words that signal a shock that can be avoided show lowered thresholds, words signaling unavoidable shock show a threshold rise. One may well speculate whether the instrumental rel-evance of objects is not a controlling factor in guiding the kind of search behavior that affects category accessibility. The problem needs much more thorough investigation than it has received.

We have touched on various conditions that might lead a person to be inappropriately set for the events he must perceive easily and quickly in his environment. Many other studies could be mentioned. But the intention has not been to review the rather sprawling literature in the field, but to propose some possible mechanism affecting readiness so that research might be given a clearer theoretical direction.

CONCLUSIONS

We have been concerned in these pages with a general view of perception that depends upon the construction of a set of organized categories in terms of which stimulus inputs may be sorted, given identity, and given more elaborated, connotative meaning. Veridical perception, it has been urged, depends upon the construction of such category systems, categories built upon the inference of identity from cues or signs. Identity, in fine, represents the range of inferences about properties, uses, and consequences that can be predicted from the presence of certain criterial cues.

Perceptual readiness refers to the relative accessibility of categories to afferent stimulus inputs. The more accessible a category, the less the stimulus input required for it to be sorted in terms of the category, given a degree of match between the characteristics of the input and the specifications of the category. In rough form, there appear to be two general determinants of category accessibility. One of them is the likelihood of occurrence of events learned by the person in the course of dealing with the world of objects and events and the redundant sequences in which these are imbedded. If you will, the person builds a model of the likelihood of events, a form of probability learning only now beginning to be understood. Again in rough terms, one can think of this activity as achieving a minimization of surprise for the organism. A second determinant of accessibility is the requirements of search dictated by need states and the need to carry out habitual enterprises such as walking, reading, or whatever it is that makes up the round of daily, habitual life.

Failure to achieve a state of perceptual readiness that matches the probability of events in one's world can be dealt with in one of two ways: either by the relearning of categories and expectancies, or by constant close inspection of events and objects. Where the latter alternative must be used, an organism is put in the position of losing his lead time for adjusting quickly and smoothly to events under varying conditions of time pressure, risk, and limited capacity. Readiness in the sense that we are using it is not a luxury, but a necessity for smooth adjustment.

The processes involved in "sorting" sensory inputs to appropriate categories involve cue utilization, varying from sensorially "open" cue searching under relative uncertainty, to selective search for confirming cues under partial certainty, to sensory "gating" and distortion when an input has been categorized beyond a certain level of certainty.

Four kinds of mechanisms are proposed to deal with known phenomena of perceptual categorizing and differential perceptual readiness: *grouping and integration, access ordering, match-mismatch signal utilization,* and *gating.* The psychological evidence leading one to infer such processes were examined and possible neurological analogues considered. The processes are conceived of as mediators of categorizing and its forms of connectivity, the phenomena of differential threshold levels for various environmental events, the guidance of cue search behavior, and lastly, the phenomena of sensory inhibition and "filtering."

Finally, we have considered some of the ways in which failure of perceptual readiness comes about—first, through a failure to learn appropriate categories for sorting the environment and for following its sequences, and second, through a process of interference whereby more accessible categories with wide acceptance limits serve to mask or prevent the use of less accessible categories for the coding of stimulus inputs. The concept of "perceptual defense" may be re-examined in the light of these notions.

In conclusion, it seems appropriate to say that the ten years of the so-called New Look in perception research seem to be coming to a close with much empirical work accomplished—a great deal of it demonstrational, to be sure, but with a promise of a second ten years in which hypotheses will be more rigorously formulated and, conceivably, neural mechanisms postulated, if not discovered. The prospects are anything but discouraging.

REFERENCES

1. Allport, F. H., *Theories of Perception and the Concept of Structure.* New York: John Wiley & Sons Inc., 1955.

2. Asch, S. E., *Social Psychology.* Englewood Cliffs, N. J.: Prentice-Hall, Inc., 1952.

3. Bartlett, F. C., *Remembering.* Cambridge, England: Cambridge University Press, 1932.

4. Binder, A., "A Statistical Model for the Process of Visual Recognition," *Psychological Review*, **62** (1955), 119-29.

5. Bitterman, M. E. and C. W. Kniffin, "Manifest Anxiety and 'Perceptual Defense,'" *Journal of Abnormal Social Psychology*, **48** (1953), 248-52.

6. Bricker, P. D. and A. Chapanis, "Do Incorrectly Perceived Tachistoscopic Stimuli Convey Some Information?" *Psychological Review*, **60** (1953), 181-88.

7. Brown, D. R., "Stimulus Similarity and the Anchoring of Subjective Scales," *American Journal of Psychology*, **66** (1953), 199-214.

8. Bruner, J. S., "Personality Dynamics and the Process of Perceiving," in *Perception: An Approach to Personality*, eds. R. R. Blake and G. V. Ramsey, pp. 121-47. New York: The Ronald Press Company, 1951.

9. Bruner, J. S., J. J. Goodnow, and G. A. Austin, *A Study of Thinking*. New York: John Wiley & Sons, Inc., 1956.

10. Bruner, J. S., G. A. Miller, and C. Zimmerman, "Discriminative Skill and Discriminative Matching in Perceptual Recognition," *Journal of Experimental Psychology*, **49** (1955), 187-92.

11. Bruner, J. S. and A. L. Minturn, "Perceptual Identification and Perceptual Organization," *Journal of Genetic Psychology*, **53** (1955), 21-28.

12. Bruner, J. S. and L. Postman, "Emotional Selectivity in Perception and Reaction," *Journal of Personality*, **16** (1947), 69-77.

13. ———, "Perception, Cognition, and Behavior," *Journal of Personality*, **18** (1949), 14-31.

14. ———, "On the Perception of Incongruity: A Paradigm," *Journal of Personality*, **18** (1949), 206-23.

15. Bruner, J. S., L. Postman, and W. John, "Normalization of Incongruity." Research memorandum. Cognition project, Harvard University, 1949.

16. Bruner, J. S., L. Postman, and J. Rodrigues, "Expectation and the Perception of Color," *American Journal of Psychology*, **64** (1951), 216-27.

17. Brunswik, E., *Systematic and Representative Design of Psychological Experiments*. Berkeley: University of California Press, 1949.

18. Bush, R. R. and C. F. Mosteller, *Stochastic Models for Learning*. New York: John Wiley & Sons, Inc., 1955.

19. Chapman, D. W., "Relative Effects of Determinate and Indeterminate *Aufgaben*," *American Journal of Psychology*, **44** (1932), 163-74.

20. Cowen, E. L. and E. G. Beier, "The Influence of 'Threat Expectancy' on Perception," *Journal of Personality*, **19** (1951), 85-94.

21. Eccles, J. C., *The Neurophysiological Basis of Mind*. London: Oxford University Press, 1953.

22. Edwards, W., "The Theory of Decision Making," *Psychological Bulletin*, **51** (1954), 380-417.

23. Estes, W. K., "Individual Behavior in Uncertain Situations: An Interpretation in Terms of Statistical Association Theory," in *Decision Processes*, eds. R. M. Thrall, C. H. Coombs, and R. L. Davis, pp. 127-37. New York: John Wiley & Sons, Inc., 1954.

24. Fry, D. P. and P. Denes, "Mechanical Speech Recognition," in *Communication Theory*, ed. W. Jackson. New York: Academic Press, 1953.

25. Galanter, E. and M. Gerstenhaber, "On Thought: Extrinsic Theory of Insight," *American Psychologist*, **10** (1955), 465.

26. Gibson, J. J., *The Perception of the Visual World*. Boston: Houghton Mifflin Company, 1950.

27. Gibson, J. J. and E. J. Gibson, "Perceptual Learning: Differentiation or Enrichment?" *Psychological Review*, **62** (1955), 32-41.

28. Golambos, R., G. Sheatz, and V. G. Vernier, "Electrophysiological Correlates of a Conditioned Response in Cats," *Science*, **123** (1956), 376-77.

29. Goodnow, J. J., "Determinants of

Choice-Distribution in Two-Choice Situations," *American Journal of Psychology,* **68** (1955), 106-16.

30. Goodnow, J. J. and T. E. Pettigrew, "Some Difficulties in Learning a Simple Pattern of Events." Paper presented at annual meeting of the Eastern Psychological Association, Atlantic City, March 1956.

31. Graham, C. H., "Perception and Behavior." Presidential address to the Eastern Psychological Association, Atlantic City, March 1956.

32. Granit, R., *Receptors and Sensory Perception.* New Haven, Conn.: Yale University Press, 1955.

33. Haire, M. and W. F. Grunes, "Perceptual Defenses: Processes Protecting an Organized Perception of Another Personality," *Human Relations,* **3** (1950), 403-12.

34. Hake, H. W. and R. Hyman, "Perception of the Statistical Structure of a Random Series of Binary Symbols," *Journal of Experimental Psychology,* **45** (1953), 64-74.

35. Harper, R. S. and E. G. Boring, "Cues," *American Journal of Psychology,* **61** (1948), 119-23.

36. Hebb, D. O., *The Organization of Behavior.* New York: John Wiley & Sons, Inc., 1949.

37. Helson, H., "Adaptation-Level as a Basis for a Quantitative Theory of Frames of Reference, *"Psychological Review,* **55** (1948), 297-313.

38. Hernandez-Péon, R., R. H. Scherrer, and M. Jouvet, "Modification of Electric Activity in the Cochlear Nucleus during 'Attention' in Unanesthetized Cats," *Science,* **123** (1956), 331-32.

39. Hornbostel, E. M. von, "Unity of the Senses," *Psyche,* **7** (1926), 83-89.

40. Howes, D., "On the Interpretation of Word Frequency as a Variable Affecting Speed of Recognition," *Journal of Experimental Psychology,* **48** (1954), 106-12.

41. Irwin, F. W., "Stated Expectations as Functions of Probability and Desirability of Outcomes," *Journal of Personality,* **21** (1953), 329-35.

42. Ittleson, W. H., *The Ames Demonstration in Perception.* Princeton, N. J.: Princeton University Press, 1952.

43. Jarrett, J., "Strategies in Risk-taking Situations." (Unpublished Doctoral dissertation, Harvard University Library, 1951.)

44. Jarvik, M. E., "Probability Learning and a Negative Recency Effect in the Serial Anticipation of Alternative Symbols," *Journal of Experimental Psychology,* **41** (1951), 291-97.

45. Jenkin, N., "Two Types of Perceptual Experience," *Journal of Clinical Psychology,* **12** (1956), 44-49.

46. Klein, G. S., "The Personal World through Perception," in *Perception: An Approach to Personality,* eds. R. R. Blake and G. V. Ramsey, pp. 328-55. New York: The Ronald Press Company, 1951.

47. Kohler, I., "Rehabituation in Perception." Published separately in three parts, in German, in *Die Pyramide,* 1953, Heft 5, 6, and 7 (Austria). Trans. Henry Gleitman; ed. J. J. Gibson. Privately circulated by the editor.

48. Köhler, W., *Dynamics in Psychology.* New York: Liveright Publishing Corp., 1940.

49. Kuffler, S. W., C. C. Hunt, and J. P. Quillian, "Function of Medullated Small-Nerve Fibers in Mammalian Ventral Roots: Efferent Nervous Regulation of Muscle Spindle Innervation, *Journal of Neurophysiology,* **14** (1951), 29-54.

50. Kuffler, S. W. and C. C. Hunt, "The Mammalian Small Nerve Fibers: A System for Efferent Nervous Regulation of Muscle Spindle Discharge," *Proceedings of the Association for Research in Nervous and Mental Diseases,* **30** (1952).

51. Lashley, K. S., "Experimental Analysis of Instinctive Behavior," *Psychological Review,* **45** (1938), 445-71.

52. ———, "In Search of the Engram," *Symposium of the Society for Experimental Biology,* **4** (1950), 454-82.

53. Lazarus, R. S., C. W. Eriksen, and C. P. Fonda, "Personality Dynamics and

Auditory Perceptual Recognition," *Journal of Personality*, **19** (1951), 471-82.

54. Lazarus, R. S. and R. A. McCleary, "Autonomic Discrimination without Awareness: A Study of Subception," *Psychological Review*, **58** (1951), 113-222.

55. Leksell, L., "The Action Potential and Excitatory Effects of the Small Ventral Root Fibers to Skeletal Muscles," *Acta Physiol. Scand.*, **10**, Suppl. 31 (1945).

56. Lenneberg, E. H., "An Empirical Investigation into the Relationship between Language and Cognition." (Unpublished Doctoral dissertation, Harvard University Library, 1956.)

57. Lorente De No, R., "Transmission of Impluses through Cranial Motor Nuclei," *Journal of Neurophysiology*, **2** (1939), 402-64.

58. McGinnies, E., "Emotionality and Perceptual Defense," *Psychological Review*, **56** (1949), 244-51.

59. MacKay, D. M., "Toward an Information-flow Model of Human Behavior," *British Journal of Psychology*, **47** (1956), 30-43.

60. Marks, R. W., "The Effect of Probability, Desirability, and 'Privilege' on the State of Expectations of Children," *Journal of Personality*, **19** (1951), 332-51.

61. Miller, G. A., J. S. Bruner, and L. Postman, "Familiarity of Letter Sequences and Tachistoscopic Identification," *Journal of Genetic Psychology*, **50** (1954), 129-39.

62. Miller, G. A., G. A. Heise, and W. Lichten, "The Intelligibility of Speech as a Function of the Context of the Test Materials," *Journal of Experimental Psychology*, **41** (1951), 329-55.

63. Peirce, C. S., "How to Make Our Ideas Clear," *Popular Science Monthly*, **12** (1878), 286-302.

64. Penfield, W., "Memory Mechanisms," *Archives of Neurology and Psychiatry*, **67** (1952), 178-91.

65. Piaget, J., *Play, Dreams, and Imitation in Childhood*. New York: W. W. Norton & Company, Inc., 1951.

66. Pratt, C. C., "The Role of Past Experience in Visual Perception," *Journal of Psychology*, **30** (1950), 85-107.

67. Prentice, W. C. H. Paper read at the Symposium on Conceptual Trends in Psychology, at the American Psychological Association, New York, September 1954.

68. Postman, L. and J. S. Bruner, "Perception under Stress," *Psychological Review*, **55** (1948), 314-23.

69. Postman, L., J. S. Bruner, and R. D. Walk, "The Perception of Error," *British Journal of Psychology*, **42** (1951), 1-10.

70. Postman, L., and R. S. Crutchfield, "The Interaction of Need, Set, and Stimulus Structure in a Cognitive Task," *American Journal of Psychology*, **65** (1952), 196-217.

71. Selfridge, O., "Pattern Recognition and Learning." Memorandum of Lincoln Laboratory, Massachusetts Institute of Technology, 1955.

72. Solomon, R. L. and L. Postman, "Frequency of Usage as a Determinant of Recognition Thresholds for Words," *Journal of Experimental Psychology*, **43** (1952), 195-201.

73. Smith, J. W. and G. S. Klein, "Cognitive Control in Serial Behavior Patterns." Dittoed manuscript, available from author, 1951.

74. Stevens, S. S., Chapter I in *Handbook of Experimental Psychology*, ed. S. S. Stevens. New York: John Wiley & Sons, Inc., 1951.

75. Stevens, S. S., "The Direct Estimation of Sensory Magnitudes—Loudness," *American Journal of Psychology*, **69** (1956), 1-25.

76. Tanner, W. P., Jr. and J. A. Swets, "A Decision-making Theory of Human Detection," *Psychological Review*, **61** (1954), 401-409.

77. Tinbergen, N., *The Study of Instinct*. London: Oxford University Press, 1951.

78. Titchener, E. B., *A Beginner's Psychology*. New York: The Macmillan Company, 1916.

79. Tolman, E. C., "Discussion," *Journal of Personality*, **18** (1949), 6-13.

80. Uttley, A. M., *The Conditional Probability of Signals in the Nervous System*. Radar Research Establishment, British Ministry of Supply, February 1955.

81. Vernon, M. D., *A Further Study of Visual Perception*. Cambridge, England: Cambridge University Press, 1952.

82. Volkman, J., in *Social Psychology at the Crossroads*. New York: Harper & Row, Publishers, 1951.

83. Wallach, H., "Some Considerations Concerning the Relation between Perception and Cognition," *Journal of Personality*, **18** (1949), 6-13.

84. White, M., *The Age of Analysis*. New York: New American Library, 1955.

85. Woodworth, R. S., "Re-enforcement of Perception," *American Journal of Psychology*, **60** (1947), 119-24.

86. Wyatt, D. F. and D. T. Campbell, "On the Liability of Stereotype or Hypothesis, *Journal of Abnormal Social Psychology*, **46** (1951) 496-500.

87. Yokoyama, J., reported in E. G. Boring, *A History of Experimental Psychology* (2nd ed.). New York: Appleton-Century-Crofts, Inc., 1954.

88. Young, J. Z., *Doubt and Certainty in Science*. London: Oxford University Press, 1951.

On Psychological Similarity *

Michael A. Wallach

When Hume spoke of composite ideas, such as *table* or *chair,* as being compounded from simple ideas, such as *brown* or *hard,* he found himself facing the question of how one simple idea could resemble a second one more than a third one. He could handle the question of similarity between

* From M. A. Wallach, "On Psychological Similarity," *Psychological Review,* **65** (1958), 103-16. Reprinted by permission of the author and the American Psychological Association.

The writer is greatly indebted to Jerome S. Bruner for invaluable encouragement and aid in the preparation of this paper. Thanks are also due Albert J. Caron and George Mandler for critical readings of the manuscript. Preliminary research for this paper was done while the writer held a Westengard Travelling Fellowship from Harvard University to the Department of Psychology, University of Cambridge, England.

composite ideas easily enough; the degree of similarity of two composite ideas depended on the number of simple ideas they had in common. But what about similarity between simple ideas themselves? What does it mean to say blue is more similar to green than to red? Hume could not answer this beyond suggesting that similarity between simple ideas is somehow given to us directly—a capitulation that could never satisfy a British empiricist (1; 11, pp. 585–689).

Let us take Hume's predicament as our starting point. Whence does his problem arise? Its origin lies in two omissions: a failure to note the full range of attributes in terms of which objects and events can be grouped and a failure to separate the question of *potential* similarity from that of *psy-*

chological similarity. Consider the first matter. What are the attributes in terms of which objects and events can be grouped or separated? Hume limited himself here—for a reason noted below—to considering simple sensory attributes displayed by the object itself —for example, the brownness or hardness of a table. But a table can be defined in terms of many more attributes than these. To mention but a few possibilities, it can be defined in terms of use (the things done upon it), of location (the places where it is found), or of construction (how it is built). Such attributes as these are no less reducible to a sensory basis than the ones mentioned by Hume, and they suggest a possible answer to Hume's question. We may say green seems more similar to blue than to red because there indeed *are* more attribute-values that green and blue but not red have in common, while there are fewer that green and red but not blue have in common. Hume may, that is to say, be able to retain his common attribute view of similarity by accepting a wider definition of the term "attribute." Thus, for instance, green and blue— but not red—have in common the attribute-value of being colors of grass in the country, colors of water and hence cool colors, summer landscape colors, and so on.

But we have not fully answered the question yet. Some people may *not* say that green and blue are more similar than green and red. The attributive basis for a judgment of similarity may be present and yet the judgment not be made; and, on the other hand, an attributive basis for such a judgment may be lacking and yet the items may be judged similar. There would seem to be a difference, then, between potential similarity and psychological similarity. Part of Hume's difficulty seems to arise from equating the two.

This leads him to fill the perceiver's head with similacral (that is, photographic) representations of environmental attribute-values, and hence to ignore the possibility that the observer may perform a selecting and ignoring function with regard to attribute-values which are environmentally available. Indeed, it is this view that leads him to the first omission we noted—his failure to specify the full range of environmental attributes. For insofar as one assumes the organism to register in similacral fashion what the environment offers, one must conceive of that environment as relatively meager in its offerings, or else the organism would be swamped with information. If, however, one conceives of the organism as selecting some attributes by which to compare items and ignoring other attributes, then it becomes reasonable to suggest a difference between potential and psychological similarity. Potential similarity may well be most usefully measured in terms of the number of common environmental features that two objects or events are found to display—using the broad definition of attribute noted above, and determining the commonalities by reliable means.[1]

This definition has its basis in the old view of similarity as common stimulus elements, to be sure—but it is very different from that view, since the common-stimulus-elements approach used the narrow definition of attribute for which we criticized Hume, and that view was thought to apply to psychological similarity, which we shall

---

[1] The problem of just what means to use and how, has been treated at length by Brunswik (3) in his discussions of ecological validity. The means are, basically, responses of a sample of judges—and they may be responses as varied as reading a light meter or judging a painting's colors to be warm or cool. The validation, then, is consensual in nature.

see is often not the case. Establishment of the degree of potential similarity between two things provides us with an important baseline: It lets us validate or contravalidate individual reports of similarity. A person may, for instance, report that two problems are similar in the sense that the same solution is thought to be applicable to both; to ask whether this feeling of similarity is valid is to ask whether the same solution is in fact applicable to both problems; are they potentially similar in the sense of having this property in common? Or a person may report that two objects are similar in the sense that both are thought usable for driving a nail into a board. To validate or contravalidate this impression of similarity, we determine whether both objects can in fact be used this way.

Broadening the definition of "attribute" and recognizing that potential and psychological similarity are distinct but related issues, suggest that the question of psychological similarity may lie at the basis of diverse kinds of psychological research on cognition that have hitherto usually been considered apart from each other—ranging from studies on stimulus generalization to studies on learning and thinking. We submit it may be fruitful to inquire how some of this research bears on the issues we have raised, and this for two reasons. First of all, we have not yet examined the possible ways in which psychological similarity might be defined, although we have suggested what seems to us a tenable definition for potential similarity. Insofar as this research really bears on psychological similarity, it may help us weigh alternative definitions of the term. Secondly, such exploration of definitions may well have experimental implications for further research in these diverse areas.

SOME DEFINITIONS OF PSYCHOLOGICAL SIMILARITY

One may suggest at least four ways of defining psychological similarity. The first derives from Hume's approach. Hume, in equating potential and psychological similarity, supposes that if common properties are present in the environment, they will be perceived by the person. Hence, impressions of similarity can be directly controlled by varying the environment's potential similarity in the sense of the common values of attributes it displays. The selecting and ignoring capacities of the organism are neglected, and psychological similarity is defined in terms of *common environmental properties*. An alternative approach is to recognize the organism's selective functions and suggest that recognition of common environmental properties depends upon making a common response to instances that share this attribute-value. The attribute-value may be environmentally present in two items, and yet the person may not offer a common response to them; or the attribute-value may be absent, and yet a common response be made. There is not necessarily a direct relation between psychological and potential similarity. Psychological similarity here, then, is defined in terms of *common responses*. Yet another possible approach is to suggest there are neural traces laid down along various dimensions when a stimulus impinges, and psychological similarity depends on how far a new stimulus is from the old stimulus on such a dimension— the view of *primary stimulation gradients*.

A fourth view may also be proposed. It is related, to be sure, to the view of common responses but seeks to separate the process of recognizing similarity from making a common response.

Yet this fourth approach is not that of stimulation gradients, for it does not assume that there is necessarily an inverse relationship between degree of recognized similarity and distance of new from old stimuli along some dimensions. The position may be put somewhat as follows. Although a common response may be forthcoming to signal the recognition of similarity when two events occur, this response is itself a rather trivial matter (it may be made with the big toe as well as with the vocal cords, and need not be of fixed character), and its being made depends on the prior learning of a rule for categorizing events as equivalent. This rule specifies what property (attribute-value) or properties must be conjointly found in order to assign events to the same class, and also tells us the nature of the contrast being made—the relevant alternative class whose members are to be judged nonexemplars of the class of interest.[2] We construct this contrast class in such ways as the following. (*a*) By implication, from the degree of complexity of the class of interest; since the more complex that class is, the more likely we are to consider small deviations from it as the only relevant alternative class or classes, and to totally neglect large deviations.[3] Thus, for instance, we are likely to contrast cocker spaniels with setters or poodles and not with all other animals, whereas "all other animals" would be a relevant contrast class if we were interested in dogs rather than cocker spaniels. (*b*) By experience with all the instances,

positive and negative, to which we are exposed, for these establish the domain of material relevant to us. Construction of a contrast class in turn suggests which properties we may best use for discriminating positive from relevant negative instances. For example, while the attribute of size will not let us discriminate dogs from all other animals, it does suffice to separate setters from cocker spaniels.

The classification rule that we learn, then, has two aspects: it tells us on what basis we are to group two events in one class and also tells us the range of other events with which we are contrasting positive instances of the class of interest—it tells us what negative instances are relevant. The rule serves to delimit a particular domain of events and to draw a *contrast* between two subsets within that domain: positive and negative instances of the class in question. This rule stipulates that certain properties must be found compresent, that is, together, in order to place an instance in a given class. Such a rule for class-inclusion becomes harder to attain, the greater the number of properties which the rule requires to be compresent before inclusion in the given class is warranted. This is the case because the larger the number of properties whose compresence is required in this way for class-inclusion, the greater is the number of properties which are found compresent in at least some of the relevant negative instances as well as in all positive instances of the class in question, thus making it more difficult to locate the difference between positive and negative instances.

In brief, then, this fourth proposal suggests that recognition of similarity depends on applying a rule which leads one to *assign items to a common category*. There is much more to similarity than the response of making this as-

---

[2] See Bruner, Goodnow, and Austin (2), p. 38; and Kelley (13), pp. 303-305.

[3] The "implication" in question here is not one of logical necessity, but rather a strategy that people tend to use—and indeed a valuable one—for determining the level of classificategory discriminations to make in particular situations.

signment. For prior to that, one must learn the rule which guides the response.[4]

Each of these ways of defining psychological similarity has much to be said in its favor, but no one of them seems able to account for all the evidence. Our aim in the following pages is to suggest some possible limitations which various of these views face and to sketch the possible fruitfulness of exploring more fully the one of these approaches that defines psychological similarity in terms of assigning events to a common category.

If, as we have suggested, diverse areas of psychological research all concern psychological similarity, one is led to ask whether these areas may be using the same kind of procedure, since a common concern sometimes intimates a common procedure of inquiry. This seems indeed to be the case here, and the procedure in question is that of transfer—the influence of experience in one situation on the handling of a subsequent situation. Insofar as something learned in a first situation will aid performance in a second one, then the subject will show positive transfer if he recognizes the two situations to be similar; while insofar as something learned in that first situation will hinder performance in the second, then he will show **negative** transfer if he recognizes the two situations as similar. Transferability of learning thus provides a set of opera-

tions for determining whether recognition of similarity occurred. As we turn to various experiments now, in further considering the definitions of psychological similarity that we have reviewed, we shall find that all of them in effect use this transferability procedure.

COMMON ENVIRONMENTAL PROPERTIES

Since this is, perhaps, the most familiar and earliest view as to the nature of psychological similarity, we need not dwell on the many kinds of evidence from which it arose—for instance, motor learning studies, of which the work by Lewis, McAllister, and Adams (20, 21) provides a recent example. Commonality of the environmental properties is established by the identity of measurement readings of the centimeters-grams-seconds variety in the two situations being compared (call them Original Learning, OL, and Transfer Learning, TL). The evidence indicates that frequently, to be sure, transferability of learning, and hence psychological similarity, is related to presence of common environmental properties in these two situations. But there are, on the other hand, cases where presentation of common properties in OL and TL does not result in psychological similarity of the two and hence in greater transfer.

Consider, for instance, a study by Schwarz (27). In the OL task, the subject learned to attach a certain response to a certain stimulus. In the TL task, he had to learn to link a different response to that old stimulus. If transfer here depends on common environmental properties, one would expect associative interference—that is, the old stimulus should tend to elicit

---

[4] If one prefers to argue that such a rule is simply a complex response, it is incumbent upon one to specify the responses constituting that rule. The suggestion often made at this juncture is that the rule is no more than the verbal responses which express it. But in animal learning studies discussed later—where one cannot, therefore, say the rule is nothing more than verbal responses—we shall note that the common responses which are present do not in fact constitute the basis of the rule that is learned.

the old response; it should be transferred to the TL task despite its inappropriateness there. Actually, such associative interference occurred only if the subject was forced to pay attention to something other than this particular task; if allowed to attend to this task, the old response was not transferred despite identity of stimulus. When the subject was "paying attention" he was grouping environmental events differently than when he was "not paying attention." When not paying attention, stimulus identity was allowed to become the attributive basis for classification; but when paying attention, the temporal difference between "stimulus in the OL task" and "stimulus in the TL task" was effective in directing the subject to assign the OL and TL stimuli to different classes based on this temporal distinction, even though they were physically identical. Assigning them to different classes meant that negative transfer was avoided.

Or consider a study by Ellis (4) in which college students learned finger mazes. Three different mazes were used in all, Maze 3 consisting of Mazes 1 and 2 linked together. One group learned Mazes 1 and 3, another learned Mazes 2 and 3, and a third learned Maze 3 alone. Whereas an identical-stimulus-elements approach would predict marked positive transfer for the first two groups in their learning of Maze 3, in actuality those two groups were not significantly better in their learning of Maze 3 than the group learning that maze *de novo*. Objectively identical stimulus elements did not per se lead to recognition of similarity.

Common environmental attributes, then, do not seem to be an infallible indicator of psychological similarity. Such similarity may, under these conditions, be present for the person— but then again it may not.

COMMON RESPONSES

It was perhaps the Kantian revolution in philosophy that first called into question Hume's conception of the organism as a mirror of environmental stimulation and suggested instead that the organism is a filterer and arranger of environmental events. The "mentalism" of Kant's approach banned it from having direct repercussions in American psychology until it was realized that considering the organism an active mediator does not require descent into its depths but rather can be achieved by noting how the organism responds to its environment. One need not go beyond the relation between environmental stimuli and a person's responses. If, according to this view, a person was found to respond the same way to two objectively different situations, then those two situations were psychologically similar for him. And if, on the other hand, a person responded differently despite repetition of the same situation (common environmental properties), then no such psychological similarity obtained. Such an approach constituted a tremendous advance. The Humian assumption of man as capable merely of similacral representations of his environment was overcome, and in its place the capacities of the organism to select, ignore, and emphasize environmental attributes were recognized. The exciting effects of this idea can be seen, for example, in the early work by Shipley (28, 29). In one experiment, linking an eyewink response to both light and shock, where shock elicited finger withdrawal, resulted in light becoming adequate to elicit finger withdrawal too. The common response of winking made to both light and shock indicated their psychological similarity for the subject. Whereas we would say this response was a signal of this similarity, proponents of the common response view would hold that this response itself constitutes that similarity. The implications of this kind of approach are ably developed by Osgood (25), among others, and its applicability to many questions of psychological similarity is clear.

The common-response view leaves us, however, with some uneasiness. For one thing, those who maintain it sometimes seem to rely on the magical efficacy of the term *response* to provide an aura of explanation where none really exists. The premise of the approach is that transfer will occur, and hence two events will seem similar, to the extent to which the organism makes the same response to both. But from here on the going becomes less simple. Paradoxically enough, the insufficiency of this premise seems to be tacitly recognized, for the full view consists of an attempt to defend the premise's lacks. Since the hypothesized common response that supposedly mediates the transfer sometimes cannot be located even though transfer is found, one meets the rationalization that sometimes the common response linked to disparate stimuli is not observable, but in all such cases these unobservable responses are supposed to have developed as fractional anticipations of observable ones. This is an empty-organism theory with a new twist. The organism gets filled eventually, but only with fractions of things that were overt responses once.

It seems relevant to remember that much of the impetus behind this view derives not from considerations of scientific adequacy as such, but rather from the cultural milieu of an earlier behaviorism in which the model of the organism as capable of transformed representations of its environment was still held in disrepute, as "mentalistic." The common response theory hence

sought to make this model acceptable to the scientific community by framing it in the language of responses. This end has been accomplished long since, however, so it would perhaps be advisable now to restrict more carefully use of the term "response" to its usual meaning: muscular and glandular reactions. We would note that the restraints imposed by the nature of muscles and glands imply that behavior must be more limited and have fewer dimensions about it than what goes on inside the organism.[5] Why, then, limit on a priori grounds one's conception of what goes on in the organism to fractions of behavior? It does not make constructs more scientific to frame them in the same terms as observables. Rather, the reason we postulate constructs is that the relations among observables are extremely complex, and it often proves necessary to invest our constructs with properties different from those of behavior in order the better to predict that very behavior. The interests of explanation are not served simply by filling the organism with analogues of behavior. Hospers (9) and other philosophers have well pointed out that such reduction to the familiar is not what we really mean by scientific explanation.

But were our uneasiness over the common-response approach to stem only from general considerations such as these, it might well be dismissed. Dismissal becomes more difficult, however, when one notes the gradual accumulation of experimental evidence that questions the sufficiency of response identity for mediating transfer

---

[5] One way to indicate this difference between behavior and what goes on inside the organism, is in combinatorial terms: there are more elements that can be combined, and hence a greater variety of possible outcomes, at the neuron level, than at the level of muscles and glands.

of learning. Consider, for instance, a recent study by Bruner, Mandler, O'Dowd, and Wallach.[6] Rats were overtrained to run left-right-left-right at successive choice points of a linear maze, and then were faced with the task of learning to run right-left-right-left in the same maze. The object was to find whether there was positive transfer from learning the first turn sequence to learning its mirror-image reversal.

According to the response-mediation approach, transfer is said to depend on identity of response, and the greatest identity of response between OL and TL here is the single-alternation weaving motion whereby the rat alternates from one side to the other at successive choice points. The faster a rat runs from start box to goal box, the more of a weaving motion he learns. Insofar, then, as transfer depends on the identity of a weaving-alternation response in OL and TL, rats running faster should show more positive transfer than rats running more slowly. The results do not support this prediction. There was no correlation between speed of running during OL and degree of positive transfer on TL, within any of the groups run. Furthermore, considering differences in running speed between groups—differences that were created by varying hunger conditions—groups whose drive conditions resulted in their running slowly during either OL or TL or both showed positive transfer, while the group whose drive conditions resulted in its running fast during both OL and TL showed no transfer. Apparently, therefore, something other than a common response of weaving single alternation causes the transfer in the present experiment.

Or take North's finding (23, 24) that the performance of rats on discrimination reversals was no better when the rat was made to correct overtly his mistakes than when mistakes were left uncorrected. It was expected that reversal learning would be better in the former condition, since it permitted a correct response to occur after a wrong choice, and this correct response was supposed to become associated to the present maze stimuli, and hence be evoked by these stimuli on the next trial, thereby mediating a fullfledged overt correct response. Identity of response thus was expected to mediate reversal learning. Much positive transfer in the learning of successive reversals occurred, but it was not due to response mediation. It occurred, rather, only when there was a sufficient amount of overtraining on each reversal—a result also obtained in the study on single alternation cited above. Apparently, for the animal to classify initial and later situations in terms of the more abstract property which they in fact have in common, he must be given enough practice on the former situation so that its more concrete properties no longer require all his attention. The abstract property in question was single alternation in the case of the first study noted; reversal of position response on encountering an error, in the case of the second study. The concrete properties involved were particular sorts of muscular kinesthesis that occur in relation to particular olfactory and visual cues from various parts of the maze.

To be sure, insofar as one broadens the definition of "response" to include anything going on inside the organism, as some theorists such as Osgood (25) and Mandler (22) advise, evidence of the above sorts does not run counter to the common-response view. But broad-

---

[6] J. S. Bruner, Jean M. Mandler, D. O'Dowd, and M. A. Wallach. "The Role of Overlearning and Drive Level in Reversal Learning." To be published.

ening the definition in this way would seem more to cloud than to clarify the issues. There are grounds, then, for suggesting that presence or absence of common responses is not an infallible indication of presence or absence of psychological similarity, although there are certainly cases where such responses do serve in this manner.

PRIMARY STIMULATION GRADIENTS

Many studies have been done in support of a view of psychological similarity which may be stated somewhat as follows. When a stimulus impinges on a receptor and becomes associated to a response, a neural gradient is laid down such that other stimuli will also elicit this response but to lesser degree, response elicitability decreasing with increasing distance of the new stimulus from the training stimulus along some dimension of stimulus differences—for instance, intensity or pitch of tones. The dimension of primary stimulus generalization need not be innate, as was assumed by those proponents of this approach who were most directly in the Pavlovian tradition, like Hull (10); but rather may be the product of learned differentiation (that is, discrimination training)—a coming into closer contact with stimulus differences —as in the manner suggested by Gibson and Gibson (5). But however the dimensions are thought to arise, the position in question assumes the shape of the gradient laid down upon them to fall off on either side of the point of stimulation along these dimensions; and, if training and test stimuli are presented at discriminably separate points along a dimension which the individual has learned to discriminate, or can innately discriminate, then generalization is expected to occur along that dimension.

These ideas of a normal distribution of intensity of excitation about a point of stimulation, and the automatic fashion in which generalization is expected to occur between discriminable points on any discriminable dimension when these points are stimulated in succession, were derived from an earlier era of physiological research in which spatial representations of sensory qualities in the cortex were a prime concern— we may see it in such apparently opposed currents of thought as Pavlov (26) on the one hand, and Köhler (19) on the other. And some work, to be sure, does seem best interpretable in terms of such ideas (for example, Guttman and Kalish, 8). But there appear to be other studies which, although ostensibly dealing with the same processes, may perhaps be better interpreted in different terms. In a number of experiments on "stimulus generalization" in humans, psychological similarity may be mediated not by that process but rather by the class to which the subject assigns various inputs. The magnitude of the subject's response to a test stimulus can depend, one may suggest, on whether or not he places both training and test stimuli in a common class. There may well be individual differences as to whether these two stimuli are placed in the same category or not; and in addition, experimental conditions may be set up in such a manner as to induce or discourage the placement of those two stimuli in the same class without varying these stimulus presentations themselves. If such diffuse factors as these were to cause differences in magnitude of response to the test stimulus—despite the facts that the dimension along which the training and test stimuli fall and the differences along that dimension are easily discriminable by the subject, and the training and test stimuli presented are the same for all these subjects—then the sufficiency of a stimulus-generalization explanation for such data would be called into question. And, in fact, there do seem to be cases where differences of these kinds occur.

We may note, for example, a study by Wickens, Schroder, and Snide (32), using the GSR. Adult subjects in one group received shock-reinforced presentations of a particular tone and then were given extinction trials with one of three tones at varying frequency distances from the training tone. Subjects in another group underwent the same regimen, except they heard a nonreinforced click interspersed among the reinforced tone presentations during training. The group not hearing clicks—qua group—yielded a gradient of decreasing GSR magnitude as distance between training and test stimuli increased; but the height and shape of the gradient differed on different extinction trials, and only by averaging the results of large number of subjects (24 in each extinction subgroup) could one tease out even these not very great consistencies. The group hearing clicks showed no clear gradients at all, even as a group.

Why the different results from these two conditions? Recall what we noted earlier concerning the two aspects of rules for classing events as equivalent: that they specify the range of negative instances we are seeking to discriminate, as well as the nature of positive exemplars of the class of interest. We would suggest that presence versus absence of clicks during training resulted in the learning of different rules for the classification of test stimuli during extinction. The group hearing clicks used the property "tones" as definitive for class-inclusion, and excluded clicks. All test tones were assigned to one class. Because of what they experienced during the training series, the domain of

instances for this group consisted of "tones" and "clicks." The group not hearing clicks, on the other hand, used the properties "tones, and within such-and-such range of pitch" as definitive for class-inclusion, and excluded tones of other pitch—these latter being the relevant negative exemplars for them. Only some test tones met the specifications for this class. Because, then, this group experienced only the repeated tone during training—that is, heard no clicks—this group's domain of instances consisted of "tones of various pitches." Hence, we would expect the GSR to the test tones far from the training tone to be much less than that to the test tone closest to the training tone for the group not hearing clicks —and this was in fact the case. These subjects assigned only the nearest test tones to the same class as the training tone, further-away test tones being excluded. But we would expect no clear trends of differences in GSR among the test tones for the group hearing clicks—and this also was the case. These subjects assigned all test tones to the same class as the training tone, clicks being the items which were excluded from the class. The difference between the click and no-click conditions, then, seems to be that the subject was induced to classify the tones differently in each case.

It may be that many other "generalization" experiments also involve a categorization process like that we postulate for the "no-click" group in the above study: Test stimuli close to the training stimulus are placed in one class with the latter, those further from the training stimulus being excluded. The widths of the class in question vary across individuals, and hence one finds a smooth normal-curve type of gradient only when one averages all subjects together. But there are further individual differences in classification, and, what is more, classifications may change as a test series proceeds. Hence one finds, for instance, nonconsistent results over extinction trials taking groups of subjects as wholes—as in a study by Grant and Schiller (7). That these effects are due to categorization differences seems a reasonable hypothesis when one considers work like that by Wickens *et al.*, where, on our interpretation, the probabilities of alternative rules for classification were varied, and this was found to cause differences in magnitude of response to a test stimulus.

Although primary stimulation gradients seem able to account for some cases of psychological similarity, then, there are others in which a different process may well be at work.

ASSIGNMENT TO A COMMON CATEGORY

Each of the three definitions of psychological similarity noted above has been found to have only limited applicability. Such is also the case with this fourth definition. Since, however, it is younger than the others, its implications have not yet been thoroughly explored; and since it seems relevant in many cases where the other definitions cannot easily be applied, it seems advisable to examine it further with regard to its range of utility.

According to this fourth definition, when we have attained a rule which bisects a domain of events into a set that exemplifies a certain property or conjunction of properties and a particular contrasting set that does not, then we will transfer behavior from one to another of two events that fall into the former set, but will tend not to transfer behavior from either of them to an event in the latter set. Again, then, the relation has two aspects: It tells us the range of negative instances which are relevant to our purposes of dis-

crimination, as well as the basis on which we are to declare events positive exemplars of the class of interest. In short, recognition of the similarity of two events depends on their being classed as equivalent—as exemplifying the property or conjunction of properties in question, and as standing in contrast to a particular range of non-exemplars.[7] We learn to take one or more particular properties as criterial for sorting a domain of events.

There would seem to be two main determinants of the kinds of classification rules we attain: the nature of the instances presented (that is, the environmental properties to which we have been exposed); and our predilections for some bases of classification and prejudices against others. Varying either the nature of the instances or our classification preferences hence should influence psychological similarity in predictable ways.[8] Let us see if this approach seems to contribute anything in considering two psychological issues: the first, transposition—a matter around which much empirical study has centered; and the second, distinctive similarity—Köhler's demonstration of the importance of similarity in guiding attempts at more complex human problem-solving.

Transportation

Some years ago, Köhler (17, pp. 217-227) and Koffka (15) argued that

[7] This view is related to those of Goodman (6) and Kelley (13), and was first approached in Klüver's early work (14).

[8] Since the present paper's aim is to compare this fourth approach to psychological similarity with the other three and to provide initial indications of that approach's empirical utility, we cannot discuss this approach in greater detail than is provided in the present paragraphs and in the earlier section where this view was introduced. More detailed discussion of this view in particular will be provided in a subsequent paper.

discriminating in terms of such relations as "brighter than" or "larger than" is more primitive, more basic, than discriminating in terms of absolute sensory qualities such as brightnesses and sizes. Spence (30) argued just as insistently, however, that responding on the basis of absolute stimulus qualities such as brightness or size is more primitive, and relational responding is a result of the algebraic summation of response tendencies to absolute stimuli. But one may suggest a third alternative. Perhaps higher organisms (and certainly humans) can learn to respond either in terms of relations between stimuli or in terms of absolute stimulus qualities, and which selection they will make depends largely on the conditions instituted concerning classification preferences and the nature of the instances.

Consider, for example, the nature of the instances. We would predict a greater tendency for subjects to respond relationally on a transfer test, when trained on couplets of one large and one small form apiece, and when the particular forms used vary in size (but not shape) across couplets, than if the same amount of training were given on one repeated couplet of a large and small form; in both cases response to the larger form is always rewarded during training. In the former condition, the nature of the instances is such as to permit the subject to rule out the possibility of classifying the data in terms of the absolute stimulus quality of size, and the only class into which all data fit is one defined by the relational property of "larger than"; whereas in the latter condition, the kinds of instances presented permit classification on the basis of absolute size or relative size. We could just as well, of course, arrange our instances so as to rule out the possibility of classifying on the basis of relative size, simply by always rewarding choice of the same particular stimulus form, and having it appear sometimes paired with a larger form, sometimes with a smaller form. In a like manner, whether the subject will classify on an absolute, relational, or even some other basis depends on his biases for or against particular bases of classification, as induced by instructions or other means. Given variation in the nature of the instances and in such biases, it would seem one can create conditions that will induce the subject to classify the training instances, and hence to transfer, on any basis we desire.

Thus, work with children by Jackson and Jerome (12), for instance, indicates that how the child categorizes the training instances depends on whether he is asked to decide which stimulus is correct after the presentation of both, or rather is required to indicate, after each stimulus is presented, whether it is the correct or incorrect stimulus. As we would expect from the differing emphases on relational versus absolute classifying implied by these different conditions of instance presentation, relational choices were preponderant when the child gave one over-all response after simultaneous or successive presentation of both stimuli, whereas absolute choices were in the majority when the child had to respond to one stimulus before the second was presented. Requiring the subject to make a separate response to each stimulus favors classifying on an absolute basis, whereas requiring the subject to make a single response to both stimuli as a pair favors classifying on a relational basis.

Stevenson, Iscoe, and McConnell (31) found that college students varied in the basis they used for responding on the first transposition test trial; many, to be sure, responded on a relational basis, but some responded on an absolute basis. Apparently, different subjects received different impressions about what was required of them, and hence classified the data presented to them in different ways. What seem needed in this area, then, are studies analyzing the conditions of instance presentation and biases concerning particular attributes that influence the basis the subject chooses for classifying the training stimuli—conditions which therefore influence the kind of transposition shown.

Distinctive Similarity

Köhler (16) uses the term "distinctive similarity" for denoting that particular items resemble each other more than they resemble the rest of the situation. The nature of this greater or lesser resemblance is itself, however, left unanalyzed, although an earlier experiment by Köhler and von Restorff (18) had explored the effects of such similarity on complex human problem-solving. Two groups were taught a principle for solving an arithmetic problem, and transfer was measured later to the solution of a new arithmetic problem on which that principle—an arithmetic shortcut—could also be used. Between these two occurrences, one group was given arithmetic problems to which, however, this principle was not applicable, whereas the other group was given entirely different tasks to do—the solution of matchstick puzzles. The latter group showed greater transfer of the principle to the new problem than did the former group. Thus similarity of the first to the last problem, in particular, was greater for the latter group than for the former group; in one case it was "distinctive," in the other case it was not. But of what does this psychological similarity consist?

One may suggest that analysis of the classification tasks facing the sub-jects in Köhler and von Restorff's groups casts light on something which these authors really left shrouded in mystery—the nature of distinctive similarity. After being shown the application of the principle to the initial arithmetic problem, the task of the subject became, essentially, that of attaining the rule specifying what property or properties must be conjointly found in order to assign problems to the class to which this principle is applicable, and specifying the relevant range of negative instances with which the subject must concern himself. The group performing better on the transfer test learned but a simple rule for classification: only one obvious property made an item a positive exemplar of the class of items to which the shortcut principle was applicable—namely, that the item be an arithmetic problem; and the degree of overlap of positive and relevant negative instances in terms of compresence of properties was minimal—no more than that they were all "problems." The group performing less well on the transfer test was given the task of learning a more complex rule for classification; a conjunction of properties was required to make an item a positive exemplar of the class in question: the item had to be an arithmetic problem *and also* had to exhibit certain additional features. For this group there are more properties compresent for positive and relevant negative instances (for example, that the task be not only a problem but also an *arithmetic* problem is compresent for both) than for the other group. In the first case, the domain of relevant events is "arithmetic and matchstick problems," and the contrast is between these two types. In the second case, the domain is "arithmetic problems," and the contrast is between arithmetic problems with certain features and arithmetic problems with other features. Again, the nature of the instances presented to the subject determines the kind of classification attempted. In short, "distinctive similarity" of two events means that the rule for assigning them to the same class provides for a minimum number of properties to be found compresent in at least some of the relevant negative instances, as well as all the positive instances of that class. The difference between positive and relevant negative exemplars is easier to locate.

Could the rule for the group that does poorly be rendered easier by a change in biases of the subjects toward particular attributes? Let us consider the following variation on the Köhler and von Restorff experiment. Suppose we give another group all mathematics problems and in the same order as the original group, but tell them, after the shortcut has been explained, that not all the subsequent problems are amenable to the shortcut, but that some will be. We have thereby set these subjects to remain vigilant throughout the series for the features of later problems that are the same as those in the initial one—the features that hence permit the principle to be applied—and would expect them to apply the shortcut to the last problem more often than did the group not given this set. Without changing the problems, then, we would expect the percentage of shortcut solutions to increase because of this change in set; these subjects have been more sharply tuned to try to find what features of arithmetic problems permit application of the shortcut. They have been encouraged to try to take a particular conjunction of properties as criterial for sorting events.

If one wishes to study distinctive similarity in the transfer of principles for problem-solving, then, the recommendation would seem to be this. Let us determine the conditions of instance presentation and attribute biases that aid or hinder the arrival of the subjects at rules for classifying tasks in terms of properties which they potentially have in common—conditions which aid or hinder, in other words, a match between psychological similarity and potential similarity.

CONCLUSION

The aim of this discussion has been twofold. First, after pointing out the ubiquitousness of the issue of psychological similarity in various areas of research on cognition to note the way in which a common procedure, that of the transfer experiment, tends to unite them, and to urge that they be conceptualized in an integrated manner. Second, to consider the values and difficulties of four conceptions of psychological similarity, defined in terms of common environmental properties, common responses, primary stimulation gradients, and assignment to a common category. All four definitions are, to be sure, of limited applicability—but the last of them appears to apply in many instances where the first three do not. Several experimental implications of defining psychological similarity in terms of assignment to a common category were explored, and were taken to indicate that further work with this approach may well prove fruitful.

REFERENCES

1. Aaron, R. I., *The Theory of Universals*. London: Clarendon Press, 1952.

2. Bruner, J. S., J. J. Goodnow, and G. A. Austin, *A Study of Thinking*. New York: John Wiley & Sons, Inc., 1956.

3. Brunswik, E., *Perception and the Representative Design of Psychological Experiments*. Berkeley: University of California Press, 1956.

4. Ellis, W. D., "Memory for Physically Identical Elements in Human Maze Learning: A Transfer Problem," *Psychological Bulletin,* **36** (1939), 545-46.

5. Gibson, J. J. and Eleanor J. Gibson, "Perceptual Learning: Differentiation or Enrichment?" *Psychological Review,* **62** (1955), 32-41.

6. Goodman, N., *Fact, Fiction, and Forecast.* Cambridge, Mass.: Harvard University Press, 1955.

7. Grant, D. A. and J. J. Schiller, "Generalization of the Conditioned Galvanic Skin Response to Visual Stimuli," *Journal of Experimental Psychology,* **46** (1953), 309-13.

8. Guttman, N. and H. I. Kalish, "Discriminability and Stimulus Generalization," *Journal of Experimental Psychology,* **51** (1956), 79-88.

9. Hospers, J., "On Explanation," *Journal of Philosophy,* **43** (1946), 337-56.

10. Hull, C. L., "The Problem of Stimulus Equivalence in Behavior Theory," *Psychological Review,* **46** (1939), 9-30.

11. Hume, D., "An Enquiry Concerning Human Understanding," in *The English Philosophers from Bacon to Mill,* ed. E. A. Burtt, pp. 585-689. New York: Modern Library, 1939.

12. Jackson, T. A. and E. A. Jerome, "Studies in the Transposition of Learning by Children: VI. Simultaneous vs. Successive Presentation of the Stimuli to Bright and Dull Children," *Journal of Experimental Psychology,* **33** (1943), 431-39.

13. Kelley, G. A., *The Psychology of Personal Constructs:* Vol. I. *A Theory of Personality.* New York: W. W. Norton & Company, 1955.

14. Klüver, H., *Behavior Mechanisms in Monkeys.* Chicago: University of Chicago Press, 1933.

15. Koffka, K., *The Growth of the Mind.* New York: Harcourt, Brace & World, Inc., 1928.

16. Köhler, W., *Dynamics in Psychology.* New York: Liveright Publishing Corp., 1940.

17. ———, "Simple Structural Functions in the Chimpanzee and in the Chicken," in *A Source Book of Gestalt Psychology,* ed. W. D. Ellis, pp. 217-27. New York: Humanities Press, 1950.

18. Köhler, W. and Hedwig von Restorff, "Analyse von Vorgangen in Spurenfeld: II. Zur Theorie der Reproduktion," *Psychol. Forsch.,* **21** (1935), 56-112.

19. Köhler, W. and H. Wallach, "Figural After-effects: An Investigation of Visual Processes," *Proceedings of the American Philosophical Society,* **88** (1944), 269-357.

20. Lewis, D., Dorothy E. McAllister, and J. A. Adams, "Facilitation and Interference in Performance on the Modified Mashburn Apparatus: I. The Effects of Varying the Amount of Original Learning," *Journal of Experimental Psychology,* **41** (1951), 247-68.

21. McAllister, Dorothy E. and D. Lewis, "Facilitation and Interference in Performance on the Modified Mashburn Apparatus: I. The Effects of Varying the Amount of Interpolated Learning," *Journal of Experimental Psychology,* **41** (1951), 356-63.

22. Mandler, G., "Response Factors in Human Learning," *Psychological Review,* **61** (1954) 235-44.

23. North, A. J., "Improvement in Successive Discrimination Reversals," *Journal of Comparative Physiological Psychology,* **43** (1950), 442-60.

24. ———, "Performance during an Extended Series of Discrimination Reversals," *Journal of Comparative Physiological Psychology,* **43** (1950), 461-70.

25. Osgood, C. E., *Method and Theory in Experimental Psychology.* New York: Oxford University Press, 1953.

26. Pavlov, I. P., *Conditioned Reflexes.* London: Oxford University Press, 1927.

27. Schwarz, G., "Über Rückfalligkeit bei Umgewohnung, *Psychol. Forsch.,* **9** (1927), 86-158.

28. Shipley, W. C., "An Apparent Transfer of Conditioning," *Journal of Genetic Psychology,* **8** (1933), 382-90.

29. ———, "Indirect Conditioning," *Journal of Genetic Psychology*, **10** (1935), 337-57.

30. Spence, K. W., "The Differential Response in Animals to Stimuli Varying within a Single Dimension," *Psychological Review*, **44** (1937), 278-80.

31. Stevenson, H. W., I. Iscoe, and Claudia McConnell, "A Developmental Study of Transposition," *Journal of Experimental Psychology*, **49** (1955), 278-80.

32. Wickens, D. D., H. M. Schroder, and J. D. Snide, "Primary Stimulus Generalization of the GSR under Two Conditions," *Journal of Experimental Psychology*, **47** (1954), 52-56.

The Identification of Recurrent Regularity *

Jerome S. Bruner, Michael A. Wallach, and E. H. Galanter

Much of what we classify as learning, recognition, and problem-solving consists of being able to identify recurrent regularities in the environment.[1] What makes such a task a problem is that recurrent regularities—be they turns in a maze, elements in a temporal pattern, or a pattern in successive events—may either be masked by factors that are irrelevant to the regularity, or the regularity itself may be of such a complexity that it exceeds the memory span that an observer brings to the task.

One may think of the task involved in identifying recurrent regularity as requiring the observer to construct a model that is isomorphic with the redundancy of the environment. The case is easily illustrated by reference to the identification of language sequences. If the individual knows a language, that is, has a model of the recurrent regularity of letters or words in the language, his task of identification is rendered easy in proportion to the degree to which a linguistic display approximates the typical sequences of the language.[2] So, too, for the rat learning a single alternation-pattern; he must construct an adequate, predictive model of the environmental regularity to be identified over time.

Model-construction involves the elimination of irrelevancies where such exist or the evolving of methods of recoding stimulus-events in such a way as to bring them within the compass of attentional or immediate memory-span. An illustration of the first kind of

* From J. S. Bruner, M. A. Wallach, and E. H. Galanter, "The Identification of Recurrent Regularity," *American Journal of Psychology,* **72** (1959), 200-209. Reprinted by permission of the authors and publisher.

This research was supported in part by the Cognition Project of Harvard University and in part by the Air Force under Contract No. AF41 (657)-118.

[1] J. S. Bruner, "Going Beyond the Information Given," in *Cognitive Approaches to Psychology*, eds. J. S. Bruner, Egon Brunswik, *et al.* (1957), pp. 1-34. E. H. Galanter and M. Gerstenhaber, "On Thought: The Extrinsic Theory," *Psychological Review*, **63** (1956), 218-227.

[2] G. A. Miller, J. S. Bruner, and Leo Postman, "Familiarity of Letter Sequences and Tachistoscopic Identification," *Journal of Genetic Psychology*, **50** (1954), 129-39.

operation is the strategy employed in attaining concepts; the second is exemplified by the recoding of stimulus-inputs to conform to the limits imposed on memory.[3]

The present study is concerned with the sources of interference that prevent rapid and efficient identification of recurrent regularities in the environment. We shall confine ourselves exclusively to regularities of a simple kind that are well within the capacity of people to identify when no interference is present. To illustrate the approach, let us imagine a sequence of events, each of which may take one of two forms—for example, a sequence of binary digits. The sequence is made up of a series of recurrent, fixed, sub-series, such as 001001001 . . . or 100-110011001 . . . and the subject's (*S*'s) task is to predict each event before it occurs. His task is to identify the regularity by constructing such models as "001 repeated" or "1001 repeated" and thereby to predict subsequent events in the series perfectly. At the outset he knows neither that there is a recurrent sequence nor that it is of any particular length. He is told only whether each of his single predictions is correct or not.

What are the factors that prevent adequate construction of a model in such a simple task? In general terms, we can specify three.

Stimulus-interference. If the sequence is interfered with by single events that do not conform to the recurrent series, if an element of randomness is added to the series, it is likely that the task of model construction will be difficult in proportion to the amount of randomness introduced. This is a seemingly banal point, but it will appear otherwise when examined later in con-

nection with other matters. Moreover, the variation of irrelevant aspects of the stimuli that do *not* interfere with the series will have the effect of slowing model construction. Such variation may require *S* to take time and trials to get information regarding such irrelevancies sufficient to eliminate them from the prediction of the series—as in the case, for example, where the binary digits are presented in different colors.

Interference by responses and hypotheses. Heidbreder proposed some years ago a distinction between "spectator"-behavior and "participant"-behavior in problem-solving, the former being simple watching or observing without hypotheses or responses, the latter involving the formulation and test-by-response of hypotheses about the nature of events before one.[4] Participant-behavior in this sense serves to generate response-produced stimuli that may interfere with or mask the recurrent regularity in a problem to be solved. In a gambling experiment with a pattern of pay-off of RLRL . . . , we had one *S* who responded for a long series of trials with an alternating response out of phase with the rewarded choice, LRLR, and who finally announced earnestly that he guessed the machine was broken! To use a phrase designed to describe the disrupting effects of premature hypotheses in tachistoscopic recognition, there is a "liability in an hypothesis."[5]

Organismic interference. There is obvious interference from inappropriate sets, such as assuming that a series of recurrent regularity is a ran-

---

[3] G. A. Miller, "The Magical Number Seven, Plus or Minus Two: Some Limits on Our Capacity for Processing Information," *Psychological Review,* **63** (1956), 81-97.

[4] Edna Heidbreder, "An Experimental Study of Thinking," in *Archives of Psychology,* **11,** No. 73 (1924), 1-175.

[5] D. F. Wyatt and D. T. Campbell, "On the Liability of Stereotype or Hypothesis," *Journal Abnormal Social Psychology,* **46** (1951), 496-500.

dom series and acting accordingly, but it is not these that are intended here. Rather, we take these as instances of response-interference. Our concern here is with nonspecific states of the organism, nonspecific with respect to the recurrent pattern with which an *S* must deal. A trivial example is inattention or fatigue, or a toxic state, but beyond such examples of "white noisy" organismic variables, one may also expect to find some "colored noises" operating.

Chief among these is the set of factors usually labeled motivation. Riopelle found, for example, that a reward with food introduced at the beginning of each of a series of discriminative problems had the effect of distracting monkeys from the mastering of later discriminative tasks.[6] It was as if growing preoccupation with the reward interfered with looking for appropriate cues.[7] We should prefer to narrow the issue somewhat by considering the effect of the cost and value of making false and true predictions of events in the sequence. If the cost of error is high relative to the value of correct prediction, it is conceivable that the anxiety generated by the task may be high enough either to goad the person into good performance or to disrupt him. Similarly, a high value for correct prediction relative to the cost of erroneous prediction may serve to concentrate a problem-solver on his own response and to distract him from proper attention to stimulus-events.

Indeed, the point can and has been made that a "problem" exists only when the cost of error reaches a certain level.[8]

Obviously, the three kinds of interference just described interact. Errors that are costly may lead the individual to test and eliminate more rapidly hypotheses about irrelevant features of a sequence; but these are empirical matters to which we must turn now.

To sum up, to construct a model adequate to predict a recurrent environmental regularity of a length well within immediate memory span, an *S* must overcome sources of disruption and interference of three kinds: stimulus-interference, response-interference, and organismic interference.

EXPERIMENT

The *S*s employed in the experiment, 92 in number, were summer students at Harvard. They were given the basic task of predicting whether a light would appear in the left or the right window of an apparatus. They did this by pressing a key beneath one or the other window. Whichever button was pressed, the light would then appear in one or the other window for 4 sec and then be extinguished by the automatic programmer that controlled the sequence of lights.

Instructions. S was told that his task was to predict as many times as he could on which side the light would appear, and that he would be permitted to bet each time, indicating his wager by the button he pressed. He was told that he would have 40 tries at predicting and that the number of points he earned would determine how much more than his base pay of one dollar he would earn.

[6] A. J. Riopelle, "Rewards, Preferences and Learning Sets," *Psychological Report,* **1** (1955), 167-73.

[7] So too in a study of J. S. Bruner, Jean Matter, and M. L. Papanek (Breadth of Learning as a Function of Drive Level and Mechanization, *Psychological Review,* **62** (1955), 1-10), where drive-state seemed to prevent the rats from picking up "superfluous" cue-regularities in the learning-situation which might be used later.

[8] D. M. Johnson, *The Psychology of Thought and Judgment,* 1955. 1-515.

The following variations in procedure were used with our eight groups:

(*1*) *Degree of stimulus-interference.* Half of the groups received the sequential recurring pattern LLR for 40 trials (one trial more than 13 cycles) with no interference. The remaining groups received the same pattern but with some uncertainty added. That is to say, 2 of the 40 appearances of the light, the 14th and the 25th, were out of the pattern. Thus the 5th cycle of the LLR pattern became LRR, and the 9th cycle RLR. In the remaining 11 cycles, the basic pattern was left intact.

(*2*) *Degree of response-interference.* Half of the groups began immediately by responding—pressing the button. The other half was permitted to watch the sequence of lights without responding for the first three presentations. For

ton were placed two numbers, the upper one of which indicated how many points S would win if he predicted that side correctly, the lower indicating the cost in points if he predicted wrongly. Half of the groups worked under high error-cost: an error on either side costing five points, a correct prediction earning one point. The groups operating under low error-cost earned five points for a correct prediction, lost one point for one error.

RESULTS

The eight groups are summarized in Table 1. The first and most general result is that the larger the number of sources of disruption operative in a group, the greater the difficulty in identifying the recurrent regularity of the series. The simplest way to represent this is to consider the number of erroneous predictions in the 40 presen-

TABLE 1

COMPOSITION AND SIZE OF THE
EIGHT GROUPS IN THE EXPERIMENT

N = stimulus-noise; S = no stimulus-noise;
R = responding from first; W = waiting at
first; H = high error-cost; L = low error-cost

Group	No. Ss
SWH	12
SWL	12
NWH	12
NWL	12
SRH	11
SRL	11
NRH	11
NRL	11

these Ss, the light-pattern was exhibited by the E's pressing the right hand button three times in a row. They were also instructed by E to pay attention to the lights, rather than to their button-pressing activities. The other Ss were given no such instructions.

(*3*) *Cost of error.* Above each but-

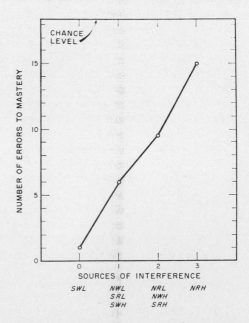

FIG. 1. *Median errors made by groups with different amounts of potential interference.*

tations of the lights in the one group operating with all three possible sources of disruption (stimulus-inter- ference, response-interference, and high cost for error), the groups with two sources of disruption, with one source, and with none. The median errors for these groups are, respectively, 15.0 errors in 37 presentations, 9.5 errors, 6.0, and 1.0.[9] Figure 1 presents the results in graphic form.

A better picture is provided by considering the eight groups separately and comparing levels of performance among them. Necessary data on errors and trials for such comparisons are contained in Tables 2 and 3.[10]

[9] Error-computations are based on the last 37 of the 40 presentations, for the groups that did not respond on the first three presentations had no opportunity for error on these presentations.

[10] We see in Table 3 that the learning-speed for groups SRH and SRL in the present experiment is considerably more rapid than that in a related experiment reported by J. J. Goodnow and T. F. Pettigrew

Effect of stimulus-interference

Comparison of the first row of Table 2 with the second row indicates that in all four comparisons, the group without stimulus-interference per- formed with fewer errors. In three of the four comparisons, the difference obtained is highly reliable, the excep- tion being the comparison of the two groups under conditions of response- interference (no wait) and low error- cost.

The first and not very surprising conclusion, then, is that even a small amount of noise thrown into a reg-

("Some Sources of Difficulty in Solving Simple Problems," *Journal of Experimental Psychology,* **51** (1956), 385-92. We be- lieve this difference is due to the fact that in the present experiment S always receives direct information about the correct side since the light appears on the correct side after each response, whereas in Goodnow and Pettigrew's experiment S receives indi- rect information when he errs, since errors are indicated by a chip's failing to drop down a chute in the panel's center.

TABLE 2

MEDIAN ERRORS IN EACH OF THE EIGHT GROUPS MADE
DURING 37 FINAL PRESENTATIONS OF LIGHTS

	—— High Cost ——		—— Low Cost ——	
	No Wait	*Wait*	*No Wait*	*Wait*
Stimulus-noise	15.0	10.5	12.0	9.0
No noise	3.0	1.5	8.0	1.0

NRH vs. NWH, NRL vs. NWL, and SRH vs. SRL are significant at the 5% level; NWH vs. SWH, NRH vs. SRH, NWL vs. SWL, and SRL vs. SWL are significant at the 1% level. Computations made by the Mosteller-Bush version of the Mann-Whitney test, see Gardner Lindsey's (ed.) *Handbook of Social Psychology,* 1, 1954, 315 ff.

TABLE 3

MEDIAN TRIALS UNTIL THE LAST ERROR WAS MADE, IN EACH OF THE EIGHT GROUPS
If an S in a "wait" group makes no errors, his trial of last error is taken as 3.

	—— High Cost ——		—— Low Cost ——	
	No Wait	*Wait*	*No Wait*	*Wait*
Stimulus-noise	37.0	37.0	35.0	33.0
No noise	11.0	4.5	25.0	4.5

SRH vs. SRL is significant at the 5% level; NWH vs. SWH, NRH vs. SRH, NWL vs. SWL, NRL vs. SRL, SRH vs. SWH, and SRL vs. SWL are significant at the 1% level.

ularly recurrent pattern seriously interferes with the identification of that regularity or, as we would prefer to put it, interferes with the task of constructing a model of this recurrent regularity.

In what does the interference consist? Figure 2 shows graphically the

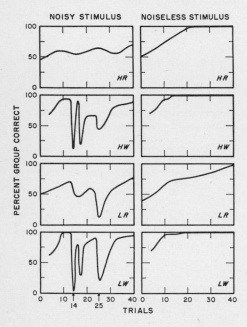

FIG. 2. *Learning-curves for each of the eight groups. Neighboring pairs are equated on all conditions save the nature of the stimulus-series to which exposed.*

learning-curves over the 40 trials of all eight groups. Side by side are curves for groups differing only in whether the stimulus-series contained two off-pattern stimuli. The introduction of the off-pattern lights on Trials 14 and 25 sharply decreases the percentage of Ss predicting correctly, following which there is more or less rapid recovery. Up to the point of the first interference, the parallel groups show very similar functions.

Interestingly enough, the interfer-

ence by the first off-pattern stimulus-sequence disrupts the group with an initial period of observation more than the group without it. The explanation is not far to seek; an off-pattern stimulus-sequence is more disruptive to an S who has already perfected a model of what the stimulus should be. Table 4 shows this difference clearly. The observing groups are doing better than the responding groups by Trial 14 and consequently make more errors when the required response is changed, 96 per cent as opposed to 59 per cent, a statistically reliable difference.

Now for the recovery from the first interference. There is no reliable difference between the groups, the responding and the observing Ss, between the first and second disruptions, errors being almost identical (Table 4).

Comes the second interfering, off-pattern sequence on Trial 25. This time there is nothing to choose in the degree of disruption: errors on this trial are about the same for both groups. Now, however, in the remaining 15 trials (Trials 26-40), the observing group shows a statistically reliable increase in mastery, or recovery, in comparison with the noise-producing responding group. Again, the data are contained in Table 4.

In sum, given the presence of stimulus-noise, the addition of response-noise may have the effect of preventing as rapid initial identification of recurrent regularity, and then prevents rapid recovery from the disruption introduced by an irregular or surprise stimulus.

Effect of response-interference

A comparison of the first with the second, and the third with the fourth column of Table 2 contains the relevant comparisons between groups alike in treatment save for difference in re-

TABLE 4
COURSE OF LEARNING, DISRUPTION, AND RECOVERY IN Ss PRESENTED WITH A
NOISY STIMULUS-SERIES WHO INTIALLY RESPONDED TO OR
SIMPLY OBSERVED THE STIMULUS-SERIES
Responding group = NRL + NRH = 22; observing group = NWL + NWH = 24

	Responding group	Observing group
Median errors: trials 4–13 *	5.0	2.0
Errors on trial 14 †	59%	96%
Median errors: trials 15–24	4.0	3.0
Errors on trial 25	68%	75%
Median errors: trials 26–40 *	5.5	3.0

* Significant at or beyond 1% level by Mosteller-Bush version of Mann-Whitney test.
† Significant at 1% level, by test of difference between two percentages.

sponding. In all comparisons, the group which responded from the outset and was not warned to attend to the stimulus made erroneous predictions more often. In three of the four comparisons, the difference is statistically reliable at least at the 5 per cent level; but the effect of response-interference is considerably less than the effect of noise in the stimulus-series. The mean difference in errors of groups with and without noise in the stimulus-series is 8.2, the difference when groups paused to observe three trials was 4.0.

Figure 2 suggests that the effects of not observing were persistent throughout the learning. The observing group shows a more sharply rising learning-curve; the responding group reached perfect performance more gradually.

Effect of error-cost

A comparison of the right and left halves of Table II reveals immediately that error-cost does not operate as a simple source of interference, if indeed it may be regarded as a source of interference at all. Neither these figures nor the forms of the learning-curves in Fig. 2 suggest that there is anything interfering about high error-cost. The only significant difference between matched groups runs counter

to the prediction that high error-cost would interfere with identification of a recurrent regularity. Indeed, we are inclined to favor the view that in this condition—where the stimulus-series was without interference and S had to overcome the interference of his own responses—high error-cost provided incentive to more careful scanning of the stimulus-situation.

DISCUSSION

We have presented here what is, in effect, a demonstrational experiment. The point of view may be briefly recapitulated: Much of learning and problem-solving can be viewed as a task in identifying recurrent regularities in the environment and this requires either the construction of a model of this regularity or the employment of a model that has previously been constructed by the person. Identification of recurrent regularity is the recognition of pattern complicated by one of two possible factors. Either the recurrent regularity is of a complexity that exceeds the limited cognitive span of the individual, or there are sources of interference either in the stimulus-input, in the required pattern of responding, or in the organism that in effect mask the recurrent regularity to be recognized. Learning, given these interferers, consists, in part, in separating the recurrent regularity to be identified from these interferers. The greater the number of interferers—the more noise there is in the stimulus, the more masking are the responses, the more difficult will identification of regularity be. When these sources are minimized, we have shown, learning is a matter of immediate recognition, provided the pattern can be handled in immediate memory-span. No stimulus-noise and minimal response-interference lead to recognition of a pattern almost immediately.

It seems unlikely to us that the explanation of how a person cuts through the interfering properties of the environment when such exist and when identification is not immediate is to be found in theories of reinforcement. Rather, the answer probably lies in how the organism learns to use techniques for weighing the relevance of different features of input for regularity-to-be-discovered. The simple instruction "Pay attention to the stimulus and disregard your past responses," for example, is highly effective advice to oneself in identifying environmental regularities that are invariant with respect to the overt responses of the problem-solver. It is conceivable that *after* such techniques have been mas-

tered a simple law of frequency might work, but not before. Essentially, as in the case of concept-attainment, the first steps in identifying a recurrent regularity require the development of strategies for utilizing potential information from the environment.[11] The greater part of contemporary learning theory has tended to overlook this feature of the learning-process or has treated such information-using strategies as just another kind of response that gets reinforced, if it happens to be followed by tension-reduction. It should be said, however, that those who, in recent years, have worked more directly with problem-solving behavior and thinking have become increasingly more mindful of the importance of methods of information-utilization.

This study gives evidence, then, that learning and problem-solving may be more profitably viewed as identification of temporally or spatially extended patterns and that the process of learning or problem-solving be viewed as the development of means for isolating such regularities from the flow of irrelevant events that originate either in the environment, in the organism, or are produced by the organism's response to the environment.

[11] J. S. Bruner, J. J. Goodnow, and G. A. Austin, *A Study of Thinking,* 1956, 1-330.

The Role of Overlearning and Drive Level in Reversal Learning *

Jerome S. Bruner, J. M. Mandler, D. O'Dowd, and

Michael A. Wallach

If one trains an organism to traverse a four-unit T maze, following the pattern of LRLR, the animal learns a series of specific turning responses of the sort "Choice Point 1, turn left; Choice Point 2, turn right; Choice Point 3, turn left; Choice Point 4, turn right." It is unnecessary to learn more for mastery of the situation. It is possible in this type of maze, however, for the organism to learn as well what might be called "the principle of single alternation." By "learning a principle" we mean merely a recording of information such that the number of decisions the organism must make in the task situation is reduced "Choice Point 1, turn left; then keep reversing sides."

One way in which to test whether or not the organism has been able to code information in terms of the principle of single alternation would be to reverse the pattern to its mirror image, RLRL, and determine the animal's ability to handle this new form of the same pattern. If there are substantial savings in learning the reversed pattern, this indicates the animal has indeed learned more than a series of

specific turning responses, and we may tentatively say that the principle of single alternation has been learned.

It should be possible to look for factors which might affect the likelihood of an organism's attaining such "principle" learning. Two such factors have been utilized in the present experiments. The first is degree of overlearning of the original task; the second is degree of motivation. Consider overlearning first: At least two studies indicate that original overlearning has the effect of increasing positive transfer from the original task to its reversal. One of these is a study by McClelland on serial verbal discrimination (3). The other is a study by Reid (4). These findings seem somehow at odds with such well known experiments as the one by Krechevsky and Honzik (2), which indicated that overtraining produced the sort of rigidity that makes organisms adapt poorly to any changes in the learning situation. The McClelland and Reid studies are, however, in keeping with the brunt of the results in the field of retroactive interference where overtraining on either original or interpolated learning has been shown to have the effect of reducing interference.

Yet there are known conditions in which overlearning has a rigidifying effect, rendering behavior stereotyped. Here it is necessary to introduce the

* From J. S. Bruner, J. Mandler, D. O'Dowd, and M. A. Wallach, "The Role of Overlearning and Drive Level in Reversal Learning," *Journal of Comparative Physiological Psychology*, 51 (1958), 607-613. Reprinted by permission of the authors and the American Psychological Association.

role of motivation. Perhaps drive level is the critical variable in resolving this seeming contradiction. It may well be that overlearning under mild motivational conditions has the effect of increasing the tendency to learn by principle, whereas overlearning under conditions of harsh motivation leads more to rigidification—that is, inability to go beyond the learning of specific responses.

Why should this be the case? Let us operate on the reasonable assumption for the moment that under high drive conditions, the organism seeks to maximize speed of goal attainment. In a previous paper (1), the point was made that under these conditions the range of alternative cues to which the organism responded would be reduced, given the equal reliability of several possible goal-pointing cues. By the same token, we should expect that high drive would have the effect of reducing the operation of *any processes not essential to attaining the immediately present goal as rapidly as possible*. This would presumably include any processes that go beyond simple response learning. Since speed of goal attainment is in no way increased by recoding the learned pathway to the goal in terms of a principle —like the principle of single alternation—we may expect that learning under high drive conditions would not be of the "principle" type.

EXPERIMENT I

Method

Fifty-four naïve male albino rats, between the ages of 80 and 100 days, served as Ss in the experiment. All animals were originally trained to various levels of mastery in running a four-unit straight-alley T maze (1) in a single-alternation pattern, half the animals learning LRLR, the remainder

RLRL. Having reached a specific criterion, animals were then transferred to a single-alternation pattern that was the reverse of what they had originally learned. Throughout the experiment, all animals were run five trials per night, and the nights of running were spaced 48 hr apart. Reward for each run consisted of 10 sec of feeding on a rich, wet food mash placed in the goal box at the end of the maze, and 1 min was spent in a waiting box between trials. The animals were divided into six groups of nine rats each. Half of the animals were run throughout the experiment—both on original learning and reversal learning—with 12 hr of food deprivation. The other half operated with 36 hr of deprivation. Animals were fed to satiety on the reward mash on a feeding table at 12-hr intervals, three omitted feedings prior to running constituting 36 hr of deprivation.

The remaining variation in treatment has to do with amount of training given on the original task. One-third of the animals was trained to a criterion of 80 per cent correct—not more than four wrong turns in the 5 trials given on a single night. Upon attaining this criterion, the animals were run on the reversed pattern starting on the next night of runs and trained again to criterion. A second third of the animals was taken to 80 per cent criterion on original learning and then given an additional four nights, or 20 trials, of overlearning. Following the 20 overlearning trials, reversal was carried out as in the other group. The final third of the animals was carried 80 trials beyond the 80 per cent criterion on original learning, 16 additional nights of training. They were then reversed. A correction method was employed, an animal being permitted to try the wrong side as many times as it chose before shifting to the correct side. Only one error per choice was recorded.

Results

The mean numbers of *errors* made by animals in all groups in reaching a criterion of 80 per cent in original learning and in reversal learning are presented in Table 1. As amount of original training increases, more positive transfer occurs. This tendency is much more notable in the group that operates under mild motivation than amongst those that operate under 36-hr deprivation. There is marked savings in the learning of reversal by the group that operates with 12-hr of deprivation and receives the maximum amount of original learning. Their counterparts in the 36-hr group do not show positive transfer.

The picture is much the same when one considers the number of *trials* necessary to reach criterion (Table 1). The same trend toward greater positive transfer with more original learning is present, and again the effect is more marked for the moderately motivated animals.

To test the significance of these findings it is necessary to equate the performance of different groups on general speed and efficiency of learning, since it is apparent from the data that speed of learning on reversal is correlated with performance on the original task regardless of the treatment given the animals. The equating operation is particularly necessary if one is to compare the performance of highly and moderately motivated groups, since we see from the data that, as one would expect, highly motivated animals learn the original task somewhat (but not significantly) more quickly. The appropriate procedure for achieving such equalization is, of course, analysis of covariance whereby the scores on reversal are corrected for correlation with scores on original learning, in effect equating all groups on general learning speed.

Consider each of the motivational conditions separately first. We have three groups of animals that operate at 12 hr of food deprivation throughout the experiment, differing only in amount of learning, and three groups that operate at 36 hr of deprivation. There are two hypotheses to be tested. One of them is, simply: Do the two levels of motivation affect the benefit derived from overlearning? Specifically, is there positive transfer under moderate motivation but not under high motivation? To test this hypothesis, we perform two one-way analyses of covariance, one on the 12-hr deprived animals, the other on those deprived for 36 hr. Such one-way analyses of covariance on each of these sets of groups show that in the case of 12-hr animals, overlearning is a significant source of variance; for the 36-hr

TABLE 1

MEAN NUMBER OF ERRORS AND TRIALS TO ATTAIN 80% CRITERION
ON ORIGINAL LEARNING (OL) AND TRANSFER LEARNING (TL)

Hours of Deprivation		— Criterion —		— Criterion — +20		— Criterion — +80	
		Errors	Trials	Errors	Trials	Errors	Trials
12	OL	11.7	9.6	16.2	10.2	15.6	11.3
	TL	17.7	12.2	16.4	10.9	6.9	6.3
36	OL	8.6	7.4	13.8	11.2	11.7	9.0
	TL	18.6	13.1	15.7	11.7	12.9	9.0

animals it is not. The data for trials to reach an 80 per cent criterion, and converted to $\sqrt{x}$ for homogeneity, resulted in $F = 7.1$ ($p < .01$, df 2, 23) for the 12-hr groups, and $F = 1.4$ (N.S., df 2, 23) for the 36-hr groups. Essentially the same findings are obtained using errors to criterion as the relevant data for analysis, again with the square-root transformation ($F = 8.9$ and 0.7, respectively).

There is a second hypothesis, whether or not the slopes describing degree of savings as a function of overlearning in the moderately and strongly motivated groups are significantly different. To test this hypothesis, a two-way analysis of covariance is required. Such an analysis yields an insignificant interaction term, although the difference is in the expected direction. There are various technical reasons why such an analysis of covariance on all six groups combined happens to come out with an insignificant interaction of motivation and overlearning—notably the increase in error term that results from combining animals operating at different drive levels. But these need not concern us here. It suffices to note only that where a high drive prevails, overlearning does not help transfer; where a moderate drive prevails, it does.

There are other differences that are of central importance as well. The first of these has to do with the amount of time spent by the animals in the different groups in the first unit of the maze on the first transfer trial—a measure of the disturbance created by being introduced to the transfer situation. A second related measure is the amount of vicarious trial and error (VTE) on the first unit of the maze following transfer. This, too, provides a measure of disturbance or "doubt." Finally, we may consider repeated errors, repeating an error in a unit of the maze be-

fore making the correct response in that unit.

In observing the animals during performance, it was evident that the animals that had received maximum overlearning under moderate motivation were the most "surprised" when put into the maze with mirror-image turns. Upon finding the first, previously correct door locked on the first transfer trial, they withdrew, showed signs of emotional disturbance, and, in general, showed a marked increase in latency before finally going through the correct door. Indeed, their geometric mean time spent in the first unit was 203.8 sec, four times as great as that of any other 12-hr group. The 36-hr groups showed no differences. The data are contained in Table 2. Again, one-way analyses of covariance were employed to test whether overlearning under one motivational condition produced effects not obtainable under the other. Amount of overlearning was a significant source of variance in affecting the latency times under discussion for the moderately motivated groups (data transformed to $\log_{10}$, $F = 10.7$, $p < .01$, df 2, 23), but not for those operating under strong motivation ($F = 0.3$, N.S., df 2, 23).

Considerable, though statistically unreliable, differences were found for the VTE responses of the various groups on the first trial on the first unit of the mirror-image version of the maze. While one-way analyses of covariance on the groups deprived for 12 and for 36 hr show that overlearning is not a significant source in either set of groups, inspection of the data (Table 2) reveals that the one group that showed the greatest transfer also showed a very marked increase in VTE.

We come finally to repeated errors made on the first unit of the maze on the first transfer trial. These data are

TABLE 2

TIME,* *VTE*,† AND REPEATED ERROR MEASURE ‡

Hours of Depri-vation		—— Criterion ——			—— Criterion —— +20			—— Criterion —— +80		
		Time	VTEs	Errors	Time	VTEs	Errors	Time	VTEs	Errors
12	Last night of OL	12.1	1.9		14.0	2.2		5.8	1.7	
	First trial of TL	47.1	2.7	1.6	49.0	2.4	2.6	203.8	6.8	6.0
36	Last night of OL	7.4	1.6		2.4	1.0		1.4	.3	
	First trial of TL	13.7	.5	2.3	9.5	.8	1.6	10.2	1.2	1.7

* Geometric means (in seconds) of time spent in first unit of maze on last trial of original training and first trial of transfer.

† Mean number of VTE responses in the first unit of the maze on the first trial of the last night before transfer and the first trial after transfer.

‡ Mean number of repeated errors in the first unit of the maze in the first trial following transfer. An error is scored when an animal physically touched the incorrect release door barring the path.

also presented in Table 2, and by now it will be a familiar pattern to the reader. The one group with notable positive transfer persists in trying the formerly correct door. For the moderately motivated groups in a one-way analysis of covariance, amount of overlearning was a significant source of variance in affecting the number of repeated errors (data transformed to $\sqrt{x + .5}$, $F = 15.8$, $p < .01$, df 2, 23), but not so for the strongly motivated animals ($F = 0.7$, N.S., df 2, 23).

Now we must say a word in a naturalistic vein about the behavior of the animals in the group with maximum transfer—the moderately motivated animals with maximum overlearning. Most of the animals, following a long delay in the first unit marked by the "doubt" of VTE, and repeated errors on all four units of that first reversal trial, then proceeded to thread their way through the reversed maze without error and thenceforth made only two or three errors in the succeeding trials before attaining criterion. Their behavior for the first few trials remained highly "tense": much rapid approach-withdrawal behavior directed toward the first set of doors. The usual emotional signs—defecation, urination, crouching in the back corners of the first unit—were also present. But the performance, once they got started, was definitely superior to the other groups'.

Compare these animals with the members of the highly motivated group that had had as much opportunity for overlearning. They charged the formerly correct door, were repelled, and paused briefly. Very quickly they shifted to the other door. And so it went in the second, third, and fourth units and on subsequent trials.

It would appear on the basis of what has been presented thus far that moderate motivation provides a condition in which frequently repeated exposure to a specific pattern aids an organism in converting that pattern into a generic, and thus more transferable, form. But before we can explore this matter further, a second experiment must be considered.

EXPERIMENT II

Method

The object of the experiment to be reported now was to discern more clearly why a large quantity of over-learning led to effective transfer in a group of moderately motivated animals and none at all in a group that was highly motivated.

The hypothesis, presented in the introduction of the present paper, was that *acquisition* occurring with over-learning under moderate motivation would tend to be more generic, involving a recoding of specific learning into a form approximating a "principle." The turns LRLR would more likely be recoded into "single alternation," thus making the mirror image, RLRL, easier to learn as another instance of the general case. High drive, for reasons already stated, would be inimical to such generic recoding.

The difficulty with the hypothesis is that it is not propertly tested by the two groups that had received large doses of overlearning. One of them acquired the original learning under high drive conditions, but was also tested for transfer under high drive. So, too, with the moderately motivated group: it was their condition both during acquisition and transfer. Could the effect be due to drive condition during transfer learning and have nothing to do with the nature of drive during acquisition?

To test the matter, two further groups of animals were run, 23 in all, identical in all but one respect to the two groups that had received 80 trials

of overlearning after attaining criterion. One of them acquired its original learning under 36 hr of food deprivation and was tested for transfer to a reverse pattern under 12 hr of deprivation. The other acquired under a 12-hr regimen of deprivation and was tested for transfer under a 36-hr regimen. In all other respects, treatment was the same.

Results

The first result serves to remind that nature rarely takes sides unequivocally about hypotheses. Scores for original learning and transfer learning are set forth in Table 3, which presents both *errors* made and number of *trials* before animals attained an 80 per cent learning criterion. In effect, the 12-36, 36-12, and 12-12 animals do equally well, all showing significant positive transfer. The 36-36 animals show no transfer. Highly motivated animals again learn the original task somewhat more quickly, but not significantly so. Analysis of covariance was performed on the data of the four groups. Both for errors and for trials to reach criterion, the interaction of original and transfer motivation was found to be significant. Error scores were transformed for homogeneity to ($\sqrt{x} + \sqrt{x + 1}$), and the interaction of drive levels before and after transfer yielded an F of 34.8, $p < .01$, df 1, 31. Trials to criterion, transformed in the same

TABLE 3

MEAN ERRORS AND TRIALS TO 80% CRITERION OF LEARNING
IN FOUR GROUPS GIVEN 80 TRIALS OF OVERLEARNING

Transfer Deprivation		DEPRIVATION DURING ORIGINAL LEARNING			
		12 hr		36 hr	
		Errors	Trials	Errors	Trials
12 hr	OL	15.6	11.3	12.6	9.7
	TL	6.9	6.3	4.5	5.3
36 hr	OL	15.3	11.2	11.7	9.0
	TL	4.7	5.5	12.9	9.0

way, yielded an *F* ratio for interaction of 59.50, $p < .01$, *df* 1, 31.

We may ask what such a constellation of results signifies. Given initial overlearning of a pattern, positive transfer to its obverse will occur provided *either* that original learning occurs under conditions of moderate drive *or* that transfer is effected under moderate drive conditions. High drive during *both* original acquisition *and* transfer seems to prevent transfer from occurring.

What the finding suggests, to pursue the general point with which this paper was introduced, is that apparently generic recoding could occur *either* during acquisition *or* when an organism is faced with the task of mastering a new instance of the principle contained in the old set of specific turns, that is, the principle of alternation. What is necessary in any case, it appears, is that there be considerable overlearning of the original task before transfer is undertaken. Before considering the difference between our four overlearning groups, several performance variables need closer inspection.

The first of these is a time measure. Table 4 sets forth the amount of time spent by animals in the four groups, expressed as geometric means, in the various units of the maze on the first run of the night preceding transfer and on the first run following transfer.

We see, first of all, that at the terminal stages of overlearning, the proportion of time spent in the first unit is roughly a quarter. The animals in all groups, in short, are passing through the maze at a quite even clip. Now comes transfer. The ratios change notably, and each group shows a distinctive pattern: 59.4 per cent for the 12-12 group; 48.4 per cent for the 12-36 group; but 30.1 per cent for the 36-36 group; and 26.8 per cent for the 36-12 group. In short, the groups that originally acquire the response pattern under moderate drive conditions spend proportionately more time in making decisions at the *beginning of the maze*; whereas the animals whose original learning occurred under high drive conditions distribute decision time in the maze after transfer in almost the same ratio as before transfer.

The time results just mentioned are statistically reliable. An analysis of covariance carried out on the proportion of time spent in the first unit of the maze, based on the data from which Table 4 is constructed, yields the following results: Using arc-sine transformed data, we find that drive level during original learning is a significant source of variance, and nothing

TABLE 4

GEOMETRIC MEAN TIME (IN SECONDS) SPENT BY OVERLEARNING GROUPS IN VARIOUS UNITS OF THE MAZE ON THE FIRST RUN OF THE NIGHT PRECEDING TRANSFER AND ON THE FIRST RUN FOLLOWING TRANSFER

Transfer Deprivation		DEPRIVATION DURING ORIGINAL LEARNING			
		12 hr		36 hr	
		Unit 1	Units 2–4	Unit 1	Units 2–4
12 hr	OL	5.8 (21.2%)	21.6	2.2 (25.9%)	6.3
	TL	203.8 (59.4%)	139.2	113.0 (26.8%)	303.0
36 hr	OL	6.3 (21.4%)	23.2	1.4 (25.9%)	4.0
	TL	140.2 (48.4%)	149.3	10.2 (30.1%)	23.7

else is—neither post-transfer drive level, nor interaction. (*F* for drive level during original learning = 7.9, *p* < .01; *F* for post-transfer drive level = 0.4, N.S.; *F* for interaction = 0.1, N.S.; *df* 1, 31 in each case.)

Further presumptive evidence of the "concept-learning" view being here presented is provided by examination of the VTEs observed in the four over-learning groups. The relevant data are in Table 5, where VTE scores are presented for the first ten trials of original learning, for the first trial of the night before transfer, and for the first transfer

the 12-12 group, and 53 per cent for the 12-36 group. The group that learned with a high drive and showed positive savings, the 36-12 group, allocates but 40 per cent of VTE responses to the first unit.

The data on time allocation and VTE seem to suggest an interesting difference between animals that learn and overlearn under high and low drive conditions—a difference in "deliberation," perhaps. Put anthropomorphically, it is as if the rats that had learned under low drive were spending their time in the first transfer trial trying

TABLE 5

MEAN NUMBER OF VTE RESPONSES IN THE VARIOUS UNITS OF THE MAZE FOR THE
FIRST TEN TRIALS OF ORIGINAL LEARNING, THE FIRST TRIAL OF THE NIGHT
BEFORE TRANSFER, AND THE FIRST TRIAL AFTER TRANSFER

Transfer Deprivation		DEPRIVATION DURING ORIGINAL LEARNING			
		12 hr		36 hr	
		Unit 1	Units 2–4	Unit 1	Units 2–4
12 hr	OL: 1–10	1.4	2.2	0.4	1.3
	OL: 76	1.7	3.7	0.0	0.2
	TL: 1	6.8	2.1	11.2	17.0
36 hr	OL: 1–10	1.2	2.3	0.8	1.0
	OL: 76	0.5	1.3	0.3	0.4
	TL: 1	7.2	6.5	1.2	1.0

trial, again divided into first unit and remaining three units of the maze. There are no striking differences among the four groups during original learning save that, as we know, more highly motivated animals show somewhat less VTE behavior. Interesting differences emerge at the time of transfer. All the groups that show positive savings show a marked increase in VTE on the first trial after transfer. Paralleling the time data, the two groups that learned originally with a low drive, show a majority of their VTE responses in the first unit of the maze: 76 per cent for

to figure out, *in advance of full testing*, what the nature of the new maze might be. The first error, an error on the first unit, leads to a high proportion of time being spent in the first unit, as if the animals could "figure out" from this error something beyond how it, the specific error, might be corrected. Animals that learned originally operating at high drive, while they too are slowed down generally, seem as we have seen to be treating the different units much as before. This is true for both groups of such animals. Perhaps the difference between them—one of them shows notable positive transfer, the other not—is that exposure to the reverse pattern now leads one group to recode learning in terms of the "principle of single alternation," the other group not. That is to say, for the group that learned with a high drive and transferred under low drive, providing *two instances of single alternation,* LRLR and RLRL, leads to attainment of the concept "single alternation." Not so the 36-36 group. For the groups operating at 12 hr of deprivation during original learning, generic recoding seems to be effected at least in part *before* transfer.

One final result wants reporting, for it will be necessary in evaluating alternative ways of interpreting the data. It has to do with running speed. Older views of the learning of single alternation held that such learning consists of the linking of successive kinesthetic patterns as the animal threads its way through the four units of the maze. It is often argued that fast running gives a more "noiseless" kinesthetic pattern, with no interfering pauses to break up the kinesthetic training. Product-moment correlations were computed for all animals in the four highly overtrained groups between (*a*) mean running speed on the first 15 trials of original learning and errors made in reaching the 80 per cent criterion in *original* learning, and (*b*) this mean running time and errors before reaching the 80 per cent criterion on *transfer* learning. No significant correlations were found for any of these groups. Neither the learning of a specific alternating path nor the learning of single alternation is related to running speed.

DISCUSSION

We have presented a not unfamiliar approach to the problem of transfer: that transfer more easily occurs when learning becomes "genericized" or recoded into a principle that can be applied to a new instance of the principle. This recoding is greatly aided, we have found, by a considerable amount of overlearning. Where the acquisition and overlearning occur under mild drive conditions, generic recoding occurs then, and transfer is simply a matter of applying the generic principle to new instances. If the principle is relevant, positive savings occur. When acquisition and overlearning occur under high drive conditions, positive savings may occur by reducing drive at the time of transfer, which permits the animal to "attain the concept" on the basis of encountering a second instance of the pattern. If high drive persists after transfer, no savings occur, which probably means some negative transfer, for there should be a certain amount of saving from sheer maze wiseness. We have marshalled a variety of evidence on time allocation in the maze, repeated errors, and the pattern of VTE behavior in suport of this view.

There is a variety of alternative explanations that are nourished by the present data, but it is not our object to pass them in review. The only point we would make is that one may state specifiable conditions that affect what may be interpreted as transfer by conceptual extension of original learning. We would urge, in the light of the relevance of such interpretations to human problem solving and high-level human intellectual performance, that an effort be made further to pursue this less fashionable approach to transfer. Efficient recoding of information in terms of a generic principle is affected by a host of factors. The present study provides an analysis of two such factors: drive level and degree of overlearning.

SUMMARY

Two experiments were reported. In the first, 54 rats were originally trained to one of three levels of mastery in running a four-unit straight-alley T maze in a single-alternation pattern, and then were transferred to a single-alternation pattern that was the reverse of what they had originally learned. Half the animals were run both on original and transfer learning with 12 hr of food deprivation, the other half with 36 hr of deprivation. There were marked savings in the learning of reversal by the group that operated with 12 hr of deprivation and received the maximum amount of original learning, while their counterparts in the 36-hr group showed no transfer. All animals receiving the minimum amount of original learning, in turn, exhibited negative transfer, while all receiving the intermediate degree of original learning showed no transfer.

In the second experiment, 23 rats were treated in the same fashion as those rats in the above experiment given the highest level of mastery on original learning, the difference being that half the animals were trained originally with 12 and transferred at 36 hr of food deprivation, while the other half had the reverse deprivation schedule. Marked positive transfer in learning the reversal was exhibited by both groups.

Thus, given initial overlearning of a pattern, positive transfer to its obverse occurred provided that either original learning or transfer learning took place under moderate drive conditions. High drive during both original learning and transfer, on the other hand, prevented such savings from occurring. From these findings plus further evidence on time in the maze and VTE behavior, an interpretation was offered in terms of the "genericizing" of learning into a principle applicable to new instances.

REFERENCES

1. Bruner, J. S., J. Matter, and M. L. Papanek, "Breadth of Learning as a Function of Drive Level and Mechanization," *Psychological Review*, **62** (1955), 1-10.

2. Krechevsky, I. and C. H. Honzik, "Fixation in the Rat," *University of California Publ. Psychology*, **6** (1932), 13-26.

3. McClelland, D. C., "Studies in Serial Verbal Discrimination Learning: IV. Habit Reversal after Two Degrees of Learning," *Journal of Experimental Psychology*, **33** (1943), 457-70.

4. Reid, L. S., "The Development of Noncontinuity Behavior through Continuity Learning," *Journal of Experimental Psychology*, **46** (1953), 107-12.

What Social Scientists Say About Having an Idea *

Jerome S. Bruner

I have been asked to address myself to the topic, "On having an idea," to concern myself with it in a manner that is at once general and yet relevant to the preoccupations of those professionally concerned with creativity in advertising.

Let me begin by trying to rescue a few obvious points from the dustbin of familiarity. Ideas—creative ones or whatever other kinds there may be— are not images nor are they gadgets or gimmicks. They are ways to do things. If an idea is worth its salt, it will have a generic property that makes it possible, by virtue of having the idea, of doing something more than what is called for by the task immediately before one's nose. A "good" idea is one that permits us to cope at one fell swoop with a lot of situations that, prior to having the idea, seemed unrelated, disparate and insoluble.

When I say that an idea is a way to do something, I mean it in a rather technical sense. For what ideas do is show us how to combine and recombine information in such a way that, having done so, we are able to go beyond the information with which we have worked.

* From J. S. Bruner, "What Social Scientists Say About Having an Idea," *Printers' Ink Magazine,* **260** (1957), 48-52. Reprinted by permission of the author and publisher.

COMBINATORIAL IDEAS

Galileo, for example, had a classic idea put together out of a wilderness of data. He put the data together in an idealized form such that $S = \frac{1}{2} gt^2$. Once this was done, it was possible to go beyond the data to predict the distance fallen by *any* body, whether yet observed or not. It describes the data for vacua.

This is one combinatorial idea, a powerful one. Join it with Priestley's ideas about the spring of the air (a way of combining information about pressure in gases and atmospheres), and between the two one can go even further beyond what is known to good predictions of the unknown.

Let me take an idea in painting and see whether the rule applies. The birth of Italian Renaissance painting provides an example. Let me symbolize it by the change in conception from Cimabuë to Giotto.

Twelfth-century Italian painting is, on the whole, deeply religious in a stylized, rather ikonic manner. As the century moved to the climax of Cimabuë, one senses a significant series of changes in convention. The Christs of the crucifix begin to show suffering, there is weight now on the nails that hold Christ to the cross. His eyes open, and suffering is there. Yet it is an ikon, this Christ—in the work of Cimabuë, an exquisitely wrought one.

Shift now to the Arena Chapel in Padua at the close of the century to the work of Giotto. Here is a Christ, a heavy-boned head, coarse hair, the suffering not just of an ascetic diety who has tasted gall and been crowned with thorns, but also of a man.

The combinatorial genius of Giotto was to join together the plight of man and the suffering of Christ in a way that gave a new breadth to the meaning of Christ and to the meaning of man. The achievement is a metaphoric one, a joining together metaphorically of man and God that enriches the conception of both and creates the possibility of going beyond conceptions that existed the moment before. This is how ideas are forged—great ideas— whether in art or science—or in any sphere.

What is striking about both examples, I think, is that the ideas involved were combinations that would not readily have been produced in a manner that mathematicians call algorithmic. You could not likely have spun out all possible combinations and then chosen by inspection the one that did the trick. For we do not use algorithms in our combinatorial thinking. We operate by other rules concerning combinations. These rules are the laws of thought, laws of fruitful and predictive combinatorial activity.

APPLICATION FOR "AD" MEN

Now how does all this concern advertising men? In what sense can it be said that the solution to problems that you encounter in your practical pursuits depends upon combinatorial thinking that permits you to go beyond present information? The copy writer and the artist seek to bring together conceptions combinatorially that produce a metaphoric going-beyond in the beholder. This is a controlled effect that links a state of mind or a situation or a value with a particular product. The advertising man's intent is to create metaphoric connections and linkages between things that he does not necessarily love. In this sense the "ad" man works with intention and not really with an impulse at all—save in a few rare cases.

In the eyes of the artist and the poet, you advertising men prostitute yourselves and your creativity to an intention. This need not concern you if you are not totally preoccupied with art and poetry. I would only note in passing that you pay a price in creativity for operating in this vein, an inevitable and a very high price, and we shall say more of this later.

Obviously, it is not simply in this artistic sense that the advertising mind works. There are plenty of practical problems to be solved. The difference is in the relatively limited degree that advertising men enter into the creation of generalizations that cover more than the immediate case. Much market research is of a highly empirical nature without aspiration to generality; this product here and now for distribution here and now. I think that this concreteness, empiricism, and practicality is one of the enemies of creative enterprise.

How then does the advertising mind work? I should like to discuss the matter from three points of view:

How Ideas and Hypotheses Arise

This is, unfortunately, one of the most obscure areas in the psychology of thinking. But there are several interesting points that can be made.

The foremost of these is that good operational ideas very often have their origin in highly personal metaphors that have about them some of the character of great myths and legends. It would seem as if the arousal of an impulse is in its full expression. It is, perhaps, even a kind of wishful action of the kind Freud referred to as primary process—almost as in dreaming.

One of the great sources of ideas seems to be the taming of such metaphoric flow. Let me give you an example from what may seem to you an unlikely field, mathematics:

We all have experienced the frustration dream, the unquieting type in which we try to reach some objective but somehow never manage to get there. The dream has its mythic counterpart in Sisyphus pushing his rock up the endless hill.

Now, there is a set of functions in mathematics called asymptotes, illustrated by the graphing of a quantity that increases gradually to some limit without reaching the limit. The invention of the asymptotic function is lost in the history of mathematics, but I would not be surprised if some day we found an ancient scroll that tells us that the inspiration of the inventor came about when his quandary during attempted solution made contact with the very personal metaphor of trying to arrive but never getting there.

Another example of this taming process is provided by Niels Bohr, who has contributed so magnificently to nuclear and atomic physics. He formulated the principle of complementarity: that viewing a state of a system in physics in one way makes it impossible to view it another way. Bohr says the idea came to him by considering the complementarity that separates viewing another person in the light of love and viewing him in the light of justice.

The man who is constructing an advertisement for a new eggbeater, a new fabric, a loaf of bread, would do well in the early stages of his effort to forget the specific product. He might well let himself wander not around the edges of a fabric to be sold, but about the deeper meaning of fabric and of covering oneself for warmth and for modesty. Or he might explore the tactual imagery that comes when one runs a hand over a rought or a smooth fabric surface. Suspension of the objective of the search may bring you, as Goethe put it, into the happy condition where you go into the forest looking for nothing and find the beautiful wood violets.

What Are the Conditions That Seem to Lead to the Production of Good Ideas?

It is characteristic of living beings that they have a highly limited attention and memory span and one of the purposes of recoding or repackaging information is to spare this limited span from being overtaxed by particulars. The best technique that has ever been invented for serving this function is to generalize.

I can present you with a 500-page book giving the distances fallen by bodies in different gravitational fields with different times of free fall, and you will be overwhelmed. Or I can give you the lot in the formula $S = \frac{1}{2} gt^2$, and you have a device for grasping a huge array of data in such a way that you can generate any value-distance you choose.

It is in this sense that a theory is the most practical thing you can have. Many of your ills and difficulties in working out problems in the business world, I suspect, stem from an embarrassment about dealing in generalizations. This is particularly true in advertising where one is preoccupied with an account, for you feel you must deal with *this* particular product rather than beginning with the more general case. The generalization is about the only economical method there is for coping with multiplicity and complexity: you are suspicious of it at your own peril.

Let me say a word about the conditions that produce good ideas, or at least help the thinner ones out. There is a well-known principle called Yerkes-Dodson Law which shows that optimum problem-solving behavior occurs in animals under conditions where drive level is neither too high nor too low. The gain in problem-solving acumen that results from moderate as compared to extreme or overly lax motivation is greatest for problems of the highest complexity, and indeed it makes little difference for very simple problems.

I would add to this law some animal studies of my own: Rats are taught to traverse a 4-unit maze. In each unit there is an option of turning right or left. The correct pattern to be learned is *left-right-left-right*. If the animal has a "good idea" as a result of learning, he will not simply have learned a series of turns but also have grasped the principle of single alternation. The easy way to determine what has been learned, a specific or a general solution, is to reverse the order of correct turns to *right-left-right-left*. An animal that has grasped the principle will be able to cope with the new situation. If it has not, it will have to learn the mirror-image turns anew.

Two groups of animals were used in my experiments. One group was deprived of food for 36 hours before being run, the other for 12 hours—the difference between real hunger and pleasant appetite. The results were clear-cut. The 36-hour animals had to learn the mirror-image pattern with no benefit from earlier learning, the 12-hour animals took it in stride.

What one may conclude is that we would do better to think not of a maximum of motivation for problem-solving, but of an *optimum*. One need

not rest the case on the behavior of animals. We know enough by now of the nature of blocks in learning and thinking in humans to recognize that the stress of too high a drive state can produce the kind of freezing that produces neither good generalizations nor a fruitful flow of metaphor-to-be-tamed.

Why Is It That Good Ideas Always Have a Long List of Unsuccessful Predecessors?

I have during the past year been studying an invention and design group at one of the great American engineering consulting firms, recording our discussions on tape. We play back the tape during the last hour or so of our sessions. What is striking is that after a good solution has been achieved, often a very original one, we find that, upon going back over the tapes, the idea has come up three or four times before—seemingly unheard, surely uncelebrated and clearly ignored.

What is the principle of ripeness that leads to a good idea being recognized later but not before? I do not think it is the matter of an open mind, nor a matter of some sort of principle of incubation. It takes a tuned organism, working with a certain kind of set, to recognize the appropriateness of an idea.

The open mind, the suspension of motive and directedness are essential for stimulating the flow of hypothesis and metaphor, but for recognizing the fitness or adequacy of a particular hypothesis, the appropriately closed mind is required.

What makes something "obvious" is that at last we understand it. To understand means to fit something into a structure. Being set, narrowing down to a few alternative structures seems to be what is required.

There is a cycle that runs from the

open state of having an idea to the more disciplined one of recognizing it as good or fitting or appropriate. At the one end, there is the taming of personal metaphor to the purpose of the problem at hand, using it as a guide for constructing new and potentially fruitful combinatorial hypotheses. At the other end is the rigorous business of recognizing the worth of an idea.

Between the two, between origination and verification, there lie many complex variables. The problem for the creative "ad" man (or for any other creative person) is to find the combination of old ideas that will lead to new solutions.

On Going Beyond the Information Given *

Jerome S. Bruner

More than thirty years ago, Charles Spearman (1923) undertook the ambitious task of characterizing the basic cognitive processes whose operations might account for the existence of intelligence. He emerged with a triad of noegenetic principles, as he called them, the first of these being simply an affirmation that organisms are capable of apprehending the world they live in. The second and third principles provide us with our starting point. One of these, called, as you know, "the eduction of relations," holds that there is an immediate evocation of a sense of relation given the mental presentation of two or more things. "White" and "black" evoke "opposite" or "different." The third principle, the "eduction of correlates," states that in the presence of a thing and a relation one immediately educes another thing. "White" and "opposite

* From J. S. Bruner, "On Going Beyond the Information Given," in *Contemporary Approaches to Cognition* (Cambridge, Mass.: Harvard University Press, 1957), pp. 41-69. Reprinted by permission of the author and publisher.

of" evokes "black." I think that Spearman was trying to say that the most characteristic thing about mental life, over and beyond the fact that one apprehends the events of the world around one, is that one constantly goes beyond the information given. With this observation I find myself in full agreement, and it is here that my difficulties start. For, as Professor Bartlett (1951, p. 1) put it in a recent paper,

. . . whenever anybody interprets evidence from any source, and his interpretation contains characteristics that cannot be referred wholly to direct sensory observation or perception, this person thinks. The bother is that nobody has ever been able to find any case of the human use of evidence which does not include characters that run beyond what is directly observed by the senses. So, according to this, people think whenever they do anything at all with evidence. If we adopt that view we very soon find ourselves looking out upon a boundless and turbulent ocean of problems.

Bother though it be, there is little else than to plunge right in.

SOME INSTANCES
OF GOING BEYOND
THE INFORMATION GIVEN

It may help to begin with some rather commonplace examples of the different ways in which people go beyond information that is given to them. The first of these represents the simplest form of utilizing inference. It consists of learning the defining properties of a class of functionally equivalent objects and using the presence of these defining properties as a basis of inferring that a new object encountered is or is not an exemplar of the class. The first form of "going beyond," then, is to go beyond sense data to the class identity of the object being perceived. This is the more remarkable an achievement when the new object encountered differs from in more respects than it resembles other exemplars of the class that have been previously encountered. A speck on the horizon surmounted by a plume of smoke is identified as a ship, so too a towering transatlantic liner at its dock, so too a few schematic lines in a drawing. Given the presence of a few defining properties or cues, we go beyond them to the inference of identity. Having done so, we infer that the instance so categorized or identified has the other properties characteristic of membership in a category. Given the presence of certain cues of shape, size, and texture, we infer that the thing before us is an apple: *ergo,* it can be eaten, cut with a knife, it relates by certain principles of classification to other kinds of fruits, and so on. The act of rendering some given event equivalent with a class of other things, placing it in an identity class, provides then one of the most primitive forms of going beyond information given.

William James (1890) wrote picturesquely of this process, remarking that cognitive life begins when one is able to exclaim, "Hollo! Thingumbob again." The adaptive significance of this capacity for equivalence grouping is, of course, enormous. If we were to respond to each event as unique and to learn anew what to do about it or even what to call it, we would soon be swamped by the complexity of our environment. By last count, there were some 7.5 million discriminable differences in the color solid alone. Yet for most purposes we get by treating them as if there were only a dozen or two classes of colors. No two individuals are alike, yet we get by with perhaps a dozen or so "types" into which we class others. Equivalence categories or concepts are the most basic currency one can utilize in going beyond the sensory given. They are the first steps toward rendering the environment generic.

Consider a second form of going beyond the information given, one that involves learning the redundancy of the environment. I present the word, P*YC*OL*GY, and with no difficulty at all you recognize that the word is PSYCHOLOGY. Or the finding of Miller, Heise, and Lichten (1951) that words masked by noise are more easily recognized when they are in a meaningful or high-probability context than when they are presented in isolation. Indeed, the missing word in the sentence, "Dwight ———— is currently President of the United States" can be completely masked by noise and yet "recognized" correctly by anybody who knows the subject matter. Or we find that subjects in some experiments currently in progress check off about an average of thirty trait words from the Gough list as being characteristic of a person who is only described as being either "intelligent," or "independent," or "considerate." Any one of these key traits has at least thirty possible avenues for going beyond it, based on learned probabilities of what things are likely to go with what in another person. Once one learns the probability texture of the environment, one can go beyond the given by predicting its likely concomitants.

We move one step beyond such probabilistic ways of going beyond the information given and come now to certain formal bases for doing so. Two propositions are presented:

$$A > B$$
$$B > C$$

and with very little difficulty most people can readily go beyond to the inference that

$$A > C.$$

Or I present a series of numbers, with one missing one to be supplied:

$$2, 4, 8, *, 32, 64$$

and as soon as you are able to see that the numbers are powers of two, or that they represent successive doublings, you will be able to provide the missing number 16. Or in an experiment by Bruner, Matter, and O'Dowd, rats are taught to find their way through a four-unit T maze by threading the path LRLR. Given the proper conditions (and to these we will return later), an animal readily transfers to the mirror-image pattern of RLRL—provided he has learned the path as an instance of single alternation and not as a set of specific turns.

What it is that one learns when one learns to do the sort of thing just described, whether it be learning to do syllogisms or learning the principle of single alternation, is not easily described. It amounts to the learning of certain formal schemata that may be

fitted to or may be used to organize arrays of diverse information. We shall use the expression *coding* to describe what an organism does to information under such circumstances, leaving its closer examination until later. Thus, we can conceive of an organism capable of rendering things into equivalence classes, capable of learning the probabilistic relationships between events belonging to various classes, and capable of manipulating these classes by the utilization of certain formal coding systems.

We often combine formal codes and probability codes in making inferences beyond the data. Studies such as those by Wilkins (1928) provide instructive examples. One finds, for example, that a typical deduction made from the proposition "If all A are B" is that "All B are A," and to the proposition "If some A are not B" a typical conclusion is that "Some B are not A." Yet none of the subjects ever agrees with the proposition that "If all men are mammals, then all mammals are men," or with the proposal that "If some men are not criminals, then some criminals are not men." In sum, it may often be the case that "common sense"—the result of inductive learning of what is what and what goes with what in the environment—may often serve to correct less well learned formal methods of going beyond information given. In short, one may often have alternative modes of going beyond, sometimes in conflict with each other, sometimes operating to the same effect.

One final case before we turn to the difficult business of trying to specify what is involved in utilizing information in this soaring manner. This time we take a scientist, and we shall take him unprepared with a theory, which, as we know, is a rare state for both the scientist and the layman alike. He has, let us say, been working on the effects of sound sleep, and in pursuit of his inquiries has hit on the bright idea of giving his subjects a complete rest for five or six days—"just to see what happens." To add to their rest, he places them on a soft bed, covers their eyes with translucent ground-glass goggles, lulls their ears with a soft but persistent homogeneous masking noise, and in general makes life as homogeneously restful as possible for them. At the end of this time, he tests them and finds, lo and behold, that they are incapable of doing simple arithmetic problems, that they cannot concentrate, that their perceptual constancies are impaired, and so on down the list of findings that have recently been reported from McGill by Bexton, Heron, Scott (1954), and their collaborators. (Please note that the McGill investigators started with a hypothesis about sensory deprivation; our example is a fiction, but it will serve us and may even relate to our Canadian colleagues before they are through.) Once one has got some data of this order, one is in a funk unless one can go beyond them. To do so requires a theory. A theory, of course, is something we invent. If it is a good theory—a good formal or probabilistic coding system—it should permit us to go beyond the present data both retrospectively and prospectively. We go backward—turn around on our own schemata—and order data that before seemed unrelated to each other. Old loose ends now become part of a new pattern. We go forward in the sense of having new hypotheses and predictions about other things that should be but that have not been tested. When we have finished the reorganizing by means of the new theoretical coding system, everything then seems obvious, if the thing fits. We mention theory construction as a final example of coding processes largely because it highlights

several points that are too easily overlooked in the simpler examples given earlier. Coding may involve inventive behavior and we must be concerned with what is involved in the construction of coding systems. And coding systems may be effective or ineffective in permitting one to go beyond information. Later we shall inquire into the conditions that make for construction of new coding systems and what may lead to the construction of adequate ones.

ON CODING SYSTEMS

A coding system may be defined as a set of contingently related, nonspecific categories. It is the person's manner of grouping and relating information about his world, and it is constantly subject to change and reorganization. Bartlett's memory *schemata* are close to what is intended here, and the early work of Piaget (1930) on the child's conception of nature represents a naturalistic account of coding systems in the child.

Let it be clear that a coding system as I describe it here is a hypothetical construct. It is inferred from the nature of antecedent and consequent events. For example, in the rat experiment cited earlier, I teach an organism to wend a course that goes LRLR through a maze. *I wish to discover how the event is coded.* I transfer the animal to a maze that goes RLRL. He transfers with marked savings. I infer now that he has coded the situation as single alternation. But I must continue to test for the genericalness of the coding system used. Is it alternation in general or alternation only in spatial terms? To test this I set up a situation in the maze where the correct path is defined by taking alternate colors, now a black, now a white member of black-white pairs, without regard to their position.

If there is saving here too, I assume that the original learning was coded not as positional alternation but as alternation in general. Of course, I use the appropriate control groups along the way. Note that the technique I am using is identical with the technique we use to discover whether children are learning proper codes in school. We provide training in addition, then we move on to numbers that the child has not yet added, then we move to abstract symbols like $a + a + a$ and see whether $3a$ emerges as the answer. Then we test further to see whether the child has grasped the idea of repeated addition, which we fool him by calling multiplication. We devise techniques of instruction along the way to aid the child in building a generic code to use for all sorts of quantities. If we fail to do this, we say that the child has learned in rote fashion or that, in Wertheimer's (1945) moralistic way of putting it, we have given the child "mechanical" rather than "insightful" ways of solving the problem. The distinction is not between mechanical and insightful, really, but whether or not the child has grasped and can use the generic code we have set out to teach him.

You will sense immediately that what I have been describing are examples of "transfer of training," so-called. But nothing is being transferred, really. The organism is learning codes that have narrower or wider applicability.

Let me give you some examples of how one uses the transfer paradigm to investigate what kind of coding systems are being learned. William Hull, a teacher in a Cambridge school, raised the question whether the learning of spelling involved simply the learning by rote of specific words or whether instead it did not also involve learning the *general coding system* for English

words from which the child might then be able to reconstruct the letters of a word. He took children of the fifth grade and separated them into those who had done well and those who had done poorly on a standard spelling achievement test, taking as subjects those who fell in the highest and lowest quartile of the class. He then presented these children brief exposures of pseudowords, which they were to write down immediately after the card bearing each word was removed. Some of the words were first-order approximations to English, essentially random strings of letters that had the same frequency distribution of letters as does English. Some were third- and fourth-order approximations to English constructed by Miller, Bruner, and Postman (1954) in connection with another experiment, words like MOSSIANT, VERNALIT, POKERSON, ONETICUL, APHYSTER, which reflected the probability structure of English very closely and which, but for the grace of God, might have been in the dictionary. Take the case for five-letter and six-letter pseudowords. For the first-order or random words, there was little difference between good and poor spellers. But for nonsense approximations to English, there was a great difference between the two, the good spellers showing a much superior performance.

The difference between the two groups is in *what* they had been learning while learning to spell English words. One group had been learning words more by rote, the others had been learning a general coding system based on the transitional probabilities that characterize letter sequences in English. Along the same lines, Mr. Robert Harcourt of Cambridge University and I used the occasion of an international seminar at Salzburg to test Italian, German, Swedish, French,

Dutch, and English speakers on their ability to reproduce random strings of letters presented briefly (that is, zero-order approximations to any language), and third-order approximations to each of these languages. As you would expect, there was no difference in ability to handle random strings, but a real difference in ability, favoring one's mother tongue, in reproducing nonsense in one's own language. You will sense immediately to what language stock each of the following nonsense words belongs: MJÖLKKOR, KLOOK, GERLANCH, OTIVANCHE, TRIANODE, FATTOLONI, and so on. When one learns a language one learns a coding system that goes beyond words. If Benjamin Lee Whorf is right, the coding system goes well beyond even such matters as we have described.

Let us sum up the matter to this point. We propose that when one goes beyond the information given, one does so by virtue of being able to place the present given in a more generic coding system and that one essentially "reads off" from the coding system additional information either on the basis of learned contingent probabilities or learned principles of relating material. Much of what has been called transfer of training can be fruitfully considered a case of applying learned coding systems to new events. Positive transfer represents a case where an appropriate coding system is applied to a new array of events, negative transfer being a case either of misapplication of a coding system to new events or of the absence of a coding system that may be applied. It follows from this that it is of the utmost importance in studying learning to understand systematically *what it is* that an organism has learned. This is the cognitive problem in learning.

There is perhaps one additional thing

that is learned by an organism when he acquires information generically, and this must be mentioned in passing although it is not directly germane to our line of inquiry. Once a situation has been mastered, it would seem that the organism alters the way in which new situations are approached in search of information. A maze-wise rat, for example, even when put into a new learning situation, seems not to nose about quite so randomly. In an experiment by Goodnow and Pettigrew (1955), for example, once their subjects have learned one pattern of pay-off on a "two-armed bandit," they approach the task of finding other patterns by responding more systematically to the alternatives in the situation. Even when they are trying to discover a pattern in what is essentially a random series of pay-offs, their sequential choice behavior shows less haphazardness. It is interesting that this acquired regularity of response makes it possible for them to locate new regularities in pay-off pattern when these are introduced after a long exposure to random positional pay-offs. Even though the behavior is designed to discover whether the old pattern will recur again, its regularity makes it possible to discover new patterns.

Three general problems now emerge. The first problem concerns the conditions under which efficient and generalizable coding systems will be acquired. What will lead a rat to learn the sequence LRLR in such a generic way that it will be transferable to the sequence of turns RLRL? What will lead a child to learn the sequence 2, 4, 8, 16, 32 . . . in such a way that it transfers to the sequence 3, 9, 27, 81. . . ? This we shall call *the conditions of code acquisition*.

The second we may label the *problem of creativity*. It has two aspects. The first has to do with the *inventive* activity involved in constructing highly generic and widely appropriate coding systems, armed with which a person will subsequently, in a highly predictive way, be able to deal with and go beyond much of the information he encounters in his environment. The other aspect of the problem of creativity is the development of a readiness to *utilize* appropriately already acquired coding systems. James long ago called this "the electric sense of analogy" and it consists in being able to recognize something before one fits it into or finds it to be a case of some more generic class of things that one has dealt with before—being able to see, for example, that laws that were originally related to statistical physics also fit the case of the analysis of transmitted information, the leap that carries us from Boltzmann's turn-of-the-century conception of entropy to modern theories of communication as initiated by Claude Shannon (1948). The equation of entropy with information was a creative analogical leap indeed, even if it did not require any new invention. Very well, the problem of creativity involves then the invention of efficient and applicable coding systems to apply to the information given and also the proper sense of knowing when it is appropriate to apply them.

The third and final problem to be considered is the *problem of instruction,* and it is a practical one. It concerns the best coding system in terms of which to present various subject matters so as to guarantee maximum ability to generalize. For example, the statement $S = \frac{1}{2} gt^2$ is an efficient and highly generalizable coding system for learning about falling bodies, and by using the code one can go beyond any partial data given one about falling bodies. But how does one teach somebody "about a country" in general so

that given some new specific knowledge about the country he can effectively "go beyond it" by appropriate inferences based on an effective coding system?

We consider each of these problems in turn.

CONDITIONS AFFECTING THE ACQUISITION OF CODING SYSTEMS

Essentially, we are asking under what conditions will an organism learn something or, as we put it, code something in a generic manner so as to maximize the transferability of the learning to new situations?

Let me propose four general sets of conditions that may be relevant here. The first of these is *set* or *attitude.* The second is *need state.* The third is *degree of mastery* of the original learning from which a more generic coding system must be derived. The fourth is *diversity of training.*

The Role of Set

It is a perennial source of embarrassment to psychologists interested in the learning process that "set to learn" is such a massive source of variance in most experiments on human learning. We make the distinction between incidental learning and intentional learning. What is the difference between the two?

Take typical experiments in the field of concept attainment as a case in point. In most such experiments since Hull's classic study (1920), the subject is given the task of *memorizing* what nonsense syllables go with what figures or pictures or words. One subset of pictures in the array presented —ones that all contain unbeknownst to the subject a certain common defining property—will have the label CIV and another subset, let us say, will have the label DAX. The task as presented is one in which the subject is to learn which label goes with which pictures. Insofar as the task is understood as one involving the memorization of labels, the subject is engaged in what can only be called incidental concept attainment. An interesting experiment by Reed (1946) shows that when subjects operate under such a set, they attain concepts more slowly and remember them less well than under instructional conditions where the subject is told frankly what is the real objective of the experiment—that is, to find what makes certain designs CIV's and others DAX's. In an extensive series of experiments by Bruner, Goodnow, and Austin (1955), moreover, it is evident that the search for the defining attributes of a class of objects—the search for a generic code in terms of which a class of objects may be rendered equivalent—leads to certain forms of behavior strategies or learning sets that are absent when the task is seen as one of rote memorization. The subject learns ways of testing instances to gather an optimum amount of information leading him to final discovery of the defining attributes of CIV's and DAX's. Once success has been achieved in this way, new instances can be recognized with no further learning and the memory of the instances already encountered need no longer depend upon sheer retention. For now, knowing the code, the subject can reconstruct the fact that all positive instances encountered were all marked by certain critical attributes.

In short, an induced set can guide the person to proceed nongenerically and by rote or to proceed as if what was to be learned was a principle or a generic method of coding events. Instructions serve, if you will, as a switching mechanism or set producer that brings different forms of coding into

play and tunes the organism to the kind and level of generic activity that seem appropriate to the situation.

Obviously, the principal giver of instruction is our own past history. For by virtue of living in a certain kind of professional or social setting, our approach to new experience becomes constrained—we develop, if you will, a professional deformation with respect to ways of coding events. The mathematician tends with time to code more and more events in terms of certain formal codes that are the stock in trade of his profession. The historian has his particular deformations, and so too the psychologist. With experience, Harlow's (1949) monkeys gradually develop a deformation, too, and attempt to solve all discrimination problems as exemplars of the oddity principle.

It is perhaps Kurt Goldstein (1939) who has insisted most strongly that one may in general characterize the typical sets a person brings to problems along the dimensions of abstractness and concreteness. The person who is high in concreteness deals with information or events in terms of their own specific identity and does not tend to genericize what is learned. The abstract attitude is one in which the individual can not only tear himself away from the given, but actually may not deal with the given save as an exemplar of more generic categories. How people "get to be" one way and the other or how they maintain an ability to operate at both levels is something we do not understand with any clarity, although some tentative proposals will be put forth in the following section.

To sum up: the manner and the degree with which newly learned knowledge is coded generically can be influenced in a transient way by situational instruction and in a more permanent way by the regimen of one's past experience. One's "attitude" toward learning, whether a transient or an enduring thing, will then determine the degree to which one is equipped with coding systems that can be brought to bear on new situations and permit one to go beyond them.

Need State

I should like to dust off the Yerkes-Dodson Law at this point and propose that the generality of the coding system in terms of which newly acquired information is organized depends upon the presence of an optimum motivational state. Very high and very low drive lead, I think, to an increase in concreteness of cognitive activity. There is a middle state of drive level that produces the strongest tendency toward generic learning.

Let me illustrate this by going back to the experiment of Bruner, Matter, and O'Dowd previously referred to. Consider two of their groups. Each group was given enough training to reach a criterion in learning the turn pattern LRLR and then given eighty additional trials of overlearning. The only difference between the groups was that one group did its learning under 36 hours of food deprivation, the other under 12 hours of deprivation. When the two groups were then transferred to the reversal pattern, RLRL, the moderately motivated group showed positive transfer, learning the new single alternation pattern significantly faster than they had learned the original pattern. The very hungry group showed marked negative transfer.

The behavior of the two groups at the time of transfer is revealing. When transferred, the moderately motivated groups showed much more disturbance in behavior. When these highly trained animals found the old reliable door at the first turn blocked, they drew back

from the choice-point and sometimes took as long as 20 minutes before they could make up their minds about what to do next. They defecated, seemed upset, and spent a great deal of time looking back and forth at the two doors. Several of the animals, at the end of this period of delay, then charged through the now correct first door and continued to charge right through the now correct single alternation pattern and made no errors from then on. Others made somewhat more errors, but on the whole, their learning was rapid.

The other group, the highly skilled and highly motivated rats of the 36-hour deprived group, showed quite different behavior. Finding the first door locked, they barged right over and took the alternative door, and then attempted unsuccessfully at each successive alley to make their old turn. Some of these animals persisted in this for many trials and then shifted to other forms of systematic response—such as one-sided position habits—that were not single alternation. In sum, it seemed as if they had to unlearn the old pattern of LRLR responses and then relearn a new one.

There is one particular feature of the behavior of the animals in the two groups that wants special attention. It is the amount of "looking around" or VTE-ing or scanning that went on in the two groups. As Tolman (1938) has observed, highly motivated organisms show less VTE behavior, less looking back and forth at choice points. So, too, our 36-hour hungry animals during original learning in contrast with the 12-hour ones. The difference in VTE was particularly marked during the early transfer trials as well, and it was exhibited by the less hungry rats predominantly in the first unit of the maze, at the choice-point that was the only real alternative, for once the first turn was correctly mastered, the rest of the pattern followed.

It would seem, then, that under conditions of high drive, if a path to the goal has been learned, it is learned, so to speak, as "*this* path to *this* goal" and is not coded or acquired as an example of a more generic pattern, "this *kind* of path to this *kind* of goal." In consequence, when a new situation arises, the driven creature does not have a generic coding system that permits him to go beyond it "insightfully." It is as if one of the students of geometry in Wertheimer's study (1945) had learned to do the operations necessary for solving the area of *this* parallelogram but had not generalized the knowledge into a coding system for handling parallelograms of slightly different size, shape, or position.

Impelling drive states seem also to affect the extent to which a person is able to apply already very firmly acquired coding systems to new material encountered, permitting him to go appropriately beyond the information given. An illustrative study is provided by the experiment of Postman and Bruner (1948) on perception under stress. Two groups of subjects were used. They began by having to recognize brief, three-word sentences presented tachistoscopically under usual laboratory conditions. Then the stress group was given an impossible perceptual recognition task to perform (reporting on the details of a complex picture presented at an exposure level too brief in duration for adequate performance). During these stress trials they were rather mercilessly badgered by the experimenter for performing so poorly and were urged to try harder. The other group was given a simple task of judging the illumination level at which the same picture was pre-

sented at the same exposure levels. And they were not badgered. Then additional sentences were given subjects in both groups. The stress group showed no further improvement in their sentence- and word-recognition thresholds, the nonstress group continued to improve. What was striking about the performance of the two groups in the latter half of the experiment was that the stress subjects either overshot the information given and made wild inferences about the nature of the briefly presented words, or they undershot and seemed unable to make words out of the briefly presented data at all. In terms of the Jamesian electric sense of analogy, it was as if the stress introduced either too many ohms of resistance into the circuit or removed too many of them. The stress subjects, let it be noted, did not behave consistently in the overshoot or the undershoot fashion, but seemed to go back and forth between the two.

Let me note finally in connection with code acquisition and/or the transfer of acquired codes to new situations that there is one interesting feature of the Harlow (1948) experiments on the acquisition of learning sets that is not often enough remarked. Recall that in the typical experiment of this kind, an animal is trained to choose the odd member of a set of stimuli, and that after training on a variety of such problems he is able to do so regardless of what characteristics the stimuli have: the odd one of several shapes, of several colors, of several junk stimuli, and so on. These experiments are carried out with animals who are only very lightly motivated. They are well fed before they are run, the reward used consists of a half or even a quarter of a peanut, and it would almost be fair to say that the most impelling drive operative is the manipulative-curiosity drive that Harlow has rightly made so much of in his recent writing. The use of such a mild motivational regimen is well advised. The fact of the matter is that one does not get such elegant principle learning in more highly motivated animals. A very hungry monkey may not develop such learning sets at all. Again, more generic coding seems to be inhibited by a condition in which the information to be acquired has too great instrumental relevance to a need state then in being.

Let me conclude this section on the role of need states in acquiring and utilizing coding systems with an important caveat, one that has been insisted upon particularly by George Klein (1951). *One cannot specify the cognitive or behavioral resultants of need states without specifying the manner in which the organism has learned to deal with his need states.* The resultant of "learning to deal with needs" is the establishment in behavior of what Klein calls *general regulatory systems.* In a sense, we have been implying such systems in the rat and monkey when we speak of the fact that a high need state has the effect of specializing the organism to deal with the here-and-now without regard to the more generic significance of what is being learned. It is conceivable that in some higher organisms this may not always be the case.

Degree of Mastery and Its Relationship to Generic Coding

Let me begin again with that overworked species, the rat. Starling Reed (1954) reports that animals who have been overtrained on a black-white discrimination, with black the positive stimulus, are able to transfer more easily to a black-white discrimination with white positive than are animals trained simply to criterion and then

reversed. In the Bruner, Matter, and O'Dowd study already referred to, three groups of 12-hour and three groups of 36-hour hungry animals were used. High- and low-motivation groups were paired in terms of amount of original training given. One pair of groups was given original training on an LRLR pattern until they just reached criterion; a second pair was given twenty additional trials of practice beyond criterion; and the third pair was given eighty additional overtraining trials. The biggest effect in the study was in the interaction of drive level and amount of overtraining. For the 12-hour groups, the more their overtraining, the better they did on transfer to the reverse pattern. But only the highly overtrained group showed positive transfer. All the strongly motivated animals showed about the same amount of negative transfer. We may take as a tentative conclusion that overtraining and mastery aids generic coding provided motivation is not severe.

We are in the midst of a controversial area, for the wisdom of common sense and of the psychologist divides sharply on the matter of practice and drill. "Practice makes perfect" is a well-thumbed proverb and the darling of practically all S-R learning theory. To be sure, it is a moot point in these theories just *what* it is that practice makes one perfect at. Nobody denies that it makes one perfect at the thing being practiced, but there is still debate on whether it also improves one at things beyond what one has practiced. The position of most stimulus-response theorists has been that it does not make one perfect at anything save the thing itself and that transfer to other things depends upon whether the other things contain elements identical to those that existed in the first task. We shall leave aside the question of how fast and loose one can play with the word "identical" in the expression "identical elements," for it is obvious that exploring its usage will be a discouraging venture. Even in the original monograph of Thorndike (1903) it was claimed that one form of identical element shared by two problems was that they could be solved by the same principle!

In any case, to return to the main issue at hand, there is another school of thought that proposed insight and understanding as a more important factor than drill in improving both performance of a particular task and in guaranteeing wider generalization of the learning to other situations. The names of Wertheimer (1945), Katona (1940), Duncker (1945), and Köhler (1925) are associated with this position, and the modern proverb has been provided by International Business Machines: THINK. The progressive school and its apostles have perhaps been the chief carriers of the practical banner.

I think the issue is a pseudoissue. The nature and effect of drill and overtraining is a function of what has to be learned. Moreover, one cannot speak of drill without specifying the nature of the set and the drive conditions under which it takes place. We cannot talk about practice or training as if it were being administered to an indifferently constructed black box.

First about the nature of materials to be learned. Take Katona's example of the string of numbers:

58121519222629

If subjects are asked to remember it, the amount of practice required to become perfect depends upon their method of recoding the numbers. If they recognize that the numbers are grouped as follows

5–8–12–15–19–22–26–29

and that this series begins with 5 and is made up of successive additions of 3 and 4, then what they had better practice is "5 then add 3 and then 4 and keep repeating this alternation." Mastering this coding system requires less practice and it is different practice than trying to remember the series by rote. As George Miller (1951) puts it in his delightful discussion of recoding systems, "Suppose that we want to know how far a body falls through space when it has been falling freely for a given number of seconds. One way to tackle this problem is to make measurements, summarize the measurements in a table, and then memorize the table. . . . This is a very stupid way to proceed because we memorize each number as if it were unrelated to all the other numbers. . . . All the measurements can be recoded into a simple rule that says the distance fallen at the end of t seconds is $gt^2/2$. The value of g is about 32. All we need remember is $16t^2$. Now we store all the measurements away in memory by storing this simple formula" (p. 234). Again, we had better practice remembering the formula and the value of g, and never mind practicing on the table of measurements from which it was produced.

But yet this fails to meet the question squarely. For where we do not know the appropriate coding system in advance, what is the best practice procedure for discovering it? Our rats and those of Starling Reed obviously had to do a fair amount of drilling at their task before they learned it in a generic way. And it seems to be frequently the case that a certain amount of skill development is necessary at a simpler level of coding before more generic recording of the learning can occur. The earliest studies of code learning, the classic study by Bryan and Harter (1897) of telegraphic code learning, can be reproduced in many later studies: one first learns to code the messages in terms of letters, then in terms of words, then in terms of sentences. Later methods of regrouping or recoding depend upon prior mastery of less generic methods of coding. One's limited immediate memory span requires one to deal first with the dits and dahs of single letters. Then gradually when the dit-dah arrangement of a letter takes on unitary properties, that is, can be categorized as a unit, it may be grouped with other unitary dit-dah arrangements into words. When words are codable as units, then one goes to sentences. So too with the rats: they must master the regularity of a set of turns before it becomes possible to reorganize or recode in terms of a single alternation principle.

In sum, then, the question of mastery comes down to this. Learning often cannot be translated into a generic form until there has been enough mastery of the specifics of the situation to permit the discovery of lower-order regularities which can then be recombined into higher-order, more generic coding systems. Once a system of recoding has been worked out whereby information is condensed into more generic codes, the problem of mastery becomes one of mastering the recoding system rather than mastering the original set of events. Moreover, the nature of practice cannot be simply specified in terms of repetition to and beyond mastery of a specific task. Rather, one must specify the conditions under which practice takes place, whether with the auxiliary intention to search out a generic coding system or whether simply with a rote learning intention. Finally, the need level at which the organism is practicing a task

must also be specified. Practice at a high rate of drive may produce no generic learning. Low-drive practice may.

Diversity of Training

I think that we know intuitively that if we wish to make a group of students understand the Pythagorean theorem in plane geometry, it helps to illustrate the intuitive proof of the theorem to use several right triangles of different dimensions, and indeed it might also help to demonstrate that the theorem does not apply to nonrectilinear triangles. It also seems intuitively right, does it not, that if monkeys are to be taught Harlow's oddity problem it helps or indeed may be essential to give them training choosing the odd member of several *different* arrays? So too when we play the original word game with children, we point to several exemplars of the word "dog" and several exemplars of "cat" in demonstrating the linguistic code utterance "cats and dogs are different." The quantitative informational importance of diversity of instances in concept attainment has been dealt with elsewhere and I would only like to consider some of the common-sense implications of the matter here.

The process of finding out what is generic about a given situation so that one can then deal with similar situations later—know their solution without having to go through the tedious business of learning all over again—consists essentially of being able to isolate the defining properties of the class of events to which the present situation belongs. In a concept-formation experiment, for example, if a subject is trying to discover what makes certain cards "positive" and certain ones "negative," his task is to discover which of the discriminable attributes or which combination of discriminable attributes are present in the positive instances and absent in the negative ones. I think one can think of the matter of diversity in terms of the interesting old proverb, "The fish will be the last to discover water," as indeed man was very late in discovering the atmosphere. Unless one is exposed to some changes, genericizing does not seem to be stimulated. Kurt Lewin had a subtle point when he urged that the best way to understand the nature of a social process was to try to change it, for only in the face of changes in events does one begin to have the information necessary to abstract generic properties.

This suggests a rather simple but rather startling conclusion. If we are to study the conditions under which generic learning occurs, the pattern of much of present learning research needs drastic change. The present approach is to study the speed of acquisition of new learning and, possibly, to study the conditions that produce extinction. When we have carried our experimental subjects through these steps, we either dismiss them or, if they are animal subjects, dispose of them. The exception, of course, is the clinician, but even his research on learning and cognition is of the cross-sectional type. We have been accustomed to speaking of maze-wise rats and test-wise human beings, but in the spirit of being annoyed by an inconvenience. The fact of the matter is, as Beach (1954) has recently pointed out, that early and diverse training of lower organisms seems to be one of the conditions for producing "intelligent" behavior in the more mature organism. If we really intend to study the conditions of generic learning by the use of the transfer-of-training paradigm I have proposed, then we shall have to keep our organisms far longer and teach them original tasks

of greater diversity than we now do if we are to discover the conditions affecting generic learning.

THE INVENTION OR CREATION OF CODING SYSTEMS

The past half-century has witnessed a profound revolution against the conception of science inherited from the Newtonian period. Newton saw the task of the scientist as a journey on the sea of discovery whose objective was to discover the islands of truth. The conception was essentially Baconian. Newton's *Principia* was not proposed as a theoretical system but as a description of discoveries about nature. His *Opticks* was in like vein a disquisiton into the secrets of light. Indeed, Jonathan Edwards preached to his parishioners in Western Massachusetts on Newton's discovery of the spectral composition of white light as an instance of the fact that God had given man sufficient capacities to see through to some of the deepest secrets of God's design. To a considerable extent, the layman's view of science is still dominated by the spirit of discovery, by the spirit of naturalistic realism.

The temper of modern science is more nominalistic. The scientist constructs formal models or theories that have predictive value, that have a value in going beyond the information available. One works with sets of observations that one fits into a theory. If the theory cannot take one beyond one's observations, if it does not have the "surplus value" that is demanded of a theory, then the theory is trivial. The universe is a set of perspectives devised by scientists for understanding and rendering predictable the array of observations that are possible. Whoever has read Robert Oppenheimer's account of "Lord Rutherford's World" in his Rieth Lectures (1954) or whoever has read Max Wertheimer's account (1945) of his conversation with Einstein on the formulation of the special and general theories of relativity cannot but be struck by the emphasis on the constructive, nominalistic, and essentially subjective conception of science-making that prevails in modern physical theory.

The activity of constructing formal models and theoretical constructs is a prototype of what we mean by the creation of generic coding systems that permits one to "go beyond" the data to new and possibly fruitful predictions.

Let us consider the creative acts by which a person constructs a "theory" for dealing with a problem. The given, let us say, is as it is in a Duncker-type problem. Here is X-ray apparatus capable of destroying a tumor in the center of a body. The difficulty is that the amount of radiation sufficient to destroy the tumor is also sufficient to destroy the healthy tissue through which it must pass in reaching the tumor. How solve the difficulty? Let us assume that the problem-solver did not learn a routine technique in medical school for dealing with this problem.

We will assume (and it is not an outrageous assumption, as we shall see) that the person has had experiences that provide the elements out of which a solution may be fashioned. The child knows, for example, that if a plank is too weak to take two chilren across a gap simultaneously, the children can get across one at a time in successive order or get across the gap at the same time if they can find two planks to throw across it. This is highly relevant knowledge. But this is not a "theory" nor by remembering it does one either solve the problem or create a relevant coding system.

Suppose now that the person comes, through whatever processes are involved, to a solution of the problem: using two X-ray beams, each of less than lethal dose, to converge at some angle upon the tumor. This solution, insofar as it is specific to the single problem at hand, is still not a theory; indeed it is not altogether clear that anything new has been "produced" or "created." What we mean by a theory or model or generic coding system is a representation of the criterial characteristics of the situation just described, a contentless depiction of the ideal case, empty in the sense that geometry is empty of particulars. It is this emptying operation, I would propose, that constitutes the creative step in inventing or producing a coding system. It is also the step that is involved when one learns something generically. In this sense there is only a difference in degree between what we have spoken of as generic learning and what we here call the production of a generic coding system.

Pursue the matter a bit further. The problem-solver says to himself, "This must be a general characteristic of loads, media, and destinations within the medium. Every medium has an array of paths to a destination within it and each path has a capacity. The number of paths required for the simultaneous transmission of a load to a destination is the size of the load divided by the capacity of any single path." Now we say the person has a theory: he has to some degree emptied the problem of specific content.

When we ask what leads to such an emptying operation (or abstraction, if one prefers the more conventional term), we are forced to answer by describing the conditions that inhibit it. What then inhibits "theory construction"? I would submit that the conditions inhibiting theory construction of this kind are the same ones that inhibit generic learning—the conditions of code acquisition described in the preceding section. For generic learning and the abstracting or "emptying" operation are, I think, the same thing.

But consider one other aspect of the creation or acquisition of generic coding systems. It consists of a form of combining activity that is made possible by the use of abstracted or "empty" codes. Take the formulation just given—the theory of loads, media, destinations, and path capacities. It now becomes possible to combine *this* formalized system with other formalized systems to generate new predictions. For example, suppose the problem-solver goes on to combine his new formulation with the equally abstract formulations of analytic geometry. The number of paths converging through a medium to an enclosed destination is infinity. Therefore, the combined path capacity of an over-all medium is infinity, and therefore, in principle, an infinite load (radiation or whatnot) can be delivered to a destination. In principle, then, one may go beyond to the hypothesis that *no* load is too large to deliver simultaneously across a medium, given the solution of technical limitations.

It seems to me that the principal creative activity over and beyond the construction of abstracted coding systems is the combination of different systems into new and more general systems that permit additional prediction. It is perhaps because of this that, in Whitehead's picturesque phrase, progress in science seems to occur on the margins between fields. There is virtually no research available on this type of combinatorial creativity. How, for example, do physiological psychologists combine the coding systems of biology and psychology, or biophysicists their component disciplines to de-

rive a new emergent? We might begin by looking.

THE PROBLEM OF INSTRUCTION

What we have said thus far obviously has implications for educational practice, and it is with one of these that we wish to conclude. How shall we teach a subject matter? If the subject matter were geometry we readily answer that we teach the person those axioms and theorems—a formal coding system—that will maximize the ability of the individual to go beyond the information given in any problem he might encounter. A problem in geometry is simply an incomplete statement, one that has unknowns in it. We say, "Here is a three-sided figure: one side measures x, and the other y, the angle between them is z degrees, and the problem is to find the length of the other side and the size of the other two angles as well as the area of the triangle." One must, in short, go beyond what is given. We know intuitively that if the person has learned the formal coding system, he will be able to perform such feats.

But how describe the history of a people or, say, Navaho culture? I would propose that much the same criterion should prevail here as we apply to geometry. The best description of a people's history is that set of propositions that permits a given individual to go beyond the information given to him. This, if you will, is *"the"* history of a people, the information that is necessary to make all other information as redundant or predictable as possible. So too in characterizing Navaho culture: that minimum set of propositions that will permit the largest reconstruction of unknowns by people to whom the propositions are revealed.

Let me in general propose this test as a measure of the adequacy of any set of instructional propositions—that once they are grasped, they permit the maximum reconstruction of material unknown to the reconstructor. My colleague Morton White (1950) argues persuasively for this position when he says (pp. 718–719),

> We ought to start by observing that a history contains true statements about the whole course of . . . [an] object's existence. True statements about the future of the object will be as much part of its history as true statements about its remote past. We must observe that some of these statements have causal implications whereas others do not . . . The next thing to observe is that there are two kinds of historians, two kinds of students who *want* to approximate the whole truth about a given object. First there are those who conceive it as their task to amass as many true singular statements as can be amassed at a given moment, and in this way approximate the ideal of the historian. Clearly this seems like the way to approach an infinite or very large number of statements—gather as many as you can. But then there are historians who are more discriminating, who recognize that some singular statements are historically more important than others, not because they fit in with some moral point of view, but because they are more useful for achieving the history of the object as here defined. The first group is near-sighted. It tries to amass everything in sight on the theory that this is a sure method of getting close to the whole truth. But it fails to realize that those who select facts which seem to have causal significance are more apt to come to know things about the future and past of the object.

White then goes on to compare the criterion of "causal fertility" in history with the criterion of "deductive fertility" in logic, noting that "both attempts at brevity . . . are motivated by a desire for intellectual economy." In the broadest sense, the economy is a predictive economy—to be able to go beyond givens to a prediction of unknowns.

I would submit, I think, that it is only by imparting "causally fertile" propositions or generic codes that general education in the broad range of human knowledge is made possible. General education does best to aim at being generic education, training men to be good guessers, stimulating the ability to go beyond the information given to probable reconstructions of other events.

CONCLUSION

This has been a programmatic essay on the conditions by which it becomes possible for people to go beyond the information given them, or as Bartlett (1951) has put it, to go beyond evidence, to fill in gaps, to extrapolate. We have posed the problem as one involving the learning of coding systems that have applicability beyond the situation in which they were learned. In essence, our proposal is that we emphasize those conditions that maximize the transferability of learning and in pursuit of that we have urged that psychologists examine more closely what is involved when we learn generically—the motivational conditions, the kinds of practice required, the nature of the set designed for gaining an optimally generic grasp of materials. Rate of acquisition and rate of extinction in learning have occupied us for a generation. Perhaps in the coming generation we can concern ourselves more directly with the utility of learning: whether, one thing having been learned, other things can be solved with no further learning required. When we have achieved this leap, we will have passed from the psychology of learning to the psychology of problem solving.

REFERENCES

1. Bartlett, F. C., "Thinking," *Manchester Memoirs*, **93,** No. 3 (The Clayton Memorial Lecture, 1951).

2. Beach, F. A. and J. Jaynes, "The Effects of Early Experience on the Behavior of Animals," *Psychological Bulletin,* **51** (1954), 239-63.

3. Bexton, W. H., W. Heron, and T. H. Scott, "Effects of Decreased Variation in the Sensory Environment," *Canadian Journal of Psychology,* **8** (1954), 70-76.

4. Bruner, J. S., J. J. Goodnow, and G. A. Austin, *A Study of Thinking.* New York: John Wiley & Sons, Inc., 1956.

5. Bryan, W. L. and N. Harter, "Studies on the Telegraphic Language. The Acquisition of a Hierarchy of Habits," *Psychological Review,* **6** (1897), 345-75.

6. Duncker, K., "On Problem Solving," *Psychology Monograph,* **58** (1945), 1-112.

7. Goldstein, K., *The Organism.* New York: American Book Company, 1939.

8. Goodnow, J. J. and T. Pettigrew, "Responding to Change and Regularity in Environmental Events," 1955. (In preparation.)

9. Harlow, H. F., "The Formation of Learning Sets," *Psychological Review,* **56** (1949), 51-65.

10. Hull, C. L., "Quantitative Aspects of the Evolution of Concepts," *Psychology Monograph,* **123** (1920).

11. Humphrey, G., *Thinking.* New York: John Wiley & Sons, Inc., 1941.

12. James, W., *The Principles of Psychology.* New York: Holt, Rinehart & Winston, Inc., 1890.

13. Katona, G., *Organizing and Memorizing.* New York: Columbia University Press, 1944.

14. Klein, G. S., "The Personal World Through Perception," in *Perception: An Approach to Personality,* eds. R. R. Blake and G. V. Ramsey. New York: The Ronald Press Company, 1951.

15. Köhler, W., *The Mentality of Apes.* New York: Harcourt, Brace & World, Inc., 1925.

16. Miller, G. A., *Language and Communication.* New York: McGraw-Hill Book Company, Inc., 1951.

17. Miller, G. A., J. S. Bruner, and L. Postman, "Familiarity of Letter Sequences and Tachistoscopic Identification," *Journal of Genetic Psychology,* **50** (1954), 129-39.

18. Miller, G. A., G. A. Heise, and W. Lichten, "The Intelligibility of Speech as a Function of the Context of the Test Materials," *Journal of Experimental Psychology,* **41** (1951), 329-35.

19. Oppenheimer, J. R., *Science and the Common Understanding.* New York: Simon and Schuster, Inc., 1954.

20. Piaget, J., *The Child's Conception of Physical Causality.* London: Routledge & Kegan Paul, Ltd., 1930.

21. Postman, L. and J. S. Bruner, "Perception under Stress," *Psychological Review,* **55** (1948), 314-23.

22. Reed, H. B., "Factors Influencing the Learning and Retention of Concepts: I. The Influence of Set." *Journal of Experimental Psychology,* **36** (1946), 71-87.

23. Reed, S., "The Development of Noncontinuity Behavior through Continuity Learning," *Journal of Experimental Psychology,* **46** (1953), 107-12.

24. Shannon, C. E., "A Mathematical Theory of Communication," *Bell System Technical Journal,* **27** (1948), 379-423, 623-56. Also in C. E. Shannon and W. Weaver, *The Mathematical Theory of Communication.* Urbana: University of Illinois Press, 1949.

25. Smith, S., "Studies of Recoding," reported by A. A. Miller, "The Magic Number 7 ± 2." Address given at the 1955 meetings of the Eastern Psychological Association, Philadelphia (1955).

26. Spearman, C., *The Nature of Intelligence and the Principles of Cognition.* London: Macmillan & Co., Ltd., 1923.

27. Thorndike, E. L., *Educational Psychology.* New York: Lencke and Buechner, 1903.

28. Tolman, E. C., "The Determiners of Behavior at a Choice Point," *Psychological Review,* **45** (1938), 1-41.

29. Wertheimer, M., *Productive Thinking.* New York: Harper & Row, Publishers, 1945.

30. White, M. G., "Toward an Analytic Philosophy of History," in *Philosophical Thought in France and the United States,* ed. M. Farber. Buffalo, N. Y.: University of Buffalo Press, 1950.

31. Wilkins, M. C., "The Effect of Changed Material on Ability to Do Formal Syllogistic Reasoning," *Archives of Psychology,* **102** (1928).

Recent Developments in Piaget's Work *

D. E. Berlyne

INTRODUCTION

Piaget is known to English-speaking psychologists mainly for his early writings, with their thought-provoking but, according to some critics, disputable accounts of the quaint notions of young children. Doubts have been expressed about the validity of the method of interrogation used for these studies and about the generality of the findings. Repetitions with other populations have not always produced the results that Piaget's works would lead one to expect. At least one writer was moved to dismiss his "subjective approaches to the analysis of child behavior" as "little removed from ordinary literary speculation." [1]

Since the 1930's, however, Piaget's researches have been undergoing some gradual but profound changes. He has been turning to more exact and behavioristic methods of collecting data: close observation of infants, setting older children practical tasks or putting precise questions to them about events enacted in front of them, and psychophysical experiments with both child and adult subjects. His theory has become more detailed and more ambitious in scope, drawing on his knowledge of biology, logic and history of science, all of them fields to which he has contributed. These developments can be summed up by saying that he has changed from one of the most celebrated *developmental* psychologists into one of the most important of contemporary *general* psychologists. But this does not mean that his work has lost any of its importance for those faced with the practical problems of childhood in their everyday work.

Like most contemporary psychologists, Piaget starts from the biological concept of "adaptation." He sees adaptation as an interplay of two complementary processes, which he calls "assimilation" and "accommodation." Assimilation occurs when an organism uses something in its environment for some activity which is already part of its repertoire. At the physiological

---

* From D. E. Berlyne, "Recent Developments in Piaget's Work," *British Journal of Educational Psychology,* **27** (1957), 1-12. Reprinted by permission of the author and publisher.
[1] Pratt, K. C.: "The Neonate," in *A Handbook of Child Psychology,* ed. C. Murchison (Worcester, Mass.: Clark University Press, 1933).

level, it is exemplified by the ingestion of food, and, at the psychological level, it embraces a variety of phenomena. Piaget sees assimilation at work, for example, whenever a situation evokes a particular pattern of behavior because it resembles situations that have evoked it in the past, whenever something new is perceived or conceived in terms of something familiar, whenever anything is invested with value or emotional importance. Accommodation, on the other hand, means the addition of new activities to an organism's repertoire or the modification of old activities in response to the impact of environmental events.

Psychologists accustomed to other conceptual schemes may wonder whether it really helps to group together such multifarious processes under the same rubrics. Is the role played by a cow appearing as roast beef on a horse really analogous to that played by a cow appearing as roast beef on the child's dinner plate? Although Piaget discusses assimilation and accommodation at great length, some readers may feel that the concepts need to be analyzed more minutely before they can yield unequivocal predictions rather than describe facts already discovered. At all events, assimilation seems to include what learning theorists call "generalization" and "discrimination," processes determining which response a particular stimulus will elicit, while accommodation covers "differentiation of responses" and the learning of new responses.

As the child's development proceeds, a more and more complete balance and synthesis between assimilation and accommodation is achieved. The child is able to take account of stimuli more and more remote from him in space and time, and to resort to more and more composite and indirect methods of solving problems.

Piaget agrees with many other theorists in distinguishing "affective" and "cognitive" factors. The former release energy, while the latter determine how the energy will be applied. Piaget's writings have concentrated on the "cognitive" aspect of behavior rather than on motivation and emotion, but he insists that neither aspect must be overlooked. The child does not undergo separate intellectual and emotional developments. The most dispassionate pursuit of knowledge must be driven by some motive, and the directions in which drives and emotions impel behavior must depend on the structures made available by the growth of intelligence.

THE PERIOD OF SENSORI-MOTOR INTELLIGENCE (BIRTH TO TWO YEARS)

During his first two years, the child gradually advances towards the highest degree of intelligence that is possible without language and other symbolic functions. He begins life with innate reflexes, but these are, from the start, modified and made more effective by learning. New responses are soon acquired, and then complex solutions to problems are achieved by piecing together familiar responses in novel combinations. By the end of the second year, the first signs of the human capacity for symbolization appear: he invents new patterns of behavior which show him to be representing the results of his actions to himself before they occur. In short, the sensori-motor period sees attainments comparable to the highest found in subhuman animals.

This growing ingenuity in the face of practical problems goes hand in hand with the formation of a less "egocentric" and more "objective" conception of the world. For some weeks after birth, the world must consist of a succession of visual patterns, sounds, and other sensations. The infant comes naturally to pay attention to those external events which are associated with satisfactions or which are brought about by his own actions. Gradually, he builds up a view of the world as a collection of objects continuing to exist even when they are out of his sight and generally preserving the same sizes and shapes, despite the changes in their appearance that come with changes in position. Whereas no distinction between himself and what is outside him can have any meaning for him at first, he comes to conceive of himself as one object among the many that people the world, most of them unaffected by his activities.

The concept of an *object* is bound up with objective notions of *space, time,* and *causality,* which the child does not possess as part of his native endowment but has to build up gradually through interaction with the world. After learning to select appropriate spatial directions and temporal successions for his actions, he comes to respond to the positions and times of occurrence of events outside himself, using his own body and his own actions as reference points. Finally, he conceives of a space and a time in which both he himself and external objects are located. He learns, for example, to distinguish occasions when objects are moving independently of him from occasions when they merely appear to be changing positions because he is moving among them. Similarly, he progresses from an understanding of the relationship between his responses and their consequences to an understanding of the causal influence inanimate objects can exert on one another and even on him.

THE ORIGIN OF SYMBOLIC PROCESSES

Anything the child has achieved during the sensori-motor period is dwarfed by the prospects introduced by signs and symbols, particularly words and images. They expose him to a world of real and imaginary entities extending far beyond his momentary range of vision or even his life span. It is a stable and consistent world, whereas the objects he perceives come and go.

Piaget deprecates the long-established belief that images are mere reactivations of traces of past experiences, passively registered by the nervous system. He insists that imagery is an extremely complex and active process, as can be seen from the time it takes to appear after birth. It grows out of the child's imitative capacities and is, in fact, "internalized imitation." The gradual extension of imitation during the sensori-motor period proceeds from a tendency to reproduce sounds and visual effects which have just been produced by the infant himself or by somebody else to an ability to copy an increasing range of new responses from an increasing range of models. It reaches its climax and the point at which it can perform symbolic functions with "deferred imitation," the imitation of the behavior of an absent person of whom the child is "reminded."

Inanimate objects also can evoke imitation, as, for example, when a child opens his mouth on finding it difficult to open a match box. Imagery consists of just such symbolic imitation "internalized" that is, so reduced in scale that only the subject himself is aware of it. It consists, in other words, of what behaviorists call "implicit" or "fractional" responses. When the first indications of imagery emerge about the middle of the second year, the child is beginning, significantly enough, to turn from "practice" games, in which pleasure is derived from exercising simple activities, to "symbolic games," which involve make-believe or role-playing. The child understands, however, the nature of the relation between a symbol and what it signifies; he knows that the doll is not really a baby or that he is not really a cowboy.

Having learned to use actions and images as symbols and having by now acquired a sufficient vocabulary, he finds himself using words in a similar way. But words, more than images, are responsible for the progressive socialization of thought. Words and the concepts corresponding to them are taken over from the social group. They are, therefore, bound to edge the child's thoughts into line with those of other persons. He can influence and be influenced by, benefit from or suffer from, the beliefs and values of other members of his group and so arrive at an equilibrium and harmony with his social as well as his physical environment.

RELATIONS BETWEEN PERCEPTION AND THOUGHT

In recent years, Piaget has been spending a great deal of time, together with Lambercier and other collaborators, on the painstaking investigation of visual illusions and related phenomena. This area of research, a time-honored preserve of the more prosaic type of experimental psychology, may seem remote from the work for which he is best known. It has, nevertheless, given rise to some of his most original and comprehensive ideas, forming the kernel of his whole theory of intellectual functions. Whereas writers influenced by Gestalt psychology or by certain trends in American social psychology have tended to lump all "cognitive"

processes together, Piaget finds the differences between perceptual and conceptual processes illuminating.

There are two obvious ways in which perception contrasts with thought. One arises from the fact, emphasized by the Gestalt school, that the perceived properties of a stimulus vary according to the pattern of which it is a component. The concepts participating in thought do not share this instability. The essential nature of a number does not change, no matter what the structure into which a mathematician fits it. A journey between two towns may seem longer or shorter in different circumstances, but the distance separating the towns according to our knowledge or our calculations does not fluctuate.

Secondly, perceptions are notoriously variable from person to person and from moment to moment. If we take 1,000 subjects, show them a line three inches long and another two inches long, and ask them to select a third line equal in length to the two combined, we shall expect a distribution of results with a high variance. We shall even expect each subject's response to vary from trial to trial, especially if the two lines are shown in different arrangements. On the other hand, if we take the same 1,000 subjects, show them the figure 2 and the figure 3, and ask them to select a third figure, equal to the sum of the two, the uniformity of the responses will be remarkable.

These differences can be traced back to two related factors which inevitably distort all perception. First, perception is always "centered" (centré). Sense-organs have to be oriented in one direction at once, and the optical apparatus in particular is so constructed that the center of the visual field is seen more clearly and in more detail than other parts. As some of Piaget's psychophysical experiments show, the size of a fixated object is overestimated in comparison with the sizes of peripheral objects. The various parts of the visual field expand and shrink in turn as the gaze wanders from one point to another. The second source of error is the fact that larger portions of a figure are likely to catch the eye more often than others, with the result that the distortions that arise when they are the center of attention play a disproportionately large part in the net impression of the figure. What we have is, in fact, a biased sample of all possible fixations. From these assumptions, Piaget has derived a formula predicting the direction and extent of "primary" visual illusions, that is, those which are found in infants and lower animals as much as, if not more than, in adult human beings and which can be ascribed to the inherently "probabilistic" nature of perception.

Perception is analogous to certain processes in physics, notably in statistical mechanics, which are likewise governed by probability. These processes are irreversible, since they always lead from a less probable to a more probable state. For example, when a hot body is brought into contact with a cool body, heat is transmitted from the former to the latter and not vice versa. A spoonful of sugar diffuses evenly through a cupful of tea, but particles of sugar in a mixture do not forgather at one spot. Similarly, the distortions to which perceived figures are subject work predominantly in one direction. They cannot be relied on to balance out.

Thinking can escape from these limitations, because it is comparable with physical systems of a different type, namely those possessing *reversibility*. An example is a balance with equal weights in the two pans. The depression of one pan is followed by an upward swing which restores the original situation. Such systems are in stable equilibrium precisely because a change can be cancelled by an equal change in the opposite direction. A balance, however, is inflexible in the sense that there is one state to which it invariably reverts. Thought processes require structures which permit of more mobility without threatening disequilibrium. They must be free to flit rapidly from one idea to another and to arrange ideas in new combinations. But systems of concepts must preserve their organization, despite this mobility, if thoughts are to be consistent and if they are to produce a stable conception of the world. The "dynamic equilibrium" which Piaget attributes to thought can perhaps best be compared with that of a lift and its counterweight. The lift can move freely up and down, and the system remains intact and in equilibrium, no matter what floor is reached. This is because of its reversibility: any movement of the lift is compensated by an equal and opposite movement of the counterweight, and it can also be nullified by an equal and opposite movement of the lift.

The reversibility of logical thought is acclaimed by Piaget as the acme in which the growth of intelligence culminates. The spoken word and the performed action can never be recalled. The influence of something which has been perceived and then disappears from view lingers to infect subsequent perceptions. But a thought can be entertained and then unthought, and everything is as if it had never occurred. We are consequently able to conceive possible solutions for problems which it would be costly, dangerous, or impossible to test by action. And no matter how extravagant an idea is considered and then rejected, the coherence of conceptual systems is not threatened. The world represented by thought, unlike that presented by perception, is relatively free from "centering" (*centration*). It does not change with the location of the thinker or the direction of his attention.

These contrary characteristics are found in a pure form only in the naïve perception of the infant on the one hand and in the rigorous thought of the scientist, mathematician, or logician on the other. The principal merit of this part of Piaget's work, as far as child psychology is concerned, is the light it sheds on certain processes forming compromises between perception and thought. As we shall see when we return to the chronological sequence, the first attempts at thinking are still contaminated with the shortcomings of perception. And perception, after the first months of life, is usually accompanied by "perceptual activities," which mitigate its imperfections. There is no way of removing distortion completely from perception, but one distortion can be set against another. The focus of attention can be systematically varied, so that information from a succession of fixations is compared and collated to yield something approaching an objective impression. What appears from one point of view can be related to the perseveration or anticipation of what has been or will be seen from a different angle. "Perceptual activities" thus contribute to the "decentering" (*decentration*) of perception and the achievement of "semireversibility," so called because errors are not corrected exactly but merely tend to cancel out in the long run. Although these activities generally enhance accuracy of perception, they can on occasion lead to "secondary illusions," which are less pronounced in younger than in older children. An example is the "size-weight illusion," which makes a small object seem heavier than a larger one of equal weight.

THE PERIOD OF PRECONCEPTUAL THOUGHT (TWO TO FOUR YEARS)

Before his use of symbolic processes can reach fruition, the child has to relearn on a conceptual level some of the lessons he has already mastered on the sensori-motor level. For instance, he may have learned to recognize transient stimulus patterns as shifting appearances assumed by enduring objects. But this does not immediately make him at home with the *concept* of an object. Adults are familiar with the concept of a particular *object* (*"this table," "Socrates"*), with the concept of a *class* (*"all four-legged tables," "all men"*), and with the relation of *class-membership* which joins them (*"This is a four-legged table," "Socrates is a man."*). These underlie our deductive reasoning, since having, for example, placed Socrates in the class of men, we can infer that Socrates has all the properties characteristic of this class.

The three-year-old child still lacks this equipment and has to use something midway between the concept of an object and that of a class, which Piaget calls the "preconcept." On a walk through the woods, for example, he does not know whether he sees a succession of different snails or whether the same snail keeps reappearing. The distinction, in fact, means nothing to him; to him they are all "snail." Similar phenomena are, in some hazy way, identified, so that a shadow under a lamp in a room has something to do with the shadows under the trees in the garden. Contrariwise, a person in new clothes may be thought to require a new name.

Unlike adults, who reason either *de*ductively from the general to the particular or *in*ductively from the particular to the general, the child at the preconceptual stage reasons *trans*ductively from the particular to the particular. It is a form of argument by analogy: "A is like B in one respect, therefore A must be like B in other respects." Transduction may often lead to valid conclusions, that is, that if Daddy is getting hot water he must be going to shave, since he shaved after getting hot water yesterday. But it will at other times lead the child into errors of a sort said to be common in psychotics but certainly not unknown in intellectual circles.

THE PERIOD
OF INTUITIVE THOUGHT
(FOUR TO SEVEN YEARS)

When the child's reasoning has overcome these deficiencies, other limitations remain, mainly because thought has not yet freed itself from perception and become "decentered." Intuitive thought can best be understood from an experiment Piaget is fond of quoting. The child sees some beads being poured out of one glass into a taller and thinner glass. It is made clear to him that all the beads that were in the first glass are now in the second; none has been added or removed. He is asked whether there are now more or fewer beads in the second glass than there were in the first. The usual answer at this stage is either that there are more (because the level has risen) or that there are fewer (because the second glass is narrower).

To explain such errors, it may be worth asking why we, as adults, are able to avoid them. The first reason is that we are told by our thought processes that the number of objects in a set, if nothing is added or subtracted, must necessarily remain the same. We usually regard our thought processes as more trustworthy than our perceptions whenever the two conflict. At a con-

jurer's performance, for example, we do not really believe that the rabbit has been created *ex nihilo* or the lady has been sawn in half. The child at the intuitive stage is, on the other hand, still dominated by his perceptions. His conclusions are still at the mercy of the changes resulting from successive "centerings." The second reason is that we take into account several aspects of the situation at once or in turn. We can see that the height of the column of beads has increased and that the width has decreased just enough to compensate for the increase in height. But the child focusses on one aspect and overlooks others. In his reasoning as in his perception, "centering" causes one element to be overemphasized and others to be relatively ignored. The instructiveness of such examples for adults, who might smile at the child's mistakes in the bead experiment but be liable to precisely the same sort of misjudgment in relation to, say, political or social problems, need hardly be labored.

THE PERIOD
OF CONCRETE OPERATIONS
(SEVEN TO ELEVEN YEARS)

We come at last to the first reasoning processes that would satisfy logicians. Logical (or, as Piaget calls it, "operational") thought emerges when a certain basic stock of concepts has been acquired and when these concepts have been organized into coherent systems. The concepts which figure in operational thought are called "operations" because they are *internalized responses*. They grow out of certain overt actions in exactly the same way as images grow out of imitation. Three sorts in particular are of importance:

(1) Classes. The concept of a

"class" or operation of "classification" is an internalized version of the action of grouping together objects recognized as similar. Having learned to pick out all the yellow counters in a heap and *place* them together in one spot, the child acquired the ability to *think of* all yellow objects together and thus form the concept of the "class of all yellow objects." This means that some part of what happens in the nervous system and musculature when yellow objects are manually gathered together occurs whenever yellow objects are grouped together in thought. Once formed, classes can be joined to form more inclusive classes, so that elaborate systems of classification are built up, the one used by biologists being the clearest illustration.

(2) *Relations.* Asymmetrical relations, such as "a is longer than b" or "x is the father of y," derive by internalization from *ordering* activities, for example, from placing objects in a row in order of increasing size. The best example of the complex systems which ordering relations can form is the family tree.

(3) *Numbers.* The number system is the joint product of classification and ordering. The number 17, for instance, depends on the operation of grouping 17 objects together to form a class and that of placing 17 between 16 and 18 in the sequence of natural numbers.

Systems of operations are called "groupings" (*groupments*), and their stability depends on their having five properties. Unless these properties are present, the relations between the elements of a grouping will change as attention is directed to different parts of them, as happens with perceptual patterns, and thought will not be immune from inconsistency. The five properties are as follows:

(1) *Closure.* Any two operations can be combined to form a third operation (e.g., $2 + 3 = 5$; *all men and all women = all human adults; A is 2 miles north of B and B is 1 mile north of C = A is 3 miles north of C.*

(2) *Reversibility.* For any operation there is an opposite operation which cancels it (e.g., $2 + 3 = 5$ but $5 - 3 = 2$; *all men and all women = all human adults,* but *all human adults except women = all men; A is 2 miles north of B and B is 1 mile north of C = A is 3 miles north of C,* but *A is 3 miles north of C and C is 1 mile south of B = A is 2 miles north of B*).

(3) *Associativity.* When three operations are to be combined, it does not matter which two are combined first. This is equivalent to the possibility of arriving at the same point by different routes (e.g., $(2 + 3) + 4 = 2 + (3 + 4)$; *all vertebrates and all invertebrates = all human beings and all subhuman animals; a is the uncle of b and b is the father of c = a is the brother of d and d is the grandfather of c*).

(4) *Identity.* There is a "null operation" formed when any operation is combined with its opposite (e.g., $2 - 2 = 0$; *all men except those who are men = nobody; I travel 100 miles to the north and I travel 100 miles to the south = I find myself back where I started*).

(5) The fifth property has two versions, one for classes and relations and the other for numbers:

(a) *Tautology.* A classification or relation which is repeated is not changed. This represents the fact, recognized by logicians but not always by conversationalists, that saying something over and over again does not convey any more information than saying it once (e.g., *all men and all men = all men; a is longer than b and a is longer than b = a is longer than b*).

(b) *Iteration.* A number combined

with itself produces a new number (e.g., $3 + 3 = 6$; $3 \times 3 = 9$).[2]

THE PERIOD
OF FORMAL OPERATIONS
(ELEVEN TO FIFTEEN YEARS)

The eleven-year-old can apply "operational" thinking to practical problems and concrete situations. The adolescent takes the final steps towards complete "decentering" and "reversibility" by acquiring a capacity for abstract thought. He can be guided by the *form* of an argument or a situation and ignore its *content*. He need no longer confine his attention to what is real. He can consider hypotheses which may or may not be true and work out what would follow if they were true. Not only are the hypothetico-deductive procedures of science, mathematics and logic open to him in consequence but also the role of would-be social reformer. The adolescent's taste for theorizing and criticizing arises from his ability to see the way the world is run as only one out of many possible ways it could be run and to conceive of alternative ways that might be better.

Quite a variety of new intellectual techniques become available at the same time. The most important new equipment of all is the *calculus of propositions*. At the concrete-operations stage, he was able to use the branches of logic, known as the *algebra of classes* and the *algebra of relations*. Now he can supplement these with forms of reasoning bearing on the relations between propositions or sen-

tences. Propositional calculus uses "second-order operations" or operations on operations. An example would be *"either sentence p is true or sentence q is true."* Another would be *"if sentence r is true, then sentence s must be true"* or, in the parlance favored by logicians, *"r implies s."*

A large part of Piaget's information on this period comes from Inhelder's ingenious experiments, in which children were invited to discover elementary laws of physics for themselves with the help of simple apparatus. Children at the intuitive-thought stage vary conditions haphazardly and observe what happens in particular cases without deriving any general principles. At the concrete-operations stage, one factor at a time is varied, and its effects are duly noted. Not before the formal-operations stage does the child plan truly scientific investigations, varying the factors in all possible combinations and in a systematic order. The pedagogical implications of Inhelder's work are unmistakeable. Children with no previous instruction appear to be capable of learning scientific laws in this way, with, presumably, more motivation and more understanding than are produced by traditional teaching methods. But, according to Piaget and Inhelder, they are not capable of the sort of thinking that makes use of such laws before the advances of the formal-operations stage have been completed.

Piaget asks why so many new ways of thinking become available about the same time, despite their superficial dissimilarity. It is, he concludes, because they all require systems of operations with similar structures, and the child is not able to organize his thinking in accordance with such structures before adolescence. He has recently been much impressed with the possibilities of modern symbolic logic and

---

[2] Readers with mathematical interests will notice that, insofar as these properties refer to numbers, they are equivalent to the defining characteristics of a *group*. Groupings of classes and relations, on the other hand, are almost, but not quite, *groups* and almost, but not quite, *lattices*.

certain non-numerical branches of mathematics as means of describing the structures common to apparently different intellectual processes. This is not one of the ways in which logic has usually been used by psychologists in the past; Piaget is interested in using "logical models" for much the same purpose as other psychologists have begun to use "mathematical models."

One new acquisition is the ability to use systems of operations in which each operation has two distinct opposites. A class (for example, *"all vertebrate animals"*) has the sort of opposite called an *inverse* (*"all invertebrate animals"*). A relation (for example, *"a is twice as heavy as b"*) has a *reciprocal* (*"b is twice as heavy as a"*). But *"p implies q"* has both an inverse (*"p does not imply q"*) and a reciprocal (*"q implies p"*). Likewise, when the adolescent experiments with a balance, he discovers that the effects of one operation (for example, increasing the weight in the right-hand pan) can be cancelled either by the inverse operation (reducing the weight in the right-hand pan to its original value) or by the reciprocal operation (increasing the weight in the left-hand pan by the same amount.) Such systems with two opposites have a structure known to mathematicians as the *"four group."*

The four group can be shown to provide the operations necessary for dealing with *proportionality.* It is no accident that the laws governing equilibrium between weights in the pans of a balance are understood at about the same age as the laws governing the sizes of shadows. In one of Inhelder's experiments, the subject is given two vertical rings of different diameters and has to place the rings between a candle and a screen in such a way that their shadows will coincide. Adolescents discover that the problem is solved when the ratio between the distances of the two rings from the candle is the same as the ratio between their diameters. Understanding proportionality opens the way to understanding *probability,* since, when we speak of the probability of a six in a game of dice, we mean the proportion of throws that will produce sixes in the long run.

Combinatorial analysis, depending on the structures mathematicians call *"lattices,"* is another equally fruitful new attainment. Suppose that we have two ways of dividing up animals—into "vertebrates (V)" and "invertebrates (v)" and into flying (F)" and "nonflying (f)." A child at the concrete-operations stage is capable of allotting a particular animal to one of the four possible classes, $(V.F.)$, $(V.f.)$, $(v.F.)$, and $(v.f.)$. An adolescent at the formal-operations stage is capable of going further and considering all the sorts of animals that there are in the world or the sorts there conceivably could be. There are now *sixteen* possibilities: there might be no animals at all, there might be animals of all four classes, there might be $(v.F.)$ only, there might be $(V.F.)$, $(V.f.)$ and $(v.f.)$ animals but no $(v.F.)$, and so on. Now each of these sixteen combinations corresponds to one of the sixteen relations between two propositions recognized by modern logic. For example, *"if an animal can fly, it must be a vertebrate"* would correspond to $(V.F.)$ *or* $(V.f.)$ *or* $(v.f.)$, that is, the $(v.F.)$ possibility is excluded. We can understand, therefore, why permutations and combinations and complex logical relations are mastered more or less simultaneously.

The mastery of logical relations between propositions is well illustrated in Inhelder's experiments. All attempts to study the relations between the phenomena of nature, whether in the laboratory or in practical life, must use them: *"If I put the kettle on the stove and light the gas, the water will boil"; "It will rain or snow tomorrow unless the forecast was wrong or unless I read a description of today's weather and thought it was the forecast for tomorrow,"* and so on. The ability to think in terms of all possible combinations, which appears together with the ability to use complex statements like these, is clearly revealed when adolescents are set one of Inhelder's most instructive problems. Five vessels, all containing colorless liquids, are provided; A, B, and C, when mixed, will turn pink, D will remove the color, and E will have no effect. The properties of the liquids can be discovered only by systematically examining mixtures of every possible pair, every possible trio, etc., in turn.

AFFECTIVE DEVELOPMENT

The child's physiological constitution makes him liable, right from birth, to emotional and drive states. These pleasant and unpleasant states come to be aroused, through some sort of conditioning, by the external stimulus patterns which regularly accompany them, and, when he had learned to perceive in terms of objects, he comes to like or dislike these. Human beings are naturally more important sources of satisfaction and distress than other objects, and so their actions and they themselves will have especially strong positive and negative values attached to them.

The social influences to which the appearance of language and other symbols makes the child amenable are manifested particularly clearly in the formation of "interindividual feelings." The ability to picture how the world looks from another person's point of view includes the power to represent to oneself the feelings aroused in him by one's own actions. The child takes over other people's evaluations of his own behavior and builds up an attitude to himself derived from his estimates of their attitudes to him. The stage is then set, during the preconceptual and intuitive periods, for the first moral feelings. These take the form of a belief in absolute prohibitions and prescriptions, derived from parental orders but somehow enjoying an existence and validity in their own right. Acts are felt to deserve punishment according to how far they depart from what is permitted, without reference to intentions or other mitigating circumstances.

When he reaches the period of concrete operations, the child can form groupings of values, as of other classifications and orderings. He can systematize his values according to their relative priorities and their mutual affinities, so that his evaluations and his motives may be consistent with one another. He can subordinate his actions to future needs, thereby achieving that "decentering" from the present which we call *will*. His addiction to "games with rules," which replace "symbolic games" about this time, shows him to have arrived at a less primitive conception of moral rules. He now sees them as conventions, accepted by a social group for the benefit of all, capable of being changed by common consent, and arising out of mutual respect between equals.

By the end of the formal-operations stage, feelings become "decentered" still further, as they are released from the domination of what is known to be actually true. Motivation and evaluation now depend on *ideals,* and everything tends to be judged by how far it approximates to or falls short of the theoretical states of affairs that would fulfil these ideals. The adolescent views his own activities and plans as part of the total activity of the social group. He begins to think of himself as a fully fledged member of society, free to imitate or criticize adults. With the "decentering" which implants the individual in the community and subordinates his activities to collective goals, the formation of the personality is complete.

CONCLUSIONS

It is evident that Piaget's latest work will not silence his critics altogether. He still does not pay much attention to questions of sampling. Some projects, for example, Inhelder's on adolescents, seem to have used a large part of the school population of Geneva. The data on the sensori-motor period, on the other hand, come mainly from observation of Piaget's own three children, hardly the children of the Average Man. But Piaget might well retort, like Kinsey, that such bodies of data, however imperfect, are all we have of comparable density.

Except for some means and mean deviations in his reports of perceptual experiments, he provides few statistics. There are generally no measures of variance, which one suspects must be considerable, no tests of significance, just a categorical statement that at such and such an age children do such and such, with a few specific illustrations. He is not much affected by the growing vogue for rigorous theories, with precise statement of assumptions, derivation of predictions and operational definition of concepts.

Be that as it may, Piaget is, without any doubt, one of the outstanding figures in contemporary psychology, and his contributions will eventually have to be reckoned with much more than they are both in the management of children and in many areas which may not seem directly connected with child psychology. His ideas are closely tied

to observation of behavior, and this makes them the sort of psychology which moves science forward because it is testable by reference to the facts of behavior. At the same time, it goes beyond the facts just sufficiently to open up new lines of research and to attempt the sort of synthesis which is one of the chief aims of science.

Not the least reason for paying attention to Piaget's work is the relation it bears to trends followed by English-speaking psychologists. At times, his conclusions parallel those reached independently by other investigators; at other times, they serve to correct or supplement what psychologists with other approaches have to say. Like those influenced by Gestalt psychology, Piaget affirms that perceptions and thoughts cannot be understood without reference to the wholes in which they are organized. He disagrees with them in denying that wholes are unanalyzable into component relations and in insisting that the wholes figuring in thought are radically different from those figuring in perception. There are, throughout his writings, many reminders of psychoanalytic concepts—the "omnipotence" and "oceanic feeling" of infancy, "functional pleasure," the formation of the ego and the superego, the advance from the pleasure principle to the reality principle. But he makes many detailed criticisms of psychoanalytic theories, and the child as described by him certainly seems tranquil and studious by comparison with the passion-torn "polymorphous pervert" that emerges from Freudian writings.

But Piaget's closest affinities are undoubtedly with the neobehaviorists. He does not hold with early attempts to explain everything by "conditioned reflexes" or "association." But many of his observations and many aspects of his theory harmonize extremely well with conceptions of learning based on studies of what has come to be called "instrumental" or "operant conditioning." The sequence of more and more complex behavior patterns which he depicts as outgrowths of simple reflexes and habits parallels Hull's list of progressively more intricate "adaptive behavior mechanisms," found in animals.[3] And Piaget's view of images and thought operations as "internalized" overt responses approximates very closely the view prevalent among stimulus-response learning theorists.

One body of work which has grown up in Great Britain and the U.S.A. and which Piaget is eagerly endeavoring to bring into relation with his own findings is that centering on cybernetics, information theory and game theory.[4] But it is to be hoped that other common ground between his psychology and others with different starting-points will be explored. It is certainly high time that the national self-sufficiencies which disfigure psychology in contradistinction to other branches of science were left behind.

[3] Hull, C. L.: *A Behavior System* (New Haven: Yale University Press, 1952, pp. 347-50.)

[4] Bibliography, item 17.

REFERENCES

A. — In English

1. Mays, W., "How We Form Concepts," *Science News,* **35** (1955), 11-23.

2. ———, "Professor Piaget's Epistemologie Genetique." Proceedings of the Second International Congress of Philosophical Science (1954), pp. 94-99.

3. Piaget, J., *The Origin of Intelligence in the Child.* London: Routledge and Kegan Paul, Ltd., 1953.

4. ———, *The Child's Construction of Reality.* London: Routledge and Kegan Paul, Ltd., 1955.

5. ———, *Play Dreams and Imitation in Childhood.* London: William Heinemann, Limited, 1951.

6. ———, *The Psychology of Intelligence.* London: Routledge and Kegan Paul, Ltd., 1950.

7. ———, *Logic and Psychology.* Manchester, England: University Press, 1953.

8. ———, "Genetic Psychology and Epistemology," *Diogenes,* **1** (1952), 49-63.

B. — In French

9. Inhelder, B., "Les attitudes expérimentales de l'enfant et de l'adolescent," *Bull. de Psychol.,* **7** (1954), 272-82.

10. Inhelder, B. and J. Piaget, *De la logique de l'enfant à la logique de l'adolescent.* Paris: Presses Universitaries de France, 1955.

11. Piaget, J., *Traité de logique.* Paris: Colin, 1949.

12. ———, *Introduction à l'épistémologie génétique.* Tome I: *La pensée mathématique,* Tome II: *La pensée physique,* Tome III: *La pensée biologique, La pensée psychologique, La pensée sociologique.* Paris: Presses Universitaries de France, 1950.

13. ———, "Les relations entre l'intelligence et l'affectivité dans le développement de l'enfant," *Bull. de Psychol.,* **7** (1953-54), *passim.*

14. ———, "Le développement de la perception de l'enfant à l'adulte," *Bull. de Psychol.,* **8** (1954-55), *passim.*

15. ———, "La période des opérations formelles et le passage de la logique de l'enfant à celle de l'adolescent," *Bull. de Psychol.,* **7** (1954), 247-53.

16. ———, "Le probléme neurologique de l'intériorisation des actions en opérations réversibles," *Arch. de Psychol.,* **32** (1949), 241-58.

17. ———, "Structures opérationelles et cybernétique," *Année Psychol.,* **53** (1953), 379-388.

18. ———, "Les lignes générales de l'épistémologie génétique," *Proc. II. Int. Cong. Phil. Sci.,* **1** (1954), 26-45.

PART FOUR

COMPUTER MODEL

There are many apparent reasons why a computer has been labeled an electronic "brain." Superficially a fast computer appears to behave like a living brain; it accepts, stores, processes, and transmits information. Similarities also appear when a comparison is made between a newly finished computer and a newborn child—both have extremely limited possibilities of receiving, processing, and transmitting information notwithstanding the fact that the input devices (sense organs in the case of the human) are capable of transducing information. Another reason why computers have been referred to as "brains" is that these electronic machines have provided solutions for problems previously provided only through the cognitive activity of the living brain, for example, bookkeeping, registration of students, solving trigonometric identities, and finding square roots. Thus the products of cortical and computer activity are the same, but is the activity itself similar?

Two types of computers can be easily distinguished. The first, the *digital computer,* processes information which is represented within the machine by a sequence of binary symbols. The symbols are usually given the values of "1" or "0," and each is referred to as a binary "bit" or digit. An electronic circuit associated with processing data may be in state "1" when it is capable of transmitting information, while an electronic circuit capable of storing information may be in the same state when a small magnet is polarized in a particular direction. Thus a series of nine binary digits such as 110001011 may represent a number, a word, or more generally, information which the computer is designed to store, manipulate, or use to set internal switching circuits which control the flow and manner in which the information is to be processed. When the binary sequence is used to control the nature of the processing, the loss of a single digit becomes extremely serious and usually results in a breakdown of the processing. In addition, the length of each binary series representative of certain specific information must be recognized by the computer, or at least the computer must be capable of dividing up without error a long series of "bits" into interpretable units.

The second type of computer, referred to as an *analogue computer,* processes information which is represented by a voltage of varying magnitude rather than a series of digits. Thus instead of information being represented as discrete units in a series, information for the analogue computer is represented by a continuous but variable voltage with respect to any base chosen. For this reason the analogue computer is not readily adaptable to processing large amounts of information which takes the form of a discrete and unordered flow of digits or units. On the other hand, the analogue computer is admirably suited for simultaneously processing information, which may come from several different sources, conveyed to it through the magnitude of some continuous medium such as a voltage. Since it is possible to have information conveyed in terms of a continuous but rapidly varying voltage to an analogue computer, one may argue that information of a binary form can be approximated in this manner and that the distinction between both types of computers is unnecessary. It must be remembered however, that for the digital computer each of the two binary symbols and the length of each unit of information is of crucial importance, while for the analogue the absence of one cycle in, say, twenty of the voltage over a given time interval does not cause a breakdown of the processing, although it may cause some error to appear in the results. Typically this error results in very little error when interpretations of the processed information are made. No breakdown in processing occurs because the analogue computer does not make extensive use of the technique of modifying its methods of processing as a function of the information being analyzed.

In addition to differences in the type of information that each computer processes, the manner of processing is quite different in both. The digital computer actually "counts" digits whereas the analogue computer "measures" electrical quantities. An abacus may be considered to belong to a class of digital computers, while a slide rule belongs to the analogue class. The term *analogue* best describes the fact that this type of computer contains structural components which, capable of specific functions, are arranged in a manner analogous to the relationships existing among parameters and variables found in the problem to be analyzed. In the case of the slide rule, distances are analogous to the magnitude of numbers, and processing proceeds on the basis of addition of distances marked along the rule.

The digital computer is the machine to which most people apply the term "electronic brain," but consideration of the analogue type must also be made when a computer model of cognitive activity is postulated.

Conceptually, one may consider the digital computer as consisting of a number of specialized units such as input, processing, memory, logic, and output. For example, the input of information may occur via a photoelectric reader which senses light passing through a certain configuration of holes in a paper tape; processing units may be considered as those units which are "wired" to carry out the basic operations such as looking up table of information correctly, addition, subtraction, multiplication, and division. Logic units permit the computer to make decisions such as "do X" if the result of the last calculation is positive or zero, and "do Y" if it is negative. Memory units are self-explanatory. The output units generally provide access to the results of the processing along the same modes as that of input. This type of computer can solve only those problems for which there exists a set of instructions or a strategy called a program, planned and written for it by a human coder and stored in the computer memory. The program contains the special sequence of instructions which, when interpreted by the computer, results in the execution of certain elementary processes or basic operations.

A conceptual analysis of the analogue computer is not as readily made. Specialized units such as those employed in the digital computer are absent. Since an analogue computer is designed for optimum efficiency in analyzing the information represented by a continuous medium, it is best used for studying problems which can be stated as mathematical equations requiring, in addition to arithmetic operations, differentiation, and integration. Given the mathematical function to be investigated, components of the computer are so arranged as to mirror the mathematical equation in terms of processes, variables, and parameters required. Automatic variation of the independent variables is made by the computer or by the operator without interrupting the simultaneous evaluation of the dependent variable. Thus the functional components of analogue computers are electronic components capable of, in addition to multiplication (amplification), summation, division, subtraction, integration, and differentiation. (The latter two operations are relatively poorly handled on the digital computer, for example, Simpson's rule for integration might be used, requiring the separate evaluation of discrete sections of an area under a curve.) The function of the human coder relative to the analogue computer is to arrange the electronic components in correct relationship to one another. It might also be pointed out that the analogue computer has a very limited capacity to store information concerning a discrete variable and is therefore not useful where large amounts of information are to be stored.

The analogue computer can be very efficiently used to solve equations of the following type:

$$X(t) = {}_0\int{}^t E(t) \, dt,$$

where $X(t)$ is in millimeters of pen deflection of the output device as a function of time, and $E(t)$ is the input voltage also as a function of time. The equation when solved, given $E(t)$ as a continuous EEG voltage, provides the total accumulated area under the EEG curve, and thus a measure of over-all neural activity within some given time interval 0 to t.

The student should consider the possibilities of coupling an analogue system to a digital system. For example, given that the rate of neuron firing in a neural system has reached a critical value, a second neural system is activated. The student might also compare the problem encountered in optics with that encountered when an analogue and digital system is used to explain cognitive phenomena. In the field of optics the propagation of light energy may be interpreted on the basis of wave theory or on the basis of a corpuscular theory, both of which are useful models. Similarly, both computer models may be required to account for cognitive phenomena effectively.

The readings which follow consider the second comparison, that is of computer simulation of cognitive activity. Investigations of cognitive activities by means of computer simulation postulate the existence of a small number of elementary processes, which, when properly organized into some integrated activity, will provide a solution to problems belonging to a certain domain of content. Hovland points out the types of questions simulation is attempting to answer, and the human characteristics which computer simulation must take account of if the simulation is to be truly one of human cognitive activity. Beginning with the premise that a solution of a problem involving cognitive activity in a given content area is a function of a number of properly combined elementary processes, Newell, Shaw, and Simon show that the behavior of the computer in terms of intermediate and end products appears in some ways comparable to a human behavior in a similar situation. The problem of how the processes are combined (strategies) is indicated, although no attempt is made to show structural comparisons. The reader should note the similarities between the strategies required in computer simulation and those postulated by Bruner as being required in concept formation tasks. One might consider, for example, comparing the strategies employed by the human and those required in systematizing elementary operations in a computer for isolating the concept "all mammals."

The problem of defining elementary processes and their strategies can be of crucial importance to teachers. Consider for example, how a proof in geometry for the teacher is simple because of a predetermined strategy or plan of attack, while the student, even if all previously proven theorems are given, encounters considerable difficulty in solving the problem.

Readers should read the first two articles consecutively, making repeated comparisons between the behavior of the computer and human behavior in similar situations. Computer simulation of cognitive activity is only an approximation to the understanding of cortical activity—such human variables as imperfect reception, transmission, and utilization of available information and the unpredictable variation of subjective probabilities used in ascertaining what strategies or combinations of elementary processes are to be used must for the present render the computer model an inaccurate representation. There are more specific problems. For example, the human may accept verbal information which is not fully comprehended. Again, the human may read off information beyond that conveyed by the symbols observed.[1] Finally, there is the

---

[1] Readers interested in incorporating the latter problem in computer simulation are referred to: C. E. Osgood, and T. A. Sebeok, eds., "Psycholinguistics: A Survey of Theory and Research Problems," *Journal of Abnormal Social Psychology*, **49** (1954), 1-49.

problem of maintenance of homeostasis by the human in relation to the environment. Readers interested in the latter problem should refer to Ashby,[2] who describes an electromechanical model which, involving both an analogue and digital system, seeks a state of equilibrium when forced into a state of imbalance.

An explanation of the tremendous capacity of the living brain to store information has challenged computer theorists. Oldfield's article presents a model which suggests, through a number of coding sequences, how a massive amount of information may be stored. The storage and accessibility of memories is of concern not only for recall of specific facts but also for the selection of strategies in processing. Given that one basic prerequisite for a memory is a unit capable of providing a time delay for information passing through it, the reader might conceive of hierarchically coded information being stored in "reverberating neural circuits" containing a measure of time delay at least equivalent to the length of time required for the message to pass through.

The final paper by Guilford presents the basis of the factor analytic model, treated more extensively by Harmon.[3] The reader is asked to notice that this model is useful for describing the common dimensions of behavior as defined by a number of processes the subjects must bring to bear on several related tasks. If Guilford's model of the intellect is an accurate representation of the elementary cognitive processes, consideration of computer simulation of cognitive activity using his factorially defined processes might be profitable. The reader might also consider the relationship between factorially defined cognitive abilities and the effective use of various problem-solving strategies.

---

[2] W. R. Ashby, *Design for a Brain* (New York: John Wiley & Sons, Inc., 1960).

[3] H. H. Harmon, *Modern Factor Analysis* (Chicago: University of Chicago Press, 1960).

Computer Simulation of Thinking *

Carl I. Hovland

It is commonplace in the history of science for developments in one field of knowledge to have profound effects on other related areas. The dramatic influence of advances in atomic physics on biology, genetics, and medicine is a good case in point. We are currently witnessing a similar phenomenon in the repercussions of high-speed computer technology on research in the behavioral sciences. The initial impact came from the computational efficiency of these devices which permitted calculations formerly prohibitive in terms of time and effort. A more recent and less direct effect has been in stimulating machine-like methods of analysis of human thought and behavior through simulation on high-speed computers. It is these newer techniques and their applicability to psychological problems that is the topic of the present paper.

The analogy between the high-speed computer and human thinking has long been noted. We frequently see the Univacs, Johniacs, Illiacs referred to in the popular press as "giant brains" or "thinking machines." In most uses of high-speed computers, however, there is an attempt to attain objectives be-

yond the scope of human capabilities, either because of their speed or their extensive storage capacity (called, interestingly enough, their "memory"). But in the investigations I shall be describing, the utilization is quite different. Here we are primarily concerned with the use of computing machines to simulate in exact fashion the way a human solves a problem. Both human weaknesses, such as limited and fallible memory, and strengths, such as the ability to choose an efficient solution out of innumerable alternatives, must be represented. We say that we can simulate human problem-solving when we are able to specify both the prior information a human possesses and the sequence of steps by which he utilizes this information in the solution of the problem. We are then able to set up a computing machine to carry out this same sequence of operation.

Those familiar with the operation of high-speed computers will readily understand the way in which simulation proceeds. Just as in ordinary operations of a computer, one gives the machine a set of "instructions" to execute. These constitute a "program." In arithmetical operations these are sentences like the following: "square the product of the first and second number," "store the product in memory," "compare the first and second number," "select the larger of the two numbers compared." Or such instructions as: "find the number of

* From C. I. Hovland, "Computer Simulation of Thinking," *American Psychologist*, **15** (1960), 687-93. Reprinted by permission of the author and the American Psychological Association.

Adapted from a talk given over the *Voice of America* in September 1959. Unrestricted use of this material is available to the United States Government without cost.

dollars paid to the individual last month," "add to this amount the number of dollars earned this month," and so forth. The machine then executes each of these instructions through an intricate electronic system, printing out its answers on an electric typewriter. Sequences of instructions can then solve the most complicated numerical problems, such as making out a payroll with each individual working different numbers of hours, at different wage rates, with advance payments to some workers, with different deductions for subscriptions to health and accident insurance, different income tax credits, and so forth. The nub of the simulation problem involves the use of similar types of "programs" of "instructions" to the machine in order to reproduce the steps an individual goes through in thinking out the solution to a difficult problem. One specifies the steps the individual uses by stating them in an unambiguous way so that a computing machine is able to carry them out. These may be instructions like: "store the answer to the last problem," "determine whether you have stored in memory any similar problems," "if so, what are the differences between the past problem and the present problem," "see if applying Rule *a* will convert the old problem into the new one," and "apply Rule *b*" to convert the answer to the former problem into the solution to the present one. Thus the computer can be given information which is exactly equivalent to that of the human problem-solver, as well as a specification of the way the human goes about processing that information to reach a solution.

The obvious point is that if we can be precise enough about a process to describe it in terms which can be programmed and executed by a machine, we indeed know quite a bit about that process. And if we can specify singly each of the subprocesses involved, we can determine the effects of combinations of them and of variations in order of execution of the steps. The outcomes are almost impossible to foresee without actually carrying out the combinations and variations.

Let me begin by giving a concrete example of the new techniques, namely, simulation of the solving of geometry problems. We certainly think of the solving of theorems in Euclidian geometry by a high school sophomore as constituting a clear-cut example of intelligent human behavior. But Gelernter and Rochester (1958) of the International Business Machines Company have now successfully developed a program whereby a high-speed computer is able to solve many of the theorems in Euclid's geometry, for example, that the diagonals of a parallelogram bisect one another. A human learner who tries to solve such a problem has usually been taught a series of fundamental principles, or axioms, together with a set of rules for inferring relationships by which the basic symbols in the system may be manipulated. He is then asked to prove a new theorem. He tries to find a way of transforming and combining previous axioms through the set of rules until he achieves the proof of the new theorem. Typically, he starts out in rather routine fashion, then has a flash of insight as to a possible means of solution, and then methodically tests the adequacy of the solution. The geometry computing machine is set up to operate in an analogous fashion. It is given a set of basic formulas and axioms, together with rules as to possible ways of manipulating them in order to form new theorems. The new theorem is then presented to the machine to prove. The machine is equipped with a number of rules of thumb for possible ways of solving problems. For example, it is instructed that if the proposition to be proved involves parallel lines and equality of angles, there is a good chance that it may be useful to try the theorem: "If two parallel lines are intersected by a third line, the opposite interior angles are equal." This instruction constitutes a short cut which often works well but is by no means sure to be of value. Successful solution typically involves setting up a series of subgoals which are then worked on in succession. For example, in the problem cited earlier the machine ascertains that it can solve the theorem if it can establish the fact that the distance from one corner of the base of the parallelogram to the point of intersection must equal the distance from the intersection to the opposite corner of the parallelogram. This is then a subgoal, which in turn can be proved if the triangle formed by the bisecting lines and one of the sides of the parallelogram is equal to the triangle formed by the opposite side and the corresponding bisects. A device which makes constructions and measures lines and angles is incorporated into the computer. This operates by means of co-ordinate geometry. Once the sequence of subgoals leads from the initial axioms to the theorem to be proved, the machine routinely tests the accuracy of the proof. This it can do in an exhaustive manner since, once one has a possible proof, checking it is largely clerical. The chief problem is to find a possible method of proceeding, out of the almost infinite number of alternatives. It is here that the short-cut methods operate. They permit the use of likely and plausible methods of solution, just the way a clever high school student would proceed. Once the proof has been verified, the machine prints QED. Throughout the entire operation, the machine prints out on paper a complete tracing of the steps it tries—this is analogous to an individual's account of the way he solves a problem in geometry. Some of the machine's failures in finding proofs closely resemble those made by beginning geometry students.

It will be noted that the methods of solution built into the computer closely resemble those used by humans solving similar problems. Let me again call attention to the fact that in this way they differ from the usual uses of high-speed computers which methodically go through every possible solution in a deliberate way. The complete methods guarantee that if there is a solution it will be found, although an extraordinary number of trials may be required. Solutions of this type are referred to as "algorithms." These are used here to check proofs. In contrast, finding a possible solution is facilitated by short cuts and rules of thumb programmed into the machine. In this way it simulates a human subject in making leaps in the solution and trying out schemes which have been successful in the past, rather than exhaustively trying out each possible alternative. Mathematicians call these short-cut solutions "heuristics."

One may wonder whether we have gained anything by the simulation, since we initially derive processes from study of how students work and then program into the computer their ways of proceeding. In fact, at the outset, we may operate in a somewhat circular fashion—that is, we may only get out of the machine what we put into it. But as one proceeds, new combinations are tested which could not have been predicted from the individual steps. Some results, although strictly determined by the processes programmed, are impossible to foresee because so many complex operations interact in the final solution. One can find out the effect of increased complexity of problems and then determine with human subjects whether the order of difficulty is the same that would be predicted from the computer's information-processing routines. In this way one is constantly working back and forth from experiments with human subjects to simulation on the computing machine. Furthermore, one frequently finds that one must make assumptions about certain steps in the process to get the computer to execute its program correctly. Here the simulation comes first and suggests later experiments with human subjects.

The geometry machine just described involves solving problems rather than learning how to solve them, in the sense that the computer would solve the same problem in the same way on a second trial. Humans, of course, do learn and improve through practice. So the interesting task is to build into the computer this capability as well. Simulation of learning is one of the most interesting potential applications of computer simulation techniques, since the ability to learn is one of the clear-cut differences between human and machine performance. A number of different types of learning are currently being simulated. The first involves stimulus-response learning. It is rather simple to simulate this type of learning with rewards ("reinforcements") given when certain types of behavior occur and not given when other types of responses are made. The probability that the response followed by reward will occur on later trials can then be made to increase. Failure of reward, or punishment, can be made to lead to a decreased probability of response ("extinction"). The studies of Herman, a computing machine, carried

out by Friedberg (1958), and of the Perceptron, investigated by Rosenblatt (1958), are interesting examples of artificial learning machines. Other related possibilities are discussed in Miller, Galanter, and Pribram (1960).

At a somewhat more complex level is the type of learning involved in recognizing patterns imbedded in complex stimuli. It seems a simple thing for a human to respond to a triangle as a triangle whether it is large or small, short or tall, tilted or upright, and to distinguish it clearly from a square. But to specify rigorously the criteria in such a way that a machine can learn to recognize it invariably is quite a job. And the difficulty clearly hints that there is a lot we do not understand about the phenomenon even at the human level where we take the process for granted. Selfridge (1955) and Dinneen (1955) have worked most extensively on this problem and have been able to develop methods for getting the salient features of patterns to stand out so that some uniform response is given to a particular pattern. With two techniques, one of "averaging," to get rid of random elements, and a second, of "edging," to maximize the most distinctive features, they are able to insure that a variety of different ways of writing the letter *A,* for example, are registered as the same letter in the computer as a basis for further processing.

The third type of learning is made possible by keeping records of success and failure attained when different methods are pursued, and using these records to improve performance. Thus, in the case of the geometry computer, it is possible to store theorems which have already been proved. Similar mechanisms have been incorporated into the General Problem Solver developed by Newell, Shaw, and Simon (1958). It is also possible for these machines to be selective in their choice of theorems for permanent storage, rejecting those which do not seem sufficiently general to be useful later on. The most highly developed simulation of this type of learning is that incorporated in a checker-playing machine developed by Samuel (1959). His machine utilizes a type of rote learning which stores all of the checkerboard positions it encounters in play, together with the outcomes following each move. In addition, this machine has some capacity to generalize on the basis of past experience and to store the generalizations themselves. With these learning mechanisms it appears possible for the computer to learn in a short period of time to play a better game of checkers than can be played by the person who wrote the program.

Many of the formulations of learning are made without any special assumptions that learning processes are consistent with known neurophysiological mechanisms. A number of students are attempting to close this gap by simulation studies of the way in which nerve networks become organized into systems and are then modified through use. There is quite extensive investigation along these lines, some of it instigated by the speculations of Hebb about the nature of nervous organization. Suffice it to say that a number of researchers have been able to program computers to simulate the changing of neural organization patterns as a result of repeated stimulation of nerve fibers and further work of a similar type is in progress (cf. Clark and Farley, 1955, and Rochester, Holland, Haibt, and Duda, 1956).

In the work in our laboratory the emphasis is on understanding and simulating the processes involved in acquiring complex concepts through experience (Hovland and Hunt, 1960). The learner acquires a particular concept when he is told which of a series of specific instances presented to him belong in the concept class and which do not. This is similar to the way in which a child learns the concept of "animate" through some experiences in which parents and teachers label a given stimulus as "animate" and others in which they label it as "inanimate" (Hovland, 1952).

Our type of problem is illustrated by a situation in which there are a large number of slides of cancer cells, some of which are known to be malignant and others nonmalignant. The task of the individual (or the machine) is one of inducing the base of difference between the two types and subsequently labeling correctly new slides previously unidentified. Medical pathologists have just such a task and have achieved considerable success, although not 100 per cent accuracy, in making such distinctions. It is of interest in passing that there is a machine available which can make such a distinction on the basis of slides presented to it, but here the combination of characteristics (the "concept") was formulated by the scientist who developed the instrument (Tolles and Bostrom, 1956). The machine's task is to see wether the new specimen conforms to certain specifications, that is, whether on the basis of density and structure the cell belongs in the "malignant" or "normal" category. Thus it has the "concept" built into it, obviating the need to start from the beginning in order to induce it.

The input to the type of concept-learning in which we are interested is a series of pictures, say, flower designs (Hovland, 1953), some of which are labeled "positive" instances (examples of the concept) and some "negative" instances (examples of what the concept *is not*). The characteristics of the instances are represented as symbols for processing by the machine. It is hoped later to have this transformation automatic through the use of techniques developed at the Bell Telephone Laboratories which employ a television camera to convert the visual representation into electrical impulses as input to the computer. Thus the picture would become converted into one set of symbols representing the characteristics which constitute the instances of the concept (like A1B2C1D1E2-F1G1H2), while another string of symbols will represent instances of what the concept *is not* (like A2B1C1-D2E1F1G1H2).

Potentially, a machine can then consider combinations of all of these characteristics as possible ways of categorizing and distinguishing between the class of "A" and of "not A." Typically, human learners only attend to part of the potential set of characteristics because of perceptual limitations. We have devoted considerable research effort toward determining just how attention and perception vary during the course of learning. We have incorporated in the machine simulation a selective scanning of possible aspects of the complex stimuli with provision for the fact that some individuals see only some of the characteristics while other individuals pay attention to different aspects.

Human subjects, at least at the adult level, operate on material of this type by developing strategies involving some generalization as to what concepts are like. Some details of these strategies have been investigated by Bruner, Goodnow, and Austin (1956). The strategies may be different for different types of concepts. Logicians describe some concepts as being of the *conjunctive* type, where all the members of the class share certain common

characteristics. For example, rubies share the characteristics of hardness, translucence, and redness. A second type of concept is called *disjunctive*, in which possession of either one characteristic or possession of a different characteristic makes the instance subsumable under the general class. This is illustrated by the concept of "strike" in American baseball, which is either a pitched ball across the plate and between the batter's knees and shoulders *or*, alternatively, any pitch at which the batter strikes but fails to send into the field. A third type of concept is *relational*, where the instances of the concept share no common fixed characteristics but do have certain relationships in common. A sample would be the concept of "isosceles triangles." All instances of this concept involve triangles with two equal sides. But any fixed characteristics, such as lengths of the equal sides, lengths of the third side, or sizes of angles, are not an adequate basis for inclusion or exclusion in the concept class.

In preparation for later simulation, we have carried out extensive experimentation to determine the order in which these various types of concepts are considered by human learners. We find that for our type of stimulus materials, conjunctive and relational concepts are considered much more commonly than disjunctive ones (Hunt and Hovland, 1960). So our present machine will have built into it a hierarchy of responses in which the first attempts to organize the material will be in terms of shared characteristics —conjunctive-type concepts. Alternatively the machine will consider concepts which are based on relationships between the stimuli. Only when these have been extensively and unsuccessfully explored will the machine try disjunctive concept patterns.

At present, then, we have the program for a machine which is able to receive drawings having a number of different dimensions. It is then able to try a number of possible ways of organizing into a concept the prior information it has received regarding confirming and nonconforming instances. First, it considers possibilities of concepts which have various combinations of features. When none of these suffice, it considers relational concepts. When these are not successful, it considers various disjunctive concepts where one set of features or another alternative set defines the concept. When a solution is reached, the description of what constitutes a concept is printed out on tape and subsequent unlabeled instances are classified "A's" or "non-A's." A scanning device is built into the machine to take into account only certain of the characteristics available for consideration. The present machine remembers all that has been presented to it. We are currently considering various devices to simulate the gradual loss of information, or forgetting, which is all too human a characteristic. Our experimental studies have indicated the over-all mathematical form which the loss should take, but there are alternative means of producing such a loss (Cahill and Hovland, 1960). Each alternative represents a different theory of the way in which forgetting occurs, and investigation of the different theories is of fundamental importance. Simulation again provides a powerful tool for specifying the operation of the process of forgetting.

A high proportion of our research effort goes into new experimentation with human learners to determine their methods of handling various aspects of the problem, as compared to other efforts which stress programing the actual simulation. It is expected that this type of imbalance in effort will continue, but we are perennially hopeful that as more and more information becomes available an increasing amount of our effort will go into the simulation itself.

Work has now progressed to the point where I think we can see more clearly both the opportunities provided by these methods and some of the difficulties involved. I hope that the foregoing discussion has suggested some of the advantages of these new techniques. Let me briefly summarize the potentialities. First, simulation methods have a tremendous role in sharpening our formulations concerning mental processes and phenomena. It is one thing to say, as earlier students have said, that problem-solving involves a number of different stages, for example, those of preparation, incubation, illumination, and verification, and quite another thing for one to specify exactly what is involved in each stage. The pioneering studies by Newell, Shaw, and Simon (1958) on the General Problem Solver indicate the great forward strides which result from specifying the nature of these processes in such complete detail that a computer is able to solve problems by following the sequence of steps programed into the machine.

Closely related is the second advantage of the computer, the emphasis which it places on developing theories that have both descriptive and predictive power. Many of the theories which exist in psychology and sociology are so general and vague that they have little real predictive power. The program written for the computer to describe a particular process constitutes a theory which, if successful in carrying out the process in the same way as the human, is highly efficient in predicting the effects of changes in conditions and in specifying what other individuals will do under particular conditions.

Lastly, the simulation of human responses has the same overwhelming advantages for our understanding of behavioral phenomena as similar methods in other sciences. For example, the use of the wind tunnel represents a complex set of interacting conditions in actuality which could not be duplicated and whose effects could not be predicted from theory alone. Analogously in the present case, for single factors one can analyze effects without simulation, but when one seeks to understand the combined action of a number of factors interacting in complex ways, no satisfactory way of predicting the exact outcome may be possible. Those working on the geometry simulator, the General Problem Solver, and the chess- and checker-playing machines, all testify to the fact that many of the moves made by the computer greatly surprised their inventors.

I hope that my remarks on the importance of simulation methods do not give rise to the feeling that these methods automatically lead to quick success in areas which have been investigated for decades using other techniques. Two examples of the difficulties confronting us may be mentioned. The first is the complexity of the process to be simulated. At present we consider ourselves fortunate if we can simulate on a machine the typical performance of a single individual in solving a particular problem. This is indeed a great step forward. But for simulation to be maximally effective we would like to be able to predict machine solutions which simulate not only a single individual under some specified condition, but also the effects for different individuals under different environmental conditions, and after various amounts of experience. To date, most simulation has been of the performance of one individual, either real or an imaginary average individual. It may prove to be extremely difficult to carry out the next step, that of specifying which characteristics must be known about each individual to be able to simulate the way he varies from the typical pattern. In addition, the effects of environmental variables, such as the effects of drugs on performance, or of pressure to complete a task, should then be simulated. Finally, the effects of experience should be specified, so that the way in which a problem is attacked is appropriately changed as a result of the machine's ability to learn. This leaves for the future such a complex problem as analysis of the interactions between type of individual and amount of learning under different environmental conditions. It is apparent that a long and difficult road lies ahead before we can accomplish successful simulation of a single type of task which has all of these variables programmed. But when they can be successfully specified we will know a great deal about the problem. Most research generalizations in the social sciences are only true for a group of people, not for each individual. Computer methodology may make possible a broadening of our understanding of behavior by emphasizing the simulation of single individuals and then studying variations between them. The integration of these complementary approaches in new computer work will help us to reduce the gap between group averages and individual processes.

A second example of the difficulties of machine simulation is attributable to the nature of the process with which we are concerned. Simulation methods have most successfully been employed where it is possible to define the final performance of a task as an outcome of a succession of single steps. Thus where the mental process involves steps in a sequence one can synthesize the process by having the computing machine work first on stage one, then stage two, and so on. Much more difficult are those processes where a number of stages are going on simultaneously, in parallel fashion. It certainly appears that much of our perceptual and thought process operates in this way. Under these conditions it is much more difficult to untangle the processes at work prior to simulation. In addition, present machines are not as suitable for these purposes as they are for sequential operation. New and radically different machines may ultimately be required to cope with this problem. Most of our present work is being carried out with computers which were built for quite other purposes, namely, high-speed arithmetical computation. It would be possible to design machines more closely simulating thought processes and more flexible in their operation, but they would be expensive to construct and would not have the large number of potential purchasers who ordinarily defray the costs of development.

Despite the difficulties mentioned, work on simulation of complex psychological processes is yielding results of increasing importance. Processes which were thought to be understood turn out to require much more explicit statement. But along with the increased explicitness comes new understanding and precision. At present most computer programs grapple with only one phase of complex processes, but we are beginning to see common features in a number of different programs, permitting the construction of comprehensive programs from simpler subprograms. Work on simulation has also had a stimulating effect on research on the higher thought processes

themselves. Attempts to program computers have repeatedly revealed that we lacked much information as to how humans carry out seemingly simple thought operations. This has led to the return of workers to the laboratory which in turn has further enriched our knowledge of the human thought process.

Let not this enthusiastic report on the scientific potentialities of simulation research arouse anxieties of the sort raised by Norbert Wiener (1960) and other writers that machines will take over our civilization and supplant man in the near future. Rather, I think, there is great hope that detailed knowledge of how humans learn, think, and organize will redound to human welfare in removing much of the mystery which surrounds these processes and in leading to better understanding of the limitations of current ways of solving problems. It may, of course, become possible for us to then build machines which will work out solutions to many problems which we now consider distinctively human and to do so in a manner surpassing present human performance. But that this will lead to the machine becoming master and the designer, slave, seems to me most unlikely. Rather, it will free man for novel creative tasks which are progressively beyond the capability of machines designed by man.

REFERENCES

Bruner, J. S., Jacqueline J. Goodnow, and G. A. Austin, *A Study of Thinking.* New York: John Wiley & Sons, Inc., 1956.

Cahill, H. and C. I. Hovland, "The Role of Memory in the Acquisition of Concepts," *Journal of Experimental Psychology,* **59** (1960), 137-44.

Clark, W. A. and B. G. Farley, "Generalization of Pattern Recognition in a

Self-organizing System," in *Proceedings of the Joint Western Computer Conference*, pp. 86-91. Institute of Radio Engineers, 1955.

Dinneen, G. P., "Programming Pattern Recognition," in *Proceedings of the Joint Western Computer Conference*, pp. 94-100. Institute of Radio Engineers, 1955.

Friedberg, R. M., "A Learning Machine," Part I, *IBM Journal of Research Development*, **2** (1952), 461-72.

Gelernter, H. L. and N. Rochester, "Intelligent Behavior in Problem-solving Machines," *IBM Journal of Research Development*, **2** (1958), 336-45.

Hovland, C. I., "A Communication Analysis of Concept Learning," *Psychological Review*, **59** (1952), 461-72.

————, "Set of Flower Designs for Concept Learning Experiments," *American Journal of Psychology*, **66** (1953), 140-42.

Hovland, C. I. and E. B. Hunt, "Computer Simulation of Concept Attainment," *Behavioral Science*, **5** (1960), 265-67.

Hunt, E. B. and C. I. Hovland, "Order of Consideration of Different Types of Concepts," *Journal of Experimental Psychology*, **59** (1960), 220-25.

Miller, G. A., E. Galanter, and K. H. Pribram, *Plans and the Structure of Behavior*. New York: Holt, Rinehart & Winston, Inc., 1960.

Newell, A., J. C. Shaw, and H. A. Simon, "Elements of a Theory of Human Problem-solving," *Psychological Review*, **65** (1958), 151-66.

Rochester, N., J. H. Holland, L. H. Haibt, and W. L. Duda, "Tests on a Cell Assembly Theory of the Action of the Brain, Using a Large Digital Computer," *Trans. Info. Theory*, **IT-2** (3) (1956), 80-93.

Rosenblatt, F., "The Perceptron: A Probabilistic Model for Information Storage and Organization in the Brain," *Psychological Review*, **65** (1958), 386-408.

Samuel, A. L., "Some Studies in Machine Learning Using the Game of Checkers," *IBM Journal of Research Development*, **3** (1959), 211-29.

Selfridge, O. G., "Pattern Recognition and Modern Computers," in *Proceedings of the Joint Western Computer Conference*, pp. 91-93. Institute of Radio Engineers, 1955.

Tolles, W. E. and R. C. Bostrom, "Automatic Screening of Cytological Smears for Cancer: The Instrumentation," *Annals of New York Academy of Science*, **63** (1956), 1211-18.

Wiener, N., "Some Moral and Technical Consequences of Automation," *Science*, **131** (1960), 1355-58.

Elements of a Theory of Human Problem-Solving *

Allen Newell, J. C. Shaw, and Herbert A. Simon

In this paper we shall set forth the elements of a theory of human problem-solving, together with some evidence for its validity drawn from the currently accepted facts about the nature of problem-solving. What questions should a theory of problem-solving answer? First, it should predict the performance of a problem-solver handling specified tasks. It should ex-

* From A. Newell, J. C. Shaw, and H. A. Simon, "Elements of a Theory of Human Problem-Solving," *Psychological Review*, **65** (1958), 151-166. Reprinted by permission of the author and the American Psychological Association.

plain how human problem-solving takes place: what processes are used, and what mechanisms perform these processes. It should predict the incidental phenomena that accompany problem-solving, and the relation of these to the problem-solving process. For example, it should account for "set" and for the apparent discontinuities that are sometimes called "insight." It should show how changes in the attendant conditions—both changes "inside" the problem-solver and changes in the task confronting him—alter problem-solving behavior. It should explain how specific and general problem-solving skills are learned, and what it is that the problem-solver "has" when he has learned them.

Information-Processing Systems

Questions about problem-solving behavior can be answered at various levels and in varying degrees of detail. The theory to be described here explains problem-solving behavior in terms of what we shall call *information processes*. If one considers the organism to consist of effectors, receptors, and a control system for joining these, then this theory is mostly a theory of the control system. It avoids most questions of sensory and motor activities. The theory postulates:

1. A control system consisting of a number of *memories,* which contain symbolized information and are interconnected by various ordering relations. The theory is not at all concerned with the physical structures that allow this symbolization, nor with any properties of the memories and symbols other than those it explicitly states.

2. A number of *primitive information processes,* which operate on the information in the memories. Each primitive process is a perfectly definite operation for which known physical mechanisms exist. (The mechanisms are not necessarily known to exist in the human brain, however—we are only concerned that the processes be described without ambiguity.)

3. A perfectly definite set of rules for combining these processes into whole *programs* of processing. From a program it is possible to deduce unequivocally what externally observable behaviors will be generated.

At this level of theorizing, *an explanation of an observed behavior of the organism is provided by a program of primitive information processes that generates this behavior.*

A program viewed as a theory of behavior is highly specific: it describes one organism in a particular class of situations. When either the situation or the organism is changed, the program must be modified. The program can be used as a theory—that is, as a predictor of behavior—in two distinct ways. First, it makes many precise predictions that can be tested in detail regarding the area of behavior it is designed to handle. For example, the theory considered in this paper predicts exactly how much difficulty an organism with the specified program will encounter in solving each of a series of mathematical problems: which of the problems it will solve, how much time (up to a proportionality constant) will be spent on each, and so on.

Second, there will be important qualitative similarities among the programs that an organism uses in various situations, and among the programs used by different organisms in a given situation. The program that a human subject uses to solve mathematical problems will be similar in many respects to the program he uses to choose a move in chess; the program one subject uses for any such task will resemble the programs used by other subjects possessing similar training and abilities. If there were no such similarities, if each subject and each task were completely idiosyncratic, there could be no theory of human problem-solving. Moreover, there is some positive evidence, as we shall see, that such similarities and general characteristics of problem-solving processes do exist.

In this paper we shall limit ourselves to this second kind of validation of our theory of problem-solving. We shall predict qualitative characteristics of human problem-solving behavior and compare them with those that have already been observed and described. Since all of the available data on the psychology of human problem-solving are of this qualitative kind, no more detailed test of a program is possible at present. The more precise validation must wait upon new experimental work.[1]

In succeeding sections we shall describe an information-processing program for discovering proofs for theorems in logic. We shall compare its behavior qualitatively with that of human problem-solvers. In general, the processes that compose the program are familiar from everyday experience and from research on human problem-solving: searching for possible solutions, generating these possibilities out of other elements, and evaluating partial solutions and cues.

---

[1] Several studies of individual and group problem-solving behavior with logic problems have been carried out by O. K. Moore and Scarvia Anderson (5). The problems Moore and Anderson gave their subjects are somewhat different from those handled by our program, and hence a detailed comparison of behavior is not yet possible. We are now engaged, with Peter Houts, in replicating and extending the experiments of Moore and Anderson with human subjects and at the same time modifying our program to predict the human laboratory behavior in detail.

From this standpoint there is nothing particularly novel about the theory. It rests its claims on other considerations:

1. It shows specifically and in detail how the processes that occur in human problem-solving can be compounded out of elementary information processes, and hence how they can be carried out by mechanisms.

2. It shows that a program incorporating such processes, with appropriate organization, can in fact solve problems. This aspect of problem-solving has been thought to be "mysterious" and unexplained because it was not understood how sequences of simple processes could account for the successful solution of complex problems. The theory dissolves the mystery by showing that nothing more need be added to the constitution of a successful problem-solver.

Relation to Digital Computers

The ability to specify programs precisely, and to infer accurately the behavior they will produce, derives from the use of high-speed digital computers. Each specific theory—each program of information processes that purports to describe some human behavior—is coded for a computer. That is, each primitive information process is coded to be a separate computer routine, and a "master" routine is written that allows these primitive processes to be assembled into any system we wish to specify. Once this has been done, we can find out exactly what behavior the purported theory predicts by having the computer "simulate" the system.

We wish to emphasize that we are not using the computer as a crude analogy to human behavior—we are not comparing computer structures with brains, nor electrical relays with synapses. Our position is that the appropriate way to describe a piece of problem-solving behavior is in terms of a program: a specification of what the organism will do under varying environmental circumstances in terms of certain elementary information processes it is capable of performing. This assertion has nothing to do—directly—with computers. Such programs could be written (now that we have discovered how to do it) if computers had never existed.[2] A program is no more, and no less, an analogy to the behavior of an organism than is a differential equation to the behavior of the electrical circuit it describes. Digital computers come into the picture only because they can, by appropriate programming, be induced to execute the same sequences of information processes that humans execute when they are solving problems. Hence, as we shall see, these programs describe both human and machine problem solving at the level of information processes.[3]

With this discussion of the relation of programs to machines and humans behind us, we can afford to relax into convenient, and even metaphoric, uses of language without much danger of misunderstanding. It is often conven-

ient to talk about the behavior implied by a program as that of an existing physical mechanism doing things. This mode of expression is legitimate, for if we take the trouble to put any particular program in a computer, we have in fact a machine that behaves in the way prescribed by the program. Similarly, for concreteness, we will often talk as if our theory of problem-solving consisted of statements about the ability of a computer to do certain things.

THE LOGIC THEORIST

We can now turn to an example of the theory. This is a program capable of solving problems in a particular domain—capable, specifically, of discovering proofs for theorems in elementary symbolic logic. We shall call this program the Logic Theorist (LT).[4] We assert that the behavior of this program, when the stimulus consists of the instruction that it prove a particular theorem, can be used to predict the behavior of (certain) humans when they are faced with the same problem in symbolic logic.

The program of LT was not fashioned directly as a theory of human behavior; it was constructed in order to get a program that would prove theorems in logic. To be sure, in constructing it the authors were guided by a firm belief that a practicable program could be constructed only if it used many of the processes that humans use. The fact remains that the program was not devised by fitting it directly

[2] We can, in fact, find a number of attempts in the psychological literature to explain behavior in terms of programs—or the prototypes thereof. One of the most interesting, because it comes relatively close to the modern conception of a computer program, is Adrian de Groot's analysis of problem-solving by chess players (2). The theory of de Groot is based on the thought-psychology of Selz, a somewhat neglected successor to the Wurzburg school. Quite recently, and apparently independently, we find the same idea applied by Jerome S. Bruner and his associates to the theory of concept formation (1). Bruner uses the term "strategy," derived from economics and game theory, for what we have called a program.

[3] For a fuller discussion of this point see (9).

[4] In fact, matters are a little more complicated, for in the body of this paper we will consider both the basic program of LT and a number of variants on this program. We will refer to all of these variants, interchangeably, as "LT." This will not be confusing, since the exact content of the program we are considering at any particular point will always be clear from the context.

to human data. As a result, there are many details of LT that we would not expect to correspond to human behavior. For example, no particular care was exercised in choosing the primitive information processes to correspond, point by point, with elementary human processes. All that was required in writing the program was that the primitive processes constitute a sufficient set and a convenient set for the type of program under study.

Since LT has been described in detail elsewhere (6, 8), the description will not be repeated here. It will also be unnecessary to describe in detail the system of symbolic logic that is used by LT. For those readers who are not familiar with symbolic logic, we may remark that problems in the sentential calculus are at about the same level of difficulty and have somewhat the same "flavor" as problems in high school geometry.[5]

Design of the Experiments

First we will describe the overt behavior of LT when it is presented with problems in elementary symbolic logic. In order to be concrete, we will refer to an experiment conducted on a digital computer. We take an ordinary general-purpose digital computer,[6]

---

[5] LT employs the sentential calculus as set forth in Chapters 1 and 2 of A. N. Whitehead and Bertrand Russell, *Principia Mathematica* (10)—the "classic" of modern symbolic logic. A simple introduction to the system of *Principia* will be found in (3).

[6] The experiments described here were carried out with the RAND JOHANNIAC computer. The JOHANNIAC is an automatic digital computer of the Princeton type. It has a word length of 40 bits, with two instructions in each word. Its fast storage consists of 4,096 words of magnetic cores, and its secondary storage consists of 9,216 words on magnetic drums. Its speed is about 15,000 operations per second. The programming techniques used are described more fully in (6). The experiments are reported in more detail in (7).

and store in its memory a program for interpreting the specifications of LT. Then we load the program that specifies LT. The reader may think of this program as a collection of techniques that LT has acquired for discovering proofs. These techniques range from the ability to read and write expressions in symbolic logic to general schemes for how a proof might be found.

Once we have loaded this program and pushed the start button, the computer, to all intents and purposes, *is* LT. It already knows how to do symbolic logic, in the sense that the basic rules of operation of the mathematics are already in the program (analogously to a human's knowing that "equals added to equals give equals" in elementary algebra).

We are now ready to give LT a task. We give it a list of the expressions (axioms and previously proved theorems) that it may take as "given" for the task at hand. These are stored in LT's memory. Finally, we present LT with another expression and instruct it to discover a proof for this expression.

From this point, the computer is on its own. The program plus the task uniquely determines its behavior. It attempts to find a proof—that is, it tries various techniques, and if they don't work, it tries other techniques. If LT finds a legitimate proof, it prints this out on a long strip of paper. There is, of course, no guarantee that it will find a proof; after working for some time, the machine will give up—that is, it will stop looking for a proof.

Now the experimenters know exactly what is in the memory of LT when it starts—indeed, they created the program. This, however, is quite different from saying that the experimenters can predict everything LT will do. In principle this is possible;

but in fact the program is so complex that the only way to make detailed predictions is to employ a human to simulate the program by hand. (A human can do anything a digital computer can do, although it may take him considerably longer.)

1. As the initial experiment, we stored the axioms of *Principia Mathematica,* together with the program, in the memory of LT, and then presented to LT the first 52 theorems in Chapter 2 of *Principia* in the sequence in which they appear there. LT's program specified that as a theorem was proved it was stored in memory and was available, along with the axioms, as material for the construction of proofs of subsequent theorems. With this program and this order of presentation of problems, LT succeeded in proving 38 (73 per cent) of the 52 theorems. About half of the proofs were accomplished in less than a minute each; most of the remainder took from one to five minutes. A few theorems were proved in times ranging from 15 minutes to 45 minutes. There was a strong relation between the times and the lengths of the proofs— the time increasing sharply (perhaps exponentially) with each additional proof step.

2. The initial conditions were now restored by removing from LT's memory the theorems it had proved. (Translate: "A new subject was obtained who knew how to solve problems in logic but was unfamiliar with the particular problems to be used in the experiment.") When one of the later theorems of Chapter 2 (Theorem 2.12) was presented to LT, it was not able to find a proof, although when it had held the prior theorems in memory, it had found one in about ten seconds.

3. Next, an experiment was performed intermediate between the first

two. The axioms and Theorem 2.03 were stored in memory, but not the other theorems prior to Theorem 2.12, and LT was again given the task of proving the latter. Now, using Theorem 2.03 as one of its resources, LT succeeded—in fifteen minutes—where it had failed in the second experiment. The proof required three steps. In the first experiment, with all prior theorems available, the proof required only one step.

Outcome of the Experiments

From these three series of experiments we obtain several important pieces of evidence that the program of LT is qualitatively like that of a human faced with the same task. The first, and most important, evidence is that LT does in fact succeed in finding proofs for a large number of theorems.

Let us make this point quite clear. Since LT can actually discover proofs for theorems, its program incorporates a *sufficient* set of elementary processes arranged in a sufficiently effective strategy to produce this result. Since no other program has ever been specified for handling successfully these kinds of problem-solving tasks, no definite alternative hypothesis is available. We are well aware of the standard argument that "similarity of function does not imply similarity of process." However useful a caution this may be, it should not blind us to the fact that specification of a set of mechanisms sufficient to produce observed behavior is strong confirmatory evidence for the theory embodying these mechanisms, especially when it is contrasted with theories that cannot establish their sufficiency.

The only alternative problem-solving mechanisms that have been completely specified for these kinds of tasks are simple algorithms that carry out exhaustive searches of all possibilities, substituting "brute force" for the selective search of LT. Even with the speeds available to digital computers, the principal algorithm we have devised as an alternative to LT would require times of the order of hundreds or even thousands of years to prove theorems that LT proves in a few minutes. LT's success does not depend on the "brute force" use of a computer's speed, but on the use of heuristic processes like those employed by humans.[7] This can be seen directly from examination of the program, but it also shows up repeatedly in all the other behavior exhibited by LT.

The second important fact that emerges from the experiments is that LT's success depends in a very sensitive way upon the order in which problems are presented to it. When the sequence is arranged so that before any particular problem is reached some potentially helpful intermediate results have already been obtained, then the task is easy. It can be made progressively harder by skipping more and more of these intermediate stepping-stones. Moreover, by providing a single "hint," as in the third experiment (that is, "Here is a theorem that might help"), we can induce LT to solve a problem it had previously found insoluble. All of these results are easily reproduced in the laboratory with humans. To compare LT's behavior with that of a human subject, we would first have to train the latter in symbolic logic (this is equivalent to reading the program into LT), but without using the specific theorems of Chapter 2 of *Principia Mathematica* that are to serve as problem material. We would then present problems to the human subject in the same sequence

as to LT. For each new sequence we would need naïve subjects, since it is difficult to induce a human subject to forget completely theorems he has once learned.

PERFORMANCE PROCESSES IN THE LOGIC THEORIST

We can learn more about LT's approximation to human problem-solving by instructing it to print out some of its intermediate results—to work its problems on paper, so to speak. The data thus obtained can be compared with data obtained from a human subject who is asked to use scratch paper as he works a problem, or to think aloud.[8] Specifically, the computer can be instructed to print out a record of the subproblems it works on and the methods it applies, successfully and unsuccessfully, while seeking a solution. We can obtain this information at any level of detail we wish, and make a correspondingly detailed study of LT's processes.

To understand the additional information provided by this "thinking aloud" procedure, we need to describe a little more fully how LT goes about solving problems. This description has two parts: (*a*) specifying what constitutes a proof in symbolic logic; (*b*) describing the methods that LT uses in finding proofs.

---

[7] A quantitative analysis of the power of the heuristics incorporated in LT will be found in (7).

[8] Evidence obtained from a subject who thinks aloud is sometimes compared with evidence obtained by asking the subject to theorize introspectively about his own thought processes. This is misleading. Thinking aloud is just as truly behavior as is circling the correct answer on a paper-and-pencil test. What we infer from it about other *processes* going on inside the subject (or the machine) is, of course, another question. In the case of the machine, the problem is simpler than in the case of the human, for we can determine exactly the correspondence between the internal processes and what the machine prints out.

Nature of a Proof

A proof in symbolic logic (and in other branches of logic and mathematics) is a sequence of statements such that each statement: (*a*) follows from one or more of the others that precede it in the sequence, or (*b*) is an axiom or previously proved theorem.[9] Here "follows" means "follows by the rules of logic."

LT is given four rules of inference:

Substitution. In a true expression (for example, "[p or p] implies p") there may be substituted for any variable a new variable or expression, provided that the substitution is made throughout the original expression. Thus, by substituting p or q for p in the expression "(p or p) implies p," we get: "([p or p] or [p or q]) implies (p or q)" but *not:* "([p or q] or p) implies p."

Replacement. In a true expression a connective ("implies," and so on) may be replaced by its definition in terms of other connectives. Thus "A implies B" is defined to be "not-A or B";

---

[9] The axioms of symbolic logic and the theories that follow from them are all tautologies, true by virtue of the definitions of their terms. It is their tautological character that gives laws of logic their validity, independent of empirical evidence, as rules of inductive inference. Hence the very simple axioms that we shall use as examples here will have an appearance of redundancy, if not triviality. For example, the first axiom of *Principia* states, in effect, that "if any particular sentence (call it p) is true, or if that same sentence (p) is true, then that sentence (p) is indeed, true,"—for example, "if frogs are fish, or if frogs are fish, then frogs are fish." The "if . . . then" is trivially and tautologically true irrespective of whether p is true, for in truth frogs are not fish. Since our interest here is in problem-solving, not in logic, the reader can regard LT's task as one of manipulating symbols to produce desired expressions, and he can ignore the material interpretations of these symbols.

hence the two forms can be used interchangeably.

Detachment. If "A" is a true expression and "A implies B" is a true expression, then B may be written down as a true expression.

Syllogism (Chaining). It is possible to show by two successive applications of detachment that the following is also legitimate: If "a implies b" is a true expression and "b implies c" is a true expression, then "a implies c" is also a true expression.

Proof Methods

The task of LT is to construct a proof sequence deriving a problem expression from the axioms and the previously proved theorems by the rules of inference listed above. But the rules of inference, like the rules of any mathematical system or any game, are permissive, not mandatory. That is, they state what sequences *may* legitimately be constructed, not what particular sequence should be constructed in order to achieve a particular result (that is, to prove a particular problem expression). The set of "legal" sequences is exceedingly large, and to try to find a suitable sequence by trial and error alone would almost always use up the available time or memory before it would exhaust the set of legal sequences.[10]

To discover proofs, LT uses *methods* which are particular combinations of information processes that result in co-ordinated activity aimed at progress in a particular direction. LT has four methods (it could have more): *substitution, detachment, forward chaining,* and *backward chaining.* Each method

---

[10] See (7). The situation here is like that in chess or checkers where the player knows what moves are legal but has to find in a reasonable time a move that is also "suitable"—that is, conducive to winning the game.

focusses on a single possibility for achieving a link in a proof.

The substitution method attempts to prove an expression by generating it from a known theorem employing substitutions of variables and replacements of connectives.

The detachment method tries to work backward, utilizing the rule of detachment to obtain a new expression whose proof implies the proof of the desired expression. This possibility arises from the fact that if B is to be proved, and we already know a theorem of the form "A implies B," then proof of A is tantamount to proof of B.

Both chaining methods try to work backward to new problems, using the rule of syllogism, analogously to the detachment method. Forward chaining uses the fact that if "a implies c" is desired and "a implies b" is already known, then it is sufficient to prove "b implies c." Backward chaining runs the argument the other way: desiring "a implies c" and knowing "b implies c" yields "a implies b" as a new problem.

The methods are the major organizations of processes in LT, but they are not all of it. There is an executive process that co-ordinates the use of the methods, and selects the subproblems and theorems upon which the methods operate. The executive process also applies any learning processes that are to be applied. Also, all the methods utilize common subprocesses in carrying out their activity. The two most important subprocesses are the *matching* process, which endeavors to make two given subexpressions identical, and the *similarity test,* which determines (on the basis of certain computed descriptions) whether two expressions are "similar" in a certain sense (for details, cf. 8).

LT can be instructed to list its attempts, successful and unsuccessful, to use these methods, and can list the new subproblems generated at each stage by these attempts. We can make this concrete by an example:

Suppose that the problem is to prove "p implies p." The statement "(p or p) implies p" is an axiom; and "p implies (p or p)" is a theorem that has already been proved and stored in the theorem memory. Following its program, LT first tries to prove "p implies p" by the substitution method, but fails because it can find no similar theorem in which to make substitutions.

Next, it tries the detachment method. Letting B stand for "p implies p," several theorems are found of the form "A implies B." For example, by substitution of not-p for q, "p implies (q or p)" becomes "p implies (not-p or p)"; this becomes, in turn, by replacement of "or" by "implies": "p implies (p implies p)." Discovery of this theorem creates a new subproblem: "Prove A"—that is, "prove p." This subproblem, of course, leads nowhere, since p is not a universally true theorem, hence cannot be proved.

At a later stage in its search LT tries the chaining method. Chaining forward, it finds the theorem "p implies (p or p)" and is then faced with the new problem of proving that "(p or p) implies p." This it is able to do by the substitution method, when it discovers the corresponding axiom.

All of these steps, successful and unsuccessful, in its proof—and the ones we have omitted from our exposition, as well—can be printed out to provide us with a complete record of how LT executed its program in solving this particular problem.

SOME CHARACTERISTICS OF THE PROBLEM-SOLVING PROCESS

Using as our data the information provided by LT as to the methods it tries, the sequence of these methods, and the theorems employed, we can ask whether its procedure shows any resemblance to the human problem-solving process as it has been described in psychological literature. We find that there are, indeed, many such resemblances, which we summarize under the following headings: set, insight, concept formation, and structure of the problem-subproblem hierarchy.

Set

The term *set*, sometimes defined as "a readiness to make a specified reponse to a specified stimulus" (4, p. 65), covers a variety of psychological phenomena. We should not be surprised to find that more than one aspect of LT's behavior exhibits "set," nor that these several evidences of set correspond to quite different underlying processes.

1. Suppose that after the program has been loaded in LT, the axioms and a sequence of problem expressions are placed in its memory. Before LT undertakes to prove the first problem expression, it goes through the list of axioms and computes a description of each for subsequent use in the "similarity" tests. For this reason, the proof of the first theorem takes an extra interval of time amounting, in fact, to about 20 seconds. Functionally and phenomenologically, this computation process and interval represent a *preparatory set* in the sense in which that term is used in reaction-time experiments. It turns out in LT that this preparatory set saves about one-third of the computing time that would otherwise be required in later stages of the program.

2. *Directional set* is also evident in LT's behavior. When it is attempting a particular subproblem, LT tries first to solve it by the substitution method. If this proves fruitless, and only then, it tries the detachment method, then chaining forward, then chaining backward. Now when it searches for theorems suitable for the substitution method, it will not notice theorems that might later be suitable for detachment (different similarity tests being applied in the two cases). It attends singlemindedly to possible candidates for substitution until the theorem list has been exhausted; then it turns to the detachment method.

3. Hints and the change in behavior they induce have been mentioned earlier. Variants of LT exist in which the order of methods attempted by LT, and the choice of units in describing expressions, depend upon appropriate hints from the experimenter.

4. Effects from directional set occur in certain learning situations—as illustrated, for example, by the classical experiments of Luchins. Although LT at the present time has only a few learning mechanisms, these will produce strong effects of directional set if problems are presented to LT in appropriate sequences. For example, it required about 45 minutes to prove Theorem 2.48 in the first experiment because LT, provided with all the prior theorems, explored so many blind alleys. Given only the axioms and Theorem 2.16, LT proved Theorem 2.48 in about 15 minutes because it now considered a quite different set of possibilities.

The instances of set observable in the present program of LT are natural and unintended by-products of a program constructed to solve problems in an efficient way. In fact, it is difficult to see how we could have avoided such effects. In its simplest aspect, the problem-solving process is a search for a solution in a very large space of possible solutions. The possible solutions must be examined in *some* particular sequence, and if they are, then certain possible solutions will be examined before others. The particular rule that induces the order of search induces thereby a definite set in the ordinary psychological meaning of that term.

Preparatory set also arises from the need for processing efficiency. If certain information is needed each time a possible solution or group of solutions is to be examined, it may be useful to compute this information, once and for all, at the beginning of the problem-solving process, and to store it instead of recomputing it each time.

The examples cited show that set can arise in almost every aspect of the problem-solving process. It can govern the sequence in which alternatives are examined (the "method" set), it can select the concepts that are used in classifying perceptions (the "viewing" set), and it can consist in preparatory processes (the description of axioms).

None of the examples of set in LT relate to the way in which information is stored in memory. However, one would certainly expect such set to exist, and certain psychological phenomena bear this out—the set in association experiments, and so-called "incubation" processes. LT as it now stands is inadequate in this respect.

Insight

In the psychological literature, *insight* has two principal connotations: (*a*) "suddenness" of discovery, and (*b*) grasp of the "structure" of the problem, as evidenced by absence of trial and error. It has often been pointed out that there is no necessary connection between the absence of overt trial-and-error behavior and grasp of the problem structure, for trial and error may be perceptual or ideational, and no obvious cues may be present in behavior to show that it is going on.

In LT an observer's assessment of how much trial and error there is will depend on how much of the record of its problem-solving processes the computer prints out. Moreover, the amount of trial and error going on "inside" varies within very wide limits, depending on small changes in the program.

The performance of LT throws some light on the classical debate between proponents of trial-and-error learning and proponents of "insight," and shows that this controversy, as it is usually phrased, rests on ambiguity and confusion. LT searches for solutions to the problems that are presented it. This search must be carried out in some sequence, and LT's success in actually finding solutions for rather difficult problems rests on the fact that the sequences it uses are not chosen casually but do, in fact, depend on problem "structure."

To keep matters simple, let us consider just one of the methods LT uses —proof by substitution. The number of valid proofs (of *some* theorem) that the machine can construct by substitution of new expressions for the variables in the axioms is limited only by its patience in generating expressions. Suppose now that LT is presented with a problem expression to be proved by substitution. The crudest trial-and-error procedure we can imagine is for the machine to generate substitutions in a predetermined sequence that is independent of the expression to be proved, and to compare each of the resulting expressions with the problem expression, stopping when a pair are identical (cf. 7).

Suppose, now, that the generator of substitutions is constructed so that it is *not* independent of the problem expression—so that it tries substitutions in different sequences depending on the nature of the latter. Then, if the dependence is an appropriate one, the amount of search required on the average can be reduced. A simple strategy of this sort would be to try in the axioms only substitutions involving variables that actually appear in the problem expression.

The actual generator employed by LT is more efficient (and hence more "insightful" by the usual criteria) than this. In fact, it works backward from the problem expression, and takes into account necessary conditions that a substitution must satisfy if it is to work. For example, suppose we are substituting in the axiom "p implies (q or p)," and are seeking to prove "r implies (r or r)." Working backward, it is clear that *if* the latter expression can be obtained from the former by substitution at all, then the variable that must be substituted for p is r. This can be seen by examining the first variable in each expression, without considering the rest of the expression at all (cf. 7).

Trial and error is reduced to still smaller proportions by the method for searching the list of theorems. Only those theorems are extracted from the list for attempted substitution which are "similar" in a defined sense to the problem expression. This means, in practice, that substitution is attempted in only about 10 percent of the theorems. Thus a trial-and-error search of the theorem list to find theorems similar to the problem expression is substituted for a trial-and-error series of attempted substitutions in each of the theorems.

In these examples, the concept of proceeding in a "meaningful" fashion is entirely clear and explicit. Trial-and-error attempts take place in some "space" of possible solutions. To approach a problem "meaningfully" is to have a strategy that either permits the search to be limited to a smaller subspace, or generates elements of the space in an order that makes probable the discovery of one of the solutions early in the process.

We have already listed some of the most important elements in the program of LT for reducing search to tolerable proportions. These are: (*a*) the description programs to select theorems that are "likely" candidates for substitution attempts; (*b*) the process of working backwards, which uses information about the goal to rule out large numbers of attempts without actually trying them. In addition to these, the executive routine may select the sequence of subproblems to be worked on in an order that takes up "simple" subproblems first.

Concepts

Most of the psychological research on concepts has focussed on the processes of their formation. The current version of LT is mainly a performance program, and hence shows no concept formation. There is in the program, however, a clear-cut example of the use of concepts in problem-solving. This is the routine for describing theorems and searching for theorems "similar" to the problem expression or some part of it in order to attempt substitutions, detachments, or chainings. All theorems having the same description exemplify a common concept. We have, for example, the concept of an expression that has a single variable, one argument place on its left side, and two argument places on its right side: "p implies (p or p)" is an expression exemplifying this concept; so is "q implies (q implies q)."

The basis for these concepts is purely pragmatic. Two expressions having the same description "look alike" in some undefined sense; hence, if we are seeking to prove one of them as a theorem, while the other is an axiom or theorem already proved, the latter is likely construction material for the proof of the former.

Hierarchies of Processes

Another characteristic of the behavior of LT that resembles human problem-solving behavior is the hierarchical structure of its processes. Two kinds of hierarchies exist, and these will be described in the next two paragraphs.

In solving a problem, LT breaks it down into component problems. First of all, it makes three successive attempts: a proof by substitution, a proof by detachment, or a proof by chaining. In attempting to prove a theorem by any of these methods, it divides its task into two parts: first, finding likely raw materials in the form of axioms or theorems previously proved; second, using these materials in matching. To find theorems similar to the problem expression, the first step is to compute a description of the problem expression; the second step is to search the list of theorems for expressions with the same description. The description-computing program divides, in turn, into a program for computing the number of levels in the expression, a program for computing the number of distinct variables, and a program for computing the number of argument places.

LT has a second kind of hierarchy in the generation of new expressions to be proved. Both the detachment and chaining methods do not give proofs directly but, instead, provide new alternative expressions to prove. LT keeps a list of these subproblems, and, since they are of the same type as the original problem, it can apply all its problem-solving methods to them. These methods, of course, yield yet other subproblems, and in this way a large network of problems is developed during the course of proving a given logic expression. The importance of this type of hierarchy is that it is not fixed in advance, but grows in response to the problem-solving process itself, and shows some of the flexibility and transferability that seem to characterize human higher mental processes.

The problem-subproblem hierarchy in LT's program is quite comparable with the hierarchies that have been discovered by students of human problem-solving processes, and particularly by de Groot in his detailed studies of the thought methods of chess players (2, pp. 78–83, 105–111). Our earlier discussion of insight shows how the program structure permits an efficient combination of trial-and-error search with systematic use of experience and cues in the total problem-solving process.

SUMMARY OF THE EVIDENCE

We have now reviewed the principal evidence that LT solves problems in a manner closely resembling that exhibited by humans in dealing with the same problems. First, and perhaps most important, it is in fact capable of finding proofs for theorems—hence incorporates a system of processes that is sufficient for a problem-solving mechanism. Second, its ability to solve a particular problem depends on the sequence in which problems are presented to it in much the same way that a human subject's behavior depends on this sequence. Third, its behavior exhibits both preparatory and directional set. Fourth, it exhibits insight both in the sense of vicarious trial and error leading to "sudden" problem solution, and in the sense of employing heuristics to keep the total amount of trial and error within reasonable bounds. Fifth, it employs simple concepts to classify the expressions with which it deals. Sixth, its program exhibits a complex organized hierarchy of problems and subproblems.

COMPARISON WITH OTHER THEORIES

We have proposed a theory of the higher mental processes, and have shown how LT, which is a particular exemplar of the theory, provides an explanation for the processes used by humans to solve problems in symbolic logic. What is the relation of this explanation to others that have been advanced?

Associationism

The broad class of theories usually labelled "associationist" share a generally behaviorist viewpoint and a commitment to reducing mental functions to elementary, mechanistic neural events. We agree with the associationists that the higher mental processes can be performed by mechanisms—indeed, we have exhibited a specific set of mechanisms capable of performing some of them.

We have avoided, however, specifying these mechanisms in neurological or pseudo-neurological terms. Problem solving—at the information-processing level at which we have described it—has nothing specifically "neural" about it, but can be performed by a wide class of mechanisms, including both human brains and digital computers. We do not believe that this functional equivalence between brains and computers implies any structural equivalence at a more minute anatomical level (for example, equivalence of neurons with circuits). Discovering what neural mechanisms realize these information-processing functions in the human brain is a task for another level of theory construction. Our theory is a theory of the information processes involved in problem solving, and not a theory of neural or electronic mechanisms for information processing.

The picture of the central nervous system to which our theory leads is a picture of a more complex and active system than that contemplated by most associationists. The notions of "trace," "fixation," "excitation," and "inhibition" suggest a relatively passive electrochemical system (or, alternatively, a passive "switchboard"), acted upon by stimuli, altered by that action, and subsequently behaving in a modified manner when later stimuli impinge on it.

In contrast, we postulate an information-processing system with large storage capacity that holds, among other things, complex strategies (programs) that may be evoked by stimuli. The stimulus determines what strategy or strategies will be evoked; the content of these strategies is already largely determined by the previous experience of the system. The ability of the system to respond in complex and highly selective ways to relatively simple stimuli is a consequence of this storage of programs and this "active" response to stimuli. The phenomena of set and insight that we have already described and the hierarchical structure of the response system are all consequences of this "active" organization of the central processes.

The historical preference of behaviorists for a theory of the brain that pictured it as a passive photographic plate or switchboard, rather than as an active computer, is no doubt connected with the struggle against vitalism. The invention of the digital computer has acquainted the world with a device—obviously a mechanism—whose response to stimuli is clearly more complex and "active" than the response of more traditional switching networks. It has provided us with operational and unobjectionable interpretations of terms like "purpose," "set," and "insight." The real importance of the digital computer for the theory of higher mental processes lies not merely in allowing us to realize such processes "in the metal" and outside the brain, but in providing us with a much profounder idea than we have hitherto had of the characteristics a mechanism must possess if it is to carry out complex information processing tasks.

Gestalt Theories

The theory we have presented resembles the associationist theories largely in its acceptance of the premise of mechanism, and in few other respects. It resembles much more closely some of the Gestalt theories of problem-solving, and perhaps most closely the theories of "directed thinking" of Selz and de Groot. A brief overview of Selz's conceptions of problem-solving, as expounded by de Groot, will make its relation to our theory clear.

1. Selz and his followers describe problem solving in terms of processes or "operations" (2, p. 42). These are clearly the counterparts of the basic processes in terms of which LT is specified.

2. These operations are organized in a strategy, in which the outcome of each step determines the next (2, p. 44). The strategy is the counterpart of the program of LT.

3. A problem takes the form of a "schematic anticipation." That is, it is posed in some such form as: Find an X that stands in the specified relation R to the given element E (2, pp. 44–46). The counterpart of this in LT is the problem: Find a *sequence of sentences* (X) that stands in the relation of *proof* (R) to the given *problem expression* (E). Similarly, the subproblems posed by LT can be described in terms of schematic anticipations:

for example, "Find an expression that is 'similar' to the expression to be proved." Many other examples can be supplied of "schematic anticipations" in LT.

4. The method that is applied toward solving the problem is fully specified by the schematic anticipation. The counterpart in LT is that, upon receipt of the problem, the executive program for solving logic problems specifies the next processing step. Similarly, when a subproblem is posed —like "prove the theorem by substitution"—the response to this subproblem is the initation of a corresponding program (here, the method of substitution).

5. Problem-solving is said to involve (*a*) finding means of solution, and (*b*) applying them (2, pp. 47–53). A counterpart in LT is the division between the similarity routines, which find "likely" materials for a proof, and the matching routines, which try to use these materials. In applying means, there are needed both *ordering* processes (to assign priorities when more than one method is available) and *control* processes (to evaluate the application) (2, p. 50).

6. Long sequences of solution methods are coupled together. This coupling may be *cumulative* (the following step builds on the result of the preceding) or *subsidiary* (the previous step was unsuccessful, and a new attempt is now made) (2, p. 51). In LT the former is illustrated by a successful similarity comparison followed by an attempt at matching; the latter by the failure of the method of substitution, which is then followed by an attempt at detachment.

7. In cumulative coupling, we can distinguish *complementary* methods from *subordinated* methods (2, p. 52). The former are illustrated by successive substitutions and replacements in

successive elements of a pair of logic expressions. The latter are illustrated by the role of matching as a subordinate process in the detachment method.

We could continue this list a good deal further. Our purpose is not to suggest that the theory of LT can or should be translated into the language of "directed thinking." On the contrary, the specification of the program for LT clarifies to a considerable extent notions whose meanings are only vague in the earlier literature. What the list illustrates is that the processes that we observe in LT are basically the same as the processes that have been observed in human problem-solving in other contexts.

PERFORMANCE AND LEARNING

LT is primarily a performance machine. That is to say, it solves problems rather than learning how to solve problems. However, although LT does not learn in all the ways that a human problem-solver learns, there are a number of important learning processes in the program of LT. These serve to illustrate some, but not all, of the forms of human learning.

Learning in LT

By *learning*, we mean any more or less lasting change in the response of the system to successive presentations of the same stimulus. By this definition —which is the customary one—LT does learn.

1. When LT has proved a theorem, it stores this theorem in its memory. Henceforth, the theorem is available as material for the proof of subsequent theorems. Therefore, whether LT is able to prove a particular theorem depends, in general, on what theorems it has previously been asked to prove.

2. LT remembers, during the course of its attempt to prove a theorem, what subproblems it has already tried to solve. If the same subproblem is obtained twice in the course of the attempt at a proof, LT will remember and will not try to solve it a second time if it has failed at first.

3. In one variant, LT remembers what theorems have proved useful in the past in conjunction with particular methods and tries these theorems first when applying the method in question. Hence, although its total repertory of methods remains constant, it learns to apply particular methods in particular ways.

These are types of learning that would certainly be found also in human problem-solvers. There are other kinds of human learning that are not yet represented in LT. We have already mentioned one—acquiring new methods for attacking problems. Another is modifying the descriptions used in searches for similar theorems, to increase the efficiency of those searches. The latter learning process may also be regarded as a process for concept formation. We have under way a number of activities directed toward incorporating new forms of learning into LT, but we will postpone a more detailed discussion of these until we can report concrete results

What is Learned

The several kinds of learning now found in LT begin to cast light on the pedagogical problems of "what is learned?" including the problems of transfer of training. For example, if LT simply stored proofs of theorems as it found these, it would be able to prove a theorem a second time very rapidly, but its learning would not transfer at all to new theorems. The storage of *theorems* has much broader transfer value than the storage of *proofs*, since, as already noted, the proved theorems may be used as stepping stones to the proofs of new theorems. There is no mystery here in the fact that the transferability of what is learned is dependent in a very sensitive way upon the form in which it is learned and remembered. We hope to draw out the implications, psychological and pedagogical, of this finding in our subsequent research on learning.

CONCLUSION

We should like, in conclusion, only to draw attention to the broader implications of this approach to the study of information-processing systems. The heart of the approach is describing the behavior of a system by a well specified program, defined in terms of elementary information processes. In this approach, a specific program plays the role that is played in classical systems of applied mathematics by a specific system of differential equations.

Once the program has been specified, we proceed exactly as we do with traditional mathematical systems. We attempt to deduce general properties of the system from the program (the equations); we compare the behavior predicted from the program (from the equations) with actual behavior observed in experimental or field settings; we modify the program (the equations) when modification is required to fit the facts.

The promise of this approach is severalfold. First, the digital computer provides us with a device capable of realizing programs, and hence, of actually determining what behavior is implied by a program under various environmental conditions. Second, a program is a very concrete specification of the processes, and permits us to see whether the processes we postulate are realizable, and whether they are sufficient to produce the phenomena. The

vaguenesses that have plagued the theory of higher mental processes and other parts of psychology disappear when the phenomena are described as programs.

In the present paper we have illustrated this approach by beginning the construction of a thoroughly operational theory of human problem-solving. There is every reason to believe that it will prove equally fruitful in application to the theories of learning, of perception, and of concept formation.

REFERENCES

1. Bruner, J. S., J. Goodnow and G. Austin, *A Study of Thinking.* New York: John Wiley & Sons, Inc., 1956.

2. De Groot, A., *Het Denken van den Schaker.* Amsterdam: Noord-Hollandsche Uitgevers Maatschappij, 1946.

3. Hilbert, D. and W. Ackermann, *Principles of Mathematical Logic.* New York: Chelsea Publishing Co., 1950.

4. Johnson, D. M., *The Psychology of Thought and Judgement.* New York: Harper & Row, Publishers, 1955.

5. Moore, O. K. and S. B. Anderson, "Search Behavior in Individual and Group Problem Solving," *American Sociological Review,* **19** (1955), 702-14.

6. Newell, A. and J. C. Shaw, "Programming the Logic Theory Machine," *Proceedings of the Joint Western Computer Conference,* pp. 230-40. Institute of Radio Engineers, 1957.

7. Newell, A., J. C. Shaw, and H. A. Simon, "Empirical Explorations with the Logic Theory Machine," *Proceedings of the Joint Western Computer Conference,* pp. 218-30. Institute of Radio Engineers, 1957.

8. Newell, A. and H. A. Simon, "The Logic Theory Machine: A Complex Information Processing System," *Transactions on Information Theory.* Institute of Radio Engineers, **IT-2,** No. 3 (1956), 61-79.

9. Simon, H. A. and A. Newell, "Models, Their Uses and Limitations," in *The State of the Social Sciences,* ed. L. D. White, pp. 66-83. Chicago: University of Chicago Press, 1956.

10. Whitehead, A. N. and B. Russell, *Principia Mathematica* (2nd ed.), Vol. 1. Cambridge, England: Cambridge University Press, 1925.

Memory Mechanisms and The Theory of Schemata *

R. C. Oldfield

INTRODUCTION

The conception that, underlying the power of recalling past experiences, there exist *traces* in the mind or brain is not only a very old one but by its simplicity gained wide acceptance among philosophers and psychologists until quite recently.[1] The idea that, as a necessary condition of reproduction, some *simulacrum* of the past occasion must be preserved carried with it the implication that the alterations in the matter of recall must be quantitative, comparable to the gradual erasure of an inscription on stone, or to the fading of a photograph. Thus many important features of recall were disregarded, though from a theoretical point of view a number of attempts were made to cope with the difficulties of "fixed, lifeless traces." [2] Many, however (especially physiologists and neurologists), who had occasion to make use of the conception showed themselves notably blind to the explanatory pitfalls entailed.[3]

The experimental work of Bartlett (1932), following that of Phillippe, disclosed a number of features in the process of recall which ill-accorded with the doctrine of fixed, lifeless and independent traces. With some of these difficulties the Gestalt school, especially Koffka (1935), attempted to deal by a relaxation of the original doctrine of traces, in the sense of postulating dynamic interaction between them. Within certain relatively simple and delimited fields this extension of the doctrine may be said to have been heuristically valuable. But intolerable complexities and uncertainties arise when the attempt is made to extend the theory generally, as students of Koffka (1935) will note. Bartlett, seeking a fresh approach based upon the theoretical views of Head (1921),[4] interpreted his experimental findings

---

* From R. C. Oldfield, "Memory Mechanisms and the Theory of Schemata," *British Journal of Psychology,* 45 (1954), 14-23. Reprinted by permission of the author and publisher. Read at meetings of the Northern Branch, British Psychological Society, May 16, 1953, and of the Bristol University Psychologcal Society, May 8, 1953.

[1] Gomulicki (1953) gives a useful account of the history of trace theories.

[2] For example, the "apperceptive mass" of Wundt, and the "dispositions" of Stout.

[3] Cf., for example, Munk (1890).

[4] For reviews of Bartlett's theory and its relation to that of Head, see Oldfield and Zangwill (1942-43), and Northway (1940). Brain (1950) has considered some wider applications of the theory.

in terms of a conception which he named the *schema*. This assuredly raises its own problems but dispenses with the trace as the basic element in the mechanism of remembering.

The trace is a theoretical conception whose concrete exemplar may be any one of those more or less permanent modifications of material substance which, in some more or less direct sense, represent an object or occasion, and which play so large a part in our everyday existence. For all its limitations as a model, it is simple and, as a conception, easily handled in thought. If, however, it may be rejected on account of demonstrated impotence to order empirical findings, it may well be asked what shall replace it. Now it may be noted, that the corresponding method of storing information in terms of permanent traces is equally out of favor with designers of modern computing machines, although for different reasons. In this latter case, a quite novel principle of storage has been evolved. And suggestions have been often made that such a device might form a better model for human memory than does the older one based upon the photograph or gramophone record. Some color is lent to proposals of this kind by the demonstration of structures in the central nervous system which incorporate interconnections similar in kind to those required in the memory-circuits of a modern computing machine. It should be noted, however, that the *known* functions of these structures relate to the temporal prolongation of inhibitory and excitatory effects. No direct connection with the mechanism of memory as such has been demonstrated. It has been urged, too, that there are grave objections to such a view of the physiological basis of memory (for example, Eccles, 1953).

The suggestion that the memory circuit of a computing machine might afford a better analogy for the consideration of remembering has generally been made upon the basis that such a device possesses greater functional flexibility than does the semipermanent trace. So far as I am aware, however, no effort has ever been made to work out the conception in more detail. In particular, it has not been asked whether a memory founded on this kind of basic element could go any further than does the trace in providing a theoretical formulation agreeable to empirical findings of the kind expounded by Bartlett and his followers. To make this effort is the object of this paper, but discussion will be confined to certain specific points, and no attempt will be made to formulate a general theory of remembering in these terms.

I will first very briefly recapitulate the relevant points of Bartlett's findings and try to indicate the vital features of theory. Secondly, the principle of the "memory circuit" as used in modern computing machines will be stated and will be illustrated by a simple example. We shall then consider whether the latter can be regarded as a suitable element out of which a memory mechanism could be built—a mechanism which would show at least some of the properties required by the known facts.

THE CHARACTER OF RECALL

Bartlett, convinced that the experimental constraints employed by Ebbinghaus in the interests of simplicity and quantification in fact prevented the emergence of the salient phenomena of recall, studied the recall of everyday material in the form of pictures and prose. The conditions in which the subject became acquainted with this material approximated to those of ordinary life. His conclusions were, briefly, as follows:

1. Only in exceptional instances is recall *literal*. In general, changes of various kinds are introduced into the material. One exception, in which recall may be literal, in effect exactly reproducing the original, is that of word-perfect recitation. Another, not mentioned by Bartlett, is that of immediate reproduction of a quantity of material which falls within the immediate memory span of the subject. In all other cases, change is the rule.

2. Such changes include not only omissions but also qualitative alterations, and even importations. Moreover, these changes are not arbitrary but occur in accordance with the general principle that the material is converted into a form more in keeping with the cognitive conventions, logical and causal, which are current in the social *milieu* to which the individual belongs. There is *conventionalization* and *rationalization*. As Bartlett views it, the function of this kind of change is to render the material more easily handled in recall.

3. There is a change in the relative emphasis of different parts of the material. Some elements, particularly details such as names, or other features which in the original are outstanding to the individual and attract his interest, possess special survival-value. They may, indeed, be elaborated or exaggerated. These dominant details may be preserved in the form of a specific image, and they are thought by Bartlett to act, so to speak, as *labels* which identify the original experience, and as *starting points* around which the rest of it may be rebuilt when the individual is faced with the need to recall.

4. Recall is thus essentially *reconstructive,* not *reproductive*. Most of our experience is not retained as such, in explicit or concrete form but is assimilated into the *schemata,* contrib-

uting its quota to the remolding of their structure and adaptive capacity. Some fragments of experience, on the other hand, survive in a relatively unchanged and explicit form. Recall consists in reconstruction, based upon these latter, by the operation of the schemata, which themselves incorporate general laws and principles expressing the uniformities of experience.

Such a view, it is clear, suggests many special problems. But it is at once evident that, if we seek to interpret it in accordance with a mechanical analogy (and the trace theory itself is a form of mechanical analogy), one important question will arise. How can information be stored in some general or abstracted form, and still allow some explicit, if incomplete, reconstruction of the original? It is sometimes suggested that *no* form of mechanical device could achieve this. But before this can be accepted, more detailed consideration of the question is desirable. Accordingly, we shall state and illustrate the general principle according to which the memory circuit of a modern computing machine operates. We shall then consider the extent to which a system built of such elements could be expected to store information in a generalized form, and subsequently reconstruct the original messages fed into it. It should perhaps be emphasized that such an attempt, though made in specific terms, can do no more than elucidate the basic requirements of the problem. It can, in itself, offer no direct suggestions as to the actual mechanisms, physiologically or otherwise, which are involved in memory.

CIRCUITAL STORAGE DEVICES

The general principle of the storage devices used in modern computing machines is most simply stated by describing an actual instance. The first requirement is that the information to be stored should be suitably coded. We may, without loss of generality,[5] suppose that all messages consist of sequences of the scale-of-two digits 0 and 1. In this form the message can be propagated in an electrical circuit as a sequence of impulses. So, for instance, the message 101100011011 will appear as the wave shown in Fig. 1.

Now consider Fig. 2. *AB* is a tube filled with mercury. At the end *A* is a transducer element which converts electrical into mechanical changes. These are propagated down the mercury and reach *B*. Here is situated a receptor element which converts them back into electrical changes. The electrical message sequence from *B* can now pass along either or both of two

routes. In the first, it passes to and may be used in other parts of the apparatus. In the second, it passes back to *A*, to be retransmitted down the tube. Deterioration in the form of the impulses, occasioned by the transmission and conversions, is corrected in the unit *X*, which also makes good incidental energy losses in the system. If, now, we pass into the system a given message, it will circulate indefinitely and is effectively stored. If the electrical circuit *BXA* is broken for a period corresponding to the time taken for the message to pass down the tube, the system is completely "cleared" and can be used again to store another message. If the information contained in the message is to be made use of elsewhere in the apparatus, it can be passed out along *BC* and can be used any number of times in this way. The length of the message which can thus be stored is approximately equal to the number of digits in a sequence which

---

[5] It can be shown that anything that is "information," in the sense that it can be explicitly formulated and represented in symbolic terms, can always be recoded completely in this form.

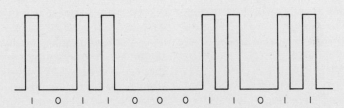

FIG. 1. *Pulse-coded version of message 101100011011.*

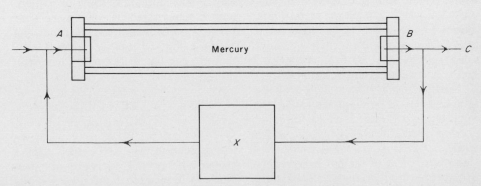

FIG. 2. *Mercury circuital storage element.*

occupies the time taken for one impulse to pass down the tube. The time of transmission in the electrical parts of the circuit may be regarded as negligible.

The general principle of storage is thus a novel one and possesses several outstanding features. Among these are (1) the ease with which the message can be constantly repaired, so that it can be preserved unchanged over long periods of time; (2) the ease with which it can be annulled and wholly disposed of when it is no longer required; and (3) the ease with which it can be made available to other parts of the apparatus when required without affecting its continued storage. The particular device just described is but one of many possible ones operating upon the same circuital principle. It happens to be a relatively poor version so far as storage capacity is concerned, and although others have been developed which are much more favorable in this respect, economy in such devices is of basic importance, and is not irrelevant to our further discussion.

MEMORY SYSTEMS
BASED UPON
CIRCUITAL STORAGE ELEMENTS

So far our discussion offers nothing novel as an analogue for the mechanism of recall. For if we merely postulate a number of independent circuital storage elements, we have only returned to another, if perhaps more entertaining and recondite, form of the hypothesis of fixed lifeless traces. The question to be discussed is whether such storage elements could be imagined as built into a system in which there would be some economy of storage without loss of the power to reconstitute the original messages. It does not seem impossible to see, broadly,

how this might be done. Consideration of this question raises a number of further points, admittedly speculative, which are of some interest in wider connexions.

We have a "black box" capable of taking in messages in the form of sequences of 0's and 1's, and storing them. At some future time, on receipt of an appropriate stimulus, the box is to redeliver the original message. For a start we shall suppose that it is to redeliver it in exactly the original form—though we shall later consider relaxation of this condition. The question of what is meant by an "appropriate" stimulus, and of how it operates to "pick out the correct message stored in the box, of course, one of great interest and importance. But we shall not, in the first instance, try to answer it. All we wish to do at this stage is to demonstrate the possibilities of economical storage and of reconstruction.

It seems fairly clear that unless the various messages received by the box incorporate *some* detectable elements of common pattern, there is no possibility of economy in their storage. If, however, *any* common patterns run through them, there arises the possibility of recoding them in briefer form, and so of storing more messages in a given storage space. *One* simple way in which community of pattern might manifest itself, which we may take as an example, is the following. Suppose that all messages handled by the box consist of thirty-six digits, and that the following is one of these:

100100011011100011100100011100100011.

On inspection, it can be seen that if broken up into sub-sequences of three digits each, all of them are of two kinds only, namely 100 and 011:

100.100.011.011.100.011.100.100.-
.011.100.100.011.

If we make 1 stand for 100, and 0 stand for 011, we can recode the message completely as follows:

110010110110.

In fact, in this particular case, further recoding is possible in sequences of three, the only patterns in this case being 110 and 010, and the second recoded version, if 110 = 1 and 010 = 0 is

1011.

Neglecting, however, for the moment, this possibility of a second recoding, we may consider how the first recoding can introduce economy of storage. Suppose that we store the sub-sequences 100 and 011 in two storage elements, and the recoded version in a third. The original message can now be reproduced by causing this latter element to draw out the sub-sequences in appropriate order as given by the sequence of digits in the recoded version. Thus, when the output from the third tube is 1, the sequence 100 is fed out of the box, and when the output of the third tube is 0, 011. The original message can, in principle, therefore, be reconstituted. Now the recoded message is only a third as long as the original, and requires only a third of the storage space. If, therefore, one storage element was just able to store one *original* message, we can store three recoded versions in the same space. For nine messages, all susceptible of recoding on the same basis, only five storage elements are required—three for the recoded versions, and two for the sub-sequences, in place of nine. It is clear that the advantage will be the greater, the greater the amount of common pattern

manifested, and the larger the number of messages possessing this community.

Before we proceed any further a few subsidiary points should be cleared up. The digits 0 and 1 only allow for the recoding of two types of sub-sequence. If there are more than two, scale-of-two numbers containing more than one digit will have to be used. Thus, if the sub-sequences 1001,0101, and 0010 are found to constitute all messages, code numbers of two digits will have to be used for each, for instance 10, 11 and 01. Hence twice as much storage space will be required for the recoded versions as in the case where only two types are present. Secondly, if a number of recoded versions are to be stored in a single tube, some indication must be provided to serve as a full stop at the end of each message. This can be any sequence not used as a code for any of the sub-sequences. This circumstance, again, makes some slight extra demand on storage space.

On assumptions such as these it is possible to derive an expression for the economy of storage. This would, however, only be valid for the rather special type of pattern assumed in the incoming messages, and its actual form would be of less interest than is the general principle that economy can be effected without impairing accuracy of reproduction. A number of further questions now require consideration.

FIVE QUESTIONS ARISING

1. As we have already remarked, recoding with consequent economy is only possible if there are some recurrences, uniformities or common patterns in the incoming messages. This is the case in the information from the environment received by the human organism. On the other hand, it is not, of course, suggested that the type of

pattern is that very simple one suggested above. By comparison with this latter, the patterns of human experience are complex and subtle. They may only reveal themselves when some amount of abstraction and elimination of irrelevant detail has been carried out, which would correspond with a recoding process in our analogy. Thus, for instance, the messages 100111011-101100110011101 and 1100010011-10110001 do not present any obvious similarity of pattern until both have been suitably recoded, by putting 1001 = 1 and 1101 = 0 in the first message, and 110 = 1 and 001 = 0 in the second, when the same recoded version, 100110, is obtained.

2. How would the performance of such a mechanism as we have considered compare with the use of Bartlett's schemata in recall? Suppose that the box has had considerable "experience" of incoming messages, and has acquired a store of type sub-sequences. These represent common elements in the events in its "environment." Treated as a total organized system, which they form in virtue of the various connections between them which could be generated by recodings of higher orders, they might be said to form its "schemata." For it is upon the basis of them that reconstruction of particular past messages is possible. Furthermore, we may suppose that, once acquired, the system is used to filter fresh incoming messages in accordance with the hierarchical organization which it possesses. Thereby each new message could be recoded in such a way that only a certain minimum of storage space is occupied. This minimum is that needed to represent the individual features of the message which cannot be subsumed in more general terms derived from the past experience of the box. Some messages will be banal, in the sense that they incorporate little that cannot be subsumed under the schemata. These will demand little storage space, and will induce little reorganization of the schemata. Viewed in terms of the schemata they may be said to be highly probable, and to contain but little information. Other messages, on the other hand, will present novelty, be improbable, and contain much information. These will only to a small degree be capable of reduction and subsumption by the prevailing schemata. They will demand relatively large storage space. On the other hand, they may induce the operation of fresh coding principles, and thus lead to reorganization of the schemata. In this sense it might be said that the box's schemata form an active organization of past experiences. The demands of novel messages of high information content might be supposed to maintain within the schemata persistently active searching for fresh ways of reorganizing the existing system by exploration of the various alternative possibilities of recoding. In this way complex, clumsy ways of storing information might, sometimes suddenly, be replaced by much simpler and more economical modes of coding and handling the same information. Perhaps in somewhat similar fashion "insight" may bring about widespread reorganization of a human individual's response tendencies.

3. We have spoken, in this last paragraph, of two supposed processes which require some further comment. These are first the "filtering" of fresh incoming messages through storage elements which contain type sub-sequences, and secondly, a spontaneous activity of searching for fresh methods of recoding material already stored, whether type sequences or abbreviated, that is, recoded, versions of messages.

The filtering process is, in principle, not difficult to conceive, since type sequences already stored are available for comparison with fresh material, without jeopardizing their continued storage. To take a very simple instance, suppose that the box contains only two stored type sequences, 010 and 110, and that a fresh message,

010010110010110110,

is received and stored temporarily as it stands. The output from this storage element is fed to two discriminator units, to one of which is also fed 010, and to the other 110. When the two messages fed to a discriminator unit are identical it responds by sending out a characteristic signal, say, 1 for the 010 unit, and 0 for the 110 unit. If the messages are not identical, then the unit does not respond. A sequence of digits is therefore formed by the combined output signals of the two discriminators, in this case 110100, is stored in a further storage element and constitutes the recoded version. Once the recoding is complete, the units used for the temporary storage of the original message are cleared and made available for use again.

As to the spontaneous activity of searching for fresh methods of recoding material already stored, this might be conceived in the following terms. Given a sufficient number of spare storage units for holding temporarily the results of its operation, there is no particular difficulty in supposing the mechanism to explore all the possibilities of recoding, since this is a type of operation familiar in computing machines. But the mechanism must be controlled in such activities by some general principle, and it must have some criterion according to which it accepts or rejects the results of operations, and continues or ceases its searching activities. Such a general principle might be that of tending to reduce the total amount of storage space occupied by the material stored to date. If this were reduced by any set of recoding operations, the results would be accepted and stored, and older, now redundant, material annulled. Further activity along these lines would continue until no further economy of storage was produced.

4. We have suggested that recoding activities are dependent upon the possession of stored type-sequences, and it might well be asked how, since these must themselves be derived from messages received by the machine, the latter "gets a start," so to speak, in laying down its "schemata." It may, perhaps, be as well not to broach the discussion of this problem, which bears a considerable resemblance to a more famous, but equally troublesome, psychological puzzle. We may remark, however, that if the memory mechanism we are considering forms part of a more complex machine which interacts with its environment, it may be reasonably supposed that it is endowed with certain "innate" simple type sequences.

5. So far we have been concerned principally to indicate that memory-mechanisms incorporating circuital storage elements could, in theory, effect economy in the storage of incoming information, and that such economy would take the form of storing general patterns common to a number of messages separately from the special features peculiar to each message. A somewhat similar principle would seem, to judge by the experimental findings of Bartlett and his followers, to operate in the mechanisms of human memory, but in this case a further notable feature is the imperfection of the process, as judged against the standard of literal recall. Repro-

duction, as we have seen, is rarely literal and we should consider to what this feature would correspond in the model memory mechanism we have outlined.

The "defects" in the products of human memory consist in omissions, alterations, and importations. These changes take place in accordance with the principles of conventionalization and rationalization. The stage in the whole process at which these changes occur has been the subject of some dispute. Bartlett, it would seem (and also the Gestalt school), thought of them as being brought about chiefly as a result of reorganization of material during the period between the original presentation and the act of reproduction. That the reproduction itself introduces changes cannot be denied, but these have often been regarded as taking an accidental form, rather than as representing the activities of the schemata. The possibility that an important and characteristic part of the change occurs at the time of presentation, and during the immediate process of storage, has been closely considered by Gomulicki (1952) in a number of pertinent investigations. His conclusion is that a very considerable amount of "editing" takes place at this stage, so that what is stored has the character of a précis of the original material.

Now consider the situation of the mechanism in the face of a message which does not entirely conform to the patterns already incorporated in the machine's "schemata." We might suppose it to act in one of three ways. In the first place, it might simply not store the offending material at all. Secondly, it might condone small departures from pre-existing patterns. Thirdly, it might store those parts of the message which do not conform "in clear," while recoding those parts which

do. The first alternative is not of interest to us. The second would involve the possession of a criterion by the sequence discriminators, according to which they would treat as an instance of a type sequence any sequence which did not depart from type by more than a certain number of digits. So, for instance, if the criterion was "not more than one digit wrong," and the existing type sequences were 11001 and 00010, the message

$$11001010100001011011110000100010$$

will be recoded 100110, the offending sequences, namely 01010 and 11011, differing from the types by only one digit each, and being coded and stored as the types themselves. If reproduction of this message is called for, it will, of course, appear in a form different from the original, and the alterations could reasonably be said to be ones of "conventionalization" inasmuch as the material is brought into a form which conforms to the machine's "past experience" in general.

The third alternative way of handling nonconformatory parts of the material was, it was suggested, by storing such parts in their original form, in much the same way as users of some codes must sometimes leave "in clear" unusual words not provided for in the code book. It would be necessary in this case to enclose the sequence in question in a pair of (coded) parentheses to indicate that this material is in clear, so that in the reproductive process such sequences are run straight off without being decoded. If sequences which cannot be assimilated are treated in this way, some points of interest arise. In the first place, the material in question is preserved unchanged and is not subject to processes of "conventionalization" which may occur in the processes of coding and decoding. Secondly, such outstanding features could act as "labels," by which such messages might be identified in the course of the further transactions of the system. It seems possible, for instance, that such a label might be operative in the appropriate selection of the message when there is a demand for reproduction. In these respects it might be said that sequences which cannot be assimilated into the schemata resemble the dominant details and images which, in Bartlett's formulation are carried along relatively unchanged, and seem to afford the starting point for reconstruction.

SUMMARY

An attempt is made to decide whether the memory model suggested by circuital storage devices in modern computing machines [6] is better adapted to meet the empirical data on recall brought to light by Bartlett and others, than is the type of model which postulates storage in the form of *simulacra,* or traces impressed upon a medium. It is pointed out that unless the cir-

---

[6] It has been pointed out to me, and it should be emphasized, that the considerations of this paper are by no means dependent upon the *sequential* aspect of processes of storing information encountered in modern computing machines. A type of machine which stored incoming messages on punched cards, automatically searched through these and punched recoded versions on fresh cards, rejecting the original cards into a waste-paper basket, would do as well in principle as an exemplar. In fact, this paper might, instead of having its present title, have been called "Sketch-design for an automatic filing system incorporating a principle of storage-space minimization." The mechanical details of such a model would, of course, be more difficult to imagine, and for this reason the electrical sequential processes we have considered afford a more helpful picture.

cuital storage-elements are functionally organized in such a way as to allow of recoding of the stored messages, they offer in themselves no advance upon the ordinary trace hypothesis. However, the flexibility of the circuital device might be used to achieve systematic reloading upon the basis of common patterns in the incoming messages. These common patterns would then be stored separately from the particular arrangements of them which constitute different messages. Not only could there be economy of storage space, but the original messages could be reproduced in their original forms. Furthermore, when we consider how such a mechanism might handle messages which contain patterns not already held stored, possible analogies to the processes of rationalization and conventionalization, and to the part played by "dominant detail," emerge. It is suggested that such a system would have some of the properties of schemata as postulated by Bartlett.

Although such a model is not immediately applicable to laboratory experimentation upon memory processes, it might prove useful in reorienting our conception of memory mechanisms over a wide field, including problems of recognition and "set," of perceptual equivalence, of retroactive inhibition and immediate memory span, and of amnesias and paramnesias.

REFERENCES

Bartlett, F. C., *Remembering*. Cambridge, England: Cambridge University Press, 1932.

Brain, W. R., "The Concept of the Schema in Neurology and Psychiatry," in *Perspectives in Neuropsychiatry,* ed. Richter. London, 1950.

Eccles, J. C., *The Neurophysiological Basis of Mind*. London: Oxford University Press, 1953.

Gomulicki, B., "Recall as an Abstractive Process." (Unpublished Doctoral dissertation, Oxford University, 1952.)

Head, B., *Studies in Neurology, II.* Oxford University Press, 1921.

Koffka, K., *Principles of Gestalt Psychology.* London, 1935.

Munk, H., "Über die Functionen der Grosshirnrinde." 2 Aufl. Berlin, 1890.

Northway, M. L., "The Concept of the 'Schema.'" *British Journal of Psychology,* 30 (1940), 316-25; 31 (1940), 22-36.

Oldfield, R. C. and O. L. Zangwill, "Head's Concept of the Schema and its Application in Contemporary British Psychology," *British Journal of Psychology,* 32 (1942), 267-86; 33 (1943), 58-64, 113-29, 143-49.

Factorial Angles to Psychology *

J. P. Guilford

Very rarely has it been recognized that factor analysts have anything to contribute toward the resolution of general, systematic issues in psychology. It must be admitted at the beginning that there is no unified body of psychological theory, as such, that has been developed by factor analysts. What I shall say on the subject is the opinion of one person and cannot be represented as an expression for any group.

The average factor analyst has delayed theory building because systematic thinking requires information concerning a rather large number of psychological factors before the most significant interrelationships become apparent and systems can take shape.[1]

The writer had felt no particular call to consider the relation of psychological factors to behavior theory until he recently faced the need to present in book form an organized picture of personality from the point of view of factors (Guilford, 1959a). As for the systematists in psychology who are not factor analysts, probably none has regarded the method of factor analysis as a scientific tool by which psychological knowledge can be advanced very much; certainly not as a tool by which a comprehensive model of the behaving organism could be derived.

Objectives of This Paper

It is the purpose of this paper to show how factor theory and factor-analytic methods and results can provide the models and the information upon which a comprehensive theory of

* From J. P. Guilford, "Factorial Angles to Psychology," *Psychological Review,* 68 (1961), 1-20. Reprinted by permission of the author and the American Psychological Association.

Based upon a paper presented at the University of Florida, Gainesville, March 9, 1959, as a part of a symposium on points of view in psychology.

[1] An early attempt to develop anything like a system of psychology based upon

factor analysis was that of Spearman (1923, 1927). More recently Cattell (1957) has applied factorial findings to behavior theory, culminating in a rather elaborate presentation. Neither has dealt with many of the major issues that have divided schools of thought.

behavior could be based. To this end, it will be necessary to present the logical foundation for factor analysis as a scientific method and to see how we can go logically from factors to the kinds of concepts that are more familiar to psychological theory. It is much too early to say that a system of psychology has been worked out from this point of view. All I can do is to indicate some of the implications of the knowledge of factors and their interrelationships for the understanding of the behavior of individuals and some of the more general ideas that follow from these implications. The conclusions have some bearing upon many of the perennial, systematic issues, such as that of associationism. Thus, some of the lines of a factorial system can be drawn, and certain comparisons can be made with the major schools of psychology.

Why Factors Have Not Contributed to Psychological Theory

One of the reasons the findings of factor analysis have not contributed more to psychological theory is that many analyses have not been basic studies of the properties of human nature, either by intention or by way of outcome. One practical use of factor analysis is the reduction of correlational data, in order to transform them into simpler form for inspection. The chances of revealing anything of fundamental psychological interest under these circumstances are rather remote.

Even when the objective is to discover something of general interest regarding human nature, the outcomes are often disappointing. Many factorial studies of this type are poorly planned because they are forced to be simply exploratory. In this instance, there is not enough prior information as a basis for setting up fruitful hypotheses. Even a single, prior exploratory analysis in the same area of behavior would be of considerable help. Without good hypotheses there is limitation as to the wise choice of experimental variables. The choice of variables to be analyzed together is all important for success. We cannot go into the technical reasons for this statement here, but the well-worn cliché "You get out of a factor analysis what you put into it" does apply, if it is revised to say: "You *cannot* get out of an analysis what you do *not* put into it."

Another reason for some failures of factor-analytical studies is the lack of good experimental design. More will be said about this point later, but I should like to add here that the fact that we have an elaborate computational procedure for treating data does not relieve us of the necessity of observing the ordinary requirements of experimental logic and experimental controls.

But results from the better factor analyses are also commonly rejected as contributions to general psychological knowledge. The reason is probably that the method has been most often used for the study of individual differences. The fact that these studies have often been inspired more by the interests of vocational psychologists than by interest in basic facts of behavior is relatively coincidental. The basic data with which the factor analyst starts are measurements of numerous individuals in a large number of experimental variables. In other words, the emphasis is upon individual differences. Factors, when interpreted psychologically, are also conceived as ways in which individuals differ from one another. Psychological theorists, on the other hand, are primarily interested in how individuals are *alike* and only in-

368   COMPUTER MODEL

cidentally in how they *differ*. It is actually very easy to bridge the gap, but there has been little effort to do so.

In this connection, the factorist could well charge the general theorist with being negligent for not bringing individual differences into the picture when he, constructs a system of psychology. No well-known system, with the exception of Tolman's purposive behaviorism, has anything of significance to say about individual differences. Individual differences are recognized as empirical facts, but they have been generally treated as nuisances by the experimental psychologist, and as phenomena of little or no interest by the theorist. The fact that reasonably satisfying systems could be built ignoring individual differences is an important reason for not bringing them into the picture.

One consequence of this general state of affairs is that the theorist who is concerned with personality often finds such systems inadequate for his purposes. Consequently he builds his own theory. But even such a theory often recognizes only implicitly the need for a significant emphasis upon individual differences. It rarely does justice to this aspect of the meaning of personality. Such a theorist recognizes that each person is unique, but he does not sufficiently appreciate the fact that it is individual differences that make him unique.

SOME FACTOR MODELS
FOR PERSONALITY

Factor theory has provided the only rigorous models of any consequence that have been proposed to make intelligible the many facets of the phenomena of individual differences. I shall mention three of those models because they are especially relevant to this paper.[2] A multidimensional model is used to represent personality in general. A hierarchical model represents interrelationships among traits within typical individuals. A matrix model represents systematic relationships among factors within a certain domain of behavior.

A Dimensional Model

The most common, basic model is a multidimensional Euclidian space, each dimension of which represents a unique trait. A unique trait can be discovered as a common factor by factor analysis. To the extent that an individual's personality can be accounted for in terms of a limited number of common factors, each person can be represented as a point in *n*-dimensional space.

Figure 1 illustrates this kind of

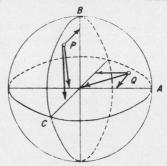

FIG. 1. *Example of a dimensional model involving three unique traits, or common factors,* A, B, *and* C, *showing characteristic point positions of two individuals,* P *and* Q, *with respect to the three personality traits.*

model, showing only three dimensions, for obvious reasons. Each axis is a linear dimension representing a unique trait along which individuals have characteristic trait positions. Let us say that axes A, B, and C represent the disparate traits of gregariousness,

---

[2] Still other models have been presented by Guttman (1954) and Lazarsfeld (1954).

meticulousness, and emotional stability, with their positive extreme qualities at the labeled ends of the axes. So far as these three traits go, Individual P is described quantitatively by his projections on the three axes. His three projections define a point, which is his characteristic position in this three-dimensional space. The point for Person P tells us that he is a bit below average in gregariousness and that he is very meticulous and also moderately strong in emotional stability, the average for each trait being at the origin.

Person Q has another combination of three projections, defining another point location in the same space. In n-dimensional space each person has n different projections defining a point in that n-dimensional space. The fact that he probably changes his trait positions somewhat from time to time need not concern us in this discussion. Such changes are the reason for the expression "characteristic position" used above. If it is difficult to think of a space of a large number of dimensions, one can think instead of a profile chart, in which the dimensions are laid side by side.

The fact that the axes shown in Fig. 1 are orthogonal (at right angles) is incidental. Actually, factorists generally agree that the best-representing axes more often than not depart from right angles. They do not agree as to how the angular separations shall be determined empirically.

A Hierarchical Model

Although the dimensional model just seen provides for the description of individuals, it is better as a representation of variables within populations than as a picture of personality structures within individuals. There is also the circumstance that factor

traits are of different degrees of generality, in the sense that some are related to wide ranges of behavior and some to narrower ranges.

A brief example will illustrate. Let us say that Student Z declined an opportunity to cheat while taking a certain examination. This is a specific action; there is no necessary implication concerning Z's traits from this one observable event. Over a run of 20 consecutive examinations, card games, and purchases Z also passed up 18 opportunities to cheat. We may infer that over this range of behavior Z has a rather high position on a trait of resistance to cheating. So far as we know from these observations, the trait is not a very broad or general one. Further observations show that Z's conduct is similar in situations that offer opportunities for deceiving and stealing. From this information we may conclude that he is strong on a more general trait that we may call "honesty." But Z has an even more general tendency toward ethical conduct of other varieties, which justifies our placing him above the average on a still broader trait of "strength of character." Furthermore, he exhibits an even more general restraint and self-control that goes beyond behavior that has ethical implications, suggesting a still broader disposition or syndrome.

Because of the appearance of traits at different levels of generality, a few writers feel the need of a second model to supplement the first (Burt, 1949; Eysenck, 1951; Guilford, 1959a; Vernon, 1950). This is a hierarchial model, which serves to relate the factorial dimensions logically to one another and to a single personality. Figure 2 is an example of a segment of such a model. In the illustration of traits just given, the particular acts of resistance, in whatever area of be-

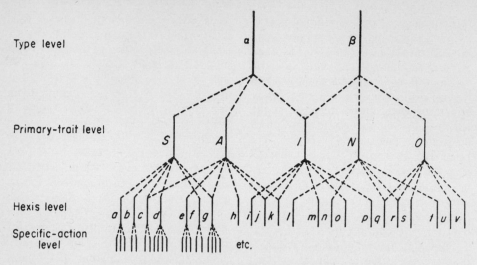

Type level

Primary-trait level

Hexis level

Specific-action level

etc.

FIG. 2. *Segment of a hierarchical model representing an area of personality, with three levels of traits of differing generality and the specific-action level.*

havior—cheating, deceiving, or stealing—are at the specific-action level. Traits of cheating, or of deceiving, or of stealing may be regarded as being at the "hexis" level. A hexis is about the same as a habit but the term "hexis" is preferred because it is not so committed to the idea that traits are determined by learning only. A trait of honesty, for which there is factor-analytical evidence (Guilford, 1959a), may be considered to be at the primary-trait level. Strength of character and general self-restraint would be considered syndrome types at two still higher levels.

Factor analysis can be applied at various levels in the hierarchy of traits. From information concerning intercorrelations of measured specific actions we can derive conclusions regarding the existence of unique traits at the hexis level. From information concerning intercorrelations of trait positions of individuals for traits at the hexis level, we can derive conclusions regarding the existence of unique traits at the primary-trait level; and so on, for higher levels. Probably

most of the psychologically meaningful factors thus far discovered have been at the primary-trait level.

Many of the apparent disagreements in results from different analysts should be attributed to the fact that they are analyzing at different levels in the hierarchy. The kind of factors one obtains depends upon the level or levels at which he obtains his information concerning individuals. In some analyses, factors of different levels are undoubtedly confused. From the standpoint of clarity of results the best general strategy would have been to start with information from the lower levels and work upward. Before we can collect clear evidence regarding status of individuals on unique traits at a certain level, we need to know what are the unique traits at that level.

The Matrix Type of Model

The third model is of recent origin and comes about from attempts to discern logical interrelationships among the known factors. Since the factors concerned are probably at the primary-trait level, the resulting models apply within that level. The results at the primary-trait level reveal organizations of the factors that suggest relations to higher levels. Hence the general outcome of this kind of model building may serve as guiding hypotheses concerning the completion of the hierarchial picture of personality. The best evidence concerning interrelationships of the levels will be empirical information regarding intercorrelations of factors. As yet we have no adequate experimental procedures for estimating these correlations.

Attempts have been made to classify the known factors in certain areas of personality, with some success in a few of them, including the psychomotor abilities, the intellectual abilities, the temperament traits, and some of the simpler traits of pathology (Guilford, 1959a). The typical outcome is a matrix of factors that places them in columns and rows according to their common properties. That is, the factors of each row have something in common and the factors of each column. In the case of the intellectual abilities, of which about 55 are known at the present time, a third dimension is necessary. They have been organized in a solid figure, known as the structure of intellect, which is shown in Fig. 3 (see Guilford, 1959b).

For our present purposes, we need to note only the general features of the model of the structure of intellect. First, the factors are classified according to the kind of operation performed: *cognition, memory, divergent production, convergent production,* and *evaluation*. Second, the factors are classified according to the kind of content or material on which the operations are performed—*figural, symbolic, semantic,* and *behavioral*. Of the four content categories we might say that the first represents concrete

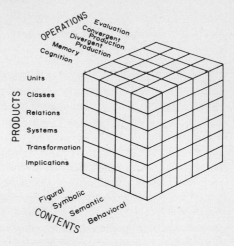

FIG. 3. *Cubical model of the structure of intellect, representing categories of primary abilities with respect to three modes of variation.*

intelligence, the next two represent two varieties of abstract intelligence, and the fourth represents social intelligence. The latter has been included on a purely theoretical basis; no factors of social intelligence are as yet known. The third basis of classification is in terms of the kinds of products resulting from the operations on the contents—*units, classes, relations, systems, transformations,* and *implications*. Theoretically, there should be a different primary intellectual ability in each cell of Fig. 3, in other words, about 120 instead of the 55 presently recognized.

We shall have occasion to refer back to the structure of intellect, for I shall draw heavily upon the principles that it demonstrates and upon the implications drawn from it in connection with discussion of general psychological theory. This is so, not only because intellect looms large among the things to be accounted for but also because our knowledge from the factorial approach is extensive in this area of personality.

FACTOR ANALYSIS AS A TOOL IN SCIENCE

Factor analysis is a potent instrument for extracting information from data, but it has no magical power to reveal anything regarding information that is not inherent in the data. The scientist who uses the method for the discovery of psychological information should start out by asking certain questions before he collects his data. In other words, a factor-analytic study must be carefully planned, with clearly stated hypotheses to be tested, if one is to use the method effectively.

The more experimental features the investigator can bring into his planning the better. This practice reduces ambiguity in the interpretation of results. In evaluating the scientific use of factor analysis, therefore, we need to be clear as to the kind of hypotheses that can be set up, the ways in which those hypotheses are tested, the kinds of variations of conditions introduced, and the kinds of controls exerted. Many psychologists are probably unaware that these experimental features are possible in factor-analytical investigations, perhaps because in publications regarding the method so much attention is given to computational steps and so little to experimental uses of it.

A Typical Factorial Study

Let us illustrate an experimental design for a factorial investigation by reference to a study of intellectual abilities. Suppose we have selected for study the area of problem-solving. Suppose that we had no prior information regarding primary abilities involved in problem-solving. Our preliminary thinking about problem-solving would first probably suggest two alternative hypotheses. One would be that there is a single, universal ability to solve problems and the alternative would be that there are a number of distinctly different abilities involved. If these were the only hypotheses that we wished to test in our first analysis, we would simply select a list of tests, each of which presents problems of a different type. The types would be varied considerably, covering a great range. The analysis should give us the answer as to whether individual differences in success in solving these many different kinds of problems can be accounted for on the basis of one common factor or whether we are led by the results to reject this idea.

Let us say that the results indicate the acceptance of the multiple-factor hypothesis to account for problem-solving ability. The next study would normally be directed toward answering the question of how many factors are needed and the question of the properties of each factor. The hypotheses set up in the second investigation would probably involve a prediction that a certain number of factors is needed and that each expected factor has certain properties. The investigator would be aided considerably in this hypothesis formation from the way in which the tests were classified among the factors in the first analysis. But there might be ambiguities regarding the properties of each factor. Hypothesized factor Q might be expected to have properties a, d, and f, or it might have properties c, d, and f, or even properties a, c, and g. From the hypothesized properties arise ideas as to the kinds of tests that will be needed to measure the factor. Experimental tests are accordingly constructed, differing systematically along the lines of the supposed properties, with the hope that when a hypothesized factor does come out in the analysis, tests with one kind of specification will be found related to it and tests with the other specifications will not. In this manner we hope to obtain clarification of the nature of a factor.

Statistical Tests and Factor Analysis

At this point the rigorously inclined investigator is quick to remind us that there are no adequate statistical tests that can be applied, either to help us decide how many common factors obtain in the particular analysis or whether factor loadings are significantly different from zero or from one another. There is no use denying this state of affairs. It is also true that there is some degree of looseness connected with rotational procedures, which also contributes to the uncertainty of conclusions. Conclusions must therefore be made on a permissive rather than a compulsory basis, in spite of the fact that an accepted rotational solution appears to be compulsory.[3] To be completely objective, we can only say that yes, we may tolerate the idea that there is a unique psychological trait having such and such properties, in line with preliminary hypotheses, or we may say that no, we cannot reasonably do so. In the latter event we may conclude that the factor has other properties not suspected before and a new analysis is called for.

The reaction of some psychologists to this state of affairs may be to reject the results from factor analysis completely. To such a person it can be said that much more important to a scientific psychologist than statistical tests are psychological ideas. Sciences generally, including psychology, originally developed and went a long way without the aid of statistical tests. The lack of statistical tests is not fatal, but the lack of ideas would be. This is not to say that we should not wish to have both if we can. But there should be no prohibition against applying a method that seems fruitful, while waiting for statistical tests to be developed.[4] I suggest that we let the results of factor analysis speak for themselves and that they be judged on the basis of how much they contribute to psychological understanding, prediction, and control.

Experimental Controls in Factor Analysis

To return to other experimental features of a factorial study, what conditions are systematically varied? The most conspicuous kind of variation is in the types of tests, or other experimental variables, used. For the most part these variations are qualitative. From test to test we find variations in kind of material—figures, pictured objects, letters, numbers, and words being the most common varieties in printed form. We find variations in item format—multiple choice, matching, completion, and their derivatives. We find variations in instruction as to what is to be done and how it is to be done. In some of our more recent analyses we have introduced a few *quantitative* variations, such as the number of restrictions of a certain kind, the number of responses called for per item, and difficulty level of tests with the same kind of items. In connection with the quantitative variations we sometimes predicted that the factor loading for a certain factor would rise systematically and that for

[3] A number of proposals have been made for rotation according to rigorously defined criteria by analytical methods. Although some of them are very attractive in principle, they usually fail to achieve fully satisfactory solutions from an intuitive point of view. The difficulty is that the selection of experimental variables must be nearly ideal in order to achieve the "right" solution from an interpretive standpoint.

[4] Some progress is being made with regard to statistical tests of certain aspects of factor-analytical results (see Maxwell, 1959).

another factor would fall system- atically, or that there would be an intermediate optimal level for the vari- ation concerned. A great deal has to be known about the nature of a factor before this much refinement in ex- perimental variation can be effectively introduced.

Certain conditions are at least par- tially controlled, or should be. The selection of population of individuals is important. In the study of intellectual abilities, there should be relative ho- mogeneity in age, education, sex, and general intellectual level. Ideally, one should like to equate individuals on all other factors than those under in- vestigation, but this would be prohibi- tive in terms of effort, and fortunately it is not essential. We can tolerate in- complete controls, as must be true of any experiment, allowing the effects to go into the error components. Factor analysis has a way of segregating er- ror variance from the variances in which we are interested, not perfectly, but within practical limits. So long as the non-error variance is of sufficient potency, we can obtain a fair picture of the common factors.

FROM FACTORS TO FUNCTIONS

Our next need in this discussion is to establish a logical bridge between factors and general psychological the- ory. Present psychological theory has arisen mainly in connection with the traditional experimental approach, hence in constructing the bridge we should profit by giving some attention to a comparison of that approach with the factor-analytical approach, in cer- tain respects.

Individual Differences vs. Functioning Individuals

The main operational difference is that the traditional experimentalist

focuses his interest upon stimulus- response relationships. The stimulus- response model is basic to his thinking and to his planning of investigations. The factorist, on the other hand, di- rects his attention primarily upon re- sponses and the concomitances among responses. From the intercorrelation of response values the factorist looks for signs of traits, not for stimulus- response relations. Traits are prop- erties of individuals. To the student of personality, their determination of behavior is just as real a phenomenon as the determination by stimuli. Some experimentalists are now recognizing this general principle, as indicated in studies of the relation of characteristic anxiety levels to various measured ef- fects in behavior. In such an experi- ment, one independent variable is not a stimulus variable or even a transi- tory personal variable such as a mental set. It is individual differences on an enduring attribute, in other words a trait.

The key to the bridge, therefore, is the concept of "trait." In the context of personality theory, a trait is any relatively enduring way in which one person differs from others. On a scalable trait, which can be represented by a straight line, each person has a characteristic position. If individuals have different positions on a common scale, the scale represents some qual- ity or property that each person pos- sesses to some degree, in common with other persons. If the quality is a unique one, such as may be discovered by factor analysis, it is some significant component of the individual's consti- tution.

There is nothing in this line of reasoning to force us to any conclusion as to the fundamental nature of this component. It might be a unique skill, a unique motive, or a unique attitude of some kind. It might be dependent upon some particular organic structure or upon some combination of structures functioning together. There is nothing in ordinary factor-analytic results to tell us about the origins of a factor or to give us sufficient basis for its automatic classification.

Traits and Functions

If we consider the primary abilities represented in the structure of intellect (Fig. 3), however, and ask ourselves what kinds of components they are, we obtain a little help. Examination of the list of intellectual abilities tells us that represented in one particular cell is an ability to cognize (discover, know, or rediscover) semantic systems and that this is distinctly different from an ability to evaluate the logical soundness of conclusions involving relations between symbols. If each person has a characteristic level of ability to perform in each of these two respects, he certainly is performing in these two ways. In other words, we may say that he has *functions* of these two types. The primary intellectual abilities may therefore be conceived as ways of functioning within individuals as well as ways in which individuals differ from one another. Thus, by the study of how persons differ we also discover how they are alike.

Traits other than abilities are not so readily conceived as functions, but it is possible to see that some of them are the *directions* that the functioning individual takes (in the case of motivational traits) and others are connected with the *manner* in which the functioning proceeds (in the case of temperamental traits). As in the case of abilities, other primary traits should give us ideas about the functioning of the individual as a going concern. Information regarding the factors and their properties should therefore help us to build up a picture of the behav-

ing organism, and hence contribute to psychological theory.

SOME IMPLICATIONS OF FACTORS FOR PSYCHOLOGICAL THEORY

It has just been suggested that from the psychologically meaningful factors that we know, and from their interrelationships, we can make progress toward the general description of behavior of individuals and account for the determination of behavior by internal sources. The primary traits that are recognized as needs, interests, and attitudes, provide potentially useful concepts for understanding the varieties of general motives operating within the individual. Forty or more years ago it was common for psychologists to draw up lists of instincts. In later years this kind of exercise has been replaced by a somewhat less common effort to draw up a list of fundamental human motives. McDougall, for example, took this kind of objective very seriously. If the point of view adopted in psychology calls for such an analysis of motivation into component urges, propensities, needs —call them what you will—factor analysis offers a very natural empirical method for arriving at such a goal.

Information, Operations, and Products

From the intellectual factors as organized in the structure of intellect, some of the most significant implications for psychological theory may be seen at this time. The first general principle is that we should conceive of a human being as an instrument or agent whose psychological purpose is to deal with information. In saying this, it is necessary to interpret information in a very broad sense. For our present purposes, "information" may be defined as anything that the individual discriminates. He need only show that he discriminates or can do so by means of differential reactions of a sufficiently consistent character.

This principle regarding information and the definition of information do not follow directly from the structure of intellect, but they are strongly suggested by it. The structure of intellect does indicate that the individual cognizes, which means that he discovers or rediscovers or recognizes information. The information may be in figural form, which is a form that can be perceived through the senses. It may be in symbolic form, which may involve letters, digits, or other conventional signs. It may be in the form of meanings, ideas, or concepts, or what I have called semantic content. If the behavioral column is appropriately included in the structure of intellect, the information may be in terms of such things as the intentions, feelings, and attitudes of other individuals and of ourselves.

The individual not only cognizes all these kinds of things, he also retains information for future use. According to the structure of intellect, for every cognitive ability there should be a corresponding ability to retain information. Eight such memory factors are known. The individual also generates new information from given information, in accordance with the two categories of productive operations—divergent and convergent. Finally, the individual evaluates information, whether it is merely cognized or whether remembered or produced from other information. He decides whether the information is correct, adequate, suitable, and so on. A negative decision provides the occasion for new activity involving the same kinds of operations, with the individual probably arriving at new products.

The kinds of products achieved are as indicated by the six categories of factors known at present. Units are relatively segregated items of information, and they are sometimes articulations or integrations of parts. The latter characteristic is best seen in the symbolic column of factors, in connection with which units may be in the form of syllables, words, or number combinations. By virtue of common properties among the units, classes can be formed. Units also enter into relations with one another, for example, relations such as larger than, attached to, or inside of. One might think that systems are merely complex sets of relations, but analysis shows that abilities needed to cope with them are different from the abilities needed to cope with relations. Transformations include changes of various kinds, for example, changes in spatial order or arrangement, in letter combinations, and in the uses or functions of objects. Implications are in the form of extrapolations from given information, such as extensions of the information in space or in time. Thus, the six kinds of products seem to pertain to varieties of knowledge when knowledge is reduced to elemental terms.

An Informational Theory of Learning

A psychological system should provide the principles by which the facts of various areas may be ordered and comprehended. As an example of how the factorial view would account for an area of behavior, let us consider the subject of learning. Each point of view should have something to say regarding this most important subject. What kind of theory of learning would be consistent with the known outcomes of factor analysis or would be implied by this information?

Taking our cue from the structure of intellect, we find that the theory of learning suggested is in the general category of cognitive theories. Furthermore, from the list of cognitive factors we see the classes into which such cognitions fall. Learning, then, is essentially discovery. The particular discovery may be achieved completely and suddenly, an instance of learning that has been called "insight," or it may be achieved in a series of approximations. The discovery may be in any of the six forms recognized as products in the structure of intellect. The achieved cognition may be an acquaintance with a new unit, the formation of a new class, the formation of a new relationship or a new system, the awareness of a transformation, or the extension to new implications.

It is possible to give an associative interpretation to some of these events but not all. Perhaps the most obvious type of product that may be interpreted as an association is that of relation. But when we recognize that two things bear some relationship to one another, it is not just that when one comes we think of the other. The relation itself is something additional. It may be a difference along some continuum, as when we say that X is taller than Y, P is older than Q, or J is softer than K. The relation might be in terms of spatial or temporal position. Or it might be in terms of opposition, friendship, status, or of whole and part. One particular relation may be of very general importance, namely, the relation to the effect that "this belongs with that" merely because the two things occur in temporal or spatial proximity. There may be no other basis, for example, in terms of properties of the two things, for justifying the formation of a relationship.

It is possible to apply the concept of association in connection with the cognition of classes. Classes can be formed because units have something in common. We could say that Aristotle's concept of association by simi-larity applies. But being aware that a class exists and knowing a class concept would seem to go well beyond a mere association by virtue of the similarity of two things.

The more modern interpretation of class recognition brings such an event under the concept of "equivalence of stimuli." But there seems to be a genuine psychological difference between failing to discriminate stimuli, on the one hand, and cognizing that discriminated stimuli have properties in common and therefore belong in the same class, on the other. We could think of all such events, of course, as belonging on a continuum of lower to higher levels of cognition of classes. The implication of this discussion is that class recognition, however primitive or sophisticated, is still a unique kind of psychological event.

A third possible place for applying the associative principle is in connection with the product of implication. One of the natural conditions for developing a cognition of implication would seem to be temporal sequences of stimulations. It seems likely that what some learning theorists refer to as "expectations" come within the category of implications.

In connection with the other three kinds of products—units, systems, and transformations—the association principle seems *entirely* inappropriate. Wundt and others failed in their attempts to account for perceived objects in terms of association. An important natural consequence was the development of Gestalt psychology. Units, systems, and transformations all pertain to things that have totality properties that defy associative interpretations. As a matter of fact, it can be maintained that even in the products of relations, classes, and implications, totality properties are also involved. Two things in relation constitute a kind of unitary structure, as Spearman pointed out. Classes are conceived groups of units and to each group a single class concept is applied. The emergence of a class idea is hardly to be accounted for as the formation of an association. In connection with implications we often have *continuities* of various kinds. Since it is possible to conceive of totality properties for all six kinds of products, it is small wonder that the Gestalt psychologists felt considerable confidence in applying their principles to all kinds of mental functioning, with complete discard of the principle of association.

As a particular example of human learning, let us take the case of memorizing a series of nonsense syllables, so popular traditionally in the laboratory. From the factorial point of view, each syllable is a symbolic *unit,* and the learner becomes more and more familiar with it as exposures are repeated. In learning to associate each syllable with the one following in the list, the learner, we may say, is seeking for and perhaps discovering a *relation* (or relations) where none existed before; a relationship may be formed involving two units of information. Two syllables offer very little in the way of properties that can be utilized for this purpose, as compared with words. But each pair of syllables does offer some possibility of the formation of some kind of relationship.

Another aspect may be that the learner is acquiring new expectations or *implications.* This may be indicated by the fact that forward connections are stronger than backward associations. We may also hypothesize that the learner is developing a new *system* of units. At least two primary abilities that we know indicate that order is an important kind of system. Some indication that a system is being formed can be seen in what are commonly called remote forward associations and backward associations. The beginning and end units of the series of syllables seem to serve as anchoring points for the whole system and hence have much to do with the relative ease of learning units in different positions in the series.

This line of reasoning suggests that in memorizing a list of syllables several of the primary abilities come into play, including the cognition of symbolic units, of symbolic relations, of symbolic systems, and of symbolic implications. Since the testing of progress in learning involves lapse of time, there is probably also involvement of the corresponding memory factors. If the series were composed of figures or of words, the corresponding cognitive and memory factors in the figural and semantic columns, respectively, should be involved. Still other intellectual resources may come into play, depending upon the strategy of the learner. The hypotheses concerning the roles of various common factors in a particular learning task can be tested by factor analysis of scores obtained at different stages of learning along with sufficient marker tests for the factors probably involved. Fleishman and Hempel (1954, 1955) have already conducted studies of this kind.

Reinforcement

Most theories of learning have some provision to account for the fact that practical changes in behavior have some degree of permanence, in other words, some concept to account for what is called "fixation." The concepts usually invoked for this purpose are some form of a law of effect or of reinforcement. In an informational theory of learning based upon the structure of intellect, the key to fixation is to be found in the category of evaluation. In this connection, feedback information is very important.

Thorndike seemed to favor the interpretation that effect is in the form of a confirming reaction, a conception that seems close to that of evaluation. The idea of confirming reaction is not comprehensive, however, because it does not give significance to *failure* of confirmation. In stressing the positive aspect of evaluation, Thorndike was reflecting the experimental findings, as he thought, that only positive effect seemed to change the strength of learned connections. He did recognize that a failure leads to new learning activity, which is equivalent to saying that an evaluation of failure is the occasion for new learning effort.

The conception of an evaluative aspect to learning is broad enough to embrace most current interpretations of effect. When primary reinforcement is equated to drive reduction, we can say that the organism is using feedback information regarding his internal condition. Secondary reinforcement may be said to involve *implications* cognized by the organism. Lest these statements raise objections that there cannot be unconscious cognitions and evaluations, as a sort of contradiction of terms, let us refer back to the definition of information that was given earlier—information is that which the organism discriminates. The conscious-unconscious distinction is therefore irrelevant.

The evaluative view of effect just expressed suggests the extension of the application of the concept of information to the phenomena of motivation and emotion generally. This extension leads to some new ways of looking at old problems. Both motives and emotions, including feelings, can be regarded as information concerning the internal conditions of the organism; concerning its needs and its states of well-being or ill-being.

In this connection we need to recognize another property of information. When motives become at all strong, there is a sense of urgency about them and about the accompanying emotional aspects. This suggests the need for the concept of "loading." We can say that information carries different degrees of loading or weight. Feelings of pleasure and of displeasure are in themselves information that is more or less loaded, positively or negatively. There is increasing evidence that in themselves these feelings can be reinforcing (Miller, 1955). They are not infallible: information and evaluation may sometimes go against them because they are outweighed by other information, but they nevertheless can be regarded as kinds of evaluative information. In this connection, it may be of more than incidental significance that in the work of Osgood and others on the dimensions of meaning, the pleasant-unpleasant or evaluative dimension seems to be the strongest and most universal (Osgood, 1957).[5]

Another thought on "loading" would be that the basis for it is to be found in the behavioral column of the structure of intellect. Information regarding our own internal conditions and our relation to external situations is evaluated as being vital to some degree. The degree of recognized vitalness determines the loading or *is* the loading. We are thus brought to the conclusion that loading is a matter of evaluation and that it may apply not only to behavioral products but quite generally.

---

[5] It is also significant that J. P. Seward (1958) has recently assembled considerable evidence in support of the cognitive interpretation of learning and also that there is evidence pointing toward need satisfaction that arises merely from acquiring new cognitions.

Transfer

The general problem of transfer of learning takes on a different complexion in view of our information concerning factors. G. A. Ferguson (1954) has proposed the unique theory that factors of ability are produced by the fact that transfer of learning takes place along the lines of the common factors. It has long been recognized that psychological similarity of tasks is a key to the direction and extent of transfer. Similarity of tasks depends upon common kinds of content, operations, and products, or of combinations of these features. We interpret common factors in terms of the common properties of the tests that indicate them.

Ferguson's theory does not necessarily mean that all the effects of learning are general. It is possible to deduce from factor theory, as applied to abilities, the principle that each instance of learning has both general and specific components. Fleishman and Hempel (1954, 1955) have provided evidence to support this principle from more than one investigation. Each time, they found a specific component, whose relative importance for individual differences systematically increased with practice; in addition to the common-factor components—each of which tended to undergo some systematic changes in importance. The common factors were identifiable with those found in testing apart from the learning experiment.

Although the Fleishman and Hempel experiments give us no information regarding progressive improvements in any of the common factors, they demonstrate that common factors do play roles in learning and they find no evidence of the existence of a unique, general learning-ability factor. These and other factorial learning studies should nail in its coffin for all time the notion that there is a single, general learning ability. Abilities to learn are apparently at least as numerous as there are intellectual factors. The writer often feels that psychologists would do well to banish the term *learning* entirely and instead talk about changes in behavior, their conditions and consequences.

Factors in Problem-Solving

The same fate is in store for the notion that there is a single problem-solving ability. As I have pointed out elsewhere (Guilford, 1954), the variety of problems is enormous. Each type of problem, like each type of task, is presented in the form of a certain kind of content; it calls for its own kinds of operations, and certain kinds of products are needed in order to achieve a solution. A problem exists for an individual when to cope with a given situation he has no adequate, previously learned and remembered device ready to deal with the situation. From this definition we see that problem-solving is as broad as behavior itself. It is likely, therefore, to tax any of the resources of intellect that may be pertinent.

Each type of problem should draw upon its own pattern of resources in the average person in a certain population. The importance of each factor for individual differences in problem-solving scores can be indicated by a factor analysis of those scores along with scores from appropriate marker tests of the factors. In our Aptitudes Project at the University of Southern California,[6] we have just completed

---

[6] Under Contract Nonr-228(20) with the Office of Naval Research, monitored by the Personnel and Training Branch. This particular study was under the direct supervision of Philip R. Merrifield (Merrifield, Guilford, Christensen, & Frick, 1960).

this type of study for one type of problem. Five factors appeared to be of some importance: *sensitivity to problems, verbal comprehension, ideational fluency, originality,* and *conceptual foresight.* The conditions, as represented by the problem tasks and the intellectual status of the subjects and their strategies, were evidently right for emphasizing these five factors.

Motor and Sensori-motor Aspects of Learning

Many readers will recognize that the account of learning is limited in a number of ways, because only the intellectual factors have been considered, and it needs certain supplementations. The theory of learning presented is not considered a complete one by any means. There are questions of how sequences of cognitions and actions are developed and how complex motor patterns are organized as a consequence of activity. Two individuals who have the same cognition may not do the same thing or do it in the same manner. Adequate motor responses are not always available on demand, and new ones must often be developed.

From a cognitive point of view, sensori-motor learning can be conceived as the formation of cognition-response sequences instead of stimulus-response sequences. If we knew the individual's cognitions, we should be better able to predict his responses than we can from knowledge of the stimulating conditions. He responds overtly to his cognitions rather than to the experimenter's "real" world. For a long time the Gestalters have been attempting to convince us of the validity of this principle. If the learner's cognitions nearly coincide with the experimenter's, of course, the experimenter's knowledge of stimulating conditions is sufficient for practical purposes. But where there are notable differences between the two views, it should pay to attempt to learn what we can regarding the learner's cognitions. The learner's evaluations would be other important sources of information regarding what he will do and with what energy.

The other problem, that of development of motor patterns, can possibly be approached profitably by giving attention to kinesthetic cognitions as a subject for study. The learner has a flood of information from himself as well as from his external environment, information of which the experimenter is unaware. A systematic factorial exploration of the individual's use of his kinesthetic content should be fruitful. It should tell us whether information from this general source also comes in the form of the six kinds of products and what sorts of things these products are in the kinesthetic domain. The individual's information concerning his responding equipment, its potentialities and limitations, from this source, should have an important bearing upon what he does with that equipment.

RELATIONS TO OTHER POINTS OF VIEW

Some Major Issues

Before comparing the point of view presented here with particular schools of thought, let us consider its position on a few of the major issues that divide those schools. One of the issues is sometimes called "mentalism," and it is concerned with the question whether conscious experience is accepted as a phenomenon and whether it plays a significant role in a system. My impression is that a system developed from factorial information and thinking need not take sides on this issue; the issue is not so very relevant. Actually, a completely objective system could be worked out, as one can see from the way in which the application to phenomena of learning and problem solving needed no reference to conscious experience or to concepts necessarily implying it. But if conscious experience is admitted as a necessary problem for psychologists, the factorial approach has much to offer in determining the dimensions of that experience and hence in finding descriptive concepts for it.

The assertion that the factorial view can generate an objective system needs additional defense, for the terms "cognition" and "thinking," particularly, arose in the context of mentalistic psychology. In spite of their origin, these terms, and others used in connection with the structure of intellect, can be given entirely objective interpretations, for the reason that they have observable referents. The referents are the test materials used in factorial investigations. The factors, and in turn the factor categories, are interpreted in terms of the kinds of test content, the kinds of operations demanded by the instructions and the items, and the kinds of responses needed to make good scores.

In one sense, factor analysis is analogous to the atomic physicist's cloud-chamber procedures. The physicist draws a conclusion regarding things that he cannot observe, from observed events remotely connected with them. From such scattered sources of observation he builds up a model of the atom and of its nucleus. From test scores and the ways in which they are interrelated, the factor analyst constructs conceptions of human nature. The one seems as objective as the other.

The issue of associationism has already been touched upon in discussing the nature of learning and it will be recalled that the outcome was to reject association as a principle that would account for the products of information. There are important areas of intellectual functioning in which development of understanding has been seriously handicapped by our staking so much on one principle. Because the principle has served in so many places, in spite of objections and necessary qualifications and omissions, over-reliance on the principle has continued. When the further restriction of recognizing only stimulus-response associations is imposed, psychology is further limited. This brings us to another issue.

A third general issue may be called "centralism vs. peripheralism." The extreme peripheralist not only restricts his observation to stimuli and responses but also chooses to limit himself to descriptive concepts that pertain only to those events. The centralist, on the other hand, although recognizing that we are limited to observations of stimuli and responses, does not hesitate to attempt to infer something regarding processes that take place between those events. Hull and others have seen the need for inferring a few intervening events or conditions (called intervening variables), but they attempt to get along with a bare minimum.

It is my conviction that a psychology that restricts itself entirely to the task of correlating stimuli and responses and that avoids attempts to build up a picture of what goes on between them will fall far short of complete success. The most significant things happen between stimuli and responses. It is these things that make known stimulus-response correlations most significant. In predicting behavior we need to know about internal conditions, including traits, as well as about the external situation. The same is true concerning the control of behavior. The factor-analytic approach is aimed at a conceptualization of psychological properties of a central nature. Whether it can supply all the kinds of concepts that are needed for this purpose remains to be seen.

Comparisons with Some Major Schools

From the preceding discussion it should be clear that a psychology based upon factor analysis agrees with behaviorism in achieving an objective science but it finds the behaviorist's exclusive dependence upon the association principle to be a serious deficiency, and behaviorism's restriction to peripheralism also seriously limiting.

A factor psychology finds in the Gestalt point of view quite a number of congenial features. As pointed out earlier, it finds the Gestalt emphasis upon totalities to be useful as a replacement for associationism. It finds, however, that Gestalt psychology failed to carry through its own program. In part this might have been due to its rapt admiration for totalities and to its aversion to analysis. Gestalt psychologists, by further elaboration in their thinking and by experimental approaches might have achieved a set of concepts such as those that describe the structure of intellect, but perhaps for lack of a method like factor analysis they would not have succeeded. Factor theory, with its additive equations, is no doubt anathema to Gestalt psychologists if they pay any attention at all to that theory. In spite of the summative equations of factor theory, factor analysis has not destroyed totalities but has discovered what many of them are like, for example, the products of information mentioned earlier.

In terms of general views and ways of thinking, the kind of factorial psychology of which I have been speaking comes closest to the traditional point of view of functionalism. The easy transition from factors to functions is the simplest indication of this similarity in type of fundamental thinking. Functional psychology never became very systematic, but through factor-analytic findings it could do so. One difference in the two views is that the functionalist has often emphasized Darwinian concepts as explanatory principles. This kind of explanation is not essential to a factorial point of view.

And what of the "dynamic" psychologies? Among this group we generally recognize the psychoanalysts, hormic psychologists, and the Lewinian psychologists. The strong intellectualistic bias of the discussion in this paper, which took its start from the structure of intellect, should not mean that factor analysis has nothing to offer regarding dynamic aspects of behavior. I have skirted this aspect, suggesting that motivation and emotion can be related to the domain of intellect in connection with evaluation. Another important point of contact would be the category of hypothesized behavioral abilities.

A more direct approach to dynamic aspects of behavior, however, is through the analysis of factors of motivation and emotion. Very much has already been done in this direction and Cattell (1957), in particular, has generated considerable theory from factorial information concerning needs, interests, and attitudes. The integration of such theory with that derived from intellectual factors is something still to be done.

SUMMARY

In explaining how factor analysis and its findings can contribute to general psychological theory, the writer described three models, derivable from factor theory or from the results of factor analysis, that apply to personality. Personality is defined as a matter of individual differences with respect to traits. One model is a space of n dimensions, each dimension representing a unique trait that is discoverable by factor analysis. Another model that emphasizes the structure of a typical personality represents traits at several distinct levels of generality, one of the levels being devoted to primary traits. A third model arises from the logical classification of known primary traits in columns and rows to form two- and three-dimensional matrices.

It is also necessary to discuss the adequacy of factor analysis as a method adaptable to the discovery of psychological concepts having theoretical significance. Used in an appropriate type of experimental design and applied to the appropriate kinds of experimental variables, factor analysis can be a powerful tool for the meaningful discrimination among traits. Hypothesis testing of a kind is possible, in spite of inadequate statistical tests of significance.

Although factor analysis starts with data regarding individual differences in behavior and comes out with primary traits that also refer to modes of individual differences, we find it possible to deduce corresponding ways of functioning in behaving organisms. In this manner we see a bridge between factors and functions. The classes of factors, as derived from the third kind of model, suggest general concepts that seem to have theoretical significance for psychology.

From the organization of intellectual factors we derive the impression that the organism is an agent that acquires information, retains it, uses it in generating new information, and evaluates information in connection with any of these steps. Learning is the achieving of information, and the various intellectual abilities are abilities to learn. Similarly, problem-solving rests upon certain combinations of primary abilities, depending upon the circumstances. Reinforcement or effect in learning is accounted for by the operations of evaluation. Drive reduction and effect supply information as bases for evaluation, along with other feedback information. Motives and emotions, too, may be brought under the heading of information that concerns the organism's internal states.

The concept of association is very inadequate in accounting for the kinds of products with which the intellectual abilities are concerned. The products, such as units, systems, transformations, and implications, have about them a totality aspect that calls for something like the concept of Gestalt. The factorial approach offers a form of analysis that should be useful to the Gestalt psychologist as well as to the functional psychologist.

Like behaviorism, the proposed factor psychology applies a completely objective approach and yields objective descriptions. Unlike behaviorism, it aims at the construction of a model of what goes on between stimulus and response rather than a model emphasizing stimulus-response correlations. Also unlike behaviorism, it finds no use for the concept of association and would substitute the concept of cognition-response sequences for that of stimulus-response associations.

From a systematic standpoint, factor psychology is best described as a type of functional psychology, without any close affiliation with the traditional functional school. With further extensions of factor-analytical efforts in the area of dynamics of behavior, we should be able to develop a more complete system than it is possible to present today.

REFERENCES

Burt, C., "The Structure of Mind: A Review of the Results of Factor Analysis," *British Journal of Psychology,* **19** (1949), 100-111, 176-99.

Cattell, R. B., *Personality and Motivation Structure and Measurement.* New York: Harcourt, Brace & World, Inc., 1957.

Eysenck, H. J., "The Organization of Personality," *Journal of Personality,* **20** (1951), 101-17.

Ferguson, G. A., "On Learning and Human Ability," *Canadian Journal of Psychology,* **8** (1954), 95-112.

Fleishman, E. A. and W. E. Hempel, Jr., "Changes in Factor Structure of a Complex Psychomotor Test as a Function of Practice," *Psychometrika,* **19** (1954), 239-52.

———, "The Relation between Abilities and Improvement with Practice in a Visual Discrimination Reaction Time Task," *Journal of Experimental Psychology,* **49** (1955), 301-12.

Guilford, J. P., "Factors in Problem Solving," *ARTC Instructors Journal,* **4** (1954), 197-204.

———, *Personality.* New York: McGraw-Hill Book Company, Inc., 1959. (a)

———, "Three Faces of Intellect," *American Psychologist,* **14** (1959), 469-79. (b)

Guttman, L., "A New Approach to Factor Analysis: The Radex," in *Mathematical Thinking in the Social Sciences,* ed. P. F. Lazarsfeld. New York: Free Press of Glencoe, Inc., 1954.

Lazarsfeld, P. F., "A Conceptual Introduction to Latent Structure Analysis," in *Mathematical Thinking in the Social Sciences,* ed. P. F. Lazarsfeld. New York: Free Press of Glencoe, Inc., 1954.

Maxwell, A. E., "Statistical Methods in Factor Analysis," *Psychological Bulletin,* **56** (1959), 228-35.

Merrifield, P. R., J. P. Guilford, P. R. Christensen, and J. W. Frick, "A Factor-Analytic Study of Problem Solving," *University of Southern California Report of the Psychology Laboratories,* No. 22 (1960).

Miller, N. E., "Shortcomings of Food Consumption as a Measure of Hunger: Results from Other Behavioral Techniques," *Annals of the New York Academy of Science,* **63** (1955), 141-43.

Osgood, C. E., G. J. Suci, and P. H. Tannenbaum, *The Measurement of Meaning.* Urbana: University of Illinois Press, 1957.

Seward, J. P., "Basic Issues in Learning Theory," in *Current Psychological Issues,* eds. G. S. Seward and J. P. Seward. New York: Holt, Rinehart & Winston, Inc., 1958.

———, *The Nature of "Intelligence" and Principles of Cognition.* New York: The Macmillan Company, 1923.

Spearman, C., *Abilities of Man.* New York: The Macmillan Company, 1927.

Vernon, P. E., *The Structure of Abilities.* New York: John Wiley & Sons, Inc., 1950.

PART FIVE

COGNITION, MOTIVATION
AND PERSONALITY

The articles in this section are concerned with the interaction between motivational and cognitive variables. Interesting attempts have been made to specify more clearly the relationship between these two sets of variables: that behavior is a joint function of motivation, and cognition is a major determinant of motivation remain possibilities to be clarified by further research.

A traditional approach is taken by Henle in her discussion of "how needs and attitudes influence cognitive processes." She advances cogent arguments to support the thesis that motivation affects cognition, but equally plausible is the almost diametrically opposite thesis, advanced by Prentice, that "what we call motives are really a particular kind of perceptual or cognitive event." Prentice also calls attention to the almost virtual neglect "of acts that are carried on for their own sake." He suggests that esthetics could be a fruitful area of study.

Writing independently of Prentice's suggestion, Wallach does much to make explicit the interaction between cognition and motivation in esthetic experiences. Perhaps educators more than psychologists, have ignored esthetic experiences and other "activities for their own sake." And yet no one can, and surely an educator would not want to, argue that esthetic experiences are unimportant or irrelevant aspects of human behavior.

Schachter and Singer advance the hypothesis and offer experimental evidence that emotional states are a joint function of physiological arousal and cognition. The crucial role played by cognition in motivation can be seen in the ease with which emotional states can be induced when the individual's cognitions are inappropriate to, or conflicting with, the physiological activity. Their research raises questions about the adequacy of the arousal or activation theory of motivation, however elegant and unifying that theory may be.

Still another and important approach to the relationship between cognitive functions and personality characteristics has been the study of categorizing styles, by Pettigrew, Wallach, and Caron, and by Bruner and Tajfel. They have identified broad and narrow categorizers of stimuli and have shown that this categorizing style is closely associated with nonintellectual factors.

Rhine indicates in his article how mediational and concept-formation theory can be used to explain attitude development. In a similar fashion Berkowitz applies the principles of judgmental contrast and assimilation from psychophysics to "personality functioning." These two articles support the contention that cognitive processes are significant aspects of motivation, but they also suggest that there may be a greater unity underlying all psychological processes than has been observed in the past.

The remaining articles are all concerned with the motivating properties of cognitive dissonance, or symbolic conflict. Festinger's concept of cognitive dissonance and the consequent striving to reduce dissonance is useful in explaining diverse behaviors including resistance to extinction as a result of partial and delayed reward. Secord and Bachman make use of a similar concept with reference to interpersonal behavior. They hypothesize that an individual is motivated to obtain congruency among three cognitive elements: (1) beliefs about self, (2) observation of one's behavior, and (3) beliefs about others. Much of human behavior is viewed by these authors as attempts to reduce dissonance or incongruities. Berlyne takes a somewhat more general view, summarizes much of the literature, and relates conceptual conflict to the arousal theory of motivation. In addition, Berlyne develops a theory explaining the acquisition of knowledge in terms of resolutions of symbolic conflicts.

The above remarks are but a few hints of the viable ideas that can be found in the articles selected for this section. The reader may wish to disagree with the major trend that we think emerges from the writings. This concerns the unity of psychological processes, a unity that becomes periodically apparent through the diversity of contemporary approaches to cognitive processes. Teachers have a tendency to think that the motivation of the student must be changed before his thoughts and beliefs will be changed. In the light of recent research and theory, it might be more fruitful to think in terms of changing thoughts and beliefs—this in turn will affect motivation. A careful consideration of this material should generate a host of hypotheses that the teacher can explore in the classroom.

Some Effects of Motivational Processes on Cognition *

Mary Henle

Work on the influence of needs and attitudes on perception and other cognitive processes has proceeded with insufficient analysis of the problem. It is the purpose of the present paper to outline a number of possible effects of motivational processes on cognitive ones. The influences to be described are regarded neither as established nor as exhaustive, but are offered as hypotheses for future research.

Frequently it seems to be tacitly assumed that the mere presence of a need or attitude is sufficient to account for an observed effect. The task of research has become, therefore, one of relating the presence or absence of particular motivational conditions to quantitative variations in performance on cognitive tasks. The point of view to be presented here is, rather, that the finding of such a correlation only opens up a problem: that of understanding *how* motivation influences cognition (cf. 44; also 6, p. 139).

The point may be illustrated by reference to the question of the effect of attitudes on recall of controversial material. There is some evidence to indicate that we remember material we agree with better than apparently equivalent material with which we disagree (for example, 14, 32). That we

agree with certain points is no explanation of their superiority in recall. But if we take this finding as a point of departure, it is indeed possible to find plausible reasons why material we agree with should be favored in memory. These are, of course, only hypotheses which require independent testing. (*a*) It may be suggested that an attitude functions as context for related material (cf. 5, p. 582). Presented data are understood in relation to the subject's existing attitudinal structure. Items which are in harmony with the attitude find their place in the structure in a simpler and more direct manner than does opposing material. There seems to be little doubt—although it needs to be demonstrated for material comparable to that used in the studies on recall of controversial material—that structured material is better recalled than unrelated items (24). The superior recall of items we agree with might follow, then, from the advantage of structured over unstructured data in memory. (*b*) Material we agree with may be better recalled because it is better understood than material which opposes our own attitude. Material which is understood is known to fare better in memory than that which we do not understand (24). A point we agree with is not, of course, better understood just *because* we agree with it, but because we have thought about it, have placed it in context, and so forth. Nor are data

* From Mary Henle, "Some Effects of Motivational Processes on Cognition," *Psychological Review*, **62** (1955), 423-52. Reprinted by permission of the author and the American Psychological Association.

that confirm our attitudes always better understood; an insult may be very well understood. (*c*) Facts and arguments we agree with may have an advantage in memory over opposing ones when they are, to start with, more familiar. (*d*) Material we agree with may be received in a more friendly manner, while that with which we disagree may be rejected at the outset, regarded as nonsense, and so forth. The former condition is, very likely, the more favorable for recall. Other things being equal, material to which we have given attention is favored in memory. (*e*) Intention to recall, a factor known to be important for memory, may operate to favor items with which we agree.[1] We may try to remember certain points because we wish to refer to them again, to use them in argument, because they are flattering to us, and so forth.

Repression will not be discussed in the present connection because, even if it operates in the experiments under consideration, there would seem to be no way of knowing that it does. It would be necessary to have detailed knowledge of the repressions of individual subjects in order to guess what new data might be repressed by association with them. It is, in addition, highly unlikely that the experiments which deal with the recall of controversial material have set up the conditions necessary to produce repression.

While there is evidence that makes the above hypotheses seem plausible, it is also becoming recognized that

[1] We are not concerned here with the problem of how intention operates in memory. It should be pointed out, however, that the intention does not impose itself on recall, but seems to act by altering other known conditions of recall. The problem of the influence of intentions on cognitive processes may be of the same order as the problem here under consideration.

there are conditions under which material which opposes our attitudes is favored in recall (cf. 2, 4). We may begin to define these conditions too. (*a*) We may remember something that disturbs us precisely because it does not fit into our schema. It might be that when an attitudinal structure is ripe for change, such disturbing, contradictory material is favored, while the organizing effects of attitudes enhance recall of confirming material at other times. (*b*) Points we disagree with may stand out, in contrast to repeated evidence for something we believe. It is known that such outstandingness can favor recall. The fact that outstanding items within a system are favored does not, of course, contradict the statement made earlier that structured data are more likely than unorganized ones to be well recalled. (*c*) We may remember something in order to refute it, to accuse somebody of it, in some way to cope with it, and so on. Intention to recall, in the service of some other need, may also favor the opposing material.

Finally, certain attitudes may operate to produce about equal recall of material we agree with and of that with which we disagree—for example, an objective attitude, a desire to be fair, to hear both sides of the case, a wish to recall as much as possible so as to do well in the recall test, and so forth (2).

It is clear from the variety of hypotheses presented above that it is necessary to have detailed information about a particular subject's understanding of, and attitude toward, the presented material if we are to attempt any predictions about the kind of material which will be favored in recall. It will also be clear that the really interesting problems about motivational factors in recall are not confined to the favoring of some particular kind of material, but concern also the qualitative dimensions of the individual subject's pattern of recall, involving the kinds of processes suggested here. It may even be that the individual's pattern of recall of personally relevant material is so distinctive that, in the hands of a skilled clinician, it may yield projective data which agree well with personal information derived from interview and projective methods.[2]

The above hypotheses, it will be noted, seek the effects of attitudes on remembering *in terms of factors known to favor or inhibit recall*. They introduce no new determinants, but are largely statements of ways in which attitudes might alter the structural conditions of recall.

By contrast, much of the interest of current research in this field has been to find distortions of cognitive processes by needs and attitudes. Such distortions undoubtedly occur, although their frequency under normal conditions may be questioned. But it is here suggested that the influence of motivational processes on cognitive ones is not limited to distortions, and that such effects are not necessarily the ones most likely to give us an understanding of the processes involved. Rather, as has been pointed out elsewhere (22), a possibly more fruitful starting point for research would seem to be to look for changes by motivational processes *in accordance with*

the nature of the material on which they act.[3] The present paper will seek to describe ways in which needs and attitudes may alter cognitive processes in a manner that does not violate the presented structure.

As is implied in the above remarks, it is maintained here that motivational processes may influence, but do not produce, cognitive organization. A vector (for example, a need, expectation, intention, or attitude) or a trace system can influence a perceived form or another memory trace only if the latter already exists. The problem, as Wallach (52) has pointed out, is to determine the stage of organization to which a visual process must develop before central factors can influence it.[4]

To see motivational processes as operating through the presented structure is not, however, to deny the influence of needs and attitudes on cognition. In a recent paper, Postman (38) seems to reduce such influences to others which are not themselves motivational, viz., set and past experience. Certainly the latter processes have important influences on cognitive ones, and motivation *may* act on cognition through them. Furthermore, they seem to cut across a number of the other influences of needs and attitudes; but it will be maintained in the paragraphs that follow that they by no means fully account for the effects in question.

[2] I am indebted to Florence R. Miale for a preliminary demonstration of this kind.

Alper and Korchin (4, p. 35) make a similar suggestion: ". . . selective recall may well function here as it does in the so-called projective tests: the subject reacts to the material selectively in terms of his needs and tension-systems, the products of his recall being themselves projections of these needs and tension-systems." These authors fail, however, to follow up their suggestion with detailed comparisons of recall and personality data of individual subjects.

[3] The theoretical consequences of taking distortions as the paradigm of the influence of needs and attitudes on cognition have been shown elsewhere (22).

[4] The present writer fails to see how the assumption of *unbewusster Schluss* (for example, 9) solves this problem. In order to initiate processes of inference or recall, perceptual data must already be organized. We cannot make inferences about an object until we can perceive it; the inferences thus do not account for, but presuppose, the perception.

We are not concerned here with imagination, wishing, and so forth, which for present purposes may be considered to be very largely determined by motivational factors.[5] Rather, the present discussion is limited to some of the interactions which occur between motivational and structural determinants of cognition.

The following hypotheses are offered as possible modes of influence of needs and attitudes on cognitive processes. They may guide, but they do not, of course, take the place of concrete analysis of particular problems. Some of these hypotheses are already to be found in the literature. Others seem to derive some support from existing studies, even though these were not specifically designed to test them. In the case of still other hypotheses, the task of testing them remains for the future.

1. A need or attitude may operate as a vector, pointing in one direction rather than other. It is sometimes possible, under the influence of a need or attitude, to find an item which would otherwise be unnoticed in the perceptual field. This is easy to demonstrate with camouflaged items. Likewise, a recall vector may bring things to mind that do not occur spontaneously. (Of course the search refers to memory traces established in the past. The vector, to be effective, must have something to point to; aroused traces, supplying this, enable the vector to be effective. Here, as in other effects to be discussed below, the attitude or need operates in cooperation with the individual's past experience.)

It is likely that effects of pointing

may be demonstrated with other vectors besides simple search vectors in perception and memory. It seems that, under the influence of a need or attitude, we are attuned to events to which we would not otherwise be sensitive. Under the pressure of an unresolved need, we find things to be angry or worried or hurt about.

This hypothesis seems to be essentially the same as earlier views of Bruner and Postman, and others (for example, 9, 42) on selective sensitization to valued or needed aspects of the environment. In later writings these authors seem to regard this process as a function of expectancies or "hypotheses" only. Postman, for example, states that "There is little evidence for direct sensitizing effects of motivational conditions on perception" (38, p. 99). It is here suggested that this function needs to be re-examined with respect to motivational states.

Some experimental work on the relation of recognition thresholds to motivational states seems to be relevant. If these studies have indeed demonstrated a lowering of threshold for need-related material that cannot be accounted for by differential frequency or the operation of specific expectancies, a process of pointing may be operating. For example, Postman and Brown (39) have shown that experiences of success attune the individual to tachistoscopically presented goal words (for example, "succeeded"), while after failure the subject is relatively more sensitive to deprivation words (for example, "obstacle," "failure"). A possible interpretation of this finding is that the persisting mood attunes the individual to material congruent with it. McClelland and Liberman (34) report comparable results for individuals differing in the strength of their need for achievement. For example, subjects

---

[5] This is probably an oversimplification. It would be worth knowing to what extent even these processes are limited by our knowledge, experience and assumptions—both conscious and unconscious—about ourselves and about reality.

(Ss) with a strong need for achievement recognized goal and instrumental words relating to achievement (for example, "success," "achieve") faster than those whose need was weak. Two studies on the influence of hunger on perceptual sensitivity to need-related material seem also to be relevant. Lazarus, Yousem, and Arenberg (31) report that recognition thresholds for photographs of food objects declined with increasing hours of food deprivation (within limits set by the habitual eating cycle), and Wispé and Drambarean (54) found that need-related words were recognized more rapidly than neutral ones under conditions of food and water deprivation, but not when Ss were satisfied.

These experiments need to be repeated under conditions where possible sets for need-related items are not allowed to develop during the experimental series. For example, the relative sensitivity to the *first* need-related item in the series should be studied (cf. 28). If the findings should be confirmed under these conditions, they would suggest the operation of the kind of sensitization to need-related material here described as pointing.

2. Closely related to pointing may be the organizing effects of needs and attitudes. Within certain limits we can voluntarily influence organizations in the perceptual field, grouping together items which would not spontaneously go together. Likewise in recall, interaction between a process and a trace which would not occur spontaneously may take place under the influence of a vector (27). In the case of other cognitive processes, the same organizing effects of needs suggest themselves. It is a fact of common observation that when a strong need or interest is aroused, the facts of experience organize themselves around it. When I am working on a scientific problem, for example, everything I read appears to bear on the issues with which I am concerned. It seems that under the influence of an aroused need we perceive similarities not otherwise noticeable. These vectors, I repeat, operate in conjunction with the individual's knowledge and previous experience. But here, as in the cases that follow, it is insufficient to refer to past experience alone.

3. The perception of other relations is likewise influenced by needs and attitudes. It has been suggested that under the influence of an aroused need, the psychological field may be restructured so that learning occurs (1). For example, an object previously seen as unrelated to a goal may come to be perceived as the means to attaining it, one event may acquire the meaning of a signal for another, etc.

4. An aroused need or attitude may act on cognition by selection among the various possibilities presented. This hypothesis has frequently appeared in the literature. It has not, however, customarily been separated from sensitization or pointing, as discussed above (for example, 9, 42).

The following example, among the many possible, illustrates the selective effect of an attitude in cognition. If two individuals who hold opposed attitudes are presented with a given fact, they do not necessarily perceive the same fact, but each may select for it a different meaning out of several possibilities it presents. As Asch puts it (5, p. 584): "One can observe much adroitness in the manipulation of meanings in the interests of an undisturbed outlook." Selective effects of needs and attitudes are most familiar from the projective methods. In the Rorschach, for instance, a variety of interpretations may be given to a similarly perceived portion of a blot; consider, for example, the variety of actions attributed by different individuals to the animals in the side details in Card VIII. Examples of this kind could be multiplied.

The experimental literature provides comparable examples. Sanford (46, 47) and Levine, Chein, and Murphy (33) found that hungry subjects gave more food responses in the interpretation of incomplete or ambiguous pictures than did satisfied ones, and that the effect increased (within limits) as hunger increased. (The effect of the need cannot, however, be separated from possible selective effects of a food set, in the experiment of Levine, Chein, and Murphy.) There appears to be a selection of need-relevant interpretations from among the many meanings the ambiguous material could be given.

5. The need or attitude may supply context. Since the context may influence decisively the manner in which an item is experienced, it follows that a given item may be differently viewed in accordance with the need or attitude aroused. This effect of attitudes was illustrated above in the case of a problem of memory. Needs may be expected to have comparable effects, since they function typically in need-object organizations or "sentiments."

6. One particular effect of the fact that needs and attitudes function as temporally extended organizations deserves special mention: memory traces relevant to these organizations may be aroused. Past experience has important effects on cognitive processes, of which the more relevant in the present connection may be such effects as the contributing of meanings, the establishing of norms or adaptation levels (20), and the rendering commonplace of some item of experience so that it is overlooked or its significance lessened in the cognitive field. Past experience likewise facilitates perception under conditions of reduced stimulation (37, 21, 23, 49, 50; but cf. also 17, 29). It probably acts also as a selective factor, favoring certain possibilities among those which are structurally given (for example, 13, 53).

These effects of past experience have been demonstrated in cognitive situations having little bearing on subjects' needs and attitudes. The work on the role of past experience needs to be extended to other cognitive situations which have motivational relevance.

7. A need may arouse an expectation, which is known to have certain effects on cognitive processes. For example, Titchener long ago formulated a principle of prior entry. "The stimulus for which we are predisposed requires less time than a like stimulus, for which we are unprepared, to produce its full conscious effect" (51, p. 251). The sensitizing, organizing, and selective effects of sets have been mentioned above. Bruner has suggested that the function of expectancies "is to re-order the availability of traces" (7, p. 307; cf. previous hypothesis). A number of recent experiments have dealt with the effects of sets on cognitive processes and the conditions under which they operate (for example, 41, 10, 11). It is clearly important to distinguish between direct effects of motivational processes on cognition and their indirect effects through the arousal of expectations, which frequently have similar consequences (cf. 38).

Postman and Crutchfield (43) have recently discussed the arousal of expectations by a state of need. These authors presented incomplete words for completion, varying the intensity of hunger of their Ss and the degree of selective set for food responses. They found the effects of set in determining food responses to be larger than those of differing intensities of hunger; the relationship between the latter and frequency of food responses depended largely on S's expectation for such responses. They conclude (p. 217): *"Intensity of need is one of the variables which modifies the operation of such general principles of cognition as selective 'set' within limits defined by the characteristics of the stimulus-materials."*

8. Needs or attitudes may make us unwilling to ask certain questions, discourage the desire to understand, keep us from considering relevant evidence or from seeing the relevance of presented evidence. They may narrow the mental field (1, 5), with significant consequences for cognition. Much current work has been concerned with such influences (for example, the effects of prejudice, the clouding of judgment by strong emotion). These effects are not, at the outset, to be dismissed as entirely automatic evasions. Reasons are frequently used in these instances to give them at least the appearance of sense. The cognitive processes involved need to be understood.

9. Needs or attitudes, in a manner closely related to the last-mentioned effect, may cause us to overlook differences, to fail to make distinctions, just as in the perceptual field a great contrast may make us fail to see a lesser one. For example, several years ago the writer heard a debate on a perceptual problem held before a group which was bitterly opposed to the use of the experimental method in psychology. The audience seemed not to know that a debate was going on but attacked both speakers alike for dissecting their human subject matter. They saw no important difference between the two positions presented. Common experience suggests similar phenomena in the realm of social and political attitudes. To a conservative person everything

left of center may seem to be radical, while the more radical individual may regard everything right of center as reactionary. The range over which fine distinctions can be made appears to be shortened.

10. A possible effect of needs and attitudes is a specific disturbance of recognition and recall. Some evidence suggests that individuals who are shown, by independent methods, to differ in the extent to which given experimental material is disturbing to them, show corresponding differences in their recognition thresholds for such material (15, 16, 30). If these findings are confirmed, and if alternative explanations (for example, differential readiness to report) can be eliminated, a disturbance of the recognition of certain kinds of threatening material suggests itself. Again, the facts of repression, insofar as this mechanism involves forgetting, raise a similar problem.

How might such a disturbance of recognition and recall operate? The phenomena of repression suggest that it is not a matter of destruction of memory traces; for repressed material to express itself in dreams, symptoms, and other disguises requires that the corresponding traces be intact. The disturbance seems, rather, to concern that interaction between process and trace, based on their similarity, which underlies recognition and is the first step in the process of recall by association. (For a discussion of the selective influence of similarity in recognition and recall, cf. Köhler, 26, pp. 126 ff.)

It is very tentatively suggested, then, that a vector may operate to prevent that interaction between a present process and a memory trace which is necessary for recognition and recall.

11. Needs and attitudes may act on the physiognomic properties of experience. Consider, for example, the

change which can sometimes be noted in a person's appearance for us with the change from acquaintance to friendship. That the change is not a matter of familiarity alone is suggested by the fact that such physiognomic changes seem to be much less pronounced when increasing acquaintance is not accompanied by friendship. It is true that the friend looks upon us with a more kindly eye than the mere acquaintance, may be happier and more relaxed with us, and so forth, so that some of the perceived change is accounted for by actual changes in his appearance. It is worth considering, however, whether changes in the person's physiognomic properties— changes which transcend differences in mood—may not be, in part, a function of the attitudes and sentiments we have for him.

It might be that, if Murray (35) has demonstrated a genuine influence of fear on judgments of maliciousness, it is of the nature of an effect on physiognomic properties. (Other interpretations, however, are possible.)

12. Needs or attitudes may animate, enliven, activate, or give outstanding position to relevant parts of the cognitive field. These effects, in turn have certain consequences for cognition.[6] In a very real sense the significant person stands out in a group. The effects of outstanding position in per-

ception, memory, and thinking are well known. As another example the possibility is suggested that Zeigarnik's main result—the favoring of incomplete over completed tasks in recall (55)—may be accounted for if it can be assumed that need tension may in some way make a trace more lively or more active and thus increase its availability. Gilchrist and Nesberg (18) have reported an experiment which suggests an interpretation in these terms. Hungry and thirsty subjects were asked to match the illuminance of just previously projected pictures of need-relevant objects. Increasing need gave rise to increasingly bright matches. In the case of thirsty subjects, the error dropped to its starting level immediately after drinking. If such a result should be confirmed, it could be viewed as an instance of the enlivening effect of need in immediate memory.

13. A strong need or interest leads us to exert efforts in its service. These may show themselves in increased efficiency in cognitive tasks, while a relaxation of effort reduces efficiency. In the case of excessive effort there may be a disruption of performance. A number of studies seem to permit interpretation in these terms rather than in terms of actual perceptual change.

Bruner and Postman (8) found that when Ss were given electric shock during a task, they judged the size of a disc which figured in the task as accurately as control Ss; but when the shock was removed, their size judgments increased. Since magnification in size is here equivalent to increased inaccuracy, it is suggested that this effect is not a matter of "posttension expansion" in perception, but of relaxation of efforts in a judging task. In another study (40) the same authors found that Ss who had been

[6] This hypothesis does not depend upon a principle of "prior entry" (9, p. 96). It sounds like some of Bruner and Postman's statements about perceptual "accentuation" (for example, 9, p. 100). In practice, however, these authors have used accentuation only to mean increase in preceived size. As such, it comes under the heading of perceptual distortions, which are not being discussed here. In the present writer's opinion, accentuation of perceived size has, in any case, not been demonstrated as a function of value, with autochthonous factors properly controlled (cf. 2, 12, 19, 25, 36).

harassed and badgered during an impossible perceptual task showed higher recognition thresholds in another perceptual situation than control Ss, as well as premature and frequently nonsensical prerecognition hypotheses. It seems plausible to regard these findings as indications of disruption of test performance as a result of the actually reported excessive efforts of the experimental Ss. Rosen (45), on the other hand, found that Ss who were able to avoid an electric shock by correct perception had lower recognition thresholds for nonsense syllables than members of a control group who did not receive shock. Here it would seem that added, but not excessive, effort increased efficiency of test performance.

Other reports suggest comparable effects of attitudes in perception and memory. Allport and Kramer (3) found that anti-Semitic individuals were able to identify photographs of Jewish and non-Jewish faces more accurately than Ss free of prejudice. The result is attributed to the greater importance of racial identity to prejudiced persons. Similarly Seeleman (48) found that different attitudes led to different degrees of effort and attention to an exposure series, with consequent differences of performance in a recognition test. Thus individuals with favorable attitudes toward the Negro correctly recognized more Negro photographs than did anti-Negro Ss.

Such differences in performance are, of course, to be distinguished from actual cognitive change under the influence of a need or attitude.[7]

------

[7] Postman (38) has discussed other motivational influences on performance in perceptual experiments, including the matter of selective reporting, which is a serious problem for all attempts to study possible differences in the perception of emotional and neutral material.

SUMMARY

This paper has been concerned with the question of how needs and attitudes influence cognitive processes. The attempt has been made to describe ways in which motivational processes alter cognitive ones in accordance with the nature of the material on which they act. It was suggested that needs and attitudes may act by pointing or sensitizing, organizing and reorganizing, selecting, supplying context, arousing relevant memory traces, arousing expectations, discouraging the desire to understand, obscuring differences, disturbing the recognition process, altering the physiognomic properties of experience, and animating or enlivening aspects of experience. In addition, strength of motivation may influence performance on perceptual or other cognitive tasks without producing actual cognitive change.

REFERENCES

1. Adams, D. K., "A Restatement of the Problem of Learning," *British Journal of Psychology,* **22** (1931), 150-78.

2. Adelman, C. *et al.,* "An Investigation of the Influence of Needs and Attitudes on Perception and Memory." (Unpublished research, New School for Social Research, 1951.)

3. Allport, G. W. and B. M. Kramer, "Some Roots of Prejudice," *Journal of Psychology,* **22** (1946), 9-39.

4. Alper, Thelma G. and S. J. Korchin, "Memory for Socially Relevant Material," *Journal of Abnormal Social Psychology,* **47** (1952), 25-37.

5. Asch, S. E., *Social Psychology.* Englewood Cliffs, N. J.: Prentice-Hall, Inc., 1952.

6. Bruner, J. S., "Personality Dynamics and the Process of Perceiving," in *Perception: An Approach to Personality,* eds. R. R. Blake and G. V. Ramsey. New York: The Ronald Press Company, 1951.

7. ———, "One Kind of Perception: A Reply to Professor Luchins," *Psychological Review,* **58** (1951), 306-12.

8. Bruner, J. S. and L. Postman, "Tension and Tension Release as Organizing Factors in Perception," *Journal of Personality,* **15** (1947), 300-308.

9. ———, "An Approach to Social Perception," in *Current Trends in Social Psychology.* Pittsburgh: University of Pittsburgh Press, 1948.

10. ———, "On the Perception of Incongruity: A Paradigm," *Journal of Personality,* **18** (1949), 206-23.

11. Bruner, J. S., L. Postman, and J. Rodrigues, "Expectation and the Perception of Color," *American Journal of Psychology,* **64** (1951), 216-27.

12. Carter, L. and K. Schooler, "Value, Need, and Other Factors in Perception," *Psychological Review,* **56** (1949), 200-207.

13. Djang, S., "The Role of Past Experience in the Visual Apprehension of Masked Forms," *Journal of Experimental Psychology,* **20** (1937), 29-59.

14. Edwards, A. L., "Political Frames of Reference as a Factor Influencing Recognition," *Journal of Abnormal Social Psychology,* **36** (1941), 34-50.

15. Eriksen, C. W., "Perceptual Defense as a Function of Unacceptable Needs," *Journal of Abnormal Social Psychology,* **46** (1951), 557-64.

16. ———, "Defense Against Ego-threat in Memory and Perception," *Journal of Abnormal Social Psychology,* **47** (1952), 230-35.

17. ———, "The Case for Perceptual Defense," *Psychological Review,* **61** (1954), 175-82.

18. Gilchrist, J. C. and L. S. Nesberg, "Need and Perceptual Change in Need-related Objects," *Journal of Experimental Psychology,* **44** (1952), 369-76.

19. Golden, S., "An Experimental Investigation into Some Factors that Determine the Perception of Size." (Unpublished Master's thesis, New School for Social Research, 1950.)

20. Helson, H., "Adaptation-level as a Basis for a Quantitative Theory of Frames of Reference," *Psychological Review,* **55** (1948), 297-313.

21. Henle, Mary, "An Experimental Investigation of Past Experience as a Determinant of Visual Form Perception," *Journal of Experimental Psychology,* **30** (1942), 1-22.

22. Henle, Mary and M. Michael, "The Influence of Attitudes on Syllogistic Reasoning," *Journal of Social Psychology.* (In press.)

23. Howes, D. H. and R. L. Solomon, "Visual Duration Threshold as a Function of Word-probability," *Journal of Experimental Psychology,* **41** (1951), 401-10.

24. Katona, G., *Organizing and Memorizing.* New York: Columbia University Press, 1940.

25. Klein, G., H. Schlesinger, and D. Meister, "The Effect of Personal Values on Perception: An Experimental Critique," *Psychological Review,* **58** (1951), 96-112.

26. Köhler, W., *Dynamics in Psychology.* New York: The Liveright Corp., 1940.

27. Köhler, W. and H. von Restorff, "Zur Theorie der Reproduktion," *Psychol. Forsch.,* **21** (1935), 56-112.

28. Lacy, O. W., N. Lewinger, and J. F. Adamson, "Foreknowledge as a Factor Affecting Perceptual Defense and Alertness," *Journal of Experimental Psychology,* **45** (1953), 169-74.

29. Lazarus, R. S., "Is There a Mechanism of Perceptual Defense? A Reply to Postman, Bronson, and Gropper," *Journal of Abnormal Social Psychology,* **49** (1954), 396-98.

30. Lazarus, R. S., C. W. Eriksen, and C. P. Fonda, "Personality Dynamics and Auditory Perceptual Recognition," *Journal of Personality,* **19** (1951), 471-82.

31. Lazarus, R. S., H. Yousem, and D. Arenberg, "Hunger and Perception," *Journal of Personality,* **21** (1953), 312-28.

32. Levine, J. M. and G. Murphy, "The Learning and Forgetting of Contro-

versial Material," *Journal of Abnormal Psychology,* **38** (1943), 507-17.

33. Levine, R., I. Chein, and G. Murphy, "The Relation of the Intensity of a Need to the Amount of Perceptual Distortion: A Preliminary Report," *Journal of Psychology,* **13** (1942), 283-93.

34. McClelland, D., and A. Liberman, "The Effect of Need for Achievement on Recognition of Need-related Words," *Journal of Personality,* **18** (1949), 236-51.

35. Murray, H. A., "The Effect of Fear upon Estimates of the Maliciousness of Other Personalities," *Journal of Social Psychology,* **4** (1933), 310-29.

36. Norton, E. N., "Is Symbolic Value an Organizing Factor in Perception?" (Unpublished Master's thesis, New School for Social Research, 1950.)

37. Ortner, A., "Nachweis der Retentionsstörung beim Erkennen," *Psychol. Forsch.,* **22** (1937), 59-88.

38. Postman, L., "The Experimental Analysis of Motivational Factors in Perception," in *Current Theory and Research in Motivation.* Lincoln: University of Nebraska Press, 1953.

39. Postman, L. and D. Brown, "Perceptual Consequences of Success and Failure," *Journal of Abnormal Social Psychology,* **47** (1952), 213-21.

40. Postman, L. and J. S. Bruner, "Perception Under Stress," *Psychological Review,* **55** (1948), 314-23.

41. ———, "Multiplicity of Set as a Determinant of Perceptual Behavior," *Journal of Experimental Psychology,* **39** (1949), 369-77.

42. Postman, L., J. S. Bruner, and E. McGinnies, "Personal Values as Selective Factors in Perception," *Journal of Abnormal Psychology,* **43** (1948), 142-54.

43. Postman, L. and R. S. Crutchfield, "The Interaction of Need, Set and Stimulus-structure in a Cognitive Task," *American Journal of Psychology,* **65** (1952), 196-217.

44. Prentice, W. C. H., "Conceptual Trends in Perception." Paper read at the American Psychological Association, New York, 1954.

45. Rosen, A. C., "Change in Perceptual Threshold as a Protective Function of the Organism," *Journal of Personality,* **23** (1954), 182-94.

46. Sanford, R. N., "The Effects of Abstinence from Food upon Imaginal Processes: A Preliminary Experiment," *Journal of Psychology,* **2** (1936), 129-36.

47. ———, "The Effects of Abstinence from Food upon Imaginal Processes: A Further Experiment," *Journal of Psychology,* **3** (1937), 145-59.

48. Seeleman, V., "The Influence of Attitude upon the Remembering of Pictorial Material," *Archives of Psychology,* **258** (1940).

49. Solomon, R. L. and D. H. Howes, "Word Frequency, Personal Values, and Visual Duration Thresholds," *Psychological Review,* **58** (1951), 256-70.

50. Solomon, R. L. and L. Postman, "Frequency of Usage as a Determinant of Recognition Thresholds for Words," *Journal of Experimental Psychology,* **43** (1952), 195-201.

51. Titchener, E. B., *Lectures on the Elementary Psychology of Feeling and Attention.* New York: The MacMillan Company, 1908.

52. Wallach, H., "Some Considerations Concerning the Relation between Perception and Cognition," *Journal of Personality,* **18** (1949), 6-13.

53. Wallach, H., D. N. O'Connell, and U. Neisser, "The Memory Effect of Visual Perception of Three-dimensional Form," *Journal of Experimental Psychology,* **45** (1953), 360-68.

54. Wispé, L. G. and N. C. Drambarean, "Physiological Need, Word Frequency, and Visual Duration Thresholds," *Journal of Experimental Psychology,* **46** (1953), 25-31.

55. Zeigarnik, B., "Das Behalten erledigter und underledigter Handlungen," *Psychol. Forsch.,* **9** (1927), 1-85.

Some Cognitive Aspects of Motivation *

William C. H. Prentice

Ideally, a presidential address should be a contribution to knowledge. Unfortunately, we are not always wise enough to choose presidents who can provide such a contribution. In my case, I can plead circumstance and thereby assure you without what might seem like false modesty that I am a president who cannot supply you with new and exciting facts. For reasons that are unimportant to you, I have been unable to get back into the laboratory for a number of years. Instead I dream about what I would like to do were I free to enter a new field of research and explore a new set of techniques. Perhaps I shall regain that freedom. In the meantime, I should like to share with you some of my dreams and hope that you may be inspired to do some of the exploring yourselves.

Off and on for a number of years, I have been identified with a controversial point of view, namely, the view that perception is not governed by motivation. Today I shall introduce a new element of controversy by turning the topic upside down and asking you to consider the possibility that what we call motives are really a particular

kind of perceptual or cognitive event. To some of you that may sound like nonsense or worse, but let me see if I cannot make some kind of sense out of it for you. Certainly motivational theory is in the doldrums, and if I can suggest a new slant on old problems, some good may result even from views that you ultimately reject, just so long as you reject them on empirical grounds—which will mean doing new research and adding to our pathetically small store of facts in the field of human motivation.

Partly because scientists are intelligent and versatile and diligent in their search for chinks in the armor of nature through which to peer for understanding, partly because of the extraordinary complexity of human psychological problems, and partly through accidents of the history of our discipline, we have come to mean several different things when we refer to understanding or explanation in psychology. To some of us, it is clear that a satisfactory explanation of a human activity must be made in neurological terms; to others, the explanatory framework can only be that of depth psychology; to still others, introspection or self-description may provide satisfactory accounts; and finally, a large group of us feels that some kind of formal theoretical model ultimately provides the only satisfactory clarification of the question "Why?" as it relates to human behavior. The approaches I have listed

* From W. C. H. Prentice, "Some Cognitive Aspects of Motivation," *American Psychologist,* 16 (1961), 503-11. Reprinted by permission of the author and the American Psychological Association.

Delivered September 1960 in Chicago, Illinois, as the address of the retiring President of the Division of General Psychology of the American Psychological Association.

are not mutually exclusive, some combinations and overlap are possible; or some of us may hold to one for certain kinds of problem and another for certain others, depending on the stage of development of information in the particular case.

What I wish to suggest, however, is that our stage of development in the field of motivation is so primitive that none of these implicit definitions of "understanding" in psychology is appropriate, and that instead we should be searching for laws of behavior in what I can only call, with gratitude to (but also with apology to) Kurt Lewin, cognitive structure.

Consider with me a single case. Smith has struck Jones a violent blow. The psychologist is called on to tell why he did it.

In our present state of ignorance, no neurological answer is possible, and if it were, it would merely push the question back one step: why did that set of neurological patterns occur?

An account in terms of unconscious wishes and fears or of struggles between ego and superego may provide some intellectual satisfaction, but it leaves us in doubt about how we may ever predict such outbreaks in the future or how we may prevent them. In short, it gives us an idiosyncratic account that cannot be generalized very usefully. Moreover, there are systematic difficulties resulting from our ignorance and the consequent necessity of our relying on a large number of highly questionable assumptions.

If we turn instead to the culprit's own account of his motivation, we may get some interesting information, but we are very likely to get one of the following answers or some variant of it. "I don't know." "I don't like him." "I was angry." "It seemed like a good idea at the time." None of these helps much. Even the three last, which

seem to hint at something useful, inspire primarily the further question, "But why?" When we ask it in such cases, we increase our chances of finally getting the inevitable, "I don't know."

Formal models are appealing. Modern behavior theory in its several forms does give at its best the possibility of deducing from antecedent conditions the behavior that must occur. A highly satisfactory kind of "understanding" to be sure, and probably for most of us an ultimate one. The trouble is that behavior theory is based on very primitive postulates, ones drawn from research on sharply limited kinds of behavior, and in 1960 it simply is not capable of encompassing our problems. It will not be able to help us until the complexities of human adult behavior have been reduced to manageable dimensions by careful descriptive investigation. Only then will we be able to discover whether or not the dimensions of maze and Skinner box can be adapted to fit the psychological problems of everyday life. And it is in the hope of stimulating your interest in that task that I stand before you today.

We desperately need to discover the dimensions of motivated behavior, and I think we are ready to make a start on that voyage of discovery if we will only take a careful and systematic but unbiased look at the phenomena of motivation. I think we can find there clues for a structural approach to our common problems that can lead in time to the construction of genuinely helpful formal models and deductive systems.

Let me return to Smith. There is one kind of comment the psychologist might make that strikes me as helpful. He may say, "He was jealous." There is a surprising amount of psychological content and tentative understanding of Smith's behavior embedded in that simple statement. We at least think we understand what it means to be jealous and what sort of behavior can be expected to ensue. By saying he was jealous, we are describing in a crude way a moderately complex psychological pattern. Jealousy can only be understood as involvement in a particular kind of interpersonal relationship and the holding of certain kinds of cognitive attitude and belief about it.

Now, to be sure, the kind of understanding is partial and incomplete, but I am suggesting that it carries with it the seeds of a progressively more complete and more satisfying understanding, if we are willing to do the requisite research. We are in somewhat the same intellectual position as the man who explains the origin of a fire as spontaneous combustion in a pile of oily rags on the cellar floor. The fire is explained very satisfactorily for certain purposes, but since not all piles of oily rags burst into flames, we are given insufficient information to let us predict where the next fire will occur or to tell householders exactly when such conditions are or are not dangerous. But merely knowing that the heat was generated in that place under those roughly describable conditions gives us a start and suggests numerous experiments with the variables of temperature, moisture, pressure, materials, etc. which should in principle give us detailed and generalizable answers to our questions.

Clearly my example of Smith hitting Jones because of jealousy is a randomly chosen example. Innumerable other situations would illustrate the same methodological point. In everyday discourse we treat each other as having chosen or avoided particular activities because they appear to be attractive or threatening, respectively; because they look easy or hard; because they appear to belong to (or be antithetical to) a particular social role. But we do not probe further to try to discover what, in detail, it means for something to seem "difficult" or "threatening" or "appropriate to my role." Systematic analysis of the phenomena of motivation has been almost entirely omitted from psychology. We recognize dimly that our understanding of Smith is furthered somehow by knowing that he was jealous, but we do not really know why or how, because we have not tried to dissect the thing called jealousy and classify it. And the same is true of almost every other motivational situation.

It is interesting though ironic that we know much more about motivation as a set of techniques than we do about motivational principles. In various ways, we do successfully create for others psychological situations that lead them to do what we hoped and predicted they would do. Almost never are we able to give a systematic account of why our efforts were effective. Salesmen and advertisers, teachers and political leaders, parents and orchestra directors, friends and neighbors, and husbands and wives dimly understand and certainly use a principle that has never been part of scientific theory, namely, that you can influence another person, create motives in him, if you like, by manipulating his conception of the situation in which he finds himself.

The admirable parsimony of behavior theories like Hull's, or the learning theory of Thorndike to which it owes so much, has led several generations of academic theorists to persist in the attempt to deal with motivation without reference to cognition as such. We have, in fact, continued to hope that we could do away with motivational problems by explaining all behavior in terms of instigation by stimuli, merely noting that the conditions of instigation include the prior influence of what we call positive and negative reinforcement on the formation of habits. But the system has not worked. The motivational problems will not go away. Let me remind you of two roughly symmetrical ones dealing respectively with the long-term effects of positive and negative reinforcement.

One way of asking the question I have in mind, would be in terms of behavior theory itself. "Can the conditions of reinforcement (either positive or negative) be themselves changed by training?" Or, a bit less obscurely, "May learned responses take on permanently the character of what Thorndike called states that the animal will seek or avoid."

In everyday language, the problem is this. When we repeatedly reward a kind of behavior, do we ever reach a state where that behavior is now permanently attractive in its own right and as predictable and characteristic an aspect of the organism as was the tendency to repeat responses followed by (for example) food in the first place? Of course, this is the problem of what Gordon Allport calls functional autonomy. Is it really true that states of affairs to be sought or prolonged by the organism can be *created* by training, or does training only strengthen the probability of responses leading to states innately sought by that animal?

As long ago as 1937, Allport provided us with convincing examples of just such acquired motives, and all the attempts of alternative theories to explain them away have failed. We must take as a fact of nature the finding that, in man at least, genuine and permanent "reinforcers" may be acquired during the individual's lifetime.

Some adult motives do seem to have all the characteristics of bodily needs despite having obviously been acquired through some kind of training or experience. The grave difficulty is that we know nothing about the conditions of such training, if indeed the training is to be held responsible. Some acts long performed in the service of a basic satisfaction ultimately seem to become self-sustaining; others do not. Which are the differences among them? Does the difference really lie, as is so often proposed, in the nature of the reinforcement or in its frequency? Or should we not ask whether it lies in the nature of the acts themselves?

Functional autonomy has, of course, a parallel case on the negative side. When certain behavior is followed repeatedly by unsatisfactory states and finally ceases to occur, have we created new motives or merely created a habit that is inconsistent with the old response? When we reduce the frequency of a particular response by punishing it, have we weakened the instigation to that response or merely blocked its expression? There is a brand of radical behaviorism that would claim my question is trivial or meaningless or both, but that is a mistaken view. We cannot shrug off as merely verbal the question of whether the psychological nature of the organism may be so changed that a state of affairs natively satisfying becomes permanently discomforting. Our question is roughly equivalent to asking of a physical system whether we prevented an explosion by building thicker walls and thus containing the pressure or whether we got rid of the pressure. The two answers have genuinely different consequences for many uses to which we might wish to put the system. And so they do for the psychological parallel. Psychoanalytic theory emphasizes this problem, and clinical evidence of continued strong tendencies toward acts long suppressed by punishment is pretty impressive. Rats which are taught to press a bar for food, then shocked for the same response, and finally allowed to return to the bar pressing situation without shock sometimes show comparatively little loss of the originally learned instigation toward bar pressing, though the shock may have temporarily reduced the response level to zero.

But what about the cases where the opposite appears to occur? A child becomes ill after eating a favorite food and later finds that food permanently distasteful. A game or a place of residence or a companion once loved is made hateful by continual disappointment or injustice and thereafter serves as a negative reinforcement for activities connected with it, though it used to play a positive role. If indeed such things really occur, they raise the same kinds of questions as those raised by claims for functional autonomy. Under what conditions does such fundamental psychological change occur? And under what conditions does mere suppression of a response occur? Is it only the strength and frequency of the punishment that are important, as traditional theories would hold? Or are not other more complex matters worth investigating?

Surely it is naive, for example, to persist in using Thorndike's "state of affairs which the animal avoids and abandons" as the definition of negative reinforcement and to treat it without differentiation. It is one thing to abandon a bad tasting food; it is quite another to abandon an unhappy marriage; and it is still another to abandon a burning building. Even a simple slap from a parental hand can be a very different matter taken in play from what it is when set in the context of deterrence.

I have probably digressed far enough in trying to make clear some illustrations of my conviction that we have persisted too long in the use of artificial unidimensional concepts instead of investigating the variety and richness that we know exists within what we call reward or punishment. We will not answer the fundamental questions about how motives are acquired until we give up the fiction that the psychological consequences of an act may vary only in one dimension, ranging from strongly negative to strongly positive. We must start with a more naturalistic approach and try to discover what are the true dimensions of effect and then proceed to manipulate experimental situations in terms of those dimensions. Perhaps we will thus finally begin to throw some light on the differences between habitual responses that become autonomous and those that extinguish, between punished responses that bounce back with all their original vigor when threat of punishment is removed and those that become instead the basis of phobic reactions, motivating in turn new complexes of behavior.

I may have seemed to imply that it is only the behavior theorists whose treatment of motivation is inadequate. But of course physiological psychology, comparative psychology, and clinical psychology all have their own inadequacies in this respect. All have failed to make clear what kind of answers we are seeking in the study of motivation.

Everyone's explanations have tended to attempt to reduce motives to something else. Almost no attempt has been made to study the unique properties of acts that are carried on for their own sake. Esthetics and play offer an almost infinitely fertile field for such investigation. What is satisfying about looking at something we call "beautiful?" What properties must the object have? What properties must the observer have? What other properties must be present in the situation? How could any part of the total be changed so as to make it discomforting instead of satisfying? Or take games and unorganized play. What are the properties that make a game or a hobby enjoyable? Clearly those properties are not entirely objective, since the game may be exciting to me and boring to you, or deeply satisfying to you and irritating to me. What kinds of interaction are involved? What dimensions of the person are important, and how do they relate to the structure of the objective situation?

Let me suggest a few examples of what I have in mind, taking my first examples from games. Most games involve built-*difficulty*. It is no fun to move pieces across a chessboard without constraint or to fill up blanks in a crossword puzzle with any old letters that come into our heads. One of the things we seek from games is somehow related to the overcoming of obstacles or barriers or competition from an opponent. But "difficulty" is not a property of objects or situations; it is a property of interactions between objects or sets of objects and a person. The degree of difficulty depends on the person as well as the task. We must develop a technique for quantifying the degree of difficulty of a task that makes it attractive or gives it reinforcing properties, and the measure will clearly have to be one that involves personal parameters of some sort.

Novelty is another positive factor in games. Satiation, boredom, ennui result from sameness. A game that does not offer new situations does not hold one's attention or provide continuing satisfaction. But novelty is also "in the eye of the beholder" in some sense. What is new to me may be old to you.

Or the newness may result only from a subtle change that you are bright enough to detect while I miss what charms you. Or the reverse may occur. Your superior intelligence may lead you to notice that despite superficial variations, the game in question really offers only one or two basic problems endlessly repeated with perfectly predictable variations, and you may then find the game no longer appealing, while I remain enchanted with what I consider infinite novelty. We shall never be in a position to discover to what extent novelty is an important factor in human choosing until we discover how to define novelty as an interaction between a particular observer and a situation.

Suppose that a research program were to be undertaken along these lines. What other properties of motivational situations would we wish to investigate? If I suggest a few, I think you will find others springing to mind in large numbers.

For instance, in the same general category as novelty will be *change, unpredictability,* and *surprise.* The McGill studies on sensory deprivation and some early explorations of satiation in Lewin's laboratory suggest that the most discomforting of all conditions other than severe sensory pain may turn out to be lack of change. Prolonged periods with only a little change may be more than enough to counteract the initial attractiveness of any activity. I am here distinguishing change from novelty in the sense that church on Sunday is a change from the rest of the week though by no means a novelty; mere alternation between two perfectly familiar patterns may be a great deal more satisfying (or less discomforting) than complete lack of change. Experiments should be designed to explore this relationship.

Unpredictability seems to have

charms of its own. It would be interesting to inquire whether church, for
example, would be even more inviting
if we never knew which day was going
to be appointed church-going day or
whether a job would be more attractive
if our day off sometimes came on
Thursday, sometimes on Monday, etc.
without predictable pattern.

Surprise is still different. Surprise
appears when the predictable does not
occur. We make a prediction in confidence, and something goes awry.
Some interesting quantitative problems
arise here. How do we establish the
kind of expectation that can be surprised? Must the expected event have
invariably occurred in the past, or in
what proportion of cases, and how
often? Once the expectation is established, under what conditions of timing
is surprise attractive? For, though
some surprises can surely be unattractive, there is considerable evidence of a
homely kind that surprise as such,
stripped of everything but the formal
relation of an expected event that does
not appear, is a "state that the organism will tend to prolong or repeat."
Small children are delighted by any
form of repeated behavior that is suddenly replaced by something else. Much
of our humor is based on such a switch
in the direction of thought: the humor-
ist or clown leads you to expect one
kind of idea or action and then hands
you something else. It is funny, and it
is fun. The fun lies partly in proper
timing, and another interesting quantitative problem here presents itself. Both
the "suddenness," or rate of exposure
of the switch, and the properly dramatic
moment for producing it are relationally determined. When we come to
study them systematically, we must, of
course, deal not with a simple measure
like a number of seconds from part
of the sequence to another but instead
with a second—or higher—order re-

lationship among time intervals. I am
not proposing that the content of the
surprise is without importance, but it
is striking that proper timing can often
change what seems to be inherently
frightening or distasteful into something pleasurable.

Within the more general category of
difficulty, already alluded to, we need
to investigate the seemingly desirable
qualities of barriers having certain
properties. What follows is speculation,
but careful observation should lead to
specific hypotheses that are subject to
empirical study. It appears to be true
that barriers, in order to be enticing,
must seem not to be insuperable but
must nevertheless seem to offer a test
and a challenge to one's self-esteem.
No adult would spend much time
jumping over a stick raised 2 feet off
the ground, nor would he spend time
trying to jump over one 10 feet up. But
quite a few young men spend many
afternoons trying to jump over ones
between 4.5 and 7.5 feet high.

If you watch a small child involved
in spontaneous play, you will recognize that so simple a matter as opening
a door or turning a faucet on and off
can be a source of interest and enjoyment so long as it is both new and a
bit difficult. When it becomes too easy,
it is abandoned; but we can also lead
the child to abandon it by making it
too hard. Lock the door, and the
struggle with it soon ceases. Think
how helpful it would be if we could
uncover the laws that operate on such
ranges of difficulty. Sporting activities,
college courses, professional problems,
and social roles can all be made more
or less attractive within limits by adjusting their difficulty. We know in a
general way that they may be unattractive because they are too easy,
offering no sense of achievement, or
because they are too difficult, permitting either no achievement at all

or too little to compete successfully with other activities. We must learn to identify optimum ranges of difficulty for different tasks. The problem will, of course, be a tough one, because the measures we need will have to take account of the abilities of the person himself and deal with information available to him about the task. Still, since the research problem is difficult but not insuperable, it should fall in an optimum range for someone and seem attractive to a psychologist or two.

Perhaps the same psychologists will also take up a closely related set of problems. The setting of personal goals seems to be enhanced by the opportunity to see a graded series of achievements. It would take a bolder theorist than I to assert that as a general law of human motivation, but I think we have the tools to find out whether or not it is one. The first step must be to learn how to measure the kind of graded goals that lead to choice behavior and how to distinguish them from ones that lead to avoidance. Let me illustrate. If I asked a 15-year-old boy to attempt to high jump 7 feet, he would almost certainly give up very soon. But if I let him start with a height that can be achieved and show him how practice and training can help him to inch his way upward over a period of years, I may be able to make a high jumper out of him. Or suppose I invite you to run for President. A realistic view of what that would mean were you to set out on your own would probably make the program unappealing. It would fall in the "too difficult" category. But the apparent degree of difficulty might change if I presented you with a series of stratagems leading to successive subgoals of precinct leader, city chairman, governor, etc.

Our knowledge in this area is slight, indeed, but we do have a few facts. Studies of levels of aspiration show that success typically leads to the setting of higher sights but that success also leads to more realistic goals than failure does. Apparently it is important to permit the aspirant to very distant goals an opportunity to avoid the cognitive confusion that can be produced by failure. It is necessary not only for a properly graded series of steps to exist, but also for them to be apprehended. And that fact emphasizes the importance of recognizing the motivational differences that may exist between clearly presented situations and less clearly presented ones, but also between people capable of understanding what lies ahead and those unable to do so. The attractive progression from subgoal to subgoal can occur only when it is cognitively available to the actor.

It may be valuable in this connection to note that in games we typically arrange things so that the direction of the paths to the goal is much clearer than it is likely to be in life's ordinary tasks. Even in a game like chess or bridge, where uncountable combinations of steps are available, the game provides strict constraints, and the shrewd player may know within reasonably narrow limits the probabilities of success on any one play. The dull player will probably find the same game confusing and, therefore, unattractive. It seems likely that the clarity of paths toward the goal is a part of the attractiveness of the entire enterprise. At least we may note that people who are skillful in handling human beings make regular use of this motivational principle (if it can be dignified with that title). The salesman or politician will typically attempt to diminish uncertainies for you with respect to the next step and where it will lead, while at the same time showing you the magnificent possibilities of the steps to come. Any theory of motivation will have to find room for an assessment of the clarity with which the path to the goal is delineated.

Earlier I spoke of the charms of uncertainty and surprise; now I am asking you to consider the attractiveness of a diminution of alternatives and a maximizing of clarity. There is really no contradiction. It is simply a fact of life that the attractiveness of most situations increases with uncertainty up to some recognizable point and then decreases. If we can learn to measure such things, we can discover empirically the optimum ranges of uncertainty just as I have proposed that we seek the optimum ranges of difficulty.

The observation of games and recreations, activities that are seemingly without extrinsic goals but are instead indulged in for their own attractive properties, suggests still another kind of pattern that seems to create attractiveness. That is the pattern of tension followed by release. The playground roller coaster is a classic example. So is a horror movie. So is the game of hide-and-seek between parent and small child. So to some extent are skiing, mountain climbing, automobile racing, and others. I should certainly not maintain that any of these occupations has as its only charm the building up of fear or tendencies like fear only to find out that one comes out safely in the end. But the fact is that the tension release pattern appears over and over again throughout observations of human motivation, taking forms as various as the taking of snuff, the seeking of sexual arousal that it may then be dispelled, and the half-serious tales of women who buy shoes that are too tight because it feels so good to take them off. What we do not know, and what so desperately needs careful study, is the objective meaning

of what we call tension. The word has been used by psychologists to refer to physical changes (as in muscle), to experiences (like anxiety), to conditions of the nervous system, and to purely formal constructs (as in the writings of Lewin). In general we tend to feel that these uses are not unrelated, that there is a kind of basic common sense to justify the same word's being assigned in the different contexts. But the common core, if any, has not been identified. And we should not continue trying to use the word for scientific purposes until it is. All the uses seem to have in common a reference to some kind of constriction of behavioral possibilities combined with a probability, increasing with time, that the constriction will be replaced by relatively diffuse and undirected expenditure of energy. Can we find a mathematical statement of those relationships that is adequate to enable us to try it for size on the various things called tension?

Another formal problem has to do with the rates at which tension is built up and released. It seems likely that the explosive relief of the sneeze is a very important part of the snuff-taker's pleasure and that if the nasal tickle merely faded slowly away, the point would be lost. Conversely, the fear and uncertainty of the roller-coaster- or horror-movie-type of thrill can sometimes be built up for so long that the fun is destroyed. Genuine problems of temporal patterning exist here, and I see no reason why they should not be amenable to experimental investigation.

We have made here only a small beginning. We have hardly scratched the surface of the things that people do "for their own sake." The afternoon of a small child is a gold mine of suggestions for research on the structural properties of situations that motivate behavior. What are the structural properties of the task of taking apart and putting together a simple object that make it attractive? How could we make it more attractive, or less so? What are the *temporal* characteristics of that same task? How long can play continue before interest flags? After what might be likened to experimental extinction does take place, does spontaneous recovery occur? How soon? Under what conditions does permanent extinction occur?

We have tended to think of extinction only in terms of inhibition by a competing response or in terms of the weakening of a stimulus-response bond by punishment or by reactive inhibition. But the problem is bigger than that. Human beings do, after all, find that block piling and percolator dismantling permanently pall before adulthood. When I became a man, I put away childish things. What, psychologically speaking, are childish things?

Visitors from other cultures often strike us as childish because of their delight with what is new to them but old to us. Adults who "discover" a new art form go rapidly through stages of excitement followed by boredom with particular styles in the art until, as we say, their taste matures. Perhaps maturing taste means only that increasing opportunity to experience the various sensory relationships inherent in an art form leads to a gradual recognition of the difference between experiences that are, for some inherent structural reason, readily satiated and those that are not. As in games, *difficulty* may play a part in maintaining interest. Or sheer complexity may provide a sense of unending novelty and variety within a familiar framework. We do not know what is important here, but someone ought to be finding out. Experimental esthetics seems to hold little interest

for the artist or art historian, but it may hold the key to many important motivational issues and should thus be of great interest to psychologists.

In fact, nowhere is the cognitive approach to motivation so clearly promising as in aesthetics. Successive re-exposures to a work of art produce genuine cognitive changes that are in turn clearly related to changes in aesthetic satisfaction and value. A work seen or heard for the sixth or sixtieth time comes to be more familiar, perhaps more orderly, sometimes more complex as we begin to appreciate details that escaped us at first, and finally in at least some cases to be apprehended so differently from the first time that we genuinely have difficulty believing that we are dealing with the same work of art. These cognitive changes affect the degree of satisfaction or dissatisfaction that we have with the experience and determine whether or not we seek to experience that work again.

But to return to the matter of maturing taste and putting away childish things, it should be apparent that some kinds of experience do lose their charm after numerous exposures. If the process is a cognitive one, it would not be surprising that adults develop more rapidly than children and, if started at the same stage, run faster through the various delights that (for whatever reason) seem not to hold experienced human beings despite their early charm.

The problem gains added interest when we look at it from the point of view of the now classic problem of functional autonomy. Allport supplied us many years ago with numerous examples of human activities first engaged in as a way of reaching some more distant goal and later accepted as attractive in their own right. A typical example is that of the fisherman who first went to sea to earn a living but who now finds that the ocean exerts an irresistible pull when he no longer makes his living that way. Or consider the man who first learned to play the violin in order to win the favor of his parents and now, though parental favor is no longer an issue, seeks out the violin as his favorite relaxation. Why is it true that in both cases only part of the activity acquires motivational force? The fisherman has given up all the things he used to do on the boat as a commercial fisherman; he does not feel the need to cast nets and clean fish. The violinist has given up doing his homework before dinner, riding his bicycle to music lessons, and all the other things he used to do as part of the same activity. Our problem is to discover what factors select out the particular parts that become and remain intrinsically attractive. It is important that we investigate the properties of activities which drop out as well as the properties of the activities that remain.

The idea that one may "discover" in a genuinely cognitive sense the undesirability of a course of action that appeared superficially to be desirable is, so far as I know, an unexplored one. But the cognitive approach might conceivably clear up the present mystery and confusion about the role of punishment. Let us, in a purely speculative way, consider the possibility that punishment produces three distinguishable results.

In one case, punishment may deter the attractive response. A child, knowing that he will have his hands slapped if he steals the cake, eyes it greedily from afar but does not touch it. Continued contemplation does not diminish the desirability of the forbidden object. Indeed, in some cases, deterrence may result in just such opportunity for contemplation as will bring out hitherto unforeseen attractions in the forbidden response.

In the second case, punishment having deterred the response itself, study and contemplation of the .total situation may follow and have the opposite result. That is, a child punished for playing in the street may live to understand the situation as his parents understood it and thus find it no longer inviting. The punishment may serve primarily to focus attention on the problem and to provide a respite from the activity that was indulged in so automatically that suitable contemplation never occurred.

The third case, that in which a relatively strong response tendency seems to be permanently destroyed, may come about not through the discovery of unsuspected properties in the original situation, but more directly by the addition of punishment to that situation. Perhaps there, too, hypothetical answers can be proposed in terms of cognitive structure. At least two aspects deserve investigation. To what extent is punishment made to appear intrinsic to the situation? Touching a hot stove or walking into areas posted for dangerous radiation provides a deterrent very different psychologically from the intrinsic fear of detection and punishment by a policeman. If an activity can be made to appear *inherently* painful or destructive or sinful, that may in itself be sufficient to produce permanent withdrawal and distaste. Secondly, the structural characteristics of the punishment itself, already hinted at above, deserve the most careful investigation. To be scolded by Mother and to be scolded by Teacher are two different matters. Mother's scolding when angry is itself different from her scolding when she is apparently otherwise in a good mood. A punishment accepted as personal rejection is different from mere retributive payment of a symmetrical kind such as blows or angry words exchanged by boys on a playground.

Obviously we do not have the theoretical tools for dealing with such differences in cognitive pattern, and we must begin to forge them. I have seemed to describe all motivation in terms free of self-reference, and many of you will be uneasy about the seeming disappearance of the self from the motivational stage. There is not time to develop the thesis fully, but I want to suggest that the self too is a cognition and that it appears as a single factor in relation to others in experience. The kinds of relationship between self and others or between self and objects that lead to particular kinds of action simply need the same kind of careful descriptive account that we need in dealing with other cognitive facts. "Self-realization," "self-esteem," and similar words describe cognitions. When we recognize certain kinds of failure or opportunity or threat involving ourselves we behave in particular ways. We must seek the regularities in such self-involved behavior as we would seek those in more objective situations.

To summarize: The sizes and shapes and colors of objects determine in part their attractiveness. Temporal patterns of stimulation may be pleasant or unpleasant. Invitations from persons in one social role produce a different response from those in another. The clarity with which we grasp the details of a situation may affect our interest or lack of interest in dealing with it in a particular way. Complex matters of cognitive organization that can only be described crudely by words like novelty and difficulty and threat seem to play a critical part in the selection of playful activities. Choice of particular foods, particular mates, and particular vocations seems to depend on characteristics of patterns of sensory stimulation or relations between such patterns and memories or ideas. In short, the cognitive contribution to why we do what we do is an important one. It is also one that we know very little about. I have tried to present some suggestions for ways of looking at these problems, ways that might lead to empirical research of the kind we need so badly.

It is my hope that the establishment of lawful relationships among cognitive variables and patterns of choice may some day give us a genuine theory of motivation at a prephysiological level. I have no objection to physiology. In fact, I look forward to the day when we will have a physiological account of every behavioral fact or relationship, but the behavioral facts and relationships must come first. And we must not delay longer in finding out what kinds of psychological situation produce what kinds of behavior, writing first approximations to laws about the structure of such situations, and then beginning to seek the biological substrate.

Art, Science, and Representation: Toward an Experimental Psychology of Aesthetics *

Michael A. Wallach

Perhaps the most distinctively human of all man's products are his works of art. It is therefore especially curious that most experimental psychologists have shown so little interest in the study of aesthetics—with such noteworthy exceptions as Arnheim, Farnsworth, Munro, and Schoen.[1] Such, of course, has not been the case with philosophers, who, however, typically do not proceed to infer particular experimental consequences from their discussions. The present essay seeks to join philosophical and psychological approaches to aesthetics. Using a philosophical examination of art, science, and representation as its starting point, questions about the nature of art, talent, and preference are suggested which can be answered by psychological experiments. Several such experiments are proposed. Our aim is to suggest one frame of reference, and not necessarily the only one, within which philosophers and psychologists can join forces fruitfully in work on aesthetics.

A DEFINITION

We begin by proposing a definition. A work of art, we would suggest, may be defined as an organization of information according to a set of rules, where the construction, tracing, or observation of this organization (composing, performing, and perceiving or hearing an art work, respectively) serves to alter a person's motivational state in a way sought by the individual. What do we mean by information? Anything that impinges on a sense organ and/or that can be entertained in the mind. This hence includes colors, sounds, words, numbers—whatever can modify behavior. And the set of rules? By these we mean postulates, whether explicit or implicit, about what kinds of information are deemed relevant and how they are to be related to one another. Consider, for instance, the following postulates: "only lines at right angles and parallels to such lines shall appear on the canvas"—an unwritten assumption of certain Mon-

* From M. A. Wallach, "Art, science, and representation: Toward an Experimental Psychology of Aesthetics," *Journal of Aesthestics and Art Criticism,* **18** (1959), 159-173. Reprinted by permission of the author and publisher.

This research is supported in part by a grant from the Laboratory of Social Relations, Harvard University; and in part by grant M-2269 from the United States Public Health Service, Michael A. Wallach, principal investigator. Thanks are due Gordon W. Allport, Roderick Firth, Norbett L. Mints, and Walter Mischel for readings of the manuscript.

[1] See, for example, R. Arnheim, *Art and Visual Perception* (Berkeley, Calif.: University of California Press, 1954); P. R. Farnsworth, *The Social Psychology of Music* (New York: The Dryden Press, 1958); T. Munro, *Toward Science in Aesthestics* (New York: Liberal Arts Press, Inc., 1956); and M. Schoen, *The Psychology of Music* (New York: The Ronald Press Company, 1940).

drian paintings; "parallel fifths and parallel octaves shall not appear"—a postulate of classical counterpoint stating that two or more musical voices a fifth or an octave apart may not move simultaneously the same number of notes in the same direction; "every sentence shall contain a subject and a predicate"—a postulate of English grammar that tells us how words are to be organized; or "through every point not on a given line there exists one and only one parallel to that line"—a postulate of Euclidean geometry which we must never violate in our manipulations of geometrical terms.

There was a further part to our definition. Information organized according to a set of postulates, so we suggested, has to perform a motivation alteration function before it qualifies as art. This change must be one sought after by the individual, whether its direction be to arouse or reduce a motive state. Our view of art implies that what may be aesthetic for one person may not be so for another. Information organized according to a set of rules—for example, the rectilinear structure of a Mondrian painting, the interlacing of voices in a Bach fugue, or a theorem in geometry—may placate a motive state which had possessed one person, create one where none existed before in a second person (both changes being sought by the respective people), and leave a third person cold. Thus a mathematician will be undergoing an aesthetic experience if he feels a motivational lift when he demonstrates a theorem; while the student of his who then learns the same demonstration may receive no such motivational charge from this work. Further, although Stravinsky's *Sacred Rite of Spring,* for example, may cause a motivational change in each of two listeners, this change may be of a kind sought after by one person but not by

the other. For instance, the piece may arouse the first listener sexually, which he likes; but instigate the second to aggression, which he dislikes. It is art for the former person, but not for the latter, who stamps out of the concert hall in a huff.

On the other hand, sought-after motivational changes may occur without mediation by rule systems, and in such cases we do not call the phenomenon aesthetic. Eating reduces one's hunger; yet we do not consider an infant's mouthing of food to constitute art. But eating can become an art; as when individuals permit their hunger to be satisfied only if certain prescriptions are followed concerning the use of particular eating instruments, the order in which particular foods should be served, how the foods are to be prepared. The alcoholic's drinking likewise is not considered aesthetic: it has no restrictions about it; he will down anything that will intoxicate him. But drinking can be an art: we consider it so in the case of a wine connoisseur who follows rules as to what particular intoxicants shall be taken with different kinds of foods, at different points in the meal, at different times of the day. The wine connoisseur permits himself tension reduction (that is, motivational change) from drinking alcohol only if he achieves this end while following a set of injunctions about what is permitted and what is not.

Or take love-making. As one goes up the phylogenetic scale, and, among humans, perhaps as one goes up the intellectual scale, there is an increase in the number and complexity of self-imposed requirements before individuals permit themselves sexual intercourse: requirements concerning who will constitute an appropriate partner, ranging from more tangible attributes of looks and education, to less tangible ones of emotional support, sympathy, and understanding; and concerning nature and duration of courtship. It is such requirements that turn sex into the art of love.

We have proposed a definition which seems reasonably to fit, at least in large measure, what we consider aesthetic and what not. It is most closely related to expressionist theories of art, and the present essay will propose psychological ways of exploring such theories. Our definition's utility can perhaps best be further evaluated first by comparing art with other forms of knowledge.

ART AND SCIENCE

Suppose we try to describe our phenomenal experience. If we consider the individual experiencer, it becomes evident that no particular kind of experience is more "primary" than another. We may, on the one hand, sense things whose origins are outside the body, as when we report "I see a brownness with a darker outline around it"; or we may sense things originated by bodily changes, as when we report feeling short of breath and hot. (Call the first an external percept, and the second an internal percept.) Both reports are relatively direct readings of our experience. But to say "I see a table," or "I feel angry," are inferences from the first and second statements respectively. Perceptions of our subjective states are thus no less basic than perceptions of data originating outside ourselves; and statements about objects in an outer world are no less inferential than those about particular motives.[2]

In some sense man wants to gain control over these phenomenal experiences of his—wants to be able to bring about or avoid particular experiences at will. We posit such an interest in controlling percepts for two reasons: it is a basic way of bringing order out of the chaos of experience that would otherwise continually swamp and surprise us;[3] and it insures that pleasurable experiences or ones remembered to lead to pleasure will occur, while painful experiences or ones recalled as mediating pain will be avoided. In what does control consist? It involves predicting an experience (call it "y") from some other information (call it "x")—and being right. In the sentence "If x, then y," the business of both art and science is to develop information-systems, the "x" term above, that predict the occurrence of the phenomenal experiences abbreviated by "y."

It is our view that both science and art are methods for trying to control experiences, but they differ in that science involves the consensual validation of its predictions, while art as such does not. In other words, while science's predictions must be public, those of art remain private. What does it mean to suggest that science consists of consensually validated predictions of experiences, while art's predictions are not consensually validated? It means that in the last analysis, the predictions of science must concern external percepts—percepts

---

[2] See A. J. Ayer, *Language, Truth and Logic* (London, 1951); A. J. Ayer, *The Foundations of Empirical Knowledge* (London, 1951); H. H. Price, *Perception* (London, 1932).

[3] This point is experimentally supported in M. A. Wallach, "On Psychological Similarity," *Psychological Review,* 65 (1958), 103-16; M. A. Wallach, "The Influence of Classification Requirements on Gradients of Response," *Psychological Monographs,* 73 (1959), No. 478; and J. S. Bruner, M. A. Wallach, and E. H. Galanter, "The Identification of Recurrent Regularity," *American Journal of Psychology,* 72 (1959), 200-209.

that can be reported by anyone else situated at the same vantage point. Only in their case can we validate—that is, can we furnish reliably the stimuli that should cause similar percepts (and hence similar perceptual reports) in different observers. We are not thereby implying that science cannot study internal percepts, for indeed the study of motivation is a central part of psychology and physiology. But changes in motivational states can be validated only by inference from external percepts that are taken as signs of such changes. While, for example, no one else can get inside an angry person and experience his rapid breathing and his hotness, any number of observers can observe his panting and sweating, or the fact that he shouts.

Art's predictions, on the other hand, remain more ambiguous and intuitive: they concern effects on the artist's or appreciator's own feelings, and stop there. The individual appreciator comes to know how various works of art make him feel, and the individual artist learns the moods that result from his process of creating. But art *itself* is not concerned with explicating the nature of these feelings, nor the relations which various kinds of information-systems may have to them. Such explication is the task of a science of aesthetics or art criticism. It requires, first of all, attaching externally perceivable signs of motivational states so that their presence and degree can be agreed upon by more than one observer. Then its task is to discover the relations between differences in individuals, differences in art, and sought-after motivational changes.

In sum, then, we have been proposing that the difference between science and art is not as great as one may first imagine. Both aim to control percepts, but only science is concerned with the public validation of such attempts at control. Since validation requires arranging for external percepts to be had by more than one observer, scientific prediction of sought-after internal percepts, that is, of desired motives, requires finding symptoms of them which are externally perceivable. Other branches of science, of course, are directly concerned with predicting external percepts: for example, physics and chemistry. Art, on the other hand, is a kind of unconscious version of the first aspect of science: control or prediction of sought-after internal percepts which are not publicly described, by means whose relations to these percepts are not public.

But we would suggest further that the similarity between art and science extends beyond their both being attempts to control percepts. For they both seem to involve systems of information organized by various rules, and it is these systems that constitute predictions of particular percepts, internal or external. Such rules, by stipulating the initial information and how it is to be organized—which catalyst to unite with which compound because of the properties of each; or what kind of music to play, with its particular admissible harmonies, counterpoint, rhythms, and tempos—guide the construction of information structures designed to bring about certain sights or motive states.

If science is the public prediction of any kinds of percepts, and art is the private prediction of internal percepts, then the criterion for adequacy in both science and art depends on the predictions made, rather than on the sets of information which furnish the predictions. It is an arbitrary matter as to what rules are used for the organization and content of information, so long as, in science, these rules validly permit the control of percepts; and, in art, they yield results that bring about particular internal percepts or motive states. We feel that an understanding of this arbitrariness in the choice of rules sheds further light on the nature of both science and art.

In science, it was not until recently that such arbitrariness was realized. An important aid was the insight that Euclidean geometry started from postulates whose assumption was arbitrary, rather than from postulates that were intuitively true to the nature of physical space.

POSTULATE-INFERENCE SYSTEMS IN GEOMETRY AND SCIENCE

A long time ago, Euclid started theorizing about the nature of space. This in itself was not novel, since others had thought about space before him. What was new, however, was the clarity of the logical form he used. Certain postulates or rules were given that stipulated how various concepts about space, such as "point" and "straight line," were related. From these postulates, theorems were derived which were not completely self-evident, but which nevertheless were dependent on the postulates alone (at least in Hilbert's version of Euclidean geometry). Thus, if the theorems could be proven true of physical space, then the postulates were true also. But the truth or falsity of theorems and postulates was quite independent of the necessity with which the former could be deduced from the latter—a matter that confused geometers for a long time. Since the necessity in such deduction conferred no validity on the postulates themselves, there was no *self-evident* reason for preferring Euclidean postulates in geometry to others, once self-consistent alternative postulate sets were invented.[4]

To transform an *a priori* logical system like Euclidean geometry into a science, requires changing the theorems into hypotheses about conditions under which a scientist will receive certain external percepts. If these hypotheses turn out to be validated, *then* the postulates from which they were derived do become more true than alternative possible postulates. Interestingly enough, experiments involving astronomical space ranges have shown Euclidean theorems, based on their assumption that a straight line always has one parallel to it through any point not on that straight line, to be false for such great distances. Tests demonstrating the curved path followed by light rays in the sun's gravitational field support rather the theorems of a non-Euclidean geometry developed by Riemann, based on the assumption that straight lines always meet somewhere; that a straight line has no parallel to it through any point not on that straight line.[5]

In geometry as a branch of logic, then, there is no basis for choosing among alternative postulate sets: no one set of postulates is more true than another. In geometry as a science of space, on the other hand, treating the theorems as hypotheses about the nature of space—for example, defining "straight line" to mean "light ray"—turns them into predictions of external percepts which may or may not occur—for instance, percepts of meter readings and oscilloscope waves. Since their occurrence supports the postulates from which these hypotheses

[4] C. G. Hempel, "On the Nature of Mathematical Truth," in *Readings in Philosoph-*

ical Analysis, eds. H. Feigl and W. Sellars (New York, 1949); J. Nicod, "Geometry in the Perceived World," in *Readings in Philosophy of Science,* ed. P. P. Wiener (New York, 1953).

[5] W. K. Clifford, "On the Bending of Space," and C. G. Hempel, "Geometry and Empirical Science," in P. P. Wiener, ed., *op. cit.*

were derived, the basis for preference among postulates consists in discovering which set predicts the scientist's external percepts more accurately.[6,7] A scientist, of course, also may gain aesthetic pleasure from his work: his theory-construction can have desired motivational effects for him, as well as predicting external percepts.

Science thus is concerned with constructing theories which generate veridical representations of nature; which generate descriptions of external percepts that turn out to match what happens in reality when the conditions specified in the theory are met. All this seems quite close to the nature of representationalism in art. In graphic representationalism, for example, postulates as to how to mix colors, how to draw objects in perspective, how to indicate shadow, textures, atmospheric effects, foreshortening of limbs, and so forth, stipulate ways of painting people and things that should yield pictures which are veridical descriptions or portrayals of the external world. The pictures that result are themselves the conditions under which the observer is expected to experience certain external percepts: percepts describable as houses, people, animals, objects of various kinds. The more closely identifiable is the individual's external percept with what it would be were he viewing the real object in question—this house, rather than a picture of it; this man, rather than a picture of him; and so on—then the more highly verified is this painting

as a theorem deduced from, that is, painted in accordance with, postulates concerning how to achieve veridicality. And thus also, the more highly validated are those particular postulates.

The painting hence is an attempt accurately to describe or match reality —to predict, as it were, that the observer will perceive this particular bowl of fruit rather than a signification of it; and the painting itself embodies the conditions which are supposed to bring about this external percept. While a hypothesis in physical science thus might read "If you perform such-and-such operations, then this meter's needle will point to 50," a representational picture stipulates that "If you follow such-and-such rules of painting, your picture will look like this particular chair." Just as the relation between the phrase "this meter's needle will point to 50" and perception of the meter needle's crossing 50 is one of match, mediated by conventions of linguistic reference, so the relation between perception of the picture of the chair and perception of the actual chair is that of matching—but without any mediating conventions. Thus graphic representationalism, for example, reaches its epitome in the stereoscopic color photograph: the supreme in representational art is a picture providing the illusion that the observer is looking at the real thing.

If rules as to how to paint are postulates, and particular paintings are theorems derived from those postulates, then we can check as to whether the painting in question is or isn't consistent with these postulates—whether, for instance, the perspective in such-and-such painting was portrayed according to the rules set down by Leonardo da Vinci. Such checking is analogous to the logician's proving that his geometry theorem follows from such-and-such postulates, but is harder

[6] If two alternative postulate sets have equal predictive value—which is not often the case—then the simpler of the two will be preferred.
[7] See C. G. Hempel, *Fundamentals of Concept Formation in Empirical Science* (Chicago, 1952); and C. L. Hull, "The Hypothetico-deductive Methods," in *Psychological Theory*, ed. M. H. Marx (New York, 1951).

in art than in mathematics or science because knowledge of the postulates used by a particular artist usually is difficult to obtain. If representationalism is a goal, however, then our task is not only to find out if an artist can paint products that reflect the rules he purports to use, but also if his paintings match the real world with high veridicality. Insofar as his painting achieves this objective, then we have grounds for urging the use of his rules rather than others—just as validation of any theorem by empirical test supports the particular postulates from which that theorem was derived.

The point of view just elaborated leads us to question whether a goal of representationalism really belongs to art rather than to science. For to require of postulates that they generate results which match or describe the external world is exactly the task of science, and different from our discussion of what constitutes art. That representation is not an artistic issue seems even more apparent when one considers music rather than visual art; for, except in the case of program music, postulates of musical style usually have nothing to do with representation of external phenomena. Even with program music, we tend to consider it good art only if it arouses motivational states in us which do not necessarily depend on the device of imitating natural sounds, although they also may be elicited by association with such sounds.[8] It is never veridicality of representation as such that makes for art, but rather the successful use of representation as a possible device for causing motivational changes in artists and their audience, by means of the subject matter and postures depicted.

The artist, however, may well think his goal is representation when it isn't.

Thus da Vinci, for example, defined painting as "the sole imitator of all visible works of nature,"[9] and his books about painting were instructions on how best to achieve veridicality in depicting, for example, perspective and light. One look at his work is enough to indicate that he failed to communicate what made his paintings great. Rather than treating representation as an end, it functioned as a means for presenting content that would affect us motivationally: particular figures engaged in particular activities.

We would suggest, then, that representational accuracy as an objective belongs more to the realm of science, with its interest in constructing hypotheses that match or depict happenings in the external world, than to that of art. Regarding art, representationalism may serve as one among many devices that can function to control the motivational states of artists and observers.

POSTULATE-INFERENCE SYSTEMS IN ART

Works of art thus may be viewed as theorems derived from one or another set of postulates as to how painting, for instance, ought to be done, or how music should be composed. We have, further, proposed that such a derivation becomes aesthetic if it performs the function of changing an individual's motivational state in a way sought by him.

Artistic talent in part may concern an individual's degree of sensitivity to what constitutes consistency vs. inconsistency in the art work derived from given or implied postulates. A more talented listener hence ought to be better able to select the one continuation which is a stylistically consistent

[8] J. W. N. Sullivan, *Beethoven* (New York, 1949).

[9] E. G. Holt, ed., *A Documentary History of Art* (New York, 1957), p. 284.

extrapolation from the part of a musical composition which he has already heard, and to discriminate it from extrapolations which are inconsistent with that prior part. (The more talented composer, in turn, should be better able to continue composing in a style consistent with a set of measures he has just heard.) Talent in art hence would be like the talent of the mathematician in being better able to "see" intuitively that a particular theorem in Euclidean geometry, for instance, is or isn't consistent with the initial postulates. Individuals vary, of course, in the kinds of rule systems to which they are sensitive. Not everyone has the insight of a mathematician into the implications of geometry postulates, nor of a musician into the fact that a wily psychologist began a passage of music in one style and then continued it with the omission of passing notes which previously had been characteristic of the accompaniment.[10]

Our earlier discussion of art's nature raises the further question of whether such differences in talent are gratuitous, or rather serve a motivational function. We would propose the latter possibility, since never yet have evolutionary developments flourished without performing some function for the organism. May not a person talented regarding a particular art form be one for whom that kind of art work is better able to control particular motive states in a manner sought by him?

Consider the following experimental proposal. We have suggested that a listener talented regarding a particular musical style is a person who knows what to expect when listening to that music; not because he has memorized the piece and simply remembers what comes next, but rather because he suf-

ficiently understands the postulates underlying this music's composition that he can tell whether the further music he hears is or isn't consistent with those assumptions. Our question: Does talent, thus defined, serve a motivational function? Suppose we restrict our inquiry for now to talent concerning music of Baroque style. We select unfamiliar music of that period and assess talent in the following manner. Part of each selection is played, and then the individual is provided with various possible alternative continuations which he must rate for degree of appropriateness to the initial section of the piece. The set of multiple-choice continuations of each piece includes the actual continuation, plus others which deviate from the music's stylistic assumptions along such dimensions as the pattern and degree of complexity of passing notes between harmonically important chords, type of embellishments used, and where embellishments are placed. The initial section is repeated with each continuation, different initial sections following each other so that the same one doesn't occur twice in a row.

Our hypothesis is that individuals who tend to rate the correct completion as the most appropriate one, will undergo greater sought-after motivational modifications from experiencing music of this kind. Since exploration of all motives is a lifetime task, the experimental program described below makes a start by considering one general aspect of motivation: rhythmic and movement arousal. Our further use of the term *motivation* in this paper hence is shorthand for these motives. One procedure for assessing motivational change of this sort is the content analysis of imaginative stories written by the listener and inspired by the music. In a technique we are currently using,

---

[10] There is another aspect of talent that we are not considering here: the ability to invent new postulate-systems.

the participant is asked to listen to a musical selection first, and then to let its mood guide him in the writing of a four-minute story. These stories are scored for degree of rhythmic and movement arousal by noting the presence or absence of imagery concerning bodily motion, rhythm, rise to a climax followed by a decline in the intensity of action, and forceful penetration.[11] Individuals more sensitive to the stylistic postulates of Baroque music also should exhibit more rhythmic and movement arousal, as defined by the scoring categories just described, when we later present other examples of such music and have them write the imaginative stories which this music inspires.[12]

Let us look in more detail at an example indicating the presence in art of postulate systems not unlike those

[11] Although Beardslee and Fogelson (D. C. Beardslee and R. Fogelson, "Sex Differences in Sexual Imagery Aroused by Musical Stimulation," in *Motives in Fantasy, Action and Society,* ed. J. W. Atkinson (New York, 1958), who developed these categories, use them as indicators of specifically sexual arousal, the link to sex is sufficiently indirect that we prefer to consider them in their own right as rhythmic and movement arousal. Further research will be done later on their relation to sexual motivation. This measure of arousal, by the way, has been found more effective with women than men. The proposed studies involving it hence use women as the listeners.

[12] Although our initial discussion of art's motivational functions included both drive-arousing and drive-reducing aspects, our current experimental program concentrates on the former. It may well be that optimal levels of motivation are between extremes, so that the same person will seek drive-arousal if his initial motivational level is low, and drive-reduction if that initial level is high. Since no particular prior motivational arousal is provided in the experiments described, it seems reasonable to assume that the initial drive level of participants with respect to rhythm and movement is low, and hence that arousal is the direction of change most sought.

underlying geometry and science. Compare traditional classical music with that of Schoenberg. Among the postulates for composing traditional classical music were certain principles of harmony and counterpoint. The chords of this music, for example, were constructed in terms of the addition of thirds. Consonance was defined mainly in terms of that interval, and this definition was thought to follow from what innately pleased the ear rather than being a matter of convention. Such a belief seems quite similar to the feeling that Euclidean geometry's postulates were self-evidently true to the nature of physical space, rather than being assumptions that could be abandoned. So strong was classical harmony's postulate as to the nature of consonance, that use of a discord such as a fourth had to be ameliorated, according to the rules, by having it appear as a transition between thirds.[13]

Schoenberg, on the other hand, used quite different postulates for composing. Assuming that all twelve tones within the octave should be given equal importance, he objected to classical harmony's emphasis on one basic tone and the triad of thirds built upon it. Having discovered that one passes through all twelve tones and returns to one's starting place if one proceeds up the keyboard in fourths, Schoenberg hence decided that this interval was a more appropriate building block for musical composition than the third. His compositions contain a theme of all twelve chromatic tones arranged in some order without repetition, and he permits himself several further rules as to how the basic theme of twelve tones is to be used: it can be played in reverse order,

[13] D. F. Tovey, *The Forms of Music* (New York, 1957).

inverted, and its inversion played in reverse. Further, these tone sequences may appear successively to form a melody, or simultaneously to form harmonies.[14]

Just as Euclidean geometry was assumed necessarily to be true by virtue of how the world looked, so also the traditional classicists felt that their harmonic and contrapuntal postulates were true by virtue of what pleased the ear. Although the fallacy of the geometers was effectively indicated by the development of consistent non-Euclidean geometries, the development of a nonclassical system of musical composition such as that of Schoenberg has not had a parallel effect because Schoenberg, no less than the classicists, believes his postulates to be more true to the "essential" nature of music! Thus Tovey criticizes Schoenberg's system of composition on the ground that music constructs its chords in terms of thirds, and therefore "Schoenberg's theory rests on no observation at all."[15] But Tovey hence is assuming that the postulates of classical harmony cannot be questioned, while Schoenberg simply favors his own postulates. He justifies his preference by declaring that music's essence is to be concentrated and economical, and his postulates are certainly in line with this ideal; for example, every chromatic tone being used once and only once in the basic theme. The classical tradition's composition postulates, on the other hand, encouraged the redundancy of emphasizing a triad of thirds based on one or another tonality.

Since different cultures have produced music based on different chord intervals (for example, the fourth is a consonant in the music of India, while the third is not[16]), Tovey's argument for classical harmony in terms of thirds necessarily being the most pleasing intervals seems without force. Since, on the other hand, the redundancy of classical music appeals to most Western ears, and even Schoenberg himself admits some redundancy by permitting reversals and inversions of the twelve-tone theme (the extreme of nonredundancy being to play nothing but the twelve tones once each in the same order), Schoenberg cannot argue that complete economy in composition necessarily should be music's goal. Rather, the answer seems to be that just as non-Euclidean geometries are possible, so also are various sets of postulates as to how music should be composed.

Schoenberg and Tovey obviously become aroused by music based on different postulates. The immediate explanation probably is that Tovey hasn't exposed himself much to twelve-tone music; although *why* Schoenberg chose to invent and become familiar with music based on a new postulate system is a matter beyond our present scope. Just as a mathematician couldn't be motivationally affected by tracing the proof of a theorem based on a non-Euclidean geometry unless he were familiar with that geometry's postulates, so also one cannot be motivationally influenced by Schoenberg's music unless one is familiar with the assumptions on which it rests. The very familiarity to Western ears of traditional classical music's assumptions tends to push them into a background and confuse us into thinking that they are intuitively based on nature.

If art comes into existence when the product of a rule-system takes on

[14] A. Schoenberg, *Structural Functions of Harmony* (New York, 1954); A. Schoenberg, *Style and Idea* (New York, 1950).

[15] Tovey, *op. cit.*, p. 70.

[16] A. Bake, "The Music of India," in *Ancient and Oriental Music*, ed. E. Wellesz (London, 1957).

the power of controlling a person's motives in a sought-after manner, then the question arises of whether teaching a person the postulates of a new method for composing music—thoroughly familiarizing the person with them over a period of time—will result in that music's coming to have such motivational control value for him. Our suggestion hence is that a person can become motivationally affected by hitherto unfamiliar music which initially left him unmoved, if one teaches him its postulates of composition thoroughly enough through exposing him to selections constructed according to those rules.

A second experiment hence seems indicated. Our procedure, in collaborations with N. Mintz, is to subject listeners to a particular kind of musical education. Suppose, for example, we work with individuals who, by the measure of talent described earlier, show talent for Baroque music but are totally unfamiliar with the music of Schoenberg. (We want listeners who are sensitive to traditional classical music, since we must know that they possess the general ability to become aware of the postulates underlying a particular style of music.) Various examples of Schoenberg's music are heard by these individuals at regular intervals: once a week for a semester. Motivational effects, in turn, are assessed in the manner described earlier; the listeners being told to write imaginative stories stimulated by the music on the first, seventh, and fourteenth weeks of the experiment. We would expect the rhythmic and movement arousal value of Schoenberg's music, as reflected in story content, to increase with the amount of time spent listening to it. But part of this effect might be due to story-writing practice as such. The necessary control hence is provided by similar persons who

write stories stimulated by Schoenberg's music upon hearing it for the first time, after having written stories both seven and fourteen weeks ago to Baroque music. They are thus equated regarding experience in writing stories to music, and their degree of arousal upon first exposure to Schoenberg should be less than that of the experimental group on their fourteenth exposure.

MOTIVATION AND ART

The preceding considerations raise still further questions that can be approached experimentally. Is it the case, for instance, that the effectiveness of an art work in modifying the individual's motivation in a sought-after manner is a factor influencing judgments of aesthetic value? In the experiment just described, we might well expect our listeners not only to be more aroused, but also to like Schoenberg more on the fourteenth presentation than on the first. We would propose the following study. Suppose we find three otherwise similar musical selections which judges agree as rating low, medium, and high respectively in rhythmic and movement arousal value. We play first the low, then the medium, and then the high arousal pieces to persons who are told to let each selection inspire them to write a story—yielding the measure of arousal discussed above. Later we have these individuals rank order the pieces for degree of preference, and also indicate in absolute terms the degree to which each is liked or disliked. In general, we would expect the mean arousal value of each piece, as inferred from the story content, to increase from the first to the third selection; and predict that the mean degree of preference will increase in the same order. But we well might expect these results to hold only for those persons who had a reasonably high absolute level of liking for all the pieces played; people who, hence, probably were more sensitive to the postulates governing composition of this music. Again only considering persons in general liking this music, however, some may show the highest arousal in their stories to the second piece rather than the third—and we would expect such individuals to follow suit in their preference pattern. Their highest rank of preference should be assigned to the second rather than for third selection. Further, persons with high vs. low degrees of preference for a particular piece should reveal a corresponding difference in arousal to that selection. And those, finally, with stronger preferences for all the pieces should show a higher total arousal effect.

But will everybody be equally open to the rhythmic and movement arousal potential of the music? Motivational openness to music—the willingness to let oneself be aroused by it— is a kind of risk, since it involves exposing one's feelings to oneself, and possibly to the view of others with the chance of injury at their hands. The safer approach is to remain motivationally constricted: not to let the music move one at all. Such openness also may be more likely in an extroverted than an introverted individual—extroversion meaning that the person is more given to communication with others and/or to overt expression of himself.[17] We hence may

well expect our listeners to vary in their degree of openness to musical arousal: some showing progressively more arousal in their story content as one proceeds from first, to second, to third selection; others showing some arousal increase from first to second selections, perhaps, but then dropping off with the threat of more obvious arousal-relevance in the third selection; still others being completely closed motivationally to all three pieces. Rhythmic and movement arousal, in other words, may not be sought by everyone.

Can we predict the person's degree of motivational openness to music from more general aspects of his personality? We would hypothesize that tendencies toward risk-taking or conservatism in one's over-all behavior, and tendencies toward extroversion or introversion, will influence the individual's willingness to take risks in the motivational sphere; the high general risk-taker and the extrovert being more open to musical arousal.[18] There is also the possibility of an alternative trend: some individuals who are very conservative and/or introverted in their general conduct may use music as a displacement or compensation at the fantasy level, and be all the more arousable to music because of their avoidance of risk and/or their introversion in other aspects of their lives. Two points may be made about this latter possibility. First, generally constricted people may well be quite closed against arousal by music too, because our measure of arousal requires the use of at least some kinds of story imagery that would probably

---

[17] For typical research on this dimension of personality, see H. J. Eysenck, *The Structure of Human Personality* (London, 1953); A. J. Caron and M. A. Wallach, "Personality Determinants of Recall and Perception under Failure-stress," *Journal of Abnormal and Social Psychology,* in press. The concept of extroversion-introversion stems from C. G. Jung, *Psychological Types* (London, 1923).

[18] For related work on risk, see M. A. Wallach and A. J. Caron, "Attribute Criteriality and Sex-linked Conservatism as Determinants of Psychological Similarity," *Journal of Abnormal and Social Psychology,* **59** (1959), 43-50.

threaten them. Second, if the alternative trend described does occur, we shall be able to detect it. Such a result would mean that persons either very high or very low in general risk-taking tendencies or at the extremes of extroversion-introversion should be most open to motivational arousal by music, with those in the middle of the risk-taking or extroversion-introversion distributions being less subject to musical arousal.

For assessing these hypotheses, a measure of general risk-taking has been constructed in which the person is presented with dilemmas of choice regarding a number of everyday life situations. The central person in each situation is faced with a choice between two courses of action, one of which is more risky than the other but also is more rewarding if successful. The reader must indicate how desirable he feels it would be for the person to follow the more risky course of action, by selecting the probability of success that he would deem necessary to warrant following the risky alternative. The content of the situations varies widely, ranging from an electrical engineer who must decide whether to continue with his secure but modest income job, or accept a higher paying job with a new firm that has an uncertain future; and a chess player who must decide whether to attempt a risky stratagem which would bring quick victory if a success, but sure defeat if a failure; to a couple wondering if they should marry despite sharp difference of opinion in the way each views certain matters. Preliminary results on the questionnaire alone indicate that different kinds of items reliably measure different kinds of risks; ego risks concerning prestige and failure, for example, having a different psychological meaning than financial investment risks. Measures of extro-

version-introversion also are available to us: for instance, Eysenck's Maudsley inventory and the Minnesota TSE questionnaire.[19] The next experimental step, then, is to determine the relationships between responses to these questionnaires and arousal content in stories written to music.

The personality dimensions of risk-taking and extroversion may also prove fruitful for understanding aesthetic reactions in spheres other than the musical. Take, for example, architectural preferences. We would hypothesize that the high risk-taker or the extreme extrovert is the person who wants to live in larger spatial areas, while the conservative or introverted individual prefers a more constricted living area. We expect the low risk-taker or the introvert, in other words, to be less willing to extend himself into the environment: to feel frightened and overwhelmed by larger spatial areas, and hence to avoid the cause of such feelings.[20] This size difference in the envelope of space within which the individual prefers to operate also would be expected to manifest itself in other ways—the low risk-taker or introvert, for example, conceiving of a "short distance" as being much shorter in mileage than a high risk-taker or extrovert, wanting a house with fewer rooms in it (when told to assume money is no object), and spending more of his leisure time in the house than outside of it. In experiments cur-

[19] H. J. Eysenck, "The Questionnaire Measurement of Neuroticism and Extraversion," *Revista di Psicologia*, **50** (Oct.-Dec. 1956), 113-40. C. Evans and T. R. McConnell, "A New Measure of Introversion-Extroversion," *Journal of Psychology*, **12** (1941), 111-24.

[20] The central role of space preferences in architectural design is evident from such diverse writings as H. Adams, *Mont-Saint-Michel and Chartres* (Boston, 1913), and B. Zevi, *Architecture as Space* (New York, 1957).

rently underway, we are estimating the preferred living area size by having the participant draw a rectangle around a little figure that stands on a cross-grid board; the instructions being to imagine that you are this figure and to indicate the size of the living room most appropriate for you (again assuming money is no object). This and other indices of space preferences are being related to the measures of general risk-taking and extroversion discussed above.

Finally, we would propose that spatial expansiveness and motivational openness to arousal by music also may well be related—something the above sets of hypotheses would lead us to expect. Openness or constriction, in other words, may be a general personality style with ramifications for various aspects of aesthetics.

THE EXPERIMENTAL APPROACHES IN OVERVIEW

The aim of this essay is to propose an approach to aesthetics which will generate questions answerable by psychological experimentation. From an exploration of the relations between art, geometry, and science, and of the role of representation in art and science, we arrived at various suggestions concerning the nature of art, talent, and preference. A number of experiments were described as examples of means for validating these suggestions. Some of these are now in progress, and the others are soon to begin. Just as important as the particular empirical studies described, however, is the general idea of moving from a philosophical considerations of aesthetics to specific hypotheses that can be tested by psychological methods. It is hoped that this paper will serve not only as a description of certain psychological hypotheses about art—hypotheses which

could be false as well as true—but also as a demonstration of how one can move from the philosophy of aesthetics to its psychology; how one can operationalize and test views on the nature and functions of art.

In conclusion, we shall summarize the experimental questions to which our discussion has led, each of which will require extensive psychological investigation to evaluate. These are, of course, not the only experiments suggested by our approach, but rather constitute an exploration of several possibilities as examples.

1. Does musical talent serve a motivational function for the individual? We hypothesize that greater sensitivity to the musical continuations that are most consistent with the stylistic postulates of a particular musical idiom, will lead to greater rhythmic and movement arousal by music of this kind.

2. Does teaching a person the hitherto unfamiliar postulates of a new style of music cause that kind of music to take on motivational arousal value which it previously lacked? Our hypothesis: as various examples of Schoenberg's music are heard with increasing frequency, thereby revealing the stylistic postulates of this music by example, music of this idiom will increase in rhythmic and movement significance for individuals who show ability to sense the stylistic assumptions of traditional classical music.

3. Does an individual's preferences among musical selections reflect the extent to which each arouses him motivationally? We suggested that people will show the greatest preference among a group of musical pieces for the one which arouses them most regarding rhythm and movement, assuming that in general all these selections are liked. Further, we proposed that different levels of preference for one or

more pieces will be reflected in corresponding differences in arousal.

4. Do a person's general tendencies toward risk-taking or conservatism and toward extroversion-introversion influence his degree of openness to rhythmic and movement arousal by music? We proposed that either of two trends may be possible. On the one hand, there may be a direct relationship between general tendencies to take risks or to be extroverted, and willingness to let oneself be motivationally aroused by music. On the other hand, there may be a curvilinear relationship; very high and very low risk-takers and extreme extroverts and introverts all being most open to musical arousal, with moderate risk-takers and those in the middle on extroversion-introversion being least open—a direct expression for the extreme risk-takers and extroverts, and a fantasy compensation for the extreme conservatives and introverts.

5. Do risk-taking and extroversion, as dimensions of personality, have further aesthetic consequences? We proposed the following hypothesis in the field of architecture: that the high risk-taker and the extrovert may prefer to dwell in larger architectural spaces; may wish to be surrounded by a larger space envelope. Further, we suggested that degree of spatial expansiveness and of motivational openness to musical arousal may well be related.

Cognitive, Social, and Physiological Determinants of Emotional State *

Stanley Schachter and Jerome E. Singer

The problem of which cues, internal or external, permit a person to label and identify his own emotional state has been with us since the days that

* From S. Schachter & J. E. Singer, "Cognitive, Social, and Physiological Determinants of Emotional State," *Psychological Review,* **69** (1962), 379-399. Reprinted by permission of the authors and the American Psychological Association.

This experiment is part of a program of research on cognitive and physiological determinants of emotional state which is being conducted at the Department of Social Psychology at Columbia University under PHS Research Grant M-2584 from the National Institute of Mental Health, United States Public Health Service. This experiment was conducted at the Laboratory for Research in Social Relations at the University of Minnesota.

James (1890) first tendered his doctrine that "the bodily changes follow directly the perception of the exciting fact, and that our feeling of the same changes as they occur *is* the emotion" (p. 449). Since we are aware of a variety of feeling and emotion states, it should follow from James' proposition that the various emotions will be accompanied by a variety of differentiable bodily states. Following James' pronouncement, a formidable number of studies were undertaken in search of the physiological differentiators of the emotions. The results, in these

The authors wish to thank Jean Carlin and Ruth Hase, the physicians in the study, and Bibb Latané and Leonard Weller who were the paid participants.

early days, were almost uniformly negative. All of the emotional states experimentally manipulated were characterized by a general pattern of excitation of the sympathetic nervous system but there appeared to be no clear-cut physiological discriminators of the various emotions. This pattern of results was so consistent from experiment to experiment that Cannon (1929) offered, as one of the crucial criticisms of the James-Lange theory, the fact that "the same visceral changes occur in very different emotional states and in non-emotional states" (p. 351).

More recent work, however, has given some indication that there may be differentiators. Ax (1953) and Schachter (1957) studied fear and anger. On a large number of indices both of these states were characterized by a similarly high level of autonomic activation but on several indices they did differ in the degree of activation. Wolf and Wolff (1947) studied a subject with a gastric fistula and were able to distinguish two patterns in the physiological responses of the stomach wall. It should be noted, though, that for many months they studied their subject during and following a great variety of moods and emotions and were able to distinguish only two patterns.

Whether or not there are physiological distinctions among the various emotional states must be considered an open question. Recent work might be taken to indicate that such differences are at best rather subtle and that the variety of emotion, mood, and feeling states are by no means matched by an equal variety of visceral patterns.

This rather ambiguous situation has led Ruckmick (1936), Hunt, Cole, and Reis (1958), Schachter (1959) and others to suggest that cognitive factors may be major determinants of emotional states. Granted a general

pattern of sympathetic excitation as characteristic of emotional states, granted that there may be some differences in pattern from state to state, it is suggested that one labels, interprets, and identifies this stirred-up state in terms of the characteristics of the precipitating situation and one's apperceptive mass. This suggests, then, that an emotional state may be considered a function of a state of physiological arousal [1] and of a cognition appropriate to this state of arousal. The cognition, in a sense, exerts a steering function. Cognitions arising from the immediate situation as interpreted by past experience provide the framework within which one understands and labels his feelings. It is the cognition which determines whether the state of physiological arousal will be labeled as "anger," "joy," "fear," or whatever.

In order to examine the implications of this formulation let us consider the fashion in which these two elements, a state of physiological arousal and cognitive factors, would interact in a variety of situations. In most emotion inducing situations, of course, the two factors are completely interrelated. Imagine a man walking alone down a dark alley, a figure with a gun suddenly appears. The perception-cognition "figure with a gun" in some fashion initiates a state of physiological arousal; this state of arousal is interpreted in terms of knowledge about dark alleys and guns and the state of arousal is labeled "fear." Similarly a

---

[1] Though our experiments are concerned exclusively with the physiological changes produced by the injection of adrenalin, which appear to be primarily the result of sympathetic excitation, the term physiological arousal is used in preference to the more specific "excitation of the sympathetic nervous system" because there are indications, to be discussed later, that this formulation is applicable to a variety of bodily states.

student who unexpectedly learns that he has made Phi Beta Kappa may experience a state of arousal which he will label "joy."

Let us now consider circumstances in which these two elements, the physiological and the cognitive, are, to some extent, independent. First, is the state of physiological arousal alone sufficient to induce an emotion? Best evidence indicates that it is not. Marañon [2] (1924), in a fascinating study, (which was replicated by Cantril and Hunt, 1932, and Landis and Hunt, 1932) injected 210 of his patients with the sympathomimetic agent adrenalin and then simply asked them to introspect. Seventy-one percent of his subjects simply reported their physical symptoms with no emotional overtones; 29 percent of the subjects responded in an apparently emotional fashion. Of these the great majority described their feelings in a fashion that Marañon labeled "cold" or "as if" emotions, that is, they made statements such as "I feel *as if* I were afraid" or *"as if* I were awaiting a great happiness." This is a sort of emotional "déjà vu" experience; these subjects are neither happy nor afraid; they feel "as if" they were. Finally a very few cases apparently reported a genuine emotional experience. However, in order to produce this reaction in most of these few cases, Marañon (1924) points out:

> One must suggest a memory with strong affective force but not so strong as to produce an emotion in the normal state. For example, in several cases we spoke to our patients before the injection of their sick children or dead parents and they responded calmly to this topic. The same topic presented later, during the adrenal commotion, was sufficient to trigger

emotion. This adrenal commotion places the subject in a situation of "affective imminence" (pp. 307-308).

Apparently, then, to produce a genuinely emotional reaction to adrenalin, Marañon was forced to provide such subjects with an appropriate cognition.

Though Marañon (1924) is not explicit on his procedure, it is clear that his subjects knew that they were receiving an injection and in all likelihood knew that they were receiving adrenalin and probably had some order of familiarity with its effects. In short, though they underwent the pattern of sympathetic discharge common to strong emotional states, at the same time they had a completely appropriate cognition or explanation as to why they felt this way. This, we would suggest, is the reason so few of Marañon's subjects reported any emotional experience.

Consider now a person in a state of physiological arousal for which no immediately explanatory or appropriate cognitions are available. Such a state could result were one covertly to inject a subject with adrenalin or, unknown to him, feed the subject a sympathomimetic drug such as ephedrine. Under such conditions a subject would be aware of palpitations, tremor, face flushing, and most of the battery of symptoms associated with a discharge of the sympathetic nervous system. In contrast to Marañon's (1924) subjects he would, at the same time, be utterly unaware of why he felt this way. What would be the consequence of such a state?

Schachter (1959) has suggested that precisely such a state would lead to the arousal of "evaluative needs" (Festinger, 1954), that is, pressures would act on an individual in such a state to understand and label his bodily feelings. His bodily state grossly resembles the condition in which it has been at

---

[2] Translated copies of Marañon's (1924) paper may be obtained by writing to the senior author.

times of emotional excitement. How would he label his present feelings? It is suggested, of course, that he will label his feelings in terms of his knowledge of the immediate situation.[3] Should he at the time be with a beautiful woman he might decide that he was wildly in love or sexually excited. Should he be at a gay party, he might, by comparing himself to others, decide that he was extremely happy and euphoric. Should he be arguing with his wife, he might explode in fury and hatred. Or, should the situation be completely inappropriate he could decide that he was excited about something that had recently happened to him or, simply, that he was sick. In any case, it is our basic assumption that emotional states are a function of the interaction of such cognitive factors with a state of physiological arousal.

This line of thought, then, leads to the following propositions:

1. Given a state of physiological arousal for which an individual has no immediate explanation, he will "label" this state and describe his feelings in terms of the cognitions available to him. To the extent that cognitive factors are potent determiners of emotional states, it could be anticipated that precisely the same state of physiological arousal could be labeled "joy" or "fury" or "jealousy" or any of a great diversity of emotional labels depending on the cognitive aspects of the situation.

2. Given a state of physiological arousal for which an individual has a completely appropriate explanation (for example, "I feel this way because I have just received an injection of adrenalin") no evaluative needs will arise and the individual is unlikely to label his feelings in terms of the alternative cognitions available.

Finally, consider a condition in which emotion inducing cognitions are present but there is no state of physiological arousal. For example, an individual might be completely aware that he is in great danger but for some reason (drug or surgical) remain in a state of physiological quiescence. Does he experience the emotion "fear"? Our formulation of emotion as a joint function of a state of physiological arousal and an appropriate cognition, would, of course, suggest that he does not, which leads to our final proposition.

3. Given the same cognitive circumstances, the individual will react emotionally or describe his feelings as emotions only to the extent that he experiences a state of physiological arousal.[4]

PROCEDURE

The experimental test of these propositions requires (a) the experimental manipulation of a state of physiological arousal, (b) the manipulation of the extent to which the subject has an appropriate or proper explanation of his bodily state, and (c) the creation of situations from which explanatory cognitions may be derived.

In order to satisfy the first two experimental requirements, the experiment was cast in the framework of a study of the effects of vitamin supple-

---

[3] This suggestion is not new for several psychologists have suggested that situational factors should be considered the chief differentiators of the emotions. Hunt, Cole, and Reis (1958) probably make this point most explicitly in their study distinguishing among fear, anger, and sorrow in terms of situational characteristics.

[4] In this critique of the James-Lange theory of emotion, Cannon (1929) also makes the point that sympathectomized animals and patients do seem to manifest emotional behavior. This criticism is, of course, as applicable to the above proposition as it was to the James-Lange formulation.

ments on vision. As soon as a subject arrived, he was taken to a private room and told by the experimenter:

In this experiment we would like to make various tests of your vision. We are particularly interested in how certain vitamin compounds and vitamin supplements affect the visual skills. In particular, we want to find out how the vitamin compound called "Suproxin" affects your vision.

What we would like to do, then, if we can get your permission, is to give you a small injection of Suproxin. The injection itself is mild and harmless; however, since some people do object to being injected we don't want to talk you into anything. Would you mind receiving a Suproxin injection?

If the subject agrees to the injection (and all but 1 of 185 subjects did) the experimenter continues with instructions we shall describe shortly, then leaves the room. In a few minutes a physician enters the room, briefly repeats the experimenter's instructions, takes the subject's pulse and then injects him with Suproxin.

Depending upon condition, the subject receives one of two forms of Suproxin—epinephrine or a placebo.

Epinephrine or adrenalin is a sympathomimetic drug whose effects, with minor exceptions, are almost a perfect mimicry of a discharge of the sympathetic nervous system. Shortly after injection systolic blood pressure increases markedly, heart rate increases somewhat, cutaneous blood flow decreases, while muscle and cerebral blood flow increase, blood sugar and lactic acid concentration increase, and respiration rate increases slightly. As far as the subject is concerned the major subjective symptoms are palpitation, tremor, and sometimes a feeling of flushing and accelerated breathing. With a subcutaneous injection (in the dosage administered to our subjects),

such effects usually begin within 3–5 minutes of injection and last anywhere from 10 minutes to an hour. For most subjects these effects are dissipated within 15–20 minutes after injection.

Subjects receiving epinephrine received a subcutaneous injection of ½ cubic centimeter of a 1:1000 solution of Winthrop Laboratory's Suprarening, a saline solution of epinephrine bitartrate.

Subjects in the placebo condition received a subcutaneous injection of ½ cubic centimeter of saline solution. This is, of course, completely neutral material with no side effects at all.

Manipulating an Appropriate Explanation

By "appropriate" we refer to the extent to which the subject has an authoritative, unequivocal explanation of his bodily condition. Thus, a subject who had been informed by the physician that as a direct consequence of the injection he would feel palpitations, tremor, etc. would be considered to have a completely appropriate explanation. A subject who had been informed only that the injection would have no side effects would have no appropriate explanation of his state. This dimension of appropriateness was manipulated in three experimental conditions which shall be called: Epinephrine Informed (Epi Inf), Epinephrine Ignorant (Epi Ign), and Epinephrine Misinformed (Epi Mis).

Immediately after the subject had agreed to the injection and before the physician entered the room, the experimenter's spiel in each of these conditions went as follows:

Epinephrine informed.

I should also tell you that some of our subjects have experienced side effects from the Suproxin. These side effects are transitory, that is, they will only last for about 15 or 20 minutes.

What will probably happen is that your hand will start to shake, your heart will start to pound, and your face may get warm and flushed. Again these are side effects lasting about 15 or 20 minutes.

While the physician was giving the injection, she told the subject that the injection was mild and harmless and repeated this description of the symptoms that the subject could expect as a consequence of the shot. In this condition, then, subjects have a completely appropriate explanation of their bodily state. They know precisely what they will feel and why.

Epinephrine ignorant. In this condition, when the subject agreed to the injection, the experimenter said nothing more relevant to side effects and simply left the room. While the physician was giving the injection, she told the subject that the injection was mild and harmless and would have no side effects. In this condition, then, the subject has no experimentally provided explanation for his bodily state.

Epinephrine misinformed.

I should also tell you that some of our subjects have experienced side effects from the Suproxin. These side effects are transitory, that is, they will only last for about 15 or 20 minutes. What will probably happen is that your feet will feel numb, you will have an itching sensation over parts of your body, and you may get a slight headache. Again these are side effects lasting 15 or 20 minutes.

And again, the physician repeated these symptoms while injecting the subject.

None of these symptoms, of course, are. consequences of an injection of epinephrine and, in effect, these instructions provide the subject with a completely inappropriate explanation of his bodily feelings. This condition was introduced as a control condition of sorts. It seemed possible that the description of side effects in the Epi Inf condition might turn the subject introspective, self-examining, possibly slightly troubled. Differences on the dependent variables between the Epi Inf and Epi Ign conditions might, then, be due to such factors rather than to differences in appropriateness. The false symptoms in the Epi Mis condition should similarly turn the subject introspective, and so forth, but the instructions in this condition do not provide an appropriate explanation of the subject's state.

Subjects in all of the above conditions were injected with epinephrine. Finally, there was a placebo condition in which subjects, who were injected with saline solution, were given precisely the same treatment as subjects in the Epi Ign condition.

Producing an Emotion-Inducing Cognition

Our initial hypothesis has suggested that given a state of physiological arousal for which the individual has no adequate explanation, cognitive factors can lead the individual to describe his feelings with any of a diversity of emotional labels. In order to test this hypothesis, it was decided to manipulate emotional states which can be considered quite different—euphoria and anger.

There are, of course, many ways to induce such states. In our own program of research, we have concentrated on social determinants of emotional states and have been able to demonstrate in other studies that people do evaluate their own feelings by comparing themselves with others around them (Schachter 1959; Wrightsman 1960). In this experiment we have attempted again to manipulate emotional state by social means. In one set of conditions, the subject is placed together with a stooge who has been trained to act euphorically. In a second set of conditions the subject is with a stooge trained to act in an angry fashion.

Euphoria

Immediately [5] after the subject had been injected, the physician left the room and the experimenter returned with a stooge whom he introduced as another subject, then said:

> Both of you have had the Suproxin shot and you'll both be taking the same tests of vision. What I ask you to do now is just wait for 20 minutes. The reason for this is simply that we have to allow 20 minutes for the Suproxin to get from the injection site into the bloodstream. At the end of 20 minutes when we are certain that most of the Suproxin has been absorbed into the bloodstream, we'll begin the tests of vision.

The room in which this was said had been deliberately put into a state of mild disarray. As he was leaving, the experimenter apologetically added:

> The only other thing I should do is to apologize for the condition of the room. I just didn't have time to clean it up. So, if you need any scratch paper or rubber bands or pencils, help yourself. I'll be back in 20 minutes to begin the vision tests.

As soon as the experimenter had left, the stooge introduced himself again, made a series of standard icebreaker comments, and then launched his routine. For observation purposes,

_____
[5] It was, of course, imperative that the sequence with the stooge begin before the subject felt his first symptoms for otherwise the subject would be virtually forced to interpret his feelings in terms of events preceding the stooge's entrance. Pretests had indicated that, for most subjects, epinephrine-caused symptoms began within 3-5 minutes after injection. A deliberate attempt was made then to bring in the stooge within 1 minute after the subject's injection.

the stooge's act was broken into a series of standard units, demarcated by a change in activity or a standard comment. In sequence, the units of the stooge's routine were the following:

1. Stooge reaches for a piece of paper and starts doodling saying, "They said we could use this for scratch, didn't they?" He doodles a fish for some 30 seconds, then says:

2. "This scrap paper isn't even much good for doodling" and crumples paper and attempts to throw it into wastebasket in far corner of the room. He misses but this leads him into a "basketball game." He crumples up other sheets of paper, shoots a few baskets, says "Two points" occasionally. He gets up and does a jump shot saying, "The old jump shot is really on today."

3. If the subject has not joined in, the stooge throws a paper basketball to the subject saying, "Here, you try it."

4. Stooge continues his game saying, "The trouble with paper basketballs is that you don't really have any control."

5. Stooge continues basketball, then gives it up saying, "This is one of my good days. I feel like a kid again. I think I'll make a plane." He makes a paper airplane saying, "I guess I'll make one of the longer ones."

6. Stooge flies plane. Gets up and retrieves plane. Flies again, and so forth.

7. Stooge throws plane at subject.

8. Stooge, flying plane, says, "Even when I was a kid, I was never much good at this."

9. Stooge tears off part of plane saying, "Maybe this plane can't fly but at least it's good for something." He wads up paper and making a slingshot of a rubber band begins to shoot the paper.

10. Shooting, the stooge says, "They [paper ammunition] really go better if you make them long. They don't work right if you wad them up."

11. While shooting, stooge notices a sloppy pile of manila folders on a table. He builds a tower of these folders, then goes to the opposite end of the room to shoot at the tower.

12. He misses several times, then hits and cheers as the tower falls. He goes over to pick up the folders.

13. While picking up, he notices, behind a portable blackboard, a pair of hula hoops which have been covered with black tape with a few wires sticking out of the tape. He reaches for these, taking one for himself and putting the other aside but within reaching distance of the subject. The stooge tries the hula hoop, saying, "This isn't as easy as it looks."

14. Stooge twirls hoop wildly on arm, saying, "Hey, look at this—this is great."

15. Stooge replaces the hula hoop and sits down with his feet on the table. Shortly thereafter the experimenter returns to the room.

This routine was completely standard, though its pace, of course, varied depending upon the subject's reaction, the extent to which he entered into this bedlam and the extent to which he initiated activities of his own. The only variations from this standard routine were those forced by the subject. Should the subject originate some nonsense of his own and request the stooge to join in, he would do so. And, he would, of course, respond to any comments initiated by the subject.

Subjects in each of the three "appropriateness" conditions and in the placebo condition were submitted to this setup. The stooge, of course, never knew in which condition any particular subject fell.

Anger

Immediately after the injection, the experimenter brought a stooge into the subject's room, introduced the two and after explaining the necessity for a 20-minute delay for "the Suproxin

to get from the injection site into the bloodstream," he continued, "We would like you to use these 20 minutes to answer these questionnaires." Then handing out the questionnaires, he concludes with, "I'll be back in 20 minutes to pick up the questionnaires and begin the tests of vision."

Before looking at the questionnaire, the stooge says to the subject,

I really wanted to come for an experiment today, but I think it's unfair for them to give you shots. At least, they should have told us about the shots when they called us; you hate to refuse, once you're here already.

The questionnaires, five pages long, start off innocently requesting face-sheet information and then grow increasingly personal and insulting. The stooge, sitting directly opposite the subject, paces his own answers so that at all times subject and stooge are working on the same question. At regular points in the questionnaire, the stooge makes a series of standardized comments about the questions. His comments start off innocently enough, grow increasingly querulous, and finally he ends up in a rage. In sequence, he makes the following comments.

1. Before answering any items, he leafs quickly through the questionnaire saying, "Boy, this is a long one."

2. Question 7 on the questionnaire requests, "List the foods that you would eat in a typical day." The stooge comments, "Oh for Pete's sake, what did I have for breakfast this morning?"

3. Question 9 asks, "Do you ever hear bells? ____. How often? ____." The stooge remarks, "Look at Question 9. How ridiculous can you get? I hear bells every time I change classes."

4. Question 13 requests, "List the childhood disease you have had and the age at which you had them" to which the stooge remarks, "I get an-

noyed at this childhood disease question. I can't remember what childhood diseases I had, and especially at what age. Can you?"

5. Question 17 asks "What is your father's average annual income?" and the stooge says, "This really irritates me. It's none of their business what my father makes. I'm leaving that blank."

6. Question 25 presents a long series of items such as "Does not bathe or wash regularly," "Seems to need psychiatric care," and so on and requests the respondent to write down for which member of his immediate family each item seems most applicable. The question specifically prohibits the answer "None" and each item must be answered. The stooge says, "I'll be damned if I'll fill out Number 25. 'Does not bathe or wash regularly'— that's a real insult." He then angrily crosses out the entire item.

7. Question 28 reads:
"How many times each week do you have sexual intercourse?" 0-1 —— 2-3 —— 4-6 —— 7 and over ——. The stooge bites out, "The hell with it! I don't have to tell them all this."

8. The stooge sits sullenly for a few moments then he rips up his questionnaire, crumples the pieces and hurls them to the floor, saying, "I'm not wasting any more time. I'm getting my books and leaving" and he stamps out of the room.

9. The questionnaire continues for eight more questions ending with: "With how many men (other than your father) has your mother had extramarital relationships?"
4 and under ——: 5-9 ——: 10 and over ——.

Subjects in the Epi Ign, Epi Inf and Placebo conditions were run through this "anger"-inducing sequence. The stooge, again, did not know to which condition the subject had been assigned.

In summary, this is a seven-condition experiment which, for two differ-

ent emotional states, allows us (a) to evaluate the effects of "appropriateness" on emotional inducibility and (b) to begin to evaluate the effects of sympathetic activation on emotional inducibility. In schematic form the conditions are the following:

EUPHORIA	ANGER
Epi Inf	Epi Inf
Epi Ign	Epi Ign
Epi Mis	Placebo
Placebo	

The Epi Mis condition was not run in the Anger sequence. This was originally conceived as a control condition and it was felt that its inclusion in the Euphoria conditions alone would suffice as a means of evaluating the possible artifactual effect of the Epi Inf instructions.

Measurement

Two types of measures of emotional state were obtained. Standardized observation through a one-way mirror was the technique used to assess the subject's behavior. To what extent did he act euphoric or angry? Such behavior can be considered in a way as a "semiprivate" index of mood for as far as the subject was concerned, his emotional behavior could be known only to the other person in the room— presumably another student. The second type of measure was self-report in which, on a variety of scales, the subject indicated his mood of the moment. Such measures can be considered "public" indices of mood for they would, of course, be available to the experimenter and his associates.

Observation

EUPHORIA. For each of the first 14 units of the stooge's standardized routine an observer kept a running chronicle of what the subject did and said. For each unit the observer coded the subject's behavior in one or more of the following categories:

Category 1: Joins in activity. If the subject entered into the stooge's activities, for example, if he made or flew airplanes, threw paper basketballs, hula-hooped, and so on, his behavior was coded in this category.

Category 2: Initiates new activity. A subject was so coded if he gave indications of creative euphoria, that is, if, on his own, he initiated behavior outside of the stooge's routine. Instances of such behavior would be the subject who threw open the window and, laughing, hurled paper basketballs at passersby; or, the subject who jumped on a table and spun one hula hoop on his leg and the other on his neck.

Categories 3 and 4: Ignores or watches stooge. Subjects who paid flatly no attention to the stooge or who, with or without comment, simply watched the stooge without joining in his activity were coded in these categories.

For any particular unit of behavior, the subject's behavior was coded in one or more of these categories. To test reliability of coding two observers independently coded two experimental sessions. The observers agreed completely on the coding of 88 percent of the units.

ANGER. For each of the units of stooge behavior, an observer recorded the subject's responses and coded them according to the following category scheme:

Category 1: Agrees. In response to the stooge the subject makes a comment indicating that he agrees with the stooge's standardized comment or that he, to, is irked by a particular item on the questionnaire. For example, a subject who responded to the stooge's comment on the "father's income" question by saying, "I don't like that kind of personal question either" would be so coded (scored $+2$).

Category 2: Disagrees. In response to the stooge's comment, the subject makes a comment which indicates that he disagrees with the stooge's meaning or mood; for example, in response to the stooge's comment on the "father's income" question, such a subject might say, "Take it easy, they probably have a good reason for wanting the information" (scored -2).

Category 3: Neutral. A noncommittal or irrelevant response to the stooge's remark (scored 0).

Category 4: Initiates agreement or disagreement. With no instigation by the stooge, a subject, so coded, would have volunteered a remark indicating that he felt the same way or, alternatively, quite differently than the stooge. Examples would be "Boy I hate this kind of thing" or "I'm enjoying this" (scored $+2$ or -2).

Category 5: Watches. The subject makes no verbal response to the stooge's comment but simply looks directly at him (scored 0).

Category 6: Ignores. The subject makes no verbal response to the stooge's comment nor does he look at him; the subject, paying no attention at all to the stooge, simply works at his own questionnaire (scored -1).

A subject was scored in one or more of these categories for each unit of stooge behavior. To test reliability, two observers independently coded three experimental sessions. In order to get a behavioral index of anger, observation protocol was scored according to the values presented in parentheses after each of the above definitions of categories. In a unit-by-unit comparison, the two observers agreed completely on the scoring of 71 percent of the units jointly observed. The scores of the two observers differed by a value of 1 or less for 88 percent of the units coded and in not a single case did the two observers differ in the direction of their scoring of a unit.

Self-Report of Mood and Physical Condition

When the subject's session with the stooge was completed, the experimenter returned to the room, took pulses and said:

> Before we proceed with the vision tests, there is one other kind of information which we must have. We have found, as you can probably imagine, that there are many things beside Suproxin that affect how well you see in our tests. How hungry you are, how tired you are, and even the mood you're in at the time—whether you feel happy or irritated at the time of testing will affect how well you see. To understand the data we collect on you, then, we must be able to figure out which effects are due to causes such as these and which are caused by Suproxin.

> The only way we can get such information about your physical and emotional state is to have you tell us. I'll hand out these questionnaires and ask you to answer them as accurately as possible. Obviously, our data on the vision tests will only be as accurate as your description of your mental and physical state.

In keeping with this spiel, the questionnaire that the experimenter passed out contained a number of mock questions about hunger, fatigue, and so on, as well as questions of more immediate relevance to the experiment. To measure mood or emotional state the following two were the crucial questions:

1. How irritated, angry or annoyed would you say you feel at present?

2. How good or happy would you say you feel at present?

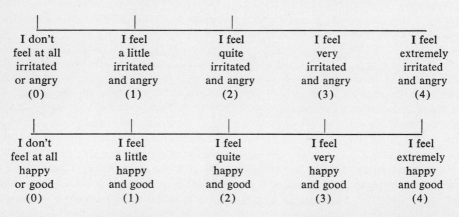

I don't feel at all irritated or angry (0)	I feel a little irritated and angry (1)	I feel quite irritated and angry (2)	I feel very irritated and angry (3)	I feel extremely irritated and angry (4)

I don't feel at all happy or good (0)	I feel a little happy and good (1)	I feel quite happy and good (2)	I feel very happy and good (3)	I feel extremely happy and good (4)

To measure the physical effects of epinephrine and determine whether or not the injection had been successful in producing the necessary bodily state, the following questions were asked:

1. Have you experienced any palpitation (consciousness of your own heart beat)?

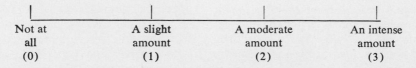

Not at all (0)	A slight amount (1)	A moderate amount (2)	An intense amount (3)

2. Did you feel any tremor (involuntary shaking of the hands, arms or legs)?

Not at all (0)	A slight amount (1)	A moderate amount (2)	An intense amount (3)

To measure possible effects of the instructions in the Epi Mis condition, the following questions were asked:

1. Did you feel any numbness in your feet?
2. Did you feel any itching sensation?
3. Did you experience any feeling of headache?

To all three of these questions was attached a four-point scale running from "Not at all" to "An intense amount."

In addition to these scales, the subjects were asked to answer two open-end questions on other physical or emotional sensations they may have experienced during the experimental session. A final measure of bodily state was pulse rate which was taken by the physician or the experimenter at two times—immediately before the injection and immediately after the session with the stooge.

When the subjects had completed these questionnaires, the experimenter announced that the experiment was over, explained the deception and its necessity in detail, answered any questions, and swore the subjects to secrecy. Finally, the subjects answered a brief questionnaire about their experiences, if any, with adrenalin and their previous knowledge or suspicion of the experimental setup. There was no indication that any of the subjects had known about the experiment beforehand but 11 subjects were so extremely suspicious of some crucial feature of the experiment that their data were automatically discarded.

Subjects

The subjects were all male, college students taking classes in introductory psychology at the University of Minnesota. Some 90 percent of the students in these classes volunteer for a subject pool for which they receive two extra points on their final exam for every hour that they serve as experimental subjects. For this study the records of all potential subjects were cleared with the Student Health Service in order to insure that no harmful effects would result from the injections.

Evaluation of the Experimental Design

The ideal test of our propositions would require circumstances which our experiment is far from realizing. First, the proposition that: "A state of physiological arousal for which an individual has no immediate explanation will lead him to label this state in terms of the cognitions available to him" obviously requires conditions under which the subject does not and cannot have a proper explanation of his bodily state. Though we toyed with such fantasies as ventilating the experimental room with vaporized adrenalin, reality forced us to rely on the disguised injection of Suproxin—a technique which was far from ideal for no matter what the experimenter told them, some subjects would inevitably attribute their feelings to the injection. To the extent that subjects did so, differences between the several appropriateness conditions should be attenuated.

Second, the proposition that: "Given the same cognitive circumstances the individual will react emotionally only to the extent that he experiences a state of physiological arousal" requires for its ideal test the manipulation of states of physiological arousal and of physiological quiescence. Though there is no question that epinephrine effectively produces a state of arousal, there is also no question that a placebo does not prevent physiological arousal. To the extent that the experimental situation effectively produces sympathetic stimulation in placebo subjects, the proposition is difficult to test, for such a factor would attenuate differences between epinephrine and placebo subjects.

Both of these factors, then, can be expected to interfere with the test of our several propositions. In presenting the results of this study, we shall first present condition by condition results and then evaluate the effect of these two factors on experimental differences.

RESULTS

Effects of the Injections on Bodily State

Let us examine first the success of the injections at producing the bodily state required to examine the propositions at test. Does the injection of epinephrine produce symptoms of sym-

pathetic discharge as compared with the placebo injection? Relevant data are presented in Table 1 where it can be immediately seen that on all items subjects who were in epinephrine conditions show considerably more evidence of sympathetic activation than do subjects in placebo conditions. In all epinephrine conditions pulse rate increases significantly when compared with the decrease characteristic of the placebo conditions. On the scales it is clear that epinephrine subjects experience considerably more palpitation and tremor than do placebo subjects. In all possible comparisons on these symptoms, the mean scores of subjects in any of the epinephrine conditions are greater than the corresponding scores in the placebo conditions at better than the .001 level of significance. Examination of the absolute values of these scores makes it quite clear that subjects in epinephrine conditions were, indeed, in a state of physiological arousal, while most subjects in placebo conditions were in a relative state of physiological quiescence.

The epinephrine injection, of course, did not work with equal effectiveness for all subjects; indeed for a few subjects it did not work at all. Such sub-

TABLE 1

THE EFFECTS OF THE INJECTIONS ON BODILY STATE

Condition	N	PULSE		SELF-RATING OF				
		Pre	Post	Palpitation	Tremor	Numbness	Itching	Headache
Euphoria								
Epi Inf	27	85.7	88.6	1.20	1.43	0	0.16	0.32
Epi Ign	26	84.6	85.6	1.83	1.76	0.15	0	0.55
Epi Mis	26	82.9	86.0	1.27	2.00	0.06	0.08	0.23
Placebo	26	80.4	77.1	0.29	0.21	0.09	0	0.27
Anger								
Epi Inf	23	85.9	92.4	1.26	1.41	0.17	0	0.11
Epi Ign	23	85.0	96.8	1.44	1.78	0	0.06	0.21
Placebo	23	84.5	79.6	0.59	0.24	0.14	0.06	0.06

jects reported almost no palpitation or tremor, showed no increase in pulse and described no other relevant physical symptoms. Since for such subjects the necessary experimental conditions were not established, they were automatically excluded from the data and all further tabular presentations will not include such subjects. Table 1, however, does include the data of these subjects. There were four such subjects in euphoria conditions and one of them in anger conditions.

In order to evaluate further data on Epi Mis subjects it is necessary to note the results of the "numbness," "itching," and "headache" scales also presented in Table 1. Clearly the subjects in the Epi Mis condition do not differ on these scales from subjects in any of the other experimental conditions.

Effects of the Manipulations on Emotional State

EUPHORIA. *Self-report.* The effects of the several manipulations on emotional state in the euphoria conditions are presented in Table 2. The scores recorded in this table are derived, for each subject, by subtracting the value of the point he checks on the irritation scale from the value of the point he checks on the happiness scale. Thus, if a subject were to check the point "I feel a little irritated and angry" on the irritation scale and the point "I feel very happy and good" on the happiness scale, his score would be $+2$. The higher the positive value, the happier and better the subject reports himself as feeling. Though we employ an index for expositional simplicity, it should be noted that the two components of the index each yield results completely consistent with those contained by use of this index.

Let us examine first the effects of the appropriateness instructions. Comparison of the scores for the Epi Mis and Epi Inf conditions makes it immediately clear that the experimental differences are not due to artifacts resulting from the informed instructions. In both conditions the subject was warned to expect a variety of symptoms as a consequence of the injection. In the Epi Mis condition, where the symptoms were inappropriate to the subject's bodily state the self-report score is almost twice that in the Epi Inf condition where the symptoms were completely appropriate to the subject's bodily state. It is reasonable, then, to attribute differences between informed subjects and those in other conditions to differences in manipulated appropriateness rather than to artifacts such as introspectiveness or self-examination.

It is clear that, consistent with expectations, subjects were more susceptible to the stooge's mood and consequently more euphoric when they had no explanation of their own bodily states than when they did. The means of both the Epi Ign and Epi Mis conditions are considerably greater than the mean of the Epi Inf condition.

It is of interest to note that Epi Mis subjects are somewhat more euphoric than are Epi Ign subjects. This pattern repeats itself in other data shortly to be presented. We would attribute this difference to differences in the appropriateness dimension. Though, as in the Epi Ign condition, a subject is not provided with an explanation of his bodily state, it is, of course, possible that he will provide one for himself which is not derived from his interaction with the stooge. Most reasonably he could decide for himself that he feels this way because of the injection. To the extent that he does so he should be less susceptible to the stooge. It seems probable that he would be less likely to hit on such an explanation in the Epi Mis condition than in the Epi

440   COGNITION, MOTIVATION AND PERSONALITY

TABLE 2

SELF-REPORT OF EMOTIONAL STATE IN THE EUPHORIA CONDITIONS

Condition	N	Self-Report scales	Comparison	p[a]
Epi Inf	25	0.98	Epi Inf vs. Epi Mis	$<.01$
Epi Ign	25	1.78	Epi Inf vs. Epi Ign	.02
Epi Mis	25	1.90	Placebo vs. Epi Mis,	ns
Placebo	26	1.61	Ign, or Inf	

[a] All p values reported throughout paper are two-tailed.

Ign condition for in the Epi Mis condition both the experimenter and the doctor have told him that the effects of the injection would be quite different from what he actually feels. The effect of such instructions is probably to make it more difficult for the subject himself to hit on the alternative explanation described above. There is some evidence to support this analysis. In open-end questions in which subjects described their own mood and state, 28 percent of the subjects in the Epi Ign condition made some connection between the injection and their bodily state compared with the 16 percent of subjects in the Epi Mis condition who did so. It could be considered, then, that these three conditions fall along a dimension of appropriateness, with the Epi Inf condition at one extreme and the Epi Mis condition at the other.

Comparing the placebo to the epinephrine conditions, we note a pattern which will repeat itself throughout the data. Placebo subjects are less euphoric than either Epi Mis or Epi Ign subjects but somewhat more euphoric than Epi Inf subjects. These differences are not, however, statistically significant. We shall consider the epinephrine-placebo comparisons in detail in a later section of this paper following the presentation of additional relevant data. For the moment, it is clear that, by self-report manipulating appropriateness has had a very strong effect on euphoria.

Behavior. Let us next examine the extent to which the subject's behavior was affected by the experimental manipulations. To the extent that his mood has been affected, one should expect that the subject will join in the stooge's whirl of manic activity and initiate similar activities of his own. The relevant data are presented in Table 3. The column labeled "Activ-

TABLE 3

BEHAVIORAL INDICATIONS OF EMOTIONAL STATE IN THE EUPHORIA CONDITIONS

Condition	N	Activity index	Mean number of acts initiated
Epi Inf	25	12.72	.20
Epi Ign	25	18.28	.56
Epi Mis	25	22.56	.84
Placebo	26	16.00	.54

p value

Comparison	Activity index	Initiates[a]
Epi Inf vs. Epi Mis	.05	.03
Epi Inf vs. Epi Ign	ns	.08
Plac vs. Epi Mis, Ign, or Inf	ns	ns

[a] Tested by X^2 comparison of the proportion of subjects in each condition initiating new acts.

ity index" presents summary figures on the extent to which the subject joined in the stooge's activity. This is a weighted index which reflects both the nature of the activities in which the subject engaged and the amount of time he was active. The index was devised by assigning the following weights to the subject's activities: 5—hula-hooping; 4—shooting with sling-shot; 3—paper airplanes; 2—paper basketballs; 1—doodling; 0—does nothing. Pre-test scaling on 15 college students ordered these activities with respect to the degree of euphoria they represented. Arbitrary weights were assigned so that the wilder the activity, the heavier the weight. These weights are multiplied by an estimate of the amount of time the subject spent in each activity and the summed products make up the activity index for each subject. This index may be considered a measure of behavioral euphoria. It should be noted that the same between-condition relationships hold for the two components of this index as for the index itself.

The column labeled "Mean number of acts initiated" presents the data on the extent to which the subject deviates from the stooge's routine and initiates euphoric activities of his own.

On both behavioral indices, we find precisely the same pattern of relationships as those obtained with self-reports. Epi Mis subjects behave somewhat more euphorically than do Epi Ign subjects who in turn behave more euphorically than do Epi Inf subjects. On all measures, then, there is consistent evidence that a subject will take over the stooge's euphoric mood to the extent that he has no other explanation of his bodily state.

Again it should be noted that on these behavioral indices, Epi Ign and Epi Mis subjects are somewhat more euphoric than placebo subjects but not significantly so.

ANGER. *Self-report.* Before presenting data for the anger conditions, one point must be made about the anger manipulation. In the situation devised, anger, if manifested, is most likely to be directed at the experimenter and his annoyingly personal questionnaire. As we subsequently discovered, this was rather unfortunate, for the subjects, who had volunteered for the experiment for extra points on their final exam, simply refused to endanger these points by publicly blowing up, admitting their irritation to the experimenter's face, or spoiling the questionnaire. Though, as the reader will see, the subjects were quite willing to manifest anger when they were alone with the stooge, they hesitated to do so on material (self-ratings of mood and questionnaire) that the experimenter might see, and only after the purposes of the experiment had been revealed were many of these subjects willing to admit to the experimenter that they had been irked or irritated.

This experimentally unfortunate situation pretty much forces us to rely on the behavioral indices derived from observation of the subject's presumably private interaction with the stooge. We do, however, present data on the self-report scales in Table 4. These figures are derived in the same way as the figures presented in Table 2 for the euphoria conditions, that is, the value checked on the irritation scale is subtracted from the value checked on the happiness scale. Though, for the reasons stated above, the absolute magnitude of these figures (all positive) is relatively meaningless, we can, of course, compare condition means within the set of anger conditions. With the happiness-irritation index employed, we should, of course, anticipate precisely the reverse results from those obtained in the euphoria conditions; that is, the Epi Inf subjects in the anger conditions should again be less susceptible to the stooge's mood

TABLE 4

SELF-REPORT OF EMOTIONAL STATE IN THE ANGER CONDITIONS

Condition	N	Self-Report scales	Comparison	p
Epi Inf	22	1.91	Epi Inf vs. Epi Ign	.08
Epi Ign	23	1.39	Placebo vs. Epi Ign or Inf	ns
Placebo	23	1.63		

and should, therefore, describe themselves as in a somewhat happier frame of mind than subjects in the Epi Ign condition. This is the case; the Epi Inf subjects average 1.91 on the self-report scales while the Epi Ign subjects average 1.39.

Evaluating the effects of the injections, we note again that, as anticipated, Epi Ign subjects are somewhat less happy than Placebo subjects but, once more, this is not a significant difference.

Behavior. The subject's responses to the stooge, during the period when both were filling out their questionnaires, were systematically coded to provide a behavioral index of anger. The coding scheme and the numerical values attached to each of the categories have been described in the methodology section. To arrive at an "Anger index" the numerical value assigned to a subject's responses to the stooge is summed together for the several units of stooge behavior. In the coding scheme used, a positive value to this index indicates that the subject agrees with the stooge's comment and is growing angry. A negative value indicates that the subject either disagrees with the stooge or ignores him.

The relevant data are presented in Table 5. For this analysis, the stooge's routine has been divided into two phases—the first two units of his behavior (the "long" questionnaire and "What did I have for breakfast?") are considered essentially neutral revealing nothing of the stooge's mood; all of the following units are considered "angry" units for they begin with an irritated remark about the "bells" question and end with the stooge's fury as he rips up his questionnaire and stomps out of the room. For the neutral units, agreement or disagreement with the stooge's remarks is, of course, meaningless as an index of mood and we should anticipate no difference between conditions. As can be seen in Table 5, this is the case.

For the angry units, we must, of course, anticipate that subjects in the Epi Ign condition will be angrier than subjects in the Epi Inf condition. This is indeed the case. The Anger index for the Epi Ign condition is positive and large, indicating that these subjects have become angry, while in the Epi Inf condition the Anger index is slightly negative in value indicating

TABLE 5

BEHAVIORAL INDICATIONS OF EMOTIONAL STATE IN THE ANGER CONDITIONS

Condition	N	Neutral units	Anger units
Epi Inf	22	+0.07	−0.18
Epi Ign	23	+0.30	+2.28
Placebo	22[a]	−0.09	+0.79

Comparison for anger units	p
Epi Inf vs. Epi Ign	<.01
Epi Ign vs. Placebo	<.05
Placebo vs. Epi Inf	ns

[a] For one subject in this condition the sound system went dead and the observer could not, of course, code his reactions.

that these subjects have failed to catch the stooge's mood at all. It seems clear that providing the subject with an appropriate explanation of his bodily state greatly reduces his tendency to interpret his state in terms of the cognitions provided by the stooge's angry behavior.

Finally, on this behavioral index, it can be seen that subjects in the Epi Ign condition are significantly angrier than subjects in the Placebo condition. Behaviorally, at least, the injection of epinephrine appears to have led subjects to an angrier state than comparable subjects who received Placebo shots.

Conformation of Data to Theoretical Expectations

Now that the basic data of this study have been presented, let us examine closely the extent to which they conform to theoretical expectations. If our hypotheses are correct and if this experimental design provided a perfect test for these hypotheses, it should be anticipated that in the euphoria conditions the degree of experimentally produced euphoria should vary in the following fashion:

$$\text{Epi Mis} \geqq \text{Epi Ign} > \text{Epi Inf} = \text{Placebo}$$

And in the anger conditions, anger should conform to the following pattern:

$$\text{Epi Ign} > \text{Epi Inf} = \text{Placebo}$$

In both sets of conditions, it is the case that emotional level in the Epi Mis and Epi Ign conditions is considerably greater than that achieved in the corresponding Epi Inf conditions. The results for the Placebo condition, however, are ambiguous for consistently the Placebo subject fall between the Epi Ign and the Epi Inf subjects. This is a particularly troubling pattern

for it makes it impossible to evaluate unequivocally the effects of the state of physiological arousal and indeed raises serious questions about our entire theoretical structure. Though the emotional level is consistently greater in the Epi Mis and Epi Ign conditions than in the Placebo condition, this difference is significant at acceptable probability levels only in the anger conditions.

In order to explore the problem further, let us examine the experimental factors identified earlier, which might have acted to restrain the emotional level in the Epi Ign and Epi Mis conditions. As was pointed out earlier, the ideal test of our first two hypotheses requires an experimental setup in which the subject has flatly no way of evaluating his state of physiological arousal other than by means of the experimentally provided cognitions. Had it been possible to physiologically produce a state of sympathetic activation by means other than injection, one could have approached this experimental ideal more closely than in the present setup. As it stands, however, there is always a reasonable alternative cognition available to the aroused subject—he feels the way he does because of the injection. To the extent that the subject seizes on such an explanation of his bodily state, we should expect that he will be uninfluenced by the stooge. Evidence presented in Table 6 for the anger condition and in Table 7 for the euphoria conditions indicates that this is, indeed, the case.

As mentioned earlier, some of the Epi Ign and Epi Mis subjects in their answers to the open-end questions clearly attributed their physical state to the injection, e.g., "the shot gave me the shivers." In Tables 6 and 7 such subjects are labeled "Self-informed." In Table 6 it can be seen that the self-informed subjects are considerably less angry than are the remaining subjects; indeed, they are not angry at all. With these self-informed subjects eliminated the difference between the Epi Ign and the Placebo

TABLE 6

THE EFFECTS OF ATTRIBUTING BODILY STATE TO THE INJECTION ON ANGER IN THE ANGER EPI IGN CONDITION

	N	Anger index
Self-informed subjects	3	−1.67
Others	20	+2.88
Self-informed versus Others		$p = .05$

conditions is significant at the .01 level of significance.

Precisely the same pattern is evident in Table 7 for the euphoria conditions. In both the Epi Mis and the Epi Ign conditions, the self-informed subjects have considerably lower activity indices than do the remaining subjects. Eliminating self-informed subjects, comparison of both of these conditions with the Placebo condition yields a difference significant at the .03 level of significance. It should be noted, too, that the self-informed subjects have much the same score on the activity index as do the experimental Epi Inf subjects (Table 3).

It would appear, then, that the experimental procedure of injecting the subjects, by providing an alternative cognition, has, to some extent, obscured the effects of epinephrine. When account is taken of this artifact, the evidence is good that the state of physiological arousal is a necessary component of an emotional experience for when self-informed subjects are removed, epinephrine subjects give consistent indications of greater emotionality than do Placebo subjects.

Let us examine next the fact that

TABLE 7

THE EFFECTS OF ATTRIBUTING BODILY STATE TO THE INJECTION ON EUPHORIA IN THE EUPHORIA EPI IGN AND EPI MIS CONDITIONS

EPI IGN		
	N	Activity index
Self informed subjects	8	11.63
Others	17	21.14
Self-informed versus Others		$p = .05$

EPI MIS		
	N	Activity index
Self-informed subjects	5	12.40
Others	20	25.10
Self-informed versus Others		$p = .10$

consistently the emotional level, both reported and behavioral, in Placebo conditions is greater than that in the Epi Inf conditions. Theoretically, of course, it should be expected that the two conditions will be equally low, for by assuming that emotional state is a joint function of a state of physiological arousal and of the appropriateness of a cognition we are, in effect, assuming a multiplicative function, so that if either component is at zero, emotional level is at zero. As noted earlier this expectation should hold if we can be sure that there is no sympathetic activation in the Placebo conditions. This assumption, of course, is completely unrealistic for the injection of placebo does not prevent sympathetic activation. The experimental situations were fairly dramatic and certainly some of the placebo subjects gave indications of physiological arousal. If our general line of reasoning is correct, it should be anticipated that the emotional level of subjects who give indications of sympathetic activity will be greater than that of subjects who do not. The relevant evidence is presented in Tables 8 and 9.

TABLE 8

SYMPATHETIC ACTIVATION AND EUPHORIA IN THE EUPHORIA PLACEBO CONDITION

Subject whose:	N	Activity index
Pulse decreased	14	10.67
Pulse increased or remained same	12	23.17
Pulse decreasers versus pulse increasers or same		$p = .02$

TABLE 9

SYMPATHETIC ACTIVATION AND ANGER IN ANGER PLACEBO CONDITION

Subject whose:	N[a]	Anger index
Pulse decreased	13	+0.15
Pulse increased or remained same	8	+1.69
Pulse decreasers versus pulse increasers or same		$p = .01$

[a] N reduced by two cases owing to failure of sound system in one case and experimenter's failure to take pulse in another.

As an index of sympathetic activation we shall use the most direct and unequivocal measure available—change in pulse rate. It can be seen in Table 1 that the predominant pattern in the Placebo condition is a decrease in pulse rate. We shall assume, therefore, that those subjects whose pulse increases or remains the same give indications of sympathetic activity while those subjects whose pulse decreases do not. In Table 8, for the euphoria condition, it is immediately clear that subjects who give indications of sympathetic activity are considerably more euphoric than are subjects who show no sympathetic activity. This relationship is, of course, confounded by the fact that euphoric subjects are considerably more active than noneuphoric subjects—a factor which independent of mood could elevate pulse rate. However, no such factor operates in the anger condition where angry subjects are neither more active nor talkative than calm subjects. It can be seen in Table 9 that Placebo subjects who show signs of sympathetic activation give indications of considerably more anger than do subjects who show no such signs. Conforming to expectations, sympathetic activation accompanies an increase in emotional level.

It should be noted, too, that the emotional levels of subjects showing no signs of sympathetic activity are quite comparable to the emotional level of subjects in the parallel Epi Inf conditions (see Tables 3 and 5). The similarity of these sets of scores and their uniformly low level of indicated emotionality would certainly make it appear that both factors are essential to an emotional state. When either the level of sympathetic arousal is low or a completely appropriate cognition is available, the level of emotionality is low.

DISCUSSION

Let us summarize the major findings of this experiment and examine the extent to which they support the propositions offered in the introduction of this paper. It has been suggested, first, that given a state of physiological arousal for which an individual has no explanation, he will label this state in terms of the cognitions available to him. This implies, of course, that by manipulating the cognitions of an individual in such a state we can manipulate his feelings in diverse directions. Experimental results support this proposition for, following the injection of epinephrine, those subjects who had no explanation for the bodily state thus produced gave behavioral and self-report indications that they had been readily manipulable into the disparate feeling states of euphoria and anger.

From this first proposition, it must follow that given a state of physiological arousal for which the individual has a completely satisfactory explanation, he will not label this state in terms of the alternative cognitions available. Experimental evidence strongly supports this expectation. In those conditions in which subjects were injected with epinephrine and were told precisely what they would feel and why, they proved relatively immune to any effects of the manipulated cognitions. In the anger condition, such subjects did not report or show anger; in the euphoria condition, such subjects reported themselves as far less happy than subjects with an identical bodily state but no adequate knowledge of why they felt the way they did.

Finally, it has been suggested that given constant cognitive circumstances, an individual will react emotionally only to the extent that he experiences a state of physiological arousal. Without taking account of experimental artifacts, the evidence in support of this proposition is consistent but tentative. When the effects of "self-informing" tendencies in epinephrine subjects and of "self-arousing" tendencies in placebo subjects are partialed out, the evidence strongly supports the proposition.

The pattern of data, then, falls neatly in line with theoretical expectations. However, the fact that we were forced, to some extent, to rely on internal analyses in order to partial out the effects of experimental artifacts

inevitably makes our conclusions somewhat tentative. In order to further test these propositions on the interaction of cognitive and physiological determinants of emotional state, a series of additional experiments, published elsewhere, was designed to rule out or overcome the operation of these artifacts. In the first of these, Schachter and Wheeler (1962) extended the range of manipulated sympathetic activation by employing three experimental groups—epinephrine, placebo, and a group injected with the sympatholytic agent, chlorpromazine. Laughter at a slapstick movie was the dependent variable, and the evidence is good that amusement is a direct function of manipulated sympathetic activation.

In order to make the epinephrine-placebo comparison under conditions which would rule out the operation of any self-informing tendency, two experiments were conducted on rats. In one of these Singer (1961) demonstrated that under fear-inducing conditions, manipulated by the simultaneous presentation of a loud bell, a buzzer, and a bright flashing light, rats injected with epinephrine were considerably more frightened than rats injected with a placebo. Epinephrine-injected rats defecated, urinated, and trembled more than did placebo-injected rats. In non-fear control conditions, there were no differences between epinephrine and placebo groups, neither group giving any indication of fear. In another study, Latané and Schachter (1962) demonstrated that rats injected with epinephrine were notably more capable of avoidance learning than were rats injected with a placebo. Using a modified Miller-Mowrer shuttlebox, these investigators found that during an experimental period involving 200 massed trials, 15 rats injected with epinephrine avoided shock an average of 101.2 trials while 15 placebo-injected rats averaged only 37.3 avoidances.

Taken together, this body of studies does give strong support to the propositions which generated these experimental tests. Given a state of sympathetic activation, for which no immediately appropriate explanation is available, human subjects can be readily manipulated into states of euphoria, anger, and amusement. Varying the intensity of sympathetic activation serves to vary the intensity of a variety of emotional states in both rats and human subjects.

Let us examine the implications of these findings and of this line of thought for problems in the general area of the physiology of the emotions. We have noted in the introduction that the numerous studies on physiological differentiators of emotional states have, viewed en masse, yielded quite inconclusive results. Most, though not all, of these studies have indicated no differences among the various emotional states. Since as human beings, rather than as scientists, we have no difficulty identifying, labeling, and distinguishing among our feelings, the results of these studies have long seemed rather puzzling and paradoxical. Perhaps because of this, there has been a persistent tendency to discount such results as due to ignorance or methodological inadequacy and to pay far more attention to the very few studies which demonstrate *some* sort of physiological differences among emotional states than to the very many studies which indicate no differences at all. It is conceivable, however, that these results should be taken at face value and that emotional states may, indeed, be generally characterized by a high level of sympathetic activation with few if any physiological distinguishers among the many emotional states. If

this is correct, the findings of the present study may help to resolve the problem. Obviously this study does *not* rule out the possibility of physiological differences among the emotional states. It is the case, however, that given precisely the same state of epinephrine-induced sympathetic activation, we have, by means of cognitive manipulations, been able to produce in our subjects the very disparate states of euphoria and anger. It may indeed be the case that cognitive factors are major determiners of the emotional labels we apply to a common state of sympathetic arousal.

Let us ask next whether our results are specific to the state of sympathetic activation or if they are generalizable to other states of physiological arousal. It is clear that from our experiments proper, it is impossible to answer the question for our studies have been concerned largely with the effects of an epinephrine created state of sympathetic arousal. We would suggest, however, that our conclusions are generalizable to almost any pronounced internal state for which no appropriate explanation is available. This suggestion receives some support from the experiences of Nowlis and Nowlis (1956) in their program of research on the effects of drugs on mood. In their work the Nowlises typically administer a drug to groups of four subjects who are physically in one another's presence and free to interact. The Nowlises describe some of their results with these groups as follows:

At first we used the same drug for all 4 men. In those sessions seconal, when compared with placebo, increased the checking of such words as expansive, forceful, courageous, daring, elated, and impulsive. In our first statistical analysis we were confronted with the stubborn fact that when the same drug is given to all 4 men in a group, the N that has to be entered into the analysis is 1, not 4. This increases the cost of an already expensive experiment by a considerable factor, but it cannot be denied that the effects of these drugs may be and often are quite contagious. Our first attempted solution was to run tests on groups in which each man had a different drug during the same session, such as 1 on seconal, 1 on benzedrine, 1 on dramamine, and 1 on placebo. What does seconal do? Cooped up with, say, the egotistical benzedrine partner, the withdrawn, indifferent dramimine partner, and the slightly bored lactose man, the seconal subject reports that he is distractible, dizzy, drifting, glum, defiant, languid, sluggish, discouraged, dull, gloomy, lazy, and slow! This is not the report of mood that we got when all 4 men were on seconal. It thus appears that the moods of the partners do definitely influence the effect of seconal (p. 350).

It is not completely clear from this description whether this "contagion" of mood is more marked in drug than in placebo groups, but should this be the case, these results would certainly support the suggestion that our findings are generalizable to internal states other than that produced by an injection of epinephrine.

Finally, let us consider the implications of our formulation and data for alternative conceptualizations of emotion. Perhaps the most popular current conception of emotion is in terms of "activation theory" in the sense employed by Lindsley (1951) and Woodworth and Schlosberg (1958). As we understand this theory, it suggests that emotional states should be considered as at one end of a continuum of activation which is defined in terms of degree of automatic arousal and of electroencephalographic measures of activation. The results of the experiment described in this paper do, of course, suggest that such a formulation is not completely adequate. It is possible to have very high degrees of activation without a subject either appearing to be or describing himself as "emotional." Cognitive factors appear to be indispensable elements in any formulation of emotion.

SUMMARY

It is suggested that emotional states may be considered a function of a state of physiological arousal and of a cognition appropriate to this state of arousal. From this follows these propositions:

1. Given a state of physiological arousal for which an individual has no immediate explanation, he will label this state and describe his feelings in terms of the cognitions available to him. To the extent that cognitive factors are potent determiners of emotional states, it should be anticipated that precisely the same state of physiological arousal could be labeled "joy" or "fury" or "jealousy" or any of a great diversity of emotional labels depending on the cognitive aspects of the situation.

2. Given a state of physiological arousal for which an individual has a completely appropriate explanation, no evaluative needs will arise and the individual is unlikely to label his feelings in terms of the alternative cognitions available.

3. Given the same cognitive circumstances, the individual will react emotionally or describe his feelings as emotions only to the extent that he experiences a state of physiological arousal.

An experiment is described which, together with the results of other studies, supports these propositions.

REFERENCES

Ax, A. F., "Physiological Differentiation of Emotional States," *Psychosmatic Medicine,* **15** (1953), 433-42.

Cannon, W. B., *Bodily Changes in Pain, Hunger, Fear and Rage* (2nd ed.). New York: Appleton-Century-Crofts, Inc., 1929.

Cantril, H., and W. A. Hunt, "Emotional Effects Produced by the Injection of Adrenalin," *American Journal of Psychology,* **44** (1932), 300-307.

Festinger, L., "A Theory of Social Comparison Processes," *Human Relations,* **7** (1954), 114-40.

Hunt, J. McV., M. W. Cole, and E. E. Reis, "Situational Cues Distinguishing Anger, Fear, and Sorrow," *American Journal of Psychology,* **71** (1958), 136-51.

James, W., *The Principles of Psychology.* New York: Holt, Rinehart & Winston, Inc., 1890.

Landis, C. and W. A. Hunt, "Adrenalin and Emotion," *Psychological Review,* **39** (1932), 467-85.

Latané, B. and S. Schachter, "Adrenalin and Avoidance Learning," *Journal of Comparative Physiological Psychology,* **65** (1962), 369-72.

Lindsley, D. B., "Emotion," in *Handbook of Experimental Psychology,* ed. S. S. Stevens, pp. 473-516. New York: John Wiley & Sons, Inc., 1951.

Marañon, G., "Contribution à l'étude de l'action émotive de l'adrénaline," *Rev. Française Endocrinol.,* **2** (1924), 301-25.

Nowlis, V. and H. H. Nowlis, "The Description and Analysis of Mood," *Annals of New York Academy of Science,* **65** (1956), 345-55.

Ruckmick, C. A., *The Psychology of Feeling and Emotion.* New York: McGraw-Hill Book Company, Inc., 1936.

Schachter, J., "Pain, Fear, and Anger in Hypertensives and Normotensives: A Psychophysiologic Study," *Psychosomatic Medicine,* **19** (1957), 17-29.

Schachter, S., *The Psychology of Affiliation.* Stanford, Calif.: Stanford University Press, 1959.

Schachter, S. and L. Wheeler, "Epinephrine, Chlorpromazine, and Amusement," *Journal of Abnormal Social Psychology,* **65** (1962), 121-28.

Singer, J. E., "The Effects of Epinephrine, Chlorpromazine and Dibenzyline upon the Fright Responses of Rats under Stress and Non-stress Conditions." (Unpublished Doctoral dissertation, University of Minnesota, 1961.)

Wolf, S. and H. G. Wolff, *Human Gastric Function.* New York: Oxford University Press, 1947.

Woodworth, R. S. and H. Schlosberg, *Experimental Psychology.* New York: Holt, Rinehart & Winston, Inc., 1958.

Wrightsman, L. S., "Effects of Waiting with Others on Changes in Level of Felt Anxiety," *Journal of Abnormal Social Psychology,* **61** (1960), 216-22.

The Measurement and Correlates of Category Width as a Cognitive Variable *

Thomas F. Pettigrew

Bruner and Rodrigues (2) have demonstrated that Ss reveal marked individual consistency in the range or width of their cognitive categories. Using standard laboratory equipment, such as color mixing wheels and audio-oscillators, these investigators asked their Ss to select the extremes, for example, the darkest and lightest or highest and lowest, of a wide variety of categories. For such diverse categories as the brightness of an overcast sky and the pitch of a female singing voice, Ss in this situation tended to be consistently broad, medium, or narrow in their category widths relative to the total sample.

Such consistency suggests that category width may be fruitfully thought of as an *Anshauung* (5), complementing Klein's dimensions of leveling–sharpening and tolerance–resistance

* From T. F. Pettigrew, "The Measurement and Correlates of Category Width as a Cognitive Variable," *Journal of Personality*, 26 (1958), 532-44. Reprinted by permission of the author and publisher.

The author wishes to express his appreciation to Professor Jerome S. Bruner for his initial theoretical impetus and his continuing encouragement of this project. Gratitude is also extended to Professors Dorothy C. Adkins and Gordon W. Allport for their assistance, and to Mr. Edward Johnson of the University of North Carolina for his invaluable computational help. The project was supported by a grant from the Social Science Research Council.

to the unstable (4, 5). Several interpretations can be made as to precisely what this category width *Anshauung* is tapping. It can be thought of as measuring S's typical equivalence range for classifying objects. This would make category width an important factor in similarity problems. Wallach (12), for instance, has recently suggested that psychological similarity can be effectively studied in terms of factors influencing equivalence ranges. Another not incompatible possibility is that category width is tapping a "risk-taking" dimension. Broad categorizers seem to have a tolerance for type I errors: they risk negative instances in an effort to include a maximum of positive instances. By contrast, narrow categorizers are willing to make type II errors. They exclude many positive instances by restricting their category ranges in order to minimize the number of negative instances. It will require further research before these two possible interpretations can be properly evaluated.

The extensive cognitive and personality implications of this consistency of range phenomenon have led first to the development of an objectively scored, paper and pencil measure of category width. The present paper introduces the scale (*C-W* scale), lists its properties and correlates, and suggests its future research possibilities.

SCALE DEVELOPMENT

The first form of the *C-W* scale consisted of 14 items which supplied each category's average and required open-ended estimates of each category's extremes. Thus, one item stated that an average of 58 ships enter New York harbor daily, and *S* was asked to write down his guesses as to what were the largest number and the smallest number of ships to enter New York harbor in a single day. Two later forms replaced items with low item-test correlations and enlarged the scale. On all of these forms *S*s revealed significant consistency from one item to another in the breadth of their estimates. That is, when *S*s were ranked as to their category widths on each item, Kendall's *W* statistic repeatedly indicated for five college and high school samples significant concordance in rankings. *S*s proved to be reliably broad, medium, or narrow in their estimated ranges of such varied categories as speed of birds in flight, length of whales, and annual rainfall in Washington, D. C.

Following these paper and pencil replications of the Bruner and Rod-

rigues phenomenon, a final and more easily scored 20-item form of the scale was devised with fixed alternatives. This is reproduced in Table 1. The alternatives offered were empirically derived by choosing the 10th, 35th, 65th, and 90th percentile choices of the 750 college students who took the earlier, open-ended forms of the *C-W* scale.[1] Scoring of the items is based on how far from the given mean of the category is the particular alternative: $+3$ is assigned the alternative farthest from the mean, $+2$ for the next farthest, etc. Table 1 provides in parentheses the points assigned each alternative. The orders of these alternatives are varied to minimize response sets. Scores for questions *a* and *b* of each item are added together to obtain the total item score. Hence, the higher the score, the broader is the category width.

Properties of the Scale

CHIEF CORRELATES AND TENTATIVE COLLEGE DISTRIBUTIONS. *C-W* relates

---

[1] When the correct alternatives were available—as in items 15 and 19—they were supplied in place of the nearest alternative that would otherwise have been used.

TABLE 1

THE CATEGORY WIDTH SCALE ITEMS [a]

---

1. It has been estimated that the average width of windows is *34 inches*. What do you think:
   a. is the width of the widest window . . .

1.	1,363 inches . . . . . (3)[b]	3.	48 inches . . . . . (0)
2.	341 inches . . . . . (2)	4.	81 inches . . . . . (1)

   b. is the width of the narrowest window . . .

1.	3 inches . . . . . (2)	3.	11 inches . . . . . (1)
2.	18 inches . . . . . (0)	4.	1 inch . . . . . . (3)

2. Ornithologists tell us that the best guess of the average speed of birds in flight would be about *17 m.p.h.* What do you think:
   a. is the speed in flight of the fastest bird . . .

1.	25 m.p.h. . . . . . (0)	3.	73 m.p.h. . . . . . (2)
2.	105 m.p.h. . . . . . (3)	4.	34 m.p.h. . . . . . (1)

   b. is the speed in flight of the slowest bird . . .

1.	10 m.p.h. . . . . . (1)	3.	12 m.p.h. . . . . . (0)
2.	2 m.p.h. . . . . . (3)	4.	5 m.p.h. . . . . . (2)

TABLE 1 (*Continued*)

3. The average length of whales in the Atlantic Ocean has been estimated by zoologists to be roughly *65 feet*. What do you think:
   a. is the length of the longest whale in the Atlantic Ocean . . .
      1.   120 ft. . . . . (2)   3.   86 ft. . . . . (1)
      2.   190 ft. . . . . (3)   4.   75 ft. . . . . (0)
   b. is the length of the shortest whale in the Atlantic Ocean . . .
      1.   6 ft. . . . . (3)   3.   52 ft. . . . . (0)
      2.   43 ft. . . . . (1)   4.   21 ft. . . . . (2)
4. Shipping authorities have calculated that the average weight of merchant ships registered with the U.S. Maritime Commission in 1946 was *5,705 tons*. What do you think:
   a. is the weight of the heaviest ship registered with the commission . . .
      1.   10,500 tons . . . . . (1)   3.   23,000 tons . . . . . . (2)
      2.   62,000 tons . . . . . (3)   4.   7,500 tons . . . . . . (0)
   b. is the weight of the lightest ship registered with the commission . . .
      1.   3,900 tons . . . . . (0)   3.   2,700 tons . . . . . . (1)
      2.   1,100 tons . . . . . (2)   4.   2 tons . . . . . . (3)
5. Weather officials report that during this century Washington, D.C. has received an average rainfall of *41.1 inches* annually. What do you think:
   a. is the largest amount of rain that Washington has received in a single year during this century . . .
      1.   82.4 inches . . . . . (3)   3.   63.7 inches . . . . . (2)
      2.   45.8 inches . . . . . (0)   4.   51.2 inches . . . . . (1)
   b. is the smallest amount of rain that Washington has received in a single year during this century . . .
      1.   20.2 inches . . . . . (2)   3.   9.9 inches . . . . . (3)
      2.   36.3 inches . . . . . (0)   4.   29.7 inches . . . . . (1)
6. An average of *58 ships* entered or left New York harbor daily during the period from 1950 through 1955. What do you think:
   a. was the largest number of ships to enter or leave New York in a single day during this period . . .
      1.   69 ships . . . . . . (0)   3.   76 ships . . . . . (1)
      2.   153 ships . . . . . . (3)   4.   102 ships . . . . . (2)
   b. was the smallest number of ships to enter or leave New York in a single day during this period . . .
      1.   34 ships . . . . . (1)   3.   16 ships . . . . . (2)
      2.   3 ships . . . . . (3)   4.   43 ships . . . . . (0)
7. For the past twenty years, Alaska's population has increased an average *3,210 people* per year. What do you think:
   a. was the greatest increase in Alaska's population in a single year during these twenty years . . .
      1.   6,300 . . . . (2)   3.   3,900 . . . . (0)
      2.   21,500 . . . . (3)   4.   4,800 . . . . (1)
   b. was the smallest increase in Alaska's population in a single year during these twenty years . . .
      1.   470 . . . . (3)   3.   980 . . . . (2)
      2.   1,960 . . . . (1)   4.   2,520 . . . . (0)
8. Boating experts estimate that the average speed of all sailing craft in America is around *4.1 knots*. What do you think:
   a. is the speed of the fastest sailing boat in America . . .
      1.   8.2 knots . . . . . (1)   3.   5.9 knots . . . . . (0)
      2.   30.7 knots . . . . . (3)   4.   21.3 knots . . . . . (2)
   b. is the speed of the slowest sailing boat in America . . .
      1.   3.3 knots . . . . . (0)   3.   2.2 knots . . . . . (1)
      2.   0.6 knots . . . . . (3)   4.   1.2 knots . . . . . (2)
9. Book review editors guess that around *300 new American novels* have appeared annually since World War II. What do you think:
   a. is the largest number of novels to be published in America in a single year during this period . . .

TABLE 1 (*Continued*)

1.	380 novels .....(0)	3.	870 novels .....(3)
2.	495 novels .....(1)	4.	620 novels .....(2)

b. is the smallest number of novels to be published in America in a single year during this period . . .

1.	145 novels .....(2)	3.	90 novels .....(3)
2.	205 novels .....(1)	4.	260 novels .....(0)

10. Between 1900 and 1940 there was an average of *48 lynchings* per year in the United States. What do you think:

a. was the largest number of lynchings in any one year during this period in the United States . . .

1.	79 ....(2)	3.	53 ....(0)
2.	63 ....(1)	4.	135 ....(3)

b. was the smallest number of lynchings in any one year during this period in the United States . . .

1.	1 ....(3)	3.	33 ....(0)
2.	11 ....(2)	4.	19 ....(1)

11. It has been calculated that the average time for all trains in 1953 from New York City to Washington, D.C. was *285 minutes* (4 hours and 45 minutes). What do you think:

a. was the time of the slowest train from New York City to Washington in 1953 . . .

1.	337 minutes ....(1)	3.	396 minutes ....(2)
2.	304 minutes ....(0)	4.	483 minutes ....(3)

b. was the time of the fastest train from New York City to Washington in 1953 . . .

1.	236 minutes ....(1)	3.	268 minutes ....(0)
2.	202 minutes ....(2)	4.	145 minutes ....(3)

12. The average number of births in the world per day during 1955 has been computed to be *27,440*. What do you think:

a. was the largest number of births in the world in any one day during 1955 . . .

1.	36,501 ....(2)	3.	49,876 ....(3)
2.	28,207 ....(0)	4.	30.023 (1)

b. was the smallest number of births in the world in any one day during 1955 . . .

1.	26,340 ....(0)	3.	14,330 ....(3)
2.	24,725 ....(1)	4.	19,704 ....(2)

13. When all of the world's written languages are considered, linguists tell us that the average number of verbs per language must be somewhere around *15,000*. What do you think:

a. is the largest number of verbs in any single language . . .

1.	21,000 ....(1)	3.	50,000 ....(3)
2.	18.000 (0)	4.	30,000 ....(2)

b. is the smallest number of verbs in any single language . . .

1.	1,000 ....(3)	3.	5,000 ....(2)
2.	13,000 ....(0)	4.	10,000 ....(1)

14. The average muzzle to tail length of a sample of 1,000 German Shepherd dogs is *40.3 in.* What do you think:

a. is the length of the longest Shepherd dog in the sample . . .

1.	60.4 inches .....(3)	3.	44.1 inches .....(0)
2.	47.8 inches .....(1)	4.	54.2 inches .....(2)

b. is the length of the shortest Shepherd dog in the sample . . .

1.	34.6 inches .....(1)	3.	19.7 inches .....(3)
2.	28.4 inches .....(2)	4.	36.9 inches .....(0)

15. The average population of South American countries is approximately *8.6 million* people each. What do you think:

a. is the population of the most populated country in South America . . .

1.	11.2 million ....(0)	3.	23.6 million ....(1)
2.	54.7 million ....(2)	4.	129.1 million ....(3)

b. is the population of the least populated country in South America . . .

1.	7,000 ....(3)	3.	2.4 million ....(1)
2.	6.2 million ....(0)	4.	29,000 ....(2)

TABLE 1 (*Continued*)

16. A Stanford University home economists has estimated that the average American spends around *55 minutes* of his day eating. What do you think:
    a. is the longest eating time of any single American . . .

1.	185 minutes . . . . (2)	3.	245 minutes . . . . (3)
2.	125 minutes . . . . (1)	4.	90 minutes . . . . (0)

    b. is the shortest eating time of any single American . . .

1.	16 minutes . . . . (2)	3.	38 minutes . . . . (0)
2.	4 minutes . . . . (3)	4.	27 minutes . . . . (1)

17. In 1946 the average number of births per state was *68,000*. What do you think:
    a. was the highest number of births in a single state . . .

1.	87,000 . . . . (1)	3.	71,000 . . . . (0)
2.	122,000 . . . . (2)	4.	254,000 . . . . (3)

    b. was the lowest number of births in a single state . . .

1.	29,000 . . . . (1)	3.	14,000 . . . . (2)
2.	53,000 . . . . (0)	4.	900 . . . . (3)

18. Immediately after World War II, the average number of submarines owned by the largest seven navies in the world was *58*. What do you think:
    a. was the largest number of submarines owned by *one* of these navies . . .

1.	159 . . . . (3)	3.	118 . . . . (2)
2.	91 . . . . (1)	4.	69 . . . . (0)

    b. was the smallest number of submarines owned by *one* of these navies . . .

1.	22 . . . . (2)	3.	36 . . . . (1)
2.	9 . . . . (3)	4.	47 . . . . (0)

19. The average number of churches per religious denomination in the United States is estimated to be *511*. What do you think:
    a. is the largest number of churches of a single religious denomination in the U.S.A. . . .

1.	4,833 . . . . (2)	3.	1,219 . . . . (1)
2.	757 . . . . (0)	4.	39,801 . . . . (3)

    b. is the smallest number of churches of a single religious denomination in the U.S.A. . . .

1.	313 . . . . (0)	3.	1 . . . . (3)
2.	146 . . . . (1)	4.	23 . . . . (2)

20. In the years 1916 through 1946, according to the U.S. Weather Bureau, there was an average of *140 tornadoes* a year in the United States. What do you think:
    a. was the largest number of tornadoes in a single year in the United States during this period . . .

1.	154 . . . . (0)	3.	312 . . . . (3)
2.	243 . . . . (2)	4.	197 . . . . (1)

    b. was the smallest number of tornadoes in a single year in the United States during this period . . .

1.	103 . . . . (1)	3.	61 . . . . (2)
2.	122 . . . . (0)	4.	28 . . . . (3)

[a] Presented to all *S*'s with the title "Estimation Questionnaire," instruction stressing accuracy, and a simple example.

[b] Indicates the weights assigned to each item alternative.

significantly to both sex and quantitative (*Q*) scores on the ACE with University of North Carolina student samples. Table 2 shows that *C-W* has a significant, though low, correlation of +.17 with total ACE scores which is chiefly due to a higher +.26 co-efficient between *C-W* and the ACE *Q* score.

The sharp difference between the sexes on *C-W* is indicated in Table 3. Since these male and female populations do not differ on ACE *Q* scores, the males' typically broader category

TABLE 2
CORRELATIONS BETWEEN CATEGORY WIDTH AND ACE SCORES [a]

Variables	Product-moment r	p
C-W and total ACE	+.17	<.05
C-W and ACE L (linguistic)	+.07	n.s.
C-W and ACE Q (quantitative)	+.26	<.01

[a] Based on a sample of 200 college undergraduates.

TABLE 3
SEX AND CATEGORY WIDTH SCORE

Sex	N	C-W Mean	Range	SD	t	p	Narrows	Mediums	Broads
Males	218	71.87	23-117	17.32			0-66	67-78	79-120
					4.55	<.001			
Females	116	64.46	34- 99	12.04			0-58	59-70	71-120

(Last three columns: LIMITS OF DISTRIBUTION'S THIRDS)

estimates cannot be accounted for in terms of the quantitative variable. Both sex distributions do not significantly deviate from normality. Separate limits for the thirds of these distributions are provided in Table 3 for each sex. Using a children's form of the C-W scale, Wallach and Caron report equally striking sex differences among sixth-graders (12).

Over-time Reliability

Odd and even item split-half forms of the C-W were given to 97 University of North Carolina undergraduates at intervals of at least six weeks (the even and odd item forms were reversed as to order of presentation to two groups of Ss). The Spearman-Brown corrected coefficient proves to be + .72.

Internal Consistency

Five college samples varying in size from 42 to 66 yield Spearman-Brown corrected even-odd reliabilities ranging from + .86 to + .93. When the total 281 Ss are combined, the Spear-

man-Brown even-odd coefficient is + .90.

The 190 inter-item tetrachoric correlations calculated on 270 Ss for factor analytic purposes also give some indication of the scale's internal consistency.[2] Over 98 percent of these relationships are positive, with 87 percent of these significant at better than the 1 percent level and with 5 percent significant at better than the 5 percent level. The median tetrachoric coefficient is + .27 (p < .01).

Factorial Structure

A 21 x 21 tetrachoric correlation matrix was constructed for each item score and the Q score of the ACE of 270 college Ss. Employing Thurstone's complete centroid method (11), the four factors shown in Table 4 emerge. Orthogonal rotation yields the results in Table 5. It had been expected that the scale would have two important factors: one a verisimilitude factor

[2] Item dichotomization for the tetrachoric correlations was made by splitting each item as near its median as possible.

with heavy loadings on items with categories close to everyday experience, and the other a fantasy factor with heavy loadings on items with categories quite removed from common experience.

TABLE 4

ORIGINAL FACTOR MATRIX

C-W Items	FACTORS			
	I	II	III	IV
1	.45	—.35	.13	—.22
2	.57	—.21	—.14	—.14
3	.40	.14	—.20	—.40
4	.47	.32	.37	—.35
5	.35	.35	—.19	.16
6	.68	.12	.19	.23
7	.46	.18	.15	.10
8	.75	—.13	.13	.13
9	.47	.33	—.07	.14
10	.66	.04	.09	—.07
11	.54	.18	—.21	—.12
12	.43	.31	.11	.31
13	.46	—.11	—.27	.11
14	.50	.20	—.06	—.11
15	.46	—.28	.14	.08
16	.49	—.22	—.47	.18
17	.60	—.34	.18	—.07
18	.57	—.32	.24	.09
19	.69	—.26	.11	—.16
20	.56	.06	—.12	.16
ACE Q	.42	.15	—.09	—.01

Two major factors do evolve, but they bear no close resemblance to the verisimilitude-fantasy differentiation. Rather, they vary in their content and in their relationships with the ACE measure of quantitative ability (Q). Factor I is primarily a time and speed dimension: the scale's four-time or speed items—2, 8, 11, and 16—all have heavy loadings on it. Moreover, Q is weighted more heavily on factor I than on any of the remaining factors. By contrast, the other major dimension, factor II, is more general in its content and is the least related to Q of all the factors. Most of the items

with large factor II loadings—15, 17, 18, and 19—require direct judgments (as opposed to indirect judgments in terms of minutes or miles per hour) of such varied categories as births, submarines, and churches.

Only slightly related to Q, the smaller factors III and IV tend to have their heaviest loadings on relatively poor items. That is, such items as 3, 4, 7, 9, and 12 have been found to be among those with the least criterion

TABLE 5

ROTATED ORTHOGONAL FACTOR MATRIX

C-W Items	FACTORS			
	I	II	III	IV
1	.28	.50	—.14	.20
2	.52	.29	—.04	.22
3	.33	.00	.04	.52
4	—.01	.34	.41	.55
5	.33	—.15	.41	.08
6	.39	.39	.51	.02
7	.22	.23	.41	.10
8	.51	.52	.29	.05
9	.34	.00	.47	.12
10	.40	.37	.29	.26
11	.47	.03	.24	.32
12	.23	.11	.56	—.06
13	.55	.08	.06	.00
14	.35	.10	.29	.31
15	.32	.46	.05	—.04
16	.73	.01	—.05	—.09
17	.38	.60	.01	.11
18	.34	.61	.09	—.03
19	.46	.55	.04	.25
20	.50	.15	.29	.04
ACE Q	.33	.06	.25	.18

validity (Table 6). It appears, then, that these factors in large part constitute error.

Criterion Validity

The scale's criterion is defined as the category width rankings determined from laboratory procedures similar to those employed in the original Bruner and Rodrigues work. Twenty-six undergraduate Ss were individually tested on five categories not contained in the C-W scale. Presented with drawn lines of the average lengths of pheasants and turtles, they chose between lines drawn on a blackboard the longest and shortest instances of these categories. Similarly, they estimated the weight extremes of ostrich eggs with fixed sets of weights, and the pitch extremes of women's singing voices and factory whistles from fixed alternatives generated by an audio-oscillator. Rankings of the Ss according to their range estimates across these five categories prove to be significantly consistent (Kendall's $W = .334$,

TABLE 6

CRITERION VALIDITY OF C-W ITEMS [a]

Item	Mean of 9 Narrows	Mean of 9 Broads	t	One-tail p
19	2.11	4.22	2.75	.01
1	2.33	4.56	2.72	.01
8	3.33	4.11	2.58	.02
6	2.67	4.33	2.36	.02
15	1.78	3.44	2.24	.02
5	3.33	4.44	2.09	.05
16	3.00	4.00	2.00	.05
14	1.67	3.22	1.88	.05
13	2.89	4.00	1.65	.10
2	2.67	3.56	1.60	.10
17	3.33	4.22	1.44	.10
11	3.11	3.78	1.10	.15
3	2.78	3.78	1.08	.15
20	2.78	3.22	0.91	.20
4	3.22	3.78	0.73	.25
9	2.44	2.89	0.65	.30
12	4.22	4.56	0.62	.30
18	3.67	4.11	0.55	.30
7	3.44	3.67	0.34	.40
10	4.00	3.44	—0.05	—

[a] The criterion rankings were independently determined by laboratory procedures. The item analysis of this table indicates the discriminatory powers of each C-W item in separating the laboratory's narrow and broad thirds. The total C-W scale yields a rank order correlation with the criterion rankings of $+.57$, $p<.01$.

$p < .02$). This provides both a laboratory replication of Bruner and Rodrigues's finding and an independent ranking of the 26 Ss according to their category widths for criterion validity purposes.

The Ss were later administered C-W scales. Table 6 presents the item and total scale relationships with the criterion rankings. Of the 20 C-W items, 19 correctly discriminated between the criterion's broad and narrow thirds, 14 of these differences surpassing the 20 percent level of confidence and 8 surpassing the 5 percent level. Many of the poorer items in this table have been noted previously in the factorial structure discussion. The rank order correlation between the total C-W scale and the total criterion rankings is $+ .57$ ($p < .01$). Allowing for error in both sets of rankings, we may conclude that the C-W scale is measuring much the same phenomenon as that originally obtained in the laboratory.

C-W and Other Cognitive Variables

Four other cognitive tasks have been compared with C-W in an effort to define more precisely the category width dimension: Rokeach's "narrow-mindedness" task (8), a self-concept span instrument, the F scale (1), and the D scale (9).

Rokeach has delineated three types of categorizers on his task—comprehensive, narrow, and isolated (8). Comprehensive categorizers group all of Rokeach's ten political and religious labels under one concept, while narrows use more than one concept, and isolated categorizers omit labels. Those who categorize comprehensively in these terms were predicted to score higher on C-W than the narrow and isolated categorizers taken together. Both measures were administered to 68 college Ss. The 31 Ss who grouped

the ten terms comprehensively averaged 73.5 on the *C-W* as compared
with the remaining 37 narrow and isolated *S*s' average of 68.9. With a one-
tail *t* test, this difference is significant
at the 5 percent level of confidence.

Mayzner and Tresselt (7) have
studied value concept spans by defining span as the number of words in a
standard list checked by the respondent as being related to a particular
value area. Employing this definition
of span, the 300-word *Gough Adjective Check List* was administered to
106 male student *S*s who had previously taken the *C-W*. The "self-concept span"—the number of adjectives
checked as self-descriptive—was predicted to be related positively to *C-W*.
A product-moment correlation of
$+ .30$ supports the hypothesis at the
1 percent level of confidence. The
broader the categorizer, the more adjectives he tends to see as related to
himself.

The 30-item forms 40 and 45 of the
F scale (1) and the 40-item short
form of the *D* scale (9) were administered together with the *C-W* to 49
female college *S*s. While the authoritarian *F* measure correlated $+ .82$
with Rokeach's Dogmatism instrument, neither of these scales correlated
significantly with the *C-W*. *F* and *C-W*
yielded only a $+ .03$ coefficient, and
D and *C-W* produced only a $-.08$
relationship. The category width and
authoritarian variables apparently are
quite independent.

DISCUSSION

The scale properties of *C-W* seem
to be very adequate for further
research purposes. With both satisfactory reliabilities and substantial criterion validity, this objectively scored
measure has but one major limitation.
C-W is not a one dimensional test: it

is composed of two important, orthogonal factors—one a moderately
quantitative, time-and-speed dimension, the other a nonquantitative,
general dimension.

The scale's relationships with quantitative ability and sex have two
possible interpretations. They may be
artifacts of the procedures. The intensive use of numbers and the particular
choice of categories may lead the quantitatively gifted and males to score
higher. Alternatively, however, these
relationships may indicate that highly
quantitative people and males do tend
to be more broadly tuned to their
environment. As suggested by Wheeler's interesting work (14), individuals
with developed mathematical skills
may achieve a uniquely broad sense
of category variance. Males, too, may
be more reinforced than females in
our culture for wide category ranges.
Studies by Komarovsky (6), Diggory
(3), and Sears *et al.* (10) hint at such
a possibility, and Wallach and Caron's
work with children indicates that this
sex difference develops early in life
(13). Further work with the scale will
be necessary before a choice can be
made between these two possibilities.

The comparison between *C-W* and
the four other cognitive measures aid
in determining the nature of category
width. Both tasks revealing significant
association with *C-W*—Rokeach's narrow-mindedness technique and the
self-concept span measure—involve
categorizing behavior, too. Since comprehensive categorizers on Rokeach's
instrument tend to have wide category
ranges, and *C-W* broads judge more
adjectives on Gough's check list as
being self-descriptive, it appears that
breadth of categorizing generalizes to
a variety of procedures. This finding
lends support to the interpretation of
category width as a given *S*'s typical
equivalence range for classifying ob-

jects. Further research might check on this possibility more rigorously by observing how high and low *C-W* scorers differ in the building-up process of attaining a new category in an experimental setting.

The failure of the *F* and *D* scales to correlate with *C-W* indicates that authoritarianism, dogmatism, and their related concept, rigidity, are not helpful in understanding category width. The independence of these dimensions (and how many variables have ever been shown to be *un*related to *F*?) raises some interesting questions. Perhaps much of the heterogeneity frequently noted among high *F* scorers and especially among low *F* scorers can be partly accounted for in terms of *C-W* variance within each of these clusters. Future authoritarianism research could test this possibility by employing both *F* and *C-W* to sort their *S*s.

The risk-taking interpretation of *C-W* also deserves further research. Are broad categorizers different from narrow categorizers chiefly in their willingness to accept type I errors and tolerate negative instances? This explanation can be tested with both personality scale work and experimental studies employing *C-W* and known risk-taking procedures.

Another set of questions revolves around the developmental factors in childhood that make the phenomenon of range consistency possible. Whatever these factors are—independence training, inconsistent training, and so on—they must vary considerably in the training of the sexes. A children's form of the *C-W* has been constructed now for future research use in this area (13).

SUMMARY

When *S*s are asked to estimate the extremes of a number of diverse categories—from length of whales to annual rainfall in Washington, D. C.—they evidence a significant tendency to be consistent in their category ranges. That is, they are consistently broad, medium, or narrow in their category widths relative to the total sample.

Based on this phenomenon, a 20-item, objectively scored measure of category width (*C-W*) is presented together with its properties. With adequate overtime reliability and internal consistency, the scale yields a rank order correlation of + .57 with a laboratory-established criterion. It is not, however, an undimensional instrument. Two major orthogonal factors describe *C-W*'s inter-item matrix: one a moderately quantitative, time-and-speed dimension, the other a nonquantitative, general dimension.

C-W is positively related to the quantitative score of the ACE (+ .26), and males generally score higher than females. The scale is also significantly associated with two other categorizing tasks. It does not correlate, however, with either authoritarianism (*F* scale) or dogmatism (*D* scale).

Several interpretations of the scale are offered and future research suggested.

REFERENCES

1. Adorno, T. W., Else Frenkel-Brunswik, D. Levinson, and N. Sanford, *The Authoritarian Personality*. New York: Harper & Row, Publishers, 1950.

2. Bruner, J. S., J. J. Goodnow, and G. A. Austin, *A Study of Thinking*. New York: John Wiley & Sons, Inc., 1956.

3. Diggory, J. C. "Sex Differences in the Organization of Attitudes," *Journal of Personality*, **22** (1953), 89-100.

4. Holzman, P. S. and G. S. Klein, "Cognitive System-principles of Leveling and Sharpening: Individual Differ-

ences in Assimilation Effects in Visual Time-error," *Journal of Psychology*, **37** (1954), 105-22.

5. Klein, G. S., "The Personal World through Perception," in *Perception: An Approach to Personality*, eds. R. R. Blake and G. V. Ramsey, pp. 328-55. New York: The Ronald Press Company, 1951.

6. Komarovsky, Mirra, "Functional Analysis of Sex Roles," *American Sociological Review*, **15** (1950), 508-16.

7. Mayzner, M. S. and Margaret Tresselt, "Concept Span as a Composite Function of Personal Values, Anxiety, and Rigidity," *Journal of Personality*, **24** (1955), 20-33.

8. Rokeach, M., "A Method for Studying Individual Differences in 'Narrow-Mindedness,'" *Journal of Personality*, **20** (1951), 219-33.

9. ———, "Political and Religious Dogmatism: An Alternative to the Authoritarian Personality," *Psychology Monograph*, **70** (1956), No. 18 (Whole No. 425).

10. Sears, R. J. Whiting, V. Nowlis, and Pauline Sears, "Some Child-rearing Antecedents of Aggression and Dependency in Young Children," *Genetic Psychology Monograph*, **47** (1953), 135-236.

11. Thurstone, L. L., *Multiple Factor Analysis*. Chicago: University of Chicago Press, 1947.

12. Wallach, M., "On Psychological Similarity," *Psychological Review*, **65** (1958), 103-16.

13. Wallach, M. and J. Caron, "Attribute Criteriality and Sex-linked Conservatism as Determinants of Psychological Similarity," *Journal of Abnormal Psychology*. (In press.)

14. Wheeler, J. A., "A Septet of Sibyles: Aids in the Search for Truth," *American Scientist*, **44** (1956), 360-77.

Attribute Criteriality and Sex-linked Conservatism as Determinants of Psychological Similarity *

Michael A. Wallach and Albert J. Caron

In a recent paper, Wallach (1958) has suggested that an important determinant of whether a person will recog-

* From M. A. Wallach & A. J. Caron, "Attribute Criteriality and Sex-linked Conservatism as Determinants of Psychological Similarity," *Journal of Abnormal Social Psychology*, **59** (1959), 43-50. Reprinted by permission of the authors and the American Psychological Association.

This research is part of a project supported by Grant M-1324 from the United States Public Health Service, and under the general direction of Jerome S. Bruner, whom the authors wish to thank for his encouragement and aid. We are also indebted to Rhea Diamond for a critical reading of the manuscript, to Leonard Green for aid in constructing stimulus materials, and to Jean Yeomans for scheduling the Ss and for administering paper-and-pencil tests.

nize a second event as similar to a first is the nature of the contrast class he is implicitly or explicitly considering when presented with that first event.[1] Suppose, for example, that a person is learning to identify Boston Brahmins. He comes across various instances of this class of persons— some are old, others younger; some rich, others not as rich; and so on. In each case he finds out that the person

[1] The antecedents of this view are treated at length in the paper cited.

is of old aristocratic Yankee stock, and eventually he learns to make appropriate identifications. But how is he defining this class to himself? Does he accept every attribute of Boston Yankees as equally important or criterial to the class definition, so that he now has learned such people must be Anglo-Saxon in appearance, enunciate a flat "a," dress conservatively, express themselves with terseness and restraint, and so on? Very likely not. It is more probable that a person learns to define this class of persons mainly in terms of those characteristics which have been *absent* from contrasting negative instances—that is, from people that he had in mind as part of the non-Yankee class.

Consider two middle-class individuals of recent immigrant extraction, one from New York, the other from Boston. Suppose each sees a certain number of Boston Brahmins—the former in New York, the latter in Boston. Both also think about certain other kinds of people in contrast to Boston Brahmins, but these are likely to be different for each. Our New Yorker will think of middle-class, second-generation New Yorkers, and our Bostonian, of middle-class, second-generation Bostonians: in each case, people like himself. As a result, these two individuals should regard different attributes as crucial for identifying Boston blue bloods: for the New Yorker, a Boston accent and expressive terseness and restraint should be most criterial (in combination, of course, with physical appearance); for the Bostonian, more subtle aspects of manner and dress (for example, language idiom, drinking habits, etc.) would be most important. In sum, then, the characteristics we take as criterial for defining a class depend not only on the positive exemplars of that class to which we have been ex-

posed, but also on the particular sorts of negative exemplars that have been considered as a contrast. What one takes as a contrast, in turn, may depend on a host of factors—including one's social background.

But what has all this to do with psychological similarity? The paper cited above also suggested that we consider two events similar insofar as we place them in the same class. And this we will do, in turn, only if both exemplify the property or properties that are criterial for defining that class. It follows, then, that if a second event deviates from a first along an attribute regarded as criterial, it is more likely to be judged different from the first than if it deviates along an attribute regarded as noncriterial. When judging similarity, in other words, there should be less tolerance for deviation along an attribute viewed as criterial than along the same attribute when viewed as noncriterial; there should be greater "conceptual conservatism" in the former case than in the latter.

If we assume, then, that attribute criteriality depends on the contrasting negative instances present during learning, and that criteriality in turn affects psychological similarity, we should be able to predict a person's judgments of similarity or dissimilarity of other events to some key event if we know what contrasts were present when he first learned about that key event. Thus, returning to our New Yorker and Bostonian, suppose each is now exposed to an upper middle-class Bostonian of immigrant origin and of ambiguous appearance, but whose speech carries the immigrant idiom, and is asked if this person is a Boston Brahmin type. If our hypothesis about contrast and similarity is correct, then the New Yorker (sensitized to accent and restraint) will tend to say yes, while the Bostonian (sensitized to speech patterns) will tend to say no. And we expect this even though both persons have seen the same number and variety of Boston blue bloods.

But another aspect of the similarity question yet remains. Suppose we take a large number of middle-class, second-generation Bostonians—people who should tend to use speech patterns as criterial for defining Boston Brahmins—and let them see a variety of upper middle-class Bostonians of immigrant origin, ranging from one who speaks in Ivy League idiom to one who retains most of the immigrant idiom. We ask our sample of judges whether each such upper middle-class Bostonian seems like a Boston Brahmin or not. Since we postulate greater conceptual conservatism for criterial than for noncriterial attributes, we expect these persons to refuse to acknowledge similarity between the various upper middle-class Bostonians and Boston Brahmins much more often than middle-class immigrant New Yorkers (who in turn should be maximally "liberal" in acknowledging similarity). But will all the idiom-sensitive Bostonians be equally adamant in denying the upper middle-class Bostonians a resemblance to Brahmins? Or, stated differently, might there not be individual differences in conceptual conservatism?

A strong hint in this regard comes from recent work by Pettigrew [2] on category width. This investigator reports substantial and reliable differences between males and females in the range of attribute-values one is willing to assign to a category when given the *average* attribute-value of the category, males tending to be "broad" categorizers and females to be "narrow" categorizers. The disposition to bind concepts to their most frequent or most familiar instances—to be a narrow categorizer—seems very close to the notion of conceptual conservatism (intolerance of attribute deviation) advanced above. If this is the case, then, when faced with deviation along a criterial dimension, females, that is, people who tend to categorize narrowly, should also tend to perceive less similarity than males, that is, people who tend to categorize broadly.

The foregoing discussion hence has led us to two hypotheses concerning the relationship between conceptual conservatism and psychological similarity. The first assumes that tendencies toward conceptual conservatism should be greater for criterial attributes; and the second, that there are persistent individual differences in conceptual conservatism. The two hypotheses may be stated as follows:

1. Attribute criteriality: One event is more likely to be judged similar to a standard event if the two differ on some property which, although always present in the standard, has *not* been learned as criterial for defining it, than if this property *has* been learned as criterial for its definition.

2. Categorizing style: When presented with events of varying criterial difference from a standard, females should judge fewer of these events as similar to the standard than males, on the ground that the former tend to categorize more narrowly—that is, to be more conceptually conservative—than the latter.

The present experiment provides a test for each of these predictions.

METHOD

Seventy-eight public school children in the sixth grade [3] served as *S*s in a

---

[2] A paper-and-pencil measure of category width is presented in Pettigrew (1958).

[3] We are greatly indebted to Ernest R. Caverly, Superintendent of Schools, James

procedure based on the paradigm we have just discussed. They were taught about "poggles": a nonsense name for geometric forms with certain characteristics. For all of the children, exactly the same figures were called poggles. For half the Ss, however, the contrasting figures that were not poggles differed on one attribute, while for the other half they differed on another attribute.

In brief, the experiment involved three parts: (I) an initial concept attainment session in which differential criteriality for poggles was established; (II) a similarity judgment session involving reports of whether figures of varying deviation from poggles were similar to poggles or not; and (III) a perceptual discrimination session entailing an estimation of the number of different figures presented during the similarity judgment session.

Establishment of "Angle" and "Cutout" Criteriality Groups

In the concept attainment session, all Ss were given the task of learning to predict accurately whether each of a series of figures is or isn't a poggle. The following instructions were provided:

I'm going to show you some cards, one at a time. Each one has a different figure on it that looks something like this. (E showed S the bottom one of a stack of 32 cards.) These figures differ in several ways. Now, I have named some of these figures "poggles," and the rest are not poggles. Which are poggles and which not depends on one or more of the differences in the

R. Hobson, Director of Child Placement, and Elgie Clucas, Principal of the Michael Driscoll School in Brookline, Massachusetts, for making available the pupils and facilities of the Michael Driscoll School for this research.

figures. Your job is to figure out how to tell which are poggles and which not—and there's a definite way of telling. After I show you each card, you tell me whether you think it's a poggle or not and I'll tell you whether you're right or wrong. You'll name some incorrectly at the start because you won't have any clues, but after a while you should be able to name them all correctly.

The array of 32 cards was then presented one at a time in a prearranged but random order, the series being continued through a second runthrough if necessary, until S had attained the learning criterion of 16 correct predictions of "poggle" or "not poggle" in a row. All Ss were exposed to the same four noncriterial or noisy attributes. Thus, half the poggles and half the nonpoggles were blue, and half of each were red; likewise, half of each were large figures and half of each were small; half of each were pointing upward and half of each were pointing to S's right; and half of each had a hole punched near the base while the other half did not. For half the Ss, however (hereafter called the "angle" group or simply Group A), angularity was made criterial for poggles, in that all poggles had a stubby point and nonpoggles a sharp point. For the remaining Ss, on the other hand (called the "cutout" group or Group C), cutouts were made criterial by providing all poggles with square cutouts at their base corners, while nonpoggles had no cutouts. The criterial attribute for each group, moreover, remained constant for the other group (that is, in Group A all figures had cutouts, and in Group C all figures had stubby points). In the figures for each group, then, there were five attributes with two values each, and an additional attribute that was constant.

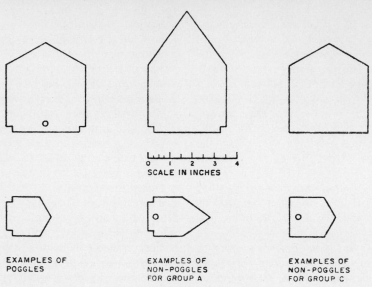

SCALE IN INCHES

EXAMPLES OF
POGGLES

EXAMPLES OF
NON-POGGLES
FOR GROUP A

EXAMPLES OF
NON-POGGLES
FOR GROUP C

FIG. 1. *Examples of poggles for both contrast groups, and examples of nonpoggles for each of the contrast groups, as used in Part I of the experiment.*

The 32 figures used for each group consisted of all possible combinations of attribute-values. Figure 1 presents examples of poggles, of nonpoggles for Group A, and of nonpoggles for Group C.

Similarity Judgment and Discrimination Report Sessions

The second part of the experiment ensued after S had learned the poggle concept to criterion. E introduced this next task in these words:

Now I am going to show you some figures one at a time. None of them, some of them, or all of them, may seem like poggles to you. You just learned what a poggle is, and a poggle is still the same thing. For each of the figures, I want you to tell me whether it seems like a poggle to you or not.

In this series 11 new cards were used, presented one at a time. The figures on all of these cards had square cutouts from the two corners of their

base, were red, large, pointed to S's right, and had no hole punched near the base. The way they varied was in the degree of stubbiness or sharpness of their angle point. The 11 degrees of angle variation used were equal differences in angle starting with one just a bit sharper than the stubby point that had been present in all poggles for both groups, and ending with one just a bit stubbier than the sharp point that had been present in all the contrast instances for Group A. Figure 2 shows these figures superimposed on one another in order of increasing sharpness of angle point. Let us refer to the stubby angle point exemplified by all poggles as Angle 1, and the sharp angle point exemplified by all of Group A's nonpoggles as Angle 13. The angle points used in this second part of the experiment, then, ranged from Angle 2 to Angle 12 inclusive. The first figure presented to S was Angle 7—that is, the angle degree midway between 2 and 12; thereafter the order of the series was identically random for

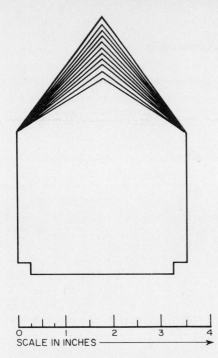

FIG. 2 *The eleven test figures used in Part II of the experiment, superimposed in order of increasing sharpness of angle point.*

everyone and was gone through twice, for a total of 22 presentations.

To determine whether any differences obtained in similarity judgments might arise from differences in the number of perceptually discriminated angle sizes (Group C perhaps not "seeing" as much angle variation as Group A), *E* asked this final question: "By the way, how many different figures do you think there were in the series I just showed you?"

Our major index for assessing individual differences in conceptual conservatism was the sex of the subject. Nineteen boys and 20 girls constituted Group A, while Group C consisted of 20 boys and 19 girls. Our expectation, on the basis of Pettigrew's findings for adults, that girls would be narrower in category width—or more conceptually

conservative—than boys, was confirmed by our finding of a significant sex difference in this direction on the children's form of Pettigrew's "category width" questionnaire,[4] employed as an accessory index in our study.

This written test contained 12 two-part items, and each part of an item was to be answered by choosing from among four alternatives. The questionnaire was called a "Guessing Game" and was introduced with the following instructions, which were both read by the children and repeated orally by the test administrator:

This game asks you to guess about a lot of things in our world. For instance, if you knew that most grown-up men in the world are around five feet seven inches tall, how tall would you guess the tallest man in the world is? Seven feet tall? Eight feet tall? And how tall would you guess the shortest man in the world is? Three feet tall? Four feet tall? Circle your guesses for each of the things printed below.

The first item was as follows:

Most birds fly at the speed of about 17 miles per hour.
A. How fast does the fastest bird fly?
   1. 30 miles per hour.
   2. 21 miles per hour.
   3. 60 miles per hour.
   4. 18 miles per hour.
B. How fast does the slowest bird fly?
   1. 15 miles per hour.
   2. 5 miles per hour.
   3. 10 miles per hour.
   4. 2 miles per hour.

Subsequent items concerned the length of whales, the ships in New York harbor, the length of dogs, the speed of cars, the width of roads, the population of states, the height of

---

[4] We are indebted to T. F. Pettigrew for the development and use of a children's form of his category width questionnaire.

buildings, the width of windows, the speed of sailboats, schoolbooks written in a year, and amount of daily time spent eating. Each S's category width was measured in the following way: "A" and "B" choices were first coded from 0 to 3, the greater the deviation from the average, the larger the code number; S's score on each item was the sum of his "A" and "B" coded scores for that item, and his total score was the sum of his item scores.

As previously noted, there was a highly significant difference in category width scores between boys and girls in our sample (the medians were 45 and 35, respectively, with $p < .001$ by a two-tail Mann-Whitney test).

Dependent Measures and Hypotheses

Let us consider now the measures provided by our experimental procedure, and the specific predictions implicit in our two hypotheses. The similarity judgment session provides several indices of the range of variation in angle point that a person will tolerate as being similar to a poggle: one measure is the number of trials on which S reported the figure was like a poggle (hereafter called frequency or F score), the maximum possible number here being, of course, 22; another measure is the angle of that figure which stands at the median of all the figures which S reported as being like a poggle (hereafter called angle or A score); and yet another is whether S judged the first figure presented in Part II—namely, the figure whose point was intermediate in angle degree—to be like a poggle (hereafter called the initial figure or I score).

Our attribute criteriality hypothesis leads us to expect that the extent of angle deviation which is still called similar to a poggle, will be greater for Group C than for Group A by each of the three similarity measures just

noted. Our hypothesis concerning categorizing style suggests that, for Group A, the extent of angle deviation that is still judged similar to a poggle will be greater for boys than for girls, and be positively correlated with the category width measure, by all measures of similarity. For Group C, on the other hand, where angularity is not criterial, there should be no relation between any differences in similarity range and sex or category width, since the group as a whole should be extreme.

Attempts to reduce any obtained relationship between sex or category width and similarity judgments to some other basis, and hence to imply that the effect is something other than motivational, also had to be evaluated. We had to deal with the possible objection that individual differences in similarity judgments were basically a function of intellectual differences. A measure of general intelligence and a measure of quantitative ability were used in this connection: the Kuhlmann-Anderson IQ (1942), and the average arithmetic achievement score from the Metropolitan Achievement Test (Allen, Bixler, Conner, and Graham, 1946). Both were obtained from our sixth-grade children when they were in the spring term of their fifth-grade year.

RESULTS

Attribute Criteriality and Similarity Judgments

We find from Table 1 that Groups A and C were not significantly different in their learning of the initial poggle concept (median number of trials to criterion), and also discriminated the same number of different figures during the similarity judgment series (median number of different figures discriminated, or D score). This finding suggests that the attributes used as criterial for defining the concept in each group were of about equal difficulty; and further, that Group A, for whom angle-difference was criterial during concept attainment, was not thereby made more perceptually sensitive to that attribute than Group C. Differences in similarity judgments between the groups, then, cannot be an effect of differing perceptual sensitivities to degree of angle but, rather, must be of conceptual origin.

Further examination of Table 1 indicates such differences in similarity judgments to be considerable. By each of our three measures of similarity (median frequency of similarity calls, or F score; median angle size of the figure standing at the median of all

TABLE 1

COMPARISON OF GROUPS A AND C ON
VARIOUS EXPERIMENTAL MEASURES

Measure	Group A	Group C	p
F score			
median	9	22	<.001*
RFM[a]	7/39	27/39	<.001**
A score			
median	4	7	<.001*
RFM	14/39	31/39	<.001**
I score			
frequency	10/39	38/39	<.001**
RFM	29/39	38/39	n.s.**
Trials to criterion			
median	27	22	n.s.*
RFM	9/39	5/39	n.s.**
D score			
median	3	3	n.s.*
RFM	19/39	21/39	n.s.**

* Mann-Whitney two-tail test, with corrections for ties, as described by Siegel (1956).
** Chi square two-tail test, with correction for continuity, as described by Siegel (1956).
[a] Relative frequency of the modal score.

figures S reported as being like a poggle, or A score; and number of Ss judging the initial figure presented in Part II to be like a poggle, or I score), the range of acceptance along the angle dimension is significantly greater for Group C than for Group A. Moreover, the degree of deviation tolerance is not only almost maximal for Group C, but quite low in variability, since we note from Table 1 that the relative frequency of the modal score (or RFM) —a measure that increases as individual differences decrease—is significantly higher in Group C than in Group A for two of the three similarity measures, and in the predicted direction for the third. This smaller variability for Group C than Group A in similarity range indicates that there is but a minimal tendency to consider events nonsimilar when a criterial property is present in both, even though they differ greatly on a noncriterial attribute.

Since these differences occur even though the characteristics present in all positive instances of the poggle class have been the same for both groups, we may conclude that the objective degree of attribute difference between two events does not suffice to determine whether they will appear similar. Rather, psychological similarity depends on whether or not the attribute that varies is criterial for defining either event.

Categorizing Style and Similarity Judgments

Turning to our major indicator of categorizing style—the sex of the child —Table 2 shows the sex breakdown for each of the similarity measures. We find that, for Group A, females tolerate less deviation than males by every index. This sex difference in similarity judgments for Group A occurs despite the fact that there is no sex difference in number of trials to attain the poggle concept (and hence no heightened sensitivity to angle due to a difference in number of exposures) nor in the number of figures actually discriminated during the judgment trials. There is no significant sex difference for any measure of similarity in Group C, on the other hand, indicating that what little variance appeared in that condition was due to factors other than conceptual conservatism.

With regard to our accessory index of categorizing style, examination of Table 3 reveals that, for Group A, the correlations between the category width scale and two of our similarity measures (F score and A score) are significant and in the predicted direction, while the correlation of category width with the more conservative I measure,

TABLE 3

CORRELATIONS * BETWEEN THE
CATEGORY WIDTH MEASURE
AND SIMILARITY JUDGMENTS
IN THE EXPERIMENT

Measure	Boys and Girls Combined	Boys	Girls
F score			
Group A	$r = .36, p < .03$	n.s.	n.s.
Group C	n.s.	n.s.	n.s.
A score			
Group A	$r = .34, p < .04$	n.s.	n.s.
Group C	n.s.	n.s.	n.s.
I score			
Group A	$r = .30, p < .07$	n.s.	n.s.
Group C	n.s.	n.s.	n.s.

* Spearman two-tail rank correlation, with corrections for ties, as described by Siegel (1956).

although in the predicted direction, just misses significance. Thus, wide categorizers tend to be more tolerant of deviation in criterial attributes when judging similarity. As with the sex index, there is no significant relationship with category width for any measure of similarity in Group C.

Finally, neither sex nor the category width score is related to IQ or to arithmetic achievement, indicating that the relationships of sex and category width to similarity judgments are not reducible to general intelligence or quantitative factors. (Spearman rank correlations between sex and IQ, sex and arithmetic achievement, category width and IQ, and category width and arithmetic achievement, are all nonsignificant.) Indeed, the Spearman rank correlations between the F measure of similarity (the most representative index) and IQ, and between the F measure and arithmetic achievement, are also nonsignificant for Group A and Group C. Further, category width does not reflect any factor critical for similarity other than the sex difference, since, as Table 3

TABLE 2

COMPARISON OF BOYS AND GIRLS
WITHIN GROUP A AND WITHIN GROUP
C, ON VARIOUS EXPERIMENTAL
MEASURES

Measure	Boys	Girls	p
F score, median			
Group A	10	7.5	<.02*
Group C	22	22	n.s.*
A score, median			
Group A	4	3.25	<.03*
Group C	7	7	n.s.*
I score, frequency			
Group A	8/19	2/20	.05**
Group C	20/20	18/19	n.s.**
Trials to Criterion, median			
Group A	26	27	n.s.*
Group C	21.5	26	n.s.*
D score, median			
Group A	3	3	n.s.*
Group C	3	3	n.s.*

* Mann-Whitney two-tail test, with corrections for ties, as described by Siegel (1956).
** Fisher exact probability test, two-tail, as described by Siegel (1956).

indicates, correlations *within* sex between category width and similarity measures are all nonsignificant.

It thus seems warranted to conclude that individual differences in similarity judgments for Group A were clearly a function of some such factor as conceptual conservatism, while the limited variance in Group C was not a function of this factor.

DISCUSSION

We have found, then, that psychological similarity depends on attribute criteriality and on individual differences in conceptual conservatism. Let us consider each in turn.

With regard to attribute criteriality, it appears that similarity or dissimilarity of one event to another does not merely depend on the objective degree of difference between them, but rather on whether the one or more properties in whose terms the events differ have been made criterial to S for defining either event or not. If criterial, the events are more likely to be judged dissimilar; if not criterial, similar. Criteriality of a property for defining an event, in turn, is established by contrasting that event with others which differ regarding the property in question, so that S learns a classification rule to the effect that events exemplifying one value of the property belong in one class and events exemplifying another value in another.

Secondly, we have found that individual differences in conceptual conservatism come into play only when the attribute in question is criterial. What factors determine the limited variance that occurs when the deviating attribute is noncriterial, we cannot say for sure. Considering that for Group C all comparison events contained the attribute-value learned as criterial of poggles (cutout base corners), re-jection of similarity would have to involve a shifting of emphasis to a noncriterial property. Whether such rejectors had a clearer perceptual image of the original poggle or became suspicious of E's intention, or were motivated by a need to be different, we can only conjecture at this point. The one positive statement we can make about this variance is that it had nothing to do with conceptual conservatism.

The relation of sex (and nonrelation of intelligence and quantitative ability measures) both to the range of criterial deviation judged similar and to category width, suggest other factors that may possibly underlie our inferred dimension of conceptual conservatism. There is much evidence in the literature (Komarovsky, 1950; Milner, 1949; Sears, 1951; Sears, Maccoby, and Levin, 1957; Sears, Whiting, Nowlis, and Sears, 1953) indicating that, at least in Western culture, boys in general are more aggressive, more independent and less docile than girls. While boys tend to be encouraged for independent and aggressive behavior outside the home, girls are usually punished for such behavior. Whereas boys are generally free to choose their own activities and are allowed more privacy in personal affairs, girls tend to be more closely supervised. It seems reasonable to assume that such conditions, implying, as they do, drastic consequences to girls for free expression, render them more restrained and cautious as well as more dependent on external standards.

It is quite possible that such a factor as fear of independent expression may have acted in the present situation to limit the range of similarity acceptance for girls and, also, in Pettigrew's and our own sample, to narrow their category width. In the subculture of experimenter and subject established in our study, a poggle was defined as a form with a particular angle-point (Group A). To allow deviant angle-points into this category is actually to violate the prescriptions of the culture, to take a step beyond convention and authority. Likewise, in Pettigrew's procedure, to assign values to a category beyond those with which one is most familiar, is to rely more on one's own judgment than on accepted standards.

Some corroboration for this position comes from the studies of Witkin, Lewis, Hertzman, Machover, Meissner, and Wapner (1954) and Sandström (1953), which indicated that girls were much more dependent on external context, and much more disturbed by its absence in perceptual situations. The same tendency appears in Sweeney's data (1953) showing that girls are poorer in problem-solving because of a failure to restructure the field, that is, to move away from the given.

In sum, we are hypothesizing that for girls there has been a generalization of fear of independence from the sphere of action to that of cognition. Concepts are subject to social regulation as much as behavior, and because girls have been made reluctant to overstep the behavioral boundaries prescribed by authority, so also they are loathe to be expansive in the realm of concepts.

SUMMARY

Two hypotheses were proposed: 1. *Attribute Criteriality:* One event is more likely to be judged similar to a standard event if the two differ on some property which, although always present in the standard, has *not* been learned as criterial for defining it, than if this property *has* been learned as criterial for its definition. 2. *Categor-izing Style:* When presented with events of varying criterial difference from a standard, females should judge fewer of these events as similar to the standard than males, on the ground that the former tend to categorize more narrowly (that is, conservatively) than the latter.

Attribute criteriality was varied by changing the nature of the negative instances with which positive exemplars of a class were contrasted, and categorizing style was assessed from the sex of the child and also by an independent measure of category width in an experiment involving a concept attainment task and similarity judgments with nonsense figures. Seventy-eight sixth-grade school children served as *S*s, and both hypotheses were sustained. It was concluded that recognition of similarity depends on learned classification rules and on individual differences in conceptual conservatism. The latter in turn seemed due to a sex difference in fear of independent expression.

REFERENCES

Allen, R. S., H. H. Bixler, W. L. Conner, and F. B. Graham, *Metropolitan Achievement Tests: Intermediate Battery*. New York: Harcourt, Brace & World, Inc., 1946.

Komarovsky, Mirra, "Functional Analysis of Sex Roles," *American Sociological Review*, **15** (1950), 508-16.

Kuhlmann, F. and Rose G. Anderson, *Kuhlmann-Anderson Intelligence Tests*. Minneapolis, Minn.: Educational Publishers, 1942.

Milner, Esther, "Effects of Sex Role and Social Status on the Early Adolescent Personality," *Genetic Psychology Monograph*, **40** (1949), 231-325.

Pettigrew, T. F., "The Measurement and Correlates of Category Width as a Cognitive Variable," *Journal of Personality*, **26** (1958), 532-44.

Sandström, C. I., "Sex Differences in Localization and Orientation," *Acta Psychol.,* **9** (1953), 82-96.

Sears, Pauline S., "Doll Play Aggression in Normal Young Children: Influence of Sex, Age, Sibling Status, Father's Absence," *Psychology Monograph,* **65**, No. 6 (1951).

Sears, R. R., Eleanor E. Maccoby, and H. Levin, *Patterns of Child Rearing.* Evanston, Ill.: Row-Peterson & Company, 1957.

Sears, R. R., J. W. M. Whiting, V. Nowlis, and Pauline S. Sears, "Some Child-rearing Antecedents of Aggression and Dependency in Young Children,"

Genetic Psychology Monograph, **47** (1954), 135-234.

Siegel, S., *Nonparametric Statistics for the Behavioral Sciences.* New York: McGraw-Hill Book Company, Inc., 1956.

Sweeney, E. J., "Sex Differences in Problem Solving," *Stanford University Department of Psychology Technical Report,* No. 1 (1953).

Wallach, M. A., "On Psychological Similarity," *Psychological Review,* **65** (1958), 103-16.

Witkin, H. A., Helen B. Lewis, M. Hertzman, Karen Machover, P. B. Meissner, and S. Wapner, *Personality through Perception.* New York: Harper & Row, Publishers, 1954.

Cognitive Risk and Environmental Change *

Jerome S. Bruner and Henri Tajfel

It is the objective of the present paper to examine wherein breadth of categorizing reflects the manner in which people deal with the risk of errors of judgment—specifically, the risk of saying that things are similar when they might be different, or that they are different when they might be similar.

Breadth of category—or, as it has sometimes been called, equivalence range—refers to the range of stimuli that are placed in the same class or category and share a common label.

* From J. S. Bruner and H. Tajfel, "Cognitive Risk and Environmental Change," *Journal of Abnormal Social Psychology,* **62** (1961), 231-241. Reprinted by permission of the authors and the American Psychological Association.
This research was done as part of a research project in cognition, supported in part by USPHS Grant M-1324.

The criteria for placing objects in a common category may be many or few, explicit or implicit. In psychophysical experiments using unidimensional continua, such as length, breadth of category defines the limits beyond which stimuli are no longer classified as X, or "long," but either as non-X, "not long," or as Y, "short." In more complex arrays of stimuli, there is no such unidimensional simplicity, and the criteria for classification are often combined relationally or disjunctively in the process of deciding whether something does or does not belong in a class —as, for example, in classifying men as "competent" or "eligible to vote."

In recent years, individual differences in categorizing, particularly in breadth of categorizing, have been thought to reflect important general differences in cognitive functioning.

Four trends of research on this problem can be distinguished: the investigation of changes in breadth of category as a function of changes in categorizing conditions, the study of individual consistencies in breadth of categorizing in different judging situations, the search for relationships between various emotional and personality factors and the individual's general preference for broad or narrow classifications, and the exploration of relationships between breadth of categorizing and various forms of abnormal mental functioning.

A word about each of these trends as they relate to the present study. It is apparent that when one alters the conditions of decision breadth of category changes. Thus, a sentry, deciding whether approaching figures in the twilight are friends or foes will have a broader inclusion category of "foes" than will an inspector judging machine parts as defective or not. For the consequences obviously vary in the two instances and one can control the severity of these consequences by altering breadth of category (see Bruner, Goodnow, and Austin, 1956). In general, it can be said that when the perceived consequences of overinclusion are more severe than the consequences of overexclusion, inclusion categories narrow. When overexclusion leads to more severe consequences, inclusion categories broaden.

We mention this line of research for two reasons. In the first place, it underlines the risk-regulating character of categorizing. But beyond that, it points to the possible meaning of consistencies in categorizing breadth that appear to be associated with different personality characteristics—the subject matter of the last three of the four lines of inquiry mentioned above. Thus, Gardner (1953), Hamilton (1957), Klein (for example, 1958), and others remark

that obsessive, anxious doubters tend to prefer narrow inclusion categories in their sensory judgments. Perhaps they have a tendency to minimize risk of error by the nay-saying route, preferring the consequences of error that come from avoiding contact with threatening objects. It has been shown, too, that the ambivalent, ethnocentric personalities studied by Frenkel-Brunswik (1949) and Rokeach (1951) show a tendency to narrow categorizing. Yet, on the other hand, Arnhoff (1956) has noted among ethnocentrics a tendency to overgeneralization— which is indeed what ethnocentrism implies. Interestingly enough, Arnhoff (1957) obtained completely negative results in an attempt to replicate his study. This negative replication, while one must be cautious in interpreting it, may be revealing in the sense that there may be two opposing tendencies operative in the ethnocentric personality: a tendency toward overgeneralization under certain conditions, and toward narrow categorizing under others. Zaslow (1950) suggests, and perhaps his suggestion is relevant in this connection, that normal subjects, in contrast to schizophrenics, tend to use middling wide categories, whereas schizophrenics veer either toward overnarrowness or overgeneralization.

In any case, it seems patent that experiments seeking to relate categorizing breadth either to conditions of judgment or to personality cannot get very far unless and until we understand much more about the intimate texture of the act of categorizing itself. This is not to say that we do not recognize the degree to which categorizing is affected by these two sets of determinants. Rather, we feel that an examination of the underlying judgmental processes involved in categorizing is necessary for a fuller understanding of the role played by motivational and personality variables.

We turn now to the series of experiments with which the present paper is concerned. Our central interest is in the specific behavior of broad and narrow categorizers in a highly simplified judging task. Two questions concern us. The first has to do with consistency of preference for broad and narrow categorizing in a stable stimulus situation. But consistency is not as simple as it might at first appear. There is an equally important question concerning reactions to a changing stimulus environment. Is there some consistent manner in which broad and narrow categorizers alter their judgments in the face of changes in the stimulus situations with which they must cope?

With respect to the second question, some predictions can be made. If we assume that a narrow categorizer is one who is compelled to attend to differences in stimuli, whereas a broad categorizer tends to overlook differences, then it should follow that narrow categorizers will be more likely to *alter the breadth of their categorizing* to conform to changes in the stimulus world. Thus, narrow categorizers should show more susceptibility to anchoring effects in psychophysical judgment than do broad categorizers by virtue of being more sensitive or reactive to change and contrast. Indeed, we would say, it is precisely this sensitivity to change that constitutes the hedge against risk that characterizes the narrow categorizer. For to the narrow categorizer, differences and change are highly relevant, and, as Tajfel shows (1959), these relevant differences tend to be accentuated. And if this is the case, not only should the narrow categorizer alter his breadth of category more readily in response to stimulus changes, but he should also adapt more quickly

when the change persists and becomes a new steady state of stimulation.

There is another way of stating our prediction, one taken from the language of anchoring experiments. When a subject has been judging a range of stimuli in terms of categories of absolute magnitude, the introduction of new stimuli larger than the range has either a "contrast" or an "assimilation" effect. A contrast effect is responding strongly to the newly-introduced stimulus—say a stimulus larger than any previously encountered—by judging previous stimuli as contrastingly smaller. Assimilation, both in common sense terms and technically, is "not heeding" the new anchoring stimulus, that is, judging it as no larger than the stimuli previously encountered. We might well predict that narrow subjects, sensitive to differences, will be subject to contrast effects. Broad subjects, on the other hand, should by virtue of their less acute reactiveness to change, show less of the contrast effect and may indeed assimilate the stimuli of the extended range to the psychophysical scale established with the smaller range of stimuli.

With these predictions in mind, we may turn now to the experiments proper.

EXPERIMENT I

Subjects and Procedure

Forty-eight fifth grade school children served as subjects in this experiment. They were tested individually.

Stimuli consisted of projected slides containing clusters of dots, cast on a bended screen at an exposure time of .5 second per cluster. The subject, facing the screen 12 feet away, was seated next to the table on which the 35-millimeter Bell and Howell projector was placed. At the beginning of the session, each subject was told that his task would be to decide whether each of the clusters to be flashed on the screen contained 20 dots or did not contain 20 dots. If he thought that there were 20 dots in the cluster he was to say "yes"; if he thought that the cluster did not contain 20 dots, he was to say "no." The subject was then told that 20 would be the smallest number of dots in any of the clusters that he would see, and was shown two sample clusters of 20 dots each, as demonstrations.

The presentation of the experimental series followed immediately. In order to avoid the possibility that the decision about the number of dots might be determined by the recognition of the shape of a cluster once seen, four clusters with different dispositions of dots in them were used for each number of dots, and, in addition, each of these slides was shown in different positions at its successive presentations.

The experimental presentations were divided into two parts. First, a series of clusters containing from 20–26 dots was presented eight times successively —a total of 56 presentations. The presentations were randomized in such a way that each cluster of the series appeared once before the whole series was repeated in a different random order. Following this, in the second part of a session, four series of clusters containing from 20–30 dots were presented in varying random orders—a total of 44 presentations.

The session was interrupted by two periods of rest of approximately two minutes, the first after three presentations of the series; the next, three presentations later.

The scoring was based on the percentage of yes responses, representing for each subject the proportion of the stimuli which for him fell into the category "20." These percentages were taken for each subject for three separate phases of the presentations of stimuli: for the initial range of 20–26 dots in its eight consecutive presentations (Phase I), for the stimuli 20–26 of the extended range in its first two presentations (Phase II), for the stimuli 20–26 of the extended range in its last two presentations (Phase III). Breadth of category was defined as the proportion of stimuli assigned by a subject to the inclusion category 20 in Phases I, II, and III, and a comparison of these phases provides us with comparative data for testing our hypotheses.

Results

Before the results are reported and discussed, the hypothesis stated in general terms earlier should be stated specifically in the context of the procedure just described. It was assumed that during the initial eight presentations of the stimuli in the original range, each subject would settle to his characteristic pattern of assigning a certain proportion of stimuli to the inclusion category of 20. The subjects could, thus, be divided, by means of ranking, into three groups: a group of broad categorizers with the largest proportions of number of calls of 20; a middle group, and a group of narrow categorizers with the smallest number of calls of 20.

Extending the series of stimuli from clusters ranging from 20–26 dots to clusters ranging from 20–30 dots was conceived as a form of anchoring, introducing a larger difference between the two extremes of the range. According to the argument outlined previously, this change should have been more salient and effective for the narrow than for the broad categorizers. In other words, after the introduction of the additional larger stimuli, the narrow categorizers should, in their responses to this part of the new range which constituted the original range (clusters from 20–26 dots), increase the proportion of clusters called 20 more than the broad categorizers. The narrow categorizers should, moreover, adapt back to their old narrow pattern with the continued experience of the new range provided by Phase III.

1. *Initial breadth of category.* The range in breadth of category for the original series of stimuli was wide: from 85.5 percent–30.3 percent, with the median proportion of calls of 20 being about 55 percent, with six subjects calling 40 percent or fewer 20, and eight calling more than 70 percent of the stimuli 20.

The division of subjects into three groups was made at "cut-off" points nearest to 27 percent of the distribution (Kelly, 1939) for the upper and lower ends of the distribution. This resulted in 12 subjects with the largest percentages of yes responses being assigned to the broad group, (with breadths ranging from 64.3 percent–89.5 percent), and 13 subjects with the lowest percentages of yes responses being assigned to the narrow group (with breadths ranging from 30.3 percent–44.6 percent). The difference between the number of subjects in the groups is due to a run of ties at the upper end of the distribution. Assigning all the remaining 23 subjects to the middle group seemed the least arbitrary procedure.

2. *Change in breadth of category as a function of extending the range.* As a first test of the general hypothesis, a rank correlation was run between breadth of category in Phase I and the shift from Phase I to Phase II in the percentage of calls of 20. This correlation was of the order of rho = —.433; with 46 df this is significant at $p < .005$. Thus, the larger the number of stimuli initially assigned to the cate-

gory 20 by a subject, the less did he tend to increase this number for stimuli of 20–26 dots in the first two presentations of the extended range.

As Hamilton (1957) rightly points out, however, "there are few forms of behavior, especially in the cognitive sphere, which cannot be shown to vary with intelligence. In fact, it might be thought that intelligence is maximally involved in any process requiring perceptual judgments" (p. 203). In pursuit of this point, a rank correlation between IQ and breadth of category in Phase I was obtained. It was of the order of —.53. The initial breadth of category appears then to be determined, in part at least by the subjects' intelligence—more intelligent subjects tended to use narrower categories. The mean IQ of the broad group was 107.4; of the middle group, 113.6; and of the narrow group, 122.7. The difference between the broad and narrow groups is significant at $p < .002$.

The testing of predictions outlined above depended, however, on the relationships found between the breadth of category shown by the subjects in Phase I and the amount of shift from Phase I to Phase II. A rank correlation between the amount of shift and IQ was obtained, and found to be .27, reflecting the fact that narrow subjects shifted more. However, a partial correlation between IQ and shift, holding breadth of category constant, reduced this figure to .05. A complementary finding is that the partial correlation between breadth of category and amount of shift, this time holding IQ constant, remained as high as —.35. Thus, it would seem that, though breadth of category is consistently related to intelligence, the amount of judgmental shift that occurs when the environment changes is related not to intelligence but to breadth of category.

The Wilcoxon matched-pairs signed-ranks test (Siegel, 1956) was applied to assess the significance of the increase in the percentage of yes responses to stimuli 20–26 after the extension of the range for each of the groups. The results for the broad group were not significant. Out of 12 subjects in this group, 6 actually shifted in the direction of *decreasing* the proportion of their yes responses after the extension of the range. In the middle group the shift was significant at $p < .005$ (19 out of 23 subjects increased the proportion of their yes responses). In the narrow group, all 13 subjects increased their proportion of yes responses. The mean increase in percentages of yes responses from Phase I to II for broad categorizers was $+.45$, the range being from $- 21.4 – + 21.4$. The comparable increase for the narrow categorizers was $+ 20.1$, with a range from $+ 3.6 – + 37.5$. The middle categorizers were in between: mean increase in percentage of yes responses being 12.3 with a range from $— 12.5 – + 30.4$. Mann-Whitney U tests were then applied to compare the amount of shift found in the different groups. All of them were found to be significantly different from each other (broad vs. narrow, $p < .01$; broad vs. middle, $p < .02$; narrow vs. middle, $p = .05$).

It might also be said parenthetically that the broad and narrow groups behaved consistently in their placement of dot clusters ranging in number from 27–30 in Phase II. Some 40.6 percent of these were called 20 by the broad categorizers in contrast to 20.2 percent called 20 by the narrow categorizers, a difference significant at $p < .025$ by the U test.

3. *Changes in breadth of category as a function of adaptation to the extended range of stimuli.* Let us now compare the change from Phase II to Phase III —the subjects now having had experience with two presentations of the

extended range and confronting the two additional series. In the narrow group, out of 12 subjects (data for this shift for one of the subjects were not available), 8 subjects shifted back towards fewer yes responses for the 20–26 part of the range, 1 did not shift, and 3 shifted towards more yes responses. The comparable figures for the broad group are interesting. Only 2 subjects in this group showed a decrease in yes responses in Phase III in comparison with Phase II; 7 subjects increased their yes responses and the remaining 3 subjects showed no shift at all. A comparison of means tells the same story. On the average, subjects in the broad group *increased* their yes responses by 7.0 percent between Phase II and III. Narrow categorizers *decreased* theirs 9.7 percent. The difference between the two groups tested by the Mann-Whitney U test is significant at a $p < .025$.

Here again there is a correlation of .37 between the initial breadth of category and the amount of shift from Phase II to Phase III, indicating that broad categorizers tend to broaden their range more as they get more exposure to the changed stimulus situation, the narrow categorizers having done most of their changing when the stimulus situation was first altered. A correlation of —.29 was found to hold between IQ and the amount of shift, an obvious consequence of the fact that the more intelligent subjects had already done their shifting in Phase II. A partial correlation was computed between IQ and the amount of shift, from II to III, holding breadth of category constant. It was found to be —.12. But a partial correlation between breadth of category and amount of shift, holding IQ constant this time, is .27. It can be argued then, that the amount of shift from Phase II to Phase III, reflecting adaptation to the new range, is related to the initial breadth of category but not to intelligence, though intelligence and the initial breadth of category are related to each other.

The data for all subjects in the three phases of experiment are summarized in Table 1 in the form of percentage of yes responses given.

Figure 1 summarizes the findings.

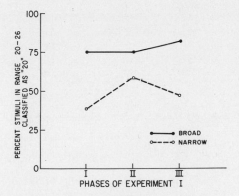

FIG. 1. *Mean percentage of stimuli in range 20-26 classified as 20 (yes responses) by broad and narrow categorizers in the three phases of Experiment I.*

The feature of the results is the relative stability of performance in the broad group and the sharp changes from phase to phase in the narrow group. This is congruent with the general conception of broad and narrow categorizers as outlined in this paper and in others (for example, Gardner, 1953). The broad categorizers do not react to change markedly or rapidly; the small and insignificant amount of shift that they show after the extension of the range maintains a slow and steady increase as the new range continues to be presented. Narrow categorizers react to change strongly, but then they seem to revert rapidly to their preferred mode of response as soon

as there is habituation to the new situation.

Our main hypothesis—that the narrow categorizers are more sensitive to change than broad ones—is confirmed.

There is one other point to be made in connection with cognitive risk. One can conceive of risk regulation in terms of a cost-for-gain reckoning. That is to say, for a gain in accuracy or security or some other "good," one pays a cost. In the case of the broad categorizers in Experiment I, we see that they do in fact call more of the stimuli containing 20 dots correctly. The cost of this is calling many more of the other dot clusters incorrectly. The narrow categorizers show a considerably sharper slope in their discrimination function. The price they pay for *not* being wrong about the excluded items is missing some of those that should be included among the 20s. Broad subjects, in short, pay their price for being right; narrow subjects seem to pay theirs for not being wrong.

But before these, or any other conclusions are finally drawn from the results, some very obvious artifactual possibilities must be dealt with. The results may have been due not to the narrow group's more abrupt reaction to change, but to the fact that by definition the narrow categorizers have more room to expand their proportion of yes responses. A broad categorizer who started out with 80 percent of yes responses cannot, of course, achieve an increase of 25 percent. This "ceiling effect" may account for the broad group showing less increase in yes responses than the narrow group. Yet, the reversal of trends in shift from Phase II to Phase III argues in some measure against this artifactual explanation; so does the fact that half of the broad subjects *decreased* their proportion of yes responses from Phase I

TABLE 1

PERCENTAGE OF YES RESPONSES GIVEN BY SUBJECTS IN THE THREE PHASES OF
EXPERIMENT I AND IN EXPERIMENT III

	EXPERIMENT I					
Group	Phase I (20-26)	Phase II (20-26)	Phase III (20-26)	Phase II (27-30)	Phase III (27-30)	Experiment III
Broad						
1	89.5	71.4	78.6	62.5	62.5	58.9
2	85.7	100.0	100.0	37.5	75.0	64.3
3	83.9	78.6	100.0	0	37.5	69.5
4	80.3	64.3	85.7	37.5	50.0	71.4
5	80.3	92.8	100.0	100.0	100.0	100.0
6	75.0	71.4	85.7	25.0	37.5	75.0
7	71.4	50.0	78.6	62.5	50.0	94.6
8	71.4	78.6	50.0	62.5	75.0	58.9
9a	69.6					64.3
10	67.8	85.7	70.1	37.5	37.5	83.9
11	67.8	50.0	78.6	25.0	75.0	58.9
12a	64.3					62.5
13a	64.3					62.5
14	64.3	78.6	78.6	25.0	25.0	58.9
15	64.3	85.7	85.7	12.5	50.0	58.9
Mb	75.1	75.6	82.6	40.6	56.2	
Md	73.3					69.5
Middle						
1	62.5	64.3	71.4	25.0	0	55.4
2	62.5	64.3	85.7	62.5	25.0	57.1
3	62.5	50.0	64.3	37.5	0	58.9
4	60.7	78.6	85.7	25.0	25.0	53.6
5	58.9	78.6	57.1	12.5	25.0	51.8
6	57.1	85.7	78.6	25.0	25.0	41.1
7	57.1	71.4	57.1	12.5	50.0	50.0
8	57.1	64.3	57.1	37.5	25.0	92.9
9	57.1	85.7	71.4	12.5	12.5	44.6
10	57.1	71.4	78.6	62.5	50.0	66.1
11	57.1	85.7	78.6	50.0	25.0	60.7
12	55.3	42.8	35.7	37.5	50.0	55.4
13	53.6	71.4	50.0	37.5	12.5	73.2
14c	53.6	78.6	71.4	37.5	12.5	
15a	51.8					57.1
16	51.8	50.0	50.0	37.5	12.5	48.3
17	51.8	64.3	85.7	25.0	62.5	41.1
18	51.8	71.4	64.3	0	12.5	57.1
19	50.0	64.3	78.6	37.5	12.5	50.0
20a	50.0					50.0
21	48.2	50.0	57.1	12.5	25.0	39.3
22	48.2	78.6	64.3	0	0	55.4
23e	46.4	57.1	35.7	0	37.5	57.1
24c	46.4	42.9	50.0	25.0	12.5	
25e	46.4	64.3	57.1	62.5	50.0	44.6
Mb	54.5	66.8	64.6	29.4	24.5	
Md	55.3					55.2

TABLE 1 (*Concluded*)

| | EXPERIMENT I | | | | | |
Group	Phase I (20-26)	Phase II (20-26)	Phase III (20-26)	Phase II (27-30)	Phase III (27-30)	Experiment III
Narrow						
1	44.6	78.6		12.5		51.8
2	42.8	57.1	71.4	0	12.5	48.3
3	41.1	71.4	50.0	12.5	25.0	51.8
4	41.1	50.0	42.9	25.0	12.5	64.3
5	41.1	64.3	50.0	0	0	60.7
6c	41.1	78.6	78.6	87.5	87.5	
7	41.1	57.1	21.4	0	0	62.5
8	39.3	64.3	78.6	25.0	25.0	39.3
9c	39.3	42.9	35.7	0	0	
10	35.7	50.0	14.3	87.5	87.5	64.3
11	33.9	57.1	64.3	0	25.0	46.4
12	32.1	57.1	35.7	12.5	0	35.7
13	30.3	35.7	28.5	0	0	46.4
Mb	38.7	58.8	47.6	20.2	22.9	
Md	39.7					51.8

a Subjects not included in the analysis of Experiment I, and added subsequently for comparison of their performance in Experiments I and III.

b Means for Experiment I, not including subjects marked a.

c Subjects taking part in Experiment I, and not available for Experiment III.

d Means for comparison of performance in Experiments I and III, not including subjects marked c.

e Subjects falling in the lower part of the distribution (narrow group) for comparison between Experiments I and III, and included in means for narrow group (d).

to Phase II, some of them quite considerably. The results, at least the shift from Phase I to Phase II it might also be argued, could have been due to regression effects. Experiment II was conducted to test further the validity of interpretation given to the results of Experiment I, particularly with respect to ceiling effects and regression effects.

Another artifact, possibly lurking in the results, is that the narrow group is "narrow" not because of its preferred mode of taking cognitive risks, but simply because, for one reason or another (such as, for example, interest in the task), the capacity of narrow subjects to discriminate was better than that of the broad group. The relationship between intelligence and breadth of category, previously reported, increases the likelihood of some

such interpretation. Under the conditions of Experiment I and with the small number of yes responses that we obtained, the narrow group could by definition get closer to the actual leptokurtic distribution of the "correct" stimuli than the broad group. Thus, in Phase I, the proportion of clusters containing 20 dots was 14.3 percent, and decreased to 9.1 percent in Phases II and III. But note, however, that 7 out of 13 subjects in the narrow group *increased* their proportion of yes responses to the new range presented to them in Phase II, while only 3 out of 12 subjects in the broad group did so, a difference that is significant at the .02 level as estimated by a *U* test. There remains the possibility, however, that there is some intrinsic relationship between intelligence test scores and narrow categorizing based on the possible bias of intelligence tests in favor of the precise or narrow categorizers. Yet this is not borne out by the indifferent partial correlation between IQ and shift from Phase II to Phase III. But such indirect evidence is not sufficient. Consequently, Experiment III was conducted in order to explore further the question of accuracy.

EXPERIMENT II

In Experiment I, change was introduced by extending the series beyond its initial range. Using the same series of stimuli, it should be possible to shift judgments in the opposite direction by biasing the distribution of stimuli through *cutting off* a part of the range. The order of presentation used in Experiment I was reversed in Experiment II: The subjects were first confronted with the range of 20–30 dots, then the larger end of the series was eliminated and only the 20–26 range presented. If it is true that change has a greater effect on narrow than on broad categorizers, then in Experiment II the narrow categorizers should *decrease* their proportion of yes responses in the 20–26 range from the original to the reduced series more than the broad categorizers.

Twenty-four new subjects were used in this experiment, this time drawn from the fifth grade. The initial series of 20–30 dot clusters was run through randomly eight times (a total of 88 presentations), and then followed by four presentations of the reduced range of 20–26 dots for a total of 28 presentations. Apart from this difference, the procedure was the same as in Experiment I. The subjects were ranked in the order of their percentage of yes responses to the 20–30 initial

range to establish broad, middle, and narrow groups.

Results

The range in breadth of category for Phase I (now 20–30 dots) was from 95.4 percent to 21.6 percent. The 27 percent cut-off point resulted in six subjects being assigned to each of the two extreme groups: the broad and the narrow. The range in breadth of category for the broad group was 95.4 percent–59 percent; for the narrow group, 36.4 percent–21.6 percent.

This time, as one shifts from Phase I to Phase II, one finds the narrow subjects *decreasing* their calls of 20 in response to the narrowing of the range—all of them doing so with a mean shift in percentage of yes responses of − 13.7 (Table 2). The broad group again hardly reacts to change: three of the subjects decrease their proportion of yes responses, one does not change, and two increase the number of yes responses. The mean percentage decrease of yes responses for the broad group is − 1.4. The difference, as measured by a *U* test, is significant at the .03 level.

The shift from Phase I to II goes counter to what would be expected by virtue of "ceiling" and "floor" effects, or, indeed, according to the effect of regression. Those who have been calling few of the clusters 20 decrease the number of their calls much more markedly than those who have been calling many clusters 20. While these results provide an effective answer to the query raised in the last section about the possible contribution of artifacts to the results of Experiment I, they also raise some interesting questions of interpretation.

Take first the narrow categorizers. When the range of stimuli to which they are exposed broadens, their categorizing broadens. It is, if you will,

TABLE 2

PERCENTAGE OF YES RESPONSES GIVEN BY SUBJECTS IN THE THREE PHASES OF EXPERIMENT II

Group	Phase I (20-30)	Phase I (27-30)	Phase I (20-26)	Phase II (20-26)	Phase III (20-26)
Broad					
1	95.4	90.6	98.2	100.0	100.0
2	80.7	53.1	96.4	85.7	64.3
3	67.0	40.6	82.1	78.6	71.4
4	62.5	31.2	80.4	64.3	57.1
5	62.5	71.9	57.1	57.1	85.7
6	59.0	34.4	73.2	92.9	71.4
M	71.2	53.6	81.2	79.8	75.0
Middle					
1	56.8	37.5	67.9	57.1	50.0
2	55.6	37.5	66.1	78.6	85.7
3	54.4	34.4	66.1	71.4	42.9
4	52.3	28.1	66.1	42.9	42.9
5	50.0	25.0	64.3	42.9	57.1
6	50.0	37.5	57.1	78.6	57.1
7	47.7	12.5	67.9	64.3	42.9
8	46.6	15.6	64.3	57.1	57.1
9	46.6	50.0	44.6	35.7	57.1
10	42.0	28.1	50.0	42.9	57.1
11	40.9	40.6	41.1	57.1	57.1
12	37.5	9.4	53.6	57.1	57.1
M	48.4	29.7	59.1	57.1	55.3
Narrow					
1	36.4	12.5	50.0	28.6	50.0
2	35.2	3.1	53.6	42.9	21.4
3	32.9	34.4	32.1	21.4	21.4
4	32.9	9.4	46.4	42.9	42.9
5	31.8	34.4	30.4	14.3	14.3
6	21.6	12.5	26.8	7.1	14.3
M	31.8	17.7	39.9	26.2	27.4

now safer to take positive fliers on doubtful stimuli, and more dot clusters are labeled as 20. When the universe of stimuli narrows in range, narrow categorizers show a response of caution, and the bounds of their inclusion class are narrowed. Interestingly enough, both reactions go counter to the "reality" situation. That is to say, in Experiment I the proportion of actual clusters of 20 dots decreases from Phase I to Phase II—yet the yes responses of narrow subjects increase. In Experiment II it is the reverse: the proportion of clusters of 20 dots increases from Phase I to Phase II, but the calls of 20 decrease for narrow subjects. It seems plain then, that while these subjects are responding to change in the environment, they are doing so in terms of *internal* requirements, not *external* ones. What is also interesting is that whereas in Experiment I narrow subjects reverted to narrow categorizing after they had habituated to the extended range, in Experiment

II they do *not* change in Phase III after they have narrowed their categorizing in response to a narrowed range of stimuli. There is no change in the percentage of yes responses from Phase II to Phase III (Table 2). In short, a change in categorizing in the preferred direction sticks, a change in the nonpreferred direction (toward greater breadth) habituates out.

Now consider the broad categorizers. In Experiment I we show that they did not respond on the average to an extension of the range of stimuli to which they were exposed in shifting from Phase I to Phase II. But in Phase III, habituation to the extended series, or possibly an insignificant and delayed reaction to the change of stimulation, led to a moderate increase in the breadth of their 20 category. They, too, respond to increased diversity in environmental stimulation, but more slowly and more modestly. In Experiment II, the picture is very similar: as before, and in contrast to narrow categorizers, their response to change is slow and insignificant.

One last check on possible artifacts in Experiment I is provided by the design of Experiment II—a check on regression effects. In Experiment I, the transition from the initial to the extended range occurred after 8 successive presentations of the 7 stimuli of the initial range—a total of 56 presentations. This was followed by Phase II which consisted of a series of 11 stimuli repeated twice—22 presentations. As Phase I in Experiment II consisted of 11 stimuli repeated 8 times, it was possible to ascertain whether any regression effect (which would consist of an increase in the proportion of yes responses for the narrow group and of a decrease for the broad group) had occurred at the point of presentations nearest to the transition point between Phases I and II in Experiment I. This was done by comparing the percentages of yes responses for the first 5 presentations of the series (a total of 55) with the same percentages for the 2 following presentations (a total of 22). There was no evidence of any trend towards increase for the narrow categorizers, or towards decrease for the broad ones.

EXPERIMENT III

This experiment was conducted in order to ascertain whether the results of Experiment I were due to consistent differences between the broad and the narrow categorizers in their preferred mode of dealing with an uncertain cognitive situation, rather than to a tendency of the narrow group to be more accurate, presumably under any conditions. A subject who is in the group of narrow categorizers in Experiment I because he might be intent to perform as accurately as possible should become a broad categorizer in a situation where the distribution of stimuli is such that most stimuli fall into the inclusion or target category. The converse is, of course, not necessarily true: if a broad categorizer performed as he did because he was bored and was paying very little attention to the task, he might still perform in a similar manner when confronted with any distribution of stimuli—assuming that yes responses are easier for maintaining an attitude of nondiscriminating boredom.

Though we have spoken of "accuracy," there is one general question concerning it that is difficult to answer in these experiments. In most cognitive situations flexibility and avoidance of extreme response tendencies probably lead in the end to most "adaptive" responses—that is, to responses which keep in closest touch with the normally distributed and continuously changing environment. There may be situations, however, in which either a very narrow or a very broad type of response is the most useful. This, as Bruner, Goodnow, and Austin (1956) have shown, is a function of the "payoff matrix" in the situation, of the respective consequences that errors of overinclusion or of overexclusion may have. It is, therefore, impossible to state *a priori* which of the two extreme forms of categorizing is the "better" or the most useful save in a restricted way applying to specific situations.

The arrangement of stimuli in Experiment I favored the narrow categorizer in the sense that few stimuli were in fact 20s. We decided, therefore, to run another experiment in which a broad style of categorizing would lead to performance corresponding more closely to the actual distribution of stimuli. This time, the great majority of stimuli would belong in the inclusion class and the preferred response distribution of broad categorizers would conform to the distribution of "correct" or inclusion stimuli.

Subjects and Procedure

Experiment III was conducted with 45 subjects who took part in Experiment I plus 4 subjects who were added subsequently. The latter were first subjected to the procedure of Experiment I, and then, a few days later, took part in Experiment III. Stimuli consisted of straight lines drawn on rectangles of white cardboard, 11 by 14 in. in size. The inclinations and positions of lines on the rectangles were varied randomly. There were 56 rectangles: on 48 of them (6 out of 7) lines 5 in. long were drawn, one to a rectangle. The remaining 8 rectangles contained lines varying in length from 5¼ to 5¾ in. The subjects, tested individually, were seated at one end of a table, the experimenter at the other, separated by a distance of 3 feet. The lines were shown one by one, the order of presentation so arranged that one line longer than 5 in. appeared in each successive series of six 5 in. lines, the serial position of the longer line varying at random. Subjects were told to decide whether a line was 5 in. long or not. If they thought that it was, they should say "yes"; if they thought not, "no." They were duly informed that some of the lines would be 5 in. long, some slightly longer. Two 5 in. lines were shown first, and the subjects told what they were. The presentation of the experimental series followed immediately. Time of exposure was not limited, the cardboard rectangle being held up until the subject made his decision.

Scores again consist of the percentages of yes responses given to the total of 56 stimuli presented—a number equal to the number of clusters of dots presented in Phase I of Experiment I. The prediction, of course, is that if the subjects' performance in Experiment I reflected their preferred mode of categorizing, they should perform in a similar manner in Experiment III, despite the radical change in the frequency of stimuli belonging to the inclusion class—that is, broad categorizers should respond more broadly in both experiments.

Results

The range of percentage of yes responses was from 100 percent to 35.7 percent with a median of 57.1 percent. Table 2 sets out the distribution of the subjects according to the percentage of their yes response.

1. *Comparison of breadth of category in Experiment I and Experiment III.* The subjects were ranked according to their breadth of category

in both experiments. A rank correlation was run between their performances in the two experiments. This was found to be of the order of rho = .572, significant at $p < .0005$.

A further assessment of the similarity of performance in the two tasks was made by selecting the subjects who in Experiment I belonged to the broad and narrow groups, and comparing the difference in the performance of these two groups in Experiment III. The cutoff point for the groups in Experiment I was slightly different from the one used in the previous analysis of results for this experiment, as some subjects dropped out and some were added. Taking ties into account, the nearest point to 27 percent now included 15 subjects in the broad group, the narrow group consisting as previously of 13 subjects. The difference, as assessed by a U test, is highly significant, the confidence level being less than .001. The mean percentage of yes responses in the previously defined broad group is 69.5. The percentage of yes responses in Experiment III of the previously defined narrow group is 51.8.

2. *Comparison of accuracy of performance in Experiment I and Experiment III.* The group of narrow categorizers performed more accurately in Phase I of Experiment I than the group of broad categorizers. Accuracy of performance was assessed by assigning to each subject a score that consisted of the proportion of his number of yes responses assigned by him to clusters containing 20 and 21 dots. The percentage of accurate calls for the narrow group was 45.9, as compared with 33.4 for the broad group, a difference significant at the .001 level.

The same measure of accuracy could not be applied in Experiment III, as almost all subjects gave all correct no responses to the eight lines that were longer than 5 in. Therefore, the assessment of accuracy here was made by summating *all* incorrect responses made by a subject: no responses given to 5 in. lines, and yes responses given to the longer lines. Of the 25 subjects belonging to the broad and narrow groups in Experiment I whose accuracy of performance in that experiment had been originally compared, 23 were still available in Experiment III. Their accuracy of performance in the new task was compared and the broad subjects were found to have 81.5 percent of their calls accurate, in contrast to 71.4 percent for the narrow subjects—a difference significant at the .01 level.

To sum up Experiment III, then, subjects maintain their relative positions with respect to breadth of categorizing when they shift from a situation where few stimuli fit the specifications of an inclusion class to one where many stimuli fit that specification: ones who are narrow in the first situation tend to be narrow in the second, and so, too, for those who are at the broad end of the distribution. One finds, moreover, that whereas in a situation where few stimuli fit the specifications for inclusion in the target class, narrow categorizers are more accurate, whereas when many stimuli fit, the broad categorizer turns out more accurate. Accuracy, in brief, seems more a function of a happy fit between response preference and stimulus properties than of discrimination capacity, much as in an experiment of Tagiuri, Bruner, and Blake (1958), where accuracy of social perception was a systematic resultant of two response patterns that had nothing to do with discriminative finesse. It would seem, then, that *not* only does discriminative capacity not determine categorizing breadth, but that, in a paradoxical way, it is the other way round.

CONCLUSIONS

Several things appear quite plain. To begin with, there appear to be consistencies in breadth of categorizing. We find, moreover, that narrow categorizers tend to be more sensitive to changes in the stimulus environment. They show more alteration in their categorizing breadth in response to change and show it more swiftly—though in a way that is not necessarily "rational." That is to say, when the range of stimuli to which they must respond *broadens,* they broaden their equivalence range for stimuli of a target class, although the specifications of the target class have not changed, and although their response may lead to more errors. It is as if they were "exploring" the new and wider range. Broad categorizers, on the other hand, do not change as much in response to an increase in the range of stimuli to which they must respond. They appear to be "holding on" to old methods in the face of a new situation. When the changed stimulus situation persists and becomes a steady state, the narrow categorizer reverts to his more precise and narrow mode of categorizing and reduces error. The broad categorizer, slower to react in the first place, begins to respond to change only when the change becomes more permanent.

An analogous picture holds when the stimulus world to which broad and narrow categorizers are exposed is constricted and becomes less varied. The narrow categorizer "follows" the change more swiftly by narrowing his categorizing range for the target class. Again even though logically it may lead to more error, for the specification of the target class has not changed. This time his response seems to be in the direction of closer analysis of a narrower range. The broad categorizer responds with no discernible change,

as if he were riding out the narrowing of the stimulus world that runs counter to his preference for breadth rather than changing with it.

It should not be surprising then—although we were taken unawares—that breadth of category is associated with intelligence, the narrow categorizers having a higher average IQ than the broad ones. Interestingly enough, though, shift in categorizing in the face of stimulus change is found to be related to breadth of categorizing but not to intelligence. Regardless of intelligence, the narrow categorizer handles change by shifting, by reacting to contrast; the broad categorizer shifts much less and later. In sum, reaction to change appears to be a strategy of dealing with the consequences of error. The narrow categorizer appears to prefer the risk of *reacting* and possibly being wrong. The broad categorizer prefers the risk of *not reacting* to change and possibly being wrong. Now we are in a position to ask about personality. What personality characteristics produce such preferences?

REFERENCES

Arnhoff, F. N., "Ethnocentrism and Stimulus Generalization," *Journal of Abnormal Social Psychology,* **53** (1956), 138-39.

———, "Ethnocentrism and Stimulus Generalization: A Replication and Further Study," *Journal of Abnormal Social Psychology,* **55** (1957), 393-94.

Bruner, J. S., J. J. Goodnow, and G. A. Austin, *A Study of Thinking.* New York: John Wiley & Sons, Inc., 1956.

Frenkel-Brunswik, Else, "Intolerance of Ambiguity as an Emotional and Perceptual Personality Variable," *Journal of Personality,* **18** (1949), 108-43.

Gardner, R. W., "Cognitive Styles in Categorizing Behavior," *Journal of Personality,* **22** (1953), 214-33.

Hamilton, V., "Perceptual and Personality Dynamics in Reactions to Ambiguity," *British Journal of Psychology*, **48** (1957), 200-15.

Kelly, T. L., "The Selection of Upper and Lower Groups for the Validation of Test Items," *Journal of Educational Psychology*, **30** (1939), 17-24.

Klein, G. S., "Cognitive Control and Motivation," in *Assessment of Human Motives*, ed. G. Lindzey, pp. 87-115. New York: Holt, Rinehart & Winston, Inc., 1958.

Rokeach, M., " 'Narrow-mindedness' and Personality," *Journal of Personality*, **20** (1951), 234-51.

Siegel, S., *Nonparametric Statistics for the Behavioral Sciences*. New York: McGraw-Hill Book Company, Inc., 1956.

Tagiuri, R., J. S. Bruner, and R. R. Blake, "On the Relation between Feelings and Perception of Feelings among Members of Small Groups," in *Readings in Social Psychology*, eds. Eleanor E. Maccoby, T. Newcomb, and E. Hartley, pp. 110-16. New York: Holt, Rinehart & Winston, Inc., 1958.

Tajfel, H., "The Anchoring Effects of Value in a Scale of Judgments," *British Journal of Psychology*, **50** (1959), 294-304.

Zaslow, R. W., "A New Approach to the Problem of Conceptual Thinking in Schizophrenia," *Journal of Consulting Psychology*, **14** (1950), 335-39.

A Concept-formation Approach to Attitude Acquisition *

Ramon J. Rhine

The purpose of this paper is to attempt a theoretical formulation of attitude development from a concept-formation point of view. Mediating responses have been employed by Osgood (21) to explain concept formation, and a mediating or implicit response has also been used as a main theoretical construct in Doob's (8) outline of attitude theory. To this extent, there is already an established theoretical link between concepts and attitudes.

Doob calls attitude "an implicit drive producing response considered

* From R. J. Rhine, "A Concept-formation Approach to Attitude Acquisition," *Psychological Review*, **65** (1958), 362-70. Reprinted by permission of the author and the American Psychological Association.

socially significant in the individual's society" (8, p. 136). This viewpoint has been criticized by Chein for a number of reasons, including the fact that it does not clearly indicate the evaluative nature of attitudes. Chein would rather call attitude a "disposition to evaluate certain objects, actions and situations in certain ways" (3, p. 177). Although many researchers in the field of attitudes might concur with Chein on this last point, a single meaning of attitude upon which there is close agreement is not available. Nelson's (20) review of the literature disclosed 23 more or less different definitions of attitude, and more recent statements could expand the list even further. No one definition seems clearly superior solely on logical grounds; if it were otherwise, there would not be so many alternatives.

The various definitions name constructs, and presumably some constructs have more scientific value than others. The psychologist, seeking a guide for his research among many alternatives, looks for a construct with heuristic and predictive value, particularly a construct which leads to informative research. Insofar as attitude change is concerned, Doob's type of approach has stimulated considerable research. But in the area of attitude development, very little carefully controlled experimentation has been done. Besides the research of Eisman (9), there is little experimentation available on attitude acquisition, although studies such as those by Horowitz (13) and by Clark and Clark (4) provide information about attitude growth. If it is possible to explain attitude learning in terms of concept formation, then attitude development is opened to controlled experimentation through concept-formation methods. A concept-formation approach to attitude learning also enables any systematic viewpoint which can account for concept formation to account at the same time for attitude formation.

THE GENERAL MEANING OF AN ATTITUDE

A concept is sometimes thought of as a psychological mechanism that represents a set of stimulus patterns; that is, a concept is considered a mental principle through which an individual can classify a number of objects in his stimulus world. Thus, redwood, elm, pine, fir, and oak fall into the class of "tall, nonanimal, living things," and *tree* is the name given to this principle. Similarly, the concept "a person who speaks with a drawl and has dark skin, thick lips, and kinky hair" classi-

fies American Negroes for some people. Of course, the concepts learned in real life are not always verbalized into a precise principle. In fact, behavior in laboratory studies (19) indicates that a concept can be learned even though S is unaware of it and is unable to verbalize the principle on which the concept is based. The same phenomenon probably occurs with attitudes. People often betray by their behavior attitudes which they do not recognize as their own.

On a common-sense level, concepts are developed over a period of time through a series of experiences. The child learns the concept *cow* because his parents and others point to objects in the field or in pictures and call them by that name. He learns that color alone is not the key to cow-ness, but that it is helpful. All black objects are not called cow, but green objects are never called by that name. The child soon learns to discriminate between cows and other objects as he learns that cow-ness is a feature of not one stimulus pattern but of a whole class of patterns.

The child learns about people in much the same manner. He discovers that one dimension of Negro-ness is dark skin, but that a deep suntan does not make one a Negro. He gradually learns that Negro-ness involves other dimensions such as facial characteristics and hair properties. This learning eventually enables him to make fairly accurate discriminations between Negroes and other persons. So far, the child has a concept of a Negro but not an attitude, because an attitude involves an evaluative dimension. Suppose, however, he has some unpleasant personal experiences with Negroes or receives adverse information about them from his parents. Then the child's concept might be based on the dimensions, "dark skin, kinky hair, thick lips, speaks with a drawl, and *bad."* Since an evaluative dimension now appears in the concept, he has acquired an attitude.

This approach to attitudes is not an arbitrary substitute for other meanings of attitude, but is representative of commonly used meanings, as may be seen from the following quotations:

"Most researchers in attitudes agree that one of the functions of attitudes is to integrate social perceptions and experiences. Thus our experiences with our mothers, sisters, girl friends and maiden aunts are integrated . . . into an attitude toward women" (16, p. 292). ". . . attitude [is] a more or less permanently enduring state of readiness of mental organization which predisposes an individual to react in a characteristic way to any object or situation with which it is related" (1, p. 13). "The attitude is a way of conceiving an object; it is the mental counterpart of an object" (10, p. 11). ". . . the *meaning* of a concept is its location in a space defined by some number of factors or dimensions, and *attitude* toward a concept is its projection onto one of these dimensions defined as 'evaluative' " (22, p. 42). "An attitude, roughly, is a residuum of experience, by which further activity is conditioned and controlled . . . an inner mental organization takes place which predisposes the person to a certain type of activity towards objects, persons, and situations" (17, p. 238).

The thread which runs through these quotations — "experiences integrated into an attitude," "mental organization," "mental counterpart," "a way of conceiving"—is that an attitude is a kind of mental organization that is built through many experiences. In a sense, as a result of varied contacts with a class of objects, a concentrated representation of a set of stimuli is left within the person, which is the essence

of what is generally meant by a concept.

AN EXPLANATION OF ATTITUDE

If an attitude is taken to be a concept with an evaluative dimension, its meaning may be derived from an explanation of concept formation. Consequently, any theory which can explain concept formation can also help to explain attitude development. One of several possible explanations of concept formation is provided by S–R Theory.

Borrowing from Osgood (21), a concept may be defined as the associations between a common response (often verbal) and a set of stimuli. These stimuli frequently comprise a class of phenomena which display certain common characteristics. The common characteristic of the set of phenomena may be the identical elements with which Hull (14) worked, such as a common shape embedded in each of several different Chinese characters. Or, as Smoke (30) has demonstrated, it may be common perceptual relations when, for instance, *S*s view a series of different figures and classify together all those having perpendicular lines in them. Although the stimuli mentioned in the definition of a concept often fall into a class, Osgood suggests that the only essential condition for concept formation is the associations between a common response and a variety of stimuli. There are no obvious stimulus characteristics common to hourglass, ruler and mental test, all of which are *measuring instruments;* or to file cabinet, typewriter, and desk, all of which are *office equipment.* These items have in common the overt response of naming them, and, of greater theoretical importance, a common mediating process.

The mediating response, Hull's pure

stimulus act, can be any fraction of a total response pattern. Partly as a result of the organism's capacity to discriminate, the mediating response will tend to become as fractionated as possible without destroying its cue function.

The greater the discriminatory capacity of an organism, the more reduced and implicit can become the ("detachable") reactions finally included in the stable mediation process. The higher the organism in the evolutionary scale, the finer the discriminations it can usually make and the less gross its representing processes. Similarly, the more mature and intelligent the human individual, the less overt his symbolic processes. The hosts of fine discriminations that characterize language behavior are Nature's farthest step in this direction (21, p. 398).

Of all possible human mediators, probably the most significant are verbal mediators. Research by Cofer and Foley and associates (5, 6, 7, 12), Riess (28, 29), and others demonstrates the significance for language behavior of mediating responses. Other investigations by Reed (23, 24, 25), Kendler and Karasik (15), and by Goss and associates (2, 11) show the importance of verbal mediators in concept formation. Studies by Eisman (9), Rhine (26, 27), and Staats and Staats (31) show how verbal mediators enter into attitudes.

The general model for a simple, first-order concept based on either verbal or nonverbal mediators is illustrated in Part A of Fig. 1. Many stimuli are conditioned to a common mediating response. By virtue of the common mediator, these stimuli become organized into one system. It is this system of associations between the stimuli and the common mediating process which is the concept. For the concept *gray,* the stimuli of Part A of Fig. 1 would be various acromatic shades all of which arouse the same mediating response. This response provides a stimulus generally conditioned in adults to the overt, verbal label *gray.*

A more complex or second-order concept is illustrated in Part B of Fig. 1. Each set of stimuli with their associated mediators (r_1's) are first-order concepts. In the second-order concept, the stimuli produced by the first-order mediators are themselves associated with another common mediator. One set of first-order stimuli in Part B of Fig. 1 might be different skin shades leading to the mediator representing *dark skin;* the second set of first-order stimuli might be various lip thicknesses which are associated with the mediator for *thick lips;* and each of the stimuli from these mediating responses may

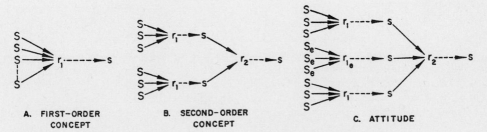

A. FIRST—ORDER CONCEPT   B. SECOND-ORDER CONCEPT   C. ATTITUDE

FIG. 1. *A stimulus-response explanation of concepts and attitude.* S_e = *evaluative stimuli;* r_2 = *a first-order mediator;* r_{1e} = *a first-order evaluative mediator;* r_2 = *a second-order mediator;* s = *the stimulus produced by a mediator.*

be associated with the mediator for *Negro* (r_2). This illustrates a second-order concept, but there is no attitude as yet because no evaluation is involved.

There is an attitude when the mediator of at least one of the first-order concepts is an evaluative reaction. Thus, attitudes are equivalent to that special class of concepts which is distinguished by the inclusion of an evaluative dimension. Part C of Fig. 1 is a simplified illustration of an attitude. Suppose, as in the example of a second-order concept, that one r_1 of this figure is the mediator for *thick lips,* that the second r_1 represents *dark skin,* and that r_2 is the mediator for *Negro.* Suppose also that the stimuli (S_e) of the evaluative dimension are *dirty, stupid,* and *rude* and that r_{1e}, the evaluative reaction, is *bad.* Now the stimuli associated with Negro are *dark skin, thick lips,* and *bad.* The inclusion of an evaluative dimension identifies Part C of Fig. 1 as an attitude.

The mediating response produces a stimulus which may then become conditioned to other mediating or instrumental reactions. Part A of Fig. 2 shows some of the major associations possible between the attitude and these other mediating responses. It indicates how instrumental responses may depend upon a chain of associations involving two major types of mediators,

namely, affective and verbal. Part A of Fig. 2 is not meant to imply that in any given instance all the illustrated associations between the attitude and verbal or affective mediators will be formed. Instead, it indicates that one or more of the associations may be learned by a given individual. For instance, as is shown in Part B-1 of Fig. 2, only some of the relations between the attitude, affect, and the instrumental response may be learned in an individual case.

One implication of Fig. 2 is particularly interesting. A reaction conditioned to the attitude may be aroused by a stimulus which is associated with affect but not with the attitude. This situation suggests an explanation for prejudiced responses through displaced aggression. Suppose an individual has a negative attitude towards Negroes. Suppose further that the affect of Part B of Fig. 2 is the mediator for *anger* and the instrumental response is aggression toward Negroes. Assume also, as Part B-1 of Fig. 2 indicates, that the attitude leads to the simultaneous arousal of anger and of aggression against Negroes. Eventually, through conditioning, anger alone can lead to aggression. Now, as indicated by Part B-2 of Fig. 2, any stimulus (S_n) which arouses anger will also have a tendency to evoke aggression towards Negroes, depending upon the degree to which

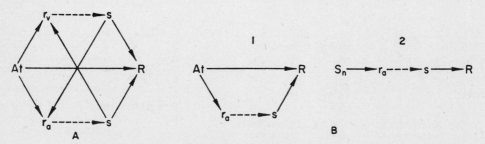

FIG. 2. *A: Major associations between the attitude* (At = *the attitude as shown in Part A of Fig. 1), and verbal* (r_v) *and affective* (r_a) *mediators. B: A stimulus-response explanation of prejudice through displaced aggression.*

this stimulus is supported by other stimuli. As a result, there is a tendency to displace aggression from S_n, the real source of anger, to Negroes.

Other specific predictions follow from the general relations shown in Part A of Fig. 2. The relationship between verbal mediating responses and affect suggests one reason why attitudes are commonly accompanied by affective reactions. If a given verbal mediator, through past experience, has become associated with affect, then the arousal of this mediator by an attitude will also lead to an affective response: the attitude leads to the verbal mediator and the verbal mediator is associated with affect. Suppose, for instance, that an attitude supplies the conditioned stimulus which evokes the verbal mediator for *green vomit*. Then, insofar as this mediator evokes an emotional reaction, the attitude will be accompanied by affect. This particular verbal mediator was used as an example because in some cases it will make the illustration more vivid by actually arousing an emotional reaction in the reader.

There is probably a more important reason why attitudes are commonly linked to affect. It is quite often true that the experiences through which the attitude is developed occur in a charged atmosphere. In this case, the mediating response of the attitude is continuously aroused in conjunction with an emotional reaction, and the stimulus produced by the mediating response becomes a conditioned stimulus capable of evoking affect. As a result, the expression of this attitude is accompanied by an emotional response.

A METHOD FOR STUDYING
ATTITUDE DEVELOPMENT

One of the main values of the concept-formation approach to attitude is that it suggests a simple laboratory method for studying attitude development. If an attitude is a kind of concept, then its acquisition may be investigated by the methods of concept formation. Such a method, depending on an evaluative dimension in the concept, has been employed by the writer. In order to construct an evaluative dimension, 100 Ss were asked to rate a large number of descriptive traits in terms of their desirability in a person. Some example traits are: ambitious, boring, calm, intelligent, obedient, and vain. All traits showing less than 90 percent agreement as to their desirability were discarded. The remaining traits can be employed to study the development of an attitude and to measure its strength and resistance to change. To do this, a group of Ss is told that anthropologists, missionaries and physicians have visited a group of people about which little is known, and that all the visitors agree on certain characteristics of this group of people. When these instructions are concluded, Ss are shown a number of traits, one by one, and are asked to predict whether each trait is or is not characteristic of the people. After each prediction they are told whether or not the word is indeed characteristic. For example, to develop a positive attitude, E would say "characteristic" after presenting each trait previously rated as desirable and "not characteristic" for words previously rated undesirable.

If S has learned the positive attitude, which might be labeled "pro-ness," he would be expected to respond accordingly. Hence, when he has completed the first list of traits, S is asked to continue responding in the previous manner to a second list of words without being told which traits are characteristic or not characteristic. Responses under this condition are taken as a measure of attitude strength. It is assumed that a strongly acquired, positive attitude will lead to a high proportion of positively rated traits being called "characteristic" and to most negatively rated traits being called "not characteristic."

Finally, resistance to attitude change is measured by using a third list of traits with E again saying "characteristic" or "not characteristic" after each prediction. But this time E's responses are reversed. For example, if S has previously acquired a positive attitude, change may be accomplished by calling "not characteristic" all positive traits in the third list and "characteristic" all negative traits.

This method is derived from the concept-formation approach to attitudes. The meaning of the many traits seen in a single session varies considerably, as can be observed from the examples given above. Although the traits are not synonyms, they do exhibit one common aspect, the evaluative element. The Ss are able to respond correctly when this evaluative element is consistently reinforced by E because the traits are stimuli which are capable of arousing a common, evaluative mediating response. The mediating process, in turn, determines S's further predictions of "characteristic" or "not characteristic."

The stimulus function of mediating responses in attitude development is demonstrated by two experiments which also illustrate the mediating response approach as applied through the concept-attitude method. A negative attitude was developed in both investigations. In one study (27), consistency of reinforcement was defined as the sum of the number of positive traits called "not characteristic" by E and the number of negative traits called "characteristic," divided by the total number of traits used during atti-

tude development. Using five levels of consistency, it was shown that both attitude development and strength increase as a function of consistency of reinforcement, as would be predicted from the approach to attitude development based on mediating responses. The results for attitude change also suggest that attitudes exhibit properties of mediating responses. Research on acquired distinctiveness of cues (18) indicates that strong habits reverse more easily than weak ones when the cues arousing them have become distinct through learning. The distinctiveness of the stimulus dimension is believed to be related to the degree to which the stimuli are conditioned to a mediating process. The evaluative element of the stimulus traits should be most distinct when reinforcement is fully consistent; consequently, attitude change should be easiest under this condition. The Ss receiving the greatest consistency of reinforcement did in fact show least resistance to change.

A second experiment (26) illustrating the concept-attitude method investigated the effect on attitude development of peer responses. The traits were used with 100 percent and 84 percent consistency of reinforcement to develop a negative attitude. Some Ss made their predictions after first hearing the responses of three fellow students who were E's confederates, and other Ss made their predictions in private. The confederates' responses prior to S's predictions were always or almost always in contradiction with the statement E made after each prediction. Thus, when the confederates said a trait was characteristic, it was pretty certain that E would say the trait was not characteristic. The Ss who heard the confederates' responses learned the attitude with greater ease than those who responded in private.

Apparently, peer responses provided cues which were an aid to S in attaining the attitude. This seemed to occur mainly with high consistency of reinforcement. With less than full consistency of reinforcement, peer responses were predictive of E's behavior for a majority of the traits, but not all of them. When this ambiguity is introduced, cues from peer responses do not affect attitude development at a statistically significant level, although there is a slight trend in this direction.

These results may be explained by considering the effect of peer responses upon the arousal of the common, evaluative mediating response. With 100 percent consistency of reinforcement, a negative mediating reaction is aroused by a trait just prior to reinforcement and in conjunction with peer responses of "characteristic." Similarly, a positive mediating reaction is aroused in conjunction with peer responses of "not characteristic." In time, as a result of conditioning, the peer responses can be expected to help cue the appropriate positive or negative mediating response. With 84 percent consistency of reinforcement, the trend of conditioning is the same, but a minority of trials tend to establish competing, mediating responses: the same peer reactions are sometimes associated with positive mediating responses and sometimes with negative. Under these conditions, peer responses are a less stable and less predictive aspect of the stimulus environment. This would account for the statistically significant effect from peer responses with high consistency of reinforcement, which is diminished with lesser consistency.

Staats and Staats (31) have also studied attitudes using an approach similar to that employed in the preceding two studies. They associated given names, Tom or Bill, and nationalities, Dutch or Swedish, with positive or negative evaluative words. Subsequent ratings indicate that the given names and nationalities took on the same evaluative flavor as the words with which they were associated. The researchers explain their results by pointing to the common, evaluative mediating response made to the words which are paired with the nationalities and names. It is assumed that through conditioning the names (or nationalities) would also lead to the mediating response aroused by the words with which they were paired. This was reflected when the names (or nationalities) were rated on the evaluative scale.

The studies derived from the concept theory of attitudes illustrate the possibility of bringing attitude development under laboratory scrutiny. Despite the generally recognized significance of attitude development, as distinguished from attitude change, the literature reveals relatively little laboratory evidence bearing upon its nature. It is hoped that the concept theory of attitudes and the method it implies will help provide a means through which attitude development will be more accessible to experimental investigations.

SUMMARY

A theory of attitude development based upon concept formation was discussed, and similarities between this view and earlier meanings of attitude were pointed out. An attitude was defined as a concept with an evaluative dimension, and the mediating response was employed to explain attitude learning. A method for inducing an attitude in the laboratory was described along with illustrative studies employing this method.

REFERENCES

1. Cantril, H., "Attitudes in the Making," *Understanding the Child,* **4** (1934), 13-14, 18.

2. Carey, J. E. and A. E. Goss, "The Role of Verbal Labeling in the Conceptual Sorting Behavior of Children," *Journal of Genetic Psychology,* **90** (1957), 69-74.

3. Chein, I., "Behavior Theory and the Behavior of Attitudes: Some Critical Comments," *Psychological Review,* **55** (1948), 175-88.

4. Clark, K. B. and Mamie P. Clark, "Racial Identification and Preference in Negro Children," in *Readings in Social Psychology,* eds. G. E. Swanson, T. M. Newcomb, and E. L. Hartley. New York: Holt, Rinehart & Winston, Inc., 1952.

5. Cofer, C. N. and J. P. Foley, "Mediated Generalization and the Interpretation of Verbal Behavior: I. Prolegomena," *Psychological Review,* **49** (1942), 513-40.

6. ———, "Mediated Generalization and the Interpretation of Verbal Behavior: II. Experimental Study of Certain Homophone and Synonym Gradients," *Journal of Experimental Psychology,* **32** (1943), 168-75.

7. Cofer, C. N., Marjorie E. Janis, and Mary M. Rowell, "Mediated Generalization and the Interpretation of Verbal Behavior: III. Experimental Study of Antonym Gradients," *Journal of Experimental Psychology,* **32** (1943), 266-69.

8. Doob, L. W., "The Behavior of Attitudes," *Psychological Review,* **54** (1947), 135-56.

9. Eisman, Bernice S., "Attitude Formation: The Development of a Color Preference Response through Mediated Generalization," *Journal of Abnormal Social Psychology,* **50** (1955), 321-26.

10. Faris, E., "The Concept of Social Attitudes," in *Social Attitudes,* ed. K. Young. New York: Holt, Rinehart & Winston, Inc., 1931.

11. Fenn, J. D. and A. E. Goss, "The Role of Mediating Verbal Responses in the Conceptual Sorting Behavior of Normals and Schizophrenics," *Journal of Genetic Psychology,* **90** (1957), 59-67.

12. Foley, J. P., Jr. and M. A. Mathews, "Mediated Generalization and the Interpretation of Verbal Behavior: IV. An Experimental Study of the Development of Interlinguistic Synonym Gradients," *Journal of Experimental Psychology,* **33** (1943), 188-200.

13. Horowitz, E. L., "The Development of Attitude toward the Negro," *Archives of Psychology,* No. 194 (1936).

14. Hull, C. L., "Quantitative Aspects of the Evolution of Concepts," *Psychology Monograph,* **28**, No. 1 (Whole No. 123 [1920]).

15. Kendler, H. H. and A. D. Karasik, "Concept-formation as a Function of Competition between Response-produced Cues," *Journal of Experimental Psychology,* **55** (1958), 278-83.

16. Krech, D., "Attitudes and Learning: A Methodological Note," *Psychological Review,* **53** (1946), 290-93.

17. Krueger, E. T. and W. C. Reckless, *Social Psychology.* New York: David McKay Co., Inc., 1931.

18. Lawrence, D. H., "Acquired Distinctiveness of Cues: II. Selective Association in a Constant Stimulus Situation," *Journal of Experimental Psychology,* **40** (1950), 175-88.

19. Leeper, R., "Cognitive Processes," in *Handbook of Experimental Psychology,* ed. S. S. Stevens. New York: John Wiley & Sons, Inc., 1951.

20. Nelson, E., "Attitudes: I. Their Nature and Development," *Journal of Genetic Psychology,* **21** (1939), 367-99.

21. Osgood, C. E., *Method and Theory in Experimental Psychology.* New York: Oxford University Press, 1953.

22. Osgood, C. E. and P. H. Tannenbaum, "The Principle of Congruity in the Prediction of Attitude Change," *Psychological Review,* **62** (1955), 42-55.

23. Reed, H. B., "Factors Influencing the Learning and Retention of Concepts: I. The Influence of Set," *Journal of Experimental Psychology,* **36** (1946), 71-87.

24. ———, "The Learning and Retention of Concepts: II. The Influence of Length of Series. III. The Origin of Concepts," *Journal of Experimental Psychology,* **36** (1946), 166-79.

25. ———, "The Learning and Retention of Concepts: IV. The Influence of Complexity of the Stimuli," *Journal of Experimental Psychology,* **36** (1946), 252-61.

26. Rhine, R. J., "The Effect of Peer Group Influence upon Concept-attitude Development and Change," *Journal of Social Psychology.* (In press.)

27. Rhine, R. J. and B. A. Silun, "Acquisition and Change of a Concept Attitude as a Function of Consistency of Reinforcement," *Journal of Experimental Psychology,* **55** (1958), 524-29.

28. Riess, B. F., "Semantic Conditioning Involving the GSR," *Journal of Experimental Psychology,* **26** (1940), 238-40.

29. ———, "Genetic Changes in Semantic Conditioning," *Journal of Experimental Psychology,* **36** (1946), 143-52.

30. Smoke, K. L., "An Objective Study of Concept Formation," *Psychology Monograph,* **42,** No. 4 (Whole No. 191 [1932]).

31. Staats, A. W. and Carolyn K. Staats, "Attitudes Established by Classical Conditioning," *Journal of Abnormal Social Psychology,* **57** (1958), 37-40.

The Judgmental Process in Personality Functioning *

Leonard Berkowitz

Consistent with their general cognitive bias, many psychologists have actively been engaged in extending judgmental principles from the psychophysics laboratory to the social world. Sherif, for example, who has devoted much of his professional life to this endeavor (1935, 1936, 1945–1946, 1956), continually has emphasized the importance of judgmental processes in social phenomena. Thus, writing some fourteen years ago in this journal, he and Cantril attempted to apply the psychology of perception and judgment to the concept of "attitude" (1945, 1946). From their point of view, these areas were intimately bound together. When an individual forms an attitude, they maintained, he learns to make a class of judgments in the course of which an issue or object is related to an appropriate frame of reference. More recently, Helson (1948) has suggested the relevance of his adaptation-level theory for a wide range of behavioral data. The present paper, in a sense, follows the same tradition. Here, as in the earlier works, the focus is upon cognitive processes. But more than this, together with these writers, we assume the underlying unity of psychological principles. To paraphrase Sherif and Cantril (1945, pp. 299–300), judgments made in the experimental laboratory and judgments in the most complicated social situation follow the same laws,

* From L. Berkowitz, The Judgmental Process in Personality Functioning," *Psychological Review,* **67,** (1960), 130-42. Reprinted by permission of the author and the American Psychological Association.

". . . the basic psychological substrata functioning in both instances are the same in nature." [1]

CATEGORIZATION AND JUDGMENT

In each case, regardless of the situation in which the judgment is made, the "psychological substratum" involves the act of categorization. As Bruner has put it, when "we stimulate an organism with some appropriate input . . . he responds by referring the input to some class of things or events" (1957, p. 123); ". . . whatever is perceived is placed in and achieves its 'meaning' from a class of percepts with which it is grouped" (p. 124). For our present purposes it is worth considering these groupings as categories and supracategories within which the smaller sets can be ordered. Confront the S with a number of small metallic

---

[1] This thesis, obvious though it may seem to many readers, is not universally shared in social psychology. Tagiuri and Petrullo (1958) prefer to emphasize the differences rather than the similarities between the "person perception" and "thing perception." They point out that in responding to people we frequently assume that they are "capable of watching, perceiving, remembering, and waiting for opportune circumstances." We experience them as directing themselves to us, "with intentions, attitudes and feelings," and these experiences affect the interaction between them and ourselves (p. xi). However, these experiences and assumptions concerning the cognitions and motivations of other stimulus objects serve only to complicate rather than to transform the picture. By and large, the assumptions are our "laws of nature" by means of which we make inferences as to the future behavior of the people concerned, but similarly we utilize other "laws" (more or less naïve depending upon our sophistication) to predict the behavior of inanimate objects. Furthermore, these assumptions at times become relatively unimportant in affecting reactions to others. Just as money may become valued because it is instrumental to need satisfaction, so do we often learn to value other people for their instrumental significance.

objects and he may classify them as weights, with some being relatively light and others heavier. The supracategory defines the continuum, or continua, along which the smaller categories are placed. It establishes the relationships that may exist among the smaller sets (for example, heavier or lighter). Judgment, then, is a function of these relationships.

Two familiar kinds of judgmental phenomena are of particular concern to us here: contrast and assimilation. Without attempting to account for these phenomena (explanatory hypotheses have been offered by Helson [1948] and Peak [1958]), this paper will try to show that conditions analogous to those producing either contrast or assimilation in the psychophysics laboratory will yield essentially similar results with self- and other-evaluations. If the distinction can be made, our purpose is description rather than explanation. This being the case, a crude model of the judgmental process will suffice. Translating the fact that all judgments are made with respect to a frame of reference, we can say these evaluations are a function of the relationship between some standard or anchorage category [2] and the category in which the evaluated stimulus would be placed by an observer who had not experienced the standard. If the distance between these two categories is relatively small there is *assimilation,* that is, the S locates the stimulus in some category *between* the standard and the observer's judgment, or even *in* the standard category. On the other hand, *contrast* takes place when this distance is relatively great. In this case, the S places the evaluated stimulus

---

[2] Helson (1948) maintains that an "adaptation-level, defined operationally in terms of the stimulus evoking a neutral or indifferent response" (p. 298), serves as this frame of reference.

further away from the standard than does the observer not affected by the standard (Peak, 1958, pp. 335–336, cites the experimental evidence for these propositions).

Two experiments by Hovland and Sherif illustrate the relevance of contrast and assimilation for social psychology. In the first of these (Hovland and Sherif, 1952) groups of strongly involved judges, some pro-Negro, others anti-Negro in their attitudes, were asked to sort 114 opinion statements in terms of their favorableness toward Negroes. The rather indefinite statements in the middle of the scale were displaced away from the judges' own positions (that is, there was contrast), contrary to Thurstone's assumption that the judges' attitudes would not effect their item sorting in his "equal-appearing intervals" scaling technique. It is likely, as I will attempt to show later, that the strongly involved S perceived a clear difference between his own position, the anchorage, and the beliefs reflected in the items. In other words, the distance between these categories was relatively great. Since the items' true position was indefinite, contrast could take place readily.

The second study (Hovland, Harvey, and Sherif, 1957) demonstrates both contrast and assimilation. Three communications dealing with the then locally important issue of prohibition were delivered to Ss in Oklahoma and Texas, one communication advocating the strong "wet" position, another strongly "dry," and the third being moderately "wet." The investigators report that the Ss' evaluations of the communicator's position was a function of the distance between their own attitude and the communicator's "true" position. The Ss closest to the communicator reported his beliefs relatively accurately; those not too far

from the communicator tended to judge his opinion on being more like their own than it actually was (assimilation); while those furthest from the communicator saw him as advocating a view further away from themselves than it really was (contrast).

On the basis of these studies, then, there would seem to be little doubt that contrast and assimilation effects take place in social judgments. A more pressing problem is the necessity of showing the usefulness of the present categorization model for the understanding of these phenomena, and this can be done by citing two additional experiments. The first of these is mentioned by Bruner (1957):

. . . Helson's law of adaptation level states that the subjective magnitude of a singly presented stimulus depends upon the weighted geometric mean of the series of stimuli that the subject has worked with, and the ingenious experiments of Donald Brown have indicated that this adaptation level is influenced only by those stimuli that the subject considers to be within the category of objects being considered. Ask the subject to move a weight from one side of the table to the other with the excuse that it is cluttering up the table, and the weight does not serve as an anchor to the series, although it will show a discernible effect if it is directly included in the series being judged (p. 128).

Apparently, for a stimulus to be included in and affect the nature of the standard category it has to be seen as appropriate to that category. It has to be grouped with the other anchorage stimuli. This grouping process obviously also can influence the perceived distance between the standard and the evaluated stimuli. Richard Schilling conducted an experiment under the writer's supervision in which the Ss had to judge the over-all "goodness"

of 11 personality traits by orally assigning ratings on a 13-point scale.
The first seven traits (all "good" or
all "bad" depending on the condition)
served as the anchorage. After giving
a judgment for each of these traits, all
of the Ss then evaluated four neutral
traits one at a time. Half of the Ss
had been informed at the beginning
of the study that the traits all referred
to one person, while the remaining Ss
were told the traits did not describe
any one individual. The results showed
a significant contrast effect; the evaluation of the neutral traits was displaced
away from the evaluations of the preceding seven stimuli. However, the
interaction of "good-or-bad anchorage" with the "same person-different
people" instruction also was significant; there was a smaller difference
between the "good" and "bad" anchorage Ss in the evaluations of the
neutral traits under the "same person"
instruction than under the "different
people" condition. In the former treatment the Ss presumably were more
likely to group the neutral traits together with the preceding seven traits.
This placing of the traits in one larger
category ("all describe one person")
apparently then served to lessen the
psychological distance between the
anchorage and neutral traits, thereby
lessening the contrast effect.

If this interpretation is correct, the
results of this experiment can clarify
some of the findings obtained by the
Yale Attitude Change Project. Working under the auspices of this project,
Luchins replicated the essential features of Asch's study of the primacy
effect in first impressions (Asch,
1952). The information presented first
was found to be more influential in
shaping the total impression of a stimulus person than the material presented
later. In commenting upon these findings, Hovland notes that most of

Luchins' Ss failed to see any incompatibility between the earlier and later
information, and he suggests that a
primacy effect is most likely to occur
under these conditions (Hovland,
1958, pp. 144–146). Using the present terminology, we would say that
Asch's primacy effect refers to the
assimilation of the later material into
the first presented category. When
people recognize the incompatibility
between the earlier and later information, they place the sets of information
in separate categories relatively far
apart psychologically, thus making
assimilation unlikely.

SELF- AND OTHER-EVALUATIONS IN PSYCHOANALYTIC PROJECTION AND PARANOIA

There is no necessary reason, as far
as the writer can see, why the social
analogues of contrast and assimilation
should be limited to opinion statements
or even isolated judgments of other
people. Conceivably, self-other relationships also should be subject to
these effects. Furthermore, I would
like to propose that part of the phenomenon usually referred to as projection can be understood as a contrast
effect in the judgment of others relative to one's self.

In his famous study of projection,
Sears (1936) defines this process in
these terms: "A wish, attitude, or
habit hierarchy which is not compatible with other attitudes or habits of an
individual may be attributed by that
individual to other persons rather than
to himself providing he lacks insight
into the fact that he himself possesses
the trait in question" (p. 151). College
men in three fraternities were asked to
rate their fraternity brothers and themselves on four bipolar traits (for example, stingy–generous). Two effects

were noted. First, consistent with psychoanalytic theory, Ss who lacked insight into the amount of a given trait they themselves possessed (that is, whose self-ratings disagreed with the group consensus on them) attributed more of this trait to others than did the insightful Ss. By the way, and as psychanalytic theory does *not* suggest, this occurred whether the trait was socially desirable or not. Thus, a generous person who supposedly did not realize he actually was generous tended to attribute more generosity to his fraternity brothers than an equally generous person who knew he possessed this trait. The second effect was limited by Sears to the insightful Ss. These people exhibited "contract-formation." For example, the more generous the individual knew he was the more he tended to see the others as stingy.

Sears seems to have regarded these as two distinct processes because he was concerned with the individual's insight into his *actual possession* of a trait. However, if our focus of attention is shifted to the Ss' *self*-descriptions we can see there is only one effect here: judgmental contrast. In this case we have to assume that an individual's self concept (his category, "me") serves as his judgmental standard and that he perceives most of the others in his group as being somewhat different from him. "Projection" then becomes "contrast-formation." The actually generous person who perceives himself as stingy judges his fellow group members in reference to this self-anchorage, stingy, and the resulting contrast gives rise to the evaluation, generous. From this viewpoint, the important feature in the supposedly insightful Ss is that they also utilize their self concept as the judgmental standard. As far as their evaluations of others is concerned, how

these others see them is largely irrelevant (except perhaps in that the self-anchorage might be affected by knowing the opinions of others). Here too, the person judges others in reference to his image of himself, and contrast results to the extent that there is some perceived difference between the anchorage category, self, and evaluated category, others.

More recently, Goldings (1954) has reported a study whose findings can readily be reconciled with the Sears' results. Judges were asked to rate their own degree of happiness and also to evaluate the happiness or unhappiness of people shown in a series of 30 pictures. Among other things, Goldings concluded: "At the extremes of happiness and unhappiness, *contrast projection* occurs: those who avow extreme happiness tend to attribute unhappiness to others and those who avow extreme unhappiness tend to attribute happiness to others. In more moderate degrees of happiness and unhappiness, regular supplementary projection occurs" (p. 42), that is, the Ss attributed their own feelings to the pictured individuals.

Although Goldings explicitly states that Sears' concepts cannot account for his findings (pp. 44–45), it seems to me that the two studies are easily brought together. To explain the later results we first have to assume that the pictured individuals on the average are located towards the middle of the happiness–unhappiness continuum. The judges who anchor themselves at the extremes of this continuum then perceive relatively great dissimilarity between themselves and the stimulus objects, and there is a contrast effect. On the other hand, for the judges whose self-standard is moderate happiness or moderate unhappiness, the distance between this anchorage and the evaluated category, others, is relatively small. The result is assimilation, or what Goldings, following H. A. Murray, terms supplementary projection.

In both experiments, therefore, the nature of the projection exhibited depends upon the psychological distance between the self-standard and the category of others being evaluated. If this distance is relatively great (as was the case for some of Goldings' Ss and, presumably, most of Sears') we find contrast in the judgment of the others. However, when the distance is small (again, as was the case for some of Goldings' Ss but few, if any, of those utilized by Sears) there is assimilation, or supplementary projection, in the judgment of others. Clearly, Sears' results parallel the previously cited findings obtained by Hovland and Sherif (1952) regarding the evaluations of opinion statements as a function of the judges' own strong attitudes on these issues, while the Goldings results essentially are close to the findings mentioned earlier in the study by Hovland, Harvey, and Sherif (1957).

This is not to say that psychoanalytic projection is entirely accounted for by the present judgmental phenomena; evaluation of others is only part of the process of projection. As Sears has pointed out, the psychoanalytic concept also involves lack of insight into (or the repression of knowledge of) the possession of undesirable traits, wishes, or ideas. His data suggest, furthermore, that these "undesirable" responses need not always be socially "bad." Some of his Ss apparently did not realize they had "good" attributes such as generosity. If this lack of awareness is motivated, it may be, as Rogers has proposed (1951, Ch. 11), that the repression stems from a perceived inconsistency between the given trait and the indi-

vidual's self concept.[3] At any rate, regardless of the nature of repression, there is an additional component to this process that also must be considered: reaction formation. Frequently, when a person projects his own characteristics onto others, he not only lacks awareness that he has these characteristics, he leans over backward in denying them and insists to himself and others that he is just the opposite. All this can be illustrated by taking the case of the person most likely to exhibit projection, the paranoid.[4] According to psychoanalytic theory, the paranoid's basic problem involves latent homosexuality (Freud, 1925; Zamansky, 1958). This characteristic is threatening to him, he represses the drive, and projects it onto important others. However, even the attribution of homosexual desires to another supposedly provokes anxiety, so the idea is transformed from "he loves me" to "he hates me."

I would like to offer tentatively a somewhat different explanation for the dynamics of paranoia. As in analytic theory, the process commences when the individual judges himself (his "real" self) as being located towards the homosexual end of the heterosexual-homosexual continuum, while his

---

[3] Rogers here has anticipated recent theoretical developments in social psychology, such as the Osgood and Tannenbaum (1955) incongruity hypotheses and Festinger's (1957) dissonance theory. In terms of this latter view, for example, knowledge of the possession of a trait incompatible with beliefs regarding the nature of the self is likely to produce psychologically uncomfortable "cognitive dissonance." Since the individual is motivated to reduce dissonance, he may repress (exclude from awareness) knowledge of his possession of the incompatible trait.

[4] The ideas given in this section were stimulated to a considerable extent by discussions with Norman S. Greenfield.

ideals ("ideal" self) are anchored towards the extreme opposite end. The ideal self then serves as the standard by which others as well as the real self are evaluated. Several things then happen. First, the relatively great gap between the ideal and real selves upsets the individual, and in defense he (a) represses knowledge of his real self-evaluation, as well as (b) strongly insists, to himself and others, that he really is the way he would like to be. In this latter process he has not only repressed his homosexual attributes, he has exhibited reaction formation in characterizing himself as extremely nonhomosexual. At the conscious level his ideals and his self-image both are strongly heterosexual,[5] and it is from this extreme viewpoint that he judges others. The consequence, of course, is a contrast effect; other people are evaluated as more homosexual than they actually are. (But only people important to him are so evaluated because he does not bother to judge everyone he encounters.)

However, this judgment of others also may be threatening. The very idea, homosexuality, may arouse anxiety, and subsequent avoidance responses, so that even the characterization of another as possessing this disapproved motive is repressed. The emotion aroused by the initial judgment remains; the person is hated for possessing the evil trait, but the basis for the hatred is kept from awareness. Festinger (1957, pp. 235–243) has

suggested that this state of affairs, strong emotion without a conscious explanation for it, is upsetting (produces dissonance) and motivates the individual to invent reasons for his feeling. (According to Festinger [cf. his citation on p. 235], Freud had recognized this phenomenon, but he nevertheless goes on to provide additional support for his thesis.) Following this lead, we would propose that to a considerable extent, the paranoid's ideas of being persecuted are the reasons he invents to give conscious meaning to his hatred for others.

Undoubtedly also contributing to this persecution complex are the paranoid's assimilative tendencies. As will be discussed more fully later, the discrepancy between his ideals and his unverbalized self-image probably produces an extremely unfavorable self-evaluation. Since the basis for this evaluation is not known, it is easy for him to attribute this evaluation to others. In essence, he unconsciously dislikes himself and, as a result, consciously expects others also to dislike him. To employ the Postman-Bruner terminology of the early 1950's, he has an hypothesis of reproof, dislike, and even aggression from others. As a consequence, ambiguous events or acts that are not too obviously at variance from this hypothesis are assimilated into it. The paranoid expects this behavior from others and interprets appropriate stimulus situations in a manner consistent with his hypothesis. Postman and Brown (1952) have obtained evidence that is of some relevance here. They have shown that threat-associated stimuli are perceived readily by Ss trained to have a failure self-hypothesis. Thus, not only would the paranoid assimilate ambiguous situations into his threat hypothesis; his threshold for the recognition of

[5] Extrapolating some of Festinger's observations (1957), we might say that the greater the uncertainty felt by the individual that he really is the way he thinks he is (that is, the greater the dissonance regarding his conscious beliefs about himself)— up to some maximum level of doubt—the more strongly he will consciously deny these doubts and insist that the self-belief is correct.

these threats also would be low.

Psychoanalytic theory obviously has contributed a great deal to this interpretation of paranoia. The major difference is that the present scheme weights the judgmental process much more heavily, particularly with regard to projection. According to this view, projection is not a defense in the usual meaning of this term, but rather, is a consequence of the evaluation of others. When the paranoid attributes disapproved traits to another he does so because there is a relatively great distance, psychologically, between the anchorage, his ideals and conscious self-characterization, and the indeterminate location of the other on the trait continuum.

Much of this analysis admittedly is speculation, but there are a number of implications here that seem to be consistent with quantitative evidence. It has been reported, for example, that judges tend to assume their friends are more like themselves than are persons they dislike (Fiedler, Warrington, and Blaisdell, 1952; Lundy, et al., 1955). Thus, a paranoid might tend to view others as being dissimilar to himself, increasing the psychological distance between these others and himself, not only because of his reaction formation-produced extreme self-evaluation, but also because of his dislike for the others. The result is that contrast projection becomes more likely, and additional fuel is thrown on the fire of hatred.

Fensterheim and Tresselt (1953) report some data that are pertinent here. They found that college students tended to attribute their least preferred values to strangers, and that this tendency was strongest for those strangers who were least liked. Since most of the Ss saw themselves as possessing the values they preferred, it may well be that this preferred self-image served

as the anchorage in the judgmental process. The results of this study then suggest: (a) that strangers often are regarded as fairly distant psychologically from the self, giving rise to a contrast effect ("they are different from me") and (b), as was proposed above, that feelings of unfriendliness toward the evaluated object serve to increase this distance, further heightening the contrast. Extrapolating from the Fensterheim-Tresselt findings, we can readily predict that the paranoid, hating other people, would be all too prone to attribute his least preferred characteristics to them. In his case this would appear to the psychoanalytically biased observer as projection.

The present analysis also proposes that there is a considerable discrepancy between the paranoid's ideals (the way he would like to be) and his unverbalized image of his actual characteristics (his perceived real self). Rogers and his colleagues have shown (Butler and Haigh, 1954) that this ideal self-real self discrepancy frequently is found in people with personality disorders. It is easy to see why this discrepancy would have harmful effects: to the extent that the ideal self is utilized as the standard category, the contrast effect produced by a relatively great discrepancy between this and the real self results in the latter being evaluated even more unfavorably.

There is support for this prediction in a recent exploratory study conducted by the writer. Half of 52 Ss in two psychology classes were asked to describe themselves on an adjective check list as they believed they "really were." The remaining Ss performed this self-description task after first describing their ideals (what they wished they were like) on this check list. The saliency of the ideal self was thereby increased in this latter condition, and presumably, it therefore was more likely to have served as an anchorage affecting the subsequent judgments of the real self. The nature of this effect, of course, depends upon the distance between the ideal self anchorage and the evaluated object, the real self, and we assumed this distance would be greater the more dissatisfied the *S*s were with themselves. Each of the adjectives in the check list had been classified earlier as either "good" or "bad" (based upon the evaluations of a pool of judges), making it possible to score the favorableness of each *S*'s ideal self and real self descriptions. In addition, the *S*s in both conditions indicated on a graphic rating scale how satisfied they were with themselves. These latter self-satisfaction ratings supported the assumption regarding the discrepancy between ideal and real selves; for the *S*s who described their ideals, the greater the rated dissatisfaction with the self the greater the discrepancy in the favorableness of the ideal and real self descriptions. Each of the two experimental conditions was then dichotomized at the condition median on the self-satisfaction ratings, and the number of favorable adjectives attributed to the real self [6] on the check list was computed in each of the four resulting conditions. As expected, when their ideals had been made more salient, the *S*s who were relatively satisfied with themselves (and, it will be remembered, whose real selves were close to their ideals) evaluated their real selves significantly more favorably than the *S*s in any other condition. Similarly, the dissatisfied *S*s (whose real selves were far from their ideals) described themselves

most unfavorably of all four groups of *S*s when put in the condition enhancing the likelihood of their ideals serving as a judgmental anchorage. Apparently, when our *S*s became more aware of their ideals, the subsequent evaluations of their real selves were affected. Those whose real selves were close to their ideals seemed to show assimilation, that is, the favorableness of the real self-evaluation presumably was increased bringing it closer to the ideal self. On the other hand, the people whose real selves were relatively far from their ideals manifested a contrast-like effect; they evaluated themselves more unfavorably. [7]

It makes sense, therefore, to regard one of the principle aims of psychotherapy, at least in some instances, as the reduction of the ideal self-real self discrepancy, and Butler and Haigh (1954) and Rudikoff report (1954) such a discrepancy reduction in their investigation of psychotherapeutic results. Evaluating himself with an unrealistic set of ideals (Freud's harsh "superego") as the standard, the individual who sees himself as not living up to these ideals also is likely to judge himself, by contrast, as more of a failure than he actually is (for example, as might be determined by an independent observer).

---

[6] In actuality, the dependent variable was the number of favorable adjectives attributed to the real self *plus* the number of unfavorable adjectives that were said to be not characteristic of the person.

[7] These results do not seem to be due to a situation-induced correlation between the self-satisfaction ratings and ideal self-real self discrepancy in the case of the subjects describing their ideals, and the absence of such a correlation in the other condition. The *S*s in the former condition were much more likely to be at both extremes of the favorableness of real self description continuum, while the remaining subjects tended to be in the middle of this continuum. In other words, the variance was greater in the former condition, as if the *S*s had been made to move out toward the extremes. However, in the absence of proof that their self-judgments had indeed changed, this conclusion must be tentative.

Of course, one of the major difficulties here, at least as far as research is concerned, is the frequent inaccessibility of the individual's unfavorable self-image to verbal report. That is, these unfavorable self-attitudes often are repressed. For example, we already have proposed that the paranoid is not consciously aware of his negative self-evaluation but instead describes himself in a highly positive manner. The previously cited investigations by Rogers and his colleagues, on the other hand, clearly imply that many neurotics are aware of their unfavorable self-portrayal. There is evidence supporting this interpretation in a paper published by Friedman (1955). Normal, psychoneurotic, and paranoid schizophrenic subjects described themselves and their ideals utilizing the Q sort. For the paranoids the discrepancy between the real and ideal self was only slightly less than that for the normals (the statistically significant median r's were .42 and .62 respectively), but there was no relationship between these self-concepts in the case of the neurotics (median $r = .03$). Friedman concludes:

. . . normals tends to see themselves as they would like to be, reflecting positive attitudes toward the self. The psychoneurotic group tended to regard their self qualities as being very much different from the way they would like to be . . . (but the positive self concept) of the paranoid schizophrenic group is based upon unrealistic self appraisal (p. 613).

This study also contains data consistent with other aspects of our analysis of paranoia. According to the present scheme, the paranoid is relatively unlikely to exhibit judgmental assimilation of others to his perceived positive values because his hostility towards others, as well as his reaction formation, increases the psychological distance between himself (the standard category) and these others. Thus, he does not attribute his perceived self characteristics (as he consciously believes he is) to other people. Friedman's findings indicate that this is indeed the case. Both the normal and psychoneurotic groups tended to attribute their consciously perceived characteristics to the figures depicted in TAT cards (apparently in this case there wasn't the alienation or strangeness felt by the Fensterheim-Tresselt Ss), but the paranoids did not.

INDIVIDUAL DIFFERENCES IN CATEGORIZING TENDENCIES, THE AUTHORITARIAN PERSONALITY, AND HOSTILITY DISPLACEMENT

Up to this point we have seen that a variety of judgmental situations give rise to contrast or assimilation effects depending upon the distance between the standard category and the evaluated object or issue. This distance, in many cases, obviously can be determined objectively prior to the evaluation task. In other instances, however, it appears that this determination may be made more difficult by the characteristic categorizing behavior of the Ss involved in the task. For example, the distance between the standard and the evaluated stimulus can be coordinated to the number of discrete categories the person can establish between them. Defining a category, with Bruner (1957), "as a set of specifications regarding what (stimuli) will be grouped as equivalent" (p. 133), Ss who typically have broad equivalence ranges (that is, utilize broad categories) are likely to perceive the anchor and the evaluated stimulus as more similar than Ss who customarily establish narrow categories. Gardner (1953) and Pettigrew

(1958) have shown that there are reliable individual differences in category width. In the former experiment people who established relatively small categories in an object-sorting test were less subject to brightness, size and shape constancy effects than people who adopted relatively large categories in this test. The former apparently made finer discriminations in their sensory judgments. Although Gardner did not test this possibility, we also would expect the people who typically set up narrow categories in their object sorting to be less likely than others to demonstrate judgmental assimilation and be quicker to manifest judgmental contrast with an objectively defined increasing distance between the anchor and the evaluated stimulus.

To complicate matters still further, individual differences in these judgmental effects may become evident in some evaluation situations but not in others. This is indicated in the research on the relationship between personality rigidity and problem-solving. If a person were to go about solving all the problems given him in the same manner, even though the experimenter knows many types of solutions were available, conceivably, for this individual, the problems are equivalent. They are placed in the same category

of problems and the same responses are made to them. In this sense, then, rigidity is a function of the breadth of an individual's categories. Roger Brown (1953) has demonstrated that highly authoritarian individuals (as defined by the California F scale) tend to exhibit greater problem-solving rigidity than less authoritarian subjects, but only when placed in a mildly stressful, ego-involving situation. Translating this finding, we might say the authoritarian's categorizations generally become broader under mild stress. To put it another way, he does not make fine discriminations among the stimulus tasks confronting him in this type of situation.

Recently, the present writer has observed that some instances of hostility displacement may stem from an essentially similar process. An experiment was carried out to test the hypothesis that characteristically prejudiced people are more likely to displace frustration-instigated aggression upon an innocent bystander than are less prejudiced people. High and low anti-Semitic female college students were selected on the basis of their scores on a prejudice-assessing questionnaire, with half of each group later exposed to harsh and frustrating individual treatment by the experimenter. After this each S was required to work for

TABLE 1

MEAN EVALUATIONS OF THE FOUR NEUTRAL TRAITS FOLLOWING THE SEVEN ANCHORING TRAITS

| | HIGH F SCALE SCORE | | LOW F SCALE SCORE | |
	Ego-involved	Nonego-involved	Ego-involved	Nonego-involved
Anchorage:				
"Good"	6.68_{bc}	7.45_a	7.10_{ab}	6.15_{cd}
"Bad"	6.12_{cd}	6.02_{de}	5.42_e	6.72_{bc}

Note.—(High Score = "Unfavorable" Evaluation; $N = 10$ in each condition).
Cells containing the same subscript are not significantly different from each other at the .05 level by Duncan multiple-range test.

a brief period with a peer (the experimenter's confederate) and then rate her degree of liking for the peer. For the nonangered Ss, there was no difference between the high and low anti-Semitic girls in their rated friendliness toward the other girl. However, in comparison to these neutral-situation ratings, the angered less prejudiced girls became friendlier toward the peer, while the angered more highly prejudiced subjects tended to become more hostile (Berkowitz, 1959).

If we assume that the S's experience with the anger-arousing experimenter served as a judgmental anchorage, the reaction of the less prejudiced (less authoritarian) girls become a contrast effect: in contrast to the annoying experimenter, the peer seemed to be friendly and was so evaluated. On the other hand, if the stress of the frustrating situation served to broaden the highly prejudiced (more authoritarian) girls' categories, their hostility displacement is due to assimilation: the annoying experimenter and the peer were grouped together in the same category so that the hostility aroused by the former was generalized readily to the latter.

A judgment experiment conducted by the writer and Pauline Schoenberg tested this interpretation. As in Schilling's study, described above, the students were asked to judge the "goodness" of eleven personality traits, with the first seven traits, all clearly "good" or all clearly "bad," providing the anchorage, and the remaining four being relatively neutral. Schilling's investigation had shown, it will be recalled, that contrast is relatively unlikely to occur when the traits all refer to the same individual. These instructions were utilized throughout in the present experiment; the Ss were told the adjectives described traits possessed by one person, Joe, and each trait was introduced by the phrase, "Joe is ————."

Eight conditions were created in a factorial design for the study. Half of the Ss, taken from a pool of previously tested volunteers, came from the upper third of the distribution of F scale scores, with the remaining Ss coming from the lowest third. Half of each of these groups then was made to be ego involved in the experiment by telling the Ss their judgments were a test of them, while the other Ss presumably were less ego-involved. Finally, within each of these resulting four conditions, half of the Ss had the "good" anchorage and the others the "bad" anchorage.

The mean judgments of the neutral traits in each condition are shown in Table 1. Beginning at the right with the nonego-involved low authoritarian Ss, it can be seen that the neutral traits were judged on the whole somewhat (but not significantly) more favorably when preceded by the "good" rather than the "bad" anchorage. In other words, there is an indication here of an assimilation effect. Moving on to the next column, the mildly stressful ego-involving instruction served to eliminate this judgmental tendency in the less authoritarian Ss and there is a significant contrast effect. Presumably, the stress tended to narrow the categories established by these people resulting in a sharp differentiation between the seven anchoring stimuli and the four more neutral traits. This finding seems to parallel the results obtained for the angered less prejudiced girls in the hostility-displacement study. As mentioned earlier, these girls under stress also had tended to sharpen their differentiation between the frustrating experimenter and their neutral peer co-worker.

This discrimination apparently is

the "normal" state of affairs for the highly authoritarian Ss. As shown in the table, these Ss differentiated the anchoring stimuli from the more neutral traits and displayed a significant contrast effect. However, as predicted mild stress apparently weakened this judgmental tendency somewhat. Table 1 indicates there was a reliable decrease in the contrast effect manifested in the evaluations of the neutral stimuli following the "good" anchorage. It may be, as we have hypothesized, that the conceptual categories set up by the authoritarian tend to broaden under stress, thereby reducing the psychological distance between the standard and the evaluated stimuli [8] and, as a consequence, weakening the

_____

[8] Note that the highly authoritarian Ss under stress still tended to rate the neutral traits somewhat more unfavorably after the "good" anchorage than after the "bad" anchorage. This moderate contrast effect indicates they still were not acting in conformity to the instruction that the traits all referred to one individual, so that the decrease in the magnitude of this contrast probably was not due to a stress-induced adherence to the instructions. Furthermore, since the instruction on this point was very explicit and each trait was introduced by a phrase reminding the S of the single-person referent, there is little doubt that the Ss in every condition were aware of the instruction. Similarly, the lower evaluation scores in this condition probably were not caused by an increase in rating conservatism (an increased desire to "play it safe" in their evaluations by avoiding extremely "good" ratings). The authoritarian Ss under the mild stress rated the anchoring traits in as extreme a manner as the other groups of Ss. On the other hand, if they had decided "safety" lay in being consistent in their evaluations, they would have shown a much stronger "assimilation" effect than actually occurred.

At any rate, a more recent investigation completed after this paper had gone to press, employing the same procedures but without the "all-one-person" instruction, obtained essentially the same pattern of differences between the high and low authoritarian Ss.

judgmental contrast. If so, this broadening can account for at least some of the hostility displacement shown by the angered highly prejudiced girls. In this case stress caused them not to differentiate the frustrator from the available bystander so that the aggression aroused by the former generalized to the latter.

SUMMARY

Assuming the underlying unity of psychology, the present paper has attempted to show that judgmental principles uncovered in the psychophysics laboratory and recently extended to social evaluation situations can also be applied to personality functioning. These principles deal with judgmental contrast and assimilation, and it is proposed, for example, that psychoanalytic projection is readily understood as a special instance of these phenomena.

The theme of the unity of psychological science also runs strongly through the tentative theory of paranoia presented here. From psychoanalytic theory, we assume that much of the paranoid's behavior stems from repressed homosexuality. However, our description of the reactions to this disapproved drive leans heavily on recent social psychological theorizing, particularly Festinger's theory of cognitive dissonance. Whether the details of this analysis are correct or not is relatively unimportant. As far as the writer is concerned, it is much more important to demonstrate that the laboratory researcher does deal with material of relevance to the clinician and that this is true even when he studies judgments of lifted weights. Aberrant phenomena are not in a world entirely apart from the normal. In many respects they can profitably be regarded as special cases of more general psychological principles.

REFERENCES

Asch, S., *Social Psychology,* Chap. 8. Englewood Cliffs, N. J.: Prentice-Hall, Inc., 1952.

Berkowitz, L. "Anti-Semitism and the Displacement of Aggression," *Journal of Abnormal Social Psychology,* **59** (1959), 182-87.

Brown, R., "A Determinant of the Relationship between Rigidity and Authoritarianism," *Journal of Abnormal Social Psychology,* **48** (1953), 469-76.

Bruner, J. S., "On Perceptual Readiness," *Psychological Review,* **64** (1957), 123-52.

Butler, J. and G. Haigh, "Changes in the Relation between Self-conc~pts and Ideal-concepts Consequent upon Client-centered Counseling," in *Psychotherapy and Personality Change,* eds. C. Rogers and Rosalind Dymond. Chicago: University of Chicago Press, 1954.

Fensterheim, H. and Margaret Tresselt, "The Influence of Value Systems on the Perception of People," *Journal of Abnormal Social Psychology,* **48** (1953), 93-98.

Festinger, L., *A Theory of Cognitive Dissonance.* Evanston, Ill.: Row, Peterson & Company, 1957.

Fiedler, F. W., Warrington, and F. Blaisdell, "Unconscious Attitudes as Correlates of Sociometric Choice in a Social Group," *Journal of Abnormal Social Psychology,* **47** (1952), 790-97.

Freud, S., *Collected Papers.* London: The Hogarth Press, 1925.

Friedman, I., "Phenomenal, Ideal, and Projected Conceptions of Self," *Journal of Abnormal Social Psychology,* **51** (1955), 611-15.

Gardner, R., "Cognitive Styles in Categorizing Behavior," *Journal of Personality,* **23** (1953), 214-33.

Goldings, H., "On the Avowal and Projection of Happiness," *Journal of Personality,* **23** (1954), 30-47.

Helson, H., "Adaptation-level as a Basis for a Quantitative Theory of Frames of Reference," *Psychological Review,* **55** (1948), 297-313.

Hovland, C., "The Role of Primacy and Recency in Persuasive Communication," in *Readings in Social Psychology* (3rd ed.), eds. Eleanor Maccoby, T. Newcomb, and E. Hartley. New York: Holt, Rinehart & Winston, Inc., 1958.

Hovland, C., O. Harvey, and M. Sherif, "Assimilation and Contrast Effects in Reactions to Communication and Attitude Change," *Journal of Abnormal Social Psychology,* **55** (1957), 244-52.

Hovland, C. and M. Sherif, "Judgmental Phenomena and Scales of Attitude Measurement: Item Displacement in Thurston Scales," *Journal of Abnormal Social Psychology,* **47** (1952), 822-32.

Lundy, R., W. Katkovsky, R. Cromwell, and D. Shoemaker, "Self Acceptability and Descriptions of Sociometric Choices," *Journal of Abnormal Social Psychology,* **51** (1955), 260-62.

Osgood, C. and P. Tannenbaum, "The Principle of Congruity in the Prediction of Attitude Change," *Psychological Review,* **62** (1955), 42-55.

Peak, Helen, "Psychological Structure and Psychological Activity," *Psychological Review,* **65** (1958), 325-47.

Pettigrew, T., "The Measurement and Correlates of Category Width as a Cognitive Variable," *Journal of Personality,* **26** (1958), 532-44.

Postman, L. and D. Brown, "The Perceptual Consequences of Success and Failure," *Journal of Abnormal Social Psychology,* **47** (1952), 213-21.

Rogers, C., *Client-centered Therapy.* Boston: Houghton Mifflin Company, 1951.

Rudikoff, Esselyn, "A Comparative Study of the Changes in the Concepts of the Self, the Ordinary Person, and the Ideal in Eight Cases," in *Psychotherapy and Personality Changes,* eds. C. Rogers and Rosalind Dymond. Chicago: University of Chicago Press, 1954.

Sears, R., "Experimental Studies of Projection: I. Attribution of Traits," *Journal of Social Psychology,* **7** (1936), 151-63.

Sherif, M., "A Study in Some Social

Factors in Perception," *Archives of Psychology,* 187 (1935).

———, *The Psychology of Social Norms.* New York: Harper & Row, Publishers, 1936.

Sherif, M. and H. Cantril, "The Psychology of 'Attitudes': Part I," *Psychological Review,* **52** (1945), 295-319.

———, "The Psychology of 'Attitudes': Part II," *Psychological Review,* **53** (1946), 1-24.

Sherif, M. and C. Sherif, *An Outline of Social Psychology.* New York: Harper & Row, Publishers, 1956.

Tagiuri, R. and L. Petrullo, eds., *Person Perception and Interpersonal Behavior.* Stanford, Calif.: Stanford University Press, 1958.

Zamansky, H., "An Investigation of the Psychoanalytic Theory of Paranoid Delusions," Journal of Personality, **26** (1958), 410-25.

The Motivating Effect of Cognitive Dissonance *

Leon Festinger

Since this paper represents a contribution to a conference on the Assessment of Human Motives, I feel a particular responsibility to say something about my conception of psychological motivation—how should motives be defined and conceptualized, how should theories about human motives be stated, how should research on human motives be carried forward? Regrettably, when I started to write this paper and tried to formulate my ideas about human motivation, it turned out to be an incredibly difficult task. The major source of this difficulty was, I think, that my conceptions of human motivation have all been implicit rather than explicitly and coherently verbalized to myself. Furthermore, I could not, and still cannot see any satisfactory, clear-cut distinctions between concepts concerning human motivations and other psychological concepts with respect to either theory construction or research planning. In the light of this situation, there seemed two courses which I could follow. I could try to infer from my own work and my thinking the nature of my implicit conceptions of motivation, or I could exemplify these implicit notions by presenting here some of the recent theoretical and empirical work I have been doing which concerns a hypothesized human motive. Rather than choose between these alternatives, I decided to do a little of both.

MOTIVATION AS A THEORETICAL CONCEPT

Any specifically defined human motive must, it seems to me, be treated as a hypothetical construct. The specified motive is nothing more than a notion which the psychologist invents

* From Festinger, "The Motivating Effect of Cognitive Dissonance," in *Assessment of Human Motives,* ed. G. Lindsley (New York: Grove Press, 1958), pp. 65-86. Reprinted by permission of the author and Holt, Rinehart & Winston, Inc., New York.

in an attempt to explain certain behavior which he observes. For example, we may observe in our own culture that people frequently expend considerable energy to do something well, that is, to do it better than they had done before or to do it better than someone else. In an attempt to explain this kind of behavior one might postulate the existence of an "achievement need." Someone else might try to explain the same phenomena by postulating the existence of an "ego-protection need." Still another person, somewhat more ambitious than the first two, might contend that he can derive the whole thing by postulating a "survival need." All three of these would be hypothetical constructs, and the choice among them would have to be on the basis of which one explains the most data most efficiently. One cannot, and must not, choose on the basis of questions such as, "Are people aware of the existence of such needs or motives?", "Is there a physiological basis for such a need or motive?" or "Does it sound plausible?" These are all irrelevant issues to raise. The only valid issue is whether or not the hypothetical construct is useful, that is, functions better than other constructs in explaining the data.

Before anyone agrees too readily with what I have just said, I want to point out that I have been talking virtual nonsense, because what I have said so far is incomplete. I have stated that the choice among different postulated human needs which attempt to deal with the same behavioral phenomena should be guided by which of them explains the data best. But no single hypothetical construct can explain anything. Before it can do any explaining it must be part of a theory or at least part of a hypothesis. Thus it turns out that one cannot choose among alternative hypothetical human

needs apart from the theory in which these constructs are imbedded. And if a postulated human need is not part of a theory or hypothesis, one cannot evaluate it at all. Indeed, if it is not part of a theory it is not performing any explanatory function and, apart from perhaps adding a gratifying technical ring to our language, it is useless. If someone, for example, postulates the existence of an "affiliation need," this means nothing unless he also tells us what this need is supposed to do, that is, how this need, as an independent variable, is related to some dependent variable, or, to state it another way, how this need state motivates behavior. If the person who postulates such an "affiliation need" says, "By giving a questionnaire or a projective test I can measure individual differences with respect to this need, and these measures relate to how much time the person spends with other people," it is still not satisfactory. In essence, one would then be saying only that the stronger the "affiliation need," the greater was the amount of affiliative behavior. Surely this does not constitute a hypothesis with much explanatory power.

What kind of things then does one want to say about human needs and motives? On a general level, the answer to this question is simple. If one is going to postulate some specific need which is part of a theoretical system, one would like to include the following things:

1. Some hypotheses in which the hypothetical need appears as a dependent variable. These hypotheses, in essence, state theories about the variables which affect the magnitude of the need. These variables, let us call them antecedent variables, should ideally be conceptually defined with sufficient clarity to make possible two kinds of empirical operation. One of these is

the identification of measurable aspects of the life history of a person which would affect the magnitude of the antecedent variables, thus affecting the magnitude of the need in that person. The other is the identification of immediate situational factors which affect the magnitude of the antecedent variables, thus enabling experimental manipulation.

2. Some hypotheses in which the hypothetical need appears as an independent variable. These hypotheses state theories concerning the consequences for behavior of the existence of the need in different situations.

If one looks at the problem in this way, a number of things become clear. The greater the number of different antecedent conditions which affect the magnitude of the need, and the greater the number of consequent behaviors which are motivated *by* the need, the greater is the usefulness, as an explanatory device, of the postulated need and of the theory concerning it. If there is only one behavioral consequence, then postulating the existence of the need does not help. At this level there would be an unlimited number of possible needs one could postulate which would simply duplicate exactly the chaos of the empirical world.

Another point to be made is that it is essential to define and deal with both antecedent variables and consequent behaviors. It is highly unsatisfactory simply to show that two consequent behaviors relate to one another. If I obtain verbal responses in a given situation and show that this verbal behavior bears a relation to some nonverbal behavior, I have merely shown that both behaviors are dependent in part on the same variables. Calling one of these behaviors a "measure of the need" does not help the situation at all. Both are dependent variables and sooner or later one must show a relation between dependent and independent variables.

I have one last general point to discuss. How can one measure the magnitude of a human need? From the preceding discussion it is clear that one cannot measure it directly. One can measure antecedent conditions which supposedly affect the magnitude of the need, or one can measure behavioral consequences motivated by the need. The situation is precisely similar to the problem of measuring any hypothetical construct. One can measure it only through the variables which affect it or through the effects it has on other variables. To obtain a measure of the magnitude of some hypothetical need one should, then, first demonstrate a relation between the hypothesized antecedent and consequent variables. One can then regard measures of any of these variables as, at least in part, a measure of the magnitude of the need. What one usually tries to do is to select as a measure some consequent behavior which is most closely related to the postulated need in the sense that it is least affected by other variables.

The preceding remarks conclude what I have to say, in general, about human motivation. They represent neither an exhaustive analysis nor a profound discussion of the problem. Rather, they almost border on truisms and platitudes from philosophy of science. Let us, however, keep this discussion in mind for a while.

COGNITIVE DISSONANCE AS A MOTIVATING STATE

I shall now turn to a consideration of one particular hypothetical concept on which I have been working for some years (Festinger, 1957). I hope that this example will illustrate concretely many of the general remarks I have made. First of all, I should like to postulate the existence of *cognitive dissonance* as a motivating state in human beings. Since most of you probably never heard of cognitive dissonance, I assume that so far I have been no more informative than if I had said that I wish to postulate X as a motivating state. I will try, then, to provide a conceptual definition of cognitive dissonance. Let me start by trying to convey, in a loose way, what I have in mind. Afterward we can arrive at a more formal conceptual definition.

Definition of Dissonance

The word "dissonance" was not chosen arbitrarily to denote this motivating state. It was chosen because its ordinary meaning in the English language is close to the technical meaning I want to give it. The synonyms which the dictionary gives for the word "dissonant" are "harsh," "jarring," "grating," "unmelodious," "inharmonious," "inconsistent," "contradictory," "disagreeing," "incongruous," "discrepant." The word, in this ordinary meaning, specifies a relation between two things. In connection with musical tones, where it is usually used, the relation between the tones is such that they sound unpleasant together. In general, one might say that a dissonant relation exists between two things which occur together, if, in some way, they do not belong together or fit together.

Cognitive dissonance refers to this kind of relation between cognitions which exist simultaneously for a person. If a person knows two things, for example, something about himself and something about the world in which he lives, which somehow do not fit together, we will speak of this as cognitive dissonance. Thus, for example, a person might know that he is a very intelligent, highly capable person. At the same time, let us imagine, he knows that he meets repeated failure. These two cognitions would be dissonant— they do not fit together. In general, two cognitions are dissonant with each other if, considering these two cognitions alone, the obverse of one follows from the other. Thus, in the example we have given, it follows from the fact that a person is highly capable that he does not continually meet with failure.

The phrase "follows from" that was used in the previous two sentences needs some explaining. Without going into it in too great detail here, I should like to stress that we are concerned with psychological implication and not necessarily logical implication. The psychological implication which one cognition can have for another cognition can arise from a variety of circumstances. There can be psychological implications because of experience and what one has learned. Thus, if a person is out in the rain with no umbrella or raincoat, it follows from this that he will get wet. There can also be psychological implication because of cultural mores and definition. If one is at a highly formal dinner party, it follows from this that one does not pick up the food with one's fingers. I do not have the time to be thorough or exhaustive in my discussion here, but I hope I have sufficiently explained the concept of dissonance so that we can proceed.

How Cognitive Dissonance Resembles Other Need States

Thus far I have said nothing about the motivating aspects of cognitive dissonance. This is the next step. I wish to hypothesize that the existence of cognitive dissonance is comparable to any other need state. Just as hunger is motivating, cognitive dissonance is motivating. Cognitive dissonance will give rise to activity oriented toward reducing or eliminating the dissonance. Successful reduction of dissonance is rewarding in the same sense that eating when one is hungry is rewarding.

In other words, if two cognitions are dissonant with each other there will be some tendency for the person to attempt to change one of them so that they do fit together, thus reducing or eliminating the dissonance. There are also other ways in which dissonance may be reduced but, not having the time to go into a complete discussion of this, I would rather confine myself to this one manifestation of the motivating character of cognitive dissonance.

Data Needed to Demonstrate the Motivating Character of Cognitive Dissonance

Before proceeding, let us consider for a moment the kinds of data one would like to have in order to document the contention that cognitive dissonance is a motivating state. One would like to have at least the following kinds of data:

1. Determination at Time 1 that a state of cognitive dissonance exists. This could be done either by measurement or by experimental manipulation.
2. Determination at Time 2 that the dissonance has been eliminated or reduced in magnitude.
3. Data concerning the behavioral process whereby the person has succeeded in changing some cognition, thus reducing the dissonance.

Actually, the above three items are minimal and would probably not be sufficient to demonstrate cogently the validity of the theory concerning cognitive dissonance. Consider the following example. We have determined for a certain person that at one time he believes that tomatoes are poisonous

and also knows that his neighbor eats them continually with apparently no ill effect. A dissonance between these two cognitions certainly exists. We then observe that he talks to people about it, shows evidence of being bothered by it, and at a later time, no longer believes that tomatoes are poisonous. The dissonance has been eliminated. But this example would not be very convincing. There are too many alternative ways of understanding this change in the person's belief about tomatoes. He is simply, someone might say, being responsive to the real world.

The kind of data that would be more convincing concerning the motivating aspects of dissonance would be data concerning instances where the dissonance was reduced in the other direction, such as is exemplified in the old joke about the psychiatrist who had a patient who believed he was dead. After getting agreement from the patient that dead men do not bleed, and being certain that the patient understood this, the psychiatrist made a cut on the patient's arm and, as the blood poured out, leaned back in his chair, smiling. Whereupon the patient, with a look of dismay on his face, said, "Well, what do you know, dead men *do* bleed." This kind of thing, if it occurred actually, would be harder to explain in alternative ways.

In other words, one has to demonstrate the effects of dissonance in circumstances where these effects are not easily explainable on the basis of other existing theories. Indeed, if one cannot do this, then one could well ask what the usefulness was of this new notion that explained nothing that was not already understood. Consequently, in order to persuade you of the validity of cognitive dissonance and its motivating characteristics I will give two examples where dissonance reduction produced results somewhat contrary to what one would expect on the basis of the operation of other human motives.

Some Examples of Unusual Manifestations of Dissonance Reduction

Example 1: One rather intriguing example comes from a pair of studies of rumors following disasters. Prasad (1950) systematically recorded rumors which were widely current immediately following an especially severe earthquake in India, in 1934. The quake itself, a strong and prolonged one, was felt over a wide geographical area. Actual damage, however, was quite localized and, for a period of days, communication with the damaged area was very poor. The rumors were collected in the area which felt the shock of the earthquake but which did not suffer any damage. We are, then, dealing with communication of rumors among people who felt the shock of the earthquake but who did not see any damage or destruction.

While Prasad reports little concerning the emotional reactions of people to the quake, it is probably plausible to assume that these people who knew little about earthquakes had a strong reaction of fear to the violent and prolonged shaking of the ground. We may also assume that such a strong fear reaction does not vanish immediately but probably persists for some time after the actual shock of the quake is over.

Let us speculate about the content of the cognition of these persons. When the earthquake was over they had this strong, persistent fear reaction but they could see nothing different around them, no destruction, no further threatening things. In short, a situation had been produced where dissonance existed between cognition corresponding to the fear they felt and the knowledge of what they saw around them

which, one might say, amounted to the cognition that there was nothing to be afraid of.

The vast majority of the rumors which were widely circulated were rumors which, if believed, provided cognition consonant with being afraid. One might even call them "fear-provoking" rumors, although, if our interpretation is correct, they would more properly be called "fear-justifying" rumors. The following are a fair sample of the rumors which Prasad collected:

> *There will be a severe cyclone at Patna between January 18 and January 19. (The earthquake occurred on January 15.)*

> *There will be a severe earthquake on the lunar eclipse day.*

> *A flood was rushing from the Nepal borders to Madhubani.*

> *January 23 will be a fatal day. Unforseeable calamities will arise.*

Here, then, is an instance where the reduction of dissonance produced results which looked like fear arousal.

If this explanation is correct in accounting for the prevalence of these "fear-justifying" rumors, there is one clear implication, namely, that if rumors had been collected among persons living *in* the area of destruction, few, if any, of such rumors would have been found. Those persons directly in the area of destruction caused by the earthquake were, undoubtedly, also frightened. Indeed, their fear reaction would very likely have been even stronger than that of the persons who merely felt the shock of the quake. But for the people in the area of destruction, no cognitive dissonance would have created. The things they could see around them, the destruction, the wounded and killed, would produce cognition which would certainly be consonant with feeling afraid. There would be no impulse or desire to acquire additional cognitions which fit with the fear, and fearful rumors of the type so prevalent outside the area of destruction should have been absent.

Unfortunately, Prasad presents no data on rumors which circulated inside the area of destruction following the earthquake. There is, however, another study reported by Sinha (1952) which bears on this. This study reports a careful collection of rumors following a disaster in Darjeeling, India, a disaster which was fully comparable to the earthquake in terms of destruction and loss of life but which, unfortunately, for purposes of comparison, did not arise from an earthquake but from a landslide. Nevertheless, it must have produced considerable fear among the people. Sinha directly compares the two when, in describing the landslide disaster he states:

> There was a feeling of instability and uncertainty similar to that which followed the Great Indian Earthquake of 1934. (p. 200)

There is, however, one important difference between the study reported by Prasad and the one reported by Sinha. While the rumors following the earthquake were collected among persons outside of the area of destruction, the rumors which Sinha reports were collected from persons in Darjeeling who actually were in the area and witnessed the destruction. Since for these people there would have been no dissonance—what they saw and knew was quite consonant with being afraid —we would not expect disaster rumors to arise and spread among them.

Actually, in Sinha's report, there is a complete absence of rumors predicting further disasters or of any type of rumor that might be regarded as sup-

plying cognition consonant with being afraid. The contrast between the rumors reported by Sinha and those reported by Prasad is certainly strong.

Example 2: Another intriguing example of the reduction of dissonance in a startling manner comes from a study I did together with Riecken and Schachter (1956) of a group of people who predicted that, on a given date, a catastrophic flood would overwhelm most of the world. This prediction of the catastrophic flood had been given to the people in direct communications from the gods and was an integral part of their religious beliefs. When the predicted date arrived and passed there was considerable dissonance established in these people. They continued to believe in their gods and in the validity of the communications from them, and at the same time they knew that the prediction of the flood had been wrong. We observed the movement as participants for approximately two months preceding and one month after this unequivocal disproof of part of their belief. The point of the study was, of course, to observe how they would react to the dissonance. Let me give a few of the details of the disproof and how they reacted to it.

For some time it had been clear to the people in the group that those who were chosen were to be picked up by flying saucers before the cataclysm occurred. Some of the believers, these mainly college students, were advised to go home and wait individually for the flying saucer that would arrive for each of them. This was reasonable and plausible, since the data of the cataclysm happened to occur during an academic holiday. Most of the group, including the most central and most heavily committed members, gathered together in the home of the woman who received the messages from the gods to wait together for the arrival of the saucer. For these latter, disproof of the prediction, in the form of evidence that messages were not valid, began to occur four days before the predicted event was to take place. A message informed them that a saucer would land in the back yard of the house at 4:00 P.M. to pick up the members of the group. With coat in hand they waited, but no saucer came. A later message told them there had been a delay—the saucer would arrive at midnight. Midst absolute secrecy (the neighbors and press must not know), they waited outdoors on a cold and snowy night for over an hour, but still no saucer came. Another message told them to continue waiting, but still no saucer came. At about 3:00 A.M. they gave up, interpreting the events of that night as a test, a drill, and a rehearsal for the real pickup which would still soon take place.

Tensely, they waited for the final orders to come through—for the messages which would tell them the time, place, and procedure for the actual pickup. Finally, on the day before the cataclysm was to strike, the messages came. At midnight a man would come to the door of the house and take them to the place where the flying saucer would be parked. More messages came that day, one after another, instructing them in the passwords that would be necessary in order to board the saucer, in preparatory procedures such as removal of metal from clothing, removal of personal identification, maintaining silence at certain times, and the like. The day was spent by the group in preparation and rehearsal of the necessary procedures and, when midnight came, the group sat waiting in readiness. But no knock came at the door, no one came to lead them to the flying saucer.

From midnight to five o'clock in the morning the group sat there struggling

to understand what had happened, struggling to find some explanation that would enable them to recover somewhat from the shattering realization that they would not be picked up by a flying saucer and that consequently the flood itself would not occur as predicted. It is doubtful that anyone alone, without the support of the others, could have withstood the impact of this disproof of the prediction. Indeed, those members of the group who had gone to their homes to wait alone, alone in the sense that they did not have other believers with them, did not withstand it. Almost all of them became skeptics afterward. In other words, without easily obtainable social support to begin reducing the dissonance, the dissonance was sufficient to cause the belief to be discarded in spite of the commitment to it. But the members of the group that had gathered together in the home of the woman who received the messages could, and did, provide social support for one another. They kept reasuring one another of the validity of the messages and that some explanation would be found.

At fifteen minutes before five o'clock that morning an explanation was found that was at least temporarily satisfactory. A message arrived from God which, in effect, said that He had saved the world and stayed the flood because of this group and the light and strength this group had spread throughout the world that night.

The behavior of these people from that moment onwards presented a revealing contrast to their previous behavior. These people who had been disinterested in publicity and even avoided it, became avid publicity seekers. For four successive days, finding a new reason each day, they invited the press into the house, gave lengthy interviews, and attempted to attract the public to their ideas. The first day they called all the newspapers and news services, informed them of the fact that the world had been saved and invited them to come and get interviews. The second day, a ban on having photographs taken was lifted, and the newspapers were once more called to inform them of the fact and to invite them to come to the house and take pictures. On the third day they once more called the press to inform them that on the next afternoon they would gather on their front lawn singing and that it was possible a space man would visit them at that time. What is more, the general public was specifically invited to come and watch. And on the fourth day, newspapermen and about two hundred people came to watch the group singing on their front lawn. There were almost no lengths to which these people would not go to attract publicity and potential believers in the validity of the messages. If, indeed, more and more converts could be found, more and more people who believed in the messages and the things the messages said, then the dissonance between their belief and the knowledge that the messages had not been correct could be reduced.

These examples, while they do illustrate attempts to reduce dissonance in rather surprising directions, still leave much to be desired. One would also like to be able to show that such dissonance-reduction phenomena do occur under controlled laboratory conditions and that the magnitude of the effect does depend upon the magnitude of the dissonance which exists. Consequently, I will describe for you a laboratory experiment which we have just completed at Stanford, one in which we investigated the reduction of dissonance following experimental manipulation of the magnitude of dissonance. The obtained results are, in my opinion, not easily interpreted in terms of other existing theories.

An Experimental Investigation

In this experiment, we created dissonance in the subjects by inducing them to say something which was at variance with their private opinion. It is clear that this kind of situation does produce dissonance between what the person believes and what he knows he has said. There are also cognitive consonances for the person. His cognitions concerning the things that induced him to make the public statement are consonant with his knowledge of having done it. The total magnitude of the dissonance between all other relevant cognitions taken together and the knowledge of what he has publicly said will, of course, be a function of the number and importance of the dissonances in relation to the number and importance of the consonances. One could, then, manipulate the total magnitude of dissonance experimentally by holding everything constant and varying the strength of the inducement for the person to state something publicly which was at variance with his private opinion. The *stronger* the inducement to do this, the *less* would be the overall magnitude of dissonance created.

Let us imagine a concrete situation. Suppose a number of people have had an experience to which they reacted negatively. Each of these persons, then, let us say, is offered a different amount of money to tell someone else that the experience was very pleasant and enjoyable. In each case, let us further imagine, the amount of money offered is at least large enough so that the person accepts the money and engages in the overt behavior required. Certainly, after telling someone that the experience was enjoyable, there is a dissonance between his cognition of what he has said and his own private opinion.

This dissonance could, clearly, be

reduced if the person persuades himself that the experience was, indeed, fairly pleasant and enjoyable, that is, if he changes his private opinion so that it corresponds more closely with what he has said. The greater the dissonance, the more frequently should one observe such subsequent attitude change. We would expect then that, after the person had told someone else that the experience was pleasant and enjoyable, he would change his private opinions concerning the experience to some extent. We would further expect that the more money he was given to induce him to make the public statement, the smaller would be the subsequent opinion change, because less dissonance had been created initially.

Now for the details of the experiment. I will describe it as it proceeded for the subject, with occasional explanatory comments. Each subject had signed up for a two-hour experiment on "measures of performance." The subjects were all students from the Introductory Psychology course at Stanford where they are required to serve a certain number of hours as subjects in experiments. When the student arrived he was met by the experimenter and, with a minimum of explanation, was given a repetitive motor task to work on. He packed a frameful of little spools, then emptied it, then packed it again, and so on for a half hour. He was then given another task to do in which he turned rows of pegs, each a quarter turn, then turned them all another quarter turn, and so on for another half hour. When he had finished, the experimenter informed him that the experiment was over, thanked him for his participation, and proceeded to explain to him what the experiment was about and what its purpose was.

From our point of view, the purpose of this initial part was to provide for each subject an experience which was rather dull, boring, and somewhat fatiguing. The student, however, believed this to be the whole experiment. The explanation of the experiment given to the student was that the experiment was concerned with the effect of preparatory set on performance. He was told that there were two conditions in the experiment, one of these being the condition he had experienced where the subject was told nothing ahead of time. The other condition, the experimenter explained, was one in which the subject, before working on the tasks, was led to expect that they were very enjoyable, very interesting, and lots of fun. The procedure for subjects in this other condition, the experimenter explained, proceeded in the following manner. A person working for us is introduced to the waiting subject as someone who has just finished the experiment and will tell the prospective subject a little about it. This person who works for us then tells the waiting subject that the experiment is very enjoyable, interesting, and lots of fun. In this way, the subjects in the other condition are given the set we want them to have. This concluded the false explanation of the experiment to the student and, in the control group, nothing more was done at this point.

In the experimental groups, however, the experimenter continued by telling the subject that he had a rather unusual proposal to make. It seems that the next subject is scheduled to be in that condition where he is to be convinced in advance that the experiment is enjoyable and a lot of fun. The person who works for us and usually does this, however, although very reliable, could not do it today. We thought we would take a chance and ask him (the student) to do it for us. We would like, if agreeable to him, to hire him on the same basis that the other person was hired to work for us. We would like to put him on the payroll and pay him a lump sum of money to go tell the waiting subject that the experiment is enjoyable, interesting, and fun; and he was also to be on tap for us in case this kind of emergency arises again.

There were two experimental conditions which we actually conducted. The procedure was absolutely identical in both except for the amount of money that the subjects were paid as "the lump sum." In one condition they were paid one dollar for their immediate and possible future services. In the other condition they were paid twenty dollars. When the student agreed to do this, he was actually given the money and he signed a receipt for it. He was then taken into the room where the next subject was waiting and introduced to her by the experimenter, who said that the student had just been a subject in the experiment and would tell her a bit about it. The experimenter then went out, leaving student and the waiting subject together for two and a half minutes. The waiting subject was actually a girl in our employ. Her instructions were very simple. After the student had told her that the experiment was interesting, enjoyable and lots of fun, she was to say something like, "Oh, a friend of mine who took it yesterday told me it was dull and that if I could I should get out of it." After that she was simply supposed to agree with whatever the student said. If, as almost always happened, the student reaffirmed that the experiment was fun, she was to say that she was glad to hear it. The following is a typical record of this interchange, which was recorded on a tape recorder for all subjects.

STUDENT: It's quite a deal.
GIRL: Is it?
STUDENT: Yeah—it's kind of fun. You play with pegs and spools. I don't know what it's supposed to test, but it's a lot of fun.
GIRL: I'm living over at Moore. I have a friend who took the experiment last week and she wouldn't tell me what she did but she said it was very boring.
STUDENT: I don't know—it's kind of fun when you get going at it.
GIRL: Oh, really? Well, I'm relieved to hear you say that in a way. Gosh, I was kind of worried.
STUDENT: It's kind of interesting to play with those things. I can't figure out what they're trying to test but it's kind of fun.
GIRL: You sit there trying to figure out what it is, huh?
STUDENT: (laughs) I guess so. It's kind of fun—fun to work on. It's interesting to do something with your hands. Lots of fun. What class you in—sophomore?
GIRL: No, senior.
STUDENT: Senior? (laughs) Quite a difference.
GIRL: Yeah. I wanted to get some Psych in before I graduate. (few seconds silence)
STUDENT: Quite a challenge. Yeah. Some of them are fun—some of them don't seem to have much point to them. (Here the subject talked for a few seconds about other experiments he had taken.)

When the experimenter returned, after two and a half minutes, he sent the girl into the experimental room, telling her he would be there in a few minutes. He then obtained the student's phone number in order to continue the fiction that the student was to be available for future services of like nature. The experimenter then thanked the subject and made a brief speech in which he said that most subjects found the experimental tasks very interesting and enjoyed them, and that, when he thinks about it, he will probably agree. The purpose of this brief speech is to provide some cognitive material which the subject can use to reduce dissonance, assuming that such dissonance exists. The identical speech is, of course, made to the control subjects, too.

The only remaining problem in the experiment was to obtain a measure of what each subject honestly thought privately about the tasks on which he had worked for an hour. It seemed desirable, naturally, to obtain this measure in a situation where the subject would be inclined to be very frank in his statements. It also seemed desirable to obtain these measures quite independently of the actual experiment. This was done in the following manner. It had previously been announced by the instructor in the Introductory Psychology class that, since students were required to participate in experiments, the Psychology Department was going to do a study to assess the value of the experiences they had. The purpose of this, the instructor had explained, was to help improve the selection of experiments in the future. They were told that a sample of them, after serving in experiments, would be interviewed about them. It would be to their advantage, and to the advantage of future students in the course, for them to be very frank and honest in these interviews.

In our experiment, the student was told that someone from Introductory Psychology probably wanted to interview him. The experimenter confessed ignorance about what this impending interview was about but said he had been told that the subject would know about it. Usually at this point the subject nodded his head or otherwise indicated that he did, indeed, know what it was about. The experimenter then took him to an office where the interviewer was waiting, said good-bye to the subject, and left.

The interview itself was rather brief. Four questions were asked, namely, how interesting and enjoyable the experiment was, how much the subject learned from it, how important he thought it was scientifically, and how much he would like to participate in a similar experiment again. The important question, for us, is the first one concerning how interesting and enjoyable the experiment was, since this was the content area in which dissonance was established for the experimental subjects. The subject was encouraged to answer the question in some detail and then was asked to rate, on a scale running from — 5 to + 5, how he felt about it. The other questions were included to make the interview realistic and also to provide a comparison, since there seemed little reason to believe that there would or should be any difference among the three conditions on the questions concerning how much they learned and how important the experiment was. There might, of course, be differences on the question concerning their desire to participate in a similar experiment, the answers to which would undoubtedly reflect, in part, how much they liked this one.

Needless to say, since it is standard practice, after the interview was concluded, the experimenter, the student, and the girl who posed as the waiting subject were brought together, and the truth about the whole experiment was explained in detail to the subject's satisfaction.

Some of you may wonder about the effectiveness of the experimental procedure. Were the subjects really taken in by all of it? Actually, if you have been wondering about this, let me assure you that it is a legitimate thing to wonder about. It took us several months of preliminary work to get the procedure in a form so that subjects did not become suspicious. In its present form, the procedure I have described works well. Of the forty subjects, twenty in each of the two experimental conditions (there were, of course, also twenty control subjects, but here there is no problem) only five gave evidence of suspecting that the experiment really dealt with having him talk to the waiting subject. These few subjects, of course, had to be omitted from the data.

Let us look, then, at what the results show. Figure 1 shows the average

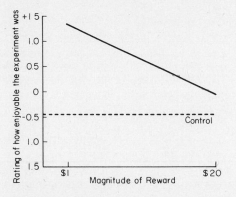

FIG. 1. *Relation between magnitude of reward used to elicit compliance and subsequent rating of how enjoyable the experiment was.*

rating, for each of the three conditions, for the question concerning how interesting and enjoyable the experiment was. A rating of — 5 meant extremely dull and boring, + 5 meant extremely interesting and enjoyable, and 0 meant neutral. The subject could, of course, rate his reaction to the experiment anywhere between — 5 and + 5. The average rating for the control group is represented as a horizontal dotted line across the figure. It is done this way since the data from the control group actually provide a base line. This is how subjects reacted to the experiment

after having gone through it and having been told exactly the same things that the experimental subjects were told. They simply were never asked to, and never did, tell the waiting subject that the experiment was interesting, enjoyable, and lots of fun. It turns out that, on the average, the control group rates the experiment —.45 for how enjoyable it was, slightly below neutral. In the One Dollar experimental condition there is a definite increase over the control group. Here the average rating is + 1.35, definitely on the positive side of the scale and significantly different from the control group at the 1 percent level of confidence. In other words, in the One Dollar condition the dissonance between their private opinion of the experiment and their knowledge of what they had said to the waiting subject was reduced significantly by changing their private opinion somewhat, to bring it closer to what they had overtly said.

But now let us turn our attention to the Twenty Dollar condition. Here the magnitude of dissonance experimentally created was less than in the One Dollar condition because of the greater importance of the cognition that was consonant with what they knew they had done. It seems undeniable that twenty dollars is a good deal more important than one dollar. There should hence be less pressure to reduce the dissonance, and indeed, the average rating for the Twenty Dollar condition is —.05, only slightly above the Control condition and significantly different from the One Dollar condition at the 2 percent level of confidence.

While I will not take the time to present the data on the other questions in detail, I will say that there were no significant differences on any of the other questions among the three conditions in the experiment. On the scale concerning how much they feel they learned from the experiment, the three means are virtually identical. On their desire to participate again in a similar experiment and on how scientifically important they think it is, the results are in the same direction as those we have shown, but the differences are smaller and not significant.

There is just one other point I would like to discuss about the data from this experiment. What are the possible alternative interpretations? Clearly, any interpretation which seeks to explain the opinion change in terms of reward or reinforcement is doomed to failure, since the smaller reward led to the larger opinion change. Janis and King (1954; King and Janis, 1956) have published two experiments in which they show that opinion change occurs after a person has made a speech favoring a particular point of view. They offer an explanation of their results mainly in terms of rehearsal of arguments, thinking up new arguments, and in this way convincing themselves. Could this be an explanation of the difference between the One and Twenty Dollar conditions? On the surface it appears implausible, since such an explanation would demand that the subjects in the One Dollar condition would have tried harder to be persuasive when talking to the waiting girl than the subjects in the Twenty Dollar condition. This would seem unlikely since, if anything, having received more money, they should be *more* motivated to do a good job in the Twenty Dollar condition. However, strange things sometimes happen; with this possibility in mind, we obtained recordings of the discussion between the subjects and the waiting girl. These have been rated for persuasiveness, number of different things the subject says, and other conceivably relevant variables. The ratings were, of course, done in ignorance of the experimental condition by two separate raters. The reliability of the independent ratings varies between .6 and .9. The ratings used in the actual analysis of the data were settled on by discussion of disagreements between the two raters. It turns out that there are no large differences between the two experimental conditions in what the subject said or how he said it. As one might expect, the small differences which do exist are in the direction favoring the $20 condition. In the $20 condition the subjects are a bit more emphatic about saying the experiment was interesting and enjoyable. Personally, I have not been able to think of any very satisfactory alternative explanation of the results. It is precisely this difficulty of devising alternative explanations that makes these results strongly supportive of the dissonance interpretation.

SUMMARY AND CONCLUSIONS

I should like to summarize a bit before concluding. I started out, as you will recall, by making a number of rather general remarks about human motivation. In these general remarks I did not discuss the nature of human motives but rather the circumstances under which hypothesizing the existence of a specific motive was fruitful and useful. I then proceeded to propose to you that the existence of cognitive dissonance was a motivating state and I attempted to illustrate the validity and usefulness of this concept. The evidence for the validity and usefulness of conceiving cognitive dissonance as motivating is as follows:

1. Evidence that the existence of cognitive dissonance sometimes leads to behavior that appears very strange indeed when viewed only from the standpoint of commonly accepted motives. Here I have had time only to give two examples illustrating this phenomenon.

2. Evidence that the amount of reduction of dissonance is a direct function of the magnitude of dissonance which exists. I illustrated this by describing a laboratory experiment where, under controlled conditions, the magnitude of dissonance was experimentally manipulated.

There is at least one further point that I would have liked to have made, and would have if I had supporting data. If cognitive dissonance is indeed a motivating state, one would like to be able to show that, assuming that individual differences exist, which they almost certainly do, those persons for whom it is more highly motivating react more strongly. In order to do this one would first have to have some way of measuring the degree to which cognitive dissonance is painful or uncomfortable for the individual. This I do not as yet have. It is, though, one of the clearly important goals of the future.

I stress this lack, not so much to emphasize that a measure of individual differences is missing, but rather to re-emphasize what I consider an important procedural point. I do not think it will be maximally fruitful in the long run to begin by developing tests to give measures of the strength of some hypothesized human need, and then to attempt to discover how this need operates. I believe strongly that it is better to proceed in the reverse order. After one has demonstrated the validity and usefulness of some hypothesized need is the time to start measuring individual variation. One then knows much more clearly what one is trying to measure, why one is trying to measure it, and to what the individual measure should relate.

REFERENCES

Festinger, Leon, *A Theory of Cognitive Dissonance*. Evanston, Ill.: Row, Peterson & Company, 1957.

Festinger, Leon, H. W. Riecken, and S. Schachter, *When Prophecy Fails*. Minneapolis: University of Minnesota, 1956.

Janis, I. L. and B. T. King, "The Influence of Role-playing on Opinion Change," *Journal of Abnormal Psychology*, **49** (1954), 211-18.

King, B. T. and I. L. Janis, "Comparison of the Effectiveness of Improvised versus Non-improvised Role-playing in Producing Opinion Changes," *Human Relations*, **9** (1956), 177-86.

Prasad, J., "Comparative Study of Rumors and Reports in Earthquakes," *British Journal of Psychology*, **41** (1950), 129-44.

Sinha, D., "Behavior in a Catastrophic Situation: A Psychological Study of Reports and Rumors," *British Journal of Psychology*, **43** (1952), 200-209.

The Psychological Effects of Insufficient Rewards *

Leon Festinger

Some fields of psychology have for many years been dominated by ideas concerning the importance of rewards in the establishment and maintenance of behavior patterns. So dominant has this notion become, that some of our most ingenious theoretical thinking has been devoted to imagining the existence of rewards in order to explain behavior in situations where, plausibly, no rewards exist. It has been observed, for example, that under some circumstances an organism will persist in voluntarily engaging in behavior which is frustrating or painful. To account for such behavior it has, on occasion, been seriously proposed that the cessation of the frustration or pain is rewarding and thus reinforces the tendency to engage in the behavior.

I want to maintain that this type of explanation is not only unnecessary but also misleading. I certainly do *not* wish to say that rewards are unimportant, but I propose to show that the absence of reward or the existence of inadequate reward produces certain specific consequences which can account for a variety of phenomena which are difficult to deal with if we use our usual conceptions of the role of reward.

Before I proceed, I would like to say that most of the thinking and most of the experimental work which I will present are the result of collaboration between Douglas H. Lawrence and myself. Indeed, whatever you find interesting in what I say you may safely attribute primarily to him.

I will start my discussion in a rather roundabout manner with some remarks which concern themselves primarily with some aspects of the thinking processes of human beings. Human thinking is sometimes a strange mixture of "plausible" and "magical" processes. Let us examine more closely what I mean by this. For example, imagine that a person knows that some event is going to occur, and that the person can do something to prepare himself to cope more adequately with the impending event. Under such circumstances it is very reasonable (perhaps you might even want to use the word "rational") for the person to do whatever is necessary in preparation for the coming event. Human thinking, however, also works in reverse. Consider a person who goes to a lot of trouble to prepare himself for a future event which might possibly occur. Such a person will subsequently tend to persuade himself that the event is rather likely to occur. There is nothing very plausible or rational about this kind of mental process—rather, it has almost a magical quality about it. Let me illustrate this briefly by describing an experiment recently conducted by Ruby Yaryan.[1]

* From L. Festinger, "The Psychological Effects of Insufficient Rewards," *American Psychologist*, 16 (1961), 1-11. Reprinted by permission of the author and the American Psychological Association.

[1] R. B. Yaryan and L. Festinger, The Effect of Preparatory Action on Belief in the Occurrence of Possible Future Events. Unpublished paper.

Under the pretext of investigating the manner in which students study for examinations she asked subjects to study a list of arbitrary definitions of symbols in preparation for a possible test. Two conditions were experimentally created for the subjects. Half of the subjects were told that, if they actually took the test, this list of definitions of the symbols would be in their possession during the test, and so, all that was necessary in preparation was to familiarize themselves with the list. This was, essentially, an "easy preparation" condition. That is, not much effort was required of the subjects in advance preparation for the test.

The other half of the subjects were told that, if they actually took the test, they would *not* have the list of definitions with them and so it was necessary for them to memorize the symbols and their definitions in preparation for the test. It is clear that this constitutes a much more "effortful preparation" condition. Considerable effort was required of these subjects in advance preparation for the possible test.

It was carefully explained to each subject that not everyone would actually have to take the test. Specifically, they were told that only half of the people in the experiment *would* take the test. It was also carefully explained that the selection of who would, and who would not, have to take the test had already been made in consultation with their teachers (the subjects were all high school girls). Nothing that happened during the experiment would affect whether or not they took the test —this had already been decided in advance for each of them.

After they finished studying the list of definitions, they were asked a number of questions to preserve the fiction that the experiment was concerned with study habits. Each subject was also asked to indicate how likely she thought it was that she, personally, would have to actually take the test. The results show, quite clearly, that subjects in the effortful preparation condition, on the average, thought it was more likely that they would have to take the test than did subjects in the easy preparation condition. In other words, those who were experimentally induced to engage in a lot of preparatory effort, persuaded themselves that the thing they were preparing for would actually occur.

The relevance of this experiment to the problem of the effects of inadequate rewards will become clearer in the following example which illustrates the same psychological process. Consider some person who is strongly attracted to some goal. It is quite reasonable for this person to be willing to expend more effort, or to endure more pain, in order to reach the goal than he would be if he were less attracted. Once more, however, one finds the same process of reasoning in reverse. That is, if a person exerts a great deal of effort, or endures pain, in order to reach some ordinary objective, there is a strong tendency for him to persuade himself that the objective is especially valuable or especially desirable. An experiment conducted by Elliot Aronson and Judson Mills (1959) shows the effect quite nicely.

The subjects in the experiment by Aronson and Mills were college girls who volunteered to join small discussion groups. Each subject, when she appeared for the discussion group, was told that, instead of being put into a new group, she was being considered for inclusion in an ongoing group which had recently lost one of its members. However, the subject was told, because of the group's concern that the replacement be someone who would be able to discuss things freely and openly, the experimenter had agreed to test the replacement before admitting her to the group. Some subjects were then given a very brief and not painful test while others were given a rather extended and embarrassing test. The experimenter then, of course, told each subject that she had done well and was admitted to the group. Thus, there were some subjects who had attained membership in the group easily and some subjects who had endured a painful experience in order to be admitted to the group.

The experimenter then explained to the subject that the discussion was carried on by means of an intercommunication system, each girl being in a separate room. She was brought into her room, which contained a microphone and earphones. The experimenter told her that the others had already started and perhaps it would be best for her not to participate in the discussion this time but just to listen. Next meeting, of course, she would participate fully. Speaking into the microphone the experimenter then went through the illusion of introducing her to the three other girls in the group. He then "disconnected" the microphone and gave the subject the earphones to wear. The subject then listened for about 25 minutes to a tape recording of a rather dull and halting discussion. All subjects, of course, heard exactly the same tape recording, thinking they were listening to the actual live group discussion.

When the discussion was finished, the experimenter explained to the subject that, after each meeting, each of the girls filled out a "post-meeting reaction form." She was then given a questionnaire to complete which asked a variety of questions concerning how interesting she had found the discussion to be, how much she liked the other members of the group, and other similar questions. The results show, as

anticipated, that those subjects who had gone through a painful procedure in order to be admitted to the group thought the discussion was more interesting and liked the other group members better than did those who had gained admission to the group easily. In other words, we see the same process operating here as we noted in the previous experiment. If someone is somehow induced to endure embarrassment in order to achieve something, she then persuades herself that what she has achieved is valuable.

In both of the examples which I have discussed (and one could present many more examples of similar nature) a situation has been produced where the organism has two pieces of information (or cognitions) which do not fit together. In the first example, these two pieces of information were: (a) I have worked hard in preparation for an event. (b) The event is not too likely to occur. In the second example, the two cognitions which did not fit together were: (a) I have endured pain to attain an objective. (b) The objective is not very attractive. This kind of "nonfitting" relationship between two pieces of information may be termed a dissonant relation (Festinger, 1957). The reason, of course, that dissonance exists between these cognitions is that, psychologically, the obverse of one follows from the other. Psychologically, if an objective *is* very attractive, it follows that one would be willing to endure pain to attain it; or if the objective is *not* attractive, it follows that one does *not* endure pain to attain it. This specification of why a given relation between cognitions is dissonant also provides the clues to predicting specifically how the organism will react to the existence of the dissonance. Assuming that the organism will attempt to reduce the dissonance between the cognitions, there are obviously two major classes of ways in which this can be done. He can attempt to persuade himself that the pain which he endured was not really painful or he can attempt to persuade himself that the objective *is* very attractive.

I will not spend any more time than this in general theoretical discussion of the theory of dissonance and the reduction of dissonance. I hope that this small amount of general theoretical discussion will be enough to give context to the specific analysis of the psychological effects of insufficient rewards.

Let us consider in more detail what is suggested by the example of the experiment by Aronson and Mills and by the theory of cognitive dissonance. In that experiment the dissonance which was created was reduced by enhancing the value of the goal. This suggests that organisms may come to like and value things for which they have worked very hard or for which they have suffered. Looking at it from another aspect, one might say that they may come to value activities for which they have been inadequately rewarded. At first glance this may seem to contradict a widely accepted notion in Psychology, namely, that organisms learn to like things for which they *have* been rewarded. In a sense it is contradictory, but not in the sense that it denies the operation of this widely assumed process. It does, however, state that another process also operates which is rather of an opposite character.

Let us analyze the situation with which we are concerned somewhat more carefully and more precisely. We are concerned with the dissonance between two possible cognitions. One of these is a cognition the organism has concerning his behavior, namely, I have voluntarily done something which, all other things being equal, I would avoid doing. The other is a cognition about the environment or about the result of his action, namely, the reward that has been obtained is inadequate. As we mentioned before, this dissonance can be reduced if the organism can persuade himself that he really likes the behavior in which he engaged or if he enhances for himself the value of what he has obtained as a result of his actions.

There is, of course, another way to reduce the dissonance, namely, for the organism to change his behavior. That is, having done something which resulted in an inadequate reward the organism can refuse to perform the action again. This means of reducing the dissonance is undoubtedly the one most frequently employed by organisms. If the organism obtains information which is dissonant with his behavior, he usually modifies his behavior so that it fits better what he knows concerning his environment. Here, however, I am going to consider only situations in which this means of reducing dissonance is not available to the organism. That is, I will consider only situations in which the organism is somehow tricked or seduced into continuing to engage in the activity in spite of the dissonance which is introduced. Under these circumstances we would expect one of the two previously mentioned dissonance reduction mechanisms to be used.

If one thinks for a while about the possible behavioral consequences of such a psychological process as we have described, an explanation suggests itself for the well-known finding that resistance to extinction is greater after partial reward than after complete reward.

Before I explain this more adequately, I would like to digress for a moment. Since much of the research on the effects of partial reward has been done on rats, and since the experiments that Lawrence and I have done are also on rats, the question will inevitably arise as to whether or not I really think that rats have cognitions and that rats reduce dissonance the way humans do.

First, for the matter of cognitions in rats: All that is meant by cognition is knowledge or information. It seems to me that one can assume that an organism has cognitions or information if one can observe some behavioral difference under different stimulus conditions. If the organism changes his behavior when the environment changes, then obviously he uses information about the environment and, equally obviously, can be said to have cognitions.

Now, for the question of whether or not rats reduce dissonance as humans do: Although Lawrence keeps telling me that rats are smarter than humans, I suspect that the rat is a rather stupid organism and does not reduce dissonance nearly as effectively as the human being does. I suspect that the mechanisms available to the rat for dissonance reduction are very limited and that the amount of dissonance which gets effectively reduced is relatively small. Still, I suspect that they *do* reduce dissonance. At any rate, if we find that the theory of dissonance can make valid predictions for rat behavior, this will be evidence that they do, indeed, reduce dissonance.

Now to return to the matter of the increased resistance to extinction following partial reward. Let us examine what occurs, psychologically, during a series of trials on which the behavior of an organism is only occasionally rewarded. Imagine a hungry animal who dashes frantically down some runway and into some so-called "goal box," only to find that there is nothing there. The cognition that he has ob-

tained nothing is dissonant with the cognition that he has expended effort to reach the goal box. If this state of affairs were continually repeated, as we all know, the animal would reduce the dissonance by refusing to go to the goal box, that is, he would change his behavior. But, in a partial reward situation, the animal is tricked into continuing to run to the goal box because an appreciable number of times that he goes there he does find food. But, on each nonrewarded trial dissonance is introduced when the animal finds the goal box empty. The assumed process of dissonance reduction would lead us to expect that, gradually, the animal develops some extra preference either for the activity or for the goal box itself. A comparable animal that was rewarded every time he ran to the goal box would not develop any such extra preference.

Consider the situation, then, when extinction trials began. In addition to realizing that food is no longer present, the partially rewarded animal also has to overcome his extra preference before he stops going to the goal box. We would thus expect "extinction" to take longer for a partially rewarded animal than for an animal that was always rewarded. The magnitude of the difference should be far greater than just the slight effect which would exist if the 100 percent animal discovers more rapidly that the situation has changed.

If this explanation is correct, then the greater resistance to extinction following partial reward is a direct consequence of the process of dissonance reduction. This, of course, immediately suggests an extension of this line of reasoning to situations other than those involving partial reward. *Any* procedure which introduces dissonance during the training trials should similarly be expected to increase resistance to extinction since the same kind of dissonance reduction process should operate.

Let us, however, try to be precise about what kinds of procedures would introduce dissonance for an organism during training trials in an experiment. It is, fortunately, possible to define this operationally in a precise manner. Let us imagine that we test an organism in a single-choice situation. In the case of a rat, for example, this might be simply an apparatus where, from the starting point the animal can turn either right or left. Let us further imagine that the organism we are testing is quite hungry and that, whichever alternative he chooses, he obtains food. We can, then, vary one at a time a variety of factors to discover what the organism will ordinarily avoid doing. One would, of course, find many such factors which would lead the organism not to choose the alternative with which that factor is associated. Dissonance will be created for the organism if he is somehow tricked into consistently engaging in an activity involving such a factor.

This may sound very involved so let me try to say it again, this time, a bit less abstractly. Imagine that we test rats in a simple left-right choice apparatus and, no matter whether the animal goes left or right, he obtains food. But, imagine that, if he goes left, the animal must swim through water to get to the food but, if he goes right, there is simply a short run down an alley to the food. Let us further imagine that, under such circumstances, the animal will consistently choose to go to the right, that is, he will avoid swimming through water. Armed with this knowledge concerning the behavior of the rat, we can then assert the following: if one puts a rat in a situation where we somehow trick the rat into consistently swimming through water, dissonance will have been created.

Remembering what we have already said about the ways in which dissonance can be reduced in this kind of situation (provided that we are successful in tricking the organism into continuing to engage in the activity), we would then arrive at the following statement: any condition which the animal will avoid in the above mentioned test situation will increase resistance to extinction in a nonchoice situation.

Let us look at some of the data which exist which are relevant to this statement. We know that if a hungry rat is put in a situation where he has a choice between a goal box where he is rewarded 100 percent of the time and a goal box where he is rewarded only part of the time, he will fairly consistently go to the place where he is rewarded 100 percent of the time. And, of course, we also know that where no choice is involved, partial reward increases resistance to extinction. But there are other variables or conditions which should increase resistance to extinction in a similar manner if our theoretical analysis is correct.

Consider the question of delay of reinforcement. Once more, thinking of our hypothetical test situation, we can be reasonably certain that a rat, if faced with a choice where one alternative led to immediate reward while the other alternative involved an appreciably delay before the rat was allowed to continue to the goal box to obtain food, the rat would rather consistently choose the alternative that led to immediate reward. We should then expect that, in a nonchoice situation, delay of reward should lead to greater resistance to extinction. Appreciable delay of reward does lead to greater resistance to extinction. I will briefly review some of the data which exist on delay of reward to give you some idea of the effect which is obtained.

The usual experiment that has been done on extinction following delay of reinforcement compares one condition in which the rats encounter no enforced delay between starting down a runway and obtaining food in the goal box with other conditions in which, on some trials, the rats are detained in a delay chamber before being allowed to proceed to the food. The usual period of delay which has been used has been about 30 seconds. Crum, Brown, and Bitterman (1951) and Scott and Wike (1956) both find that a group of rats delayed on half the trials shows much greater resistance to extinction than a group which was never delayed. In another experiment, Wike and McNemara (1957) ran three groups which differed in the percentage (and of course, number) of trials on which they were delayed. They find that the larger the percentage or number of trials on which the animal experiences delay, the greater is the resistance to extinction. The same kind of result is obtained by Fehrer (1956) who compared rats who were delayed for 20 seconds on *every* trial with ones who were never delayed. She also finds that delay results in increased resistance to extinction.

Before we proceed to other matters, I would like to briefly raise a question concerning one kind of explanation that has frequently, in one form or another, been offered to account for increased resistance to extinction after partial reward. The basis of this kind of explanation, whether it be in terms of expectancy, or conditioning of cues, or any of a number of other varieties, rests in pointing out that there is more similarity between acquisition and extinction for partial reward conditions than for 100 percent reward conditions. I would like to point out that

this type of explanation is clearly not very useful in explaining the increased resistance to extinction after delay of reward. From the point of view of the explanation I am here proposing, however, partial reward and delay of reward clearly involve the same psychological processes.

Let us go now to examine the matter of work and effort. I am sure it is fairly obvious to all of you now what I want to say about work and effort. If we return to a consideration of our hypothetical test situation we know that, given a choice between an effortless path to food and a path requiring expenditure of effort, the hungry animal will choose the effortless path rather regularly. Hence, in accordance with our analysis concerning dissonance and dissonance reduction, we would expect the requirement of greater effort during acquisition to lead to increased resistance to extinction.

It is surprising that, in spite of the relative consistency of results among the studies which exist in the literature, the effect of effort during acquisition on resistance to extinction has not been generally noted. People have rather tended to note the finding that the greater the effort required during extinction, the faster does extinction occur. But the data are also clear with respect to the effect of effort during acquisition. They show quite clearly that, holding effort during extinction constant, the more effort required during acquisition, the more resistance there is to extinction. The data from one of the more adequately controlled experiments will suffice to illustrate the effect.

Aiken (1957) reports an experiment in which the animal was required to press a panel in order to gain access to food. Some rats were required to exert little effort while others were required to exert considerable effort during training. Half of the animals in each condition were extinguished with the low-effort requirement and half with the high-effort requirement. Holding effort during extinction constant, the results show clearly that the average number of trials to a criterion of extinction was considerably greater for the high-effort acquisition condition than for the low-effort acquisition condition. Other experiments in the literature also show this same effect if one examines the data carefully. It should once more be pointed out that any explanation of this effect which depends upon a notion of similarity between acquisition and extinction conditions is clearly inadequate.

One could list many other specific conditions which, analyzed in the same way, would be expected to increase resistance to extinction. I have chosen the three preceding ones to discuss because reasonably good data concerning them exist in the literature. Now, however, I would like to return to a more thorough consideration of the partial reward situation.

I have stated that, on nonrewarded trials in a partial reward situation, dissonance is introduced into the animal's cognition when he realizes that there is no food available. The amount of dissonance can, of course, vary in magnitude. It is important for us to consider the operational variables which will affect the total magnitude of dissonance which is introduced in this manner. This total magnitude of dissonance, of course, will determine how much dissonance reduction occurs through the development of extra preferences (always assuming that the animal does not change his behavior) and hence will determine the resistance to extinction.

In the past, it has generally been assumed that the major operational variable affecting resistance to extinc-

tion is the ratio of reward. That is, the smaller the proportion of rewarded trials, the greater the resistance to extinction. However, one might reason that since dissonance is created for the animal on every nonrewarded trial, it seems plausible to suppose that the major operational variable which will affect the resistance to extinction is, rather, to sheer total number of nonrewarded trials which the animal has experienced rather than the ratio of nonreward. From the data in published experiments it is impossible to assess whether or not this is correct since these two variables are completely confounded in the literature. Experiments on partial reward have always held constant either the number of rewarded trials or else the total number of trials that the animal experiences. It is clear, of course, that when either of these quantities is held constant, the number of nonrewarded trials is perfectly correlated with the ratio of nonreward and so the effects cannot be separated.

It is possible, perhaps, to get some hunch about this, however, from examining the results of experiments which have used rather few training trials. If we are correct, these experiments should show very weak effects of partial reward on resistance to extinction. Sheffield (1949), for example, using a total of 30 trials (only 15 nonrewarded trials) found very small differences between extinction after partial and complete reward. Wilson, Weiss, and Amsel (1955) and also Lewis (1956), replicating the Sheffield experiment almost exactly, also find such small differences that it requires an analysis of covariance to make them appear significant. However, Weinstock (1954), using a similar apparatus, but employing 75 training trials, finds huge and unmistakable differences.

It is unnecessary to belabor the matter by quoting many studies here since it is all a matter of hunch and impression. In general, when one goes through the literature one gets the impression that the experiments which show small effects after partial reward have tended to employ rather few trials. But comparison of this kind between different experiments done by different experimenters is a very shabby business at best since the variation from experimenter to experimenter can be quite large for unknown reasons. The question seemed important enough, however, so that Lawrence and I thought it worthwhile to do a study which could answer the question. The study was carried out through the kind efforts of John Theios. I would like to describe it to you briefly.

The general design of the study is very simple and does not differ in any essential way from the usual study which has been done on the effects of partial reward. The major difference was that we were primarily concerned with seeing the effects of the absolute number of nonrewarded trials and with being able to separate these effects from the effects of ratio of reward. We employed four different conditions of "number of unrewarded trials." Some groups experienced 0 unrewarded trials; some groups of animals experienced a total of 16 unrewarded trials in the apparatus; still other groups experienced a moderate number of unrewarded trials, namely 27; and finally some groups were run who experienced very many unrewarded trials, namely, 72.

Within these conditions, by varying the total number of trials, different conditions of ratio of reward were set up. Some animals were run with 33 percent reward, others with 50 percent reward, and still others with 67 percent reward. Of course, it was not possible to vary the ratio of reward for

animals in the condition of 0 unrewarded trials, but the animals were run for varying numbers of trials anyhow. Figure 1 shows the total design.

Reward Schedule	NUMBER OF UNREWARDED TRIALS			
	0	*16*	*27*	*72*
33%		24	43	108
50%		31	54	144
67%		48		216
100%	0 54 216			

FIG. 1. *Total number of trials after preliminary training in partial reward experiment.*

The numbers in the cells indicate the total number of trials after preliminary training which the animals in that condition ran. During preliminary training, of course, all groups were rewarded 100 percent of the time. There were between 11 and 16 animals in each condition. It will be noted that we did not run a condition of 67 percent reward and 27 unrewarded trials. The reason for this is simple. We ran out of patience and decided this condition was not essential.

It will also be noted that three groups of 0 unrewarded trials were run so that the total number of trials brackets the entire range for the other groups.

Figure 2 shows the results of the experiment. Along the horizontal axis of the figure are indicated the various values of number of unrewarded trials which we employed and along the ordinate are the average number of trials to reach a criterion of extinction. Each circle on the figure represents the results for one of our experimental conditions. The empty circles represent the data for those with the fewest total

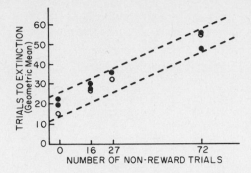

FIG. 2. *Number of trials to extinction after partial reward.*

number of trials. Thus, except for the 0 unrewarded trials conditions, these empty circles represent the data for the 33 percent reward conditions. Similarly, the dark circles represent the longest number of total trials and hence, for the partial reward groups, represent the 67 percent reward conditions.

It is clear from an examination of the figure that, holding constant the number of unrewarded trials, there were only slight differences among the different conditions of ratio of reward. On the other hand, the variable of total number of unrewarded trials has a large and significant effect. It would, indeed, seem that in these data the only variable affecting resistance to extinction after partial reward is the number of unrewarded trials. The results of the experiment are, hence, quite consistent with the interpretations which we have made from the theory of dissonance.

These data are, of course, encouraging but certainly not conclusive. It would be nice to be able to have more direct evidence that nonreward tends to result in the development of extra preferences. From the point of view of obtaining such more direct evidence concerning the validity of our theoretical interpretation, the partial reward situation is not very adequate. For one

thing, our theoretical analysis states that quite different processes occur, psychologically, on rewarded and on unrewarded trials. In a partial reward situation, however, the animal experiences both kinds of trials and, hence, an attempt to separate the effects of the two kinds of trials is bound to be indirect. And, of course, the possibility always exists that the increased resistance to extinction may depend upon some more or less complicated interaction between rewarded and unrewarded trials.

It would then be desirable to be able to compare pure conditions of reward and nonreward. That is, we could test the theory more adequately if we could compare the resistance to extinction of two groups of animals, one of which had always been rewarded in a given place, and the other of which had *never* been rewarded in that same place. This, of course, presents technical problems of how one manages to induce an animal to consistently go to a place where he never gets rewarded. This problem, however, can be solved by employing a variation of what is, essentially, a delay of reward experiment. With the very able assistance and hard work of Edward Uyeno we proceeded to do a series of such experiments in an attempt to get more direct validation of our theoretical derivations. I would like to describe some of these experiments for you.

The apparatus we used was a runway with two boxes in addition to the starting box. The two boxes were, of course, quite easily distinguishable. We will refer to one of them as the end-box and to the other as the mid-box. From the starting place, the animal was to run through a section of alley to the mid-box and then through another section of alley to the end-box. One group of rats was fed on every trial in the mid-box and also fed on every trial in the end-box. We will refer to this group as the 100 percent reward condition. Another group of rats was never fed in the mid-box but, instead, was delayed there for the same amount of time that it took the other to eat its food. These animals then continued to the end-box where they were also fed on every trial. We will refer to this group as the 0 percent reward condition. The designations of 100 percent and 0 percent reward refer, of course, to the reward in the mid-box. Both groups were rewarded on every trial in the end-box and this, of course, is what induced the animals in the 0 percent reward condition to run consistently to a place where they were never rewarded.

The procedure which was employed in extinction was also somewhat different from the usual procedure in a delay of reward experiment. Because we were interested in comparing the two groups of animals in their willingness to go to the mid-box where one group had always, and the other group had never, been fed, we ran extinction trials only from the starting position to the mid-box. During extinction, of course, no food was present for either condition and after a short period of time in the mid-box the animals were returned to their home cage. Thus, from this experiment we have a better comparison of the effects of reward and of nonreward. Figure 3 shows the average running times for the two groups during extinction.

The figure shows the data for the first 30 extinction trials averaged in groups of 3 trials each. It is clear from the figure that there is a very marked difference between the two groups of animals. Those who were always fed in the mid-box start off running quite fast (reflecting their speed of running during acquisition) but slow down very rapidly. Those animals that were never

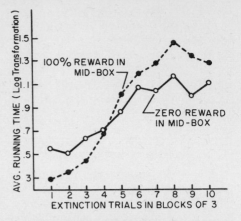

FIG. 3. *Running time during extinction in single mid-box experiment.*

fed in the mid-box start off more slowly (again reflecting their speed of running during acquisition) but they do not show as rapid a rate of extinction. Indeed, between the fourth and fifth blocks of trials the two curves cross over and thereafter the animals run considerably faster to a place where they have never been rewarded than they do to a place where they have always been rewarded.

One may certainly conclude from these data that increased resistance to extinction results from nonreward and that an explanation of the partial reward effect in terms of some interaction between reward and nonreward is not very tenable. Actually, in the experiment I have just described we ran a third group of animals which was rewarded 50 percent of the time in the mid-box and the results for these animals during extinction fall nicely midway between the two curves in Figure 3. The resistance to extinction of those who were never fed in the mid-box is greater than that of either of the other two groups of animals.

At the risk of being terribly repetitious, I would like to remind you at this point of the explanation I am offering for these data. Briefly, dissonance is introduced as a result of the insufficient reward or absence of reward. As long as the organism is prevented from changing his behavior, the dissonance tends to be reduced by developing some extra preference about something in the situation. The existence of this extra preference leads to the stronger inclination to continue running during extinction trials.

If this explanation is correct, however, one should be able to observe the effects of this extra preference even in a situation where all the motivation for food was removed. Indeed, it would seem that this would be a better test of this theoretical explanation. We consequently repeated the experiment I have just described to you, with one modification. Three days were allowed to elapse between the end of acquisition and the beginning of extinction. During these 3 days food was always present in the cages so that by the time the extinction trials started the animals were quite well fed and not hungry. Food remained always available in their cages during the extinction period. In addition, during the 3 intervening days, each animal was placed for periods of time in the end-box without food being available there. In other words, there was an attempt to communicate to the animal that food was no longer available in the apparatus and anyhow the animals were not very motivated for food.

Extinction trials were, of course, run just from the starting box to the mid-box. Three trials were run each day and Fig. 4 shows the results for the first 10 days of extinction. It is clear from an examination of the figure that the results are very similar to the previous results and are, in a sense, even stronger. Those animals who were always fed in the mid-box start off relatively fast and as extinction trials pro-

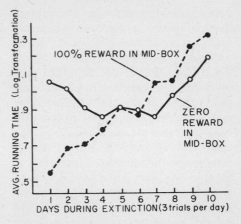

FIG. 4. *Running time while satiated during extinction in single mid-box experiment.*

gress the curve shows steady and rather rapid increase in running time. In short, one obtains a familiar kind of extinction curve for these animals.

The group that was never fed in the mid-box, however, shows a very different pattern of behavior. They start off much more slowly than the other group but, for the first 4 days of extinction, they actually run faster than at the beginning. By the seventh day the two curves have crossed and thereafter the 0 percent reward group runs faster than the 100 percent reward group. It is also interesting to note that, for the 0 percent reward group, through the eighth day, one can see no evidence of any extinction having occurred at all. If one is inclined to do so, one can certainly see in these data some evidence that an extra preference of rather weak strength exists for the animals that were never rewarded in the mid-box.

We were sufficiently encouraged by these results so that we proceeded to perform what I, at least, regarded as a rather ambitious experiment. Before I describe the experiment, let me briefly explain the reasoning which lay behind it. It is plausible to suppose that the extra preference which the organism develops in order to reduce dissonance may be focussed on any of a variety of things. Let me explain this by using the experiment I have just described as an illustration. Those animals who were never fed in the mid-box, and thus experienced dissonance, could have developed a liking for the activity of running down the alley to the mid-box, they could have developed a preference for some aspect of the mid-box itself, or they could have developed a preference for any of the things they did or encountered subsequent to leaving the mid-box. Experimentally, of course, there was no control over this.

It occurred to us, in thinking about this, that if the dissonance were reduced, at least to some extent, by developing a preference for something about the *place* where the dissonance was introduced, then it would be possible to show the same effects in a very well-controlled experiment. In other words, if the dissonance introduced by absence of reward were reduced, at least in part, by developing some liking for the place where they were not rewarded, then one could compare two groups of animals, both of which experienced the identical amount of dissonance, but who would be expected to develop preferences for different places.

To do this we used the same basic technique as in the previous two experiments I have described but with an important modification. Instead of one mid-box, two mid-boxes were used. From the starting box the animals went to Mid-box A, from there to Mid-box B, and from there to the end-box where all animals received food on every trial. Two groups of animals were run in this experiment. Group A was delayed in Mid-box A

for a period of time and then was allowed to run directly through Mid-box B to the end-box. Group B was allowed to run directly through Mid-box A but was delayed for a period of time in Mid-box B before being allowed to go to the end-box. In other words, both groups of animals had identical experience. The only difference between the groups lay in the particular box in which they were delayed. (All three boxes were, of course, quite distinctive.) For the extinction trials the animals were satiated as in the preceding experiment. For the extinction trials, the animals were run only from Box A to Box B. That is, during extinction the animals were placed directly into Box A, the door was then opened, and when they ran to Box B were removed to their home cage.

Thus, Group A during extinction was running away from the place where they had been delayed, while Group B was running to the place where they had been delayed. If some extra preference had developed for the place where they had been delayed, we would expect Group B to show more resistance to extinction than Group A. In short, during extinction, Group B should behave like the 0 percent reward groups in the previous experiments. Group A, however, should behave during extinction more like the 100 percent reward animals in the preceding experiments.

Figure 5 shows the data for these two groups of animals for the first 10 days of extinction, three trials having been run on each day. The two curves in the figure must, by now, look very familiar to you. The same result is obtained as in the two previous experiments. The initial difference between the two groups again reflects their previous running speed in that section of the apparatus. During acquisition,

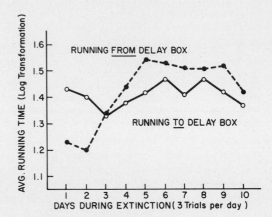

FIG. 5. *Running time while satiated during extinction in double mid-box experiment.*

Group B ran more hesitantly in the section between the two mid-boxes than did Group A. This difference, of course, still exists at the start of the extinction trials. Thereafter, however, Group A, which was running away from its delay box, rapidly increases its running time. Group B, which was running to its delay box, does not increase its time at all and shows no evidence of any extinction during 30 trials. By the fourth day of extinction, the two curves have crossed and thereafter Group B consistently runs faster than Group A.

If one looks carefully at all the data, I think one finds reasonable evidence that insufficient reward does lead to the development of extra preference. This extra preference, at least in the white rat, seems to be of a rather mild nature, but the magnitude of the effect is quite sufficient to account for the increased resistance to extinction after partial reward or after delay of reward.

Let us then briefly examine the implications of these findings and of the theory of dissonance for our traditional conception of how reward functions. It seems clear that the inclination to engage in behavior after extrinsic rewards are removed is not so much a function of past rewards themselves. Rather, and paradoxically, such persistence in behavior is increased by a history of nonrewards or inadequate rewards. I sometimes like to summarize all this by saying that rats and people come to love things for which they have suffered.

REFERENCES

Alken, M. G., "The Effort Variable in the Acquisition, Extinction and Spontaneous Recovery of an Instrumental Response," *Journal of Experimental Psychology,* **53** (1957), 47-51.

Aronson, E. and J. Mills, "The Effect of Severity of Initiation on Liking for a Group," *Journal of Abnormal Social Psychology,* **59** (1959), 177-81.

Crum, J., W. L. Brown, and M. E. Bitterman, "The Effect of Partial and Delayed Reinforcement on Resistance to Extinction," *American Journal of Psychology,* **64** (1951), 228-37.

Fehrer, E., "Effects of Amount of Reinforcement and of Pre- and Postreinforcement Delays on Learning and Extinction," *Journal of Experimental Psychology,* **52** (1956), 167-76.

Festinger, L., *A Theory of Cognitive Dissonance.* Evanston, Ill: Row, Peterson & Co., 1957.

Lewis, D. J., "Acquisition, Extinction, and Spontaneous Recovery as a Function of Percentage of Reinforcement and Intertrial Intervals," *Journal of Experimental Psychology*, **51** (1956), 45-53.

Scott, E. D. and E. L. Wike, "The Effect of Partially Delayed Reinforcement and Trial Distribution on the Extinction of an Instrument Response," *American Journal of Psychology*, **69** (1956), 264-68.

Sheffield, V. F., "Extinction as a Function of Partial Reinforcement and Distribution of Practice," *Journal of Experimental Psychology*, **39** (1949), 511-26.

Weinstock, S., "Resistance to Extinction of a Running Response Following Partial Reinforcement under Widely Spaced Trials," *Journal of Comparative Physiological Psychology*, **47** (1954), 318-22.

Wike, E. L. and H. J. McNemara, "The Effects of Percentage of Partially Delayed Reinforcement on the Acquisition and Extinction of an Instrumental Response," *Journal of Comparative Physiological Psychology*, **50** (1957), 348-51.

Wilson, W., E. J. Weiss, and A. Amsel, "Two Tests of the Sheffield Hypothesis Concerning Resistance to Extinction, Partial Reinforcement, and Distribution of Practice," *Journal of Experimental Psychology*, **50** (1955), 51-60.

Personality Theory and The Problem of Stability and Change in Individual Behavior: An Interpersonal Approach *

Paul F. Secord and Carl W. Backman

Clinical psychologists, personality theorists, and most other students of individual behavior commonly assume that a person gradually forms characteristic behavior patterns which become more and more resistant to change with the passage of time. These patterns are usually thought of as reflections of intra-individual structures or mecha-

* From P. F. Secord and C. W. Backman, "Personality Theory and the Problem of Stability and Change in Individual Behavior: An Interpersonal Approach," *Psychological Review*, **68** (1960), 21-32. Reprinted by permission of the authors and the American Psychological Association.

This investigation was supported in part by a grant (M-1892) from the National Institute of Mental Health, United States Public Health Service.

nisms: for example, habits, needs, cognitive structures, or traits. Because these intrapersonal determinants of behavior are, in effect, accepted as given, observable consistency over a period of time tends to remain unexplained— it is simply a manifestation of these structures. From this point of view, a person behaves as he does because of what he is.

Thus, Allport (1937), Cattell (1950), and Eysenck (1953) attribute enduring structure to personality, a structure in which the concept of trait is central. Murray (1938) conceives of personality as an organizing and integrating force having a neural locus in the organism. In spite of his field emphasis, Lewin (1935) conceives of personality structure as characterized by certain differentiations and articulations of regions, which correspond to aspects of personal character. Murphy (1947) includes physiological dispositions, canalizations, conditioned responses, and cognitive and perceptual habits as components of personality. Two cognitive orientations are those of Rogers (1951), and Combs and Snygg (1959), who conceive of behavior as organized around and guided by a relatively enduring self-concept. Finally, almost all forms of personality assessment are based upon the assumption that the individual undergoing appraisal has a stable personality structure which the investigator is attempting to describe, in part or in whole. Murphy (1947) has summed up this attitude succinctly. He states:

> The laboratory psychologist and the clinician have both conceived the individual as a system of events and tendencies carried around within the skin of the individual subject. They have both assumed that his delinquencies or his triumphs, his interests or nervous maladjustments, result fully and simply from structured dispositions within him (p. 877).

For all of these theorists, then, personality has a certain stability of structure which in turn maintains continuity in behavior over time. This is not to assert that behavior is viewed by these theorists as unchanging or unresponsive to varying stimulus situations. On the contrary, many of these personologists often give careful attention to stimulus situations as modifiers of behavior. But, sometimes explicitly and sometimes implicitly, they do appear to make the assumption that when behavioral stability occurs, it is a function of stability in personality structure. A closely related assumption is that personality structure has a strong resistance to change; in the absence of special change-inducing forces or conditions, it remains constant.

These assumptions have two consequences. The first is that continuity in individual behavior is not a problem to be solved; it is simply a natural outcome of the formation of stable structure. The second is that either behavioral change is not given systematic attention, or change is explained independently of stability. Whereas behavioral stability is explained by constancy of structure, change tends to be explained by environmental forces and fortuitous circumstances. A more parsimonious approach would be to account for both stability and change by means of a single set of explanatory principles. The following theoretical statement abandons the assumption that internal stabilizing mechanisms are inherently resistant to change and are the sole source of stability in individual behavior.

The present paper places the locus of stability and change in the interaction process rather than in intrapersonal structures. At the same time, the importance of habit, cognitive structure, and similar concepts is not denied, but these mechanisms do not by themselves establish necessary conditions for behavioral stability. Stable patterns in the interaction process, which constitute the essential condition for consistency in individual behavior, may be thought of as deriving from two major sources. One source is the cultural, normative, and institutional forces which stabilize the behavior of persons with whom a particular individual interacts, as well as his behavior toward them. With this important source the present paper is not concerned; social psychologists, sociologists, anthropologists, and others have analyzed these forces in extensive detail.

The other source of stability, although it has been given some attention by social psychologists, has been relatively neglected by students of individual behavior. It has been customary to think of the two classes of behavioral determinants: cultural and normative forces, and those forces stemming from the individual. The present paper attempts to identify a third class of determinants, which have their locus neither in the individual nor the culture, but in the interaction process itself. In a general sense, this third class may be characterized as the tendencies of the individual and the persons with whom he interacts to shape the interaction process according to certain requirements, that is, they strive to produce certain patterned relations. As will be seen, the principles governing this activity are truly interpersonal; they require as much attention to the behavior of the other as they do to the behavior of the individual, and it cannot be said that one or the other is the sole locus of cause.

Because of limitations of space and in the interests of clarity, the theory will be presented without attempting to specifically examine the empirical evidence, but those familiar with the literature will recognize that much supporting evidence exists. For definitive support, however, an extensive research program guided by the theory needs to be carried out.

SOURCES OF STABILITY IN INDIVIDUAL BEHAVIOR

Definition of Interpersonal Matrix and Matrix Congruency

The locus of behavioral stability and change lies in the interpersonal matrix, which has three components: an aspect of the self-concept of the subject (S), S's interpretation of those elements of his behavior related to that aspect, and S's perception of related aspects of the other person (O) with whom he is interacting. An interpersonal matrix is a recurring functional relation between these three components. The behavior of a particular person is episodic in character, in that he shifts from one matrix to another over varying periods of time. A matrix is referred to as the same if, on two or more occasions, the same self-component, S-behavior, and O-component are present in the same functional relation. The present theoretical treatment focusses mainly on the discussion of single matrices. Also, only aspects of self and behavior which are valued by S are dealt with, and these are assumed to maintain relatively constant values.

S strives to achieve congruency [1] among the components of the matrix. Congruency is a cognitive phenomenon: that is, each component enters into a state of congruency only as a perceptual cognitive experience on the part of S: All three components of the matrix are in a state of congruency when the behaviors of S and O imply definitions of self congruent with relevant aspects of the self-concept. In a nurturant-dependent relation, for example, a dependent S has conceptions of self containing elements of inadequacy and need for support. His behavior is consistent with these aspects of cognitive structure, for it is hesitant and compliant, reaffirming his self-definition. Since the behavior of O is perceived as providing assistance and as reassuring and decisive, it implies a matching definition of S's self-concept

---

[1] Congruency as used here has some similarities to the following: Abelson's (1958) resolution of belief dilemmas, Cartwright and Harary's (1956) concept of structure balance, Festinger's (1957) theory of cognitive dissonance, Heider's (1958) theory of balance, and Osgood and Tannenbaum's (1955) concept of congruence.

and behavior. In the above example, S's interpretation of his behavior is congruent with a relevant aspect of the self, S's perception of O is congruent with the self-respect, and S's interpretation of his behavior is congruent with his perception of O. Thus, any two components of a matrix may be congruent with each other, with the third either congruent with both of them, or not congruent with either.

Implications for self-definitions may take three forms: S may perceive O's behavior as directly confirming a component of self, O's behavior may enable S to behave in ways that would confirm a component of self, O's behavior may (by comparison) lead other Os to confirm a component of S's self-concept. Examples of each form are:

> An S who regards himself as mature and responsible perceives that Os respect him for these characteristics.
> An S who regards himself as nurturant encounters an O in need of help; this allows him to behave toward O in a manner which supports his nurturant aspect of self.
> A girl who regards herself as popular and well liked keeps company with an unpopular girl; Os are viewed by her as judging her favorably by contrast.

REALITY-ORIENTED VS. COGNITIVELY DISTORTED MATRICES. A matrix is reality-oriented if the S-behavior component and O-component are correctly interpreted or perceived. On the other hand, a matrix which involves misinterpretation of S's behavior or misperception of O is not reality-oriented; it involves some form of cognitive distortion. It is obvious that congruency would sometimes be achieved by means of cognitive distortion. Presumably a congruency achieved by this means would be less stable than a reality-oriented congruency. At least this would be true if there were forces tending to produce accurate interpretations and perceptions. On the other hand, *in*congruencies which might be made congruent simply by correcting cognitive distortions to fit reality are not regarded as particularly stable or significant, and thus are not further discussed.

THE TENDENCY TO ACHIEVE AND MAINTAIN CONGRUENT STATES. A number of general principles may be presented concerning the maintenance of congruent states. In many instances these will be elaborated later.

1. S tends to repeat and perpetuate those interpersonal relations which were previously characterized by congruency.

2. An S involved in a matrix which is not in a state of congruency will tend to modify the matrix in the direction of greater congruency.

3. The engagement of S and O in congruent interaction develops mutual affect toward each other, which tends to perpetuate the interaction.

4. Because of the tendency to establish congruent matrices, S gradually builds up an increasingly greater repertory of such matrices.

5. The more the O-component of a congruent matrix is valued, the greater the tendency of the matrix to be perpetuated.

RELATIONS AMONG THE MATRICES AND THE PERPETUATION OF CONGRUENT STATES. A given matrix may be considered *relevant* to those matrices which contain one or more of the same or similar components as the given matrix. For example, for an S who considers himself to be a kind person, there will be many S-behaviors and O-behaviors which are perceived as forming congruencies and incongruencies with this aspect of self. The various matrices formed by distinctive S-behaviors and O-behaviors in connection with the aspect of self, kindness, are all considered relevant to each other.

A relevant matrix may be either *supportive* or *nonsupportive* with respect to a given matrix. Supportiveness between two matrices is determined by whether or not the component(s) common to them has the same relation (one of congruency or one of incongruency) to the other unique components in each matrix. If the common component has the same relation in both matrices, they are said to be supportive.

> For example, suppose a woman regards herself as unattractive to men. Her mother continually calls her attention to the fact that women in her family were seldom noted for their attractiveness. Our S also finds that a man she likes at work avoids her as much as possible. In the one matrix, unattractiveness is congruent with her mother's direct definition of her as unattractive and, in the other, the avoidance behavior of the man leads her to perceive his behavior as defining her as unattractive. Thus, one matrix supports the other. On the other hand, if her mother perceived many good features in her appearance and stressed these, and the man professed admiration for her, both matrices would be incongruent with her notion of self as unattractive. These two matrices would also support each other—they agree in denying an aspect of self. These might be termed incongruent supportive matrices, and the former type, congruent supportive matrices.

A statement may now be made with respect to the role of a complex of matrices in perpetuating a given matrix. Matrices vary with respect to *centricality*. The centricality of a matrix is a function of the number of other matrices which stand in a supportive relation to it, and the value of the O-components in these matrices. The greater the centricality of a matrix, the more resistant it is to change, and,

should it change, the greater the resultant shifts in other matrices.

Interpersonal Processes Contributing to Congruent States

Congruency is continually threatened by the changing nature of interpersonal relations due to: (*a*) normative patterns of change, which result in changes in the behavior of others towards *S,* for example, changes in the behavior of others as the child grows older, or as a person changes occupations, gets married; (*b*) fortuitous changes, for example, death of a parent, loss of a friend, induction into the military; and (*c*) the fact that O's means of establishing congruency for himself often create incongruencies for S. A number of interpersonal processes may be suggested which counter these pressures for change and which perpetuate previous matrices.

The first five interpersonal processes restore congruency through some transformation of the O-component of the matrix:

1. *Selective interaction with Os. S* tends to maximize engagement in congruent patterns of interpersonal behavior by selecting and interacting with those Os whose behavior requires a minimum change from previously congruent interpersonal situations in which *S* has engaged. For example, if *S* regards himself as especially intelligent, he tends to interact frequently with Os who respect his intelligence or who allow him to exercise it, or he interacts in such a way as to make himself appear intelligent by comparison.

2. *Selective evaluation of Os. S* tends to maximize congruency by altering the evaluation of selected Os in a positive or negative direction, depending upon whether they are behaving congruently or incongruently with certain aspects of self. The more an

O is valued by *S,* either positively or negatively, the more important his role is in maintaining congruency. This provides a means of increasing the effects of congruency or reducing the effects of incongruency. Thus, *S* tends to increase his liking for Os who behave toward him in a congruent fashion, and to decrease his liking for those who have in an incongruent manner.

3. *Selective comparison with aspects of O. S* tends to maximize congruency by selectively attending to behaviors of O which are congruent, and selectively ignoring those which are incongruent. For example, a patient in therapy particularly notes those behaviors on the part of the therapist which confirm aspects of his self-concept and behavior, and tends to ignore those which are incongruent.

4. *Evocation of congruent responses from O. S* develops techniques for eliciting from O behavior which will be congruent with components of his self-concept and behavior. For example, a feminine woman plays a helpless role in order to elicit dominance from men.

5. *Misperception of O. S* may misperceive O's behavior so as to achieve congruency with aspects of his behavior and self-concept. Thus, an *S* has a high regard for himself as a lover and perceives other women as more interested in him than they really are.

The sixth and seventh interpersonal processes restore congruency by a transformation of the S-behavior component of the matrix:

6. *Selective behavior-matching.* In interacting with a particular O, *S* tends to maximize congruency by selecting from his total behavioral repertoire those behaviors which are most congruent with his perception of O. This principle reflects William James' (1890, Vol. 1, p. 294) notion that each person has as many "social selves" as there are classes of persons whose opinion he cares about.

7. *Misinterpretation of own behavior. S* may misinterpret his behavior so as to achieve maximum congruency with an aspect of his self-concept and his perception of O. For example, a dutiful mother spanks her child because of anger and frustration but convinces herself that she is doing it for the child's own good.

Certain combinations of these principles may sometimes operate under a single rubric. For example, an individual may select a *social role* which enables him to achieve maximum congruency among the three components. This involves interaction with selected Os who will engage in certain desired reciprocal behavior, and also permits behaviors which validate the self. Thus, a woman who regards herself as intelligent, independent, and ambitious may reject the marital role in favor of a career role. A second example is found in *circular interaction systems.* In these, response evocation tends to become an activity mutual to two persons: the actions of *S* give rise to behavior on the part of O which in turn evoke further actions of the type initially displayed by the individual. For example, aggressive actions on the part of the mother, initiated in the attempt to control or eliminate undesirable aggressive behavior in her child, raise his frustration level, which in turn gives further impetus to his tendency to respond in aggressive ways.

FORCES TOWARD CHANGE AND THE RESOLUTION OF THESE FORCES

States of Incongruency and Their Consequences

Any theory of stability in self and behavior must also be able to explain change. There are three steps leading to change: the creation of an incongruency, the formation of a new congruent matrix which involves a different component of self or behavior from that existing prior to the change, and the adjustment of relevant matrices which have been affected by the changes made in resolving the incongruent matrix. As mentioned earlier, incongruencies arise from several sources: from cultural, normative, and institutional forces, from fortuitous factors, and from O's attempts to establish congruency for himself. Incongruencies occur frequently, but are often followed by restoration of a congruent matrix which does not involve a change in self or behavior. Whether or not change occurs, resolution of the newly formed incongruency occurs through utilization of one or more of the interpersonal processes previously discussed. Thus, a single set of interpersonal processes are presumed to underlie both behavioral stability and the direction of behavioral change.

Four types of incongruency are identified in the following discussion. Of considerable interest and importance is the manner in which the various types of incongruency may be resolved. As already noted, there are two general classes of resolution. One of these results in restoration of the original matrix, leaving self and behavior unchanged (although cognitive distortions may occur), and the other leads to a new matrix in which self or behavior are changed. In order to avoid being tedious, only a brief, informal discussion of the forms of resolution will be presented. Table 1, however, presents in symbolic form a complete set of resolutions for the first three types of incongruency. The fourth is omitted since it is mainly of academic interest and is probably quite rare.

Type I. The behavior of O is perceived as incongruent with a component of self and with S's behavior, the latter two elements being congruent with each other.

For example, S, an alcoholic, who regards himself as a "weak," inadequate person, neglects his family by going on extensive binges, implying a definition of self as inadequate. O, his wife, behaves toward S as if he were capable of controlling his drinking.

In this type of incongruency, S may employ any one of the first five interpersonal processes to transform the incongruent O- component, and thereby maintain self and behavior unchanged. Thus, he may reduce interaction with his wife, may devaluate her, may avoid selective comparison by declaring her opinion irrelevant, may evoke new responses from her, or may falsely perceive her as trying to give him a pep talk.

Other forms of achieving congruency require a change in self or behavior. S may change both components, or he may change self but not behavior by misinterpreting his behavior.

Type II. An aspect of self is incongruent with S's behavior and with the perceived behavior of O, the latter two elements being congruent with each other.

For example, a woman behaving seductively gets matching responses from O, but regards herself as morally conservative.

One form of resolution involves maintenance of self and behavior. Since behavior is incongruent, it would have to be misinterpreted if self is to be maintained, and in addition, the five interpersonal processes which transform the incongruent O component would be employed here. For example, behavior is misinterpreted if S regards her behavior as casually flirtatious, or as "not me" because she had

TABLE 1

RESOLUTION OF BASIC TYPES OF INCONGRUENCY

Let E represent the self-component of matrix
     B represent S-behavior as a reality-oriented matrix component
     O represent O-behavior as a reality-oriented matrix component
     B′ represent a matrix component based on misinterpretation of S-behavior
     O′ represent a matrix component based on misperception of O-behavior
     $\bar{X}$ represent an incongruent form of a component X
     X_c represent a change in a component X

		TYPE OF RESOLUTION		
Type of Incongruency	Maintenance of Self and Behavior	Change in Self-Concept	Change in Behavior	Change in Self-Concept and Behavior
I. $SB\bar{O}$	SB SB SBO_c SBO_c $SBO′$	$S_cB′O$	Not applicable	S_cB_cO
II. $\bar{S}BO$	SB′ SB′ $SB′O_c$ $SB′O_c$ $SB′O′$	S_cBO	SB_c SB_c SB_cO_c SB_cO_c $SB_cO′$	Not applicable
III. $S\bar{B}O$	SB′O	S_cB S_cB S_cBO_c S_cBO_c $S_cBO′$	SB_cO	Not applicable

Note. Resolutions involving O are listed in order of the five interpersonal processes which apply to O: (a) reduced interaction—SB. (b) devaluation—SB. (c) O-behavior selection—SBO_c. (d) response evocation—SBO_c, and (e) misperception—$SBO′$.

been drinking, and, with respect to O, S might reduce interaction with him, regard his behavior as harmless flirtation, or she might make her own behavior irrelevant by defining him as a man who would try to seduce any woman, etc.

A simple change in self would result in a congruent matrix. Or, finally, S might change her behavior and transform the O-component.

Type III. S's behavior is incongruent with a component of self and with the perceived behavior of O, the latter two elements being congruent with each other.

For example, a wife regards herself as loving, but realizes that she is often hostile toward her husband. Her husband fails to recognize much of the hostility and behaves toward her as if he perceives her as loving.

If, in this instance, S changes her self-concept to match her unchanged behavior, she may employ the five interpersonal processes to transform the O-component. Thus, she may leave her husband, devaluate him, emphasize occasions on which he has been angry with her, evoke hostility from him, or think that he secretly does recognize her hostility. If she maintains self-concept and behavior, she must necessarily misinterpret her behavior in order to achieve congruency.

Type IV. All three matrix components are incongruent with each other. Two general forms of resolution are: (*a*) any two of the components may be changed to match the third; (*b*) all three may be modified to achieve a new matrix congruency. Type IV incongruency is thought to be rare and is not discussed further.

Factors Governing the Probable Direction of Resolution

The various forms of resolution of incongruent matrices are not equally probable. Which ones are more likely to occur is in part a matter for empirical study. In the meantime, however, a number of factors relating to the probability of change in the various components may be identified. In the first place, O's behavior toward S may be systematic and consistent because it stems from certain factors external to the dyad, such as role expectations— for example, O may be S's therapist, or he may be a parent socializing his child. An obvious second consideration is the ease with which S may leave the dyad. A patient may readily leave therapy, but a child cannot usually leave his family. A third condition pertains to the extent to which an individual's congruent relations are reality-oriented, that is, to what degree misinterpretation and misperception are required for congruency. Matrix components which are not reality-oriented tend to be less stable. A fourth point is that the greater the number and value of supportive congruent matrices which are relevant to a component, the more resistant is that component to change. Finally, it may be postulated that the individual learns to utilize selectively the various modes of resolution. For a particular individual, certain types of component-transformation are more practiced and are preferred to others.

DISCUSSION

An important difference between the present approach and earlier ones should be re-emphasized. Such traditional concepts as cognitive structure, self-concept, trait, and habit are products of earlier social interaction. But the assumption is *not* made that persons strive to maintain either their self-concept or various habitual behaviors by virtue of some inherent "gyroscopic" force residing in these dispositions. Maintenance of intrapersonal structure occurs only when such maintenance is consistent with an ongoing interaction process which is in a state of congruency. That most individuals do maintain intrapersonal structure is a function of the fact that the behavior of others toward the individuals in question is normally overwhelmingly consistent with such maintenance. This fact has often been overlooked. It should be made clear that the concept of structure continues to have a place in the present theory. Matrices are structures; they are aspects of perceptual-cognitive experience. Unlike habit and trait, however, they tend to be more integrated with certain behaviors of O. Even the self-concept, employed in the present theory as a matrix component, is always tied to certain behaviors of S and O.

The interpersonal environment is not always stable and familiar. The present approach predicts that were the interpersonal environment to suddenly undergo drastic change, with others uniformly behaving toward the individual in markedly new and strange ways, an individual held in such an environment would rapidly modify his own behavior and internal structure to produce a new set of congruent matrices. As a result, he would be a radically changed person. This prediction is consistent with the experiences of some soldiers imprisoned and "brainwashed" by Chinese communists. Some investigators have emphasized as a key factor in successful brainwashing the isolation of the individual from his normal interpersonal relations. Marked changes in an individual may also occur as a result of shifts in a single matrix, if that matrix involves a highly valued O, for example, a therapist. As noted earlier, there are complexes consisting of matrices relevant to each other because they contain at least one common component, and a shift in one highly valued matrix may have ramifications throughout the structure of relevant matrices. In a word, the differences in emphasis between the present and previous approaches to behavioral stability is that the individual strives to maintain interpersonal relations characterized by congruent matrices, rather than to maintain a self, habits, or traits. Some of the advantages of this approach are the following:

1. The approach provides a place in theory for the variability of individual behavior in different interpersonal situations. For example, it does not make the questionable assumption that an individual belongs at fixed points with respect to each of a variety of personality traits in all interpersonal situations. A given individual is unlikely to be equally aggressive in interaction with every other person or in every situation involving the same person. Yet, a typical personality appraisal instrument yields a single score on "aggressive" for an individual. In the present view, trait behaviors such as aggressiveness tend to appear only when they are congruent with certain O-behaviors and certain components of

self. This idea calls for an overhaul of our traditional methods of personality assessment.

2. While self-theory emphasizes that self emerges out of social interaction, it is rather vague on details. In fact it implies that the only role of the behavior of others in supporting the self is that expressed by the first type of congruent O-behavior, namely, behavior which directly defines an S-component of S in the same way as S does. Moreover, the organism is often assumed to be passive in this process. For example, the fact that S may actively seek out those who support components of self, may evoke certain responses on the part of the other, and so forth is often ignored.

3. The interpersonal framework makes the process of individual change less mysterious and less difficult to explain. Individual behavior is always linked to the behavior of others, and the key to deliberate change lies in creating shifts in the perception of the behavior of Os toward S. This is accomplished either through bringing about actual changes in the behavior of Os toward S, or by blocking various techniques that S uses to distort or to evoke certain O-behaviors which tend to support his current perceptions. Socialization and psychotherapy will shortly be discussed in order to illustrate the application of the theory to problems of change.

4. It is believed that variables on the perceptual-cognitive level are more directly assessable in view of the ability of Ss to directly describe their self-concept, their behavior, and the behavior of Os. In addition, the question of cognitive distortion can be checked by obtaining information by direct observation of the interaction, or by obtaining descriptive information from O. In contrast, such concepts as need, habit, and trait must be inferred,

and there has been considerable controversy over the validity of various procedures of inference in regard to these variables. Another advantage stems from the fact that, in the experience of the present investigators, matrix variables are readily manipulable when using conventional experimental procedures in social psychology. For example, an incongruency can be readily created in the laboratory by false test protocol reports to *S*s concerning aspects of self and behavior, or by placing *S* in the laboratory with an O who has been instructed by the experimenter to behave in an incongruent fashion.

5. The present point of view should be helpful in integrating concepts of personality with those of social psychology. At present there is a tendency to conceptualize each of these disciplines in such a way as to make difficult, if not impossible, the simultaneous application of concepts from both areas to consideration of any particular behavioral phenomenon. Dyadic relations will be briefly touched upon to indicate how a rapprochement between these areas might be initiated. Also, by examining the role of culture in establishing congruencies and incongruencies, light may be thrown on variations in individual strain from culture to culture, and on a source of cultural change, namely, the attempt of individuals to resolve such strains.

Socialization and Psychotherapy

The process of socialization involves those changes occurring as a result of movement through the social structure. Psychotherapy has a less systematic relation to social structure and may be thought of as a process of change resulting from highly significant interaction between patient and therapist. Both socialization and psychotherapy may be examined briefly to determine whether or not the process of change can be conceptualized in terms of the present interpersonal theory.

Socialization may be viewed as a process in which the person moves through a succession of changing patterns of O-behaviors over a long period of time. These changing patterns are culturally induced, and create incongruencies for S. In this process there is a certain amount of resistance to change on the part of *S*, arising out of the fact that typically the changing behavior of Os toward him requires continual reorganization of previously established matrices. Behaviors which previously led readily to congruent matrices now bring forth incongruent reactions from O. Take, for example, the small child who has an overprotective mother. Here self-cognitions are rudimentary and limited, but if existing components were phrased in adult language, they might include the following: "I am the baby of the family." "Daily family life revolves around me." "I can get most anything I want." When this child moves out of his mother's sphere of control, however, and plays with other children, he meets many responses incongruent with these components of self. Other children are likely to thwart his needs rather than meet them; he is unlikely to be the center of play activities. These incongruencies force change in self-components and behavior. To the extent that an overprotective mother limits a child's contacts with other children, and reduces the extent to which other children are valued, components of self inappropriate to interaction outside the family develop in the child.

Normal development in the socialization process involves removing incongruency by changing components of self and behavior so that they correspond with the definitions made by significant Os. Because of the difficulty of changing S-components which are relevant to an increasingly larger number of congruent matrices, however, the individual also learns to use other ways of handling incongruency: for example, misperception, misinterpretation, response evocation, changing valuations of others, and so forth. These latter actions delay or prevent changes in self or behavior. It is probable that early adjustment to incongruency involves changing the self-concept and behavior, but as the individual develops these other techniques, he frequently handles incongruency by means of them. Disturbances of the developmental sequence may frequently occur as a result of overuse of modes of reducing incongruency which involve distortion of reality instead of change in self or behavior. This may be expected to result in the establishment of a somewhat precarious stability of self at a low level of maturity. This is a social psychological interpretation of the Freudian phenomenon of fixation.

The interpersonal theory as outlined also seems to point to a crucial process in psychotherapy. The modes of reducing incongruency spelled out in an earlier section suggest that the primary problem facing a psychotherapist is the necessity for blocking all modes which permit the maintenance of the undesirable aspects of self and behavior, and facilitating those which involve change in these components. The advantage of a systematic theory providing an exhaustive classification of the various forms of reducing incongruency is that it allows the therapist to anticipate various ways in which the individual may fail to change. There are two directions, however, in which the theory must be further elaborated. One involves spelling out the behaviors required of the change agent for successful facilitation of modes of reso-

lution leading to desired changes in the self-concept and behavior of the S. The other requires the elaboration of techniques for blocking those modes leading to maintenance of undesirable aspects of self and behavior.

Dyadic Relations

So far the focus has been on stability and change in *individual* behavior. Emphasis has been placed on the point that stability and change in individual behavior is in part a product of a reciprocal process having its locus in the interactions between the individual and those around him. This reciprocal process may also be applied to an understanding of both members of the dyad. The instability of adolescent love relations would appear to be initiated by the confronting of the adolescent with marked and frequent changes in the behavior of peers and adults which are incongruent with components of self and his behavior. These changes lead to shifts in self-concept and behavior, and in turn new relations are sought to establish congruency with these modified aspects of self and behavior. The disruptive effect of separation on a friendship or a marriage is another case in point. The new interpersonal environment contains Os who define the individual's self and behavior differently, and he gradually changes so as to establish congruency in this new interpersonal situation. On the other hand, old relations become less congruent, and consequently progressively weaker in affect. These changes are dramatically illustrated by the disappointment so often experienced at the reunion after long separation of boyhood friends or ex-army buddies. In a similar fashion, induced changes in personality, such as those which occur in psychotherapy, and fortuitous ones which arise as a result of entering a new job, obtaining more formal education, and so forth may well result in drastic shifts in dyadic relations.

SUMMARY AND CONCLUSIONS

Most students of individual behavior comonly assume that when behavioral stability occurs, it is a function of stability in personality structure, and that in the absence of special change-inducing forces, structure remains constant. Thus continuity in individual behavior is not a problem to be solved; it is simply a natural outcome of the formation of stable structure. Behavioral change, moreover, either is not given systematic attention, or is explained independently of stability, in terms of environmental forces and fortuitous circumstances. The present interpersonal theory attempts to account for both stability and change in terms of a single set of explanatory principles.

In the present view, the locus of behavioral stability and change lies in the interpersonal matrix, which has three components: an aspect of the self-concept of S, S's interpretation of those elements of his behavior related to that aspect, and S's perception of related aspects of the person with whom he is interacting (O). S strives to achieve congruency among the components of the matrix, a state which is achieved when the behaviors of S and the other imply definitions of self which are consistent with relevant aspects of the self-concept. Congruency is continually threatened by the changing nature of interpersonal relations due to: (a) normative patterns of change, which result in changes in the behavior of Os toward S, for example, changes in the behavior of Os as the child grows older, or as a person changes occupations or gets married; (b) fortuitous changes, for example, death of a parent, loss of a friend, induction into the military; and (c) the fact that O's means of establishing congruency for himself often creates incongruencies for S.

When incongruencies arise, a variety of interpersonal processes which have been carefully described here often acts to restore congruency without change in self or behavior. Sometimes, however, these same interpersonal processes operate to form a new congruent matrix which involves a change in self or behavior. The circumstances under which either of these effects take place are a function of the type of incongruency which occurred and of a variety of other conditions which have been discussed in some detail. Thus, a single set of principles is utilized to offer a systematic explanation of the reasons for stability or change in individual behavior.

The advantages of adopting such an interpersonal theory are spelled out, and a brief discussion is included to illustrate how it might be applied to such processes as socialization, psychotherapy, and dyadic relations.

REFERENCES

Abelson, R. P., "Modes of Resolution of Belief Dilemmas." Paper read at Western Psychological Association, Monterey, Calif., April 1958.

Allport, G. W., *Personality: A Psychological Interpretation.* New York: Holt, Rinehart & Winston, Inc., 1937.

Cartwright, D. and F. Harary, "Structural Balance: A Generalization of Heider's Theory," *Psychological Review,* **63** (1956), 277-93.

Cattell, R. B., *Personality: A Systematic, Theoretical, and Factual Study.* New York: McGraw-Hill Book Company, Inc., 1950.

Combs, A. W. and D. Snygg, *Individual Behavior: A Perceptual Approach to Behavior.* New York: Harper & Row, Publishers, 1959.

D. E. BERLYNE   551

Eysenck, H. J., *The Structure of Human Personality*. New York: John Wiley & Sons, Inc., 1953.

Festinger, L., *A Theory of Cognitive Dissonance*. Evanston, Ill.: Row, Peterson & Company, 1957.

Heider, F., *The Psychology of Interpersonal Relations*. New York: John Wiley & Sons, Inc., 1958.

James, W., *Principles of Psychology*, 2 vols. New York: Holt, Rinehart & Winston, Inc., 1890.

Lewin, K., A Dynamic Theory of Personality. New York: McGraw-Hill Book Company, Inc., 1935.

Murphy, G., *Personality: A Biosocial Approach to Origins and Structure*. New York: Harper & Row, Publishers, 1947.

Murray, H. A., *Explorations in Personality*. New York: Oxford University Press, 1938.

Osgood, C. E. and P. H. Tannenbaum, "The Principle of Congruity in the Prediction of Attitude Change," *Psychological Review*, **62** (1955), 42-55.

Rogers, C. R., *Client-Centered Therapy: Its Current Practice, Implications, and Theory*. Boston: Houghton Mifflin Company, 1951.

Uncertainty and Conflict: A Point of Contact Between Information-Theory and Behavior-Theory Concepts *

D. E. Berlyne

Information theory, originally designed to handle certain problems in communications engineering (41), needs to be distinguished from *psychological information theory,* which is one of its offshoots. The former consists of a mathematical language, incorporating a number of distinctive

* From D. E. Berlyne, "Uncertainty and Conflict: A Point of Contact Between Information-Theory and Behavior-Theory Concepts," *Psychological Review*, **64** (1957), 329-39. Reprinted by permission of the author and the American Psychological Association.

This article owes a great deal to discussions with Dr. I. R. Savage and several other colleagues at the Center for Advanced Study in the Behavioral Sciences. It was written while the author was on leave of absence from the University of Aberdeen, Scotland.

measuring techniques. Psychological information theory is, in contrast, a type of theory in the scientific sense: it applies information-theory measures to phenomena within the purview of psychology and uses information-theory language to formulate laws or hypotheses with testable implications about behavior.

Recent literature contains several sketches of such theory (for example, 1, 26, 35), mostly concerned with how human beings code information or with how much information can pass through them in particular situations. There are many unmistakable affinities between this kind of psychological theory and S-R behavior theory (learning theory): they have overlapping interests in such matters as discrimination, remembering, and reaction time, they share a predilection for operationally definable and quantitative concepts, and they start out, respectively, from the closely related "black-box" and "neobehaviorist" points of view. It is therefore rather disappointing that so little integration between theories of the two types has yet taken place. We can regard two theories as "integrated" if one can be deduced from the other or if both can be deduced from a third theory. Before any integration can be attempted, the scope of information-theory language within the domain of behavior theory must be examined, which means considering to what extent recourse to it is *possible* and to what extent, if possible, it is *useful.*

The use of information-theory measures is *possible* whenever we have a *partition,* that is, a set of phenomena that can be divided into non-overlapping subsets, and a *probability distribution,* i.e., a way of associating with each subset a number of 0 to 1, such that the numbers associated with all the subsets in the partition add up to 1. Whenever these two requirements are fulfilled, such measures as "amount of information," "uncertainty," and "relative uncertainty" can be applied. As soon as we have *two* sets of phenomena satisfying both requirements, the two can jointly be regarded as a "transducer," and the relations between them described in terms of "transmitted information," "noise," and "equivocation."

The phenomena that concern behavior theory consist, in fact, of two sets that can be partitioned into subsets with associated probabilities, namely *stimuli* and *responses.* The language of information theory is therefore, in principle, applicable to everything within the competence of behavior theory. Two limitations to its appro-

priateness have often been pointed out (14, 47). One is that the behavior theorist is especially interested in learning, that is, in situations where probabilities of responses are changing. The other is that information-theory measures take no account of any ordering of the subsets in the partition or, more particularly, of the fact that stimuli and responses are not confined to nominal scaling (44). But these limitations are not insuperable. Information-theory measures can be derived from response probabilities at different stages of a learning process and compared, or else they can be applied when learning is near its asymptote. Stimuli and responses can be successively described in information-theory terms and in terms of physical or psychophysical dimensions, and the different measures can be related. For example, a response-class can have attached to it both a mean reaction time and a rate of transmitted information, and connections between the two can be explored.

If the possibility of describing the domain of behavior theory in information-theory language is accepted, the question of its *usefulness* still remains. One of the principal functions of any language is to make secondary or mediated generalization and discrimination possible. A language incorporates classifications, of which measures are special cases. Classifications are procedures for attaching certain descriptive terms (values in the case of measures) as verbal responses to certain items in the universe of discourse but not to others. Items bearing a common verbal label come to evoke similar behavior in the users of the language. A classification is useful only as long as the items allotted the same label share some important quality, such that a common response to them will be rewarded (or reinforced) despite other qualities that might distinguish them. Information-theory measures are useful for the description of behavior, therefore, if these measures are closely related to other variables that have proved to be important for psychology.

A large body of data demonstrating that such is the case has been amassed within the last ten years. Reaction time, retention of verbal material, and accuracy of psychophysical judgment, to cite examples, appear to be functions of "uncertainty" and "amount of transmitted information." The situations in which such associations have been found have, however, been situations in which *subjects have some knowledge of the range of alternative stimuli that might occur and of their probabilities.* This knowledge is provided by E's instructions, or by the presentation of a sufficient sample of material for estimates to be made, or, as in experiments using natural languages, by previous training. It has, indeed, been contended by Cronbach (14) that information-theory measures in psychology should be confined to cases where "the receiver knows the probabilities and joint probabilities of the source." As Cherry reminds us, information theory is part of the "metalanguage of an external observer; it is not a description of the process of communication as it appears to one of the participants" (13, p. 170). An observer can compute information-theory measures from data not accessible to the individuals he is observing. But there is not likely to be much connection between these measures and variables of psychological importance, unless there is some isomorphism between the situation as viewed by the observer and the situation as it impinges on the observed organism.

The situations in which the use of information-theory terminology has had

some success can be analyzed further as follows:

1. There is an antecedent stimulus-pattern, S_x. It may consist of the background conditions of the experiment, of an E's warning signal or, in sequential studies, of any item in a sequence.

2. Whenever S_x occurs, it is followed by one and only one of a set of consequent stimuli $\{S_1 \ldots S_n\}$.

3. Whenever one of the consequent stimuli occurs, a particular response corresponding to it is performed.

4. The responses corresponding to the consequent stimuli are such that no more than one of them can be performed at once, whether because of the E's instructions or because of some physiological incompatibility between them.

In such situations, one can predict that all the n responses corresponding to the n consequent stimuli will become conditioned to S_x. No more than fractional components of these responses can be expected to occur immediately after the onset of S_x, both because simultaneous performance of the complete responses is precluded by the conditions of the experiment and because performance of any of them before the consequent stimulus appears will not be reinforced, so that the conditions for inhibition of delay will be fulfilled (38). S_x will thus come to evoke *competing response tendencies.* For Hull's theory (27, 28), these response tendencies will be "reaction potentials." Cognitive behavior theories (for example, 45) would describe them as "expectations" of the consequent stimuli, and the "expectation" resembles the "reaction potential" insofar as both imply the occurrence of a particular response, if certain additional conditions are met.

Furthermore, the relative *strengths* of the competing response tendencies will reflect the probabilities of the corresponding stimuli. Whether one regards the number of reinforced trials (27, 28), the variety of stimulus situations that have been contiguous with the response (23), or the number of times an expectation has been confirmed (45) as the decisive factor, responses associated with more frequent consequent stimuli will become more strongly associated with S_x. There is, in fact, experimental evidence (17, 21) that the strength of a predictive verbal response (which is especially relevant here), as judged by the asymptote of response probability, increases with the probability of the corresponding stimulus.

To sum up, the situations in which information-theory language has been of value are ones in which *conflict* is an important factor, and the theory of conflict seems to be one area where linkages between information theory and behavior theory may hopefully be sought.

DEGREE OF CONFLICT (C)

If the study of conflict is to progress beyond noting the effects of its presence or absence, some way of distinguishing *degrees of conflict* will have to be adopted. The degree of conflict is, of course, not necessarily the same as the *severity of the effects of conflict,* of which it is likely to be merely one determinant. Other determinants would be the nature of the conflicting response tendencies (for example, whether they are approach or avoidance tendencies [36]) and the conflict tolerance of an individual organism. Brown and Farber (11) suggest two conditions for the degree-of-conflict function (or, as they call it, "frustration"), viz., that it increase with the *absolute strengths* of the competing tendencies, and that it increase as their strengths approach

equality. They, like most writers who have considered psychological conflict, confine their attention to conflicts between two response tendencies. If conflicts involving three or more alternatives are to be included in the treatment, as would seem desirable, the *number* of competing tendencies can be proposed as a third variable with which degree of conflict increases (4).

We can thus state the conditions for a degree-of-conflict function a little more precisely, as follows. Let us assume that response tendencies corresponding to a set of responses $\{R_1 \ldots R_n\}$ occur in an organism, that the responses in the set are such that no two of them can be performed at once, and that some non-negative quantity E (for example, Hull's "reaction potential") can be associated with each response tendency (as a measure of its strength).

It should be noted that, although the *responses* cannot occur simultaneously, we are assuming that their corresponding *response tendencies* can. Second, there is no reason why several independent sets of competing response tendencies should not be aroused in the same organism at once. Third, we are considering cases where there is complete incompatibility, whether innate or learned, between alternative responses. It is, however, conceivable that two responses may be *partially* antagonistic, that is, the evocation of one may reduce the amplitude or probability of the other without excluding its performance altogether. This may suggest *degree of incompatibility* between responses as an additional determinant of degree of conflict (4), which would complicate any mathematical treatment. Possible ways of reducing degree of incompatibility to other variables, when learned incompatibility is involved, are considered elsewhere (7).

The degree-of-conflict function $C(E_1 \ldots E_n)$ should then have the following properties:

1. C is continuous and symmetric in the E_i;
2. $C \geqq 0$;
3. if $n = 1$, $C = 0$;
4. with $\sum_{i=1}^{n} E_i$ held constant, C reaches an absolute maximum when $E_1 = E_2 = \ldots = E_n$;
5. if $E_1 = E_2 = \ldots = E_n$, and a response R_{n+1} with strength $E_{n+1} = E_1$ is added to the set $\{R_1 \ldots R_n\}$, C increases;
6. if every E_i is multiplied by $k > 1$, C increases.

Now, let us suppose that we have a way of translating the E value for each response in a p value, or measure of probability, such that

1. $0 \leqq p \leqq 1$;
2. $\sum_{i=1}^{n} p_i = 1$;
3. if $E_1 = E_2 = \ldots = E_n$, then $p_1 = p_2 = \ldots p_n = 1/n$;
4. if one E_i increases with the others held constant, then the corresponding p increases and the other p's decrease.

Some theorists (for example, 12, 16) content themselves with probability as a sole measure of response strength. Others (for example, 27, 42, 43) recognize additional ones, such as latency, frequency, resistance to extinction, amplitude and vigor. Of these, mean latency and mean frequency are merely the reciprocal of the probability that a response of the class in question will occur during one unit of time. Resistance to extinction may be regarded as the rate at which response probability decreases when reinforcement is withdrawn. But other measures of response strength, expressing the energy with which the response is performed, are not the same as probabilities. Hull (28, pp. 25 ff.) and Spence (43, App. A) present methods for transforming Es into probabilities, when E is the Hullian reaction potential. Doing this means, however, losing information, since many sets of E values can be represented by the same set of p values. Whenever we have two or more independently defined response classes, as distinct from one response class and its complement, probability is a measure of *relative* and not absolute response strength. The distinction may be important. For example, Mr. A. may be torn between his duty to the community and his duty to his family, while Mr. B. may have difficulty in deciding whether or not to spend a small sum on a newspaper. Both of them have two response tendencies with probabilities of .5, but in other respects the effects of the two conflicts may be radically different.

Be that as it may, the use of probabilities to express response strengths provides us with the partition and the probability distribution that are necessary conditions for recourse to information-theory measures. And if we examine the information theorist's formula for "uncertainty" or "entropy" ($-\Sigma_i \, p_i \, log_2 \, p_i$), we find that it satisfies the first five of our requirements for a degree-of-conflict function, but not the sixth. It increases with the number of alternative responses and is at a maximum when their strengths are equal. But it does not vary with their absolute strengths. In order to make "uncertainty" fulfill all our conditions, we can multiply it by some such quantity as the mean E. French's hypothesis (20) that the frustrating effects of a binary conflict are a function of the weaker of the two opposing forces suggests that "uncertainty" should be multiplied by the minimum rather than the mean E. But this would produce rather anomalous results in higher-order conflicts when there are one very weak and several very strong response tendencies in competition. Our expression for degree of conflict then becomes $- \bar{E} \Sigma_i \, p_i \log p_i \ldots 1$. Put somewhat differently, "uncertainty" can be regarded as an indication of the "complexity" of a conflict, or of the difficulty that an observer would have in predicting which of the conflicting responses will be the first to occur. It does not reflect the "scale" of the conflict, which depends on the energy invested in the competing response tendencies. There may be a temptation to relate these two components to the *utility* and *probability-of-outcome* factors that must be taken into account in decision theory, or to the *motivational* and *structural* factors that often have been distinguished in psychological literature. But any such correspondence would be misleading. Both the "uncertainty" and the $\bar{E}$ are determined by absolute response strengths, which depend on both motivational (utility) and structural (probability-of-outcome) variables; for example, Hull's "reaction potential" (28) depends on "drive" and "amount of reinforcement" on the one hand and on "number of reinforcements" (habit-strength) on the other. It is interesting to observe that Shannon (41, p. 19) gives $- K \Sigma_i \, p_i \log p_i$ as the only function satisfying his assumptions, and goes on to describe K as amounting to a "choice of a unit of measure" or, in other words, to some scaling factor comparable to our $\bar{E}$.

Expression 1 is, however, by no means the only one that will accord with our requirements. Another function, for example, that will do so without necessitating a transformation of E, is $\Sigma_i \, E_i \, (\log \Sigma_j \, E_i) - \log E_i) \ldots 2$. If E represents Hull's reaction potential, this function will not, in general,

have the same values as Expression 1, because probabilities are not proportional to reaction potentials. It will, however, be an increasing monotonic transform of Expression 1.

We are not even confined to logarithmic functions, since we lack the additivity requirement that makes them mandatory for Shannon's purposes. A nonlogarithmic function that will pass muster is

$$\frac{(\Sigma \, E_i)^2 (n-1)}{1 + \Sigma_i \, (E_i - \bar{E})^2} \ldots 3.$$

Our requirements are, in fact, very weak ones, which a large number of functions will fit. Further research will, no doubt, add stipulations, allowing the range of possible functions to be narrowed down. For instance, one additional requirement that may be held reasonable, in view both of everyday observation of persons confronted with choices and of the logarithmic relation that obtains between number of alternative stimuli and choice reaction time, is that C should be a negatively accelerated increasing function of n. If this were adopted, then Expression 1 would be among those still meriting consideration, but Expressions 2 and 3 would be ruled out.

CORRELATES OF DEGREE OF CONFLICT

A degree-of-conflict measure, like an information-theory measure, can be justified as a classificatory device only if situations that have a common value assigned to them by the measure result in similar behavior, much as they may differ in other respects. The following are some psychological variables that appear likely, in the light of present knowledge, to depend on degree of conflict. They may actually turn out to be closely interrelated, but they are here separated for convenience.

1. *Emotional Disturbance*

Various writers, from Dewey (15) on, have mentioned conflict as a cause of "emotion." Both the special reaction patterns (24) and the disruption of habitual behavior (31) that are characteristic of "emotional disturbance" have been ascribed to the occurrence of divergent neural processes. The power of conflict to precipitate neurotic behavior was pointed out independently by Pavlov and by Freud, employing very different research techniques. So far, merely the dependence of these phenomena on relatively severe conflict has been noted, but future progress may well demand a quantitative treatment, in which intensities of disturbance are differentiated and related to degrees of conflict.

2. *Reaction Time*

A lengthening of reaction time (or decision time or choice time) has often been reported as a consequence of conflict (see Berlyne [7]). A link with information theory presents itself in the finding that reaction time increases linearly, at least in some conditions, with "uncertainty" (26, 29); mean reaction time has been found to increase when alternative stimuli approach equiprobability and when they become more numerous. If, as we concluded, the number of competing response tendencies corresponds to the number of alternative stimuli, and if the relative strengths of those tendencies reflect the probabilities of the corresponding stimuli, we can infer that two of the suggested determinants of C affect reaction time.

Both traditional experimental psychology and psychological information theory have hitherto concentrated on *"forced-choice"* situations, in which only one response is appropriate to each alternative stimulus, and selection of a response depends on identification of the stimulus. A recent investigation by the writer (7) compared forced choices with *free choices*. For the latter, two or more stimuli were presented together, and the response corresponding to any *one* of them was to be performed. Both kinds of choice can be assumed to entail conflict: the free choice means a conflict between response tendencies of about equal strength evoked by the stimuli that are simultaneously present, while the forced choice means an unequal and therefore relatively mild conflict between a strong tendency to respond correctly to the one stimulus that occurs and weak tendencies to make responses appropriate to other stimuli, resulting from generalization. The usual information-theory analysis of the forced choice, in which the S is viewed as a transducer with a limited channel capacity, is not helpful for the treatment of the free choice.

Free-choice reaction times invariably exceeded forced-choice reaction times, and both were longer when the number of alternative stimuli and responses was increased from two to four, as the hypothesis that reaction time increases with degree of conflict would lead one to expect. Furthermore, when the absolute strengths of the response tendencies—the determinant of degree of conflict that is disregarded by uncertainty—were manipulated by changing the intensity or extensity of the stimuli, changes in free-choice reaction time resulted.

3. *Drive*

Various considerations and observed phenomena have led a number of writers (for example, 11, 30, 46) to conclude that conflict may be a drive condition. The drive resulting from conflict as such must, of course, be distinguished from other drives that may be at a high level because conflict blocks the behavior that would normally reduce them.

A certain amount of evidence for a conflict drive was obtained by Lowell (30), who found approach-approach conflict to produce a greater speed of running in rats than a single approach tendency. A supplementary observation fitting our conception of C was that the conflict drive was not so much in evidence when the stimuli were unequal in intensity or when learning was incomplete (and the competing response tendencies presumably relatively weak).

Wyckoff's experiment (48, 49) provides other data that might be predicted from our assumptions. His pigeon Ss were rewarded with food when they pecked at a key of a certain color and not rewarded when the key was of another color. They were then tested with the key white, but the color indicating whether pecking would be reinforced or not appeared if the animal stepped on a pedal. The pedal response was rapidly learned, even though it did not affect the probability of receiving food. It merely diminished the pigeon's "uncertainty" by one bit. The white key is reminiscent of the stimulus that made the dog neurotic in the famous Shenger-Krestovnikova experiment (38, pp. 290 ff:). This stimulus, intermediate in shape between the reinforced circle and the nonreinforced ellipse, was thought by Pavlov (38, p. 318) to produce a "conflict between excitation and inhibition." If the white key produced a conflict in Wyckoff's pigeons between tendencies to peck and to refrain from pecking, or between tendencies to expect and not to expect food, the coloring of the key that was a consequence of stepping on the pedal must have reduced the conflict by strengthening one response tendency and weakening the other. If a conflict drive is proportional to C,

reduction of the drive can be expected to reinforce the pedal-stepping response. When the discrimination was reversed, Wyckoff found that the frequency of the pedal response would temporarily decrease. This also fits our interpretation, as each color would then go through a stage of evoking both tendencies, and seeing the colored key would thus increase rather than reduce conflict. Wyckoff himself offers an alternative explanation in terms of secondary reinforcement, but this leads into difficulties, as Prokasy points out in his report of a somewhat similar experiment (39).

Yet another relevant experiment is one by Fonberg (19). She trained dogs to perform a certain response (R_1) as a way of terminating stimuli that had been associated with puffs of air or electric shocks. The animals then received training in quite a different response (R_2), which was followed by food reinforcement in the presence of a loud tone but not in the presence of a faint tone. When they were later subjected to a Shenger-Krestovnikova type of conflict by exposure to tones intermediate in intensity between the positive and negative alimentary conditioned stimuli, they reverted to their defensive response (R_1). This finding indicates that the physiological state produced by a conflict, even when noxious stimuli have played no part in it, may be sufficiently similar to the physiological state (fear or anxiety) resulting from a noxious stimulus for generalization between the two to occur.

4. Curiosity

There is currently a good deal of interest in certain sorts of behavior whose main function seems to be the provision of information, and information theory might reasonably be expected to throw some light on them. The behavior under discussion includes the "exploratory" activities that bring about opportunities to perceive objects more readily; the verbal activities, including asking questions, that elicit informative verbal behavior from other individuals; and the symbolic activities that allow thought processes to feed on information other than that supplied by the immediate environment.

"Novelty" has often been mentioned as a distinguishing mark of situations that provoke such activities (2, 6). But something can either be relatively novel, in the sense that it has never been encountered before in its present context, or absolutely novel, in the sense that it has never been encountered at all. In both cases, we have situations in which "amount of information" is high, since this measure is inversely related to the probability of an event, and the probability of particular novel occurrence must be low in the light of an individual's past experience. We can also speak of conflict in connection with the same occurrences. A relatively novel stimulus pattern is one in which perception conflicts with the expectations aroused by the context. Moreover, at least as far as human beings are concerned, any absolutely novel object is bound to consist of an unfamiliar combination of familiar elements or to possess characteristics intermediate between those of several well-known objects. Such an object can be expected to induce conflict, since it will inevitably evoke, by generalization, responses appropriate to a number of discrepant familiar objects.

Other words that seem apposite to situations that call for investigatory behavior are "doubt," "perplexity," and "ambiguity." These words likewise imply some degree of behavioral conflict; they indicate that different aspects of a situation evoke discordant reactions or else that a particular reaction is called forth by one aspect and inhibited by another. They are opposite in meaning to words like "clear" and "distinct," which generally imply that certain response tendencies have come, through discriminatory learning, to predominate over their competitors. "Doubtful," "perplexing," or "ambiguous" stimulus situations are usually also cases of high "uncertainty" in the information-theory sense, both because the subject cannot predict very successfully what the future behavior or the hidden properties of the entities will be, and because observers will not be able to predict very successfully how he will react to them. Nevertheless, curiosity is by no means always commensurate with "uncertainty"; there are many events whose outcomes are uncertain and yet which leave us completely indifferent. For knowledge of the outcome to be rewarding, the event must be of some "interest" to us, which usually means that strong habits or drives must be aroused. In other words, curiosity seems to be a matter of conflict rather than of "uncertainty" alone; "uncertainty" may be high, but there will not be much conflict if the absolute response strengths are low. That human beings, like Wyckoff's pigeons, find relief from doubt about vital matters rewarding, even when the truth is unpleasant, is attested by common experience. Of the convicts studied by Farber (18), those who did not know how much time they would have to serve suffered more than those who were certain that they would never be paroled.

The writer suggested a few years ago (4) that at least some forms of human curiosity spring from the drive-producing properties of conflict. The conflicts that seem especially pertinent are those between implicit, most often symbolic, responses, such as "beliefs," "ways of thinking," and "ways of perceiving," whose incompatibility is largely an effect of learning. There are experimental data supporting the conclusion that curiosity, measured in various ways, is an increasing function of C (5, 8, 9).

5. Stimulus Complexity

Among the various properties by which stimulus patterns can be classified, there is a group that can only be described collectively by some such term as "complexity." They are hard to define rigorously, and a number of quite distinct dimensions will, in all likelihood, be unraveled by attempts to do so. But the influence of this aspect of perceived material is revealed in several contexts: the special properties attributed to less complex (more "prägnant") figures by the Gestalt school, the bearing of degree of complexity on aesthetic preferences, and, more recently, the influence of stimulus complexity on exploratory behavior on animals (see 10).

Attneave (1) has related the "complexity" dimension in visual figures to information theory through the concept of "redundancy," the inverse of "relative uncertainty." His treatment suggests a possible link between these variables and conflict. More "complex" stimulus patterns might well be those arousing more conflict, for example, between perception of one part and expectations of redintegrative perceptual responses (3, 24, 37) aroused by other parts, between verbal or other classificatory responses, or between ocular and other orienting movements. If this hypothesis is well founded, we should expect more "complex" (or less "redundant") figures, like figures arousing conflict in other ways, to elicit more investigatory behavior. Experimental data confirming this prediction are available (8, 9).

6. Reward

While the punishing or drive producing role of conflict is more evident and has received more attention, the possibility that conflict and uncertainty may at times be rewarding is suggested by gambling and aesthetic behavior. Similarly, journalistic practice seems to indicate a positive relation between the reward value of a piece of news and the "amount of information" it contains, which depends on its improbability or surprisingness (40). Surprise, like novelty, seems to mean some sort of clash between the reactions occasioned by an unexpected situation and those evoked anticipatorily through previously established habits (3). Surprising statements are, at least in certain circumstances, recalled more readily than others (5), and maze-learning experiments (see 10) show that exposure to a more complex environment (which, as we have seen, may mean a more conflictful environment) can be more reinforcing than exposure to a simpler one.

If conflict is usually an aversive condition but occasionally functions as a reward, it resembles fear, which likewise seems to be actively sought at times, for example, at fairgrounds and in dangerous sports. The analogy with fear suggests two hypotheses to account for the paradox. One is that drive arousal may be rewarding at a moderate level. Hebb refers to "the *positive attraction of risk-taking,* or mild fear, *and of problem-solving,* or mild frustration," and speculates that "when arousal or drive is at a low level . . . a response that produces increased stimulation and greater arousal will tend to be repeated" (25, p. 250). McClelland *et al.* (33) propound a rather similar hypothesis, whose bearing on conflict is a little more conspicuous: "positive affect is the result of smaller discrepancies of a sensory or perceptual event from the adaptation of the organism; negative affect is the result of larger discrepancies." There have been a number of recent studies (for example, Marx *et al.* [32]) showing that an increase in illumination up to a certain intensity will reinforce a bar-pressing response in a rat, while light of much greater intensity is known to be aversive.

The second hypothesis is that such states as fear or conflict are sought only when their arousal in similar circumstances has reliably and speedily been followed by drive reduction in the past. Two recent works by empirically minded aestheticians provide some corroboration for these hypotheses. Graves (22) contends that the appeal of a visual design depends on variety, but that one part or quality must be made to dominate the others if the effect is to be satisfying. This would keep within bounds any conflict aroused. In accord with the second hypothesis, Meyer (34) shows that music owes much of its savor to continual departures from what preceding or accompanying patterns lead the listener to expect. But what is initially heard as an incongruity is invested with a new meaning by what follows, so that the momentary conflict is promptly resolved.

SUMMARY

The use of information-theory measures is possible whenever there is a partition and a probability distribution. The stimuli and responses of behavior theory fulfill these conditions, but the situations in which information-theory language has proved useful to psychology have been ones in which conflict is an important factor. The "uncertainty" function satisfies some of the requirements that may reasonably be laid down for a meas-ure of "degree of conflict." But it does not satisfy them all without some modification, because it depends on the relative but not the absolute strengths of competing response tendencies.

A discussion of six psychological variables that appear to depend on degree of conflict reveals several further links with information theory. The variables are emotional disturbance, reaction time, drive, curiosity, stimulus, complexity, and reward.

REFERENCES

1. Attneave, F., "Some Informational Aspects of Visual Perception," *Psychological Review,* **61** (1954), 183-93.

2. Berlyne, D. E., "Novelty and Curiosity as Determinants of Exploratory Behavior," *British Journal of Psychology,* **41** (1950), 68-90.

3. ———, "Knowledge and Stimulus-Response Psychology?" *Psychological Review,* **61** (1954), 245-54.

4. ———, "A Theory of Human Curiosity," *British Journal of Psychology,* **45** (1954), 180-91.

5. ———, "An Experimental Study of Human Curiosity," *British Journal of Psychology,* **45** (1954), 256-65.

6. ———, "The Arousal and Satiation of Perceptual Curiosity in the Rat," *Journal of Comparative Physiological Psychology,* **48** (1955), 238-46.

7. ———, "Conflict and Choice Time," *British Journal of Psychology,* **48** (1957), 106-18.

8. ———, "Conflict and Information-Theory Variables as Determinants of Human Perceptual Curiosity," *Journal of Experimental Psychology,* **53** (1957), 399-404.

9. ———, "The Influence of Complexity and Change in Visual Figures on Orienting Responses," *Journal of Experimental Psychology* (1958). (In press.)

10. Berlyne, D. E. and J. Slater, "Perceptual Curiosity, Exploratory Behavior

and Maze Learning," *Journal of Comparative Physiological Psychology,* **50** (1957), 228-32.

11. Brown, J. S. and I. E. Farber, "Emotions Conceptualized as Intervening Variables—with Suggestions toward a Theory of Frustration," *Psychological Bulletin,* **48** (1951), 465-95.

12. Bush, R. R. and F. Mosteller, *Stochastic Models for Learning.* New York: John Wiley & Sons, Inc., 1955.

13. Cherry, C., *On Human Communication.* New York: John Wiley & Sons, Inc., 1957.

14. Cronbach, L. J., "On the Nonrational Application of Information Measures in Psychology," in *Information Theory in Psychology,* ed. H. Quartler. New York: Free Press of Glencoe, Inc., 1955.

15. Dewey, J., "The Theory of Emotion: II. The Significance of Emotion," *Psychological Review,* **2** (1895), 13-32.

16. Estes, W. K., "Toward a Statistical Theory of Learning," *Psychological Review,* **57** (1950), 94-107.

17. ———, "Individual Behavior in Uncertain Situations: An Interpretation in Terms of Statistical Association Theory," in *Decision Processes,* eds. R. M. Thrall *et al.* New York: John Wiley & Sons, Inc., 1954.

18. Farber, M. L., "Suffering and the Time Perspective of the Prisoner," *University of Iowa Studies in Child Welfare,* **20** (1944), 155-227.

19. Fonberg, E., "On the Manifestation of Conditioned Defensive Reactions in Stress," *Bull. Soc. Sci. et Lett.,* de Lódz, **7** (1956), 1-8.

20. French, J. R. P., "Organized and Unorganized Groups under Fear and Frustration," *University of Iowa Studies in Child Welfare,* **20** (1944), 231-308.

21. Grant, D. A., H. W. Hake, and P. Hornbeth, "Acquisition and Extinction of a Verbal Conditioned Response with Differing Percentages of Reinforcement," *Journal of Experimental Psychology,* **42** (1951), 1-5.

22. Graves, M. E., *Art of Color and Design* (2nd ed.). New York: McGraw-Hill Book Company, Inc., 1951.

23. Guthrie, E. R., *The Psychology of Learning.* New York: Harper & Row, Publishers, 1935.

24. Hebb, D. O., *The Organization of Behavior.* New York: John Wiley & Sons, Inc., 1949.

25. ———, "Drives and the C.N.S. (Conceptual Nervous System)," *Psychological Review,* **62** (1955), 243-54.

26. Hicks, W. E., "On the Rate of Gain of Information," *Quarterly Journal of Experimental Psychology,* **4** (1952), 11-26.

27. Hull, C. L., *Principles of Behavior.* New York: Appleton-Century-Crofts, Inc., 1943.

28. ———, *A Behavior System.* New Haven, Conn.: Yale University Press, 1952.

29. Hyman, R., "Stimulus Information as a Determinant or Reaction Time," *Journal of Experimental Psychology,* **45** (1953), 188-96.

30. Lowell, E. L., "The Effect of Conflict on Motivation." (Unpublished Doctoral dissertation, Harvard University, 1952.)

31. Luria, A. R., *The Nature of Human Conflicts.* New York: Liveright Publishing Corp., 1932.

32. Marx, M. H., R. L. Henderson, and C. L. Roberts, "Positive Reinforcement of the Bar-pressing Response by a Light Stimulus following Dark Operant Pre-tests with No Aftereffect," *Journal of Comparative Physiological Psychology,* **48** (1955), 73-76.

33. McClelland, D., J. W. Atkinson, R. A. Clark, and E. L. Lowell, *The Achievement Motive.* New York: Appleton-Century-Crofts, Inc., 1953.

34. Meyer, L. B., *Emotion and Meaning in Music.* Chicago: University of Chicago Press, 1956.

35. Miller, G. A., "The Magical Number Seven, Plus or Minus Two: Some limits on Our Capacity for Processing Information," *Psychological Review,* **63** (1956), 81-97.

36. Miller, N. E., "Experimental Studies of Conflict," in *Personality and the Behavior Disorders,* ed. J. McV. Hunt. New York: The Ronald Press Company, 1944.

37. Osgood, C. E., "Behavior Theory and the Social Sciences," *Behavioral Science,* **1** (1956), 167-85.

38. Pavlov, I. P., *Conditioned Reflexes.* London: Oxford University Press, 1927.

39. Prokasy, W. F., "The Acquisition of Observing Responses in the Absence of Differential External Reinforcement," *Journal of Comparative Physiological Psychology,* **49** (1956), 131-34.

40. Samson, E. W., *Fundamental Natural Concepts of Information Theory.* AFCRL Rep. E5079 (1951).

41. Shannon, C. E. and W. Weaver, *The Mathematical Theory of Communication.* Urbana: University of Illinois Press, 1949.

42. Skinner, B. F., *The Behavior of Organisms.* New York: Appleton-Century-Crofts, Inc., 1938.

43. Spence, K. W., *Behavior Theory and Conditioning.* New Haven, Conn.: Yale University Press, 1956.

44. Stevens, S. S., "Mathematics, Measurement and Psychophysics," in *Handbook of Experimental Psychology,* ed. S. S. Stevens. New York: John Wiley & Sons, Inc., 1951.

45. Tolman, E. C., *Purposive Behavior in Animals and Man.* New York: Appleton-Century-Crofts, Inc., 1932.

46. Whiting, J. W. M. and I. L. Child, *Child Training and Personality.* New Haven, Conn.: Yale University Press, 1953.

47. Wilson, K., "The Information Theory Approach," in *Psycholinguistics, Journal of Abnormal Social Psychology,* **49** (4, Part 2—Suppl. [1954]), 35-49.

48. Wyckoff, L. B., "The Role of Observing Responses in Discrimination Learning: Part I," *Psychological Review,* **59** (1952), 431-42.

49. ———, "The Role of Observing Responses in Discrimination Learning: Part II." (Unpublished Doctoral dissertation, University of Indiana, 1951.)

Toward a Theory of Epistemic Behavior: Conceptual Conflict and Epistemic Curiosity*

D. E. Berlyne

Experimental studies of conflict between overt responses are difficult enough to conduct and have been scanty, considering the importance of the topic. To extend the notion of conflict to implicit responses thus amounts to quite a bold scouting expedition. It is not unreasonable, however, to suppose that there can be incompatibilities between symbolic responses and that the conflict engendered by them, which we shall call *conceptual conflict,* may affect the central nervous system in much the same way as other forms of conflict.

Among a number of recent writers who have recognized something like

* From D. E. Berlyne, *Conflict, Arousal, and Curiosity* (Toronto: McGraw-Hill Book Company, Inc., 1960), pp. 283-303. Reprinted by permission of the author and publisher.

our conceptual conflict (for example, Heider 1946, Osgood and Tannenbaum 1955, Cartwright and Harary 1956), Festinger (1957) and Abelson (Abelson and Rosenberg 1958, Abelson 1958) have come closest to our concept, while concentrating on different aspects of the phenomenon.

Festinger's "dissonance" is a relation that can obtain between two "cognitive elements" (beliefs, evaluations, perceptions) or between a cognitive element and an overt action that the subject either is contemplating or has already executed. He actually subsumes the second case under the first by referring to the cognitive element corresponding to the action (that is, the memory or the thought of performing it). Most of his discussion is, however, devoted to the second case. He also deals preponderantly with dissonances between evaluations rather than between factual beliefs. Dissonance is defined in terms of logical contradiction ("p implies not-q"), but, taken strictly, this definition does not fit many of the instances that are analyzed. The statement, "Car A is superior to car B," and the statement, "I have bought car B," are certainly not contradictory in the usual sense that they cannot both be true. It seems better to invoke the more general notion of conflict.

When dissonance is present, there is held to be a drive toward its reduction, with a strength depending on the importance of the areas between which the clash occurs and the proportion (suitably weighted) of all relations between these areas that happen to be dissonant.

Dissonance can be reduced in a variety of ways, for example, by changing evaluations of conflicting elements, by reducing the importance attached to them, by propagating rumors to justify hard-pressed beliefs or evalua-

tions, or by seeking social support from other persons who share them. Most interesting of all, in view of our current interest in stimulus selection, is Festinger's prediction that dissonance will help to determine what stimuli are sought out, favoring pursuit of those which are likely to moderate dissonance and avoidance of those which are apt to aggravate it. In harmony with this prediction, it was found that motorists tend to expose themselves to advertisements that commend the make of car that they have bought rather than to advertisements extolling the virtues of other makes that they might have chosen. There are, however, other hypotheses that might explain such phenomena differently.

Abelson's theory of "cognitive imbalance" is even more frankly focused on discrepancies among evaluations rather than factual beliefs. Cognitive elements can be valued positively, negatively, or neutrally, and between any two of these elements there can be an associative relation (expressed by words like "is," "has," "includes," "likes," "helps," "produces," "implies") or a dissociative relation (expressed by words like "avoids," "hates," "hinders," "defeats," "destroys," "is incompatible with"). Imbalance is said to exist when two positively or two negatively valued elements are dissociatively linked or when a positively valued and a negatively valued element are associatively linked, and there is assumed to be a "pressure toward the attainment of cognitive balance."

Imbalance can be reduced by reorganizing attitudes and belief in any of the following four ways:

1. *Denial.* The evaluation of one of the elements involved is changed. For example, a man who would like both to be slim and to eat rich foods, but

realizes that it is impossible to satisfy both likes, professes that he never liked rich foods anyway.

2. *Bolstering.* One of the elements is linked with other ideas that are associated with strong attitudes and with whose assistance the opposing belief or evaluation can be outweighed. For example, the smoker who is worried about lung cancer decides that smoking is a bad habit and costs too much money.

3. *Differentiation.* A distinction is made within one of the conflicting elements, such that some aspect of it is valued positively and the other negatively. For example, a tendency to believe in the truth of the Bible and a tendency to believe in the theory of evolution are reconciled by differentiating literal truth and figurative truth and attributing only the latter to the Bible.

4. *Transcendence.* The conflicting elements are combined into some larger unit which is collectively viewed with favor or disfavor. For example, a partiality for both science and religion, perceived as leading in opposing directions, may give rise to the feeling that a well-rounded life requires the cultivation of both.

Our own concern with conceptual conflict leads us in different directions from those pursued by Festinger and Abelson. We are interested primarily in conflicts arising out of the denotative content rather than the affective tone of beliefs or thoughts and also in the relations between such conflicts and the pursuit of knowledge.

Nevertheless, there is much in common between these conceptions, despite their divergent emphases. The ways in which dissonance or imbalance can be removed, according to these other authors, parallel the ways in which the acquisition of knowledge can relieve conflict, as we shall see. Fur-

thermore, all these theories are alike in recognizing that the beliefs, attitudes, and other symbolic processes of an individual do not exist in isolation but interact, that there can be discrepancies between them that the individual is motivated to remedy.

This is one respect in which the human nervous system differs from the electronic computer, with which it is so often compared. The computer is apt to come to a halt as soon as any obstacle is placed in the way of its functioning, for example, when it is given some instruction that it cannot execute or when the information that is necessary for a particular operation is lacking. The human nervous system does not accept such situations passively. On the other hand, computers may one day be programmed to react constructively to conflicts between instructions or deficiencies in information. They will then be able to raise and solve problems of their own formulation and exercise control over the information that they take in.

VARIETIES OF CONCEPTUAL CONFLICT

Conceptual conflict can presumably result, like other forms of conflict, from innate antagonism, learned antagonism, or occlusion. In so far as symbolic representations embody evaluations—characterizations of things as good or bad, pleasant or unpleasant—they may well involve autonomic processes, glandular processes, or processes in the limbic system of the lower brain. If an individual is subjected simultaneously to conditions that lead him to evaluate the same entity both favorably and unfavorably, physiological processes that are innately antagonistic may be aroused at once.

When muscular activities are represented in thought, weak action currents are detectable in the muscles that these activities would bring into play. It is thus possible, here again, that there would be some physiological incompatibility when activities that would mean contraction and relaxation of the same muscles are called to mind at once.

The possibilities for occlusion that arise from the ramification of associations are impossible to overlook. Whether it is practicable to think two thoughts at once is a question that is inherently difficult to settle. But let us suppose that each thought is, on the average, associated with n other thoughts, and let us even suppose that n thoughts could be entertained simultaneously. Each of these n thoughts would then arouse n other thoughts in the next unit of time, producing a total of n^2, then n^3, and so on. The limits of channel capacity, however capacious, must rapidly be overstepped.

Most conceptual conflict will, however, fall clearly into the learned-antagonism class. Training in the use of language, in the facts of external nature, and in the techniques of thinking will have made the subject averse to, or incapable of, fusing certain elements into one symbolic unit. He will have learned that the various stimulus properties that populate the universe and form the substance of his own thoughts are not independent of one another. Some occur together more often and some less often. Some are invariably found in juxtaposition and some never. There may thus arise an acquired mutual inhibitory relation between the concepts, or their combination may become drive inducing. Some of the major types of conceptual conflict that can come about in this way may be enumerated as follows, without maintaining that the list is complete or that the boundaries between them are sharp.

Doubt. There is, first of all, the conflict between tendencies to believe and to disbelieve the same statement. Doubt will presumably create maximum conflict when the tendencies to believe and to disbelieve are equal in strength, and when maximally strong but incompatible overt responses are associated with them. The agonies of Othello illustrate the point admirably.

We class doubt provisionally as learned antagonism. It is, however, entirely possible that it involves some kind of excitatory and inhibitory neural processes with an innate physiological opposition between them.

Perplexity. When there are factors inclining the subject toward each of a number of mutually exclusive beliefs, for example, when there is some evidence favoring each of them but no way of knowing for certain which is true, we have the second type of conceptual conflict. This is the kind of situation for which the information-theory measure of uncertainty was originally designed and to which it can be most naturally applied. Perplexity must encompass doubt, since there will be factors simultaneously supporting and inhibiting each of the alternative beliefs when it is contemplated separately.

Contradiction. It was long believed among philosophers that the ability to recognize logical contradictions is inborn and one of the peculiar glories of the human mind. This view is now much less prevalent for several reasons: the demonstration by logicians and mathematicians that what is and is not a contradiction varies with the axiom system that is under consideration, the studies of developmental psychologists like Piaget who show that the logical capacities necessary for avoidance of contradiction are acquired gradually, and, finally, a mass of experimental and anecdotal evidence that few adults are infallibly immune to illogicality. It seems reasonable, therefore, to suppose that human beings eschew fallacious thinking, in so far as they do so, as a result of learning, because the overt expression of thinking that violates the laws of thought leads to disapproval and ridicule from parents, teachers, and peers, or otherwise that illicit deduction comes to be associated with sad disappointments in the course of attempts to predict and control events. Either way, symbolic sequences that make for contradiction will come to arouse a drive, provided that the contradiction is recognized as such.

Conceptual Incongruity. The fourth type of conceptual conflict occurs when a subject has learned to believe that property *A* is unlikely to be found together with property *B*, and yet sources of knowledge indicate that a certain object or event has both *A* and *B*. Earlier chapters have dealt with perceptual incongruity, which occurs when properties regarded as incompatible are perceived together. In that case, the conflict is between the perceptual responses evoked through stimulation of receptors and those evoked centrally through redintegration. Conceptual incongruity, on the other hand, arises out of learned conflict between symbolic responses. Perceptual incongruity would occur when a person who expects all swans to be white first sees a black swan. Conceptual incongruity would occur when a person who has hitherto believed that all swans are white hears, reads, or deduces that black swans exist.

Confusion. Stimulus patterns that are ambiguous or can be confused with one another may give rise to conflicting symbolic responses in much the same way as they arouse conflicting identifying or overt responses. When we first see a hybrid animal like the tigon, the stimulus pattern is sufficiently similar to those produced by a lion and a tiger to evoke responses corresponding to both and yet not so much nearer the one than the other that one set of responses will predominate.

An experience of this kind might leave one wondering which the animal could have been. But conceptual and perceptual ambiguity or confusion is probably most frequently a product of symbolic stimuli—drawings, letters of the alphabet, verbal descriptions— either because the person creating them has not succeeded in conveying his intent unequivocally or because the symbolic pattern undergoes distortion between leaving him and impinging on the recipient's receptors. In information-theory language, there is apt to be noise at several points along the channel.

Irrelevance. This is by far the hardest kind of conceptual dissonance conflict to define, let alone to explain. But there is no doubt about the strength of the learned aversive quality that it can have. In any form of psychotherapy that uses free association, the patient invariably takes a few days to accustom himself to flitting inconsequentially from topic to topic and, in fact, rarely succeeds in doing so to more than a minor extent. His previous training to speak and think coherently provokes resistance long before his free association has led him to touch on anything delicate or anxiety-laden.

The learning process involved may be partly the same as that responsible for the clustering of words belonging to a common category in recall: we learn to connect thoughts with certain supraordinate concepts or topics, and there is a disinclination to entertain ideas on a different topic until all available ideas pertaining to the topic of the moment have been exhausted. It may be partly a matter of learning to distinguish the ways in which thoughts conducive to successful thinking are related to the problem on hand. Finally, we are all so thoroughly taught to follow threads in other people's conversation that severe frustration and arousal are apt to result when efforts to connect one utterance with the last meet with difficulty. Generalization or punishment will explain why similar discomfort supervenes when our own utterances or thoughts are not linked together perspicuously.

In information-theory terms, doubt and ambiguity are states of high uncertainty, since the subject is faced with a number of alternative states of affairs leading to different expectations with regard to future events, and he must treat them as more or less equally probable. Conceptual incongruity means a state of affairs with a low initial probability and thus a high information content, while contradiction means a state with a probability of zero and bearing an infinite amount of information (see Bar Hillel and Carnap, 1953). Irrelevant thoughts correspond to signals that are statistically independent of important events and consequently bear no information about them, leaving high uncertainty undiminished. So in all cases, we have the makings of intense arousal.

THE SEQUENCE OF EVENTS

We have noted how both cue stimuli and motivational or drive-inducing stimuli are required both to propel a quest for knowledge and to control its course. It is plain that some pattern including stimuli of both sorts will be needed to set the quest in motion in the first place.

The clearest example of such a pattern is a question. Some quests for knowledge start out with an explicit question, either put to the subject by

another person or formulated to himself as a consequence of his own thoughts or observations. But this does not always seem to be the case. There are even instances of divertive epistemic curiosity, when somebody is eager to learn something new without much caring what. All specific epistemic behavior must, however, be launched by the equivalent of a question.

In the grammatical structure of a question, the cue and motivational components are fairly distinct. The yes-or-no question, for example, "Has the train for London left yet?" contains a reference to an event which serves as a cue, confining associations to a narrowly restricted section of the individual's repertoire. The interrogative word order supplies the motivation, indicating that conflict between expectations of affirmation and denial exists in the questioner. In the kind of question that begins with an interrogative adverb, for example, "When does the next train for London leave?" there is a similar cue element, but the interrogative adverb provides a motivating perplexity conflict; it implies an information space, with some attendant uncertainty in the questioner. He must know the kinds of answers that are given to questions beginning with "when," especially to questions about the times of trains. He may even be able to assign probabilities to the various times that the train might depart, making it possible to work out a measure of his uncertainty.

There is ample testimony in everyday life to the power with which questions can impel the delivery of an answer if known, or a search for an answer otherwise. The gruffest and surliest of crosspatches finds it hard to ignore a direct question to the point of saying nothing at all. Persistent interrogation, even without accompanying physical and psychological pressures, has led many a criminal to make revelations very much opposed to his interests. The skillful lecturer or writer excites curiosity and an eagerness to remain with him by putting questions which have never occurred to his listeners or readers. Celebrated thinkers have not infrequently been stimulated to a lifetime's inquiry through thinking of questions about matters that ordinary men take for granted.

Once the quest for an answer has begun, the uncertainty and conflict implicit in the question will inevitably be augmented by conceptual conflicts of other kinds:

1. The question itself may embody conceptual incongruity. For example, "What crops do some ants cultivate in underground farms?" is especially likely to stimulate curiosity in a person who has never heard of fungus-growing ant colonies, since it embodies the assertion, contrary to his prior beliefs, that insects can engage in agriculture.

2. In a subject who is versed in entomology, any utterance that juxtaposes "ants" with "farms" will, through patterning, evoke associations peculiar to fungus-growing ants. In one who is not, there will be no associations peculiar to the combination. But, knowing how difficult it is to keep the mind blank, we shall expect some thoughts to emerge. The thoughts that are most likely to come up are those which are associated with the separate elements. The word *ants* will give rise to thoughts about small, black, busy insects and the word *farming* to thoughts of life in human rural communities. The two trains of thought will not fit in with each other, and the resultant associations will not help in the discovery of an answer to the question, so that irrelevance conflict will grow. We may, in fact, advance the hypothesis that

the arousal value of situations where a subject is completely baffled by a problem comes partly from frustration and partly from the fact that, in default of others, irrelevant thoughts obtrude themselves.

3. After a period of thought or other epistemic behavior, the subject may light upon a number of possible answers. But as long as they all seem worth considering and there is no cause for preferring one to the others, there will be perplexity conflict.

4. Finally, one answer may be singled out as the most plausible one. But if the subject has no way of being sure that it is correct, there will be doubt conflict.

Thus conflict from a variety of sources will be present to keep epistemic curiosity alive, to keep the epistemic process moving, and to determine in what direction it will turn at each choice point.

THE REDUCTION OF CONFLICT BY THE ACQUISITION OF KNOWLEDGE

Incompatible beliefs, like incompatible habits generally, can lie dormant in the nervous system without generating any disturbance or impelling any change in the network of knowledge. Conceptual conflict and its attendant disequilibrium will not emerge until some external stimulus pattern, verbal or nonverbal, or some thought process causes incompatible symbolic responses to be aroused in combination.

There are, of course, plenty of learned responses that are capable of alleviating conceptual conflict besides those that augment knowledge. Stimulus patterns that may not square with the subject's established beliefs, or thoughts that may detonate their latent inconsistencies, can often simply be avoided. Psychoanalytic writers (for example, Freud 1913, Abraham 1921) have vividly described the sort of person who goes about in terror of knowing and understanding, who enjoys mysteries and decries anything that might possibly foist clarity or certainty onto him.

How likely an individual is to behave in these ways will depend on his personality and on how unsuccessful he has previously been in disposing of puzzles by facing them. The policy of safeguarding beliefs by shielding them from possible jolts is, however, apt to postpone trouble rather than eliminate it, which must militate against recourse to it.

Beliefs may likewise change passively, especially in their evaluative aspects, under the pressure of conceptual conflict, in much the same way as they can be tugged out of shape by the forces that make for rationalization and wishful thinking. Changes of this sort are among the processes discussed by Festinger and Abelson. But the forms that beliefs assume in this manner will reflect the interplay of internal stresses and strains more than they will correspond to external reality. The replacement of one belief by another that is less troublesome will aggravate rather than lessen conflict in a person of adequate psychological health, intelligence, and intellectual training, unless it is sanctioned by logical thinking or new external evidence.

A new belief that assuages conflict may be fostered by external stimuli that impinge on the subject through no effort of his own. As many social-psychological studies (for example, Cantril 1941, Allport and Postman 1947) have graphically depicted, periods of political and social upheaval are apt to bring with them a barrage of unprecedented experiences that unseat established expectations and beliefs. In such circumstances, human beings are extraordinarily suggestible and liable to be taken in by propaganda, to espouse any fanatical social movement that forces itself on their attention, or to accept and spread rumors, provided only that they can derive from these sources the explanations and predictions that their prior beliefs are at a loss to supply.

The conception of knowledge that we have outlined obliges us to consider all these processes as ways in which knowledge can be modified. Some would refuse to regard any but a true belief as an item of knowledge. But this is essentially an extrapsychological criterion; to use the subdivisions of *semiotic* (the science of signs and symbols) proposed by Morris (1938, 1946), this is a matter of *semantics* (the study of the relations between signs and what they stand for), whereas the psychology of symbolic processes is directly concerned only with *pragmatics* (the study of the relations between signs and the organisms that use them). Whether a belief is true or not may well affect the domain of psychology in the long run, since it determines the likelihood that a subject will encounter stimulus situations that run counter to his beliefs. Apart from this consideration, however, and with regard to events outside the present stimulus field, a false belief must affect behavior in exactly the same way as a valid one.

But even if they are classifiable as changes in knowledge, the mechanisms that we have just been reviewing do not count as epistemic behavior as long as the stimuli that generate the new belief are independent of what the subject himself does. Epistemic responses bring about knowledge-furnishing stimulus patterns that would not have been available without them.

Whatever the means by which conceptual conflict is reduced—whether it be through knowledge accruing as a consequence of epistemic behavior, through knowledge acquired independently of epistemic behavior, or through any other of the mechanisms that we have mentioned—there would seem to be only three ways in which the reduction in conflict can be effected, namely, by making the competing response tendencies less incompatible, by introducing a new response tendency that is stronger than those which are in competition, or by strengthening or weakening one or more of the competing response tendencies and thus rendering the conflict unequal. We shall refer to these three ways as *conciliation, swamping,* and *disequalization.*

Conciliation

Since the incompatibilities that make for acquired-antagonism conflict are products of learning, other learning should be able to undo them. Inhibitory bonds can be disinhibited, and acquired drive-inducing power can be removed.

To make the incompatible compatible is evidently the principal function of knowledge of the strange and wonderful, whether of the useless kind found in the odd-facts features of magazines or of the kind that can herald undreamed-of practical gains. It is discovered that, after all, black swans exist, that there are ants that cultivate crops, that somebody once wrote a full-length novel without using the letter *e* even once, that there is a mule receiving a pension from the Italian government, or that yaws can be cured by the injections that the white man administers.

Such knowledge is welcomed with eagerness, presumably because high arousal is induced when anything suggestive of a bizarre or astonishing fact is first encountered, and the arousal is diminished by exposure to evidence that convinces of its truth. The process thus follows the pattern of the arousal jag.

Swamping

In the second case, the subject acquires a new response tendency that is much stronger than the conflicting tendencies and is thus able to dominate them. In this way uncertainty ($- \Sigma_i\ p_i\ \log_2 p_i$) will be cut down to a subthreshold quantity, since we end up with one very strong, and two or more very weak, response tendencies, and conflict will be eliminated.

This process is especially likely when a subject is faced with novel combinations of concepts or with irrelevances. Irrelevant responses are almost bound to be fairly feeble. So when a new reponse that is associated with the combination as such or that is otherwise relevant to the problem is hit upon, it will readily preponderate over them.

It may be best to take a specific example. If a person with no special knowledge of marine biology is asked, or asks himself, "How does the starfish eat?" he will have no associations available that are peculiar to the thought of a starfish eating. The most likely responses are thus going to be those associated with eating, and those associated with the starfish. "Eating" will predominantly evoke thoughts about vertebrates inserting edible objects into holes in their faces, and this will be recognized as inapplicable to the starfish, which does not appear to have a face. "Starfish" will evoke thoughts derived from memories of pictures of starfishes, which are usually of the dorsal surface and so include no feature that seems pertinent to eating. The subject may even find himself completely at a loss and allow his fancy to wander farther and farther from any line of thought that could lead to a solution. When, however, he has ascertained that the starfish has an aperture on its ventral surface and that its stomach emerges through this aperture to envelop prey, he has some strong associations that will in future be called up by the unified concept of an eating starfish and will exclude the less apposite thoughts that would have occurred earlier in the same context.

The emergence of a new prepotent line of association may mitigate not only conflicts due to irrelevance but also conflicts due to contradiction or occlusion. Swamping by a new response sequence will, of course, be most easily established when the other, conflicting responses have yielded to some degree of extinction through failure to bring a solution nearer.

Disequalization

Conceptual conflicts, like other conflicts, can be reduced by increasing the difference in strength between competing response tendencies, that is, strengthening one, weakening the other, or both. In other words, one of the contestants is made to win the competition or, at least, to have the upper hand. Situations where perplexity conflicts are attenuated by eliminating some of the alternatives are cases in point. Disequalization is, no doubt, the commonest way in which conceptual conflicts are allayed by the absorption of new knowledge. There is usually some measure of perplexity commingled with conflicts of the other types.

More often than not, a fact of which one becomes newly aware is one that could have been specified as a possibility beforehand. A sophisticated human adult probably meets few problems in his everyday life for which he cannot supply guesses at a solution. To acquire knowledge and to feel the lack of knowledge, one must generally have some knowledge to begin with. Only the expert in a field can tell where information is lacking and use observations or verbal formulas which would mean nothing to the uninitiated to fill in the gaps.

Information, in the technical sense, cannot be received without having an information space already set up; the signal that appears must belong to one of a number of alternative classes that might have appeared, and it must have a probability allotted to it. But one must already be in possession of information before one can establish an information space, since the space must itself be selected from a set of alternative information spaces.

So knowledge relieves uncertainty by strengthening one expectation at the expense of the others and relieves doubt by confirming or discounting the belief in question.

Herein may lie the answer to the problem about the explorer that we raised in the last chapter. It is true that the explorer can immediately picture himself on the other side of the stream, as the logician or mathematician can, from the start, repeat to himself the expression that is to be proved. But these thoughts cannot be entertained with conviction, that is, the corresponding symbolic responses are overlaid with conflict-inducing inhibition, unless they can be preceded by the discovery of a valid solution. Only when the explorer has conceived of a chain of events that would in fact place him and his party beyond the stream, or the logician has worked out a valid proof, can the representation of the desired result be released from inhibition and conflict eliminated.

Confusion may be resolved similarly. Knowledge about hidden properties of an object may make clear to which class it should be assigned and which symbolic label should be attached to it to govern secondary generalization and discrimination. Knowledge of measurements that cannot be estimated at a glance may show where an entity should be placed in an ordering (Berlyne 1960).

Disequalization can plainly be achieved by other means than the acquisition of knowledge, some of which are analyzed by Abelson and by Festinger, for example, denial, bolstering, obtaining social support for beliefs that are held with some misgiving, seeking out stimulus situations that are likely to reinforce such beliefs and keeping away from those that might implant doubt.

EXPERIMENTAL EVIDENCE

Conceptual Conflict and Indexes of Arousal

There is evidence that indexes of arousal, like alpha-wave blocking and the GSR, are especially marked when subjects meet with experiences that are surprising or hard to understand. It is usually impossible to say how far conflict between symbolic responses may be behind this reaction and how far it is due to the interplay of other, more immediate and primitive, responses.

Conflict among symbolic responses can be identified with more confidence as the responsible agent when manifestations of high arousal accompany intellectual effort. Setting subjects intellectual tasks, such as problems in mental arithmetic, produces GSR (Sears 1933), the breakup of alpha activity (Berger 1930), and increased muscular tension (Courts 1942). Wechsler (1925) said that the GSR is most prominent when an arithmetical problem is first attacked and sub-

sides during later stages of calculation. Toman (1943) likewise claimed that alpha blocking marks only the presentation of a problem and not the actual problem-solving work. Other workers have not corroborated this claim (see Ellingson 1956), but it would fit in with our hypotheses, since conflict should be most acute when the initial impact of a problem arouses perplexities and divergent lines of attack. It should be quite mild when a clear-cut computing procedure has been selected and is being put into effect.

There have been two experiments in which the degree of conceptual conflict has been manipulated. In one of them, Cooper and Siegel (1956) asked students to indicate their attitudes to each of twenty social groups with the help of a rating scale ranging from "like intensely" to "dislike intensely." Each of them then heard three statements expressing favorable evaluations of groups that fell near the middle of his order of preference and a fourth statement praising the group that ranked lowest in his esteem. This fourth statement, which will, of course, have been most incompatible with the subject's own beliefs, produced significantly greater GSRs than the other three.

The second of these experiments was performed by Berlyne (unpublished). Thirty-two adjective-noun pairs were selected from a list, kindly supplied by Dr. J. T. Jenkins, in such a way that half of the pairs (for example, "devilish butter," "beautiful abortion") had components that were far apart in Osgood's "semantic space," that is, they produced highly divergent responses on the semantic-differential test of meaning (Osgood, Suci, and Tannenbaum 1957). The other half (for example, "green butter," "beautiful lady") had components that were close together, that is, they produced highly similar semantic-differential responses. Each subject was given eight high-distance and eight low-distance pairs in a random order. He was instructed to treat each pair as a unified concept and carry out the semantic-differential test on it.

It was found that subjects took slightly but significantly longer to complete the ratings for the high-distance pairs. We can presume that the adjective and the noun in high-distance pairs induced conflict by inclining each rating response in discrepant directions, and, as we have noted before, a lengthening of reaction time is known to result from other types of conflict. At the end of the experiment, each pair was presented to a subject who had not had it in his list during the earlier phase, and he was asked to estimate how likely it was that the adjective would apply to the noun, for example, how likely, in some sense, butter is to be green or an abortion to be beautiful. The likelihoods were rated significantly lower for high-distance pairs, verifying that their components were related in a way that should make for conceptual conflict of the incongruity type.

Conceptual Conflict and Intrinsic Epistemic Curiosity

An endeavor to explore some relations between conceptual conflict and epistemic curiosity was made in another experimental project by Berlyne (1953, 1954b, 1954c). The first objective was to verify that curiosity can be intensified simply by putting questions to subjects. There was an experimental group that received (1) a prequestionnaire of forty-eight questions about invertebrate animals, each followed by two alternative answers between which a choice had to be made, (2) a list of seventy-two statements about invertebrate animals, including

answers to all the questions in the prequestionnaire, and (3) a postquestionnaire consisting of the questions of the prequestionnaire in a re-randomized order but without the answers, so that answers had to be supplied by the subjects. A control group underwent exactly the same procedure except that the prequestionnaire was omitted.

The outcome was that the experimental group supplied a mean of 32.4 correct answers in the postquestionnaire, as compared with 27.2 for the control group. The difference was significant and was taken as evidence that questions heighten epistemic curiosity, facilitating the retention of facts that answer the questions when they are subsequently encountered.

The exact mechanism by which this takes place is impossible to specify with present knowledge. The recognition of the answer may cause the question to be recalled, rearousing the curiosity, the curiosity may be revived in some other manner, or it may persist in some form between the putting of the question and the receipt of the answer. Be that as it may, the rehearsal of the answer by the subject will reduce the curiosity to a subthreshold value, furnishing reinforcement for the learning process. The higher the initial level of curiosity, the greater the curiosity reduction and thus the more effective the learning is likely to be.

There was evidence that questions intensify, not only specific curiosity directed at their answers, but more general curiosity about their topic. At the end of the experiment, subjects were asked to indicate which of the twelve animals that had figured in the questions they would like to know more about. The experimental group, which, it will be remembered, differed only in having had the prequestionnaire, marked off significantly more animals than the control group (a mean of 5.4 as compared with 3.4).

The next objective was to ascertain which classes of questions aroused more curiosity than others. This was done in two ways. The proportions of correct answers retained by the experimental group were compared for different classes, and the subjects were also required to mark the three questions out of each consecutive set of twelve in the prequestionnaire whose answers they would most like to know. These two measures of curiosity, which we shall call the *retention test* and the *marking test* respectively, turned out to have a highly significant measure of agreement.

The disturbing effects of previous knowledge were controlled for by two expedients. First, subjects in the experimental group were told to indicate which questions they felt they could answer with certainty; these questions were then omitted from consideration. The data for the control group were likewise adjusted on the assumption that they would, on the average, have known the same numbers of answers. Secondly, half of the answers provided in the list of statements were untrue, the subjects being dehoaxed afterwards, so that previous knowledge would hinder retention as often as it would help.

Predictions concerning the effects on curiosity of two of the determinants of degree of conflict (C), namely the number of competing response tendencies and their degree of incompatibility, were supported.

Number. If questions give rise to divergent and conflicting trains of thought, the concepts figuring in the question must have associations already attached to them, that is, they must be familiar to the subject. Starting from this assumption, it was hypothesized that questions about animals that subjects had heard of would arouse more

curiosity than those about unfamiliar animals. This hypothesis was examined by presenting subjects of both groups with a list of the twelve animals that would figure in the experiment, before it began, and having them rate them for familiarity. Questions about more familiar animals aroused significantly more curiosity according to both tests. The control group showed a tendency to recall statements about more familiar animals more readily, but statistical analysis confirmed that there was a curiosity-increasing effect of questions about more familiar animals over and above this tendency.

The number-of-competing-response-tendencies variable received a more direct test in an earlier experiment that used the same general procedure. There the retention test showed multiple-choice questions with four alternatives to arouse more curiosity than ones with two alternatives.

Degree of Incompatibility. During the prequestionnaire, experimental-group subjects were instructed to indicate which questions surprised them, and the marking test showed subjects to be more desirous of knowing the answers to these than to other questions.

A further test was made by calling on a group of thirty judges, taken from the same population as the subjects. They received a list of eight of the animals figuring in the experiment (two fictitious and two highly unfamiliar animals were omitted). Opposite the name of each animal were four phrases, representing the predicates implied by the four questions about each animal in the questionnaire. The judges had to mark off the two phrases that seemed least likely of the four to fit the animal concerned. The marking test revealed that the two questions per animal incorporating the predicates that the judges deemed least applicable were more curiosity-arousing than the others.

Conceptual Conflict and Extrinsic Epistemic Curiosity

An experiment by Irwin and Smith (1957) is highly instructive with respect to the part that conceptual conflict plays when knowledge is sought for the sake of some extraneous reward. They used packs of cards, each bearing a positive or a negative number. Subjects were allowed to see as many cards as they wished, but a small charge (½ cent in some cases and 1 cent in others) was made for each card that they saw. After seeing as many or as few cards as they chose, they were to conclude the session by guessing whether the mean of the numbers in the whole pack was positive or negative. A prize, amounting to 50 cents for some and $1 for others, was received if the guess was correct.

At each point in the experiment, therefore, subjects had to decide between seeing one more card, which meant a gain in information but a slight monetary loss, or venturing a guess about the mean and thus securing or forfeiting the prize. The motivation to see a card can be classified as epistemic curiosity, since the resulting stimulus pattern was clearly sought neither for its own sake nor, in most cases, for the guidance of some immediate response. The information the card bore was generally stored in the form of a modification of internal symbolic representations which determined overt behavior, i.e., a guess, after quite a lapse of time.

The response of looking at a card was obviously actuated by the perplexity conflict between guessing "positive" and guessing "negative." When a guess had been formulated, there was also conflict between the tendency to voice it, motivated by hope of win-

ning the prize, and the tendency to withhold it, motivated by fear of losing. The additional conflict, between asking for another card and stating a guess, was not one that could be resolved by acquiring more knowledge.

The only way to reduce the first two conflicts would be to see all the cards, and subjects would undoubtedly have waited to see them all, were it not for the cost imposed. It is only to be expected, therefore, that more cards would be looked at when the cost was ½ cent than when it was 1 cent, and this was indeed found.

But, if the cost is held constant, the number of cards looked at tells us how much information it took to reduce epistemic curiosity to the point where it could no longer outweigh the reluctance to pay. Since degree of conflict depends on the absolute strength of competing response tendencies, the prospect of a $1 prize should induce a more intense desire to win and a more intense fear of losing than a 50-cent prize, which means a higher level of initial conflict and curiosity. It is not surprising, therefore, that the higher prize led subjects to look at significantly more cards.

The rate at which perplexity is relieved by disequalization would vary inversely with the absolute value of the mean (its distance from zero) and the standard deviation of the numbers on the cards. And more cards were, in fact, seen when the mean was (plus or minus) 0.5 than when it was (plus or minus) 1.5 and when the standard deviation was 7.5 than when it was 2.0.

Irwin and Smith also arranged for their subjects to rate the confidence with which they made their guesses. This is of particular interest to us because of the likelihood that a rating of confidence reflects the degree of doubt conflict. Subjects who paid ½ cent per card recorded more confidence than those who paid 1 cent; they could afford to pay for enough information to reduce their doubt and curiosity to a lower level before committing themselves to a guess. It is even more instructive that confidence was greater when the mean was farther from zero and when the standard deviation had the lower value, which means when the numbers borne by the cards were able to diminish uncertainty more effectively.

Other pertinent data are yielded by a somewhat similar experiment carried out by Becker (1958). The epistemic response consisted of pressing a switch, which caused one or the other of two counters to advance a unit. Subjects were provided with descriptions of two to five populations, from one of which, they were told, the items of information (that is, the movements of the counters) were selected. The populations differed in the proportions of left-counter and right-counter items that they contained.

After pressing the switch as many times as they wished, the subjects were to guess which population the items actually came from. They were put through a series of such problems and were given to understand that their chances of winning a monetary bonus depended on the ratio that the excess of correct over incorrect guesses bore to the number of items of information drawn.

More epistemic responses were performed when the problem was a hard one, requiring discrimination between a population with 3,000 left-counter items and 3,000 right-counter items and a 4,000/2,000 population, than with an easy problem, involving discrimination between a 3,000/3,000 and a 1,000/5,000 population. Furthermore, the number of epistemic responses increased with the number of alternative populations to be con-

sidered. These are conditions in which, respectively, the opposing guessing responses would be more nearly equal in strength and more numerous, and thus conflict would be more intense.

Both experiments thus corroborate our supposition that collative variables will not only govern intrinsic epistemic behavior but even contribute to the motivation of extrinsic epistemic behavior.

CONCLUSIONS

The study of exploratory behavior, as we have already seen, forces on our consideration a whole spate of basic theoretical questions relating to motivation and learning in general. Epistemic behavior, forming an even more uncharted region, must likewise raise wider issues and, in particular, make us conscious of the deplorable neglect from which the motivational aspects of intellectual activity have suffered.

Some reconsideration of the motivations and reinforcements affecting symbolic learning is demanded, to cite an illustrative experiment, by Porter's (1957) finding that the learning of a verbal response is not facilitated when it is immediately followed by cessation of an electric shock. Pain reduction is, of course, known to be quite a powerful reinforcing agent for nonverbal responses in human beings and animals. And many motivational conditions, for example, monetary rewards and social approval, are capable of affecting verbal learning (see Young 1936). But the corresponding motivational states must work through symbolic representations, which means that such factors as uncertainty and conceptual conflict might play their part.

In case we may seem to be hankering unnecessarily after new problems, we may cite some recent conclusions of Piaget (1957), inspired by long investigation of intellectual development in children. Intellectual development embraces a number of attainments, amounting to new ways of organizing responses, symbolic and nonsymbolic. The child arrives at more and more roundabout techniques for solving practical problems, at perceptual constancies (for example, of shape, size, and brightness), and at conceptual constancies (for example, of the object, of quantity, of space, of time). He acquires the practice of systematically varying his fixations so as to counteract the illusions and distortions to which the nonhomogeneity of the perceptual field is apt to lead. Most important and striking of all, he gradually builds up more and more powerful and coherent logical structures, permitting him to conduct his thought processes with maximum flexibility, combined with consistency of outcome. It is noteworthy that, once a child is in possession of a logical structure, he does not usually justify a conclusion by mentioning experiences of external events that show that it happens to be true; he appeals to inference from general principles and evinces a conviction that what he says has to be true.

Piaget contends that the nature of these phenomena compels the conclusion that the course of development is governed not only by maturation and by pressure of environmental events but by a further class of factors that he calls "equilibrium." Equilibrium can exist in varying degrees, but there is an inexorable, autonomous movement toward better and better equilibrium as the child matures. He gives up his earlier and cruder ways of perceiving and thinking because he finds that they lead to surprises and frustrations, since the expectations which they generate often turn out to be erroneous and frequently leave him unable to anticipate what is going to

happen next. As his nervous system develops, he is able to adopt more advanced ways of perceiving and thinking which permit him to have greater confidence in his judgments and to make predictions in more and more contexts.

We may reinterpret Piaget's view by regarding what he calls equilibrium as a class of hitherto overlooked sources of drive and reward propelling the learning processes that give rise to generalized habits of perception and thought. The drive states that are fomented by disequilibrium arise not out of visceral disturbances or aversive external stimuli, but out of unsatisfactory relations between the subject's own responses. Changes in behavior that remove disequilibrium are ones that avert surprise and uncertainty. Ability to recognize and respond to invariants amid the shifting appearances of objects must diminish complexity and moderate the impact of change. So, once more, we find testimony to the importance of conceptual conflict.

Work on simulation of intellectual processes with computers furnishes another view of the matter. Pursuit of the analogies between computers and brains has helped to obscure the necessity of considering motivational aspects of thinking, since current computers, like human subjects in psychological laboratories, have the experimenter's motives artificially instilled in them. But the recent movement toward a more flexible use of the computer, approaching the more creative forms of human thought, must unavoidably bring up the problem.

For example, Shaw, Newell, Simon, and Ellis (1958) have discussed how a machine should be constructed to function as a general problem solver, a device that would simulate a wide range of intellectual feats from proving theorems to playing chess. The machine, as conceived by them, and the programs with which they have successfully converted existing computers to such uses, involve the following elements: (1) a representation of the essential properties of a solution, (2) a representation of the data that are initially given, (3) a means of selecting some of these initial data and performing specifiable operations on them to yield new data, and (4) a device for comparing the products of these operations with the representation of the solution, and noting wherein they fail to match.

Element 4 is what corresponds to the mechanism of epistemic curiosity. It works through the equivalent of conceptual conflict, and its function is an eminently motivational one; its recognition of match or mismatch determines whether the search for a solution ends or continues, and its characterization of the mismatch determines the direction in which the search for a solution is pursued. Future research may well be aimed at devising a problem-solving machine that will improve its technique in the light of its experience. The reduction of mismatch or conflict would then have to be the reinforcing agent, causing the immediately preceding operations to move up in the machine's order of precedence.

It is, after all, fairly obvious that conceptual conflict must underlie the notions of truth and falsity. Modern philosophers have emphasized that truth and falsity are properties not of facts but of sentences, that is, of representations of facts. They have also distinguished two senses in which a sentence can be true (for example, Carnap 1936–1937). It is *synthetically* true or *P-valid* if, like the truths of science, it agrees with external reality. It is *analytically* true or *L-valid* if, like the truths of mathematics or logic, it cannot be denied without contradicting rules that govern the use of language. Neither of these notions could have arisen, nor could have any value, if discrepancies between symbolic processes—between the response to an empirical statement and the response to an observation of nature, or between the response to a logicomathematical formula and the response to an axiom or rule of inference—did not produce special psychological discomforts and impel a quest for other, less dissatisfying representational patterns.

The doubts that several writers (for example, Pap 1953, Apostel, Mays, Morf, and Piaget 1957) have, on both logical and psychological grounds expressed about the sharpness of the analytic-synthetic dichotomy can only lend further weight to our contention that the two criteria of truth have roots in related motivational processes.

REFERENCES

Abelson, R., "Modes of Resolution of Belief Dilemmas." Paper read to Western Psychological Association, Monterey, Calif., 1958.

Abelson, R. and H. Rosenberg, "Symbolic Psychologic: A Model of Attitudinal Recognition," *Behavioral Science,* **3** (1958), 1-13.

Abraham, K., "Über Einschrankungen und Umwandlunger der Schaulust bei den Psychoneurotikern nebst Bermerkungen über analoge Erscheinungen in der Völkerpsychologie," in *Klinische Beiträge zur Psychoanalyse aus den Jahren 1907-1920.* Internationaler Psychoanalytischer Verlag, Leipzig, Vienna, and Zurich. ("Restrictions and Transformations of Scoptophilia in Neurosis with Remarks on Analogous Phenomena in Folk Psychology," in *Selected Papers.* London: Hogarth, 1921.

Allport, G. W. and L. J. Postman, *The Psychology of Rumour.* New York: Holt, Rinehart & Winston, Inc., 1947.

Apostel, L., W. Mays, A. Morf, and J. Piaget, "Les liaisons analytiques et synthetiques dans le comportement du sujet," *Études d'Epistémologie Génétique,* IV. Paris: Presses Universitaires de France, 1957.

Becker, G. M., "Sequential Decision-making: Wald's Model and Estimates of Parameter," *Journal of Experimental Psychology,* **55** (1958), 628-36.

Berger, H., "Über das Elektrenkephalogramm des Menschen: II," *Journal of Psychological Neurology,* **40** (1930), 160-79.

Berlyne, D. E., "Some Aspects of Human Curiosity." (Unpublished Doctoral dissertation, Yale University, 1953.)

————, "An Experimental Study of Human Curiosity," *British Journal of Psychology,* **45** (1954c), 256-65.

————, "A Theory of Human Curiosity," *British Journal of Psychology,* **45** (1954b), 180-91.

————, "Les équivalences psychologiques et les notions quantitatives," in *Études d'Epistémologie Génétique: XII.* Paris: Presses Universitaires de France, 1960.

Cantril, H., *The Psychology of Social Movements.* New York: John Wiley & Sons, Inc., 1941.

Carnap, R., "Testability and Meaning," *Philosophical Science,* **3** (1936), 419-71; **4** (1937), 1-40.

Cartwright, D. and F. Harary, "Structural Balance: A Generalization of Heider's Theory," *Psychological Review,* **63** (1956), 277-93.

Cooper, J. B. and H. E. Siegel, "The Galvanic Skin Response as a Measure of Emotion in Prejudice," *Journal of Psychology,* **42** (1956), 149-55.

Courts, F. A., "Relations between Muscular Tension and Performance," *Psychological Bulletin,* **39** (1942), 347-67.

Ellingson, R. R., "Brain Waves and Problems of Psychology," *Psychological Bulletin,* **53** (1956), 1-34.

Festinger, L., *Theory of Cognitive Dissonance.* Evanston, Ill.: Row, Peterson & Company, 1957.

Freud, S., "Bemerkungen über einen Fall von Zwangsneurose," in *Sammlung kleiner Schriften zur Neurosenlehre,* 3. Folge, Leipzig and Vienna: Deuticke; 1913. ("Notes upon a Case of Obsessional Neurosis," in S. Freud, *Collected Papers,* III. London: The Hogarth Press, 1924.)

Heider, F., "Attitudes and Cognitive Organization," *Journal of Psychology,* **21** (1946), 107-12.

Irwin, F. and W. A. S. Smith, "Value, Cost and Information as Determiners of Decision," *Journal of Experimental Psychology,* **54** (1957), 229-32.

Morris, C. R., "Foundations of the Theory of Signs," *International Encyclopedia of Unified Science,* **1,** No. 2 (1938).

————, *Signs, Language and Behavior.* Englewood Cliffs, N. J.: Prentice-Hall, Inc., 1946.

Osgood, C. E., G. J. Suci, and P. H. Tannenbaum, *The Measurement of Meaning.* Urbana, Ill.: University of Illinois Press, 1957.

Osgood, C. E. and P. H. Tannenbaum, "The Principle of Congruity in the Prediction of Attitude Change," *Psychological Review,* **62** (1955), 42-55.

Pap, A., "Reduction-sentences and Open Concepts," *Methods,* **5** (1953), 3-30.

Piaget, J., "Logique et equilibre dans les comportements du sujet," in *Logique et Equilibre,* eds. L. Apostel, B. Mandelbrot, and J. Piaget, *Études d'Epistémologie Génétique,* II. Paris: Presses Universitaires de France, 1957.

Porter, L. W., "Effect of Shock-cessation as an Incidental Reward in Verbal Learning," *American Journal of Psychology,* **70** (1957), 421-26.

Sears, R., "Psychogalvanic Responses in Arithmetical Work," *Archives of Psychology,* **155** (1933).

Shaw, J. C., A. Newell, H. A. Simon, and T. O. Ellis, "A Command Structure for Complex Information-processing." Paper read at Joint Western Computer Conference, Los Angeles, California, 1958.

Toman, J. E. P., "The Electroencephalogram during Mental Effort," *Fed. Proc.*, **2** (1943), 49.

Wechsler, D., "Measurement of Emotional Reactions," *Archives of Psychology*, **76** (1925).

Young, P. T., *Motivation of Behavior.* New York: John Wiley & Sons, Inc., 1936.

PART SIX

COGNITION IN CHILDREN
AND COGNITIVE DEVELOPMENT

An understanding of the nature and development of cognitive processes is of primary importance to the classroom teacher. The articles in this section reflect some of the major theoretical and research trends in this area of psychology.

Kendler and Kendler, whose article serves as an introduction to cognitive development, utilize the neobehavioristic construct of the response-produced cue as a mediator between external stimulus and external response in problem-solving. In very young children this mediator is virtually absent and instead, direct associations are formed between stimuli and responses. With age and experience these single-stage associations give way to the establishment of central controls which are variably associated with the external stimulus on the one hand and the overt response on the other. Kendler and Kendler lay considerable stress on the role of language in mediating processes in behavior, a point that is taken up by Luria in his article on the role of speech as a regulator of behavior. This eminent Soviet psychologist argues that internalized speech assumes the major role in self-directed behavior. Luria argues that adult verbalizations can initiate behavior in a two-year-old child but cannot inhibit ongoing response sequences. By the age of three or four the child's own speech begins to assume a directive role in behavior, but the inhibitory factor is still absent. At this stage the child reacts to his own verbalizations as he would to other exteroceptive stimuli. By about five years, speech is used not only to initiate behavior but to program its course through time and space.

The relationship between language and behavior, discussed by Kendler and Kendler, is further clarified by Kuenne's experiment. She proposes two developmental stages. In the first stage the child responds verbally to characteristics of stimuli, but this does not determine overt behavior. In the second stage overt behavior comes under the control of verbalizations.

583

Reese reviews several studies that indicated less verbal mediation in younger children than older children. He is doubtful that verbal mediation is a function of age and proposes that it is a function of how well a concept is learned.

Brown provides evidence that cognitive development does not necessarily proceed from concrete to abstract and lack of differentiation to increased differentiation. Development can occur in both directions. He also points to the influence of adult's choice of words on the development of cognitive processes in children. Utility or function probably determines the adult's choice.

The last six articles in this part report research on probability learning in children. This research is concerned with the relationship between the probability of occurrence of an event, for example, reinforcement, and the probability of a response (learning). Responses of three- and four-year-old children are influenced by the probability of reinforcement, demonstrating that young children have an understanding of probability and behave accordingly. Some of the findings are similar to those obtained with adults, for example, acquisition of behavior is more rapid with continuous reinforcement while partial reinforcement results in less rapid extinction. Probability of reward has a different effect at different age levels. The student's attention is called to the theoretical and methodological differences between the papers on probability learning and those at the beginning of this section. The former represent an attempt either to avoid the use of hypothetical constructs altogether or to anchor them as closely to observables as possible. Such an approach calls for the maximum degree of specification of stimulus and response variables. It will be readily appreciated that the experimenter pays a price for this rigor in terms of the nature and scope of the problems he can investigate. The validity and promise of this highly quantitative orientation to the study of cognitive behavior, however, is not to be denied.

Vertical and Horizontal Processes
in Problem-Solving *

Howard H. Kendler and Tracy S. Kendler

The present paper is concerned with *an* approach—and not *the* approach—to the universally appealing but nevertheless unpopular research area of problem-solving. Problems of problem-solving have proved to be particularly refractory to psychologists. More often than not the uncommon researcher with the temerity to attack some aspect of reasoning retreats to more secure and conventional problems when he discovers that his sorties fail to achieve any impressive victory. As a result the literature of problem-solving is almost chaotic because it is so heavily sprinkled with isolated bits of information (Duncan, 1959).

Perhaps the present stage of development of psychology does not justify the strategy of investigating such a complex phenomenon. Fortunately, or not, science has no built-in traffic lights to inform investigators when to proceed. It may be a risky and potentially unfruitful gambit to investigate problem-solving but then again it may not be. In addition to the intrinsic interest of the area it does offer a challenge to those psychologists who are interested in testing the generality of any set of theoretical principles stemming from other areas of behavior (for example, learning, perception).

This paper initially will make fleeting references to some methodological problems with which a researcher in the field of reasoning must contend. Then a simple pretheoretical model of problem-solving will be described, followed by a report of research which the model generated, and which in turn is shaping the model itself.

METHODOLOGICAL PROBLEMS IN PROBLEM-SOLVING RESEARCH

Anybody who does research is—or should be—aware that every decision he makes cannot be justified by facts or logic. Some decisions must be made on the basis of personal intuition. This is particularly true for the researcher in problem-solving who must make three strategic decisions which cannot help but have profound influences on his research and the ideas they generate (Kendler, 1961). These decisions, which are not completely independent, are related to the place of problem-solving in psychology, the use of complex or simple experimental tasks, and the selection of a pretheoretical model

* From H. H. Kendler and T. S. Kendler, "Vertical and Horizontal Processes in Problem-Solving," *Psychological Review,* **69** (1962), 1-16. Reprinted by permission of the authors and the American Psychological Association.

An earlier version of this paper was delivered by Howard H. Kendler as an invited address to the 1960 meeting of the Eastern Psychological Association, which was held in New York City. The authors are indebted to the Office of Naval Research and the National Science Foundation for their support of the research reported in this paper.

to guide research. Considering the volitional nature of these problems, as well as the current status of psychological knowledge, it would be both inappropriate and erroneous to consider these methodological problems as offering only one sensible alternative. Adopting this point of view would do much to minimize the needless disputation that seems to perennially surround matters of research strategy.

Accepting the principle that a basic research strategy is not simply an outgrowth of logical and factual considerations does not reduce one to making decisions in either a haphazard or random manner. A given strategy can be adopted on the basis of rational considerations as long as it is realized that other reasonable attitudes might lead to the adoption of different decisions.

The history of problem-solving in particular and psychology in general suggests that problem-solving can best be conceptualized not as a basic psychological process, but instead as one that reflects the interaction of more fundamental processes (for example, learning, perception, and motivation).

If problem-solving is not viewed as a unitary process, how is an appropriate experimental situation selected to investigate it? One possibility is that a problem can be selected from a "true life" situation such as troubleshooting electronic equipment. Or problems can be invented (Duncker, 1945; Maier, 1930) that capture the flavor, if only partially, of problems we meet in everyday life.

A more analytical approach can be taken to the selection of an experimental situation to investigate problem-solving. If problem-solving is compounded of elementary behavioral processes, then it may be more strategic to devise some simple problems in which the relationships of fundamental psychological mechanisms to problem-solving are highlighted. That is, tasks should be devised not to duplicate or imitate everyday problems, but instead to isolate and magnify the basic mechanisms that operate in such complex tasks.

This analytical approach which is favored by the authors suffers from one major drawback. How is it possible to know the basic mechanisms of problem-solving prior to their discovery? Obviously, excepting divination, there is no method. But this does not prevent the analytical approach from operating. The researcher can prejudge theoretical issues by formulating a model of what he guesses problem-solving to be like. The model can guide the investigator in selecting the hypotheses to test, as well as the experimental situations in which to test them.

This brings us to the third and most important decision a problem-solving researcher has to make: his choice of a pretheoretical model (Koch, 1959). A pretheoretical model is not equivalent to a theory. The criterion of validity cannot properly be applied to it because essentially a pretheoretical model is an informal conception that operates as an analogy (Lachman, 1960). It is conceivable that different models (for example, learning, perception, information theory) can all lead to fruitful and valid theories of problem-solving.

Psychologists have many possibilities from which to choose their model. These models can be conveniently divided into two main categories: the empirical model that springs primarily from experimental data, and the formal model that is usually generated by mathematical or logical systems. Among the empirical models that have achieved some acceptance are those that are based on introspective findings (for example, the four successive stage model of "preparation," "incubation," "inspiration," and finally "verification"), the facts of perception, and those of learning. Some formal models used are those dependent upon stochastic models, game theory, and the operation of computers.

The present authors adopted an S-R learning pretheoretical model. The decision no doubt was influenced by professional training and past research efforts. But other considerations entered. For the past four decades S-R learning psychologists have probably been the most active experimental and theoretical group in psychology. To some, if not a large, extent this can be attributed to the fruitful and cleansing effect S-R language has upon designing, reporting, and interpreting research. S-R language forces the psychologist to focus his attention on objectively defined environmental and behavioral variables and thus encourages the collection of data and the testing of ideas. The efforts of S-R learning psychologists have supplied a host of facts, concepts, and hypotheses that can be exploited in an exploratory excursion into the realm of problem-solving.

The facts and theories of learning, however, do not spontaneously coalesce to form a model that can guide research in problem-solving. Some selection must be made. S-R learning theory does not represent a single organized formulation. Anyone who is familiar with the systematic orientations of Hull (1952), Guthrie (1952), Spence (1956), and Skinner (1953) is aware of this. Many of these systematic differences, however, become attenuated and some even disappear when viewed from the distance of problem-solving behavior. It is possible and perhaps even profitable to develop a learning model for problem-solving that ignores many of the points of disagreement among S-R theories.

Much of the objection to S-R language stems from the apparent discrepancy between active, flowing behavior and the inert, static, single S-R association. Using S-R language does not mean that complex behavior *actually* consists of S-R connections. After analyzing the concept of light, Toulmin (1953) concludes: "We do not *find* light atomized into individual rays: we *represent* it as consisting of such rays" (p. 29). Applying the same idea to the concept of the S-R association: "We do not *find* behavior atomized into individual S-R associations: we *represent* it as consisting of such S-R associations." The concept of the S-R association, therefore, must be judged not in terms of its ability to provide a clear image of behavior, but rather in its capacity to represent the facts of behavior.

PRETHEORETICAL MODEL OF PROBLEM-SOLVING

An S-R model needs to represent two important characteristics of problem-solving behavior. These characteristics are: behavior is continuous, and at any one time behavior consists of several habits. The terms "horizontal" and "vertical" are used to refer to these processes; horizontal to the continuity of behavior against the dimension of time, and vertical to the assumption that independent levels of behavior (that is, S-R units) occur simultaneously.

The assumption that S-R associations do not occur in isolation, but instead are linked together to form integrated, continuous behavior, goes back many years (for example, Watson, 1913). Today the process is most commonly referred to as chaining. Skinner (1953) and his associates have developed powerful techniques that shape behavior into long, complicated chains. The mass of data they have collected suggests important principles governing habit chaining. There is little doubt that when their quasi-theoretical system is exploited fully with autoinstructional devices that important insights into problem-solving behavior will emerge, particularly in relation to how an added bit of knowledge can trigger problem solution. The kind of chaining with which the Skinnerians have dealt (that is, adding new S-R units to an already functioning chain) does not exhaust all the problems associated with the horizontal processes of problem-solving. Of particular importance to problem-solving is the *spontaneous* integration of separate habits which occurs when an organism infers the consequences of combining previously independent S-R units. This kind of chaining was investigated in Kohler's (1925) classical studies of insight and in the more controlled reasoning experiments of Maier (1930). More recently the authors (Kendler and Kendler, 1956, 1961; Kendler, Kendler, Pliskoff, and D'Amato, 1958) have tried to identify some of the important variables that enable children to combine separate experiences in order to solve an inference-type problem. Much of the research reported in this paper will be concerned with how mediated stimulus and response events aid in the formation of problem-solving chains.

The assumption of vertical processes, that is, the organism responds several different ways at any one time, is also not a novel one. Every psychologist is aware that organisms make several different responses simultaneously, although typically only one is attended to. Sometimes the different responses are interrelated, as is the case between the heart and respiration rates of a fearful organism. In other cases the different responses are independent, for example, a person's conversation is uninfluenced by his tugging at his ear lobe. The best laboratory example of vertical processes, and one that has much relevance to problem-solving, is shown in Fig. 1. Those

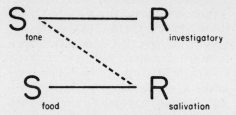

FIG. 1. *An S-R representation of classical conditioning.*

familiar with introductory psychology textbooks will recognize this diagram as representing classical conditioning. Notice that the two solid lines indicate independent S-R units which are operating simultaneously. One is the tone that initiates the "investigatory" response, and the other is the food which elicits salivation. Initially these two associations operate in a *parallel* fashion, but as a result of their simultaneous occurrence an *interaction* takes place which is expressed by the broken line representing the acquired conditioned response.

Obviously the brief reference to horizontal and vertical processes in which it is assumed fundamental S-R principles operate (for example, discrimination, generalization, etc.) presents at best the barest skeleton of a model of problem-solving. It needs the flesh and skin of experimental facts to give it solidity and theoretical principles to clothe it in scientific respectability. Let us now review some of the progress that has been made in this direction.

CONCEPT LEARNING AND UTILIZATION

Although the primitive model just described fails to generate any research by itself, it does suggest that individual experiments cannot be directed at *problem-solving in its entirety*. There are too many aspects to this phenomenon. The researcher, in designing an experiment, must scan the entire problem-solving process and then focus upon that segment that promises to yield fruitful results and is also amenable to investigation.

For reasons that will become evident, it was decided to compare reversal and nonreversal shifts in a simple concept learning task. Figure 2 characterizes each kind of shift by

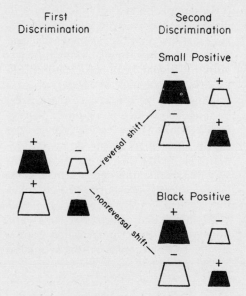

First Discrimination   Second Discrimination

FIG. 2. *Examples of a reversal and a nonreversal shift.*

showing a *simplified* version of an experimental situation used with children. The stimuli (cups) for their first discrimination differ simultaneously on two dimensions (size and brightness). The subject is rewarded for responses to one dimension (for example, large cup is positive, small cup is negative). The other dimension is irrelevant. After learning the first dis-

crimination, the subject is forced to shift to another response. In a reversal shift the subject is required to respond to the same dimension on which he was originally trained, but his overt choice has to be reversed, for example, he has to shift from a *large* cup to a *small* one. For a nonreversal shift the previously irrelevant dimension becomes relevant, for example, black becomes positive after large had been positive.

Buss (1953) reported that college students executed a reversal shift more rapidly than a nonreversal shift. He attributed this superiority to the intermittent reinforcements that retard the progress of a nonreversal shift. For example, in Fig. 2 [1] when a subject is making a nonreversal shift from large positive to black positive, he is reinforced when choosing the large black cup in preference to the small white cup. This fortuitous reinforcement of the choice of the large cup helps maintain the size discrimination and hence retards the learning of the brightness discrimination. The reversal shift group, on the other hand, receives no reinforcement of the previously correct responses, since they are 100 percent *non*reinforced.

This analysis is at best incomplete. The work of Kendler and Vineberg (1954) suggested that adult human concept learning cannot be represented adequately by a single unit S-R theory in which the external stimulus is directly connected to the overt response. Instead, a mediational mechanism

---

[1] The purpose of Fig. 2 is to clarify the meaning of both a reversal and nonreversal shift. It would be misleading to believe that it represents *exactly* the methodology of "reversal-nonreversal" studies reported in this paper. For all experiments reported, except that of Buss (1953), designs were used that controlled for fortuitous intermittent reinforcements effects in a nonreversal shift.

(see Fig. 3) is required which assumes

FIG. 3. *A schematic representation of the mediational hypothesis.*

that the external stimulus evokes an implict response which produces an implicit cue that is connected to the overt response.

It would be useful to digress for a moment to comment about the epistemological status of these inferred stimulus and response events which are enclosed in the rectangle to emphasize their hypothetical character. Although not directly observable, they are "tied to" environmental and behavioral events. The basic assumption of the mediational hypothesis, at least for the time being, is that the implicit stimulus and response events obey the same principles that operate in observable S-R relationships.

The mediational hypothesis has generated confusion. Perhaps the following brief statements will clarify some possible areas of misunderstanding.

1. The mediational hypothesis is neither new nor revolutionary. Meyer (1911) and Watson (1913) referred to it, and Hull (1930) gave it a more formal status by coining the concept of the "pure stimulus act." Guthrie (1952) has always laid heavy stress on a mediational-type hypothesis when emphasizing the importance of proprioceptive stimulation in learning.

2. The implicit stimulus and response events *need not* be conceived as having an existence independent of their relation to independent and dependent variables. These implicit events are theoretical constructs. Their epistemological status is closer to such

concepts as drive and habit than to directly observable stimulus and response events.

Some mediating events can conceivably and probably will be coordinated to introspective reports, language behavior, muscular movements, and other observable events. Co-ordinations of this sort can be useful in developing mediational theory. But such co-ordinations are not *essential* to mediational theory. The fact that genes are not directly observable (at least according to the geneticists consulted) does not interfere with their theoretical and practical usefulness. Even if it were possible to observe a gene directly, it would be necessary to distinguish between it as an observable entity and as a concept within a nomological network. It would be unwise, and strategically shortsighted, to *identify* mediational events with introspective reports or language behavior, or other observable events. The "validity" of the mediational mechanism does not depend on being co-ordinated with observable events, but depends instead on being utilized in a successful explanatory system.

Figure 4 characterizes reversal and nonreversal shifts in terms of both a single unit S-R analysis and a media-

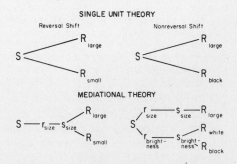

FIG. 4. *A single unit and mediational S-R analysis of a reversal and nonreversal shift.*

tional one.[2] It would be predicted, according to a single unit hypothesis, that if fortuitous intermittent reinforcements were eliminated from a nonreversal shift, it would occur more rapidly than a reversal shift. The reason for this is that at the time of the shift the difference between the strength of the dominant incorrect habit and the to-be-correct habit is much greater for the reversal, as compared to the nonreversal shift. Consequently more training will be required to make the correct habit dominant in a reversal shift. According to the mediational theory the situation is entirely different. A reversal shift enables the subject to utilize the same mediated response. Only the overt response has to be changed. A nonreversal shift, on the other hand, required the acquisition of a *new* mediated response, the cues of which have to be attached to a *new* overt response. Because the old mediational sequence has to be discarded and a new one formed, the nonreversal

---

[2] Figure 4 highlights the problem of what are the effective stimuli that are associated to the overt response in both a reversal and nonreversal shift. It is not intended to be a detailed analysis of which there may be several alternatives. For example, in a single unit theory the habit to choose the large container might result from learning two separate specific habits (for example, the choice of a large black container when coupled with a small white one and the selection of a large white container when paired with a small black one). Another possibility, which would be consistent with Spence's theory (1936), is that the response is to the effective stimulus *large* since responses to the other features of the environment are not consistently reinforced. Similarly adult subjects in a reversal shift might use the mediator *size* or *large* or both. The effective stimulus which is controlling the organism's response must be determined by experimentation. The point made here is that the general implications of the single unit and mediational theories, as discussed in this paper, would be the same for a number of different effective stimuli.

shift should be executed more slowly than a reversal shift.[3] Thus, if it were possible to eliminate fortuitous intermittent reinforcements, then the stage would be set for a crucial experiment testing the conflicting implications of the single unit and mediational S-R theories. The results of a series of such crucial experiments (Buss, 1956; Harrow and Friedman, 1958; Kendler and D'Amato, 1955) have been consistent with the mediational formulation in showing that college students execute a reversal shift more rapidly than a nonreversal shift. It is important to

TABLE 1

MEAN NUMBER OF TRIALS TO CRITERION ON TEST DISCRIMINATION FOR SUBJECTS SCORING ABOVE AND BELOW THE MEDIAN ON THE TRAINING DISCRIMINATION

| Group | PERFORMANCE ON TRAINING DISCRIMINATION | |
	Above Median (slow learners)	Below Median (fast learners)
Reversal	24.4	6.0
Nonreversal	9.0	15.5

note that in a similar kind of problem rats find a nonreversal shift easier than a reversal shift (Kelleher, 1956). Thus, one is forced to conclude that a single unit S-R theory accurately represents the behavior of rats, while mediational S-R theory is required for

---

[3] There are two possible ways of analyzing the superiority of a reversal shift over a nonreversal shift within an S-R mediational framework. One is to simply count the number of new associations that have to be formed. As Fig. 4 indicates only one new association has to be formed in a reversal shift while two have to be formed for a nonreversal shift. Another possibility is that a mediating response is more difficult to extinguish than is an overt response. For the present the formulation can remain open-ended until information relevant to these two alternatives is gathered.

the concept learning of articulate humans.

The discontinuity between the behavior of rats and college students directs one's attention toward the conditions responsible for the development of mediational processes. Somewhere on a hypothetical evolutionary dimension between the rat and college student there should be a point where a transition is made from a single unit to mediational control. An obvious place to locate this point would be in the behavior of young children.

A study with kindergarten children (Kendler and Kendler, 1959) showed that these children as a group executed a reversal and nonreversal shift at approximately the same rate. One might conclude that the point in human development was discovered which was psychologically halfway between the white rat and the college student, since the kindergarten children were neither responding in a single unit nor mediational manner, but instead in some compromise fashion. Another possibility is that the children had reached a transitional stage in development, in which the task to which they were subjected led some to function on a single unit basis, and others to operate with a mediational mechanism. If half of the subjects respond in each way, the total results would have revealed no difference between the two kinds of shifts.

The second alternative seems to fit the data. When the kindergarten children were divided into fast and slow learners on the basis of their performance in the first problem (training discrimination), slow learners performed during the second problem (test discrimination) according to the single unit theory; like rats they found a nonreversal shift easier. Fast learners, on the other hand, performed in accordance with the mediational theory;

like college students, they found a reversal shift easier. These results were interpreted as demonstrating that these kindergartners, taken as a group, were in the process of developing mediating responses relevant to this task, and that some were further along than others.

If this interpretation be correct, then it would follow that for a group of younger (that is, preschool) children a still smaller proportion should develop appropriate mediating responses. It would be expected that such a group, taken as a whole, would show clearcut evidence of the superiority of a nonreversal over a reversal shift. An experiment (Kendler, Kendler, and Wells, 1960) designed to test this hypothesis produced results consistent with this prediction; like rats, nursery school children found a nonreversal shift to be easier than a reversal shift.

In a very recent study the experimental procedure was modified so that after learning the initial discrimination, the children of 3, 4, 6, 8, and 10 years of age who served as subjects had a choice of either responding in a reversal or a nonreversal manner. Under such circumstances, it would be expected that the proportion of children who respond in a reversal manner would increase with age. Figure 5 shows that the percentage of children who chose a reversal shift rose gradually from 37.5 at 3 to 62.5 at 10.

Generalizing from all of these results, it would seem that in their early development, children tend to respond in a manner consistent with a single unit S-R theory. With age, they develop a tendency to respond in a mediational manner. The last study cited suggests that it is, or will soon be, possible to ascertain the lawful relationship governing the course of this development.

The point of these experiments is

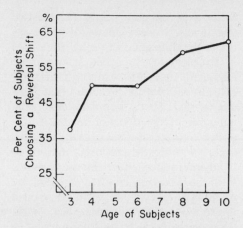

FIG. 5. *Percentage of children responding in a reversal shift manner as a function of age.*

not to classify children into one of two categories: rat-like or human-like. Their aim is to lay the groundwork for experiments designed to investigate the mediational process itself. If one wants to investigate mediational processes, does it not seem sensible to scrutinize them at the time when they are developing? Answering this question in the affirmative, it was decided to investigate the relationship between the hypothesized mediational processes and verbal behavior—a relationship everybody assumes to be intimate and important.

Particularly relevant to this attempt to co-ordinate verbalization with mediation were observations that during the course of the experiments just described, it was not uncommon for children to verbalize spontaneously the correct solution while simultaneously making an incorrect choice. A few children did this for many consecutive trials. This observation is relevant to the concept of vertical processes. Two chains of habits are occurring simultaneously. One has to do with verbal response; the other with the overt choice. For these children the two

chains are parallel, that is, they do not interact.

Luria (1957), the Russian psychologist, made somewhat similar observations in his research with children. He explains this sort of phenomenon in the following way:

> In the early stages of child development, speech is only a means of communication with adults and other children. . . . Subsequently it becomes also a means whereby he organizes his own experience and regulates his own actions. So the child's activity is mediated through words (p. 116).

These observations and their interpretations of noninteracting parallel processes point to the complex interrelationships existing between verbal behavior on the one hand and problem-solving on the other. If nothing else, they destroy the illusion that it is reasonable to describe an organism as verbal or nonverbal without considering the problem with which it is confronted. The terms verbal and nonverbal become meaningful—and fruitful—when related to specific problem-solving tasks.

It would seem fruitful to investigate the cue function of words for children of two age levels. One possibility is that age influences problem-solving only in so far as it leads to the acquisition of words. If younger children, say 4 years of age, could acquire the same words as 7-year-olds, they would solve a simple concept-learning problem the same way. The other possibility is that the acquisition of the verbal label by itself is not sufficient; the word must be integrated with other behavioral chains to influence problem-solving behavior. And for this to happen some developmental changes must first take place.

In order to test these two alternatives, children of 4 and 7 years of age were presented with another variation

First
Discrimination

Second
Discrimination

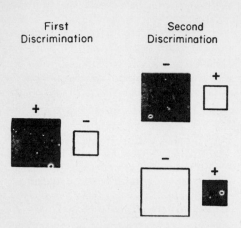

FIG. 6. *The experimental procedure used to study the influence of verbal habits on a reversal shift.*

of the reversal shift problem as shown in Fig. 6. They initially learned a simple discrimination between a pair of stimuli that varied simultaneously in size and brightness. In the illustration provided in Fig. 6, the large black square is correct. While they were learning, the children were required to verbalize aloud the stimuli to which they were responding. One-third learned to say "large" (or "small" as the case may be) by the simple device of instructing them to tell the experimenter which was correct, the large or the small one. Another third learned to say "black" (or "white") in a corresponding way. The remaining third was not required to say anything. After learning the discrimination, all subjects were presented with a reversal shift. In the example depicted in Fig. 6, the shift is to small regardless of size. Thus, the group that initially described the correct stimulus as "large" had verbalized the relevant dimension. The verbal response of "black" was irrelevant to this reversal shift.

Figure 7 shows the results of the

three experimental groups for the two age levels. If developmental processes affect the utilization of verbal responses in problem-solving, then it would be expected that the three verbalization conditions (which produced a significant main effect) would influence the behavior of the two age groups differently. These results suggest, but not quite at a significant level, that there is an interaction effect. Figure 7 shows that the younger children profited by making the kind of verbal response appropriate to a reversal shift, while they were hindered by learning inappropriate verbal responses. With no verbalization the 7-year-old children, who presumably were responding largely in a mediational manner, accomplished a reversal shift much more rapidly than their younger counterparts. But unlike the 4-year-olds, they did not profit from being trained to make the relevant responses. At 7 years of age they are capable of making the response themselves and out-

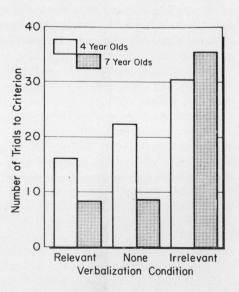

FIG. 7. *The effect of verbalizations on a reversal shift for 4- and 7-year-old children.*

side help appears to be of little use. In contrast, the influence of irrelevant verbalizations is marked. The performance of the 7-year-olds was even poorer than that of the 4-year-olds, suggesting that the interfering effects of being given an inappropriate mediated response are greater when one is capable of spontaneously generating the correct one (7-year-olds) than when one is not (4-year-olds).

How are these data to be explained? Attributing differences to developmental factors is not sufficient. It is necessary to represent developmental differences in terms of the concepts of the behavior model that is being used. That is, if a verbal label for a young child does not possess the same cue function as it does for an older child, then it becomes necessary to specify how and why this comes about. To some extent this has been done by emphasizing the transition from a single unit to a mediational system, as well as suggesting that with age an increase occurs in interaction among chains of different vertical levels. But obviously this analysis of the developmental process demands further theoretical and empirical development.

These studies are intimately related to the oft-reported finding that many species of subhuman animals are able to make a fairly rapid reversal shift *if* they receive a previous series of such shifts. Rats (Buytendijk, 1930; Krechevsky, 1932) show a marked improvement in executing successive reversals. They finally reach a point (Dufort, Guttman, and Kimble, 1954), in a T maze, where they learn to go to a new rewarded goal after making only one error. Even more dramatic are the rapid discrimination reversals exhibited by Harlow's (1949) monkeys. But fish (Wodinsky and Bitterman, 1957) exhibit only a slight improvement in successive reversals,

while isopods (invertebrates) show no improvement (Thompson, 1957).

Because of the necessity to use somewhat different experimental procedures for different species, it is difficult to draw an unqualified conclusion about the ability of different species to transfer what has been learned from previous reversal shifts to a new one. But the suggestion is strong that as you ascend the evolutionary scale organisms acquire a greater capacity to generate cues that enable them to make rapid reversal shifts. This behavior, according to our analysis, borders on the language responses of humans. The main difference is that our human subjects, except those of a very young age, exhibit rapid reversals without any previous reversal training. Whereas the human automatically seems to generate a mediated response that provides the basis for his rapid reversal, the animal subject must gradually acquire an ability to respond appropriately to some response-produced cue resulting from nonreinforcement of a previously correct response.

Up to now, the reversal and nonreversal technique has been used to investigate mediational and developmental variables. It has proved sufficiently flexible to be used in a study (Kendler, Glucksberg, and Keston, 1961) which was designed to lengthen a problem-solving chain so that the interaction between various segments could be observed. In this study a perceptual orienting S-R unit was added on to the mediational chain already described. Figure 8 illustrates in an oversimplified manner the behavioral sequence involved in this study in which subjects had to learn to press the correct button when two physically discrete and spatially separate stimulus patterns were projected on a screen at such a rapid rate that only one could be perceived on any

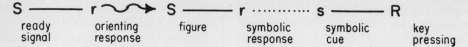

FIG. 8. *The hypothesized behavioral chain operating at the time the subject was being shifted to the second concept. (Capital letters refer to directly observable stimulus and response events, while small letters refer to those that are inferred.)*

trial. During the learning of each of two successive concepts (involving either a reversal or nonreversal shift), the subject had to pay attention to the relevant stimulus pattern while ignoring the irrelevant one. Thus, in order to make the correct overt response consistently, a subject initially had to make the appropriate orienting response in order to perceive the relevant stimulus pattern to which he had to make the correct mediational response which served as the cue for the key-pressing act.

An experimental design was used in which, at the time of the shift from the first to the second concept, one group had already learned the appropriate orienting response as well as the appropriate mediating act. They needed only to learn a new terminal key-pressing response. The shift, for them, was easy to make. In contrast, the behavior of three other experimental groups was significantly worse. One group had to learn a new orienting response, for example, look to the left instead of the right. Another group had to learn a new mediated response (that is, they were required to make a nonreversal shift). The last group had to acquire both a new orienting and mediated response. The fact that the groups which were missing one or both of the necessary behavior units (orienting and mediated responses) did not differ significantly among themselves, as well as being much poorer than the group that had both, highlights the problem of synchronizing the S-R units in a behavioral chain. The advantage

in this study of having one appropriate unit without the other is at best negligible. The reason for this is that reinforcement is only achieved consistently when both the appropriate orienting and mediating responses are operating. This particular study points to the need for discovering laws associated with the strengthening and weakening of independent S-R units in a problem-solving chain, as well as the principles governing their synchronization.

This study also highlighted a very basic problem in all of these reversal studies. This problem has to do with the very first correct response following the reversal shift. After discovering that the previous mode of responding is erroneous, what makes the subject change his response, that is, push the button that was previously wrong? Introspective reports fail to provide any clearcut answer and even if they did they would be in need of explaining (Kendler, 1961).

One hypothesis is that the selection of the new correct response is due to the operation of a behavioral chain in addition to the one described in Fig. 8. The first nonreinforcement in a reversal shift sets off a chain, the consequence of which is to select the response other than the one that was previously correct. This may result from a number of different reasons (for example, logical considerations, forgetting, and so forth). The important point, however, is that the new key-sorting response occurs contiguously with the implicit mediational response appropriate to a reversal shift. As a result, a new association is formed between the old implicit cue and the new key-pressing response.

In essence, what is being stated is that adult subjects, when making or deciding to make the first correct post-shift response, do not adopt the *principle* underlying a reversal shift. Instead, it is assumed processes are operating which encourage the selection of the correct response while an implicit cue appropriate to a reversal shift is operating. This sort of an analysis was described previously (Kendler and Mayzner, 1956) as

> sort of a James-Lange theory of problem solving . . . one makes the overt correct . . . response and if the appropriate symbolic cue is present, then problem solution will occur (pp. 247-248).

Guthrie (1959) says the same thing more neatly: *"What is being noticed becomes a signal for what is being done"* (p. 186).

Again the authors would like to guard against giving the impression of oversimplifying a terribly complex problem. They do not believe the contiguous occurrence of an implicit cue from one chain with the correct overt response from another tells the whole story. This new association in order to persist must be reinforced and in some manner "fit into" the subject's ongoing behavioral chains.

The emphasis on this vertical connection between a cue and a response from different chains is related in a distant way to Hebb's (1958) stressing the role of "chance" in problem-solving:

> There are few scientists who have not had the experience of setting out to solve problem A and ending up instead with the solution to B. . . . This is serendipity, the art of finding one

thing while looking for another (p. 215).

According to the present analysis, serendipity results from the adventitious and contiguous occurrence of a cue and a response which are themselves segments from different behavior chains. Theoretically it should be possible to demonstrate this point experimentally by training subjects to respond simultaneously to two separate tasks. A problem then would have to be presented that requires for its solution the combination of a stimulus from one chain with the response from the other. In such an experimental situation, controlling the time relationship between the two should have an important effect on problem-solving. Presumably contiguity between the two should provide the most optimal conditions for problem-solving (Underwood, 1952). The development of this kind of experimental procedure should allow for parametric studies of the basic variables of the phenomenon which has commonly been called "insight," as well as throw light upon issues raised by others (for example, Cofer, 1957; Maltzman, 1955; Saugstad, 1957).

The pretheoretical model that guides the present research has many more facets that can be exploited. Only one will now be mentioned. Glucksberg (1962), for example, extended neo-behavioristic drive theory (Spence, 1956) to problem-solving. He used a functional-fixedness problem (Adamson, 1952, Duncker, 1945) in which the correct response in the habit hierarchy could either be made to be low or high. If the correct habit was low, it would be expected that a strong drive would retard problem-solving because it would retard the extinction of the dominant incorrect response (Kendler and Lachman, 1958; Perin, 1942). Since drive energizes behavior, a high drive should facilitate problem-solving performance when the correct habit is dominant. The findings were consistent with this analysis.

Because functional-fixedness problems are often represented in perceptual terms, Glucksberg was interested in seeing whether the same drive model could be applied to a simple perceptual recognition problem in which subjects were instructed to identify tachistoscopically presented words as rapidly as possible. The results were similar to those reported for the functional-fixedness study: when the correct response was dominant, an increase in drive improved performance, that is, the visual duration threshold was lowered. In contrast, increasing drive when the correct response was low in the hierarchy raised the threshold.

There is obviously still much more work, both empirical and theoretical, needed to develop the model that has been described. At this point it may be appropriate to summarize the major points of this paper.

There is not just one way to investigate problem-solving. The researcher who is interested in problem-solving has several different pretheoretical models from which to choose. This paper reported the results of a research program based on an S-R model in which the importance of horizontal and vertical processes were emphasized. Horizontal processes refer to the linking of successive S-R units into a behavioral chain, while vertical processes refer to the assumption that independent chains occur simultaneously. A series of experiments was reported, the implications of which supported postulating a mediational mechanism within a behavioral chain. By comparing the behavior of human subjects of different ages, as well as relating their results to lower animals,

it was possible to infer that as a child matures he makes a transition from responding on the basis of a single unit S-R mechanism to a mediational one. Additional data were cited that suggest the full impact of verbal behavior on problem-solving depends on developmental processes that encourage interaction between chains at different vertical levels. It was also suggested that problem-solving begins in a simple concept learning task when a correct overt response from one behavioral chain occurs contiguously and adventitiously with the appropriate implicit cue from another chain. The paper was concluded by citing findings that suggested the neobehavioristic drive theory which assumes that the effect of different levels of drive depends on the position of the correct response in the habit hierarchy is applicable to a functional-fixedness problem as well as a perceptual-recognition task.

If nothing else, it is hoped that the present paper demonstrates that it is possible to investigate problem-solving in a systematic fashion. If more psychologists accepted this possibility and were willing to expend their research energies in the field of problem-solving, progress in this area would be greater than it is today.

REFERENCES

Adamson, R. E., "Functional-fixedness as Related to Problem Solving," *Journal of Experimental Psychology*, **44** (1952), 288-91.

Buss, A. H., "Rigidity as a Function of Reversal and Nonreversal Shifts in the Learning of Successive Discrimination," *Journal of Experimental Psychology*, **45** (1953), 75-81.

———, "Reversal and Nonreversal Shifts in Concept Formation with Partial Reinforcement Eliminated," *Journal of*

Experimental Psychology, **52** (1956), 162-66.

Buytendijk, F. J. J., "Über das Umlernen," *Arch. Neerl. Physiol.,* **15** (1930), 283-310.

Cofer, C. N., "Reasoning as an Associative Process: III. The Role of Verbal Responses in Problem Solving," *Journal of Genetic Psychology,* **57** (1957), 55-58.

Dufort, R. H., N. Guttman, and G. A. Kimble, "One Trial Discrimination Reversal in the White Rat," *Journal of Comparative Physiological Psychology,* **47** (1954), 248-49.

Duncan, C. P., "Recent Research on Human Problem Solving," *Psychological Bulletin,* **56** (1959), 397-429.

Duncker, K., "On Problem Solving," *Psychology Monograph,* **58** (5, Whole No. 270 [1945]).

Glucksberg, S., "The Influence of Strength of Drive on Functional Fixedness and Perceptual Recognition," *Journal of Experimental Psychology* (1962). (On press.)

Guthrie, E. R., *The Psychology of Learning* (rev. ed.). New York: Harper & Row, Publishers, 1952.

―――, "Association by Contiguity," in *Psychology: A Study of a Science,* Vol. 2, ed. S. Koch, pp. 158-95. New York: McGraw-Hill Book Company, Inc., 1959.

Harlow, H. F., "The Formation of Learning Sets," *Psychological Review,* **56** (1949), 51-65.

Harrow, M. and G. B. Friedman, "Comparing Reversal and Nonreversal Shifts in Concept Formation with Partial Reinforcement Controlled," *Journal of Experimental Psychology,* **55** (1958), 592-97.

Hebb, D. O., *A Textbook of Psychology.* Philadelphia: W. B. Saunders Co., 1958.

Hull, C. L., "Knowledge and Purpose as Habit Mechanisms," *Psychological Review,* **37** (1930), 511-25.

―――, *A Behavior System.* New Haven, Conn.: Yale University Press, 1952.

Kelleher, R. T., "Discrimination Learning as a Function of Reversal and Nonreversal Shifts," *Journal of Experimental Psychology,* **51** (1956), 379-84.

Kendler, H. H., "Problems in Problem Solving Research," in *Current Trends in Psychological Theory: A Bicentennial Program.* Pittsburgh: University of Pittsburgh Press, 1961.

Kendler, H. H. and M. F. D'Amato, "A Comparison of Reversal Shifts and Nonreversal Shifts in Human Concept Formation Behavior," *Journal of Experimental Psychology,* **49** (1955), 165-74.

Kendler, H. H., S. Glucksberg, and R. Keston, "Perception and Mediation in Concept Learning," *Journal of Experimental Psychology,* **61** (1961), 186-91.

Kendler, H. H. and T. S. Kendler, "Inferential Behavior in Preschool Children," *Journal of Experimental Psychology,* **51** (1956), 311-14.

Kendler, H. H., T. S. Kendler, S. S. Pliskoff, and M. F. D'Amato, "Inferential Behavior in Children: I. The Influence of Reinforcement and Incentive Motivation," *Journal of Experimental Psychology,* **55** (1958), 207-12.

Kendler, H. H. and R. Lachman, "Habit Reversal as a Function of Schedule of Reinforcement and Drive Strength," *Journal of Experimental Psychology,* **55** (1958), 584-91.

Kendler, H. H. and M. S. Mayzner, Jr., "Reversal and Nonreversal Shifts in Card Sorting Tests with Two or Four Sorting Categories," *Journal of Experimental Psychology,* **51** (1956), 244-48.

Kendler, H. H. and R. Vineberg, "The Acquisition of Compound Concepts as a Function of Previous Training," *Journal of Experimental Psychology,* **48** (1954), 252-58.

Kendler, T. S. and H. H. Kendler, "Reversal and Nonreversal Shifts in Kindergarten Children," *Journal of Experimental Psychology,* **58** (1959), 56-60.

Kendler, T. S. and H. H. Kendler,

"Inferential Behavior in Children: II. The Influence of Order of Presentation," *Journal of Experimental Psychology,* **61** (1961), 442-48.

Kendler, T. S., H. H. Kendler, and D. Wells, "Reversal and Nonreversal Shifts in Nursery School Children," *Journal of Comparative Physiological Psychology,* **53** (1960), 83-88.

Koch, S., *Psychology: A Study of a Science.* Vol. I, *Sensory, Perceptual and Physiological Formulations.* New York: McGraw-Hill Book Company, Inc., 1959.

Kohler, W., *The Mentality of Apes.* New York: Harcourt, Brace & World, Inc., 1925.

Krechevsky, I., "Antagonistic Visual Discrimination Habits in the White Rat," *Journal of Comparative Psychology,* **14** (1932), 263-77.

Lachman, R., "The Model in Theory Construction," *Psychological Review,* **67** (1960), 113-29.

Luria, A. R., "The Role of Language in the Formation of Temporary Connections," in *Psychology in the Soviet Union,* ed. B. Simon, pp. 115-29. Stanford, Calif.: Stanford University Press, 1947.

Maier, N. R. F., "Reasoning in Humans: I. On Direction," *Journal of Comparative Psychology,* **10** (1930), 115-43.

Maltzman, I., "Thinking: From a Behavioristic Point of View," *Psychological Review,* **62** (1955), 275-76.

Meyer, M. F., *The Fundamental Laws of Human Behavior.* Boston: Gorham Company, 1911.

Perin, C. T., "Behavior Potentiality as a Joint Function of the Amount of Training and the Degree of Hunger at the Time of Extinction," *Journal of Experimental Psychology,* **30** (1942), 93-113.

Saugstad, P., "An Analysis of Maier's Pendulum Problem," *Journal of Experimental Psychology,* **54** (1957), 169-79.

Skinner, B. F., *Science and Human Behavior.* New York: The Macmillan Company, 1953.

Spence, K. W., "The Nature of Discrimination Learning in Animals," *Psychological Review,* **43** (1936), 427-49.

————, *Behavior Theory and Conditioning.* New Haven, Conn.: Yale University Press, 1956.

Thompson, R., "Successive Reversal of a Position Habit in an Invertebrate," *Science,* **126** (1957), 163-64.

Toulmin, S., *The Philosophy of Science.* London: Hutchinson University Library, 1953.

Underwood, B. J., "An Orientation for Research on Thinking," *Psychological Review,* **59** (1952), 209-20.

Watson, J. B., "Psychology as the Behaviorist Sees It," *Psychological Review,* **20** (1913), 158-77.

Wodinsky, J. and M. E. Bitterman, "Discrimination-reversal in the Fish," *American Journal of Psychology,* **70** (1957), 569-75.

The Development of the Regulatory Role of Speech *

A. R. Luria

We have seen that speech enters integrally into the structure of mental processes and that it is a powerful means of regulation of human behavior.

However, the following questions inevitably arise: how is the regulatory function of speech formed? What stages of development does it pass through? How is it converted from a means by which the adult shapes the child's behavior into the very complex mechanism thanks to which, in Pavlov's terminology, man can be considered "the highest self-regulating system"?

Let us examine these questions and by means of experimental investigations analyze the stages through which speech passes before it gradually becomes the main mechanism of conscious voluntary behavior.

To tackle the problem successfully one must first select a very simple model which embodies all the principal characteristics of the form of conscious voluntary regulation of behavior that interests us, and which at the same time is readily susceptible to exact and, if possible, psycho-physiological investigation.

It would not be wrong to state that *the accomplishment of a simple action on verbal instruction* can be regarded as the core of voluntary behavior regulated by speech.

There is every reason to believe that the old experiments on so-called "simple reactions," which played such a great role in the early development of experimental psychology may acquire new significance if we approach them from this standpoint.

Indeed, these very experiments with simple and complex reactions may prove very helpful in our investigation. In such cases we study reflex processes of a specific kind: they begin with the experimenter's verbal instructions, which bring about a definite conditioned connection in the child's cerebral cortex; they make the child obey precisely this conditioned connection which (throughout the experiment) must predominate over all other extraneous stimuli not included in this system. Later, in more complex forms, the conditioned connection linked to the verbal instructions can be supplemented and maintained by the child's own speech: he is able to formulate the required principle of reaction and to convert it into a regulator of his future behavior. Can a thorough, genetic analysis of the child's behavior in experiments with simple reactions allow us, therefore, to aproach these experiments afresh and throw new light on them?

* From A. R. Luria, *The Role of Speech in the Regulation of Normal and Abnormal Behavior* (New York: The Liveright Publishing Corp., 1961). Reprinted by permission of the publishers.

Let us try to uncover the real source of the phenomenon in question: let us see how the child becomes capable of subordinating his actions to the adult's verbal instructions, what forms this ability, and how, in gradually developing his ability to obey the adult's instruction, the child at the same time acquires the faculty of subordinating his actions to the connections formed *in his own speech.*

There are, in the literature, accounts of many detailed factual investigations carried out in many different countries, of the way in which the adult's verbal instruction first begins to influence the child's active behavior.

We know, from numerous Soviet studies by Shchelovanov, Rosengardt, Koltsova and others, that the adult's verbal instructions are not themselves immediately separated off from more general and direct affective forms of contact with the child. Only such verbal instructions (for instance "Give me your hands") as are uttered in a certain tone of voice as part of a definite, active situation can produce an appropriate reaction in the child. The affective and active situation as a whole still plays a decisive part at this early stage; a considerable time has yet to pass before the adult's speech becomes separated off from this situation and can call forth the required reactions in the child independently.

This very simple *impellant or initiating function of speech* may appear to develop as early as the beginning of the child's second year; it is indeed quite easy to get the required movements from a child of 18 months by verbal instructions only, such as "Give me your hands" or "Clap hands." Careful analysis, however, shows that the influence of this speech-function is still very limited here and that speech is quite useless when it conflicts with

an action already begun. Try, for example, giving a child of 20 months to 2 years verbal instructions to take its stockings *off* while it is pulling them *on* (this test was made in the Shchelovanov laboratory), or to put rings *on* a bar while it is taking them *off,* and you will see that your verbal instructions are unable to alter the action already begun; on the contrary, they will merely intensify it. Thus at this stage of development the child's action still predominates: although the adult's speech has already assumed an initiating function, it cannot yet inhibit an action once started, much less *switch the child from one action to another.*

This can quite easily be analyzed by a very simple experiment.

Give a child of 18 months to 2 years a rubber balloon with instructions to squeeze it. As Fig. 1 shows, the instructions readily bring about the required movement, but once having started, the child cannot *stop* the movement; the continual kinesthetic stimulation of the palm by the balloon will intensify the child's diffuse nervous excitation, and will induce further pressing movements. Though we have started the action by verbal instructions, we cannot similarly inhibit it; the added verbal instruction "That's enough" will not serve to discontinue the widely irradiating excitation process, but in many cases still further intensifies the now dominant motor-reaction system.

Thus at this early stage, while the initiating function of speech is manifestly already developed, its inhibitory function has not yet been defined. The third or preparatory function of speech, that is, its *regulatory function proper,* is of a still more complex kind, and develops at a still later age. This function is best illustrated by a very ordinary experiment with a "simple reaction." It might seem that when we

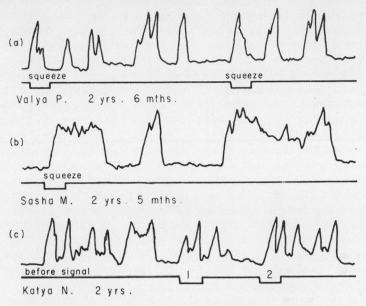

(a)

squeeze   squeeze

Valya P.   2 yrs . 6 mths .

(b)

squeeze

Sasha M.   2 yrs . 5 mths .

(c)

before signal   1   2

Katya N.   2 yrs .

Fig. 1. *Unregulated motor reactions in a child of pre-school age. Generalized action of verbal order or instruction. (Experiments by S. V. Yakovleva)*

say to a child "When you see the light squeeze the balloon" we do not demand any complex form of activity. This is not so however. In actual fact such a verbal instruction is a good deal more complex than was the previous direct instruction just to squeeze the balloon. To carry it out the child has to be able to link the symbol of the future stimulus (that is, the light) with that of the consequent response (the movement); but this movement must not be made at once but only after the real stimulus (the light) has appeared. Thus in this case the verbal stimulus *inhibits* both the direct search for the signal, and the actual movement. The essence of the instruction is that it demands a *synthesis* of the two verbal elements: it is this creation of *a preliminary system regulating a subsequent course of action* that is the principal distinguishing feature of such verbal instructions.

Can a child of 18 months to 2 years, with an initiating speech-function al-

ready developed, readily subordinate his actions to such a preliminary conditioned system of verbal connections?

Yakovleva's experiments in our laboratory have shown that a child often finds that to perform such a task is beyond him. The experiments show that in such cases the conditioned verbal instructions do not yet present a synthetic system; they still act in piecemeal fashion; the words "when you see the light" produce direct orienting reactions in the child, who begins looking for the light signal; the words "squeeze the ball" produce direct motor reactions which—owing to the conditions mentioned—become diffused and persist as a cycle of movements not controlled by speech. Because of the direct initiating action of the separate parts of the verbal instructions, the presentation of the stimulus itself (the light signal) may produce not the conditioned motor reaction of squeezing the ball, but a direct orienting reaction; the presentation of the light signal fails to take on the required signalling property, and the light begins to act as an external inhibitory agent and paradoxically causes the reaction to be discontinued (Fig. 2).

Typically, the inhibitory action of speech in such cases is incapable of producing a regulatory effect; both the generalizing verbal instructions ("Don't squeeze when there is no light") and the repeated inhibitions ("Don't squeeze, don't squeeze") will either act unspecifically and result in even more intense squeezing (Fig. 3) or will at best result in complete irradiated inhibition and the discontinuance of all motor reactions (Fig. 4).

Only through protracted and consistent training aimed at mastering each link in the verbal instructions separately, and based on practical demonstration and active reproduction of the action in question, can the connection required by the verbal instructions be formed and the child's conditioned reaction to the signal become more firmly established. Even then, however, we do not obtain a stable and distinct system of reactions to the conditioned signals. The action

of squeezing the balloon persists for some time after the light has ceased to appear as a cycle of reflex movements not co-ordinated with the signal. This demonstrates the diffuse nature of the motor excitation since the child is virtually unconscious of the fact that he is continuing to squeeze the balloon and the movements remain uncontrollable (Fig. 4 shows a record of such an experiment, typical of children aged 2½ to 3 years).

We have described the period in a child's development when his behavior is influenced solely by the very elementary initiating function of speech and when any attempt to use adult verbal instructions to inhibit motor activity already begun is unsuccessful.

Does this mean that it is quite impossible to get a young child to perform a voluntary action consisting of the inhibition of a motor action already begun and the subordination of movement to inhibitory verbal impulses? The fact that at this age the direct inhibitory function of speech is not yet developed, and that adult speech which attempts to inhibit nonvolitional motor reactions often operates unspecifically

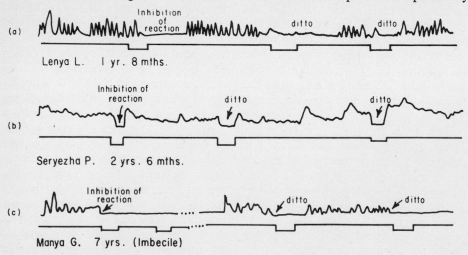

FIG. 2. *The inhibition of motor reactions by orientation to a signal: (a) and (b) are normal children, (c) is an imbecile.*

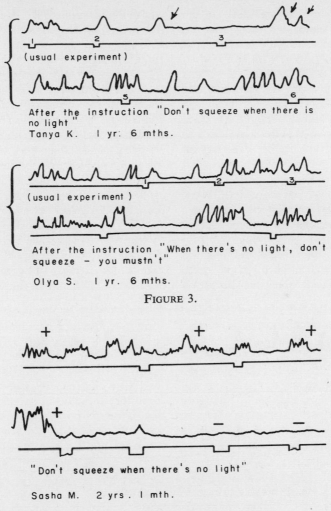

(usual experiment)

After the instruction "Don't squeeze when there is no light"

Tanya K.   1 yr: 6 mths.

(usual experiment)

After the instruction "When there's no light, don't squeeze — you mustn't"

Olya S.   1 yr. 6 mths.

FIGURE 3.

"Don't squeeze when there's no light"

Sasha M.   2 yrs. 1 mth.

FIGURE 4.

and only intensifies the motor reaction, does not prevent us from seeking the beginnings of the organization of volitional movement.

Some assumptions by Sechenov, later reproduced by Anokhin, help us in tackling this problem. These scientists maintained that the inhibition of a given action usually results from conflict between two excitations, the one inhibiting the other. Is it then possible to make use of the impelling, initiating action which adult speech already has for the child, and on this basis to produce a conflict between two excitations which would result in the inhibition of the reaction already begun?

With this aim in mind, we performed a very simple experiment, the results of which fully came up to our expectations. Having failed to stop the child's continual "extra-signal" squeezing of the ball by inhibitory verbal instructions, we asked him to perform two simple actions in succession: to squeeze the ball at the flash of an electric-light signal and then move his hand away at once (for instance, put it on his knee). When he had obeyed this double set of starting instructions (which did not present any difficulty to him), we gradually reduced the distance he had to move his hand after pressing the bulb. First he was told to put it not on his knee but on the table by the ball; then we reduced the distance still further, and at last, after some time, we were able to cut out the second and intermediary part of the instructions altogether. Having learned through performing the second action to thus inhibit the first, the child was now able to cope quite easily with a task which he had previ-

ously found impossible. He was able to co-ordinate his movements strictly with the signal and no longer produced any extra-signal squeezings of the bulb. Verbal instructions, previously ineffective, could now produce the required effect, thanks to the inhibitory influences prepared by the preliminary conflict between the two successive excitations. This effect was obtained in the great majority of children aged 18 months to 2 years, and in all children aged 2½ to 3 years. Figure 5 shows the definite effect obtained by this method.

The very fact that we have obtained the first and earliest model of organized action capable of overcoming the diffuseness of the motor impulses, can-

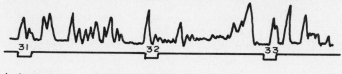

(a) Motor reaction to the signal (ball in hands)

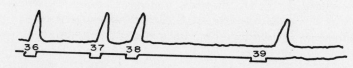

(b) Hand moves away every time

(c) Ball in hands again

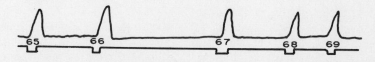

(d) do. after lengthy development of the inhibitory link (ball in hands again)

Pavel A.   2 yrs.   4 mths.

FIG. 5. *Experiment with the development in infants of the inhibitory link of reaction.*

not but encourage us in our further research. It shows once again how right Sechenov was when he regarded the voluntary movements of man as movements "acquired by learning." This impels us to continue and to intensify our work in this direction.

However, the organized movement obtained in this experiment, arose from a collision of two excitations, each of which had been called forth by the experimenter from the outside. Can we not make a new step forward and attempt to obtain a true voluntary movement—one in which the inhibition of inadequate motor impulses proceeds from the child himself.

To attempt such an experimental elaboration of an elementary voluntary act with its inherent inhibitory function it was necessary to make some basic changes in the experiment.

In the experiments so far described the verbal instructions served only as an impelling signal, while inhibitory verbal signals, to extinguish superfluous motor reactions, were not included in the experiment at all; their function was taken by the kinesthetic stimulations produced by the contractions of the muscles of the finger. It was these, in our experiment, which had to act as signals to inhibit further movements. However, we could not expect the still immature motor system of the child to ensure that these kinesthetic signals would serve an inhibitory function as well as an excitatory one and the inhibitory function of speech also proved insufficient for this purpose. Therefore the experiment remained imperfect: receiving no distinct signal of the *fulfillment* of the task, the child did not stop its motor reactions and instead produced superfluous pressures of the bulb. We were compelled to reshape the experiment radically and to find conditions which would bring about not only a beginning, but also an end, to the child's motor reaction.

Analysis of the reflex structure of the motor act showed the way here. Many outstanding neurophysiologists have repeatedly pointed out that the regulation of action requires a system of "feedback" afferentations which give a signal for the discontinuance of the action after its accomplishment; and they have also stated that without such a system of signals, arising from the effect of the action, movement cannot become controllable. These propositions, which are accepted in present-day cybernetics, have been frequently expounded in the works of British and American psychologists and have been substantiated in Soviet physiology by L. A. Orbeli, N. A. Bernstein, and P. K. Anokhin.

Following this line of thought is it possible to arrange our experiments in such a way as to make *the very movement of the child,* which has been initiated by the verbal instruction, *produce also a distinct (and possibly exteroceptive) signal sufficient to mark the end of the action, exert an influence according to the principle of "feedback" afferentation and extinguish the irradiated motor impulses?*

To obtain such a "self-regulating" model of action, we rearranged the scheme of our experiment. All the conditions of the experiment remained unchanged, but the infant was instructed to press the bulb at the flash of light and thereby *to put out the light* or, in the course of a more complex experiment, to press the bulb and thereby to ring a bell. Simple mechanical devices made it possible in this way to turn off the signalling light in the first case, and to bring an electric bell into action in the second. In this experiment the stimulation of movement was not discontinued at its beginning; the very movement of the child called forth a distinct exteroceptive signal, and this signal served as a sanctioning afferentation which signalized the fulfillment of the required action.

Experiments on these lines performed by S. V. Yakovleva yielded very interesting results: in 50 percent of all the children tested at 18 months to 2 years, and in 75 percent of children at the age of 2 to 3 years, this change in the instructions resulted in the complete disappearance of accidental intersignal pressures of the bulb and produced clear-cut reactions coordinated with the conditioned signal (Figs. 6 and 6a); on the other hand

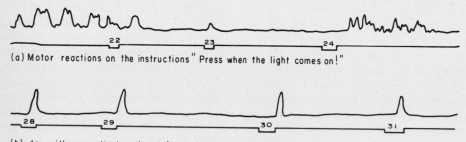

(a) Motor reactions on the instructions "Press when the light comes on!"

(b) do. with a sanctioning signal (each pressure extinguishes the lamp).

Experiment on Seryezha S.   2 yrs.

FIGURE 6.

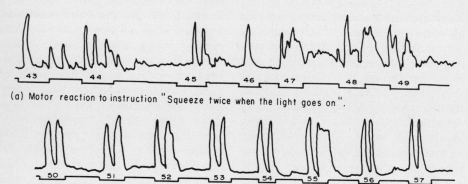
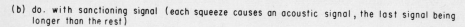

(a) Motor reaction to instruction "Squeeze twice when the light goes on".

(b) do. with sanctioning signal (each squeeze causes an acoustic signal, the last signal being longer than the rest)

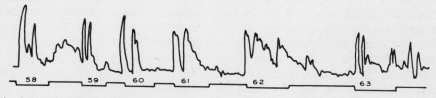

(c) do. but again without sanctioning signal

Experiment on Monya B.   3 yrs. 11 mths.

FIG. 6a. *The role of a sanctioning afferentation in the execution of a voluntary movement.*

the removal of the sanctioning afferentation led, in the overwhelming majority of children, to the recovery of the original diffusiveness of the motor reactions. Only one-third of the older children (at the age of 2 to 3) still continued to co-ordinate their movements in time with the signals.

These experiments cannot but prove that *we have obtained the first and simplest model of a voluntary movement in a very young child.* This movement is started by verbal instruction and is stopped by visual exteroceptive signals which arise from the child's own movement. While preserving its reflex nature, it acquires all the features of a voluntary, self-regulating act. What could not be achieved through the action of the experimenter's inhibitory speech proved quite attainable through the introduction of a sanctioning signal arising from the movement. Is not this the simplest model of the self-regulating act, the analysis of which has been recently given so much attention? And does not this method of experimentation already produce an effect in children so young that one could hardly expect to obtain a real voluntary movement?

The obtaining of a very simple model of voluntary action in a child at the age of 2 to 2½ opens up new prospects for our further research.

The first and simplest voluntary action of the child was regulated by an external sanctioning signal, which arose from the movement of the child itself. Is it possible, however, to ensure the organization of the experiment in such a way that self-regulation proceeds from the child itself without the help of any external regulating signal?

To this end we can quite naturally utilize the speech of the adult, which has from the first served to organize the child's behavior, and later the child's own speech. Will not both these factors help us to solve our problem and provide us with a means for the formation of true voluntary actions?

Let us recall the features which characterize both the further development of the child's ability to obey clear verbal instructions, as well as the regulatory functions of the child's own speech.

As we have already seen, at the age of 3 to 4 years substantial changes take place in the speech behavior of the child. Experience shows that an initiating system of connections can easily be established through verbal instructions in a child of 3 to 3½ years; this can be achieved by suggesting to the child that he does not act at once but waits till the conditioned signal appears. An even more complex system of connections can be produced in this way—for example, by suggesting to the child that he press a bulb in response to a red signal and does not press in response to a green signal. However, as shown by the investigation carried out in our laboratory by N. P. Paramonova, here the excitatory part of the verbal instruction still remains considerably stronger than the inhibitory part, and the motor excitation evoked by the verbal instruction is still highly diffuse; as a rule, a child of 3 to 3½, will readily produce a motor reaction in response to a positive signal, but will often continue to exhibit uncontrolled inter-signal reactions. Moreover, following verbal instructions, he is able to abstain from pressing the bulb at the appearance of the inhibitory signal for only a very short time. The direct, stimulating influence of this signal is here so strong, and the inhibitory property imparted to it by the verbal instruction is so weak that it is not long before a motor reaction to the inhibitory signal begins to appear (Fig. 7). In such cases

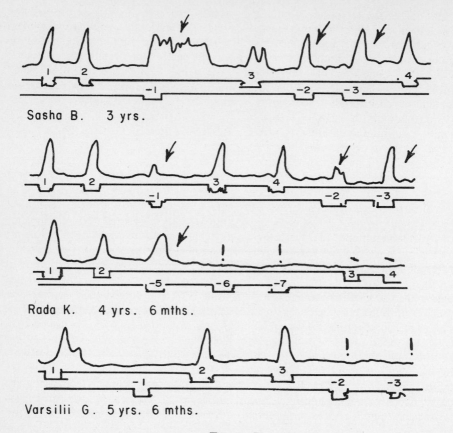

Sasha B.   3 yrs.

Rada K.   4 yrs. 6 mths.

Varsilii G. 5 yrs. 6 mths.

FIGURE 7.

therefore it is necessary to apply a different method and to reinforce each signal by a special verbal instruction in order to strengthen the inhibitory property of the signal and thus gradually to elaborate the required system of differentiated reactions.

Figure 8 shows that such a task, which cannot be accomplished by preliminary verbal instruction, can easily be carried out with the help of continuous verbal reinforcement, and that the experimenter's speech which, by this time has acquired a firmly established inhibitory property, leads to the concentration of the diffuse excitation of the child and to the formation of a complete, differentiated reaction.

However, the fourth year in the life of the child, that is, the first year of preschool childhood, is characterized not only by the ability of the child to fulfill rather complicated instructions of the adult, but also by the fact that the child's own speech becomes rather more rich, fluent and mobile.

Can we not use this newly developed skill in the formation of further methods of instruction?

We have seen that, at the first stage of development, the regulation of the movements of the child could only be obtained when the motor reaction itself produced a distinct exteroceptive signal indicating the effect of the action; we have also seen that at the next stage of development such a regulatory influence can proceed from the

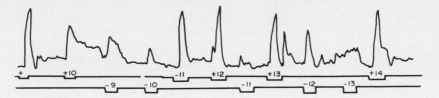

(a) The evolution of a system from a positive and inhibitory reaction to a preliminary verbal instruction

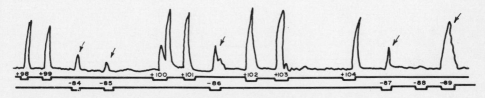

(b) Verbal reinforcement "correct!" Do. with continuous verbal reinforcement

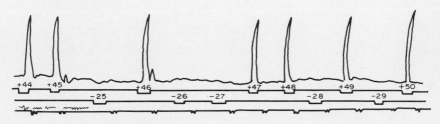

(c) Do. after cessation of continuous verbal reinforcement

Natasha B.   3 yrs. 6 mths.

FIG. 8. *The development of differentiated reactions in a 3½-yr.-old child, using verbal instruction and continuous verbal reinforcement.*

sanctioning verbal reinforcement of each reaction by the adult.

But can this regulatory function be assumed by the *child's own speech?*

To answer this question, let us change once again the form of our experiment. Let us ask the child to reinforce its motor reactions by its own speech, accompanying each motor response to the signal by its own verbal command "Go!", "Go!"

Is it possible that the child's speech is now well enough developed, and that the neurodynamic processes governing it are now sufficiently perfect to enable him to regulate his motor re-

actions through speech rather than through other influences of a more constant and direct nature, such as the kinesthetic stimulation proceeding from the contact with the bulb?

All attempts to make use of the regulatory role of the child's own speech at the age of 2 to 2½ ended in failure. The speech system of children at this age is still imperfect, and to obtain even the simplest verbal reactions to conditioned signals proved impossible: moreover, such attempts impeded the organized motor reactions of the child. It is true that in these experiments children at the age of 2 or

2½ at first reacted to the signals with the word "Go!" (or with any other phonetically simple vocal reaction); however, these reactions proved very unstable: the child soon showed himself unable to pronounce the word "Go!" and simultaneously to press the bulb. The verbal reactions either became rapidly extinct, or were produced stereotypically, without any connection with the signal; finally in some cases they began to inhibit the motor reactions by way of negative induction. Figure 9 shows pictorially how this

experiments demanding motor reactions, these experiments resulted in practically no perseverating verbal behavior produced independently of the signal, nor on the other hand did the responses become extinct. All the data obtained showed that *the neurodynamics of simple verbal reactions at this age become much more perfect than the neurodynamics of the motor reactions and prove to be quite concentrated and mobile.*

Is it possible, therefore, to make use of this neurodynamically quite perfect

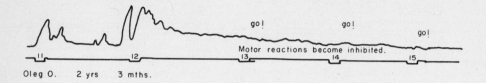

Oleg O.   2 yrs   3 mths.

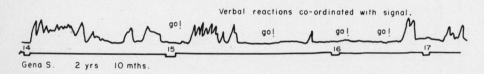

Gena S.   2 yrs   10 mths.

FIG. 9. *The negative influence of verbal accompaniment of motor reactions in infants.*

highly complicated task deranges organized motor reactions in children at the age of 2 to 2½.

Quite different results were obtained in children of 3 to 4 years, especially in those whose speech had been thoroughly trained in the kindergarten.

Unlike 2-year-old children, they did not experience any appreciable difficulties in fulfilling the instruction to react to each signal with the words "Go!", "Go!" This task interested them greatly; their verbal reactions were always strictly co-ordinated with the signals, the latent periods being much more stable than those in the motor reactions. In contrast to the

and, consequently, controllable system, to substitute it for the additional sanctioning signals, and thus obtain with its help the required regulatory effect?

Let us recall the distinct change that is produced in the course of the motor reactions by the introduction into the experiment of sanctioning exteroceptive signals; the effect of these signals becomes still more perfect and distinct in children at the age of 3 to 3½.

Whereas, in the course of our usual experiments with motor responses produced by verbal instruction we did not succeed in extinguishing the diffuse motor reactions, the introduction of additional sanctioning signals led to their complete discontinuance. If, in our usual experiments, the child's motor reactions exhibited a direct dependence on the character of the stimulus, as a result of which protracted stimulations produced a long tonic pressure of the bulb or repeated pressures during the entire period of action of the stimulus, the introduction of additional sanctioning afferentation made the movement no longer dependent on the character of the stimulus.

Instead, the child began to be able to obey the verbal instruction (Fig. 10).

However, the most essential and fundamental fact, characteristic of this stage of the child's development, is that *similar results can be obtained if we replace the external sanctioning afferentation by the child's own speech.* We suggest that the child himself says "Go!" in response to each flash of light and simultaneously presses the bulb; thereby *we replace the regulatory action of the external signal* by

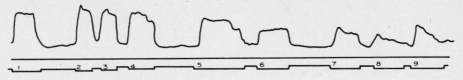

Instruction "Press when light goes on" (in silence).

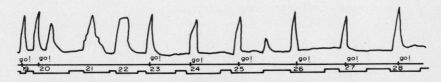

Do. accompanied by reactions to speech impulses.

Valya S.   3 yrs.

FIG. 10. *The regulation of motor reactions by speech impulses.*

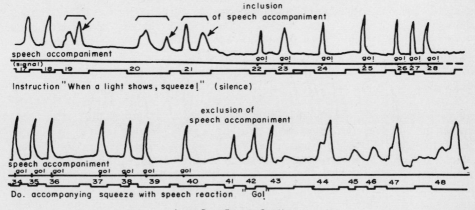

inclusion of speech accompaniment

speech accompaniment (signal)

Instruction "When a light shows, squeeze!" (silence)

exclusion of speech accompaniment

speech accompaniment

Do. accompanying squeeze with speech reaction "Go!"

Lena D.   3 yrs. 9 mths.

FIG. 10a. *The regulation of motor reactions by verbal impulses.*

the child's own verbal command, which, owing to its more perfect neurodynamics and greater controllability, now becomes a good regulating mechanism.

Let us cast a glance at Figs. 11 and 12 which demonstrate the results of such experiments performed in our laboratory by M. P. Peskovskaya and O. N. Tikhomirova. The first of these figures clearly shows that the introduction by the child of speech into the

experiment fully eliminates the diffuseness of the motor processes, strictly co-ordinates the movements with the signals and imparts to them a distinct and organized character; we can also see that with the abolition of this verbal reinforcement the motor reactions of the child again acquire a diffuse character and become poorly controlled. The second figure shows that the introduction of the child's own verbal reactions into the experiment

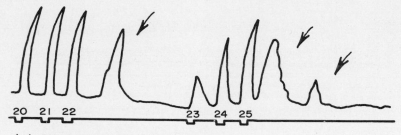

(a) Simple reactions (Speechless)

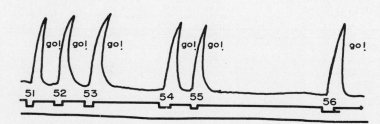

(b) do. with speech reactions go!

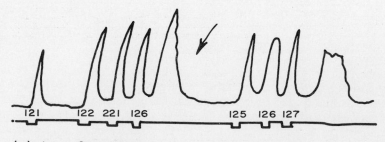

(c) do. — Speechless

Lena P.   3 yrs. 6 mths.

FIGURE 11.

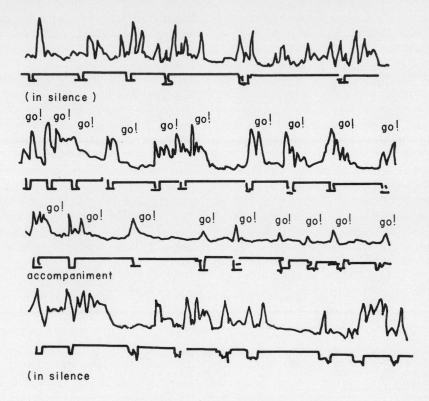

(in silence)

go! go!
go!
go!
go! go!
go! go!
go!
go!

go!
go!
go!
go! go! go! go! go!
go!

accompaniment

(in silence

Olya B.   3 yrs. 9 mths.

FIGURE 12

puts an end to the dependence of the motor reactions on the character of the stimulus and subordinates them to the task formulated in the verbal instruction; the child, whose motor responses during the action of short and protracted stimuli were not of an equally distinct character, begins to accomplish the task quite easily; he subordinates his movement to his own abruptly pronounced command "Go!" which turns into a link between the conditioned stimulus and the reaction that controls the movements.

The regulatory role of the child's own speech can be still better illustrated, if we make our experiment somewhat more complicated.

Let us give a child of 3 or 4 years the following verbal instructions: "When the light appears, press twice!"; we will be able to see that the child is unable to cope with this task. Even knowing the meaning of the word "twice" perfectly well, the child will fulfill the task only once or twice and even then provided that the signal is not too protracted. The motor excitation produced in the child easily irradiates and no longer obeys the instruction; instead of pressing the balloon twice, the child presses it three times, four times and, finally, many times in succession. But as soon as we pass to another form of experiment in which the motor reactions to the signal are accompanied by the verbal reaction "Go!" "Go!", the irradiation of excitation stops, and the child begins to produce the required double pressures; with the discontinuance of these verbal reactions the motor reactions of the child once again acquire a diffuse character (Fig. 13).

It is difficult to overestimate the fundamental significance of these facts. In our experiments with the action of additional exteroceptive signals we succeeded in obtaining the first, although artificial, model of the simplest voluntary action of the child. But the experiments with the introduction of the child's own speech allowed us to study the *initial stages* of formation of *the natural self-regulating system* in which *the neurodynamically most perfect and developed link assumes the* *role of a regulating mechanism* reinforced by the verbal instruction which makes possible the accomplishment of a real voluntary act.

Let us now try to characterize the mechanism which determines the regulatory influence of the child's own speech at this stage. Is this regulatory effect of the child's own speech due to the fact that the motor reactions are included in the system of elective, significative connections produced by speech, or is the influence of the child's own speech observed in the course of our experiments even more elementary, and therefore considerably more limited?

When analyzing different forms of the influence of speech we have al-

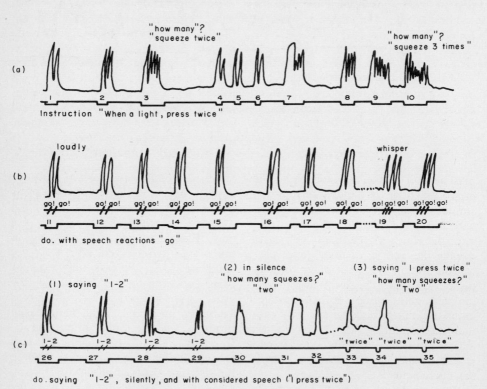

Sasha Sh.   Experiment 12.1.56.

FIGURE 13.

ready, at the beginning of this lecture, described the impelling or starting function of verbal instruction, as well as its inhibition and specific coupling function (or regulatory function proper). Is it possible to make use of these differentiated criteria and with their help discover which aspect of the child's own reactions performs a regulatory function in our case?

There is no doubt that the verbal reaction "Go!", which acts according to the feedback principle, is a complex stimulus for the child itself. On the one hand, the child's subsequent behavior can be influenced by the *innervating verbal impulse* which consists in the innervation of definite speech organs and creates a center of excitation in the motor speech area of the cerebral cortex. On the other hand, it includes also the system of *elective significative connections which are called forth by speech* and which turn it into a complex signal; the latter produces a certain system of reactions already in the previous experiment shown to be closely bound up with speech. Which of these two aspects— the unspecific—impulse aspects or the specifically significative one—appears as the regulator of motor reactions at this early stage of organization of the child's behavior?

The experiments just mentioned do not provide any answer to this question. Since the impulse function and the significative function coincide in the verbal reaction of the child, it is necessary to separate them, and thus obtain an answer to the question.

A very simple method may be of help in this respect. Let us slightly alter the conditions of the experiment just described. Let us suggest to a 3- or 4-year-old child, who has just successfully fulfilled the task of pressing the balloon twice in response to the signal, not to produce two separate verbal impulses—"Go!" "Go!" simultaneously, but to react to each light flash by the generalized verbal command "I shall press twice!"

It might seem that the alteration introduced by us into the experiment is insignificant. In reality, however, we have fundamentally changed the conditions of the experiment. While in the first variant the regulatory influence of the verbal reaction could proceed from two isolated impulses ("Go!" "Go!"), these two isolated impulses are now fully removed, and the regulatory influence can proceed only from the *significative* side of the self-instruction, in other words, from the elective system of connections which was firmly established by these words in the course of the previous experiment. Moreover, in the new variant of the experiment, the impulse side of the verbal self-instruction even comes into conflict with its significative side: according to the latter, the child has to press the balloon twice, while the impulse side of the words "I shall press twice!" contains only a single, protracted, innervating signal.

To what does the child subordinate his motor reaction in this case?

Experiments performed by O. K. Tikhomirov with children 3 to 4 years old produced a very definite answer to this question. If the verbal command of the child himself—"Go!" "Go!"—was a successful regulator of the motor reactions in all cases without exception, the verbal command "I shall press twice!" did not call forth the necessary effect altogether; the child, as a rule, accompanied this command by a *single protracted movement*. This clearly shows that it is the impulse aspect of speech which played a regulatory role here rather than the system of elective significative connections. Figure 14 gives an example of the results obtained.

(a) Simple reaction. "When a light - press twice"

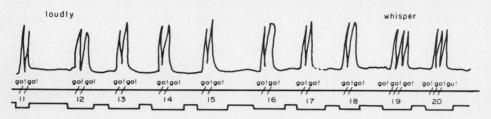

(b) do. - with speech reactions "go - go!"

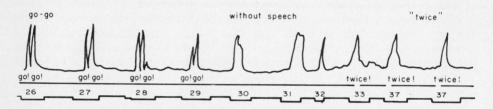

(c) Sasha 1.   3 yrs. 6 mths.

FIGURE 14.

There is, however, another even more convincing experiment which shows that the regulatory influence proceeds here from the impulse side of speech, rather than from the elective connections produced by the child's speech.

Up to now we have studied the regulatory role of speech only in experiments in which a simple reaction to the signal was required, experiments that is where the verbal impulse of necessity possessed only an impelling, starting property.

We are able, however, just as successfully, to carry out experiments on *the formation of differentiated systems of connections,* in which one signal possesses a positive property and another an inhibitory one. We have already seen how difficult it is for a child of this age to inhibit its direct, impulsive reaction to a signal which, according to the verbal instruction, was to acquire a conditioned inhibitory property.

Is it possible to inhibit this impulse reaction with the help of the child's own speech, if this accompanies each presentation of the stimulus and thus reinforces its signalling property? For this purpose we could suggest to the child that each positive signal is accompanied by the word "Press!" and each inhibitory signal by the words "Don't press!"

Experiments have shown that the

elaboration of such a differentiated verbal reaction to different signals does not present any difficulty to children of 3 or 4 years. However, in the light of what we have just said, the regulatory influence of such verbal reactions is in this appreciably impeded.

Indeed, the verbal reaction "Press!" accompanying each positive signal is of an impelling character both in its significative and impulsive aspects. The matter is quite different with the reaction "Don't press!" which accompanies the inhibitory signals. Whereas, in its significative aspect it must be of an inhibitory character, in its impulsive aspect it still retains as well the same innervation property as the positive signal "Press!" Which side of this complex verbal reaction—the impulse side, or the significative one—will take the upper hand and influence the motor reaction? In this case, too, experiments performed with children of 3 to 4 years of age have yielded very

definite results. While the verbal reaction of the child "Press!" which accompanied the positive signals, led to a concentration of excitation and produced distinct motor reactions co-ordinated with the signals, the verbal reaction "Don't press!" accompanying the inhibitory signals resulted not in the inhibition, but in the disinhibition of the motor reactons which, as shown in Fig. 15, are still further stimulated by the verbal impulse that accompanied the given signals. According to statistical data obtained by Tikhomirov, experiments on the elaboration of differentiated reactions, carried out in silence by children of 3 to 4 years of age, resulted in 42 percent of impulsive motor reactions to inhibitory signals; but when the presentation of these signals was accompanied by the child's own verbal command "Don't press!", the number of such disinhibited reactions increased to 70 percent.

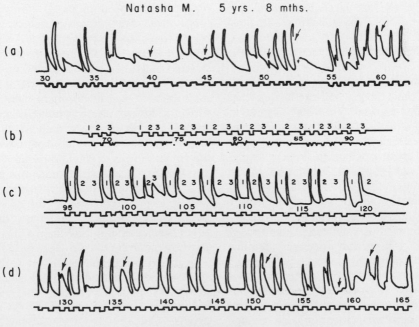

FIGURE 15.

Only when we suggested to the child that at each positive signal he should say the word "Press!" and simultaneously press the balloon, and in response to each inhibitory signal he should refrain from pressing the balloon *without uttering a single word* was conflict eliminated: the child, previously unable to elaborate a stable system of differentiated reactions by preliminary instruction, proved capable of attaining it with the help of its own regulatory speech.

From this it follows that it is perfectly possible for a child of 3 to 4 years of age to regulate his motor reactions with the help of his own speech which reinforces the action of the preliminary verbal instruction and subsequently acts in accordance with the principle of feedback afferentation. However, at this early stage—at least in conditions of our laboratory experiments—this regulatory influence proceeds *from the nonspecific, impulse aspect of the child's own speech rather than from its elective, significative aspect*. And if by this time the nonspecific influence of the speech of others is almost fully overcome in the child, it still persists with regard to the child's own speech.

We have considered the earliest and least investigated stages of formation of voluntary actions in the child and have described the specific and simplest forms in which the speech of the child appears as a regulatory of its behavior.

It remains for me to say a few words about the subsequent stages of development of this regulatory function of speech. The most essential feature characterizing these stages will appear unexpected to us; it is as follows: *the regulatory function is steadily transferred from the impulse side of speech to the analytic system of elective significative connections which are pro-*

duced by speech. Moreover, and this is most interesting, it simultaneously shifts *from the external to the internal speech of the child*.

Here we can manage many special experiments; but every experimenter naturally desires to investigate the genesis of the given phenomenon as thoroughly as possible, and prefers to accomplish it in one and the same series of experiments.

Experimental facts prove that the radical change just mentioned takes place in the child at the age of 4½ to 5½. Before this age it is absolutely impossible to elaborate in the child a stable system of motor reactions by means of verbal instruction only. Now the child easily grasps even such a complicated instruction as "Press in response to one signal and do not press in response to the other"; it regulates its further behavior by the internally retained verbal rule, and no longer produces any impulse reactions to the signal to which a conditioned inhibitory property has been imparted. Only in those cases when the conditions of the experiment are complicated, for example, when the presentation of the signals is accelerated or the differentiation between the two signals is made more difficult, can the inhibitory stimuli still produce impulse reactions; in such cases it is often observed that the child begins to pronounce the meaning of the signal; however, the verbal reaction of the child "Don't press!" here acts not from its impulse side but from its specific significative side—it does not disinhibit the impulse reactions, but, on the contrary, inhibits them. This is why in children at the age of 5 to 6 years the introduction of a verbal reinforcement of the inhibitory signal, as shown by the experiments of O. K. Tikhomirov, halves the number of impulse reactions in these relatively complex conditions. A similar influence of the child's own external speech is observed at this age in cases when, owing to the complexity of the experimental conditions, the traces of the verbal instruction begin to lose their regulatory function. This can be clearly seen, for example, in those cases when we offer the child a difficult task, the accomplishment of which requires most complex forms of internal inhibition—say, to press twice in response to short signals and to abstain from pressing in response to long signals, or to press in response to two successive similar signals and to abstain from pressing in response to a similar third signal. The proper accomplishment of such a task often proves impossible for a 5-year-old child if it tries to do it silently, merely by following the traces of the preliminary verbal instruction; however, the child proves able to cope with such a task easily if its fulfillment is accompanied by the child's own verbal reaction, which in this case reinforces the internal inhibition or fixes the sequence of the positive and inhibitory reactions.

But even in such cases a constant verbal regulation of the motor reactions is not always indispensable to normal children; it begins to play its role only in some special cases on which we shall dwell later. Therefore it often suffices to strengthen the verbal analysis of the signals presented to the child, and the internal verbal connections created by such training prove to be adequate for the further regulation of the child's motor reactions.

I have reviewed in general outline the long path of development of the regulatory role of speech in the formation of the child's behavior.

My review began at the stage when speech, being insufficiently developed, cannot serve as a regulator of the child's motor reactions; we have seen that at this stage the regulatory role

is played only by the separation of the action itself, as well as by the system of practical, exteroceptive afferentations which arise from the child's own movements. It may be assumed that the system of reverse connections, developing on a practical basis and acting in accordance with the feed-back principle, is the main form of regulation of the child's behavior at the early stages of its development.

We have also considered the second stage, when the role of these external reverse signals is assumed by the child's own speech, and when the latter begins to play a regulatory role. However, we could see that at this stage the new means still acts in the old way, and that its regulatory influence in our experiments proceeds not from the system of the significative connections which are produced by speech, but from the direct, impellant or initiating action of the speech itself.

It is only at the third stage, which is characterized by the development and enrichment of the child's speech, that this "impellant" action of speech recedes into the background and the leading role passes to the regulatory influence of the system of significative connections produced by speech. This stage, however, is followed by another, final stage: the external developed forms of speech become reduced, and the decisive influence is now exerted by that higher form of internal speech which constitutes an essential component both of thought and volitional action and whose objective study still remains the task of the rising generation of scientific psychologists.

This formation of internal speech, which is closely bound up with thought, leads to a new, specifically human, stage of development. The verbal analysis of the situation begins to play an important role in the establishment of new connections; the child orients himself to the given signals with the help of the rules he has verbally formulated for himself; this abstracting and generalizing function of speech mediates the stimuli acting upon the child and turns the process of elaboration of temporary connections into the complex, "highest self-regulating system" whose peculiar properties were described in my first lecture.

Experimental Investigation of the Relation of Language to Transposition Behavior in Young Children *

Margaret R. Kuenne

The phenomenon of transposition in the discrimination behavior of animals and young children has received a considerable amount of attention from psychological theorists. The Gestalt psychologists, in particular, have made much of this ability of Ss to transfer a learned differential response, for example, a response to the larger of two stimuli, to a new combination of stimulus objects differing in the same property (for example, size), and they have cited it as conclusive evidence that the response was to the relative properties of the stimulus situation.

* From M. R. Kuenne. "Experimental Investigation of the Relation of Language to Transposition Behavior in Young Children," *Journal of Experimental Psychology*, **36** (1946), 471-90. Reprinted by permission of the author and publishers.

This article is based on a dissertation submitted in partial fulfillment of the requirements for the degree of Doctor of Philosophy in the Iowa Child Welfare Research Station, in the Graduate College of the State University of Iowa. The writer is deeply indebted to Professor Kenneth W. Spence for his advice and assistance throughout the course of the study.

Relational theories of transposition, as has been pointed out by others (5, 27), fall into two groups. According to one type (1, 13, 15, 20, 22) the organism perceives the relationship between the training stimuli and employs this "relational-perception" in responding differentially to the transposed stimulus situation. Thus, Kinnaman, the earliest investigator of this problem, wrote regarding the results in his brightness experiment with monkeys: "It would appear then that if the monkey managed to choose with measurable correctness, he very likely had a general notion of a low order which might be represented by *food-always-in-the-lighter*" (15, p. 143).

The second type of relational theory conceives of the organism as responding differentially to the training stimuli as a stimulus whole. The formulations of Köhler (17, 18) and Gulliksen and Wolfle (5) fall into this category. Thus, Köhler, in explaining his brightness experiments, stresses the "togetherness" of the stimuli, recognizing that this togetherness may occur independently either as *color-wholes* or as *perceived color-relations.* He regards the two processes as distinct but their functions as similar, and so he chooses to ignore the differences. In either case, the colors (brightnesses) are assumed to attain an "inner union" in which their role "depends not upon their absolute qualities, but upon their places in the system they compose. If their places with respect to each other are held constant, but a variation is made in their absolute quality, the Gestalt and the perceived relationship will be transposed" (17, p. 221). The occurrence of transposition is then regarded as evidence of such a configural response.

Köhler has made no further attempt to elaborate his theory so as to explain the occurrences of failure of transposition which have been found under a number of experimental conditions. A configuration theory more adequate in this respect is the recent one of Gulliksen and Wolfle (5). They conceive of the animal in the discrimination situation as responding directionally to the total stimulus configuration consisting of the stimuli varying in a single dimension and presented simultaneously in a given spatial order. Thus, in the two-choice size discrimination situation, the animal learns to respond differentially (left or right) to the two configurations, small on left and large on right, small on right and large on left. They assume, further, the operation of the law of effect and generalization of the effects of the learning on the training-stimulus configuration to similar configurations. On the basis of this theoretical schema, these writers were able to deduce a number of implications which are in agreement with existing experimental data. An outstanding exception is the failure of the theory to deduce one of the most well-established experimental findings concerning transposition—the tendency for it to decrease as the distance between the training and test stimuli is increased.

Contrasting sharply with these two types of relational theories of transposition phenomena is the stimulus-response theory suggested by Spence (23, 24, 25, 26). Based on principles derived from experimental studies of conditioning, his theory represents an extension of an earlier theoretical treatment of the nature of discrimination learning in animals. According to this latter formulation, discrimination learning is a cumulative process in which reinforcement strengthens the excitatory tendency or association of the positive stimulus cue to the response of approaching it as compared with the response of approaching the negative stimulus cue which receives only nonreinforcement, hence developing an opposing inhibitory tendency. When the difference between the excitatory strengths of the two cue aspects is sufficiently large, so as always to be greater than any differences in the excitatory strengths of other stimulus aspects that may happen to be allied in their response-evoking action with one or another of the cue stimuli on a particular trial, the S will consistently respond to the positive stimulus; in other words, he will have learned.

In extending the theory to the problem of transposition, Spence assumes that the excitatory tendency to respond to the positive cue aspect generalizes to other members of the stimulus dimension according to the exponential function $E = Ae^{-cX^d}$, where X is the distance in logarithmic units between the positive stimulus and that stimulus point under consideration on the dimension. Similarly, the inhibitory tendency to respond to the negative cue aspect is assumed to generalize to other members of the stimulus dimension according to the function $I =$

Be^{-kX^d}, X being the distance in logarithmic units between the negative stimulus and that stimulus point under consideration on the dimension. The excitatory and inhibitory tendencies to respond to a stimulus cue at any point on the dimension are assumed further to summate algebraically, yielding the effective excitatory strength at that point. Which of a pair of any stimulus members of a dimension will be chosen by an organism after training on a particular pair will depend upon the magnitude of the difference in the effective excitatory strengths of the competing stimulus cues as calculated from the values of the generalization curves.

The accompanying diagram, Fig. 1,

that transposition will occur on pairs 256 vs. 160 and 100 vs. 62, but that transposition should fail to occur in the case of stimulus pairs farther removed from the training pair.

While insufficient knowledge as to the nature of the variation of generalization curves from individual to individual precludes the possibility of making specific deductions as to the exact results to be expected from individual Ss at each point on the stimulus dimension, nevertheless the theory does lead to certain more general implications which are experimentally testable. One of these, that the amount of transfer will be less the farther removed the test pair from the original training pair, is of particular

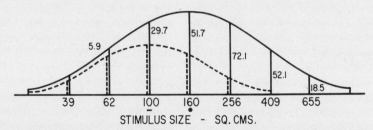

FIG. 1. *Diagrammatic representation of the relations between the hypothetical generalization curves, positive and negative, after training on the stimulus combination 160(+) and 100(—).*

taken from one of Spence's (27) recent papers, illustrates the workings of the theory. The S is assumed to have been trained to choose a square of 160 sq cm, in preference to one of 100 sq cm. The stimulus members indicated on the base line are placed at equal intervals on a logarithmic scale, and for each of these there is calculated the effective excitatory strength, determined by summing algebraically the excitatory and inhibitory generalization values for the given member. Comparing these hypothetical effective strengths for pairs of stimuli on the dimension, one would be led to predict

importance for the present investigation.

STATEMENT OF THE PROBLEM

The present study takes its point of departure from the theoretical formulation of transposition phenomena proposed by Spence. This theory was developed in relation to the behavior of nonarticulate organisms and is assumed to represent the underlying mechanisms (variables and laws) operating in infrahuman subjects and possibly in human Ss prior to the advent of verbal processes. In the case of an organism possessing verbal responses, however, behavior in discrimination situations presumably becomes cued to some extent to such words as "bigger," "longer," "brighter," and so forth. Observation and phenomenological reports suggest that verbal processes dominate such behavior in the case of the human adult. The relational theories originally proposed by the early American experimenters provide excellent examples of the recognition of the role of verbal processes in the human S. In line with the existing tendency to anthropomorphize, these writers projected their own processes into their animal Ss, although they usually acknowledged that such abstractions could function only as "more general notions," whatever that might mean.

As a basis for an attempt to extend our understanding of discrimination behavior and the phenomenon of transposition in human Ss, *the working hypothesis is here adopted that the mechanisms assumed by Spence to underlie this behavior in animals are also operative in the young child, and that with the development in older children of the capacity to employ verbal responses in such behavior situations, a shift occurs to the verbal type of control.*

According to this assumption, the child who has not yet learned the terms "bigger" or "smaller," or who has not yet learned to control his overt behavior by means of such verbal responses or their implicit equivalents in a size discrimination problem, would learn the discrimination in much the same way as the animal S. Transfer of the learned response to another set of stimuli differing from the training set only with respect to size would depend upon the generalization of excitation and inhibition from the positive and negative members of the training pair,

respectively, to these other members of the size dimension. With increasing distance on the continuum of the test stimuli from the training pair, the differential effects of generalization would be expected to decrease until a point is eventually reached at which the difference would be too small to produce a differential response to the test stimuli. Noncue factors would then be decisive and should produce a response which, except in the case of an original size preference, would be unrelated to the size aspect of the stimuli. A group of nonverbal Ss would, in such a case, be expected to respond in a manner consistent with original training only a chance number of times.[1]

The child whose discrimination behavior is controlled by verbalization of the cue aspect of the stimulus situation should, on the other hand, generalize equally well to all other pairs of test stimuli differing from the training stimuli in the same dimension. For example, if he learns to respond to the "smaller" of a stimulus pair during training and is then tested on a new stimulus pair also maintaining the relationship "smaller-larger," it is expected that he will abstract the relationship in the new pair and respond on the basis of it to the smaller stimulus of the pair, whatever the distance of the test stimuli from the training stimuli. His choice behavior, in other words, will be controlled by some such verbal response as "always in the smaller."

Studies of transposition of response in children thus far reported in the literature consistently show that transposition occurs in a large proportion of cases, but they have employed only test stimuli near to the original training

---

[1] The size dimension has been used for illlustrative purposes, but any other stimulus continuum, such as brightness, weight, and so on, would be equally applicable.

pair. Transposition would be expected under this condition whether the child used verbal responses effectively or not: in the first instance through generalization on a verbal basis; in the second, through generalization on a simple conditioning basis. Thus, the findings are not critical so far as the present hypothesis is concerned. Evidence for or against it can be obtained only on transposition tests with stimuli that are at a considerable distance from the training pair. This investigation attempts to provide such evidence.

In the absence of a measure of the extent to which the child employs the type of verbal concepts demanded by the theory, mental age has been taken as a rough indicator of the degree to which verbal or symbolic responses control behavior. *The implications of our working hypothesis are, then, that (mentally) very young children trained in a discrimination situation and in whom, presumably, verbal mechanisms are not highly developed, will respond on the distant transposition test in a chance manner, not in a manner consistent with training, while (mentally) older children, in whom the verbal-type mechanism is presumably well established, will exhibit transposition, that is, will respond in the distant test situation in a manner consistent with the original training.* It is probable that intermediate age groups will, as groups, fall somewhere between these two extremes, for some individuals will still be in the nonverbal stage, some will have progressed to the verbal level, while still others might possibly be in a stage of transition.

REVIEW OF PREVIOUS STUDIES

Comparatively few transposition experiments have employed child Ss, and none has treated the variables under consideration in the present study, namely: (1) the relation of the choice

to the distance of the two test stimuli from the training pair on the stimulus dimension, and (2), the relation of choice to verbal development. Köhler (18), Frank (3), Klüver (16), and Jackson *et al.* (12) have demonstrated the predominance in children of relative choices on critical tests with stimuli one step [2] distant from the training pair on a size, brightness, or weight dimension, even under the condition of overtraining. Other transposition experiments with children (7, 8, 9, 10, 11) have employed conditions irrelevant to the present problem.

In the animal field, a number of investigators have studied the relation of transposition to the distance of the test stimuli from the training stimuli on a single dimension. Gulliksen (4) and Flory (2) working with white rats, and Klüver (16) and Spence (25) working with chimpanzees have consistently found that, in the size dimension, as the distance between the training and test stimuli increases from one to five steps, the frequency of relative choices decreases from a significantly high toward a chance level. Kendler (14), employing hooded rats, conducted a similar experiment in the brightness dimension through four step intervals. She found a progressive decrease in the relative choice through the first three steps, but a rise or leveling off thereafter, depending on whether training was to the brighter or duller stimulus. Thus, the findings with respect to the distance variable in transposition experiments with ani-

[2] "Step," a term introduced by Kendler (14), refers to the distance on the stimulus dimension of the test stimuli from the training stimuli, such that the members of the test set have the same relation to the corresponding members of the training set, as the members of the training set have to each other. One step interval is represented by the distance between a training pair 10 vs. 5, for example, and a test pair 20 vs. 10.

mals tend to be in line with the theory based on conditioning principles.

EXPERIMENT

A. Subjects

Thirty-eight children from the preschools of the University of Iowa and 18 children from the kindergarten of the Horace Mann Public School in Iowa City were Ss in this experiment. They were selected on the basis of mental age scores within the range 3 to 6 years, and intelligence quotients of average or higher. In all, 12 who had from 140 to 630 training trials left school before they reached the learning criterion. Those who completed the study ranged in CA at the start of the experiment from 30 to 70 months, in MA from 36 to 83 months, and in IQ from 89 to 151.

Mental age and intelligence scores were obtained for all Ss on the New Revised Stanford-Binet Tests of Intelligence, Form L, within 6 months preceding the first day of training. With two exceptions, the investigator administered the tests. On the basis of the scores the children within each of the mental age levels 3, 4, 5, and 6 years, were divided into pairs matched for MA and IQ, and for sex whenever possible. One member of each pair was randomly assigned to one test group, and the other automatically fell into the alternate group.

B. Apparatus

The apparatus, shown in Fig. 2, consisted of a stand 22 in. in height, on which rested a panel inclined at a 60-degree angle. Two 10-in.-square openings were cut 10 in. apart in the panel, and covered with hinged lids. Behind these openings boxes were constructed. A thin strip of metal ⅜ in. wide was attached to the lower edge of the lid of each box to hold the stimuli in place. The metal extended over the inner edge of the lids and was bent slightly

FIG. 2. *Photograph of the apparatus with the training stimuli in position.*

to form tabs for opening the boxes. Locks invisible to the *S* and manipulated from behind the apparatus were arranged so that the lid under the negative stimulus was always locked. Notched blocks of wood attached to the front legs of the table held a pressed-wood screen in place between trials. A large variety of colorful toys, one of which was hidden each trial in the box on which the positive stimulus lay, served to motivate the child. The entire apparatus was painted flat black.

Stimuli were white-enameled ¼-in. pressed-wood squares with the areas 2.0, 3.6, 21.0, 37.8, and 68.0 sq. in. These will be referred to by the numbers 1, 2, 5, 6, and 7, respectively. Numbers 3 and 4 are omitted to emphasize the links needed to complete the stimulus series whose successive members have areas maintaining the ratio 1.8:1 between them. A duplicate of stimulus 6, the positive training stimulus, was used for transposition tests as a control over responses on the near test to some specific characteristic (other than size) of the original training stimulus.

C. Experimental Procedures

TRAINING SERIES. The procedure was identical for both experimental groups. *S*s were trained to choose the box with the smaller of the two stimuli, 6 and 7. Fig. 2 shows these stimuli in position. In the event of a correct response, the box opened and a toy was found inside, while in the event of an incorrect response, the box was found to be locked. The *S* was never permitted to try both boxes. Toys were collected in a cardboard box which the child held on his lap.

Training began on the first day with a preliminary set of two trials during which *E* demonstrated the response. Instructions, uniform for all *S*s, included no mention of the stimuli. On

the first trial, the positive stimulus appeared on the left box, the negative on the right. The positions were reversed on the second trial. Following the demonstration the regular training session was begun. In no case was the preliminary series repeated. Any spontaneous verbalization of the cue aspect of the stimuli was recorded throughout the experiment.

Ten trials were presented the *S* each school day. On odd-numbered days the position of the positive stimulus for the 10 trials was LRLLRLRRLR. The order on even-numbered days was RLLRLRLRRL. Training was continued until the *S* chose the positive stimulus on at least the last 9 of the 10 trials. In instances in which a child responded nine consecutive times on the basis of position, *E,* on the ninth trial, indicated the correct box, saying, "Look! This box opens!" Trials were then given with the positive stimulus on the nonpreferred side until the child chose correctly once.

If, after 450 standard training trials, the *S* showed no indication of approaching the learning criterion, he was given at the start of the next session 5 to 10 trials in which no stimuli were present, followed immediately by the regular training trials. Five trials without stimuli were given after 470 and 490 trials if learning still had not occurred. After 500 trials, the daily session opened with 10 trials in which the positive stimulus was presented alone. This series was followed immediately by 10 regular trials. Single stimulus presentation was continued on alternate days until there was evidence of learning.

TEST SERIES. Twenty-four hours after reaching the learning criterion the *S* was given a transposition test of 10 trials, during which all choices were rewarded. Group I was tested on the stimulus pair 5 vs. 6, while Group II was tested on the pair 1 vs. 2. If the child was not in school on the day after reaching the criterion, he was given training trials on his first day back. If he was able to choose the correct stimulus on 5 trials in 5, he was given a 24-hour interval and then tested for transposition. If he failed on one of the 5 training trials, he was presented a total of 10 regular training trials that day and every day thereafter until he again reached the original criterion of nine consecutive correct choices in 10 trials. He was then given a 24-hour interval before the transposition series.

On the day following the first transposition series, 10 trials were presented with the training stimuli. If the child reached the original learning criterion, he was given a 24-hour interval and then presented with the other pair of test stimuli. For this test, Group I had the stimulus pair 1 vs. 2, while Group II had the pair 5 vs. 6. If, on the other hand, the child failed to reach the criterion, he was given 10 trials each day until he could reach it. As before, a transposition test was given after a 24-hour interval.

ELICITATION OF VERBALIZATION.

Following the final transposition test trial on the last day of the experiment, the screen was placed in position and the child was asked how he knew which box to open. If there was no response, the training blocks were placed in position, the screen was removed, and the S was asked how he knew which block to choose. If there was still no response he was asked how the blocks differed.

It was recognized, of course, that failure of the child to verbalize the size aspect aloud does not indicate that he also failed to verbalize internally; nor does failure to state a generalization in response to questioning indicate a similar failure during the course of the experiment. Furthermore, verbalizing at the conclusion of the experiment gives no cue as to the time the child actually formulated his generalization. On the other hand, the occurrence of spontaneous verbalization aloud is evidence of the presence of a verbal mechanism at least at that time. Verbalization in response to questioning indicates capacity for such a process and the possibility that it did occur during the learning period.

TABLE 1

LEARNING AND TEST DATA FOR SUBJECTS AT THE 3-YEAR LEVEL

Subjects	CA Mos.	MA Mos.	IQ	No. Trials	No. "Smaller" Responses in 10 Trials	
					Near Test	Far Test
GROUP I (Ss given near test first)						
1	34	36	107	590	9	6
2	43	38	89	320	9	4
3	40	42	105	190	10	6
4	30	44	148	40	10	4
GROUP II (Ss given far test first)						
5	37	37	100	540	7	5
6	40	42	105	170	10	5
7	39	46	119	500	10	5
Means	37.6	40.7	110.4	335.7	9.3	5.0
Medians	39	42	105	320	9.5	5.0

D. Results

The various data obtained on the 44 Ss divided into four mental age levels are presented in Tables 1 to 4. The first column of each table identifies the S by number, and the next three contain data on CA, MA, and IQ, respectively, for each individual. The fifth column gives the total number of standard trials required to attain the criterion of learning in the discrimination situation. Finally, the last two columns show the number of responses consistent with the original training made in the 10 trials on the near test and the 10 trials on the far test. Each of the tables has been divided into an upper and lower part. The former includes those Ss (Group I) who were given the near test first; the latter, those Ss (Group II) who had the far test first. At the bottom of each table appear the means and medians of these various measures for each mental age group.

LEARNING. An examination of the data showing the number of trials to reach the learning criterion of nine consecutive correct choices in 10 reveals that the individual Ss ranged from 10 to 590 trials. There is evident a marked tendency for the low scores (fast learning) to be concentrated at the older age levels and the high scores (slow learning) to be found at the younger age levels. Both measures of central tendency for the four age groups reveal a decrease in the number of trials with increasing age, the means showing a consistent downward trend and the medians a single inversion between ages 4 and 5. Further support for this relation between speed of learning and mental age is provided by the product-moment coefficient of correlation of —.62 found between these variables. For a significant relationship at the .1 percent level with this number of cases, a coefficient of only .47 is needed. Speed of learning is also highly correlated with chrono-

TABLE 2

LEARNING AND TEST DATA FOR SUBJECTS AT THE 4-YEAR LEVEL

Subjects	CA Mos.	MA Mos.	IQ	No. Trials	No. "Smaller" Responses in 10 Trials	
					Near Test	Far Test
Group I (Ss given near test first)						
8	43	48	112	360 ·	9	7
9	41	53	129	40	10	5
10	59	58	98	90	1	5
11	41	58	142	400	10	10
12	45	59	131	230	10	4
13	44	59	133	170	10	10
Group II (Ss given far test first)						
14	52	54	104	90	10	3
15	42	56	134	190	10	6
16	37	56	151	380	0	10
17	39	58	149	176*	1	6
18	46	59	128	380	10	6
Means	44.5	56.2	128.3	227.8	7.4	6.5
Medians	43	58	131	190	10	6

* On one training day, only 6 trials were given for reasons beyond E's control.

TABLE 3

LEARNING AND TEST DATA FOR SUBJECTS AT THE 5-YEAR LEVEL

Subjects	CA Mos.	MA Mos.	IQ	No. Trials	No. "Smaller" Responses in 10 Trials	
					Near Test	Far Test
GROUP I (Ss given near test first)						
19	61	60	98	290	10	10
20	64	65	102	270	10	7
21	65	65	100	50	10	8
22	68	66	97	160	10	4
23	66	70	106	110	10	2
24	62	70	113	200	10	10
GROUP II (Ss given far test first)						
25	63	65	103	200	10	7
26	64	65	102	210	10	9
27	62	66	107	30	10	10
28	67	67	100	250	10	10
29	65	70	108	310	10	8
30	63	71	113	220	10	9
Means	64.2	66.7	104.1	191.7	10	7.8
Medians	64	66	102.5	205	10	8

TABLE 4

LEARNING AND TEST DATA FOR SUBJECTS AT THE 6-YEAR LEVEL

Subjects	CA Mos.	MA Mos.	IQ	No. Trials	No. "Smaller" Responses in 10 Trials	
					Near Test	Far Test
GROUP I (Ss given near test first)						
31	60	72	120	50	10	10
32	67	74	111	130	10	9
33	70	75	107	130	10	10
34	61	77	126	100	10	10
35	61	78	128	190	10	10
36	67	81	121	10	10	10
37	64	83	130	50	10	10
GROUP II (Ss given far test first)						
38	63	72	115	40	10	10
39	66	73	111	60	10	10
40	68	74	109	20	10	10
41	65	75	116	10	10	10
42	67	78	117	80	10	10
43	68	80	118	10	10	10
44	63	80	127	120	10	10
Means	65.0	76.6	118.3	71.4	10	9.9
Medians	65.5	76.0	117.5	55	10	10

logical age as shown by the r of —.55 between these two measures.

In addition to the regular training trials, special trials ranging in number from 2 to 199 were given to eight 3- and 4-year-old Ss and one 5-year-old in an attempt to modify position habits. In line with the plan described in Section C, three 3-year-old Ss—Nos. 1, 5, and 7—were given 5 to 20 trials without the stimuli present, and Ss 1 and 5 also received single-stimulus trials numbering 15 and 10, respectively. These data serve to add to the evidence that the problem was relatively much more difficult for the young Ss than for the older ones.

The majority of Ss, 28 in all, spontaneously commented on the size of the stimuli at some time during learning. Of these, nine mentioned the size aspect for the first time on the day they reached the criterion, or the day just preceding it, and 12 others verbalized the concept on one of these two days in addition to some earlier day or days. A number of other children talked about the "big block" or "little block" but never reached the learning criterion.

RELEARNING. Only three Ss of the 44 required more than the minimum of 10 trials to reach the learning criterion the second time.[3] Two of these three, Ss 8 and 22, met the criterion after 20 trials. Both, it is interesting to note, were among the three Ss who at no time during the experiment verbalized the size aspect of the stimuli. S 30 took 40 trials to relearn the discrimination, but the conditions in this case were exceptional in that a period of over three weeks elapsed between the first transposition test and the start of the relearning. With no other S was the interval greater than four days.

[3] The relearning series, it will be recalled, came at least 24 hours after the first transposition test.

TRANSPOSITION TESTS. The results of the near transposition test show that with very few exceptions the children tended to respond in a manner consistent with the original training, that is, to choose the smaller stimulus. Thus, if we select a score of 9 or more such responses in 10 as a significant one (a score of 9 would be expected on a chance basis only 10 times in 1024), it will be seen that there were only four Ss in all who did not choose the smaller stimulus a statistically significant number of times, that is, did not demonstrate transposition. One of these, S 5, was in the 3-year-old group, while the other three, Ss 10, 16, and 17, were in the 4-year-old group. The results for these latter three Ss on the near transposition test were quite different from those of the other children, their responses being predominantly (beyond chance) to the absolute stimulus cue.[4]

The findings of the far transposition tests present a somewhat different picture from those of the near test, particularly in the case of the younger Ss. Thus, none of the Ss at the 3-year level behaved on this test in a manner consistent with original training. Rather, all seven responded to the two stimuli in more or less chance fashion, as may be seen from the data in the last column of Table 1. The percent

[4] The results for these individuals are discussed in some detail in the original thesis, deposited in the library of the State University of Iowa. The behavior of Ss 10 and 16 are not necessarily contrary to the proposed theory. Both appear to have learned the discrimination on a nonverbal basis. Their responses on the near test could possibly be explained as resulting from very narrow generalization curves. Such an assumption would require that the responses on the far test be random, which is in line with the experimental results. The absolute choice of S 17 on the near test, after transposing on the far test, is contrary to the theoretical expectation.

of Ss responding a statistically significant number of times (nine or more)
to the smaller stimulus on this far test
increased at each of the subsequent
age levels. Thus, 27.3 percent (three
Ss) of the 4-year-old group, 50 percent
(six Ss) of the 5-year-old group, and
100 percent (14 Ss) of the 6-year-old
group chose in accord with their original training in nine or more of the 10
far test trials.

The differences in the results for
the two transposition tests are also revealed by the measures of central
tendency included at the bottom of
Tables 1 to 4. Figure 3 brings together

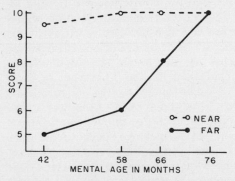

FIG. 3. *Graphic representation of the
relation between mental age and median
scores on near and far transposition tests.*

in graphic form the median near and
far transposition scores made by Ss at
various age levels. The number of
transposition responses in 10 trials appears on the ordinate, while the median
mental age in months for each of the
four groups is plotted on the abscissa.
Inspection of the almost horizontal near
test curve reveals that all four age
groups showed transposition to a very
high degree. The far curve, on the other
hand, begins at chance (5) for the
youngest group and rises to 10 for the
oldest group, with the intermediate
age groups falling at 6 and 8.

We turn now to the consideration of
the relation of these experimental facts
to the theoretical formulation elaborated at the beginning of this paper.
It will be recalled that the implications
of this theory were that the far transposition test would reveal significant
differences between children of different age levels, whereas the near
transposition test would not. In the
first instance the theoretical expectation was that at some point in the
age range, presumably at a very young
level, the responses of the Ss on the far
transposition test would approximate a
chance result. At an older age, on the
other hand, presumably when the stage
of verbal abstraction and control of
behavior is attained, the response of
the child on this far test would be
highly consistent with the direction of
original training.

That the results of the experiment
were in agreement with these theoretical expectations is readily apparent.
The children of different age levels
showed little, if any, difference in the
near transposition test. In the far
transposition test, however, the 3-year-
olds responded in a purely chance
manner, while the 6-year-olds showed
practically 100 percent transposition.
There now remains the task of ascertaining the degree of confidence we
may have that these differences did
not arise purely by accident.

Because of the nature of the data,
for example, the skewed character of
the distributions of the transposition
scores and the inequality of the variances at different age levels, it was not
possible to apply analysis of variance,
or to apply, in most instances, the usual
t-test of significance between means.
The main theoretical implications may,
nevertheless, be tested for significance
in the following manner. If we set up
the null hypothesis with respect to
differences on the two tests, near and

far, for both the 3- and 6-year mental-age groups, then our theory would require that the experimental results for the 3-year-old group would lead to the rejection of the null hypothesis of no difference between the two tests at this age, while the results for the 6-year mental-age group would lead to acceptance of that hypothesis.

In the case of the 3-year-old group, we can apply the t-test for differences in the means of related measures (21). The resulting t is 8.25, which far exceeds the value of 5.96 required for a significant difference at the .1 percent level. From this we would be led, as our theory demands, to reject the hypothesis that there is no difference in the results on the two tests for this age group.

Unfortunately, a similar statistical test of the differences between the near and far transposition scores for the 6-year-old group cannot be made because of the almost complete lack of variability in these test scores. The nature of the results is such, however, that one can readily accept the null hypothesis that no difference exists. All Ss but one responded 10 times on both tests to the smaller stimulus and, in the case of the single exception, the transposition scores were 10 on the near test and 9 on the far. Thus, there are 13 cases of zero difference and a single case of a difference of 1. The probability that one would obtain on the basis of chance 13 instances of zero in 14 is extremely remote.

As was true at the 6-year level, the distributions of transposition scores at the intermediate ages 4 and 5 do not justify the assumptions of normality and homogeneous variability that are necessarily made in applying the t-test for differences between means. There are too few Ss to permit a chi-square test of independence on these two groups alone, but by combining the 3-

with the 4-year group and the 5- with the 6-year one, the application of that test is made possible. We are interested in testing the hypothesis that there is no relationship between mental age and the occurrence of transposition (score of 9 or 10 in 10 trials) in the far test situation. The resulting chi-square, corrected for continuity by Yates' method, is 13.1, which, for one degree of freedom, exceeds the value required for significance at the .1 percent level. The hypothesis can, therefore, be rejected even if some reservation is made for the relatively small number of Ss. Further evidence against the hypothesis of no relation between mental age and far transposition scores is furnished by the product-moment correlation of .66 obtained between these variables for the 44 Ss. This coefficient is far in excess of the value .47 required for significance at the .1 percent level.

A chi-square test of independence could not be applied to the near transposition measures to test their relationship to mental age, because the data fail to satisfy the requirement that there be a theoretical (expected) frequency of at least 5 in each of the cells of the contingency table. The correlational approach is likewise not applicable to these results, for the transposition scores show almost no variability. Examination of the data, however, should make one extremely hesitant about rejecting the null hypothesis of the relation between mental age and near transposition.[5]

---

[5] Analysis of transposition scores based on only the first test trial gave results which corroborate those for 10 test trials. No significant differences were found between the different mental age groups on the near transposition test, whereas the percent of Ss who transposed on the far test increased from 14.3 percent for the 3-year-old group to 100 percent for the 6-year-olds. The 4- and 5-year-old groups fell in between these values, with 72.7 of the former and 86.7

TABLE 5

NUMBER AND PERCENT OF SUBJECTS AT EACH AGE LEVEL
IN THE FOUR VERBALIZATION CATEGORIES

| | MENTAL AGE | | | | | | | |
| | 3 | | 4 | | 5 | | 6 | |
Category	N	%	N	%	N	%	N	%
A	0	0	2	18.2	1	8.3	0	0
B	7	100.0	2	18.2	1	8.3	0	0
C	0	0	4	36.4	5	41.7	5	35.7
D	0	0	3	27.3	5	41.7	9	64.3

VERBALIZATION. An analysis of the recorded verbalizations of the stimulus cue suggested the classification of the Ss into four mutually exclusive categories—A, B, C, and D. A includes those Ss who at no time, either spontaneously or in response to questioning, verbalized the size aspect. In category B are those who did spontaneously mention the size variable at least once at any time during the experiment, but who failed to state the relation of size to the sucess or failure of choice behavior. Typical verbalizations of Ss in this group are: "This one is big and this one is little." "What a nice little block!" "This time I'll take the big one." Ss in the third class, C, verbalized the general principle of solution, but only in response to questioning at the conclusion of the experiment. Many of these individuals also mentioned the size of the stimuli during the training or transposition trials, but in no instance did they express generalizations at that time. Examples of replies judged as adequate generalizations are: "It's (toy) always in the little one," or "The big one doesn't open." Category D includes those children who verbally generalized with

percent of the latter showing transposition. Application of the chi-square test of independence permits one to reject, at a confidence level between 2 and 5 percent, the hypothesis of no difference in the percent of transposition for the four groups.

respect to the size aspect of the stimuli at some time prior to the routine questioning at the conclusion of the experiment. All except three of these Ss repeated the principle in reply to the experimenter's questions following the last 10 trials.

The number and percent of Ss at each age level who fall in the four verbalization categories are shown in Table 5. It is apparent that the 3- and 4-year-old children tend to be in the nongeneralizing groups (A and B), while the 5- and 6-year-old children are predominantly in the generalizing ones. A chi-square test of the null hypothesis of no relationship between mental age and classification in the combined A-B or combined C-D categories yields a corrected chi-square of 12.22, permitting the rejection of the hypothesis at the .1 percent level of confidence. This result lends support to our proposed use of mental age as an indicator of the ability to make verbal generalizations in such situations.

Table 6 indicates the median transposition scores in 10 trials for Ss in the four verbalization categories, and the median number of trials to learn the discrimination originally. It is evident that Ss who failed to verbalize the size aspect of the stimuli explicitly, or who merely noted the size without stating the relationship of the size aspect to the solution of the problem, behaved differently on the far trans-

TABLE 6

MEDIAN TRANSPOSITION SCORES FOR SUBJECTS IN THE FOUR
VERBALIZATION CATEGORIES

Category	N	Median Trials	MEDIAN TRANSPORTATION RESPONSES (10 TRIALS)	
			Near Test	Far Test
A	3	176.0	9.0	6.0
B	10	250.0	10.0	5.0
C	14	100.0	10.0	10.0
D	17	130.0	10.0	10.0

position test from Ss who did formulate and state the relationship. On the near test, responses were similar from group to group.

It is possible to test the significance of the apparent relationship by using the chi-square test of independence. The obtained corrected chi-square of 18.37 permits us to reject at the .1 percent level the hypothesis of no relationship between the occurrence of transposition (a score of 9 or 10 in 10 trials) in the far test and the tendency to verbalize the solution of the discrimination problem. As in previous applications of this test, a chi-square of only 10.83 is needed for significance at this level for one degree of freedom. The chi-square test is not applicable to the near transposition data for the reason, before discussed, of too small theoretical frequencies in the nontransposing categories. There seems to be no occasion for doubting, however, that the null hypothesis is tenable for the relation between near transposition and tendency to verbalize the principle.

Analysis of individual data with respect to the relation of verbalization to the phenomenon of transposition suggests the possibility that there are several verbal stages. There appears to be one stage in which the child verbally identifies the stimuli as "little" and "big," but he fails to verbalize the relation of size to the success or failure of his choice responses. This occurred predominantly in the younger Ss and was associated in every case with chance performance on the far transposition test series. There is another stage—presumably a later one because of its much greater incidence in older Ss—in which the child states aloud or to himself that the little stimulus always leads to success and the big one to failure. The occurrence out loud of such verbal behavior in the learning or transposition series invariably was followed by transposition on the far test, regardless of the mental age of the child. In contrast, 43 percent of those who made such verbalizations only upon questioning at the conclusion of the experiment transposed on the far series with this consistency. In the case of three Ss who had failed to transpose in the far test and a few seconds later, upon questioning, verbalized the principle, there seemed to be no apparent recognition of the discrepancy between this verbal formulation of the solution and their failure to act in a manner consistent with it in the immediately preceding test trials.

While the data on verbalization are not sufficiently clear-cut to permit any definite conclusions, there is, however, the suggestion that there are at least two developmental stages so far as the relation of verbal responses to overt choice behavior is concerned. In the first, the child is able to make differential verbal responses to appropriate aspects of the situation, but this verbalization does not control or influence his overt choice behavior. Later, such verbalizations gain control and dominate choice behavior.

SUMMARY AND CONCLUSIONS

Taking its point of departure from a theoretical formulation of discrimination learning based on the findings of conditioning experiments, this study hypothesizes that the simple mechanisms mediating transposition of response infrahuman organisms are identical with those responsible for similar behavior in children in the preverbal stage of development. With the acquisition of verbal processes, however, and the transition to behavior dominated by such processes, it is hypothesized that the child's responses in the discrimination-learning situation become keyed to words relating to the cue aspect of the stimuli. Implications of this theory are that the preverbal child, like the animal S, will transpose consistently on test stimuli near on the dimension to the training pair, but will show only chance response on transposition tests with distant stimuli. The verbal child, on the other hand, would be expected to show transposition on both far and near stimulus tests.

As an empirical test of the proposed hypothesis, an experiment was conducted in which mental age was used as a rough indicator of verbal level. Ss were 44 Iowa City preschool and kindergarten children distributed over the mental age range 3 to 6 years and divided into two matched groups at each year level. Both groups were trained to select the smaller of a pair of squares whose areas were 37.8 and 68.0 sq in. They were tested in counterbalanced order after learning, with two pairs of still smaller stimuli (21.0 vs. 37.8 sq in., and 2.0 vs. 3.6 sq in.). All spontaneous verbalizations of the size aspect of the stimuli were recorded throughout the experiment, and attempts were made at the conclusion, through questioning, to elicit verbalization of the general principle of solution.

Analysis of the results revealed a highly significant relationship between mental age and the occurrence of far transposition, and a low relationship between mental age and near transposition. The median number of responses on the far transposition test increased with age from 50 percent at mental age 3 years to 100 percent at 6 years. The corresponding value for the near transposition test was 90 percent or above at all four age levels.

With regard to verbalization, Ss tended to fall into four categories: (1) failure to verbalize the size aspect of the problem; (2) verbal identification of the size difference between the stimuli without explicit association of size with the success or failure of choice behavior; (3) verbalization of the principle of solution in response to questioning at the conclusion of the experiment; and (4) verbalization of the principle spontaneously during training or transposition trials. Ss in the first two categories were significantly younger in mental age than those in the last two. No S in the first two categories transposed on the far test, while 73 percent of the individuals in the last two categories transposed. Analysis of the individual data suggests the possibility of two developmental stages so far as the relation of verbal responses to overt choice behavior is concerned.

On the whole, the experimental results were found to be in close accord with the proposed hypothesis.

638 COGNITION IN CHILDREN AND COGNITIVE DEVELOPMENT

REFERENCES

1. Bingham, H. C., "Visual Perception in the Chick," *Behavior Monogram*, **4**, No. 20 (1922), 1-104.

2. Flory, R. M., "A Study of the Factors Determining Discrimination of Size by the White Rat." (Unpublished Master's thesis, University of Virginia, 1938.)

3. Frank, Helene, "Untersuchung über Schgrössenkonstanz bei Kindern," *Psychol. Forsch.*, **7** (1926), 137-45.

4. Gulliksen, H., "Studies of Transfer of Response: I. Relative versus Absolute Factors in the Discrimination of Size by the White Rat," *Journal of Genetic Psychology*, **40** (1932), 37-51.

5. Gulliksen, H. and D. L. Wolfle, "A Theory of Learning and Transfer," *Psychometrika*, **3** (1938), 127-49, 225-51.

6. ———, "Correction of an Error in 'A Theory of Learning and Transfer,'" *Psychometrika*, **4** (1939), 178.

7. Jackson, T. A., "Studies in the Transposition of Learning by Children: III. Transpositional Response as a Function of the Number of Transposed Dimensions," *Journal of Experimental Psychology*, **25** (1939), 116-24.

8. Jackson, T. A. and K. Dominguez, "Studies in the Transposition of Learning by Children: II. Relative vs. Absolute Choice with Multi-dimensional Stimuli," *Journal of Experimental Psychology*, **24** (1939), 630-39.

9. Jackson, T. A. and M. E. Eckhardt, "Studies in the Transposition of Learning by Children: V. The Number of Stimuli in the Training Series as a Factor in Generalization," *Journal of Experimental Psychology*, **27** (1940), 303-12.

10. Jackson, T. A. and E. A. Jerome, "Studies in the Transposition of Learning by Children: IV. A Preliminary Study of Patternedness in Discrimination Learning," *Journal of Experimental Psychology*, **26** (1940), 432-39.

11. ———, "Studies in the Transposition of Learning by Children: VI. Simultaneous vs. Successive Presentation of the Stimuli to Bright and Dull Children," *Journal of Experimental Psychology*, **33** (1943), 431-39.

12. Jackson, T. A., E. Stonex, E. Lane, and K. Dominguez, "Studies in the Transposition of Learning by Children: I. Relative vs. Absolute Response as a Function of Amount of Training," *Journal of Experimental Psychology*, **23** (1938), 578-600.

13. Johnson, H. M., "Visual Pattern Discrimination in the Vertebrates," *Journal of Animal Behavior*, **4** (1914), 319-39, 340-61; **6** (1916), 169-88.

14. Kendler, Sylvia T. S., "Experimental Investigation of the Effect of Difference between Training and Test Stimuli on the Amount of Transposition." (Unpublished Doctoral dissertation, State University of Iowa, 1943.)

15. Kinnaman, A. J., "Mental Life of Two *Macacus rhesus* Monkeys in Captivity," *American Journal of Psychology*, **13** (1902), 98-148, 173-218.

16. Klüver, H., *Behavior Mechanisms in Monkeys.* Chicago: University of Chicago Press, 1933.

17. Köhler, W., *Gestalt Psychology.* New York: Liveright Publishing Corp., 1929.

18. ———, "Simple Structural Functions in the Chimpanzee and in the Chicken," in *A Source Book of Gestalt Psychology*, ed. W. D. Ellis, pp. 217-27. New York: Harocurt, Brace & World, Inc., 1938.

19. Koffka, K., The Growth of the Mind (2nd ed., rev.). New York: Harcourt, Brace & World, Inc., 1928.

20. Lashley, K. S., "The Mechanism of Vision: XV. Preliminary Studies of the Rat's Capacity for Detail Vision," *Journal of Genetic Psychology*, **18** (1938), 123-93.

21. Lindquist, E. F., *Statistical Analysis in Educational Research.* Boston: Houghton Mifflin Company, 1940.

22. Perkins, F. T. and R. H. Wheeler, "Configural Learning in the Goldfish," *Comparative Psychology Monograph*, **7**, No. 31 (1930), 1-50.

23. Spence, K. W., "The Nature of Discrimination Learning in Animals," *Psychological Review*, **43** (1936), 427-49.

24. ———, "Analysis of Formation of Visual Discrimination Habits in Chimpanzee," *Journal of Comparative Psychology*, **23** (1937), 77-100.

25. ———, "The Differential Response in Animals to Stimuli Varying within a Single Dimension," *Psychological Review*, **44** (1937), 430-44.

26. ———, "Failure of Transposition in Size-discrimination of Chimpanzees," *American Journal of Psychology*, **54** (1941), 223-29.

27. ———, "The Basis of Solution by Chimpanzees of the Intermediate Size Problem," *Journal of Experimental Psychology*, **31** (1942), 257-71.

28. Warden, C. J. and Jean B. Rowley, "The Discrimination of Absolute versus Relative Brightness in the Ring Dove, *Turtur Risorius*," *Journal of Comparative Psychology*, **9** (1929), 317-37.

Verbal Mediation as a Function of Age Level *

Hayne W. Reese

On the basis of her study of transposition in the two-stimulus problem in young children, Kuenne (1946) proposed that

> there are at least two developmental stages so far as the relation of verbal responses to overt choice behavior is concerned. In the first, the child is able to make differential verbal responses to appropriate aspects of the situation, but this verbalization does not control or influence his overt choice behavior. Later, such verbalizations gain control and dominate choice behavior (p. 488).

Similarly, Kendler, Kendler, and Wells (1960) suggested in a study of reversal and nonreversal shifts in discrimination learning in preschool subjects (*S*s) that

> there is a stage in human development in which verbal responses, though

available, do not readily mediate between external stimuli and overt responses (p. 87)

and noted that Luria (1957) had reached essentially the same conclusion. This suggestion that there is a stage of development in which verbal responses do not serve as mediators is designated the "mediational deficiency hypothesis" in the present paper. The evidence regarding this hypothesis is reviewed in the following sections.

REVERSAL AND NONREVERSAL

Kendler and Kendler (1959) reasoned that, if verbal mediation occurs, performance on a reversal shift (in which the previously positive stimulus becomes negative; and the previously negative stimulus, positive) should be superior to that on a nonreversal shift (in which the previously relevant dimension becomes irrelevant; and the previously irrelevant dimension, rele-

* From H. W. Reese. "Verbal Mediation as a Function of Age Level," *Psychological Bulletin*, **59** (1962), 502-9. Reprinted by permission of the author and publishers.

vant). In the reversal shift, appropriate verbal labels developed during the original discrimination remain relevant and facilitate learning; whereas in the nonreversal shift, new labels must be acquired and the old labels, developed in the original discrimination, interfere with learning. The verbal labels function like the "internal orienting responses" of Goodwin and Lawrence (1955), which involve the "identification of and reaction to" the relevant dimensions.

Kendler and Kendler (1959) reported that kindergarten Ss who learned the initial discrimination rapidly, compared with those who learned it more slowly, were superior on the reversal condition and slightly inferior on the nonreversal shift. They concluded that the Ss were in the process of developing mediating responses relevant to the task, and that some Ss were further along than others, since the fast initial learners responded as though they were mediating, and the slow initial learners responded as though mediation did not occur. Kendler, Kendler, and Wells (1960) found that preschool Ss performed like the slow-learning kindergarten Ss, and that instructions to verbalize their choices on the last 10 trials of the initial discrimination had no effect on reversal or nonreversal shifts, leading to their statement of the mediational deficiency hypothesis.

O'Connor and Hermelin (1959) found that imbeciles learned a reversal faster than normal preschool Ss except when the imbeciles were required to verbalize their choices on the initial discrimination. Verbalization interfered with reversal by imbeciles. The imbeciles in the verbalization group and the normal preschool Ss performed in essentially the same way as those of Kendler et al. (1960). O'Connor and Hermelin interpreted their results

as indicating that the use of verbal labels interferes with reversal shifts, because the S must inhibit not only the association between the overt choice response and the previously positive stimulus, but also the association between the choice response and the *name* of the previously positive stimulus. This interpretation does not conflict with that of Kendler and Kendler (1959) if it is assumed that in normal Ss the mediator is an orienting response, usually verbally directed, which involves identification of and reaction to the appropriate dimension, and that in imbeciles it is a verbal response functionally equivalent to a nonsense-syllable name (as in studies of acquired distinctiveness of cues). Kendler and Kendler assumed that S names both stimuli as members of a single dimension, and O'Connor and Hermelin assumed that the imbecile names only one stimulus. It should be emphasized that the performance of O'Connor and Hermelin's normal preschool Ss supports the mediational deficiency hypothesis, since it is in line with the findings of Kendler et al. (1959, 1960).

DISCRIMINATION SET

In the preceding section it was assumed that the mediator in reversal shifts is a verbal orienting response. Two studies of discrimination set (orienting responses, identification of relevant dimensions, and so forth) provide somewhat conflicting evidence regarding the assumption. Weiss (1954) found that set-inducing instructions (informing Ss that the reward was always behind the same stimulus in a discrimination task) were more effective in older than in younger preschool Ss. This finding supports the assumption, since it supports the mediational deficiency hypothesis. On the other hand, Spiker (1959) found that although pretraining with distinctive stimuli facilitated learning a discrimination with similar stimuli, there was no significant age difference in the effectiveness of the pretraining. If the pretraining resulted in the acquisition of a discrimination set, the data contradict the mediational deficiency hypothesis or the assumption that discrimination set (orienting response) involves verbal mediators. However, as Spiker noted, the pretraining may serve only to minimize failure-produced responses by minimizing failures. The failure-produced responses are incompatible with efficient discrimination performance and their occurrence results in inferior performance. His results, then, do not necessarily contradict the mediational deficiency hypothesis.

TRANSPOSITION

Kuenne (1946) hypothesized that possession of a concept of the relation between the stimuli in a discrimination task would facilitate transposition because the concept would mediate correct responses. Using the two-stimulus problem, she found that the frequency of transposition on a "far" test, several steps removed from the training stimuli on the stimulus continuum, increased with increasing age level, but her data suggested that possession of the concept by younger preschool Ss did not facilitate transposition as much as it did in older preschool Ss. Alberts and Ehrenfreund (1951) obtained essentially the same results in a similar study. Both of these studies, as well as others (Jackson, Stonex, Lane, and Dominguez, 1938; Terrell, 1958; Terrell and Kennedy, 1957), found a high frequency of transposition on the "near" tests (one step removed) in the two-stimulus problem, with no significant age differences. According to

Spence's (1936) theory, mediation is not required for transposition on the near test; and Jackson et al. (1938) noted that

> although the subjects [3-6 years of age] may readily understand the concept "bigger than," they do not transfer by such verbal analysis on critical trials [on a near test] (pp. 581-582).

Hunter's (1952) study, designed to test absolute versus relative theories of transposition, apparently demonstrated transposition in preschool Ss who did not have the relevant concept. Hunter attempted to design the tasks in such a way that absolute theories would predict no transposition, but the Ss may have acquired a discrimination learning set (violating the boundary conditions of absolute theories of transposition) since he trained them on three discrimination tasks before giving them the transposition test. Shepard (1957) found that discrimination learning set was maximal in preschool Ss after they were trained to criterion on one problem. Hunter's results might be attributed to a discrimination learning set, but they might also be accounted for by Stevenson and Bitterman's (1955) hypothesis that S transposes if he fails to discriminate between the training and test sets of stimuli. The latter possible explanation is less plausible than the former, since Hunter had marked differences between the training and test stimuli in some conditions.

Plenderleith (1956) found no significant differences between normal and feebleminded Ss (mean mental age about 69 months) in the acquisition of a discrimination learning set or in the subsequent acquisition of a discrimination reversal set (except when there was a long interval between sessions). Although other studies (Ellis, 1958; Kaufman and Peterson,

1958; Koch and Meyer, 1959; Stevenson and Swartz, 1958) have found a relationship between mental age and speed of acquisition of discrimination learning set, there is no evidence that verbal ability is directly involved. Therefore, if the transposition in Hunter's (1952) Ss resulted from discrimination learning set rather than the usually postulated mechanisms, his finding that preverbal Ss transposed would not be relevant to the present topic. In support of this conclusion, Levinson and Reese (1961) found no significant age difference in the speed of acquisition of discrimination learning set, indicating that it is at least less dependent on age level than verbal mediation is.

Three studies of transposition in the intermediate-size problem tested the distance effect (that is, the decrease in frequency of transposition with increasing separation between the training and test stimuli on the stimulus continuum) in young children. Reese (on press) and Rudel (1960) found no significant difference between preschool Ss who had the concept of middle-sizedness, or at least the concept name, and those who did not. A significant distance effect was obtained in both studies. Similarly, Reese (1961) found that on a far test (three steps removed from the training stimuli) younger (preschool) Ss transposed only when the area ratio of the stimuli was small, that is, when the transposition did not theoretically require mediation (Stevenson and Bitterman, 1955), though older (kindergarten) Ss transposed on the far test even when the area ratio of the stimuli was large, when mediation was presumably required. The results of the last study support the mediational deficiency hypothesis and the Stevenson-Bitterman hypothesis. The obtaining of the distance effect in both "concept" and "no-concept" groups in the first

two studies can be explained by the Stevenson-Bitterman hypothesis if it is assumed that mediation did not occur in the concept Ss.

Spiker, Gerjuoy, and Shepard (1956) interpreted their results as indicating a greater frequency of transposition in concept than in no-concept Ss, but their procedure was such that mediation need not be assumed to have occurred, since acquired distinctiveness of cues could account for their findings. That is, in their study learning could have been facilitated by acquired distinctiveness in the concept group, even if mediation did not occur, but there would be no acquired distinctiveness in the no-concept group.

ACQUIRED DISTINCTIVENESS

Studies of acquired distinctiveness of cues (stimulus pretraining) in young children have uniformly found no significant deficiency in the effectiveness of the pretraining for the younger Ss. Norcross and Spiker (1957) found that younger preschool Ss made fewer correct responses than older ones, but stimulus pretraining was equally effective in both groups, that is, age did not interact significantly with experimental conditions. Spiker (1956) found that stimulus pretraining was more effective in younger than older preschool Ss. The younger control group was inferior to the other groups, but the other groups performed at about the same high level. Weir and Stevenson (1959) obtained a similar result with their preschool Ss, but the interaction between age and experimental conditions was apparently not significant. Finally, Cantor (1955) found no significant effects of age levels in his study of stimulus pretraining in preschool Ss.

The interpretation of the results of these studies must take possible ceiling effects into account. The maximum mean percentages correct responses in the studies were: Norcross and Spiker, 83 percent; Spiker, 86 percent; Weir and Stevenson, about 90 percent; and Cantor, 79 percent. It appears that there were ceiling effects, particularly in Spiker and Weir and Stevenson. If there were ceiling effects, the effectiveness of stimulus pretraining for the older experimental groups would have been obscured. It is also possible that the older control Ss used pre-experimentally acquires names for the stimuli, obscuring the stimulus pretraining effect in the older experimental groups. In either case, no definite conclusion could be made about the relative effectiveness of the pretraining in younger and older preschool Ss.

Acquired distinctiveness does not involve mediation, according to Dollard and Miller's (1950) interpretation, and therefore a failure to find a deficiency in younger preschool Ss would not contradict the mediational deficiency hypothesis. However, Spiker (1956) has suggested that acquired distinctiveness may result from the use of the stimulus names for rehearsal of the stimulus-response connections during the inter-stimulus interval. His interpretation requires mediation, since the rehearsal would not facilitate performance unless the stimulus name mediated the appropriate response when the stimulus was presented. According to his interpretation, then, a failure to find a deficiency in younger Ss would contradict the mediational deficiency hypothesis. Since the results of the previous studies are inconclusive because of the possibility of ceiling effects and the possible occurrence of pre-experimentally acquired stimulus names, it is apparent that further study of the acquired distinctiveness of cues is required.

There is no clear-cut evidence regarding the mechanisms which have been assumed to underlie acquired distinctiveness. Jeffrey (1958a) found that learning names for two stick figures, one pointing to the right and the other to the left, was facilitated in preschool Ss by learning to push buttons toward which the figures pointed. The response unit was present during the transfer task, and Jeffrey reported that one S lifted the appropriate shoulder before naming, but other Ss "would look at the appropriate button before supplying the name of the figure" (p. 274). Whether mediation or acquired distinctiveness was involved is not clear. Jeffrey (1958b) has also obtained facilitation of learning to associate buttons with piano tones by pretraining Ss to match the tones with a piano or by singing. In this study, however, the facilitation may have resulted from the development of a discrimination set. In studies in which the response unit was not present during the transfer task, pretraining with motor responses has not produced facilitation. For example, Murdock (1958) found that motor pretraining did not produce facilitation in college students; and Reese, in an unpublished study, found no facilitation of fifth-graders' learning to associate buttons with colored stimuli following pretraining in which the stimuli were associated with switch throwing responses. Although Ss of the former and latter pairs of studies differ in age, the presence or absence of the response unit during the transfer task may be the critical variable determining whether or not facilitation occurs on the transfer task.

ACQUIRED EQUIVALENCE

There have been only two studies of the acquired equivalence of cues in preschool Ss, and both of these also involved acquired distinctiveness. In both studies it was impossible to separate the effects of acquired equivalence and distinctiveness experimentally or statistically. Jeffrey (1953) reported that pretraining with verbal and motor responses led to greater facilitation of performance in older than in younger preschool Ss (the groups were divided on the basis of MA, which apparently also yielded a division on the basis of CA); and Shepard's (1954) data implied a similar result, since she obtained a correlation of .70 between errors on a transfer task and trials to criterion on the name learning task. Although she did not report the correlation between age level and trials to criterion, age level should be negatively correlated with trials to criterion and therefore negatively correlated with errors on the transfer task. Since studies of acquired distinctiveness, which does not necessarily involve mediation, have found no deficiency in younger Ss (see above), the Jeffrey and Shepard studies may be interpreted as indicating a deficiency in younger Ss in acquired equivalence, which does require mediation, supporting the mediational deficiency hypothesis.

DOUBLE ALTERNATION

Although it is usually considered that a series of double alternations requires meditation, Hunter and Bartlett (1948) found that of eleven Ss below the age of 48 months, 9 failed to reach criterion on a double alternation (the 2 who reached criterion were 43 and 45 months of age), but no S younger than 60 months gave the basis of responding either spontaneously or in response to questions asked at the end of training. Stolurow and Pascal (1950), studying double alternation in mental defectives, also reported that the solution of the problem did not always indicate ability to verbalize the

correct pattern of response. The implications of these results are inconclusive, however, since Bugelski and Scharlock (1952) have shown that even college students may mediate without being able to verbalize the process, that is, without awareness. If mediation occurred without awareness in the younger Ss who reached criterion in the Hunter and Bartlett (1948) and Stolurow and Pascal (1950) studies, and if the other younger Ss also possessed the concepts required ("left" and "right"), the results may be interpreted as supporting the mediational deficiency hypothesis.

CONCLUSION

Studies of reversal and nonreversal learning, transposition in the two-stimulus and intermediate-sized problems, acquired equivalence of cues, and possibly other problems indicate that there is a deficiency in mediation in young children, compared with older children. The studies reviewed above indicate that the critical age for the occurrence of mediation may be different for different experimental situations and for different concepts. It seems likely that in some cases the deficiency is a characteristic of an early stage of human development, but that in others it may be a characteristic of an early stage of concept formation. There is some evidence that inadequately learned stimulus names, if used for rehearsal (as suggested by Spiker, 1961), produce interference. Reese's (1960) data suggest such a trend in fourth, fifth, and sixth-grade school children, and McCormack's (1958) study suggests it in college students. It is proposed, then, that with a well-learned concept there is no necessary deficiency in mediation as a function of age, but with a less well-established concept there is a deficiency at any age. (For a discussion of the possible sources of deficiency with inadequately learned concepts, see Spiker, 1961).

If mediation is a "voluntary" process, as rehearsal is, there may be a stage of development in which Ss have typically not yet learned to use it, and instruction in the use of the process should facilitate the learning of these Ss. If it is an involuntary or automatic process, instructions should have no effect.

REFERENCES

Alberts, E. and D. Ehrenfreund, "Transposition in Children as a Function of Age," *Journal of Experimental Psychology*, **41** (1951), 30-38.

Bugelski, B. and D. Scharlock, "An Experimental Demonstration of Unconscious Mediated Association," *Journal of Experimental Psychology*, **44** (1952), 334-38.

Cantor, G. N., "Effects of Three Types of Pretraining on Discrimination Learning in Preschool Children," *Journal of Experimental Psychology*, **49** (1955), 339-42.

Dollard, J. and N. E. Miller, *Personality and Psychotherapy*. New York: McGraw-Hill Book Company, Inc., 1950.

Ellis, N. R., "Object-quality Discrimination Learning Sets in Mental Defectives," *Journal of Comparative Physiological Psychology*, **51** (1958), 79-81.

Goodwin, W. R. and D. H. Lawrence, "The Functional Independence of Two Discrimination Habits Associated with a Constant Stimulus Situation," *Journal of Comparative Physiological Psychology*, **48** (1955), 437-43.

Hunter, I. M. L., "An Experimental Investigation of the Absolute and Relative Theories of Transposition Behavior in Children," *British Journal of Psychology*, **43** (1952), 113-28.

Hunter, W. S. and C. Bartlett, "Double Alternation Behavior in Young Children," *Journal of Experimental Psychology*, **38** (1948); 558-67.

Jackson, T. A., E. Stonex, E. Lane, and K. Dominguez, "Studies in the Transposition of Learning by Children: I. Relative vs. Absolute Choice as a Function of the Amount of Training," *Journal of Experimental Psychology*, **23** (1938), 578-99.

Jeffrey, W. E., "The Effects of Verbal and Nonverbal Responses in Mediating an Instrumental Act," *Journal of Experimental Psychology*, **45** (1953), 327-33.

————, "Variables in Early Discrimination Learning: I. Motor Responses in the Training of a Left-right Discrimination," *Child Development*, **29** (1958), 269-75. (a)

————, "Variables in Early Discrimination Learning: II. Mode of Response and Stimulus Difference in the Discrimination of Tonal Frequencies," *Child Development*, **29** (1958), 531-38. (b)

Kaufman, M. E. and W. M. Peterson, "Acquisition of a Learning Set by Normal and Mentally Retarded Children," *Journal of Comparative Physiological Psychology*, **51** (1958), 619-21.

Kendler, T. S. and H. H. Kendler, "Reversal and Nonreversal Shifts in Kindergarten Children," *Journal of Experimental Psychology*, **58** (1959), 56-60.

Kendler, T. S., H. H. Kendler, and D. Wells, "Reversal and Nonreversal Shifts in Nursery School Children," *Journal of Comparative Physiological Psychology*, **53** (1960), 83-88.

Koch, M. B. and D. R. Meyer, "A Relationship of Mental Age to Learning-set Formation in the Preschool Child," *Journal of Comparative Physiological Psychology*, **52** (1959), 387-89.

Kuenne, M. K., "Experimental Investigation of the Relation of Language to Transposition Behavior in Young Children," *Journal of Experimental Psychology*, **36** (1946), 471-90

Levinson, B. and H. W. Reese, "Discrimination Learning Set in Preschool Children." Paper read at Midwestern Psychological Association, Chicago, May 1961.

Luria, A. R., "The Role of Language in the Formation of Temporary Connections," in *Psychology of the Soviet Union*, ed. B. Simon. Stanford, Calif.: Stanford University Press, 1957.

McCormack, P. D., "Negative Transfer in Motor Performance following a Critical Amount of Verbal Pretraining," *Perceptual Motor Skills*, 8 (1958), 27-31.

Murdock, B. B., Jr., "Effects of Task Difficulty, Stimulus Similarity, and Type of Response on Stimulus Predifferentiation," *Journal of Experimental Psychology*, 55 (1958), 167-72.

Norcross, K. J. and C. C. Spiker, "The Effects of Type of Stimulus Pretraining on Discrimination Performance in Preschool Children," *Child Development*, 28 (1957), 79-84.

O'Connor, N. and B. Hermelin, "Discrimination and Reversal Learning in Imbeciles," *Journal of Abnormal Social Psychology*, 59 (1959), 409-13.

Plenderleith, M., "Discrimination Learning and Discrimination Reversal Learning in Normal and Feeble-minded Children," *Journal of Genetic Psychology*, 88 (1956), 107-12.

Reese, H. W., "Motor Paired-associate Learning and Stimulus Pretraining," *Child Development*, 31 (1960), 505-13.

————, "The Distance Effect in Transposition in the Intermediate-size Problem." Paper read at Ontario Psychological Association, Hamilton, Ontario, February 1961.

————, "Transposition in the Intermediate-size Problem by Preschool Children," *Child Development*. (In press.)

Rudel, R. G., "The Transposition of Intermediate Size by Brain Damaged and Mongoloid Children," *Journal of Comparative Physiological Psychology*, 53 (1960), 89-94.

Shepard, W. O., "The Effects of Verbal Pretraining on Discrimination Learning in Preschool Children." (Unpublished Doctoral dissertation, State University of Iowa, 1954.)

————, "Learning Set in Preschool Children," *Journal of Comparative Physiological Psychology*, 50 (1957), 15-17.

Spence, K. W., "The Nature of Discrimination Learning in Animals," *Psychological Review*, 43 (1936), 427-49.

Spiker, C. C., "Stimulus Pretraining and Subsequent Performance in the Delayed Reaction Experiment," *Journal of Experimental Psychology*, 52 (1956), 107-11.

————, "Performance on a Difficult Discrimination following Pretraining with Distinctive Stimuli," *Child Development*, 30 (1959), 513-21.

————, "Verbal Factors in the Discrimination Learning of Children." Paper read at the Conference on Cognitive Processes, Minneapolis, April 1961.

Spiker, C. C., I. R. Gerjuoy, and W. O. Shepard, "Children's Concept of Middle-sizedness and Performance on the Intermediate-size Problems," *Journal of Comparative Physiological Psychology*, 49 (1956), 416-19.

Stevenson, H. W. and M. E. Bitterman, "The Distance-effect in the Transposition of Intermediate Size by Children," *American Journal of Psychology*, 68 (1955), 274-79.

Stevenson, H. W. and J. D. Swartz, "Learning Set in Children as a Function of Intellectual Level," *Journal of Comparative Physiological Psychology*, 51 (1958), 755-57.

Stolurow, L. M. and G. R. Pascal, "Double Alternation Behavior in Mental Defectives," *American Psychologist*, 5 (1950), 273-74. (Abstract.)

Terrell, G., Jr., "The Role of Incentive in Discrimination Learning in Children," *Child Development*, 29 (1958), 231-36.

Terrell, G., Jr., and W. A. Kennedy, "Discrimination Learning and Transposition in Children as a Function of the Nature of Reward," *Journal of Experimental Psychology*, 53 (1957), 257-60.

Weir, M. W. and H. W. Stevenson, "The Effect of Verbalization in Children's Learning as a Function of Chronological Age," *Child Development*, 30 (1959), 143-49.

Weiss, G., "Discrimination Learning in Preschool Children under Three Levels of Instruction." (Unpublished Master's thesis, State University of Iowa, 1954.)

How Shall a Thing Be Called? *

Roger Brown

The most deliberate part of first-language teaching is the business of telling a child what each thing is called. We ordinarily speak of *the* name of a thing as if there were just one, but in fact, of course, every referent has many names. The dime in my pocket is not only a *dime*. It is also *money,* a *metal object,* a *thing,* and, moving to subordinates, it is a *1952 dime,* in fact a *particular 1952 dime* with a unique pattern of scratches, discolorations, and smooth places. When such an object is named for a very young child how is it called? It may be named *money* or *dime* but probably not *metal object, thing, 1952 dime, or particular 1952 dime.* The dog out on the lawn is not only a *dog* but is also a *boxer,* a *quadruped,* an *animate being;* it is the *landlord's dog,* named *Prince.* How will it be identified for a child? Sometimes it will be called a *dog,* sometimes *Prince,* less often a *boxer,* and almost never a *quadruped,* or *animal being.* Listening to many adults name things for many children, I find that their choices are quite uniform and that I can anticipate them from my own inclinations. How are these choices determined and what are their consequences for the cognitive development of the child?

Adults have notions about the kind of language appropriate for use with children. Especially strong and universal is the belief that children have trouble pronouncing long names and so should always be given the shortest possible names. A word is preferable to a phrase and, among words, a monosyllable is better than a polysyllable. This predicts the preference for *dog* and *Prince* over *boxer, quadruped,* and *animate being.* It predicts the choice of *dime* over *metal object* and *particular 1952 dime.*

Zipf (10) has shown that the length of a word (in phonemes or syllables) is inversely related to its frequency in the printed language. Consequently the shorter names for any thing will usually also be the most frequently used names for that thing, and so it would seem that the choice of a name is usually predictable from either frequency or brevity. The monosyllables *dog* and *Prince* have much higher frequencies according to the Thorndike-Lorge list (8) than do the polysyllables *boxer, quadruped,* and *animate being.*

It sometimes happens, however, that the frequency-brevity principle makes the wrong prediction. The thing called a *pineapple* is also *fruit. Fruit* is the shorter and more frequent term, but adults will name the thing *pineapple.* Similarly they will say *apple, banana, orange,* and even *pomegranate;* all of them longer and less frequent words than the perfectly appropriate *fruit.* Brevity seems not to be the powerful determinant we had imagined. The frequency principle can survive this

* From R. Brown. "How Shall a Thing Be Called?" *Psychological Review,* **65** (1958), 14-21. Reprinted by permission of the author and publishers.

kind of example, but only if it is separated from counts like the Thorndike-Lorge of over-all frequency in the printed language. On the whole the word *fruit* appears more often than the word *pineapple* (and also is shorter), but we may confidently assume that, when pineapples are being named, the word *pineapple* is more frequent than the word *fruit*. This, of course, is a kind of frequency more directly relevant to our problem. Word counts of general usage are only very roughly applicable to the prediction of what will be said when something is named. What we need is referent-name counts. We don't have them, of course, but if we had them it is easy to see that they would improve our predictions. Bananas are called *banana,* apples *apple,* and oranges *orange* more often than any of them is called *fruit.* The broad frequency-brevity principle predicts that *money* and *dime* will be preferred to *metal object, 1952 dime,* and *particular 1952 dime,* but it does not predict the neglect of the common monosyllable *thing.* For this purpose we must again appeal to imagined referent-name counts, according to which dimes would surely be called *dime* or *money* more often than *thing.*

While the conscious preference for a short name can be overcome by frequency, the preference nevertheless affects the naming act. I have heard parents designate the appropriate objects *pineapple, television, vinegar,* and *policeman;* all these to children who cannot reproduce polysyllabic words. Presumably they use these names because that is what the referents ·are usually called, but the adult's sense of the absurdity of giving such words to a child is often evident. He may smile as he says it or remark, "That's too hard for you to say, isn't it?"

Some things are named in the same way by all adults for all children. This is true of the apple and the orange. Other things have several common names, each of them used by a specifiable group of adults to specifiable children. The same dog is *dog* to most of the world and *Prince* in his own home and perhaps on his own block. The same man is a *man* to most children, *policeman* to some at some times, *Mr. Jones* to the neighborhood kids, and *papa* to his own. Referent-name counts from people in general will not predict these several usages. A still more particular name count must be imagined. The name given a thing by an adult for a child is determined by the frequency with which various names have been applied to such things in the experience of the particular adult. General referent-name counts taken from many people will predict much that the individual does, but, for a close prediction, counts specific to the individual would be needed.

The frequencies to which we are now appealing have not, of course, been recorded. We are explaining imagined preferences in names by imagined frequencies of names. It is conceivable, certainly, that some of these specific word counts might be made and a future naming performance independently predicted from a past frequency. Probably, however, such frequencies will never be known, and if we choose to explain particular naming performances by past frequencies we shall usually have to infer the frequency from the performance.

BEYOND THE FREQUENCY PRINCIPLE

A frequency explanation is not very satisfying even when the appeal is to known frequencies. The question will come to mind: "Why is one name more common than another?" Why is a dog called *dog* more often than *quadruped* and, by some people, called *Prince* more often than *dog?* Perhaps it just happened that way, like driving on the right side of the road in America and on the left in England. The convention is preserved but has no justification outside itself. As things have worked out, coins are usually named by species as *dime, nickel,* or *penny* while the people we know have individual names like *John, Mary,* and *Jim.* Could it just as easily be the other way around? Might we equally well give coins proper names and introduce people as types?

The referent for the word *dime* is a large class of coins. The name is equally appropriate to all members of this class. To name a coin *dime* is to establish its equivalence, for naming purposes, with all other coins of the same denomination. This equivalence for naming purposes corresponds to a more general equivalence for all purposes of economic exchange. In the grocery one dime is as good as another but quite different from any nickel or penny. For a child the name given an object anticipates the equivalences and differences that will need to be observed in most of his dealings with such an object. To make proper denotative use of the word *dime* he must be able to distinguish members of the referent category from everything else. When he learns that, he has solved more than a language problem. He has an essential bit of equipment for doing business. The most common names for coins could not move from the species level to the level of proper names without great alteration in our nonlinguistic culture. We should all be numismatists preparing our children to recognize a particular priceless 1910 dime.

Many things are reliably given the same name by the whole community. The spoon is seldom called anything but *spoon,* although it is also a piece of *silverware,* an *artifact,* and a *particular ill-washed restaurant spoon.* The community-wide preference for the word *spoon* corresponds to the community-wide practice of treating spoons as equivalent but different from knives and forks. There are no proper names for individual spoons because their individuality seldom signifies. It is the same way with pineapples, dimes, doors, and taxicabs. The most common name for each of these categorizes them as they need to be categorized for the community's nonlinguistic purposes. The most common name is at the level of usual utility.

People and pets have individual names as well as several kinds of generic name. The individual name is routinely coined by those who are disposed to treat the referent as unique, and is available afterwards to any others who will see the uniqueness. A man at home has his own name to go with the peculiar privileges and responsibilities binding him to wife and child. But the same man who is a one-of-a-kind *papa* to his own children is simply a *man* to children at large. He is, like the other members of this large category, someone with no time to play and little tolerance for noise. In some circumstances, this same man will be given the name of his occupation. He is a *policeman* equivalent to other policemen but different from *bus drivers* and *Good Humor men.* A policeman is someone to "behave in front of" and to go to when lost. To the kids in the neighborhood the man is *Mr. Jones,* unique in his way—a crank, bad-tempered, likely to shout at you if you play out in front of his house. It is the same way with dogs as with people. He may be a unique *Prince* to his owners, who feed and house him, but he is just a *dog* to the rest of the world. A homeless dog reverts to namelessness, since there is none to single him out from his species. Dimes and nickels have much the same significance for an entire society, and their usual names are fixed at this level of significance. People and pets function uniquely for some and in various generic ways for others. They have a corresponding variety of designations, but each name is at the utility level for the group that uses it. Our naming practices for coins and people correspond to our nonlinguistic practices, and it is difficult to imagine changing the one without changing the other.

The names provided by parents for children anticipate the functional structure of the child's world.[1] This is not, of course, something parents are aware of doing. When we name a thing there does not seem to be any process of choice. Each thing has its name, just one, and that is what we give to a child. The one name is, of course, simply the usual name for us. Naming each thing in accordance with local frequencies, parents unwittingly transmit their own cognitive structures. It is a world in

which *Prince* is unique among dogs and *papa* among men, *spoons* are all alike but different from *forks*. It may be a world of *bugs* (to be stepped on), of *flowers* (not to be picked), and *birds* (not to be stoned). It may be a world in which *niggers,* like *spoons,* are all of a kind. A division of caste creates a vast categorical equivalence and a correspondingly generic name. *Mr. Jones* and *Mr. Smith* do not come out of racial anonymity until their uniqueness is appreciated.

Adults do not invariably provide a child with the name that is at the level of usual utility in the adult world. An effort is sometimes made to imagine the utilities of a child's life. Some parents will, at first, call every sort of coin *money*. This does not prepare a child to buy and sell, but then he may be too young for that. All coins are equivalent for the very young child in that they are objects not to be put into the mouth and not to be dropped down the register, and *money* anticipates that equivalence. A more differentiated terminology can wait upon the age of storegoing. Sometimes an adult is aware of a child's need for a distinction that is not coded in the English lexicon. A new chair comes into the house and is not going to be equivalent to the shabby chairs already there. A child is permitted to sit on the old chairs but will not be permitted on the new one. A distinctive name is created from the combinational resources of the language. *The new chair* or *the good chair is* not to be assimilated to *chairs* in general.

Eventually, of course, children learn many more names for each thing than the one that is most frequent and useful. Sometimes a name is supplied in order to bring forward an immediately important property of the referent. A child who starts bouncing the coffee pot needs to be told that it is *glass*.

---

[1] The equivalence of dimes and their distinctiveness as a class from nickels and pennies is strongly suggested by the appearance of individual coins as well as by their names. Variations in size, weight, and hue are far greater between classes than within a class. This, of course, is because coins are manufactured in accordance with a categorical scheme which is also represented in our names for coins. It is possible, then, that a child might structure coins in the culturally approved manner if he never heard them named at all. However, we cannot be sure that an untutored child would not put all shiny new coins into one class and all the dingy specimens into another. When the referents are not manufactured articles but are such things as dogs, people, flowers, and insects, it is clear that autochthonous factors in perception do not force any single scheme of categorization. The names applied must be the child's principal clue to the locally functioning scheme.

Sometimes a name is supplied to satisfy the child's curiosity as to the place of a referent in a hierarchy of categories. Chairs are *furniture* and so are tables; carrots are a *vegetable,* but apples are not. Probably, however, both children and adults make some distinction among these various names. *The* name of a thing, the one that tells what it "really" is, is the name that constitutes the referent as it needs to be constitued for most purposes. The other names represent possible recategorizations useful for one or another purpose. We are even likely to feel that these recategorizations are acts of imagination, whereas the major categorization is a kind of passive recognition of the true character of the referent.

THE CHILD'S CONCRETE
VOCABULARY

It is a commonplace saying that the mind of a child is relatively "concrete" and the mind of an adult "abstract." The words "concrete" and "abstract" are sometimes used in the sense of subordinate and superordinate. In this sense a relatively concrete mind would operate with subordinate categories and an abstract mind with superordinate categories. It is recorded in many studies of vocabulary acquisition (for example, 2, 6) that children ordinarily use the words *milk* and *water* before the word *liquid;* the words *apple* and *orange* before *fruit; table* and *chair* before *furniture; mamma* and *daddy* before *parent* or *person;* etc. Very high-level superordinate terms like *article, action, quality,* and *relation,* though they are common in adult speech (8), are very seldom heard from preschool children (2). Presumably this kind of vocabulary comparison is one of the sources of the

notion that the child's mind is more concrete than the mind of the adult.[2] However, the vocabulary of a child is not a very direct index of his cognitive preferences. The child's vocabulary is more immediately determined by the naming practices of adults.

The occasion for a name is ordinarily some particular thing. In the naming it is categorized. The preference among possible names seems to go to the one that is most commonly applied to the referent in question. That name will ordinarily categorize the referent so as to observe the equivalences and differences that figure in its usual utilization. There are not many purposes

----

[2] From the facts of vocabulary acquisition alone it is not possible to draw safe conclusions about cognitive development. Such conclusions rely on something like the following set of assumptions. A subject, whether animal or human, is ordinarily credited with a cognitive category when he extends some distinctive response to new instances of the category and withholds it from noninstances. Words, when used to denote new referents, are such a distinctive response. If children speak words they probably can make correct denotative use of them, and so the presence of the word in a child's vocabulary may be taken as evidence that he possesses the category to which the word makes reference. The instances of the category are presumed not to be differentiated by the child unless he uses words for such differentiations. If all of these assumptions are made it would seem to follow that the direction of vocabulary growth (from subordinate to superordinate or vice versa) reveals the direction of cognitive development. When the assumptions of such an argument are explicitly stated, it is clear that they are too many and too doubtful. Obviously words may be spoken but not understood; objects may be differentiated by nonlinguistic response even though they are not differentiated linguistically. However, it is not my purpose here to quarrel with these assumptions but rather to show that, even when they are accepted, the facts of vocabulary growth do not compel the conclusion that cognitive development is from the concrete to the abstract.

for which all liquids are equivalent or all fruits, furniture, or parents; and so the names of these categories are less commonly used for denotation than are the names of categories subordinate to them. It is true that words like *article, action, quality,* and *relation* are rather common in adult written English, but we can be sure that these frequencies in running discourse are not equaled in naming situations. Whatever the purposes for which all articles are equivalent, or all actions or qualities, they are not among the pressing needs of children.

It is not invariably true that vocabulary builds from concrete to abstract. *Fish* is likely to be learned before *perch* and *bass; house* before *bungalow* and *mansion; car* before *Chevrolet* and *Plymouth* (6). The more concrete vocabulary waits for the child to reach an age where his purposes differentiate kinds of fish and makes of cars. There is much elaborately concrete vocabulary that is not introduced until one takes courses in biology, chemistry, and botany. No one has ever proved that vocabulary builds from the concrete to the abstract more often than it builds from the abstract to the concrete. The best generalization seems to be that each thing is first given its most common name. This name seems to categorize on the level of usual utility. That level sometimes falls on the most concrete categories in a hierarchy (proper names for significant people), and vocabulary then builds toward the more abstract categories (names for ethnic groups, personality types, social classes). Utility sometimes centers on a relatively abstract level of categorization (fish) and vocabulary then builds in both directions (perch and vertebrate). Probably utility never centers on the most abstract levels (thing, substance, and so on), and so probably there is no hierarchy within which

vocabulary builds in an exclusively concrete direction.

In the literature describing first-language acquisition (5) there is much to indicate that children easily form large abstract categories. There are, to begin with, the numerous cases in which the child overgeneralizes the use of a conventional word. The word *dog* may, at first, be applied to every kind of four-legged animal. It sometimes happens that every man who comes into the house is called *daddy*. When children invent their own words, these often have an enormous semantic range. Wilhelm Stern's (7) son Günther used *psee* for leaves, trees, and flowers. He used *bebau* for all animals. Lombroso (9) tells of a child who used *qua qua* for both duck and water and *afta* for drinking glass, the contents of a glass, and a pane of glass. Reports of this kind do not suggest that children are deficient in abstracting ability. It even looks as if they may favor large categories.

There are two extreme opinions about the direction of cognitive development. There are those who suppose that we begin by discriminating to the limits of our sensory acuity, seizing each thing in its uniqueness, noting every hair and flea of the particular dog. Cognitive development involves neglect of detail, abstracting from particulars so as to group similars into categories. By this view abstraction is a mature rather than a primitive process. The contrary opinion is that the primitive stage in cognition is one of a comparative lack of differentiation. Probably certain distinctions are inescapable; the difference between a loud noise and near silence, between a bright contour and a dark ground, etc. These inevitable discriminations divide the perceived world into a small number of very large (abstract) categories. Cognitive development is increasing differentiation. The more distinctions we make, the more categories we have and the smaller (more concrete) these are. I think the latter view is favored in psychology today. While there is good empirical and theoretical support (1, 3, 4) for the view that development is differentiation, there is embarrassment for it in the fact that much vocabulary growth is from the concrete to the abstract. This embarrassment can be eliminated.

Suppose a very young child applies the word *dog* to every four-legged creature he sees. He may have abstracted a limited set of attributes and created a large category, but his abstraction will not show up in his vocabulary. Parents will not provide him with a conventional name for his category, for example, *quadruped,* but instead will require him to narrow his use of *dog* to its proper range. Suppose a child calls all elderly ladies *aunt.* He will not be told that the usual name for his category is *elderly ladies* but, instead, will be taught to cut back *aunt* to accord with standard usage. In short, the sequence in which words are acquired is set by adults rather than children and may ultimately be determined by the utility of the various categorizations. This will sometimes result in a movement of vocabulary toward higher abstraction and sometimes a movement toward greater concreteness. The cognitive development of the child may nevertheless always take the direction of increasing differentiation or concreteness.

The child who spontaneously hits on the category four-legged animals will be required to give it up in favor of dogs, cats, horses, cows, and the like. When the names of numerous subordinates have been mastered, he may be given the name *quadruped* for the superordinate. This abstraction is not the same as its primitive forerunner.

The schoolboy who learns the word *quadruped* has abstracted from differentiated and named subordinates. The child he was abstracted through a failure to differentiate. Abstraction after differentiation may be the mature process, and abstraction from a failure to differentiate the primitive. Needless to say, the abstractions occurring on the two levels need not be coincident, as they are in our quadruped example.

SUMMARY

Though we often think of each thing as having a name—a single name—in fact, each thing has many equally correct names. When some thing is named for a child, adults show considerable regularity in their preference for one of the many possible names. This paper is addressed to the question: "What determines the name given to a child for a thing?" The first answer is that adults prefer the shorter to the longer expression. This gives way to the frequency principle. Adults give a thing the name it is most commonly given. We have now come full circle and are left with the question, "Why is one name for a thing more common than another?"

It seems likely that things are first named so as to categorize them in a maximally useful way. For most purposes Referent A is a spoon rather than a piece of silverware, and Referent B a dime rather than a metal object. The same referent may have its most useful categorization on one level (*Prince*) for one group (the family) and on another level (*dog*) for another group (strangers). The categorization that is most useful for very young children (*money*) may change as they grow older (*dime* and *nickel*).

With some hierarchies of vocabulary the more concrete terms are learned before the abstract; probably the most abstract terms are never learned first, but it often happens that a hierarchy develops in both directions from a middle level of abstraction. Psychologists who believe that mental development is from the abstract to the concrete, from a lack of differentiation to increased differentiation, have been embarrassed by the fact that vocabulary often builds in the opposite direction. This fact need not trouble them, since the sequence in which words are acquired is not determined by the cognitive preferences of children so much as by the naming practices of adults.

REFERENCES

1. Gibson, J. J. and Eleanor J. Gibson, "Perceptual Learning: Differentiation or Enrichment?" *Psychological Review,* **62** (1955), 32-41.

2. International Kindergarten Union, *A Study of the Vocabulary of Children before Entering the First Grade.* Baltimore: The Williams & Wilkins Co., 1928.

3. Lashley, K. S. and Marjorie Wade, "The Pavlovian Theory of Generalization," *Psychological Review,* **53** (1946), 72-87.

4. Lewin, K., *A Dynamic Theory of Personality.* New York: McGraw-Hill Book Company, Inc., 1935.

5. McCarthy, Dorothea, "Language Development in Children," in *Manual of Child Psychology,* ed. L. Carmichael, pp. 477-581. New York: John Wiley & Sons, Inc., 1946.

6. Smith, M. E., "An Investigation of the Development of the Sentence and the Extent of Vocabulary in Young Children," *State University of Iowa Studies in Child Welfare,* **3,** No. 5 (1926).

7. Stern, Clara and W. Stern, *Die Kindersprache.* Leipzig: Barth, 1920.

8. Thorndike, E. L. and I. Lorge, *The Teacher's Word Book of 30,000 Words.* New York: Bureau of Publications, Teachers College, Columbia University, 1944.

9. Werner, H., *Comparative Psychology of Mental Development.* Chicago: Follett Publishing Company, 1948.

10. Zipf, G. K., *The Psycho-biology of Language.* Boston: Houghton Mifflin Company, 1935.

Nonverbal Probability Judgments by Young Children *

Patricia A. Yost, Alberta E. Siegel, and Julia M. Andrews

Although few adults would be able to define probability with any precision, and, in fact, definitions of probability are a matter for dispute among logicians and mathematicians, most adults are able to behave effectively in probabilistic situations involving quantitative proportions of independent elements. Piaget has studied the behavior of children in a probabilistic situation and from their behavior has concluded that young children (say, up to age 7) are unable to utilize a concept of probability. The present study is a

* From P. A. Yost, A. E. Siegel, and J. M. Andrews, "Nonverbal Probability Judgments by Young Children," *Child Development,* **33** (1962), 769-80. Reprinted by permission of the authors and the Society for Research in Child Development Inc.

The authors, members of the Department of Child Development and Family Relationships, Pennsylvania State University, University Park, are grateful to the late Professor Sidney Siegel for his interest and help in the planning and execution of this study. Support for the study was provided in part by a grant to him from the National Science Foundation (G-7071), in part by a National Science Foundation Graduate Fellowship (20297) to P. A. Y., and in part by a Public Health Service Research Fellowship (MF-10, 157-C1) to J. M. A. from the National Institute of Mental Health. We appreciate the cooperation of Professors Winona L. Morgan and Mary Alice Russell and of Miss Aurelia Way in making available the facilities of the Pennsylvania State University Nursery School. Thanks are extended to Miss JoAnne Evans for assistance in data collection.

demonstration that young children are able to behave in terms of the probability concept under appropriate conditions. It is an experiment in which Piaget's technique for assessing the probability concept in young children is compared with a decision-making technique.

PIAGET'S WORK

Piaget (3) studied the concept of probability in 14 boys and girls between the ages of 5 and 12 years. Since his paper is not available in English and since his results are central to the present study, we present them in some detail here.

Each S was seen individually. For each judgment, an assortment of tokens in various colors was put into an opaque bag and shaken. An identical assortment of tokens was placed in a row on the table before S. He was then asked which color he would be "most likely" to get if he reached into the bag without looking and withdrew one token. In addition, older Ss were asked to predict the colors of successive pairs of tokens which were drawn from the bag. Tokens withdrawn from the bag remained on the table in S's view.

Piaget found that young children (ages 5 to 7) do not make their predictions consistently on the basis of the quantitative proportions of the elements, but rather use various other criteria. Thus, the child might make his choice on the basis of the initial order of the tokens on the table ("I'll get red because it's first") ignoring the mixing (randomizing) of elements in the bag. He might base his choice on the exact number of tokens of a particular color, disregarding their quantitative proportion in the total number of elements ("I'll get two red because there are [exactly] two red ones"). He might justify his prediction on the basis of the intrinsic characteristics of the elements ("I'll get pink because pink goes with red"). Or his choice might reflect his preference ("I'll get red because I like red").

From such behavior of young children, Piaget concludes that children at this developmental level do not understand the idea of mixing (randomness) and are unable to utilize information about the quantitative proportions of elements because they do not yet possess a system of numerical and combinatorial operations.

Somewhat older children (roughly, ages 8 to 10) base their choices on the quantitative proportions of elements but fail to consider the implications of drawing tokens from the bag without replacement. Still older children, Piaget concludes, succeed in recognizing the change in probabilities in the situation after each new drawing of chips.

PROBABILITY LEARNING IN YOUNG CHILDREN

Some doubts about the meaning of Piaget's observations stem from several criticisms of his technique and also from the findings of studies of children in probability learning situations. Thus, Siegel and Andrews (6) studied the performance of 24 4-year-old boys in a probabilistic situation, using amount of reinforcement as a critical variable in testing the predictions of the Siegel model of choice behavior (5). Each S was asked to predict which of two identical containers placed before him contained an object. The container in one of the two positions held the object on 75 percent of the trials in a randomized series; the container in the other position held the object on the remaining 25 percent of the trials.

Two conditions of reinforcement were used. Under the low reinforcement condition, the object was an uninteresting button, and knowledge of the outcome of each trial was the only systematic reinforcement. Under the condition of higher reinforcement, the object was a small prize which the child received each time he correctly predicted the container holding it. The prizes were a variety of small toys, candies, trinkets, crayons, balloons, etc.—such an assortment has been shown to have high reinforcement value for preschool children (1).

Siegel and Andrews found that under the low reinforcement condition the 4-year-olds tended to choose the position in which the container most frequently held the object on about 75 percent of the trials, i.e., Ss tended to match their response output probabilities to the stimulus input probability. Under the condition of greater reinforcement, on the other hand, Ss tended to choose the container in the more frequent position on more than 75 percent of the trials, i.e., they tended to maximize the probability of being rewarded. These results are consistent with the predictions of the Siegel model for each condition of reinforcement.

Evidence of learning by young children in probabilistic situations also emerged from the work of Messick and Solley (2), Stevenson and Zigler (9), and Stevenson and Weir (8).

The tendency of children to adopt a maximizing strategy in a probabilistic situation led to the hypothesis that young children may have a greater understanding of probabilities than would be attributed to them by Piaget. An examination of his evidence led to the following criticisms of his technique and to the development of a technique which is not subject to these criticisms:

1. The method relies heavily on verbal skills, in two ways: (a) the child is required to understand the meaning of the term "most likely," and (b) the child is required to demonstrate his own grasp of the concept by verbalization—naming the color he expects to draw. Since the intent is not to study the child's verbal skillfulness with the concept of probability, this seems inappropriate.

2. The method confounds color preference with color expectation. When a child says "I'll get red because I like red," it is not clear whether he is stating a prediction (expectation) or a preference.

3. Placing before S an assortment identical to that in the bag, in the interests of aiding his memory, may be confusing because the assortment before S is not randomized, and position preferences may be confounded with expectations: "I'll get red because it's nearest," or "I'll get red because it's first."

4. The method involves no special incentive for a correct response; there is no reward contingent upon the child's exhibiting or not exhibiting probability understanding. Thus there is no provision for maintaining motivation in the Ss.

5. In Piaget's study, no provision was made for analyzing the results statistically. Conclusions are drawn from single or noncomparable responses, rather than from response frequencies for repeated comparable events.

A DECISION-MAKING TECHNIQUE

For the present study, a decision-making method was developed for assessing understanding of probability.

Technique

The first step of the procedure, under which each S is seen individually, is to determine S's most-preferred and least-preferred of three colors of chips, by the method of paired comparisons. Only chips of these two colors are used in the session.

The child is asked to make choices on a large number of trials. At the start of each trial, he is shown a small assortment of prizes and asked to select one which he would like to win. (The prizes are trinkets, balloons, candies, crayons, etc.) The prize he chooses is placed before him, and he is told that in order to win that prize to keep he must draw a chip of a certain color. A chip of this payoff color is then placed next to the prize, as a reminder.

Next, two clear plastic boxes are placed before S. An equal number of chips of the most-preferred color are placed in both boxes simultaneously by E. Then chips of the least-preferred color are placed in both boxes. The numbers of chips of the latter color are not equal.

Both plastic boxes are then shaken at the same time to randomize the position of the chips, and S is asked to choose the box from which he wants to draw (without looking) in order to get a chip of the payoff color. A response is considered correct if S chooses the box for which the objective probability of getting a chip of the payoff color is greater.

Thus, for a child having red as his

thinks he will draw from the box. Like the decision-making technique, this approach is nonverbal. Moreover, with the use of the transparent container, there is no necessity for arranging an identical assortment of chips on the table before S. The only reinforcement received by S is knowledge of the color he has drawn.

After S's color preference has been determined, one chip of each of the two colors (most-preferred and least-preferred) is placed before him; these two chips remain before him throughout the session. Next a predetermined number of chips of the two colors is put into the box all at once, the lid is closed, and the box is shaken to randomize the position of the chips. He is then asked to indicate, by pointing to one of the two chips on the table, which color he thinks he will draw from the box.

For example, on trial 1, for a child whose most-preferred color is blue and least-preferred is white, the probability under study is $\frac{1}{3}$. Four blue chips and two white are placed in the box and shaken, and S is asked to indicate, by pointing, which color he expects to draw from the box. On trial 2, the probability under study is $\frac{1}{5}$. Four white chips and one blue are placed in the box, and the child is asked to indicate which color he expects to draw this time.

Then S is told to "hide your eyes" and is allowed to do this in his own way. (Some Ss close their eyes tightly, some cover their eyes with their hands, some hold a cardboard before their faces, and some lean forward and rest their foreheads on the edge of the table.) The box is shaken a second time, the lid is removed, and S (still hiding his eyes) is instructed to reach into the box and select one chip. After the selection is made, S opens his eyes to see what he has drawn. E empties the box, returns the chips to her apron pockets, and selects the chips for the next trial.

Condition DM. Under condition *DM,* S is first asked to select a prize which he would like to have from an assortment of five or six items on a small tray. This assortment is different for each trial. The S's selection is placed on the table, and the rest of the prizes are hidden from view. Then E tells S that a chip of a certain color is needed to get the prize. She places a chip of this color on the table near the prize.

Next, two identical plastic boxes of the type already described are placed on the table. Chips of the preferred color are put into the two boxes simultaneously by E; then chips of the least-preferred color are put into them. Both boxes are shaken at the same time and replaced on the table. The child is then asked to indicate, by pointing to one of them, from which box he wants to draw in order to try to get a chip of the payoff color. He hides his eyes while E shakes the box he has chosen and then draws one chip from it.

For example, consider trial 1 for a child whose preferred color is blue and least-preferred color is white. The probability under study is $\frac{1}{3}$. S is told that he must draw a white chip in order to win the prize; to remind him, a white chip is placed next to the prize he has selected to try for. Two blue chips are placed in each box; then four white chips are placed in the left box while one is placed in the right. Then S is asked to point to one box, either right or left, from which he wishes to draw in order to try to get a white chip.

After each trial, E comments as follows on the outcome: (a) when S chooses the correct box and draws a chip of the payoff color, "You may keep the prize; that was a good try";

(b) when *S* chooses the correct box but does not draw a chip of the payoff color, "You don't get the prize; but that was a good try"; (c) when *S* chooses the incorrect box but draws a chip of the payoff color, "You may keep the prize"; and (d) when *S* chooses the incorrect box and does not draw the payoff color, "You don't get to keep the prize." Thus, verbal reinforcements are always given for correct choices; prize reinforcements are given for choices according to the probabilities built into the situation.

If *S* wins a prize by drawing a chip of the payoff color, he puts his prize into a small paper bag marked with his name. If he does not win a prize on a given trial, the prize is replaced in the tray and appears in the assortment used in the next trial.

The two conditions—*P* and *DM*—are summarily described and compared in Table 1.

P would not expect to receive prizes in their first session. Some of the children in group DM were somewhat reluctant to participate in condition P_2 after having been rewarded with prizes in the DM_1 session; however, it was possible to observe every *S* in a complete series of trials under both conditions.

A session under condition *P* usually lasted from 15 to 30 minutes; a session under condition *DM* lasted from 20 to 35 minutes. These figures include the brief rest period which was typically taken after the first 12 trials.

The first two trials in each session were practice trials. However, no distinction was made for *S* between these trials and the initiation of the experimental series of 24 trials.

In both condition *P* and condition *DM,* a series of 24 trials was presented to *S*. These trials were based upon the probabilities ⅓, ¼, and ⅕. Four

TABLE 1

DESCRIPTION OF CONDITIONS

Condition P	Condition DM
Modified Piaget method	Decision-making technique
One box	Two boxes
Color choice	Container choice
No control for color preference	Control for color preference
No reinforcement other than knowledge of outcome	Reinforcement

EXPERIMENTAL CONTROLS. As has been mentioned, each *S* participated in both kinds of sessions. The two sessions with a given *S* were separated by several days: from four to ten, with a median and mode of seven days.

In order to minimize the effects of communication among *S*s concerning the sessions, all *S*s in group P were observed under condition P_1 (*see* Table 3) before any *S* in either group was observed under condition *DM*. This was necessary so that *S*s in group

different trials (A, B, C, and D) were derived from each of the three probabilities, according to a predesigned pattern, making a total of 12 different trials. The order of these 12 was randomized in advance, and the same random order was used for trials 1 through 12 and again for trials 13 through 24.

Table 2 represents the trials schematically. The reader will observe that in the *DM* condition the payoff colors were counterbalanced over trials be-

TABLE 2
DESCRIPTION OF TRIALS

P = Most-Preferred Color N = Least-Preferred Color R = Right Box L = Left Box

| | CONDITION P | | | CONDITION DM | | | | |
Trial No. and Type	Number of P Chips	Number of N Chips	Correct Response	Number of P Chips in Each Box	Number of N Chips in L Box	Number of N Chips in R Box	Payoff Color	Correct Response
Probability 1/3 (Ratio 2:1)								
8 A	2	1	P	2	1	4	P	L
5 B	1	2	N	2	4	1	P	R
11 C	2	4	N	2	1	4	N	R
1 D	4	2	P	2	4	1	N	L
Probability 1/4 (Ratio 3:1)								
3 A	3	1	P	3	1	9	P	L
7 B	1	3	N	3	9	1	P	R
4 C	3	9	N	3	1	9	N	R
12 D	9	3	P	3	9	1	N	L
Probability 1/5 (Ratio 4:1)								
9 A	4	1	P	4	1	16	P	L
2 B	1	4	N	4	16	1	P	R
10 C	4	16	N	4	1	16	N	R
6 D	16	4	P	4	16	1	N	L

NOTE. Trials No. 13 through 24 simply repeat trials No. 1 through 12. Thus, trial 1 is also trial 13, trial 2 is also trial 14, etc.

tween the most-preferred and least-preferred colors (P and N). Further, in the *DM* condition the positional locations of the correct box, whether left or right (L or R), were counterbalanced. Analogously, in the *P* condition the more probable colors were counterbalanced. In addition, in the *DM* condition the payoff color was equally often in the box containing the larger and the smaller total number of chips, and this factor was counterbalanced with respect to the other factors. Finally, the reader will note that under the *DM* condition the number of chips of the most-preferred color (P) was the same in both boxes.

Results

A child's score was the number of correct responses he made in the series of 24 trials. For each child, a score under condition *P* and a score under condition *DM* were obtained. A score of 12 represents performance at only a chance level, while a score of 24 is taken to represent consistent use of the probability concept in responding.

The hypothesis that children exhibit a greater understanding of probability under condition *DM* than under condition *P* was tested in two ways.

First, the *S*s were considered as two independent groups, and a nonparametric sum of ranks procedure (7) was used to test whether scores under condition DM_1 were significantly greater than scores under condition P_1. That is, only scores for first sessions were used. As Table 3 shows, the median number of correct responses under condition P_1 was 12 (just chance performance) while the median number of correct responses under condition DM_1 was 18. The difference in location betwen the two distributions was highly significant: $p = .0052$, one-tailed test.

Since, in fact, all *S*s were observed under both conditions, having been randomly assigned to two groups so that order of condition could be counterbalanced, it was possible to consider each *S* as his own control and to analyze difference scores representing the difference between each *S*'s

TABLE 3

MEDIAN NUMBER OF CORRECT RESPONSES

Experimental Group	First Session	Second Session
Group P (N = 10)	Condition P_1: 12	Condition DM_2: 19
Group DM (N = 9)	Condition DM_1: 18	Condition P_2: 18

Hypothesis test. The median scores of *S*s under the two conditions and in the two groups are presented in Table 3.[2]

[2] The scores of one *S* in group DM were not included in the analysis of the data. While performing under condition P_2, this *S* pointed to chips of the appropriate color inside the box (rather than to the chip of the appropriate color on the table, as instructed). However, when she was asked to indicate her choice by pointing to one of the two chips on the table, she consistently pointed to the chip of the opposite (incorrect) color. Thus her score did not seem to

performance under conditions *P* and *DM*. The Wilcoxon matched-pairs signed-ranks test for two related samples (4, pp. 75-83) was employed, and again the difference was highly significant: $p = .0048$, one-tailed test.

Thus both modes of analysis provide support for the hypothesis.

Other findings. The reader will ob-

be a valid measure of her understanding of probability. Since the scores for this *S* would have supported the hypothesis, their omission leads to a conservative analysis.

called *response output probability* or, equivalently, just *output probability*. Depending upon the purpose of the experiment and on the complexity of the stimulus choices, the experimenter may utilize only these probability definitions, or he may choose to work with expectation values of a log transformation of the probabilities, usually called "bits of information." The present authors propose to use only the probability definitions in this series of studies.

The systematic change in output probability as a function of having more and more experience with an input probability is called *probability learning*. Studies in this area have used either adult college students (3, 6, 8, 9) or subhuman species such as rats (1) or goldfish (4). Differences obtained between studies could well be due to (*a*) different mathematical models being required for different experimental designs, (*b*) instructions given Ss, (*c*) motivational variables, or (*d*) developmental differences between or within species. Human maturational and learning differences at different age levels could be investigated by using children as Ss in these probability learning experiments, and the present studies attempt such an investigation of developmental differences at an exploratory level. These studies were designed to explore children's behavior in situations similar to those used with adults. Rather than use a large number of children in an extremely restricted set of conditions, it was decided to use a small number of children in a large number of different conditions for probability learning, with long enough time delays between conditions to avoid correlation of error components.

One purpose of the present experiments was to see whether or not young children would tend to "maximize probability" of reward in their guessing behavior. For example, if one stimulus is correct 75 percent of the time and a second, alternative stimulus is correct the other 25 percent of the time, then S will usually obtain as much reward as possible in the situation if he chooses the most frequently correct stimulus all of the time. *Maximizing probability,* then, means that S chooses the most frequently correct stimulus all of the time. If the young children tend to maximize probability of reward, then their output probability curves will converge toward a probability of 1.00, even though the input probability level is much lower.

A second question asked in these experiments was "How near chance probability (.50 in the two-choice situation used) could children discriminate a deviation from chance probability?" Brunswik (1) suggests that this "probability threshold" for rats is near .70. Data for humans (5) indicate that adults can at least discriminate a probability of .62 from .50 in a two-choice situation. In the present study the input values of 1.00, .90, .75, and .60 were used to bracket roughly the "probability threshold" for children. It was felt that the discrimination threshold for children would probably be higher than for adults and, hence, that they would not discriminate an input of .60 from chance. It was also felt that thresholds might vary as a function of the children's chronological age.

Three studies were done in an attempt to answer these questions. In the first study the questions concerning "maximizing probability" and "probability thresholds" were investigated. In the second study a stimulus with "social" characteristics was used —stick-men drawings with happy and sad faces. It was felt that perhaps the Ss would split into two or more groups with respect to initial probability bias and rate of learning, with the curves of both groups increasing to an asymptote at the input probability. This notion was based upon an expectation that there would be more variation in the frequency with which such characteristics as "happy" and "sad" are experienced among children than for such physical characteristics as "big" and "little." In the third study the effect of adding an incentive to the reinforcement word *right* was investigated, that is, in addition to telling S "right," he was given a small piece of candy as well. Experiment III was set up on the basis of the results of Experiment I. It was felt that with increased incentive the children would "maximize probability" of getting a reward.

METHOD

Subjects

Subjects consisted of one 8-year-old child, one 7-year-old, three 5-year-olds, one 4-year-old, and one 3-year-old. All of these children were judged to be above average in intelligence, although no *IQ* test was given, and they were all normal and healthy.

Materials

EXPERIMENT I. The materials consisted of 4 x 6 index cards, upon which drawings of kangaroos, horses, and stick-men were mounted. In this study the figures varied only with respect to size (big-little). Decks of 20 cards were arranged, and samples of "big" and "little" stimuli were shown to the children before the learning task. One deck (horses) had an input probability of 1.00 for "big" and .00 for "little." Another deck (stick-men) had an input probability of .90 for "big" and .10 for "little." A third deck (also stick-men) had an input proba-

bility of .75 for "big" and .25 for "little." A fourth deck (kangaroos) had inputs of .60 and .40 for "big" and "little," respectively. Different kinds of stimuli—horses, stick-men, and kangaroos—were used to keep up the children's interest and to make the tasks appear different.

EXPERIMENT II. The only stimuli in this study were stick-men with happy and sad faces. The characteristic "happy" had an input probability of .75, while "sad" had an input probability of .25.

EXPERIMENT III. In this study the stimuli were the same stick-men used in Exp. I for the .75 condition. The characteristic "big" occurred 75 percent of the time, and "little" occurred the other 25 percent of the time, thus reproducing exactly the input conditions for the .75 level of Exp. I. However, in addition to telling S "right" when he guessed the card correctly, he was also given a small piece of candy.

Procedure

All of the children were tested separately, usually in their own homes. The children were told that they were about to play a guessing game. The procedure was essentially the same for all the three experiments. Before each experiment S was shown an example of each of the two figures, for example, a "big" kangaroo and a "little" kangaroo. He was then asked to guess which figure would be on top of the deck. S was instructed to guess either "big" or "little" in Exps. I and III and to say either "happy" or "sad" in Exp. II. The deck of cards was then shuffled and placed face down on the table.

After S made each guess, the top card was turned over for his inspection. S was told "right" if he had guessed it correctly and "wrong" if he had guessed it incorrectly. In Exp.

III S was also given a piece of candy if he was correct and nothing if he was wrong. When all 20 cards in the deck had been guessed, the deck was shuffled and the procedure repeated until S had gone through the deck 10 times for a total of 200 guesses. These 200 guesses were then arbitrarily divided into 10 trial units of 20 guesses each. The proportion of times S guessed "big" out of the 20 guesses in each trial unit was taken as his response probability for that trial (in Exp. II the measure was for "happy").

Rest periods were permitted whenever Ss appeared to be tiring. Frequently the children would stop spontaneously, talk, walk around, get a drink of water, and so forth, before completing the task. The 3- and 4-year-old children stopped most frequently, were the most distractible, and often seemed to pay no attention whatever. Each series of 200 guesses was completed in a single session, and at least one day and not more than three weeks elapsed between sessions.

RESULTS

Experiment I

The results of Exp. I are summarized in Figs. 1 and 2. Figure 1 shows that the median response probabilities reach an asymptote at the input probability level. Individual curves for all seven Ss reached the same asymptote for a given input level; there were no differences between age levels with respect to asymptotes reached. Thus the children did not tend to maximize probabilities, that is, the curves did not converge to a probability of 1.00 but to the input levels. Thus, the children operated exactly like adults in similar studies (6, 8), in that their response probabilities approached the stimulus input probabilities. It should

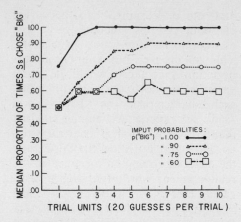

FIG. 1. *Probability learning curves for four stimulus input levels: All ages pooled, N = 7 for each curve.*

be noted that the response curve for an input of .60 also stabilizes at that level, indicating that children successfully discriminate .60 from chance.

Figure 2 repeats some of the infor-

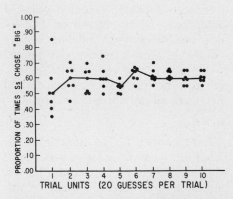

FIG. 2. *Change in score distribution at .60 input level for seven subjects.*

mation in Fig. 1 in that it shows that the median response probability curves for the input level of .60 did stabilize at .60. In addition, Fig. 2 shows how the distribution of response probabilities changes as a function of practice. The variance systematically decreases with practice—another indication that children can discriminate .60 from chance probability in a two-choice situation. Even the 3- and 4-year-olds discriminated this small deviation. Thus the threshold for probability discrimination in children would appear to be approximately the same as for adults (5).

In the data collected in Exp. I, only the slightest hint was found that the rate of learning was positively related to chronological age, and even this slight indication of slower learning for the younger children may be accounted for by their greater distractibility and inattention.

Experiment II

The results of Exp. II are summarized in Fig. 3. Although it was felt

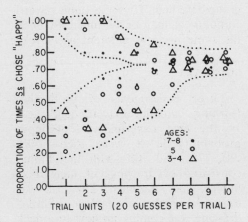

FIG. 3. *Probability learning curve for the characteristic "happy" at an input level of .75.*

that Ss might divide into two or more discrete groups with distinct initial biases toward saying "happy" or "sad" and that there might be marked differences in rates of learning, the extreme effects illustrated in Fig. 3 were not anticipated. One group of children showed an almost complete bias toward

saying "happy" initially and actually had to *extinguish* their "happy" response *down to* the input level of .75. A second group exhibited a slight bias toward perceiving the stick-men as "sad" initially and *learned* (in the usual sense) to say "happy" *up to* the .75 input level.

Experiment III

Experiment III was designed as an attempt to obtain experimentally the maximizing of probability that was not found in Exp. I. It might be argued that people maximize the probability of reinforcement only if the reward is desirable enough and that merely telling Ss "right" in Exp. I was not sufficient incentive. Since E's verbal approval in Exp. I might not have been sufficient incentive for the children to maximize the probability of reward, the effect of increasing the incentive was studied. For this purpose a candy reward was also given for being correct.

The results of Exp. III are summarized in Fig. 4. The increased incentive

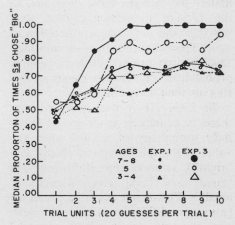

FIG. 4. *Median probability learning curves at an input level of .75 under conditions of verbal approval (Exp. I) and verbal approval with candy reward (Exp. III).*

did produce a reward maximizing tendency, but it was only partially effective. Over all Ss, the asymptote for the .75 input probabilities used in this experiment did shift upwards significantly, but the most interesting effect was an interaction between age levels and change in incentive. The output curves for the 7- and 8-year-olds converged to 1.00 (perfect maximization of reward), those for the 5-year-olds stabilized at approximately .90 (a compromise between input level and maximization of reward level), and those for the 3- and 4-year-olds stabilized at the input level again. This interaction and general upward shift will be discussed in the section to follow.

DISCUSSION

In Exp. I it was found that children operate in a manner similar to adults in that (a) their response probability curves reach an asymptote at the stimulus input level; and (b) their discrimination thresholds for probabilities deviating from chance are approximately the same as those of adults. In the present experiments, these two variables did not vary as a function of age. This experiment also indicated that children can and do learn relative probabilities of stimulus events occurring in their environments.

In Exp. III it was observed that there is a marked tendency to maximize probability of reward when the value of the reinforcement (being told "right") is increased (to being told "right" and being given a piece of candy). This result could be predicted from several theoretical points of view. For example, in the Hullian model (7) an increase of drive multiplied by a specific level of habit strength (D. $_sH_r$) should raise the level of performance.

The results of Exp. III also indicated a relationship between age level and tendency to maximize probability. There are at least two possible explanations of this result, which can perhaps be differentiated in future research. It is possible, first, that the results reflect a "learning to learn" phenomenon in that children learn how to maximize the probability of reward with increased age and maturation. Thus when a reward strong enough to evoke this potential is introduced, the older children maximize the probability, the younger children do not perfectly maximize the probability of reward, and the youngest children cannot maximize the probability of reward. An alternative and perhaps complementary explanation is that the incentive value of candy increases with chronological age, at least for those age groups studied. Thus the same reward stimulus cannot be assumed to elicit the same drive at different age levels.

SUMMARY

Three experiments of probability learning in children were conducted. In the first experiment, four input probability levels were used—1.00, .90, .75, and .60—with the stimuli consisting of drawings of kangaroos, horses, and stick-men. The task was to guess whether a "big" or a "little" drawing was coming up next in a deck of 20 cards. The results of this study suggested that (a) children's response output curves converge to an asymptote equal to the input probability level, a parallel of the performance of adults in other studies; and (b) children's thresholds for discriminating probabilities deviating from chance in a two-choice situation appears to be close to those obtained from adults. In Exp. II stick-men figures were used which had "happy" or "sad" faces, with an input probability of .75 for "happy" and .25 for "sad." The children split into two discrete groups— one showing an extreme initial bias toward perceiving "happy" stick-men and extinguishing down to the .75 input level and one showing a slight initial bias toward "sad" and learning up to the input level. In Exp. III a candy reward was added to verbal approval for correct guesses of "big" and "little" stick-men (input probability .75 for "big" and .25 for "little"). The 7- and 8-year-olds maximized probability, that is, their response probability curves converged to 1.00; the 5-year-olds stabilized at .90; and the 3- and 4-year-olds converged to the .75 input level for "big."

REFERENCES

1. Brunswik, W., "Probability as a Determiner of Rat Behavior," *Journal of Experimental Psychology*, **25** (1939), 175-97.

2. ———, "Organismic Achievement and Environmental Probability," *Psychological Review*, **50** (1943), 255-72.

3. Brunswik, E. and H. Herma, "Probability Learning of Perceptual Cues in the Establishment of a Weight Illusion," *Journal of Experimental Psychology*, **41** (1951), 281-90.

4. Bush, R. R., "Mathematical Models for Two-choice Experiments." Talk delivered to the psychological colloquium, University of Illinois, 1954.

5. Detambel, M. H., "A Test of a Model for Multiple-choice Behavior," *Journal of Experimental Psychology*, **49** (1955), 97-104.

6. Hake, H. W. and R. Hyman, "Perception of the Statistical Structure of a Random Series of Binary Symbols," *Journal of Experimental Psychology*, **45** (1953), 64-74.

7. Hull, C. L., *"Principles of Behavior."* New York: Appleton-Century-Crofts, Inc., 1943.

8. Humphreys, L. G., "Acquisitions and Extinction of Verbal Expectations in a Situation Analogous to Conditioning," *Journal of Experimental Psychology*, **25** (1939), 294-301.

9. Jarvik, M. E., "Probability Learning and a Negative Recency Effect in the Serial Anticipation of Alternative Symbols," *Journal of Experimental Psychology*, **41** (1951), 291-97.

The Effects of Differential Reinforcement and Motivation on Prediction Responses of Children *

Sidney Rosenblum

Since the early 1930's the effects on behavior of varied patterns of partial and continuous reinforcement have received steadily increasing attention from psychologists. Although new and ingenious procedures are being devised for the study of this problem at the human level, the major emphasis continues to be on animal experimentation. A survey of partial reinforcement literature by Jenkins and Stanley (6) reveals that of the thirty studies reported during the years 1939-1949 few used humans as subjects. No significant change in this tendency is apparent from a review of the published research of the past five years. This fact has concerned some psychologists who have argued seriously for the greater utilization of human subjects in the testing of various aspects of learning theory. It is their contention

* From S. Rosenblum, "The Effects of Differential Reinforcement and Motivation on Prediction Responses of Children," *Child Development,* **27** (1956), 99-108. Reprinted by permission of the Society for Research in Child Development Inc.

This article is based on a dissertation submitted to the Iowa Child Welfare Research Station, State University of Iowa, in partial fulfillment of the requirements for the Ph.D. degree, June 1953. The writer is indebted to Dr. B. R. McCandless under whose direction the research was performed, and to Drs. C. C. Spiker, A. Castaneda, I. E. Farber, and H. Bechtoldt for their helpful criticisms and suggestions.

that although constructs and laws coming from the animal laboratory have been shown to predict the behavior of infrahuman organisms with accuracy and usefulness, the time has come for a "validation" of some of these principles at the human level.

Although studies with humans in the area of partial reinforcement have supported, for the most part, results of animal research, a survey of the literature has disclosed two general characteristics of such experiments. First, very few have used the normal child as a subject. Apart from the fact that children can be conceived loosely as representing an "intermediary level" between inarticulate organisms and the ubiquitous college undergraduate, and, as such, constitute another valuable source of data, their use in learning studies seems vital for the development of a systematic approach in the field of child psychology, an area characterized until somewhat recently by a notable lack of sound, theoretically oriented research (7). Second, virtually no studies have been reported in which the effects of motivation have been intentionally introduced and systematically varied. Such situations as have been used [for example, conditioning of the eyelid response (5), lever-pulling (3), and making predictions about the occurrence or nonoccurrence of a light (4)] would appear to lack "importance" to the subject, in the sense that nothing has been done to make them "ego-involving."

The present study was designed to investigate the effects on children's behavior of various reinforcement patterns in combination with motivational factors. Specifically, it concerns the effects of three schedules of reinforcement (100 percent, 50 percent, and 0 percent) at two levels of motivation (high and low) on the acquisition and extinction of a "certainty of prediction" response (CPR), that is, the degree of certainty with which a child makes a prediction concerning the occurrence of a success experience for himself.

The investigation can be conceived as having five stages. Stage one consists of determining an initial response measure (trial 1). During stage two (trials 1 to 10) changes in the CPR under high and low motivation conditions during 100 percent, 50 percent, and 0 percent reinforcement are determined. Stage three involves observation of the CPR at the end of trial 10. During stage four (trials 11 to 20) the effects of a 0 percent reinforcement series on the CPR are measured. And stage five (trial 20) consists of obtaining the terminal CPR.

The following hypotheses were formulated for testing.

1. Increase in mean CPR's during trials 1 to 10 would be significantly greater for the 100 percent group than either the 50 percent or 0 percent groups, with the 50 percent evincing reliably greater increments than the 0 percent group.

2. Decrease in mean CPR's during trials 11 to 20 would be significantly greater for the 0 percent group than either the 100 percent or 50 percent groups, with the 100 percent group demonstrating reliably greater decrements than the 50 percent group.

3. Increase in mean CPR's during trails 1 to 10 would be greater for high in comparison to low motivation groups, except for the 0 percent group, where no significant differences would manifest themselves.

4. Decrease in mean CPR's from trials 11 to 20 would be greater for low in comparison to high motivation groups, except for the 0 percent group, where no significant differences would manifest themselves.

It should be noted with regard to the motivational variables that there is no systematic framework from which it is possible to derive hypotheses concerning the performance of humans. Although some work has been done with adults (3), there is no general agreement as to whether increased motivational factors "help" or "hinder" a specific response. Hypotheses 3 and 4, then, were conceived purely as matters for empirical investigation.

METHOD

Materials

A series of "stimulus cards"—20 simple geometric designs drawn with a rule in black india ink on 4 by 5 in. index cards, a series of "comparison cards"—the same 20 designs drawn freehand in pencil on 4 by 5 in. yellow index cards, and a box of 15 red poker chips constituted the materials utilized in this experiment. The figures on the yellow cards were actually drawn by the experimenter, but were presented to each subject as the work of a "fourth- (or fifth-) grader just like yourself." The reason for this procedure is discussed below.

Subjects

The subjects used in this investigation were 120 white fourth- and fifth-grade children, 60 boys and 60 girls, with a mean CA of 10 years, 0 months, a mean IQ of 110.4, and a mean grade equivalent of 4.5. They were all obtained from one elementary school in Cedar Rapids, Iowa. Only "normal" children were included in the study; that is, children who were, according to the principal's report, not undergoing any kind of psychological treatment procedure, were not crippled, and so forth. A superficial analysis of fathers' occupations revealed that the children came from predominantly middle-class homes.

Experimental Design

The subjects were assigned randomly to three major reinforcement groupings, and again randomized into motivational subgroups within each of the main groups. Group I received continuous positive reinforcement for trials 1 to 10, followed by a series of 10 nonreinforced trials; Group II received positive reinforcement only on trials 1, 4, 5, 7, and 10, followed by a series of 10 nonreinforced trials; and Group III received a continuous series of 20 nonreinforced trials.

Procedure

Each subject was seen individually in a private office and was read the following instructions:

> I'd like to play a game with you today. Other boys and girls have played this game with me and have liked it a lot. I'd like to see how you do at it.
> On this sheet of paper I'd like you to draw a design which I shall show you in just a moment. You can draw it anywhere at all on the page, and you can make it any size you want. Many other children in the fourth (fifth) grade have drawn these designs for me, and each time I present a new design to you on a white card like this (demonstrated with blank card), I'll show you on a yellow card like this (demonstrated) what kind of a job a fourth- (fifth-) grader just like yourself can do. Now, if you do a better job than this (pointing to yellow comparison card) I'll put a big plus mark on your paper like this (demonstrated), and if you do a poorer job I'll put a minus like this (demonstrated). And if you do just about as well I won't put anything on your paper. Get it? A plus mark for a better job, a minus mark for a poorer job, and nothing at all if you do just about as well. Draw these designs as quickly as you can, but work carefully since you won't be allowed to erase.
> Before you begin, though, I'd like you to tell me what you honestly think you'll get for this first drawing, and to make it more fun for you I want you to use these chips to tell me. (Box and chips moved to center of table in front of subject.) Here is a pile of 15 chips which you are to use to tell me how certain you are of getting a *plus* mark on your paper. You can bet with as many or as few chips as you like to tell me how certain you are of getting a *plus*. For example, you can bet up to 15 of the chips if you're absolutely 100 percent certain you're going to get a plus; or you can bet just *one* of the chips if you're not certain at all of getting it. Or you might want to bet somewhere in between, like 5, 6, 7, 8, or 9. Remember, the more certain you are of getting a plus on your paper the more chips you will want to bet. The less certain you are of a plus the fewer chips you'll want to bet. You can use from none at all to all 15 of them. You will make a bet every time before you draw. Count out your chips carefully, and put them in this box. Any questions? [1]

---

[1] This betting method is a modification of one used by Castaneda (1). With this technique direct verbalization of prediction is avoided. Providing the child with chips that must be manipulated requires him to do some "subjective scaling" and careful thinking regarding each bet he makes. Nothing

If the subject was part of a low motivation group he was then asked: "How certain are you of getting a plus mark on this first design?" If he was a high motivation subject he was read the following set of motivating (that is, "ego-involving") instructions:

Now I'm interested in knowing who shall do better in your class, the boys or the girls. I know you'd like to see the boys (girls) come out on top, wouldn't you? All right, then, I want you to try to do the *very best* job you can. Also, I'm interested in knowing which fourth (or fifth) grade is best in Cedar Rapids. I'm sure you'd like your class to come out on top, so remember—do your very best! Now, how certain are you of getting a plus mark on this first design?

The subject then indicated the certainty of his prediction of receiving a plus mark for the first performance by counting out into the box whatever amount of poker chips he desired, after which a sheet of paper and the first pair of stimulus and comparison cards were presented. The comparison card was removed from the subject's vision after about a 4-second exposure, and then placed where only the experimenter could see it. The purpose of introducing such a card in the first place was to provide some "face validity" to the drawing game in general and to prevent the subject from feeling the experimenter's evaluations were merely arbitrary.

After the subject had copied the stimulus figure the experimenter would pick up the paper, glance at it carefully, look over with a definite head movement to where the comparison card lay, glance back again at the subject's drawing, and place either a large red

is won or lost with these chips. They were introduced solely as a technique of slowing down the subject so as to make him think more carefully about his response.

plus mark on the paper or do nothing at all. A fresh sheet would then be put in front of the subject and the entire procedure begun again. While the child was busy copying the stimulus card, the experimenter would remove the chips counted out into the box and replace them in a single symmetrical pile with the rest of the chips on the table. After completion of the 20 trials each child was told he had done, on the whole, a very excellent job.

RESULTS

The criterion measures used for testing the hypotheses of this study were the numbers of poker chips bet by a subject to indicate the degree of certainty with which he made a prediction of success for himself on each of the 20 trials constituting the experimental session.

Figure 1 represents schematically the results obtained on the three experimental groups. Each point on the curve is based on the mean number of chips bet (mean CPR's) by all 40 subjects in one group. An inspection of the curves at trial 1 reveal that mean CPR's do not differ significantly at that point, but that differences do manifest themselves with the advent of subsequent trials.

Trials 1 to 10

Using the technique of trend analysis for the data obtained for trials 1 to 10 the following results were obtained: (1) Fs of 25.15 for the 100 percent group, 3.93 for the 50 percent group, and 5.01 for the 0 percent group (all significant at less than the .001 level of confidence) revealed there were highly significant increments in mean CPR's from trials 1 to 10 under the three reinforcement schedules. (2) Tests for differences between pairs of curves revealed that significantly greater increments in mean CPR's were demonstrated under the 100 percent in comparison to the 50 percent or 0 percent schedules (significant at less than the .001 level of confidence), with no significant difference appearing between the 50 percent and 0 percent schedules. (3) No statistically significant differences appeared between the high and low motivation groupings.

Trials 11 to 20

It will be remembered that 10 successive nonreinforcements were presented to all subjects after they had been administered either 100 percent,

50 percent, or 0 percent reinforcement for trials 1 to 10. Analysis of variance of the data revealed that the trials by reinforcement interaction (a test of whether the three groups manifested differential decrements over trials 11 to 20) barely missed statistical significance at the .05 level of confidence. This may have been due to the fact that the 50 percent and 0 percent groups, though evidencing no extinction trends in and of themselves, were contributing additional sources of variance to the total extinction data. Because of this insignificant T × R interaction it was not deemed feasible to test for differences between pairs of curves as

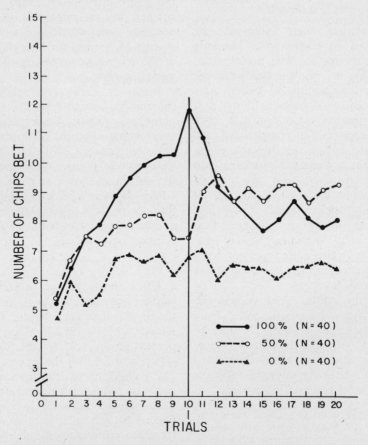

FIG. 1. *Mean certainty of prediction responses for all groups.*

had been done with the data obtained for trials 1 to 10. However, since an inspection of the empirical curve for the 100 percent group revealed a decided decline in mean CPR's from trials 11 to 20, whereas the 50 percent curve did not, it was decided to test for the presence of a 100 percent extinction curve. A sigma of the difference between the means of trials 11 and 20 netted a critical ratio of 3.48, which is significant at the .002 level of confidence. Thus, it appears a significant decrement does manifest itself for the 100 percent group, but this finding must be viewed with caution in light of the insignificant T × R interaction.

As with data for trials 1 to 10, comparisons of motivation results for trials 11 to 20 proved statistically insignificant.

DISCUSSION

Results, then, supported that part of hypothesis 1 which posited that a group receiving 100 percent reinforcement would evidence greater increments in mean CPR's during trials 1 to 10 than would a group receiving either 50 percent or 0 percent reinforcement. This result conforms to those obtained from more conventional partial reinforcement studies using adult humans as subjects (2, 4, 5), which have demonstrated that acquisition of a response is directly proportional to the frequency of reinforced trials, proceeding, generally speaking, somewhat more rapidly under continuous than partial reinforcement.

On the basis of the findings of such studies it was further hypothesized that the group receiving 0 percent reinforcement during the first 10 trials would evidence statistically weaker increments in mean CPR's than would be the case with either the 50 percent or 100 percent groups. That this is not

true is evident from an inspection of the curves in Fig. 1. Not only was a significant increment trend demonstrated, but also there was no reliable difference between it and that of the 50 percent group.

Post hoc considerations of this somewhat paradoxical result lead to two tentative hypotheses, the first being that a state of anxiety was produced in these 0 percent subjects by the continuing series of nonreinforced trials (which may have been construed by the subjects as failure). If (*a*) anxiety is thought of as a drive, (*b*) it is considered that increased drive interacts with existing tendencies-to-respond so as to increase probability of strong response, and (*c*) the CPR can be thought of as a response of this nature, then the results for the 0 percent group can perhaps be considered from the point of view of such current psychological formulations as the Spence-Taylor type (9). Second, it might be that the increased CPR was due to some anxiety-reducing mechanism, perhaps of the "denial" variety. That is, it is possible these subjects tended to reject the reality aspects of the situation in which they were involved, steadily increasing their CPR's in spite of continued nonreinforcement. Because of a lack of opportunity to contrast positive and nonreinforcement, as was possible for the 50 percent group, the entire experimental situation was highly ambiguous for 0 percent subjects. Hence, for them an anxiety-reducing mechanism such as denial would be more "available" than for the 50 percent group subjects, who have experienced both positive and nonreinforcement, and who would not be as likely to respond negatively to the reality aspects of the situation.

Results offered no statistical support to hypothesis 2, which predicted significantly greater decrements in mean

CPR's during trials 11 to 20 for the 100 percent group than for either the 50 percent or 0 percent groups. There is a suggestion, however, from an inspection of the 100 percent and 50 percent curves and a consideration of the significant extinction test for the 100 percent data that results of these two groups are not completely deviant from the general conclusion reached in more conventional partial reinforcement research on human and animal subjects, namely, that a response will be more resistant to extinction if acquired under a schedule of partial rather than continuous reinforcement.

As was stated above, there was no systematic framework from which it was possible to predict the performance of high vs. low motivation groupings. The two motivation hypotheses in this study, therefore, were almost purely speculative, and were devised solely for purposes of empirical investigation. It will be remembered that an attempt was made to induce a high state of motivation in certain subjects by presenting a set of what were considered "ego-involving" instructions. It seems likely these instructions did not serve the purpose for which they were intended. Instructing a child at the beginning of the experimental situation to do his very best so that his sex will win top position in his class and his class top position among other similar classes in the city's schools apparently does not induce or sustain the desired state of motivation or drive. Were this experiment replicated it would perhaps be better first to match high and low anxiety groups on the basis of a technique such as the Iowa Anxiety Scale for Children and then induce motivation with a set of instructions geared to be more highly ego-involving. Such instructions could perhaps tell the child that the results of his performance during the experiment would be reported to his teacher, who would then incorporate them in a final grade for him.

To summarize, what has been demonstrated in this experiment is that Child A, instructed that three physical events are possible of occurrence during the course of the experimental situation (receipt of a plus, a minus, or nothing at all for a performance), will, significantly, become increasingly more confident that future success will occur as he receives a series of continuing successful experiences than will Child B, who is administered a number of success experiences interspersed with an equal number of nonsuccess experiences (defined as the receipt of neither a plus nor a minus), or Child C, who receives a series of continuous nonreinforcements. This is interpreted as a function of the greater frequency of successes experienced by Child A. Though not statistically significant, there is a tendency for certainty to diminish somewhat more rapidly for Child A than for B or C as each is administered the same number of continuous nonreinforcements after the first series of trials, with the latter two children manifesting no significant decrements in response whatsoever. Child C, who does not experience success at all during the entire course of the experiment will, nonetheless, evidence steady increments in the certainty with which he predicts the occurrence of potential success for himself from trial 1 to 10. This is interpreted as a function of the presence of anxiety factors which are operating in this child.

SUMMARY

This research was devised to investigate the acquisition and extinction of a response, namely, the degree of certainty with which a child makes a prediction concerning the occurrence of a success experience for himself, under three schedules of reinforcement (100 percent, 50 percent, and 0 percent) and two levels of motivation (high and low).

One hundred and twenty normal fourth- and fifth-grade children were assigned randomly to three major reinforcement groups and again divided into six motivational subgroups. Group I (100 percent) was administered a series of continuous positive reinforcements during trials 1 to 10, followed by a series of 10 nonreinforced trials; Group II (50 percent) received positive reinforcements on only five randomly selected trials during acquisition, followed by 10 nonreinforced trials; and Group III (0 percent) received a continuous series of 20 nonreinforced trials.

Each subject, seen individually, was presented with a "game" involving the copying of a series of 20 geometric designs. Before starting, he was informed that one of three possible events would occur after the completion of each individual drawing, the receipt of a plus, a minus, or nothing at all. Before copying each design he was instructed to "make a bet" from a pile of 15 poker chips to indicate how certain he was of the occurrence of a success experience for himself (that is, the receipt of a plus). Any number of chips from zero to 15 could be bet, zero indicating a success prediction of least and 15 a success prediction of most certainty. Nothing was won or lost with these chips; they were introduced solely as a nonverbal technique of obtaining a child's certainty of prediction responses (CPR's), and of getting him to do some "subjective scaling" regarding each bet. All subjects in "high motivation" subgroups were provided, additionally, with a set of specially prepared "ego-involving" instructions to induce a state of drive.

The criterion measures used in statistical analyses were the numbers of poker chips bet by each subject to indicate the degree of certainty with which he made a prediction of success for himself on each of the 20 trials constituting the experiment. In general, results yielded by the acquisition data are considered consistent with the findings of continuous and partial reinforcement research (using animals and adult humans as subjects) of somewhat more rapid acquisition of behavior under continuous than partial reinforcement. Though missing statistical significance slightly, results of the 100 percent and 50 percent extinction data are in the same direction as the general conclusion reached in these same studies, indicating greater resistance to extinction when behavior has been acquired under a schedule of partial as compared to continuous reinforcement. No significant differences between high and low motivation groups were demonstrated.

REFERENCES

1. Castaneda, A., "A Systematic Investigation of the Concept Expectancy as Conceived with Rotter's Social Learning Theory of Personality." (Unpublished Doctoral dissertation, Ohio State University, 1953.)

2. Grant, D. A., H. W. Hake, and J. P. Hornseth, "Acquisition and Extinction of a Verbal Conditioned Response with Differing Percentages of Reinforcement," *Journal of Psychology*, **42** (1951), 1-5.

3. Grosslight, J. J. and I. L. Child, "Persistence as a Function of Previous Experience of Failure Followed by Success," *American Journal of Psychology*, **60** (1947), 378-87.

4. Humphreys, L. G., "Acquisition and Extinction of Verbal Expectations in a

Situation Analogous to Conditioning," *Journal of Experimental Psychology*, **25** (1939), 294-301.

5. ――――, "The Effects of Random Alternation of Reinforcement on the Acquisition and Extinction of Conditioned Eyelid Response," *Journal of Experimental Psychology*, **25** (1939), 141-58.

6. Jenkins, W. O. and J. C. Stanley, "Partial Reinforcement: A Review and Critique," *Psychological Bulletin*, **47** (1959), 193-234.

7. McCandless, B. R. and S. Rosen-

blum, "Psychological Theory as a Determiner of Experimental Pattern in Child Study," *Review of Educational Research*, **25** (1952), 496-525.

8. Mosteller, F. and P. Nogee, "Measurement of Utility in a Gambling Situation." Reported in Jenkins and Stanley (see 6).

9. Spence, K. W. and Janet A. Taylor, "Anxiety and Strength of the UCS as Determiners of the Amount of Eyelid Conditioning," *Journal of Experimental Psychology*, **42** (1951), 183-88.

Variables Affecting Children's Performance In a Probability Learning Task [1]

Harold W. Stevenson and Morton W. Weir

It was found in a recent study (Stevenson and Zigler, 1958) that children's performance in a probability learning task differed for normal and institutionalized feeble-minded children and for normal children given pretraining on games involving high and low degrees of success. It was hypothesized that these differences were related to the children's different expectancies for frequency of reinforcement. These expectancies were assumed to affect performance by determining the degree to which the child would accept a solution in the probability learning task which yielded

less than 100 percent reinforcement. It was predicted that Ss with low expectancies would show a greater frequency of choice of the reinforcing stimulus than would Ss with higher expectancies. This would result from the attempt by Ss with higher expectancies to seek, through variable behavior, a means by which they could obtain a frequency of reinforcement corresponding to the frequency which they expect.

In the present study three experiments are reported investigating the effects of three variables on probability learning in children: CA, incentive conditions, and shifts in percentage of reinforcement. It is assumed that older children have expectancies for a higher percentage of reinforcement than do younger children and that the performance of these groups will differ in the manner outlined above. In the experiment involving incentive condi-

[1] From H. W. Stevenson and M. W. Weir, "Variables Affecting Children's Performance in a Probability Learning Task," *Journal of Experimental Psychology*, **57** (1959), 403-412. Reprinted by permission of the authors and publishers.

This study was supported by a grant from the National Science Foundation (Grant 3280) to the first author.

tions, the same general hypothesis is tested; however, it is assumed that the degree to which the child will accept a particular frequency of reinforcement is a function in part of the value of the reinforcement to S. In the third experiment, the effects of shifts in percentage of reinforcement during the experimental trials are investigated. The hypotheses tested in each experiment are discussed in greater detail in later sections.

EXPERIMENT I

The purpose of this experiment was to investigate the behavior of young children of different chronological ages in a probability learning task. There is some basis for assuming that performance in such a task would differ as a function of CA. It has been suggested (Goodnow, 1955) that one of the conditions influencing performance in a probability learning task is the level of success S will accept in the task. It seems reasonable to assume that older Ss' greater familiarity with soluble problems and their greater desire to master adult-controlled tasks would result in their being less likely than younger children to accept low levels of success. It is assumed that when less than 100 percent reinforcement is available older children would seek a solution which would provide a level of success more acceptable than that attainable by the consistent choice of the reinforcing stimulus. The variable behavior resulting from their attempts would reduce the frequency of choice of the reinforcing stimulus below that found with younger Ss. It is predicted, therefore, that with levels of reinforcement below 100 percent there is an inverse relationship between frequency of choice of the reinforcing stimulus and chronological age. It is further predicted that under conditions of 100 percent reinforcement the

asymptotic frequency of correct response will be comparable at all CA levels, since 100 percent reinforcement provides a level of success acceptable to all Ss.

Method

SUBJECTS. The Ss were 120 children attending nursery and elementary schools in Austin, Texas.[2] The Ss were selected at random from among children of the appropriate CA's enrolled in the schools. Children at four age levels were used: 3–0 to 3–11, 5–0 to 5–11, 7–0 to 7–11, and 8–9 to 10–2. There were 30 Ss at each CA level.

APPARATUS. The apparatus has been described previously (Stevenson and Zigler, 1958). It consisted of a yellow panel containing a horizontal row of three knobs. Above the knobs was a signal light and below the knobs was a delivery hole for marbles. The marbles fell into an enclosed plastic container.

PROCEDURE. The S was seated in front of the apparatus and was told that he was to play a game. The E demonstrated the apparatus, and said, "When the light comes on, you push one of the knobs. If you push the correct knob a marble comes out here, like this. Now every time the light comes on you push the knob that you think will get you the marble. Remember, just push one knob each time the light comes on." The S was told that he was to get as many marbles as he could and when

[2] The writers wish to thank Larry Schmucker for testing Ss in Exp. I, Mary Bess Whidden for testing Ss in Exp. II, and Martin Steigman for testing Ss in Exp. III, and the directors or principals of All Saints Nursery School, Austin High School Child Development Laboratory, University of Texas Nursery School, Tarrytown Methodist Nursery School, and St. Louis School, St. Austin School, St. Mary's School, and Trinity Lutheran School for their cooperation in making Ss available.

the game was over he could choose two toys from a selection of toys including balloons, plastic figures, and so forth, which *E* showed him.

Three conditions which differed in the percentage of reinforcement of correct response were used. For each *S*, one of the three knobs (either L, M, or R) was designated as the correct knob. The knob which was to be correct for a patricular *S* was deterdminded by a prearranged random sequence. An equal number of *S*s was tested with each knob. The correct knob yielded reinforcement; choices of the other two knobs were never reinforced. Depending upon the condition, the correct knob yielded 100 percent, 66 percent, or 33 percent reinforcement. In other words, a contingent procedure of reinforcement was employed whereby *S* was reinforced for a certain percentage of the times

that he chose the correct knob. For example, in the 33 percent condition reinforcement was delivered on 33 percent of *S*'s choices of the correct stimulus rather than on 33 percent of the trials. Ten *S*s at each CA level were assigned at random to each of the three conditions. In the 66 percent and 33 percent conditions the trials on which a choice of the correct knob was reinforced were determined by a random sequence of 30 trials. This sequence was repeated when *S* pressed the correct knob on more than 30 trials. The *S*s were given a total of 80 trials each.

Results and Discussion

The average numbers of correct responses in blocks of 10 trials for the four age levels and the three percentages of reinforcement are presented in Fig. 1. An examination of the

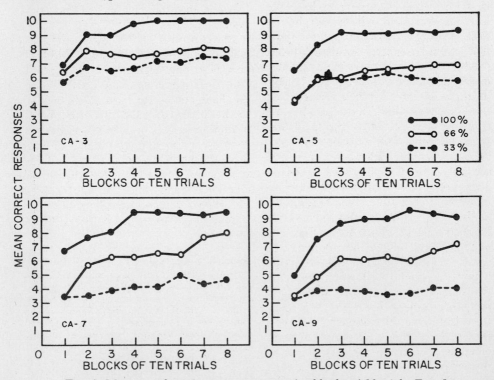

FIG. 1. *Mean number of correct responses for blocks of 10 trials: Exp. I.*

curves for the 33 percent and 66 percent groups reveals that performance differed as a function of CA. As predicted, there is a tendency for older Ss to choose the reinforcing stimulus less frequently than younger Ss. An analysis of variance of the results of the total 80 trials indicates a significant difference associated with CA ($F = 4.43$, $df = 3$ and 72, $P < .01$). A significant difference is found also for percentage of reinforcement ($F = 7.37$, $df = 1$ and 72, $P < .01$). The interaction between CA and percentage of reinforcement is not significant ($F < 1$).

Performance in the groups receiving 100 percent reinforcement was similar at each age level. It was predicted that asymptotic level of response would be comparable in all four groups. This was found to be true, for all but six Ss chose the correct stimulus on all of the last 20 trials. There were two Ss in each age group except CA 3 who did not consistently choose the correct knob during the last 20 trials.

There are several additional features of Ss' performance which are of interest. The Ss initially had strong postion preferences. On Trial 1, 15 percent of the Ss chose the left knob, 50 percent the middle knob, and 35 percent the right knob. As a control for possible knob preferences, each knob was correct for an equal number of Ss at each CA level. Knob preferences did not operate throughout all the trials, however, for of the total number of correct responses made on the 80 trials, .33 were made when the left knob was correct, .35 when the middle knob was correct, and .32 when the right knob was correct.

In order to determine whether the poor performance of older Ss was a result of their developing patterns of response, each individual's performance was examined. A high frequency of LMR and RML patterns of response appeared. The Ss at CA 3 had an average of 8.4 repetitions of these patterns, Ss at CA 5 an average of 14.8, Ss at CA 7 an average of 14.5, and Ss at CA 9 an average of 14.0. No other patterns of response were readily apparent. The behavior of Ss at CA's 5, 7, and 9, therefore, was not random since approximately 50 percent of the responses were made in the form of one of the patterns analyzed. This may indicate that the performance of these Ss is attributable in part to the fact that they were more likely than were the youngest Ss to form complex hypotheses resulting in the patterning of their responses.

The high level of performance of the 3-year-old Ss indicates that a task of this type is within the level of ability of young nursery-school children. These Ss, as are most children attending private nursery schools, were highly selected. The older children, however, were also from private schools and were above average in their performance on group intelligence tests.

EXPERIMENT II

The purpose of this study was to investigate the effect of two incentive conditions upon performance of children in a probability learning task. The hypothesis to be tested was that, under conditions of less than 100 percent reinforcement, the frequency of choice of the reinforcing stimulus will vary inversely with the value of the incentive. The hypothesis is derived in the following manner. In simple probability learning tasks such as the one used, children should learn rather quickly that the reinforcing stimulus does not pay off 100 percent of the time. If S accepts this frequency of reinforcement, S should choose the reinforcing stimulus with a high degree of consistency. If this frequency of reinforcement is not acceptable, *S* must attempt to find a solution to increase the frequency with which he is rewarded. This attempt leads to variable behavior, with the result that the frequency of choice of the reinforcing stimulus is lower than that occurring if such an attempt is not made. It is assumed that incentives affect performance by determining the degree to which *S* would attempt to find such solutions. It is further assumed that if incentives are of high value *S* is more likely to seek a solution yielding consistent reinforcement than if incentives are of low value. In this manner incentives of high value would produce more variable behavior than would incentives of lower value, with the consequence that there would be an inverse relationship between frequency of choice of the reinforcing stimulus and incentive value.

Under conditions of 100 percent reinforcement no differences between incentive groups should appear, except perhaps in the rate at which an asymptotic level of response is approached.

Method

SUBJECTS. The *S*s consisted of 60 5-year-old children attending nursery schools in Austin, Texas. The *S*s were selected at random from among children of the appropriate CA enrolled in the schools.

APPARATUS. The apparatus was the same as that described in Exp. I.

PROCEDURE. High and low incentive conditions were used. In the high incentive condition, the choice of the reinforcing knob resulted in the delivery of a trinket. A wide assortment of small plastic trinkets was provided. In the low incentive condition, the choice of the reinforcing knob resulted in the delivery of a marble. The *S* was told that at the end of the experiment the marbles could be exchanged for three trinkets of the types used in the high incentive condition.

As in Exp. I, reinforcement was delivered on 33 percent, 66 percent, or 100 percent of the choices of the correct knob. The procedure was the same as that in Exp. I except for the reinforcements used.

Results

The average numbers of times that the correct knob was selected in each incentive condition under the three percentages of reinforcement are presented in Fig. 2. The curves for the 100 percent reinforcement groups are

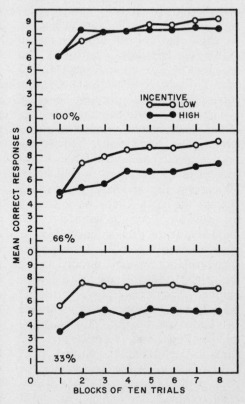

FIG. 2. *Mean number of correct responses for blocks of 10 trials: Exp. II.*

highly similar and do not differ significantly $(t = .12)$. The data in Fig. 2 support the prediction that the low incentive groups in the 66 percent and 33 percent conditions would choose the correct knob more frequently than the high incentive groups. An analysis of variance of these data results in an F of 6.71 $(P = .05, 1$ and 36 $df)$. The difference in frequency of choice of the correct knob in the groups receiving 66 percent and 33 percent reinforcement is not significant $(F = 2.70, P > .05, df = 1$ and 36). The interaction between percentage of reinforcement and incentive condition is not significant $(F < 1)$.

The higher level of performance in the low incentive, compared to the high incentive groups in the 33 percent and 66 percent conditions is an inversion of the results typically found in learning situations. It has been noted earlier (Stevenson and Zigler, 1958) that even though Ss in the present type of problem may not choose the reinforcing stimulus consistently, they do know which stimulus has provided reinforcemnt. This suggests that performance in this situation does not mirror the learning that has taken place; rather, it indicates the degree to which S will accept the percentage of reinforcement provided by the reinforcing stimulus.

The two incentive conditions appeared to operate in the anticipated manner; Ss in the high incentive groups seemed to be much more pleased to get the trinkets than were Ss in the low incentive groups to get the marbles.

These results differ from those of Messick and Solley (1957), who report exploratory data indicating an increase in frequency of choice of the reinforced stimulus when candy was compared to verbal reinforcement as the incentive. It is difficult to compare the results of the two studies because of differences in

procedure and because of the descriptive nature of their results.

The results may be interpreted as providing support for the suggestion by Goodnow (1955) that one of the conditions affecting the distribution of choices in a probability learning task is S's ability to overlook losses. If the reward has significance for S, he may be less likely to overlook loss than when the reward has less significance. The S's inability to overlook losses, as Goodnow suggests, would lead to more variable behavior than when S is less concerned about the failure of a response to lead to reinforcement. Behavior would become more variable as S attempts to seek a solution to minimize the frequency of nonreinforced responses.

EXPERIMENT III

The purpose of this experiment was to investigate the performance of Ss in a probability learning task when the probability of reinforcement is changed during the course of the experimental trials. Several recent studies have been concerned with this problem. Estes and Straughan (1954) found that Ss matched the stimulus probabilities with their choices, regardless of whether or not Ss had prior experience with different stimulus probabilities in the task. This was interpreted as providing support for Estes' statistical learning theory, which predicts that after a series of trials Ss' choices depend upon the present stimulus probabilities and are independent of earlier experience with different stimulus probabilities. On the other hand, Parducci (1957), using different shifts in probability from those employed by Estes and Straughan, found in two experiments that Ss differed in their final performance as a function of an initial experience with different stimulus probabilities. Differences in terminal performance were also found by Goodnow and Pettigrew (1955) in a "gambling" task involving several shifts in probabilities of reinforcement during initial periods of training. The Goodnow and Pettigrew study was designed to determine whether a number of shifts in the probabilities and patterns of reinforcement would have an effect upon the strategies employed in the solution of subsequent problems.

The purpose of the present study was to investigate the effects on performance of a wide range of systematic changes in stimulus probabilities. A three-stimulus task was used in this study in order to investigate the effects of prior probability of reinforcement and to determine some of the characteristics of the variability of response found in this type of task.

Method

SUBJECTS. The Ss consisted of 225 elementary school children ranging in CA from 7.5 to 10.3 yr.[2] All Ss within these age levels attending the schools visited were tested.

APPARATUS. The apparatus was the same as that used in Exp. I and II.

PROCEDURE. The general procedure was the same as that used in Exp. I and II and reinforcements were the same as those used in Exp. I.

The procedure differed from that in the previous experiments in that different reinforcement probabilities were used. During the first 40 trials Ss received either 0 percent, 33 percent, 66 percent, or 100 percent reinforcement of the correct response. During the last 40 trials Ss either continued to receive the percentage of reinforcement obtained during the first 40 trials, or were switched to a different per-

---

[2] See Footnote 1.

centage of reinforcement. The two sets of 40 trials were presented in an uninterrupted sequence. The same knob was correct for a particular S throughout the experiment; only the percentage of choices on which this knob was reinforced was changed. This procedure resulted in a 4×4 design containing all combinations of initial and final percentages of reinforcement. For example, Ss receiving 33 percent reinforcement during the first 40 trials could receive either 0 percent, 33 percent, 66 percent, or 100 percent reinforcement during the last 40 trials, depending upon the condition to which they were assigned. Fifteen Ss were assigned at random to all but one cell of this design. One cell, 0 percent to 0 percent, was not filled. It was felt to be impractical to test children for 80 trials during which no reinforcement was received. Previous experience indicated that it is difficult to maintain children's motivation during protracted periods of 0 percent reinforcement. Among Ss receiving 33 percent, or 66 percent reinforcement, the trials on which a choice of the correct knob was reinforced were determined by 10 random sequences of 40 trials. These sequences were randomized among Ss tested in these conditions.

Results

When a contingent procedure of reinforcement is used in conditions involving other than 0 percent and 100 percent reinforcement it is impossible to be assured that Ss will receive exactly the designated percentage of reinforcement of correct responses. In the present experiment, for example, the proportions of correct responses on which Ss in the 33 percent and 66 percent conditions were reinforced were .35 and .64, respectively. The designation of groups as 33 percent or 66 percent does not, therefore, represent exactly the proportion of trials on which reinforcement was received.

During the first 40 trials the average numbers of choices of the reinforcing stimulus made under conditions of 0 percent, 33 percent, 66 percent, and 100 percent reinforcement differed from each other consistently. An analysis of variance of these data reveals a highly significant difference among the groups ($F = 92.8$, $df = 3$ and 221, $P < .001$).

By the end of the first 40 trials, Ss in each group appeared to be approaching an asymptotic level of response. The question of whether an asymptote was reached may be answered by determining whether there was a significant change in performance between Trials 21–40 and 61–80 by groups for

whom the probability of reinforcement remained constant throughout the experiment. The differences between Trials 21–40 and Trials 61–80 in the average numbers of choices of the reinforcing stimulus are not significant at the 0.5 level ($F = 3.83$ $df = 1$ and 42).

The results for Trials 41–80 are presented in blocks of 10 trials in Fig. 5. In this figure Ss are classified according to the percentage of reinforcement received on Trials 1–40 and 41–80. For example, the notation, 33 percent–0 percent, indicates that this group received 33 percent reinforcement of choices of the correct response during Trials 1–40 and 0 percent reinforcement during Trials 41–80.

In Fig. 3 the frequencies of choice

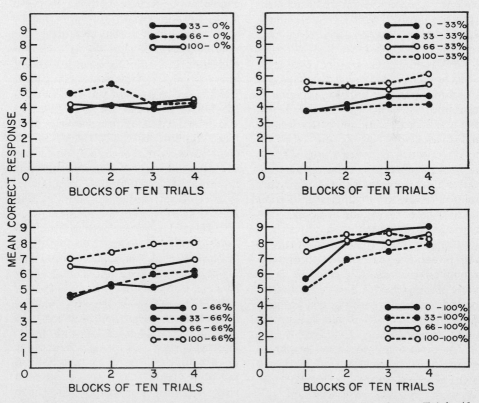

FIG. 3. *Mean number of correct responses in blocks of 10 trials during Trials 41–80: Exp. III.*

of the reinforcing stimulus appear to vary both with the stimulus probabilities of Trials 41–80 and with the stimulus probabilities of Trials 1–40. It is clear from Fig. 3 that there are differences in the average number of choices of the reinforcing stimulus by Ss receiving 0 percent, 33 percent, 66 percent, and 100 percent reinforcement during the last 40 trials. During the terminal trials there is an increase in the average frequency of choice of the reinforcing stimulus as the proportion of reinforcement received during these trials increases from 0 percent to 100 percent. It is also apparent that there are differences among the groups receiving the same percentage of reinforcement during Trials 41–80. These differences are related to the percentage of reinforcement received during Trials 1–40. No simple relationship between the performance on the last 40 and the first 40 trials is apparent. There was no consistent tendency for Ss changed from high to low or from low to high probabilities of reinforcement to fall above or below the level of response shown by Ss who had consistently been reinforced at the level to which Ss were shifted. There is some tendency for the groups receiving 33 percent and 66 percent reinforcement during the last 40 trials to be ordered according to the percentage of reinforcement received during the first 40 trials. In the groups receiving 0 percent and 100 percent reinforcement during the last 40 trials there is no tendency for the groups to be ordered in any fashion, and terminal levels of response in all groups are quite similar.

To determine whether the differences are statistically significant, an analysis of variance of performance on Trials 61–80 was performed. For this analysis Ss were classified according to the probability of reinforcement under which they had been tested on Trials 1–40 and 41–80. A significant difference among the groups as a function of level of reinforcement during Trials 41–80 was found ($F = 57.2$, $df = 3$ and 210, $P < .001$). (The entry for the 0 percent–0 percent cell in the analysis of variance was selected at random from one of the other cells in which 0 percent reinforcement was received during Trials 41–80.) A significant difference was also obtained as a function of the levels of reinforcement Ss had received during Trials 1–40 ($F = 3.96$, $df = 3$ and 210, $P < .01$). The interaction term was not significant ($F = 1.17$, $df = 9$ and 210, $P > .05$). It is concluded, therefore, that performance on Trials 61–80 differed significantly, both as a function of current and previous reinforcement probabilities.

A question of recent interest is the relative frequency with which Ss choose nonreinforced stimuli in a probability learning task (Anderson and Grant, 1957). An analysis of the distributions of choices by Ss in the present study was made possible by the use of a three-stimulus task. The data from all conditions were combined, since the stimulus which was reinforced was randomized among all conditions. When the left knob was correct, the middle knob was chosen on an average of 20.7 trials and the right knob on an average of 18.5 trials. The difference in the average frequency with which the two knobs were chosen is significant at beyond the .001 level ($t = 4.64$, $df = 85$). When the middle knob was correct, the left knob was chosen on an average of 14.7 trials, and the right knob on 16.0 trials ($t = 3.59$, $df = 72$, $P < .001$). When the right knob was correct, the left knob was chosen on an average of 16.7 trials, and the middle knob on 20.8 trials ($t = 6.96$, $df = 65$, $P < .001$).

The Ss, therefore, did not distribute their choices of nonreinforced stimuli equally. The tendency to prefer the middle knob was also found when the initial response of each S in this experiment was examined. On Trial 1, 56 percent of Ss chose the middle knob, 23 percent chose the right knob, and 21 percent chose the left knob. These tendencies were not found, however, when the total frequencies of choice of the reinforcing stimulus were considered. Individual t tests comparing the proportion of times the correct stimulus was chosen under conditions where the left, middle, and right stimuli were correct indicate no significant differences ($t \leq 1.41$).

These results are consistent with those of experiments showing that the terminal level of response in a probability learning task is affected by earlier experience with other stimulus probabilities. The results do not support the conclusion of Estes and Straughan that asymptotic level of response is independent of prior experience with different probabilities of reinforcement. The significance of the present finding for Estes' theory is not clear, for Estes has not made predictions concerning the three-choice case with contingent reinforcement of only one response. The problem facing a statistical learning theory in making such a prediction is that of determining some basis of distributing the effects of a nonreinforced trial between two incorrect stimuli. The present study provides evidence related to this problem: Ss did not distribute their choices equally between the two nonreinforcing stimuli. The results indicate a hierarchy of response tendencies such that one of the nonreinforcing knobs was more likely to be chosen than another.

Even though the results indicate that previous experience does affect final level of response, their similarity to those found in other probability learning tasks is striking, in that the level of response was dependent on the probability of reinforcement provided by the reinforcing stimulus and in that an asymptotic level of response was rapidly reached. The high dependence of the response level upon probability of reinforcement was seen in the rapid changes in performance that occurred following the change in probability of reinforcement. The rapidity with which the change in level of response occurred following the change in reinforcement indicates that Ss readily discriminated the change in reward probability.

SUMMARY

Three experiments are reported concerning the effects of differences in CA, incentive, and prior experience with different probabilities of reinforcement on children's performance in a probability task.

In Exp. I, Ss at CA's 3, 5, 7, and 9 were tested in a three-stimulus situation with reinforcement of only one of the three responses. Reinforcement was delivered on 33 percent, 66 percent, or 100 percent of Ss' choices of the correct stimulus. An inverse relationship between frequency of choice of the reinforced stimulus and CA was found in the 33 percent and 66 percent groups. No differences appeared among the age groups with 100 percent reinforcement.

In Exp. II, Ss at CA 5 were tested under the same conditions employed in Exp. I with incentives of high or low value. In the 66 percent and 33 percent groups the frequency of choice of the reinforcing stimulus was significantly lower for the high incentive than for the low incentive groups. With 100 percent reinforcement no difference between the high and low incentive groups in the frequency of choice

on every trial), and this belief persisted throughout 80 trials for some of the *S*s. If *S* performs in accordance with an hypothesis of this nature, variability of response and a lack of maximization behavior is not surprising and should, in fact, be considered the rational way to play the game.

The present study is an attempt to vary instructions in order to lead some *S*s to believe that there is a solution which yields 100 percent reinforcement and others to believe that there is no way they can receive 100 percent reinforcement. A third group given neutral instructions will be compared with these two groups. A three-choice probability learning task will be used in which one of the choices is reinforced 50 percent of the time, and the other two are never reinforced. It is predicted that *S*s told there is a way to get 100 percent reinforcement and *S*s given neutral instructions will not differ in the frequency with which they choose the reinforcing stimulus, since it is assumed that all *S*s enter this task with the idea that there is a solution and telling them there is a solution will only reinforce this self-instruction. The group told there is *no* way to get 100 percent reinforcement, however, should choose the reinforcing knob more often than the other two groups, since they should no longer be expecting a perfect solution and should therefore show less variable behavior.

Two age groups in each of the instructional conditions are also included to investigate the effectiveness of instructions at different age levels. It is predicted that older children will choose the reinforcing stimulus less often than younger children, since older children are more likely to expect a solution which will yield 100 percent reinforcement. It is also possible that older *S*s will be affected less

by any instructional conditions, since they will have stronger pre-experimental sets concerning the outcome of any problem-solving task.

METHOD

Subjects

The *S*s were 96 children selected from two different age ranges, 5.0 to 7.3 years and 9.2 to 13.0 years. They were divided into six experimental groups of 16 *S*s each. Subjects in each age range were selected and assigned to experimental groups at random from nursery schools and groups of children attending summer Bible School classes at various churches in Austin, Texas.

Apparatus

The apparatus has previously been described in detail (11). It consisted of a vertical yellow panel containing a horizontal row of three knobs. Above the knobs was a signal light and below the knobs a delivery hole for marbles. The marbles fell into an enclosed plastic container.

Procedure

The *S* was seated in front of the apparatus and was told that he was to play a game. The *E* demonstrated the apparatus and instructed *S:* "Whenever the light comes on you push one of these knobs. If you push on the correct knob, a marble will fall out of this hole right here, like this." (*E* dropped a marble through the hole into the plastic container.) "Now every time the light comes on, you push the knob that you think will get you the marble."

After the preliminary instructions, which were the same for all *S*s, different experimental groups were given differing instructions. *S*s receiving neutral instructions (group N) were told:

"Remember, just push one knob each time the light comes on." Subjects in the group told there was a solution to the task (group S) were told: "Now let me tell you something about this game. There *is* a way that you can get a marble on every single push. There's a way that you can get a marble every single time. Remember, just push one knob each time the light goes on, and also remember that there *is* a way that you can get a marble on every single push." Subjects in the no-solution group (group NS) were told: "Now let me tell you something about this game. There is *no* way you can get a marble on every single push. It's impossible for *anybody* to get a marble on every single push. But let's just see how you do. Remember, just push one knob each time the light comes on, and also remember that there is *no* way you can get a marble on every single push." The experimental trials were then begun.

All Ss received 50 percent reinforcement of their choices of one of the three knobs and 0 percent on the other two. The 50 percent reinforcement schedule was determined prior to the experiment and was randomized in blocks of 10 trials with the following restrictions: No S was allowed to have more than one nonreinforcement on the reinforcing knob prior to his first reinforcement on that knob. Actually, half the Ss were reinforced on their first choice of the reinforcing knob, and half were reinforced on their second choice. No S was allowed to receive more than three consecutive nonreinforcements of his choices of the correct knob. Nine of these 10-trial blocks were constructed, and Ss in each group were randomly started with one of these nine blocks in order to minimize further the effects of particular sequences. All reinforcement was of a contingent nature. That is, S was reinforced 50 percent of the times he pushed the correct knob. Reinforcement was thus available 50 percent of the time he made the correct response, rather than on 50 percent of the total trials.

For each S, one of the three knobs (either left, middle, or right) was designated as the correct knob. In each group five Ss were reinforced for their choices of the left knob, five for their choices of the middle knob, and six for their choices of the right knob.

RESULTS AND DISCUSSION

An analysis of variance was performed on the total number of correct responses throughout the 80 experimental trials. A significant age effect was found ($F = 8.93$, 1 and 90 *df*, $p < .01$). This difference was in the predicted direction, with the younger Ss choosing the reinforcing knob more often (mean = 41.1) than the older Ss (mean = 33.1). This finding adds support to an earlier finding of the same nature (8), as well as that of a recent study by Jones and Liverant (6) using a two-choice task. This result is interpreted as indicating that older Ss enter the task with an expectancy for some solution to the task which will yield a high percentage of reinforcement; consequently they employ variable behavior in an attempt to obtain a frequency of reinforcement more compatible with their expectancy. The younger Ss, on the other hand, do not have this expectancy to as great a degree and are willing to settle for lower frequencies of reinforcement. This variable behavior on the part of the older Ss results in less frequent choice of the reinforcing knob than is exhibited by the younger Ss.

Analysis of variance of the total number of choices of the reinforced knob did not provide support for the prediction that Ss instructed that there was no way they could be correct every time would choose the reinforcing knob more often than Ss told there was a solution and Ss given neutral instructions. There was no main effect associated with the instruction variable ($F < 1$), nor was the interaction of age with instructions significant ($F = 2.04$, 2 and 90 df). It is possible, however, that a simple frequency count of the number of times the reinforcing knob was chosen is not sensitive to certain response tendencies which may be affected by instructions. For example, the experimental variables might influence the frequency with which Ss would exhibit certain dominant response patterns which have been observed in this task in the previously cited investigation by Stevenson and Weir (10). The two most frequently occurring patterns observed in this earlier study involved all three knobs and took the form of right, middle, left (RML) and left, middle, right (LMR) sequences. In this earlier study, Ss who believed there was a solution to the task also believed this solution would involve some sort of pattern and appeared to search across all three knobs in an attempt to find this solution.

In order to determine if the frequency of pattern responses of an RML or LMR nature was influenced by either of the experimental variables in the present study, several analyses of these types of pattern responses were performed. An analysis of variance of the total number of pattern responses for all 80 trials revealed no differences associated with age or instructions, but the age $\times$ instructions interaction was significant ($F = 5.11$, 2 and 90 df, $p < .01$). Inspection of the data indicates that this interaction is the result of the fact that the younger children in group S averaged about twice as many pattern responses as the older children in group S, while in the other two instruction groups the younger Ss made slightly fewer pattern responses (see Table 1).

Examination of pattern responses also revealed that the younger Ss had · a greater initial tendency to make these types of responses. For 15 of the 48 younger Ss, the first three responses in the task were of a pattern (RML or LMR) nature, while only four of the older Ss made pattern responses during the first three trials. A chi-square test performed on these frequency data showed this difference to be significant ($\chi^2 = 7.94$, $df = 1$, $p < .01$). In order to determine if there was any tendency for the younger or older Ss to be making more pattern responses at the end of the task, the number of Ss making pattern responses during the last four trials was examined. Although the number of younger Ss making pattern responses ($N = 19$) was still larger than the number of older Ss making pattern responses ($N = 12$), this difference did not result in a significant chi square ($\chi^2 = 2.33$, $df = 1$, $p > .05$). It appears that the younger Ss have a definite tendency to enter the

TABLE 1

MEAN NUMBER OF PATTERN RESPONSES FOR SIX EXPERIMENTAL GROUPS
(All 80 Trials)

	INSTRUCTIONS		
Age	Neutral	Solution	No Solution
5- 7 years	14.2	19.7	12.9
9-13 years	14.3	10.4	15.9

task with a set to respond in a pattern manner, while older *S*s show this initial tendency to a lesser degree. This could be interpreted as indicating that the younger *S*s approach an experimental task with simpler and more stereotyped tendencies than do older *S*s with more varied experiences in learning tasks. No differences in the frequency of pattern responses during the first three or last four trials was found to be associated with the instruction variable.

Another indication of the "qualitative" response differences between the older and younger *S*s in this task is the tendency to change to another knob following the first reinforcement or nonreinforcement in the task. In an earlier study (9) it was noted that the proportion of *S*s changing response after the first reinforcement or nonreinforcement increased as a function of age. Apparently, then, older *S*s have a greater tendency to show negative recency than do younger *S*s. In this earlier study the oldest *S*s examined were 9 years of age. The present study will extend these findings somewhat, since the average age of the *S*s in the older group was 10.8 years. When the tendency to change response after the first reinforcement was examined, it was found that 47 of the 48 older *S*s switched to another knob, while only 37 of the 48 younger *S*s switched. This difference is significant at beyond the .01 level ($\chi^2 = 9.6$, $df = 1$). Following the first nonreinforcement, 45 of the 48 older *S*s changed response, and 40 of the younger *S*s changed. This difference is not significant ($\chi^2 = 2.58$, $df = 1$, $p > .10$). Again, no differences were found which were associated with the instruction variable. When these data are combined with those from the previous experiment (9), it becomes apparent that, as age increases, so does the tendency to

change response after both the first reinforcement and the first nonreinforcement. The tendency to show this negative recency effect following the first nonreinforcement appears to reach its peak at about 5 years of age and remain at this peak at 7, 9, and 11 years of age. The same tendency following the first reinforcement does not reach its height until about 11 years, since the 9-to-13-year-old *S*s in this study changed response following the first reinforcement significantly more often than did the 9-year-olds in the previous study and the younger *S*s in the present study.

The most striking feature of this study was the difficulty encountered in changing *S*s' performance by differing instructions. None of the older *S*s maximized their choice of the reinforcing stimulus even though telling some of them there was no solution to the task was intended to give this effect. The results are even more surprising when the comments made to *E* during postexperimental questioning are considered. All *S*s questioned knew which knob was paying off and that choices of the other knobs had not resulted in reinforcement. Nevertheless, they frequently continued to choose the nonreinforcing knobs throughout the 80 experimental trials. Moreover, many of the *S*s questioned were quite sure that these knobs would never pay off, but still felt they had some function in the task.

Since some *S*s believed that choices of the nonreinforcing knobs would never be reinforced, these choices must have had some other utility for them. It seems likely that older *S*s in this task may realize rather quickly that there is no way they can achieve 100 percent reinforcement and search instead for a solution which will result in perfect predictability of when a reinforcement will occur. Thus, the solution sought for in this task may at first be one involving 100 percent reward, but may change to a solution which will allow perfect predictability of the occurrence of a reinforcement. If instructions are to change performance in a task of this sort, it appears that S must discard the notion of perfect predictability as well as that of 100 percent success. Obviously, the instructions given in the present study were not sufficient to produce this result. It may be that the only way maximization behavior will appear consistently in this type of task is for S to believe that the only criterion of success is the number of reinforcements obtained and that no "solution" of the type most Ss appear to expect is possible.

SUMMARY

A three-choice probability learning task was employed in which one of the three choices was reinforced 50 percent of the times it was chosen and the other two were never reinforced. Children at two age levels (5 to 7 years and 9 to 13 years) served as Ss. One-third of the Ss at each age level were instructed that it was possible to be correct on every trial, one-third were told that it was not possible to be correct on every trial, and one-third were given neutral instructions. Results indicated that the younger Ss chose the reinforcing knob more often than did the older Ss, while the instructional conditions did not influence the number of choices of the reinforcing knob. Analysis of the number of pattern responses revealed an age $\times$ instructions interaction. Younger Ss were also found to have a greater tendency to make pattern responses at the beginning of the task, and the older Ss showed a greater negative recency effect following the first reinforcement. The failure to find differences related to the instructional variable was interpreted as indicating that Ss search for a solution which will allow them accurately to predict the occurrence of a reinforcement, rather than a solution which will yield 100 percent reinforcement.

REFERENCES

1. Anderson, N. H., "Effect of First-order Conditional Probability in a Two-choice Learning Situation," *Journal of Experimental Psychology,* **59** (1960), 73-93.

2. Estes, W. K. and J. H. Straughan, "Analysis of a Verbal Conditioning Situation in Terms of Statistical Learning Theory," *Journal of Experimental Psychology,* **47** (1954), 225-34.

3. Flood, M. M., "One Game-learning Theory and Some Decision-making Experiments," in *Decision Processes,* eds. R. M. Thrall, C. H. Coombs, and R. L. Davis. New York: John Wiley & Sons, Inc., 1954.

4. Goodnow, J. J., "Determinants of Choice-distribution in Two-choice Situations," *American Journal of Psychology,* **68** (1955), 106-16.

5. Grant, D. A., H. W. Hake, and J. P. Hornseth, "Acquisition and Extinction of a Verbal Conditioned Response with Differing Percentages of Reinforcement," *Journal of Experimental Psychology,* **42** (1951), 1-5.

6. Jones, M. H. and S. Liverant, "Effects of Age Differences on Choice Behavior," *Child Development,* **31** (1960), 673-80.

7. Simon, H. A., "A Comparison of Game Theory and Learning Theory," *Psychometrika,* **21** (1956), 267-72.

8. Stevenson, H. W. and M. W. Weir, "Variables Affecting Probability Learning in Children," *Journal of Experimental Psychology,* **57** (1959), 403-13.

9. ————, "Development Changes in the Effects of Reinforcement and Nonreinforcement of Single Response," *Child Development,* **32** (1961), 1-5.

10. ———, "The Role of Age and Verbalization in Probability Learning," *American Journal of Psychology.* (On press.)

11. Stevenson, H. W. and E. F. Zigler, "Probability Learning in Children," *Journal of Experimental Psychology,* **56** (1958), 185-92.

Magnitude of Reward and Probability Learning *

Y. Brackbill, M. S. Kappy and R. H. Starr

At first concern in studies of probability learning—and still a persistent one—is the "matching" choice behavior that Ss show when confronted with events of unequal occurrence. Instead of behaving like rational game theorists by learning to respond at unity, Ss tend to match the relative frequencies of their responses to the relative frequencies of the stimulus events (Grant, Hake, and Hornseth, 1951). Goodnow (1955) has advanced an interesting set of hypotheses concerning factors that lead to matching; she cites intolerance for boredom, inability to overlook losses, and so on. Statistical learning theories provide a more formal approach to the prediction of probability matching (cf. Bush and Estes, 1959).

In terms of experimental evidence,

* From Y. Brackbill, M. S. Kappy, and R. H. Starr, "Magnitude of Reward and Probability Learning," *Journal of Experimental Psychology, 63* (1962), 32-35. Reprinted by permission of the authors and publishers.

This investigation was carried out during the term of a postdoctoral fellowship awarded to the first author by the National Institute of Mental Health. The authors are grateful for the co-operation of Mary Adams, Dorothy Rawlings, and the staff of the Barclay Elementary School, Baltimore, Maryland.

one variable that appears to be of no small importance in predicting and manipulating relative response frequencies is the nature of tangible reinforcing contingencies offered by the experimental procedure. First, the mere introduction of reward for correct predictions has been shown to increase maximum gain responding. Money may not be everything, but it can do a lot toward alleviating the boredom that comes from making the same verbal response for 100 trials or more (Siegel and Goldstein, 1959). Further, it has been found that maximum gain responding is increased by the use of both reward for correct prediction and punishment for incorrect prediction (as in the "risk" condition of Siegel and Goldstein 1959), by a previous history of infrequent rewards (or low "expectancy for success," Stevenson and Zigler, 1958), and by higher frequencies of reward in a contingent procedure (Stevenson and Weir, 1959).

In the present study, the effect of amount of reward was investigated, with the expectation that Ss will maximize gain to the extent that there is something tangible to be gained by so doing. In other words, the hypothesis was that in the typical noncontingent probability learning situation maximum gain strategy is a direct function of the amount of reward offered for correct predictions.

METHOD

Subjects

The Ss were 24 boys and 24 girls from the second grade classes of a single elementary school. Mean age was 95.5 mo., $SD = 9.4$. Mean IQ was 85.8, $SD = 18.9$, by the SRA test. The sample was relatively homogeneous in terms of socioeconomic background; modal occupation level for fathers corresponded to Class 5 of Warner's (1949) 7-point scale. Thirty-four Ss were white, 13 were Negro, and 1 was Oriental.

Experimental Material

This consisted of 3×5 in. cards cut from green, lightweight cardboard stock. On each card was printed the picture of either a cat or a dog. Two packs of 200 cards each were prepared, in order that dog or cat would appear equally as the more frequent event over treatment levels, sex of Ss, and sequence of running Ss. In preparing these packs, the relative proportions of the two stimulus events were held constant for all treatment levels at .75:.25. A randomized series of events was prepared (and recorded) in blocks of 20 trials each, with the over-all objective probability split of .75:.25 maintained within each block. There was no other restriction on randomization. Twenty such 20-trial blocks were prepared. Then, for each S, a 10-block sequence was randomly drawn from the 20-block pool.

In addition to the pack of 200 cards, a box containing approximately 750 marbles and a cup with a 100-marble capacity in which S accumulated his winnings were also on the table at which E and S worked. On display in another part of the room was a standard array of ten $10¢$ toys. These were high-preference toys, selected on the basis of previously obtained rankings from same-age Ss.

Procedure

Forty-eight Ss were randomly assigned to four experimental groups, with the single restriction that each group of 12 contain equal numbers of boys and girls. The four groups were given 5, 3, 1, or 0 units of reward (marbles) for each correct response. One hundred marbles could be exchanged for one toy.

At the beginning of a series, the pack of 200 cards was face down; S was instructed to guess before E turned each card over, whether the card would show a dog or a cat. Both at the beginning of the experiment and subsequently, whenever he had accumulated 100 marbles, S was asked if he wanted to try to win a toy (or another toy). If he responded negatively at any choice point, the procedure was discontinued. One prospective S was discarded at the beginning of the experiment after stating that none of the available toys interested her.

RESULTS AND DISCUSSION

Figure 1 shows the mean proportions of predictions of the more frequent event ($S_{.75}$) in successive 20-trial blocks for the four groups. As a test of the hypothesis that maximum gain responding increases as a function of magnitude of reward for correct predictions, the Jonckheere (1954) test against ordered alternatives was applied to the data from the last three blocks. The resulting statistic of 2.65 is significant at the .004 level by a one-tailed test. (Scores from three

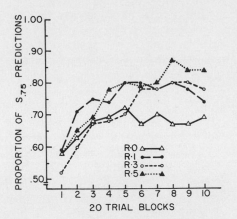

R·0 △——△
R·1 ●——●
R·3 ○----○
R·5 ▲······▲

20 TRIAL BLOCKS

FIG. 1. *Mean proportions of* $S_{.75}$ *predictions in successive 20-trial blocks for four experimental groups differing in number of units of reward offered for every correct prediction. (Each plotted point is a Group × Block mean based on 12 cases.)*

blocks were used in order to minimize the number of tied scores. If one used the same test on scores of the last block only and split the ties, the resulting statistic of 1.83 would still be significant at the .02 level.)

Inspection of Fig. 1 shows that, for the last half of the trials, the most noticeable difference among treatment levels is between nonreward and any value of reward. This suggests that the performance function under amount of reward is not linear for these data. The same suggestion has been made by Pubols (1960), who concluded from his review of studies on amount of reward in learning and performance in animals, that the performance function ". . . is negatively accelerated, and possibly logarithmic . . ." (p. 111). If one prefers a technique more sophisticated than simple visual inspection, the same question may be considered from the standpoint of utility theory. On the basis of Siegel's (1959) Model I (Equation 1), it is possible to calculate the ratio of the utility of making correct responses to that of varying responses (assuming constant utility of varying responses). The resulting a values for R-0 through R-5 (and interpolating for R = 2 and R = 4) would be .72, 1.08, 1.13, 1.16, 1.29, and 1.40. Clearly, the largest increment in utility value follows the introduction of any material reward; subsequent additions in reward produce relatively less effect on utility value, so that the resulting utility curve becomes negatively accelerated.

Sequence Analysis

A first-order sequence analysis was performed on the last 100 trials for each S. Such an analysis yields the probability of Ss prediction on Trial n, given two items of information about Trial n-1: (a) the event that S had predicted previously, and (b) the event that had actually occurred previously. Since the Jonckheere (1954) analysis had already shown tangible rewards to have a significant effect on responding, it is reasonable to expect that previous actual occurrence rather than previous prediction would emerge from a sequence analysis as the more dependable predictor from Trial n-1 to n. This expectation finds support in a comparison of Columns A and B, Table 1; the average difference between the two sets of probabilities is a mere .04. Further, the ordering within the two sets of probabilities reflects with fair accuracy the effect of the experimental variable, magnitude of reward.

However, comparison of Columns C and D reveals a different outcome. Prediction to Trial n is not a simple function of previous actual occurrence on Trial n-1, as it appears to be for the A-B comparison. In fact, the mean difference between the two sets of 48 correlated proportions is significantly different from zero ($CR = 2.82$, $P < .01$). This means that, for those trials on which the less frequent event actually occurred, not only that occurrence but also Ss own previous prediction determined his next prediction. Specifically, S was much more willing to revert to a maximum gain strategy on his next prediction *if* he had just successfully predicted the less frequent event than if he had not predicted it and it had occurred. This effect appears to be independent of the experimental variable, since there is no systematic trend among C-D difference scores as a function of treatment level.

What is the interpretation of this effect, and how does it relate to the experimental variable? Obviously, the best strategy to maximize tangible reward is for S to predict the more frequent event on every trial. Further, this strategy is the more compelling the more the reward. That Ss do behave in accordance with this strategy was shown by the Jonckheere (1954) analysis. What the sequence analysis shows is that there is a second source of reinforcement at work: the utility to S of correctly predicting the occurrence of the less frequent event. Where the investigators had intended only one game, Ss discovered two.

Whether or not one agrees with this interpretation, the fact remains that the net result of this secondary effect is to subtract from maximum gain responding. In effect, it constitutes a response that is competing with the criterion response. However, in contrast with the results of studies in which incentive magnitude has been found to affect both criterion response and competing responses (Pereboom and Crawford, 1958), the present results show only the criterion response to have been influenced by magnitude of reward. The competing response appears to have been maintained by some other form of reinforcement, independent of the form under study.

SUMMARY

This study investigated probability learning in a binary choice, noncontingent procedure with 0, 1, 3, and 5 units of reward for each correct prediction, 100 units being exchangeable for one toy. The Ss were second-grade children. Maximum gain responding increased with larger values of reward, although the function relating these two variables did not appear to be linear. From a first order sequence analysis, an independent effect emerged through an unexpected source of reinforcement: the utility to S of correctly predicting the occurrence of the less frequent event.

TABLE 1

PROBABILITY OF PREDICTING S.75 ON TRIAL n, GIVEN CERTAIN INFORMATION ABOUT TRIAL n-1

| | EVENT ON TRIAL n-1 | | | |
| | A | B | C | D |
Group	S Predicted S.75 and S.75 Occurred	S Predicted S.25 and S.75 Occurred	S Predicted S.25 and S.25 Occurred	S Predicted S.75 and S.25 Occurred
R-0	.74	.82	.56	.38
R-1	.80	.83	.85	.65
R-3	.82	.87	.73	.67
R-5	.89	.87	.78	.64

NOTE. Each entry represents the mean of 12 individual proportions.

REFERENCES

Bush, R. R. and W. K. Estes (eds.). *Studies in Mathematical Learning Theory.* Stanford, Calif.: Stanford University Press, 1959.

Goodnow, J. J. "Determinants of Choice-distribution in Two-choice Situations," *American Journal of Psychology,* **68** (1955), 106-116.

Grant, C. A., H. W. Hake, and J. P. Hornseth. "Acquisition and Extinction of a Verbal Conditioned Response with Differing Percentages of Reinforcement," *Journal of Experimental Pschology,* **42** (1951), 1-5.

Jonckheere, A. R. "A Distribution-free *k*-sample Test Against Ordered Alternatives," *Biometrika,* **41** (1954), 133-145.

Pereboom, A. C. and B. M. Crawford. "Instrumental and Competing Behavior as a Function of Trials and Reward Magnitude," *Journal of Experimental Psychology,* **56** (1958), 82-85.

Pubols, B. H., Jr. "Incentive Magnitude, Learning, and Performance in Animals," *Psychological Bulletin,* **57** (1960), 89-115.

Siegel, S. "Theoretical Models of Choice and Strategy Behavior: Stable Behavior in the Two-choice Uncertain Outcome Situation," *Psychometrika,* **24** (1959), 303-316.

Siegel, S. and D. A. Goldstein. "Decision-making Behavior in a Two-choice Uncertain Outcome Situation," *Journal of Experimental Psychology,* **57** (1959), 37-42.

Stevenson, H. W. and M. W. Weir. "Variables Affecting Children's Performance in a Probability Learning Task," *Journal of Experimental Psychology,* **57** (1959), 403-412.

Stevenson, H. W. and E. F. Zigler. "Probability Learning in Children," *Journal of Experimental Psychology,* **56** (1958), 185-192.

Warner, W. L. *Social Class in America.* Chicago: Science Research Associates, 1949.

INDEX